PHILOSOPHY
OF
LAW

edited by

Joel Feinberg

and

Hyman Gross

WADSWORTH PUBLISHING COMPANY, INC.,
BELMONT, CALIFORNIA

ISBN-0-8221-0150-5

Library of Congress Catalog Card Number: 74-83950

Printed in the United States of America
Printing (last digit): 9 8 7 6 5 4

Production Editor: Linda Malevitz Hashmi   *Cover Designer: Jill Casty*

CONTENTS

PART 4 RESPONSIBILITY

PART 5 PUNISHMENT

PREFACE

There is currently a widespread and truly philosophical perplexity about law that is occasioned by the events of the day and by the legal proceedings to which they give rise. Increasing numbers of students have been attracted to courses in philosophy of law and social philosophy offered by philosophy departments, and law students, constantly challenged by the theoretical dimensions of law school subjects, are prompted more than ever to enroll in jurisprudence courses. These students often are disappointed by what seems to them an excessively abstract approach. Portentous terms such as "Law," "Morality," and "Justice," are manipulated like counters in an uncertain game, and hoary figures from the past are marched by, each with his distinctive dogmatic pronouncement and his own curious technical vocabulary. No wonder traditional jurisprudence often seems among the driest and most remote of academic subjects.

We have tried in this volume to relate the traditional themes of legal philosophy to the live concerns of modern society in a way that invigorates one and illuminates the other. The volume begins with essays by classic and contemporary figures on the essential nature of law, and on the relation of law to morality or other sources of principle outside the legal system. No attempt is made to give contending doctrines equal time, or even to give them all a day in court. We have passed over much excellent material that might have been included, though this is sure to cause some displeasure in an area of jurisprudential concern that is so marked by doctrinal partisanship. Our endeavor is not to represent all important points of view, nor to represent any in a truly comprehensive way, but instead to offer a series of selections that raise sharply the most important issues. Many of these philosophical issues debated in the first part recur later in the book where authors take up specific problems about liberty, justice, responsibility, and punishment.

Opinions in fifteen court cases, together with two literary inventions and one newspaper story, serve to illuminate more abstract discussion and to test the adequacy of principles developed in them. These materials cover such problems as the law in conflict with itself during successive regimes in a single country, how to determine the hitherto unknown scope of a manufacturer's liability, obscene public displays, compulsory medical treatment, the right to privacy, equality between the sexes, good samaritans and officious intermeddlers (and how to tell them apart), "slayers' bounties" (and how to prevent them), criminal insanity, and capital punishment. Our aim here is not to supplement the essays with further discussion but to make clear the concreteness and immediacy of matters of philosophical interest in a way that will stimulate further discussion of them.

Some few articles have been included that do not purport to be works of philosophical significance. They have been selected to balance discussions, to draw attention to neglected issues, or to provide some desirable nonphilosophical perspective on philosophical questions of public concern. Many important articles—and indeed many important problems—have been omitted, much to our regret. We claim for the included materials only that they serve to raise a good number of the great questions in the field, not that they represent anything approaching an exhaustive survey of questions or of answers. The bibliographies at the end of each Part list further materials on each topic and on other related topics of importance.

In selecting materials for this anthology we have benefited from the advice of anonymous critics well selected by the publisher. We are also grateful to Patricia Burns, Gertrude Schiller, and Oksana Wengerchuk for their cheerful and efficient help in typing, duplicating, and assembling the manuscript.

Joel Feinberg
Hyman Gross

PART 1 LAW

The question "What is law?" seems at first glance hardly to deserve a philosopher's attention. Ask a lawyer about the law, and if he is unable to give an answer on the spot he knows where to look it up, or at least where to get the ingredients for a reliable professional opinion. Statutes, judicial opinions, administrative regulations, constitutional provisions all are official pronouncements of law. When these texts leave the matter ambiguous, a lawyer knows the appropriate techniques to resolve the ambiguity, and in aid of that consults scholarly works of interpretation and other sources of authoritative opinion. The question "What is law?" then seems simply a request for a general definition that covers all those, and only those, items of official pronouncement that lawyers finally treat as law. It is true that even the best dictionary may leave us unsatisfied, for something more informative than a mere guide for word use is wanted. Still, at first sight nothing in the question appears to need the fine grinding of the philosopher's mill, and we conclude that we are adequately acquainted with the notion of something as familiar as law, only details remaining to be filled in.

Our simple belief is shattered not only by philosophical reflection but also by the common experience of those who use and are subject to the law. Professor H.L.A. Hart, whose work now dominates Anglo-American legal philosophy, has described this illusion of understanding in this way. "The same predicament was expressed by some famous words of St. Augustine about the notion of time. 'What then is time? If no one asks me I know: if I wish to explain it to one that asks I know not.' It is in this way that even skilled lawyers have felt that, though they know the law, there is much about law and its relations to other things that they cannot explain and do not fully understand. Like a man who can get from one point to another in a familiar town but cannot explain or show others how to do it, those who press for a definition need a map exhibiting clearly the relationships dimly felt to exist between the law they know and other things."[1]

[1] *The Concept of Law* (1961), pp. 13–14.

What then are the further questions left unanswered by simple definitions, and what is their importance? In theories of law, three different interpretations have been given to the question "What is law?" These different versions of the question are not always clearly distinguished, but an analogy may serve to clarify the difference.

Suppose the question were "What is a postage stamp?" One interpretation would call for a statement of *what counts as* a postage stamp, or, putting it another way, *what deserves to be called* a postage stamp. The answer would distinguish postage stamps from, and relate them to, revenue stamps, Christmas seals, postage meter imprints, postal privilege franks, and postage due stamps. A second way of viewing the question is as a request for information about *what is properly given effect* as a postage stamp. What counts as a postage stamp is not at issue, but it is recognized that a seriously torn or blemished stamp will not be treated as valid for postage, nor will a counterfeit stamp, one withdrawn from use, or a foreign stamp; and so *criteria of validity* are sought. Finally, a third way of interpreting the question stresses *the nature* of postage, requiring an explanation of the postal system of which stamps are a part and a description of the role of stamps in it. Turning to the far weightier question about law, we notice first that law is the ultimate social recoursé of civilized men when claims are in conflict. There are many other standards to which men may and often do turn in regulating their affairs, but when these fail, standards bearing the authority of the state are the last resort. It is important, therefore, for the citizen as well as for the judge weighing his claim to be able to tell exactly what is law, so that the force of law is not given to lawlike things of other sorts, such as standards of customary practice, moral precepts, by-laws and private regulations.

Once items that are properly called laws are distinguished from other lawlike pronouncements, how do we distinguish those that are valid from those that are not? Invalid licenses, arguments, coupons, and orders are not properly given effect, and neither are invalid laws (though it is important to note that in all these cases invalidity does not affect the *kind* of thing it is). What then in general supports the claim that a law may not be given effect? Suppose it is regularly disobeyed and unenforced? Suppose it is hideously unjust? Suppose it is the product of a political regime that is clearly illegitimate? Suppose there are no means for enforcing or changing the law? Here the issue is whether moral, social, or political standards of validity that are (in the first instance, at least) outside the law must be met if a law is to be valid.

A third range of questions concerns the nature of law, and particularly its relation to morality. At every turn lawyers, judges, legislators, and citizens grapple with moral questions: What is fair, who is to blame, what rights does one have, what is wrong with doing that? To make sure the law reflects the lives we live as moral creatures, we need to understand the relation between our law and our morals. In addition, another aspect of the nature of law raises questions about its formal properties: Are laws rules or standards of some other sort? And just what difference is there between what is included as an item of law and other expressions of the same form that are not part of the law?

It is a truism that no question in legal philosophy is far removed from any other, and the reader should especially *not* expect to find such closely related matters as these treated in isolation from one another. The selections from the work of Thomas Aquinas, with which the readings in this part begin, bear this out. His unifying doctrine is one of natural law. Law, in this view, is universal because it springs from reason possessed by all men, and it is this natural law that shapes the positive law that we ordinarily speak of as "the law." Positive law determined by natural law is for the common good, and it is binding upon the conscience of men because it is just. Aquinas' concept of law, then, is of an ideal to be found in laws. It is absent when unjust exercise of power produces laws only in name, and for the most part these need not be obeyed. Aquinas' views on law and morality may surprise those who think of objections to legislating morality as a modern movement. Only moral wrongs that are socially significant as harms to others properly concern the law, according to Aquinas. His idea of conscientious objection to unjust laws and his approval of a qualified civil disobedience will also seem surprising to those who think such views to be of recent origin.

Several critical questions might usefully be kept in mind while reading this selection. Is there an adequate distinction drawn between what characterizes good law and what characterizes any law whether good or bad? Is there sufficient appreciation of the difference in what appears to be just to equally rational persons whose interests or circumstances are different? Is reason really disinterested, so that everyone using reason will have the same view of what the law ought to be? Is it possible that a great many perfectly good laws make no appeal at all to conscience but are recommended by sheer expediency?

A word about form may help the reader looking into Aquinas for the first time. The method is dialectical, with the issue posed in the form of a question at the start (there are six such questions comprising this selection); then objections which make the matter problematic are presented, many of these based on pronouncements of noted authorities. Next, Aquinas gives a general statement of his own position on the question (beginning always with a supporting statement from a Church authority); and finally, there are the specific replies of Aquinas to each of the objections previously presented. The authorities cited are mostly religious, though "the Philosopher" (Aristotle) and "the jurists" (from the Code of Justinian) are secular.

The very brief excerpt from a work of Sir Ernest Barker, *Traditions of Civility*, presents concisely the "natural law" conception of law and contrasts it sharply with the view of those who reject natural law. The author also reminds us of the power of these jurisprudential ideas in political history, and particularly of their influence on the American Revolution. The contrast he presents continues to be reflected in the very different notions of constitutional principles found in the British and in the American legal systems.

John Austin's *The Province of Jurisprudence Determined* was published in England in 1832 and has long been regarded in the Anglo-American tradition as the leading work in opposition to natural law theory. It is exceedingly careful work of great range and refinement, the portions reprinted here setting forth only the essentials of Austin's views about the nature of law. Positive law is what Austin seeks to define, and this he does by distinguishing *laws properly so called* from other lawlike utterances and other things called laws. *Laws properly so called* turn out to be *commands* requiring conduct, and some, called positive law, issue from a sovereign to members of an *independent political society* over which sovereignty is exercised. *Commands* entail a purpose and a power to impose sanctions upon those who disobey; a *sovereign* is a determinate human superior (that is, one who can compel others to obey) who is not himself in a habit of obedience to such a superior and who himself receives habitual obedience; and an *independent political society* is one in which the bulk of the society habitually obeys a sovereign.

Austin's theory of law has surely called forth more abundant and more eminent criticism than any other. The reader will likely wonder whether Austin's analysis is not too much influenced by his own legal system and form of government. Can, for example, the features of a federal system like that of the United States be comfortably accommodated in Austin's model? And there are other kinds of troubling questions. Is the power-dependent notion of a command adequate, or would the authority-dependent notion of a rule prove more illuminating since it allows subtler analysis of law in terms more complex than threats of force? Has Austin taken penal laws to be the prototype for all laws, thereby distorting the features of other kinds of laws and exaggerating the role of sanctions in their operation? Are the rules that govern the validity of laws to be taken as commands by the sovereign to himself and, if so, does that account do justice to claims of invalidity that are advanced in modern legal systems? Austin's account of judge-made law is one of acquiescence by the sovereign in what a minister has decided. That seems plausible enough with reference to the case being decided. But looking at the way judicial opinions are used subsequently in legal arguments as a source of law, can they really be said to be commands of the sovereign "though not by its express declaration?" Does Austin's account of sovereignty distinguish *legitimate* exercise of political power through legislation from *effective* legislative exercise of political power, presumably only the former qualifying as law?

Hans Kelsen has in this century assumed a position in the Continental tradition of positivism corresponding to Austin's. The selections included here are from his *Pure Theory of Law*, and they address many of the same questions that Austin attempted to answer, though with a very different style and intellectual temper. Law is conceived as a system of norms whose validity derives from a basic norm. It is thus not the source of a law that certifies it as valid (as Austin would have it), but rather its membership in an authority-dependent normative order. Validity is likewise not a matter of content, and this is equally true for the system as a whole and for the norms which comprise it. In this both Kelsen and Austin identify themselves as positivists; but they soon part company. In explaining what makes a law valid, Kelsen stresses conformity to prescriptive procedures required by the basic norm, while Austin looks to the facts of social life in a sovereign political society. It is therefore easier in Kelsen's view to account, for example, for the phenomenon of international law that is not a part of national law, and indeed one tends to find Kelsen's writings on the subject of international law much more persuasive than Austin's. Though Kelsen is not entirely clear, it would seem that the presupposition of being binding which gives the basic constitutional norms their effect is a social fact much like the habit of obedience in Austin. Indeed, Kelsen's thesis that in the extreme case of revolution legitimacy is dependent upon effectiveness again stresses the paramount importance of social facts in deciding questions of validity. It is not only the abnormal condition of revolution in which effectiveness is significant. Even under normal circumstances, the validity of each norm is destroyed if (but only if) the legal order as a whole is ineffective. It is not true, however, that isolated instances of ineffectiveness of its norms destroys the validity of the legal order. Nor is it the case that isolated instances of ineffectiveness of any norm destroys its validity, though norms never applied or obeyed are indeed invalid.

The first question to ask is whether all purported legal rights are to be recognized simply because conferred by a norm that is formally valid in the system. In any modern legal system there are challenges to validity of laws based upon considerations of what the law ought to be rather than on whether the rules for creating laws have been complied with. Typically, this occurs when a law is shockingly unjust. It would be question-begging to assert that any such challenges based on content really appeal to what are part of the norms that determine validity, unless one ignores a distinction that is fundamental to Kelsen—between the status as law of the norm and its content. One may also ask whether certain standards of validity that are universal according to Kelsen's theory—for example, that laws not obeyed or enforced are invalid—are not simply rules of validity within certain legal systems rather than general criteria of validity for any legal system. Further, one may wonder whether, as Kelsen suggests, revolutionary change is necessary to overcome constitutional objections that a law is invalid. In the United States, for example, the Supreme Court has viewed its role differently at different periods in its history, and as a result, decisions affecting a law's validity that would be deemed constitutionally illegitimate in one period are considered altogether legitimate in another, though no revolution has occurred.

Suppose the question were "What is chess?" How should one go about analyzing the concept of chess so as to make clear the relation between the game he observes and the rules according to which it is played? This furnishes us with a model for the question "What is law?", particularly when the question is interpreted as an inquiry concerning validity. Alf Ross, the distinguished Danish legal philosopher, develops and analyzes the question in this way in the first part of the selection from his work. A game of chess and the law are both social phenomena. Players and judges present us with observable actions. Laws, like rules of chess, provide "an abstract set of normative ideas which serve as a scheme of interpretation for the phenomena of law in action." At first this conception seems exceedingly odd, for we normally think of laws as a means of regulating and judging the acts of the citizen. But in judging, judges do not simply apply laws, any more than the players simply apply rules of chess. The play must be *according to* the rules, and the judicial decision *according to* the law; and that is something different. But neither are rules of law merely explanations or descriptions of what the judge has done, any more than the rules of chess are mere descriptions or explanations of the play. Ross continues along this line to explain his conception of a *valid* system of norms as one in which judges feel bound by the law, or more exactly, one in which judges feel that the laws are socially binding norms and therefore to be observed by them. Each norm that is valid is felt to be socially binding in this way, and by virtue of that it is valid.

As a representation of law, Ross's model has much to recommend it; but it seems somewhat incomplete as a touchstone for law. As later selections make clear, the most difficult problem is deciding which of those norms that judges consider socially binding and rely upon in rendering decisions really are law, and which of them are simply guides for the exercise of judicial discretion. The model of chess, with its readily identifiable rules, does not help here.

The consummate contemporary statement of the positivist view is H.L.A. Hart's book, *The Concept of Law,* published in 1961. This work, above all others in the field, deserves to be read in its entirety, and because of that no attempt has been made to provide excerpts here. An article by Hart, titled "Positivism and the Separation of Law and Morals," was published three years before the book and is reprinted here. It contains an earlier version of some discussions to be found in the book and clarifies to an extraordinary degree many of the issues so far raised here in the works of the other authors. The piece speaks admirably for itself without synopsis or highlighting. By way of introduction it seems necessary only to draw special attention to two things: (1) the discussion of the "realists" in section III of the article, since that position has so far not been represented, and (2) the connection between law and morals in section V, a connection based on the " 'natural' necessity" for human survival and on a consideration of procedural justice.

In section IV of his article, Professor Hart considers the positivist's dilemma when confronted with the need to recognize as law the odious edicts of a morally depraved regime. Lon L. Fuller in "The Problem of the Grudge Informer" contrives an imaginary situation that elaborates this dilemma. In seeking a solution, it is helpful first to separate the major issues that are posed. Is it a question of whether the laws of the previous regime were valid? Whether all valid laws furnish a defense to those who acted under them? Whether criminal laws that are enacted after the crime are never to be applied retroactively? Whether prosecution or some other measure under public authority represents the better policy to be pursued now by the government?

We have noticed several times already that courts are the legal institution of greatest interest to those who want to know what law is. Within a legal system it is the judge who decides what the law is; and in the course of making that decision, he often says things that then become law, at least as his words are later interpreted by other judges. This suggests a considerable latitude of discretion for judges. True, it is a discretion limited by legislation, and it is not as great as that of the legislator, which (except for constitutional limitations pronounced by judges) is untrammeled by prior judicial decision. But, unlike the legislature's discretion, judicial discretion is exercised to decide what the law is and to give it effect, not simply to decide what the law will be. Roscoe Pound, in the chapter from *An Introduction to the Philosophy of Law* reprinted here, illuminates the discretionary activity of the judge already discussed in the Hart selection and again to be carefully explored in the work of Ronald Dworkin. Pound professes to see in the problem of the judge's discretion virtually all the problems of jurisprudence; and he makes clear the need for judicial discretion to be exercised in the interest of justice and of coherent law. He speaks of "the more or less trained intuition of experienced magistrates" in contrast to rules of law, but suggests that beyond that intuition there are standards other than rules to which discretionary decisions regularly. appeal. "Individualization" of law in the interest of justice is the constraint upon law that requires courts (juries and administrative tribunals, as well as judges) to exercise discretion.

It is the virtue of Pound's discussion to make clear that the judicial process does not consist only in application of what is established prior to, and independent of, the judge's decision. But this underscores rather than resolves the dilemma. Why is the intuition of those occupying judicial office to be given the force of law? Indeed, does it not follow that what acquires the force of law in this way is therefore itself law? Ronald Dworkin in "The Model of Rules" provides answers to these core questions of legal philosophy. Initially he argues against the "realist" view (which ironically he styles "nominalist"), denying that the questions of what law is are answered by descriptions of what courts in fact do in exercising their power. He then subjects to critical analysis the theory of law which Professor Hart presented in *The Concept of Law*. The burden of his opposition to Hart as the examplar of positivism is that rules are only one variety of standard to be invoked by a judge in deciding legal issues. There are other standards, the most important of which are principles and policies, and those other standards are not extralegal, but are law as much as rules are. Furthermore, there is no master rule, no matter how complex, which determines their validity as law. The arguments are subtle, thorough, and complex, and they have set the stage for a major current debate of this topic.

Professor Dworkin makes use of two cases—*Riggs v. Palmer* and *Henningsen v. Bloomfield Motors, Inc.*—to illustrate how standards other than rules function as law. Excerpts from the opinions in those cases are included here to allow the reader to decide himself about the character of what the court provides as support for its decision. It is useful to distinguish different kinds of standards as they appear in the opinions; to consider whether the judge is bound or has discretion in using them, and in what sense they are binding or discretionary; and to consider the origins of whatever authority they have

Among the distinguished contributions to the continuing debate is that of Professor Dworkin's Oxford colleague, Joseph Raz. Reprinted here is the second part of a recent article in which Dr. Raz defends the positivist position against Dworkin's criticism. The reader should consider Raz's view of the role of discretion, his view of the significance of judicial invocation of those social norms that count as principles, and his thesis that legal principles may be valid in the same way that legal rules are. The final selection is a portion of an article by Dworkin replying to his critics in which he addresses points made by Raz. (Not all of the points in contention have been included in the Raz selection.) In the second part of the selection Dworkin elaborates important points regarding the distinction that he developed earlier between rules and principles.

H.G.

THOMAS AQUINAS

Concerning the Nature of Law*

WHETHER LAW IS ALWAYS DIRECTED TO THE COMMON GOOD?

Objection 1. It would seem that law is not always directed to the common good as to its end. For it belongs to law to command and to forbid. But commands are directed to certain individual goods. Therefore the end of law is not always the common good.

Obj. 2. Further, law directs man in his actions. But human actions are concerned with particular matters. Therefore law is directed to some particular good.

Obj. 3. Further, Isidore says: *If law is based on reason, whatever is based on reason will be a law.* But reason is the foundation not only of what is ordained to the common good, but also of that which is directed to private good. Therefore law is not directed only to the good of all, but also to the private good of an individual.

On the contrary, Isidore says that *laws are enacted for no private profit but for the common benefit of the citizens.*

I answer that, As we have stated above, law belongs to that which is a principle of human acts, because it is their rule and measure. Now as reason is a principle of human acts, so in reason itself there is something which is the principle in respect of all the rest. Hence to this principle chiefly and mainly law must needs be referred. Now the first principle in practical matters, which are the object of the practical reason, is the last end: and the last end of human life is happiness or beatitude, as we have stated above. Consequently, law must needs concern itself mainly

*From *Summa Theologica, The Basic Writings of Saint Thomas Aquinas,* ed. Anton C. Pegis (New York: Random House, Inc., 1945), Vol. II, pp. 744–47, 777–78, 791–95. Copyright © 1945 Random House, Inc. Reprinted by permission of the publisher and The Very Rev. Prior Provincial O. P., St. Dominic's Priory, London. Footnotes appearing in the original of this edition are omitted.

with the order that is in beatitude. Moreover, since every part is ordained to the whole as the imperfect to the perfect, and since one man is a part of the perfect community, law must needs concern itself properly with the order directed to universal happiness. Therefore the Philosopher, in the above definition of legal matters mentions both happiness and the body politic, since he says that we call these legal matters *just which are adapted to produce and preserve happiness and its parts for the body politic.* For the state is a perfect community, as he says in *Politics* i.

Now, in every genus, that which belongs to it chiefly is the principle of the others, and the others belong to that genus according to some order towards that thing. Thus fire, which is chief among hot things, is the cause of heat in mixed bodies, and these are said to be hot in so far as they have a share of fire. Consequently, since law is chiefly ordained to the common good, any other precept in regard to some individual work must needs be devoid of the nature of a law, save in so far as it regards the common good. Therefore every law is ordained to the common good.

Reply Obj. 1. A command denotes the application of a law to matters regulated by law. Now the order to the common good, at which law aims, is applicable to particular ends. And in this way commands are given even concerning particular matters.

Reply Obj. 2. Actions are indeed concerned with particular matters, but those particular matters are referable to the common good, not as to a common genus or species, but as to a common final cause, according as the common good is said to be the common end.

Reply Obj. 3. Just as nothing stands firm with regard to the speculative reason except that which is traced back to the first indemonstrable principles, so nothing stands firm with regard to the practical reason, unless it be directed to the last end which is the common good. Now whatever stands to reason in this sense has the nature of a law.

WHETHER THE REASON OF ANY MAN IS COMPETENT TO MAKE LAWS?

Objection 1. It would seem that the reason of any man is competent to make laws. For the Apostle says (*Rom.* ii. 14) that *when the Gentiles, who have not the law, do by nature those things that are of the law, ... they are a law to themselves.* Now he says this of all in general. Therefore anyone can make a law for himself.

Obj. 2. Further, as the Philosopher says, *the intention of the lawgiver is to lead men to virtue.* But every man can lead another to virtue. Therefore the reason of any man is competent to make laws.

Obj. 3. Further, just as the sovereign of a state governs the state, so every father of a family governs his household. But the sovereign of a state can make laws for the state. Therefore every father of a family can make laws for his household.

On the contrary, Isodore says, and the *Decretals* repeat: *A law is an ordinance of the people, whereby something is sanctioned by the Elders together with the Commonalty.* Therefore not everyone can make laws.

I answer that, A law, properly speaking, regards first and foremost the order to the common good. Now to order anything to the common good belongs either to the whole people, or to someone who is the vicegerent of the whole people. Hence the making of a law belongs either to the whole people or to a public personage who has care of the whole people; for in all other matters the directing of anything to the end concerns him to whom the end belongs.

Reply Obj. 1. As we stated above, a law is in a person not only as in one that rules, but also, by participation, as in one that is ruled. In the latter way, each one is a law to himself, in so far as he shares the direction that he receives from one who rules him. Hence the same text goes on: *Who show the work of the law written in their hearts* (*Rom.* ii. 15).

Reply Obj. 2. A private person cannot lead another to virtue efficaciously; for he can only advise, and if his advice be not taken, it has no coercive power, such as the law should have, in order to prove an efficacious inducement to virtue, as the Philosopher says. But this coercive power is vested in the whole people or in some public personage, to whom it belongs to inflict penalties, as we shall state further on. Therefore the framing of laws belongs to him alone.

Reply Obj. 3. As one man is a part of the household, so a household is a part of the state; and the state is a perfect community, according to *Politics* i. Therefore, just as the good of one man is not the last end, but is ordained to the common good, so too the good of one household is ordained to the good of a single state, which is a perfect community. Consequently, he that governs a family can indeed make certain commands of ordinances, but not such as to have properly the nature of law.

WHETHER PROMULGATION IS ESSENTIAL TO LAW?

Objection 1. It would seem that promulgation is not essential to law. For the natural law, above all, has the character of law. But the natural law needs no promulgation. Therefore it is not essential to law that it be promulgated.

Obj. 2. Further, it belongs properly to law to bind one to do or not to do something. But the obligation of fulfilling a law touches not only those in whose presence it is promulgated, but also others. Therefore promulgation is not essential to law.

Obj. 3. Further, the binding force of law extends even to the future, since *laws are binding in matters of the future,* as the jurists say. But promulgation concerns those who are present. Therefore it is not essential to law.

On the contrary, It is laid down in the *Decretals* that *laws are established when they are promulgated.*

I answer that, As was stated above, a law is imposed on others as a rule and measure. Now a rule or measure is imposed by being applied to those who are to be ruled and measured by it. Therefore, in order that a law obtain the binding force which is proper to a law, it must needs be applied to the men who have to be ruled by it. But such application is made by its being made known to them by promulgation. Therefore promulgation is necessary for law to obtain its force.

Thus, from the four preceding articles, the definition of law may be gathered. Law is nothing else than an ordinance of reason for the common good, promulgated by him who has the care of the community.

Reply Obj. 1. The natural law is promulgated by the very fact that God instilled it into man's mind so as to be known by him naturally.

Reply Obj. 2. Those who are not present when a law is promulgated are bound to observe the law, in so far as it is made known or can be made known to them by others, after it has been promulgated.

Reply Obj. 3. The promulgation that takes place in the present extends to future time by reason of the durability of written characters, by which means it is continually promulgated. Hence Isidore says that *lex* [*law*] *is derived from legere* [*to read*] *because it is written.*

WHETHER THE NATURAL LAW IS THE SAME IN ALL MEN?

Objection 1. It would seem that the natural law is not the same in all. For it is stated in the *Decretals* that *the natural law is that which is contained in the Law and the Gospel.* But this is not common to all men, because, as it is written (*Rom.* x. 16), *all do not obey the Gospel.* Therefore the natural law is not the same in all men.

Obj. 2. Further, *Things which are according to the law are said to be just,* as is stated in *Ethics* v. But it is stated in the same book that nothing is so just for all as not to be subject to change in regard to some men. Therefore even the natural law is not the same in all men.

Obj. 3. Further, as was stated above, to the natural law belongs everything to which a man is inclined according to his nature. Now different men are naturally inclined to different things,— some to the desire of pleasures, others to the desire of honors, and other men to other things. Therefore, there is not one natural law for all.

On the contrary, Isidore says: *The natural law is common to all nations.*

I answer that, As we have stated above, to the natural law belong those things to which a man is inclined naturally; and among these it is proper to man to be inclined to act according to reason. Now it belongs to the reason to proceed from what is common to what is proper, as is stated in *Physics* i. The speculative reason, however, is differently situated, in this matter, from the prac-

tical reason. For, since the speculative reason is concerned chiefly with necessary things, which cannot be otherwise than they are, its proper conclusions, like the universal principles, contain the truth without fail. The practical reason, on the other hand, is concerned with contingent matters, which is the domain of human actions; and, consequently, although there is necessity in the common principles, the more we descend towards the particular, the more frequently we encounter defects. Accordingly, then, in speculative matters truth is the same in all men, both as to principles and as to conclusions; although the truth is not known to all as regards the conclusions, but only as regards the principles which are called *common notions.* But in matters of action, truth or practical rectitude is not the same for all as to what is particular, but only as to the common principles; and where there is the same rectitude in relation to particulars, it is not equally known to all.

It is therefore evident that, as regards the common principles whether of speculative or of practical reason, truth or rectitude is the same for all, and is equally known by all. But as to the proper conclusions of the speculative reason, the truth is the same for all, but it is not equally known to all. Thus, it is true for all that the three angles of a triangle are together equal to two right angles, although it is not known to all. But as to the proper conclusions of the practical reason, neither is the truth or rectitude the same for all, nor where it is the same, is it equally known by all. Thus, it is right and true for all to act according to reason, and from this principle it follows, as a proper conclusion, that goods entrusted to another should be restored to their owner. Now this is true for the majority of cases. But it may happen in a particular case that it would be injurious, and therefore unreasonable, to restore goods held in trust; for instance, if they are claimed for the purpose of fighting against one's country. And this principle will be found to fail the more, according as we descend further towards the particular, for example, if one were to say that goods held in trust should be restored with such and such a guarantee, or in such and such a way; because the greater the number of conditions added, the greater the number of ways in which the principle may fail, so that it be not right to restore or not to restore.

Consequently, we must say that the natural law, as to the first common principles, is the same for all, both as to rectitude and as to knowledge. But as to certain more particular aspects, which are conclusions, as it were, of those common principles, it is the same for all in the majority of cases, both as to rectitude and as to knowledge; and yet in some few cases, it may fail, both as to rectitude, by reason of certain obstacles (just as natures subject to generation and corruption fail in some few cases because of some obstacle), and as to knowledge, since in some the reason is perverted by passion, or evil habit, or an evil disposition of nature. Thus at one time theft, although it is expressly contrary to the natural law, was not considered wrong among the Germans, as Julius Cæsar relates.

Reply Obj. 1. The meaning of the sentence quoted is not that whatever is contained in the Law and the Gospel belongs to the natural law, since they contain many things that are above nature; but that whatever belongs to the natural law is fully contained in them. Therefore Gratian, after saying that *the natural law is what is contained in the Law and the Gospel,* adds at once, by way of example, *by which everyone is commanded to do to others as he would be done by.*

Reply Obj. 2. The saying of the Philosopher is to be understood of things that are naturally just, not as common principles, but as conclusions drawn from them, having rectitude in the majority of cases, but failing in a few.

Reply Obj. 3. Just as in man reason rules and commands the other powers, so all the natural inclinations belonging to the other powers must needs be directed according to reason. Therefore it is universally right for all men that all their inclinations should be directed according to reason.

WHETHER IT BELONGS TO HUMAN LAW TO REPRESS ALL VICES?

Objection 1. It would seem that it belongs to human law to repress all vices. For Isidore says that *laws were made in order that, in fear thereof, man's audacity might be held in check.* But it would not be held in check sufficiently unless all evils were repressed by law. Therefore human law should repress all evils.

Obj. 2. Further, the intention of the lawgiver is to make the citizens virtuous. But a man cannot be virtuous unless he forbear from all kinds of vice. Therefore it belongs to human law to repress all vices.

Obj. 3. Further, human law is derived from the natural law, as was stated above. But all vices are contrary to the law of nature. Therefore human law should repress all vices.

On the contrary, We read in *De Libero Arbitrio,* i: *It seems to me that the law which is written for the governing of the people rightly permits these things, and that divine providence punishes them.* But divine providence punishes nothing but vices. Therefore human law rightly allows some vices, by not repressing them.

I answer that, As was stated above, law is framed as a rule or measure of human acts. Now a measure should be homogeneous with that which it measures, as is stated in *Metaph.* x., since different things are measured by different measures. Therefore laws imposed on men should also be in keeping with their condition, for, as Isidore says, law should be *possible both according to nature, and according to the customs of the country.* Now the ability or facility of action is due to an interior habit or disposition, since the same thing is not possible to one who has not a virtuous habit, as is possible to one who has. Thus the same thing is not possible to a child as to a full-grown man, and for which reason the law for children is not the same as for adults, since many things are permitted to children, which in an adult are punished by law or at any rate are open to blame. In like manner, many things are permissible to men not perfect in virtue, which would be intolerable in a virtuous man.

Now human law is framed for the multitude of human beings, the majority of whom are not perfect in virtue. Therefore human laws do not forbid all vices, from which the virtuous abstain, but only the more grievous vices, from which it is possible for the majority to abstain; and chiefly those that are injurious to others, without the prohibition of which human society could not be maintained. Thus human law prohibits murder, theft and the like.

Reply Obj. 1. Audacity seems to refer to the assailing of others. Consequently, it belongs to those sins chiefly whereby one's neighbor is injured. These sins are forbidden by human law, as was stated.

Reply Obj. 2. The purpose of human law is to lead men to virtue, not suddenly, but gradually. Therefore it does not lay upon the multitude of imperfect men the burdens of those who are already virtuous, to wit, that they should abstain from all evil. Otherwise these imperfect ones, being unable to bear such precepts, would break out into yet greater evils. As it is written (*Prov.* xxx.33): *He that violently bloweth his nose, bringeth out blood;* again (*Matt.* ix. 17): if *new wine,* that is, precepts of a perfect life, is *put into old bottles,* that is, into imperfect men, *the bottles break, and the wine runneth out,* that is, the precepts are despised, and those men, from contempt, break out into evils worse still.

Reply Obj. 3. The natural law is a participation in us of the eternal law, while human law falls short of the eternal law. For Augustine says: *The law which is framed for the government of states allows and leaves unpunished many things that are punished by divine providence. Nor, if this law does not attempt to do everything, is this a reason why it should be blamed for what it does.* Therefore, human law likewise does not prohibit everything that is forbidden by the natural law.

WHETHER HUMAN LAW BINDS A MAN IN CONSCIENCE?

Objection 1. It would seem that human law does not bind a man in conscience. For an inferior power cannot impose its law on the judgment of a higher power. But the power of man, which frames human law, is beneath the divine power. Therefore human law cannot impose its precept on a divine judgment, such as is the judgment of conscience.

Obj. 2. Further, the judgment of conscience depends chiefly on the commandments of God. But sometimes God's commandments are made void by human laws, according to *Matt.* xv. 6: *You have made void the commandment of God for your tradition.* Therefore human law does not bind a man in conscience.

Obj. 3. Further, human laws often bring loss of character and injury on man, according to *Isa.* x. 1, 2: *Woe to them that make wicked laws, and when they write, write injustice; to oppress the poor in judgment, and do violence to the cause of the humble of My people.* But it is lawful for anyone to avoid oppression and violence. Therefore human laws do not bind man in conscience.

On the contrary, It is written (*I Pet.* ii. 19): *This is thanksworthy, if for conscience . . . a man endure sorrows, suffering wrongfully.*

I answer that, Laws framed by man are either just or unjust. If they be just, they have the power of binding in conscience from the eternal law whence they are derived, according to *Prov.* viii. 15: *By Me kings reign, and lawgivers decree just things.* Now laws are said to be just, both from the end (when, namely, they are ordained to the common good), from their author (that is to say, when the law that is made does not exceed the power of the lawgiver), and from their form (when, namely, burdens are laid on the subjects according to an equality of proportion and with a view to the common good). For, since one man is a part of the community, each man, in all that he is and has, belongs to the community; just as a part, in all that it is belongs to the whole. So, too, nature inflicts a loss on the part in order to save the whole; so that for this reason such laws as these, which impose proportionate burdens, are just and binding in conscience, and are legal laws.

On the other hand, laws may be unjust in two ways: first, by being contrary to human good, through being opposed to the things mentioned above:—either in respect of the end, as when an authority imposes on his subjects burdensome laws, conducive, not to the common good, but rather to his own cupidity or vainglory; or in respect of the author, as when a man makes a law that goes beyond the power committed to him; or in respect of the form, as when burdens are imposed unequally on the community, although with a view to the common good. Such are acts of violence rather than laws, because, as Augustine says, *a law that is not just seems to be no law at all.* Therefore, such laws do not bind in conscience, except perhaps in order to avoid scandal or disturbance, for which cause a man should even yield his right, according to *Matt.* v. 40, 41: *If a man . . . take away thy coat, let go thy cloak also unto him; and whosoever will force thee one mile, go with him other two.*

Secondly, laws may be unjust through being opposed to the divine good. Such are the laws of tyrants inducing to idolatry, or to anything else contrary to the divine law. Laws of this kind must in no way be observed, because, as is stated in *Acts* v. 29, *we ought to obey God rather than men.*

Reply Obj. 1. As the Apostle says (*Rom.* xiii. 1, 2), all human power is from God . . . *therefore he that resisteth the power,* in matters that are within its scope, *resisteth the ordinance of God;* so that he becomes guilty in conscience.

Reply Obj. 2. This argument is true of laws that are contrary to the commandments of God, which is beyond the scope of [human] power.

Therefore in such matters human law should not be obeyed.

Reply Obj. 3. This argument is true of a law that inflicts an unjust burden on its subjects. Furthermore, the power that man holds from God does not extend to this. Hence neither in such matters is man bound to obey the law, provided he avoid giving scandal or inflicting a more grievous injury.

ERNEST BARKER

Natural Law and English Positivism*

There were two ways in which the theory of natural law affected American thought and action. The first way was that of destruction. It served as a charge of powder which blasted the connection with Great Britain and cleared the way for the Declaration of Independence. The second way was that of construction. It served as a foundation for the building of new constitutions in the independent colonies from 1776 onwards, and for the addition to those constitutions (or rather to some of them) of an entrance-hall or façade called a declaration of rights. The idea of nature can be revolutionary; but it can also promote and support evolution. It worked in both ways in the American colonies. First it made revolution; and then, when that was done, it fostered evolution. In order to understand its accomplishment, we must pause to consider its principles and to examine its potentialities.

We may begin by noting (for it is a fact of crucial importance) that the English thinkers and lawyers of the eighteenth century have little regard for natural law and natural rights. Indeed, it may be said that natural law is generally repugnant to the genius of English legal thought, generally busied with a 'common law' which, however common, is still peculiar, and anyhow is sufficiently actual, sufficiently practical, sufficiently definite, to suit the English temper. To Burke any speech of natural law and natural rights is metaphysics, and not politics. To Blackstone—though he is inconsistent, writing in one way when he theorises on the nature of laws in general, and in another when he comments on the laws of England—the law of nature is not a concern of English courts, and may therefore be treated, for their purposes, as nonexistent. To Bentham, when he wrote the *Fragment on Government* in 1776, the law of nature was 'nothing but a phrase': its natural tendency was 'to impel a man, by the force of conscience, to rise up in arms against any law whatever that he happens not to like'; and a far better clue—indeed 'the only clue to guide a man through these straits'—was the principle of utility.

The general view of the English thinkers of the period may be resumed in two propositions. In

*From *Traditions of Civility* by Sir Ernest Barker (London: Cambridge University Press, 1948), pp. 310–12. Reprinted by permission of the publisher.

the first place, law is a body of rules which is recognised and enforced in courts of law; and it is simply that body of rules. Since the courts of law recognise and enforce both the judge-made law of tradition and the statute law enacted by parliament, law is these two things, and only these two things. Since, again, the judge-made law of tradition may be regarded as an *opus perfectum* (so, at any rate, Blackstone seems to think), and since law now grows only or mainly by the addition of the statutes enacted by parliament—since, in a word, it is parliament only which now gives new rules to the judges, either by amending the law of the past, both judge-made and parliament-made, or by enacting fresh law *de novo*—parliament must be acknowledged as 'the sovereign legislative', maker and author supreme of all law, an uncontrollable authority acting by its own motion, 'as essential to the body politic' (so a member of parliament declared) 'as the Deity to religion'. Such is the gist and sweep of the first of the two propositions. The second proposition is similar, and may be said to be consequential. It is a proposition affirming that constitutional law is not in any way different in kind from the rest of the law, but is merely a part of the general law. It is simply that part of the general law which, as Paley says, 'regulates the form of the legislative'. Being part of the general law, it is subject, like all other law, to the control of the sovereign legislature—which thus regulates itself and determines its own form. You can-

not therefore distinguish between constitutional law and ordinary law, or say that the one is made and amended by one process and the other by another. In origin, and in kind, the two are simply identical; and they are under the same control. You cannot say that a law is unconstitutional; if it is a law—that is to say, if it is made by parliament—it is necessarily constitutional. In a word, the legal is also the constitutional: 'the terms *constitutional* and *unconstitutional*', as Paley writes, 'mean the legal and illegal'.

In the light of these two propositions we may now turn to natural law, and note how it differs from English law in regard to both. The origin of the idea of natural law may be ascribed to an old and indefeasible movement of the human mind (we may trace it already in the *Antigone* of Sophocles) which impels it towards the notion of an eternal and immutable justice; a justice which human authority expresses, or ought to express— but does not make; a justice which human authority may fail to express—and must pay the penalty for failing to express by the diminution, or even the forfeiture, of its power to command. This justice is conceived as being the higher or ultimate law, proceeding from the nature of the universe from the Being of God and the reason of man. It follows that law—in the sense of the law of the last resort—is somehow above lawmaking. It follows that lawmakers, after all, are somehow under and subject to law.

JOHN AUSTIN

A Positivist Conception of Law*

LECTURE I

The matter of jurisprudence is positive law: law, simply and strictly so called: or law set by political superiors to political inferiors. But positive law (or law, simply and strictly so called) is often confounded with objects to which it is related by *resemblance,* and with objects to which it is related in the way of *analogy*: with objects which are *also* signified, *properly* and *improperly,* by the large and vague expression *law.* To obviate the difficulties springing from that confusion, I begin my projected Course with determining the province of jurisprudence, or with distinguishing the matter of jurisprudence from those various related objects: trying to define the subject of which I intend to treat, before I endeavour to analyse its numerous and complicated parts.

A law, in the most general and comprehensive acceptation in which the term, in its literal meaning, is employed, may be said to be a rule laid down for the guidance of an intelligent being by an intelligent being having power over him. Under this definition are concluded, and without impropriety, several species. It is necessary to define accurately the line of demarcation which separates these species from one another, as much mistiness and intricacy has been infused into the science of jurisprudence by their being confounded or not clearly distinguished. In the comprehensive sense above indicated, or in the largest meaning which it has, without extension by metaphor or analogy, the term *law* embraces the following objects:—Laws set by God to his human creatures, and laws set by men to men.

The whole or a portion of the laws set by God to men is frequently styled the law of nature, or natural law: being, in truth, the only natural law of which it is possible to speak without a meta-

phor, or without a blending of objects which ought to be distinguished broadly. But, rejecting the appellation Law of Nature as ambiguous and misleading, I name those laws or rules, as considered collectively or in a mass, the *Divine law,* or the *law of God.*

Laws set by men to men are of two leading or principal classes: classes which are often blended, although they differ extremely; and which, for that reason, should be severed precisely, and opposed distinctly and conspicuously.

Of the laws or rules set by men to men, some are established by *political* superiors, sovereign and subject: by persons exercising supreme and subordinate *government,* in independent nations, or independent political societies. The aggregate of the rules thus established, or some aggregate forming a portion of that aggregate, is the appropriate matter of jurisprudence, general or particular. To the aggregate of the rules thus established, or to some aggregate forming a portion of that aggregate, the term *law,* as used simply and strictly, is exclusively applied. But, as contradistinguished to *natural* law, or to the law of *nature* (meaning, by those expressions, the law of God), the aggregate of the rules, established by political superiors, is frequently styled *positive* law, or law existing *by position.* As contradistinguished to the rules which I style *positive morality,* and on which I shall touch immediately, the aggregate of the rules, established by political superiors, may also be marked commodiously with the name of *positive law.* For the sake, then, of getting a name brief and distinctive at once, and agreeable to frequent usage, I style that aggregate of rules, or any portion of that aggregate, *positive law*: though rules, which are *not* established by political superiors, are also *positive,* or exist *by position,* if they be rules or laws, in the proper signification of the term.

*From *The Province of Jurisprudence Determined,* Selections from Lectures I and VI. First published in 1832.

Though *some* of the laws or rules, which are set by men to men, are established by political superiors, *others* are *not* established by political superiors, or are *not* established by political superiors, in that capacity or character.

Closely analogous to human laws of this second class, are a set of objects frequently but *improperly* termed *laws,* being rules set and enforced by *mere opinion,* that is, by the opinions or sentiments held or felt by an indeterminate body of men in regard to human conduct. Instances of such a use of the term *law* are the expressions—'The law of honour'; 'The law set by fashion'; and rules of this species constitute much of what is usually termed 'International law'.

The aggregate of human laws properly so called belonging to the second of the classes above mentioned, with the aggregate of objects *improperly* but by *close analogy* termed laws, I place together in a common class, and denote them by the term *positive morality.* The name *morality* severs them from *positive law,* while the epithet *positive* disjoins them from the *law of God.* And to the end of obviating confusion, it is necessary or expedient that they *should* be disjoined from the latter by that distinguishing epithet. For the name *morality* (or *morals*), when standing unqualified or alone, denotes indifferently either of the following objects: namely, positive morality *as it is,* or without regard to its merits; and positive morality *as it would be,* if it conformed to the law of God, and were, therefore, deserving of *approbation.*

Besides the various sorts of rules which are included in the literal acceptation of the term law, and those which are by a close and striking analogy, though improperly, termed laws, there are numerous applications of the term law, which rest upon a slender analogy and are merely metaphorical or figurative. Such is the case when we talk of *laws* observed by the lower animals; of *laws* regulating the growth or decay of vegetables; of *laws* determining the movements of inanimate bodies or masses. For where *intelligence* is not, or where it is too bounded to take the name of *reason,* and, therefore, is too bounded to conceive the purpose of a law, there is not the *will* which law can work on, or which duty can incite or restrain. Yet through these misapplications of a *name,* flagrant as the metaphor is, has the field

of jurisprudence and morals been deluged with muddy speculation.

Having suggested the *purpose* of my attempt to determine the province of jurisprudence: to distinguish positive law, the appropriate matter of jurisprudence, from the various objects to which it is related by resemblance, and to which it is related, nearly or remotely, by a strong or slender analogy: I shall now state the essentials of *a law* or *rule* (taken with the largest signification which can be given to the term *properly*).

Every *law* or *rule* (taken with the largest signification which can be given to the term *properly*) is a *command.* Or, rather, laws or rules, properly so called, are a *species* of commands.

Now, since the term *command* comprises the term *law,* the first is the simpler as well as the larger of the two. But, simple as it is, it admits of explanation. And, since it is the *key* to the sciences of jurisprudence and morals, its meaning should be analysed with precision.

Accordingly, I shall endeavour, in the first instance, to analyse the meaning of *'command'*: an analysis which I fear, will task the patience of my hearers, but which they will bear with cheerfulness, or, at least, with resignation, if they consider the difficulty of performing it. The elements of a science are precisely the parts of it which are explained least easily. Terms that are the largest, and, therefore, the simplest of a series, are without equivalent expressions into which we can resolve them *concisely.* And when we endeavour to *define* them, or to translate them into terms which we suppose are better understood, we are forced upon awkward and tedious circumlocutions.

If you express or intimate a wish that I shall do or forbear from some act, and if you will visit me with an evil in case I comply not with your wish, the *expression* or *intimation* of your wish is a *command.* A command is distinguished from other significations of desire, not by the style in which the desire is signified, but by the power and the purpose of the party commanding to inflict an evil or pain in case the desire be disregarded. If you cannot or will not harm me in case I comply not with your wish, the expression of your wish is not a command, although you utter your wish in imperative phrase. If you are able and willing to harm me in case I comply not with your wish, the expression of your wish amounts to a command, although you are prompted by a spirit of courtesy to utter it in the shape of a request. *'Preces* erant, sed *quibus contradici non posset.'* Such is the language of Tacitus, when speaking of a petition by the soldiery to a son and lieutenant of Vespasian.

A command, then, is a signification of desire. But a command is distinguished from other significations of desire by this peculiarity: that the party to whom it is directed is liable to evil from the other, in case he comply not with the desire.

Being liable to evil from you if I comply not with a wish which you signify, I am *bound* or *obliged* by your command, or I lie under a *duty* to obey it. If, in spite of that evil in prospect, I comply not with the wish which you signify, I am said to disobey your command, or to violate the duty which it imposes.

Command and duty are, therefore, correlative terms: the meaning denoted by each being implied or supposed by the other. Or (changing the expression) wherever a duty lies, a command has been signified; and whenever a command is signified, a duty is imposed.

Concisely expressed, the meaning of the correlative expressions is this: He who will inflict an evil in case his desire be disregarded, utters a command by expressing or intimating his desire. He who is liable to the evil in case he disregard the desire, is bound or obliged by the command.

The evil which will probably be incurred in case a command be disobeyed or (to use an equivalent expression) in case a duty be broken, is frequently called a *sanction,* or an *enforcement of obedience.* Or (varying the phrase) the command or the duty is said to be *sanctioned* or *enforced* by the chance of incurring the evil.

Considered as thus abstracted from the command and the duty which it enforces, the evil to be incurred by disobedience is frequently styled a *punishment.* But, as punishments, strictly so called, are only a *class* of sanctions, the term is too narrow to express the meaning adequately.

I observe that Dr. Paley, in his analysis of the term *obligation,* lays much stress upon the *violence* of the motive to compliance. In so far as I can gather a meaning from his loose and inconsistent statement, his meaning appears to be this: that unless the motive to compliance be *violent* or *intense,* the expression or intimation of a wish is not a *command,* nor does the party to whom it is directed lie under a *duty* to regard it.

If he means, by a *violent* motive, a motive operating with certainty, his proposition is manifestly false. The greater the evil to be incurred in case the wish be disregarded, and the greater the chance of incurring it on that same event, the greater, no doubt, is the *chance* that the wish will *not* be disregarded. But no conceivable motive will *certainly* determine to compliance, or no conceivable motive will render obedience inevitable. If Paley's proposition be true, in the sense which I have now ascribed to it, commands and duties are simply impossible. Or, reducing his proposition to absurdity by a consequence as manifestly false, commands and duties are possible, but are never disobeyed or broken.

If he means by a *violent* motive, an evil which inspires fear, his meaning is simply this: that the party bound by a command is bound by the prospect of an evil. For that which is not feared is not apprehended as an evil: or (changing the shape of the expression) is not an evil in prospect.

The truth is, that the magnitude of the eventual evil, and the magnitude of the chance of incurring it, are foreign to the matter in question. The greater the eventual evil, and the greater the chance of incurring it, the greater is the efficacy of the command, and the greater is the strength of the obligation: Or (substituting expressions exactly equivalent), the greater is the *chance* that the command will be obeyed, and that the duty will not be broken. But where there is the smallest chance of incurring the smallest evil, the expression of a wish amounts to a command, and, therefore, imposes a duty. The sanction, if you will, is feeble or insufficient; but still there *is* a sanction, and, therefore, a duty and a command.

By some celebrated writers (by Locke, Bentham, and, I think, Paley), the term *sanction,* or *enforcement of obedience,* is applied to conditional good as well as to conditional evil: to reward as to punishment. But, with all my habitual veneration for the names of Locke and Bentham, I think that this extension of the term is pregnant with confusion and perplexity.

Rewards are, indisputably, *motives* to comply with the wishes of others. But to talk of commands and duties as *sanctioned* or *enforced* by rewards, or to talk of rewards as *obliging* or *constraining* to obedience, is surely a wide departure from the established meaning of the terms.

If *you* expressed a desire that *I* should render a service, and if you proffered a reward as the motive or inducement to render it, *you* would scarcely be said to *command* the service, nor should *I,* in ordinary language, be *obliged* to render it. In ordinary language, *you* would *promise* me a reward, on condition of my rendering the service, whilst *I* might be *incited* or *persuaded* to render it by the hope of obtaining the reward.

Again: If a law hold out a *reward* as an inducement to do some act, an eventual *right* is conferred, and not an *obligation* imposed, upon those who shall act accordingly: The *imperative* part of the law being addressed or directed to the party whom it requires to *render* the reward.

In short, I am determined or inclined to comply with the wish of another, by the fear of disadvantage or evil. I am also determined or inclined to comply with the wish of another, by the hope of advantage or good. But it is only by the chance of incurring *evil,* that I am *bound* or *obliged* to compliance. It is only by conditional *evil,* that duties are *sanctioned* or *enforced.* It is the power and the purpose of inflicting eventual *evil,* and *not* the power and the purpose of imparting eventual *good,* which gives to the expression of a wish the name of a *command.*

If we put *reward* into the import of the term *sanction,* we must engage in a toilsome struggle with the current of ordinary speech; and shall often slide unconsciously, notwithstanding our efforts to the contrary, into the narrower and customary meaning.

It appears, then, from what has been premised, that the ideas or notions comprehended by the term *command* are the following. 1. A wish or desire conceived by a rational being, that another rational being shall do or forbear. 2. An evil to proceed from the former, and to be incurred by the latter, in case the latter comply not with the wish. 3. An expression or intimation of the wish by words or other signs.

It also appears from what has been premised, that *command, duty,* and *sanction* are inseparably connected terms: that each embraces the same ideas as the others, though each denotes those ideas in a peculiar order or series.

'A wish conceived by one, and expressed or intimated to another, with an evil to be inflicted and incurred in case the wish be disregarded,' are signified directly and indirectly by each of the three expressions. Each is the name of the same complex notion.

But when I am talking *directly* of the expression or intimation of the wish, I employ the term *command*: The expression or intimation of the wish being presented *prominently* to my hearer; whilst the evil to be incurred, with the chance of incurring it, are kept (if I may so express myself) in the background of my picture.

When I am talking *directly* of the chance of incurring the evil, or (changing the expression) of the liability or obnoxiousness to the evil, I employ the term *duty,* or the term *obligation*: The liability or obnoxiousness to the evil being put foremost, and the rest of the complex notion being signified implicitly.

When I am talking *immediately* of the evil itself, I employ the term *sanction,* or a term of the like import: The evil to be incurred being signified directly; whilst the obnoxiousness to that evil, with the expression or intimation of the wish, are indicated indirectly or obliquely.

To those who are familiar with the language of logicians (language unrivalled for brevity, distinctness, and precision), I can express my meaning accurately in a breath:—Each of the three terms *signifies* the same notion; but each *denotes* a different part of that notion, and *connotes* the residue.

Commands are of two species. Some are *laws* or *rules.* The others have not acquired an appropriate name, nor does language afford an expression which will mark them briefly and precisely. I must, therefore, note them as well as I can by the ambiguous and inexpressive name of 'occasional or particular commands'.

The term *laws* or *rules* being not unfrequently applied to occasional or particular commands, it is hardly possible to describe a line of separation which shall consist in every respect with established forms of speech. But the distinction between laws and particular commands may, I think, be stated in the following manner.

By every command, the party to whom it is directed is obliged to do or to forbear.

Now where it obliges *generally* to acts or forbearances of a *class,* a command is a law or rule. But where it obliges to a *specific* act or forbearance, or to acts or forbearances which it determines *specifically* or *individually,* a command is occasional or particular. In other words, a class or description of acts is determined by a law or rule, and acts of that class or description are enjoined or forbidden generally. But where a command is occasional or particular, the act or acts, which the command enjoins or forbids, are assigned or determined by their specific or individual natures as well as by the class or description to which they belong.

The statement which I have given in abstract expressions I will not endeavour to illustrate by apt examples.

If you command your servant to go on a given errand, or *not* to leave your house on a given evening, or to rise at such an hour on such a morning, or to rise at that hour during the next week or month, the command is occasional or particular. For the act or acts enjoined or forbidden are specially determined or assigned.

But if you command him *simply* to rise at that hour, or to rise at that hour *always,* or to rise at that hour *till further orders,* it may be said, with propriety, that you lay down a *rule* for the guidance of your servant's conduct. For no specific act is assigned by the command, but the command obliges him generally to acts of a determined class.

If a regiment be ordered to attack or defend a post, or to quell a riot, or to march from their present quarters, the command is occasional or particular. But an order to exercise daily till further orders shall be given would be called a *general* order, and *might* be called a *rule.*

If Parliament prohibited simply the exportation of corn, either for a given period or indefinitely, it would establish a law or rule: a *kind* or *sort* of acts being determined by the command, and acts of that kind or sort being *generally* forbidden. But an order issued by Parliament to meet an impending scarcity, and stopping the exportation of corn *then shipped and in port,* would not be a law or rule, though issued by the sovereign legislature. The order regarding exclusively a specified quantity of corn, the negative acts or forbearances, enjoined by the command, would be determined specifically or individually by the determinate nature of their subject.

As issued by a sovereign legislature, and as wearing the form of a law, the order which I have now imagined would probably be *called* a law. And hence the difficulty of drawing a distinct boundary between laws and occasional commands.

Again: An act which is not an offence, according to the existing law, moves the sovereign to displeasure: and, though the authors of the act are legally innocent or unoffending, the sovereign commands that they shall be punished. As enjoining a specific punishment in that specific case, and as not enjoining generally acts or forbearances of a class, the order uttered by the sovereign is not a law or rule.

Whether such an order would be *called* a law, seems to depend upon circumstances which are purely immaterial: immaterial, that is, with reference to the present purpose, though material with reference to others. If made by a sovereign assembly deliberately, and with the forms of legislation, it would probably be called a law. If uttered by an absolute monarch, without deliberation or ceremony, it would scarcely be confounded with acts of legislation, and would be styled an arbitrary command. Yet, on either of these suppositions, its nature would be the same. It would not be a law or rule, but an occasional or particular command of the sovereign One or Number.

To conclude with an example which best illustrates the distinction, and which shows the importance of the distinction most conspicuously, *judicial commands* are commonly occasional or particular, although the commands which they are calculated to enforce are commonly laws or rules.

For instance, the lawgiver commands that thieves shall be hanged. A specific theft and a specified thief being given, the judge commands that the thief shall be hanged, agreeably to the command of the lawgiver.

Now the lawgiver determines a class or description of acts; prohibits acts of the class generally and indefinitely; and commands, with the like generality, that punishment shall follow transgression. The command of the lawgiver is, therefore, a law or rule. But the command of the judge is occasional or particular. For he orders a specific punishment, as the consequence of a specific offence.

According to the line of separation which I have now attempted to describe, a law and a particular command are distinguished thus:—Acts or forbearances of a *class* are enjoined *generally* by the former. Acts determined specifically, are enjoined or forbidden by the latter.

A different line of separation has been drawn by Blackstone and others. According to Blackstone and others, a law and a particular command are distinguished in the following manner: —A law obliges *generally* the members of the given community, or a law obliges *generally* persons of a given class. A particular command obliges a *single* person, or persons whom it determines *individually.*

That laws and particular commands are not to be distinguished thus, will appear on a moment's reflection.

For, *first,* commands which oblige generally the members of the given community, or commands which oblige generally persons of given classes, are not always laws or rules.

Thus, in the case already supposed; that in which the sovereign commands that all corn actually shipped for exportation be stopped and detained; the command is obligatory upon the whole community, but as it obliges them only to a set of acts individually assigned, it is not a law. Again, suppose the sovereign to issue an order, enforced by penalties, for a general mourning, on occasion of a public calamity. Now, though it is addressed to the community at large, the order is scarcely a rule, in the usual acceptation of the term. For, though it obliges generally the members of the entire community, it obliges to acts which it assigns specifically, instead of obliging generally to acts or forbearances of a class. If the sovereign commanded that *black* should be the dress of his subjects, his command would amount to a law. But if he commanded them to wear it on a specified occasion, his command would be merely particular.

And, *secondly,* a command which obliges exclusively persons individually determined, may amount, notwithstanding, to a law or a rule.

For example, A father may set a *rule* to his child or children: a guardian, to his ward: a master, to his slave or servant. And certain of God's *laws* were as binding on the first man, as they are binding at this hour on the millions who have sprung from his loins.

Most, indeed, of the laws which are established by political superiors, or most of the laws which are simply and strictly so called, oblige generally the members of the political community, or oblige generally persons of a class. To frame a system of duties for every individual of the community, were simply impossible: and if it were possible, it were utterly useless. Most of the laws

established by political superiors are, therefore, *general* in a twofold manner: as enjoining or forbidding generally acts of kinds or sorts; and as binding the whole community, or, at least, whole classes of its members.

But if we suppose that Parliament creates and grants an office, and that Parliament binds the grantee to services of a given description, we suppose a law established by political superiors, and yet exclusively binding a specified or determinate person.

Laws established by political superiors, and exclusively binding specified or determinate persons, are styled, in the language of the Roman jurists, *privilegia.* Though that, indeed, is a name which will hardly denote them distinctly: for, like most of the leading terms in actual systems of law, it is not the name of a definite class of objects, but a heap of heterogeneous objects.[1]

It appears, from what has been premised, that a law, properly so called, may be defined in the following manner.

A law is a command which obliges a person or persons.

But, as contradistinguished or opposed to an occasional or particular command, a law is a command which obliges a person or persons, and obliges *generally* to acts or forbearances of a class.

In language more popular but less distinct and precise, a law is a command which obliges a person or persons to a *course* of conduct.

Laws and other commands are said to proceed from *superiors,* and to bind or oblige *inferiors.* I will, therefore, analyse the meaning of those correlative expressions; and will try to strip them of a certain mystery, by which that simple meaning appears to be obscured.

Superiority is often synonymous with *precedence* or *excellence.* We talk of superiors in rank; of superiors in wealth; of superiors in virtue: comparing certain persons with certain other persons; and meaning that the former precede or excel the latter in rank, in wealth, or in virtue.

But, taken with the meaning wherein I here understand it, the term *superiority* signifies *might*: the power of affecting others with evil or pain, and of forcing them, through fear of that evil, to fashion their conduct to one's wishes.

For example, God is emphatically the *superior* of Man. For his power of affecting us with pain, and of forcing us to comply with his will, is unbounded and resistless.

To a limited extent, the sovereign One or Number is the superior of the subject or citizen: the master, of the slave or servant: the father, of the child.

In short, whoever can *oblige* another to comply with his wishes, is the *superior* of that other, so far as the ability reaches: The party who is obnoxious to the impending evil, being, to that same extent, the *inferior*.

The might or superiority of God, is simple or absolute. But in all or most cases of human superiority, the relation of superior and inferior, and the relation of inferior and superior, are reciprocal. Or (changing the expression) the party who is the superior as viewed from one aspect, is the inferior as viewed from another.

For example, To an indefinite, though limited extent, the monarch is the superior of the governed: his power being commonly sufficient to enforce compliance with his will. But the governed, collectively or in mass, are also the superior of the monarch: who is checked in the abuse of his might by his fear of exciting their anger; and of rousing to active resistance the might which slumbers in the multitude.

A member of a sovereign assembly is the superior of the judge: the judge being bound by the law which proceeds from that sovereign body. But, in his character of citizen or subject, he is the inferior of the judge: the judge being the minister of the law, and armed with the power of enforcing it.

It appears, then, that the term *superiority* (like the terms *duty* and *sanction*) is implied by the term *command*. For superiority is the power of enforcing compliance with a wish: and the expression or intimation of a wish, with the power and the purpose of enforcing it, are the constituent elements of a command.

'That *laws* emanate from *superiors*' is, therefore, an identical proposition. For the meaning which it affects to impart is contained in its subject.

If I mark the peculiar source of a given law, or if I mark the peculiar source of laws of a given class, it is possible that I am saying something which may instruct the hearer. But to affirm of laws universally 'that they flow from *superiors*', or to affirm of laws universally 'that *inferiors* are

bound to obey them,' is the merest tautology and trifling.

Like most of the leading terms in the sciences of jurisprudence and morals, the term *laws* is extremely ambiguous. Taken with the largest signification which can be given to the term properly, *laws* are a species of *commands*. But the term is improperly applied to various objects which have nothing of the imperative character to objects which are *not* commands; and which, therefore, are *not* laws, properly so called.

Accordingly, the proposition 'that laws are commands' must be taken with limitations. Or, rather, we must distinguish the various meanings of the term *laws*; and must restrict the proposition to that class of objects which is embraced by the largest signification that can be given to the term properly.

I have already indicated, and shall hereafter more fully describe, the objects improperly termed laws, which are *not* within the province of jurisprudence (being either rules enforced by opinion and closely analogous to laws properly so called, or being laws so called by a metaphorical application of the term merely). There are other objects improperly termed laws (not being commands) which yet may properly be included within the province of jurisprudence. These I shall endeavour to particularise:—

1. Acts on the part of legislatures to *explain* positive law, can scarcely be called laws, in the proper signification of the term. Working no change in the actual duties of the governed, but simply declaring what those duties *are*, they properly are acts of *interpretation* by legislative authority. Or, to borrow an expression from the writers on the Roman Law, they are acts of *authentic* interpretation.

But, this notwithstanding, they are frequently styled laws; *declaratory* laws, or declaratory statutes. They must, therefore, be noted as forming an exception to the proposition 'that laws are a species of commands.'

It often, indeed, happens (as I shall show in the proper place), that laws declaratory in name are imperative in effect: Legislative, like judicial interpretation, being frequently deceptive; and establishing new law, under guise of expounding the old.

2. Laws to repeal laws, and to release from existing duties, must also be excepted from the

proposition 'that laws are a species of commands'. In so far as they release from duties imposed by existing laws, they are not commands, but revocations of commands. They authorize or permit the parties, to whom the repeal extends, to do or to forbear from acts which they were commanded to forbear from or to do. And, considered with regard to *this,* their immediate or direct purpose, they are often named *permissive laws,* or, more briefly and more properly, *permissions.*

Remotely and indirectly, indeed, permissive laws are often or always imperative. For the parties released from duties are restored to liberties or rights: and duties answering those rights are, therefore, created or revived.

But this is a matter which I shall examine with exactness, when I analyse the expressions 'legal right', 'permission by the sovereign or state', and 'civil or political liberty'.

3. Imperfect laws, or laws of imperfect obligation, must also be excepted from the proposition 'that laws are a species of commands'.

An imperfect law (with the sense wherein the term is used by the Roman jurists) is a law which wants a sanction, and which, therefore, is not binding. A law declaring that certain acts are crimes, but annexing no punishment to the commission of acts of the class, is the simplest and most obvious example.

Though the author of an imperfect law signifies a desire, he manifests no purpose of enforcing compliance with the desire. But where there is not a purpose of enforcing compliance with the desire, the expression of a desire is not a command. Consequently, an imperfect law is not so properly a law, as counsel, or exhortation, addressed by a superior to inferiors.

Examples of imperfect laws are cited by the Roman jurists. But with us in England, laws professedly imperative are always (I believe) perfect or obligatory. Where the English legislature affects to command, the English tribunals not unreasonably presume that the legislature exacts obedience. And, if no specific sanction be annexed to a given law, a sanction is supplied by the courts of justice, agreeably to a general maxim which obtains in cases of the kind.

The imperfect laws, of which I am now speaking, are laws which are imperfect, in the sense of *the Roman jurists*: that is to say, laws which speak the desires of political superiors, but which

their authors (by oversight or design) have not provided with sanctions. Many of the writers on *morals,* and on the so called *law of nature,* have annexed a different meaning to the term *imperfect.* Speaking of imperfect obligations, they commonly mean duties which are *not legal*: duties imposed by commands of God, or duties imposed by positive morality, as contradistinguished to duties imposed by positive law. An imperfect obligation, in the sense of the Roman jurists, is exactly equivalent to no obligation at all. For the term *imperfect* denotes simply, that the law wants the sanction appropriate to laws of the kind. An imperfect obligation, in the other meaning of the expression, is a religious or a moral obligation. The term *imperfect* does not denote that the law imposing the duty wants the appropriate sanction. It denotes that the law imposing the duty is *not* a law established by a political superior: that it wants that *perfect,* or that surer or more cogent sanction, which is imparted by the sovereign or state.

I believe that I have now reviewed all the classes of objects, to which the term *laws* is improperly applied. The laws (improperly so called) which I have here lastly enumerated, are (I think) the only laws which are not commands, and which yet may be properly included within the province of jurisprudence. But though these, with the so called laws set by opinion and the objects metaphorically termed laws, are the only laws which *really* are not commands, there are certain laws (properly so called) which may *seem* not imperative. Accordingly, I will subjoin a few remarks upon laws of this dubious character.

1. There are laws, it may be said, which *merely* create *rights*: And, seeing that every command imposes a *duty,* laws of this nature are not imperative.

But, as I have intimated already, and shall show completely hereafter, there are no laws *merely* creating *rights.* There are laws, it is true, which *merely* create *duties*: duties not correlating with correlating rights, and which, therefore may be styled *absolute.* But every law, really conferring a right, imposes expressly or tacitly a *relative* duty, or a duty correlating with the right. If it specify the remedy to be given, in case the right shall be infringed, it imposes the relative duty expressly. If the remedy to be given be not specified, it refers tacitly to pre-existing law, and clothes the right which it purports to create with a remedy provided by that law. Every law, really conferring a right, is, therefore, imperative: as imperative, as if its only purpose were the creation of a duty, or as if the relative duty, which it inevitably imposes, were merely absolute.

The meanings of the term *right,* are various and perplexed; taken with its proper meaning, it comprises ideas which are numerous and complicated; and the searching and extensive analysis, which the term, therefore, requires, would occupy more room than could be given to it in the present lecture. It is not, however, necessary, that the analysis should be performed here. I purpose, in my earlier lectures, to determine the province of jurisprudence; or to distinguish the laws established by political superiors, from the various laws, proper and improper, with which they are frequently confounded. And this I may accomplish exactly enough, without a nice inquiry into the import of the term *right.*

2. According to an opinion which I must notice *incidentally* here, though the subject to which it relates will be treated *directly* hereafter, *customary laws* must be excepted from the proposition 'that laws are a species of commands'.

By many of the admirers of customary laws (and, especially, of their German admirers), they are thought to oblige legally (independently of the sovereign or state), *because* the citizens or subjects have observed or kept them. Agreeably to this opinion, they are not the *creatures* of the sovereign or state, although the sovereign or state may abolish them at pleasure. Agreeably to this opinion, they are positive law (or law, strictly so called), inasmuch as they are enforced by the courts of justice: But, that notwithstanding, they exist as *positive law* by the spontaneous adoption of the governed, and not by position or establishment on the part of political superiors. Consequently, customary laws, considered as positive law, are not commands. And, consequently, customary laws, considered as positive law, are not laws or rules properly so called.

An opinion less mysterious, but somewhat allied to this, is not uncommonly held by the adverse party: by the party which is strongly opposed to customary law; and to all law made judicially, or in the way of judicial legislation. According to the latter opinion, all judge-made law, or all judge-made law established by *subject* judges, is purely the creature of the judges by whom it is established immediately. To impute it to the sovereign legislature, or to suppose that it speaks the will of the sovereign legislature, is one of the foolish or knavish *fictions* with which lawyers, in every age and nation, have perplexed and darkened the simplest and clearest truths.

I think it will appear, on a moment's reflection, that each of these opinions is groundless: that customary law is *imperative,* in the proper signification of the term; and that all judge-made law is the creature of the sovereign or state.

At its origin, a custom is a rule of conduct which the governed observe spontaneously, or not in pursuance of a law set by a political superior. The custom is transmuted into positive law, when it is adopted as such by the courts of justice, and when the judicial decisions fashioned upon it are enforced by the power of the state. But before it is adopted by the courts, and clothed with the legal sanction, it is merely a rule of positive morality: a rule generally observed by the citizens or subjects; but deriving the only force, which it can be said to possess, from the general disapprobation falling on those who transgress it.

Now when judges transmute a custom into a legal rule (or make a legal rule not suggested by a custom), the legal rule which they establish is established by the sovereign legislature. A subordinate or subject judge is merely a minister. The portion of the sovereign power which lies at his disposition is merely delegated. The rules which he makes derive their legal force from authority given by the state: an authority which the state may confer expressly, but which it commonly imparts in the way of acquiescence. For, since the state may reverse the rules which he makes, and yet permits him to enforce them by the power of the political community, its sovereign will 'that his rules shall obtain as law' is clearly evinced by its conduct, though not by its express declaration.

The admirers of customary law love to trick out their idol with mysterious and imposing attributes. But to those who can see the difference between positive law and morality, there is nothing of mystery about it. Considered as rules of positive morality, customary laws arise from the consent of the governed, and not from the position or establishment of political superiors. But, considered as moral rules turned into positive laws, customary laws are established by the state:

established by the state directly, when the customs are promulged in its statutes; established by the state circuitously, when the customs are adopted by its tribunals.

The opinion of the party which abhors judge-made laws, springs from their inadequate conception of the nature of commands.

Like other significations of desire, a command is express or tacit. If the desire be signified by *words* (written or spoken), the command is express. If the desire be signified by conduct (or by any signs of desire which are *not* words), the command is tacit.

Now when customs are turned into legal rules by decisions of subject judges, the legal rules which emerge from the customs are *tacit* commands of the sovereign legislature. The state, which is able to abolish, permits its ministers to enforce them: and it, therefore, signifies its pleasure, by that its voluntary acquiescence, 'that they shall serve as a law to the governed.'

My present purpose is merely this: to prove that the positive law styled *customary* (and all positive law made judicially) is established by the state directly or circuitously, and, therefore, is *imperative.* I am far from disputing, that law made judicially (or in the way of improper legislation) and law made by statute (or in the properly legislative manner) are distinguished by weighty differences. I shall inquire, in future lectures, what those differences are; and why subject judges, who are properly ministers of the law, have commonly shared with the sovereign in the business of making it.

I assume, then, that the only laws which are not imperative, and which belong to the subject-matter of jurisprudence, are the following:—1. Declaratory laws, or laws explaining the import of existing positive law. 2. Laws abrogating or repealing existing positive law. 3. Imperfect laws, or laws of imperfect obligation (with the sense wherein the expression is used by the Roman jurists).

But the space occupied in the science by these improper laws is comparatively narrow and insignificant. Accordingly, although I shall take them into account so often as I refer to them directly, I shall throw them out of account on other occasions. Or (changing the expression) I shall limit the term *law* to laws which are imperative, unless I extend it expressly to laws which are not.

LECTURE VI

. . . The superiority which is styled sovereignty, and the independent political society which sovereignty implies, is distinguished from other superiority, and from other society, by the following marks or characters:—1. The *bulk* of the given society are in a *habit* of obedience or submission to a *determinate* and *common* superior: let that common superior be a certain individual person or a certain body or aggregate of individual persons. 2. That certain individual, or that certain body of individuals, is *not* in a habit of obedience to a determinate human superior. Laws (improperly so called) which opinion sets or imposes, may permanently affect the conduct of that certain individual or body. To express or tacit commands of other determinate parties, that certain individual or body may yield occasional submission. But there is no determinate person, or determinate aggregate of persons, to whose commands, express or tacit, that certain individual or body renders habitual obedience.

Or the notions of sovereignty and independent political society may be expressed concisely thus. —If a *determinate* human superior, *not* in a habit of obedience to a like superior, receive *habitual* obedience from the *bulk* of a given society, that determinate superior is sovereign in that society, and the society (including the superior) is a society political and independent.

To that determinate superior, the other members of the society are *subject:* or on that determinate superior, the other members of the society are *dependent.* The position of its other members towards that determinate superior, is *a state of subjection,* or *a state of dependence.* The mutual relation which subsists between that superior and them, may be styled *the relation of sovereign and subject,* or *the relation of sovereignty and subjection.*

Hence it follows, that it is only through an ellipsis, or an abridged form of expression, that the *society* is styled *independent.* The party truly independent (independent, that is to say, of a determinate human superior), is not the society, but the sovereign portion of the society: that certain member of the society, or that certain body of its members, to whose commands, expressed or intimated, the generality or bulk of its members render habitual obedience. Upon that certain person, or certain body of persons, the other members of the society are *dependent:* or to that certain person, or certain body of persons, the other members of the society are *subject.* By 'an independent political society,' or 'an independent and sovereign nation,' we mean a political society consisting of a sovereign and subjects, as opposed to a political society which is merely subordinate: that is to say, which is merely a limb or member of another political society, and which therefore consists entirely of persons in a state of subjection.

In order that a given society may form a society political and independent, the two distinguishing marks which I have mentioned above must unite. The *generality* of the given society must be in the *habit* of obedience to a *determinate* and *common* superior: whilst that determinate person, or determinate body of persons must *not* be habitually obedient to a determinate person or body. It is the union of that positive, with this negative mark, which renders that given society (including that certain superior) a society political and independent.

To show that the union of those marks renders a given society a society political and independent, I call your attention to the following positions and examples.

1. In order that a given society may form a society political, the generality or bulk of its members must be in a *habit* of obedience to a determinate and common superior.

In case the generality of its members obey a determinate superior, but the obedience be rare or transient and not habitual or permanent, the relation of sovereignty and subjection is not created thereby between that certain superior and the members of that given society. In other words, that determinate superior and the members of that given society do not become thereby an independent political society. Whether that given society be political and independent or not, it is not an independent political society whereof that certain superior is the sovereign portion.

For example: In 1815 the allied armies occupied France; and so long as the allied armies occupied France, the commands of the allied sovereigns were obeyed by the French government, and, through the French government, by the French people generally. But since the commands and the obedience were comparatively rare and transient, they were not sufficient to con-

stitute the relation of sovereignty and subjection between the allied sovereigns and the members of the invaded nation. In spite of those commands, and in spite of that obedience, the French government was sovereign or independent. Or in spite of those commands, and in spite of that obedience, the French government and its subjects were an independent political society whereof the allied sovereigns were not the sovereign portion.

Now if the French nation, before the obedience to those sovereigns, had been an independent society in a state of nature or anarchy, it would not have been changed by the obedience into a society political. And it would not have been changed by the obedience into a society political, because the obedience was not habitual. For, inasmuch as the obedience was not habitual, it was not changed by the obedience from a society political and independent, into a society political but subordinate. —A given society, therefore, is not a society political, unless the generality of its members be in a *habit* of obedience to a determinate and common superior.

Again: A feeble state holds its independence precariously, or at the will of the powerful states to whose aggressions it is obnoxious. And since it is obnoxious to their aggressions, it and the bulk of its subjects render obedience to commands which they occasionally express or intimate. Such, for instance, is the position of the Saxon government and its subjects in respect of the conspiring sovereigns who form the Holy Alliance. But since the commands and the obedience are comparatively few and rare, they are not sufficient to constitute the relation of sovereignty and subjection between the powerful states and the feeble state with its subjects. In spite of those commands, and in spite of that obedience, the feeble state is sovereign or independent. Or in spite of those commands, and in spite of that obedience, the feeble state and its subjects are an independent political society whereof the powerful states are not the sovereign portion. Although the powerful states are permanently *superior,* and although the feeble state is permanently *inferior,* there is neither a *habit* of command on the part of the former, nor a *habit* of obedience on the part of the latter. Although the latter is unable to defend and maintain its independence, the latter is independent of the former in fact or practice.

From the example now adduced, as from the example adduced before, we may draw the following inference: that a given society is not a society political, unless the generality of its members be in a *habit* of obedience to a determinate and common superior.—By the obedience to the powerful states, the feeble state and its subjects are not changed from an independent, into a subordinate political society. And they are not changed by the obedience into a subordinate political society, because the obedience is not habitual. Consequently, if they were a natural society (setting that obedience aside), they would not be changed by that obedience into a society political.

2. In order that a given society may form a society political, habitual obedience must be rendered, by the *generality* or *bulk* of its members, to a determinate and *common* superior. In other words, habitual obedience must be rendered, by the *generality* or *bulk* of its members, to *one and the same* determinate person, or determinate body of persons.

Unless habitual obedience be rendered by the *bulk* of its members, and be rendered by the bulk of its members to *one and the same* superior, the given society is either in a state of nature, or is split into two or more independent political societies.

For example: In case a given society be torn by intestine war, and in case the conflicting parties be nearly balanced, the given society is in one of the two positions which I have now supposed.— As there is no common superior to which the bulk of its members render habitual obedience, it is not a political society single or undivided.—If the bulk of each of the parties be in a habit of obedience to its head, the given society is broken into two or more societies, which, perhaps, may be styled independent political societies.—If the bulk of each of the parties be not in that habit of obedience, the given society is simply or absolutely in a state of nature or anarchy. It is either resolved or broken into its individual elements, or into numerous societies of an extremely limited size: of a size so extremely limited, that they could hardly be styled societies independent and *political.* For, as I shall show hereafter, a given independent society would hardly be styled *political,* in case it fell short of a *number* which cannot

be fixed with precision, but which may be called considerable, or not extremely minute.

3. In order that a given society may form a society political, the generality or bulk of its members must habitually obey a superior *determinate* as well as common.

On this position I shall not insist here. For I have shown sufficiently in my fifth lecture, that no indeterminate party can command expressly or tacitly, or can receive obedience or submission: that no indeterminate body is capable of corporate conduct, or is capable, as a body, of positive or negative deportment.

4. It appears from what has preceded, that, in order that a given society may form a society political, the bulk of its members must be in a habit of obedience to a certain and common superior. But, in order that the given society may form a society political and independent, that certain superior must *not* be habitually obedient to a determinate human superior.

The given society may form a society political and independent, although that certain superior be habitually affected by laws which opinion sets or imposes. The given society may form a society political and independent, although that certain superior render occasional submission to commands of determinate parties. But the society is not independent, although it may be political, in case that certain superior habitually obey the commands of a certain person or body.

Let us suppose, for example, that a viceroy obeys habitually the author of his delegated powers. And, to render the example complete, let us suppose that the viceroy receives habitual obedience from the generality or bulk of the persons who inhabit his province.—Now though he commands habitually within the limits of his province, and receives habitual obedience from the generality or bulk of its inhabitants, the viceroy is not sovereign within the limits of his province, nor are he and its inhabitants an independent political society. The viceroy, and (through the viceroy) the generality or bulk of its inhabitants, are habitually obedient or submissive to the sovereign of a later society. He and the inhabitants of his province are therefore in a state of subjection to the sovereign of that larger society. He and the inhabitants of his province are a society political but subordinate, or form a political society which is merely a limb of another.

NOTES

1. Where a *privilegium* merely imposes a duty, it exclusively obliges a determinate person or persons. But where a *privilegium* confers a right, and the right conferred *avails against the world at large,* the law is *privilegium* as viewed from a certain aspect, but is also *a general law* as viewed from another aspect. In respect of the right conferred, the law exclusively regards a determinate person, and, therefore, is *privilegium.* In respect of the duty imposed, and corresponding to the right conferred, the law regards generally the members of the entire community.

This I shall explain particularly at a subsequent point of my Course, when I consider the peculiar nature of so-called *privilegia,* or of so-called *private laws.*

HANS KELSEN

The Dynamic Aspect of Law*

THE REASON FOR THE VALIDITY OF A NORMATIVE ORDER: THE BASIC NORM

THE MEANING OF THE SEARCH FOR THE REASON FOR VALIDITY

If the law as a normative order is conceived as a system of norms that regulates the behavior of men, the question arises: What constitutes the unity of a multitude of norms—why does a certain norm belong to a certain order? And this question is closely tied to the question: Why is a norm valid, what is the reason for its validity?

A norm referring to the behavior of a human being as "valid" means that it is binding—that an individual ought to behave in the manner determined by the norm. It has been pointed out in an earlier context that the question why a norm is valid, why an individual ought to behave in a certain way, cannot be answered by ascertaining a fact, that is, by a statement that something *is;* that the reason for the validity of a norm cannot be a fact. From the circumstance that something *is* cannot follow that something *ought* to be; and that something *ought* to be, cannot be the reason that something *is.* The reason for the validity of a norm can only be the validity of another norm. A norm which represents the reason for the validity of another norm is figuratively spoken of as a higher norm in relation to a lower norm. It looks as if one could give as a reason for the validity of a norm the circumstance that it was established by an authority, human or divine; for example, the statement: "The reason for the validity of the Ten Commandments is that God Jehovah issued them on Mount Sinai"; or: "Men ought to love their enemies, because Jesus, Son of God, issued this command in his Sermon on the Mount." But in both cases the reason for the validity is not that God or his son issued a certain norm at a certain time in a certain place, but the tacitly presupposed norm that one ought to obey the commands of God or his son. To be true: In the syllogism whose major premise is the *ought*-statement asserting the validity of the higher norm: "One ought to obey God's commands," and whose conclusion is the ought-statement asserting the validity of the lower norm: "One ought to obey God's Ten Commandments," the assertion that God had issued the Ten Commandments, an "is-statement," as the minor premise is an essential link. The major premise and the minor premise are both conditions of the conclusion. But only the major premise, which is an *ought*-statement, is the *conditio per quam* in relation to the

*From *Pure Theory of Law* by Hans Kelsen, trans. by Max Knight (Berkeley and Los Angeles: University of California Press, 1967), pp. 193–95, 198–201, and 208–14. Reprinted by permission of The Regents of the University of California.

conclusion, which is also an *ought*-statement; that is, the norm whose validity is stated in the major premise is the reason for the validity of the norm whose validity is stated in the conclusion. The *is*-statement functioning as minor premise is only the *conditio sine qua non* in relation to the conclusion; this means: The fact whose existence is asserted in the minor premise is not the reason for the validity of the norm whose validity is asserted in the conclusion.

The norm whose validity is stated in the major premise ("One ought to obey God's commands") is included in the supposition that the norms, whose reason for validity is in question, originate from an authority, that is, from somebody competent to create valid norms: this norm bestows upon the norm-creating personality the "authority" to create norms. The mere fact that somebody commands something is no reason to regard the command as a valid norm, a norm binding the individual at whom it is directed. Only a competent authority can create valid norms; and such competence can only be based on a norm that authorizes the issuing of norms. The authority authorized to issue norms is subject to that norm in the same manner as the individuals are subject to the norms issued by the authority.

The norm which represents the reason for the validity of another norm is called, as we have said, the "higher" norm. But the search for the reason of a norm's validity cannot go on indefinitely like the search for the cause of an effect. It must end with a norm which, as the last and highest, is presupposed. It must be *presupposed* because it cannot be "posited," that is to say: created, by an authority whose competence would have to rest on a still higher norm. This final norm's validity cannot be derived from a higher norm, the reason for its validity cannot be questioned. Such a presupposed highest norm is referred to in this book as basic norm. All norms whose validity can be traced back to one and the same basic norm constitute a system of norms, a normative order. The basic norm is the common source for the validity of all norms that belong to the same order—it is their common reason of validity. The fact that a certain norm belongs to a certain order is based on the circumstance that its last reason of validity is the basic norm of this order. It is the basic norm that constitutes the unity in the multitude of norms by representing the reason for the validity of all norms that belong to this order.

THE REASON FOR THE VALIDITY OF A LEGAL ORDER

The norm system that presents itself as a legal order has essentially a dynamic character. A legal norm is not valid because it has a certain content, that is, because its content is logically deducible from a presupposed basic norm, but because it is created in a certain way—ultimately in a way determined by a presupposed basic norm. For this reason alone does the legal norm belong to the legal order whose norms are created according to this a basic norm. Therefore any kind of content might be law. There is no human behavior which, as such, is excluded from being the content of a legal norm. The validity of a legal norm may not be denied for being (in its content) in conflict with that of another norm which does not belong to the legal order whose basic norm is the reason for the validity of the norm in question. The basic norm of a legal order is not a material norm which, because its content is regarded as immediately self-evident, is presupposed as the highest norm and from which norms for human behavior are logically deduced. The norms of a legal order must be created by a specific process. They are posited, that is, positive, norms, elements of a positive order. If by the constitution of a legal community is understood the norm or norms that determine how (that is, by what organs and by what procedure—through legislation or custom) the general norms of the legal order that constitute the community are to be created, then the basic norm is that norm which is presupposed when the custom through which the constitution has come into existence, or the constitution-creating act consciously performed by certain human beings, is objectively interpreted as a norm-creating fact; if, in the latter case, the individual or the assembly of individuals who created the constitution on which the legal order rests, are looked upon as norm-creating authorities. In this sense, the basic norm determines the basic fact of law creation and may in this respect be described as the constitution in a logical sense of the word (which will be explained later) in contradistinction to the constitution in the meaning of positive law. The basic norm is the presupposed starting point of a procedure: the procedure of positive law creation. It is itself not a norm created by custom or by the act of a legal organ; it is not a positive but a presupposed norm so far as the constitution-establishing authority is looked upon as the highest authority and can therefore not be regarded as authorized by the norm of a higher authority.

If the question as to the reason for the validity of a certain legal norm is raised, then the answer can only consist in the reduction to the basic norm of this legal order, that is, in the assertion that the norm was created—in the last instance—according to the basic norm. In the following pages we would like to consider only a national legal order, that is, a legal order limited in its validity to a specific space, the so-called territory of the state, and which is regarded as "sovereign," that is, as not subordinated to any higher legal order. We shall discuss the problem of the validity of the norms of a national legal order, at first without considering an international legal order superordinated to or included in it.

The question of the reason for the validity of a legal norm belonging to a specific national legal order may arise on the occasion of a coercive act; for example, when one individual deprives another of his life by hanging, and now the question is asked why this act is legal, namely the execution of a punishment, and not murder. This act can be interpreted as being legal only if it was prescribed by an individual legal norm, namely as an act that "ought" to be performed, by a norm that presents itself as a judicial decision. This raises the questions: Under what conditions is such an interpretation possible; why is a judicial decision present in this case; why is the individual norm created thereby a legal norm belonging to a valid legal order and therefore ought to be applied? The answer is: Because this individual norm was created in applying a criminal law that contains a general norm according to which (under conditions present in the case concerned) the death penalty ought to be inflicted. If we ask for the reason for the validity of this criminal law, then the answer is: The criminal law is valid because it was created by the legislature, and the legislature, in turn, is authorized by the constitution to create general norms. If we ask for the reason of the validity of the constitution, that is, for the reason of the validity of the norms regulating the creation of the general norms, we may,

perhaps, discover an older constitution; that means the validity of the existing constitution is justified by the fact that it was created according to the rules of an earlier constitution by way of a constitutional amendment. In this way we eventually arrive at a historically first constitution that cannot have been created in this way and whose validity, therefore, cannot be traced back to a positive norm created by a legal authority; we arrive, instead, at a constitution that became valid in a revolutionary way, that is, either by breach of a former constitution or for a territory that formerly was not the sphere of validity of a constitution and of a national legal order based on it. If we consider merely the national legal order, not international law, and if we ask for the reason of the validity of the historically first constitution, then the answer can only be (if we leave aside God or "nature") that the validity of this constitution—the assumption that it is a binding norm—must be *presupposed* if we want to interpret (1) the acts performed according to it as the creation or application of valid general legal norms; and (2) the acts performed in application of these general norms as the creation or application of valid individual legal norms. Since the reason for the validity of a norm can only be another norm, the presupposition must be a norm: not one posited (that is, created) by a legal authority, but a presupposed norm, that is, a norm presupposed if the subjective meaning of the constitution-creating facts and the subjective meaning of the norm-creating facts established according to the constitution are interpreted as their objective meaning. Since it is the basic norm of a legal order (that is, an order prescribing coercive acts), therefore this norm, namely the basic norm of the legal order concerned, must be formulated as follows: Coercive acts ought to be performed under the conditions and in the manner which the historically first constitution, and the norms created according to it, prescribe. (In short: One ought to behave as the constitution prescribes.) The norms of a legal order, whose common reason for their validity is this basic norm, are not a complex of valid norms standing coordinatedly side by side, but form a hierarchical structure of super- and subordinate norms. This structure of the legal order will be discussed later.

LEGITIMACY AND EFFECTIVENESS

The function of the basic norm becomes particularly apparent if the constitution is not changed by constitutional means but by revolution; when the existence—that is, the validity—of the entire legal order directly based on the constitution, is in question.

It was said earlier that a norm's sphere of validity, particularly its temporal sphere of validity, may be limited; the beginning and end of its validity may be determined by the norm itself or by a higher norm regulating the creation of the lower one. The norms of a legal order are valid until their validity is terminated according to the rules of this legal order. By regulating its own creation and application, the legal order determines the beginning and end of the validity of the legal norms. Written constitutions usually contain special rules concerning the method by which they can be changed. The principle that a norm of a legal order is valid until its validity is terminated in a way determined by this legal order, or replaced by the validity of another norm of this order, is called the principle of legitimacy.

This principle is applicable to a national legal order with one important limitation only: It does not apply in case of a revolution. A revolution in the broader sense of the word (that includes a coup d'état) is every not legitimate change of this constitution or its replacement by an other constitution. From the point of view of legal science, it is irrelevant whether this change of the legal situation has been brought about by the application of force against the legitimate government or by the members of that government themselves, whether by a mass movement of the population or by a small group of individuals. Decisive is only that the valid constitution has been changed or replaced in a manner not prescribed by the constitution valid until then. Usually a revolution abolishes only the old constitution and certain politically important statutes. A large part of the statutes created under the old constitution remains valid, as the saying goes; but this expression does not fit. If these statutes are to be regarded as being valid under the new constitution, then this is possible only because they have been validated expressly or tacitly by the new constitution. We are confronted here not with a creation of new law but with the reception of norms of one legal order by another; such as the reception of the Roman Law by the German Law. But such reception too is law creation, because the direct reason for the validity of the legal norms taken over by the new revolutionary established constitution can only be the new constitution. The content of these norms remains unchanged, but the reason for their validity, in fact the reason for the validity of the entire legal order, has been changed. As the new constitution becomes valid, so simultaneously changes the basic norm, that is, the presupposition according to which are interpreted as norm-creating and norm-applying facts the constitution-creating fact and the facts established according to the constitution. Suppose the old constitution had the character of an absolute monarchy and the new one of a parliamentary democracy. Then the basic norm no longer reads: "Coercive acts ought to be carried out under the conditions and in the manner as determined by the old, no longer valid, constitution," and hence by the general and individual norms created and applied by the constitutionally functioning monarch and the organs delegated by him; instead, the basic norm reads: "Coercive acts ought to be carried out under the conditions and in the manner determined by the new constitution," and hence by the general and individual norms created and applied by the parliament elected according to that constitution and by the organs delegated in these norms. The new basic norm does not make it possible—like the old one—to regard a certain individual as the absolute monarch, but makes it possible to regard a popularly elected parliament as a legal authority. According to the basic norm of national legal order, the government, which creates effective general and individual norms based on an effective constitution is the legitimate government of the state.

The change of the basic norm follows the change of the facts that are interpreted as creating and applying valid legal norms. The basic norm refers only to a constitution which is actually established by legislative act or custom, and is effective. A constitution is "effective" if the norms created in conformity with it are by and large applied and obeyed. As soon as the old constitution loses its effectiveness and the new one has become effective, the acts that appear with the subjective meaning of creating or applying legal norms are no longer interpreted by presupposing the old basic norm, but by presupposing the new one. The statutes issued under the old constitution and not taken over are no longer regarded as valid, and the organs authorized by the old constitution no longer as competent. If the revolution is not successful there would be no reason to replace the old basic norm by a new one. Then, the revolution would not be regarded as procedure creating new law, but—according to the old constitution and the criminal law based on it and regarded as valid—would be interpreted as high treason. The principle applied here is the principle of effectiveness. The principle of legitimacy is limited by the principle of effectiveness.

VALIDITY AND EFFECTIVENESS

This limitation reveals the repeatedly emphasized connection (so important for a theory of positive law) between the validity and the effectiveness of law. The correct determination of this relationship is one of the most important and at the same time most difficult problems of a positivistic legal theory. It is only a special case of the relationship between the "ought" of the legal norm and the "is" of natural reality. Because the act by which a positive legal norm is created, too, is an "is-fact" (German: *Seinstatsache*) just as the effectiveness of the legal norm. A positivistic legal theory is faced by the task to find the correct middle road between two extremes which both are untenable. The one extreme is the thesis that there is no connection between validity as something that ought to be and effectiveness as something that is; that the validity of the law is entirely independent of its effectiveness. The other extreme is the thesis that validity and effectiveness are identical. An idealistic theory of law tends to the first solution of this problem, a realistic theory to the second. The first is wrong for it is undeniable that a legal order in its entirety, and an individual legal norm as well, lose their validity when they cease to be effective; and that a relation exists between the *ought* of the legal norm and the *is* of physical reality also insofar as the positive legal norm, to be valid, must be created by an act which exists in the reality of being. The second solution is wrong because it is equally undeniable that there are many cases—as has been shown before—in which legal norms are

regarded as valid although they are not, or not yet, effective. The solution proposed by the Pure Theory of Law is this: Just as the norm (according to which something *ought* to be) as the meaning of an act is not identical with the act (which actually *is*), in the same way is the validity of a legal norm not identical with its effectiveness; the effectiveness of a legal order as a whole and the effectiveness of a single legal norm are—just as the norm-creating act—the condition for the validity; effectiveness is the condition in the sense that a legal order as a whole, and a single legal norm, can no longer be regarded as valid when they cease to be effective. Nor is the effectiveness of a legal order, any more than the fact of its creation, the reason for its validity. The reason for the validity—that is, the answer to the question why the norms of this legal order ought to be obeyed and applied—is the presupposed basic norm, according to which one ought to comply with an actually established, by and large effective, constitution, and therefore with the by and large effective norms, actually created in conformity with that constitution. In the basic norm the fact of creation and the effectiveness are made the condition of the validity—"effectiveness" in the sense that it has to be added to the fact of creation, so that neither the legal order as a whole nor the individual legal norm shall lose their validity. A condition cannot be identical with that which it conditions. Thus, a man, in order to live, must have been born; but in order that he remain alive other conditions must also be fulfilled, for example, he must receive nutrition. If this condition is not fulfilled, he will lose his life. But life is neither identical with birth nor with being nourished.

In the normative syllogism leading to the foundation of the validity of a legal order, the major premise is the ought-sentence which states the basic norm: "One ought to behave according to the actually established and effective constitution"; the minor premise is the is-sentence which states the facts: "The constitution is actually established and effective"; and the conclusion is the ought-sentence: "One ought to behave according to the legal order, that is, the legal order is valid." The norms of a positive legal order are valid *because* the fundamental rule regulating their creation, that is, the basic norm, is presupposed to be valid, not because they are effective; but they are valid only *as long as* this legal order is effective. As soon as the constitution loses its effectiveness, that is, as soon as the legal order as a whole based on the constitution loses its effectiveness, the legal order and every single norm lose their validity.

However, a legal order does not lose its validity when a single legal norm loses its effectiveness. A legal order is regarded as valid if its norms are *by and large* effective (that is, actually applied and obeyed). Nor does a single legal norm lose its validity if it is only exceptionally ineffective in single cases. As mentioned in another connection, the possibility of an antagonism between that which is prescribed by a norm as something that ought to be and that which actually happens must exist; a norm, prescribing that something *ought* to be, which, as one knows beforehand *must* happen anyway according to a law of nature, is meaningless—such a norm would not be regarded as valid. On the other hand, a norm is not regarded as valid which is never obeyed or applied. In fact, a legal norm may lose its validity by never being applied or obeyed—by so-called *desuetude. Desuetudo* may be described as negative custom, and its essential function is to abolish the validity of an existing norm. If custom is a law-creating fact at all, then even the validity of statutory law can be abolished by customary law. If effectiveness in the developed sense is the condition for the validity not only of the legal order as a whole but also of a single legal norm, then the law-creating function of custom cannot be excluded by statutory law, at least not as far as the negative function of *desuetudo* is concerned.

The described relation between validity and effectiveness refers to general legal norms. But also individual legal norms (judicial decisions, administrative decrees) that prescribe an individual coercive act lose their validity if they are permanently unexecuted and therefore ineffective, as has been shown in the discussion of a conflict between two legal decisions.[76]

Effectiveness is a condition for the validity— but it is not validity. This must be stressed because time and again the effort has been made to identify validity with effectiveness; and such identification is tempting because it seems to simplify the theoretical situation. Still, the effort is doomed to failure, not only because even a partly ineffective legal order or legal norm may be regarded as valid, and an absolutely effective norm which cannot be violated as invalid because not being regarded as a norm at all; but particularly for this reason: If the validity, that is, the specific existence of the law, is considered to be part of natural reality, one is unable to grasp the specific meaning in which the law addresses itself to reality and thereby juxtaposes itself to reality, which can be in conformity or in conflict with the law only if reality is not identical with the validity of the law. Just as it is impossible in determining validity to ignore its relation to reality, so it is likewise impossible to identify validity and reality. If we replace the concept of reality (as effectiveness of the legal order) by the concept of power, then the problem of the relation between validity and effectiveness of the legal order coincides with the more familiar problem of the relationship between law and power or right and might. And then, the solution attempted here is merely the scientifically exact formulation of the old truism that right cannot exist without might and yet is not identical with might. Right (the law), according to the theory here developed, is a certain order (or organization) of might.

ALF ROSS

The Idea of Valid Law*

PRELIMINARY ANALYSIS OF THE CONCEPT "VALID LAW"

Let us imagine that two persons are playing chess, while a third person looks on.

If the onlooker knows nothing about chess, he will not understand what is going on. From his knowledge of other games, he will probably conclude that it is some sort of game. But he will not be able to understand the individual moves or to see any connection between them. Still less will he have any notion of the problems involved in any particular disposition of the pieces on the board.

If the onlooker knows the rules of chess, but beyond that not much about the theory of the game, his experience of the others' play changes character. He will understand that the horse's "irregular" movement is the prescribed knight's move. He is in a position to recognize the movements of the pieces in turn as moves prescribed by the rules. Within limits he is even able to predict what will take place. For he knows that the players take turns to make a move, and that each move has to fall within the total of possibilities allowed by the rules in any given disposition of the pieces. But beyond that, especially if the players are more than mere beginners, a great deal will appear puzzling. He does not understand the players' strategy, and has no eye for the tactical problems of the situation. Why, for example, does White not take the bishop? For a complete understanding of the game, a knowledge not only of the rules of chess but also of a certain amount of the theory of the game is essential. The likelihood of being able to predict the next move increases if account is taken not only of the rules of play but also of the theory of the game and the understanding each player has of it. Finally there

must also be taken into account the purpose governing the play of the individual players. It is normally assumed that a player plays to win. But there are also other possibilities (for example, to let his opponent win, or to experiment and try out the value of a certain move).

These considerations of the game of chess contain a peculiar and interesting lesson. Here before us we have a series of human actions (the movements of the hands to change the position of certain objects in space) and we may well suppose that these together with other bodily processes (breathing, psychophysical processes, etc.) constitute a course of events which follow certain biological and physiological laws. Nevertheless, it is obvious that it is beyond the limit of all reasonable possibility to give an account of this course of events in such a way that the individual moves of chess can be explained and predicted on a biological and physiological basis.

The problem presents a quite different aspect if we go to another level of observation and interpret the course of events in the light of the rules and theory of chess. Certain items of the whole series of events, namely, the moving of the pieces, stand out then as being actions relevant to chess or significant for chess. The movement of the pieces is not looked on as merely changing the position of objects in space, but as moves in the game, and the game becomes a significant coherent whole, because the moves reciprocally motivate each other and are construed as attack and defence in accordance with the theoretical principles of the game. If we watch the players, we understand each move made by each player from the point of view of their consciousness of the rules of chess together with the knowledge we assume them to have of the theory of the game, and the goal they have set themselves in the game. Further it is also possible to ignore the

*From *On Law and Justice* by Alf Ross (London: Sweet & Maxwell, Ltd., 1958), pp. 11–18 and 34–38. Reprinted by permission of the publisher.

persons of the players and understand the game on its own in its abstract significance (a game in a book of chess).

It must be noted that the "understanding" we are thinking of here is of a kind other than causal. We are not operating here with laws of causation. The moves do not stand in any mutually causal relation. The connection between them is established by way of the rules and theory of chess. The connection is one of meaning.

It can further be stated that fellowship is an essential factor in a game of chess. By this I mean that the aims and interests pursued and the actions conditioned by these can only be conceived of as a link in a greater whole which includes the actions of another person. When two men dig a ditch together, they are doing nothing that each of them could not equally well do on his own. It is quite otherwise in chess. It is not possible for one person on his own to set himself the goal of winning at chess. The actions which make up playing chess can only be performed when playing in turns with a second person. Each player has his part to play, but each part only achieves significance when the second player fulfils his role.[1]

Fellowship is also revealed in the intersubjective character of the rules of chess. It is essential that they should be given the same interpretation, at least by the two players in a given game. Otherwise there would be no game, and the separate moves would remain in isolation with no coherent meaning.

Now all this shows that the game of chess can be taken as a simple model of that which we call a social phenomenon. Human social life in a community is not a chaos of mutually isolated individual actions. It acquires the character of community life from the very fact that a large number (not all) of individual actions are relevant and have significance in relation to a set of common conceptions of rules. They constitute a significant whole, bearing the same relation to one another as move and countermove. Here, too, there is mutual interplay, motivated by and acquiring its significance from the common rules of the social "game." And it is the consciousness of these rules which makes it possible to understand and in some measure to predict the course of events.

I will now examine more closely what a rule of chess actually is, and in what way it is possible to establish what the rules are which govern the game of chess.

I have in mind here the primary rules of chess, those which determine the arrangement of the pieces, the moves, "taking," and the like, and not rules of chess theory.

As to the latter a few remarks will suffice. Like other technological rules they obviously are of the nature of hypothethetical theoretical pronouncements. They assume the existence of the primary rules of chess and indicate the consequences which different openings and gambits will lead to in the game. If a player does not have this interest, then the theory of the game is without importance to him.

The primary rules of chess, on the other hand, are directives. Although they are formulated as assertions about the "ability" or "power" of the pieces to move and "take," it is clear that they are intended to indicate how the game is to be played. They aim directly, that is, unqualified by any underlying objective, to motivate the player; they tell him, as it were: This is how it is played.

These directives are felt by each player to be socially binding; that is to say, a player not only feels himself spontaneously motivated ("bound") to a certain method of action but is at the same time certain that a breach of the rules will call forth a reaction (protest) on the part of his opponent. And in this way they are clearly distinguished from the rules of skill contained in the theory. A stupid move can arouse astonishment, but not a protest.

On the other hand, the rules of chess are not tinged with morality; this is the result of the fact that normally no one really wants to break them. The wish to cheat at a game must be due to the fact that a player has an aim other than merely to win according to the rules of the game; for example, he may want to be admired or to win a sum of money which is at stake. This latter aim is often present at a game of cards, and it is well known that the demand for honourable play here takes on a moral value.

How is it possible then to establish which rules (directives) govern the game of chess?

One could perhaps think of approaching the problem from the behaviorist angle—limiting oneself to what can be established by external observation of the actions and then finding certain regularities. But in this way an insight into the rules of the game would never be achieved. It would never be possible to distinguish actual custom, or even regularities conditioned by the theory of the game, from the rules of chess proper. Even after watching a thousand games, it would still be possible to believe that it is against the rules to open with a rook's pawn.

The simplest thing, perhaps, would be to go by certain authoritative rulings, for example, rulings given at chess congresses, or information contained in recognised textbooks on chess. But even this might not be sufficient, since it is not certain that such declarations are adhered to in practice. Sometimes games are played in fact in many varying ways. Even in a classic game like chess variations of this kind can occur (for example, the rule about "taking" *en passant* is not always adhered to). This problem of what rules govern "chess" must therefore, strictly speaking, be understood to refer to the rules which govern an actual game between two specific persons. It is their actions, and theirs alone, which are bound up in a significant whole, and governed for both of them by the rules.

Thus we cannot but adopt an introspective method. The problem is to discover which rules are actually felt by the players to be socially binding, in the sense indicated above. The first criterion is that they are in fact effective in the game and are outwardly visible as such. But in order to decide whether rules that are observed are more than just customary usage or motivated by technical reasons, it is necessary to ask the players by what rules they feel themselves bound.

Accordingly we can say: A rule of chess "is valid" means that within a given fellowship (which fundamentally comprises the two players of an actual game) this rule is effectively adhered to, because the players feel themselves to be socially bound by the directive contained in the rule. The concept of validity (in chess) involves two elements. The one refers to the actual effectiveness of the rule which can be established by outside observation. The other refers to the way in which the rule is felt to be motivating, that is, socially binding.

There is a certain ambiguity in the concept "rule of chess." The rules of chess have no reality and do not exist apart from the experience of the players, that is, their ideas of certain patterns of behaviour and, associated therewith, the emotional experience of the compulsion to obey. It is possible to abstract the meaning of an assertion purely as a thought content ("2 and 2 makes 4") from the apprehension of the same by a given person at a given time; and in just the same way it is also possible to abstract the meaning of a directive ("the king has the power of moving one square in any direction") from the concrete experience of the directive. The concept "rule of chess" must therefore in any accurate analysis be divided into two: the experienced ideas of certain patterns of behaviour (with the accompanying emotion) and the abstract content of those ideas, the norms of chess.

Thus the norms of chess are the abstract idea content (of a directive nature) which make it possible, as a scheme of interpretation, to understand the phenomena of chess (the actions of the moves and the experienced patterns of action) as a coherent whole of meaning and motivation, a game of chess; and, along with other factors, within certain limits to predict the course of the game.

The phenomena of chess and the norms of chess are not mutually independent, each of them having their own reality; they are different sides of the same thing. No biological-physical action is as such regarded as a move of chess. It acquires this quality only by being interpreted in relation to the norms of chess. And conversely, no directive idea content has as such the character of a valid norm of chess. It acquires this quality only by the fact that it can, along with others, be effectively applied as a scheme of interpretation for the phenomena of chess. The phenomena of chess become phenomena of chess only when placed in relation to the norms of chess and vice versa.

The purpose of this discussion of chess has undoubtedly become clear by now. It is a pointer toward the statement that the concept "valid norm of chess" may function as the model for the concept "valid law" which is the real object of our preliminary considerations.

The law too may be regarded as consisting partly of legal phenomena and partly of legal norms in mutual correlation.

Observing the law as it functions in society we find that a large number of human actions are interpreted as a coherent whole of meaning and motivation by means of legal norms as the scheme of interpretation. A purchases a house from B. It turns out that the house is full of termites. A asks B for a reduction in the purchase price, but B will not agree. A brings an action against B, and the judge in accordance with the law of contract orders B to pay to A a certain sum of money within a given time. B does not do this. A has the sheriff levy upon the personal property of B which is then sold in auction. A biological-physical consideration of these actions cannot reveal any causal connection between them. Such connections lie within each single individual. But we interpret them with the aid of the reference scheme "valid law" as legal phenomena constituting a coherent whole of meaning and motivation. Each one of these actions acquires its legal character only when this is done. A's purchase of the house happens by word of mouth or with the aid of written characters. But these become a "purchase" only when seen in relation to the legal norms. The various actions are mutually motivating just like the moves in chess. The judge, for example, is motivated by A's and B's parts in the deal (and the further circumstances in connection with it, the condition of the house), and by the precedents establishing the law of contract. The whole proceeding has the character of a "game," only according to norms which are far more complicated than the norms of the game of chess.

On the basis of what has been said, the following hypothesis is advanced: The concept "valid (Illinois, California, common) law" can be explained and defined in principle in the same manner as the concept "valid (for any two players) norm of chess." That is to say, "valid law" means the abstract set of normative ideas which serve as a scheme of interpretation for the phemomena of law in action, which again means that these norms are effectively followed, and followed because they are experienced and felt to be socially binding.[2]

This conclusion may perhaps be thought commonplace, and it may seem that a vast apparatus of reasoning has been employed to this end. This might be true if the problems were approached by a person with no preconceived notions. But it would not be true for an historical approach. By far the greater part of all writers on jurisprudence up to the present have maintained that the concept "valid law" cannot be explained without recourse to the metaphysical. The law according to

this view is not merely an empirical phenomenon. When we say that a rule of law is "valid" we refer not only to something factual, that can be observed, but also to a "validity" of a metaphysical character. This validity is alleged to be a pure concept of reason of divine origin or existing *a priori* (independent of experience) in the rational nature of man. And eminent writers on jurisprudence who deny such spiritual metaphysics have nevertheless been of the opinion that the "validity" of the law can only be explained by means of specific postulates.

Seen in this light our preliminary conclusion will, I trust, not be called commonplace. This analysis of a simple model is calculated to raise doubts as to the necessity of metaphysical explanations of the concept of law. Who would ever think of tracing the valid norms of chess back to an *a priori* validity, a pure idea of chess, bestowed upon man by God or deduced by man's eternal reason? The thought is ridiculous, because we do not take chess as seriously as law—because stronger emotions are bound up with the concepts of law. But this is no reason for believing that logical analysis should adopt a fundamentally different attitude in each of the two cases.

Of course many problems still remain before the concept "valid law" is satisfactorily analysed. But there is no need to go further into the matter at this point. This preliminary study is sufficient to serve as a basis for a survey of the various branches of the study of law, and for determining the proper place of "jurisprudence."

THE VALIDITY OF THE LEGAL SYSTEM

The point from which we set out is the hypothesis that a system of norms is "valid" if it is able to serve as a scheme of interpretation for a corresponding set of social actions in such a way that it becomes possible for us to comprehend this set of actions as a coherent whole of meaning and motivation, and within certain limits to predict them. This capacity within the system is based on the fact that the norms are effectively complied with, because they are felt to be socially binding.

What, now, are those social facts which as legal phenomena constitute the counterpart of the legal norms? They must be the human actions regulated by the legal norms. These, as we have seen, are in the last analysis norms determining the conditions under which force shall be exercised through the machinery of the State; or—briefly—norms for the ordering by the courts of the exercise of force. It follows that the legal phenomena as the counterpart of the norms must be the decisions of the courts. It is here that we must seek for the effectiveness that is the validity of law.

A national law system, considered as a valid system of norms, can accordingly be defined as the norms which actually are operative in the mind of the judge, because they are felt by him to be socially binding and therefore obeyed. The test of the validity is that on this hypothesis—that is, accepting the system of norms as a scheme of interpretation—we can comprehend the actions of the judge (the decisions of the courts) as meaningful responses to given conditions and within certain limits predict them—in the same way as the norms of chess enable us to understand the moves of the players as meaningful responses and predict them.

The action of the judge is a response to a number of conditions determined by the legal norms —that a contract of sale has been performed, that the seller has not delivered, that the buyer has given notice in due time, and so on. Also these conditioning facts acquire their specific meaning as legal acts through an interpretation in the light of the ideology of the norms. For this reason they might be included under the term legal phenomena in the wider sense or law in action.

Only the legal phenomena in the narrower sense, however—the application of the law by the courts—are decisive in determining the validity of the legal norms. In contrast to generally accepted ideas, it must be emphasised that the law provides the norms for the behaviour of the courts, and not of private individuals. The effectiveness which conditions the validity of the norms can therefore be sought solely in the judicial application of the law, and not in the law in action among private individuals. If, for example, criminal abortion is prohibited, the true content of the law consists in a directive to the judge that he shall under certain conditions impose a penalty for criminal abortion. The decisive factor determining that the prohibition is valid law is solely the fact that it is effectively upheld by the courts where breaches of the law are brought to light and prosecuted.[3] It makes no difference whether the people comply with or frequently ignore the prohibition. This indifference results in

the apparent paradox that the more effectively a rule is complied with in extrajudicial legal life, the more difficult it is to ascertain whether the rule possesses validity, because the courts have that much less opportunity to manifest their reaction.[4]

In the foregoing, the terms "the judge" and "the courts" have been used indiscriminately. When we are speaking of a national law system, it is assumed that we are dealing with a set of norms which are supraindividual in the sense that they are particular to the nation, varying from nation to nation, not from one individual judge to another. For this reason it makes no difference whether one refers to "the judge" or to "the courts." So far as the individual judge is motivated by particular, personal ideas, these cannot be assigned to the law of the nation, although they are a factor which must be considered by anyone interested in forecasting a concrete legal decision.

When the basis for the validity of the law is sought in the decisions of the courts, the chain of reasoning may appear to be working in a circle. For it may be adduced that the qualification of judge is not merely a factual quality but can only be assigned by reference to valid law, in particular to the rules of public law governing the organization of the courts and the appointment of judges. Before I can ascertain whether a certain rule of private law is valid law, therefore, I have to establish what is valid law in these other respects. And what is the criterion for this?

The answer to this problem is that the legal system forms a whole integrating the rules of private law with the rules of public law. Fundamentally, validity is a quality ascribed to the system as a whole. The test of the validity is that the system in its entirety, used as a scheme of interpretation, makes us to comprehend, not only the manner in which the judges act, but also that they are acting in the capacity as "judges." There is no Archimedes point for the verification, no part of the law which is verified before any other part.[5]

The fact that fundamentally the entire legal system undergoes verification need not exclude the possibility of investigating whether a definite individual rule is valid law. It merely implies that the problem cannot be solved without reference to "valid law" as a whole. These more particular problems of verification are discussed in §§ 9 and 10.

The concept of the validity of the law rests, according to the explanation offered in this section, on hypotheses concerning the spiritual life of the judge. What is valid law cannot be ascertained by purely behaviouristic means, that is, by external observation of regularity in the reactions (customs) of the judges. Throughout a lengthy period the judge may have exhibited a certain typical reaction; for example, he may have imposed penalties for criminal abortion. Suddenly this reaction changes, because a new law has been promulgated. Validity cannot be ascertained by recourse to a more general, externally observable custom, namely, that of "obeying the legislator." For it is not possible from external observation to identify the "legislator" who is being obeyed. Purely external observation might lead one to the conclusion that obedience was paid to the persons, mentioned by their names, who at the time of observation were members of the legislature. But one day this too is changed. One can continue in this way right up to the constitution, but there is nothing to prevent the constitution from being changed too one day.

A behaviouristic interpretation, then, achieves nothing. The changing behavior of the judge can only be comprehended and predicted through ideological interpretation, that is, by means of the hypothesis of a certain ideology which animates the judge and motivates his actions.

Another way of expressing the same thing is to say that law presupposes, not only regularity in the judge's mode of action, but also his experience of being bound by the rules. In the concept of validity two points are involved: partially the outward observable and regular compliance with a pattern of action, and partly the experience of this pattern of action as being a socially binding norm. Not every outward observable custom in the game of chess is an expression of a valid norm of chess, as, for example, not to open with a rook's pawn; in the same way not every outward and observable regularity in the reactions of the judge is the expression of a valid norm of law. It may be, for example, that a custom has developed of imposing only fines as the penalties for certain breaches of the law even though imprisonment is also authorised. Now it must, to be sure, be added that the customs of judges show a strong inclina-tion to develop into binding norms, and that a custom will, in that case, be construed as the expression of valid law. But this is not the case so long as it is nothing more than a factual custom.

This twofold point in the concept of validity explains the dualism which has always marked this concept in current metaphysical theory of law. According to this theory valid law means both an order which is in fact effective and an order which possesses "binding force" derived from *a priori* principles; law is at the same time something factual in the world of reality and something valid in the world of ideas. It is not difficult to see that this dualism of viewpoint may lead to both logical and epistemological complications which find expression in a number of antinomies in the theory of law. It leads consistently to a metaphysical assertion that existence itself in its innermost being is valid (Hegel). Like most metaphysical constructions, the construction of the immanent validity of positive law rests on a misinterpretation of certain experiences, in this case the experience that the law is not merely a factual, customary order, but an order which is experienced as being socially binding. The traditional conception, therefore, with the metaphysics removed, can be appropriated in support of my own view so far as it is opposed to a purely behaviouristic interpretation of the validity of the law.

NOTES

1. In his *Schachnovelle* Stephan Zweig gives an interesting description of a person who is able to play chess with himself. The explanation is that he has cultivated schizophrenia so that he is able to function as two persons.

2. By the judge and other legal authorities applying the law.

3. The term "courts" is here understood as a comprehensive term for the authorities which combine to administer the criminal prosecutions: police, prosecuting authority and court. If the police regularly omit to investigate certain breaches of the law, or if the prosecuting authority regularly omits to bring a prosecution, the penal law loses its character of valid law, notwithstanding its application at rare intervals in the courts.

4. For the application of this view in international law see Alf Ross, *Textbook of International Law* (1947), §§ 24 and 28 iv.

5. There is nothing peculiar in the fact that the system as a whole comes up for verification. The same principle also applies in natural science. The verification of one particular natural law is compatible with the hitherto accepted system. But nothing is established beyond doubt. There is nothing to prevent fresh experience compelling us to revise all hitherto accepted starting points. It is always the entire systematic whole which remains the final criterion in deciding what shall be held to be true.

H. L. A. H A R T

Positivism and the Separation of Law and Morals*

In this article I shall discuss and attempt to defend a view which Mr. Justice Holmes, among others, held and for which he and they have been much criticized. But I wish first to say why I think that Holmes, whatever the vicissitudes of his American reputation may be, will always remain for Englishmen a heroic figure in jurisprudence. This will be so because he magically combined two qualities: One of them is imaginative power, which English legal thinking has often lacked; the other is clarity, which English legal thinking usually possesses. The English lawyer who turns to read Holmes is made to see that what he had taken to be settled and stable is really always on the move. To make this discovery with Holmes is to be with a guide whose words may leave you unconvinced, sometimes even repelled, but never mystified. Like our own Austin, with whom Holmes shared many ideals and thoughts, Holmes was somtimes clearly wrong; but again like Austin, when this was so he was always wrong clearly. This surely is a sovereign virtue in jurisprudence. Clarity I know is said not to be enough; this may be true, but there are still questions in jurisprudence where the issues are confused because they are discussed in a style which Holmes would have spurned for its obscurity. Perhaps this is inevitable: Jurisprudence trembles so uncertainly on the margin of many subjects that there will always be need for someone, in Bentham's phrase, "to pluck the mask of Mystery" from its face.[1] This is true, to a preeminent degree, of the subject of this article. Contemporary voices tell us we must recognize something obscured by the legal "positivists" whose day is now over: that there is a "point of intersection between law and morals,"[2] or that what *is* and

what *ought* to be are somehow indissolubly fused or inseparable,[3] though the positivists denied it. What do these phrases mean? Or rather which of the many things that they *could* mean, *do* they mean? Which of them do "positivists" deny and why is it wrong to do so?

I.

I shall present the subject as part of the history of an idea. At the close of the eighteenth century and the beginning of the nineteenth the most earnest thinkers in England about legal and social problems and the architects of great reforms were the great utilitarians. Two of them, Bentham and Austin, constantly insisted on the need to distinguish, firmly and with the maximum of clarity, law as it is from law as it ought to be. This theme haunts their work, and they condemned the natural-law thinkers precisely because they had blurred this apparently simple but vital distinction. By contrast, at the present time in this country and to a lesser extent in England, this separation between law and morals is held to be superficial and wrong. Some critics have thought that it blinds men to the true nature of law and its roots in social life.[4] Others have thought it not only intellectually misleading but corrupting in practice, as its worst apt to weaken resistance to state tyranny or absolutism,[5] and at its best apt to bring law into disrespect. The nonpejorative name "legal positivism," like most terms which are used as missiles in intellectual battles, has come to stand for a baffling multitude of different sins. One of them is the sin, real or alleged, of insisting, as Austin and Bentham did, on the separation of law as it is and law as it ought to be.

How then has this reversal of the wheel come about? What are the theoretical errors in this distinction? Have the practical consequences of stressing the distinction as Bentham and Austin

*From 71 *Harvard Law Review* 593 (1958). Copyright © 1958 by The Harvard Law Review Association. Reprinted by permission of the author and the publisher.

did been bad? Should we now reject it or keep it? In considering these questions we should recall the social philosophy which went along with the utilitarians' insistence on this distinction. They stood firmly but on their own utilitarian ground for all the principles of liberalism in law and government. No one has ever combined, with such even-minded sanity as the utilitarians, the passion for reform with respect for law together with a due recognition of the need to control the abuse of power even when power is in the hands of reformers. One by one in Bentham's works you can identify the elements of the *Rechtstaat* and all the principles for the defense of which the terminology of natural law has in our day been revived. Here are liberty of speech, and of press, the right of association,[6] the need that laws should be published and made widely known before they are enforced,[7] the need to control administrative agencies,[8] the insistence that there should be no criminal liability without fault,[9] and the importance of the principle of legality, *nulla poena sine lege.*[10] Some, I know, find the political and moral insight of the utilitarians a very simple one, but we should not mistake this simplicity for superficiality nor forget how favorably their simplicities compare with the profundities of other thinkers. Take only one example: Bentham on slavery. He says the question at issue is not whether those who are held as slaves can reason, but simply whether they suffer.[11] Does this not compare well with the discussion of the question in terms of whether or not there are some men whom Nature has fitted only to be the living instruments of others? We owe it to Bentham more than anyone else that we have stopped discussing this and similar questions of social policy in that form.

So Bentham and Austin were not dry analysts fiddling with verbal distinctions while cities burned, but were the vanguard of a movement which laboured with passionate intensity and much success to bring about a better society and better laws. Why then did they insist on the separation of law as it is and law as it ought to be? What did they mean? Let us first see what they said. Austin formulated the doctrine:

The existence of law is one thing; its merit or demerit is another. Whether it be or be not is one enquiry; whether it be or be not conformable to an assumed standard, is a different enquiry. A law, which actually exists, is a law, though we happen to dislike it, or though it vary from the text, by which we regulate our approbation and disapprobation. This truth, when formally announced as an abstract proposition, is so simple and glaring that it seems idle to insist upon it. But simple and glaring as it is, when enunciated in abstract expressions the enumeration of the instances in which it has been forgotten would fill a volume.

Sir William Blackstone, for example, says in his "Commentaries," that the laws of God are superior in obligation to all other laws; that no human laws should be suffered to contradict them; that human laws are of no validity if contrary to them; and that all valid laws derive their force from that Divine original.

Now, he *may* mean that all human laws ought to conform to the Divine laws. If this be his meaning, I assent to it without hesitation. ... Perhaps, again, he means that human lawgivers are themselves obliged by the Divine laws to fashion the laws which they impose by that ultimate standard, because if they do not, God will punish them. To this also I entirely assent. ...

But the meaning of this passage of Blackstone, if it has a meaning, seems rather to be this: that no human law which conflicts with the Divine law is obligatory or binding; in other words, that no human law which conflicts with the Divine law *is a law.* ...[12]

Austin's protest against blurring the distinction between what law is and what it ought to be is quite general: it is a mistake, whatever our standard of what ought to be, whatever "the text by which we regulate our approbation or disapprobation." His examples, however, are always a confusion between law as it is and law as morality would require it to be. For him, it must be remembered, the fundamental principles of morality were God's commands, to which utility was an "index": besides this there was the actual accepted morality of a social group or "positive" morality.

Bentham insisted on this distinction without characterizing morality by reference to God but only, of course, by reference to the principles of utility. Both thinkers' prime reason for this insistence was to enable men to see steadily the precise issues posed by the existence of morally bad laws, and to understand the specific character of the authority of a legal order. Bentham's general recipe for life under the government of laws was simple: it was *"to obey punctually; to censure freely."*[13] But Bentham was especially aware, as an anxious spectator of the French revolution, that this was not enough: the time might come in any society when the law's commands were so evil that the question of resistance had to be faced, and it was then essential that the issues at stake at this point should neither be oversimplified nor obscured.[14] Yet, this was precisely what the confusion between law and morals had done and Bentham found that the confusion had spread symmetrically in two different directions. On the one hand Bentham had in mind the anarchist who argues thus: "This ought not to be the law, therefore it is not and I am free not merely to censure but to disregard it." On the other hand he thought of the reactionary who argues: "This is the law, therefore it is what it ought to be," and thus stifles criticism at its birth. Both errors, Bentham thought, were to be found in Blackstone: there was his incautious statement that human laws were invalid if contrary to the law of God,[15] and "that spirit of obsequious *quietism* that seems constitutional in our Author" which "will scarce ever let him recognise a difference" between what is and what ought to be.[16] This indeed was for Bentham the occupational disease of lawyers: "[I]n the eyes of lawyers—not to speak of their dupes—that is to say, as yet, the generality of non-lawyers—the *is* and *ought to be* ... were one and indivisible."[17] There are therefore two dangers between which insistence on this distinction will help us to steer: the danger that law and its authority may be dissolved in man's conceptions of what law ought to be and the danger that the existing law may supplant morality as a final test of conduct and so escape criticism.

In view of later criticisms it is also important to distinguish several things that the utilitarians did not mean by insisting on their separation of law and morals. They certainly accepted many of the things that might be called "the intersection of law and morals." First, they never denied that, as a matter of historical fact, the development of legal systems had been powerfully influenced by moral opinion, and, conversely, that moral standards had been profoundly influenced by law, so that the content of many legal rules mirrored moral rules or principles. It is not in fact always easy to trace this historical causal connection, but Bentham was certainly ready to admit its existence; so too Austin spoke of the "frequent coincidence"[18] of positive law and morality and

attributed the confusion of what law is with what law ought to be to this very fact.

Secondly, neither Bentham nor his followers denied that by explicit legal provisions moral principles might at different points be brought into a legal system and form part of its rules, or that courts might be legally bound to decide in accordance with what they thought just or best. Bentham indeed recognized, as Austin did not, that even the supreme legislative power might be subjected to legal restraints by a constitution[19] and would not have denied that moral principles, like those of the Fifth Amendment, might form the content of such legal constitutional restraints. Austin differed in thinking that restraints on the supreme legislative power could not have the force of law, but would remain merely political or moral checks;[20] but of course he would have recognized that a statute, for example, might confer a delegated legislative power and restrict the area of its exercise by reference to moral principles.

What both Bentham and Austin were anxious to assert were the following two simple things: first, in the absence of an expressed constitutional or legal provision, it could not follow from the mere fact that a rule violated standards of morality that it was not a rule of law; and, conversely, it could not follow from the mere fact that a rule was morally desirable that it was a rule of law.

The history of this simple doctrine in the nineteenth century is too long and too intricate to trace here. Let me summarize it by saying that after it was propounded to the world by Austin it dominated English jurisprudence and constitutes part of the framework of most of those curiously English and perhaps unsatisfactory productions—the omnibus surveys of the whole field of jurisprudence. A succession of these were published after a full text of Austin's lectures finally appeared in 1863. In each of them the utilitarian separation of law and morals is treated as something that enables lawyers to attain a new clarity. Austin was said by one of his English successors, Amos, "to have delivered the law from the dead body of morality that still clung to it";[21] and even Maine, who was critical of Austin at many points, did not question this part of his doctrine. In the United States men like N. St. John Green,[22] Gray, and Holmes considered that insistence on this distinction had enabled the understanding of law as a means of social control to get off to a fruitful new start; they welcomed it both as self-evident and as illuminating—as a revealing tautology. This distinction is, of course, one of the main themes of Holmes' most famous essay "The Path of the Law,"[23] but the place it had in the estimation of these American writers is best seen in what Gray wrote at the turn of the century in *The Nature and Sources of the Law.* He said:

The great gain in its fundamental conceptions which Jurisprudence made during the last century was the recognition of the truth that the Law of a State . . . is not an ideal, but something which actually exists. . . . [I]t is not that which ought to be, but that which is. To fix this definitely in the Jurisprudence of the Common Law, is the feat that Austin accomplished.[24]

II.

So much for the doctrine in the heyday of its success. Let us turn now to some of the criticisms. Undoubtedly, when Bentham and Austin insisted on the distinction between law as it is and as it ought to be, they had in mind *particular* laws the meanings of which were clear and so not in dispute, and they were concerned to argue that such laws, even if morally outrageous, were still laws. It is, however, necessary, in considering the criticisms which later developed, to consider more than those criticisms which were directed to this particular point if we are to get at the root of the dissatisfaction felt; we must also take account of the objection that, even if what the utilitarians said on this particular point were true, their insistence on it, in a terminology suggesting a general cleavage between what is and ought to be law, obscured the fact that at other points there is an essential point of contact between the two. So in what follows I shall consider not only criticisms of the particular point which the utilitarians had in mind, but also the claim that an essential connection between law and morals emerges if we examine how laws, the meanings of which are in dispute, are interpreted and applied in concrete cases; and that this connection emerges again if we widen our point of view and ask, not whether every particular rule of law must satisfy a moral minimum in order to be a law, but whether a system of rules which altogether failed to do this could be a legal system.

There is, however, one major initial complexity by which criticism has been much confused. We must remember that the utilitarians combined with their insistence on the separation of law and morals two other equally famous but distinct doctrines. One was the important truth that a purely analytical study of legal concepts, a study of the meaning of the distinctive vocabulary of the law, was as vital to our understanding of the nature of law as historical or sociological studies, though of course it could not supplant them. The other doctrine was the famous imperative theory of law—that law is essentially a command.

These three doctrines constitute the utilitarian tradition in jurisprudence; yet they are distinct doctrines. It is possible to endorse the separation between law and morals and to value analytical inquiries into the meaning of legal concepts and yet think it wrong to conceive of law as essentially a command. One source of great confusion in the criticism of the separation of law and morals was the belief that the falsity of any one of these three doctrines in the utilitarian tradition showed the other two to be false; what was worse was the failure to see that there were three quite separate doctrines in this tradition. The indiscriminate use of the label "positivism" to designate ambiguously each one of these three separate doctrines (together with some others which the utilitarians never professed) has perhaps confused the issue more than any other single factor.[25] Some of the early American critics of the Austinian doctrine were, however, admirably clear on just this matter. Gray, for example, added at the end of the tribute to Austin, which I have already quoted, the words, "He may have been wrong in treating the Law of the State as being the command of the sovereign"[26] and he touched shrewdly on many points where the command theory is defective. But other critics have been less clearheaded and have thought that the inadequacies of the command theory which gradually came to light were sufficient to demonstrate the falsity of the separation of law and morals.

This was a mistake, but a natural one. To see how natural it was we must look a little more closely at the command idea. The famous theory that law is a command was a part of a wider and more ambitious claim. Austin said that the notion of a command was "the *key* to the sciences of jurisprudence and morals,"[27] and contemporary attempts to elucidate moral judgments in terms of "imperative" or "prescriptive" utterances echo this ambitious claim. But the command theory, viewed as an effort to identify even the quintessence of law, let alone the quintessence of morals, seems breathtaking in its simplicity and quite inadequate. There is much, even in the simplest legal system, that is distorted if presented as a command. Yet the utilitarians thought that the essence of a legal system could be conveyed if the notion of a command were supplemented by that of a habit of obedience. The simple scheme was this: What is a command? It is simply an expression by one person of the desire that another person should do or abstain from some action, accompanied by a threat of punishment which is likely to follow disobedience. Commands are laws if two conditions are satisfied: First, they must be general; second, they must be commanded by what (as both Bentham and Austin claimed) exists in every political society whatever its constitutional form, namely, a person or a group of persons who are in receipt of habitual obedience from most of the society but pay no such obedience to others. These persons are its sovereign. Thus law is the command of the uncommanded commanders of society—the creation of the legally untrammelled will of the sovereign who is by definition outside the law.

It is easy to see that this account of a legal system is threadbare. One can also see why it might seem that its inadequacy is due to the omission of some essential connection with morality. The situation which the simple trilogy of command, sanction, and sovereign avails to describe, if you take these notions at all precisely, is like that of a gunman saying to his victim, "Give me your money or your life." The only difference is that in the case of a legal system the gunman says it to a large number of people who are accustomed to the racket and habitually surrender to it. Law surely is not the gunman situation writ large, and legal order is surely not to be thus simply identified with compulsion.

This scheme, despite the points of obvious analogy between a statute and a command, omits some of the most characteristic elements of law. Let me cite a few. It is wrong to think of a legislature (and a fortiori an electorate) with a changing membership, as a group of persons habitually obeyed: this simple idea is suited only to a monarch sufficiently long-lived for a "habit" to grow up. Even if we waive this point, nothing which

legislators do makes law unless they comply with fundamental accepted rules specifying the essential lawmaking procedures. This is true even in a system having a simple unitary constitution like the British. These fundamental accepted rules specifying what the legislature must do to legislate are not commands habitually obeyed, nor can they be expressed as habits of obedience to persons. They lie at the root of a legal system, and what is most missing in the utilitarian scheme is an analysis of what it is for a social group and its officials to accept such rules. This notion, not that of a command as Austin claimed, is the "key to the science of jurisprudence," or at least one of the keys.

Again, Austin, in the case of a democracy, looked past the legislators to the electorate as "the sovereign" (or in England as part of it). He thought that in the United States the mass of the electors to the state and federal legislatures were the sovereign whose commands, given by their "agents" in the legislatures, were law. But on this footing the whole notion of the sovereign outside the law being "habitually obeyed" by the "bulk" of the population must go: for in this case the "bulk" obeys the bulk, that is, it obeys itself. Plainly the general acceptance of the authority of a lawmaking procedure, irrespective of the changing individuals who operate it from time to time, can be only distorted by an analysis in terms of mass habitual obedience to certain persons who are by definition outside the law, just as the cognate but much simpler phenomenon of the general social acceptance of a rule, say of taking off the hat when entering a church, would be distorted if represented as habitual obedience by the mass to specific persons.

Other critics dimly sensed a further and more important defect in the command theory, yet blurred the edge of an important criticism by assuming that the defect was due to the failure to insist upon some important connection between law and morals. This more radical defect is as follows. The picture that the command theory draws of life under law is essentially a simple relationship of the commander to the commanded, of superior to inferior, of top to bottom; the relationship is vertical between the commanders or authors of the law conceived of as essentially outside the law and those who are commanded and subject to the law. In this picture no place, or only an accidental or subordinate place, is afforded for a distinction between types of legal rules which are in fact radically different. Some laws require men to act in certain ways or to abstain from acting whether they wish to or not. The criminal law consists largely of rules of this sort: like commands they are simply "obeyed" or "disobeyed." But other legal rules are presented to society in quite different ways and have quite different functions. They provide facilities more or less elaborate for individuals to create structures of rights and duties for the conduct of life within the coercive framework of the law. Such are the rules enabling individuals to make contracts, wills, and trusts, and generally to mould their legal relations with others. Such rules, unlike the criminal law, are not factors designed to obstruct wishes and choices of an antisocial sort. On the contrary, these rules provide facilities for the realization of wishes and choices. They do not say (like commands) "do this whether you wish it or not," but rather "if you wish to do this, here is the way to do it." Under these rules we exercise powers, make claims, and assert rights. These phrases mark off characteristic features of laws that confer rights and powers; they are laws which are, so to speak, put at the disposition of individuals in a way in which the criminal law is not. Much ingenuity has gone into the task of "reducing" laws of this second sort to some complex variant of laws of the first sort. The effort to show that laws conferring rights are "really" only conditional stipulations of sanctions to be exacted from the person ultimately under a legal duty characterizes much of Kelsen's work.[28] Yet to urge this is really just to exhibit dogmatic determination to suppress one aspect of the legal system in order to maintain the theory that the stipulation of a sanction, like Austin's command, represents the quintessence of law. One might as well urge that the rules of baseball were "really" only complex conditional directions to the scorer and that this showed their real or "essential" nature.

One of the first jurists in England to break with the Austinian tradition, Salmond, complained that the analysis in terms of commands left the notion of a right unprovided with a place.[29] But he confused the point. He argued first, and correctly, that if laws are merely commands it is inexplicable that we should have come to speak of legal rights and powers as conferred or arising under them, but then wrongly concluded that the rules of a legal system must necessarily be connected with moral rules or principles of justice and that only on this footing could the phenomenon of legal rights be explained. Otherwise, Salmond thought, we would have to say that a mere "verbal coincidence" connects the concepts of legal and moral right. Similarly, continental critics of the utilitarians, always alive to the complexity of the notion of a subjective right, insisted that the command theory gave it no place. Hägerström insisted that if laws were merely commands the notion of an individual's right was really inexplicable, for commands are, as he said, something which we either obey or we do not obey: they do not confer rights.[30] But he, too, concluded that moral, or, as he put it, commonsense, notions of justice must therefore be necessarily involved in the analysis of any legal structure elaborate enough to confer rights.[31]

Yet, surely these arguments are confused. Rules that confer rights, though distinct from commands, need not be moral rules or coincide with them. Rights, after all, exist under the rules of ceremonies, games, and in many other spheres regulated by rules which are irrelevant to the question of justice or what the law ought to be. Nor need rules which confer rights be just or morally good rules. The rights of a master over his slaves show us that. "Their merit or demerit," as Austin termed it, depends on how rights are distributed in society and over whom or what they are exercised. These critics indeed revealed the inadequacy of the simple notions of command and habit for the analysis of law; at many points it is apparent that the social acceptance of a rule or standard of authority (even if it is motivated only by fear or superstition or rests on inertia) must be brought into the analysis and cannot itself be reduced to the two simple terms. Yet nothing in this showed the utilitarian insistence on the distinction between the existence of law and its "merits" to be wrong.

III.

I now turn to a distinctively American criticism of the separation of the law that is from the law that ought to be. It emerged from the critical study of the judicial process with which American jurisprudence has been on the whole so beneficially occupied. The most skeptical of these critics—the loosely named "Realists" of the 1930s—perhaps too naïvely accepted the conceptual framework of the natural sciences as adequate for the characterization of law and for the analysis of rule-guided action of which a living system of law at least partly consists. But they opened men's eyes to what actually goes on when courts decide cases, and the contrast they drew between the actual facts of judicial decision and the traditional terminology for describing it as if it were a wholly logical operation was usually illuminating; for in spite of some exaggeration the "Realists" made us acutely conscious of one cardinal feature of human language and human thought, emphasis on which is vital not only for the understanding of law but in areas of philosophy far beyond the confines of jurisprudence. The insight of this school may be presented in the following example. A legal rule forbids you to take a vehicle into the public park. Plainly this forbids an automobile, but what about bicycles, roller skates, toy automobiles? What about airplanes? Are these, as we say, to be called "vehicles" for the purpose of the rule or not? If we are to communicate with each other at all, and if, as in the most elementary form of law, we are to express our intentions that a certain type of behavior be regulated by rules, then the general words we use—like "vehicle" in the case I consider—must have some standard instance in which no doubts are felt about its application. There must be a core of settled meaning, but there will be, as well, a penumbra of debatable cases in which words are neither obviously applicable nor obviously ruled out. These cases will each have some features in common with the standard case; they will lack others or be accompanied by features not present in the standard case. Human invention and natural processes continually throw up such variants on the familiar, and if we are to say that these ranges of facts do or do not fall under existing rules, then the classifier must make a decision which is not dictated to him, for the facts and phenomena to which we fit our words and apply our rules are as it were *dumb*. The toy automobile cannot speak up and say, "I am a vehicle for the purpose of this legal rule," nor can the roller skates chorus, "We are not a vehicle." Fact situations do not await us neatly labeled, creased, and folded, nor is their legal classification written on them to be simply read off by the judge. Instead, in applying legal rules, someone must take the responsibility of deciding that words do or do not cover some case in hand with all the practical consequences involved in this decision.

We may call the problems which arise outside the hard core of standard instances or settled meaning "problems of the penumbra"; they are always with us whether in relation to such trivial things as the regulation of the use of the public park or in relation to the multidimensional generalities of a constitution. If a penumbra of uncertainty must surround all legal rules, then their application to specific cases in the penumbral area cannot be a matter of logical deduction, and so deductive reasoning, which for generations has been cherished as the very perfection of human reasoning, cannot serve as a model for what judges, or indeed anyone, should do in bringing particular cases under general rules. In this area men cannot live by deduction alone. And it follows that if legal arguments and legal decisions of penumbral questions are to be rational, their rationality must lie in something other than a logical relation to premises. So if it is rational or "sound" to argue and to decide that for the purposes of this rule an airplane is not a vehicle, this argument must be sound or rational without being logically conclusive. What is it then that makes such decisions correct or at least better than alternative decisions? Again, it seems true to say that the criterion which makes a decision sound in such cases is some concept of what the law ought to be; it is easy to slide from that into saying that it must be a moral judgment about what law ought to be. So here we touch upon a point of necessary "intersection between law and morals" which demonstrates the falsity or, at any rate, the misleading character of the utilitarians' emphatic insistence on the separation of law as it is and ought to be. Surely, Bentham and Austin could only have written as they did because they misunderstood or neglected this aspect of the judicial process, because they ignored the problems of the penumbra.

The misconception of the judicial process which ignores the problems of the penumbra and which views the process as consisting preeminently in deductive reasoning is often stigmatized as the error of "formalism" or "literalism." My question now is, how and to what extent does the demonstration of this error show the utilitarian distinction to be wrong or misleading? Here there are many issues which have been confused, but I can only disentangle some. The charge of formalism has been leveled both at the "positivist" legal theorist and at the courts, but of course it must be a very different charge in each case. Leveled at the legal theorist, the charge means that he has made a theoretical mistake about the character of legal decision; he has thought of the reasoning involved as consisting in deduction from premises in which the judges' practical choices or decision play no part. It would be easy to show that Austin was guiltless of this error; only an entire misconception of what analytical jurisprudence is and why he thought it important has led to the view that he, or any other analyst, believed that the law was a closed logical system in which judges deduced their decisions from premises.[32] On the contrary, he was very much alive to the character of language, to its vagueness or open character;[33] he thought that in the penumbral situation judges must necessarily legislate,[34] and, in accents that sometimes recall those of the late Judge Jerome Frank, he berated the common-law judges for legislating feebly and timidly and for blindly relying on real or fancied analogies with past cases instead of adapting their decisions to the growing needs of society as revealed by the moral standard of utility.[35] The villains of this piece, responsible for the conception of the judge as an automaton, are not the utilitarian thinkers. The responsibility, if it is to be laid at the door of any theorist, is with thinkers like Blackstone and, at an earlier stage, Montesquieu. The root of this evil is preoccupation with the separation of powers and Blackstone's "childish fiction" (as Austin termed it) that judges only "find," never "make," law.

But we are concerned with "formalism" as a vice not of jurists but of judges. What precisely is it for a judge to commit this error, to be a "formalist," "automatic," a "slot machine"? Curiously enough the literature which is full of the denunciation of these vices never makes this clear in concrete terms; instead we have only descriptions which cannot mean what they appear to say: it is said that in the formalist error courts make an excessive use of logic, take a thing to "a dryly logical extreme,"[36] or make an excessive use of analytical methods. But just how in being

a formalist does a judge make an excessive use of logic? It is clear that the essence of his error is to give some general term an interpretation which is blind to social values and consequences (or which is in some other way stupid or perhaps merely disliked by critics). But logic does not prescribe interpretation of terms; it dictates neither the stupid nor intelligent interpretation of any expression. Logic only tells you hypothetically that *if* you give a certain term a certain interpretation then a certain conclusion follows. Logic is silent on how to classify particulars—and this is the heart of a judicial decision. So this reference to logic and to logical extremes is a misnomer for something else, which must be this. A judge has to apply a rule to a concrete case—perhaps the rule that one may not take a stolen "vehicle" across state lines, and in this case an airplane has been taken.[37] He either does not see or pretends not to see that the general terms of this rule are susceptible of different interpretations and that he has a choice left open uncontrolled by linguistic conventions. He ignores, or is blind to, the fact that he is in the area of the penumbra and is not dealing with a standard case. Instead of choosing in the light of social aims, the judge fixes the meaning in a different way. He either takes the meaning that the word most obviously suggests in its ordinary nonlegal context to ordinary men, or one which the word has been given in some other legal context, or, still worse, he thinks of a standard case and then arbitrarily identifies certain features in it—for example, in the case of a vehicle, (1) normally used on land, (2) capable of carrying a human person, (3) capable of being self-propelled—and treats these three as always necessary and always sufficient conditions for the use in all contexts of the word "vehicle," irrespective of the social consequences of giving it this interpretation. This choice, not "logic," would force the judge to include a toy motor car (if electrically propelled) and to exclude bicycles and the airplane. In all this there is possibly great stupidity but no more "logic," and no less, than in cases in which the interpretation given to a general term and the consequent application of some general rule to a particular case is consciously controlled by some identified social aim.

Decisions made in a fashion as blind as this would scarcely deserve the name of decisions; we might as well toss a penny in applying a rule of law. But it is at least doubtful whether any judicial decisions (even in England) have been quite as automatic as this. Rather either the interpretations stigmatized as automatic have resulted from the conviction that it is fairer in a criminal statute to take a meaning which would jump to the mind of the ordinary man at the cost even of defeating other values, and this itself is a social policy (though possibly a bad one); or much more frequently, what is stigmatized as "mechanical" and "automatic" is a determined choice made indeed in the light of a social aim but of a conservative social aim. Certainly many of the Supreme Court decisions at the turn of the century which have been so stigmatized[38] represent clear choices in the penumbral area to give effect to a policy of a conservative type. This is peculiarly true of Mr. Justice Peckham's opinions defining the spheres of police power and due process.[39]

But how does the wrongness of deciding cases in an automatic and mechanical way and the rightness of deciding cases by reference to social purposes show that the utilitarian insistence on the distinction between what the law is and what it ought to be is wrong? I take it that no one who wished to use these vices of formalism as proof that the distinction between what is and what ought to be is mistaken would deny that the decisions stigmatized as automatic are law; nor would he deny that the system in which such automatic decisions are made is a legal system. Surely he would say that they are law, but they are bad law, they ought not to be law. But this would be to use the distinction, not to refute it; and of course both Bentham and Austin used it to attack judges for failing to decide penumbral cases in accordance with the growing needs of society.

Clearly, if the demonstration of the errors of formalism is to show the utilitarian distinction to be wrong, the point must be drastically restated. The point must be not merely that a judicial decision to be rational must be made in the light of some conception of what ought to be, but that the aims, the social policies and purposes to which judges should appeal if their decisions are to be rational, are themselves to be considered as part of the law in some suitably wide sense of "law" which is held to be more illuminating than that used by the utilitarians. This restatement of the point would have the following consequence: Instead of saying that the recurrence of penumbral questions shows us that legal rules are essentially incomplete, and that, when they fail to determine decisions, judges must legislate and so exercise a creative choice between alternatives, we shall say that the social policies which guide the judges' choice are in a sense there for them to discover; the judges are only "drawing out" of the rule what, if it is properly understood, is "latent" within it. To call this judicial legislation is to obscure some essential continuity between the clear cases of the rule's application and the penumbral decisions. I shall question later whether this way of talking is salutory, but I wish at this time to point out something obvious, but likely, if not stated, to tangle the issues. It does not follow that, because the opposite of a decision reached blindly in the formalist or literalist manner is a decision intelligently reached by reference to some conception of what ought to be, we have a junction of law and morals. We must, I think, beware of thinking in a too simple-minded fashion about the word "ought." This is not because there is no distinction to be made between law as it is and ought to be. Far from it. It is because the distinction should be between what is and what from many different points of view ought to be. The word "ought" merely reflects the presence of some standard of criticism; one of these standards is a moral standard but not all standards are moral. We say to our neighbour, "You ought not to lie," and that may certainly be a moral judgment, but we should remember that the baffled poisoner may say, "I ought to have given her a second dose." The point here is that intelligent decisions which we oppose to mechanical or formal decisions are not necessarily identical with decisions defensible on moral grounds. We may say of many a decision: "Yes, that is right; that is as it ought to be," and we may mean only that some accepted purpose or policy has been thereby advanced; we may not mean to endorse the moral propriety of the policy or the decision. So the contrast between the mechanical decision and the intelligent one can be reproduced inside a system dedicated to the pursuit of the most evil aims. It does not exist as a contrast to be found only in legal systems which, like our own, widely recognize principles of justice and moral claims of individuals.

An example may make this point plainer. With us the task of sentencing in criminal cases is the one that seems most obviously to demand from the judge the exercise of moral judgment. Here the factors to be weighed seem clearly to be moral factors: society must not be exposed to wanton attack; too much misery must not be inflicted on either the victim or his dependents; efforts must be made to enable him to lead a better life and regain a position in the society whose laws he has violated. To a judge striking the balance among these claims, with all the discretion and perplexities involved, his task seems as plain an example of the exercise of moral judgment as could be; and it seems to be the polar opposite of some mechanical application of a tariff of penalties fixing a sentence careless of the moral claims which in our system have to be weighed. So here intelligent and rational decision is guided however uncertainly by moral aims. But we have only to vary the example to see that this need not necessarily be so and surely, if it need not necessarily be so, the utilitarian point remains unshaken. Under the Nazi regime men were sentenced by courts for criticism of the regime. Here the choice of sentence might be guided exclusively by consideration of what was needed to maintain the state's tyranny effectively. What sentence would both terrorize the public at large and keep the friends and family of the prisoner in suspense so that both hope and fear would cooperate as factors making for subservience? The prisoner of such a system would be regarded simply as an object to be used in pursuit of these aims. Yet, in contrast with a mechanical decision, decision on these grounds would be intelligent and purposive, and from one point of view the decision would be as it ought to be. Of course, I am not unaware that a whole philosophical tradition has sought to demonstrate the fact that we cannot correctly call decisions or behavior truly rational unless they are in conformity with moral aims and principles. But the example I have used seems to me to serve at least as a warning that we cannot use the errors of formalism as something which per se demonstrates the falsity of the utilitarian insistence on the distinction between law as it is and law as *morally* it ought to be.

We can now return to the main point. It is true that the intelligent decision of penumbral questions is one made not mechanically but in the light of aims, purposes, and policies, though not necessarily in the light of anything we would call

moral principles, is it wise to express this important fact by saying that the firm utilitarian distinction between what the law is and what it ought to be should be dropped? Perhaps the claim that it is wise cannot be theoretically refuted for it is, in effect, an *invitation* to revise our conception of what a legal rule is. We are invited to include in the "rule" the various aims and policies in the light of which its penumbral cases are decided on the ground that these aims have, because of their importance, as much right to be called law as the core of legal rules whose meaning is settled. But though an invitation cannot be refuted, it may be refused and I would proffer two reasons for refusing this invitation. First, everything we have learned about the judicial process can be expressed in other less mysterious ways. We can say laws are incurably incomplete and we must decide the penumbral cases rationally by reference to social aims. I think Holmes, who had such a vivid appreciation of the fact that "general propositions do not decide concrete cases," would have put it that way. Second, to insist on the utilitarian distinction is to emphasize that the hard core of settled meaning is law in some centrally important sense and that even if there are borderlines, there must first be lines. If this were not so the notion of rules controlling courts' decisions would be senseless as some of the "Realists" —in their most extreme moods, and, I think, on bad grounds—claimed.[40]

By contrast, to soften the distinction, to assert mysteriously that there is some fused identity between law as it is and as it ought to be, is to suggest that all legal questions are fundamentally like those of the penumbra. It is to assert that there is no central element of actual law to be seen in the core of central meaning which rules have, that there is nothing in the nature of a legal rule inconsistent with *all* questions being open to reconsideration in the light of social policy. Of course, it is good to be occupied with the penumbra. Its problems are rightly the daily diet of the law schools. But to be occupied with the penumbra is one thing, to be preoccupied with it another. And preoccupation with the penumbra is, if I may say so, as rich a source of confusion in the American legal tradition as formalism in the English. Of course we might abandon the notion that rules have authority; we might cease to attach force or even meaning to an argument that a case falls clearly within a rule and the scope of a precedent. We might call all such reasoning "automatic" or "mechanical," which is already the routine invective of the courts. But until we decide that this *is* what we want, we should not encourage it by obliterating the utilitarian distinction.

IV.

The third criticism of the separation of law and morals is of a very different character; it certainly is less an intellectual argument against the utilitarian distinction than a passionate appeal supported not by detailed reasoning but by reminders of a terrible experience. For it consists of the testimony of those who have descended into Hell, and, like Ulysses or Dante, brought back a message for human beings. Only in this case the Hell was not beneath or beyond earth, but on it; it was a Hell created on earth by men for other men.

This appeal comes from those German thinkers who lived through the Nazi regime and reflected upon its evil manifestations in the legal system. One of these thinkers, Gustav Radbruch, had himself shared the "positivist" doctrine until the Nazi tyranny, but he was converted by this experience and so his appeal to other men to discard the doctrine of the separation of law and morals has the special poignancy of a recantation. What is important about this criticism is that it really does confront the particular point which Bentham and Austin had in mind in urging the separation of law as it is and as it ought to be. These German thinkers put their insistence on the need to join together what the utilitarians separated just where this separation was of most importance in the eyes of the utilitarians: for they were concerned with the problem posed by the existence of morally evil laws.

Before his conversion Radbruch held that resistance to law was a matter for the personal conscience, to be thought out by the individual as a moral problem, and the validity of a law could not be disproved by showing that the effect of compliance with the law would be more evil than the effect of disobedience. Austin, it may be recalled, was emphatic in condemning those who said that if human laws conflicted with the fundamental principles of morality then they cease to be laws, as talking "stark nonsense."

The most pernicious laws, and therefore those which are most opposed to the will of God, have been and are continually enforced as laws by judicial tribunals. Suppose an act innocuous, or positively beneficial, be prohibited by the sovereign under the penalty of death; if I commit this act, I shall be tried and condemned, and if I object to the sentence, that it is contrary to the law of God ... the court of justice will demonstrate the inconclusiveness of my reasoning by hanging me up, in pursuance of the law of which I have impugned the validity. An exception, demurrer, or plea, founded on the law of God was never heard in a Court of Justice, from the creation of the world down to the present moment.[41]

These are strong, indeed brutal words, but we must remember that they went along—in the case of Austin and, of course, Bentham—with the conviction that if laws reached a certain degree of iniquity then there would be a plain moral obligation to resist them and to withhold obedience. We shall see, when we consider the alternatives, that this simple presentation of the human dilemma which may arise has much to be said for it.

Radbruch, however, had concluded from the ease with which the Nazi regime had exploited subservience to mere law—or expressed, as he thought, in the "positivist" slogan "law as law" *(Gesetz als Gesetz)*—and from the failure of the German legal profession to protest against the enormities which they were required to perpetrate in the name of law, that "positivism" (meaning here the insistence on the separation of law as it is from law as it ought to be) had powerfully contributed to the horrors. His considered reflections led him to the doctrine that the fundamental principles of humanitarian morality were part of the very concept of *Recht* or Legality and that no positive enactment or statute, however clearly it was expressed and however clearly it conformed with the formal criteria of validity of a given legal system, could be valid if it contravened basic principles of morality. This doctrine can be appreciated fully only if the nuances imported by the German word *Recht* are grasped. But it is clear that the doctrine meant that every lawyer and judge should denounce statutes that transgressed the fundamental principles not as merely immoral or wrong but as having no legal character, and enactments which on this ground lack the quality of law should not be taken into account in working out the legal position of any given individual in particular circumstances. The striking recantation of his previous doctrine is unfortunately omitted from the translation of his works, but it should be read by all who wish to think afresh on the question of the interconnection of law and morals.[42]

It is impossible to read without sympathy Radbruch's passionate demand that the German legal conscience should be open to the demands of morality and his complaint that this has been too little the case in the German tradition. On the other hand there is an extraordinary naïveté in the view that insensitivity to the demands of morality and subservience to state power in a people like the Germans should have arisen from the belief that law might be law though it failed to conform with the minimum requirements of morality. Rather this terrible history prompts inquiry into why emphasis on the slogan "law is law," and the distinction between law and morals, acquired a sinister character in Germany, but elsewhere, as with the utilitarians themselves, went along with the most enlightened liberal attitudes. But something more disturbing than naïveté is latent in Radbruch's whole presentation of the issues to which the existence of morally iniquitous laws give rise. It is not, I think, uncharitable to say that we can see in his argument that he has only half digested the spiritual message of liberalism which he is seeking to convey to the legal profession. For everything that he says is really dependent upon an enormous overvaluation of the importance of the bare fact that a rule may be said to be a valid rule of law, as if this, once declared, was conclusive of the final moral question: "Ought this rule of law to be obeyed?" Surely the truly liberal answer to any sinister use of the slogan "law is law" or of the distinction between law and morals is, "Very well, but that does not conclude the question. Law is not morality; do not let it supplant morality."

However, we are not left to a mere academic discussion in order to evaluate the plea which Radbruch made for the revision of the distinction between law and morals. After the war Radbruch's conception of law as containing in itself the essential moral principle of humanitarianism was applied in practice by German courts in certain cases in which local war criminals, spies, and informers under the Nazi regime were punished. The special importance of these cases is that the persons accused of these crimes claimed that what they had done was not illegal under the laws of the regime in force at the time these actions were performed. This plea was met with the reply that the laws upon which they relied were invalid as contravening the fundamental principles of morality. Let me cite briefly one of these cases.[43]

In 1944 a woman, wishing to be rid of her husband, denounced him to the authorities for insulting remarks he had made about Hitler while home on leave from the German army. The wife was under no legal duty to report his acts, though what he had said was apparently in violation of statutes making it illegal to make statements detrimental to the government of the Third Reich or to impair by any means the military defense of the German people. The husband was arrested and sentenced to death, apparently pursuant to these statutes, though he was not executed but was sent to the front. In 1949 the wife was prosecuted in a West German court for an offense which we would describe as illegally depriving a person of his freedom (rechtswidrige Freiheitsberaubung). This was punishable as a crime under the German Criminal Code of 1871 which had remained in force continuously since its enactment. The wife pleaded that her husband's imprisonment was pursuant to the Nazi statutes and hence that she had committed no crime. The court of appeal to which the case ultimately came held that the wife was guilty of procuring the deprivation of her husband's liberty by denouncing him to the German courts, even though he had been sentenced by a court for having violated a statute, since, to quote the words of the court, the statute "was contrary to the sound conscience and sense of justice of all decent human beings." This reasoning was followed in many cases which have been hailed as a triumph of the doctrines of natural law and as signaling the overthrow of positivism. The unqualified satisfaction with this result seems to me to be hysteria. Many of us might applaud the objective—that of punishing a woman for an outrageously immoral act—but this was secured only by declaring a statute established since 1934 not to have the force of law, and at least the wisdom of this course must be doubted. There were, of course, two other choices. One was to let the woman go unpunished; one can sympathize with and endorse the view that this might have been a bad thing to do.

The other was to face the fact that if the woman were to be punished it must be pursuant to the introduction of a frankly retrospective law and with a full consciousness of what was sacrificed in securing her punishment in this way. Odious as retrospective criminal legislation and punishment may be, to have pursued it openly in this case would at least have had the merits of candour. It would have made plain that in punishing the woman a choice had to be made between two evils, that of leaving her unpunished and that of sacrificing a very precious principle of morality endorsed by most legal systems. Surely if we have learned anything from the history of morals it is that the thing to do with a moral quandary is not to hide it. Like nettles, the occasions when life forces us to choose between the lesser of two evils must be grasped with the consciousness that they are what they are. The vice of this use of the principle that, at certain limiting points, what is utterly immoral cannot be law or lawful is that it will serve to cloak the true nature of the problems with which we are faced and will encourage the romantic optimism that all the values we cherish ultimately will fit into a single system, that no one of them has to be sacrificed or compromised to accommodate another.

> "All Discord Harmony not understood
> All Partial Evil Universal Good"

This is surely untrue and there is an insincerity in any formulation of our problem which allows us to describe the treatment of the dilemma as if it were the disposition of the ordinary case.

It may seem perhaps to make too much of forms, even perhaps of words, to emphasize one way of disposing of this difficult case as compared with another which might have led, so far as the woman was concerned, to exactly the same result. Why should we dramatize the difference between them? We might punish the woman under a new retrospective law and declare overtly that we were doing something inconsistent with our principles as the lesser of two evils; or we might allow the case to pass as one in which we do not point out precisely where we sacrifice such a principle. But candour is not just one among many minor virtues of the administration of law, just as it is not merely a minor virtue of morality. For if we adopt Radbruch's view, and with him the Ger-

man courts make our protest against evil law in the form of an assertion that certain rules cannot be law because of their moral iniquity, we confuse one of the most powerful, because it is the simplest, forms of moral criticism. If with the utilitarians we speak plainly, we say that laws may be law but too evil to be obeyed. This is a moral condemnation which everyone can understand and it makes an immediate and obvious claim to moral attention. If, on the other hand, we formulate our objection as an assertion that these evil things are not law, here is an assertion which many people do not believe, and if they are disposed to consider it at all, it would seem to raise a whole host of philosophical issues before it can be accepted. So perhaps the most important single lesson to be learned from this form of the denial of the utilitarian distinction is the one that the utilitarians were most concerned to teach: when we have the ample resources of plain speech we must not present the moral criticism of institutions as propositions of a disputable philosophy.

V.

I have endeavored to show that, in spite of all that has been learned and experienced since the utilitarians wrote, and in spite of the defects of other parts of their doctrine, their protest against the confusion of what is and what ought to be law has a moral as well as an intellectual value. Yet it may well be said that, though this distinction is valid and important if applied to any particular law of a system, it is at least misleading if we attempt to apply it to "law," that is, to the notion of a legal system, and that if we insist, as I have, on the narrower truth (or truism), we obscure a wider (or deeper) truth. After all, it may be urged, we have learned that there are many things which are untrue of laws taken separately, but which are true and important in a legal system considered as a whole. For example, the connection between law and sanctions and between the existence of law and its "efficacy" must be understood in this more general way. It is surely not arguable (without some desperate extension of the word "sanction" or artificial narrowing of the word "law") that every law in a municipal legal system must have a sanction, yet it is at least plausible to argue that a legal system must, to be a legal system, provide sanctions for certain of its rules. So too, a rule of law may be said to exist though enforced or obeyed in only a minority of cases, but this could not be said of a legal system as a whole. Perhaps the differences with respect to laws taken separately and a legal system as a whole are also true of the connection between moral (or some other) conceptions of what law ought to be and law in this wider sense.

This line of argument, found (at least in embryo form) in Austin, where he draws attention to the fact that every developed legal system contains certain fundamental notions which are "necessary" and "bottomed in the common nature of man,"[44] is worth pursuing—up to a point—and I shall say briefly why and how far this is so.

We must avoid, if we can, the arid wastes of inappropriate definition, for, in relation to a concept as many-sided and vague as that of a legal system, disputes about the "essential" character, or necessity to the whole, of any single element soon begin to look like disputes about whether chess could be "chess" if played without pawns. There is a wish, which may be understandable, to cut straight through the question whether a legal system, to be a legal system, must measure up to some moral or other standard with simple statements of fact: for example, that no system which utterly failed in this respect has ever existed or could endure; that the normally fulfilled assumption that a legal system aims at some form of justice colours the whole way in which we interpret specific rules in particular cases, and if this normally fulfilled assumption were not fulfilled no one would have any reason to obey except fear (and probably not that) and still less, of course, any moral obligation to obey. The connection between law and moral standards and principles of justice is therefore as little arbitrary and as "necessary" as the connection between law and sanctions, and the pursuit of the question whether this necessity is logical (part of the "meaning" of law) or merely factual or causal can safely be left as an innocent pastime for philosophers.

Yet in two respects I should wish to go further (even though this involves the use of a philosophical fantasy) and show what could intelligibly be meant by the claim that certain provisions in a legal system are "necessary." The world in which we live, and we who live in it, may one day change in many different ways; and if this change were radical enough not only would certain statements of fact now true be false and vice versa, but whole ways of thinking and talking which constitute our present conceptual apparatus, through which we see the world and each other, would lapse. We have only to consider how the whole of our social, moral, and legal life, as we understand it now, depends on the contingent fact that though our bodies do change in shape, size, and other physical properties they do not do this so drastically nor with such quicksilver rapidity and irregularity that we cannot identify each other as the same persistent individual over considerable spans of time. Though this is but a contingent fact which may one day be different, on it at present rest huge structures of our thought and principles of action and social life. Similarly, consider the following possiblity (not because it is more than a possibility but because it reveals why we think certain things necessary in a legal system and what we mean by this): suppose that men were to become invulnerable to attack by each other, were clad perhaps like giant land crabs with an impenetrable carapace, and could extract the food they needed from the air by some internal chemical process. In such circumstances (the details of which can be left to science fiction) rules forbidding the free use of violence and rules constituting the minimum form of property—with its rights and duties sufficient to enable food to grow and be retained until eaten—would not have the necessary nonarbitrary status which they have for us, constituted as we are in a world like ours. At present, and until such radical changes supervene, such rules are so fundamental that if a legal system did not have them there would be no point in having any other rules at all. Such rules overlap with basic moral principles vetoing murder, violence, and theft; and so we can add to the factual statement that all legal systems in fact coincide with morality at such vital points, the statement that this is, in this sense, necessarily so. And why not call it a "natural" necessity?

Of course even this much depends on the fact that in asking what content a legal system must have we take this question to be worth asking only if we who consider it cherish the humble aim of survival in close proximity to our fellows. Natural-law theory, however, in all its protean guises, attempts to push the argument much further and to assert that human beings are equally devoted to and united in their conception of aims (the pursuit of knowledge, justice to their fellow men) other than that of survival, and these dictate a further necessary content to a legal system (over and above my humble minimum) without which it would be pointless. Of course we must be careful not to exaggerate the differences among human beings, but it seems to me that above this minimum the purposes men have for living in society are too conflicting and varying to make possible much extension of the argument that some fuller overlap of legal rules and moral standards is "necessary" in this sense.

Another aspect of the matter deserves attention. If we attach to a legal system the minimum meaning that it must consist of general rules—general both in the sense that they refer to courses of action, not single actions, and to multiplicities of men, not single individuals—this meaning connotes the principle of treating like cases alike, though the criteria of when cases are alike will be, so far, only the general elements specified in the rules. It is, however, true that *one* essential element of the concept of justice is the principle of treating like cases alike. This is justice in the administration of the law, not justice of the law. So there is, in the very notion of law consisting of general rules, something which prevents us from treating it as if morally it is utterly neutral, without any necessary contact with moral principles. Natural procedural justice consists therefore of those principles of objectivity and impartiality in the administration of the law which implement just this aspect of law and which are designed to ensure that rules are applied only to what are genuinely cases of the rule or at least to minimize the risks of inequalities in this sense.

These two reasons (or excuses) for talking of a certain overlap between legal and moral standards as necessary and natural, of course, should not satisfy anyone who is really disturbed by the utilitarian or "positivist" insistence that law and morality are distinct. This is so because a legal system that satisfied these minimum requirements might apply, with the most pedantic impartiality as between the persons affected, laws which were hideously oppressive, and might deny to a vast rightless slave population the minimum benefits of protection from violence and theft. The stink of such societies is, after all, still in our

nostrils and to argue that they have (or had) no legal system would only involve the repetition of the argument. Only if the rules failed to provide these essential benefits and protection for anyone—even for a slave-owning group—would the minimum be unsatisfied and the system sink to the status of a set of meaningless taboos. Of course no one denied those benefits would have any reason to obey except fear and would have every moral reason to revolt.

VI.

I should be less than candid if I did not, in conclusion, consider something which, I suspect, most troubles those who react strongly against "legal positivism." Emphasis on the distinction between law as it is and law as it ought to be may be taken to depend upon and to entail what are called "subjectivist" and "relativist" or "noncognitive" theories concerning the very nature of moral judgments, moral distinctions, or "values." Of course the utilitarians themselves (as distinct from later positivists like Kelsen) did not countenance any such theories, however unsatisfactory their moral philosophy may appear to us now. Austin thought ultimate moral principles were the commands of God, known to us by revelation or through the "index" of utility, and Bentham thought they were verifiable propositions about utility. Nonetheless I think (though I cannot prove) that insistence upon the distinction between law as it is and ought to be has been, under the general head of "positivism," confused with a moral theory according to which statements of what is the case ("statements of fact") belong to a category or type radically different from statements of what ought to be ("value statements"). It may therefore be well to dispel this source of confusion.

There are many contemporary variants of this type of moral theory: according to some, judgments of what ought to be, or ought to be done, either are or include as essential elements expression of "feeling," "emotion," or "attitudes" or "subjective preferences"; in others such judgments both express feelings or emotions or attitudes and enjoin others to share them. In other variants such judgments indicate that a particular case falls under a general principle or policy of action which the speaker has "chosen" or to which he is "committed" and which is itself not a recognition of what is the case but analogous to a general "imperative" or command addressed to all including the speaker himself. Common to all these variants is the insistence that judgments of what ought to be done, because they contain such "non-cognitive" elements, cannot be argued for or established by rational methods as statements of fact can be, and cannot be shown to follow from any statement of fact but only from other judgments of what ought to be done in conjunction with some statement of fact. We cannot, on such a theory, demonstrate, for example, that an action was wrong, ought not to have been done, merely by showing that it consisted of the deliberate infliction of pain solely for the gratification of the agent. We only show it to be wrong if we add to those verifiable "cognitive" statements of fact a general principle not itself verifiable or "cognitive" that the infliction of pain in such circumstances is wrong, ought not to be done. Together with this general distinction between statements of what is and what ought to be go sharp parallel distinctions between statements about means and statements of moral ends. We can rationally discover and debate what are appropriate means to given ends, but ends are not rationally discoverable or debatable; they are "fiats of the will," expressions of "emotions," "preferences," or "attitudes."

Against all such views (which are of course far subtler than this crude survey can convey) others urge that all these sharp distinctions between is and ought, fact and value, means and ends, cognitive and noncognitive, are wrong. In acknowledging ultimate ends or moral values we are recognizing something as much imposed upon us by the character of the world in which we live, as little a matter of choice, attitude, feeling, emotion as the truth of factual judgments about what is the case. The characteristic moral argument is not one in which the parties are reduced to expressing or kindling feelings or emotions or issuing exhortations or commands to each other but one by which parties come to acknowledge after closer examination and reflection that an initially disputed case falls within the ambit of a vaguely apprehended principle (itself no more "subjective," no more a "fiat of our will" than any other principle of classification) and this has as much title to be called "cognitive" or "rational" as any other initially disputed classification of particulars.

Let us now suppose that we accept this rejection of "noncognitive" theories of morality and this denial of the drastic distinction in type between statements of what is and what ought to be, and that moral judgments are as rationally defensible as any other kind of judgments. What would follow from this as to the nature of the connection between law as it is and law as it ought to be? Surely, from this alone, nothing. Laws, however morally iniquitous, would still (so far as this point is concerned) be laws. The only difference which the acceptance of this view of the nature of moral judgments would make would be that the moral iniquity of such laws would be something that could be demonstrated; it would surely follow merely from a statement of what the rule required to be done that the rule was morally wrong and so ought not to be law or conversely that it was morally desirable and ought to be law. But the demonstration of this would not show the rule not to be (or to be) law. Proof that the principles by which we evaluate or condemn laws are rationally discoverable, and not mere "fiats of the will," leaves untouched the fact that there are laws which may have any degree of iniquity or stupidity and still be laws. And conversely there are rules that have every moral qualification to be laws and yet are not laws.

Surely something further or more specific must be said if disproof of "noncognitivism" or kindred theories in ethics is to be relevant to the distinction between law as it is and law as it ought to be, and to lead to the abandonment at some point or some softening of this distinction. No one has done more than Professor Lon Fuller of the Harvard Law School in his various writings to make clear such a line of argument and I will end by criticising what I take to be its central point. It is a point which again emerges when we consider not those legal rules or parts of legal rules the meanings of which are clear and excite no debate but the interpretation of rules in concrete cases where doubts are initially felt and argument develops about their meaning. In no legal system is the scope of legal rules restricted to the range of concrete instances which were present or are believed to have been present in the minds of legislators; this indeed is one of the important differences between a legal rule and a command.

Yet, when rules are recognized as applying to instances beyond any that legislators did or could have considered, their extension to such new cases often presents itself not as a deliberate choice or fiat on the part of those who so interpret the rule. It appears neither as a decision to give the rule a new or extended meaning nor as a guess as to what legislators, dead perhaps in the eighteenth century, would have said had they been alive in the twentieth century. Rather, the inclusion of the new case under the rule takes its place as a natural elaboration of the rule, as something implementing a "purpose" which it seems natural to attribute (in some sense) to the rule itself rather than to any particular person dead or alive. The utilitarian description of such interpretative extension of old rules to new cases as judicial legislation fails to do justice to this phenomenon; it gives no hint of the differences between a deliberate fiat or decision to treat the new case in the same way as past cases and a recognition (in which there is little that is deliberate or even voluntary) that inclusion of the new case under the rule will implement or articulate a continuing and identical purpose, hitherto less specifically apprehended.

Perhaps many lawyers and judges will see in this language something that precisely fits their experience; others may think it a romantic gloss on facts better stated in the utilitarian language of judicial "legislation" or in the modern American terminology of "creative choice."

To make the point clear Professor Fuller uses a nonlegal example from the philosopher Wittgenstein which is, I think, illuminating.

Someone says to me: "Show the children a game." I teach them gaming with dice and the other says "I did not mean that sort of game." Must the exclusion of the game with dice have come before his mind when he gave me the order?[45]

Something important does seem to me to be touched on in this example. Perhaps there are the following (distinguishable) points. First, we normally do interpret not only what people are trying to do but what they say in the light of assumed common human objectives so that unless the contrary were expressly indicated we would not interpret an instruction to show a young child a game as a mandate to introduce him to gambling even though in other contexts the word "game" would be naturally so interpreted. Second, very often, the speaker whose words are thus interpreted might say: "Yes, that's what I mean [or "that's what I meant all along"] though I never thought of it until you put this particular case to me." Third, when we thus recognize, perhaps after argument or consultation with others, a particular case not specifically envisaged beforehand as falling within the ambit of some vaguely expressed instruction, we may find this experience falsified by description of it as a mere decision on our part so to treat the particular case, and that we can only describe this faithfully as coming to realize and to articulate what we "really" want or our "true purpose"—phrases which Professor Fuller uses later in the same article.[46]

I am sure that many philosophical discussions of the character of moral argument would benefit from attention to cases of the sort instanced by Professor Fuller. Such attention would help to provide a corrective to the view that there is a sharp separation between "ends" and "means" and that in debating "ends" we can only work on each other nonrationally, and that rational argument is reserved for dicussion of "means." But I think the relevance of his point to the issue whether it is correct or wise to insist on the distinction between law as it is and law as it ought to be is very small indeed. Its net effect is that in interpreting legal rules there are some cases which we find after reflection to be so natural an elaboration or articulation of the rule that to think of and refer to this as "legislation," "making law," or a "fiat" on our part would be misleading. So, the argument must be, it would be misleading to distinguish in such cases between what the rule is and what it ought to be—at least in some sense of ought. We think it ought to include the new case and come to see after reflection that it really does. But even if this way of presenting a recognizable experience as an example of a fusion between is and is admitted, two caveats must be borne in mind. The first is that "ought" in this case need have nothing to do with morals for the reasons explained already in section III: there may be just the same sense that a new case will implement and articulate the purpose of a rule in interpreting the rules of a game or some hideously immoral code of oppression whose immorality is appreciated by those called in to interpret it. They too can see what the "spirit" of the game they are playing requires in previously unenvisaged cases. More important is this: After all is said and done we must remember how rare in the law is the phenomenon held to justify this way of talking, how exceptional is this feeling that one way of deciding a case is imposed upon us as the only natural or rational elaboration of some rule. Surely it cannot be doubted that, for most cases of interpretation, the language of choice between alternatives, "judicial legislation" or even "fiat" (though not arbitrary fiat), better conveys the realities of the situation.

Within the framework of relatively well-settled law there jostle too many alternatives too nearly equal in attraction between which judge and lawyer must uncertainly pick their way to make appropriate here language which may well describe those experiences which we have in interpreting our own or others' principles of conduct, intention, or wishes, when we are not conscious of exercising a deliberate choice, but rather of recognizing something awaiting recognition. To use in the description of the interpretation of laws the suggested terminology of a fusion of inability to separate what is law and ought to be will serve (like earlier stories that judges only find, never make, law) only to conceal the facts, that here if anywhere we live among uncertainties between which we have to choose, and that the existing law imposes only limits on our choice and not the choice itself.

NOTES

1. Bentham, *A Fragment on Government,* in 1 Works 221, 235 (Bowring ed. 1859) (preface, 41st para.).

2. D'Entrèves, Natural Law 116 (2d ed. 1952).

3. Fuller, The Law in Quest of Itself 12 (1940); Brecht, *The Myth of Is and Ought,* 54 Harv. L. Rev. 811 (1941); Fuller, *Human Purpose and Natural Law,* 53 J. Philos 697 (1953).

4. See Friedmann, Legal Theory 154, 294–95 (3d ed. 1953). Friedmann also says of Austin that "by his sharp distinction between the science of legislation and the science of law," he "inaugurated an era of legal positivism and self-sufficiency which enabled the rising national State to assert its authority undisturbed by juristic doubts." *Id.* at 416. Yet, "the existence of a highly organised State which claimed sovereignty and unconditional obedience of the citizen" is said to be "the political condition which makes analytical positivism possible." *Id.* at 163. There is therefore some difficulty in determining which, in this account, is to be hen and which egg (analytical positivism or political condition). Apart from this, there seems to be little evidence that any national State rising in or after 1832 (when the *Province of Jurisprudence Deter-*

mined was first published) was enabled to assert its authority by Austin's work or "the era of legal positivism" which he "inaugurated."

5. See Radbruch, *Die Erneuerung des Rechts,* 2 Die Wandlung 8 (Germany 1947); Radbruch, *Gesetzliches Unrecht und Übergesetzliches Recht,* I Süddeutsche Juristen-Zeitung 105 (Germany 1946) (reprinted in Radbruch, Rechtsphilosophie 347 (4th ed. 1950). Radbruch's views are discussed at pp. 617–21 *infra.*

6. Bentham, *A Fragment on Government,* in 1 Works 221, 230 (Bowring ed. 1859) (preface, 16th para.); Bentham, *Principles of Penal Law,* in 1 Works 365, 574–75, 576–78 (Bowring ed. 1859) (pt. III, c. XXI, 8th para., 12th para.).

7. Bentham, *Of Promulgation of the Laws,* in 1 Works 155 (Bowring ed. 1859); Bentham, *Principles of the Civil Code,* in 1 Works 297, 323 (Bowring ed. 1859) (pt. I, c. XVII, 2d para.); Bentham, *A Fragment on Government,* in 1 Works 221, 233 n.[*m*] (Bowring ed. 1859) (preface, 35th para.).

8. Bentham, *Principles of Penal Law,* in 1 Works 365, 576 (Bowring ed. 1859) (pt. III, c. XXI, 10th para., 11th para.).

9. Bentham, *Principles of Morals and Legislation,* in 1 Works I, 84 (Bowring ed. 1859) (c. XIII).

10. Bentham, *Anarchical Fallacies,* in 2 Works 489, 511–12 (Bowring ed. 1859) (art. VIII); Bentham, *Principles of Morals and Legislation,* in 1 Works 1, 144 (Bowring ed. 1859) (c. XIX, 11th para.).

11. *Id.* at 142 n.§ (c. XIX, 4th para. n.§).

12. Austin, The Province of Jurisprudence Determined 184–85 (Library of Ideas ed. 1954).

13. Bentham, *A Fragment on Government,* in 1 Works 221, 230 (Bowring ed. 1859) (preface, 16th para.).

14. See Bentham, *Principles of Legislation,* in The Theory of Legislation 1, 65 n.* (Ogden ed. 1931) (c. XII, 2d para. n.*).

Here we touch upon the most difficult of questions. If the law is not what it ought to be; if it openly combats the principle of utility; ought we to obey it? Ought we to violate it? Ought we to remain neuter between the law which commands an evil, and morality which forbids it?

See also Bentham, *A Fragment on Government,* in 1 Works 221, 287–88 (Bowring ed. 1859) (c. IV, 20th–25th paras.).

15. 1 Blackstone, Commentaries *41. Bentham criticized "this dangerous maxim," saying "the natural tendency of such a doctrine is to impel a man, by the force of conscience, to rise up in arms against any law whatever that he happens not to like." Bentham, *A Fragment on Government,* in 1 Works 221, 287 (Bowring ed. 1859) (c. IV, 19th para.). See also Bentham, *A Comment on the Commentaries* 49 (1928) (c. III). For an expression of a fear lest anarchy result from such a doctrine, combined with a recognition that resistance may be justified on grounds of utility, See Austin, *op. cit. supra* note 12, at 186.

16. Bentham, *A Fragment on Government,* in 1 Works 221, 294 (Bowring ed. 1859) (c. V, 10th para.).

17. Bentham, *A Commentary on Humphreys' Real Property Code,* in 5 Works 389 (Bowring ed. 1843).

18. Austin, *op. cit. supra* note 12, at 162.

19. Bentham, *A Fragment on Government,* in 1 Works 221, 289–90 (Bowring ed. 1859) (c. IV, 33d–34th paras.).

20. See Austin, *op. cit. supra* note 12, at 231.

21. Amos, The Science of Law 4 (5th ed. 1881). See also Markby, Elements of Law 4–5 (5th ed. 1896):

Austin, by establishing the distinction between positive law and morals, not only laid the foundation for a science of law, but cleared the conception of law ... of a number of pernicious consequences to which ... it had been supposed to lead. Positive laws, as Austin has shown, must be legally binding, and yet a law may be unjust. ... He has admitted that law

itself may be immoral, in which case it may be our moral duty to disobey it. . . .
Cf. Holland, Jurisprudence 1–20 (1880).

22. See Green, Book Review, 6 Am. L. Rev. 57, 61 (1871) (reprinted in Green, Essays and Notes on the Law of Tort and Crime 31, 35 (1933)).

23. 10 Harv. L. Rev. 457 (1897).

24. Gray, The Nature and Sources of the Law 94 (1st ed. 1909) (§ 213).

25. It may help to identify five (there may be more) meanings of "positivism" bandied about in contemporary jurisprudence:

(1) the contention that laws are commands of human beings, see pp. 602–06 *infra,*

(2) the contention that there is no necessary connection between law and morals or law as it is and ought to be, see pp. 594–600 *supra,*

(3) the contention that the analysis (or study of the meaning) of legal concepts is (a) worth pursuing and (b) to be distinguished from historical inquiries into the causes or origins of laws, from sociological inquiries into the relation of law and other social phenomena, and from the criticism or appraisal of law whether in terms of morals, social aims, "functions," or otherwise, see pp. 608–10 *infra,*

(4) the contention that a legal system is a "closed logical system" in which correct legal decisions can be deduced by logical means from predetermined legal rules without reference to social aims, policies, moral standards, see pp. 608–10 *infra,* and

(5) the contention that moral judgments cannot be established or defended, as statements of facts can, by rational argument, evidence, or proof ("noncognitivism" in ethics), see pp. 624–26 *infra.*

Bentham and Austin held the views described in (1), (2), and (3) but not those in (4) and (5). Opinion (4) is often ascribed to analytical jurists, see pp. 608–10 *infra,* but I know of no "analyst" who held this view.

26. Gray, The Nature and Sources of the Law 94–95 (2d ed. 1921).

27. Austin, *op. cit. supra* note 12, at 13.

28. See, *e.g.,* Kelsen, General Theory of Law and State 58–61, 143–44 (1945). According to Kelsen, all laws, not only those conferring rights and powers, are reducible to such "primary norms" conditionally stipulating sanctions.

29. Salmond, The First Principles of Jurisprudence 97–98 (1893). He protested against "the creed of what is termed the English school of jurisprudence," because it "attempted to deprive the idea of law of that ethical significance which is one of its most essential elements." *Id.* at 9, 10.

30. Hägerström, Inquiries Into the Nature of Law and Morals 217 (Olivecrona ed. 1953): "[T]he whole theory of the subjective rights of private individuals . . . is incompatible with the imperative theory." See also *id.* at 221:

The description of them [claims to legal protection] as rights is wholly derived from the idea that the law which is concerned with them is a true expression of rights and duties in the sense in which the popular notion of justice understands these terms.

31. *Id.* at 218.

32. This misunderstanding of analytical jurisprudence is to be found in, among others, Stone, The Province and Function of Law 141 (1950):

In short, rejecting the implied assumption that all propositions of all parts of the law must be logically consistent with each other and proceed on a single set of definitions . . . he [Cardozo, J.,] denied that the law is actually what the analytical jurist, *for his limited purposes,* assumes it to be.

See also *id.* at 49, 52, 138, 140; Friedmann, Legal Theory 209 (3d ed. 1953). This misunderstanding seems to depend on the unexamined and false belief that analytical studies of the meaning of legal terms would be impossible or absurd if, to reach sound decisions in particular cases, more than a capacity for formal logical reasoning from unambiguous and clear predetermined premises is required.

33. See the discussion of vagueness and uncertainty in law, in Austin, *op. cit. supra* note 12, at 202–05, 207, in which Austin recognized that, in consequence of this vagueness, often only "fallible tests" can be provided for determining whether particular cases fall under general expressions.

34. See Austin, *op. cit. supra* note 12, at 191: "I cannot understand how any person who has considered the subject can suppose that society could possibly have gone on if judges had not legislated. . . ." As a corrective to the belief that the analytical jurist must take a "slot machine" or "mechanical" view of the judicial process it is worth noting the following observations made by Austin:

(1) Whenever law has to be applied, the " 'competition of opposite analogies' " may arise, for the case "may resemble in some of its points" cases to which the rule has been applied in the past and in other points "cases from which the application of the law has been withheld." 2 Austin, Lectures on Jurisprudence 633 (5th ed. 1885).

(2) Judges have commonly decided cases and so derived new rules by "building" on a variety of grounds including sometimes (in Austin's opinion too rarely) their views of what law ought to be. Most commonly they have derived law from preexisting law by "consequence founded on analogy," *i.e.,* they have made a new rule "in *consequence* of the existence of a similar rule applying to subjects which are *analogous.* . . ." 2 *id.* at 638–39.

(3) "[I]f every rule in a system of law were perfectly definite or precise," these difficulties incident to the application of law would not arise. "But the ideal completeness and correctness I now have imagined is not attainable in fact. . . . though the system had been built and ordered with matchless solicitude and skill." 2 *id.* at 997–98. Of course he thought that much could and should be done by codification to eliminate uncertainty. See 2 *id.* at 662–81.

35. 2 *id.* at 641:

Nothing, indeed, can be more natural, than that legislators, direct or judicial (especially if they be narrow-minded, timid and unskillful), should lean as much as they can on the examples set by their predecessors.

See also 2 *id.* at 647:

But it is much to be regretted that Judges of capacity, experience and weight, have not seized every opportunity of introducing a new rule (a rule beneficial for the future). . . . This is the reproach I should be inclined to make against Lord Eldon. . . . [T]he Judges of the Common Law Courts would not do what they ought to have done, namely to model their rules of law and of procedure to the growing exigencies of society, instead of stupidly and sulkily adhering to the old and barbarous usages.

36. Hynes v. New York Cent. R.R., 231 N.Y. 229, 235, 131 N.E. 898, 900 (1921); see Pound, Interpretations of Legal History 123 (2d ed. 1930); Stone, *op. cit. supra* note 32, at 140–41.

37. See McBoyle v. United States, 283 U.S. 25 (1931).

38. See, *e.g.,* Pound, *Mechanical Jurisprudence,* 8 Colum. L. Rev. 605, 615–16 (1908).

39. See, *e.g.,* Lochner v. New York, 198 U.S. 45 (1905). Justice Peckham's opinion that there were no reasonable grounds for interfering with the right of free contract by determining the hours of labour in the occupation of a baker

may indeed be a wrongheaded piece of conservatism but there is nothing automatic or mechanical about it.

40.   One recantation of this extreme position is worth mention in the present context. In the first edition of *The Bramble Bush,* Professor Llewellyn committed himself wholeheartedly to the view that "what these officials do about disputes is, to my mind, the law itself" and that "*rules* . . . are important so far as they help you . . . predict what judges will do. . . . That is all their importance, except as pretty playthings." Llewellyn, The Bramble Bush 3, 5 (1st ed. 1930). In the second edition he said that these were "unhappy words when not more fully developed, and they are plainly at best a very partial statement of the whole truth. . . . [O]ne office of law is to control officials in some part, and to guide them even . . . where no thoroughgoing control is possible, or is desired. . . . [T]he words fail to take proper account . . . of the office of the institution of law as an instrument of conscious shaping. . . ." Llewellyn, The Bramble Bush 9 (2d ed. 1951).

41.   Austin, the Province of Jurisprudence Determined 185 (Library of Ideas ed. 1954).

42.   See Radbruch, *Gesetzliches Unrecht und Übergesetzliches Recht,* 1 Süddeutsche Juristen-Zeitung 105 (Germany 1946) (reprinted in Radbruch, Rechts-philosophie 347 (4th ed. 1950)). I have used the translation of part of this essay and of Radbruch, *Die Erneuerung des Rechts,* 2 Die Wandlung 8 (Germany 1947), prepared by Professor Lon Fuller of the Harvard Law School as a mimeographed supplement to the readings in jurisprudence used in his course at Harvard.

43.   Judgment of July 27, 1949, Oberlandesgericht, Bamberg, 5 Süddeutsche Juristen-Zeitung 207 (Germany 1950), 64 Harv. L. Rev. 1005 (1951); See Freidmann, Legal Theory 457 (3d ed. 1953).

44.   Austin, *Uses of the Study of Jurisprudence,* in The Province of Jurisprudence Determined 365, 373, 367–69 (Library of Ideas ed. 1954).

45.   Fuller, *Human Purpose and Natural Law,* 53 J. Philos. 697, 700 (1956).

46.   *Id.* at 701, 702.

L O N   L.   F U L L E R

The Problem of the Grudge Informer*

By a narrow margin you have been elected Minister of Justice of your country, a nation of some twenty million inhabitants. At the outset of your term of office you are confronted by a serious problem that will be described below. But first the background of this problem must be presented.

For many decades your country enjoyed a peaceful, constitutional and democratic government. However, some time ago it came upon bad times. Normal relations were disrupted by a deepening economic depression and by an increasing antagonism among various factional groups, formed along economic, political, and religious lines. The proverbial man on horseback appeared in the form of the Headman of a politi-

cal party or society that called itself the Purple Shirts.

In a national election attended by much disorder the Headman was elected President of the Republic and his party obtained a majority of the seats in the General Assembly. The success of the party at the polls was partly brought about by a campaign of reckless promises and ingenious falsifications, and partly by the physical intimidation of night-riding Purple Shirts who frightened many people away from the polls who would have voted against the party.

When the Purple Shirts arrived in power they took no steps to repeal the ancient Constitution or any of its provisions. They also left intact the Civil and Criminal Codes and the Code of Procedure. No official action was taken to dismiss any government official or to remove any judge from the bench. Elections continued to be held at inter-

*From *The Morality of Law,* Revised Edition, by Lon L. Fuller (New Haven: Yale University Press, 1969), pp. 245–53. Reprinted by permission of the author and the publisher.

vals and ballots were counted with apparent honesty. Nevertheless, the country lived under a reign of terror.

Judges who rendered decisions contrary to the wishes of the party were beaten and murdered. The accepted meaning of the Criminal Code was perverted to place political opponents in jail. Secret statutes were passed, the contents of which were known only to the upper levels of the party hierarchy. Retroactive statutes were enacted which made acts criminal that were legally innocent when committed. No attention was paid by the government to the restraints of the Constitution, of antecedent laws, or even of its own laws. All opposing political parties were disbanded. Thousands of political opponents were put to death, either methodically in prisons or in sporadic night forays of terror. A general amnesty was declared in favor of persons under sentence for acts "committed in defending the fatherland against subversion." Under this amnesty a general liberation of all prisoners who were members of the Purple Shirt party was effected. No one not a member of the party was released under the amnesty.

The Purple Shirts as a matter of deliberate policy preserved an element of flexibility in their operations by acting at times through the party "in the streets," and by acting at other times through the apparatus of the state which they controlled. Choice between the two methods of proceeding was purely a matter of expediency. For example, when the inner circle of the party decided to ruin all the former Socialist-Republicans (whose party put up a last-ditch resistance to the new regime), a dispute arose as to the best way of confiscating their property. One faction, perhaps still influenced by prerevolutionary conceptions, wanted to accomplish this by a statute declaring their goods forfeited for criminal acts. Another wanted to do it by compelling the owners to deed their property over at the point of a bayonet. This group argued against the proposed statute on the ground that it would attract unfavorable comment abroad. The Headman decided in favor of direct action through the party to be followed by a secret statute ratifying the party's action and confirming the titles obtained by threats of physical violence.

The Purple Shirts have now been overthrown and a democratic and constitutional government restored. Some difficult problems have, however, been left behind by the deposed regime. These you and your associates in the new government must find some way of solving. One of these problems is that of the "grudge informer."

During the Purple Shirt regime a great many people worked off grudges by reporting their enemies to the party or to the government authorities. The activities reported were such things as the private expression of views critical of the government, listening to foreign radio broadcasts, associating with known wreckers and hooligans, hoarding more than the permitted amount of dried eggs, failing to report a loss of identification papers within five days, etcetera. As things then stood with the administration of justice, any of these acts, if proved, could lead to a sentence of death. In some cases this sentence was authorized by "emergency" statutes; in others it was imposed without statutory warrant, though by judges duly appointed to their offices.

After the overthrow of the Purple Shirts, a strong public demand grew up that these grudge informers be punished. The interim government, which preceded that with which you are associated, temporized on this matter. Meanwhile it has become a burning issue and a decision concerning it can no longer be postponed. Accordingly, your first act as Minister of Justice has been to address yourself to it. You have asked your five Deputies to give thought to the matter and to bring their recommendations to conference. At the conference the five Deputies speak in turn as follows:

FIRST DEPUTY. "It is perfectly clear to me that we can do nothing about these so-called grudge informers. The acts they reported were unlawful according to the rules of the government then in actual control of the nation's affairs. The sentences imposed on their victims were rendered in accordance with principles of law then obtaining. These principles differed from those familar to us in ways that we consider detestable. Nevertheless they were then the law of the land. One of the principal differences between that law and our own lies in the much wider discretion it accorded to the judge in criminal matters. This rule and its consequences are as much entitled to respect by us as the reform which the Purple Shirts introduced into the law of wills, whereby only two witnesses were required instead of three. It is immaterial that the rule granting the judge a more or less uncontrolled discretion in criminal cases was never formally enacted but was a matter of tacit acceptance. Exactly the same thing can be said of the opposite rule which we accept that restricts the judge's discretion narrowly. The difference between ourselves and the Purple Shirts is not that theirs was an unlawful government—a contradiction in terms—but lies rather in the field of ideology. No one has a greater abhorrence than I for Purple Shirtism. Yet the fundamental difference between our philosophy and theirs is that we permit and tolerate differences in viewpoint, while they attempted to impose their monolithic code on everyone. Our whole system of government assumes that law is a flexible thing, capable of expressing and effectuating many different aims. The cardinal point of our creed is that when an objective has been duly incorporated into a law or judicial decree it must be provisionally accepted even by those that hate it, who must await their chance at the polls, or in another litigation, to secure a legal recognition for their own aims. The Purple Shirts, on the other hand, simply disregarded laws that incorporated objectives of which they did not approve, not even considering it worth the effort involved to repeal them. If we now seek to unscramble the acts of the Purple Shirt regime, declaring this judgment invalid, that statute void, this sentence excessive, we shall be doing exactly the thing we most condemn in them. I recognize that it will take courage to carry through with the program I recommend and we shall have to resist strong pressures to public opinion. We shall also have to be prepared to prevent the people from taking the law into their own hands. In the long run, however, I believe the course I recommend is the only one that will insure the triumph of the conceptions of law and government in which we believe."

SECOND DEPUTY. "Curiously, I arrive at the same conclusion as my colleague, by an exactly opposite route. To me it seems absurd to call the Purple Shirt regime a lawful government. A legal system does not exist simply because policemen continue to patrol the streets and wear uniforms or because a constitution and code are left on the shelf unrepealed. A legal system presupposes laws that are known, or can be known, by those subject to them. It presupposes some uniformity of action and that like cases will be given like treatment. It presupposes the absence of some lawless power, like the Purple Shirt Party, standing above the government and able at any time to interfere with the administration of justice whenever it does not function according to the whims of that power. All of these presuppositions enter into the very conception of an order of law and have nothing to do with political and economic ideologies. In my opinion law in any ordinary sense of the word ceased to exist when the Purple Shirts came to power. During their regime we had, in effect, an interregnum in the rule of law. Instead of a government of laws we had a war of all against all conducted behind barred doors, in dark alleyways, in palace intrigues, and prison-yard conspiracies. The acts of these so-called grudge informers were just one phase of that war. For us to condemn these acts as criminal would involve as much incongruity as if we were to attempt to apply juristic conceptions to the struggle for existence that goes on in the jungle or beneath the surface of the sea. We must put this whole dark, lawless chapter of our history behind us like a bad dream. If we stir among its hatreds, we shall bring upon ourselves something of its evil spirit and risk infection from its miasmas. I therefore say with my colleague, let bygones be bygones. Let us do nothing about the so-called grudge informers. What they did do was neither lawful nor contrary to law, for they lived, not under a regime of law, but under one of anarchy and terror."

THIRD DEPUTY. "I have a profound suspicion of any kind of reasoning that proceeds by an 'either-or' alternative. I do not think we need to assume either, on the one hand, that in some manner the whole of the Purple Shirt regime was outside the realm of law, or, on the other, that all of its doings are entitled to full credence as the acts of a lawful government. My two colleagues have unwittingly delivered powerful arguments against these extreme assumptions by demonstrating that both of them lead to the same absurd conclusion, a conclusion that is ethically and politically impossible. If one reflects about the matter without emotion it becomes clear that we did not have during the Purple Shirt regime a 'war of all against all.' Under the surface much of what we call normal human life went on—marriages were contracted, goods were sold, wills were drafted and executed. This life was attended by the usual dislocations—automobile accidents, bankruptcies, unwitnessed wills, defamatory misprints in the newspapers. Much of this normal life and most of these equally normal dislocations of it were unaffected by the Purple Shirt ideology. The legal questions that arose in this area were handled by the courts much as they had been formerly and much as they are being handled today. It would invite an intolerable chaos if we were to declare everything that happened under the Purple Shirts to be without legal basis. On the other hand, we certainly cannot say that the murders committed in the streets by members of the party acting under orders from the Headman were lawful simply because the party had achieved control of the government and its chief had become President of the Republic. If we must condemn the criminal acts of the party and its members, it would seem absurd to uphold every act which happened to be canalized through the apparatus of a government that had become, in effect, the alter ego of the Purple Shirt Party. We must therefore, in this situation, as in most human affairs, discriminate. Where the Purple Shirt philosophy intruded itself and perverted the administration of justice from its normal aims and uses, there we must interfere. Among these perversions of justice I would count, for example, the case of a man who was in love with another man's wife and brought about the death of the husband by informing against him for a wholly trivial offense, that is, for not reporting a loss of his identification papers within five days. This informer was a murderer under the Criminal Code which was in effect at the time of his act and which the Purple Shirts had not repealed. He encompassed the death of one who stood in the way of his illicit passions and utilized the courts for the realization of his murderous intent. He knew that the courts were themselves the pliant instruments of whatever policy the Purple Shirts might for the moment consider expedient. There are other cases that are equally clear. I admit that there are also some that are less clear. We shall be embarrassed,

for example, by the cases of mere busybodies who reported to the authorities everything that looked suspect. Some of these persons acted not from desire to get rid of those they accused, but with a desire to curry favor with the party, to divert suspicions (perhaps ill-found) raised against themselves, or through sheer officiousness. I don't know how these cases should be handled, and make no recommendation with regard to them. But the fact that these troublesome cases exist should not deter us from acting at once in the cases that are clear, of which there are far too many to permit us to disregard them."

FOURTH DEPUTY. "Like my colleague I too distrust 'either-or' reasoning, but I think we need to reflect more than he has about where we are headed. This proposal to pick and choose among the acts of this deposed regime is thoroughly objectionable. It is, in fact, Purple Shirtism itself, pure and simple. We like this law, so let us enforce it. We like this judgment, let it stand. This law we don't like, therefore it never was a law at all. This governmental act we disapprove, let it be deemed a nullity. If we proceed this way, we take toward the laws and acts of the Purple Shirt government precisely the unprincipled attitude they took toward the laws and acts of the government they supplanted. We shall have chaos, with every judge and every prosecuting attorney a law unto himself. Instead of ending the abuses of the Purple Shirt regime, my colleague's proposal would perpetuate them. There is only one way of dealing with this problem that is compatible with our philosophy of law and government and that is to deal with it by duly enacted law, I mean, by a special statute directed toward it. Let us study this whole problem of the grudge informer, get all the relevant facts, and draft a comprehensive law dealing with it. We shall not then be twisting old laws to purposes for which they were never intended. We shall furthermore provide penalties appropriate to the offense and not treat every informer as a murderer simply because the one he informed against was ultimately executed. I admit that we shall encounter some difficult problems of draftsmanship. Among other things, we shall have to assign a definite legal meaning to 'grudge' and that will not be easy. We should not be deterred by these difficulties, however, from adopting the only course that will lead us out of a condition of lawless, personal rule."

FIFTH DEPUTY. "I find a considerable irony in the last proposal. It speaks of putting a definite end to the abuses of the Purple Shirtism, yet it proposes to do this by resorting to one of the most hated devices of the Purple Shirt regime, the ex post facto criminal statute. My colleague dreads the confusion that will result if we attempt without a statute to undo and redress 'wrong' acts of the departed order, while we uphold and enforce its 'right' acts. Yet he seems not to realize that his proposed statute is a wholly specious cure for this uncertainty. It is easy to make a plausible argument for an undrafted statute; we all agree it would be nice to have things down in black and white on paper. But just what would this statute provide? One of my colleagues speaks of someone who had failed for five days to report a loss of his indentification papers. My colleague implies that the judicial sentence imposed for that offense, namely death, was so utterly disproportionate as to be clearly wrong. But we must remember that at that time the underground movement against the Purple Shirts was mounting in intensity and that the Purple Shirts were being harassed constantly by people with false identification papers. From their point of view they had a real problem, and the only objection we can make to their solution of it (other than the fact that we didn't want them to solve it) was that they acted with somewhat more rigor than the occasion seemed to demand. How will my colleague deal with this case in his statute, and with all of its cousins and second cousins? Will he deny the existence of any need for law and order under the Purple Shirt regime? I will not go further into the difficulties involved in drafting this proposed statute, since they are evident enough to anyone who reflects. I shall instead turn to my own solution. It has been said on very respectable authority that the main purpose of the criminal law is to give an outlet to the human instinct for revenge. There are times, and I believe this is one of them, when we should allow that instinct to express itself directly without the intervention of forms of law. This matter of the grudge informers is already in process of straightening itself out. One reads almost every day that a former lackey of the Purple Shirt regime has met his just reward in some unguarded spot. The people are quietly handling this thing in their own way and if we leave them alone, and instruct our public prosecutors to do the same, there will soon be no problem left for us to solve. There will be some disorders, of course, and a few innocent heads will be broken. But our government and our legal system will not be involved in the affair and we shall not find ourselves hopelessly bogged down in an attempt to unscramble all the deeds and misdeeds of the Purple Shirts."

As Minister of Justice which of these recommendations would you adopt?

ROSCOE POUND

The Application of Law*

Three steps are involved in the adjudication of a controversy according to law: (1) Finding the law, ascertaining which of the many rules in the legal system is to be applied, or, if none is applicable, reaching a rule for the cause (which may or may not stand as a rule for subsequent cases) on the basis of given materials in some way which the legal system points out; (2) interpreting the rule so chosen or ascertained, that is, determining its meaning as it was framed and with respect to its intended scope; (3) applying to the cause in hand the rule so found and interpreted. In the past these have been confused under the name of interpretation. It was assumed that the function of the judge consisted simply in interpreting an authoritatively given rule of wholly extrajudicial origin by an exact process of deducing its logically implied content and in mechanically applying the rule so given and interpreted. This assumption has its origin in the stage of the strict law in the attempt to escape from the overdetail on the one hand, and the vague sententiousness on the other hand, which are characteristic of primitive law. For the most part primitive law is made up of simple, precise, detailed rules for definite narrowly defined situations. It has no general principles. The first step toward a science of law is the making of distinctions between what comes within and what does not come within the legal meaning of a rule. But a body of primitive law also often contains a certain number of sententious legal proverbs, put in striking form so as to stick in the memory, but vague in their content. The strict law by means of a conception of results obtained inevitably from fixed rules and undeviating remedial proceedings seeks relief from the uncertainty inherent in the finding of a larger content for overdetailed special rules through differentiation of cases and the application of legal proverbial sayings through the "equity of the tribunal." It conceives of application of law as involving nothing but a mechanical fitting of the case with the straitjacket of rule or remedy. The inevitable adjustments and extendings and limitations, which an attempt to administer justice in this way must involve, are covered up by a fiction of interpretation in order to maintain the general security.

Philosophical rationalizing of the attempt to avoid the overpersonal administration of justice incident to the partial reversion to justice without law in the stage of equity and natural law, reinforced the assumption that judicial application of law was a mechanical process and was but a phase of interpretation. In the eighteenth century it was given scientific form in the theory of separation of powers. The legislative organ made laws. The executive administered them. The judiciary applied them to the decision of controversies. It was admitted in Anglo-American legal thinking that courts must interpret in order to apply. But the interpretation was taken not to be in any wise a lawmaking and the application was taken not to involve any administrative element and to be wholly mechanical. On the Continent interpretation so as to make a binding rule for future cases was deemed to belong only to the legislator. The maturity of law was not willing to admit that judge or jurist could make anything. It was not the least service of the analytical jurisprudence of the last century to show that the greater part of what goes by the name of interpretation in this way of thinking is really a lawmaking process, a supplying of new law where no rule or no sufficient rule is at hand. "The fact is," says Gray most truly, "that the difficulties of so-called

*From *An Introduction to the Philosophy of Law* (New Haven: Yale University Press, 1922), Chap. 3. Copyright © 1922 by Yale University Press. Reprinted by permission of the publisher.

interpretation arise when the legislature has had no meaning at all; when the question which is raised on the statute never occurred to it; when what the judges have to do is, not to determine what the legislature did mean on a point which was present to its mind, but to guess what it would have intended on a point not present to its mind had the point been present." The attempt to maintain the separation of powers by constitutional prohibitions has pointed to the same lesson from another side. Lawmaking, administration and adjudication cannot be rigidly fenced off one from the other and turned over each to a separate agency as its exclusive field. There is rather a division of labor as to typical cases and a practical or historical apportionment of the rest.

Finding the law may consist merely in laying hold of a prescribed text of a code or statute. In that event the tribunal must proceed to determine the meaning of the rule and to apply it. But many cases are not so simple. More than one text is at hand which might apply; more than one rule is potentially applicable, and the parties are contending which shall be made the basis of a decision. In that event the several rules must be interpreted in order that intelligent selection may be made. Often the genuine interpretation of the existing rules shows that none is adequate to cover the case and that what is in effect, if not in theory, a new one must be supplied. Attempts to foreclose this process by minute, detailed legislation have failed signally, as, for example, in the overgrown code of civil procedure in New York. Providing of a rule by which to decide the cause is a necessary element in the determination of a large proportion of the causes that come before our higher tribunals, and it is often because a rule must be provided that the parties are not content to abide the decision of the court of first instance.

Cases calling for genuine interpretation are relatively few and simple. Moreover genuine interpretation and lawmaking under the guise of interpretation run into one another. In other words, the judicial function and the legislative function run into one another. It is the function of the legislative organ to make laws. But from the nature of the case it cannot make laws so complete and all-embracing that the judicial organ will not be obliged to exercise a certain lawmaking function also. The latter will rightly consider this a subordinate function. It will take

it to be one of supplementing, developing and shaping given materials by means of a given technique. None the less it is a necessary part of judicial power. Pushed to the extreme that regards all judicial lawmaking as unconstitutional usurpation, our political theory, a philosophical classification made over by imperfect generalization from the British constitution as it was in the seventeenth century, has served merely to intrench in the professional mind the dogma of the historical school, that legislative lawmaking is a subordinate function and exists only to supplement the traditional element of the legal system here and there and to set the judicial or juristic tradition now and then in the right path as to some particular item where it had gone astray.

In Anglo-American law we do not think of analogical development of the traditional materials of the legal system as interpretation. In Roman-law countries, where the law is made up of codes supplemented and explained by the codified Roman law of Justinian and modern usage on the basis thereof, which stands as the common law, it seems clear enough that analogical application whether of a section of the code or of a text of the Roman law is essentially the same process. Both are called interpretation. As our common law is not in the form of authoritative texts, the nature of the process that goes on when a leading case is applied by analogy, or limited in its application, or distinguished, is concealed. It does not seem on the surface to be the same process as when a text of the Digest is so applied or limited or distinguished. Hence it has been easy for us to assume that courts did no more than genuinely interpret legislative texts and deduce the logical content of authoritatively established traditional principles. It has been easy to accept a political theory, proceeding on the dogma of separation of powers, and to lay down that courts only interpret and apply, that all making of law must come from the legislature, that courts must "take the law as they find it," as if they could always find it ready-made for every case. It has been easy also to accept a juristic theory that law cannot be made; that it may only be found, and that the process of finding it is a matter purely of observation and logic, involving no creative element. If we really believed this pious fiction, it would argue little faith in the logical powers of the bench in view of the diversity of judicially asserted doctrines on the same point which so frequently exist in our case law and the widely different opinions of our best judges with respect to them. As interpretation is difficult, when it is difficult, just because the legislature had no actual intent to ascertain, so the finding of the common law on a new point is difficult because there is no rule of law to find. The judicial and the legislative functions run together also in judicial ascertainment of the common law by analogical application of decided cases.

As interpretation on the one side runs into lawmaking and so the judicial function runs into the legislative function, on the other side interpretation runs into application and so the judicial function runs into the administrative or executive. Typically judicial treatment of a controversy is a measuring of it by a rule in order to reach a universal solution for a class of causes of which the cause in hand is but an example. Typically administrative treatment of a situation is a disposition of it as a unique occurrence, an individualization whereby effect is given to its special rather than to its general features. But administration cannot ignore the universal aspects of situations without endangering the general security. Nor may judicial decision ignore their special aspects and exclude all individualization in application without sacrificing the social interest in the individual life through making justice too wooden and mechanical. The idea that there is no administrative element in the judicial decision of causes and that judicial application of law should be a purely mechanical process goes back to Aristotle's Politics. Writing before a strict law had developed, in what may be called the highest point of development of primitive law, when the personal character and feelings for the time being of kings or magistrates or dicasts played so large a part in the actual workings of legal justice, Aristotle sought relief through a distinction between the administrative and the judicial. He conceived that discretion was an administrative attribute. In administration regard was to be had to times and men and special circumstances. The executive was to use a wise discretion in adjusting the machinery of government to actual situations as they arose. On the other hand, he conceived that a court should have no discretion. To him the judicial office was a Procrustean one of fitting each case to the legal bed, if necessary by a surgical

operation. Such a conception met the needs of the strict law. In a stage of legal maturity it was suited to the Byzantine theory of law as the will of the emperor and of the judge as the emperor's delegate to apply and give effect to that will. In the Middle Ages it had a sufficient basis in authority and in the needs of a period of strict law. Later it fitted well into the Byzantine theory of lawmaking which French publicists adopted and made current in the seventeenth and eighteenth centuries. In the United States it seemed to be required by our constitutional provisions for a separation of powers. But in practice it has broken down no less completely than the analogous idea of entire separation of the judicial from the lawmaking function.

Almost all of the problems of jurisprudence come down to a fundamental one of rule and discretion, of administration of justice by law and administration of justice by the more or less trained intuition of experienced magistrates. Controversies as to the nature of law, whether the traditional element or the imperative element of legal systems is the typical law, controversies as to the nature of lawmaking, whether the law is found by judicial empiricism or made by conscious legislation, and controversies as to the bases of law's authority, whether in reason and science on the one hand or in command and sovereign will on the other hand, get their significance from their bearing upon this question. Controversies as to the relation of law and morals, as to the distinction of law and equity, as to the province of the court and of the jury, as to fixed rule or wide judicial power in procedure, and as to judicial sentence and administrative individualization in punitive justice are but forms of this fundamental problem. This is not the place to discuss that problem. Suffice it to say that both are necessary elements in the administration of justice and that instead of eliminating either, we must partition the field between them. But it has been assumed that one or the other must govern exclusively, and there has been a continual movement in legal history back and forth between wide discretion and strict detailed rule, between justice without law, as it were, and justice according to law. The power of the magistrate has been a liberalizing agency in periods of growth. In the stage of equity and natural law, a stage of infusion of moral ideas from without into the law, the power of the magistrate to give legal force to his purely moral ideas was a chief instrument. Today we rely largely upon administrative boards and commissions to give legal force to ideas which the law ignores. On the other hand rule and form with no margin of application have been the main reliance of periods of stability. The strict law sought to leave nothing to the judge beyond seeing whether the letter had been complied with. The nineteenth century abhorred judicial discretion and sought to exclude the administrative element from the domain of judicial justice. Yet a certain field of justice without law always remained and by one device or another the balance of the supposedly excluded administrative element was preserved.

In the strict law individualization was to be excluded by hard and fast mechanical procedure. In practice this procedure was corrected and the balance between rule and discretion, between the legal and the administrative, was restored by fictions and by an executive dispensing power. Roman equity has its origin in the *imperium* of the *praetor*—his royal power to dispense with the strict law in particular situations. Also English equity has its origin in the royal power of discretionary application of law and dispensing with law in particular cases, misuse of which as a political institution was one of the causes of the downfall of the Stuarts. Thus we get a third agency for restoring the balance in the form of systematic interposition of praetor or chancellor on equitable grounds, leading to a system of equity. Carried too far in the stage of equity and natural law, overdevelopment of the administrative element brings about a reaction and in the maturity of law individualization is pushed to the wall once more. Yet this elimination of the administrative takes place more in theory and in appearance than in reality. For justice comes to be administered in large measure through the application of legal standards which admit of a wide margin for the facts of particular cases, and the application of these standards is committed to laymen or to the discretion of the tribunal. Moreover a certain judicial individualization goes on. Partly this takes the form of a margin of discretionary application of equitable remedies, handed down from the state of equity and natural law. Partly it takes the form of ascertainment of the facts with reference to the legal result desired in view of the legal rule or of choice between competing rules in effect

covering the same ground, although nominally for distinct situations. In other words, a more subtle fiction does for the maturity of law what is done for the strict law by its relatively crude procedural fictions.

Of these five agencies for preserving the administrative element in judicial justice, in periods when legal theory excludes it, two call for special consideration.

It is usual to describe law as an aggregate of rules. But unless the word rule is used in so wide a sense as to be misleading, such a definition, framed with reference to codes or by jurists whose eyes were fixed upon the law of property, gives an inadequate picture of the manifold components of a modern legal system. Rules, that is, definite, detailed provisions for definite, detailed states of fact, are the main reliance of the beginnings of law. In the maturity of law they are employed chiefly in situations where there is exceptional need of certainty in order to uphold the economic order. With the advent of legal writing and juristic theory in the transition from the strict law to equity and natural law, a second element develops and becomes a controlling factor in the administration of justice. In place of detailed rules precisely determining what shall take place upon a precisely detailed state of facts, reliance is had upon general premises for judicial and juristic reasoning. These legal principles, as we call them, are made use of to supply new rules, to interpret old ones, to meet new situations, to measure the scope and application of rules and standards and to reconcile them when they conflict or overlap. Later, when juristic study seeks to put the materials of the law in order, a third element develops, which may be called legal conceptions. These are more or less exactly defined types, to which we refer cases or by which we classify them, so that when a state of facts is classified we may attribute thereto the legal consequences attaching to the type. All of these admit of mechanical or rigidly logical application. A fourth element, however, which plays a great part in the everyday administration of justice, is of quite another character.

Legal standards of conduct appear first in Roman equity. In certain cases of transactions or relations involving good faith, the formula was made to read that the defendant was to be condemned to that which in good faith he ought to give or do for or render to the plaintiff. Thus the judge had a margin of discretion to determine what good faith called for and in Cicero's time the greatest lawyer of the day thought these *actiones bonae fidei* required a strong judge because of the dangerous power which they allowed him. From this procedural device, Roman lawyers worked out certain standards or measures of conduct, such as what an upright and diligent head of a family would do, or the way in which a prudent and diligent husbandman would use his land. In similar fashion English equity worked out a standard of fair conduct on the part of a fiduciary. Later the Anglo-American law of torts worked out, as a measure for those who are pursuing some affirmative course of conduct, the standard of what a reasonable, prudent man would do under the circumstances. Also the law of public utilities worked out standards of reasonable service, reasonable facilities, reasonable incidents of the service and the like. In all these cases the rule is that the conduct of one who acts must come up to the requirements of the standard. Yet the significant thing is not the fixed rule but the margin of discretion involved in the standard and its regard for the circumstances of the individual case. For three characteristics may be seen in legal standards: (1) They all involve a certain moral judgment upon conduct. It is to be "fair," or "conscientious," or "reasonable," or "prudent," or "diligent." (2) They do not call for exact legal knowledge exactly applied, but for common sense about common things or trained intuition about things outside of everyone's experience. (3) They are not formulated absolutely and given an exact content, either by legislation or by judicial decision, but are relative to times and places and circumstances and are to be applied with reference to the facts of the case in hand. They recognize that within the bounds fixed each case is to a certain extent unique. In the reaction from equity and natural law, and particularly in the nineteenth century, these standards were distrusted. Lord Camden's saying that the discretion of a judge was "the law of tyrants," that it was different in different men, was "casual" and dependent upon temperament, has in it the whole spirit of the maturity of law. American state courts sought to turn the principles by which the chancellors were wont to exercise their discretion into hard and fast rules of jurisdiction. They sought to re-

duce the standard of reasonable care to a set of hard and fast rules. If one crossed a railroad, he must "stop, look and listen." It was negligence *per se* to get on or off a moving car, to have part of the body protruding from a railroad car, and the like. Also they sought to put the duties of public utilities in the form of definite rules with a detailed, authoritatively fixed content. All these attempts to do away with the margin of application involved in legal standards broke down. The chief result was a reaction in the course of which many states turned over all questions of negligence to juries, free even from effective advice from the bench, while many other jurisdictions have been turning over subject after subject to administrative boards and commissions to be dealt with for a season without law. In any event, whether the standard of due care in an action for negligence is applying by a jury, or the standard of reasonable facilities for transportation is applying by a public service commission, the process is one of judging of the quality of a bit of conduct under its special circumstances and with reference to ideas of fairness entertained by the layman or the ideas of what is reasonable entertained by the more or less expert commissioner. Common sense, experience and intuition are relied upon, not technical rule and scrupulously mechanical application.

We are familiar with judicial individualization in the administration of equitable remedies. Another form, namely, individualization through latitude of application under the guise of choice or ascertainment of a rule, is concealed by the fiction of the logical completeness of the legal system and the mechanical, logical infallibility of the logical process whereby the predetermined rules implicit in the given legal materials are deduced and applied. To a large and apparently growing extent the practice of our application of law has been that jurors or courts, as the case may be, take the rules of law as a general guide, determine what the equities of the cause demand, and contrive to find a verdict or render a judgment accordingly, wrenching the law no more than is necessary. Many courts today are suspected of ascertaining what the equities of a controversy require, and then raking up adjudicated cases to justify the result desired. Often formulas are conveniently elastic so that they may or may not apply. Often rules of contrary tenor overlap, leaving a convenient no-man's-land wherein cases may be decided either way according to which rule the court chooses in order to reach a result arrived at on other grounds. Occasionally a judge is found who acknowledges frankly that he looks chiefly at the ethical situation between the parties and does not allow the law to interfere therewith beyond what is inevitable.

Thus we have in fact a crude equitable application, crude individualization, throughout the field of judicial administration of justice. It is assumed by courts more widely than we suspect, or at least, more widely than we like to acknowledge. Ostensibly there is no such power. But when one looks beneath the surface of the law reports, the process reveals itself under the name of "implication" or in the guise of two lines of decisions of the same tribunal upon the same point from which it may choose at will, or in the form of what have been termed "soft spots" in the law— spots where the lines are so drawn by the adjudicated cases that the court may go either way as the ethical exigencies of the special circumstances of the case in hand may require, with no apparent transgression of what purport to be hard and fast rules. Such has been the result of attempts to exclude the administrative element in adjudication. In theory there is no such thing except with respect to equitable remedies, where it exists for historical reasons. In practice there is a great deal of it, and that in a form which is unhappily destructive of certainty and uniformity. Necessary as it is, the method by which we attain a needed individualization is injurious to respect for law. If the courts do not respect the law, who will? There is no exclusive cause of the current American attitude toward the law. But judicial evasion and warping of the law, in order to secure in practice a freedom of judicial action not conceded in theory, is certainly one cause. We need a theory which recognizes the administrative element as a legitimate part of the judicial function and insists that individualization in the application of legal precepts is no less important than the contents of those precepts themselves.

Three theories of application of law obtain in the legal science of today. The theory which has the largest following among practitioners and in dogmatic exposition of the law is analytical. It assumes a complete body of law with no gaps and no antinomies, given authority by the state at one stroke and so to be treated as if every item was of the same date as every other. If the law is in the form of a code, its adherents apply the canons of genuine interpretation and ask what the several code provisions mean as they stand, looked at logically rather than historically. They endeavor to find the preappointed code pigeonhole for each concrete case, to put the case in hand into it by a purely logical process and to formulate the result in a judgment. If the law is in the form of a body of reported decisions, they assume that those decisions may be treated as if all rendered at the same time and as containing implicitly whatever is necessary to the decision of future causes which they do not express. They may define conceptions or they may declare principles. The logically predetermined decision is contained in the conception to which the facts are referred or involved in the principle within whose scope the facts fall. A purely logical process, exactly analogous to genuine interpretation of a legislative rule, will yield the appropriate conception from given premises or discover the appropriate principle from among those which superficially appear to apply. Application is merely formulation in a judgment of the result obtained by analysis of the case and logical development of the premises contained in the reported decisions.

Among teachers a historical theory has the larger following. If the law is in the form of a code, the code provisions are assumed to be in the main declaratory of the law as it previously existed; the code is regarded as a continuation and development of preexisting law. All exposition of the code and of any provision thereof must begin by an elaborate inquiry into the preexisting law and the history and development of the competing juristic theories among which the framers of the code had to choose. If the law is in the form of a body of reported decisions, the later decisions are regarded as but declaring and illustrating the principles to be found by historical study of the older ones; as developing legal conceptions and principles to be found by historical study of the older law. Hence all exposition must begin with an elaborate historical inquiry in which the idea that has been unfolding in the course of judicial decision is revealed and the lines are disclosed along which legal development must move. But when the content of the applicable legal precept is discovered in these ways, the method of applying it in no way differs from that which obtains under the analytical theory. The process of application is assumed to be a purely logical one. Do the facts come within or fail to come within the legal precept? This is the sole question for the judge. When by historical investigation he has found out what the rule is, he has only to fit it to just and unjust alike.

Analytical and historical theories of application of law thus seek to exclude the administrative element wholly and their adherents resort to fictions to cover up the judicial individualization which none the less obtains in practice or else ignore it, saying that it is but a result of the imperfect constitution of tribunals or of the ignorance of sloth of those who sit therein. The latter explanation is no more satisfying than the fictions, and a new theory has sprung up of late in continental Europe which may be understood best by calling it the equitable theory, since the methods of the English Chancellor had much to do with suggesting it. To the adherents of this theory the essential thing is a reasonable and just solution of the individual controversy. They conceive of the legal precept, whether legislative or traditional, as a guide to the judge, leading him toward the just result. But they insist that within wide limits he should be free to deal with the individual case so as to meet the demands of justice between the parties and accord with the reason and moral sense of ordinary men. They insist that application of law is not a purely mechanical process. They contend that it involves not logic only but moral judgments as to particular situations and courses of conduct in view of the special circumstances which are never exactly alike. They insist that such judgments involve intuitions based upon experience and are not to be expressed in definitely formulated rules. They argue that the cause is not to be fitted to the rule but the rule to the cause.

Much that has been written by advocates of the equitable theory of application of law is extravagant. As usually happens, in reaction from theories going too far in one direction this theory has gone too far in the other. The last century would have eliminated individualization of application. Now, as in the sixteenth- and seventeenth-century reaction from the strict law, come those who would have nothing else; who would turn over the whole field of judicial justice to administrative methods. If we must choose, if judicial administration of justice must of necessity be wholly mechanical or else wholly administrative, it was a sound instinct of lawyers in the maturity of law that led them to prefer the former. Only a saint, such as Louis IX under the oak at Vincennes, may be trusted with the wide powers of a judge restrained only by a desire for just results in each case to be reached by taking the law for a general guide. And St. Louis did not have the crowded calendars that confront the modern judge. But are we required to choose? May we not learn something from the futility of all efforts to administer justice exclusively by either method? May we not find the proper field of each by examining the means through which in fact we achieve an individualization which we deny in theory, and considering the cases in which those means operate most persistently and the actual administration of justice most obstinately refuses to become as mechanical in practice as we expect it to be in theory?

In Anglo-American law today there are no less than seven agencies for individualizing the application of law. We achieve an individualization in practice: (1) through the discretion of courts in the application of equitable remedies; (2) through legal standards applied to conduct generally when injury results and also to certain relations and callings; (3) through the power of juries to render general verdicts; (4) through latitude of judicial application involved in finding the law; (5) through devices for adjusting penal treatment to the individual offender; (6) through informal methods of judicial administration in petty courts, and (7) through administrative tribunals. The second and fourth have been considered. Let us look for a moment at the others.

Discretion in the exercise of equitable remedies is an outgrowth of the purely personal intervention in extraordinary cases on grounds that appealed to the conscience of the chancellor in which equity jurisdiction has its origin. Something of the original flavor of equitable interposition remains in the doctrine of personal bar to relief, and in the ethical quality of some of the maxims which announce policies to be pursued in the exercise of the chancellor's powers. But it was possible for the nineteenth century to reconcile what remained of the chancellor's discretion with its mode of thinking. Where the plaintiff's right was legal but the legal remedy was not adequate to secure him in what the legal right entitled him to claim, equity gave a concurrent remedy supplementing the strict law. As the remedy in equity was supplementary and concurrent, in case the chancellor in his discretion kept his hands off, as he would if he felt that he could not bring about an equitable result, the law would still operate. The plaintiff's right was in no wise at the mercy of anyone's discretion. He merely lost an extraordinary and supplementary remedy and was left to the ordinary course of the law. Such was the orthodox view of the relation of law and equity. Equity did not alter a jot or tittle of the law. It was a remedial system alongside of the law, taking the law for granted and giving legal rights greater efficacy in certain situations. But take the case of a "hard bargain," where the chancellor in his discretion may deny specific performance. In England and in several states the damages at law do not include the value of the bargain where the contract is for the sale of land. Hence unless specific performance is granted, the plaintiff's legal right is defeated. It is notorious that bargains appeal differently to different chancellors in this respect. In the hands of some the doctrine as to hard bargains has a tendency to become wooden, as it were. There is a hard and fast rule that certain bargains are "hard" and that equity will not enforce them. In states where the value of the bargain may be recovered at law, it may well be sometimes that the bargain might as well be enforced in equity, if it is not to be cancelled. But the chancellor is not unlikely to wash his hands of a hard case, saying that the court of law is more callous; let that court act, although that court is the same judge with another docket before him. In other hands, the doctrine tends to become ultro-ethical and to impair the security of transactions. In other words, the margin of discretion in application of equitable remedies tends on the one hand to disappear through crystallization of the principles governing its exercise into rigid rules, or on the other hand, to become overpersonal and uncertain and capricious. Yet as one reads the reports attentively he cannot doubt that in action it is an important engine of justice; that it is a needed safety valve in the working of our legal system.

At common law the chief reliance for individualizing the application of law is the power of juries to render general verdicts, the power to find the facts in such a way as to compel a different result from that which the legal rule strictly applied would require. In appearance there has been no individualization. The judgment follows necessarily and mechanically from the facts upon the record. But the facts found were found in order to reach the result and are by no means necessarily the facts of the actual case. Probably this power alone made the common law of master and servant tolerable in the last generation. Yet exercise of this power, with respect to which, as Lord Coke expressed it, "the jurors are chancellors," has made the jury an unsatisfactory tribunal in many classes of cases. It is largely responsible for the practice of repeated new trials which makes the jury a most expensive tribunal. The crude individualization achieved by juries, influenced by emotional appeals, prejudice and the peculiar personal ideas of individual jurors, involves quite as much injustice at one extreme as mechanical application of law by judges at the other extreme. Indeed the unchecked discretion of juries, which legislation has brought about in some jurisdictions, is worse than the hobbled court and rigid mechanical application of law from which it is a reaction.

Our administration of punitive justice is full of devices for individualizing the application of criminal law. Our complicated machinery of prosecution involves a great series of mitigating agencies whereby individual offenders may be spared or dealt with leniently. Beginning at the bottom there is the discretion of the police as to who and what shall be brought to the judicial mill. Next are the wide powers of our prosecuting officers who may ignore offences or offenders, may dismiss proceedings in their earlier stages, may present them to grand juries in such a way that no indictment results, or may enter a *nolle prosequi* after indictment. Even if the public prosecutor desires to prosecute, the grand jury may ignore the charge. If the cause comes to trial, the petit jury may exercise a dispensing power by means of a general verdict. Next comes judicial discretion as to sentence, or in some jurisdictions, assessment of punishment by the discretion of the trial jury. Upon these are superposed administrative parole or probation and executive power to pardon. The lawyer-politician who practices in the criminal courts knows well how to work upon this complicated machinery so as to enable the professional criminal to escape as well as those or even instead of those for whom these devices were intended. They have been developed to obviate the unhappy results of a theory which would have made the punishment mechanically fit the crime instead of adjusting the penal treatment to the criminal. Here, as elsewhere, the attempt to exclude the administrative element has brought about back-handed means of individualization which go beyond the needs of the situation and defeat the purposes of the law.

Even more striking is the recrudescence of personal government, by way of reaction from an extreme of government of laws and not of men, which is involved in the setting up of administrative tribunals on every hand and for every purpose. The regulation of public utilities apportionment of the use of the water of running streams among different appropriators, workmen's compensation, the actual duration and nature of punishment for crime, admission to and practice of professions and even of trades, the power to enter or to remain in the country, banking, insurance, unfair competition and restraint of trade, the enforcement of factory laws, of pure food laws, of housing laws and of laws as to protection from fire and the relation of principal and agent, as between farmers and commission merchants, are but some of the subjects which the living law, the law in action, is leaving to executive justice in administrative tribunals. To some extent this is required by the increasing complexity of the social order and the minute division of labor which it involves. Yet this complexity and this division of labor developed for generations in which the common-law jealousy of administration was dominant. Chiefly our revival of executive justice in the present century is one of those reversions to justice without law which are perennial in legal history. As in the case of life reversions in the past it is the forerunner of growth. It is the first form of reaction from the overrigid application of law in a period of stability. A bad adjustment between law and administration and cumbrous, ineffective and unbusinesslike legal procedure, involving waste of time and money in the mere etiquette of justice, are doing in our time what like conditions did in English law in the middle of the sixteenth century.

If we look back at the means of individualizing the application of law which have developed in our legal system, it will be seen that almost without exception they have to do with cases involving the moral quality of individual conduct or of the conduct of enterprises, as distinguished from matters or property and of commercial law. Equity uses its powers of individualizing to the best advantage in connection with the conduct of those in whom trust and confidence have been reposed. Legal standards are used chiefly in the law of torts, in the law of public utilities and in the law as to fiduciary relations. Jury lawlessness is an agency of justice chiefly in connection with the moral quality of conduct where the special circumstances exclude that "intelligence without passion" which, according to Aristotle, characterizes the law. It is significant that in England today the civil jury is substantially confined to cases of defamation, malicious prosecution, assault and battery and breach of promise of marriage. Judicial individualization through choice of a rule is most noticeable in the law of torts, in the law of domestic relations and in passing upon the conduct of enterprises. The elaborate system of individualization in criminal procedure has to do wholly with individual human conduct. The informal methods of petty courts are meant for tribunals which pass upon conduct in the crowd and hurry of our large cities. The administrative tribunals, which are setting up on every hand, are most called for and prove most effective as means of regulating the conduct of enterprises.

A like conclusion is suggested when we look into the related controversy as to the respective provinces of common law and of legislation. Inheritance and succession, definition of interests in property and the conveyance thereof, matters of commercial law and the creation, incidents and transfer of obligations have proved a fruitful field for legislation. In these cases the social interest in the general security is the controlling element. But where the questions are not of interests of substance but of the weighing of human conduct and passing upon its moral aspects, legislation has accomplished little. No codification of the law of torts has done more than provide a few significantly broad generalizations. On the other hand, succession to property is everywhere a matter of statute law and commercial law is codified or codifying throughout the world. Moreover the common law insists upon its doctrine of *stare decisis* chiefly in the two cases of property and commercial law. Where legislation is effective, there also mechanical application is effective and desirable. Where legislation is ineffective, the same difficulties that prevent its satisfactory operation require us to leave a wide margin of discretion in application as in the standard of the reasonable man in our law of negligence and the standard of the upright and diligent head of a family applied by the Roman law, and especially by the modern Roman law, to so many questions of fault, where the question is really one of good faith. All attempts to cut down this margin have proved futile. May we not conclude that in the part of the law which has to do immediately with conduct complete justice is not to be attained by the mechanical application of fixed rules? Is it not clear that in this part of the administration of justice the trained intuition and disciplined judgment of the judge must be our assurance that causes will be decided on principles of reason and not according to the chance dictates of caprice, and that a due balance will be maintained between the general security and the individual human life?

Philosophically the apportionment of the field between rule and discretion which is suggested by the use of rules and of standards respectively in modern law has its basis in the respective fields of intelligence and intuition. Bergson tells us that the former is more adapted to the inorganic, the latter more to life. Likewise rules, where we proceed mechanically, are more adapted to property and to business transactions, and standards; where we proceed upon intuitions, are more adapted to human conduct and to the conduct of enterprises. According to him, intelligence is characterized by "its power of grasping the general element in a situation and relating it to past situations," and this power involves loss of "that perfect mastery of a special situation in which instinct rules." In the law of property and in the law of commercial transactions it is precisely this general element and its relation to past situations that is decisive. The rule, mechanically applied, works by repetition and precludes individuality in results, which would threaten the security of acquisitions and the security of transactions. On the other hand, in the handmade, as distinguished from the machine-made product, the specialized skill of the workman gives us something infinitely more subtle than can be expressed in rules. In law some situations call for the product of hands, not of machines, for they involve not repetition, where the general elements are significant, but unique events, in which the special circumstances are significant. Every promissory note is like every other. Every fee simple is like every other. Every distribution of assets repeats the conditions that have recurred since the Statute of Distributions. But no two cases of negligence have been alike or ever will be alike. Where the call is for individuality in the product of the legal mill, we resort to standards. And the sacrifice of certainty in so doing is more apparent than actual. For the certainty attained by mechanical application of fixed rules to human conduct has always been illusory.

RONALD M. DWORKIN

The Model of Rules*

EMBARRASSING QUESTIONS

Lawyers lean heavily on the connected concepts of legal right and legal obligation. We say that someone has a legal right or duty, and we take that statement as a sound basis for making claims and demands, and for criticizing the acts of public officials. But our understanding of these concepts is remarkably fragile, and we fall into trouble when we try to say what legal rights and obligations are. We say glibly that whether someone has a legal obligation is determined by applying "the law" to the particular facts of this case, but this is not a helpful answer, because we have the same difficulties with the concept of law.

We are used to summing up our troubles in the classic questions of jurisprudence: What is "the law"? When two sides disagree, as often happens, about a proposition "of law," what are they disagreeing about, and how shall we decide which side is right? Why do we call what "the law" says a matter of legal "obligation"? Is "obligation" here just a term of art, meaning only "what the law says"? Or does legal obligation have something to do with moral obligation? Can we say that we have, in principle at least, the same reasons for meeting our legal obligations that we have for meeting our moral obligations?

These are not puzzles for the cupboard, to be taken down on rainy days for fun. They are sources of continuing embarrassment, and they nag at our attention. They embarrass us in dealing with particular problems that we must solve, one way or another. Suppose a novel right-of-privacy case comes to court, and there is no statute or precedent either granting or denying the particular right of anonymity claimed by the plaintiff. What role in the court's decision should

be played by the fact that most people in the community think that private individuals are "morally" entitled to that particular privacy? Suppose the Supreme Court orders some prisoner freed because the police used procedures that the Court now says are constitutionally forbidden, although the Court's earlier decisions upheld these procedures. Must the Court, to be consistent, free all other prisoners previously convicted through these same procedures?[1] Conceptual puzzles about "the law" and "legal obligation" become acute when a court is confronted with a problem like this.

These eruptions signal a chronic disease. Day in and day out we send people to jail, or take money away from them, or make them do things they do not want to do, under coercion of force, and we justify all of this by speaking of such persons as having broken the law or having failed to meet their legal obligations, or having interfered with other people's legal rights. Even in clear cases (a bank robber or a willful breach of contract), when we are confident that someone had a legal obligation and broke it, we are not able to give a satisfactory account of what that means, or why that entitles the state to punish or coerce him. We may feel confident that what we are doing is proper, but until we can identify the principles we are following we cannot be sure that they are sufficient, or whether we are applying them consistently. In less clear cases, when the issue of whether an obligation has been broken is for some reason controversial, the pitch of these nagging questions rises, and our responsibility to find answers deepens.

Certain lawyers (we may call them "nominalists") urge that we solve these problems by ignoring them. In their view the concepts of "legal obligation" and "the law" are myths, invented and sustained by lawyers for a dismal mix of

*From 35 *University of Chicago Law Review* 14 (1967). Reprinted by permission of the author and the publisher.

conscious and subconscious motives. The puzzles we find in these concepts are merely symptoms that they are myths. They are unsolvable because unreal, and our concern with them is just one feature of our enslavement. We would do better to flush away the puzzles and the concepts altogether, and pursue our important social objectives without this excess baggage.

This is a tempting suggestion, but it has fatal drawbacks. Before we can decide that our concepts of law and of legal obligation are myths, we must decide what they are. We must be able to state, at least roughly, what it is we all believe that is wrong. But the nerve of our problem is that we have great difficulty in doing just that. Indeed, when we ask what law is and what legal obligations are, we are asking for a theory of how we use these concepts and of the conceptual commitments our use entails. We cannot conclude, before we have such a general theory, that our practices are stupid or superstitious.

Of course, the nominalists think they know how the rest of us use these concepts. They think that when we speak of "the law," we mean a set of timeless rules stocked in some conceptual warehouse awaiting discovery by judges, and that when we speak of legal obligation we mean the invisible chains these mysterious rules somehow drape around us. The theory that there are such rules and chains they call "mechanical jurisprudence," and they are right in ridiculing its practitioners. Their difficulty, however, lies in finding practioners to ridicule. So far they have had little luck in caging and exhibiting mechanical jurisprudents (all specimens captured—even Blackstone and Joseph Beale—have had to be released after careful reading of their texts).

In any event, it is clear that most lawyers have nothing like this in mind when they speak of the law and of legal obligation. A superficial examination of our practices is enough to show this, for we speak of laws changing and evolving, and of legal obligation sometimes being problematical. In these and other ways we show that we are not addicted to mechanical jurisprudence.

Nevertheless, we do use the concepts of law and legal obligation, and we do suppose that society's warrant to punish and coerce is written in that currency. It may be that when the details of this practice are laid bare, the concepts we do use will be shown to be as silly and as thick with illusion as those the nominalists invented. If so, then we shall have to find other ways to describe what we do, and either provide other justifications or change our practices. But until we have discovered this and made these adjustments, we cannot accept the nominalists' premature invitation to turn our backs on the problems our present concepts provide.

Of course the suggestion that we stop talking about "the law" and "legal obligation" is mostly bluff. These concepts are too deeply cemented into the structure of our political practices—they cannot be given up like cigarettes or hats. Some of the nominalists have half-admitted this and said that the myths they condemn should be thought of as Platonic myths and retained to seduce the masses into order. This is perhaps not so cynical a suggestion as it seems; perhaps it is a covert hedging of a dubious bet.

If we boil away the bluff, the nominalist attack reduces to an attack on mechanical jurisprudence. Through the lines of the attack, and in spite of the heroic calls for the death of law, the nominalists themselves have offered an analysis of how the terms "law" and "legal obligation" should be used which is not very different from that of more classical philosophers. Nominalists present their analysis as a model of how legal institutions (particularly courts) "really operate." But their model differs mainly in emphasis from the theory first made popular by the nineteenth century philosopher John Austin, and now accepted in one form or another by most working and academic lawyers who hold views on jurisprudence. I shall call this theory, with some historical looseness, "positivism." I want to examine the soundness of positivism, particularly in the powerful form that Professor H. L. A. Hart of Oxford has given to it. I choose to focus on his position, not only because of its clarity and elegance, but because here, as almost everywhere else in legal philosophy, constructive thought must start with a consideration of his views.

POSITIVISM

Positivism has a few central and organizing propositions as its skeleton, and though not every philosopher who is called a positivist would subscribe to these in the way I present them, they do define the general position I want to examine. These key tenets may be stated as follows:

(a) The law of a community is a set of special rules used by the community directly or indirectly for the purpose of determining which behavior will be punished or coerced by the public power. These special rules can be identified and distinguished by specific criteria, by tests having to do not with their content but with their *pedigree* or the manner in which they were adopted or developed. These tests of pedigree can be used to distinguish valid legal rules from spurious legal rules (rules which lawyers and litigants wrongly argue are rules of law) and also from other sorts of social rules (generally lumped together as "moral rules") that the community follows but does not enforce through public power.

(b) The set of these valid legal rules is exhaustive of "the law," so that if someone's case is not clearly covered by such a rule (because there is none that seems appropriate, or those that seem appropriate are vague, or for some other reason) then that case cannot be decided by "applying the law." It must be decided by some official, like a judge, "exercising his discretion," which means reaching beyond the law for some other sort of standard to guide him in manufacturing a fresh legal rule or supplementing an old one.

(c) To say that someone has a "legal obligation" is to say that his case falls under a valid legal rule that requires him to do or to forbear from doing something. (To say he has a legal right, or has a legal power of some sort, or a legal privilege or immunity, is to assert, in a shorthand way, that others have actual or hypothetical legal obligations to act or not to act in certain ways touching him.) In the absence of such a valid legal rule there is no legal obligation; it follows that when the judge decides an issue by exercising his discretion, he is not enforcing a legal obligation as to that issue.

This is only the skeleton of positivism. The flesh is arranged differently by different positivists, and some even tinker with the bones. Different versions differ chiefly in their description of the fundamental test of pedigree a rule must meet to count as a rule of law.

Austin, for example, framed his version of the fundamental test as a series of interlocking definitions and distinctions.[2] He defined having an obligation as lying under a rule, a rule as a general command, and a command as an expression of desire that others behave in a particular way, backed by the power and will to enforce that expression in the event of disobedience. He distinguished classes of rules (legal, moral or religious) according to which person or group is the author of the general command the rule represents. In each political community, he thought, one will find a sovereign—a person or a determinate group whom the rest obey habitually, but who is not in the habit of obeying anyone else. The legal rules of a community are the general commands its sovereign has deployed. Austin's definition of legal obligation followed from this definition of law. One has a legal obligation, he thought, if one is among the addressees of some general order of the sovereign, and is in danger of suffering a sanction unless he obeys that order.

Of course, the sovereign cannot provide for all contingencies through any scheme of orders, and some of his orders will inevitably be vague or have furry edges. Therefore (according to Austin) the sovereign grants those who enforce the law (judges) discretion to make fresh orders when novel or troublesome cases are presented. The judges then make new rules or adapt old rules, and the sovereign either overturns their creations, or tacitly confirms them by failing to do so.

Austin's model is quite beautiful in its simplicity. It asserts the first tenet of positivism, that the law is a set of rules specially selected to govern public order, and offers a simple factual test— what has the sovereign commanded?— as the sole criterion for identifying those special rules. In time, however, those who studied and tried to apply Austin's model found it too simple. Many objections were raised, among which were two that seemed fundamental. First, Austin's key assumption that in each community a determinate group or institution can be found, which is in ultimate control of all other groups, seemed not to hold in a complex society. Political control in a modern nation is pluralistic and shifting, a matter of more or less, of compromise and cooperation and alliance, so that it is often impossible to say that any person or group has that dramatic control necessary to qualify as an Austinian sovereign. One wants to say, in the United States for example, that the "people" are sovereign. But this means almost nothing, and in itself provides no test for determining what the "people" have commanded, or distinguishing their legal from their social or moral commands.

Second, critics began to realize that Austin's analysis fails entirely to account for, even to recognize, certain striking facts about the attitudes we take toward "the law." We make an important distinction between law and even the general orders of a gangster. We feel that the law's strictures—and its sanctions—are different in that they are obligatory in a way that the outlaw's commands are not. Austin's analysis has no place for any such distinction, because it defines an obligation as subjection to the threat of force, and so founds the authority of law entirely on the sovereign's ability and will to harm those who disobey. Perhaps the distinction we make is illusory—perhaps our feelings of some special authority attaching to the law is based on religious hangover or another sort of mass self-deception. But Austin does not demonstrate this, and we are entitled to insist that an analysis of our concept of law either acknowledge and explain our attitudes, or show why they are mistaken.

H. L. A. Hart's version of positivism is more complex than Austin's, in two ways. First, he recognizes, as Austin did not, the rules are of different logical kinds (Hart distinguishes two kinds, which he calls "primary" and "secondary" rules). Second, he rejects Austin's theory that a rule is a kind of command, and substitutes a more elaborate general analysis of what rules are. We must pause over each of these points, and then note how they merge in Hart's concept of law.

Hart's distinction between primary and secondary rules is of great importance.[3] Primary rules are those that grant rights or impose obligations upon members of the community. The rules of the criminal law that forbid us to rob, murder or drive too fast are good examples of primary rules. Secondary rules are those that stipulate how, and by whom, such primary rules may be formed, recognized, modified or extinguished. The rules that stipulate how Congress is composed, and how it enacts legislation, are examples of secondary rules. Rules about forming contracts and executing wills are also secondary rules because they stipulate how very particular rules governing particular legal obligations (that is, the terms of a contract or the provisions of a will) come into existence and are changed.

His general analysis of rules is also of great importance.[4] Austin had said that every rule is a general command, and that a person is obligated

under a rule if he is liable to be hurt should he disobey it. Hart points out that this obliterates the distinction between being *obliged* to do something and being *obligated* to do it. If one is bound by a rule he is obligated, not merely obliged, to do what it provides, and therefore being bound by a rule must be different from being subject to an injury if one disobeys an order. A rule differs from an order, among other ways, by being *normative,* by setting a standard of behavior that has a call on its subject beyond the threat that may enforce it. A rule can never be binding just because some person with physical power wants it to be so. He must have *authority* to issue the rule or it is no rule, and such authority can only come from another rule which is already binding on those to whom he speaks. That is the difference between a valid law and the orders of a gunman.

So Hart offers a general theory of rules that does not make their authority depend upon the physical power of their authors. If we examine the way different rules come into being, he tells us, and attend to the distinction between primary and secondary rules, we see that there are two possible sources of a rule's authority.[5]

(a) A rule may become binding upon a group of people because that group through its practices *accepts* the rule as a standard for its conduct. It is not enough that the group simply conforms to a pattern of behavior: even though most Englishmen may go to the movies on Saturday evening, they have not accepted a rule requiring that they do so. A practice constitutes the acceptance of a rule only when those who follow the practice regard the rule as binding, and recognize the rule as a reason or justification for their own behavior and as a reason for criticizing the behavior of others who do not obey it.

(b) A rule may also become binding in quite a different way, namely by being enacted in conformity with some *secondary* rule that stipulates that rules so enacted shall be binding. If the constitution of a club stipulates, for example, that by-laws may be adopted by a majority of the members, then particular by-laws so voted are binding upon all the members, not because of any practice of acceptance of these particular by-laws, but because the constitution says so. We use the concept of *validity* in this connection: rules binding because they have been created in a manner stipulated by some secondary rule are called "valid" rules. Thus we can record Hart's fundamental distinction this way: a rule may be binding (a) because it is accepted or (b) because it is valid.

Hart's concept of law is a construction of these various distinctions.[6] Primitive communities have only primary rules, and these are binding entirely because of practices of acceptance. Such communities cannot be said to have "law," because there is no way to distinguish a set of legal rules from amongst other social rules, as the first tenet of positivism requires. But when a particular community has developed a fundamental secondary rule that stipulates how legal rules are to be identified, the idea of a distinct set of legal rules, and thus of law, is born.

Hart calls such a fundamental secondary rule a "rule of recognition." The rule of recognition of a given community may be relatively simple ("What the king enacts is law") or it may be very complex (the United States Constitution, with all its difficulties of interpretation, may be considered a single rule of recognition). The demonstration that a particular rule is valid may therefore require tracing a complicated chain of validity back from that particular rule ultimately to the fundamental rule. Thus a parking ordinance of the city of New Haven is valid because it is adopted by a city council, pursuant to the procedures and within the competence specified by the municipal law adopted by the state of Connecticut, in conformity with the procedures and within the competence specified by the constitution of the state of Connecticut, which was in turn adopted consistently with the requirements of the United States Constitution.

Of course, a rule of recognition cannot itself be valid, because by hypothesis it is ultimate, and so cannot meet tests stipulated by a more fundamental rule. The rule of recognition is the sole rule in a legal system whose binding force depends upon its acceptance. If we wish to know what rule of recognition a particular community has adopted or follows, we must observe how its citizens, and particularly its officials, behave. We must observe what ultimate arguments they accept as showing the validity of a particular rule, and what ultimate arguments they use to criticize other officials or institutions. We can apply no mechanical test, but there is no danger of our confusing the rule of recognition of a community with its rules of morality. The rule of recognition is identified by the fact that its province is the operation of the governmental apparatus of legislatures, courts, agencies, policemen, and the rest.

In this way Hart rescues the fundamentals of positivism from Austin's mistakes. Hart agrees with Austin that valid rules of law may be created through the acts of officials and public institutions. But Austin thought that the authority of these institutions lay only in their monopoly of power. Hart finds their authority in the background of constitutional standards against which they act, constitutional standards that have been accepted, in the form of a fundamental rule of recognition, by the community which they govern. This background legitimates the decisions of government and gives them the cast and call of obligation that the naked commands of Austin's sovereign lacked. Hart's theory differs from Austin's also, in recognizing that different communities use different ultimate tests of law, and that some allow other means of creating law than the deliberate act of a legislative institution. Hart mentions "long customary practice" and "the relation [of a rule] to judicial decisions" as other criteria that are often used, though generally along with and subordinate to the test of legislation.

So Hart's version of positivism is more complex than Austin's, and his test for valid rules of law is more sophisticated. In one respect, however, the two models are very similar. Hart, like Austin, recognizes that legal rules have furry edges (he speaks of them as having "open texture") and, again like Austin, he accounts for troublesome cases by saying that judges have and exercise discretion to decide these cases by fresh legislation.[7] (I shall later try to show why one who thinks of law as a special set of rules is almost inevitably drawn to account for difficult cases in terms of someone's exercise of discretion.)

RULES, PRINCIPLES, AND POLICIES

I want to make a general attack on positivism, and I shall use H. L. A. Hart's version as a target, when a particular target is needed. My strategy will be organized around the fact that when lawyers reason or dispute about legal rights and obligations, particularly in those hard cases when our problems with these concepts seem most acute, they make use of standards that do not function as rules, but operate differently as principles, policies, and other sorts of standards. Positivism, I shall argue, is a model of and for a system of rules, and its central notion of a single fundamental test for law forces us to miss the important roles of these standards that are not rules.

I just spoke of "principles, policies, and other sorts of standards." Most often I shall use the term "principle" generically, to refer to the whole set of these standards other than rules; occasionally, however, I shall be more precise, and distinguish between principles and policies. Although nothing in the present argument will turn on the distinction, I should state how I draw it. I call a "policy" that kind of standard that sets out a goal to be reached, generally an improvement in some economic, political, or social feature of the community (though some goals are negative, in that they stipulate that some present feature is to be protected from adverse change). I call a "principle" a standard that is to be observed, not because it will advance or secure an economic, political, or social situation deemed desirable, but because it is a requirement of justice or fairness or some other dimension of morality. Thus the standard that automobile accidents are to be decreased is a policy, and the standard that no man may profit by his own wrong a principle. The distinction can be collapsed by construing a principle as stating a social goal (that is, the goal of a society in which no man profits by his own wrong), or by construing a policy as stating a principle (that is, the principle that the goal the policy embraces is a worthy one) or by adopting the utilitarian thesis that principles of justice are disguised statements of goals (securing the greatest happiness of the greatest number). In some contexts the distinction has uses which are lost if it is thus collapsed.[8]

My immediate purpose, however, is to distinguish principles in the generic sense from rules, and I shall start by collecting some examples of the former. The examples I offer are chosen haphazardly; almost any case in a law school casebook would provide examples that would serve as well. In 1889 a New York court, in the famous case of *Riggs v. Palmer*,[9] had to decide whether an heir named in the will of his grandfather could inherit under that will, even though he had murdered his grandfather to do so. The court began its reasoning with this admission: "It is quite true that statutes regulating the making, proof and effect of wills, and the devolution of property, if literally construed, and if their force and effect can in no way and under no circumstances be controlled or modified, give this property to the murderer."[10] But the court continued to note that "all laws as well as all contracts may be controlled in their operation and effect by general, fundamental maxims of the common law. No one shall be permitted to profit by his own fraud, or to take advantage of his own wrong, or to found any claim upon his own iniquity, or to acquire property by his own crime."[11] The murderer did not receive his inheritance.

In 1960, a New Jersey court was faced, in *Henningsen v. Bloomfield Motors, Inc.,*[12] with the important question of whether (or how much) an automobile manufacturer may limit his liability in case the automobile is defective. Henningsen had bought a car, and signed a contract which said that the manufacturer's liability for defects was limited to "making good" defective parts—"this warranty being expressly in lieu of all other warranties, obligations or liabilities." Henningsen argued that, at least in the circumstances of his case, the manufacturer ought not to be protected by this limitation, and ought to be liable for the medical and other expenses of persons injured in a crash. He was not able to point to any statute, or to any established rule of law, that prevented the manufacturer from standing on the contract. The court nevertheless agreed with Henningsen. At various points in the court's argument the following appeals to standards are made: (a) "[W]e must keep in mind the general principal that, in the absence of fraud, one who does not choose to read a contract before signing it cannot later relieve himself of its burdens."[13] (b) "In applying that principle, the basic tenet of freedom of competent parties to contract is a factor of importance."[14] (c) "Freedom of contract is not such an immutable doctrine as to admit of no qualification in the area in which we are concerned."[15] (d) "In a society such as ours where the automobile is a common and necessary adjunct of daily life, and where its use is so fraught with danger to the driver, passengers and the public, the manufacturer is under a special obligation in connection with the construction, promotion and sale of his cars. Consequently, the courts must examine purchase agreements closely to see if consumer and public interests are treated fairly."[16] (e) " '[I]s there any principle which is more familiar or more firmly embedded in the history of Anglo-American law than the basic doctrine that the courts will not permit themselves to be used as instruments of inequity and injustice?' "[17] (f) " 'More specifically, the courts generally refuse to lend themselves to the enforcement of a "bargain" in which one party has unjustly taken advantage of the economic necessities of other. ...' "[18]

The standards set out in these quotations are not the sort we think of as legal rules. They seem very different from propositions like "The maximum legal speed on the turnpike is sixty miles an hour" or "A will is invalid unless signed by three witnesses." They are different because they are legal principles rather than legal rules.

The difference between legal principles and legal rules is a logical distinction. Both sets of standards point to particular decisions about legal obligation in particular circumstances, but they differ in the character of the direction they give. Rules are applicable in an all-or-nothing fashion. If the facts a rule stipulates are given, then either the rule is valid, in which case the answer it supplies must be accepted, or it is not, in which case it contributes nothing to the decision.

This all-or-nothing is seen most plainly if we look at the way rules operate, not in law, but in some enterprise they dominate—a game, for example. In baseball a rule provides that if the batter has had three strikes, he is out. An official cannot consistently acknowledge that this is an accurate statement of a baseball rule, and decide that a batter who has had three strikes is not out. Of course, a rule may have exceptions (the batter who has taken three strikes is not out if the catcher drops the third strike.) However, an accurate statement of the rule would take this exception into account, and any that did not would be incomplete. If the list of exceptions is very large, it would be too clumsy to repeat them each time the rule is cited; there is, however, no reason in theory why they could not all be added on, and the more that are, the more accurate is the statement of the rule.

If we take baseball rules as a model, we find that rules of law, like the rule that a will is invalid unless signed by three witnesses, fit the model well. If the requirement of three witnesses is a valid legal rule, then it cannot be that a will has been signed by only two witnesses and is valid. The rule might have exceptions, but if it does then it is inaccurate and incomplete to state the rule so simply, without enumerating the exceptions. In theory, at least, the exceptions could all be listed, and the more of them that are, the more complete is the statement of the rule.

But this is not the way the sample principles in the quotations operate. Even those which look most like rules do not set out legal consequences that follow automatically when the conditions provided are met. We say that our law respects the principle that no man may profit from his own wrong, but we do not mean that the law never permits a man to profit from wrongs he commits. In fact, people often profit, perfectly legally, from their legal wrongs. The most notorious case is adverse possession—if I trespass on your land long enough, some day I will gain a right to cross your land whenever I please. There are many less dramatic examples. If a man leaves one job, breaking a contract, to take a much higher paying job, he may have to pay damages to his first employer, but he is usually entitled to keep his new salary. If a man jumps bail and crosses state lines to make a brilliant investment in another state, he may be sent back to jail, but he will keep his profits.

We do not treat these—and countless other counter-instances that can easily be imagined—as showing that the principle about profiting from one's wrongs is not a principle of our legal system, or that it is incomplete and needs qualifying exceptions. We do not treat counter-instances as exceptions (at least not exceptions in the way in which a catcher's dropping the third strike is an exception) because we could not hope to capture these counter-instances simply by a more extended statement of the principle. They are not, even in theory, subject to enumeration, because we would have to include not only these cases (like adverse possession) in which some institution has already provided that profit can be gained through a wrong, but also those numberless imaginary cases in which we know in advance that the principle would not hold. Listing some of these might sharpen our sense of the principle's weight (I shall mention that dimension in a moment), but it would not make for a more accurate or complete statement of the principle.

A principle like "No man may profit from his own wrong" does not even purport to set out conditions that make its application necessary. Rather, it states a reason that argues in one direction, but does not necessitate a particular decision. If a man has or is about to receive something, as a direct result of something illegal he did to get it, then that is a reason which the law will take into account in deciding whether he should keep it. There may be other principles or policies arguing in the other direction—a policy of securing title, for example, or a principle limiting punishment to what the legislature has stipulated. If so, our principle may not prevail, but that does not mean that it is not a principle of our legal system, because in the next case, when these contravening considerations are absent or less weighty, the principle may be decisive. All that is meant, when we say that a particular principle is a principle of our law, is that the principle is one which officials must take into account, if it is relevant, as a consideration inclining in one direction or another.

The logical distinction between rules and principles appears more clearly when we consider principles that do not even look like rules. Consider the proposition, set out under "(d)" in the excerpts from the *Henningsen* opinion, that "the manufacturer is under a special obligation in connection with the construction, promotion and sale of his cars." This does not even purport to define the specific duties such a special obligation entails, or to tell us what rights automobile consumers acquire as a result. It merely states—and this is an essential link in the *Henningsen* argument—that automobile manufacturers must be held to higher standards than other manufacturers, and are less entitled to rely on the competing principle of freedom of contract. It does not mean that they may never rely on that principle, or that courts may rewrite automobile purchase contracts at will; it means only that if a particular clause seems unfair or burdensome, courts have less reason to enforce the clause than if it were for the purchase of neckties. The "special obligation" counts in favor, but does not in itself necessitate, a decision refusing to enforce the terms of an automobile purchase contract.

This first difference between rules and principles entails another. Principles have a dimension that rules do not—the dimension of weight or importance. When principles intersect (the policy of protecting automobile consumers intersecting with principles of freedom of contract, for example), one who must resolve the conflict has to take into account the relative weight of each. This cannot be, of course, an exact measurement, and the judgment that a particular principle or policy is more important than another will often be a controversial one. Nevertheless, it is an integral part of the concept of a principle that it has this dimension, that it makes sense to ask how important or how weighty it is.

Rules do not have this dimension. We can speak of rules as being *functionally* important or unimportant (the baseball rule that three strikes are out is more important than the rule that runners may advance on a balk, because the game would be much more changed with the first rule altered than the second). In this sense, one legal rule may be more important than another because it has a greater or more important role in regulating behavior. But we cannot say that one rule is more important than another within the system of rules, so that when two rules conflict one supersedes the other by virtue of its greater weight. If two rules conflict, one of them cannot be a valid rule. The decision as to which is valid, and which must be abandoned or recast, must be made by appealing to considerations beyond the rules themselves. A legal system might regulate such conflicts by other rules, which prefer the rule enacted by the higher authority, or the rule enacted later, or the more specific rule, or something of that sort. A legal system may also prefer the rule supported by the more important principles. (Our own legal system uses both of these techniques.)

It is not always clear from the form of a standard whether it is a rule or a principle. "A will is invalid unless signed by three witnesses" is not very different in form from "A man may not profit from his own wrong," but one who knows something of American laws knows that he must take the first as stating a rule and the second as stating a principle. In many cases the distinction is difficult to make—it may not have been settled how the standard should operate, and this issue may itself be a focus of controversy. The First Amendment to the United States Constitution contains the provision that Congress shall not abridge freedom of speech. Is this a rule, so that if a particular law does abridge freedom of speech, it follows that it is unconstitutional? Those who claim that the first amendment is "an absolute" say that it must be taken in this way, that is, as a rule. Or does it merely state a principle, so that when an abridgement of speech is discovered, it is unconstitutional unless the context presents some other policy or principle which in the circumstances is weighty enough to permit the abridgement? That is the position of those who argue for what is called the "clear and present danger" test or some other form of "balancing."

Sometimes a rule and a principle can play much the same role, and the difference between them is almost a matter of form alone. The first section of the Sherman Act states that every contract in restraint of trade shall be void. The Supreme Court had to make the decision whether this provision should be treated as a rule in its own terms (striking down every contract "which restrains trade," which almost any contract does) or as a principle, providing a reason for striking down a contract in the absence of effective contrary policies. The Court construed the provision as a rule, but treated that rule as containing the word "unreasonable," and as prohibiting only "unreasonable" restraints of trade.[19] This allowed the provision to function logically as a rule (whenever a court finds that the restraint is "unreasonable" it is bound to hold the contract invalid) and substantially as a principle (a court must take into account a variety of other principles and policies in determining whether a particular restraint in particular economic circumstances is "unreasonable").

Words like "reasonable," "negligent," "unjust," and "significant" often perform just this function. Each of these terms makes the application of the rule which contains it depend to some extent upon principles or policies lying beyond the rule, and in this way makes that rule itself more like a principle. But they do not quite turn the rule into a principle, because even the least confining of these terms restricts the *kind* of other principles and policies on which the rule depends. If we are bound by a rule that says that "unreasonable" contracts are void, or that grossly "unfair" contracts will not be enforced, much more judgment is required than if the quoted terms were omitted. But suppose a case in which some consideration of policy or principle suggests that a contract should be enforced even though its restraint is not reasonable, or even though it is grossly unfair. Enforcing these contracts would be forbidden by our rules, and thus permitted only if these rules were abandoned or modified. If we were dealing, however, not with a rule but with a policy against enforcing unreasonable contracts, or a principle that unfair contracts ought not to be enforced, the contracts could be enforced without alteration of the law.

IV. PRINCIPLES AND THE CONCEPT OF LAW

Once we identify legal principles as separate sorts of standards, different from legal rules, we are suddenly aware of them all around us. Law teachers teach them, lawbooks cite them, legal historians celebrate them. But they seem most energetically at work, carrying most weight, in difficult lawsuits like *Riggs and Henningsen.* In cases like these principles play an essential part in arguments supporting judgments about particular legal rights and obligations. After the case is decided, we may say that the case stands for a particular rule (that is, the rule that one who murders is not eligible to take under the will of his victim). But the rule does not exist before the case is decided; the court cites principles as its justification for adopting and applying a new rule. In *Riggs,* the court cited the principle that no man may profit from his own wrong as a background standard against which to read the statute of wills and in this way justified a new interpretation of that statute. In *Henningsen,* the court cited a variety of intersecting principles and policies as authority for a new rule respecting manufacturer's liability for automobile defects.

An analysis of the concept of legal obligation must therefore account for the important role of principles in reaching particular decisions of law. There are two very different tacks we might take.

(a) We might treat legal principles the way we treat legal rules and say that some principles are binding as law and must be taken into account by judges and lawyers who make decisions of legal obligation. If we took this tack, we should say that in the United States, at least, the "law" includes principles as well as rules.

(b) We might, on the other hand, deny that principles can be binding the way some rules are. We would say, instead, that in cases like *Riggs* or *Henningsen* the judge reaches beyond the rules that he is bound to apply (reaches, that is, beyond the "law") for extralegal principles he is free to follow if he wishes.

One might think that there is not much difference between these two lines of attack, that it is only a verbal question of how one wants to use the word "law." But that is a mistake, because the choice between these two accounts has the greatest consequences for an analysis of legal obligation. It is a choice between two *concepts* of a legal principle, a choice we can clarify by comparing it to a choice we might make between two concepts of a legal rule. We sometimes say of someone that he "makes it a rule" to do something, when we mean that he has chosen to follow a certain practice. We might say that someone has made it a rule, for example, to run a mile before breakfast because he wants to be healthy and believes in a regimen. We do not mean, when we say this, that he is *bound* by the rule that he must run a mile before breakfast, or even that he regards it as binding upon him. Accepting a rule as binding is something different from making it a rule to do something. If we use Hart's example again, there is a difference between saying that Englishmen make it a rule to see a movie once a week, and saying that the English have a rule that one must see a movie once a week. The second implies that if an Englishman does not follow the rule, he is subject to criticism or censure, but the first does not. The first does not exclude the possibility of a *sort* of criticism—we can say that one who does not see movies is neglecting his education—but we do not suggest that he is doing something wrong *just* in not following the rule.[20]

If we think of the judges of a community as a group, we could describe the rules of law they follow in these two different ways. We could say, for instance, that in a certain state the judges make it a rule not to enforce wills unless there are three witnesses. This would not imply that the rare judge who enforces such a rule is doing anything wrong just for that reason. On the other hand we can say that in that state a rule of law requires judges not to enforce such wills; this does imply that a judge who enforces them is doing something wrong. Hart, Austin and other positiv-

ists, of course, would insist on this latter account of legal rules; they would not at all be satisfied with the "make it a rule" account. It is not a verbal question of which account is right. It is a question of which describes the social situation more accurately. Other important issues turn on which description we accept. If judges simply "make it a rule" not to enforce certain contracts, for example, then we cannot say, before the decision, that anyone is "entitled" to that result, and that proposition cannot enter into any justification we might offer for the decision.

The two lines of attack on principles parallel these two accounts of rules. The first tack treats principles as binding upon judges, so that they are wrong not to apply the principles when they are pertinent. The second tack treats principles as summaries of what most judges "make it a principle" to do when forced to go beyond the standards that bind them. The choice between these approaches will affect, perhaps even determine, the answer we can give to the question whether the judge in a hard case like *Riggs* or *Henningsen* is attempting to enforce preexisting legal rights and obligations. If we take the first tack, we are still free to argue that because such judges are applying binding legal standards they are enforcing legal rights and obligations. But if we take the second, we are out of court on that issue, and we must acknowledge that the murderer's family in *Riggs* and the manufacturer in *Henningsen* were deprived of their property by an act of judicial discretion applied *ex post facto*. This may not shock many readers—the notion of judicial discretion has percolated through the legal community—but it does illustrate one of the most nettlesome of the puzzles that drive philosophers to worry about legal obligation. If taking property away in cases like these cannot be justified by appealing to an established obligation, yet another justification must be found, and nothing satisfactory has yet been supplied.

In my skeleton diagram of positivism, previously set out, I listed the doctrine of judicial discretion as the second tenet. Positivists hold that when a case is not covered by a clear rule, a judge must exercise his discretion to decide that case by what amounts to a fresh piece of legislation. There may be an important connection between this doctrine and the question of which of the two approaches to legal principles we must take. We shall therefore want to ask whether the doctrine is correct, and whether it implies the second approach, as it seems on its face to do. En route to these issues, however, we shall have to polish our understanding of the concept of discretion. I shall try to show how certain confusions about that concept, and in particular a failure to discriminate different senses in which it is used, account for the popularity of the doctrine of discretion. I shall argue that in the sense in which the doctrine does have a bearing on our treatment of principles, it is entirely unsupported by the arguments the positivists use to defend it.

DISCRETION

The concept of discretion was lifted by the positivists from ordinary language, and to understand it we must put it back *in habitat* for a moment. What does it mean, in ordinary life, to say that someone "has discretion"? The first thing to notice is that the concept is out of place in all but very special contexts. For example, you would not say that I either do or do not have discretion to choose a house for my family. It is not true that I have "no discretion" in making that choice, and yet it would be almost equally misleading to say that I do have discretion. The concept of discretion is at home in only one sort of context: when someone is in general charged with making decisions subject to standards set by a particular authority. It makes sense to speak of the discretion of a sergeant who is subject to orders of superiors, or the discretion of a sports official or contest judge who is governed by a rule book or the terms of the contest. Discretion, like the hole in a doughnut, does not exist except as an area left open by a surrounding belt of restriction. It is therefore a relative concept. It always makes sense to ask, "Discretion under which standards?" or "Discretion as to which authority?" Generally the context will make the answer to this plain, but in some cases the official may have discretion from one standpoint though not from another.

Like almost all terms, the precise meaning of "discretion" is affected by features of the context. The term is always colored by the background of understood information against which it is used. Although the shadings are many, it will be helpful for us to recognize some gross distinctions.

Sometimes we use "discretion" in a weak sense, simply to say that for some reason the standards an official must apply cannot be applied mechanically but demand the use of judgment. We use this weak sense when the context does not already make that clear, when the background our audience assumes does not contain that piece of information. Thus we might say, "The sergeant's orders left him a great deal of discretion," to those who do not know what the sergeant's orders were or who do not know something that made those orders vague or hard to carry out. It would make perfect sense to add, by way of amplification, that the lieutenant had ordered the sergeant to take his five most experienced men on patrol but that it was hard to determine which were the most experienced.

Sometimes we use the term in a different weak sense, to say only that some official has final authority to make a decision and cannot be reviewed and reversed by any other official. We speak this way when the official is part of a hierarchy of officials structured so that some have higher authority but in which the patterns of authority are different for different classes of decision. Thus we might say that in baseball certain decisions, like the decision whether the ball or the runner reached second base first, are left to the discretion of the second base umpire, if we mean that on this issue the head umpire has no power to substitute his own judgment if he disagrees.

I call both of these senses weak to distinguish them from a stronger sense. We use "discretion" sometimes not merely to say that an official must use judgment in applying the standards set him by authority, or that no one will review that exercise of judgment, but to say that on some issue he is simply not bound by standards set by the authority in question. In this sense we say that a sergeant has discretion who has been told to pick any five men for patrol he chooses or that a judge in a dog show has discretion to judge airedales before boxers if the rules do not stipulate an order of events. We use this sense not to comment on the vagueness or difficulty of the standards, or on who has the final word in applying them, but on their range and the decisions they purport to control. If the sergeant is told to take the five most experienced men, he does not have discretion in this strong sense because that order purports to govern his decision. The boxing referee who must decide which fighter has been the more aggressive does not have discretion, in the strong sense, for the same reason.[21]

If anyone said that the sergeant or the referee had discretion in these cases, we should have to understand him, if the context permitted, as using the term in one of the weak senses. Suppose, for example, the lieutenant ordered the sergeant to select the five men he deemed most experienced, and then added that the sergeant had discretion to choose them. Or the rules provided that the referee should award the round to the more aggressive fighter, with discretion in selecting him. We should have to understand these statements in the second weak sense, as speaking to the question of review of the decision. The first weak sense —that the decisions take judgment—would be otiose, and the third, strong sense is excluded by the statements themselves.

We must avoid one tempting confusion. The strong sense of discretion is not tantamount to license, and does not exclude criticism. Almost any situation in which a person acts (including those in which there is no question of decision under special authority, and so no question of discretion) makes relevant certain standards of rationality, fairness and effectiveness. We criticize each other's acts in terms of these standards, and there is no reason not to do so when the acts are within the center rather than beyond the perimeter of the doughnut of special authority. So we can say that the sergeant who was given discretion (in the strong sense) to pick a patrol did so stupidly or maliciously or carelessly, or that the judge who had discretion in the order of viewing dogs made a mistake because he took boxers first although there were only three airedales and many more boxers. An official's discretion means not that he is free to decide without recourse to standards of sense and fairness, but only that his decision is not controlled by a standard furnished by the particular authority we have in mind when we raise the question of discretion. Of course this latter sort of freedom is important; that is why we have the strong sense of discretion. Someone who has discretion in this third sense can be criticized, but not for being disobedient, as in the case of the soldier. He can be said to have made a mistake, but not to have deprived a participant of a decision to which he was entitled, as in the case of a sports official or contest judge.

We may now return, with these observations in hand, to the positivists' doctrine of judicial discretion. That doctrine argues that if a case is not controlled by an established rule, the judge must decide it by exercising discretion. We want to examine this doctrine and to test its bearing on our treatment of principles; but first we must ask in which sense of discretion we are to understand it.

Some nominalists argue that judges always have discretion, even when a clear rule is in point, because judges are ultimately the final arbiters of the law. This doctrine of discretion uses the second weak sense of that term, because it makes the point that no higher authority reviews the decisions of the highest court. It therefore has no bearing on the issue of how we account for principles, any more than it bears on how we account for rules.

The positivists do not mean their doctrine this way, because they say that a judge has no discretion when a clear and established rule is available. If we attend to the positivists' arguments for the doctrine, we may suspect that they use discretion in the first weak sense to mean only that judges must sometimes exercise judgment in applying legal standards. Their arguments call attention to the fact that some rules of law are vague (Professor Hart, for example, says that all rules of law have "open texture"), and that some cases arise (like *Henningsen*) in which no established rule seems to be suitable. They emphasize that judges must sometimes agonize over points of law, and that two equally trained and intelligent judges will often disagree.

These points are easily made; they are commonplace to anyone who has any familiarity with law. Indeed, that is the difficulty with assuming that positivists mean to use "discretion" in this weak sense. The proposition that, when no clear rule is available discretion in the sense of judgment must be used, is a tautology. It has no bearing, moreover, on the problem of how to account for legal principles. It is perfectly consistent to say that the judge in *Riggs,* for example, had to use judgment, and that he was bound to follow the principle that no man may profit from his own wrong. The positivists speak as if their doctrine of judicial discretion is an insight rather than a tautology, and as if it does have a bearing on the treatment of principles. Hart, for example, says that when the judge's discretion is in play, we can no longer speak of his being bound by standards, but must speak rather of what standards he "characterisitcally uses."²² Hart thinks that when judges have discretion, the principles they cite must be treated on our second approach, as what courts "make it a principle" to do.

It therefore seems that positivists, at least sometimes, take their doctrine in the third, strong sense of discretion. In that sense it does bear on the treatment of principles; indeed, in that sense it is nothing less than a restatement of our second approach. It is the same thing to say that when a judge runs out of rules he has discretion, in the sense that he is not bound by any standards from the authority of law, as to say that the legal standards judges cite other than rules are not binding on them.

So we must examine the doctrine of judicial discretion in the strong sense. (I shall henceforth use the term "discretion" in that sense.) Do the principles judges cite in cases like *Riggs* or *Henningsen* control their decisions, as the sergeant's orders to take the most experienced men or the referee's duty to choose the more aggressive fighter control the decisions of these officials? What arguments could a positivist supply to show that they do not?

(1) A positivist might argue that principles cannot be binding or obligatory. That would be a mistake. It is always a question, of course, whether any particular principle is *in fact* binding upon some legal official. But there is nothing in the logical character of a principle that renders it incapable of binding him. Suppose that the judge in *Henningsen* had failed to take any account of the principle that automobile manufacturers have a special obligation to their consumers, or the principle that the courts seek to protect those whose bargaining position is weak, but had simply decided for the defendant by citing the principle of freedom of contract without more. His critics would not have been content to point out that he had not taken account of considerations that other judges have been attending to for some time. Most would have said that it was his duty to take the measure of these principles and that the plaintiff was entitled to have him do so. We mean no more, when we say that a *rule* is binding upon a judge, than that he must follow it if it applies, and that if he

does not he will on that account have made a mistake.

It will not do to say that in a case like *Henningsen* the court is only "morally" obligated to take particular principles into account, or that it is "institutionally" obligated, or obligated as a matter of judicial "craft," or something of that sort. The question will still remain why this type of obligation (whatever we call it) is different from the obligation that rules impose upon judges, and why it entitles us to say that principles and policies are not part of the law but are merely extralegal standards "courts characteristically use."

(2) A positivist might argue that even though some principles are binding, in the sense that the judge must take them into account, they cannot determine a particular result. This is a harder argument to assess because it is not clear what it means for a standard to "determine" a result. Perhaps it means that the standard *dictates* the result whenever it applies so that nothing else counts. If so, then it is certainly true that individual principles do not determine results, but that is only another way of saying that principles are not rules. Only rules dictate results, come what may. When a contrary result has been reached, the rule has been abandoned or changed. Principles do not work that way; they incline a decision one way, though not conclusively, and they survive intact when they do not prevail. This seems no reason for concluding that judges who must reckon with principles have discretion because a set of principles *can* dictate a result. If a judge believes that principles he is bound to recognize point in one direction and that principles pointing in the other direction, if any, are not of equal weight, then he must decide accordingly, just as he must follow what he believes to be a binding rule. He may, of course, be wrong in his assessment of the principles, but he may also be wrong in his judgment that the rule is binding. The sergeant and the referee, we might add, are often in the same boat. No one factor dictates which soldiers are the most experienced or which fighter the more aggressive. These officials must make judgments of the relative weights of these various factors; they do not on that account have discretion.

(3) A positivist might argue that principles cannot count as law because their authority, and

even more so their weight, are congenitally *controversial*. It is true that generally we cannot *demonstrate* the authority or weight of a particular principle as we can sometimes demonstrate the validity of a rule by locating it in an act of Congress or in the opinion of an authoritative court. Instead, we make a case for a principle, and for its weight, by appealing to an amalgam of practice and other principles in which the implications of legislative and judicial history figure along with appeals to community practices and understandings. There is no litmus paper for testing the soundness of such a case—it is a matter of judgment, and reasonable men may disagree. But again this does not distinguish the judge from other officials who do not have discretion. The sergeant has no litmus paper for experience, the referee none for aggressiveness. Neither of these has discretion, because he is bound to reach an understanding, controversial or not, of what his orders or the rules require, and to act on that understanding. That is the judge's duty as well.

Of course, if the positivists are right in another of the doctrines—the theory that in each legal system there is an ultimate *test* for binding law like Professor Hart's rule of recognition—it follows that principles are not binding law. But the incompatibility of principles with the positivists' theory can hardly be taken as an argument that principles must be treated any particular way. That begs the question; we are interested in the status of principles because we want to evaluate the positivists' model. The positivist cannot defend his theory of a rule of recognition by fiat; if principles are not amenable to a test he must show some other reason why they cannot count as law. Since principles seem to play a role in arguments about legal obligation (witness, again *Riggs* and *Henningsen*), a model that provides for that role has some initial advantage over one that excludes it, and the latter cannot properly be inveighed in its own support.

These are the most obvious of the arguments a positivist might use for the doctrine of discretion in the strong sense, and for the second approach to principles. I shall mention one strong counterargument against that doctrine and in favor of the first approach. Unless at least some principles are acknowledged to be binding upon judges, requiring them as a set to reach particular decisions, then no rules, or very few rules, can be said to be binding upon them either.

In most American jurisdictions, and now in England also, the higher courts not infrequently reject established rules. Common law rules—those developed by earlier court decisions—are sometimes overruled directly, and sometimes radically altered by further development. Statutory rules are subjected to interpretation and reinterpretation, sometimes even when the result is not to carry out what is called the "legislative intent."[23] If courts had discretion to change established rules, then these rules would of course not be binding upon them, and so would not be law on the positivists' model. The positivist must therefore argue that there are standards, themselves binding upon judges, that determine when a judge may overrule or alter an established rule, and when he may not.

When, then, is a judge permitted to change an existing rule of law? Principles figure in the answer in two ways. First, it is necessary, though not sufficient, that the judge find that the change would advance some policy or serve some principle, which policy or principle thus justifies the change. In *Riggs* the change (a new interpretation of the statute of wills) was justified by the principle that no man should profit from his own wrong; in *Henningsen* certain rules about automobile manufacturer's liability were altered on the basis of the principles and policies I quoted from the opinion of the court.

But not any principle will do to justify a change, or no rule would ever be safe. There must be some principles that count and others that do not, and there must be some principles that count for more than others. It could not depend on the judge's own preferences amongst a sea of respectable extralegal standards, any one in principle eligible, because if that were the case we could not say that any rules were binding. We could always imagine a judge whose preferences amongst extralegal standards were such as would justify a shift or radical reinterpretation of even the most entrenched rule.

Second, any judge who proposes to change existing doctrine must take account of some important standards that argue against departures from established doctrine, and these standards are also for the most part principles. They include the doctrine of "legislative supremacy," a set of principles and policies that require the courts to pay a qualified deference to the acts of the legislature. They also include the doctrine of precedent, another set of principles and policies reflecting the equities and efficiencies of consistency. The doctrines of legislative supremacy and precedent incline toward the *status quo,* each within its sphere, but they do not command it. Judges are not free, however, to pick and choose amongst the principles and policies that make up these doctrines—if they were, again, no rule could be said to be binding.

Consider, therefore, what someone implies who says that a particular rule is binding. He may imply that the rule is affirmatively supported by principles the court is not free to disregard, and which are collectively more weighty than other principles that argue for a change. If not, he implies that any change would be condemned by a combination of conservative principles of legislative supremacy and precedent that the court is free to ignore. Very often, he will imply both, for the conservative principles, being principles and not rules, are usually not powerful enough to save a common law rule or an aging statute that is entirely unsupported by substantive principles the court is bound to respect. Either of these implications, of course, treats a body of principles and policies as law in the sense that rules are; it treats them as standards binding upon the officials of a community, controlling their decisions of legal right and obligation.

We are left with this issue. If the positivists' theory of judicial discretion is either trivial because it uses "discretion" in a weak sense, or unsupported because the various arguments we can supply in its defense fall short, why have so many careful and intelligent lawyers embraced it? We can have no confidence in our treatment of that theory unless we can deal with that question. It is not enough to note (although perhaps it contributes to the explanation) that "discretion" has different senses that may be confused. We do not confuse these senses when we are not thinking about law.

Part of the explanation, at least, lies in a lawyer's natural tendency to associate laws and rules, and to think of "the law" as a collection or system of rules. Roscoe Pound, who diagnosed this tendency long ago, thought that English-speaking lawyers were tricked into it by the fact that English uses the same word, changing only the article, for "a law" and "the law."[24] (Other languages, on the contrary, use two words: "loi" and "droit," for example, and "Gesetz" and "Recht.") This may have had its effect, with the English speaking positivists, because the expression "a law" certainly does suggest a rule. But the principal reason for associating law with rules runs deeper, and lies, I think, in the fact that legal education has for a long time consisted of teaching and examining those established rules that form the cutting edge of law.

In any event, if a lawyer thinks of law as a system of rules, and yet recognizes, as he must, that judges change old rules and introduce new ones, he will come naturally to the theory of judicial discretion in the strong sense. In those other systems of rules with which he has experience (like games), the rules are the only special authority that govern official decisions, so that it an umpire could change a rule, he would have discretion as to the subject matter of that rule. Any principles umpires might mention when changing the rules would represent only their "characteristic" preferences. Positivists treat law like baseball revised in this way.

There is another, more subtle consequence of this initial assumption that law is a system of rules. When the positivists do attend to principles and policies, they treat them as rules *manque.* They assume that *if* they are standards of law they must be rules, and so they read them as standards that are trying to be rules. When a positivist hears someone argue that legal principles are part of the law, he understands this to be an argument for what he calls the "higher law" theory, that these principles are the rules of a law above the law.[25] He refutes this theory by pointing out that these "rules" are sometimes followed and sometimes not, that for every "rule" like "no man shall profit from his own wrong" there is another competing "rule" like "the law favors security of title," and that there is no way to test the validity of "rules" like these. He concludes that these principles and policies are not valid rules of a law above the law, which is true, because they are not rules at all. He also concludes that they are extralegal standards which each judge selects according to his own lights in the exercise of his discretion, which is false. It is as if a zoologist had proved that fish are not mammals, and then concluded that they are really only plants.

THE RULE OF RECOGNITION

This discussion was provoked by our two competing accounts of legal principles. We have been exploring the second account, which the positivists seem to adopt through their doctrine of judicial discretion, and we have discovered grave difficulties. It is time to return to the fork in the road. What if we adopt the first approach? What would the consequences of this be for the skeletal structure of positivism? Of course we should have to drop the second tenet, the doctrine of judicial discretion (or, in the alternative, to make plain that the doctrine is to be read merely to say that judges must often exercise judgment). Would we also have to abandon or modify the first tenet, the proposition that law is distinguished by tests of the sort that can be set out in a master rule like Professor Hart's rule of recognition? If principles of the *Riggs* and *Henningsen* sort are to count as law, and we are nevertheless to preserve the notion of a master rule for law, then we must be able to deploy some test that all (and only) the principles that do count as law meet. Let us begin with the test Hart suggests for identifying valid *rules* of law, to see whether these can be made to work for principles as well.

Most rules of law, according to Hart, are valid because some competent institution enacted them. Some were created by a legislature, in the form of statutory enactments. Others were created by judges who formulated them to decide particular cases, and thus established them as precedents for the future. But this test of pedigree will not work for the *Riggs* and *Henningsen* principles. The origin of these as legal principles lies not in a particular decision of some legislature or court, but in a sense of appropriateness developed in the profession and the public over time. Their continued power depends upon this sense of appropriateness being sustained. If it no longer seemed unfair to allow people to profit by their wrongs, or fair to place special burdens upon oligopolies that manufacture potentially dangerous machines, these principles would no longer play much of a role in new cases, even if they had never been overruled or repealed. (Indeed, it hardly makes sense to speak of principles like these as being "overruled" or "repealed." When they decline they are eroded, not torpedoed.)

True, if we were challenged to back up our claim that some principle is a principle of law, we would mention any prior cases in which that principle was cited, or figured in the argument. We would also mention any statute that seemed to exemplify that principle (even better if the principle was cited in the preamble of the statute, or in the committee reports or other legislative documents that accompanied it). Unless we could find some such institutional support, we would probably fail to make out our case, and the more support we found, the more weight we could claim for the principle.

Yet we could not devise any formula for testing how much and what kind of institutional support is necessary to make a principle a legal principle, still less to fix its weight at a particular order of magnitude. We argue for a particular principle by grappling with a whole set of shifting, developing and interacting standards (themselves principles rather than rules) about institutional responsibility, statutory intepretation, the persuasive force of various sorts of precedent, the relation of all these to contemporary moral practices, and hosts of other such standards. We could not bolt all of these together into a single "rule," even a complex one, and if we could the result would bear little relation to Hart's picture of a rule of recognition, which is the picture of a fairly stable master rule specifying "some feature or features possession of which by a suggested rule is taken as a conclusive affirmative indicating that it is a rule. . . ."[26]

Moreover, the techniques we apply in arguing for another principle do not stand (as Hart's rule of recognition is designed to) on an entirely different level from the principles they support. Hart's sharp distinction between acceptance and validity does not hold. If we are arguing for the principle that a man should not profit from his own wrong, we could cite the acts of courts and legislatures that exemplify it, but this speaks as much to the principle's acceptance as its validity. (It seems odd to speak of a principle as being valid at all, perhaps because validity is an all-or-nothing concept, appropriate for rules, but inconsistent with a principle's dimension of weight.) If we are asked (as we might well be) to defend the particular doctrine of precedent, or the particular technique of statutory interpretation, that we used in this argument, we should certainly cite the practice of others in using that doctrine or technique. But we should also cite other general principles that we believe support that practice, and this introduces a note of validity into the chord of acceptance. We might argue, for example, that the use we make of earlier cases and statutes is supported by a particular analysis of the point of practice of legislation or the doctrine of precedent, or by the principles of democratic theory, or by a particular position on the proper division of authority between national and local institutions, or something else of that sort. Nor is this path of support a one-way street leading to some ultimate principle resting on acceptance alone. Our principles of legislation, precedent, democracy, or federalism might be challenged too; and if they were we should argue for them, not only in terms of practice, but in terms of each other and in terms of the implications of trends of judicial and legislative decisions, even though this last would involve appealing to those same doctrines of interpretation we justified through the principles we are now trying to support. At this level of abstraction, in other words, principles rather hang together than link together.

So even though principles draw support from the official acts of legal institutions, they do not have a simple or direct enough connection with these acts to frame that connection in terms of criteria specified by some ultimate master rule of recognition. Is there any other route by which principles might be brought under such a rule?

Hart does say that a master rule might designate as law not only rules enacted by particular legal institutions, but rules established by *custom* as well. He has in mind a problem that bothered other positivists, including Austin. Many of our most ancient legal rules were never explicitly created by a legislature or a court. When they made their first appearance in legal opinions and texts, they were treated as already being part of the law because they represented the customary practice of the community, or some specialized part of it, like the business community. (The examples ordinarily given are rules of mercantile practice, like the rules governing what rights arise under a standard form of commercial paper.)[27] Since Austin thought that all law was the command of a determinate sovereign, he held that

these customary practices were not law until the courts (as agents of the sovereign) recognized them, and that the courts were indulging in a fiction in pretending otherwise. But that seemed arbitrary. If everyone thought custom might in itself be law, the fact that Austin's theory said otherwise was not persuasive.

Hart reversed Austin on this point. The master rule, he says, might stipulate that some custom counts as law even before the courts recognize it. But he does not face the difficulty this raises for this general theory, because he does not attempt to set out the criteria a master rule might use for this purpose. It cannot use, as its only criterion, the provision that the community regard the practice as *morally* binding, for this would not distinguish legal customary rules from moral customary rules, and of course not all of the community's long-standing customary moral obligations are enforced at law. If, on the other hand, the test is whether the community regards the customary practice as *legally* binding, the whole point of the master rule is undercut, at least for this class of legal rules. The master rule, says Hart, marks the transformation from a primitive society to one with law, because it provides a test for determining social rules of law other than by measuring their acceptance. But if the master rule says merely that whatever other rules the community accepts as legally binding are legally binding, then it provides no such test at all, beyond the test we should use were there no master rule. The master rule becomes (for these cases) a nonrule of recognition; we might as well say that every primitive society has a secondary rule of recognition, namely the rule that whatever is accepted as binding is binding. Hart himself, in discussing international law, ridicules the idea that such a rule could be a rule of recognition, by describing the proposed rule as "an empty repetition of the mere fact that the society concerned . . . observes certain standards of conduct as obligatory rules."[28]

Hart's treatment of custom amounts, indeed, to a confession that there are at least some rules of law that are not binding because they are valid under standards laid down by a master rule but are binding—like the master rule—because they are accepted as binding by the community. This chips at the neat pyramidal architecture we admired in Hart's theory: we can no longer say that only the master rule is binding because of its acceptance, all other rules being valid under its terms.

This is perhaps only a chip, because the customary rules Hart has in mind are no longer a very significant part of the law. But it does suggest that Hart would be reluctant to widen the damage by bringing under the head of "custom" all those crucial principles and policies we have been discussing. If he were to call these part of the law and yet admit that the only test of their force lies in the degree to which they are accepted as law by the community or some part thereof, he would very sharply reduce that area of the law over which his master rule held any dominion. It is not just that all the principles and policies would escape its sway, though that would be bad enough. Once these principles and policies are accepted as law, and thus as standards judges must follow in determining legal obligations, it would follow that *rules* like those announced for the first time in *Riggs* and *Henningsen* owe their force at least in part to the authority of principles and policies, and so not entirely to the master rule of recognition.

So we cannot adapt Hart's version of positivism by modifying his rule of recognition to embrace principles. No tests of pedigree, relating principles to acts of legislation, can be formulated, nor can his concept of customary law, itself an exception to the first tenet of positivism, be made to serve without abandoning that tenet altogether. One more possibility must be considered, however. If no rule of recognition can provide a test for identifying principles, why not say that principles are ultimate, and *form* the rule of recognition of our law? The answer to the general question "What is valid law in an American jurisdiction?" would then require us to state all the principles (as well as ultimate constitutional rules) in force in that jurisdiction at the time, together with appropriate assignments of weight. A positivist might then regard the complete set of these standards as the rule of recognition of the jurisdiction. This solution has the attraction of paradox, but of course it is an unconditional surrender. If we simply designate our rule of recognition by the phrase "the complete set of principles in force," we achieve only the tautology that law is law. If, instead, we tried actually to list all the principles in force we would

fail. They are controversial, their weight is all important, they are numberless, and they shift and change so fast that the start of our list would be obsolete before we reached the middle. Even if we succeeded, we would not have a key for law because there would be nothing left for our key to unlock.

I conclude that if we treat principles as law we must reject the positivists' first tenet, that the law of a community is distinguished from other social standards by some test in the form of a master rule. We have already decided that we must then abandon the second tenet—the doctrine of judicial discretion—or clarify it into triviality. What of the third tenet, the positivists' theory of legal obligation?

This theory holds that a legal obligation exists when (and only when) an established rule of law imposes such an obligation. It follows from this that in a hard case—when no such established rule can be found—there is no legal obligation until the judge creates a new rule for the future. The judge may apply that new rule to the parties in the case, but this is *ex post facto* legislation, not the enforcement of an existing obligation.

The positivists' doctrine of discretion (in the strong sense) required this view of legal obligation, because if a judge has discretion there can be no legal right or obligation—no entitlement— that he must enforce. Once we abandon that doctrine, however, and treat principles as law, we raise the possibility that a legal obligation might be imposed by a constellation of principles as well as by an established rule. We might want to say that a legal obligation exists whenever the case supporting such an obligation, in terms of binding legal principles of different sorts, is stronger than the case against it.

Of course, many questions would have to be answered before we could accept that view of legal obligation. If there is no rule of recognition, no test for law in that sense, how do we decide which principles are to count, and how much, in making such a case? How do we decide whether one case is better than another? If legal obligation rests on an undemonstrable judgment of that sort, how can it provide a justification for a judicial decision that one party had a legal obligation? Does this view of obligation square with the way lawyers, judges and laymen speak, and is it consistent with our attitudes about moral obligation?

Does this analysis help us to deal with the classical jurisprudential puzzles about the nature of law?

These questions must be faced, but even the questions promise more than positivism provides. Positivism, on its own thesis, stops short of just those puzzling, hard cases that send us to look for theories of law. When we reach these cases, the positivist remits us to a doctrine of discretion that leads nowhere and tells nothing. His picture of law as a system of rules has exercised a tenacious hold on our imagination, perhaps through its very simplicity. If we shake ourselves loose from this model of rules, we may be able to build a model truer to the complexity and sophistication of our own practices.

NOTES

1. *See* Linkletter v. Walker, 381 U.S. 618 (1965).
2. J. Austin, The Province of Jurisprudence Determined (1832).
3. *See* H. L. A. Hart, The Concept of Law 89–96 (1961).
4. *Id.* at 79–88.
5. *Id.* at 97–107.
6. *Id. passim,* particularly ch. VI.
7. *Id.* ch. VII.
8. *See* Dworkin, *Wasserstrom: The Judicial Decision,* 75 Ethics 47 (1964), reprinted as *Does Law Have a Function?,* 74 Yale L. J. 640 (1965).
9. 115 N.Y. 506, 22 N.E. 188 *1889); [p. 93 this volume.]
10. *Id.* at 509, 22 N.E. at 189; [p. 93 this volume.]
11. *Id.* at 511, 22 N.E. at 190. [p. 94 this volume.]
12. 32 N.J. 358, 161 A.2d 69 (1960). [p. 95 this volume.]
13. *Id.* at 386, 161 A.2d at 84. [p. 96 this volume.]

14. *Id.*
15. *Id.* at 388, 161 A.2d at 86. [p. 97 this volume.]
16. *Id.* at 387, 161 A.2d at 85. [p. 96 this volume.]
17. *Id.* at 389, 161 A.2d at 86 (quoting Frankfurter, J., in United States v. Bethlehem Steel, 315 U.S. 289, 326 (1942). [p. 97 this volume.]
18. *Id.*
19. Standard Oil v. Unites States, 221 U.S. 1, 60 (1911); United States v. American Tobacco Co., 221 U.S. 106, 180 (1911).
20. The distinction is in substance the same as that made by Rawls, *Two Concepts of Rules,* 64 Philosophical Rev. 3 (1955).
21. I have not spoken of that jurisprudential favorite, "limited" discretion, because that concept presents no special difficulties if we remember the relativity of discretion. Suppose the sergeant is told to choose from "amongst" experienced men, or to "take experience into account." We might say either that he has (limited) discretion in picking his patrol, or (full) discretion to either pick amongst experienced men or decide what else to take into account.
22. H. L. A. Hart, The Concept of Law 144 (1961).
23. *See* Wellington & Albert, *Statutory Interpretation and the Political Process: A Comment on Sinclair v. Atkinson,* 72 Yale L. J. 1547 (1963).
24. R. Pound, An Introduction to the Philosophy of Law 56 (rev. ed. 1954).
25. *See, e.g.,* Dickinson, *The Law Behind Law* (pts. 1 & 2), 29 Colum. L. Rev. 112, 254 (1929).
26. H. L. A. Hart, The Concept of Law 92 (1961).
27. *See* Note, *Custom and Trade Usage: Its Application to Commercial Dealings and the Common Law,* 55 Colum. L. Rev. 1192 (1955), and materials cited therein at 1193 n.1. As that note makes plain, the actual practices of courts in recognizing trade customs follow the pattern of applying a set of general principles and policies rather than a test that could be captured as part of a rule of recognition.
28. H. L. A. Hart, The Concept of Law 230 (1961).

RIGGS v. PALMER

New York Court of Appeals, 1889*

Earl, J. On the 13th day of August, 1880, Francis B. Palmer made his last will and testament, in which he gave small legacies to his two daughters, Mrs. Riggs and Mrs. Preston, the plaintiffs in this action, and the remainder of his estate to his grandson, the defendant Elmer E. Palmer, subject to the support of Susan Palmer, his mother, with a gift over to the two daughters, subject to the support of Mrs. Palmer in case Elmer should survive him and die under age, unmarried, and without any issue. The testator, at the date of his will, owned a farm, and considerable personal property. He was a widower, and thereafter, in March, 1882, he was married to Mrs. Bresee, with whom, before his marriage, he entered into an antenuptial contract, in which it was agreed that in lieu of dower and all other claims upon his estate in case she survived him she should have her support upon his farm during her life, and such support was expressly charged upon the farm. At the date of the will, and subsequently to the death of the testator, Elmer lived with him as a member of his family, and at his death was 16 years old. He knew of the provisions made in his favor in the will, and, that he might prevent his grandfather from revoking such provisions, which he had manifested some intention to do, and to obtain the speedy enjoyment and immediate possession of his property, he willfully murdered him by poisoning him. He now claims the property, and the sole question for our determination is, can he have it?

The defendants say that the testator is dead; that his will was made in due form, and has been admitted to probate; and that therefore it must have effect according to the letter of the law. It is quite true that statutes regulating the making, proof, and effects of wills and the devolution of property if literally construed, and if their force and effect can in no way and under no circumstances be controlled or modified, give this property to the murderer. The purpose of those statutes was to enable testators to dispose of their estates to the objects of their bounty at death, and to carry into effect their final wishes legally expressed; and in consid-

ering and giving effect to them this purpose must be kept in view. It was the intention of the law-makers that the donees in a will should have the property given to them. But it never could have been their intention that a donee who murdered the testator to make the will operative should have any benefit under it. If such a case had been present to their minds, and it had been supposed necessary to make some provision of law to meet it, it cannot be doubted that they would have provided for it. It is a familiar canon of construction that a thing which is within the intention of the makers of a statute is as much within the statute as if it were within the letter; and a thing which is within the letter of the statute is not within the statute unless it be within the intention of the makers. The writers of laws do not always express their intention perfectly, but either exceed it or fall short of it, so that judges are to collect it from probable or rational conjectures only, and this is called "rational interpretation;" and Rutherford, in his Institutes, (page 420,) says: "Where we make use of rational interpretation, sometimes we restrain the meaning of the writer so as to take in less, and sometimes we extend or enlarge his meaning so as to take in more, than his words express." Such a construction ought to be put upon a statute as will best answer the intention which the makers had in view, for *qui haeret in litera, haeret in cortice.* In Bac. Abr. "Statutes," 1, 5; Puff. Law Nat. bk. 5, c. 12; Ruth. Inst. 422, 427, and in Smith's Commentaries, 814, many cases are mentioned where it was held that matters embraced in the general words of statutes nevertheless were not within the statutes, because it could not have been the intention of the law-makers that they should be included. They were taken out of the statutes by an equitable construction; and it is said in Bacon: "By an equitable construction a case not within the letter of a statute is sometimes holden to be within the meaning, because it is within the mischief for which a remedy is provided. The reason for such construction is that the law-makers could not set down every case in express terms. In order to form a right judgment whether a case be within the equity of a statute, it is a good way to suppose the law-maker present, and that you have asked him this question: Did you intend to compre-

*22 N.E. 188 (1889). A portion of the court's opinion has been omitted here.

hend this case? Then you must give yourself such answer as you imagine he, being an upright and reasonable man, would have given. If this be that he did mean to comprehend it, you may safely hold the case to be within the equity of the statute; for while you do no more than he would have done, you do not act contrary to the statute, but in conformity thereto." 9 Bac. Abr. 248. In some cases the letter of a legislative act is restrained by an equitable construction; in others, it is enlarged; in others, the construction is contrary to the letter. The equitable construction which restrains the letter of a statute is defined by Aristotle as frequently quoted in this manner: *Æquitas est correctio legis generaliter latae qua parte deficit.* If the law-makers could, as to this case, be consulted, would they say that they intended by their general language that the property of a testator or of an ancestor should pass to one who had taken his life for the express purpose of getting his property? In 1 Bl. Comm. 91, the learned author, speaking of the construction of statutes, says: "If there arise out of them collaterally any absurd consequences manifestly contradictory to common reason, they are with regard to those collateral consequences void. * * * Where some collateral matter arises out of the general words, and happens to be unreasonable, there the judges are in decency to conclude that this consequence was not foreseen by the parliament, and therefore they are at liberty to expound the statute by equity, and only *quoad hoc* disregard it;" and he gives as an illustration, if an act of parliament gives a man power to try all causes that arise within his manor of Dale, yet, if a cause should arise in which he himself is party, the act is construed not to extend to that, because it is unreasonable that any man should determine his own quarrel. There was a statute in Bologna that whoever drew blood in the streets should be severely punished, and yet it was held not to apply to the case of a barber who opened a vein in the street. It is commanded in the decalogue that no work shall be done upon the Sabbath, and yet giving the command a rational interpretation founded upon its design the Infallible Judge held that it did not prohibit works of necessity, charity, or benevolence on that day.

What could be more unreasonable than to suppose that it was the legislative intention in the general laws passed for the orderly, peaceable, and just devolution of property that they should have operation in favor of one who murdered his ancestor that he might speedily come into the possession of his estate? Such an intention is inconceivable. We need not, therefore, be much troubled by the general language contained in the laws. Besides, all laws, as well as all contracts, may be controlled in their operation and effect by general, fundamental maxims of the common law. No one shall be permitted to profit by his own fraud, or to take advantage of his own wrong, or to found any claim upon his own iniquity, or to acquire property by his own crime. These maxims are dictated by public policy, have their foundation in universal law administered in all civilized countries, and have nowhere been superseded by statutes. They were applied in the decision of the case of Insurance Co. v. Armstrong, 117 U.S. 599, 6 Sup. Ct. Rep. 877. There it was held that the person who procured a policy upon the life of another, payable at his death, and then murdered the assured to make the policy payable, could not recover thereon. Mr. Justice FIELD, writing the opinion, said: "Independently of any proof of the motives of Hunter in obtaining the policy, and even assuming that they were just and proper, he forfeited all rights under it when, to secure its immediate payment, he murdered the assured. It would be a reproach to the jurisprudence of the country if one could recover insurance money payable on the death of a party whose life he had feloniously taken. As well might he recover insurance money upon a building that he had willfully fired." These maxims, without any statute giving them force or operation, frequently control the effect and nullify the language of wills. A will procured by fraud and deception, like any other instrument, may be decreed void, and set aside; and so a particular portion of a will may be excluded from probate, or held inoperative, if induced by the fraud or undue influence of the person in whose favor it is. Allen v. McPherson, 1 H. L. Cas. 191; Harrison's Appeal, 48 Conn. 202. So a will may contain provisions which are immoral, irreligious, or against public policy, and they will be held void.

Here there was no certainty that this murderer would survive the testator, or that the testator would not change his will, and there was no certainty that he would get this property if nature was allowed to take its course. He therefore murdered the testator expressly to vest himself with an estate. Under such circumstances, what law, human or divine, will allow him to take the estate and enjoy the fruits of his crime? The will spoke and became operative at the death of the testator. He caused that death, and thus by his crime made it speak and have operation. Shall it speak and operate in his favor? If he had met the testator, and taken his property by force, he would have had no title to it. Shall he acquire title by murdering him? If he had gone to the testator's house, and by force compelled him, or by fraud or undue influence had induced him, to will him his property, the law would not allow him to hold it. But can he give effect and operation to a will by murder, and yet take the property? To answer these questions in the affirmative it seems to me would be a reproach to the jurisprudence of our state, and an offense against public policy. Under the civil law, evolved from the general principles of natural law and justice by many generations of jurisconsults, philosophers, and statesmen, one cannot take property by inheritance or will from an ancestor or benefactor whom he has murdered. Dom, Civil Law, pt. 2, bk. 1, tit. 1, § 3; Code Nap. § 727; Mack Rom. Law, 530, 550. In the Civil Code of Lower Canada the provisions on the subject in the Code Napoleon have been substantially copied. But, so far as I can find, in no country where the common law prevails has it been deemed important to enact a law to provide for such a case. Our revisers and law-makers were familiar with the civil law, and they did not deem it important to incorporate into our statutes its provisions upon his subject. This is not a *casus omissus.* It was evidently supposed that the maxims of the common law were sufficient to regulate such a case, and that a specific enactment for that purpose was not needed. For the same reasons the defendant Palmer cannot take any of this property as heir. Just before the murder he was not an heir, and it was not certain that he ever would be. He might have died before his grandfather, or might have been disinherited by him. He made himself an heir by the murder, and he seeks to take property as the fruit of his crime. What has before been said as to him as legatee applies to him with equal force as an heir. He cannot vest himself with

title by crime. My view of this case does not inflict upon Elmer any greater or other punishment for his crime than the law specifies. It takes from him no property, but simply holds that he shall not acquire property by his crime, and thus be rewarded for its commission.

Our attention is called to Owens v. Owens, 100 N.C. 240, 6 S.E. Rep. 794, as a case quite like this. There a wife had been convicted of being an accessory before the fact to the murder of her husband, and it was held that she was nevertheless entitled to dower. I am unwilling to assent to the doctrine of that case. The status provide dower for a wife who has the misfortune to survive her husband, and thus lose his support and protection. It is clear beyond their purpose to make provision for a wife who by her own crime makes herself a widow, and willfully and intentionally deprives herself of the support and protection of her husband. As she might have died before him, and "though" never have been his widow, she cannot by her crime vest herself with an estate. The principle which lies at the bottom of the maxim *volenti non fit injuria* should be applied to such a case, and a widow should not, for the purpose of acquiring, as such, property rights, be permitted to allege a widowhood which she has wickedly and intentionally created.

HENNINGSEN v. BLOOMFIELD MOTORS, INC.

Supreme Court of New Jersey, 1960*

Action by automobile buyer's wife and buyer himself against manufacturer and dealer to recover damages on account of injuries sustained by wife while she was driving allegedly defective automobile shortly after its purchase. The trial court entered judgment in favor of buyer and wife and manufacturer and dealer appealed and matter was certified by Supreme Court prior to consideration in Appellate Division. The Supreme Court, Francis. J., held that where purchase order for new automobile contained therein an express warranty by which manufacturer warranted vehicle free from defects in material or workmanship and warranty fur-

*161 A. 2d 69 (1960). The first paragraph printed here is a summary of the facts which appeared in the report of the case. It is not a part of the court's opinion. The excerpt from the opinion reprinted here is only a small portion of the whole opinion.

ther stated that it was expressly in lieu of all other warranties express or implied, and such warranty was the uniform warranty of the Automobile Manufacturers Association to which all major automobile manufacturers belonged, under circumstances, manufacturer's attempted disclaimer of an implied warranty of merchantability and of the obligations arising therefrom was so inimical to public good as to compel an adjudication of its invalidity.

... Judicial notice may be taken of the fact that automobile manufacturers, including Chrysler Corporation, undertake large scale advertising programs over television, radio, in newspapers, magazines and all media of communication in order to persuade the public to buy their products. As has been observed above, a number of jurisdictions, conscious of modern marketing practices, have declared that when a manufacturer engages in advertising in order to bring his goods and their quality to the attention of the public and thus to create consumer demand, the representations made constitute an express warranty running directly to a buyer who purchases in reliance thereon. The fact that the sale is consummated with an independent dealer does not obviate that warranty. Mannsz v. Macwhyte Co., supra; Bahlman v. Hudson Motor Car Co., supra; Rogers v. Toni Home Permanent Co., supra; Meyer v. Packard Cleveland Motor Co., 106 Ohio St. 328, 140 N.E. 118, 28 A.L.R. 986 (1922); Baxter v. Ford Motor Co., supra; 1 Williston, Sales, supra § 244a.

In view of the cases in various jurisdictions suggesting the conclusion which we have now reached with respect to the implied warranty of merchantability, it becomes apparent that manufacturers who enter into promotional activities to stimulate consumer buying may incur warranty obligations of either or both the express or implied character. These developments in the law inevitably suggest the inference that the form of express warranty made part of the Henningsen purchase contract was devised for general use in the automobile industry as a possible means of avoiding the consequences of the growing judicial acceptance of the thesis that the described express or implied warranties run directly to the consumer.

In the light of these matters, what effect should be given to the express warranty in question which seeks to limit the manufacturer's liability to replacement of defective parts, and which disclaims all other warranties, express or implied? In assessing its significance we must keep in mind the general principle that, in the absence of fraud, one who does not choose to read a contract before signing it, cannot later relieve himself of its burdens. Fivey v. Pennsylvania R. R. Co., 67 N.J.L. 627, 52 A. 472, (E.& A.1902). And in applying that principle, the basic tenet of freedom of competent parties to contract is a factor of importance. But in the framework of modern commercial life and business practices, such rules cannot be applied on a strict, doctrinal basis. The conflicting interests of the buyer and seller must be evaluated realistically and justly, giving due weight to the social policy evinced by the Uniform Sales Act, the progressive decisions of the courts engaged in administering it, the mass production methods of manufacture and distribution to the public, and the bargaining position occupied by the ordinary consumer in such an economy. This history of the law shows that legal doctrines, as first expounded, often prove to be inadequate under the impact of later experience. In such case, the need for justice has stimulated the necessary qualifications or adjustments. Perkins v. Endicott Johnson Corporation, 128 F.2d 208, 217 (2 Cir. 1942), affirmed 317 U.S. 501, 63 S.Ct. 339, 87 L.Ed. 424 (1943); Greenberg v. Lorenz, supra.

In these times, an automobile is almost as much a servant of convenience for the ordinary person as a household utensil. For a multitude of other persons it is a necessity. Crowded highways and filled parking lots are a commonplace of our existence. There is no need to look any farther than the daily newspaper to be convinced that when an automobile is defective, it has great potentiality for harm.

No one spoke more graphically on this subject than Justice Cardozo in the landmark case of MacPherson v. Buick Motor Co., 217 N.Y. 382, 111 N.E. 1050, 1053, L.R.A.1916F, 696 (Ct.App.1916):

"Beyond all question, the nature of an automobile gives warning of probable danger if its construction is defective. This automobile was designed to go 50 miles per hour. Unless its wheels were sound and strong, injury was almost certain. It was as much a thing of danger as a defective engine for a railroad. * * * The dealer was indeed the one person of whom it might be said with some approach to certainty that by him the car would not be used. * * * Precedents drawn from the days of travel by stagecoach do not fit the conditions of travel to-day. The principle that the danger must be imminent does not change, but the things subject to the principle do change. They are whatever the needs of life in a developing civilization require them to be."

In the 44 years that have intervened since that utterance, the average car has been constructed for almost double the speed mentioned; 60 miles per hour is permitted on our parkways. The number of automobiles in use has multiplied many times and the hazard to the user and the public has increased proportionately. The Legislature has intervened in the public interest, not only to regulate the manner of operation on the highway but also to require periodic inspection of motor vehicles and to impose a duty on manufacturers to adopt certain safety devices and methods in their construction. R.S. 39:3–43 et seq., N.J.S.A. It is apparent that the public has an interest not only in the safe manufacture of automobiles, but also, as shown by the Sales Act, in protecting the rights and remedies of purchasers, so far as it can be accomplished consistently with our system of free enterprise. In a society such as ours, where the automobile is a common and necessary adjunct of daily life, and where its use is so fraught with danger to the driver, passengers and the public, the manufacturer is under a special obligation in connection with the construction, promotion and sale of his cars. Consequently, the courts must examine purchase agreements closely to see if consumer and public interests are treated fairly.

What influence should these circumstances have on the restrictive effect of Chrysler's express warranty in the framework of the purchase contract? As we have said, warranties originated in the law to safeguard the buyer and not to limit the liability of the seller or manufacturer. It seems obvious in this instance that the motive was to avoid the warranty obligations which are normally incidental to such sales. The language gave little and withdrew much. In return for the delusive remedy of replacement of defective parts at the factory, the buyer is said to have accepted the exclusion of the maker's liability for personal injuries arising from the breach of the warranty, and to have agreed to the elimination of any other express or implied warranty. An instinctively felt sense of justice cries out against such a sharp bargain. But does the doctrine that a person is bound by his signed agreement in the absence of fraud, stand in the way of any relief?

In the modern consideration of problems such as this, Corbin suggests that practically all judges are "chancellors" and cannot fail to be influenced by any equitable doctrines that are available. And he opines that "there is sufficient flexibility in the concepts of fraud, duress, misrepresentation and undue influence, not to mention differences in economic bargaining power" to enable the courts to avoid enforcement of unconscionable provisions in long printed standardized contracts. 1 Corbin on Contracts (1950) § 128, p. 188. Freedom of contract is not such an immutable doctrine as to admit of no qualification in the area in which we are concerned. As Chief Justice Hughes said in his dissent in Morehead v. People of State of New York ex rel. Tipaldo, 298 U.S. 587, 627, 56 S.Ct. 918, 930, 80 L.Ed. 1347, 1364 (1936):

"We have had frequent occasion to consider the limitations on liberty of contract. While it is highly important to preserve that liberty from arbitrary and capricious interference, it is also necessary to prevent its abuse, as otherwise it could be used to override all public interests and thus in the end destroy the very freedom of opportunity which it is designed to safeguard."

That sentiment was echoed by Justice Frankfurter in his dissent in United States v. Bethlehem Steel Corp., 315 U.S. 289, 326, 62 S.Ct. 581, 599, 86 L.Ed. 855, 876 (1942):

"It is said that familiar principles would be outraged if Bethlehem were denied recovery on these contracts. But is there any principle which is more familiar or more firmly embedded in the history of Anglo-American law than the basic doctrine that the courts will not permit themselves to be used as instruments of inequity and injustice? Does any principle in our law have more universal application than the doctrine that courts will not enforce transactions in which the relative positions of the parties are such that one has unconscionably taken advantage of the necessities of the other?

"These principles are not foreign to the law of contracts. Fraud and physical duress are not the only grounds upon which courts refuse to enforce contracts. The law is not so primitive that it sanctions every injustice except brute force and downright fraud. More specifically, the courts generally refuse to lend themselves to the enforcement of a 'bargain' in which one party has unjustly taken advantage of the economic necessities of the other. * * * "

The traditional contract is the result of free bargaining of parties who are brought together by the play of the market, and who meet each other on a footing of approximate economic equality. In such a society there is no danger that freedom of contract will be a threat to the social order as a whole. But in present-day commercial life the standardized mass contract has appeared. It is used primarily by enterprises with strong bargaining power and position. "The weaker party, in need of the goods or services, is frequently not in a position to shop around for better terms, either because the author of the standard contract has a monopoly (natural or artifical) or because all competitors use the same clauses. His contractual intention is but a subjection more or less voluntary to terms dictated by the stronger party, terms whose consequences are often understood in a vague way, if at all." Kessler, "Contracts of Adhesion—Some Thoughts About Freedom of Contract," 43 Colum.L.Rev. 629, 632 (1943); Ehrenzweig, "Adhesion Contracts in the Conflict of Laws," 53 Colum.L.Rev. 1072, 1075, 1089 (1953). Such standardized contracts have been described as those in which one predominant party will dictate its law to an undetermined multiple rather than to an individual. They are said to resemble a law rather than a meeting of the minds. Siegelman v. Cunard White Star, 221 F.2d 189, 206 (2 Cir. 1955).

JOSEPH RAZ

Legal Principles and the Limits of Law*

PRINCIPLES AND THE LIMITS OF LAW

By the thesis of the "limits of law" I mean the position that there is a test which distinguishes what is law from what is not. Professor Dworkin's writings in effect contain three arguments, each of which is partly dependent on his theory of principles, against the thesis of the limits of law.[1] While only two of these arguments are explicitly directed against this thesis, all of them, if valid, undermine it. In the remainder of this article I shall show that each of Professor Dworkin's arguments must fail and that there is good reason to persevere in the attempt to construct a test for distinguishing what is law from what is not. I hope in the course of this discussion to throw some light on how such seemingly disparate matters as the thesis of the limits of law, the nature of rules and principles, the role of judicial discretion, and the criterion of the identity of a legal system are related.

A. JUDICIAL DISCRETION

Professor Dworkin's first argument is a result of his theory of judicial discretion.[2] He distinguishes three senses of discretion. In the two weak senses "discretion" means "judgment" and "finality." "Sometimes," explains Professor Dworkin,

we use "discretion" in a weak sense, simply to say that for some reason the standards an official must apply cannot be applied mechanically but demand the use of judgment. . . .

Sometimes we use the term in a different weak sense, to say only that some official has final authority to make a decision and cannot be reviewed and reversed by any other official. . . .

I call both of these senses weak to distinguish them

*Reprinted by permission of the author and of The Yale Law Journal Company and Fred B. Rothman & Company. From *The Yale Law Journal*, Vol. 81, pp. 823, 842–54.

from a stronger sense. We use "discretion" sometimes . . . to say that on some issue [an official] is simply not bound by standards set by the authority in question.[3]

The thesis that judges have discretion in the strong sense[4] means that there are cases which they are legally entitled to decide and in which no one correct decision is determined by standards of law. The thesis of judicial discretion does not entail that in cases where discretion may be exercised anything goes. Such cases are governed by laws which rule out certain decisions. The only claim is that the laws do not determine any decision as the correct one.

Professor Dworkin argues that (1) the law includes some principles as well as rules. From this he concludes that (2) the courts never have discretion in the strong sense. It follows, though he does not draw the conclusion at this point, that (3) the thesis of the limits of law is wrong. I shall argue that (3) does indeed follow from (2), but that (2) does not follow from (1) and is in any case wrong.

If courts are never entitled to exercise discretion (in the strong sense) it follows that all the reasons, rules and principles which they are entitled to rely on are part of the law. There is one important exception to this conclusion; those standards which are applied because they are the standards of some other legal system or organization, the standards of which the law respects and enforces, are not part of the law. The exception covers those laws of other states which are recognized and enforced according to the rules of private international law. It also extends to contracts and the rules of voluntary associations recognized by law, and to social, moral and religious standards of individuals and communities which are taken into account for some legal purposes (such as mitigation of punishment or exemption from military service) or as creating presumptions of fact as to the behavior or intention of litigants. When referring to such standards in their judgments the courts quite clearly do so not because they are part of the law but because the law makes it its business to recognize and give support, to a certain extent, to standards of other organizations, communities or individuals.[5]

This exception apart (and however important, it does not affect Professor Dworkin's case against the thesis of the limits of law), it follows from Professor Dworkin's views on judicial discretion that all the reasons which the courts are entitled to use in justifying decisions are part of the law. All the reasons for a decision are legal reasons for the law uniquely determines which decision is the correct one.[6] Now it seems to me true that on various occasions the courts are entitled to rely on every reason which is endorsed by part of the community for some purpose or other. It follows, therefore, from Professor Dworkin's view on judicial discretion that the thesis of the limits of law is wrong at least to the extent to which it claims that it is possible to distinguish between the law and nonlegal social standards.

If, on the other hand, courts do have discretion, then in cases in which they are entitled to exercise discretion, they act on standards which are not part of the law. Therefore, though every social standard may figure in a court's decision, it does not follow that all of them are laws. The opportunity is given to those who support the thesis of the limits of law to draw a distinction between the standards used by courts which are law and those which are not. How is one to decide whether courts do or do not have discretion?

Professor Dworkin is primarily concerned to argue that there are legally binding principles. But this has never been denied by anyone, least of all by the positivists. Indeed, Austin could not have denied that some principles are legally binding while remaining true to his theory of law. The most fundamental tenet of his theory is that the commands of a sovereign are law, and there is nothing to prevent a sovereign from commanding that a principle shall be binding. Professor Dworkin's mistake lies in assuming that when Austin was talking about commands he was referring to what Professor Dworkin calls rules. But this is not the case. Neither does Hart use "rules" in the same sense as Professor Dworkin. By "rules" he means what Professor Dworkin seems to mean by "standards," namely rules, principles or any other type of norm (whether legal or social).[7]

The crux of the argument lies in the inference that since some principles are law judicial discretion does not exist. Professor Dworkin says very little on this. The reason, I suspect, is that he rightly sees that other theorists, not only the positivists, exaggerated the scope of judicial discretion because they failed to attend to the role principles play in the law. They tended to assume that whenever a rule is vague the court has discretion and did not see that sometimes the rule when read in light of some principles is not vague and does not leave room for discretion. "A set of principles," as Professor Dworkin reminds us, "*can* dictate a result."[8] But that it sometimes can does not mean that it always does. And it is this that Professor Dworkin has to establish to make his case against judicial discretion. Unfortunately, he does not even try to establish this point.

I suppose that there might be a legal system which contains a rule that whenever the courts are faced with a case for which the law does not provide a uniquely correct solution they ought to refuse to render judgment. In such a system there would be no judicial discretion. But, whether or not such a system can exist, few if any legal systems in fact contain such a rule. In most legal systems there are at least three different sources of judicial discretion. Let me survey them briefly.

1. *Vagueness.* Vagueness is inherent in language. It is a problem courts have to face very frequently. As noted above, principles as well as rules of interpretation can sometimes solve problems of vagueness without leaving room for discretion. But principles themselves are vague, and discretion in cases of vagueness cannot be dispensed with so long as courts are entitled to render judgment in such cases.

2. *Weight.* Though principles sometimes limit the scope of the courts' discretion, they tend on the whole to expand it. For reasons noted earlier, the law usually determines with precision the relative weight of rules. Not so with principles. The law characteristically includes only incomplete indications as to their relative weight and leaves much to judicial discretion to be exercised in particular cases. The scope of discretion is in fact doubly extended, since not only must the relative importance of principles be determined, but also

the importance relative to each principle of deviating from it or of following it on particular occasions. This matter is usually entrusted to judicial discretion.

That courts have discretion as to weight does not, of course, mean that the law has nothing to contribute to the solution of the case. It contributes some of the elements for a solution, but not all the elements necessary to dictate a uniquely correct solution. In such cases the law dictates what considerations have to be taken into account, but not what weight to assign to each of them or to actions in accordance with contrary to each of them in particular cases.

3. *Laws of discretion.* Most legal systems contain laws granting courts discretion, not only as to the weight of legally binding considerations, but also to act on considerations which are not legally binding. Such discretion may be, and usually is, guided by principles. These principles, however, do not dictate the considerations to be taken into account, but merely limit the range of the considerations.

One may distinguish between substantive principles, which dictate a goal to be pursued or a value to be protected, and principles of discretion, which guide discretion by stipulating what type of goals and values the judge may take into account in exercising his discretion. Compare the following two sets of hypothetical principles. (a) "Car manufacturers have a duty to protect the public from accidents." "Increased productivity and efficiency should be the prime objective of public corporations." "The validity of standard contracts is contingent on their not taking advantages of the economic necessities of the weaker party." "The law favors security of title." (b) "The courts will not enforce unjust contracts." "Public corporations should act for the general good." "Whatever is *contra bonos mores et decorum* the principles of our law prohibit." The first group of principles set particular considerations to be acted on. They may be vague and they do not specify the weight to be given to each consideration, but the consideration prescribed is clear enough and is not a matter left to the courts' discretion. Principles of the second group, on the other hand, do not stipulate what considerations should be acted on. They merely specify the type of considerations which may be taken into account and leave the rest to the officials or the

courts addressed by the principles. Rather than negating discretion, they presuppose its existence and guide it. What is "unjust" or "for the general good" is a matter of opinion and the courts or officials concerned are instructed by law to act on their own views. The law does not impose its own views of justice or the common good. Rather it leaves the matter to the discretion of the courts or the officials. Many of the principles governing the action of the courts and the executive are principles of discretion.[9] Such principles, far from proving the absence of judicial discretion, are a manifestation of a legal policy to rely on and make use of judicial and administrative discretion in order to increase the flexibility of the law and improve the procedures for its constant review to meet changes in circumstance and opinion.

We must conclude that legal principles do not exclude judicial discretion; they presuppose its existence and direct and guide it. The argument from the absence of judicial discretion against the thesis of the limits of law must therefore be rejected. It should be noted, however, that judicial discretion is not arbitrary judgment. Courts are never allowed to act arbitrarily. Even when discretion is not limited or guided in any specific direction the courts are still legally bound to act as they think is best according to their beliefs and values. If they do not, if they give arbitrary judgment by tossing a coin, for example, they violate a legal duty. A judge must always invoke some general reasons. He has no discretion when the reasons are dictated by law. He has discretion when the law requires him to act on reasons which he thinks are correct, instead of imposing its own standards. When discretion is denied, the law dictates which standards should be applied by all the judges. When discretion is allowed, each judge is entitled to follow different reasons but he must believe that they are the best. Otherwise, discretion can be equated only with arbitrariness, whim, and caprice.

B. "SOURCES" OF LEGAL PRINCIPLES

Legal principles, like other laws, can be enacted or repealed by legislatures and administrative authorities. They can also become legally binding through establishment by the courts. Many legal systems recognize that both rules and principles can be made into law or lose their status as law through precedent. Rules and principles differ in this respect. A court can establish a new rule in a single judgment which becomes a precedent. Principles are not made into law by a single judgment; they evolve rather like a custom and are binding only if they have considerable authoritative support in a line of judgments. Like customary law, judicially adopted principles need not be formulated very precisely in the judgments which count as authority for their existence. All that has to be shown is that they underlie a series of courts' decisions, that they were in fact a reason operating in a series of cases.

This is recognized by Professor Dworkin. He does, however, add a third "source" of legally binding principles: "judgments of the community at large or some identifiable segment thereof."[10] And he adds in a footnote: "On some occasions, in some kinds of cases, moral principles accepted as standards within the community will figure as good reasons for a legal decision, just as, on other occasions, in other kinds of cases, will standards otherwise established. In this sense, such principles are part of the legal system, if it is helpful to talk about law as a system at all, and the flat statement that law and morals are separate systems in misleading."[11] The morality that Professor Dworkin has in mind consists of those moral views which became social norms in the community. No supporter of the thesis of the limits of law has ever denied that some social norms can be legal norms as well. The legislator can make a social norm into law either by direct enactment or by stipulating that social customs of a certain type should be binding as law. By the doctrine of precedent the courts can do the same. To admit as much does not weaken in the least the thesis of the limits of law.

To challenge the thesis it has to be established that all social norms are automatically (without prior legislative or judicial recognition) binding as law at least to the extent to which they do not conflict with laws created by legislation and precedent. If this were the case in all legal systems, the thesis of the limits of law would indeed be badly shaken and would need a far-reaching reformulation. In his subsequent remarks Professor Dworkin implies that this is in fact the case.[12] I think that he is mistaken, and it is worth pausing to examine the source of his mistake.

In most countries one of the most general principles restraining judicial discretion enjoins judges to act only on those values and opinions which have the support of some important segment of the population.[13] There are various grounds on which the principle can be justified, none of which in itself justifies its full scope. It can be justified on democratic grounds; it can be defended by arguing that a judge whose actions affect the fortune of many should not trust his own judgment if it is not supported by learned opinion; it can be argued that laws out of tune with community values are unlikely to achieve their aim or will have some undesirable consequences. Each of these justifications, and others that can be used, interprets the principle somewhat differently. A close study of the matter will no doubt distinguish [among] various related principles which sometimes reinforce each other and sometimes conflict, or which apply to different situations. All these principles restrain but do not exclude judicial discretion. They do not oblige the courts to enforce any specific social norms. They limit their freedom to act on what they think is right by making it conditional on their ability to show that they are not alone in that opinion. There is, therefore, no reason to regard these principles as converting all social morality into law or as undermining the thesis of the limits of law.

They have, however, a curious, though perhaps not surprising, effect on judicial rhetoric in some countries and especially in the United States. As they should, courts tend to justify judgments based on discretion by arguments designed to show that the decision is a good one,[14] and by other arguments to show that the decision conforms to the views of some segment of the population. Unfortunately, some judges like to claim that the values they endorse are not merely the values of some but embody the national consciousness, represent the national consensus, are universally acknowledged, et cetera. This is perhaps harmless rhetoric if it is understood as such. Professor Dworkin, however, urges us to give literal interpretation to such pronouncements from the bench. The courts apply what they think are community values. It follows that it is wrong to regard them as acting on their own beliefs as legislators do. They may be wrong in their views of what the values of the community are, but if so they are wrong on a point of law, for since they are bound to apply community values these are part of the law.

This literal interpretation of judicial rhetoric is made possible only if one is prepared to join the courts in endorsing two really harmful myths. One is the myth that there is a considerable body of specific moral values shared by the population of a large and modern country. The myth of the common morality has made much of the oppression of minorities possible. It also allows judges to support a partisan point of view while masquerading as the servant of a general consensus. The second myth is that the most general values provide sufficient ground for practical conclusions. This myth holds that, since we all have a general desire for prosperity, progress, culture, justice, and so on, we all want precisely the same things and support exactly the same ideals; and that all the differences [among] us result from disagreements of fact about the most efficient policies to secure the common goals. In fact, much disagreement about more specific goals and about less general values is genuine moral disagreement, which cannot be resolved by appeal to the most general value-formulations which we all endorse, for these bear different interpretations for different people.

The courts tend all too often to claim that a specific policy is entailed by belief in some general value, thus avoiding a concrete justification of their decision, maintaining the rhetoric of common goals and community values and endorsing partisan positions without admitting it. Some judges may themselves be captives of the myths they help to perpetuate. But the fact that are misled should not mislead us. Occasional deviations from the canons of good reasoning can be dismissed as mistakes, but when constant use is made of a pattern of argumentation completely devoid of logical validity, it is time to distinguish between myth and rhetoric on the one hand and reality on the other. And the law should be understood to encompass reality, not rhetoric.

C. THE POSSIBILITY OF A CRITERION OF IDENTITY

If the thesis of the limits of law is right, there must be a criterion of identity which sets necessary and sufficient conditions, satisfaction of which is a mark that a standard is part of a legal system. Austin's criterion of identity was that all

and only the general commands of one sovereign are part of one legal system. Hart has criticized this criterion and suggested another. According to his theory every legal system contains a rule of recognition directed at the courts and imposing on them an obligation to apply those standards which fulfill various criteria set out in the rule.[15] The rule of recognition is a customary rule arising out of the behavior of law-enforcing officials through a period of time. The rest of the laws of the system are valid because they fulfill the conditions set out in the rule of recognition. The general criterion of identity of all legal systems is that each contains a rule of recognition and all those laws satisfying the conditions it stipulates.

Professor Dworkin claims that no adequate criterion of identity can be formulated and that therefore the thesis of the limits of law must be rejected. He directs his attack against Hart's criterion and employs two arguments to show that neither Hart's nor any other criterion of identity can account for the existence of legal principles. I shall argue that one of Professor Dworkin's arguments contains a valid criticism of Hart but does not bear on the possibility of formulating a somewhat different criterion of identity, whereas his second argument fails altogether.

"Hart's sharp distinction between acceptance and validity," the first argument runs, "does not hold. If we are arguing for the principle that a man should not profit from his own wrong, we could cite the acts of courts and legislatures that exemplify it, but this speaks as much to the principle's acceptance as its validity. (It seems odd to speak of a principle as being valid at all, perhaps because validity is an all-or-nothing concept, appropriate for rules, but inconsistent with a principle's dimension of weight.)"[16] The concept of validity is said to be inconsistent with the principle's dimension of weight on the ground that one establishes a principle's validity by showing that it has "institutional support"; but the amount of support a principle enjoys determines its weight and is a matter of degree: "[T]he more support we found, the more weight we could claim for the principle."[17] But this is surely mistaken. A principle might have been referred to frequently by the courts as binding, but have little weight. The degree of support may sometimes be evidence for a principle's weight, but it need not be and the two notions are not logically related.

Legal principles may be valid in precisely the same way that rules are. They may, for example, be enacted in the constitution or in a statute, as some of Professor Dworkin's own examples show. It is true, though, that some legal principles are law because they are accepted by the judiciary. But this is true of rules as well as principles. It is, however, an important point which does necessitate a modification of Hart's criterion of identity. But here again Professor Dworkin claims too much. He claims that if the master rule says merely that whatever other rules the community accepts are legally binding then it fails to act as an identifying criterion distinguishing between law and social norms.[18] Had all social customs in all countries been legally binding this would have been a valid criticism. Some countries, however, do not recognize custom as a source of law at all. Those legal systems which do regard customs as legally binding do so only if they pass certain tests. These tests, if they are not set out in a statute or some other law, are laid down by the rule of recognition, which determines under what conditions social customs are binding in law.

The rule of recognition, therefore, does serve to explain the legal status of general community customs. It cannot, however, explain in the same way the legal status of judicial customs. Since it is itself a judicial custom it cannot confer any special status on other judicial customs. Judicial rule-making, as I indicated above, differs in this respect from the evolution of principles by the courts. A rule becomes binding by being laid down in one case as a precedent. It does not have to wait until it is accepted in a series of cases to be binding. It is binding because of the doctrine of precedent which is part of our rule of recognition. Principles evolved by the courts become binding by becoming a judicial custom. They are part of the law because they are accepted by the courts, not because they are valid according to the rule of recognition.

Hart's criterion of identity must be modified. A legal system consists not only of one customary rule of the law-enforcing agencies and all the laws recognized by it, but of all the customary rules and principles of the law-enforcing agencies and all the laws recognized by them.[19] This is an important modification, but it preserves the fundamental point underlying Hart's criterion and

shared by many: namely, that law is an institutionalized normative system and that the fact that the enforcement of its standards is a duty of special law-enforcing agencies is one important feature which distinguishes it from many other normative systems. The importance of this feature of law is made manifest by distinguishing between legal and nonlegal standards according to whether or not the courts have an obligation to apply them, either because they are themselves judicial custom or because judicial customs make their application obligatory.

Professor Dworkin has a second argument disputing the possibility of formulating an adequate criterion of identity. "True," he says, "if we were challenged to back up our claim that some principle is a principle of law, we would mention any prior cases in which that principle was cited, or figured in the argument. . . . Unless we could find some such institutional support, we would probably fail to make out our case. . . . Yet we could not devise any formula for testing how much and what kind of institutional support is necessary to make a principle a legal principle."[20] In this passage Professor Dworkin is rejecting not merely Hart's version of the thesis of the limits of law but all versions of this thesis. He agrees that if legal and non-legal standards can be distinguished this could only be done by relying on the fact that only legal standards have adequate institutional support in the practice of the courts. He denies, however, the possibility of a general explanation of what counts as adequate institutional support. It follows that it is impossible to provide a general account of the difference between legal and nonlegal standards and the thesis of the limits of law must be abandoned. What is the force of this argument? If a legal system consists, as I have suggested, of those standards which the courts are bound to recognize, we must agree with Professor Dworkin that we need a general explanation of what counts as adequate institutional support. For laws are binding on the courts either because judicial customs make their recognition obligatory or because they are themselves judicial customs. Thus the acceptability of the thesis of the limits of law depends on our ability to explain the concept of a judicial custom. But judicial customs are but a special case of social customs.

What we need is an adequate explanation of the concept of a customary norm. Once we have it we will know what judicial custom is and will have a complete criterion of identity. Hart has provided such an explanation. No doubt it is possible to improve on it, but there is no reason to suppose that the concept of a customary norm defies analysis. It is true that an analysis of the concept does not give us a decision procedure determining for every principle or rule whether or not it has sufficient support to be regarded as a judicial custom.[21] Borderline cases will remain; they must remain, for customary norms evolve gradually. But Dworkin's is a very weak argument, which rejects a distinction because it admits the existence of borderline cases.

NOTES

1. "The Model of Rules" is perhaps not altogether clear that all forms of the thesis of the limits of law are to be rejected, though it plainly opposes one version of the thesis by rejecting the tenet "that the law of a community is distinguished from other social standards by some test in the form of a master rule." Professor Dworkin has, however, confirmed to me in conversation that these arguments are directed against the thesis of the limits of the law generally and has taken such a position in his lectures at Oxford University in 1971.

2. *See* Dworkin, *Judicial Discretion*, 60 J. Phil. 624 (1963). Professor Dworkin has reformulated his theory in "The Model of Rules" (*see* Dworkin, *supra* note 1, at 32–46) to meet some of the objections raised by G. C. MacCallum, Jr., in his reply to Dworkin's first paper. *See* MacCallum, *Dworkin on Judicial Discretion*, 60 J. Phil. 638 (1963).

3. Dworkin, *supra* note 1, at 32–33.

4. I shall henceforth be concerned with "discretion" in this sense, and only this sense is involved in what I shall call the "thesis of judicial discretion."

5. On this problem see Raz, *The Identity of Legal Systems*, 59 Calif. L. Rev. 795 (1971).

6. The courts may occasionally rely on the wrong reasons. I am concerned here only with the reasons which they are entitled to use.

7. Of course both Austin and Hart would maintain that *some* principles are not part of the law. But this is no more than to say that they believe in the thesis of the limits of law. It should be noted that I am using "standards" to cover not only norms but also generally accepted reasons for action.

8. Dworkin, *supra* note 1, at 36 (emphasis in original).

9. Many of the principles mentioned by Professor Dworkin are of this kind.

10. Dworkin, *supra* note 2, at 635 (1963).

11. *Id.* at 635 n. 9.

12. *Id.* at 635 *et seq.*

13. The main device controlling courts' values and ideology is, of course, not this principle, but the methods of appointing or electing judges.

14. Though judges are entitled, sometimes, to act as they think best, that they believe the decision is a good one is never a reason for it; they must have reasons for their beliefs.

15. For arguments supporting this interpretation of Hart's doctrine, see Raz, *supra* note 5, at 807–08.

16. Dworkin, *supra* note 1, at 42.

17. *Id.* at 41.

18. *Id.* at 43–44.

19. For a more precise formulation of the criterion and a more detailed examination of the problem, see *Raz, supra* note 5.

20. Dworkin, *supra* note 1, at 41.

21. It is worth reminding ourselves that not every principle is evolved by the courts; many result from legislative acts.

R O N A L D   M .   D W O R K I N

Social Rules and Legal Theory*

DO JUDGES HAVE TO HAVE DISCRETION?

I must now discuss, once again, the second of the two strategies for positivism that I distinguished at the beginning of the last section. This argument that when judges disagree about matters of principle they disagree not about what the law requires but about how their discretion

*Reprinted by permission of the author and of The Yale Law Journal Company and Fred B. Rothman & Company. From *The Yale Law Journal*, Vol. 81, pp. 855, 879–888.

should be exercised. They disagree, that is, not about where their duty to decide lies, but about how they ought to decide, all things considered, given that they have no duty to decide either way.

I tried to explain, in my original article, that this argument in fact depends upon a kind of ambiguity in the concept of discretion. We use that concept, in discussions about duty, in three different ways. First, we say that a man has discretion if his duty is defined by standards that reasonable men can interpret in different ways, as a sergeant has discretion if he is told to take the five most experienced men on patrol. Second, we say that a man has discretion if his decision is final, in the sense that no higher authority may review and set aside that decision, as when the decision whether a player is offside is left to the discretion of the linesman. Third, we say that a man has discretion when some set of standards which impose duties upon him do not in fact purport to impose any duty as to a particular decision, as when a clause in a lease gives the tenant the option in his discretion to renew.

It is plain that if no social rule unambiguously requires a particular legal decision, and the profession is split on what decision is in fact required, then judges will have discretion in the first of these senses, because they will have to exercise initiative and judgment beyond the application of a settled rule. It is also plain, if these judges form the highest court of appeal, that they will have discretion in the second sense. But, unless we accept the strongest form of the social rule theory, that duties and responsibilities can be generated only by social rules, it does not follow that these judges have discretion in the third sense. A judge may have discretion in both the first and second senses, and nevertheless properly regard his decision as raising an issue of what his duty as a judge is, an issue which he must decide by reflecting on what is required of him by the varying considerations that he believes are pertinent. If so, then this judge does not have discretion in the third sense, which is the sense a positivist needs to establish if he is to show that judicial duty is defined exclusively by an ultimate social rule or set of social rules.

Raz was not persuaded by my argument.[1] He repeats the distinction that I drew among these three senses of discretion, but having repeated that distinction he ignores it. He apparently thinks that I meant to argue as follows. (i) Judges have no discretion with respect to a decision when they all agree that a particular set of principles is decisive. (ii) That is sometimes the case even when no rule of law settles the case. (iii) Therefore it is never the case that judges have discretion when no rule settles the case.

That is a fallacious argument; fortunately it is not mine. Judges are sometimes united on a set of principles. But even when they are divided on principles they sometimes treat the issue as one of judicial responsibility, that is, as one that raises

the question of what, as judges, they have a duty to do. In such a case they have discretion in the first sense I distinguished, but that is irrelevant. They nevertheless do not believe they have discretion in the third sense, which is the sense that counts.

Why should Raz ignore the distinctions I drew? He supposes that there are features of any legal system that have this consequence: If judges have discretion in the first sense, because no social rule directly or indirectly dictates the result they must reach, then they must also have discretion in the third sense, so that their decision cannot be a matter of judicial duty. Judges may be mistaken in this; they may inappropriately use the language of duty. But we must not, as Raz says, perpetuate mistakes, and Raz does not. What arguments might he make?

Raz's inclination, to convert discretion in the first into discretion in the third sense, is extraordinarily common among legal philosophers. We must try to diagnose its source. When a judge faces a difficult decision he must suppose, before beginning his research, that there are in principle these three possibilities. The set of standards that he must take into account, taken together, require him to decide for the plaintiff, or require him to decide for the defendant, or require neither decision but permit either one. He must also recognize that he might be to some degree uncertain which of these three possibilities in fact holds; in that case he must decide on the basis of the case that seems to him the strongest. But that uncertainty might apply just as much to the third possibility as to the other two; the law might grant him a discretion, in the third sense, to reach either decision, but whether it does is a matter of what the legal materials, taken together, come to, and one may be as certain whether the materials justify *that* conclusion as either of the other two.

Raz apparently thinks that if it is uncertain whether the first or the second possibility is realized, then it follows that the third is. He thinks, that is, that if a judge is uncertain whether to decide for the plaintiff or defendant it follows that he should be certain that he has discretion to decide for either. I can think of only two arguments to support that extraordinary conclusion.

The first depends on the assumption of moral philosophy I described earlier, that duties cannot be controversial in principle. Raz makes that assumption, because he argues from the fact that judges may disagree about principles, and particularly about their weight, to the conclusion that judges must have discretion in the sense I deny. That is a non sequitur unless something like that assumption holds, but we have no reason to suppose that it does, as I said, once we reject the strong version of the social rule theory.

The second argument relies on a different assumption, namely that every legal system contains a rule of decision which provides affirmatively that judges have discretion in hard cases. Some legal systems may employ such a rule. But the English and American systems do not. They contain no such explicit rule, nor as Raz agrees, does judicial behavior show that any such rule is recognized implicitly.

On the contrary, for us the proposition that judges have discretion in the third sense on some issue or other is a proposition that must be established affirmatively, on the balance of argument, and not simply by default. Sometimes judges do reach that conclusion; for example, when passing sentences under criminal statutes that provide a maximum and minimum penalty, or when framing equitable relief under a general equity jurisdiction. In such cases judges believe that no one has a right to any particular decision; they identify their task as selecting the decision that is best on the whole, all things considered, and here they talk not about what they must do but about what they should do. In most hard cases, however, judges take the different posture I described. They frame their disagreement as a disagreement about what standards they are entitled or obliged to take into account, or what relative weights they are obliged to take into account, or what relative weights they are obliged to attribute to these, on the basis of arguments like the arguments I described in the last section illustrating the theory of institutional support. In such cases, some judges argue for the first possibility I mentioned, others for the second and others are undecided; but all exclude the third. There is plainly not even the beginnings of a social rule that converts the discretion that requires judgment into the descretion that excludes duty.

ARE RULES REALLY DIFFERENT FROM PRINCIPLES?

In my article I distinguished rules from principles by distinguishing the different force that the two types of standards have in argument. My purpose was twofold: first, to call attention to a distinction which I thought was of importance in understanding how lawyers reason, and second, to call attention to the fact that some of the standards to which judges and lawyers appeal pose special problems for positivism, because these standards cannot be captured under a fundamental test for law like Hart's rule of recognition. These two purposes were distinct; even if the particular logical distinction that I claim between rules and principles can be shown to be spurious, it might still be that standards like those I mentioned, however identified, and whether or not classified as rules, cannot be captured by any such test. If I do not succeed in establishing my distinction between rules and principles, therefore, it by no means follows that the general argument I make against legal positivism is undermined.

Nevertheless, I do continue to think that the distinction that I drew between rules and principles is both genuine and important, and I should want to defend it. I do not mean, of course, that it is wrong to draw other sorts of distinctions among types of legal standards, or even that it is wrong or confusing to use the terms "rule" and "principle" to make these distinctions rather than the one I drew.

Raz's chief objection to my distinction might be put this way. I argued that principles, like those I mentioned, conflict and interact with one another, so that each principle that is relevant to a particular legal problem provides a reason arguing in favor of, but does not stipulate, a particular solution. The man who must decide the problem is therefore required to assess all the competing and conflicting principles that bear upon it, and to make a resolution of these principles rather than identifying one among others as "valid." Raz wishes to argue that it is not simply principles that properly conflict with one another in this way, but rules as well, and he believes that this fact undermines the distinction that I have drawn. He offers examples from both moral and legal argument. I shall consider each set of examples in turn.

Raz has it in mind that a man might accept, as moral rules for the guidance of his conduct, both the rule that one must never tell a lie and the rule that one must always keep his promises. He points out that on particular occasions these two rules might conflict, and require the man who accepts them both to choose between them on the basis of which under the circumstances has the greater weight, or importance, or on some other basis. He concludes that moral rules follow the logic that I described for principles, that is, that they point in one direction though they are not necessarily decisive of any moral issue.

But, in the first place, though it is possible that a man might accept moral rules for the guidance of his conduct in the way this argument assumes, it is far from the case that most men who take morality seriously do anything of the sort. For most people moral argument or decision is a matter of giving reasons for or against the morality of a certain course of conduct, rather than appealing to rules set down in advance whether by social or individual decision. It is true that a moral man may find himself in difficulty when he must choose between telling a lie or breaking a promise, but it does not follow that he has accepted rules which come into conflict over the issue. He might simply have recognized that telling lies and breaking promises are both in principle wrong.

Of course we might describe his predicament by saying that he was forced to choose between two moral standards, even if he would not put the matter that way himself. But in that case, if we use the distinction I made, we should say that he was forced to resolve competing principles, not rules, because that would be the more accurate way of describing his situation. He recognizes that no moral consideration is by itself of overwhelming and overriding effect, and that any reason that counts against an act may in some circumstances have to yield to a competing consideration. Any philosopher or sociologist who wants to report his moral practices in terms of a code of standards must therefore say that for him morality is a matter of principle and not of rule.

But it is possible that some man might accept a rule for the guidance of his conduct in the way that Raz supposes. He might say, for example, that he has undertaken a personal commitment never to tell a lie. If he can accept one flat moral rule in this way, then he can accept others, and

these may conflict in the way the example supposes. It would then be wrong to say, using my distinction, that this man has simply accepted a set of principles which might in principle conflict, because that wrongly describes his attitudes towards the several commitments he believes he has made. He believes he is committed to his different standards as rules, that is, as propositions which demand a particular course of conduct in the circumstances they name.

But I did not deny, in my original article, that conflicts in rules might exist. I said that in our legal system such conflicts would be occasions of emergency, occasions requiring a decision that would alter the set of standards in some dramatic way. Indeed this description fits the present non-legal example as well. Our moral hero, if he understands at all the concepts he has been using, cannot continue to say, after he has resolved his conflict that he has been following both of his standards as flat rules. If he still wishes to present his morality as a consistent code, he may amend one or both of them to provide for the conflict, or he may revise his attitude towards one or both so as to convert them from rules into principles. He may do neither, but rather, when a conflict appears, announce himself to be in a state of moral dilemma, and do nothing, or flip a coin or decide in some other irrational way that the legal system does not permit. In any case, the distinction between rules and principles that I drew, so far from being called into question by the behavior of this unusual man, is in fact needed to explain it.

Raz takes his other examples from law. He calls our attention, for example, to rules of criminal law like the rule that prohibits an assault; this rule, he says, is in conflict with another rule which permits assault in self-defense. Here, he concludes, we have two legal rules, both of them plainly valid which are in conflict with one another. He believes that in particular cases, when these two rules do conflict, as they will when someone commits an assault in self-defense, it is necessary for the judge to weigh the rules and decide to apply the more important, which will always be the rule that permits an assault in self-defense. He offers this as an example of two rules which conflict acceptably, and with no sense of emergency, in the way that I said rules do not.

But this example surely rests on a bizarre notion of what a conflict is. If a criminal code contains a general rule to the effect that no one shall be criminally liable for an act committed in self-defense, then that rule does not conflict with particular rules defining particular crimes, even if these particular rules make no mention of self-defense. The general rule about self-defense must be read to mean that notwithstanding the particular rules of criminal law, no act shall be a crime if committed in self-defense. Indeed, rules providing general defenses are often drafted in just this way, but even when they are not, they are understood in that way. But a rule that provides an exception to another rule is not in conflict with that other rule, at least not in the way in which two principles conflict. It would be silly to say that when a man accused of assault has proved a case of self-defense, the judge is then faced with two rules pulling in opposite directions, which he has somehow to weigh against one another in reaching his decision. The two rules taken together determine the result in a manner which does not require the judge to choose between them, or to determine their relative importance.

Why should Raz suppose that two rules are in conflict even when one has plainly the force of an exception to the other? The answer lies, I think, in what he says about the individual of laws. He supposes that I would want to answer his point, that the rule prohibiting assault conflicts with the rule permitting assult in self-defense, by arguing that these two rules are really part of the same rule. He says that I could do that only at the price of accepting an unacceptable theory about the individual of laws, and, anticipating such a mistake on my part, he says, that I pay insufficient attention to the general problem of the individuation of laws. In this he is too generous for it would be more accurate to say that I pay no attention to that problem at all. I did not in fact rely upon the argument that a rule and its exception really count as one rule, but neither would I be disposed to argue that they must be in reality two rules.

Raz is of two minds about his theory of individuation of laws. Sometimes he treats a theory of individuation as a strategy of exposition, that is to say, a theory about the most illuminating way in which the legal system of a nation may be described. Plainly, the author of a textbook on criminal law, for example, needs a strategy of exposition. He needs to distinguish the doctrine of *mens rea* from the doctrine of necessity and to

distinguish both of these general doctrines from the more particular rules which they cut across as qualifications and exemptions. But of course, though some strategies of exposition might be perverse or misguided, because they describe the law in an unmanageable or unassimilatable form, a great many different strategies might be more or less equally competent.

At other times, however, Raz seems to think that the problem of individuation of laws has to do, not with any strategy of explaining what the law is to students or lawyers, but with the more philosophical question of what law is. He says that it is a problem about the formal structure of the law, which is of importance to the legal philosopher. And not to the author of a text. He poses the central problem in this way: "What is to count as one complete law?", and he adopts Bentham's elaboration of this question: "What is a law? What the part of a law? The subject of these questions, it is to be observed, is the *logical,* the *ideal,* the *intellectual* whole, not the *physical* one. . . ."

This sort of question carries us very far away from techniques of legal exposition: it carries us to the point at which, as Dr. Raz insists, theories of law may rise or fall depending upon the right answer to the question, "What is to count as one complete law?" That seems to me much too far. Suppose that you have read a long book about geology, and I ask you to tell me what information it contains. You will do so in a series of propositions of fact. But now suppose I ask you first how many propositions of fact the book contains, and what theory you used in counting them. You would think me mad, not simply because the question is preposterously difficult, as if I had asked you how many separate grains of sand there were in a particular beach, or because it requires a difficult conceptual discrimination, as if I had asked you how many human beings there were in a group that included a woman in early pregnancy. You would think me mad because I had asked entirely the wrong sort of question about the material at hand. The book contains a great deal of information; propositions are ways of presenting that information, but the number of propositions used will depend on considerations independent of the content of the information, such as, for example, whether one uses the general term "rocks" or the names of particular sorts of rocks.

In the same way, lawyers use rules and principles to report legal information, and it is wrong to suppose that any particular statement of these is canonical. This is true even of what we call statutory rules, because it is a commonplace that lawyers will often misrepresent the rules that a statute enacted if they simply repeat the language that the statute used. Two lawyers might summarize the effect of a particular statute using different words, and one might use more rules than another; they might still both be saying the same thing.

My point was not that "the law" contains a fixed number of standards, some of which are rules and others principles. Indeed, I want to oppose the idea that "the law" is a fixed set of standards of any sort. My point was rather that an accurate summary of the considerations lawyers must take into account, in deciding a particular issue of legal rights and duties, would include propositions having the form and force of principles, and that judges and lawyers themselves, when justifying their conclusions, often use propositions which must be understood in that way. Nothing in this, I believed, commits me to a legal ontology that assumes any particular theory of individuation.

I did say that a "full" statement of a legal rule would include its exceptions, and that a statement of a rule that neglected the exceptions would be "incomplete." I would not have put the point that way had I been aware of Raz's objection. I would have made plain that an exception can be stated in the form of a distinct rule, like the rule about self-defense, as well as in the form of a revised statement of the original rule. But if I had I would also have made plain that the difference is largely a matter of exposition. The distinction between rules and principles remains untouched. I might summarize a body of law by stating a rule, like the rule that an assault is a crime, and a list of established exceptions. If my summary is complete, then anyone who commits an assault is guilty of a crime unless an exception I stated applies; if he is not guilty, then either I was wrong or the law has changed. It is otherwise in the case of a principle. If I say that in principle someone may not profit from his own wrong but someone does, because someone may properly

profit from his own wrong, as these terms must be understood, not only when a recognized exception applies, but when special features of his case invoke some other, newly-recognized, principle or policy that makes a difference; then my statement need not be corrected or even brought up-to-date.

It is his second, ontological, mood about the individuation of laws that leads Raz to his curious view about conflicts. If one takes seriously the idea that rules of law are in certain forms "whole" and "complete," then one may be tempted to think that whole and complete laws are also independent of one another, so that the rule defining assault must then be taken as a flat direction that men who do certain acts be punished. But if we take the statement of a rule of law as an attempt merely to describe the legal effect of certain institutional decisions, we are not tempted to suppose any such conflict. We shall then say merely that the rule about assault, like many of the rules about crimes, is subject to an exception in cases of self-defense; we shall not then worry about whether we have described one rule or two.

Raz has another argument against my distinction, which I do not fully understand. He argues that the distinction is undercut by the fact that rules may conflict with principles; the rules of adverse possession, for example, may be thought to conflict with the principle that no man may profit from his own wrong. I do not think it illuminating to describe the relationship between these rules and that principle as one of conflict. The fact that such rules exist, is, as I said, evidence that the principle about not profiting from one's wrong is indeed a principle and not a rule. If the rules of adverse possession are some day amended, either by explicit legislative enactment or by judicial reinterpretation, then one reason might be that the principle is then recognized as being more important than it was when the rules were adopted. Nevertheless, the rules governing adverse possession may even now be said to *reflect* the principle, rather than *conflict* with it, because these rules have a different shape than they would have had if the principle had not been given any weight in the decision at all. The long length of time generally required for acquiring title by adverse possession might have been much shorter, for example, had this not been thought to conflict with the principle. Indeed, one of my reasons for drawing the distinction between rules and principles was just to show how rules often represent a kind of compromise amongst competing principles in this way, and that point may be lost or submerged if we speak too freely about rules conflicting with principles.

In any event, I cannot see how this phenomenon casts doubt upon the distinction I want to draw between rules and principles. Raz thinks that it shows that rules as well as principles have weight, because he thinks that when rules and principles conflict a decision must be made by assigning a weight to the rule which is then set against the weight of the principle. But this description surely misrepresents the interaction between rules and principles. Suppose a court decides to overrule an established common law rule that there can be no legal liability for negligent misstatements, and appeals to a number of principles to justify this decision, including the

principle that it is unjust that one man suffer because of another man's wrong. The court must be understood as deciding that the set of principles calling for the overruling of the established rule, including the principle of justice just mentioned, are as a group of greater weight under the circumstances than the set of principles, including the principle of stare decisis, that call for maintaining the rule as before. The court weighs two sets of principles in deciding whether to maintain the rule; it is therefore misleading to say that the court weighs the rule itself against one or the other set of these principles. Indeed, when Raz describes the weighing of either a legal or a moral rule, he in fact talks about weighing the principles and policies that the rule serves, because that must be what he means when he speaks of the "goal" of the rule.

NOTE

1. Raz at 843 ff.

Suggestions for Further Reading

Ames, J. B., "Law and Morals," 22 *Harv. L. Rev.* 97 (1908).

Bentham, Jeremy, *An Introduction to the Principles of Morals and Legislation,* (ed. H. L. A. Hart, 1970).

Cairns, Huntington, *Legal Philosophy from Plato to Hegel* (1949).

Care, N. S. and T. K. Trelogan, eds., *Issues in Law and Morality* (1973).

Cardozo, Benjamin N., *The Nature of the Judicial Process* (1921).

Carrio, G., *Legal Principles and Legal Positivism* (1971).

Christie, G. C., "The Model of Principles," 1968 *Duke L. J.* 649.

Cogley, J., *et. al, Natural Law and Modern Society* (1962).

Davis, Kenneth C., *Discretionary Justice* (1969).

d'Entreves, A. P., *Natural Law* (1951).

Frank, Jerome, *Courts on Trial* (1949).

Frank, Jerome, *Law and the Modern Mind* (1930).

Friedmann, Wolfgang, *Legal Theory,* 4th ed. (1960).

Friedrich, C. J., *The Philosophy of Law in Historical Perspective,* 2nd ed. (1963).

Fuller, L. L., *Anatomy of Law* (1968).

Fuller, Lon L., "Positivism and Fidelity to Law—A Reply to Professor Hart," 71 *Harv. L. Rev.* 630 (1958).

Gierke, O. F., *Natural Law and the Theory of Society,* trans. E. Barker (1934).

Golding, Martin P., *Philosophy of Law* (1974).

Gray, John Chipman, *The Nature and Sources of the Law* (1931 ed.).

Gross, Hyman, "Standards as Law," 1968/69 *Annual Survey of American Law,* 575.

Guest, A. G., "Logic in the Law" in *Oxford Essays in Jurisprudence,* (ed. A. G. Guest, 1961).

Hägerström, A., *Inquiries into the Nature of Law and Morals,* trans. Broad. (1953).

Hart, H. L. A., *The Concept of Law* (1961).

Hoebel, E. Adamson, *The Law of Primitive Man* (1954).

Hohfeld, Wesley N., *Fundamental Legal Conceptions* (1919).

Holmes, Oliver W., Jr., "The Path of the Law," 10 *Harv. L. Rev.* 457 (1897).

Hook, Sidney, ed., *Law and Philosophy,* Parts II and III (1964).

Hughes, Graham, "Rules, Policy and Decision Making," 77 *Yale L. J.* 411 (1968).

Jones, Harry W., "Law and Morality in the Perspective of Legal Realism," 61 *Col. L. Rev.* 799 (1961).

Kantorowicz, Hermann, *The Definition of Law* (1958).

Kelsen, Hans, *General Theory of Law and State,* trans. A. Wedberg. (1949).

Leiser, Burton M., *Custom, Law, and Morality* (1969).

Levi, Edward H., *An Introduction to Legal Reasoning* (1948).

Llewellyn, K. N., *The Bramble Bush* (1930).

Llewellyn, K. N., *Jurisprudence: Realism in Theory and Practice* (1962).

Llewellyn, K. N., *The Common Law Tradition: Deciding Appeals* (1960).

Maine, Henry S., *Lectures on the Early History of Institutions,* 7th ed. (1897).

Morris, Herbert, "Verbal Disputes and the Legal Philosophy of John Austin," 7 *U.C.L.A. L. Rev.* 27 (1960).

Olivecrona, Karl, *Law as Facts,* (1939).

Salmond, John, *Jurisprudence,* 12th ed., ed. Fitzgerald. (1966).

Sartorius, Rolf, "Social Policy and Judicial Legislation," *American Philosophical Quarterly,* Vol. 8 (1971), pp. 151–70.

Selznick, Philip, "Sociology and Natural Law," *Natural Law Forum,* Vol. 6 (1961), 84–104.

Stumpf, Samuel E., *Morality and the Law* (1965).

Summers, Robert S., "Professor H. L. A. Hart's Concept of Law," 1963, *Duke L. J.* 629.

Tapper, C., "A Note on Principles," 1971 *Modern L. Rev.* 628 (1971).

Williams, Glanville, "The Controversy Concerning the Word 'Law,'" in *Philosophy, Politics, and Society* (ed P. Laslett, 1956).

Wollheim, Richard, "The Nature of Law," *Political Studies,* Vol. 2 (1954).

PART 2 LIBERTY

For what purposes can the state rightly interfere with the liberty of individual citizens to do as they please? This central question of political theory becomes a vital question in legal philosophy too in virtue of the fact that in democracies, at least, the legal system is the primary means by which restraints on liberty are imposed. Certain kinds of conduct are directly prohibited by criminal statutes which threaten punishment, typically fines or imprisonment, for noncompliance. Other kinds of undesirable behavior are controlled by regulatory devices which employ the criminal law only indirectly, as a kind of "sanction of last resort."[1] Citizens must be licensed, for example, to drive automobiles or to practice medicine, a requirement that permits the state to regulate these dangerous activities carefully and to withdraw licenses from those who fail to perform to reasonable standards. Withdrawal of license is itself an administrative penalty diminishing the liberty of those subjected to it, but it is not a criminal penalty. The criminal sanction is reserved as a backup threat to prevent persons from driving or practicing medicine without a license. Similarly, "cease and desist" orders and other injunctions restrict the liberty of those to whom they are addressed without any recourse to the criminal law, which comes into play only to prevent or to punish disobedience. Still another form of administrative or noncriminal restriction of liberty is the civil commitment procedure by which mentally disturbed persons judged dangerous to others or incompetent to govern themselves are compelled to reside in hospitals or other nonpenal institutions. For some classes of harmful conduct—for example, defamatory statements, invasions of privacy, and certain kinds of trespass and nuisance —the civil law seems better suited than the criminal law to provide threatened parties with protection. Our liberty to tell damaging lies about our neighbors, to prevent them from enjoying their property, or to tap their telephone lines, is restricted by their legal power to bring a civil suit against us which can culminate in a judgment directing us to pay compensatory or punitive damages to them. Again, the criminal law is not involved except as a backup sanction to enforce court orders.

Most writers agree that restrictions of individual liberty, whether by direct criminal prohibition or by some other legal instrumentality, always need some special justification. That is to say that other things being equal, it is always preferable that individuals be left free to make their own choices and that undesirable conduct be discouraged by such noncoercive measures as education, exhortation, taxation (on undesirable conduct) or provision of positive incentives such as economic subsidies or rewards (for alternatives to undesirable conduct). It is not easy to state the grounds of this presumption in favor of liberty. Various philosophers, in making the presumptive case for liberty, have argued that absence of coercion is a necessary (though certainly not a sufficient) condition for individual self-realization and social progress, and for such specific goods as individual spontaneity, social diversity, and the full flowering of various moral and intellectual virtues. In any case, most of us are fully convinced that our own personal liberty is a precious thing, and consistency inclines us to suppose that it is equally precious, and equally worth respecting, in others.

The value of liberty, however, is easily overstated. Liberty may be precious but it is by no means the only thing of value. Contentment and happiness, while difficult in the absence of freedom, are not impossible. Moreover, one can have perfect political liberty and yet be alienated and discontented, which also shows that no matter how intimately they may be related, freedom and contentment are distinct values not reducible one to the other. Similarly, a given society may enjoy political liberty while yet permitting large-scale social injustice, a possibility which indicates that liberty and justice are distinct social values. Failure to appreciate these distinctions has led hasty thinkers to make certain familiar errors in their discussions of liberty. Some have argued that any liberty that conflicts with contentment or with justice is not "true liberty" but rather some beguiling counterfeit. It is more accurate to say that liberty is but one value among many, that it is vitally important but not sufficient, that it can conflict with other values, and even that in some circumstances it may not be worth its price as measured against other values.

Other writers have argued that political liberty in the absence of certain specific powers and opportunities is not "true liberty" at all, but a sham and a deceit. If an invalid confined to his bed were to scoff at a legal system that grants him freedom of movement, we should no doubt reply to him that our politically guaranteed liberty to move about at will is a genuine liberty and a genuine good, even though it may be worthless to a paralyzed person. What the invalid's plight shows is that health and mobility are also important and independent goods, not that political liberty is a sham. Similarly, the political radical in a capitalist bourgeois society might deny that he has true liberty of speech on the ground that he does not have fair access to the communications media which are dominated by wealthy corporations. Again, this shows that his freedom of expression is not worth as much as a wealthier man's, and that economic power is also an important good, not that he is not "really" at liberty to speak his mind. His complaint shows us that it is possible to praise liberty too much, but if he claims further that he would be no worse off if his political opinions were criminally proscribed, he is either disingenuous or naively under-appreciative of liberty's actual value.

It must be acknowledged, however, that a given person's lack of power or opportunity—his poverty, ignorance, or poor health—may be the *indirect result* of a structure of coercive laws. To take a crude and obvious hypothetical example, racial laws on the South African model might explicitly prohibit blacks from engaging in certain remunerative occupations. As a result blacks would be poorer than other citizens, and perhaps undernourished and undereducated as well. In that case there would be a very real point in describing a given black's lack of power or opportunity to make his views heard and considered as a diminished liberty. Political liberty is best understood as the absence of political coercion (typically, the absence of criminal prohibitions and other coercive legal instrumentalities), and not simply as *de facto* ability or opportunity. But where a law preventing a class of citizens from doing X leads indirectly to an absence of ability or opportunity for members of that class to do Y, there is a clear reason to describe the latter as a negation of the *liberty* to do Y.

Under what conditions, and for what reasons, can the presumption in favor of political liberty be overridden? This is not merely an abstract question addressed to philosophers, but an unavoidable practical question to be faced by every democratic legislator. In effect, it is a question about the limits beyond which restrictive lawmaking is morally illegitimate. John Stuart Mill, the first essayist presented in this part, gives the classic liberal answer to the question. Restriction of the liberty of one citizen, he argues, can be justified only to prevent harm to others. We can refer to Mill's position as the "harm to others principle," or more succinctly, the "harm principle." Several things should be noted about this principle at the outset. First, Mill means by "harm" not only direct personal injury such as broken bones or the loss of money, but also more diffuse social harms such as air pollution or the impairment of public institutions. Second, the principle does not propose a sufficient condition for the restriction of liberty, because some harms to others are too slight to outbalance the very real harm or danger involved in the restriction of liberty. Thus, in close cases, legislators must balance the value of the interests to be restricted by proposed coercive legislation *and* the collateral costs of enforcing any coercive law on the one hand against the value of the interests to be protected by the proposed legislation on the other. It is only when the probable harms prevented by the statute are greater than those that it will cause that the legislation is justified. Finally, the harm principle should be interpreted as a claim about *reasons:* Only one *kind* of consideration is ever morally relevant to the justification of coercion, namely, that it is necessary to prevent harm to others. It is never a relevant reason that the conduct to be restricted is merely offensive (as opposed to harmful) or even that it is intrinsically immoral, nor is it relevant that coercion is necessary to prevent a person from harming himself (as opposed to others).

No one would disagree that prevention of harm to others is always *a* relevant reason for coercion, but many disagree with Mill's contention that it is the *only* relevant consideration. Thus, no one will seriously suggest that laws against battery, larceny, and homicide are unjustified, but many maintain that the state is also justified, at least in some circumstances, in prohibiting (1) "immoralities" even when they harm no one but their perpetrators (the principle of legal moralism), (2) actions that hurt or endanger the actor himself (the principle of legal paternalism), or (3) conduct that is offensive though not harmful to others (the offense principle). These rival doctrines cannot easily be proved or refuted in the abstract. Rather, they are best judged by how faithfully they reflect, and how systematically they organize, our considered judgments in particular cases; for such principles, after all, purport to be explicit renderings of the axioms to which we are committed by the most confident judgments we make in everyday discourse about problems of liberty. The main areas of controversy in which such problems arise are those concerning unorthodox expressions of opinion, "morals offenses" in the criminal law (especially when committed in private by solitary individuals or among consenting adults), pornography and obscenity (when offered or displayed to the public or to nonconsenting individuals), activities that are harmful or dangerous to those who voluntarily engage in them, voluntary suicide and euthanasia, otherwise harmless invasions of the privacy of others, and conscientious acts of civil disobedience. The cautious theorist will begin with Mill's harm principle as an account of at least one set of reasons that is always relevant in such controversies, and then apply it to the various problem areas to determine the extent, if any, to which it must be supplemented to provide solutions that are both plausible and consistent. In particular, we must decide, in each area, whether we need have recourse to the offense principle, legal moralism, or legal paternalism.

Under most of the problem area headings, there is still another kind of controversy to be settled, namely, whether even the unsupplemented harm principle can justify *too much* coercion, and whether, therefore, doing justice to our considered judgments requires also a doctrine of *natural rights* limiting the applicability of the harm principle (or for that matter of any of the other liberty-limiting principles that might apply at all). This kind of question arises most prominently perhaps in the area of free expression of opinion. There is no doubt that expressions of opinion, in speech or writing, do often cause vast amounts of harm. Politicians sometimes advocate policies that would lead to disastrous consequences if adopted, and scientists sometimes defend theories that are false and detrimental to scientific progress. If we apply the harm principle in a straightforward unqualified way by prohibiting all particular expressions which seem on the best evidence likely to cause more harm than good, we might very well justify widespread invasions of what we should naturally take to be a moral right of free speech. Quite clearly, if he is to avoid this embarrassing consequence, the partisan of the harm principle will have to propose subtle refinements and mediating norms for the application of his principle, weighing such matters as the balancing of rival interests and social costs, and the measurements of probabilities, dangers, and risks.

Mill especially wished to avoid such embarrassment since he placed an extremely high value on free expression. As a utilitarian he wished to forego all benefit in argument from the notion of a natural right, yet he insisted that, short of the usual legal boundaries of libel, slander, incitement, and fraud, *all* restrictions on the expression of opinion are illegitimate, whether in morals, politics, religion, or whatever. His strategy was to establish an extra strong presumption in favor of freedom of expression, even beyond the standing presumption in favor of liberty generally. An individual's own interest in freedom of expression, in the first place, is an especially vital one. Human beings are essentially opinion-forming and communicating animals, and to squelch a person in the expression of his opinion is to hurt him "where he lives." Moreover, each individual is in a way wronged by restrictions on the expressions of all the others, for to keep an individual in ignorance of all but officially sanctioned opinions is to violate his autonomy as a rational being who, as another author has said is "sovereign in deciding what to believe and in weighing competing reasons for action."[2] Moreover, it diminishes him as a rational thinker and decider, impairs his dignity, weakens his "moral and intellectual muscles," and so, in a subtle but real way, *harms* him. Mill gives most emphasis, however, to the powerful *social* interest in free expression. Unless all opinions are given a free airing, he argues, we can never be confident that we have the truth about anything, having heard only one side of the case. A political community that deprives itself of important sources of truth is like a ship with a defective rudder, sure to founder sooner or later on some rocky shore. That legally unhindered open debate of public issues is necessary to the pursuit of truth is a point of lasting importance never made more impressively than by Mill, but to regard the absence of legally enforced orthodoxy as sufficient guarantee of the triumph of truth would be extremely naive. Even Mill, in fact, is subject to some criticism for underemphasizing the importance of equal access to the public media for the effective operation of a "free marketplace of ideas." To tell an impecunious radical who aims to influence public policy that he enjoys political freedom of expression may be very much like congratulating a pauper on his legal right to buy a Cadillac. Free expression does not really fit Mill's description as a means of promoting knowledge and truth unless there are people about, powerful people, to listen.

In the second essay in this section, Joel Feinberg considers further how the harm principle must be qualified if it is to guarantee free expression of opinion in a morally satisfactory way. He examines first the relatively noncontroversial limits on free speech imposed by Anglo-American law: civil liability for defamatory utterances and for nondefamatory statements that reveal information which is properly private, criminal liability for irresponsible statements that cause panics or riots, laws against incitements to crime and (more controversially) sedition. They are considered in part because each raises its own questions of interest for the philosophy of law, and in part because each provides a challenge for the harm principle to provide a rationale for sensible restrictions on liberty that will not at the same time justify restrictions on free speech unacceptable to Mill and other liberals. Feinberg then attempts to provide a philosophical rationale for Justice Holmes's "clear and present danger" test, and then concludes with comments on the inevitable "balancing of interests" so central to the harm principle approach to problems of liberty.

For over a decade beginning in the mid 1950s, a committee of the American Law Institute (an elite group of lawyers, judges, and law professors) worked on a massive rewriting of the criminal law. Their goal was to produce a model penal code that might influence legislatures to rewrite the codes then in effect in most of the fifty states. The main "reporters" for this project, and the authors of the numerous tentative drafts, were Herbert Wechsler of the Columbia University Law School and Louis B. Schwartz of the University of Pennsylvania Law School. In his article included here, Professor Schwartz turns his attention to a class of crimes in our codes that are very difficult to justify by the unsupplemented harm principle. These so-called "offenses against morality" include not only tabooed sexual behavior, but also a somewhat puzzling miscellany of nonsexual conduct including mistreatment of corpses and desecration of the flag. The offense principle provides a rationale for judging some of these as crimes (for example, "open lewdness") even when they cause no one any injury, but other morals offenses (for example, homosexual relations between consenting adults in private) can be defended only by recourse to the principle of legal moralism, which maintains that the law may properly be used to enforce the prevailing morality as such, even in the absence of harm or offense.

The Model Penal Code recommendations about morals offenses are the work of a group of enlightened "would-be lawmakers" who are very much opposed to legal moralism but unwilling, if only on grounds of political realism, to urge extremely radical departures from the past ways of the law. Sexual behavior that is immoral by conventional standards should not be made criminal, according to the code, unless it involves violence or exploitation of children and other incompetents; and the traditional crimes of fornication, adultery, and sodomy are to be wiped from the books. In the absence of harm to others, Schwartz and his colleagues insist, the sexual behavior of individuals is no one else's business. "Open lewdness," on the other hand, like other "flagrant affronts" to the sensibilities of others, is another matter. Not only conventionally "immoral" sexual acts but even perfectly "normal" ones can be criminally proscribed if done in *public,* not because public sex acts harm anyone, but because they cause *offense* (quite another thing) to the unwilling observer. Thus, the Model Penal Code, while rejecting legal moralism, seems to endorse the offense principle.

This combination of principles seems to have rather clear implications in respect to obscenity control. Freely consenting adults, one would think, would be given the unfettered liberty to read or witness anything they choose, provided only that they do not display offensive materials in public or impose them on unsuspecting passersby or on children. The Model Penal Code, however, while approximating this position, prefers a more "oblique approach." The code would ban not only public exhibitions but also advertising and sale of materials "whose predominant appeal is to prurient interest." The target of this restriction, Schwartz assures us, is not "the sin of obscenity" but rather a kind of unfair business practice: "Just as merchants may be prohibited from selling their wares by appeal to the public's weakness for gambling, so they may be restrained from purveying books, movies, or other commercial exhibition by exploiting the well-nigh universal weakness for a look behind the curtain of modesty." This commercial approach to the problem of obscenity apparently influenced the Supreme Court in the famous case that sent Ralph Ginzburg to prison. With the benefit of hindsight, one can wonder whether the Model Penal Code's "oblique approach" is not simply a less direct way of accomplishing what legal moralism would do forthrightly. Is not the legal judgment that prurient interest in sex is a moral "weakness" itself a way of enveloping the conventional morality in the law?

A different aspect of the problem of obscenity was dramatically illustrated in the United States Supreme Court case of *Cohen v. California* in 1971. This case raised issues that connect the themes of the articles by Schwartz and Feinberg. Cohen was convicted by a Los Angeles municipal court for lingering in the corridors of a public building while wearing a jacket emblazoned with the words "Fuck the Draft." In his appeal to the Supreme Court of California and later to the United States Supreme Court, Cohen claimed that his right to free speech guaranteed by the First and Fourteenth Amendments had been violated, whereas the California authorities argued that they had properly applied against him a valid statute forbidding "willfully . . . offensive conduct." Now there are two ways in which a written or spoken statement can be offensive: It can express an opinion that some auditors might find offensive or it can express an opinion in language that is itself offensive independently of the "substantive message it conveys." Neither the United States Constitution nor the libertarian principles of free expression of opinion espoused by Mill and Feinberg would permit legal interference with free speech to prevent the expression of an "offensive opinion." However, restrictions on obscene, scurrilous, and incitive words, quite apart from their role in the expression of unpopular opinions, might well be justified by the offense principle, and indeed by the Constitution itself insofar as it tacitly employs the offense principle to mark out a class of exceptions to the free speech guarantee. Justice Harlan, however, rejected this approach to the case. The free expression of opinion protected by the Constitution, he argued, extends not merely to the proposition declared by a statement, but also to the speaker's (or writer's) emotions, or the intensity of his attitudes—in the case at hand "the depths of his feelings against the Vietnam War and the draft." Harlan's distinction points to an important function of what are ordinarily called obscene words. "Unseemly epithets" can shock and jolt, and in virtue of their very character as socially unacceptable, give expression to intense feelings more accurately than any other words in the language.

Unlike the authors preceding him in this section, Irving Kristol is primarily concerned not with expressions of opinion or attitude, but rather with expression in works of drama and literature and their counterfeits. Moreover, he gives a spirited defense of a kind of censorship which he claims to be quite consistent with a generally liberal attitude toward state coercion. His explicit target is the prevailing liberal view that consenting adults should be permitted to see or read anything they please and that censorship and prior restraint are justified only to protect children and unwilling witnesses. Censorship, he argues, is required for at least two additional kinds of reasons: (1) to protect the general quality of life, indeed our civilized institutions themselves (an appeal to the harm principle); and (2) to exclude practices that "brutalize and debase our citizenry" (an appeal to a kind of "moral paternalism," the need to protect even adults from moral corruption). One of the more difficult challenges Kristol poses for the liberal view he is attacking consists of an embarrassing hypothetical example. Suppose an enterprising promoter sought to stage gladiatorial contests like those of Ancient Rome in Yankee Stadium, in which well-paid gladiators fought to the death to the roars of large crowds. How could he be prevented from doing this on liberal grounds? Presumably the spectacle would be restricted to consenting adults so that interference would not be necessary to protect children and offended witnesses. The gladiators too would be consenting adults, fully prepared to shoulder enormous risks to life and limb, supposedly for the sake of money. (We can imagine that, with closed circuit TV, the promoter could offer the winning gladiator some twenty million dollars.) To interfere with the liberty of the gladiators to make agreements with promoters on the ground that the rewards they seek are not worth the risks they *voluntarily* assume would be to invoke the principle of legal paternalism, which is anathema to liberals who follow Mill. Kristol himself is not so much interested in protecting his hypothetical gladiators from death or physical harm as he is in defending the audience from a kind of moral harm, or harm to character.

The dilemma of paternalism is vividly exemplified in the New Jersey case of *Kennedy Memorial Hospital v. Heston* (1971). In his opinion reprinted here, Chief Justice Weintraub of the New Jersey Supreme Court decided in the affirmative the question whether an adult may be forced to submit against her will and against her religious convictions to a blood transfusion deemed by competent medical authority to be necessary not merely to her health but to her very life. The paternalism issue is not quite as clear in this instance as it might be since the patient was unconscious at the time the decision to proceed with the transfusion had to be made, so that it was her mother whose legal consent was solicited. Like her mother, however, the patient was a member of the Jehovah's Witnesses sect and presumably would have refused to permit the transfusion had she been conscious, and the court therefore addressed itself also to the legal consequences of her hypothetical refusal. There is no legal right to choose to die, the unanimous court concluded, suggesting that a failure to give the transfusion would be, in effect, to aid and abet an act of suicide by omission.

Under the English common law, suicide was a felony, and, unlike the law in most other American states it remains so in New Jersey, where all common law crimes are still punishable "if not otherwise provided for by act of the legislature."[3] Among the other legal consequences of the criminalization of suicide, the following were prominent: Property of the felon was forfeited to the Crown and thus denied to his heirs; life insurance was rendered void; attempted suicide was also a crime, often punished by imprisonment; all citizens had the right and duty to prevent commission of the crime by others when attempted in their presence; successful counseling of suicide, and knowing assistance in another's suicide were both murder; accidental killing of another in an attempt on one's own life was manslaughter (at least). Legal consent to one's own killing by another has always been impossible under Anglo-American law, hence even the merciful extinction of a dying patient's life in order to relieve his suffering *at his request* has been and still is a crime, usually murder. Thus, "under the present law, voluntary euthanasia [mercy killing] would, except in certain narrow circumstances, be regarded as suicide in the patient who consents and murder in the doctor who administers."[4] No doubt, some rationales of these laws are moralistic and others paternalistic, but they all agree that even when no other parties will be harmed, there can be no liberty to extinguish one's own, or another's life, even where death is ardently desired.

In a broader analysis of paternalism, Gerald Dworkin considers in a comprehensive and systematic way the question of whether paternalistic statutes (defined roughly as those interfering with a person's liberty "for his own good") are ever justified. He treats Mill's absolutistic position with respect, but points out how widespread paternalistic restrictions are, and how drastic their total elimination would be. Laws requiring hunters to wear red caps and motorcyclists to wear helmets, and those requiring medical prescriptions for certain therapeutic drugs, for example, seem innocuous to most of us. All the more so do laws actually protecting children and incompetents from their own folly, and laws which persons could regard as "social insurance" against any future decisions of their own that would be not only dangerous but irreversible. Dworkin then attempts to find criteria that can be used to separate unjustified paternalistic restrictions from those he thinks any rational man would welcome.

The relation of liberty to privacy is often obscured by subtle differences of sense and nuance in various applications of those abstract words. Privacy is often contrasted with liberty, or cited (as in Feinberg's article) as one of the moral limits to free activity. In this sense, one person's privacy is a limit to *another* person's liberty. Privacy so described is what is common to a set of claims citizens have not only against one another but also against policemen and other agents of the state. In other contexts privacy is spoken of as itself a kind of liberty—a liberty to be left alone, to enjoy one's solitude, not to be intruded upon or even known about in certain respects. Expressed in this way, privacy is a negative sort of freedom, a freedom (indeed, a right) *not* to be treated in certain ways. Thus one person's right to privacy characteristically conflicts with more active liberties of movement and surveillance by others. So conceived, privacy is not one of the "liberties" normally ascribed to the state. Some state officials and agencies, to be sure, enjoy immunities and privileges of nondisclosure, but these forms of protected secrecy characteristically have as their rationales the need to enhance efficient functioning, not the need to protect privacy. Only persons have private thoughts, inner lives, and unknown histories that in virtue of their intimate character essentially merit protection from unwanted scrutiny; and the state, as such, is not a genuine person.

The notion of privacy first entered American law in the law of torts where it served to protect a miscellany[5] of personal interests against invasions by private individuals or groups by authorizing law suits for damages. Yet in an implicit way, the idea of a private realm into which the state cannot legitimately penetrate, a domain which is simply not the state's proper business, is both ancient and ubiquitous. In the fictitious "Invitiation to Dinner Case" included in this section, all of the legal requirements for an action for breach of contract appear to have been met, yet it is questionable whether such an action should be entertained. A dinner party, the judge might well be expected to say, is a householder's private affair and no proper concern of the courts. Here in a civil context is the suggestion, normally made only with regard to criminal prohibitions, that public authority has no business interfering in private affairs.

The idea of privacy made its major entry into American constitutional law through the celebrated case of *Griswold v. Connecticut,* decided by the United States Supreme Court in 1965. The opinions in that case raise a variety of genuinely philosophical issues, and might well have been included with equal relevance in any of the first three sections of this anthology. The decision overturned a Connecticut statute making the use of contraceptives by "any person" a criminal offense. That statute was unconstitutional, Mr. Justice Douglas wrote, because it violated a right of marital privacy, "older than the Bill of Rights," but included in the "penumbra" of the First, Fourth, Fifth,

Eighth, Ninth, and Fourteenth Amendments. A "penumbra" of a right is a set of further rights not specifically guaranteed in so many words but properly inferrable from the primary right either as necessary means for its fulfillment or as implied by it in certain factual circumstances not necessarily foreseen by those who formulated it.

Still, the Constitution does not specifically spell out a right of marital privacy, and the dissenters on the Court (Justices Stewart and Black) were suspicious of the technique of finding anything a judge thinks just and reasonable in the penumbra of a specific guarantee. Justice Goldberg in his concurring opinion had rested his case for a constitutional right of marital privacy on the Ninth Amendment's reference to fundamental rights "retained by the people," and Justices Harlan and White in their concurring opinions (not reprinted here) derived the unconstitutionality of the anticontraception statute from its capriciousness, irrationality, and offensiveness to a "sense of fairness and justice." A careful reader of Part One of this book will recognize here the overtones of the natural law tradition, whereas in Justice Black's skeptical stricture on the "catchwords" of "natural justice," in his dissenting opinion, there is the powerful echo of the tradition of legal positivism.

What is this privacy which, in some cultures at least, is held so dear, and which is so easily confused with the privileges of property, the residue of shame, or the essence of personal autonomy, among other things? By sorting out various separable elements, Hyman Gross makes a strong start on a philosophical analysis of the concept. A central theme in his account is that the loss of privacy is a loss of *control* over information about and impressions of oneself. Gross then proceeds to illuminate the connections between this aspect of privacy and self-determination, self-respect, and moral responsibility—connections that help explain the high value put on privacy, both by citizens and (now) by the law.

Most of the selections in this part of the book are concerned with what the law ought to be or, in the case of basic or constitutional law, how it ought to be interpreted. Ronald Dworkin reminds us, however, that dilemmas of liberty and coercion arise also for those charged with administering and enforcing the law. Prosecutors, in particular, have discretion as to whether or not to bring criminal charges against those who have been arrested. How prosecutorial discretion should be exercised then is another question that can lead to an examination of the citizen's moral claim to liberty, its grounds, and its limits. The specific question with which Dworkin is concerned is how the government should deal with those who deliberately disobey laws for reasons of conscience. His article was written in 1968 against a background of increasing numbers of prosecutions for advocating or counseling resistance, through draft evasion or draft refusal, to the then raging Vietnam War. For that reason, it might at first sight seem to be dated. Such an impression, however, would be quite unwarranted.

All of Dworkin's arguments apply equally well to the question of amnesty for conscientious draft evaders, a moral and political question that is still very much with us in this postwar period. More importantly, the problem of how the state should respond to conscientious disobedience to law is a perennial question that has divided writers and statesmen of all political factions in all historical periods. It is not an issue that simply goes away during the brief periods between wars and other crises.

The problem of "civil disobedience" is normally taken to be an ethical problem for the individual citizen who is conscientiously opposed to some law or policy of the state. Put in a general way it has the form: "Under what conditions, if any, would I be justified in disobeying the law?" The philosophy of law, however, is at least equally concerned with the question for political officials: "Given that John Doe has conscientiously refused to obey the requirements of a legal statute, under what conditions, if any, would we be morally, or even legally, justified in permitting him to escape punishment?" For a writer with Dworkin's jurisprudential views (see his contribution to Part One of this volume), questions of law and morality are not easily separated. "In the United States at least," he writes, "almost any law which a significant number of people would be tempted to disobey on moral grounds would be doubtful—if not clearly invalid—on constitutional grounds as well." Typically, then, when conscientious disobedience occurs, the validity of the disobeyed law is itself in doubt,[6] and prosecutors must consider the fairness of prosecuting dissenters for declining to obey a statute they honestly believe to be not only immoral but probably invalid legally as well. Such cases raise a more general and basic problem still for *legislators,* for as Dworkin points out: "So long as the law appears to make acts of dissent criminal, a man of conscience will face danger. What can Congress, which shares the responsibility of leniency, do to lessen this danger?" Dworkin's answer to the question, as we might expect, is subtle and complicated. The legislature must balance numerous conflicting considerations, but by no means the least of these are the social value of respecting an individual's conscience and the unfairness of punishing violations of a doubtful law.

J. F.

NOTES

1. The phrase is Herbert Packer's. See his *The Limits of the Criminal Sanction* (Stanford, Calif.: Stanford University Press, 1968), pp. 253–56.
2. The quoted phrase is from Thomas Scanlon, "A Theory of Free Expression," *Philosophy and Public Affairs,* Vol. I (1972), p. 215. This essay is somewhat difficult, but very strongly recommended nevertheless.
3. See Glanville Williams, *The Sanctity of Life and the Criminal Law* (New York: Alfred A. Knopf, 1968), p. 289.
4. *Ibid.,* p. 318.
5. Cf. Prosser on *Torts* 2nd ed. (St. Paul, Minn.: West Publishing Co., 1955), Chap. 20.
6. This point does not apply of course to cases of "indirect civil disobedience," where an admittedly valid law is disobeyed in order to protest *another* law or policy held to be unjust or immoral.

JOHN STUART MILL

On Liberty*

The object of this Essay is to assert one very simple principle, as entitled to govern absolutely the dealings of society with the individual in the way of compulsion and control, whether the means used be physical force in the form of legal penalties, or the moral coercion of public opinion. That principle is, that the sole end for which mankind are warranted, individually or collectively, in interfering with the liberty of action of any of their number, is self-protection. That the only purpose for which power can be rightfully exercised over any member of a civilized community, against his will, is to prevent harm to others. His own good, either physical or moral, is not a sufficient warrant. He cannot rightfully be compelled to do or forbear because it will be better for him to do so, because it will make him happier, because, in the opinions of others, to do so would be wise, or even right. There are good reasons for remonstrating with him, or reasoning with him, or persuading him, or entreating him, but not for compelling him, or visiting him with any evil, in case he do otherwise. To justify that, the conduct from which it is desired to deter him must be calculated to produce evil to some one else. The only part of the conduct of any one, for which he is amenable to society, is that which concerns others. In the part which merely concerns himself, his independence is, of right, absolute. Over himself, over his own body and mind, the individual is sovereign.

It is, perhaps, hardly necessary to say that this doctrine is meant to apply only to human beings in the maturity of their faculties. We are not speaking of children, or of young persons below the age which the law may fix as that of manhood or womanhood. Those who are still in a state to require being taken care of by others, must be protected against their own actions as well as against external injury. For the same reason, we may leave out of consideration those backward states of society in which the race itself may be considered as in its nonage. The early difficulties in the way of spontaneous progress are so great, that there is seldom any choice of means for overcoming them; and a ruler full of the spirit of improvement is warranted in the use of any expedients that will attain an end, perhaps otherwise unattainable. Despotism is a legitimate mode of government in dealing with barbarians, provided the end be their improvement, and the means justified by actually effecting that end. Liberty, as a principle, has no application to any state of things anterior to the time when mankind have become capable of being improved by free and equal discussion. Until then, there is nothing for them but implicit obedience to an Akbar or a Charlemagne, if they are so fortunate as to find one. But as soon as mankind have attained the capacity of being guided to their own improvement by conviction or persuasion (a period long since reached in all nations with whom we need here concern ourselves), compulsion, either in the direct form or in that of pains and penalties for non-compliance, is no longer admissible as a means to their own good, and justifiable only for the security of others.

It is proper to state that I forego any advantage which could be derived to my argument from the idea of abstract right, as a thing independent of utility. I regard utility as the ultimate appeal on all ethical questions; but it must be utility in the largest sense, grounded on the permanent interests of man as a progressive being. Those interests, I contend, authorize the subjection of individual spontaneity to external control, only in respect to those actions of each, which concern the interest of other people. If any one does an act

*From *On Liberty*. Excerpts from Chapters I and II, and all of Chapter IV. First published in 1859.

hurtful to others, there is a *primâ facie* case for punishing him, by law, or, where legal penalties are not safely applicable, by general disapprobation. There are also many positive acts for the benefit of others, which he may rightfully be compelled to perform; such as, to give evidence in a court of justice; to bear his fair share in the common defence, or in any other joint work necessary to the interest of the society of which he enjoys the protection; and to perform certain acts of individual beneficence, such as saving a fellow creature's life, or interposing to protect the defenceless against ill-usage, things which whenever it is obviously a man's duty to do, he may rightfully be made responsible to society for not doing. A person may cause evil to others not only by his actions but by his inaction, and in either case he is justly accountable to them for the injury. The latter case, it is true, requires a much more cautious exercise of compulsion than the former. To make any one answerable for doing evil to others, is the rule; to make him answerable for not preventing evil, is, comparatively speaking, the exception. Yet there are many cases clear enough and grave enough to justify that exception. In all things which regard the external relations of the individual, he is *de jure* amenable to those whose interests are concerned, and if need be, to society as their protector. There are often good reasons for not holding him to the responsibility; but these reasons must arise from the special expediencies of the case: either because it is a kind of case in which he is on the whole likely to act better, when left to his own discretion, than when controlled in any way in which society have it in their power to control him; or because the attempt to exercise control would produce other evils, greater than those which it would prevent. When such reasons as these preclude the enforcement of responsibility, the conscience of the agent himself should step into the vacant judgment-seat, and protect those interests of others which have no external protection; judging himself all the more rigidly, because the case does not admit of his being made accountable to the judgment of his fellow-creatures.

But there is a sphere of action in which society, as distinguished from the individual, has, if any, only an indirect interest; comprehending all that portion of a person's life and conduct which affects only himself, or, if it also affects others, only with their free, voluntary, and undeceived consent and participation. When I say only himself, I mean directly, and in the first instance: for whatever affects himself, may affect others *through* himself; and the objection which may be grounded on this contingency, will receive consideration in the sequel. This, then, is the appropriate region of human liberty. It comprises, first, the inward domain of consciousness; demanding liberty of conscience, in the most comprehensive sense; liberty of thought and feeling; absolute freedom of opinion and sentiment on all subjects, practical or speculative, scientific, moral, or theological. The liberty of expressing and publishing opinions may seem to fall under a different principle, since it belongs to that part of the conduct of an individual which concerns other people; but, being almost of as much importance as the liberty of thought itself, and resting in great part on the same reasons, is practically inseparable from it. Secondly, the principle requires liberty of tastes and pursuits; of framing the plan of our life to suit our own character; of doing as we like, subject to such consequences as may follow; without impediment from our fellow-creatures, so long as what we do does not harm them, even though they should think our conduct foolish, perverse, or wrong. Thirdly, from this liberty of each individual, follows the liberty, within the same limits, of combination among individuals; freedom to unite, for any purpose not involving harm to others: the persons combining being supposed to be of full age, and not forced or deceived.

No society in which these liberties are not, on the whole, respected, is free, whatever may be its form of government; and none is completely free in which they do not exist absolute and unqualified. The only freedom which deserves the name, is that of pursuing our own good in our own way, so long as we do not attempt to deprive others of theirs, or impede their efforts to obtain it. Each is the proper guardian of his own health, whether bodily, or mental and spiritual. Mankind are greater gainers by suffering each other to live as seems good to themselves, than by compelling each to live as seems good to the rest . . .

We have now recognized the necessity to the mental well-being of mankind (on which all their other well-being depends) of freedom of opinion, and freedom of the expression of opinion, on four distinct grounds; which we will now briefly recapitulate.

First, if any opinion is compelled to silence, that opinion may, for aught we can certainly know, be true. To deny this is to assume our own infallibility.

Secondly, though the silenced opinion be an error, it may, and very commonly does, contain a portion of truth; and since the general or prevailing opinion on any subject is rarely or never the whole truth, it is only by the collision of adverse opinions that the remainder of the truth has any chance of being supplied.

Thirdly, even if the received opinion be not only true, but the whole truth; unless it is suffered to be, and actually is vigorously and earnestly contested, it will, by most of those who receive it, be held in the manner of a prejudice, with little comprehension or feeling of its rational grounds. And not only this, but, fourthly, the meaning of the doctrine itself will be in danger of being lost, or enfeebled, and deprived of its vital effect on the character and conduct: the dogma becoming a mere formal profession, inefficacious for good, but cumbering the ground, and preventing the growth of any real and heartfelt conviction from reason or personal experience . . .

OF THE LIMITS TO THE AUTHORITY OF SOCIETY OVER THE INDIVIDUAL

What, then, is the rightful limit to the sovereignty of the individual over himself? Where does the authority of society begin? How much of human life should be assigned to individuality, and how much to society?

Each will receive its proper share, if each has that which more particularly concerns it. To individuality should belong the part of life in which it is chiefly the individual that is interested; to society, the part which chiefly interests society.

Though society is not founded on a contract, and though no good purpose is answered by inventing a contract in order to deduce social obligations from it, every one who receives the protection of society owes a return for the benefit, and the fact of living in society renders it indispensable that each should be bound to observe a certain line of conduct towards the rest. This conduct consists, first, in not injuring the interests of one another; or rather certain interests, which, either by express legal provision or by tacit

understanding, ought to be considered as rights; and secondly, in each person's bearing his share (to be fixed on some equitable principle) of the labors and sacrifices incurred for defending the society or its members from injury and molestation. These conditions society is justified in enforcing, at all costs to those who endeavor to withhold fulfillment. Nor is this all that society may do. The acts of an individual may be hurtful to others, or wanting in due consideration for their welfare, without going the length of violating any of their constituted rights. The offender may then be justly punished by opinion, though not by law. As soon as any part of a person's conduct affects prejudicially the interests of others, society has jurisdiction over it, and the question whether the general welfare will or will not be promoted by interfering with it, becomes open to discussion. But there is no room for entertaining any such question when a person's conduct affects the interests of no persons besides himself, or needs not affect them unless they like (all the persons concerned being of full age, and the ordinary amount of understanding). In all such cases there should be perfect freedom, legal and social, to do the action and stand the consequences.

It would be a great misunderstanding of this doctrine, to suppose that it is one of selfish indifference, which pretends that human beings have no business with each other's conduct in life, and that they should not concern themselves about the well-doing or well-being of one another, unless their own interest is involved. Instead of any diminution, there is need of a great increase of disinterested exertion to promote the good of others. But disinterested benevolence can find other instruments to persuade people to their good, than whips and scourges, either of the literal or the metaphorical sort. I am the last person to undervalue the self-regarding virtues; they are only second in importance, if even second, to the social. It is equally the business of education to cultivate both. But even education works by conviction and persuasion as well as by compulsion, and it is by the former only that, when the period of education is past, the self-regarding virtues should be inculcated. Human beings owe to each other help to distinguish the better from the worse, and encouragement to choose the former and avoid the latter. They should be forever stimulating each other to increased exercise of their higher faculties, and increased direction of their feelings and aims towards wise instead of foolish, elevating instead of degrading, objects and contemplations. But neither one person, nor any number of persons, is warranted in saying to another human creature of ripe years, that he shall not do with his life for his own benefit what he chooses to do with it. He is the person most interested in his own well-being: the interest which any other person, except in cases of strong personal attachment, can have in it, is trifling, compared with that which he himself has; the interest which society has in him individually (except as to his conduct to others) is fractional, and altogether indirect: while, with respect to his own feelings and circumstances, the most ordinary man or woman has means of knowledge immeasurably surpassing those that can be possessed by anyone else. The interference of society to overrule his judgment and purposes in what only regards himself, must be grounded on general presumptions; which may be altogether wrong, and even if right, are as likely as not to be misapplied to individual cases, by persons no better acquainted with the circumstances of such cases than those are who look at them merely from without. In this department, therefore, of human affairs, Individuality has its proper field of action. In the conduct of human beings towards one another, it is necessary that general rules should for the most part be observed, in order that people may know what they have to expect; but in each person's own concerns, his individual spontaneity is entitled to free exercise. Considerations to aid his judgment, exhortations to strengthen his will, may be offered to him, even obtruded on him, by others; but he, himself, is the final judge. All errors which he is likely to commit against advice and warning, are far outweighed by the evil of allowing others to constrain him to what they deem his good.

I do not mean that the feelings with which a person is regarded by others, ought not to be in any way affected by his self-regarding qualities or deficiencies. This is neither possible nor desirable. If he is eminent in any of the qualities which conduce to his own good, he is, so far, a proper object of admiration. He is so much the nearer to the ideal perfection of human nature. If he is grossly deficient in those qualities, a sentiment the opposite of admiration will follow. There is a degree of folly, and a degree of what may be called (though the phrase is not unobjectionable) lowness or depravation of taste, which, though it cannot justify doing harm to the person who manifests it, renders him necessarily and properly a subject of distaste, or, in extreme cases, even of contempt: a person would not have the opposite qualities in due strength without entertaining these feelings. Though doing no wrong to anyone, a person may so act as to compel us to judge him, and feel to him, as a fool, or as a being of an inferior order: and since this judgment and feeling are a fact which he would prefer to avoid, it is doing him a service to warn him of it beforehand, as of any other disagreeable consequence to which he exposes himself. It would be well, indeed, if this good office were much more freely rendered than the common notions of politeness at present permit, and if one person could honestly point out to another that he thinks him in fault, without being considered unmannerly or presuming. We have a right, also, in various ways, to act upon our unfavorable opinion of any one, not to the oppression of his individuality, but in the exercise of ours. We are not bound, for example, to seek his society; we have a right to avoid it (though not to parade the avoidance), for we have a right to choose the society most acceptable to us. We have a right, and it may be our duty to caution others against him, if we think his example or conversation likely to have a pernicious effect on those with whom he associates. We may give others a preference over him in optional good offices, except those which tend to his improvement. In these various modes a person may suffer very severe penalties at the hands of others, for faults which directly concern only himself; but he suffers these penalties only in so far as they are the natural, and, as it were, the spontaneous consequences of the faults themselves, not because they are purposely inflicted on him for the sake of punishment. A person who shows rashness, obstinacy, self-conceit—who cannot live within moderate means—who cannot restrain himself from hurtful indulgences—who pursues animal pleasures at the expense of those of feelings and intellect—must expect to be lowered in the opinion of others, and to have a less share of their favorable sentiments, but of this he has no right to complain, unless he has merited their favor by special excellence in his social relations, and has thus established a title to their good offices, which is not affected by his demerits towards himself.

What I contend for is, that the inconveniences which are strictly inseparable from the unfavorable judgment of others, are the only ones to which a person should ever be subjected for that portion of his conduct and character which concerns his own good, but which does not affect the interests of others in their relations with him. Acts injurious to others require a totally different treatment. Encroachment on their rights; infliction on them of any loss or damage not justified by his own rights; falsehood or duplicity in dealing with them; unfair or ungenerous use of advantages over them; even selfish abstinence from defending them against injury—these are fit objects of moral reprobation, and, in grave cases, of moral retribution and punishment. And not only these acts, but the dispositions which lead to them, are properly immoral, and fit subjects of disapprobation which may rise to abhorrence. Cruelty of disposition; malice and ill-nature; that most anti-social and odious of all passions, envy; dissimulation and insincerity; irascibility on insufficient cause, and resentment disproportioned to the provocation; the love of domineering over others; the desire to engross more than one's share of advantages (the πλεονεξία of the Greeks); the pride which derives gratification from the abasement of others; the egotism which thinks self and its concerns more important than everything else, and decides all doubtful questions in his own favor—these are moral vices, and constitute a bad and odious moral character: unlike the self-regarding faults previously mentioned, which are not properly immoralities, and to whatever pitch they may be carried, do not constitute wickedness. They may be proofs of any amount of folly, or want of personal dignity and self-respect; but they are only a subject or moral reprobation when they involve a breach of duty to others, for whose sake the individual is bound to have care for himself. What are called duties to ourselves are not socially obligatory, unless circumstances render them at the same time duties to others. The term duty to oneself, when it means anything more than prudence, means self-respect or self-development; and for none of these is any one accountable to his fellow-creatures, because for none of them is it for the good of mankind that he be held accountable to them.

The distinction between the loss of consideration which a person may rightly incur by defect of prudence or of personal dignity, and the reprobation which is due to him for an offence against the rights of others, is not a merely nominal distinction. It makes a vast difference both in our feelings and in our conduct towards him, whether he displeases us in things in which we think we have a right to control him, or in things in which we know that we have not. If he displeases us, we may express our distaste, and we may stand aloof from a person as well as from a thing that displeases us; but we shall not therefore feel called on to make his life uncomfortable. We shall reflect that he already bears, or will bear, the whole penalty of his error; if he spoils his life by mismanagement, we shall not, for that reason, desire to spoil it still further: instead of wishing to punish him, we shall rather endeavor to alleviate his punishment, by showing him how he may avoid or cure the evils his conduct tends to bring upon him. He may be to us an object of pity, perhaps of dislike, but not of anger or resentment; we shall not treat him like an enemy of society: the worst we shall think ourselves justified in doing is leaving him to himself, if we do not interfere benevolently by showing interest or concern for him. It is far otherwise if he has infringed the rules necessary for the protection of his fellow-creatures, individually or collectively. The evil consequences of his acts do not then fall on himself, but on others; and society, as the protector of all its members, must retaliate on him; must inflict pain on him for the express purpose of punishment, and must take care that it be sufficiently severe. In the one case, he is an offender at our bar, and we are called on not only to sit in judgment on him, but, in one shape or another, to execute our own sentence: in the other case, it is not our part to inflict any suffering on him, except what may incidentally follow from our using the same liberty in the regulation of our own affairs, which we allow to him in his.

The distinction here pointed out between the part of a person's life which concerns only himself, and that which concerns others, many persons will refuse to admit. How (it may be asked) can any part of the conduct of a member of society be a matter of indifference to the other members? No person is an entirely isolated being; it is impossible for a person to do anything seriously or permanently hurtful to himself, without mischief reaching at least to his near connections, and often far beyond them. If he injures his property, he does harm to those who directly or indirectly derived support from it, and usually diminishes, by a greater or less amount, the general resources of the community. If he deteriorates his bodily or mental faculties, he not only brings evil upon all who depended on him for any portion of their happiness, but disqualifies himself for rendering the services which he owes to his fellow-creatures generally; perhaps becomes a burden on their affection or benevolence; and if such conduct were very frequent, hardly any offence that is committed would detract more from the general sum of good. Finally, if by his vices or follies a person does no direct harm to others, he is nevertheless (it may be said) injurious by his example; and ought to be compelled to control himself, for the sake of those whom the sight or knowledge of his conduct might corrupt or mislead.

And even (it will be added) if the consequences of misconduct could be confined to the vicious or thoughtless individual, ought society to abandon to their own guidance those who are manifestly unfit for it? If protection against themselves is confessedly due to children and persons under age, is not society equally bound to afford it to persons of mature years who are equally incapable of self-government? If gambling, or drunkenness, or incontinence, or idleness, or uncleanliness, are as injurious to happiness, and as great a hindrance to improvement, as many or most of the acts prohibited by law, why (it may be asked) should not law, so far as is consistent with practicability and social convenience, endeavor to repress these also? And as a supplement to the unavoidable imperfections of law, ought not opinion at least to organize a powerful police against these vices, and visit rigidly with social penalties those who are known to practise them? There is no question here (it may be said) about restricting individuality, or impeding the trial of new and original experiments in living. The only things it is sought to prevent are things which have been tried and condemned from the beginning of the world until now; things which experience has shown not to be useful or suitable to any person's individuality. There must be some

length of time and amount of experience, after which a moral or prudential truth may be regarded as established: and it is merely desired to prevent generation after generation from falling over the same precipice which has been fatal to their predecessors.

I fully admit that the mischief which a person does to himself, may seriously affect, both through their sympathies and their interests, those nearly connected with him, and in a minor degree, society at large. When, by conduct of this sort, a person is led to violate a distinct and assignable obligation to any other person or persons, the case is taken out of the self-regarding class, and becomes amenable to moral disapprobation in the proper sense of the term. If, for example, a man, through intemperance or extravagance, becomes unable to pay his debts, or, having undertaken the moral responsibility of a family, becomes from the same cause incapable of supporting or educating them, he is deservedly reprobated, and might be justly punished; but it is for the breach of duty to his family or creditors, not for the extravagance. If the resources which ought to have been devoted to them, had been diverted from them for the most prudent investment, the moral culpability would have been the same. George Barnwell murdered his uncle to get money for his mistress, but if he had done it to set himself up in business, he would equally have been hanged. Again, in the frequent case of a man who causes grief to his family by addiction to bad habits, he deserves reproach for his unkindness or ingratitude; but so he may for cultivating habits not in themselves vicious, if they are painful to those with whom he passes his life, or who from personal ties are dependent on him for their comfort. Whoever fails in the consideration generally due to the interests and feelings of others, not being compelled by some more imperative duty, or justified by allowable self-preference, is a subject of moral disapprobation for that failure, but not for the cause of it, nor for the errors, merely personal to himself, which may have remotely led to it. In like manner, when a person disables himself, by conduct purely self-regarding, from the performance of some definite duty incumbent on him to the public, he is guilty of a social offence. No person ought to be punished simply for being drunk; but a soldier or a policeman should be punished for being drunk on duty. Whenever, in short, there is a definite damage, or a definite risk of damage, either to an individual or to the public, the case is taken out of the province of liberty, and placed in that of morality or law.

But with regard to the merely contingent, or, as it may be called, constructive injury which a person causes to society, by conduct which neither violates any specific duty to the public, nor occasions perceptible hurt to any assignable individual except himself; the inconvenience is one which society can afford to bear, for the sake of the greater good of human freedom. If grown persons are to be punished for not taking proper care of themselves, I would rather it were for their own sake, than under pretence of preventing them from impairing their capacity of rendering to society benefits which society does not pretend it has a right to exact. But I cannot consent to argue the point as if society had no means of bringing its weaker members up to its ordinary standard of rational conduct, except waiting till they do something irrational, and then punishing them, legally or morally, for it. Society has had absolute power over them during all the early portion of their existence: it has had the whole period of childhood and nonage in which to try whether it could make them capable of rational conduct in life. The existing generation is master both of the training and the entire circumstances of the generation to come; it cannot indeed make them perfectly wise and good, because it is itself so lamentably deficient in goodness and wisdom; and its best efforts are not always, in individual cases, its most successful ones; but it is perfectly well able to make the rising generation, as a whole, as good as, and a little better than, itself. If society lets any considerable number of its members grow up mere children, incapable of being acted on by rational consideration of distant motives, society has itself to blame for the consequences. Armed not only with all the powers of education, but with the ascendency which the authority of a received opinion always exercises over the minds who are least fitted to judge for themselves; and aided by the *natural* penalties which cannot be prevented from falling on those who incur the distaste or the contempt of those who know them; let not society pretend that it needs, besides all this, the power to issue commands and enforce obedience in the personal concerns of individuals, in which, on all principles of justice and policy, the decision ought to rest with those who are to abide the consequences. Nor is there anything which tends more to discredit and frustrate the better means of influencing conduct, than a resort to the worse. If there be among those whom it is attempted to coerce into prudence or temperance, any of the material of which vigorous and independent characters are made, they will infallibly rebel against the yoke. No such person will ever feel that others have a right to control him in his concerns, such as they have to prevent him from injuring them in theirs; and it easily comes to be considered a mark of spirit and courage to fly in the face of such usurped authority, and do with ostentation the exact opposite of what it enjoins; as in the fashion of grossness which succeeded, in the time of Charles II, to the fanatical moral intolerance of the Puritans. With respect to what is said of the necessity of protecting society from the bad example set to others by the vicious or the self-indulgent; it is true that bad example may have a pernicious effect, especially the example of doing wrong to others with impunity to the wrongdoer. But we are now speaking of conduct which, while it does no wrong to others, is supposed to do great harm to the agent himself: and I do not see how those who believe this, can think otherwise than that the example, on the whole, must be more salutary than hurtful, since, if it displays the misconduct, it displays also the painful or degrading consequences which, if the conduct is justly censured, must be supposed to be in all or most cases attendant on it.

But the strongest of all the arguments against the interference of the public with purely personal conduct, is that when it does interfere, the odds are that it interferes wrongly, and in the wrong place. On questions of social morality, of duty to others, the opinion of the public, that is, of an overruling majority, though often wrong, is likely to be still oftener right; because on such questions they are only required to judge of their own interests; of the manner in which some mode of conduct, if allowed to be practised, would affect themselves. But the opinion of a similar majority, imposed as a law on the minority, on questions of self-regarding conduct, is quite as likely to be wrong as right; for in these cases public opinion means, at the best, some people's opinion of what is good or bad for other people;

while very often it does not even mean that; the public, with the most perfect indifference, passing over the pleasure or convenience of those whose conduct they censure, and considering only their own preference. There are many who consider as an injury to themselves any conduct which they have a distaste for, and resent it as an outrage to their feelings; as a religious bigot, when charged with disregarding the religious feelings of others, has been known to retort that they disregard his feelings, by persisting in their abominable worship or creed. But there is no parity between the feeling of a person for his own opinion, and the feeling of another who is offended at his holding it; no more than between the desire of a thief to take a purse, and the desire of the right owner to keep it. And a person's taste is as much his own peculiar concern as his opinion or his purse. It is easy for any one to imagine an ideal public, which leaves the freedom and choice of individuals in all uncertain matters undisturbed, and only requires them to abstain from modes of conduct which universal experience has condemned. But where has there been seen a public which set any such limit to its censorship? or when does the public trouble itself about universal experience? In its interferences with personal conduct it is seldom thinking of anything but the enormity of acting or feeling differently from itself; and this standard of judgment, thinly disguised, is held up to mankind as the dictate of religion and philosophy, by nine tenths of all moralists and speculative writers. These teach that things are right because they are right; because we feel them to be so. They tell us to search in our own minds and hearts for laws of conduct binding on ourselves and on all others. What can the poor public do but apply these instructions, and make their own personal feelings of good and evil, if they are tolerably unanimous in them, obligatory on all the world?

The evil here pointed out is not one which exists only in theory; and it may perhaps be expected that I should specify the instances in which the public of this age and country improperly invests its own preferences with the character of moral laws. I am not writing an essay on the aberrations of existing moral feeling. That is too weighty a subject to be discussed parenthetically, and by way of illustration. Yet examples are necessary, to show that the principle I maintain is of serious and practical moment, and that I am not

endeavoring to erect a barrier against imaginary evils. And it is not difficult to show, by abundant instances, that to extend the bounds of what may be called moral police, until it encroaches on the most unquestionably legitimate liberty of the individual, is one of the most universal of all human propensities.

As a first instance, consider the antipathies which men cherish on no better grounds than that persons who religious opinions are different from theirs, do not practise their religious observances, especially their religious abstinences. To cite a rather trivial example, nothing in the creed or practice of Christians does more to envenom the hatred of Mahomedans against them, than the fact of their eating pork. There are few acts which Christians and Europeans regard with more unaffected disgust, than Mussulmans regard this particular mode of satisfying hunger. It is, in the first place, an offence against their religion; but this circumstance by no means explains either the degree or the kind of their repugnance; for wine also is forbidden by their religion, and to partake of it is by all Mussulmans accounted wrong, but not disgusting. Their aversion to the flesh of the "unclean beast" is, on the contrary, of that peculiar character, resembling an instinctive antipathy, which the idea of uncleanness, when once it thoroughly sinks into the feelings, seems always to excite even in those whose personal habits are anything but scrupulously cleanly, and of which the sentiment of religious impurity, so intense in the Hindoos, is a remarkable example. Suppose now that in a people, of whom the majority were Mussulmans, that majority should insist upon not permitting pork to be eaten within the limits of the country. This would be nothing new in Mahomedan countries.* Would it be a legitimate exercise of the moral authority of public opinion? and if not, why not?

*The case of the Bombay Parsees is a curious instance in point. When this industrious and enterprising tribe, the descendants of the Persian fire-worshippers, flying from their native country before the Caliphs, arrived in Western India, they were admitted to toleration by the Hindoo sovereigns, on condition of not eating beef. When those regions afterwards fell under the dominion of Mahomedan conquerors, the Parsees obtained from them a continuance of indulgence, on condition of refraining from pork. What was at first obedience to authority became a second nature, and the Parsees to this day abstain both from beef and pork. Though not required by their religion, the double abstinence has had time to grow into a custom of their tribe; and custom, in the East, is a religion.

The practice is really revolting to such a public. They also sincerely think that it is forbidden and abhorred by the Deity. Neither could the prohibition be censured as religious persecution. It might be religious in its origin, but it would not be persecution for religion, since nobody's religion makes it a duty to eat pork. The only tenable ground of condemnation would be, that with the personal tastes and self-regarding concerns of individuals the public has no business to interfere.

To come somewhat nearer home: the majority of Spaniards consider it a gross impiety, offensive in the highest degree to the Supreme Being, to worship him in any other manner than the Roman Catholic; and no other public worship is lawful on Spanish soil. The people of all Southern Europe look upon a married clergy as not only irreligious, but unchaste, indecent, gross, disgusting. What do Protestants think of these perfectly sincere feelings, and of the attempt to enforce them against non-Catholics? Yet, if mankind are justified in interfering with each other's liberty in things which do not concern the interests of others, on what principle is it possible consistently to exclude these cases? or who can blame people for desiring to suppress what they regard as a scandal in the sight of God and man? No stronger case can be shown for prohibiting anything which is regarded as a personal immorality, than is made out for suppressing these practices in the eyes of those who regard them as impieties; and unless we are willing to adopt the logic of persecutors, and to say that we may persecute others because we are right, and that they must not persecute us because they are wrong, we must be aware of admitting a principle of which we should resent as a gross injustice the application to ourselves.

The preceding instances may be objected to, although unreasonably, as drawn from contingencies impossible among us: opinion, in this country, not being likely to enforce abstinence from meats, or to interfere with people for worshipping, and for either marrying or not marrying, according to their creed or inclination. The next example, however, shall be taken from an interference with liberty which we have by no means passed all danger of. Wherever the puritans have been sufficiently powerful, as in New England, and in Great Britain at the time of the Commonwealth, they have endeavored, with considerable success, to put down all public, and

nearly all private, amusements: especially music, dancing, public games, or other assemblages for purposes of diversion, and the theatre. There are still in this country large bodies of persons by whose notions of morality and religion these recreations are condemned; and those persons belonging chiefly to the middle class, who are the ascendant power in the present social and political condition of the kingdom, it is by no means impossible that persons of these sentiments may at some time or other command a majority in Parliament. How will the remaining portion of the community like to have the amusements that shall be permitted to them regulated by the religious and moral sentiments of the stricter Calvinists and Methodists? Would they not, with considerable peremptoriness, desire these intrusively pious members of society to mind their own business? This is precisely what should be said to every government and every public, who have the pretension that no person shall enjoy any pleasure which they think wrong. But if the principle of the pretension be admitted, no one can reasonably object to its being acted on in the sense of the majority, or other preponderating power in the country; and all persons must be ready to conform to the idea of a Christian commonwealth, as understood by the early settlers in New England, if a religious profession similar to theirs should ever succeed in regaining its lost ground, as religions supposed to be declining have so often been known to do.

To imagine another contingency, perhaps more likely to be realized than the one last mentioned. There is confessedly a strong tendency in the modern world towards a democratic constitution of society, accompanied or not by popular political institutions. It is affirmed that in the country where this tendency is most completely realized —where both society and the government are most democratic—the United States—the feeling of the majority, to whom any appearance of a more showy or costly style of living than they can hope to rival is disagreeable, operates as a tolerably effectual sumptuary law, and that in many parts of the Union it is really difficult for a person possessing a very large income, to find any mode of spending it, which will not incur popular disapprobation. Though such statements as these are doubtless much exaggerated as a representation of existing facts, the state of things they describe is not only a conceivable and possible, but a probable result of democratic feeling, combined with the notion that the public has a right to a veto on the manner in which individuals shall spend their incomes. We have only further to suppose a considerable diffusion of Socialist opinions, and it may become infamous in the eyes of the majority to possess more property than some very small amount, or any income not earned by manual labor. Opinions similar in principle to these, already prevail widely among the artisan class, and weigh oppressively on those who are amenable to the opinion chiefly of that class, namely, its own members. It is known that the bad workmen who form the majority of the operatives in many branches of industry, are decidedly of opinion that bad workmen ought to receive the same wages as good, and that no one ought to be allowed, through piecework or otherwise, to earn by superior skill or industry more than others can without it. And they employ a moral police, which occasionally becomes a physical one, to deter skilful workmen from receiving, and employers from giving, a larger remuneration for a more useful service. If the public have any jurisdiction over private concerns, I cannot see that these people are in fault, or that any individual's particular public can be blamed for asserting the same authority over his individual conduct, which the general public asserts over people in general.

But, without dwelling upon supposititious cases, there are, in our own day, gross usurpations upon the liberty of private life actually practised, and still greater ones threatened with some expectation of success, and opinions proposed which assert an unlimited right in the public not only to prohibit by law everything which it thinks wrong, but in order to get at what it thinks wrong, to prohibit any number of things which it admits to be innocent.

Under the name of preventing intemperance, the people of one English colony, and of nearly half the United States, have been interdicted by law from making any use whatever of fermented drinks, except for medical purposes: for prohibition of their sale is in fact, as it is intended to be, prohibition of their use. And though the impracticability of executing the law has caused its repeal in several of the States which had adopted it, including the one from which it derives its name,

an attempt has notwithstanding been commenced, and is prosecuted with considerable zeal by many of the professed philanthropists, to agitate for a similar law in this country. The association, or "Alliance" as it terms itself, which has been formed for this purpose, has acquired some notoriety through the publicity given to a correspondence between its Secretary and one of the very few English public men who hold that a politician's opinions ought to be founded on principles. Lord Stanley's share in this correspondence is calculated to strengthen the hopes already built on him, by those who know how rare such qualities as are manifested in some of his public appearances, unhappily are among those who figure in political life. The organ of the Alliance, who would "deeply deplore the recognition of any principle which could be wrested to justify bigotry and persecution," undertakes to point out the "broad and impassable barrier" which divides such principles from those of the association. "All matters relating to thought, opinion, conscience, appear to me," he says, "to be without the sphere of legislation; all pertaining to social act, habit, relation, subject only to a discretionary power vested in the State itself, and not in the individual, to be within it." No mention is made of a third class, different from either of these, viz., acts and habits which are not social, but individual; although it is to this class, surely, that the act of drinking fermented liquors belongs. Selling fermented liquors, however, is trading, and trading is a social act. But the infringement complained of is not on the liberty of the seller, but on that of the buyer and consumer; since the State might just as well forbid him to drink wine, as purposely make it impossible for him to obtain it. The Secretary, however, says, "I claim, as a citizen, a right to legislate whenever my social rights are invaded by the social act of another." And now for the definition of these "social rights." "If anything invades my social rights, certainly the traffic in strong drink does. It destroys my primary right of security, by constantly creating and stimulating social disorder. It invades my right of equality, by deriving a profit from the creation of a misery, I am taxed to support. It impedes my right to free moral and intellectual development, by surrounding my path with dangers, and by weakening and demoralizing society, from which I have a right to claim mutual aid and intercourse." A theory of "social rights," the like of which probably never before found its way into distinct language—being nothing short of this—that it is the absolute social right of every individual, that every other individual shall act in every respect exactly as he ought; that whosoever fails thereof in the smallest particular, violates my social right, and entitles me to demand from the legislature the removal of the grievance. So monstrous a principle is far more dangerous than any single interference with liberty; there is no violation of liberty which it would not justify; it acknowledges no right to any freedom whatever, except perhaps to that of holding opinions in secret, without ever disclosing them: for the moment an opinion which I consider noxious, passes any one's lips, it invades all the "social rights" attributed to me by the Alliance. The doctrine ascribes to all mankind a vested interest in each other's moral, intellectual, and even physical perfection, to be defined by each claimant according to his own standard.

Another important example of illegitimate interference with the rightful liberty of the individual, not simply threatened, but long since carried into triumphant effect, is Sabbatarian legislation. Without doubt, abstinence on one day in the week, so far as the exigencies of life permit, from the usual daily occupation, though in no respect religiously binding on any except Jews, it is a highly beneficial custom. And inasmuch as this custom cannot be observed without a general consent to that effect among the industrious classes, therefore, in so far as some persons by working may impose the same necessity on others, it may be allowable and right that the law should guarantee to each, the observance by others of the custom, by suspending the greater operations of industry on a particular day. But this justification, grounded on the direct interest which others have in each individual's observance of the practice, does not apply to the self-chosen occupations in which a person may think fit to employ his leisure; nor does it hold good, in the smallest degree, for legal restrictions on amusements. It is true that the amusement of some is the day's work of others; but the pleasure, not to say the useful recreation, of many, is worth the labor of a few, provided the occupation is freely chosen, and can be freely resigned. The operatives are perfectly right in thinking that if all worked on Sunday seven days' work would have to be given for six days' wages: but so long as the great mass of employments are suspended, the small number who for the enjoyment of others must still work, obtain a proportional increase of earnings; and they are not obliged to follow those occupations, if they prefer leisure to emolument. If a further remedy is sought, it might be found in the establishment by custom of a holiday on some other day of the week for those particular classes of persons. The only ground, therefore, on which restrictions on Sunday amusements can be defended, must be that they are religiously wrong; a motive of legislation which never can be too earnestly protested again. "Deorum injuriæ Diis curæ." It remains to be proved that society or any of its officers holds a commission from on high to avenge any supposed offence to Omnipotence, which is not also a wrong to our fellow-creatures. The notion that it is one man's duty that another should be religious, was the foundation of all the religious persecutions ever perpetrated, and if admitted, would fully justify them. Though the feeling which breaks out in the repeated attempts to stop railway travelling on Sunday, in the resistance to the opening of Museums, and the like, has not the cruelty of the old persecutors, the state of mind indicated by it is fundamentally the same. It is a determination not to tolerate others in doing what is permitted by their religion, because it is not permitted by the persecutor's religion. It is a belief that God not only abominates the act of the misbeliever, but will not hold us guiltless if we leave him unmolested.

I cannot refrain from adding to these examples of the little account commonly made of human liberty, the language of downright persecution which breaks out from the press of this country, whenever it feels called on to notice the remarkable phenomenon of Mormonism. Much might be said on the unexpected and instructive fact, that an alleged new revelation, and a religion founded on it, the product of palpable imposture, not even supported by the *prestige* of extraordinary qualities in its founder, is believed by hundreds of thousands, and has been made the foundation of a society, in the age of newspapers, railways, and the electric telegraph. What here concerns us is, that this religion, like other and better religions, has its martyrs; that its prophet and founder was, for his teaching, put to death by a mob; that others of its adherents lost their lives by the same lawless violence; that they were forcibly expelled, in a body, from the country in which they first grew up; while, now that they have been chased into a solitary recess in the midst of a desert, many of this country openly declare that it would be right (only that it is not convenient) to send an expedition against them, and compel them by force to conform to the opinion of other people. The article of the Mormonite doctrine which is the chief provocative to the antipathy which thus breaks through the ordinary restraints of religious tolerance, is its sanction of polygamy; which, though permitted to Mahomedans, and Hindoos, and Chinese, seems to excite unquenchable animosity when practised by persons who speak English, and profess to be a kind of Christians. No one has a deeper disapprobation than I have of this Mormon institution; both for other reasons, and because, far from being in any way countenanced by the principle of liberty, it is a direct infraction of that principle, being a mere riveting of the chains of one half of the community, and an emancipation of the other from reciprocity of obligation towards them. Still, it must be remembered that this relation is as much voluntary on the part of the women concerned in it, and who may be deemed the sufferers by it, as is the case with any other form of the marriage institution; and however surprising this fact may appear, it has its explanation in the common ideas and customs of the world, which teaching women to think marriage the one thing needful, make it intelligible that many a woman should prefer being one of several wives, to not being a wife at all. Other countries are not asked to recognize such unions, or release any portion of their inhabitants from their own laws on the score of Mormonite opinions. But when the dissentients have conceded to the hostile sentiments of others, far more than could justly be demanded; when they have left the countries to which their doctrines were unacceptable, and established themselves in a remote corner of the earth, which they have been the first to render habitable to human beings; it is difficult to see on what principles but those of tyranny they can be prevented from living there under what laws they please, provided they commit no aggression on other nations, and allow perfect freedom of departure to those who are dissatisfied with their ways. A recent writer, in some respects of considerable merit, proposes (to use his own words) not a crusade, but a *civilizade*, against this polygamous community, to put an end to what seems to him a retrograde step in civilization. It also appears so to me, but I am not aware that any community has a right to force another to be civilized. So long as the sufferers by the bad law do not invoke assistance from other communities, I cannot admit that persons entirely unconnected with them ought to step in and require that a condition of things with which all who are directly interested appear to be satisfied, should be put an end to because it is a scandal to persons some thousands of miles distant, who have no part or concern in it. Let them send missionaries, if they please, to preach against it; and let them, by any fair means (of which silencing the teachers is not one), oppose the progress of similar doctrines among their own people. If civilization has got the better of barbarism when barbarism had the world to itself, it is too much to profess to be afraid lest barbarism, after having been fairly got under, should revive and conquer civilization. A civilization that can thus succumb to its vanquished enemy must first have become so degenerate, that neither its appointed priests and teachers, nor anybody else, has the capacity, or will take the trouble, to stand up for it. If this be so, the sooner such a civilization receives notice to quit, the better. It can only go on from bad to worse, until destroyed and regenerated (like the Western Empire) by energetic barbarians.

JOEL FEINBERG

Limits to the Free Expression of Opinion

The purpose of this essay is to determine how the liberal principles that support free expression of opinion generally also define the limits to what the law can permit to be said. The liberal principle in question, put vaguely, is that state coercion is justified only to prevent personal or public harm. That more harm than good can be expected to come from suppression of dissenting opinions in politics and religion has been amply documented by experience and argument, but concentration on this important truth, despite its salutary practical effects, is likely to mislead us into thinking that the liberal "harm principle" is simple in its meaning and easy in its application. For that reason, this essay will only summarize (in Part I) the impressive case for total freedom of expression of opinions of certain kinds in normal contexts, and concentrate instead (in Part II) on the types of expressions *excluded* by the harm principle: defamation and "malicious truth," invasions of privacy, and expressions that cause others to do harm (those that cause panics, provoke retaliatory violence, or incite others to crime or insurrection). Part III will examine the traditional crime of "sedition," and conclude that it is not properly among the categories of expressions excluded by the harm principle. Among the other lessons that will emerge from these exercises, I hope, is that the harm principle is a largely empty formula in urgent need of supplementation by tests for determining the relative importance of conflicting interests and by measures of the degree to which interests are endangered by free expressions.

I THE CASE FOR FREEDOM

The classic case for free expression of opinion was made by John Stuart Mill.[1] Mill's purpose in his famous chapter "Of the Liberty of Thought

This essay has not been previously published.

and Discussion" was to consider, as a beginning, just one class of actions and how his "harm principle" applied to them. The actions in question were instances of expressing orally or in print opinions about matters of fact, and about historical, scientific, theological, philosophical, political, and moral questions. Mill's conclusion was that suppressing such expressions is always more harmful than the expressions themselves would be and therefore is never justified. But don't expressions of opinion *ever* harm others? Of course they do, and it would be silly to ascribe to Mill the absurd contrary view. Expressions of opinion harm others when they are: defamatory (libelous or slanderous), seditious, incitive to violence, malicious publications of damaging or embarrassing truths, or invasions of privacy. In fact, in classifying an expression under one of these headings, we are *ipso facto* declaring that it is harmful. Mill is not radical about this. Putting these obviously harmful expressions to one side (he is best understood as asking) is there any [further] ground for suppressing mere "opinions"? To *this* question Mill's answer is radical and absolutist: If an expression cannot be subsumed under one of these standard headings for harmfulness, then it can never be sufficiently injurious to be justifiably suppressed. Apart from direct harm to assignable persons, no other ground is ever a sufficient reason for overriding the presumption in favor of liberty. One may *never* properly suppress an expression on the grounds, for example, that it is immoral, shocking to sensibilities, annoying, heretical, unorthodox, or "dangerous," and especially not on the ground simply that it is false.

Expressions of opinion thus occupy a very privileged position, in Mill's view. That is because their suppression, he contends, is not only a private injury to the coerced party but also and inevitably a very serious harm to the public in general. The argument has two distinct branches. The first has us consider the possibility that the suppressed opinion is wholly or partially true. On this assumption, of course, repression will have the harmful social consequence of loss of truth.

The crucial contention in this wing of the argument, however, is much stronger than that. Mill contends that there is *always* a chance, for all we can know, that the suppressed opinion is at least partially true, so that the act of repression itself necessarily involves some risk. Moreover, the risk is always an unreasonable one, never worth taking, since the risk of its alternative—permitting free expression generally—to our interest in acquiring knowledge and avoiding error, is negligible. By letting every opinion, no matter how "certainly true," be challenged, we minimize the risk of permanent commitment to falsehood. In the process, of course, we allow some falsehoods to be expressed, but since the truth is not denied its champions either, there is very little risk that the tolerated falsehood will become permanently enthroned. The balance of favorable risks then is clearly on the side of absolute freedom of expression.

This argument is especially convincing in the world of science, where no hypothesis bears its evidence on its face, and old errors are continually exposed by new and easily duplicable evidence and by more careful and refined experimental techniques. Even totalitarian regimes have learned that it is in their own interest to permit physicists and plant geneticists to go their theoretical ways unencumbered by ideological restrictions. Sometimes, to be sure, the truth of a scientific theory is so apparent that it is well worth acting on even though it strains governmental priorities to do so and requires large investment of funds; but this very confidence, Mill argued, is justified only when every interested party has had an opportunity to refute the theory. In respect at least to scientific theories, the more open to attack an opinion is, the more confident we can eventually be of its truth. That "no one has disproved it yet" is a convincing reason for accepting a theory only when everyone has been free to try.

To deny that it is possible for a given opinion to be true, Mill maintained, is to assume one's own infallibility. This is no doubt an overstatement, but what does seem clear is that to deny that a given proposition can possibly be true is to assume one's own infallibility with respect to *it*, though of course not one's infallibility generally. To say that one cannot possibly be wrong in holding a given belief is to say that one knows that one's knowledge of its truth is authentic. We claim to know infallibly when we claim to know that we know. It is also clear, I think, that we are sometimes justified in making such claims. I know that I know that $2 + 3 = 5$, that I am seated at my desk writing, and that New York is in the United States. In the face of challenges from the relentless epistemological skeptic, I may have to admit that I don't know *how* I know these things, but it doesn't follow from that that I don't know them. It seems then that there is no risk, after all, in suppressing some opinions, namely, the denials of such truisms.

Yet what could ever be the point of forbidding persons from denying that $2 + 3 = 5$ or that New York is in the United States? There is surely no danger that general confidence in these true propositions would be undermined. There is no risk of loss of truth, I suppose, in suppressing their denials, but also no risk in allowing them free circulation. Conceding that we can know truisms infallibly, therefore, can hardly commit us to approve of the suppression of their denials, at least so long as we adhere, with Mill, exclusively to the harm principle. More importantly, there are serious risks involved in granting any mere man or group of men the power to draw the line between those opinions that are known infallibly to be true and those not so known, in order to ban expression of the former. Surely, if there is one thing that is *not* infallibly known, it is how to draw *that* line.

In any case, when we leave tautologies and truisms behind and consider only those larger questions of substance, doctrines about which have in fact been banned by rulers in the past as certainly false (for example, the shape of the earth, the cause of disease, the wisdom of certain wars or economic policies, and the morality of certain kinds of conduct) our own fallibility is amply documented by history. The sad fact is that at every previous stage of history including the recent past there have been questions of the highest importance about which nearly *everyone*, including the wisest and most powerful, has been dead wrong. The more important the doctrines, then, the greater the risk we run in forbidding expressions of disagreement.

Mill's account, in this first wing of his argument, of the public interest in the discovery and effective dissemination of truth has many important practical implications. Mill himself thought that we should seek out our ideological enemies and offer them public forums in which to present and defend their views, or failing that, hire "devil's advocates" to defend unpopular positions in schools and in popular debates. Mill's reasons for these proposals also provide the grounding for the so-called "adversary theory of politics." The argument is (in the words of Zechariah Chafee): "Truth can be sifted out from falsehood only if the government is vigorously and constantly cross-examined . . . Legal proceedings prove that an opponent makes the best cross-examiner."[2] This states the rationale of the two-party system exactly. The role of the out-party is like that of the prosecutor in a criminal trial, or plaintiff in a civil action. It is a vitally important role too. Numerous historical instances suggest that we are in grave danger when both parties agree. Witness, for example, the Vietnam debacle, which was the outcome of a twenty-year "bipartisan foreign policy." Foreign policy decisions are as difficult as they are important; hence the need for constant reexamination, probing for difficulties and soft spots, bringing to light new and relevant facts, and subjecting to doubt hitherto unquestioned first premises. Without these aids, we tend to drift quite complacently into dead ends and quagmires.[3]

The second branch of the argument has us assume that the unorthodox opinion we are tempted to suppress really is false anyway. Even in this case, Mill insists, we will all be the losers, in the end, for banning it. When people are not forced by the stimulus of dissent to rethink the grounds of their convictions, then their beliefs tend to wither and decay. The rationales of the tenets are forgotten, their vital direction and value lost, their very meaning altered, until at last they are held in the manner of dead dogmas rather than living truths.

No part of Mill's argument in *On Liberty* is more impressive than his case for totally free expression of opinion. It is especially ingenious in that it rests entirely on social advantages and foregoes all help that might come from appeals to "the inalienable right to say what one pleases whether it's good for society or not." But that very utilitarian ingenuity may be its Achilles heel; for if liberty of expression is justified only because it is socially useful, then some might think that it is justified only *when* it is socially useful. The possibility of special circumstances in which repression is still *more* useful is real enough to disturb allies of Mill who love liberty fully as much as he and would seek therefore a still more solid foundation for it. But even if the case for absolute liberty of opinion must rest ultimately on some theory of natural rights, Mill has given that case powerful utilitarian reinforcement.

II LIMITS TO FREEDOM

Despite the impressive case for complete liberty of expression, there are obvious instances where permitting a person to speak his mind freely will cause more harm than good all around. These instances have been lumped together in various distinct legal categories whose names have come to stand for torts or crimes and to suggest, by a powerful linguistic convention, unpermitted wrongdoing. Thus, there can be no more right to defame or to incite to riot than there can be a right way, in Aristotle's example,[4] to commit adultery. Underlying these linguistic conventions, however, are a settled residue of interest weightings as well as actual and hypothetical applications of the harm principle, often filled in or mediated in various ways by principles of other kinds. The various categories of excluded expressions are worth examining not only for the light they throw on the harm principle, but also for the conceptual and normative problems each raises on its own for political theory.

1. *Defamation and "Malicious Truth."* Defamatory statements are those that damage a person's reputation by their expression to third parties in a manner that "tends to diminish the esteem in which the plaintiff is held, or to excite adverse feelings or opinions against him."[5] The primary mode of discouraging defamers in countries adhering to the common law has been the threat of civil liability to a court-enforced order to pay cash to the injured party in compensation for the harm done his reputation. In cases of especially malicious defamation, the defendant may be ordered to pay a stiff fine ("punitive damages") to the plaintiff as well. Only in the most

egregious cases (and rarely even then) has criminal liability been imposed for defamation, but nevertheless the threat of civil suit as sufficient to entitle us to say that our law does not leave citizens (generally) free to defame one another. Here then is one clear limit to our freedom of expression.

Not all expressions that harm another's reputation, of course, are legally forbidden. Even when damaging defamation has been proved by the plaintiff, the defendant may yet escape liability by establishing one of two kinds of defense. He may argue that his utterance or publication was "privileged," or simply that it is *true*. The former defense is established by showing either that the defendant, in virtue of his public office or his special relation to the plaintiff, has been granted an absolute immunity from liability for defamation (for example, he spoke in a judicial or legislative proceeding, or he had the prior consent of the plaintiff), or that he had a prior immunity contingent on the reasonableness of his conduct. Examples of this category of privilege are the immunity of a person protecting himself or another by a warning that someone is of poor character, or of a drama, literary, or political critic making "fair comment" of an extremely unfavorable kind about a performance, a book, or a policy. These immunities are still other examples of public policies that protect an interest (in this case, the interest in reputation) just to the point where the protection interferes with interests deemed more important—either to the public in general or to other private individuals. These policies imply that a person's reputation is a precious thing that deserves legal protection just as his life, health, and property do, but on the other hand, a certain amount of rough handling of reputations is to be expected in courtrooms, in the heated spontaneous debates of legislative chambers, in reviews of works presented to the public for critical comment, and in the rough-and-tumble competition among eminent persons for power or public acclaim. To withhold immunities in these special contexts would be to allow nervous inhibitions to keep hard truths out of law courts to the detriment of justice, or out of legislatures to the detriment of the laws themselves; or to make critics overly cautious, to the detriment of those who rely on their judgments; or to make political commentators overly deferential to power and authority, to the detriment of reform.

There is, however, no public interest in keeping those who are not in these special contexts uninhibited when they speak or write about others. Indeed, we should all be nervous when we make unfavorable comments, perhaps not on the ground that feelings and reputations will simply be damaged (there may be both justice and social gain in such damage), but at least on the ground that the unfavorable comment may be *false*. In a way, the rationale for the defamation action at law is the opposite of Mill's case for the free expression of opinion. The great public interest in possessing the truth in science, philosophy, politics, and so on, is best served by keeping everyone uninhibited in the expression of his views; but there are areas where there is a greater interest in avoiding falsehood than in acquiring truth, and here we are best served by keeping people very nervous indeed when they are tempted to speak their minds.

Once the plaintiff has proved that the defendant has published a defamatory statement about him, the defendant may avoid liability in another way, namely, by showing that the statement in question is *true*. "Out of a tender regard for reputations," writes Professor Prosser, "the law presumes in the first instance that all defamation is false, and the defendant has the burden of pleading and proving its truth."[6] In the large majority of American jurisdictions, truth is a "complete defense" which will relieve the defendant of liability even when he published his defamation merely out of spite, in the absence of any reasonable social purpose. One wonders why this should be. Is the public interest in "the truth" so great that it should always override a private person's interest in his own reputation? An affirmative answer, I should think, would require considerable argument.

Most of the historical rationales for the truth defense worked out in the courts and in legal treatises will not stand scrutiny. They all founder, I think, on the following kind of case. A New York girl supports her drug addiction by working as a prostitute in a seedy environment of crime and corruption. After a brief jail sentence, she decides to reform, and travels to the Far West to begin her life anew. She marries a respectable young man, becomes a leader in civic and church affairs, and raises a large and happy family. Then twenty years after her arrival in town, her neurotically jealous neighbor learns of her past, and publishes a lurid but accurate account of it for the eyes of the whole community. As a consequence, her "friends" and associates snub her; she is asked to resign her post as church leader; gossipmongers prattle ceaselessly about her; and obscene inscriptions appear on her property and in her mail. She dare not sue her neighbor for defamation since the defamatory report is wholly true. She has been wronged, but she has no legal remedy.

Applied to this case the leading rationales for the truth defense are altogether unconvincing. One argument claims that the true gravamen of the wrong in defamation is the deception practiced on the public in misrepresenting the truth, so that where there is no misrepresentation there is no injury—as if the injury to the reformed sinner is of no account. A variant of this argument holds the reformed sinner to be deserving of exposure on the ground that he (or she) in covering up his past deceives the public, thereby compounding the earlier delinquency. If this sort of "deception" is morally blameworthy, then so is every form of 'covering up the truth,' from cosmetics to window blinds! Others have argued that a delinquent plaintiff should not be allowed any standing in court because of his established bad character. A related contention is that "a person is in no position to complain of a reputation which is consistent with his actual character and behavior."[7] Both of these rationales apply well enough to the unrepentant sinner, but work nothing but injustice and suffering on the reformed person, on the plaintiff defamed in some way that does not reflect upon his character, or on the person whose "immoralities" have been wholly private and scrupulously kept from the public eye. It does not follow from the fact that a person's reputation is consistent with the truth that it is "deserved."

The most plausible kind of argument for the truth defense is that it serves some kind of overriding public interest. Some have argued that fear of eventual exposure can serve as effectively as the threat of punishment to *deter* wrongdoing. This argument justifies a kind of endless social penalty and is therefore more cruel than a system of criminal law, which usually permits a wrongdoer to wipe his slate clean. Others have claimed that

exposure of character flaws and past sins protects the community by warning it of dangerous or untrustworthy persons. That argument is well put (but without endorsement) by Harper and James when they refer to ". . . the social desirability as a general matter, of leaving individuals free to warn the public of antisocial members of the community, provided only that the person furnishing the information take the risk of its being false."[8] (Blackstone went so far as to assert that the defendant who can show the truth of his defamatory remarks has rendered a public service in exposing the plaintiff and deserves the public's gratitude.)[9] This line of argument is convincing enough when restricted to public-spirited defamers and socially dangerous plaintiffs; but it lacks all plausibility when applied to the malicious and useless exposure of past misdeeds, or to nonmoral failings and "moral" flaws of a wholly private and well-concealed kind.

How precious a thing, after all, is this thing denoted by the glittering abstract noun, the "Truth"? The truth in general is a great and noble cause, a kind of public treasury more important than any particular person's feelings; but the truth about a particular person may be of no great value at all except to that person. When the personal interest in reputation outweighs the dilute public interest in truth (and there is no doubt that this is sometimes the case) then it must be protected even at some cost to our general knowledge of the truth. The truth, like any other commodity, is not so valuable that it is a bargain at *any* cost. A growing number of American states have now modified the truth defense so that it applies only when the defamatory statement has been published with good motives, or is necessary for some reasonable public purpose, or (in some cases) both. The change is welcome.

In summary, the harm principle would permit all harmless statements about others whether true or false (harmless statements by definition are not defamatory), but it would impose liability for all defamatory false statements and all seriously defamatory true statements except those that serve (or seem likely to serve) some beneficial social purpose.

2. *Invasions of Privacy.* Still other expressions are neither defamatory nor false, and yet they can unjustly wound the persons they describe all the same. These do not invade the interest in a good

reputation so much as a special kind of interest in peace of mind, sometimes called a sense of dignity, sometimes the enjoyment of solitude, but most commonly termed the interest in personal privacy. As the legal "right to privacy" is now understood, it embraces a miscellany of things, protecting the right-holder not only from "physical intrusions upon his solitude" and "publicity given to his name or likeness or to private information about him" without his permission, but also from being placed "in a false light [but without defamation] in the public eye" and from the "commercial appropriation of elements of his personality."[10] (Some of these are really invasions of one's property rights through unpermitted commercial exploitation of one's name, image, personality, and so on. For that reason it has been urged that the invaded right in these cases be called "the right to publicity.") What concerns us here are statements conveying true and nondefamatory information about the plaintiff, of a very intimate and properly private kind, gathered and published without his consent, often to his shame and mortification. Business advantage and journalistic profit have become ever stronger motives for such statements, and the invention of tiny, very sensitive snooping devices has made the data easier than ever to come by.

Since the "invasion of privacy" tort has been recognized, plaintiffs have recovered damages from defendants who have shadowed them, looked into their windows, investigated their bank accounts, and tapped their telephone wires. In many of these cases, the court's judgment protected the plaintiff's interest in "being let alone," but in other cases the interest protected was not merely this, or not this at all, but rather the interest in *not being known about.* If there is a right not to be known about in some respects by anyone, then *a fortiori* there is a right not to be known about, in those respects, by nearly everyone. Privacy law has also protected the interests of those who don't want details of their lives called to the public's attention and made the subject of public wonder, amusement, discussion, analysis, or debate. Hence some plaintiffs have recovered from defendants who have published embarrassing details of their illness or physical deformity; their personal letters or unpublished notes, or inventories of their possessions; their photographs in a "good looks" popularity con-

test, or in a "before and after" advertisement for baldness or obesity cures, or on the labels of tomato cans; and from defendants who have published descriptions of the plaintiffs' sexual relations, hygienic habits, and other very personal matters. No life, of course, can be kept wholly private, or immune from public inspection even in some of its most personal aspects. "No one enjoys being stared at," Harper and James remind us, yet if a person "goes out on the street he [can have] no legal objection to people looking at him."[11] On the other hand, life would be hardly tolerable if there were no secrets we could keep (away from "the street"), no preserve of dignity, no guaranteed solitude.

There would probably be very little controversy over the existence of a right to privacy were it not the case that the interest in being let alone is frequently in conflict with other interests that seem at least equally deserving of protection. Even where the right is recognized by law, it is qualified by the recognition of very large classes of privileged expressions. First of all, like most other torts and crimes, the charge of invasion of privacy is completely defeated by proof that the plaintiff gave his consent to the defendant's conduct. Secondly, and more interestingly, the right of privacy can conflict with the constitutionally guaranteed freedom of the press, which, according to Prosser, "justifies the publication of news and all other matters of legitimate public interest and concern."[12] For a court to adjudicate between a paper's right to publish and an individual's right to privacy then, it must employ some standard for determining what is of legitimate public concern or, what amounts to the same thing, which news about a person is "fit to print." Such legal standards are always in the making, never finished, but the standard of "legitimate interest" has begun to take on a definite shape. American courts have decided, first of all, that "the person who intentionally puts himself in the public eye ... has no right to complain of any publicity which reasonably bears on his activity."[13] The rationale for this judgment invokes the maxim that a person is not wronged by that to which he consents, or by that the risk of which he has freely assumed. The person who steps into the public spotlight ought to know what he is letting himself in for; hence the law presumes that he *does* know, and therefore that he is asking for it. Much the same kind of presumption lies behind the "fair comment" defense in defamation cases: The man who voluntarily publishes his own work is presumed to be inviting criticism and is therefore not entitled to complain when the criticism is adverse or harsh, providing only that it is relevant and not personally abusive. One can put oneself voluntarily into the public eye by running for or occupying public office; by becoming an actor, musician, entertainer, poet, or novelist; by inventing an interesting device or making a geographical or scientific discovery; or even by becoming wealthy. Once a person has become a public figure, he has sacrificed much of his right of privacy to the public's legitimate curiosity. Of course, one never forfeits *all* rights of privacy; even the public figure has a right to the privacy of his very most intimate affairs. (This may, however, be very small consolation to him.)

One cannot always escape the privilege of the press to invade one's privacy simply by avoiding public roles and offices, for the public spotlight can catch up with anyone. "Reluctant public characters" are nonetheless public and therefore, according to the courts, as legitimate objects of public curiosity as the voluntary public figures. Those unfortunates who attract attention unwillingly by becoming involved, even as victims, in accidents, or by being accused of crimes, or even as innocent bystanders to interesting events, have become "news," and therefore subject to the public's right to know. They maintain this unhappy status "until they have reverted to the lawful and unexciting life led by the great bulk of the community," but until then, "they are subject to the privileges which publishers have to satisfy the curiosity of the public as to their leaders, heroes, villains, and victims."[14] Again, the privilege to publish is not unlimited so that "the courts must somehow draw the distinction between conduct which outrages the common decencies and goes beyond what the public mores will tolerate, and that which the plaintiff must be expected in the circumstances to endure."[15]

When interests of quite different kinds head toward collisions, how can one determine which has the right of way? This problem, which lies behind the most puzzling questions about the grounds for liberty and coercion, tends to be concealed by broadly stated principles. The conflict between the personal interest in privacy and the public curiosity is one of the best illustrations of the problem, but it is hardly unique. In defamation cases, as we have seen, there is often a conflict between the public interest in truth and the plaintiff's interest in his own good name. In nuisance law, there is a conflict between the plaintiff's interest in the peaceful enjoyment of his land and the defendant's interest in keeping a hogpen, or a howling dog, or a small boiler factory. In suburban neighborhoods, the residents' interest in quiet often conflicts with motorcyclists' interest in cheap and speedy transportation. In buses and trains, one passenger's interest in privacy[16] can conflict with another's interest in listening to rock and roll music on a portable radio, or for that matter, with the interests of two nearby passengers in making unavoidably audible, but avoidably inane, conversation. The principle of "the more freedom the better" doesn't tell us whose freedom must give way in these competitive situations.

The invasion of privacy cases are among the very clearest examples of the inevitable clash of interests in populous modern communities. They are, moreover, examples that show that solving the problem is not just a matter of minimizing harm all around. Harm is the invasion of an interest, and invasions do differ in degree, but when interests of radically different kinds are invaded to the same degree, where is the greater harm? Perhaps we should say that some interests are more important than others in the sense that harm to them is likely to lead to greater damage to the whole economy of personal (or as the case may be, community) interests than harm to the lesser interest, just as harm to one's heart or brain will do more damage to one's bodily health than an "equal degree" of harm to less vital organs. Determining which interests are more "vital" in an analogous sense would be no easy task, but even if we could settle this matter, there would remain serious difficulties. In the first place, interests pile up and reinforce one another. My interest in peace and quiet may be more vital in my system than the motorcyclist's interests in speed, excitement, and economy are in his, but there is also the interest of the cyclist's employer in having workers efficiently transported to his factory, and the economic interest of the community in general (including me) in the flourishing of the factory owner's business; the interest of the motorcycle manufacturers in their own profits; the interest of the police and others (perhaps including me) in providing a relatively harmless outlet for adolescent exuberance, and in not having a difficult rule to enforce. There may be nowhere near so great a buildup of reinforcing interests, personal and public, in the quietude of my neighborhood.

There is still another kind of consideration that complicates the delicate task of interest-balancing. Interests differ not only in the extent to which they are thwarted, in their importance or "vitality," and the degree to which they are backed up by other interests, but also in their inherent moral quality. Some interests, simply by reason of their very natures, we might think better worth protecting than others. The interest in knowing the intimate details of Brigitte Bardot's married sex life (the subject of a sensational lawsuit in France) is a morally repugnant peeping tom's interest. The sadist's interest in having others suffer pain is a morbid interest. The interest in divulging a celebrity's private conversations is a busybody's interest. It is probably not conducive to the public good to encourage development of the character flaws from which these interests spring, but even if there were social advantage in the individual vices, there would be a case against protecting their spawned interests, based upon their inherent unworthiness. The interests in understanding, diagnosing, and simply being apprised of newsworthy events might well outbalance a given individual's reluctance to be known about, but photographs and descriptions with no plausible appeal except to the morbid and sensational can have very little weight in the scales.

3. *Causing Panic.* Defamatory statements, "malicious truths," and statements that wrongfully invade privacy do harm to the persons they are about by conveying information or falsehood to third parties. Their publication tends to instill certain beliefs in others, and the very existence of those beliefs constitutes a harm to the person spoken or written about. Other classes of injurious expressions do harm in a rather different way, namely, by causing those who listen to them (or more rarely, those who read them) to act in violent or otherwise harmful ways. In these cases, the expressions need not be about any specifiable persons, or if they are about persons, those individuals are not necessarily the victims of the subsequent harm. When spoken words cause panic, breach the peace, or incite to crime or revolt, a variety of important interests, personal and social, will be seriously harmed. Such expressions, therefore, are typically proscribed by the criminal, and not merely the civil, law.

"The most stringent protection of free speech," wrote Holmes in his most celebrated opinion, "would not protect a man in falsely shouting fire in a theatre and causing a panic."[17] In some circumstances a person can cause even more harm by *truthfully* shouting "Fire!" in a crowded theater, for the flames and smoke might reinforce the tendency of his words to cause panic, and the fire itself might block exits, leading the hysterical crowds to push and trample. But we do not, and cannot fairly, hold the excited alarm sounder criminally responsible for his warning when it was in fact true and shouted with good intentions. We can hardly demand on pain of punishment that persons pick their words carefully in emergencies, when emotions naturally run high and there is no time for judicious deliberation. A person's warning shout in such circumstances is hardly to be treated as a full-fledged voluntary act at all. Perhaps it can be condemned as negligent, but given the mitigating circumstances, such negligence hardly amounts to the gross and wanton kind that can be a basis of criminal liability. The law, then, can only punish harmful words of this class when they are spoken or written with the intention of causing the harm that in fact ensues, or when they are spoken or written in conscious disregard of a high and unreasonable risk that the harm will ensue. The practical joker in a crowded auditorium who whispers to his comrade, "Watch me start a panic," and then shouts "Fire!" could be convicted for using words intentionally to cause a panic. The prankster who is willing to risk a general panic just for the fun of alarming one particular person in the audience could fairly be convicted for the grossly reckless use of dangerous words. Indeed, his recklessness is akin to that of the motorist who drives at an excessive speed just to frighten a timorous passenger.

Suppose, however, that the theater is virtually empty, and as the lights come on at the end of the film, our perverse or dim-witted jokester shouts "Fire! Fire!" just for the sake of confusing the three or four other patrons and alarming the ushers. The ushers quickly see through the ruse and suffer only a few moments of anxiety, and the patrons walk quickly to the exits and depart. No harm to speak of has been done; nor could any have reasonably been anticipated. This example shows how very important are the surrounding circumstances of an utterance to the question of its permissibility. Given the presumptive case for liberty in general, and especially the powerful social interest in leaving persons free to use *words* as they see fit, there can be a countervailing case for suppression on the grounds of the words' dangerous tendency only when the danger in fact is great and the tendency immediate. These matters are determined not only by the particular words used, but by the objective character of the surrounding circumstances—what lawyers call "the time, place, and manner" of utterance.

The question of legal permissibility should not be confused with that of moral blameworthiness or even with civil liability. The practical joker, even in relatively harmless circumstances, is no moral paragon. But then neither are the liar, the vulgarian, the rude man, and the scandalmonger, most of whose faults are not fit subjects for penal legislation. We cannot make every instance of mendacity, rudeness, and malicious gossip criminal, but we can protect people from the serious injury that comes from fraud, battery, or defamation. Similarly, practical jokers should be blamed but not punished, unless their tricks reach the threshold of serious danger to others. On the other hand, almost all lies, bad tales, jokes, and tricks create some risk, and there is no injustice in making the perpetrator compensate (as opposed to being punished) even his unlikely victim. Thus, if a patron in the nearly empty theater described above sprains an ankle in hurrying towards an exit, there is no injustice in requiring the jokester to pay the medical expenses.

It is established in our law that when words did not in fact cause harm the speaker may nevertheless be punished for having uttered them only if there was high danger when they were spoken that serious harm would result. This condition of course could be satisfied even though the harm in fact was averted: Not everything probable becomes actual. Similarly, for a person rightly to be punished even for harm in fact caused by his words, the harm in its resultant magnitude must have been an objectively probable consequence of the spoken words in the circumstances; otherwise the speaker will be punished for an unforeseeable fluke. In either case, then, the clear and present danger that serious harm will follow a speaker's words is necessary if he is rightly to be punished.

As we have seen, punishment for the harm caused by words is proper only if the speaker caused the harm either *intentionally* or *recklessly.* Both of these "mental conditions" of guilt require the satisfaction of the clear and present danger formula, or something like it. Consider recklessness first. For there to be recklessness there must really be a substantial risk consciously and unreasonably run. A speaker is not being reckless if he utters words that have only a remote and speculative tendency to cause panics or riots.

Intentional harm-causing by words raises more complications. Suppose an evil-minded person wishes to cause a panic and believes what is false and wholly unsupported by any real evidence, namely, that his words will have that effect. Imagine that he attends a meeting of the Policemen's Benevolent Association and, at what he takes to be the strategic moment, he stands up and shrieks, "There's a mouse under my chair!" Perhaps these words would cause a panic at a meeting of Girl Scouts but it merely produces a round of contemptuous laughter here. Wanting a panic and sincerely believing that one is causing a panic by one's words, then, are not sufficient. Suppose however we complicate the story so that by some wholly unforeseeable fluke the spoken words do precipitate a panic. The story is hard to invent at this point, but let us imagine that one patrolman laughs so hard that he tips over his chair causing another to drop his pipe, starting a fire, igniting live bullets, et cetera. Now, in addition to evil desire, and conscious belief in causal efficacy, we have a third important element: The words actually do initiate a causal process resulting in the desired panic. But these conditions still are not sufficient to permit us to say that the speaker *intentionally caused* a panic. Without the antecedent objective probability that a panic would follow these words in these circumstances, we have only a bizarre but tragic coincidence.

We would say much the same thing of a superstitious lady who "attempts" to start a riot by magic means. In an inconspicuous corner of a darkened theater, she sticks pins into a doll and mutters under her breath a magic incantation designed to produce a panic. Of course this doesn't work in the way intended, but a near-sighted and neurotic passerby observes her, takes the doll to be a real baby, and screams. The hoped-for panic then really follows. The evil lady cannot be found guilty of intentionally causing a panic, even though she intended to cause one and really did cause (or at least initiate a causal process that resulted in) one. She can be condemned for having very evil motives. But if people are sufficiently ignorant and impotent, the law, applying the harm principle, allows them to be as evil as they wish.

4. *Provoking Retaliatory Violence.* Suppose a person utters words which have as their unhappy effects violence directed *at him* by his angry audience, counterviolence by his friends and protectors, and escalation into a riotous breach of the peace. This is still another way of causing harm by words. Should the speaker be punished? In almost every conceivable case, the answer should be No. There is a sense, of course, in which the speaker did not start the physical violence. He used only words, and while words can sting and infuriate, they are not instruments of violence in the same sense that fists, knives, guns, and clubs are. If the law suppresses public speech, either by withholding permits in advance or punishing afterwards, simply on the ground that the expressed views are so unpopular that some auditors can be expected to start fighting, then the law punishes some for the criminal proclivities of others. "A man does not become a criminal because someone else assaults him . . .," writes Zechariah Chafee. Moreover, he continues, on any such theory, "a small number of intolerant men . . . can prevent *any kind* of meeting . . . A gathering which expressed the sentiment of a majority of law-abiding citizens would become illegal because a small gang of hoodlums threatened to invade the hall."[18] When violent response to speech threatens, the obvious remedy is not suppression, but rather increased police protection.

So much seems evident, but there may be some exceptions. Some words uttered in public places in the presence of many unwilling auditors may be so abusive or otherwise offensive as to be "reasonably considered a direct provocation to violence."[19] The captive auditor, after all, is not looking for trouble as he walks the public streets intent on his private errands. If he is forced to

listen, as he walks past a street meeting, to speakers denouncing and ridiculing his religion, and forced to notice a banner with a large and abusive caricature of the Pope,[20] his blood might reasonably be expected to boil. Antireligious and anticlerical opinions, of course, no matter how unpopular, are entitled to the full protection of the law. Even abusive, virulent, and mocking expressions of such views are entitled to full protection if uttered to private gatherings, in private or privately reserved places. Such expressions become provocative only when made in public places to captive auditors.

What makes an expression "provocative?" Surely, if words are to be suppressed on the ground that they are provocative of violence, they must be more than merely "provoking," else all unpopular opinions will be suppressed, to the great public loss. As far as I know, the concept of provocation has received thorough legal elaboration only in the law of homicide, where provocation reduces a charge of murder to that of manslaughter, thus functioning as a kind of mitigating consideration rather than as a justification or complete excuse. In the common law, for there to be sufficient provocation to mitigate: (1) The behavior of the victim must have been so aggravating that it would have produced "such excitement and passion as would obscure the reason of an ordinary man and induce him . . . to strike the blow."[21] (2) There must not have elapsed so much time between the provocation and the violence that a reasonable man's blood would have cooled. (3) But for the victim's provocation the violence would not have occurred. In short, provocation mitigates only when it in fact produces a reason-numbing rage in the attacker and is such that it could be expected to produce such a rage in any normal person in his circumstances. Nazi emblems might be expected to have this effect on a former inmate of a Nazi death camp, but the Democratic party line cannot be sufficiently provocative to excuse a violent Republican, and similarly the other way round. Indeed, in the law of homicide, *no mere words alone,* no matter how abusive or scurrilous, can be adequate provocation to justify or totally excuse killing as a response.

There would seem to be equally good reason not to consider mere words either as justifying or totally excusing nonlethal acts of violence. The "reasonable man" in a democracy must be presumed to have enough self-control to refrain from violent responses to odious words and doctrines. If he is followed, insulted, taunted, and challenged, he can get injunctive relief, or bring charges against his tormentor as a nuisance; if there is no time for this and he is backed to the wall he may be justified in using "reasonable force" in self-defense; or if he is followed to his own home, he can use the police to remove the nuisance. But if he is not personally harrassed in these ways, he can turn on his heels and leave the provocation behind, and this is what the law, perhaps, should require of him.

Only when public speech satisfies stringent tests qualifying it as "direct provocation to violence," (if that is possible at all) will the harm principle justify its suppression. But there are many possible modes of suppression, and some are far more restrictive of liberty than others. Orders to cease and desist on pain of arrest are most economical, for they permit the speaker to continue to air his views in a nonprovocative way or else retire with his audience to a less public place. Lawful removal of the provocation (as a public nuisance) may be more satisfactory than permitting violent response to it, and is infinitely preferable to punishing the speaker. Nowhere in the law where provocation is considered as a defense do the rules deem the proven provoker (the victim) a criminal himself! At best his conduct mitigates the crime of his attacker, who is the only criminal.

One final point. While it is conceivable that some public *speech* can satisfy the common law test for provocation by being so aggravating that even a reasonable man could be expected to lose control of his reason when exposed to it, this can never be true of books. One can always escape the provocation of the printed word simply by declining to read it, and where escape from provocation is that easy, no "reasonable man" will succumb to it.

5. *Incitement to Crime or Insurrection.* In the criminal law, anyone who "counsels, commands, or encourages another to commit a crime" is himself guilty of the resultant crime as an "accessory before the fact." Counseling, commanding, and encouraging, however, must consist in more than merely uttering certain words in the presence of others. Surely there must also be serious (as op-

posed to playful) intent and some possibility at least of the words having their desired effect. It is not possible that these conditions can be satisfied if I tell my secretary that she should overthrow the United States government, or if a speaker tells an audience of bank presidents that they should practice embezzlement whenever they can. These situations are analogous to the efforts to start a panic by magical means or to panic policemen with words about mice.

The problem of interpreting the meaning of a rule making the counseling of crime itself a crime is similar, I should think, to that raised by a statute forbidding the planting of a certain kind of plant. One does not violate such a statute if he scatters the appropriate kind of seeds on asphalt pavement or in barren desert, even with evil intent. (Again, if you are stupid enough, the law—insofar as it derives from the harm principle—can allow you to be as evil as you wish.) To violate the statute, either one would have to dig a little hole in the appropriate sort of soil, deposit the appropriate seeds, cultivate, fertilize, allow for sufficient water, protect against winds, worms, and dogs; *or* one would have to find suitable conditions ready-made, where the soil is already receptive and merely dropping the seeds will create a substantial likelihood that plants will grow and thrive. By analogy, even words of advice, if they are to count as incitements to crime, must fall on reasonably receptive ears. The harm principle provides a ready rationale for this requirement. If we permit coercive repression of nondangerous words we will confer such abundant powers on the repressive organs of the state that they are certain to be abused. Moreover, we will so inhibit persons in their employment of language as to discourage both spontaneity and serious moral discussion, thus doing a great deal of harm and virtually no good at all. (The only "gain," if it is that, to be expected from looser standards of interpretation would be that nondangerous persons with evil motives could be scooped up in the state's tighter nets and punished.)

Counseling others to crime is not the only use of speech that can be described as incitement. We must also come to terms with instigating, egging on, and inflaming others to violence. Even Mill conceded that the opinion that "corn dealers are starvers of the poor," which deserves protection when published in the press, may nevertheless "justly incur punishment when delivered orally to an excited mob assembled before the house of a corn dealer ..."[22] The metaphor of planting seeds in receptive soil is perhaps less apt for this situation than the commonly employed "spark and tinder" analogy. Words which merely express legitimate though unpopular opinion in one context become "incendiary" when addressed to an already inflammable mob. As Chafee put it: "Smoking is all right, but not in a powder magazine."[23] Of course the man who carries a cigar into a powder magazine may not know that the cigar he is carrying is lighted, or he may not know that he has entered a powder magazine. He may plead his lack of intention afterward (if he is still alive) as a defense. Similarly, the man who speaks his opinion to what he takes to be a calm audience, or an excited audience with *different* axes all ground fine, may plead his ignorance in good faith as a defense. But "the law" (as judges are fond of saying) "presumes that a man intends the natural and probable consequences of his actions," so that a defendant who denies that he intended to cause a riot may have the burden of proving his innocent intention to the jury.

In summary, there are two points to emphasize in connection with the punishment of inflammatory incitements. First, the audience must really be tinder, that is to say not merely sullen, but angry to the point of frenzy, and so predisposed to violence. A left-wing radical should be permitted to deliver a revolutionary tirade before the ladies of the D.A.R., even if his final words are "to the barricades!", for that would be to light a match not in a powder magazine but in a Turkish steam bath. Second, no one should be punished for inciting others to violence unless he used words intentionally, or at least recklessly, with respect to that consequence. Otherwise at best a speaker will be punished for his mere negligence, and at worst he will be punished though perfectly innocent.

There is one further problem raised by the concept of incitement as a crime. It might well be asked how one person—the inciter—can be held criminally responsible for the free and deliberate actions of another person—the one who is incited by his words. This problem is common to both kinds of incitement, counseling and inflaming or egging on, but it seems especially puzzling in the case of advising and persuading; for the deliberate, thoughtful, unforced, and undeceived acceptance of the advice of another person is without question itself a voluntary act. Yet there may well be cases which are such that had not the advice been given, the crime would never have been perpetrated, so that the advisor can truly be said to have "got" the advisee to do something he might otherwise never have done. In this case, the initiative was the advisor's, and his advice was the crucial causal factor that led to the criminal act, so that it would be no abuse of usage to call it "the cause." And yet, for all of that, no one *forced* the advisee to act; he could have rejected the advice, but he didn't.

If there is the appearance of paradox in this account, or in the very idea of one person's causing another to act voluntarily, it is no doubt the result of an unduly restrictive conception of what a cause is. There are, of course, a great many ways of causing another person to behave in a given way by the use of words. If we sneak up behind him and shout "boo!" we may startle him so that he jumps and shrieks. In this case our word functioned as a cause not in virtue of its meaning or the mediation of the other person's understanding, but simply as a noise, and the person's startled reaction to this physical stimulus was as involuntary as an eye-twitch or a knee-jerk. Some philosophers would restrict the notion of causing behavior to cases of this kind, but there is no good reason for such a restriction, and a strong case can be built against it based both on its capacity to breed paradox and on common sense and usage. I can "get" an acquaintance to say "Good morning" by putting myself directly in his line of vision, smiling, and saying "Good morning" to him. If I do these things and he predictably responds in the way I intended, I can surely say that my behavior was the cause, in those circumstances, of his behavior; for my conduct is not only a circumstance but for which his action would not have occurred, it is also a circumstance which, when added to those already present, made the difference between his speaking and remaining silent. Yet I did not force him to speak; I did not deceive him; I did not trick him. Rather I exploited those of his known policies and dispositions that made him antecedently "receptive" to my words. To deny that I caused him to act voluntarily, in short, is either to confuse causation with compulsion (a venerable philosophical mistake) or to regard one person's initiative as incompatible with another person's responsibility.[24]

In any case, where one person causes another to act voluntarily either by giving him advice or information or by otherwise capitalizing on his carefully studied dispositions and policies, there is no reason why *both* persons should not be held responsible for the act if it should be criminal. It is just as if the law made it criminal to contribute to a human explosion either by being human dynamite or by being a human spark: either by being predisposed by one's character to crime or by one's passions to violence, or else by providing the words or materials which could fully be anticipated to incite the violent or criminal conduct of others. It is surely no reasonable defense of the spark to say that but for the dynamite there would have been no explosion. Nor is it any more reasonable to defend the dynamite by arguing that but for the spark it should have remained forever quiescent.

There is probably even less reason for excluding from responsibility the speaker haranguing an inflammable mob on the grounds that the individuals in the throng are free adults capable of refraining from violence in the circumstances. A mob might well be understood as a kind of fictitious collective person whose passions are much more easily manipulated and whose actions more easily maneuvered than those of individual persons. If one looks at it this way, the caused behavior of an inflamed mob may be a good deal less than fully voluntary, even though the component individuals in it, being free adults, are all acting voluntarily on their own responsibility.

III SEDITION

Causing panic, provoking violence, and inciting to crime or insurrection are all made punishable by what Chafee calls "the normal criminal law of words."[25] The relevant common law categories are riot, breach of the peace, solicitation, and incitement. All these crimes, as we have seen, require either intentionally harmful or reckless conduct, and all of them require, in addition— and for reasons partly derived from and explicable by the harm principle—that there be some objective likelihood that the relevant sort of harm will be produced by the words uttered in the circumstances. In addition to these traditional common law crimes, many governments have considered it necessary to create statutes making *sedition* a crime. It will be useful to consider the question of sedition against the background of the normal criminal law of words, for this will lead us quickly to two conclusions. The first is that sedition laws are wholly unnecessary to avert the harm they are ostensibly aimed at. The second is that if we must nevertheless put up with sedition laws, they must be applied by the courts in accordance with the same standards of objective likelihood and immediate danger that govern the application of the laws against provoking and inciting violence. Otherwise sedition statutes are likely to do far more social harm than good. Such laws when properly interpreted by enforcers and courts are at best legal redundancies. At worst they are corrosive of the values normally protected by freedom of expression.

The word "sedition," which in its oldest, prelegal sense meant simply divisiveness and strife, has never been the name of a crime in the English common law. Rather the adjective "seditious" forms part of the name of the common law crimes of "seditious words," "seditious libel," and "seditious conspiracy." Apparently the common ingredient in these offenses was so-called "seditious intent." The legal definition of "seditious intent" has changed over the centuries. In the beginning any spoken or written words which in fact had a tendency, however remote, to cause dissension or to weaken the grip of governmental authorities, and were spoken or published intentionally (with or without the further purpose of weakening the government or causing dissension) were held to manifest the requisite intent. In the fifteenth and sixteenth centuries, for example, publicly to call the king a fool, even in jest, was to risk capital punishment. There was to be less danger somewhat later for authors of *printed* words; for all books and printed papers had to be submitted in advance to the censorship (a practice denounced in Milton's eloquent *Areopagitica*), so that authors of politically dangerous words risked not punishment but only prior restraint. There is little evidence, however, that many of them felt more free as a consequence of this development.

The abandonment of the censorship in 1695 was widely hailed as a triumph for freedom of the press, but it was soon replaced by an equally repressive and far more cruel series of criminal trials for "seditious libel." Juries were permitted to decide only narrow factual questions, whereas the matter of "seditious intent" was left up to very conservative judges who knew well where their own personal interests lay. Moreover, truth was not permitted as a defense[26]—a legal restriction which in effect destroyed all right of adverse political criticism. Zechariah Chafee[27] has argued convincingly that the First Amendment to the United States Constitution was proposed and adopted by men who were consciously reacting against the common law of seditious libel, and in particular against the applications of that law in the English trials of the time. "Reform" (of sorts) came in England through Fox's Libel Act of 1792, which allowed juries to decide the question of seditious intent and permitted the truth defense if the opinions were published with good motives. (The ill-advised and short-lived American Sedition Act of 1798 was modeled after this act.) In the hysterical reaction to the French Revolution and the Napoleonic Wars, however, juries proved to be even more savage than judges, and hundreds were punished even for the mildest political unorthodoxy.

Throughout most of the nineteenth century, the prevailing definition of seditious intent in English law derived from a statute passed during the repressive heyday of the Fox Act sedition trials. Men were punished for publishing any words with:

the intention of (1) exciting disaffection, hatred, or contempt against the sovereign, or the government and constitution of the kingdom, or either house of parliament, or the administration of justice, *or* (2) exciting his majesty's subjects to attempt, otherwise than by lawful means, the alteration of any matter in church or state by law established, *or* (3) to promote feelings of ill will and hostility between different classes.[28]

In short, the three possible modes of seditious libel were defamation of the institutions or officers of the government, incitement to unlawful acts, and a use of language that tends toward the breach of the peace "between classes." The normal criminal law of words sufficiently covers the last two modes; and the civil law of defamation would apply to the first. The criminal law, as we have seen, employs a clear and present danger test for incitement and breach of peace, and does

so for good reasons derived from the harm principle and the analysis of "intentional causing." For other good reasons, also derived from the harm principle, the law of defamation privileges fair comment on public officials, and gives no protection at all to institutions. So there would seem to be no further need, at least none demonstrated by the harm principle, for a criminal law of sedition.[29]

Still, many have thought that the harm principle requires sedition laws, and some still do. The issue boils down to the question of whether the normal law of words with its strict standard of immediate danger is too lax to prevent serious harms, and whether, therefore, it needs supplementing by sedition laws employing the looser standards of "bad tendency" and "presumptive intent." By the standard of bad tendency, words can be punished for their dangerous propensity "long before there is any probability that they will break out into unlawful acts";[30] and by the test of presumptive intent, it is necessary only that the defendant intended to publish his words, not that he intended further harm by them. It is clear that most authors of sedition statutes have meant them to be interpreted by the courts in accordance with the tests of bad tendency and presumptive intent (although the United States Supreme Court has in recent decades declared that such interpretations are contrary to the First Amendment of the Constitution). Part of the rationale for the older tests was that if words make a definite contribution to a situation which is on its way to being dangerous, it is folly not to punish them well before that situation reaches the threshold of actual harm. There may seem to be no harm in piling up twigs as such, but if this is done with the purpose (or even the likely outcome) of starting a fire eventually, why not stop it now before it is too late? Those who favor this argument have often employed the harm principle also to defend laws against institutional defamation. The reason why it should be unlawful to bring the Constitution or the courts (or even the *flag*) into disrepute by one's words, they argue, is not simply that such words are offensive, but rather that they tend to undermine respect and loyalty and thereby contribute to more serious harm in the long run.

The focus of the disagreement over sedition laws is the status of *advocacy*. The normal law of words quite clearly outlaws counseling, urging, or demanding (under certain conditions) that others resort to crime or engage in riots, assassinations, or insurrections. But what if a person uses language not directly to counsel or call for violence but rather (where this is different) to *advocate* it? In the wake of the Russian Revolution, many working class parties in America and Europe adopted some variant of an ideology which declared that the propertied classes derived their wealth from the systematic exploitation of the poor; capitalists controlled the major media of news and opinion as well as parliaments and legislators; the grievances of the workers therefore could not be remedied through normal political channels but required instead direct pressure through such means as general strikes, boycotts, and mass demonstrations; and that the working class would inevitably be triumphant in its struggle, expropriate the exploiters, and itself run industry. Spokesmen for this ideology were known for their flamboyant rhetoric, which invariably contained such terms as "arise," "struggle," "victory," and "revolution." Such persons were commonly charged with violations of the Federal Espionage Act during and after World War I, of state sedition laws during the 1920s, and, after World War II, of the Smith Act. Often the key charge in the indictment was "teaching or advocating" riot, assassination, or the violent overthrow of the government.

Trials of Marxists for advocacy of revolution tended to be extremely difficult and problematic partly because it was never clear whether revolution in any usual sense was something taught and approved by them, and partly because it was unclear whether the form of reference to revolution in the Marxist ideology amounted to "advocacy" of it. Marxists disagreed among themselves over the first point. Many thought that forms of group pressure well short of open violence would be sufficient to overturn the capitalists; others thought that "eventually" (when is that?), when conditions were at last ripe, a brief violent seizure of power might be necessary. Does this, in any case, amount to the advocacy of revolution? If it is criminal advocacy to teach that there are conceivable circumstances under which revolution would be justified, then almost everyone, including this author, "advocates" revolution. Suppose one holds further that the "conceivable justifying

conditions" may one day become actual, or that it is even probable that they will be actual at some indeterminate future time. Is this to count as criminal advocacy?

Not according to Justice Holmes in his famous opinion in *U.S. v. Schenk.* Schenk and others had encouraged draft resistance in 1917 by mailing circulars denouncing conscription as unconstitutional and urging in very emotional prose that draft-eligible men "assert their rights." The lower court found this to be advocacy of unlawful conduct, a violation, in particular, of the Espionage Act of 1917. The Supreme Court upheld the conviction but nevertheless laid down in the words of O. W. Holmes the test which was to be applied, in a more generous spirit, in later cases: "The question in every case is whether the words . . . are used in such circumstances and are of such a nature as to create a clear and present danger that they will bring about the substantive evils that Congress has a right to prevent." Since Congress has the right to raise armies, any efforts to interfere by words or action with the exercise of that right are punishable. But the clear and present danger standard brings advocacy under the same kind of test as that used for incitement in the normal law of words. One can "advocate" draft resistance over one's breakfast table to one's daughter (though perhaps not to one's son), but not to a sullen group waiting to be sworn in at the induction center.

There is, on the other hand, never any real danger in this country in permitting the open advocacy of *revolution,* except, perhaps, as Chafee puts it, "in extraordinary times of great tension." He continues:

The chances of success are so infinitesimal that the probability of any serious attempt following the utterances seems too slight to make them punishable. . . . This is especially true if the speaker urges revolution at some future day, so that no immediate check is needed to save the country.[31]

Advocacy of assassination, on the other hand, is less easily tolerated. In the first place, the soil is always more receptive to that seed. It is not that potential assassins are more numerous than potential revolutionaries, although at most times that is true. Potential assassins include among their number persons who are contorted beyond reason by hate, mentally unstable persons, and unpredictable crackpots. Further, a successful assassination requires only one good shot. Since it is more likely to be tried and easier to achieve, its danger is always more "clear and present." There will be many circumstances, therefore, in which Holmes's test would permit advocacy of revolution but punish advocacy of assassination. Still in most contexts of utterance it would punish neither. It should no doubt be criminal for a prominent politician to advocate assassination of the president in a talk over national television, or in a letter to the *New York Times*,[32] but when a patron of a neighborhood tavern heatedly announces to his fellow drinkers that "the bum ought to be shot," the president's life will not be significantly endangered. There are times and places where it doesn't matter in the slightest how carelessly one chooses one's words, and others where one's choice of words can be a matter of life and death.

I shall, in conclusion, sketch a rationale for the clear and present danger test, as a kind of mediating standard for the application of the harm principle in the area of political expression. The natural challenge to the use of that test has been adumbrated above. It is true, one might concede, that the teaching of Communist ideology here and now will not create a clear and present danger of violent revolution. Every one knows that, including the Communists. Every trip, however, begins with some first steps, and that includes trips to forbidden destinations. The beginning steps are meant to increase numbers, add strength, and pick up momentum at later stages. To switch the metaphor to one used previously, the Communists are not just casting seeds on barren ground; their words are also meant to cultivate the ground and irrigate it. If the law prohibits planting a certain kind of shrub and we see people storing the forbidden seeds, garden tools, and fertilizer, and actually digging trenches for irrigation pipes, why wait until they are ready to plant the seed before stopping them? Even at these early stages of preparation, they are clearly attempting to achieve what is forbidden. So the argument goes.

The metaphor employed by the argument, however, is not very favorable to its cause. There is a world of difference between making plans and preparations for a future crime and actually launching an attempt, and this distinction has long been recognized by the ordinary criminal law. Mere preparations without actual steps in the direction of perpetration are not sufficient for the crime of attempt (though if preparation involves talking with collaborators, it may constitute the crime of conspiracy). Not even preliminary "steps" are sufficient; for "the act must reach far enough toward the accomplishment of the desired result to amount to the commencement of the consummation."[33] So the first faltering steps of a surpassingly difficult fifty-year trip toward an illegal goal can hardly qualify as an "attempt" in either the legal or the everyday sense.

If the journey is a collective enterprise, the participants could be charged with *conspiracy* without any violation of usage. The question is whether it would be sound public policy to suppress dissenting voices in this manner so long before they reach the threshold of public danger. The argument to the contrary has been given very clear statement in our time by Zechariah Chafee. Consider what interests are involved when the state employs some coercive technique to prevent a private individual or group from expressing an opinion on some issue of public policy, or from teaching or advocating some political ideology. Chafee would have us put these various interests in the balance to determine their relative weights. In the one pan of the scale, there are the private interests of the suppressed individual or group in having their opinions heard and shared, and in winning support and eventual acceptance for them. These interests will be effectively squelched by state suppression. In the other pan is the public interest in peace and order, and the preservation of democratic institutions. These interests may be endangered to some degree by the advocacy of radical ideologies. Now if these are the only interests involved, there is no question that the public interest (which after all includes all or most private interests) sits heavier in the pan. There is, however, another public interest involved of very considerable weight. That is the public interest in the discovery and dissemination of all information that can have any bearing on public policy, and of all opinions about what public policy should be. The dangers that come from neglecting *that* interest are enormous at all times. (See Part I above.) And the more dangerous the times—the more serious the questions before the country's decision makers (and *especially* when these are questions of war and peace)—the more important it is to keep open all the possible avenues to truth and wisdom.

Only the interest in national safety can outweigh the public interest in open discussion, but *it sits in the scale only to the degree that it is actually imperiled.* From the point of view of the public interest alone, with no consideration whatever of individual rights, it would be folly to sacrifice the social benefits of free speech for the bare possibility that the public safety may be somewhat affected. The greater the certainty and imminence of danger, however, the more the interest in public safety moves on to the scale, until at the point of clear and present danger it is heavy enough to tip the scales its way.

The scales analogy, of course, is only an elaborate metaphor for the sorts of deliberations that must go on among enforcers and interpreters of the law when distinct public interests come into conflict. These clashes of interest are most likely to occur in times of excitement and stress when interest "balancing" calls for a clear eye, a sensitive scale, and a steady hand. At such times the clear and present danger rule is a difficult one to apply, but other guides to decision have invariably gone wrong, while the clear and present danger test has hardly ever been seriously tried. Perhaps that helps account, to some degree, for the sorry human record of cruelty, injustice, and war.

NOTES

1. In Chapter Two of *On Liberty,* not reprinted in this volume.
2. Zechariah Chafee, Jr., *Free Speech in the United States* (1941), p. 33.
3. This point applies especially to discussions of moral, social, political, legal, and economic questions, as well as matters of governmental policy, domestic and foreign. "Cross-examination" in science and philosophy is perhaps less important.
4. Aristotle, *Nicomachean Ethics,* Bk. II, Chap. 6, 1107 [a]. "When a man commits adultery, there is no point in asking whether it was with the right woman or at the right time or in the right way, for to do anything like that is simply wrong."

5. William L. Prosser, *Handbook of the Law of Torts,* 2nd ed. (St. Paul: West Publishing Co., 1955), p. 584.
6. *Ibid.,* p. 631.
7. Fowler V. Harper and Fleming James, Jr., *The Law of Torts* (Boston: Little, Brown and Co., 1956), Vol. I, p. 416. The authors do not endorse this view.
8. *Ibid.*
9. William Blackstone, *Commentaries on the Laws of England,* Vol. III, 1765 Reprint (Boston: Beacon Press, 1962), p. 125.
10. Prosser, *op. cit.,* p. 644.
11. Harper and James, *op. cit.,* p. 680.
12. Prosser, *op. cit.,* p. 642.
13. *Loc. cit.*
14. American Law Institute, *Restatement of the Law of Torts* (St. Paul, 1934) § 867, comment c.
15. Prosser, *op. cit.,* p. 644.
16. "There are two aspects of the interest in seclusion. First, the interest in preventing others from seeing and hearing what one does and says. Second, *the interest in avoiding seeing and hearing what other people do and say.* ... It may be as distasteful to suffer the intrusions of a garrulous and unwelcome guest as to discover an eavesdropper or peeper." Harper and James, *op. cit.,* p. 681. (Emphasis added.)
17. Schenck v. United States, 249 U.S. 47 (1919).
18. Chafee, *op. cit.,* pp. 152, 161, 426. cf. Terminiello v. Chicago 337 U.S. 1, (1949).
19. Chafee, *op. cit.,* p. 426.
20. *Ibid.,* p. 161.
21. Toler v. State, 152 Tenn. 1, 13, 260 S.W. 134 (1923).
22. Mill, *op. cit.,* pp. 67–8.
23. Chafee, *op. cit.,* p. 397.
24. For a more detailed exposition of this view see my "Causing Voluntary Actions" in *Doing and Deserving* (Princeton, N.J.: Princeton University Press, 1970), p. 152.
25. Chafee, *op. cit.,* p. 149.
26. In the words of the great common law judge, William Murray, First Earl of Mansfield, "The Greater the Truth, the Greater the Libel," hence Robert Burns's playful lines in his poem, "The Reproof":
    "Dost not know that old Mansfield
        Who writes like the Bible,
    Says the more 'tis a truth, sir,
        The more 'tis a libel?"
27. Chafee, *op. cit.,* pp. 18–22.
28. *Ibid.,* p. 506.
29. Such things, however, as patriotic sensibilities are capable of being highly *offended* by certain kinds of language. The rationale of sedition laws, therefore, may very well derive from the "offense-principle," which warrants prohibition of offensive behavior even when it is (otherwise) harmless.
30. Chafee, *op. cit.,* p. 24.
31. *Ibid.,* p. 175.
32. In which case the newspaper too would be criminally responsible for publishing the letter.
33. Lee v. Commonwealth, 144 Va. 594, 599, 131 S.E. 212, 214 (1926) as quoted in Rollin M. Perkins, *Criminal Law* (Brooklyn Foundation Press, 1957), p. 482.

LOUIS B. SCHWARTZ

Morals Offenses and the Model Penal Code*

What are the "offenses against morals"? One thinks first of the sexual offenses, adultery, fornication, sodomy, incest, and prostitution, and then, by easy extension, of such sex-related offenses as bigamy, abortion, open lewdness, and obscenity. But if one pauses to reflect on what sets these apart from offenses "against the person," or "against property," or "against public administration," it becomes evident that sexual offenses do not involve violation of moral principles in any peculiar sense. Virtually the entire penal code expresses the community's ideas of morality, or at least of the most egregious immoralities. To steal, to kill, to swear falsely in legal proceedings —these are certainly condemned as much by moral and religious as by secular standards. It also becomes evident that not all sexual behavior commonly condemned by prevailing American penal laws can be subsumed under universal moral precepts. This is certainly the case as to laws regulating contraception and abortion. But it is also true of such relatively uncontroversial (in the Western World) "morals" offenses as bigamy and polygamy; plural marriage arrangements approved by great religions of the majority of mankind can hardly be condemned out-of-hand as "immoralities."

What truly distinguishes the offenses commonly thought of as "against morals" is not their relation to morality but the absence of ordinary justification for punishment by a nontheocratic state. The ordinary justification for secular penal controls is preservation of public order. The king's peace must not be disturbed, or, to put the matter in the language of our time, public security must be preserved. Individuals must be able to go about their lawful pursuits without fear of attack, plunder, or other harm. This is an interest

that only organized law enforcement can effectively safeguard. If individuals had to protect themselves by restricting their movements to avoid dangerous persons or neighborhoods, or by restricting their investments for fear of violent dispossession, or by employing personal bodyguards and armed private police, the economy would suffer, the body politic would be rent by conflict of private armies, and men would still walk in fear.

No such results impend from the commission of "morals offenses." One has only to stroll along certain streets in Amsterdam to see that prostitution may be permitted to flourish openly without impairing personal security, economic prosperity, or indeed the general moral tone of a most respected nation of the Western World. Tangible interests are not threatened by a neighbor's rash decision to marry two wives or (to vary the case for readers who may see this as economic suicide) by a lady's decision to be supported by two husbands, assuming that the arrangement is by agreement of all parties directly involved. An obscene show, the predilection of two deviate males for each other, or the marriage of first cousins— all these leave nonparticipants perfectly free to pursue their own goals without fear or obstacle. The same can be said of certain nonsexual offenses, which I shall accordingly treat in this paper as "morals offenses": cruelty to animals, desecration of a flag or other generally venerated symbol, and mistreatment of a human corpse. What the dominant lawmaking groups appear to be seeking by means of morals legislation is not security and freedom in their own affairs but restraint of conduct by others that is regarded as offensive.

Accordingly, Professor Louis Henkin has suggested[1] that morals legislation may contravene constitutional provisions designed to protect lib-

*From *Columbia Law Review,* Vol. 63, p. 669 (1963). Reprinted by permission of the author and the publisher.

erty, especially the liberty to do as one pleases without legal constraints based solely on religious beliefs. There is wisdom in his warning, and it is the purpose of this article to review in the light of that warning some of the Model Penal Code[2] sections that venture into the difficult area of morals legislation. Preliminarily, I offer some general observations on the point of view that necessarily governed the American Law Institute as a group of would-be lawmakers. We were sensitive, I hope, to the supreme value of individual liberty, but aware also that neither legislatures nor courts will soon accept a radical change in the boundary between permissible social controls and constitutionally protected nonconformity.

I. CONSIDERATIONS IN APPRAISING MORALS LEGISLATION

The first proposition I would emphasize is that a statute appearing to express nothing but religious or moral ideas is often defensible on secular grounds.[3] Perhaps an unrestricted flow of obscenity *will* encourage illicit sexuality or violent assaults on women, as some proponents of the ban believe. Perhaps polygamy and polyandry as well as adultery are condemnable on Benthamite grounds. Perhaps tolerance of homosexuality *will* undermine the courage and discipline of our citizen militia, notwithstanding contrary indications drawn from the history of ancient Greece. The evidence is hopelessly inconclusive. Professor Henkin and I may believe that those who legislate morals are minding other people's business, not their own, but the great majority of people believe that morals of "bad" people do, at least in the long run, threaten the security of the "good" people. Thus, *they* believe that it is their own business they are minding. And that belief is not demonstrably false, any more than it is demonstrably true. It is hard to deny people the right to legislate on the basis of their beliefs not demonstrably erroneous, especially if these beliefs are strongly held by a very large majority. The majority cannot be expected to abandon a credo and its associated sensitivities, however irrational, in deference to a minority's skepticism.

The argument of the preceding paragraph does not mean that all laws designed to enforce morality are acceptable or constitutionally valid if enough people entertain a baseless belief in their social utility. The point is rather that recognizing irrational elements in the controversy over morals legislation, we ought to focus on other elements, about which rational debate and agreement are possible. For example, one can examine side effects of the effort to enforce morality by penal law. One can inquire whether enforcement will be so difficult that the offense will seldom be prosecuted and, therefore, risk of punishment will not in fact operate as a deterrent. One can ask whether the rare prosecutions for sexual derelictions are arbitrarily selected, or facilitate private blackmail or police discriminations more often than general compliance with legal norms. Are police forces, prosecution resources, and court time being wastefully diverted from the central insecurities of our metropolitan life—robbery, burglarly, rape, assault, and governmental corruption?

A second proposition that must be considered in appraising morals legislation is that citizens may legitimately demand of the state protection of their psychological as well as their physical integrity. No one challenges this when the protection takes the form of penal laws guarding against fear caused by threat or menace. This is probably because these are regarded as incipient physical attacks. Criminal libel laws are clearly designed to protect against psychic pain;[4] so also are disorderly conduct laws insofar as they ban loud noises, offensive odors, and tumultuous behavior disturbing the peace. In fact, laws against murder, rape, arson, robbery, burglary, and other violent felonies afford not so much protection against direct attack—that can be done only by self-defense or by having a policeman on hand at the scene of the crime—as psychological security and comfort stemming from the knowledge that the probabilities of attack are lessened by the prospect of punishment and, perhaps, from the knowledge that an attacker will be condignly treated by society.

If, then, penal law frequently or typically protects us from psychic aggression, there is basis for the popular expectation that it will protect us also from blasphemy against a cherished religion, outrage to patriotic sentiments, blatant pornography, open lewdness affronting our sensibilities in the area of sexual mores, or stinging aspersions against race or nationality. Psychiatrists might tell us that the insecurities stirred by these psychic aggressions are deeper and more acute than those involved in crimes of physical violence. Physical violence is, after all, a phenomenon that occurs largely in the domain of the ego; we can rationally measure the danger and its likelihood, and our countermeasures can be proportioned to the threat. But who can measure the dark turbulences of the unconscious when sex, race, religion or patriotism (that extension of father-reverence) is the concern?

If unanimity of strongly held moral views is approached in a community, the rebel puts himself, as it were, outside the society when he arraigns himself against those views. Society owes debt to martyrs, madmen, criminals, and professors who occasionally call into question its fundamental assumptions, but the community cannot be expected to make their first protests respectable or even tolerated by law. It is entirely understandable and in a sense proper that blasphemy should have been criminal in Puritan Massachusetts, and that cow slaughter in a Hindu state, hog-raising in a theocratic Jewish or Moslem state, or abortion in a ninety-nine per cent Catholic state should be criminal. I do not mean to suggest a particular percentage test of substantial unanimity. It is rather a matter of when an ancient and unquestioned tenet has become seriously debatable in a given community. This may happen when it is discovered that a substantial, although inarticulate, segment of the population has drifted away from the old belief. It may happen when smaller numbers of articulate opinion-makers launch an open attack on the old ethic. When this kind of a beach-head has been established in the hostile country of traditional faith, then, and only then, can we expect constitutional principles to restrain the fifty-one per cent majority from suppressing the public flouting of deeply held moral views.

Some may find in all this an encouragement or approval of excessive conservatism. Societies, it seems, are by this argument morally entitled to use force to hold back the development of new ways of thought. I do not mean it so. Rather, I see this tendency to enforce old moralities as an inherent characteristic of organized societies, and I refrain from making moral judgments on group behavior that I regard as inevitable. If I must make a moral judgment, it is in favor of the individual visionaries who are willing to pay the personal cost to challenge the old moral order.

There is a morality in some lawbreaking, even when we cannot condemn the law itself as immoral, for it enables conservative societies to begin the re-examination of even the most cherished principles.

Needless to say, recognizing the legitimacy of the demand for protection against psychic discomfort does not imply indiscriminate approval of laws intended to give such protection. Giving full recognition to that demand, we may still find that other considerations are the controlling ones. Can we satisfy the demand without impairing other vital interests? How can we protect religious feelings without "establishing" religion or impairing the free exercise of proselytizing faiths? How can we protect racial sensibilities without exacerbating race hatreds and erecting a government censorship of discussion?[5] How shall we prevent pain and disgust to many who are deeply offended by portrayal of sensuality without stultifying our artists and writers?

A third aspect of morals legislation that will enter into the calculations of the rational legislator is that some protection against offensive immorality may be achieved as a by-product of legislation that aims directly at something other than immorality. We may be uneasy about attempting to regulate private sexual behavior, but we will not be so hesitant in prohibiting the commercialization of vice. This is a lesser intrusion on freedom of choice in personal relations. It presents a more realistic target for police activity. And conceptually such regulation presents itself as a ban on a form of economic activity rather than a regulation of morals. It is not the least of the advantages of this approach that it preserves to some extent the communal disapproval of illicit sexuality, thus partially satisfying those who would really prefer outright regulation of morality. So also, we may be reluctant to penalize blasphemy or sacrilege, but feel compelled to penalize the mischievous or zealous blasphemer who purposely disrupts a religious meeting or procession with utterances designed to outrage the sensibilities of the group and thus provoke a riot.[6] Reasonable rules for the maintenance of public peace incidentally afford a measure of protection against offensive irreligion. Qualms about public "establishment" of religion must yield to the fact that the alternative would be to permit a kind of violent private interference with freedom to conduct religious ceremonies.

It remains to apply the foregoing analysis to selected provisions of the Model Penal Code.

II. THE MODEL PENAL CODE APPROACH

A. FLAGRANT AFFRONTS AND PENALIZATION OF PRIVATE IMMORALITY

The Model Penal Code does not penalize the sexual sins, fornication, adultery, sodomy or other illicit sexual activity not involving violence or imposition upon children, mental incompetents, wards, or other dependents. This decision to keep penal law out of the area of private sexual relations approaches Professor Henkin's suggestion that private morality be immune from secular regulation. The Comments in Tentative Draft No. 4 declared:

The Code does not attempt to use the power of the state to enforce purely moral or religious standards. We deem it inappropriate for the government to attempt to control behavior that has no substantial significance except as to the morality of the actor. Such matters are best left to religious, educational and other social influences. Apart from the question of constitutionality which might be raised against legislation avowedly commanding adherence to a particular religious or moral tenet, it must be recognized, as a practical matter, that in a heterogeneous community such as ours, different individuals and groups have widely divergent views of the seriousness of various moral derelictions.[7]

Although this passage expresses doubt as to the constitutionality of state regulation of morals, it does so in a context of "widely divergent views of the seriousness of various moral derelictions." Thus, it does not exclude the use of penal sanctions to protect a "moral consensus" against flagrant breach. The Kinsey studies and others are cited to show that sexual derelictions are widespread and that the incidence of sexual dereliction varies among social groups. The Comments proceed to discuss various secular goals that might be served by penalizing illicit sexual relations, such as promoting the stability of marriage, preventing illegitimacy and disease, or forestalling private violence against seducers. The

judgment is made that there is no reliable basis for believing that penal laws substantially contribute to these goals. Punishment of private vice is rejected on this ground as well as on grounds of difficulty of enforcement and the potential for blackmail and other abuse of rarely enforced criminal statutes.[8] The discussion with regard to homosexual offenses follows a similar course.[9]

The Code does, however, penalize "open lewdness"—"any lewd act which [the actor] ... knows is likely to be observed by others who would be affronted or alarmed."[10] The idea that "flagrant affront to commonly held notions of morality" might have to be differentiated from other sorts of immorality appeared in the first discussions of the Institute's policy on sexual offenses, in connection with a draft that would have penalized "open and notorious" illicit relations.[11] Eventually, however, the decision was against establishing a penal offense in which guilt would depend on the level of gossip to which the moral transgression gave rise. Guilt under the open lewdness section turns on the likelihood that the lewd act itself will be observed by others who would be affronted.

Since the Code accepts the propriety of penalizing behavior that affects others only in flagrantly affronting commonly held notions of morality, the question arises whether such repression of offensive immorality need be confined to acts done in public where others may observe and be outraged. People may be deeply offended upon learning of private debauchery. The Code seems ready at times to protect against this type of "psychological assault," at other times not. Section 250.10 penalizes mistreatment of a corpse "in a way that [the actor] ... knows would outrage ordinary family sensibilities," although the actor may have taken every precaution for secrecy. Section 250.11 penalizes cruel treatment of an animal in private as well as in public. On the other hand, desecration of the national flag or other object of public veneration, an offense under section 250.9, is not committed unless others are likely to "observe or discover." And solicitation of deviate sexual relations is penalized only when the actor "loiters in or near any public place" for the purpose of such solicitation.[12] The Comments make it clear that the target of this legislation is not private immorality but a kind of public "nuisance" caused by congregation of homosexuals offensively flaunting their deviance from general norms of behavior.[13]

As I search for the principle of discrimination between the morals offenses made punishable only when committed openly and those punishable even when committed in secrecy, I find nothing but differences in the intensity of the aversion with which the different kinds of behavior are regarded. It was the intuition of the draftsman and his fellow lawmakers in the Institute that disrespectful behavior to a corpse and cruelty to animals were more intolerable affronts to ordinary feelings than disrespectful behavior to a flag. Therefore, in the former cases, but not the latter, we overcame our general reluctance to extend penal controls of immorality to private behavior that disquiets people solely because they learn that things of this sort are going on.

Other possible explanations do not satisfy me. For example, it explains nothing to say that we wish to "protect" the corpse or the mistreated dog, but not the flag itself. The legislation on its face seeks to deter mistreatment of all three. All three cases involve interests beyond, and merely represented by, the thing that is immediately "protected." It is not the mistreated dog who is the ultimate object of concern; his owner is entirely free to kill him (though not "cruelly") without interference from other dog owners. Our concern is for the feelings of other human beings, a large proportion of whom, although accustomed to the slaughter of animals for food, readily identify themselves with a tortured dog or horse and respond with great sensitivity to its sufferings. The desire to protect a corpse from degradation is not a deference to this remnant of a human being—the dead have no legal rights and no legislative lobby—but a protection of the feelings of the living. So also in the case of the flag, our concern is not for the bright bit of cloth but for what it symbolizes, a cluster of patriotic emotions. I submit that legislative tolerance for private flag desecration is explicable by the greater difficulty an ordinary man has in identifying with a country and all else that a flag symbolizes as compared with the ease in identifying with a corpse or a warm-blooded domestic animal. This is only an elaborate way of saying that he does not feel the first desecration as keenly as the others. Perhaps also, in the case of the flag, an element of tolerance is present for the right of political dissent when it goes no further than private disrespect for the symbol of authority.[14]

A penal code's treatment of private homosexual relations presents the crucial test of a legislator's views on whether a state may legimately protect people from "psychological assault" by repressing not merely overt affront to consensus morals but also the most secret violation of that moral code. As is often wise in legislative affairs, the Model Penal Code avoids a clear issue of principle. The decision against penalizing deviate sexuality is rested not merely on the idea of immunity from regulation of private morality, but on a consideration of practical difficulties and evils in attempting to use the penal law in this way.[15] The Comments note that existing laws dealing with homosexual relations are nullified in practice, except in cases of violence, corruption of children, or public solicitation. Capricious selection of a few cases for prosecution, among millions of infractions, is unfair and chiefly benefits extortioners and seekers of private vengeance. The existence of the criminal law prevents some deviates from seeking psychiatric aid. Furthermore, the pursuit of homosexuals involves policemen in degrading entrapment practices, and diverts attention and effort that could be employed more usefully against the crimes of violent aggression, fraud, and government corruption, which are the overriding concerns of our metropolitan civilization.

If state legislators are not persuaded by such arguments to repeal the laws against private deviate sexual relations among adults, the constitutional issue will ultimately have to be faced by the courts. When that time comes, one of the important questions will be whether homosexuality is in fact the subject of a "consensus." If not, that is, if a substantial body of public opinion regards homosexuals' private activity with indifference, or if homosexuals succeed in securing recognition as a considerable minority having otherwise "respectable" status, this issue of private morality may soon be held to be beyond resolution by vote of fifty-one per cent of the legislators.[16] As to the status of homosexuality in this country, it is significant that the Supreme Court has reversed an obscenity conviction involving a magazine that was avowedly published by, for, and about homosexuals and that carried on a ceaseless campaign against the repressive laws.[17] The much smaller group of American polygamists have yet to break out of the class of idiosyncratic heretic-martyrs[18] by bidding for public approval in the same group-conscious way.

B. THE OBSCENITY PROVISIONS

The obscenity provisions of the Model Penal Code best illustrate the Code's preference for an oblique approach to morals offenses, that is, the effort to express the moral impulses of the community in a penal prohibition that is nevertheless pointed at and limited to something else than sin. In this case the target is not the "sin of obscenity," but primarily a disapproved form of economic activity—commercial exploitation of the widespread weakness for titillation by pornography. This is apparent not only from the narrow definition of "obscene" in section 251.4 of the Code, but even more from the narrow definition of the forbidden behavior; only sale, advertising, or public exhibition are forbidden, and noncommercial dissemination within a restricted circle of personal associates is expressly exempt.[19]

Section 251.4 defines obscenity as material whose "predominant appeal is to prurient interest...."[20] The emphasis is on the "appeal" of the material, rather than on its "effect," an emphasis designed explicitly to reject prevailing definitions of obscenity that stress the "effect."[21] This effect is traditionally identified as a tendency to cause "sexually impure and lustful thoughts" or to "corrupt or deprave."[22] The Comments on section 251.4 take the position that repression of sexual thoughts and desires is not a practicable or legitimate legislative goal. Too many instigations to sexual desire exist in a society like ours, which approves much eroticism in literature, movies, and advertising, to suppose that any conceivable repression of pornography would substantially diminish the volume of such impulses. Moreover, "thoughts and desires not manifested in overt antisocial behavior are generally regarded as the exclusive concern of the individual and his spiritual advisors."[23] The Comments, rejecting also the test of tendency to corrupt or deprave, point out that corruption or depravity are attributes of character inappropriate for secular punishment when they do not lead to misconduct, and there is a paucity of evidence linking obscenity to misbehavior.[24]

The meretricious "appeal" of a book or picture is essentially a question of the attractiveness of the merchandise from a certain point of view: what makes it sell. Thus, the prohibition of obscenity takes on an aspect of regulation of unfair business or competitive practices. Just as merchants may be prohibited from selling their wares by appeal to the public's weakness for gambling,[25] so they may be restrained from purveying books, movies, or other commercial exhibition by exploiting the well-nigh universal weakness for a look behind the curtain of modesty. This same philosophy of obscenity control is evidenced by the Code provision outlawing advertising appeals that attempt to sell material "whether or not obscene, by representing or suggesting that it is obscene."[26] Moreover, the requirement under section 251.4 that the material go "substantially beyond customary limits of candor" serves to exclude from criminality the sorts of appeal to eroticism that, being prevalent, can hardly give a particular purveyor a commercial advantage.

It is important to recognize that material may predominantly "appeal" to prurient interest notwithstanding that ordinary adults may actually respond to the material with feelings of aversion or disgust. Section 251.4 explicitly encompasses material dealing with excretory functions as well as sex, which the customer is likely to find *both* repugnant and "shameful" and yet attractive in a morbid, compelling way. Not recognizing that material may be repellent and appealing at the same time, two distinguished commentators on the Code's obscenity provisions have criticized the "appeal" formula, asserting that "hard core pornography," concededly the main category we are trying to repress, has no appeal for "ordinary adults," who instead would be merely repelled by the material.[27] Common experience suggests the contrary. It is well known that policemen, lawyers, and judges involved in obscenity cases not infrequently regale their fellows with viewings of the criminal material. Moreover, a poll conducted by this author among his fellow law professors—"mature" and, for the present purposes, "ordinary" adults—evoked uniformly affirmative answers to the following question: "Would you look inside a book that you had been certainly informed has grossly obscene hard-core pornography if you were absolutely sure that no one else would ever learn that you had looked?"

It is not an answer to this bit of amateur sociological research to say that people would look "out of curiosity." It is precisely such shameful curiosity to which "appeal" is made by the obscene, as the word "appeal" is used in section 251.4.

Lockhart and McClure, the two commentators referred to above, prefer a "variable obscenity" concept over the Institute's "constant obscenity" concept. Under the "constant obscenity" concept, material is normally judged by reference to "ordinary adults."[28] The "variable obscenity" concept always takes account of the nature of the comtemplated audience; material would be obscene if it is "primarily directed to an audience of the sexually immature for the purpose of satisfying their craving for erotic fantasy."[29] The preference for "variable obscenity" rests not only on the mistaken view that hard-core pornography does not appeal to ordinary adults, but also on the ground that this concept facilitates the accomplishment of several ancillary legislative goals, namely, exempting transactions in "obscene" materials by persons with scholarly, scientific, or other legitimate interests in the obscene and prohibiting the advertising of material "not intrinsically pornographic as if it were hard-core pornography."[30] The Code accomplishes these results by explicit exemption for justifiable transactions in the obscene and by specific prohibition of suggestive advertising.[31] This still seems to me the better way to draft a criminal statute.

The Code's exemption for justifiable dealing in obscene material provides a workable criterion of public gain in permitting defined categories of transactions. It requires no analysis of the psyche of customers to see whether they are sexually immature or given to unusual craving for erotic fantasy. It makes no impractical demand on the sophistication of policemen, magistrates, customs officers, or jurymen. The semantics of the variable obscenity concept assumes without basis that the Kinsey researchers were immune to the prurient appeal of the materials with which they worked.[32] Would it not be a safe psychiatric guess that some persons are drawn into research of this sort precisely to satisfy in a socially approved way the craving that Lockhart and McClure deplore? In any event, it seems a confusing distortion of language to say that a pornographic picture is not obscene as respects the blasé [sexually mature?] shopkeeper who stocks it, the policeman who confiscates it, or the Model Penal Code reporter who appraises it.

As for the prohibition against suggestive advertising, this is certainly handled more effectively by explicitly declaring the advertisement criminal without regard to the "obscene" character of the material advertised than by the circumlocution that an advertisement is itself to be regarded as obscene if it appeals to the cravings of the sexually immature. That kind of test will prove more than a little troublesome for the advertising departments of some respectable literary journals.

If the gist of section 251.4 is, as suggested above, commercial exploitation of the weakness for obscenity, the question arises whether the definition of the offense should not be formulated in terms of "pandering to an interest in obscenity," that is, "exploiting such an interest primarily for pecuniary gain. . . . "[33] This proposal, made by Professor Henry Hart, a member of the Criminal Law Advisory Committee, was rejected because of the indefiniteness of "exploiting . . . primarily for pecuniary gain," and because it would clearly authorize a bookseller, for example, to procure any sort of hard-core pornography upon the unsolicited order of a customer. "Exploiting . . . primarily for pecuniary gain" is not a formula apt for guiding either judicial interpretation or merchants' behavior. It is not clear what the prosecution would have to prove beyond sale of the objectionable item. Would advertising or an excessive profit convert sale into "exploitation"? Would the formula leave a bookseller free to enjoy a gradually expanding trade in obscenity so long as he kept his merchandise discreetly under the counter and let word-of-mouth publicize the availability of his tidbits? Despite these difficulties, it may well be that the Code section on obscenity has a constitutional infirmity of the sort that concerned Professor Henkin insofar as the section restricts the freedom of an adult to buy, and thus to read, whatever he pleases. This problem might be met by framing an appropriate exemption for such transactions to be added to those now set forth in subsection (3).

The rejection of the Hart "pandering" formulation highlights another aspect of section 251.4, namely, its applicability to a class of completely noncommercial transactions that could not conceivably be regarded as "pandering." This ban on certain noncommercial disseminations results

from the fact that subsection (2) forbids every
dissemination except those exempted by subsection (3), and subsection (3) exempts noncommercial dissemination only if it is limited to "personal
associates of the actor." Thus, a general distribution or exhibition of obscenity is prohibited even
though no one is making money from it: a zealot
for sex education may not give away pamphlets
at the schoolyard gates containing illustrations of
people engaged in erotic practices; a rich homosexual may not use a billboard on Times Square
to promulgate to the general populace the techniques and pleasures of sodomy. Plainly, this is
not the economic regulation to which I have previously tried to assimilate the Code's anti-
obscenity regulations. But equally, it is not
merely sin-control of the sort that evoked Professor Henkin's constitutional doubts. Instead, the
community is merely saying: "Sin, if you must, in
private. Do not flaunt your immoralities where
they will grieve and shock others. If we do not
impose our morals upon you, neither must you
impose yours upon us, undermining the restraints
we seek to cultivate through family, church, and
school." The interest being protected is not, directly or exclusively, the souls of those who might
be depraved or corrupted by the obscenity, but
the right of parents to shape the moral notions of
their children, and the right of the general public
not to be subjected to violent psychological
affront.

C. PROSTITUTION

The prostitution provisions of the Model Penal
Code, like the obscenity provisions, reflect the
policy of penalizing not sin but commercial exploitation of a human weakness, or serious affront
to public sensibilities. The salient features of section 251.2 are as follows. Sexual activity is penalized only when carried on as a business or for
hire. The section covers any form of sexual gratification. "Promoters" of prostitution—that is,
procurers, pimps, keepers of houses of prostitution—are penalized more severely than the prostitutes. The patron of the prostitute is subject to
prosecution for a "violation" only, that is, he may
be fined but not jailed, and the offense is, by definition, not a "crime." Dependents of a prostitute
are not declared to be criminals by virtue of the
fact that they live off the proceeds of prostitution,
as under many present laws, but the circumstance

of being supported by a prostitute is made presumptive evidence that the person supported is
engaged in pimping or some other form of commercial exploitation of prostitution.

The main issues in the evolution of the Institute's position on prostitution were, on the one
hand, whether to penalize all "promiscuous" intercourse even if not for hire or, on the other
hand, whether even intercourse for hire should be
immune from prosecution when it is carried on
discreetly out of the public view. Those who favored extending the criminal law to promiscuous
noncommercial sexuality did so on secular, not
moral, grounds. They pointed to the danger that
promiscuous amateurs would be carriers of vene-
real disease, and they argued that law enforcement against hire-prostitution would be
facilitated if the law, proceeding on the basis that
most promiscuity is accompanied by hire, dispensed with proof of actual hire. Others doubted
the utility or propriety of the law's intervening in
private sexual relations on the basis of a vague
and moralistic judgment of promiscuity; and
these doubts prevailed.

It was more strenuously contended that the
Model Penal Code should, following the English
pattern, penalize prostitution only when it manifests itself in annoying public solicitation.[34] This
position was defeated principally by the argument that "call-houses" were an important cog in
the financial machine of the underworld, linked
to narcotics peddling and other "rackets." I find
more interesting and persuasive the parallel between this problem of the discreet exploitation of
sex and the suggestion in the obscenity and context that discreet sale of obscene books to patrons
who request them might not constitute "pandering." Both distinctions present the difficulty of
drawing an administrable line between aggressive
merchandising and passive willingness to make
profits by catering to a taste for spicy life or literature.

Other provisions of section 251.2 also demonstrate its basic orientation against undesirable
commerce rather than sin. The grading of
offenses under the section ranges from the classification of the patron's guilt as a noncriminal "violation," through the "petty misdemeanor"
classification (thirty-day maximum imprisonment) for the prostitute herself, and the "misdemeanor" classification (one year maximum) for

minor participation in the promotion of prostitution, to the "third degree felony" classification (five year maximum) for owning or managing a prostitution business, bringing about an association between a prostitute and a house of prostitution, or recruiting persons into prostitution. Clearly, from the point of view of the sinfulness of illicit sexual relations, the patron's guilt is equal to that of the prostitute, but it is the seller rather than the sinful customer who is labelled a criminal. And the higher the rank in the selling organization, the graver the penalty—a significant departure from the normal assimilation of accessorial guilt to that of the principal offender. This emphasis on the businessman in sex is underscored by the fact that the higher penalties applicable to him do not depend on whether he is the instigator of the relationship; if a prostitute persuades someone to manage her illicit business or to accept her in a house of prostitution, it is he, not she, who incurs the higher penalty.

In one respect, the Code's provisions against illicit sexual activity depart from the regulation of commerce. Section 251.3 makes it a petty misdemeanor to loiter "in or near any public place for the purpose of soliciting or being solicited to engage in deviate sexual relations." This extension is explained as follows in the accompanying status note:

[T]he main objective is to suppress the open flouting of prevailing moral standards as a sort of nuisance in public thoroughfares and parks. In the case of females, suppression of professionals is likely to accomplish that objective. In the case of males, there is a greater likelihood that non-professional homosexuals will congregate and behave in a manner grossly offensive to other users of public facilities.[35]

The situation is analogous to that of noncommercial dissemination of obscenity by billboard publication or indiscriminate gratuitous distribution of pornography. In a community in which assemblages of "available" women evoke the same degree of violent resentment as assemblages of homosexuals, it would be consistent with this analysis to make public loitering to solicit illicit heterosexual relations an offense regardless of proof of "hire." On the other hand, the legislator may well decide that even in such a community it is not worth risking the possibility of arbitrary police intrusion into dance halls, taverns, corner drug stores, and similar resorts of unattached adolescents, on suspicion that some of the girls are promiscuous, though not prostitutes in the hire sense . . .

NOTES

1.   See Henkin, *Morals and the Constitution: The Sin of Obscenity*, 63 Colum. L. Rev. 391 (1963), to which the present article is a companion piece. Controversy on the role of the state in the enforcement of morals has recently reached a new pitch of intensity. See Hart, *Law, Liberty, and Morality* (1963); Devlin, *The Enforcement of Morals* (1959); Devlin, *Law, Democracy, and Morality*, 110 U. Pa. L. Rev. 635 (1962). I shall not attempt to judge this debate, cf. Rostow, The Sovereign Prerogative 45–80 (1962), and I leave it to others to align the present essay with one or another of the sides. The recent controversy traverses much the same ground as was surveyed in the nineteenth century. See Mill *On Liberty* (1859); Stephen, *Liberty, Equality, Fraternity* (1873).

2.   The Model Penal Code is hereinafter cited as MPC. Unless otherwise indicated, all citations are to the 1962 Official Draft.

3.   See McGowan v. Maryland, 366 U.S. 420 (1961). The Supreme Court upheld the constitutionality of a law requiring business establishments to close on Sunday, on the ground that such regulation serves the secular goal of providing a common day of rest and recreation, notwithstanding that the statute proscribed profanation of "the Lord's day."

4.   The Model Penal Code does not make libel a criminal offense. But this decision rests upon a judgment that the penal law is not a useful or safe instrument for repressing defamation; by no means is it suggested that the hurt experienced by one who is libelled is an inappropriate concern of government. See MPC § 250.7, comment 2 (Tent. Draft No. 13, 1961).

5.   See MPC § 250.7 & comments 1–4 (Tent. Draft No. 13, 1961) ("Fomenting Group Hatred"). The section was not included in the Official Draft of 1962.

6.   See MPC §§ 250.8, 250.3 & comment (Tent. Draft No. 13, 1961).

7.   MPC § 207.1, comment at 207 (Tent. Draft No. 4, 1955).

8.   MPC § 207.1, comment at 205–10 (Tent. Draft No. 4, 1955).

9.   MPC § 207.5, comment at 278–79 (Tent. Draft NO. 4, 1955). "No harm to the secular interests of the community is involved in atypical sex practice in private between consenting adult partners. This area of private morals is the distinctive concern of spiritual authorities. . . . [T]here is the fundamental question of the protection to which every individual is entitled against state interference in his personal affairs when he is not hurting others." MPC § 207.5, comment at 277–78 (Tent. Draft No. 4, 1955).

10.   MPC § 251.1; *cf.* MPC § 213.5, which penalizes exposure of the genitals for the purpose of arousing or gratifying sexual desire in circumstances likely to cause affront or alarm. This later offense carries a heavier penalty than open lewdness, "since the behavior amounts to, or at least is often taken as, threatening sexual aggression." MPC § 213.4 & 251.1, comment at 82 (Tent. Draft No. 13, 1961).

11.   MPC § 207.1 & comment at 209 (Tent. Draft No. 4, 1955).

12.   MPC § 251.3; see text accompanying note 35 *infra.*

13.   MPC § 251.3, status note at 237.

14.   Not all legislatures are so restrained. See, e.g., Pa. Stat. Ann. tit. 18, § 4211 (1945) ("publicly or privately muti-

lates, defaces, defiles or tramples upon, or casts contempt either by words or act upon, any such flag"). Query as to the constitutionality of this effort to repress a private expression of political disaffection.

15.   MPC § 207.5, comment 278–79 (Tent. Draft No. 4, 1955).

16.   *Cf.* Robinson v. California, 371 U.S. 905 (1962) (invalidating statute that penalized addiction to narcotics).

17.   One, Inc. v. Oleson, 355 U.S. 371 (1958), *reversing* 241 F.2d 772 (9th Cir. 1957). On the "homosexual community" see Helmer, *New York's "Middle-class" Homosexuals,* Harper's, March 1963, p. 85 (evidencing current nonshocked attitude toward this minority group).

18.   See Cleveland v. United States, 329 U.S. 14 (1946); Reynolds v. United States, 98 U.S. 145 (1878).

19.   MPC § 251.4(2), (3).

20.   (1) *Obscene Defined.* Material is obscene if, considered as a whole, its predominant appeal is to prurient interest, that is, a shameful or morbid interest, in nudity, sex or excretion, and if in addition it goes substantially beyond customary limits of candor in describing or representing such matters. Predominant appeal shall be judged with reference to ordinary adults unless it appears from the character of the material or the circumstances of its dissemination to be designed for children or other specially susceptible audience. . . . MPC § 251.4(1).

21.   See MPC § 207.10, comment 6 at 19, 29 (Tent. Draft No. 6, 1957) (§ 207.10 was subsequently renumbered § 251.4).

22.   See MPC § 207.10, comment 6 at 19 n.21, 21 (Tent. Draft No. 6, 1957).

23.   MPC § 207.10, comment 6 at 20 (Tent. Draft No. 6, 1957).

24.   MPC § 207.10, comment 6 at 22–28 (Tent. Draft No. 6, 1957).

25.   See FTC v. R. F. Keppel & Brother, 291 U.S. 304 (1934) (sale of penny candy by device of awarding prizes to lucky purchasers of some pieces). The opinion of the Court declares that Section 5 of the Federal Trade Commission Act, proscribing unfair methods of competition, "does not authorize business men," *ibid.,* p. 313, but that the Commission may prevent exploitation of consumers by the enticement of gambling, as well as imposition upon competitors by use of a morally obnoxious selling appeal.

26.   MPC § 251.4(2)(e). Equivalent provisions appear in some state laws. E.g., N.Y. Pen. Law § 1141. There is some doubt whether federal obscenity laws reach such advertising. See Manual Enterprises, Inc. v. Day, 370 U.S. 478. 491 (1962). *But* see United States v. Hornick, 229 F.2d 120, 121 (3d Cir. 1956).

27.   See Lockhart & McClure, *Censorship of Obscenity: The Developing Constitutional Standards,* 45 Minn. L. Rev. 72–73 (1960).

28.   The Model Penal Code employs the "variable obscenity" concept in part, since § 251.4(1) provides that "appeal" shall be judged with reference to the susceptibilities of children or other specially susceptible audience when it appears that the material is designed for or directed to such an audience.

29.   Lockhart & McClure, *supra* note 27, at 79.

30.   *Ibid.*

31.   MPC § 251.4(2)(e), (3)(a).

32.   *Cf.* United States v. 31 Photographs, 156 F. Supp. 350 (S.D.N.Y. 1957), in which, absent a statutory exemption, the court was compelled to rely on variable obscenity in order to sanction import of obscene pictures by the [Kinsey] Institute for Sex Research.

33.   MPC § 207.10(1) (Tent. Draft No. 6, 1957) (alternative).

34.   See Street Offenses Act, 1959, 7 & 8 Eliz. 2, c. 57.

COHEN V. CALIFORNIA

United States Supreme Court, 1971*

OPINION OF THE COURT

Mr. Justice Harlan delivered the opinion of the Court.

This case may seem at first blush too inconsequential to find its way into our books, but the issue it presents is of no small constitutional significance.

Appellant Paul Robert Cohen was convicted in the Los Angeles Municipal Court of violating that part of California Penal Code § 415 which prohibits "maliciously and willfully disturb[ing] the peace or quiet of any neighborhood or person . . . by . . . offensive conduct . . . "[1] He was given 30 days' imprisonment. The facts upon which his conviction rests are detailed in the opinion of the Court of Appeal of California, Second Appellate District, as follows:

*408 U.S. 15 (1971). Some footnotes omitted.

"On April 26, 1968, the defendant was observed in the Los Angeles County Courthouse in the corridor outside of division 20 of the municipal court wearing a jacket bearing the words 'Fuck the Draft' which were plainly visible. There were women and children present in the corridor. The defendant was arrested. The defendant testified that he wore the jacket knowing that the words were on the jacket as a means of informing the public of the depth of his feelings against the Vietnam War and the draft.

"The defendant did not engage in, nor threaten to engage in, nor did anyone as the result of his conduct in fact commit or threaten to commit any act of violence. The defendant did not make any loud or unusual noise, nor was there any evidence that he uttered any sound prior to his arrest."*

In affirming the conviction the Court of Appeal held that "offensive conduct" means "behavior which has a tendency to provoke *others* to acts of violence or to in turn disturb the peace," and that the State had proved this element because, on the facts of this case, "[i]t was certainly reasonably foreseeable that such conduct might cause others to rise up to commit a violent act against the person of the defendant or attempt to forceably remove his jacket."* The California Supreme Court declined review by a divided vote. We brought the case here, postponing the consideration of the question of our jurisdiction over this appeal to a hearing of the case on the merits.* We now reverse.

I

In order to lay hands on the precise issue which this case involves, it is useful first to canvass various matters which this record does *not* present.

The conviction quite clearly rests upon the asserted offensiveness of the *words* Cohen used to convey his message to the public. The only "conduct" which the State sought to punish is the fact of communication. Thus, we deal here with a conviction resting solely upon "speech",* not upon any separately identifiable conduct which allegedly was intended by Cohen to be perceived by others as expressive of particular views but which, on its face, does not necessarily convey any message and hence arguably could be regulated without effectively repressing Cohen's ability to express himself.* Further, the State certainly lacks power to punish Cohen for the underlying content of the message the inscription conveyed. At least so long as there is no showing of an intent to incite disobedience to or disruption of the draft, Cohen could not, consistently with the First and Fourteenth Amendments, be punished for asserting the evident position on the inutility or immorality of the draft his jacket reflected.*

*Citation omitted [Eds.]

Appellant's conviction, then, rests squarely upon his exercise of the "freedom of speech" protected from arbitrary governmental interference by the Constitution and can be justified, if at all, only as a valid regulation of the manner in which he exercised that freedom, not as a permissible prohibition on the substantive message it conveys. This does not end the inquiry, of course, for the First and Fourteenth Amendments have never been thought to give absolute protection to every individual to speak whenever or wherever he pleases, or to use any form of address in any circumstances that he chooses. In this vein, too, however, we think it important to note that several issues typically associated with such problems are not presented here.

In the first place, Cohen was tried under a statute applicable throughout the entire State. Any attempt to support this conviction on the ground that the statute seeks to preserve an appropriately decorous atmosphere in the courthouse where Cohen was arrested must fail in the absence of any language in the statute that would have put appellant on notice that certain kinds of otherwise permissible speech or conduct would nevertheless, under California law, not be tolerated in certain places.* No fair reading of the phrase "offensive conduct" can be said sufficiently to inform the ordinary person that distinctions between certain locations are thereby created.[2]

In the second place, as it comes to us, this case cannot be said to fall within those relatively few categories of instances where prior decisions have established the power of government to deal more comprehensively with certain forms of individual expression simply upon a showing that such a form was employed. This is not, for example, an obscenity case. Whatever else may be necessary to give rise to the States' broader power to prohibit obscene expression, such expression must be, in some significant way, erotic.* It cannot plausibly be maintained that this vulgar allusion to the Selective Service System would conjure up such psychic stimulation in anyone likely to be confronted with Cohen's crudely defaced jacket.

This Court has also held that the States are free to ban the simple use, without a demonstration of additional justifying circumstances, of so-called "fighting words," those personally abusive epithets which, when addressed to the ordinary citizen, are, as a matter of common knowledge, inherently likely to provoke violent reaction.* While the four-letter word displayed by Cohen in relation to the draft is not uncommonly employed in a personally provocative fashion, in this instance it was clearly not "directed to the person of the hearer."* No individual actually or likely to be present could reasonably have regarded the words on appellant's jacket as a direct personal insult. Nor do we have here an instance of the exercise of the State's police power to prevent a speaker from intentionally provoking a given group to hostile reaction.* There is, as noted above, no showing that anyone who saw Cohen was in fact violently aroused or that appellant intended such a result.

Finally, in arguments before this Court much has been made of the claim that Cohen's distasteful mode of expression was thrust upon unwilling or unsuspecting viewers, and that the State might therefore legitimately act as it did in order to protect the sensitive from otherwise unavoidable exposure to appellant's crude form of protest. Of course, the mere presumed presence of unwitting listeners or viewers does not serve automatically to justify curtailing all speech capable of giving offense.* While this Court has recognized that government may properly act in many situations to prohibit intrusion into the privacy of the home of unwelcome views and ideas which cannot be totally banned from the public dialogue,* we have at the same time consistently stressed that "we are often 'captives' outside the sanctuary of the home and subject to objectionable speech."* The ability of government, consonant with the Constitution, to shut off discourse solely to protect others from hearing it is, in other words, dependent upon a showing that substantial privacy interests are being invaded in an essentially intolerable manner. Any broader view of this authority would effectively empower a majority to silence dissidents simply as a matter of personal predilections.

In this regard, persons confronted with Cohen's jacket were in a quite different posture than, say, those subjected to the raucous emissions of sound trucks blaring outside their residences. Those in the Los Angeles courthouse could effectively avoid further bombardment of their sensibilities simply by averting their eyes. And, while it may be that one has a more substantial claim to a recognizable privacy interest when walking through a courthouse corridor than, for example, strolling through Central Park, surely it is nothing like the interest in being free from unwanted expression in the confines of one's own home.* Given the subtlety and complexity of the factors involved, if Cohen's "speech" was otherwise entitled to constitutional protection, we do not think the fact that some unwilling "listeners" in a public building may have been briefly exposed to it can serve to justify this breach of the peace conviction where, as here, there was no evidence that persons powerless to avoid appellant's conduct did in fact object to it, and where that portion of the statute upon which Cohen's conviction rests evinces no concern, either on its face or as construed by the California courts, with the special plight of the captive auditor, but, instead, indiscriminately sweeps within its prohibitions all "offensive conduct" that disturbs "any neighborhood or person."*

*Citation omitted [Eds.]

II

Against this background, the issue flushed by this case stands out in bold relief. It is whether California can excise, as "offensive conduct," one particular scurrilous epithet from the public discourse, either upon the theory of the court below that its use is inherently likely to cause violent reaction or upon a more general assertion that the States, acting as guardians of public morality, may properly remove this offensive word from the public vocabulary.

The rationale of the California court is plainly untenable. At most it reflects an "undifferentiated fear or apprehension of disturbance [which] is not enough to overcome the right to freedom of expression."* We have been shown no evidence that substantial numbers of citizens are standing ready to strike out physically at whoever may assault their sensibilities with execrations like that uttered by Cohen. There may be some persons about with such lawless and violent proclivities, but that is an insufficient base upon which to erect, consistently with constitutional values, a governmental power to force persons who wish to ventilate their dissident views into avoiding particular forms of expression. The argument amounts to little more than the self-defeating proposition that to avoid physical censorship of one who has not sought to provoke such a response by a hypothetical coterie of the violent and lawless, the States may more appropriately effectuate that censorship themselves.*

Admittedly, it is not so obvious that the First and Fourteenth Amendments must be taken to disable the States from punishing public utterance of this unseemly expletive in order to maintain what they regard as a suitable level of discourse within the body politic. We think, however, that examination and reflection will reveal the shortcomings of a contrary viewpoint.

At the outset, we cannot overemphasize that, in our judgment, most situations where the State has a justifiable interest in regulating speech will fall within one or more of the various established exceptions, discussed above but not applicable here, to the usual rule that governmental bodies may not prescribe the form or content of individual expression. Equally important to our conclusion is the constitutional backdrop against which our decision must be made. The constitutional right of free expression is powerful medicine in a society as diverse and populous as ours. It is designed and intended to remove governmental restraints from the arena of public discussion, putting the decision as to what views shall be voiced largely into the hands of each of us, in the hope that use of such freedom will ultimately produce a more capable citizenry and more perfect polity and in the belief that no other approach would comport with the premise of individual dignity and choice upon which our political system rests.*

To many, the immediate consequence of this freedom may often appear to be only verbal tumult, discord, and even offensive utterance. These are, however, within established limits, in truth necessary side effects of the broader enduring values which the process of open debate permits us to achieve. That the air may at times seem filled with verbal cacophony is, in this sense not a sign of weakness but of strength. We cannot lose sight of the fact that, in what otherwise might seem a trifling and annoying instance of individual distasteful abuse of a privilege, these fundamental societal values are truly implicated. That is why "[w]holly neutral futilities . . . come under the protection of free speech as fully as do Keats' poems or Donne's sermons," Winters v New York, (1948)* (Frankfurter, J., dissenting), and why "so long as the means are peaceful, the communication need not meet standards of acceptability," Organization for a Better Austin v Keefe, (1971).*

Against this perception of the constitutional policies involved, we discern certain more particularized considerations that peculiarly call for reversal of this conviction. First, the principle contended for by the State seems inherently boundless. How is one to distinguish this from any other offensive word? Surely the State has no right to cleanse public debate to the point where it is grammatically palatable to the most squeamish among us. Yet no readily ascertainable general principle exists for stopping short of that result were we to affirm the judgment below. For, while the particular four-letter word being litigated here is perhaps more distasteful than most others of its genre, it is nevertheless often true that one man's vulgarity is another's lyric. Indeed, we think it is largely because governmental officials cannot make principled distinctions in this area that the Constitution leaves matters of taste and style so largely to the individual.

Additionally, we cannot overlook the fact, because it is well illustrated by the episode involved here, that much linguistic expression serves a dual communicative function: it conveys not only ideas capable of relatively precise, detached explication, but otherwise inexpressible emotions as well. In fact, words are often chosen as much for their emotive as their cognitive force. We cannot sanction the view that the Constitution, while solicitous of the cognitive content of individual speech, has little or no regard for that emotive function which, practically speaking, may often be the more important element of the overall message sought to be communicated. Indeed, as Mr. Justice Frankfurter has said, "[o]ne of the prerogatives of American citizenship is the right to criticize public men and measures—and that means not only informed and responsible criticism but the freedom to speak foolishly and without moderation." Baumgartner v United States, (1944).*

*Citation omitted [Eds.]

Finally, and in the same vein, we cannot indulge the facile assumption that one can forbid particular words without also running a substantial risk of suppressing ideas in the process. Indeed, governments might soon seize upon the censorship of particular words as a convenient guise for banning the expression of unpopular views. We have been able, as noted above, to discern little social benefit that might result from running the risk of opening the door to such grave results.

It is, in sum, our judgment that, absent a more particularized and compelling reason for its actions, the State may not, consistently with the First and Fourteenth Amendments, make the simple public display here involved of this single four-letter expletive a criminal offense. Because that is the only arguably sustainable rationale for the conviction here at issue, the judgment below must be reversed.

SEPARATE OPINION

Mr. Justice **Blackmun**, with whom The **Chief Justice** and Mr. Justice **Black** join.

I dissent, and I do so for two reasons:

1. Cohen's absurd and immature antic, in my view, was mainly conduct and little speech.* The California Court of Appeal appears so to have described it,* and I cannot characterize it otherwise. Further, the case appears to me to be well within the sphere of Chaplinsky v New Hampshire,* where Mr. Justice Murphy, a known champion of First Amendment freedoms, wrote for a unanimous bench. As a consequence, this Court's agonizing First Amendment values seems misplaced and unnecessary.

2. I am not at all certain that the California Court of Appeal's construction of § 415 is now the authoritative California construction . . .

NOTES

1. The statute provides in full:
"Every person who maliciously and willfully disturbs the peace or quiet of any neighborhood or person, by loud or unusual noise, or by tumultuous or offensive conduct, or threatening, traducing, quarreling, challenging to fight, or fighting, or who, on the public streets of any unincorporated town, or upon the public highways in such unincorporated town, run any horse race, either for a wager or for amusement, or fire any gun or pistol in such unincorporated town, or use any vulgar language within the presence or hearing of women or children, in a loud and boisterous manner, is guilty of a misdemeanor, and upon conviction by any Court of competent jurisdiction shall be punished by fine not exceeding two hundred dollars, or by imprisonment in the County Jail for not more than ninety days, or by both fine and imprisonment, or either, at the discretion of the Court."

2. It is illuminating to note what transpired when Cohen entered a courtroom in the building. He removed his jacket and stood with it folded over his arm. Meanwhile, a policeman sent the presiding judge a note suggesting that Cohen be held in contempt of court. The judge declined to do so and Cohen was arrested by the officer only after he emerged from the courtroom.

IRVING KRISTOL

"Pornography, Obscenity, and the Case for Censorship"*

Being frustrated is disagreeable, but the real disasters in life begin when you get what you want. For almost a century now, a great many intelligent, well-meaning, and articulate people—of a kind generally called liberal or intellectual, or both—have argued eloquently against any kind of censorship of art and/or entertainment. And within the past ten years, the courts and the legislatures of most Western nations have found these arguments persuasive—so persuasive that hardly a man is now alive who clearly remembers what the answers to these arguments were. Today, in the United States and other democracies, censorship has to all intents and purposes ceased to exist.

Is there a sense of triumphant exhilaration in the land? Hardly. There is, on the contrary, a rapidly growing unease and disquiet. Somehow, things have not worked out as they were supposed to, and many notable civil libertarians have gone on record as saying this was not what they meant at all. They wanted a world in which "Desire Under the Elms" could be produced, or "Ulysses" published, without interference by philistine busybodies holding public office. They have got that, of course; but they have also got a world in which homosexual rape takes place on the stage, in which the public flocks during lunch hours to witness varieties of professional fornication, in which Times Square has become little more than a hideous market for the sale and distribution of printed filth that panders to all known (and some fanciful) sexual perversions.

But disagreeable as this may be, does it really matter? Might not our unease and disquiet be merely a cultural hangover—a "hangup," as they say? What reason is there to think that anyone was ever corrupted by a book?

*From *The New York Times Magazine,* March 28, 1971. Reprinted by permission of the author.

This last question, oddly enough, is asked by the very same people who seem convinced that advertisements in magazines or displays of violence on television do indeed have the power to corrupt. It is also asked, incredibly enough and in all sincerity, by people—for example, university professors and school teachers—whose very lives provide all the answers one could want. After all, if you believe that no one was ever corrupted by a book, you have also to believe that no one was ever improved by a book (or a play or a movie). You have to believe, in other words, that all art is morally trivial and that, consequently, all education is morally irrelevant. No one, not even a university professor, really believes that.

To be sure, it is extremely difficult, as social scientists tell us, to trace the effects of any single book (or play or movie) on an individual reader or any class of readers. But we all know, and social scientists know it too, that the ways in which we use our minds and imaginations do shape our characters and help define us as persons. That those who certainly know this are nevertheless moved to deny it merely indicates how a dogmatic resistance to the idea of censorship can—like most dogmatism—result in a mindless insistence on the absurd.

I have used these harsh terms—"dogmatism" and "mindless"—advisedly. I might also have added "hypocritical." For the plain fact is that none of us is a complete civil libertarian. We all believe that there is some point at which the public authorities ought to step in to limit the "self-expression" of an individual or a group, even where this might be seriously intended as a form of artistic expression, and even where the artistic transaction is between consenting adults. A playwright or theatrical director might, in this crazy world of ours, find someone willing to commit suicide on the stage, as called for by the script.

We would not allow that—any more than we would permit scenes of real physical torture on the stage, even if the victim were a willing masochist. And I know of no one, no matter how free in spirit, who argues that we ought to permit gladiatorial contests in Yankee Stadium, similar to those once performed in the Colosseum at Rome—even if only consenting adults were involved.

The basic point that emerges is one that Prof. Walter Berns has powerfully argued: No society can be utterly indifferent to the ways its citizens publicly entertain themselves.* Bearbaiting and cockfighting are prohibited only in part out of compassion for the suffering animals; the main reason they were abolished was because it was felt that they debased and brutalized the citizenry who flocked to witness such spectacles. And the question we face with regard to pornography and obscenity is whether, now that they have such strong legal protection from the Supreme Court, they can or will brutalize and debase our citizenry. We are, after all, not dealing with one passing incident—one book, or one play, or one movie. We are dealing with a general tendency that is suffusing our entire culture.

I say pornography *and* obscenity because, though they have different dictionary definitions and are frequently distinguishable as "artistic" genres, they are nevertheless in the end identical in effect. Pornography is not objectionable simply because it arouses sexual desire or lust or prurience in the mind of the reader or spectator; this is a silly Victorian notion. A great many nonpornographic works—including some parts of the Bible—excite sexual desire very successfully. What is distinctive about pornography is that, in the words of D. H. Lawrence, it attempts "to do dirt on [sex] . . . [It is an] insult to a vital human relationship."

In other words, pornography differs from erotic art in that its whole purpose is to treat human beings obscenely, to deprive human beings of their specifically human dimension. That is what obscenity is all about. It is light years removed from any kind of carefree sensuality—there is no continuum between Fielding's "Tom Jones" and the Marquis de Sade's "Justine." These works have quite opposite intentions. To quote Susan Sontag: "What pornographic literature does is precisely to drive a wedge between one's existence as a full human being and one's existence as a sexual being—while in ordinary life a healthy person is one who prevents such a gap from opening up." This definition occurs in an essay *defending* pornography—Miss Sontag is a candid as well as gifted critic—so the definition, which I accept, is neither tendentious nor censorious.

Along these same lines, one can point out—as C. S. Lewis pointed out some years back—that it is no accident that in the history of all literatures obscene words—the so-called "four-letter words" —have always been the vocabulary of farce or vituperation. The reason is clear—they reduce men and women to some of their mere bodily functions—they reduce man to his animal component, and such a reduction is an essential purpose of farce or vituperation.

Similarly, Lewis also suggested that it is not an accident that we have no offhand, colloquial, neutral terms—not in any Western European language at any rate—for our most private parts. The words we do use are either (a) nursery terms, (b) archaisms, (c) scientific terms or (d) a term from the gutter (that is, a demeaning term). Here I think the genius of language is telling us something important about man. It is telling us that man is an animal with a difference: he has a unique sense of privacy, and a unique capacity for shame when this privacy is violated. Our "private parts" are indeed private, and not merely because convention prescribes it. This particular convention is indigenous to the human race. In practically all primitive tribes, men and women cover their private parts; and in practically all primitive tribes, men and women do not copulate in public.

It may well be that Western society, in the latter half of the 20th century, is experiencing a drastic change in sexual mores and sexual relationships. We have had many such "sexual revolutions" in the past—and the bourgeois family and bourgeois ideas of sexual propriety were themselves established in the course of a revolution against 18th century "licentiousness"—and we shall doubtless have others in the future. It is, however, highly improbable (to put it mildly) that what we are witnessing is the Final Revolu-

*This is as good a place as any to express my profound indebtedness to Walter Berns's superb essay, "Pornography vs. Democracy," in the winter, 1971, issue of The Public Interest.

tion which will make sexual relations utterly unproblematic, permit us to dispense with any kind of ordered relationships between the sexes, and allow us freely to redefine the human condition. And so long as humanity has not reached that utopia, obscenity will remain a problem.

One of the reasons it will remain a problem is that obscenity is not merely about sex, any more than science fiction is about science. Science fiction, as every student of the genre knows, is a peculiar vision of power: what it is really about is politics. And obscenity is a peculiar vision of humanity: what it is really about is ethics and metaphysics.

Imagine a man—a well-known man, much in the public eye—in a hospital ward, dying an agonizing death. He is not in control of his bodily functions, so that his bladder and his bowels empty themselves of their own accord. His consciousness is overwhelmed and extinguished by pain, so that he cannot communicate with us, nor we with him. Now, it would be, technically, the easiest thing in the world to put a television camera in his hospital room and let the whole world witness this spectacle. We don't do it—at least we don't do it as yet—because we regard this as an *obscene* invasion of privacy. And what would make the spectacle obscene is that we would be witnessing the extinguishing of humanity in a human animal.

Incidentally, in the past our humanitarian crusaders against capital punishment understood this point very well. The abolitionist literature goes into great physical detail about what happens to a man when he is hanged or electrocuted or gassed. And their argument was—and is—that what happens is shockingly obscene, and that no civilized society should be responsible for perpetrating such obscenities, particularly since in the nature of the case there must be spectators to ascertain that this horror was indeed being perpetrated in fulfillment of the law.

Sex—like death—is an activity that is both animal and human. There are human sentiments and human ideals involved in this animal activity. But when sex is public, the viewer does not see—cannot see—the sentiments and the ideals. He can only see the animal coupling. And that is why, when men and women make love, as we say,

they prefer to be alone—because it is only when you are alone that you can make love, as distinct from merely copulating in an animal and casual way. And that, too, is why those who are voyeurs, if they are not irredeemably sick, also feel ashamed at what they are witnessing. When sex is a public spectacle, a human relationship has been debased into a mere animal connection.

It is also worth noting that this making of sex into an obscenity is not a mutual and equal transaction, but is rather an act of exploitation by one of the partners—the male partner. I do not wish to get into the complicated question as to what, if any, are the essential differences—as distinct from conventional and cultural differences—between male and female. I do not claim to know the answer to that. But I do know—and I take it as a sign which has meaning—that pornography is, and always has been, a man's work; that women rarely write pornography; and that women tend to be indifferent consumers of pornography.* My own guess, by way of explanation, is that a woman's sexual experience is ordinarily more suffused with human emotion than is man's, that men are more easily satisfied with autoerotic activities, and that men can therefore more easily take a more "technocratic" view of sex and its pleasures. Perhaps this is not correct. But whatever the explanation, there can be no question that pornography is a form of "sexism," as the Women's Liberation Movement calls it, and that the instinct of Women's Lib has been unerring in perceiving that, when pornography is perpetrated, it is perpetrated against them, as part of a conspiracy to deprive them of their full humanity.

But even if all this is granted, it might be said —and doubtless will be said—that I really ought not to be unduly concerned. Free competition in the cultural marketplace—it is argued by people who have never otherwise had a kind word to say for laissez-faire—will automatically dispose of the problem. The present fad for pornography and obscenity, it will be asserted, is just that, a fad. It will spend itself in the course of time; people will

---

*There are, of course, a few exceptions—but of a kind that prove the rule. "L'Histoire d'O," for instance, written by a woman, is unquestionably the most *melancholy* work of pornography ever written. And its theme is precisely the dehumanization accomplished by obscenity.

get bored with it, will be able to take it or leave it alone in a casual way, in a "mature way," and, in sum, I am being unnecessarily distressed about the whole business. The New York Times, in an editorial, concludes hopefully in this vein.

"In the end . . . the insensate pursuit of the urge to shock, carried from one excess to a more abysmal one, is bound to achieve its own antidote in total boredom. When there is no lower depth to descend to, ennui will erase the problem."

I would like to be able to go along with this line of reasoning, but I cannot. I think it is false, and for two reasons, the first psychological, the second political.

The basic psychological fact about pornography and obscenity is that it appeals to and provokes a kind of sexual regression. The sexual pleasure one gets from pornography and obscenity is autoerotic and infantile; put bluntly, it is a masturbatory exercise of the imagination, when it is not masturbation pure and simple. Now, people who masturbate do not get bored with masturbation, just as sadists don't get bored with sadism, and voyeurs don't get bored with voyeurism.

In other words, infantile sexuality is not only a permanent temptation for the adolescent or even the adult—it can quite easily become a permanent, self-reinforcing neurosis. It is because of an awareness of this possibility of regression toward the infantile condition, a regression which is always open to us, that all the codes of sexual conduct ever devised by the human race take such a dim view of autoerotic activities and try to discourage autoerotic fantasies. Masturbation is indeed a perfectly natural autoerotic activity, as so many sexologists blandly assure us today. And it is precisely because it is so perfectly natural that it can be so dangerous to the mature or maturing person, if it is not controlled or sublimated in some way. That is the true meaning of Portnoy's complaint. Portnoy, you will recall, grows up to be a man who is incapable of having an adult sexual relationship with a woman; his sexuality remains fixed in an infantile mode, the prison of his autoerotic fantasies. Inevitably, Portnoy comes to think, in a perfectly *infantile* way, that it was all his mother's fault.

It is true that, in our time, some quite brilliant minds have come to the conclusion that a reversion to infantile sexuality is the ultimate mission and secret destiny of the human race. I am think-

ing in particular of Norman O. Brown, for whose writings I have the deepest respect. One of the reasons I respect them so deeply is that Mr. Brown is a serious thinker who is unafraid to face up to the radical consequences of his radical theories. Thus, Mr. Brown knows and says that for his kind of salvation to be achieved, humanity must annul the civilization it has created—not merely the civilization we have today, but all civilization —so as to be able to make the long descent backwards into animal innocence.

What is at stake is civilization and humanity, nothing less. The idea that "everything is permitted," as Nietzsche put it, rests on the premise of nihilism and has nihilistic implications. I will not pretend that the case against nihilism and for civilization is an easy one to make. We are here confronting the most fundamental of philosophical questions, on the deepest levels. But that is precisely my point—that the matter of pornography and obscenity is not a trivial one, and that only superficial minds can take a bland and untroubled view of it.

In this connection, I might also point out those who are primarily against censorship on liberal grounds tell us not to take pornography or obscenity seriously, while those who are for pornography and obscenity, on radical grounds, take it very seriously indeed. I believe the radicals— writers like Susan Sontag, Herbert Marcuse, Norman O. Brown, and even Jerry Rubin—are right, and the liberals are wrong. I also believe that those young radicals at Berkeley, some five years ago, who provoked a major confrontation over the public use of obscence words, showed a brilliant political instinct. Once the faculty and administration had capitulated on this issue— saying: "Oh, for God's sake, let's be adult: what difference does it make anyway?"—once they said that, they were bound to lose on every other issue. And once Mark Rudd could publicly ascribe to the president of Columbia a notoriously obscene relationship to his mother, without provoking any kind of reaction, the S.D.S. had already won the day. The occupation of Columbia's buildings merely ratified their victory. Men who show themselves unwilling to defend civilization against nihilism are not going to be either resolute or effective in defending the university against anything.

I am already touching upon a political aspect of pornography when I suggest that it is inherently and purposefully subversive of civilization and its institutions. But there is another and more specifically political aspect, when has to do with the relationship of pornography and/or obscenity to democracy, and especially to the quality of public life on which democratic government ultimately rests.

Though the phrase, "the quality of life," trips easily from so many lips these days, it tends to be one of those clichés with many trivial meanings and no large, serious one. Sometimes it merely refers to such externals as the enjoyment of cleaner air, cleaner water, cleaner streets. At other times it refers to the merely private enjoyment of music, painting or literature. Rarely does it have anything to do with the way the citizen in a democracy views himself—his obligations, his intentions, his ultimate self-definition.

Instead, what I would call the "managerial" conception of democracy is the predominant opinion among political scientists, sociologists and economists, and has, through the untiring efforts of these scholars, become the conventional journalistic opinion as well. The root idea behind this "managerial" conception is that democracy is a "political system" (as they say) which can be adequately defined in terms of—can be fully reduced to—its mechanical arrangements. Democracy is then seen as a set of rules and procedures, and *nothing but* a set of rules and procedures, whereby majority rule and minority rights are reconciled into a state of equilibrium. If everyone follows these rules and procedures, then a democracy is in working order. I think this is a fair description of the democratic idea that currently prevails in academia. One can also fairly say that it is now the liberal idea of democracy par excellence.

I cannot help but feel that there is something ridiculous about being this kind of a democrat, and I must further confess to having a sneaking sympathy for those of our young radicals who also find it ridiculous. The absurdity is the absurdity of idolatry—of taking the symbolic for the real, the means for the end. The purpose of democracy cannot possibly be the endless functioning of its own political machinery. The purpose of any political regime is to achieve some version of the good life and the good society. It is not at all difficult to imagine a perfectly functioning democracy which answers all questions

except one—namely, why should anyone of intelligence and spirit care a fig for it?

There is, however, an older idea of democracy —one which was fairly common until about the beginning of this century—for which the conception of the quality of public life is absolutely crucial. This idea starts from the proposition that democracy is a form of self-government, and that if you want it to be a meritorious polity, you have to care about what kind of people govern it. Indeed, it puts the matter more strongly and declares that, if you want self-government, you are only entitled to it if that "self" is worthy of governing. There is no inherent right to self-government if it means that such government is vicious, mean, squalid and debased. Only a dogmatist and a fanatic, an idolater of democratic machinery, could approve of self-government under such conditions.

And because the desirability of self-government depends on the character of the people who govern, the older idea of democracy was very solicitous of the condition of this character. It was solicitous of the individual self, and felt an obligation to educate it into what used to be called "republican virtue." And it was solicitous of that collective self which we call public opinion and which, in a democracy, governs us collectively. Perhaps in some respects it was nervously oversolicitous—that would not be surprising. But the main thing is that it cared, cared not merely about the machinery of democracy but about the quality of life that this machinery might generate.

And because it cared, this older idea of democracy had no problem in principle with pornography and/or obscenity. It censored them—and it did so with a perfect clarity of mind and a perfectly clear conscience. It was not about to permit people capriciously to corrupt themselves. Or, to put it more precisely: in this version of democracy, the people took some care not to let themselves be governed by the more infantile and irrational parts of themselves.

I have, it many be noticed, uttered that dreadful word, "censorship." And I am not about to back away from it. If you think pornography and/or obscenity is a serious problem, you have to be for censorship. I'll go even further and say that if you want to prevent pornography and/or obscenity from becoming a problem, you have to be for censorship. And lest there be any misunderstanding as to what I am saying, I'll put it as bluntly as possible: if you care for the quality of life in our American democracy, then you have to be for censorship.

But can a liberal be for censorship? Unless one assumes that being a liberal *must* mean being indifferent to the quality of American life, then the answer has to be: yes, a liberal can be for censorship—but he ought to favor a liberal form of censorship.

Is that a contradiction in terms? I don't think so. We have no problem in contrasting *repressive* laws governing alcohol and drugs and tobacco with laws *regulating* (that is, discouraging the sale of) alcohol and drugs and tobacco. Laws encouraging temperance are not the same thing as laws that have as their goal prohibition or abolition. We have not made the smoking of cigarettes a criminal offense. We have, however, and with good liberal conscience, prohibited cigarette advertising on television, and may yet, again with good liberal conscience, prohibit it in newspapers and magazines. The idea of restricting individual freedom, in a liberal way, is not at all unfamiliar to us.

I therefore see no reason why we should not be able to distinguish repressive censorship from liberal censorship of the written and spoken word. In Britain, until a few years ago, you could perform almost any play you wished—but certain plays, judged to be obscene, had to be performed in private theatrical clubs which were deemed to have a "serious" interest in theater. In the United States all of us who grew up using public libraries are familiar with the circumstances under which certain books could be circulated only to adults, while still other books had to be read in the library reading room, under the librarian's skeptical eye. In both cases, a small minority that was willing to make a serious effort to see an obscene play or read an obscene book could do so. But the impact of obscenity was circumscribed and the quality of public life was only marginally affected.*

*It is fairly predictable that someone is going to object that this point of veiw is "elitist"—that, under a system of liberal censorship, the rich will have privileged access to pornography and obscenity. Yes, of course they will—just as at present, the rich have privileged access to heroin if they want it. But one would have to be an egalitarian maniac to object to this state of affairs on the grounds of equality.

I am not saying it is easy in practice to sustain a distinction between liberal and repressive censorship, especially in the public realm of a democracy, where popular opinion is so vulnerable to demagoguery. Moreover, an acceptable system of liberal censorship is likely to be exceedingly difficult to devise in the United States today, because our educated classes, upon whose judgment a liberal censorship must rest, are so convinced that there is no such thing as a problem of obscenity, or even that there is no such thing as obscenity at all. But, to counterbalance this, there is the further, fortunate truth that the tolerable margin for error is quite large, and single mistakes or single injustices are not all that important.

This possibility, of course, occasions much distress among artists and academics. It is a fact, one that cannot and should not be denied, that any system of censorship is bound, upon occasion, to treat unjustly a particular work of art—to find pornography where there is only gentle eroticism, to find obscenity where none really exists, or to find both where its existence ought to be tolerated because it serves a larger moral purpose. Though most works of art are not obscene, and though most obscenity has nothing to do with art, there are some few works of art that are, at least in part, pornographic and/or obscene. There are also some few works of art that are in the special category of the comic-ironic "bawdy" (Boccaccio, Rabelais). It is such works of art that are likely to suffer at the hands of the censor. That is the price one has to be prepared to pay for censorship—even liberal censorship.

But just how high is this price? If you believe, as so many artists seem to believe today, that art is the only sacrosanct activity in our profane and vulgar world—that any man who designates himself an artist thereby acquires a sacred office—then obviously censorship is an intolerable form of sacrilege. But for those of us who do not subscribe to this religion of art, the costs of censorship do not seem so high at all.

If you look at the history of American or English literature, there is precious little damage you can point to as a consequence of the censorship that prevailed throughout most of that history. Very few works of literature—of real literary merit, I mean—ever were suppressed; and those that were, were not suppressed for long. Nor have I noticed, now that censorship of the written word has to all intents and purposes ceased in this country, that hitherto suppressed or repressed masterpieces are flooding the market. Yes, we can now read "Fanny Hill" and the Marquis de Sade. Or, to be more exact, we can now openly purchase them, since many people were able to read them even though they were publicly banned, which is as it should be under a liberal censorship. So how much have literature and the arts gained from the fact that we can all now buy them over the counter, that, indeed, we are all now encouraged to buy them over the counter? They have not gained much that I can see.

And one might also ask a question that is almost never raised: how much has literature lost from the fact that everything is now permitted? It has lost quite a bit, I should say. In a free market, Gresham's Law can work for books or theater as efficiently as it does for coinage—driving out the good, establishing the debased. The cultural market in the United States today is being preempted by dirty books, dirty movies, dirty theater. A pornographic novel has a far better chance of being published today than a nonpornographic one, and quite a few pretty good novels are not being published at all simply because they are not pornographic, and are therefore less likely to sell. Our cultural condition has not improved as a result of the new freedom. American cultural life wasn't much to brag about 20 years ago; today one feels ashamed for it.

Just one last point which I dare not leave untouched. If we start censoring pornography or obscenity, shall we not inevitably end up censoring political opinion? A lot of people seem to think this would be the case—which only shows the power of doctrinaire thinking over reality. We had censorship of pornography and obscenity for 150 years, until almost yesterday, and I am not aware that freedom of opinion in this country was in any way diminished as a consequence of this fact. Fortunately for those of us who are liberal, freedom is not indivisible. If it were, the case for liberalism would be indistinguishable from the case for anarchy; and they are two very different things.

But I must repeat and emphasize: What kind of laws we pass governing pornography and obscenity, what kind of censorship—or, since we are still a federal nation—what kinds of censorship we institute in our various localities may indeed be difficult matters to cope with; nevertheless the real issue is one of principle. I myself subscribe to the liberal view of the enforcement problem: I think that pornography should be illegal and available to anyone who wants it so badly as to make a pretty strenuous effort to get it. We have lived with under-the-counter pornography for centuries now, in a fairly comfortable way. But the issue of principle, of whether it should be over or under the counter, has to be settled before we can reflect on the advantages and disadvantages of alternative modes of censorship. I think the settlement we are living under now, in which obscenity and democracy are regarded as equals, is wrong; I believe it is inherently unstable; I think it will, in the long run, be incompatible with any authentic concern for the quality of life in our democracy.

JOHN F. KENNEDY MEMORIAL HOSPITAL v. HESTON

Supreme Court of New Jersey, 1971*

The opinion of the Court was delivered by WEINTRAUB, C.J.

Delores Heston, age 22 and unmarried, was severely injured in an automobile accident. She was taken to the plaintiff hospital where it was determined that she would expire unless operated upon for a ruptured spleen and that if operated upon she would expire unless whole blood was administered. Miss Heston and her parents are Jehovah's Witnesses and a tenet of their faith forbids blood transfusions. Miss Heston insists she expressed her refusal to accept blood, but the evidence indicates she was in shock on admittance to the hospital and in the judgment of the attending physicians and nurses was then or soon became disoriented and incoherent. Her mother remained adamant in her opposition to a transfusion, and signed a release of liability for the hospital and medical personnel. Miss Heston did not execute a release; presumably she could not. Her father could not be located.

Death being imminent, plaintiff on notice to the mother made application at 1:30 A.M. to a judge of the Superior Court for the appointment of a guardian for Miss Heston with directions to consent to transfusions as needed to save her life. At the hearing, the mother and her friends thought a certain doctor would pursue surgery without a transfusion, but the doctor, in response to the judge's telephone call, declined the case. The court appointed a guardian with authority to consent to blood transfusions "for the preservation of the life of Delores Heston." Surgery was performed at 4:00 A.M. the same morning. Blood was administered. Miss Heston survived.

Defendants then moved to vacate the order. Affidavits were submitted by both sides. The trial court declined to vacate the order. This appeal followed. We certified it before argument in the Appellate Division.

The controversy is moot. Miss Heston is well and no longer in plaintiff's hospital. The prospect of her return at some future day in like circumstances is too remote to warrant a declaratory judgment as between the parties. Nonetheless, the public interest warrants a resolution of the cause, and for that reason we accept the issue. (See State v. Perricone, N.J.* 1962).

In *Perricone,* we sustained an order for compulsory blood transfusion for an infant despite the objection of the parents who were Jehovah's Witnesses. In Raleigh Fitkin-Paul Morgan Memorial Hospital v. Anderson, N.J. (1964),* it appeared that both the mother, a Jehovah's Witness, and the child she was bearing would die if blood were not transfused should she hemorrhage. We held that a blood transfusion could be ordered if necessary to save the lives of the mother and the unborn child. We said:

> We have no difficulty in so deciding with respect to the infant child. The more difficult question is whether an adult may be compelled to submit to such medical procedures when necessary to save his life. Here we think it is unnecessary to decide that question in broad terms because the welfare of the child and the mother are so intertwined and inseparable that it would be impracticable to attempt to distinguish between them with respect to the sundry factual patterns which may develop. The blood transfusions (including transfusions made necessary by the delivery) may be administered if necessary to save her life or the life of her child, as the physician in charge at the time may determine.

The case at hand presents the question we thus reserved in *Raleigh Fitkin-Paul Morgan Memorial Hospital.*

It seems correct to say there is no constitutional right to choose to die. Attempted suicide was a crime at common law and was held to be a crime under N.J.S.A. 2A:85-1.* It is now denounced as a disorderly persons offense. N.J.S.A. 2A:170-25.6. Ordinarily nothing would be gained by a prosecution, and hence the offense is rarely charged. Nonetheless the Constitution does not deny the State an interest in the subject. It is commonplace for the police and other citizens, often at great risk to themselves, to use force or stratagem to defeat efforts at suicide, and it could hardly be said that thus to save someone from himself violated a right of his under the Constitution subjecting the rescuer to civil or penal consequences.

*58 N.J. 576 (1971).

*Citation omitted [Eds.]

Nor is constitutional right established by adding that one's religious faith ordains his death. Religious beliefs are absolute, but conduct in pursuance of religious beliefs is not wholly immune from governmental restraint. Mountain Lakes Bd. of Educ. v. Maas, N.J.* (1960) (vaccination of children); Bunn v. North Carolina,* (1949) (the use of snakes in a religious ritual); Baer v. City of Bend,* Or. (1956) (fluoridation of drinking water). Of immediate interest is Reynolds v. United States,* (1878), in which it was held that Congress could punish polygamy in a territory notwithstanding that polygamy was permitted or demanded by religious tenet, and in which the Court said:

* * * Laws are made for the government of actions, and while they cannot interfere with mere religious belief and opinions, they may with practices. Suppose one believed that human sacrifices were a necessary part of religious worship, would it be seriously contended that the civil government under which he lived could not interfere to prevent a sacrifice? Or if a wife religiously believed it was her duty to burn herself upon the funeral pile of her dead husband, would it be beyond the power of the civil government to prevent her carrying her belief into practice?

Complicating the subject of suicide is the difficulty of knowing whether a decision to die is firmly held. Psychiatrists may find that beneath it all a person bent on self-destruction is hoping to be rescued, and most who are rescued do not repeat the attempt, at least not at once. Then, too, there is the question whether in any event the person was and continues to be competent (a difficult concept in this area) to choose to die. And of course there is no opportunity for a trial of these questions in advance of intervention by the State or a citizen.

Appellant suggests there is a difference between passively submitting to death and actively seeking it. The distinction may be merely verbal, as it would be if an adult sought death by starvation instead of a drug. If the State may interrupt one mode of self-destruction, it may with equal authority interfere with the other. It is arguably different when an individual, overtaken by illness, decides to let it run a fatal course. But unless the medical option itself is laden with the risk of death or of serious infirmity, the State's interest in sustaining life in such circumstances is hardly distinguishable from its interest in the case of suicide.

Here we are not dealing with deadly options. The risk of death or permanent injury because of a transfusion is not a serious factor. Indeed, Miss Heston did not resist a transfusion on that basis. Nor did she wish to die. She wanted to live, but her faith demanded that she refuse blood even at the price of her life. The question is not whether the State could punish her for refusing a transfusion. It may be granted that it would serve no State interest to deal criminally with one who resisted a transfusion on the basis of religious faith. The question is whether the State may authorize force to prevent death or may tolerate the use of force by others to that end. Indeed, the issue is not solely between the State and Miss Heston, for the controversy is also between Miss Heston and a hospital and staff who did not seek her out and upon whom the dictates of her faith will fall as a burden.

Hospitals exist to aid the sick and the injured. The medical and nursing professions are consecrated to preserving life. That is their professional creed. To them, a failure to use a simple, established procedure in the circumstances of this case would be malpractice, however the law may characterize that failure because of the patient's private convictions. A surgeon should not be asked to operate under the strain of knowing that a transfusion may not be administered even though medically required to save his patient. The hospital and its staff should not be required to decide whether the patient is or continues to be competent to make a judgment upon the subject, or whether the release tendered by the patient or a member of his family will protect them from civil responsibility. The hospital could hardly avoid the problem by compelling the removal of a dying patient, and Miss Heston's family made no effort to take her elsewhere.

When the hospital and staff are thus involuntary hosts and their interests are pitted against the belief of the patient, we think it reasonable to resolve the problem by permitting the hospital and its staff to pursue their functions according to their professional standards. The solution sides with life, the conservation of which is, we think, a matter of State interest. A prior application to a court is appropriate if time permits it, although in the nature of the emergency the only question that can be explored satisfactorily is whether death will probably ensue if medical procedures are not followed. If a court finds, as the trial court did, that death will likely follow unless a transfusion is administered, the hospital and the physician should be permitted to follow that medical procedure.

The precedents are few ... With one exception, Erickson v. Dilgard, (Sup.Ct.1962), transfusions for adults were ordered despite their religious tenets.*

Two cases reached an appellate level. In *Georgetown College,* a single judge of the Court of Appeals ordered the transfusion. Thereafter a majority of the court denied a petition for rehearing en banc, without however indicating the precise basis for that denial. One dissenting opinion approached the merits. The sole appellate decision expressly reaching the merits appears to be In re Estate of Brooks.* There a conservator was appointed to authorize the transfusion for a Jehovah's

*Citation omitted [Eds.]

Witness. After the transfusion, the patient and her husband sought unsuccessfully to have the order expunged. The Supreme Court of Illinois reversed. The court could find no "clear and present danger" warranting interference with the patient's religious proscription. It has been suggested that the "clear and present danger" test, appropriate with respect to free speech, is not the appropriate criterion here, and that the relevant question is whether there is a "compelling State interest" justifying the State's refusal to permit the patient to refuse vital aid.* We think the latter test is the correct one, but it cannot be said with confidence that *Brooks* would have gone the other way if the decision had been made in its light. In fact the court there did mention conceivable interests. Thus it noted that the patient did not have minor children who might become charges of the State. But the court did not expressly consider whether the State had an interest in sustaining life, a consideration which would not be apparent when the focus is upon a "clear and present

*Citation omitted [Eds.]

danger." Nor did the court consider the sufficiency of the interest of a hospital or its staff when the patient is thrust upon them. In fact there the applicant was the patient's regular physician who had long treated her for an ulcer, knew of her religious tenet, and had assured her that he would not administer blood. The court noted, too, a fact of uncertain force in its decision, that the application was made to the trial court without notice to the patient or her husband, although time was adequate to that end.

It is not at all clear that *Brooks* would be applied in Illinois to an emergent factual pattern in which a hospital and its staff are the involuntary custodians of an adult. In any event, for the reasons already given, we find that the interest of the hospital and its staff, as well as the State's interest in life, warranted the transfusion of blood under the circumstances of this case. The judgment is accordingly affirmed. No costs.

For affirmance: Chief Justice WEINTRAUB and Justices JACOBS, FRANCIS, PROCTOR, HALL and SCHETTINO—6.

For reversal: None.

GERALD   DWORKIN

Paternalism*

*From *Morality and the Law* edited by Richard A. Wasserstrom. Copyright © 1971 by Wadsworth Publishing Company, Inc., Belmont, California 94002. Reprinted by permission of the publisher and the author.

Neither one person, nor any number of persons, is warranted in saying to another human creature of ripe years, that he shall not do with his life for his own benefit what he chooses to do with it. [Mill]

I do not want to go along with a volunteer basis. I think a fellow should be compelled to become better and not let him use his discretion whether he wants to get smarter, more healthy or more honest. [General Hershey]

I take as my starting point the "one very simple principle" proclaimed by Mill *On Liberty* . . .

That principle is, that the sole end for which mankind are warranted, individually or collectively, in interfering with the liberty of action of any of their number, is self-protection. That the only purpose for which power can be rightfully exercised over any member of a civilized community, against his will, is to prevent harm to others. He cannot rightfully be compelled to do or forbear because it will be better for him to do so, because it will make him happier, because, in the opinion of others, to do so would be wise, or even right.

This principle is neither "one" nor "very simple." It is at least two principles; one asserting that self-protection or the prevention of harm to others is sometimes a sufficient warrant and the other claiming that the individual's own good is *never* a sufficient warrant for the exercise of compulsion either by the society as a whole or by its individual members. I assume that no one, with the possible exception of extreme pacifists or anarchists, questions the correctness of the first half of the principle. This essay is an examination of the negative claim embodied in Mill's principle—the objection to paternalistic interferences with a man's liberty.

I

By paternalism I shall understand roughly the interference with a person's liberty of action justified by reasons referring exclusively to the welfare, good, happiness, needs, interests or values of the person being coerced. One is always well-advised to illustrate one's definitions by examples but it is not easy to find "pure" examples of paternalistic interferences. For almost any piece of legislation is justified by several different kinds of reasons and even if historically a piece of legislation can be shown to have been introduced for purely paternalistic motives, it may be that advocates of the legislation with an antipaternalistic outlook can find sufficient reasons justifying the legislation without appealing to the reasons which were originally adduced to support it. Thus, for example, it may be that the original legislation requiring motorcyclists to wear safety helmets was introduced for purely paternalistic reasons. But the Rhode Island Supreme Court recently upheld such legislation on the grounds that it was "not persuaded that the legislature is powerless to prohibit individuals from pursuing a course of conduct which could conceivably result in their becoming public charges," thus clearly introducing reasons of a quite different kind. Now I regard this decision as being based on reasoning of a very dubious nature but it illustrates the kind of problem one has in finding examples. The following is a list of the kinds of interferences I have in mind as being paternalistic.

II

1. Laws requiring motorcyclists to wear safety helmets when operating their machines.
2. Laws forbidding persons from swimming at a public beach when lifeguards are not on duty.
3. Laws making suicide a criminal offense.

4. Laws making it illegal for women and children to work at certain types of jobs.
5. Laws regulating certain kinds of sexual conduct, for example, homosexuality among consenting adults in private.
6. Laws regulating the use of certain drugs which may have harmful consequences to the user but do not lead to antisocial conduct.
7. Laws requiring a license to engage in certain professions with those not receiving a license subject to fine or jail sentence if they do engage in the practice.
8. Laws compelling people to spend a specified fraction of their income on the purchase of retirement annuities (Social Security).
9. Laws forbidding various forms of gambling (often justified on the grounds that the poor are more likely to throw away their money on such activities than the rich who can afford to).
10. Laws regulating the maximum rates of interest for loans.
11. Laws against duelling.

In addition to laws which attach criminal or civil penalties to certain kinds of action there are laws, rules, regulations, decrees which make it either difficult or impossible for people to carry out their plans and which are also justified on paternalistic grounds. Examples of this are:

1. Laws regulating the types of contracts which will be upheld as valid by the courts, for example, (an example of Mill's to which I shall return) no man may make a valid contract for perpetual involuntary servitude.
2. Not allowing assumption of risk as a defense to an action based on the violation of a safety statute.
3. Not allowing as a defense to a charge of murder or assault the consent of the victim.
4. Requiring members of certain religious sects to have compulsory blood transfusions. This is made possible by not allowing the patient to have recourse to civil suits for assault and battery and by means of injunctions.

5. Civil commitment procedures when these are specifically justified on the basis of preventing the person being committed from harming himself. The D.C. Hospitalization of the Mentally Ill Act provides for involuntary hospitalization of a person who "is mentally ill, and because of that illness, is likely to injure himself or others if allowed to remain at liberty." The term injure in this context applies to unintentional as well as intentional injuries.

All of my examples are of existing restrictions on the liberty of individuals. Obviously one can think of interferences which have not yet been imposed. Thus one might ban the sale of cigarettes, or require that people wear safety belts in automobiles (as opposed to merely having them installed), enforcing this by not allowing motorist to sue for injuries even when caused by other drivers if the motorist was not wearing a seat belt at the time of the accident.

I shall not be concerned with activities which though defended on paternalistic grounds are not interferences with the liberty of persons, for example, the giving of subsidies in kind rather than in cash on the grounds that the recipients would not spend the money on the goods which they really need, or not including a $1,000 deductible provision in a basic protection automobile insurance plan on the ground that the people who would elect it could least afford it. Nor shall I be concerned with measures such as "truth-in-advertising" acts and Pure Food and Drug legislation which are often attacked as paternalistic but which should not be considered so. In these cases all that is provided—it is true by the use of compulsion—is information which it is presumed that rational persons are interested in having in order to make wise decisions. There is no interference with the liberty of the consumer unless one wants to stretch a point beyond good sense and say that his liberty to apply for a loan without knowing the true rate of interest is diminished. It is true that sometimes there is sentiment for going further than providing information, for example when laws against usurious interest are passed preventing those who might wish to contract loans at high rates of interest from doing so, and these measures may correctly be considered paternalistic.

III

Bearing these examples in mind, let me return to a characterization of paternalism. I said earlier that I meant by the term, roughly, interference with a person's liberty for his own good. But, as some of the examples show, the class of persons whose good is involved is not always identical with the class of persons whose freedom is restricted. Thus, in the case of professional licensing it is the practitioner who is directly interfered with but it is the would-be patient whose interests are presumably being served. Not allowing the consent of the victim to be a defense to certain types of crime primarily affects the would-be aggressor but it is the interests of the willing victim that we are trying to protect. Sometimes a person may fall into both classes as would be the case if we banned the manufacture and sale of cigarettes and a given manufacturer happened to be a smoker as well.

Thus we may first divide paternalistic interferences into "pure" and "impure" cases. In "pure" paternalism the class of persons whose freedom is restricted is identical with the class of persons whose benefit is intended to be promoted by such restrictions. Examples: the making of suicide a crime, requiring passengers in automobiles to wear seat belts, requiring a Christian Scientist to receive a blood transfusion. In the case of "impure" paternalism in trying to protect the welfare of a class of persons we find that the only way to do so will involve restricting the freedom of other persons besides those who are benefitted. Now it might be thought that there are no cases of "impure" paternalism since any such case could always be justified on nonpaternalistic grounds, that is, in terms of preventing harm to others. Thus we might ban cigarette manufacturers from continuing to manufacture their product on the grounds that we are preventing them from causing illness to others in the same way that we prevent other manufacturers from releasing pollutants into the atmosphere, thereby causing danger to the members of the community. The difference is, however, that in the former but not the latter case the harm is of such a nature that it could be avoided by those individuals affected if they so chose. The incurring of the harm requires, so to speak, the active cooperation of the victim. It would be mistaken theoretically and hypocritical in practice to assert that our interference in such cases is just like our interference in standard cases of protecting others from harm. At the very least someone interfered with in this way can reply that no one is complaining about his activities. It may be that impure paternalism requires arguments or reasons of a stronger kind in order to be justified, since there are persons who are losing a portion of their liberty and they do not even have the solace of having it be done "in their own interest." Of course in some sense, if paternalistic justifications are ever correct, then we are protecting others, we are preventing some from injuring others, but it is important to see the differences between this and the standard case.

Paternalism then will always involve limitations on the liberty of some individuals in their own interest but it may also extend to interferences with the liberty of parties whose interests are not in question.

IV

Finally, by way of some more preliminary analysis, I want to distinguish paternalistic interference with liberty from a related type with which it is often confused. Consider, for example, legislation which forbids employees to work more than, say, forty hours per week. It is sometimes argued that such legislation is paternalistic for if employees desired such a restriction on their hours of work they could agree among themselves to impose it voluntarily. But because they do not the society imposes its own conception of their best interests upon them by the use of coercion. Hence this is paternalism.

Now it may be that some legislation of this nature is, in fact, paternalistically motivated. I am not denying that. All I want to point out is that there is another possible way of justifying such measures which is not paternalistic in nature. It is not paternalistic because, as Mill puts it in a similar context, such measures are "required not to overrule the judgment of individuals respecting their own interest, but to give effect to that judgment: they being unable to give effect to it except by concert, which concert again cannot be effectual unless it receives validity and sanction from the law." (*Principles of Political Economy*).

The line of reasoning here is a familiar one first found in Hobbes and developed with great sophistication by contemporary economists in the last decade or so. There are restrictions which are in the interests of a class of persons taken collectively but are such that the immediate interest of each individual is furthered by his violating the rule when others adhere to it. In such cases the individuals involved may need the use of compulsion to give effect to their collective judgment of their own interest by guaranteeing each individual compliance by the others. In these cases compulsion is not used to achieve some benefit which is not recognized to be a benefit by those concerned, but rather because it is the only feasible means of achieving some benefit which *is* recognized as such by all concerned. This way of viewing matters provides us with another characterization of paternalism in general. Paternalism might be thought of as the use of coercion to achieve a good which is not recognized as such by those persons for whom the good is intended. Again while this formulation captures the heart of the matter—it is surely what Mill is objecting to in *On Liberty*—the matter is not always quite like that. For example, when we force motorcyclists to wear helmets we are trying to promote a good—the protection of the person from injury—which is surely recognized by most of the individuals concerned. It is not that a cyclist doesn't value his bodily integrity; rather, as a supporter of such legislation would put it, he either places, perhaps irrationally, another value or good (freedom from wearing a helmet) above that of physical well-being or, perhaps, while recognizing the danger in the abstract, he either does not fully appreciate it or he underestimates the likelihood of its occurring. But now we are approaching the question of possible justifications of paternalistic measures and the rest of this essay will be devoted to that question.

V

I shall begin for dialectical purposes by discussing Mill's objections to paternalism and then go on to discuss more positive proposals.

An initial feature that strikes one is the absolute nature of Mill's prohibitions against paternalism. It is so unlike the carefully qualified admonitions of Mill and his fellow utilitarians on other moral issues. He speaks of self-protection as the *sole* end warranting coercion, of the individual's own goals as *never* being a sufficient warrant. Contrast this with his discussion of the prohibition against lying in *Utilitarianism:*

Yet that even this rule, sacred as it is, admits of possible exception, is acknowledged by all moralists, the chief of which is where the with-holding of some fact . . . would save an individual . . . from great and unmerited evil.

The same tentativeness is present when he deals with justice:

It is confessedly unjust to break faith with any one: to violate an engagement, either express or implied, or disappoint expectations raised by our own conduct, at least if we have raised these expectations knowingly and voluntarily. Like all the other obligations of justice already spoken of, this one is not regarded as absolute, but as capable of being overruled by a stronger obligation of justice on the other side.

This anomaly calls for some explanation. The structure of Mill's argument is as follows:

1. Since restraint is an evil the burden of proof is on those who propose such restraint.
2. Since the conduct which is being considered is purely self-regarding, the normal appeal to the protection of the interests of others is not available.
3. Therefore we have to consider whether reasons involving reference to the individual's own good, happiness, welfare, or interests are sufficient to overcome the burden of justification.
4. We either cannot advance the interests of the individual by compulsion, or the attempt to do so involves evils which outweigh the good done.
5. Hence the promotion of the individual's own interests does not provide a sufficient warrant for the use of compulsion.

Clearly the operative premise here is (4), and it is bolstered by claims about the status of the individual as judge and appraiser of his welfare, interests, needs, etcetera:

With respect to his own feelings and circumstances, the most ordinary man or woman has means of knowledge immeasurably surpassing those that can be possessed by any one else.

He is the man most interested in his own well-being: the interest which any other person, except in cases of strong personal attachment, can have in it is trifling, compared to that which he himself has.

These claims are used to support the following generalizations concerning the utility of compulsion for paternalistic purposes.

The interferences of society to overrule his judgment and purposes in what only regards himself must be grounded on general presumptions; which may be altogether wrong, and even if right, are as likely as not to be missapplied to individual cases.

But the strongest of all the arguments against the interference of the public with purely personal conduct is that when it does interfere, the odds are that it interferes wrongly and in the wrong place.

All errors which the individual is likely to commit against advice and warning are far outweighed by the evil of allowing others to constrain him to what they deem his good.

Performing the utilitarian calculation by balancing the advantages and disadvantages, we find that: "Mankind are greater gainers by suffering each other to live as seems good to themselves, than by compelling each other to live as seems good to the rest." Ergo, (4).

This classical case of a utilitarian argument with all the premises spelled out is not the only line of reasoning present in Mill's discussion. There are asides, and more than asides, which look quite different and I shall deal with them later. But this is clearly the main channel of Mill's thought and it is one which has been subjected to vigorous attack from the moment it appeared—most often by fellow utilitarians. The link that they have usually seized on is, as Fitzjames Stephen put it in *Liberty, Equality, Fraternity,* the absence of proof that the "mass of adults are so well acquainted with their own interests and so much disposed to pursue them that no compulsion or restraint put upon them by any others for the purpose of promoting their interest can really promote them." Even so sympathetic a critic as H. L. A. Hart is forced to the conclusion that:

In Chapter 5 of his essay [On Liberty] Mill carried his protests against paternalism to lengths that may now appear to us as fantastic . . . No doubt if we no longer sympathise with this criticism this is due, in part, to a general decline in the belief that individuals know their own interest best.

Mill endows the average individual with "too much of the psychology of a middle-aged man whose desires are relatively fixed, not liable to be artificially stimulated by external influences; who knows what he wants and what gives him satisfaction or happiness; and who pursues these things when he can."

Now it is interesting to note that Mill himself was aware of some of the limitations on the doctrine that the individual is the best judge of his own interests. In his discussion of government intervention in general (even where the intervention does not interfere with liberty but provides alternative institutions to those of the market) after making claims which are parallel to those just discussed, for example, "People understand their own business and their own interests better, and care for them more, than the government does, or can be expected to do," he goes on to an intelligent discussion of the "very large and conspicuous exceptions" to the maxim that:

Most persons take a juster and more intelligent view of their own interest, and of the means of promoting it than can either be prescribed to them by a general enactment of the legislature, or pointed out in the particular case by a public functionary.

Thus there are things

of which the utility does not consist in ministering to inclinations, nor in serving the daily uses of life, and the want of which is least felt where the need is greatest. This is peculiarly true of those things which are chiefly useful as tending to raise the character of human beings. The uncultivated cannot be competent judges of cultivation. Those who most need to be made wiser and better, usually desire it least, and, if they desire it, would be incapable of finding the way to it by their own lights.

. . . A second exception to the doctrine that individuals are the best judges of their own interest, is when an individual attempts to decide irrevocably now what will be best for his interest at some future and distant time. The presumption in favor of individual judgment is only legitimate, where the judgment is grounded on actual, and especially on present, personal experience; not where it is formed antecedently to experience, and not suffered to be reversed even after experience has condemned it.

The upshot of these exceptions is that Mill does not declare that there should never be government interference with the economy but rather that

. . . in every instance, the burden of making out a strong case should be thrown not on those who resist but those who recommend government interference. Letting alone, in short, should be the general practice: every departure from it, unless required by some great good, is a certain evil.

In short, we get a presumption, not an absolute prohibition. The question is why doesn't the argument against paternalism go the same way?

I suggest that the answer lies in seeing that in addition to a purely utilitarian argument Mill uses another as well. As a utilitarian, Mill has to show, in Fitzjames Stephen's words, that: Self-protection apart, no good object can be attained by any compulsion which is not in itself a greater evil than the absence of the object which the compulsion obtains." To show this is impossible, one reason being that it isn't true. Preventing a man from selling himself into slavery (a paternalistic measure which Mill himself accepts as legitimate), or from taking heroin, or from driving a car without wearing seat belts may constitute a lesser evil than allowing him to do any of these things. A consistent utilitarian can only argue against paternalism on the grounds that it (as a matter of fact) does not maximize the good. It is always a contingent question that may be returned by the evidence. But there is also a non-contingent argument which runs through *On Liberty*. When Mill states that "there is a part of the life of every person who has come to years of discretion, within which the individuality of that person ought to reign uncontrolled either by any other person or by the public collectively," he is saying something about what it means to be a person, an autonomous agent. It is because coercing a person for his own good denies this status as an independent entity that Mill objects to it so strongly and in such absolute terms. To be able to choose is a good that is independent of the wisdom of what is chosen. A man's "mode of laying out his existence is the best, not because it is the best in itself, but because it is his own mode." It is the privilege and proper condition of a human being, arrived at the maturity of his faculties, to use and interpret experience in his own way.

As further evidence of this line of reasoning in Mill, consider the one exception to his prohibition against paternalism.

In this and most civilised countries, for example, an engagement by which a person should sell himself, or allow himself to be sold, as a slave, would be null and void; neither enforced by law nor by opinion. The ground for thus limiting his power of voluntarily disposing of his own lot in life, is apparent, and is very clearly seen in this extreme case. The reason for not interfering, unless for the sake of others, with a person's voluntary acts, is consideration for his liberty. His voluntary choice is evidence that what he so chooses is desirable, or at least endurable, to him, and his good is on the whole best provided for by allowing him to take his own means of pursuing it. But by selling himself for a slave, he abdicates his liberty; he foregoes any future use of it beyond that single act. He therefore defeats, in his own case, the very purpose which is the justification of allowing him to dispose of himself. He is no longer free; but is thenceforth in a position which has no longer the presumption in its favour, that would be afforded by his voluntarily remaining in it. The principle of freedom cannot require that he should be free not to be free. It is not freedom to be allowed to alienate his freedom.

Now leaving aside the fudging on the meaning of freedom in the last line, it is clear that part of this argument is incorrect. While it is true that *future* choices of the slave are not reasons for thinking that what he chooses then is desirable for him, what is at issue is limiting his immediate choice; and since this choice is made freely, the individual may be correct in thinking that his interests are best provided for by entering such a contract. But the main consideration for not allowing such a contract is the need to preserve the liberty of the person to make future choices. This gives us a principle—a very narrow one—by which to justify some paternalistic interferences. Paternalism is justified only to preserve a wider range of freedom for the individual in question. How far this principle could be extended, whether it can justify all the cases in which we are inclined upon reflection to think paternalistic measures justified, remains to be discussed. What I have tried to show so far is that there are two strains of argument in Mill—one a straight-forward utilitarian mode of reasoning and one which relies not on the goods which free choice leads to but on the absolute value of the choice itself. The first cannot establish any absolute prohibition but at most a presumption and indeed a fairly weak one given some fairly plausible assumptions about human psychology; the second, while a stronger line of argument, seems to me to allow on its own grounds a wider range of paternalism than might be suspected. I turn now to a consideration of these matters.

VI

We might begin looking for principles governing the acceptable use of paternalistic power in cases where it is generally agreed that it is legitimate. Even Mill intends his principles to be applicable only to mature individuals, not those in what he calls "non-age." What is it that justifies us in interfering with children? The fact that they lack some of the emotional and cognitive capacities required in order to make fully rational decisions. It is an empirical question to just what extent children have an adequate conception of their own present and future interests but there is not much doubt that there are many deficiencies. For example, it is very difficult for a child to defer gratification for any considerable period of time. Given these deficiencies and given the very real and permanent dangers that may befall the child, it becomes not only permissible but even a duty of the parent to restrict the child's freedom in various ways. There is however an important moral limitation on the exercise of such parental power which is provided by the notion of the child eventually coming to see the correctness of his parent's interventions. Parental paternalism may be thought of as a wager by the parent on the child's subsequent recognition of the wisdom of the restrictions. There is an emphasis on what could be called future-oriented consent—on what the child will come to welcome, rather than on what he does welcome.

The essence of this idea has been incorporated by idealist philosophers into various types of "real-will" theory as applied to fully adult persons. Extensions of paternalism are argued for by claiming that in various respects, chronologically mature individuals share the same deficiencies in knowledge, capacity to think rationally, and the ability to carry out decisions that children possess. Hence in interfering with such people we are in effect doing what they would do if they were fully rational. Hence we are not really opposing their will, hence we are not really interfering with their freedom. The dangers of this move have been sufficiently exposed by Berlin in his *Two Concepts of Freedom*. I see no gain in theoretical clarity nor in practical advantage in trying to pass over the real nature of the interferences with liberty that we impose on others. Still the basic notion of consent is important and seems to me the only acceptable way of trying to delimit an area of justified paternalism.

Let me start by considering a case where the consent is not hypothetical in nature. Under certain conditions it is rational for an individual to agree that others should force him to act in ways which, at the time of action, the individual may not see as desirable. If, for example, a man knows that he is subject to breaking his resolves when temptation is present, he may ask a friend to refuse to entertain his requests at some later stage.

A classical example is given in the Odyssey when Odysseus commands his men to tie him to the mast and refuse all future orders to be set free, because he knows the power of the Sirens to enchant men with their songs. Here we are on relatively sound ground in later refusing Odysseus' request to be set free. He may even claim to have changed his mind but, since it is *just* such changes that he wished to guard against, we are entitled to ignore them.

A process analogous to this may take place on a social rather than individual basis. An electorate may mandate its representatives to pass legislation which when it comes time to "pay the price" may be unpalatable. I may believe that a tax increase is necessary to halt inflation though I may resent the lower pay check each month. However in both this case and that of Odysseus, the measure to be enforced is specifically requested by the party involved and at some point in time there is genuine consent and agreement on the part of those persons whose liberty is infringed. Such is not the case for the paternalistic measures we have been speaking about. What must be involved here is not consent to specific measures but rather consent to a system of government, run by elected representatives, with an understanding that they may act to safeguard our interests in certain limited ways.

I suggest that since we are all aware of our irrational propensities, deficiencies in cognitive and emotional capacities, and avoidable and unavoidable ignorance, it is rational and prudent for us to in effect take out "social insurance policies." We may argue for and against proposed paternalistic measures in terms of what fully rational individuals would accept as forms of protection. Now clearly, since the initial agreement is not about specific measures we are dealing with a more-or-less blank check and therefore there have to be carefully defined limits. What I am looking for are certain kinds of conditions which make it plausible to suppose that rational men could reach agreement to limit their liberty even when other men's interest are not affected.

Of course as in any kind of agreement schema there are great difficulties in deciding what rational individuals would or would not accept. Particularly in sensitive areas of personal liberty, there is always a danger of the dispute over agreement and rationality being a disguised version of evaluative and normative disagreement.

Let me suggest types of situations in which it seems plausible to suppose that fully rational individuals would agree to having paternalistic restrictions imposed upon them. It is reasonable to suppose that there are "goods" such as health which any person would want to have in order to pursue his own good—no matter how that good is conceived. This is an argument used in connection with compulsory education for children but it seems to me that it can be extended to other goods which have this character. Then one could agree that the attainment of such goods should be promoted even when not recognized to be such, at the moment, by the individuals concerned.

An immediate difficulty arises from the fact that men are always faced with competing goods and that there may be reasons why even a value such as health—or indeed life—may be overridden by competing values. Thus the problem with the Christian Scientist and blood transfusions. It may be more important for him to reject "impure substances" than to go on living. The difficult problem that must be faced is whether one can give sense to the notion of a person irrationally attaching weights to competing values.

Consider a person who knows the statistical data on the probability of being injured when not wearing seat belts in an automobile and knows the types and gravity of the various injuries. He also insists that the inconvenience attached to fastening the belt every time he gets in and out of the car outweighs for him the possible risks to himself. I am inclined in this case to think that such a weighing is irrational. Given his life plans, which we are assuming are those of the average person, his interests and commitments already undertaken, I think it is safe to predict that we can find inconsistencies in his calculations at some point. I am assuming that this is not a man who for some conscious or unconscious reasons is trying to injure himself nor is he a man who just likes to "live dangerously." I am assuming that he is like us in all the relevant respects but just puts an enormously high negative value on inconvenience—one which does not seem comprehensible or reasonable.

It is always possible, of course, to assimilate this person to creatures like myself. I, also, neglect to fasten my seat belt and I concede such behavior is not rational but not because I weigh the inconvenience differently from those who fasten the belts. It is just that having made (roughly) the same calculation as everybody else, I ignore it in my actions. [Note: a much better case of weakness of the will than those usually given in ethics tests.] A plausible explanation for this deplorable habit is that although I know in some intellectual sense what the probabilities and risks are I do not fully appreciate them in an emotionally genuine manner.

We have two distinct types of situation in which a man acts in a nonrational fashion. In one case he attaches incorrect weights to some of his values; in the other he neglects to act in accordance with his actual preferences and desires. Clearly there is a stronger and more persuasive argument for paternalism in the latter situation. Here we are really not—by assumption—imposing a good on another person. But why may we not extend out interference to what we might call evaluative delusions? After all, in the case of cognitive delusions we are prepared, often, to act against the expressed will of the person involved. If a man believes that when he jumps out the window he will float upwards—Robert Nozick's example—would not we detain him, forcibly if necessary? The reply will be that this man doesn't wish to be injured and if we could convince him that he is mistaken as to the consequences of his action, he would not wish to perform the action. But part of what is involved in claiming that the

man who doesn't fasten his seat-belts is attaching an incorrect weight to the inconvenience of fastening them is that if he were to be involved in an accident and severely injured he would look back and admit that the inconvenience wasn't as bad as all that. So there is a sense in which, if I could convince him of the consequences of his action, he also would not wish to continue his present course of action. Now the notion of consequences being used here is covering a lot of ground. In one case it's being used to indicate what will or can happen as a result of a course of action and in the other it's making a prediction about the future evaluation of the consequences —in the first sense—of a course of action. And whatever the difference between facts and values —whether it be hard and fast or soft and slow— we are genuinely more reluctant to consent to interferences where evaluative differences are the issue. Let me now consider another factor which comes into play in some of these situations which may make an important difference in our willingness to consent to paternalistic restrictions.

Some of the decisions we make are of such a character that they produce changes which are in one or another way irreversible. Situations are created in which it is difficult or impossible to return to anything like the initial stage at which the decision was made. In particular, some of these changes will make it impossible to continue to make reasoned choices in the future. I am thinking specifically of decisions which involve taking drugs that are physically or psychologically addictive and those which are destructive of one's mental and physical capacities.

I suggest we think of the imposition of paternalistic interferences in situations of this kind as being a kind of insurance policy which we take out against making decisions which are far-reaching, potentially dangerous and irreversible. Each of these factors is important. Clearly there are many decisions we make that are relatively irreversible. In deciding to learn to play chess, I could predict in view of my general interest in games that some portion of my free time was going to be preempted and that it would not be easy to give up the game once I acquired a certain competence. But my whole life style was not going to be jeopardized in an extreme manner. Further it might be argued that even with addictive drugs such as heroin one's normal life plans would not be seriously interfered with if an inexpensive and adequate supply were readily available. So this type of argument might have a much narrower scope than appears to be the case at first.

A second class of cases concerns decisions which are made under extreme psychological and sociological pressures. I am not thinking here of the making of the decision as being something one is pressured into—for example, a good reason for making duelling illegal is that unless this is done many people might have to manifest their courage and integrity in ways in which they would rather not do so—but rather of decisions, such as that to commit suicide, which are usually made at a point where the individual is not thinking clearly and calmly about the nature of his decision. In addition, of course, this comes under the previous heading of all-too-irrevocable decisions. Now there are practical steps which a society could take if it wanted to decrease the possibility of suicide—for example not paying social security benefits to the survivors or, as religious institutions do, not allowing persons to be buried with the same status as natural deaths. I think we may count these as interferences with the liberty of persons to attempt suicide and the question is whether they are justifiable.

Using my argument schema the question is whether rational individuals would consent to such limitations. I see no reason for them to consent to an absolute prohibition but I do think it is reasonable for them to agree to some kind of enforced waiting period. Since we are all aware of the possibility of temporary states, such as great fear of depression, that are inimical to the making of well-informed and rational decisions, it would be prudent for all of us if there were some kind of institutional arrangement whereby we were restrained from making a decision which is so irreversible. What this would be like in practice is difficult to envisage and it may be that if no practical arrangements were feasible we would have to conclude that there should be no restriction at all on this kind of action. But we might have a "cooling off" period, in much the same way that we now require couples who file for divorce to go through a waiting period. Or, more far-fetched, we might imagine a Suicide Board composed of a psychologist and another member picked by the applicant. The Board would be required to meet and talk with the person proposing to take his life, though its approval would not be required.

A third class of decisions—these classes are not supposed to be disjoint—involves dangers which are either not sufficiently understood or appreciated correctly by the persons involved. Let me illustrate, using the example of cigarette smoking, a number of possible cases.

1. A man may not know the facts—for example, smoking between one and two packs a day shortens life expectancy 6.2 years, the costs and pain of the illness caused by smoking, et cetera.
2. A man may know the facts, wish to stop smoking, but not have the requisite willpower.
3. A man may know the facts but not have them play the correct role in his calculation because, say, he discounts the danger psychologically since it is remote in time and/or inflates the attractiveness of other consequences of his decision which he regards as beneficial.

In case 1 what is called for is education, the posting of warnings, etcetera. In case 2 there is no theoretical problem. We are not imposing a good on someone who rejects it. We are simply using coercion to enable people to carry out their own goals. (Note: There obviously is a difficulty in that only a subclass of the individuals affected wish to be prevented from doing what they are doing.) In case 3 there is a sense in which we are imposing a good on someone in that given his current appraisal of the facts he doesn't wish to be restricted. But in another sense we are not imposing a good since what is being claimed—and what must be shown or at least argued for—is that an accurate accounting on his part would lead him to reject his current course of action. Now we all know that such cases exist, that we are prone to disregarding dangers that are only possibilities, that immediate pleasures are often magnified and distorted.

If in addition the dangers are severe and far-reaching, we could agree to allow the state a certain degree of power to intervene in such situations. The difficulty is in specifying in advance, even vaguely, the class of cases in which intervention will be legitimate.

A related difficulty is that of drawing a line so that it is not the case that all ultra-hazardous activities are ruled out, for example, mountain-climbing, bull-fighting, sports-car racing, etcetera. There are some risks—even very great ones—which a person is entitled to take with his life.

A good deal depends on the nature of the deprivation—for example, does it prevent the person from engaging in the activity completely or merely limit his participation—and how important to the nature of the activity is the absence of restriction when this is weighed against the role that the activity plays in the life of the person. In the case of automobile seat belts, for example, the restriction is trivial in nature, interferes not at all with the use or enjoyment of the activity, and does, I am assuming, considerably reduce a high risk of serious injury. Whereas, for example, making mountain-climbing illegal completely prevents a person from engaging in an activity which may play an important role in his life and his conception of the person he is.

In general, the easiest cases to handle are those which can be argued about in the terms which Mill thought to be so important—a concern not just for the happiness or welfare, in some broad sense, of the individual but rather a concern for the autonomy and freedom of the person. I suggest that we would be most likely to consent to paternalism in those instances in which it preserves and enhances for the individual his ability to rationally consider and carry out his own decisions.

I have suggested in this essay a number of types of situations in which it seems plausible that rational men would agree to granting the legislative powers of a society the right to impose restrictions on what Mill calls "self-regarding" conduct. However, rational men knowing something about the resources of ignorance, ill-will and stupidity available to the lawmakers of a society—a good case in point is the history of drug legislation in the United States—will be concerned to limit such intervention to a minimum. I suggest in closing two principles designed to achieve this end.

In all cases of paternalistic legislation there must be a heavy and clear burden of proof placed on the authorities to demonstrate the exact nature of the harmful effects (or beneficial consequences) to be avoided (or achieved) and the probability of their occurrence. The burden of proof here is twofold—what lawyers distinguish as the burden of going forward and the burden of persuasion. That the authorities have the burden of going forward means that it is up to them to raise the question and bring forward evidence of the evils to be avoided. Unlike the case of new drugs, where the manufacturer must produce some evidence that the drug has been tested and found not harmful, no citizen has to show with respect to self-regarding conduct that it is not harmful or promotes his best interest. In addition the nature and cogency of the evidence for the harmfulness of the course of action must be set at a high level. To paraphrase a formulation of the burden of proof for criminal proceedings—better ten men ruin themselves than one man be unjustly deprived of liberty.

Finally, I suggest a principle of the least restrictive alternative. If there is an alternative way of accomplishing the desired end without restricting liberty although it may involve great expense, inconvenience, etcetera, the society must adopt it.

HENRY M. HART, JR. and ALBERT M. SACKS

The Invitation to Dinner Case*

On the way home for lunch on Friday, January 6, 1956, Mr. Patrick met Mr. David an acquaintance of his. Mr. Patrick told Mr. David that he expected Professor Thomas for dinner and would like Mr. David to join them both for dinner and for bridge afterward. Mr. Patrick explained to Mr. David that he must be sure about coming so that there would be enough persons for bridge. Bridge, he said, was a favorite game of Professor Thomas's, and he wanted to humor the professor because he needed his help in getting a job. Mr. David asked what there would be for dinner, and Mr. Patrick promised to have planked steak, which he knew to be a favorite dish of Mr. David's. On hearing this, Mr. David promised firmly to be there at 7 P.M.

At 6:30 P.M., while Mr. David was dressing, the telephone rang. On the line was his friend, Mr. Jack, who asked him to come over for a game of poker. Mr. David agreed at once, and left soon for Jack's house, telling his wife that he was going to Patrick's.

At 9 P.M. the telephone rang in Jack's house, and a voice asked for Mr. David. Mr. David answered, fearful that it was his wife, but it was Mr. Patrick, who could hardly talk from anger. He said: "So I knew where to find you, you . . . If you do not come over to my place at once, I'll sue you in court." Mr. David hung up the phone without answering, and told the story to Jack and his friends who had a good laugh. All of them kept on playing until the early morning hours.

Mr. Patrick was as good as his word, and his lawyer filed an action against Mr. David. He claimed damages for breach of contract, including the price of a portion of planked steak specially prepared for the defendant; $2,500 compensation for not getting a job (Professor Thomas having left in dudgeon immediately after dinner); and $1,000 for mental suffering.

Mr. Patrick's lawyer claimed that there had been a legally binding contract, supported by consideration, and that the defendant had wilfully and maliciously failed to fulfill his legal and moral obligation. While acknowledging that he could find no case directly in point, he argued that the common law is elastic, and capable of developing a remedy for every wrong, especially in a case such as this where there was reliance on a promise made upon consideration, damage suffered because of malicious default, and warning to the defendant that the matter would be taken to court.

Mr. David appeared without a lawyer, telling the judge that he never thought he could be summoned to court over a social dinner invitation, and asked that the case be dismissed.

How should the judge decide?

*From *The Legal Process* by Henry M. Hart, Jr. and Albert M. Sacks (Cambridge, Mass.: Tentative Edition, 1958), pp. 477–78. Copyright © 1958 by Henry M. Hart, Jr. and Albert M. Sacks. Reprinted by permission of Albert M. Sacks. (This problem was suggested by Mr. Y. Dror, LL.M. Harvard, 1955, and a candidate for the degree of S. J. D. at the Harvard Law School during the academic year 1955–56.)

GRISWOLD v. CONNECTICUT

United States Supreme Court, 1965*

Mr. Justice Douglas delivered the opinion of the Court.

Appellant Griswold is Executive Director of the Planned Parenthood League of Connecticut. Appellant Buxton is a licensed physician and a professor at the Yale Medical School who served as Medical Director for the League at its Center in New Haven—a center open and operating from November 1 to November 10, 1961, when appellants were arrested.

They gave information, instruction, and medical advice to *married persons* as to the means of preventing conception. They examined the wife and prescribed the best contraceptive device or material for her use. Fees were usually charged, although some couples were serviced free.

The statutes whose constitutionality is involved in this appeal are §§ 53–32 and 54–196 of the General Statutes of Connecticut (1958 rev.). The former provides:

"Any person who uses any drug, medicinal article or instrument for the purpose of preventing conception shall be fined not less than fifty dollars or imprisoned not less than sixty days nor more than one year or be both fined and imprisoned."

Section 54–196 provides:

"Any person who assists, abets, counsels, causes, hires or commands another to commit any offense may be prosecuted and punished as if he were the principal offender."

The appellants were found guilty as accessories and fined $100 each, against the claim that the accessory statute as so applied violated the Fourteenth Amendment. The Appellate Division of the Circuit Court affirmed. The Supreme Court of Errors affirmed that judgment.*

We think that appellants have standing to raise the constitutional rights of the married people with whom they had a professional relationship. . . . Certainly the accessory should have standing to assert that the offense which he is charged with assisting is not, or cannot constitutionally be, a crime . . .

*381 U.S. 479 (1965). Excerpts only. Footnotes renumbered.
*Citation omitted (Eds.)

Coming to the merits, we are met with a wide range of questions that implicate the Due Process Clause of the Fourteenth Amendment. Overtones of some arguments suggest that *Lochner* v. *New York,* 198 U.S. 45, should be our guide. But we decline that invitation.* We do not sit as a super-legislature to determine the wisdom, need, and propriety of laws that touch economic problems, business affairs, or social conditions. This law, however, operates directly on an intimate relation of husband and wife and their physician's role in one aspect of that relation.

The association of people is not mentioned in the Constitution nor in the Bill of Rights. The right to educate a child in a school of the parents' choice—whether public or private or parochial—is also not mentioned. Nor is the right to study any particular subject or any foreign language. Yet the First Amendment has been construed to include certain of those rights.

By *Pierce* v. *Society of Sisters,* * the right to educate one's children as one chooses is made applicable to the States by the force of the First and Fourteenth Amendments. By *Meyer* v. *Nebraska,* * the same dignity is given the right to study the German language in a private school. In other words, the State may not, consistently with the spirit of the First Amendment, contract the spectrum of available knowledge. The right of freedom of speech and press includes not only the right to utter or to print, but the right to distribute, the right to receive, the right to read* and freedom of inquiry, freedom of thought, and freedom to teach*—indeed the freedom of the entire university community.* Without those peripheral rights the specific rights would be less secure . . .

In *NAACP* v. *Alabama,* 357 U.S. 449, 462, we protected the "freedom to associate and privacy in one's associations," noting that freedom of association was a peripheral First Amendment right. Disclosure of membership lists of a constitutionally valid association, we held, was invalid "as entailing the likelihood of a substantial restraint upon the exercise by petitioner's members of their right to freedom of association." *Ibid.* In other words, the First Amendment has a penumbra where privacy is protected from governmental intrusion. In like context, we have protected forms of "association" that are not political in the customary sense but pertain to the social, legal, and economic benefit of the members.* In *Schware* v. *Board of Bar Examiners,* 353 U.S. 232, we held it not permissible to bar a lawyer from practice, because he had once been a member of the Communist Party. The man's "association with that Party" was not shown to be "anything more than a political faith in a political party"* and was not action of a kind proving bad moral character.*

Those cases involved more than the "right of assembly"—a right that extends to all irrespective of their race or ideology.* The right of "association," like the right of belief,* is more than the right to attend a meeting; it includes the right to express one's attitudes or philosophies by membership in a group or by affiliation with it or by other lawful means. Association in that context is a form of expression of opinion; and while it is not expressly included in the First Amendment its existence is necessary in making the express guarantees fully meaningful.

The foregoing cases suggest that specific guarantees in the Bill of Rights have penumbras, formed by emanations from those guarantees that help give them life and substance.* Various guarantees create zones of privacy. The right of association contained in the penumbra of the First Amendment is one, as we have seen. The Third Amendment in its prohibition against the quartering of soldiers "in any house" in time of peace without the consent of the owner is another facet of that privacy. The Fourth Amendment explicitly affirms the "right of the people to be secure in their persons, houses, papers, and effects, against unreasonable searches and seizures." The Fifth Amendment in its Self-Incrimination Clause enables the citizen to create a zone of privacy which government may not force him to surrender to his detriment. The Ninth Amendment provides: "The enumeration in the Constitution, of certain rights, shall not be construed to deny or disparage others retained by the people."

The Fourth and Fifth Amendments were described in *Boyd* v. *United States,* 116 U.S. 616, 630, as protection against all governmental invasions "of the sanctity of a man's home and the privacies of life." We recently referred in *Mapp* v. *Ohio,* 367 U.S. 643, 656, to the Fourth Amendment as creating a "right to privacy, no less important than any other right carefully and particularly reserved to the people."* These cases bear witness that the right of privacy which presses for recognition here is a legitimate one.

The present case, then, concerns a relationship lying within the zone of privacy created by several fundamental constitutional guarantees. And it concerns a law which, in forbidding the *use* of contraceptives

*Citation omitted [Eds.]

rather than regulating their manufacture or sale, seeks to achieve its goals by means having a maximum destructive impact upon that relationship. Such a law cannot stand in light of the familiar principle, so often applied by this Court, that a "governmental purpose to control or prevent activities constitutionally subject to state regulation may not be achieved by means which sweep unnecessarily broadly and thereby invade the area of protected freedoms." *NAACP* v. *Alabama,* 377 U.S. 288, 307. Would we allow the police to search the sacred precincts of marital bedrooms for telltale signs of the use of contraceptives? The very idea is repulsive to the notions of privacy surrounding the marriage relationship.

We deal with a right of privacy older than the Bill of Rights—older than our political parties, older than our school system. Marriage is a coming together for better or for worse, hopefully enduring, and intimate to the degree of being sacred. It is an association that promotes a way of life, not causes; a harmony in living, not political faiths; a bilateral loyalty, not commercial or social projects. Yet it is an association for as noble a purpose as any involved in our prior decisions.

Reversed.

Mr. Justice Goldberg, whom The Chief Justice and Mr. Justice Brennan join, concurring . . . My Brother Stewart dissents on the ground that he "can find no . . . general right of privacy in the Bill of Rights, in any other part of the Constitution, or in any case ever before decided by this Court." He would require a more explicit guarantee than the one which the Court derives from several constitutional amendments. This Court, however, has never held that the Bill of Rights or the Fourteenth Amendment protects only those rights that the Constitution specifically mentions by name . . .

My Brother Stewart, while characterizing the Connecticut birth control law as "an uncommonly silly law," would nevertheless let it stand on the ground that it is not for the courts to " 'substitute their social and economic beliefs for the judgment of legislative bodies, who are elected to pass laws.' " Elsewhere, I have stated that "[w]hile I quite agree with Mr. Justice Brandeis that . . . 'a . . . State may . . . serve as a laboratory; and try novel social and economic experiments,'* I do not believe that this includes the power to experiment with the fundamental liberties of citizens. . . ." The vice of the dissenters' views is that it would permit such experimentation by the States in the area of the fundamental personal rights of its citizens. I cannot agree that the Constitution grants such either to the States or to the Federal Government.

The logic of the dissents would sanction federal or state legislation that seems to me even more plainly unconstitutional than the statute before us. Surely the Government, absent a showing of a compelling subordinating state interest, could not decree that all husbands and wives must be sterilized after two children have been born to them. Yet by their reasoning such an invasion of marital privacy would not be subject to constitutional challenge because, while it might be "silly," no provision of the Constitution specifically prevents the Government from curtailing the marital right to bear children and raise a family. While it may shock some of my Brethren that the Court today holds that the Constitution protects the right of marital privacy in my view it is far more shocking to believe that the personal liberty guaranteed by the Constitution does not include protection against such totalitarian limitation of family size, which is at complete variance with our constitutional concepts. Yet, if upon a showing of a slender basis of rationality, a law outlawing voluntary birth control by married persons is valid, then, by the same reasoning a law requiring compulsory birth control also would seem to be valid. In my view, however, both types of law would unjustifiably intrude upon rights of marital privacy which are constitutionally protected.

In a long series of cases this Court has held that where fundamental personal liberties are involved, they may not be abridged by the States simply on a showing that a regulatory statute has some rational relationship to the effectuation of a proper state purpose. "Where there is a significant encroachment upon personal liberty, the State may prevail only upon showing a subordinating interest which is compelling," *Bates* v. *Little Rock,* 361 U.S. 516, 524. The law must be shown "necessary, and not merely rationally related, to the accomplishment of a permissible state policy." *McLaughlin* v. *Florida,* 379 U.S. 184, 196.*

Although the Connecticut birth-control law obviously encroaches upon a fundamental personal liberty, the State does not show that the law serves any "subordinating [state] interest which is compelling" or that it is "necessary . . . to the accomplishment of a permissible state policy." The State, at most, argues that there is some rational relation between this statute and what is admittedly a legitimate subject of state concern—the discouraging of extra-marital relations. It says that preventing the use of birth-control devices by married persons helps prevent the indulgence by some in such extra-marital relations. The rationality of this justification is dubious, particularly in light of the admitted widespread availability to all persons in the State of Connecticut, unmarried as well as married, of birth-control devices for the prevention of disease, as distin-

guished from the prevention of conception.* But, in any event, it is clear that the state interest in safeguarding marital fidelity can be served by a more discriminately tailored statute, which does not, like the present one, sweep unnecessarily broadly, reaching far beyond the evil sought to be dealt with and intruding upon the privacy of all married couples.* Here, as elsewhere, "[p]recision of regulation must be the touchstone in an area so closely touching our most precious freedoms." *NAACP* v. *Button,* 371 U.S. 415, 438. The State of Connecticut does have statues, the constitutionality of which is beyond doubt, which prohibit adultery and fornication.* These statutes demonstrate that means for achieving the same basic purpose of protecting marital fidelity are available to Connecticut without the need to "invade the area of protected freedoms." *NAACP* v. *Alabama, supra,* at 307.*

Finally, it should be said of the Court's holding today that it in no way interferes with a State's proper regulation of sexual promiscuity or misconduct. As my Brother Harlan so well stated in his dissenting opinion in *Poe* v. *Ullman,*

> "Adultery, homosexuality and the like are sexual intimacies which the State forbids . . . but the intimacy of husband and wife is necessarily an essential and accepted feature of the institution of marriage, an institution which the State not only must allow, but which always and in every age it has fostered and protected. It is one thing when the States exerts its power either to forbid extra-marital sexuality . . . or to say who may marry, but it is quite another when, having acknowledged a marriage and the intimacies inherent in it, it undertakes to regulate by means of the criminal law the details of that intimacy."

In sum, I believe that the right of privacy in the marital relation is fundamental and basic—a personal right "retained by the people" within the meaning of the Ninth Amendment. Connecticut cannot constitutionally abridge this fundamental right, which is protected by the Fourteenth Amendment from infringement by the States. I agree with the Court that petitioners' convictions must therefore be reversed . . .

Mr. Justice Black, with whom Mr. Justice Stewart joins, dissenting.

I agree with my Brother Stewart's dissenting opinion. And like him I do not to any extent whatever base my view that this Connecticut law is constitutional on a belief that the law is wise or that its policy is a good one. In order that there may be no room at all to doubt why I vote as I do, I feel constrained to add that the law is every bit as offensive to me as it is to my Brethren of the majority and my Brothers Harlan, White and Goldberg who, reciting reasons why it is offensive to them, hold it unconstitutional. There is no single one of the graphic and eloquent strictures and criticisms fired at the policy of this Connecticut law either by the

*Citation omitted [Eds.]

Court's opinion or by those of my concurring Brethren to which I cannot subscribe—except their conclusion that the evil qualities they see in the law make it unconstitutional . . .

The Court talks about a constitutional "right of privacy" as though there is some constitutional provision or provisions forbidding any law ever to be passed which might abridge the "privacy" of individuals. But there is not. There are, of course, guarantees in certain specific constitutional provisions which are designed in part to protect privacy at certain times and places with respect to certain activities. Such, for example, is the Fourth Amendment's guarantee against "unreasonable searches and seizures." But I think it belittles that Amendment to talk about it as though it protects nothing but "privacy." To treat it that way is to give it a niggardly interpretation, not the kind of liberal reading I think any Bill of Rights provision should be given. The average man would very likely not have his feelings soothed any more by having his property seized openly than by having it seized privately and by stealth. He simply wants his property left alone. And a person can be just as much, if not more, irritated, annoyed and injured by an unceremonious public arrest by a policeman as he is by a seizure in the privacy of his office or home.

One of the most effective ways of diluting or expanding a constitutionally guaranteed right is to substitute for the crucial word or words of a constitutional guarantee another word or words, more or less flexible and more of less restricted in meaning. This fact is well illustrated by the use of the term "right of privacy" as a comprehensive substitute for the Fourth Amendment's guarantee against "unreasonable searches and seizures." "Privacy" is a broad, abstract and ambiguous concept which can easily be shrunken in meaning but which can also, on the other hand, easily be interpreted as a constitutional ban against many things other than searches and seizures. I have expressed the view many times that First Amendment freedoms, for example, have suffered from a failure of the courts to stick to the simple language of the First Amendment in construing it, instead of invoking multitudes of words substituted for those the Framers used.* For these reasons I get nowhere in this case by talk about a constitutional "right of privacy" as an emanation from one or more constitutional provisions. I like my privacy as well as the next one, but I am nevertheless compelled to admit that government has a right to invade it unless prohibited by some specific constitutional provision. For these reasons I cannot agree with the Court's judgment and the reasons it gives for holding this Connecticut law unconstitutional . . .

The due process argument which my Brothers Harlan and White adopt here is based, as their opinions indicate, on the premise that this Court is vested with power to invalidate all state laws that it considers to be arbitrary, capricious, unreasonable, or oppressive, or on this Court's belief that a particular state law under scrutiny has no "rational or justifying" purpose, or is offensive to a "sense of fairness and justice." If these formulas based on "natural justice," or others which mean the same thing,[1] are to prevail, they require judges to determine what is or is not constitutional on the basis of their own appraisal of what laws are unwise or unnecessary. The power to make such decisions is of course that of a legislative body. Surely it has to be admitted that no provision of the Constitution specifically gives such blanket power to courts to exercise such a supervisory veto over the wisdom and value of legislative policies and to hold unconstitutional those laws which they believe unwise or dangerous. I readily admit that no legislative body, state or national, should pass laws that can justly be given any of the invidious labels invoked as constitutional excuses to strike down state laws. But perhaps it is not too much to say that no legislative body ever does pass laws without believing that they will accomplish a sane, rational, wise and justifiable purpose. While I completely subscribe to the holding of *Marbury* v. *Madison,* and subsequent cases, that our Court has constitutional power to strike down statutes, state or federal, that violate commands of the Federal Constitution, I do not believe that we are granted power by the Due Process Clause or any other constitutional provision or provisions to measure constitutionality by our belief that legislation is arbitrary, capricious or unreasonable, or accomplishes no justifiable purpose, or is offensive to our own notions of "civilized standards of conduct."[2] Such an appraisal of the wisdom of legislation is an attribute of the power to make laws, not of the power to interpret them. The use by federal courts of such a formula or doctrine or whatnot to veto federal or state laws simply takes away from Congress and States the power to make laws based on their own judgment of fairness and wisdom and transfers that power to this Court for ultimate determination—a power which was specifically denied to federal courts by the convention that framed the Constitution. . . .

My Brother Goldberg has adopted the recent discovery[3] that the Ninth Amendment as well as the Due Process Clause can be used by this Court as authority to strike down all state legislation which this Court thinks violates "fundamental principles of liberty and justice," or is contrary to the "traditions and [collective] conscience of our people." He also states, without proof satisfactory to me, that in making decisions on this basis judges will not consider "their personal and

*Citations omitted [Eds.]

private notions." One may ask how they can avoid considering them. Our Court certainly has no machinery with which to take a Gallup Poll.[4] And the scientific miracles of this age have not yet produced a gadget which the Court can use to determine what traditions are rooted in the "[collective] conscience of our people." Moreover, one would certainly have to look far beyond the language of the Ninth Amendment[5] to find that the Framers vested in this Court any such awesome veto powers over lawmaking, either by the States or by the Congress. Nor does anything in the history of the Amendment offer any support for such a shocking doctrine. The whole history of the adoption of the Constitution and Bill of Rights points the other way, and the very material quoted by my Brother Goldberg shows that the Ninth Amendment was intended to protect against the idea that "by enumerating particular exceptions to the grant of power" to the Federal Government, "those rights which were not singled out, were intended to be assigned into the hands of the General Government [the United States], and were consequently insecure."[6] That Amendment was passed, not to broaden the powers of this Court or any other department of "the General Government," but, as every student of history knows, to assure the people that the Constitution in all its provisions was intended to limit the Federal Government to the powers granted expressly or by necessary implication. If any broad, unlimited power to hold laws unconstitutional because they offend what this Court conceives to be the "[collective] conscience of our people" is vested in this Court by the Ninth Amendment, the Fourteenth Amendment, or any other provision of the Constitution, it was not given by the Framers, but rather has been bestowed on the Court by the Court. This fact is perhaps responsible for the peculiar phenomenon that for a period of a century and a half no serious suggestion was ever made that the Ninth Amendment, enacted to protect state powers against federal invasion, could be used as a weapon of federal power to prevent state legislatures from passing laws they consider appropriate to govern local affairs. Use of any such broad, unbounded judicial authority would make of this Court's members a day-to-day constitutional convention.

NOTES

1.   A collection of the catchwords and catch phrases invoked by judges who would strike down under the Fourteenth Amendment laws which offend their notions of natural justice would fill many pages. Thus it has been said that this Court can forbid state action which "shocks the conscience," *Rochin v. California*, 342 U.S. 165, 172, sufficiently to "shock itself into the protective arms of the Constitution," *Irvine v. California*, 347 U.S. 128, 138 (concurring opinion). It has been urged that States may not run counter to the "decencies of civilized conduct," *Rochin, supra*, at 173, or "some principle of justice so rooted in the traditions, and conscience of our people as to be ranked as fundamental," *Snyder v. Massachusetts*, 291 U.S. 97, 105, or to "those canons of decency and fairness which express the notions of justice of English-speaking peoples," *Malinski v. New York*, 324 U.S. 401, 417 (concurring opinion), or to "the community's sense of fair play and decency," *Rochin, supra*, at 173. It has been said that we must decide whether a state law is "fair, reasonable and appropriate," or is rather "an unreasonable, unnecessary and arbitrary interference with the right of the individual to his personal liberty or to enter into . . . contracts," *Lochner v. New York*, 198 U.S. 45, 56. States, under this philosophy, cannot act in conflict with "deeply rooted feelings of the community," *Haley v. Ohio*, 332 U.S. 596, 604 (separate opinion), or with "fundamental notions of fairness and justice," *id.*, 607. See also, e.g., *Wolf v. Colorado*, 338 U.S. 25, 27 ("rights . . . basic to our free society"); *Hebert v. Louisiana*, 272 U.S. 312, 316 ("fundamental principles of liberty and justice"); *Adkins v. Children's Hospital*, 261 U.S. 525, 561 ("arbitrary restraint of . . . liberties"); *Betts v. Brady*, 316 U.S. 455, 462 ("denial of fundamental fairness, shocking to the universal sense of justice"); *Poe v. Ullman*, 367 U.S. 497, 539 (dissenting opinion) ("intolerable and unjustifiable"). Perhaps the clearest, frankest and briefest explanation of how this due process approach works is the statement in another case handed down today that this Court is to invoke the Due Process Clause to strike down state procedures or laws which it can "not tolerate." *Linkletter v. Walker, post*, p. 618, at 631.

2.   See Hand, The Bill of Rights (1958) 70: "[J]udges are seldom content merely to annul the particular solution before them; they do not, indeed they may not, say that taking all things into consideration, the legislators' solution is too strong for the judicial stomach. On the contrary they wrap up their veto in a protective veil of adjectives such as 'arbitrary,' 'artificial,' 'normal,' 'reasonable,' 'inherent.' 'fundamental,' or 'essential,' whose office usually, though quite innocently, is to disguise what they are doing and impute to it a derivation far more impressive than their personal preferences, which are all that in fact lie behind the decision." [Citations omitted—Eds.]

3.   See Patterson, The Forgotten Ninth Amendment (1955). Mr. Patterson urges that the Ninth Amendment be used to protect unspecified "natural and inalienable rights." P. 4. The Introduction by Roscoe Pound states that "there is a marked revival of natural law ideas throughout the world. Interest in the Ninth Amendment is a symptom of that revival." P. iii.

4.   Of course one cannot be oblivious to the fact that Mr. Gallup has already published the results of a poll which he says show that 46% of the people in this country believe schools should teach about birth control. Washington Post, May 21, 1965, p. 2, col. 1. I can hardly believe, however, that Brother Goldberg would view 46% of the persons polled as so overwhelming a proportion that this Court may now rely on it to declare that the Connecticut law infringes "fundamental" rights, and overrule the long-standing view of the people of Connecticut expressed through their elected representatives.

5.   U.S. Const., Amend. IX, provides: "The enumeration in the Constitution, of certain rights, shall not be construed to deny or disparage others retained by the people."

6.   Annuals of Congress 439.

HYMAN GROSS

Privacy and Autonomy*

Why is privacy desirable? When is its loss objectionable and when is it not? How much privacy is a person entitled to? These questions challenge at the threshold our concern about protection of privacy. Usually they are pursued by seeking agreement on the boundary between morbid and healthy reticence, and by attempting to determine when unwanted intrusion or notoriety is justified by something more important than privacy. Seldom is privacy considered as the condition under which there is *control* over acquaintance with one's personal affairs by the one enjoying it, and I wish here to show how consideration of privacy in this neglected aspect is helpful in answering the basic questions. First I shall attempt to make clear this part of the idea of privacy, next suggest why privacy in this aspect merits protection, then argue that some important dilemmas are less vexing when we do get clear about these things, and finally offer a cautionary remark regarding the relation of privacy and autonomy.

I

What in general is it that makes certain conduct offensive to privacy? To distinguish obnoxious from innocent interference with privacy we must first see clearly what constitutes loss of privacy at all, and then determine why loss of privacy when it does occur is sometimes objectionable and sometimes not.

Loss of privacy occurs when the limits one has set on acquaintance with his personal affairs are not respected. Almost always we mean not respected by *others*, though in unusual cases we might speak of a person not respecting his own privacy—he is such a passionate gossip, say, that

*From *Nomos XIII, Privacy*, ed. by John Chapman and J. Roland Pennock (New York: Lieber-Atherton, 1971), pp. 169–182. Reprinted by permission of the publisher.

he gossips even about himself and later regrets it. Limits on acquaintance may be maintained by the physical insulation of a home, office, or other private place within which things that are to be private may be confined. Or such bounds may exist by virtue of exclusionary social conventions, for example those governing a private conversation in a public place; or through restricting conventions which impose an obligation to observe such limits, as when disclosure is made in confidence. Limits operate in two ways. There are restrictions on what is known, and restrictions on who may know it. Thus, a curriculum vitae furnished to or for a prospective employer is not normally an invitation to undertake a detective investigation using the items provided as clues. Nor is there normally license to communicate to others the information submitted. In both instances there would be disregard of limitations implied by considerations of privacy, unless the existence of such limitations is unreasonable under the circumstances (the prospective employer is the CIA, or the information is furnished to an employment agency). But there is no loss of privacy when such limits as do exist are respected, no matter how ample the disclosure or how extensive its circulation. If I submit a detailed account of my life while my friend presents only the barest résumé of his, I am not giving up more of privacy than he. And if I give the information to a hundred employers, I lose no more in privacy than my friend who confides to only ten, provided those informed by each of us are equally restricted. More people know more about me, so my *risk* of losing privacy is greater and the threatened loss more serious. Because I am a less private person than my friend, I am more willing to run that risk. But until there is loss of control over what is known, and by whom, my privacy is uncompromised—though much indeed may be lost in secrecy, mystery, obscurity, and anonymity.

Privacy is lost in either of two ways. It may be given up, or it may be taken away. Abandonment of privacy (though sometimes undesired) is an inoffensive loss, while deprivation by others is an offensive loss.

If one makes a public disclosure of personal matters or exposes himself under circumstances that do not contain elements of restriction on further communication, there is loss of control for which the person whose privacy is lost is himself responsible. Such abandonment may result from indifference, carelessness, or a positive desire to have others become acquainted. There are, however, instances in which privacy is abandoned though this was not intended. Consider indiscrete disclosures while drunk which are rued when sober. If the audience is not under some obligation (perhaps the duty of a confidant) to keep dark what was revealed, there has been a loss of privacy for which the one who suffers it is responsible. But to constitute an abandonment, the loss of privacy must result from voluntary conduct by the one losing it, and the loss must be an expectable result of such conduct. If these two conditions are not met, the person who suffers the loss cannot be said to be responsible for it. Accordingly, a forced revelation, such as an involuntary confession, is not an abandonment of privacy, because the person making it has not given up control but has had it taken from him.

Regarding the requirement of expectability, we may see its significance by contrasting the case of a person whose conversation is overheard in Grand Central Station with the plight of someone made the victim of eavesdropping in his living room. In a public place loss of control is expectable by virtue of the circumstances of communication: part of what we mean when we say a place is public is that there is not present the physical limitation upon which such control depends. But a place may be called private only when there is such limitation, so communication in it is expectably limited and the eavesdropping an offensive violation for which the victim is not himself responsible. And consider the intermediate case of eavesdropping on a conversation in a public place —a distant parabolic microphone focused on a street-corner conversation, or a bugging device planted in an airplane seat. The offensive charac-

ter of such practices derives again from their disregard of expectable limitations, in this instance the force of an exclusionary social convention which applies to all except those whose immediate presence enables them to overhear.

So far there has been consideration of what constitutes loss of privacy, and when it is objectionable. But to assess claims for protection of privacy we must be clear also about *why* in general loss of privacy is objectionable. This becomes especially important when privacy and other things we value are in competition, one needing to be sacrificed to promote the other. It becomes important then to understand what good reasons there are for valuing privacy, and this is our next item of business.

II

There are two sorts of things we keep private, and with respect to each, privacy is desirable for somewhat different reasons. Concern for privacy is sometimes concern about which facts about us can become known, and to whom. This includes acquaintance with all those things which make up the person as he may become known—identity, appearance, traits of personality and character, talents, weaknesses, tastes, desires, habits, interests—in short, things which tell us who a person is and what he's like. The other kind of private matter is about our lives—what we've done, intend to do, are doing now, how we feel, what we have, what we need—and concern about privacy here is to restrict acquaintance with these matters. Together these two classes of personal matters comprise all those things which can be private. Certain items of information do indeed have aspects which fit them for either category. For example, a person's belief is something which pertains to him when viewed as characteristic of him, but pertains to the events of his life when viewed as something he has acquired, acts on, and endeavors to have others adopt.

Why is privacy of the person important? This calls mainly for consideration of what is necessary to maintain an integrated personality in a social setting. Although we are largely unaware of what influences us at the time, we are constantly concerned to control how we appear to others, and act to implement this concern in ways extremely subtle and multifarious. Models of image and behavior are noticed, imitated, adopted, so that nuances in speech, gesture, facial expression, *politesse,* and much more become a person as known on an occasion. The deep motive is to influence the reactions of others, and this is at the heart of human social accommodation. Constraints to imitation and disguise can become a pathological problem of serious proportions when concern with appearances interferes with normal functioning, but normal behavior allows, indeed requires, that we perform critically in presenting and withholding in order to effect certain appearances. If these editorial efforts are not to be wasted, we must have a large measure of control over what of us is seen and heard, when, where, and by whom. For this reason we see as offensive the candid camera which records casual behavior with the intention of later showing it as entertainment to a general audience. The victim is not at the time aware of who will see him and so does not have the opportunity to exercise appropriate critical restraint in what he says and does. Although subsequent approval for the showing eliminates grounds for objection to the publication as an offense to privacy, there remains the lingering objection to the prior disregard of limits of acquaintance which are normal to the situation and so presumably relied on by the victim at the time. The nature of the offense is further illuminated by considering its aggravation when the victim has been deliberately introduced unawares into the situation for the purpose of filming his behavior, or its still greater offensiveness if the setting is a place normally providing privacy and assumed to be private by the victim. What we have here are increasingly serious usurpations of a person's prerogative to determine how he shall appear, to whom, and on what occasion.

The same general objection applies regarding loss of privacy where there is information about our personal affairs which is obtained, accumulated, and transmitted by means beyond our control. It is, however, unlike privacy of personality in its untoward consequences. A data bank of personal information is considered objectionable, but not because it creates appearances over which we have no control. We are willing to concede that acquaintance with our reputation is in general not something we are privileged to control, and that we are not privileged to decide just what our reputation shall be. If the reputation is correct we cannot object because we do not appear

as we would wish. What then are the grounds of objection to a data bank, an objection which indeed persists even if its information is correct and the inferences based on the information are sound? A good reason for objecting is that a data bank is an offense to self-determination. We are subject to being acted on by others because of conclusions about us which we do not know and whose effect we have no opportunity to counteract. There is a loss of control over reputation which is unacceptable because we no longer have the ability to try to change what is believed about us. We feel entitled to know what others believe, and why, so that we may try to change misleading impressions and on occasion show why a decision about us ought not to be based on reputation even if the reputation is justified. If our account in the data bank were made known to us and opportunity given to change its effect, we should drop most (though not all) of our objection to it. We might still fear the danger of abuse by public forces concerned more with the demands of administrative convenience than justice, but because we could make deposits and demand a statement reflecting them, we would at least no longer be in the position of having what is known and surmised about us lie beyond our control.

Two aspects of privacy have been considered separately, though situations in which privacy is violated sometimes involve both. Ordinary surveillance by shadowing, peeping, and bugging commonly consists of observation of personal behavior as well as accumulation of information. Each is objectionable for its own reasons, though in acting against the offensive practice we protect privacy in both aspects. Furthermore, privacy of personality and of personal affairs have some common ground in meriting protection, and this has to do with a person's role as a responsible moral agent.

In general we do not criticize a person for untoward occurrences which are a result of his conduct if (through no fault of his own) he lacked the ability to do otherwise. Such a person is similarly ineligible for applause for admirable things which would not have taken place but for his conduct. In both instances we claim that he is not responsible for what happened, and so should not be blamed or praised. The principle holds true regarding loss of privacy. If a person cannot control how he is made to appear (nor could he have prevented his loss of control), he is not responsible for how he appears or is thought of, and therefore cannot be criticized as displeasing or disreputable (nor extolled as the opposite). He can, of course, be condemned for conduct which is the basis of the belief about him, but that is a different matter from criticism directed solely to the fact that such a belief exists. Personal gossip (even when believed) is not treated by others as something for which the subject need answer, because its existence defies his control. Responsible appraisal of anyone whose image or reputation is a matter of concern requires that certain private items illicitly in the public domain be ignored in the assessment. A political figure may, with impunity, be known as someone who smokes, drinks, flirts, and tells dirty jokes, so long (but only so long) as this is not the public image *he* presents. The contrasting fortunes of recent political leaders remind us that not being responsible for what is believed by others can be most important. If such a man is thought in his private life to engage in discreet though illicit liaisons he is not held accountable for rumors without more. However, once he has allowed himself to be publicly exposed in a situation which is in the slightest compromising, he must answer for mere appearances. And on this same point, we might consider why a woman is never held responsible for the way she appears in the privacy of her toilette.

To appreciate the importance of this sort of disclaimer of responsibility we need only imagine a community in which it is not recognized. Each person would be accountable for himself however he might be known, and regardless of any precautionary seclusion which was undertaken in the interest of shame, good taste, or from other motives of self-regard. In such a world modesty is sacrificed to the embarrassment of unwanted acclaim, and self-criticism is replaced by the condemnation of others. It is part of the vision of Orwell's *1984,* in which observation is so thorough that it forecloses the possibility of a private sector of life under a person's exclusionary control, and so makes him answerable for everything observed without limits of time or place. Because of this we feel such a condition of life far more objectionable than a community which makes the same oppressive social demands of loyalty and conformity but with the opportunity to be free of concern about appearances in private. In a com-

munity without privacy, furthermore, there can be no editorial privilege exercised in making oneself known to others. Consider, for example, the plight in which Montaigne would find himself. He observed that "No quality embraces us purely and universally. If it did not seem crazy to talk to oneself, there is not a day when I would not be heard growling at myself: 'Confounded fool!' And yet I do not intend that to be my definition." Respect for privacy is required to safeguard our changes of mood and mind, and to promote growth of the person through self-discovery and criticism. We want to run the risk of making fools of ourselves and be free to call ourselves fools, yet not be fools in the settled opinion of the world, convicted out of our own mouths.

III

Privacy is desirable, but rights to enjoy it are not absolute. In deciding what compromises must be made some deep quandaries recur, and three of them at least seem more manageable in light of what has been said so far.

In the first place, insistence on privacy is often taken as implied admission that there is cause for shame. The assumption is that the only reason for keeping something from others is that one is ashamed of it (although it is conceded that sometimes there is in fact no cause for shame even though the person seeking privacy thinks there is). Those who seek information and wish to disregard interests in privacy often play on this notion by claiming that the decent and the innocent have no cause for shame and so no need for privacy: "Only those who have done or wish to do something shameful demand privacy." But it is unsound to assume that demands for privacy imply such an admission. Pride, or at least wholesome self-regard, is the motive in many situations. The famous Warren and Brandeis article on privacy which appeared in the *Harvard Law Review* in 1890 was impelled in some measure, we are told, by Samuel Warren's chagrin. His daughter's wedding, a very social Boston affair, had been made available to the curious at every newsstand by the local press. Surely he was not ashamed of the wedding even though outraged by the publicity. Or consider Miss Roberson, the lovely lady whose picture was placed on a poster advertising the product of Franklin Mills with the eulogistic slogan "Flour of the family," thereby precipitating a lawsuit whose consequences included the first statutory protection of privacy in the United States. What was exploited was the lady's face, undoubtedly a source of pride.

Both these encroachments on privacy illustrate the same point. Things which people like about themselves are taken by them to belong to them in a particularly exclusive way, and so control over disclosure or publication is especially important to them. The things about himself which a person is most proud of he values most, and thus are things over which he is most interested to exercise exclusive control. It is true that shame is not infrequently the motive for privacy, for often we do seek to maintain conditions necessary to avoid criticism and punishment. But since it is not the only motive, the quest for privacy does not entail tacit confessions. Confusion arises here in part because an assault on privacy always does involve humiliation of the victim. But this is because he has been deprived of control over something personal which is given over to the control of others. In short, unwilling loss of privacy always results in the victim being shamed, not because of what others learn, but because they and not he may then determine who else shall know it and what use shall be made of it.

Defining the privilege to make public what is otherwise private is another source of persistent difficulty. There is a basic social interest in making available information about people, in exploring the personal aspects of human affairs, in stimulating and satisfying curiosity about others. The countervailing interest is in allowing people who have not offered themselves for public scrutiny to remain out of sight and out of mind. In much of the United States the law has strained with the problem of drawing a line of protection which accords respect to both interests. The result, broadly stated, has been recognition of a privilege to compromise privacy for news and other material whose primary purpose is to impart information, but to deny such privileged status to literary and other art, to entertainment, and generally to any appropriation for commercial purposes. Development of the law in New York after Miss Roberson's unsuccessful attempt to restrain public display of her picture serves as a good example. A statute was enacted prohibiting unauthorized use of the name, portrait, or picture of any living person for purposes of trade or advertising, and the legislation has been inter-

preted by the courts along the general lines indicated. But it is still open to speculation why a writer's portrayal of a real person as a character in a novel could qualify as violative, while the same account in biographical or historical work would not. It has not been held that history represents a more important social interest than art and so is more deserving of a privileged position in making known personal matters, or, more generally, that edification is more important than entertainment. Nor is the question ever raised, as one might expect, whether an item of news is sufficiently newsworthy to enjoy a privilege in derogation of privacy. Further, it was not held that the implied statutory criterion of intended economic benefit from the use of a personality would warrant the fundamental distinctions. Indeed, the test of economic benefit would qualify both television's public affairs programs and its dramatic shows as within the statute, and the reportage of *Life* Magazine would be as restricted as the films of De Mille or Fellini. But in each instance the former is in general free of the legal prohibition while the latter is not. What, then, is the basis of distinction? Though not articulated, a sound criterion does exist.

Unauthorized *use* of another person—whether for entertainment, artistic creation, or economic gain—is offensive. So long as we remain in charge of how we are used, we have no cause for complaint. In those cases in which a legal wrong is recognized, there has been use by others in disregard of this authority, but in those cases in which a privilege is found, there is not *use* of personality or personal affairs at all, at least not use in the sense of one person assuming control over another, which is the gist of the offense to autonomy. We do indeed suffer a loss of autonomy whenever the power to place us in free circulation is exercised by others, but we consider such loss offensive only when another person assumes the control of which we are deprived, when we are used and not merely exposed. Failure to make clear this criterion of offensiveness has misled those who wish to define the protectable area, and they conceive the problem as one of striking an optimal balance between two valuable interests, when in fact it is a matter of deciding whether the acts complained of are offensive under a quite definite standard of offensiveness. The difficult cases here have not presented a dilemma of selecting the happy medium, but rather the slippery job of determining whether the defendant had used the plaintiff or whether he had merely caused things about him to become known, albeit to the defendant's profit. The difference is between managing another person as a means to one's own ends, which is offensive, and acting merely as a vehicle of presentation (though not gratuitously) to satisfy established social needs, which is not offensive. Cases dealing with an unauthorized biography that was heavily anecdotal and of questionable accuracy, or with an entertaining article that told the true story of a former child prodigy who became an obscure eccentric, are perplexing ones because they present elements of both offensive and inoffensive publication, and a decision turns on which is predominant.

There remains another balance-striking quandary to be dismantled. It is often said that privacy as an interest must be balanced against security. Each, we think, must sacrifice something of privacy to promote the security of all, though we are willing to risk some insecurity to preserve a measure of privacy. Pressure to reduce restrictions on wiretapping and searches by police seeks to push the balance toward greater security. But the picture we are given is seriously misleading. In the first place we must notice the doubtful assumption on which the argument rests. It may be stated this way: the greater the ability to watch what is going on, or obtain evidence of what has gone on, the greater the ability to prevent crime. It is a notion congenial to those who believe that more efficient law enforcement contributes significantly to a reduction in crime. We must, however, determine if such a proposition is in fact sound, and we must see what crimes are suppressible, even in principle, before any sacrifice of privacy can be justified. There is, at least *in limine*, much to be said for the conflicting proposition that, once a generally efficient system of law enforcement exists, an increase in its efficiency does not result in a corresponding reduction in crime, but only in an increase in punishments. Apart from that point, there is an objection relating more directly to what has been said here about privacy. Security and privacy are both desirable, but measures to promote each are on different moral footing. Men ought to be secure, we say, because only in that condition can they live a good life. Privacy, however, like peace and prosperity, is itself part of what we mean by a good life, a part having to do with self-respect and self-determination. Therefore, the appropriate attitudes when we are asked to sacrifice privacy for security are first a critical one which urges alternatives that minimize or do not at all require the sacrifice, and ultimately regret for loss of a cherished resource if the sacrifice proves necessary.

IV

In speaking of privacy and autonomy, there is some danger that privacy may be conceived as autonomy. Such confusion has been signaled in legal literature by early and repeated use of the phrase "right to be let alone" as a synonym for "right of privacy." The United States Supreme Court succumbed completely in 1965 in its opinion in *Griswold v. Connecticut,* and the ensuing intellectual disorder warrants comment.

In that case legislative prohibition of the use of contraceptives was said to be a violation of a constitutional right of privacy, at least when it affected married people. The court's opinion relied heavily on an elaborate *jeu de mots,* in which different senses of the word "privacy" were punned upon, and the legal concept generally mismanaged in ways too various to recount here. In the *Griswold* situation there had been an attempt by government to regulate personal affairs, not get acquainted with them, and so there was an issue regarding autonomy and not privacy. The opinion was not illuminating on the question of what are proper bounds for the exercise of legislative power, which was the crucial matter before the court. It is precisely the issue of what rights to autonomous determination of his affairs are enjoyed by a citizen. The *Griswold* opinion not only failed to take up that question in a forthright manner, but promoted confusion about privacy in the law by unsettling the intellectual focus on it which had been developed in torts and constitutional law. If the confusion in the court's argument was inadvertent, one may sympathize with the deep conceptual difficulties which produced it, and if it was deliberately contrived, admire its ingenuity. Whatever its origin, its effect is to muddle the separate issues, which must be analyzed and argued along radically different lines when protection is sought either for privacy or for autonomy. Hopefully, further developments will make clear that while an offense to privacy is an offense to autonomy, not every curtailment of autonomy is a compromise of privacy.

RONALD M. DWORKIN

On Not Prosecuting Civil Disobedience*

How should the government deal with those who disobey the draft laws out of conscience? Many people think the answer is obvious: the government must prosecute the dissenters, and if they are convicted it must punish them. Some people reach this conclusion easily, because they hold the mindless view that conscientious disobedience is the same as lawlessness. They think that the dissenters are anarchists who must be punished before their corruption spreads. Many lawyers and intellectuals come to the same conclusion, however, on what looks like a more sophisticated argument. They recognize that disobedience to law may be *morally* justified, but they insist that it cannot be *legally* justified, and they think that it follows from this truism that the law must be enforced. Erwin Griswold, the Solicitor General of the United States, and the former dean of the Harvard Law School, appears to have adopted this view in a recent statement. "[It] is of the essence of law," he said, "that it is equally applied to all, that it binds all alike, irrespective of personal motive. For this reason, one who contemplates civil disobedience out of moral conviction should not be surprised and must not be bitter if a criminal conviction ensues. And he must accept the fact that organized society cannot endure on any other basis."

The New York Times applauded that statement. A thousand faculty members of several universities had signed a *Times* advertisement calling on the Justice Department to quash the indictments of the Rev. William Sloane Coffin, Dr. Benjamin Spock, Marcus Raskin, Mitchell Goodman, and Michael Ferber, for conspiring to counsel various draft offenses. The *Times* said that the request to quash the indictments "confused moral rights with legal responsibilities."

But the argument that, because the government believes a man has committed a crime, it must prosecute him is much weaker than it seems. Society "cannot endure" if it tolerates all disobedience; it does not follow, however, nor is there evidence, that it will collapse if it tolerates some. In the United States prosecutors have discretion whether to enforce criminal laws in particular cases. A prosecutor may properly decide not to press charges if the lawbreaker is young, or inexperienced, or the sole support of a family, or is repentant, or turns state's evidence, or if the law is unpopular or unworkable or generally disobeyed, or if the courts are clogged with more important cases, or for dozens of other reasons. This discretion is not license—we expect prosecutors to have good reasons for exercising it—but there are, at least *prima facie*, some good reasons for not prosecuting those who disobey the draft laws out of conscience. One is the obvious reason that they act out of better motives than those who break the law out of greed or a desire to subvert government. Another is the practical reason that our society suffers a loss if it punishes a group that includes—as a group of draft dissenters does—some of its most thoughtful and loyal citizens. Jailing such men solidifies their alienation from society, and alienates many like them who are deterred by the threat.

Those who think that conscientious draft offenders should always be punished must show that these are not good reasons for exercising discretion, or they must find contrary reasons that outweigh them. What arguments might they produce? There are practical reasons for enforcing the draft laws, and I shall consider some of these later. But Dean Griswold and those who agree with him seem to rely on a fundamental moral argument that it would be unfair, not merely impractical, to let the dissenters go unpunished. They think it would be unfair, I gather,

*Reprinted from *New York Review of Books,* June 6, 1968. Copyright © 1968, NYREV, Inc. Reprinted by permission of the author and the publisher.

because society could not function if everyone disobeyed laws he disapproved of or found disadvantageous. If the government tolerates those few who will not "play the game," it allows them to secure the benefits of everyone else's deference to law, without shouldering the burdens, such as the burden of the draft.

This argument is a serious one. It cannot be answered simply by saying that the dissenters would allow everyone else the privilege of disobeying a law he believed immoral. In fact, few draft dissenters would accept a changed society in which sincere segregationists were free to break civil rights laws they hated. The majority want no such change, in any event, because they think that society would be worse off for it; until they are shown this is wrong, they will expect their officials to punish anyone who assumes a privilege which they, for the general benefit, do not assume.

There is, however, a flaw in the argument. The reasoning contains a hidden assumption that makes it almost entirely irrelevant to the draft cases, and indeed to any serious case of civil disobedience in the United States. The argument assumes that the dissenters know that they are breaking a valid law, and that the privilege they assert is the privilege to do that. Of course, almost everyone who discusses civil disobedience recognizes that in America a law may be invalid because it is unconstitutional. But the critics handle this complexity by arguing on separate hypotheses: If the law is invalid, then no crime is committed, and society may not punish. If the law is valid, then a crime has been committed, and society must punish. This reasoning hides the crucial fact that the validity of the law may be doubtful. The officials and judges may believe that the law is valid, the dissenters may disagree, and both sides may have plausible arguments for their positions. If so, then the issues are different from what they would be if the law were clearly valid or clearly invalid, and the argument of fairness, designed for these alternatives, is irrelevant.

Doubtful law is by no means special or exotic in cases of civil disobedience. On the contrary. In the United States, at least, almost any law which a significant number of people would be tempted to disobey on moral grounds would be doubtful —if not clearly invalid—on constitutional grounds as well. The Constitution makes our con-

ventional political morality relevant to the question of validity; any statute that appears to compromise that morality raises constitutional questions, and if the compromise is serious, the constitutional doubts are serious also.

The connection between moral and legal issues is especially clear in the current draft cases. Dissent has largely been based on the following moral objections: (a) The United States is using immoral weapons and tactics in Vietnam. (b) The war has never been endorsed by deliberate, considered, and open vote of the peoples' representatives. (c) The United States has no interest at stake in Vietnam remotely strong enough to justify forcing a segment of its citizens to risk death there. (d) If an army is to be raised to fight that war, it is immoral to raise it by a draft that defers or exempts college students, and thus discriminates against the economically underprivileged. (e) The draft exempts those who object to all wars on religious grounds, but not those who object to particular wars on moral grounds; there is no relevant difference between these positions, and so the draft, by making the distinction, implies that the second group is less worthy of the nation's respect than the first. (f) The law that makes it a crime to counsel draft resistance stifles those who oppose the war, because it is morally impossible to argue that the war is profoundly immoral, without encouraging and assisting those who refuse to fight it.

Lawyers will recognize that these moral positions, if we accept them, provide the basis for the following constitutional arguments: (a) The Constitution makes treaties part of the law of the land, and the United States is a party to international conventions and covenants that make illegal the acts of war the dissenters charge the nation with committing. (b) The Constitution provides that Congress must declare war; the legal issue of whether our action in Vietnam is a "war" and whether the Tonkin Bay Resolution was a "declaration" is the heart of the moral issue of whether the government has made a deliberate and open decision. (c) Both the due process clause of the Fifth and Fourteenth Amendments and the equal protection clause of the Fourteenth Amendment condemn special burdens placed on a selected class of citizens when the burden or the classification is not reasonable; the burden is unreasonable when it patently does not serve the public interest, or when it is vastly disproportionate to the interest served. If our military action in Vietnam is frivolous or perverse, as the dissenters claim, then the burden we place on men of draft age is unreasonable and unconstitutional. (d) In any event, the discrimination in favor of college students denies to the poor the equal protection of the law that is guaranteed by the Constitution. (e) If there is no pertinent difference between religious objection to all wars, and moral objection to some wars, then the classification the draft makes is arbitrary and unreasonable, and unconstitutional on that ground. The "establishment of religion" clause of the First Amendment forbids governmental pressure in favor of organized religion; if the draft's distinction coerces men in this direction, it is invalid on that count also. (f) The First Amendment also condemns invasions of freedom of speech. If the draft law's prohibition on counseling does inhibit expression of a range of views on the war, it abridges free speech.

The principal counterargument, supporting the view that the courts ought not to hold the draft unconstitutional, also involves moral issues. Under the so-called "political question" doctrine, the courts deny their own jurisdiction to pass on matters—such as foreign or military policy—whose resolution is best assigned to other branches of the government. The Boston court trying the Coffin, Spock case has already declared, on the basis of this doctrine, that it will not hear arguments about the legality of the war. But the Supreme Court has shown itself (in the reapportionment cases, for example) reluctant to refuse jurisdiction when it believed that the gravest issues of political morality were at stake and that no remedy was available through the political process. If the dissenters are right, and the war and the draft are state crimes of profound injustice to a group of citizens, then the argument that the courts must refuse jurisdiction is considerably weakened.

We cannot conclude from these arguments that the draft (or any part of it) is unconstitutional. If the Supreme Court is called upon to rule on the question, it will probably reject some of them, and refuse to consider the others on grounds that they are political. The majority of lawyers would probably agree with this result. But the arguments of unconstitutionality are at least plausible, and a reasonable and competent

lawyer might well think that they present a stronger case, on balance, than the counterarguments. If he does, he will consider that the draft is not constitutional, and there will be no way of proving that he is wrong.

Therefore we cannot assume, in judging what to do with the draft dissenters, that they are asserting a privilege to disobey valid laws. We cannot decide that fairness demands their punishment until we try to answer the further question: What should a citizen do when the law is unclear, and when he thinks it allows what others think it does not? I do not mean to ask, of course, what it is *legally* proper for him to do, or what his *legal* rights are—that would be begging the question, because it depends upon whether he is right or they are right. I mean to ask what his proper course is as a citizen, what in other words, we would consider to be "playing the game." That is a crucial question, because it cannot be wrong not to punish him if he is acting as, given his opinions, we think he should.[1]

There is no obvious answer on which most citizens would readily agree, and that is itself significant. If we examine our legal institutions and practices, however, we shall discover some relevant underlying principles and policies. I shall set out three possible answers to the question, and then try to show which of these best fits our practices and expectations. The three possibilities I want to consider are these:

(1) If the law is doubtful, and it is therefore unclear whether it permits someone to do what he wants, he should assume the worst, and act on the assumption that it does not. He should obey the executive authorities who command him, even though he thinks they are wrong, while using the political process, if he can, to change the law.

(2) If the law is doubtful, he may follow his own judgment, that is, he may do what he wants if he believes that the case that the law permits this is stronger than the case that it does not. But he may follow his own judgment only until an authoritative institution, like a court, decides the other way in a case involving him or someone else. Once an institutional decision has been reached, he must abide by that decision, even though he thinks that it was wrong. (There are, in theory, many subdivisions of this second possibility. We may say that the individual's choice is

foreclosed by the contrary decision of any court, including the lowest court in the system if the case is not appealed. Or we may require a decision of some particular court or institution. I shall discuss this second possibility in its most liberal form, namely that the individual may properly follow his own judgment until a contrary decision of the highest court competent to pass on the issue, which, in the case of the draft, is the United States Supreme Court.)

(3) If the law is doubtful, he may follow his own judgment, even after a contrary decision by the highest competent court. Of course, he must take the contrary decision of any court into account in making his judgment of what the law requires. Otherwise the judgment would not be an honest or reasonable one, because the doctrine of precedent, which is an established part of our legal system, has the effect of allowing the decision of the courts to *change* the law. Suppose, for example, that a taxpayer believes that he is not required to pay tax on certain forms of income. If the Supreme Court decides to the contrary, he should, taking into account the practice of according great weight to the decisions of the Supreme Court on tax matters, decide that the Court's decision has itself tipped the balance, and that the law now requires him to pay the tax.

Someone might think that this qualification erases the difference between the third and the second models, but it does not. The doctrine of precedent gives different weights to the decisions of different courts, and greatest weight to the decisions of the Supreme Court, but it does not make the decision of any court conclusive. Sometimes, even after a contrary Supreme Court decision, an individual may still reasonably believe that the law is on his side; such cases are rare, but they are most likely in disputes over constitutional law when civil disobedience is involved. The Court has shown itself more likely to overrule its past decisions if these have limited important personal or political rights, and it is just these decisions that a dissenter might want to challenge.

We cannot assume, in other words, that the Constitution is always what the Supreme Court says it is. Oliver Wendell Holmes, for example, did not follow such a rule in his famous dissent in the *Gitlow* case. A few years before, in *Abrams*, he had lost his battle to persuade the court that the First Amendment protected an anarchist who had been urging general strikes against the government. A similar issue was presented in *Gitlow*, and Holmes once again dissented. "It is true," he said, "that in my opinion this criterion was departed from in [Abrams] but the convictions that I expressed in that case are too deep for it to be possible for me as yet to believe that it . . . settled the law." Holmes voted for acquitting Gitlow, on the ground that what Gitlow had done was no crime, even though the Supreme Court had recently held that it was.

Here then are three possible models for the behavior of dissenters who disagree with the executive authorities when the law is doubtful. Which of them best fits our legal and social practices?

I think it plain that we do not follow the first of these models, that is, that we do not expect citizens to assume the worst. If no court has decided the issue, and a man thinks, on balance, that the law is on his side, most of our lawyers and critics think it perfectly proper for him to follow his own judgment. Even when many disapprove of what he does—such as peddling pornography—they do not think he must desist just because its legality is subject to doubt.

It is worth pausing a moment to consider what society would lose if it did follow the first model or, to put the matter the other way, what society gains when people follow their own judgment in cases like this. When the law is uncertain, in the sense that lawyers can reasonably disagree on what a court ought to decide, the reason usually is that different legal principles and policies have collided, and it is unclear how best to accommodate these conflicting principles and policies.

Our practice, in which different parties are encouraged to pursue their own understanding, provides a means of testing relevant hypotheses. If the question is whether a particular rule would have certain undesirable consequences, or whether these consequences would have limited or broad ramifications, then, before the issue is decided, it is useful to know what does in fact take place when some people proceed on that rule. (Much anti-trust and business regulation law has developed through this kind of testing.) If the question is whether and to what degree a particular solution would offend principles of justice or fair play deeply respected by the community, it is useful, again, to experiment by testing the community's response. The extent of community indifference to anticontraception laws, for example, would never have become established had not some organizations deliberately flouted those laws in Connecticut.

If the first model were followed, we would lose the advantages of these tests. The law would suffer, particularly if this model were applied to constitutional issues. When the validity of a criminal statute is in doubt, the statute will almost always strike some people as being unfair or unjust, because it will infringe some principle of liberty or justice or fairness which they take to be built into the Constitution. If our practice were that whenever a law is doubtful on these grounds, one must act as if it were valid, then the chief vehicle we have for challenging the law on moral grounds would be lost, and over time the law we obeyed would certainly become less fair and just, and the liberty of our citizens would certainly be diminished.

We would lose almost as much if we used a variation of the first model, that a citizen must assume the worst unless he can anticipate that the courts will agree with his view of the law. If everyone deferred to his guess of what the courts would do, society and its law would be poorer. Our assumption in rejecting the first model was that the record a citizen makes in following his own judgment, together with the arguments he makes supporting that judgment when he has the opportunity, are helpful in creating the best judicial decision possible. This remains true even when, at the time the citizen acts, the odds are against his success in court. We must remember, too, that the value of the citizen's example is not exhausted once the decision has been made. Our practices require that the decision be criticized, by the legal profession and the law schools, and the record of dissent may be invaluable here.

Of course a man must consider what the courts will do when he decides whether it would be *prudent* to follow his own judgment. He may have to face jail, bankruptcy, or opprobrium if he does. But it is essential that we separate the calculation of prudence from the question of what, as a good citizen, he may properly do. We are investigating how society ought to treat him when its courts believe that he judged wrong; therefore we must ask what he is justified in doing when his judgment differs from others. We beg the question if

we assume that what he may properly do depends on his guess as to how society will treat him.

We must also reject the second model, that if the law is unclear a citizen may properly follow his own judgment until the highest court has ruled that he is wrong. This fails to take into account the fact that any court, including the Supreme Court, may overrule itself. In 1940 the Court decided that a West Virginia law requiring students to salute the Flag was constitutional. In 1943 it reversed itself, and decided that such a statute was unconstitutional after all. What was the duty, as citizens, of those people who in 1941 and 1942 objected to saluting the Flag on grounds of conscience, and thought that the Court's 1940 decision was wrong? We can hardly say that their duty was to follow the first decision. They believed that saluting the Flag was unconscionable, and they believed, reasonably, that no valid law required them to do so. The Supreme Court later decided that in this they were right. The Court did not simply hold that after the second decision failing to salute would not be a crime; it held (as in a case like this it almost always would) that it was no crime after the first decision either.

Some will say that the flag-salute dissenters should have obeyed the Court's first decision, while they worked in the legislatures to have the law repealed, and tried in the courts to find some way to challenge the law again without actually violating it. That would be, perhaps, a plausible recommendation if conscience were not involved, because it would then be arguable that the gain in orderly procedure was worth the personal sacrifice of patience. But conscience was involved, and if the dissenters had obeyed the law while biding their time, they would have suffered the irreparable injury of having done what their conscience forbade them to do. It is one thing to say that an individual must sometimes violate his conscience when he knows that the law commands him to do it. It is quite another to say that he must violate his conscience even when he reasonably believes that the law does not require it, because it would inconvenience his fellow citizens if he took the most direct, and perhaps the only, method of attempting to show that he is right and they are wrong.

Since a court may overrule itself, the same reasons we listed for rejecting the first model count against the second as well. If we did not have the pressure of dissent, we would not have a dramatic statement of the degree to which a court decision against the dissenter is felt to be wrong, a demonstration that is surely pertinent to the question of whether it was right. We would increase the chance of being governed by rules that offend the principles we claim to serve.

These considerations force us, I think, from the second model, but some will want to substitute a variation of it. They will argue that once the Supreme Court has decided that a criminal law is valid, then citizens have a duty to abide by that decision until they have a reasonable belief, not merely that the decision is bad law, but that the Supreme Court is likely to overrule it. Under this view the West Virginia dissenters who refused to salute the flag in 1942 were acting properly, because they might reasonably have anticipated that the Court would change its mind. But if the Court were to hold the draft laws constitutional, it would be improper to continue to challenge these laws, because there would be no great likelihood that the Court would soon change its mind. This suggestion must also be rejected, however. For once we say that a citizen may properly follow his own judgment of the law, in spite of his judgment that the courts will probably find against him, there is no plausible reason why he should act differently because a contrary decision is already on the books.

Thus the third model, or something close to it, seems to be the fairest statement of a man's social duty in our community. A citizen's allegiance is to the law, not to any particular person's view of what the law is, and he does not behave improperly or unfairly so long as he proceeds on his own considered and reasonable view of what the law requires. Let me repeat (because it is crucial) that this is not the same as saying that an individual may disregard what the courts have said. The doctrine of precedent lies near the core of our legal system, and no one can make a reasonable effort to follow the law unless he grants the courts the general power to alter it by their decisions. But if the issue is one touching fundamental personal or political rights, and it is arguable that the Supreme Court has made a mistake, a man is within his social rights in refusing to accept that decision as conclusive.

One large question remains before we can apply these observations to the problem of draft resistance. I have been talking about the case of a man who believes that the law is not what other people think, or what the courts have held. This description may fit some of those who disobey the draft laws out of conscience, but it does not fit most of them. Most of the dissenters are not lawyers or political philosophers; they believe that the laws on the books are immoral, and inconsistent with their country's legal ideals, but they have not considered the question of whether they may be invalid as well. Of what relevance to their situation, then, is the proposition that one may properly follow one's own view of the law?

To answer this, I shall have to return to the point I made earlier. The Constitution, through the due process clause, the equal protection clause, the First Amendment, and the other provisions I mentioned, injects an extraordinary amount of our political morality into the issue of whether a law is valid. The statement that most draft dissenters are unaware that the law is invalid therefore needs qualification. They hold beliefs that, if true, strongly support the view that the law is on their side; the fact that they have not reached that further conclusion can be traced, in at least most cases, to their lack of legal sophistication. If we believe that when the law is doubtful people who follow their own judgment of the law may be acting properly, it would seem wrong not to extend that view to those dissenters whose judgments come to the same thing. No part of the case that I made for the third model would entitle us to distinguish them from their more knowledgeable colleagues.

We can draw several tentative conclusions from the argument so far: When the law is uncertain, in the sense that a plausible case can be made on both sides, then a citizen who follows his own judgment is not behaving unfairly. Our practices permit and encourage him to follow his own judgment in such cases. For that reason, our government has a special responsibility to try to protect him, and soften his predicament, whenever it can do so without great damage to other policies. It does not follow that the government can guarantee him immunity—it cannot adopt the rule that it will prosecute no one who acts out of conscience, or convict no one who reasonably disagrees with the courts. That would paralyze the government's ability to carry out its policies; it would, moreover, throw away the most important benefit of following the third model. If the state never prosecuted, then the courts could not act on the experience and the arguments the dissent has generated. But it does follow from the government's responsibility that when the practical reasons for prosecuting are relatively weak in a particular case, or can be met in other ways, the path of fairness may lie in tolerance. The popular view that the law is the law and must always be enforced refuses to distinguish the man who acts on his own judgment of a doubtful law, and thus behaves as our practices provide, from the common criminal. I know of no reason, short of moral blindness, for not drawing a distinction in principle between the two cases.

I anticipate a philosophical objection to these conclusions: that I am treating law as a "brooding omnipresence in the sky." I have spoken of people making judgments about what the law requires, even in cases in which the law is unclear and undemonstrable. I have spoken of cases in which a man might think that the law requires one thing, even though the Supreme Court has said that it requires another, and even when it was not likely that the Supreme Court would soon change its mind. It will therefore be charged with the view that there is always a "right answer" to a legal problem to be found in natural law or locked up in some transcendental strongbox.

The strongbox theory of law is, of course, nonsense. When I say that people hold views on the law when the law is doubtful, and that these views are not merely predictions of what the courts will hold, I intend no such metaphysics. I mean only to summarize as accurately as I can many of the practices that are part of our legal process.

Lawyers and judges make statements of legal right and duty, even when they know these are not demonstrable, and support them with arguments even when they know that these arguments will not appeal to everyone. They make these arguments to one another in the professional journals, in the classroom, and in the courts. They respond to these arguments, when others make them, by judging them good or bad or mediocre. In so doing they assume that some arguments for a given doubtful position are better than others. They also assume that the case on one side of a doubtful proposition may be stronger than the case on the other, which is what

I take a claim of law in a doubtful case to mean. They distinguish, without too much difficulty, these arguments from predictions of what the courts will decide.

These practices are poorly represented by the theory that judgments of law on doubtful issues are nonsense, or are merely predictions of what the courts will do. Those who hold such theories cannot deny the fact of these practices; perhaps these theorists mean that the practices are not sensible, because they are based on suppositions that do not hold, or for some other reason. But this makes their objection mysterious, because they never specify what they take the purposes underlying these practices to be; and unless these goals are specified, one cannot decide whether the practices are sensible. I understand these underlying purposes to be those I described earlier: the development and testing of the law through experimentation by citizens and through the adversary process.

Our legal system pursues these goals by inviting citizens to decide the strengths and weaknesses of legal arguments for themselves, or through their own counsel, and to act on these judgments, although that permission is qualified by the limited threat that they may suffer if the courts do not agree. Success in this strategy depends on whether there is sufficient agreement within the community on what counts as a good or bad argument, so that, although different people will reach different judgments, these differences will be neither so profound nor so frequent as to make the system unworkable, or dangerous for those who act by their own lights. I believe there is sufficient agreement on the criteria of the argument to avoid these traps, although one of the main tasks of legal philosophy is to exhibit and clarify these criteria. In any event, the practices I have described have not yet been shown to be misguided; they therefore must count in determining whether it is just and fair to be lenient to those who break what others think is the law.

I have said that the government has a special responsibility to those who act on a reasonable judgment that a law is invalid. It should make accommodation for them as far as possible, when this is consistent with other policies. It may be difficult to decide what the government ought to do, in the name of that responsibility, in particular cases. The decision will be a matter of balance, and flat rules will not help. Still, some principles can be set out.

I shall start with the prosecutor's decision whether to press charges. He must balance both his responsibility to be lenient and the risk that convictions will rend the society, against the damage to the law's policy that may follow if he leaves the dissenters alone. In making his calculation he must consider not only the extent to which others will be harmed, but also how the law evaluates that harm; and he must therefore make the following distinction. Every rule of law is supported, and presumably justified, by a set of policies it is supposed to advance and principles it is supposed to respect. Some rules (the laws prohibiting murder and theft, for example) are supported by the proposition that the individuals protected have a moral right to be free from the harm proscribed. Other rules (the more technical anti-trust rules, for example) are not supported by any supposition of an underlying right; their support comes chiefly from the alleged utility of the economic and social policies they promote. These may be supplemented with moral principles (like the view that it is a harsh business practice to undercut a weak competitor's prices) but these fall short of recognizing a moral right against the harm in question.

The point of the distinction here is this: The judgment that someone has a moral right to be free from certain injuries is a very strong form of moral judgment, because a moral right, once acknowledged, outweighs competing claims of utility or virtue. When a law rests on such a judgment, that is a powerful argument against tolerating violations which inflict those injuries—for example, violations that involve personal injury or the destruction of property. The prosecutor may respect the dissenter's view that the law is invalid, but unless he agrees, he must honor the law's judgment that others have an overriding claim of right.

It may be controversial, of course, whether a law rests on the assumption of a right. One must study the background and administration of the law, and reflect on whether any social practices of right and obligation support it. We may take one example in which the judgment is relatively easy. There are many sincere and ardent segregationists who believe that the civil rights laws and decisions are unconstitutional, because they compromise principles of local government and of freedom of association. This is an arguable, though not a persuasive, view. But the constitutional provisions that support these laws clearly embody the view that Negroes, as individuals, have a right not to be segregated. They do not rest simply on the judgment that national policies are best pursued by preventing their segregation. If we take no action against the man who blocks the school house door, therefore, we violate the rights, confirmed by law, of the schoolgirl he blocks. The responsibility of leniency cannot go this far.

The schoolgirl's position is different, however, from that of the draftee who may be called up sooner or given a more dangerous post if draft offenders are not punished. The draft laws do not reflect a judgment that a man has a social or moral right to be drafted only after certain other men or groups have been called. The draft classifications, and the order-of-call according to age within classifications, are arranged for social and administrative convenience. They also reflect considerations of fairness, like the proposition that a mother who has lost one of two sons in war ought not to be made to risk losing the other. But they presuppose no fixed rights. The draft boards are given considerable discretion in the classification process, and the army, of course, has almost complete discretion in assigning dangerous posts. If the prosecutor tolerates draft offenders, he makes small shifts in the law's calculations of fairness and utility. These may cause disadvantage to others in the pool of draftees but that is a different matter from contradicting their social or moral rights.

It is wrong therefore to analyze draft cases and segregation cases in the same way, as many critics do when considering whether tolerance is justified. I do not mean that fairness to others is irrelevant in draft cases; it must be taken into account, and balanced against fairness to dissenters and the long-term benefit to society. But it does not play the commanding role here that it does in segregation cases, and in other cases when rights are at stake.

Where, then, does the balance of fairness and utility lie in the case of those who counsel draft resistance? If these men had encouraged violence or otherwise trespassed on the rights of others, then there would be a strong case for prosecution.

But in the absence of such actions, the balance of fairness and utility seems to me to lie the other way, and I therefore think that the decision to prosecute Coffin, Spock, Raskin, Goodman, and Ferber was wrong. It may be argued that if those who counsel draft resistance are free from prosecution, the number who resist induction will increase; but it will not, I think, increase much beyond the number of those who would resist on any event.

If I am wrong, and there is much greater resistance, then a sense of this residual discontent is of importance to policy makers, and it ought not to be hidden under a ban on speech. Conscience is deeply involved—it is hard to believe that many who counsel resistance do so on any other grounds. The case is strong that the laws making counseling a crime are unconstitutional; even those who do not find the case persuasive will admit that its arguments have substance. The harm to potential draftees, both those who may be persuaded to resist and those who maybe called earlier because others have been persuaded, is remote and speculative.

The cases of men who refuse induction when drafted are more complicated. The crucial question is whether a failure to prosecute will lead to wholesale refusals to serve. It may not—there are social pressures, including the threat of career disadvantages, that would force many young Americans to serve if drafted, even if they knew they would not go to jail if they refused. If the number would not much increase, then the state should leave the dissenters alone, and I see no great harm in delaying any prosecution until the effect of that policy becomes clearer. If the number of those who refuse induction turns out to be large, this would argue for prosecution. But it would also make the problem academic, because if there were sufficient dissent to bring us to that pass, it would be most difficult to pursue the war in any event, except under a near-totalitarian regime.

There may seem to be a paradox in these conclusions. I argued earlier that when the law is unclear citizens have the right to follow their own judgment, partly on the grounds that this practice helps to shape issues for adjudication; now I propose a course that eliminates or postpones adjudication. But the contradiction is only apparent. It does not follow from the fact that our practice

facilitates adjudication, and renders it more useful in developing the law, that a trial should follow whenever citizens do act by their own lights. The question arises in each case whether the issues are ripe for adjudication, and whether adjudication would settle these issues in a manner that would decrease the chance of, or remove the grounds for, further dissent.

In the draft cases, the answer to both these questions is negative: There is much ambivalence about the war just now, and uncertainty and ignorance about the scope of the moral issues involved in the draft. It is far from the best time for a court to pass on these issues, and tolerating dissent for a time is one way of allowing the debate to continue until it has produced something clearer. Moreover, it is plain that an adjudication of the constitutional issues now will not settle the law. Those who have doubts whether the draft is constitutional will have the same doubts even if the Supreme Court says that it is. This is one of those cases, touching fundamental rights, in which our practices of precedent will encourage these doubts. Certainly this will be so if, as seems likely, the Supreme Court appeals to the political question doctrine, and refuses to pass on the more serious constitutional issues.

Even if the prosecutor does not act, however, the underlying problem will be only temporarily relieved. So long as the law appears to make acts of dissent criminal, a man of conscience will face danger. What can Congress, which shares the responsibility of leniency, do to lessen this danger?

Congress can review the laws in question to see how much accommodation can be given the dissenters. Every program a legislature adopts is a mixture of policies and restraining principles. We accept loss of efficiency in crime detection and urban renewal, for example, so that we can respect the rights of accused criminals and compensate property owners for their damages. Congress may properly defer to its responsibility toward the dissenters by adjusting or compromising other policies. The relevant questions are these: What means can be found for allowing the greatest possible tolerance of conscientious dissent while minimizing its impact on policy? How strong is the government's responsibility for leniency in this case—how deeply is conscience involved, and how strong is the case that the law is invalid after all? How important is the policy in question—is interference with that policy too great a price to pay? These questions are no doubt too simple, but they suggest the heart of the choices that must be made.

For the same reasons that those who counsel resistance should not be prosecuted, I think that the law that makes this a crime should be repealed. The case is strong that this law abridges free speech. It certainly coerces conscience, and it probably serves no beneficial effect. If counseling would persuade only a few to resist who otherwise would not, the value of the restraint is small; if counseling would persuade many, that should be known.

The issues are more complex, again, in the case of draft resistance itself. Those who believe that the war in Vietnam is itself a grotesque blunder will favor any change in the law that makes peace more likely. But if we take the position of those who think the war is necessary, then we must admit that a policy that continues the draft but wholly exempts dissenters would be unwise. Two less drastic alternatives might be considered, however: a volunteer army, and an expanded conscientious objector category that includes those who find this war immoral. There is much to be said against both proposals, but once the requirement of respect for dissent is recognized, the balance of principle may be tipped in their favor.

So the case for not prosecuting conscientious draft offenders, and for changing the laws in their favor, is a strong one. It would be unrealistic to expect this policy to prevail, however, for political pressures now oppose it. Relatively few of those who have refused induction have been indicted so far, but the pace of prosecution is quickening, and many more indictments are expected if the resistance many college seniors have pledged does in fact develop. The Coffin, Spock trial continues, although when the present steps toward peace negotiation were announced, many lawyers had hoped it would be dropped or delayed. There is no sign of any movement to amend the draft laws in the way I have suggested.

We must consider, therefore, what the courts can and should now do. A court might, of course, uphold the arguments that the draft laws are in some way unconstitutional, in general or as applied to the defendants in the case at hand. Or it may acquit the defendants because the facts necessary for conviction are not proved. I shall not argue the constitutional issues, or the facts of any particular case. I want instead to suggest that a court ought not to convict, at least in some circumstances, even if it sustains the statutes and finds the facts as charged. The Supreme Court has not ruled on the chief arguments that the present draft is unconstitutional, nor has it held that these arguments raise political questions that are not relevant to its jurisdiction. If the alleged violations take place before the Supreme Court has decided these issues, and the case reaches that Court, there are strong reasons why the Court should acquit even if it does then sustain the draft. It ought to acquit on the ground that before its decision the validity of the draft was doubtful, and it is unfair to punish men for disobeying a doubtful law.

There would be precedent for a decision along these lines. The Court has several times reversed criminal convictions, on due process grounds, because the law in question was too vague. (It has overturned convictions, for example, under laws that made it a crime to charge "unreasonable prices" or to be a member of a "gang.") Conviction under a vague criminal law offends the moral and political ideals of due process in two ways. First, it places a citizen in the unfair position of either acting at his peril or accepting a more stringent restriction on his life than the legislature may have authorized: As I argued earlier, it is not acceptable, as a model of social behavior, that in such cases he ought to assume the worst. Second, it gives power to the prosecutor and the courts to make criminal law, by opting for one or the other possible interpretations after the event. This would be a delegation of authority by the legislature that is inconsistent with our scheme of separation of powers.

Conviction under a criminal law whose terms are not vague, but whose constitutional validity is doubtful, offends due process in the first of these ways. It forces a citizen to assume the worst, or act at his peril. It offends due process in something like the second way as well. Most citizens would be deterred by a doubtful statute if they were to risk jail by violating it. Congress, and not the courts, would then be the effective voice in deciding the constitutionality of criminal enactments, and this also violates the separation of powers.

If acts of dissent continue to occur after the Supreme Court has ruled that the laws are valid, or that the political question doctrine applies, then acquittal on the grounds I have described is no longer appropriate. The Court's decision will not have finally settled the law, for the reasons given earlier, but the Court will have done all that can be done to settle it. The courts may still exercise their sentencing discretion, however, and impose minimal or suspended sentences as a mark of respect for the dissenters' position.

Some lawyers will be shocked by my general conclusion that we have a responsibility toward those who disobey the draft laws out of conscience, and that we may be required not to prosecute them, but rather to change our laws or adjust our sentencing procedures to accommodate them. The simple Draconian propositions, that crime must be punished, and that he who misjudges the law must take the consequences, have an extraordinary hold on the professional as well as the popular imagination. But the rule of law is more complex and more intelligent than that and it is important that it survive.

NOTE

1. I do not mean to imply that the government should always punish a man who deliberately breaks a law he knows is valid. There may be reasons of fairness or practicality, like those I listed in the third paragraph, for not prosecuting such men. But cases like the draft cases present special arguments for tolerance; I want to concentrate on these arguments and therefore have isolated these cases.

Suggestions for Further Reading

American Law Institute, *Model Penal Code,* Part II, Proposed Official Draft and Comments (1962).

Amsterdam, Anthony, "Federal Constitutional Restrictions on the Punishment of Crimes of Status, Crimes of General Obnoxiousness, Crimes of Displeasing Police Officers and the Like," 3 *Crim. L. Bull.* 205 (1967).

Bayles, Michael, "Comments: Offensive Conduct and the Law," in *Issues in Law and Morality,* eds. N. Care and T. Trelogan. (1973), pp. 111–26.

Bedau, Hugo ed., *Civil Disobedience: Theory and Practice* (1969).

Benn, S. I. and R. S. Peters, *Social Principles and the Democratic State* (1959).

Berlin, Isaiah, *Four Essays on Liberty* (1969).

Brecher, Edward M., *Licit and Illicit Drugs* (1972).

Chafee, Zechariah, Jr., *Free Speech in the United States* (1941).

Chafee, Zechariah, Jr., *Three Human Rights in the Constitution* (1956).

Cohen, Carl, *Conscience, Tactics, and the Law* (1971).

Cohen, Marshall, "Liberalism and Disobedience," *Philosophy and Public Affairs,* Vol. 1 (1972).

Commission on Obscenity and Pornography, *Report* (1970).

Devlin, Patrick, "Encounter with Lord Devlin," *Listener,* Vol. 71(1964), pp. 980 ff.

Devlin, Patrick, *The Enforcement of Morals* (1965).

Dorsen, Norman, ed., *The Rights of Americans,* Sections II and III (1970).

Dworkin, Ronald, "Lord Devlin and the Enforcement of Morals," 75 *Yale L.J.* 986 (1966).

Emerson, Thomas I., *The System of Freedom of Expression* (1970).

Feinberg, Joel, " 'Harmless Immoralities' and Offensive Nuisances," in *Issues in Law and Morality,* eds. N. Care and T. Trelogan. (1973), pp. 85–109.

Feinberg, Joel, "Legal Paternalism," *Canadian Journal of Philosophy,* Vol. 1 (1971), pp. 105–24.

Feinberg, Joel, *Social Philosophy* (1973), Chaps. 2, 3.

Fortas, Abe, *Concerning Dissent and Civil Disobedience* (1968).

Frantz, Laurent B., "The First Amendment in the Balance," 71 *Yale L.J.* 1424 (1962).

Fried, Charles, "Privacy," 77 *Yale L.J.* 475 (1968).

Friedman, Milton, *Capitalism and Freedom* (1962).

Friedrich, C. J., ed., *Nomos IV: Liberty* (1962).

Ginsberg, Morris, "Law and Morals," *The British Journal of Criminology* (1964).

Goodhart, Arthur L., *English Law and the Moral Law* (1953).

Gross, Hyman, "The Concept of Privacy," 42 *N.Y.U. L. Rev.* 34 (1967).

Gussfield, J., "On Legislating Morals: The Symbolic Process of Designating Deviancy," 56 *Cal. L. Rev.* 54–59 (1968).

Hall, Robert, *The Morality of Civil Disobedience* (1971).

Harnett, B. and J. Thornton, "The Truth Hurts: A Critique of a Defense to Defamation," 35 *Va. L. Rev.* 425 (1949).

Hart, Harold H., ed., *Censorship, For and Against* (1971).

Hart, H. L. A., "Immorality and Treason," *Listener,* Vol. 62 (1959), pp. 162 ff.

Hart, H. L. A., *Law, Liberty, and Morality* (1963).

Hart, H. L. A., "Social Solidarity and the Enforcement of Morality," 35 *U. Chi. L. Rev.* 1 (1967).

Henkin, L., "Morals and the Constitution: The Sin of Obscenity," 63 *Col. L. Rev.* 391 (1963).

Hobhouse, L. T., *The Elements of Social Justice* (1922), Chap. 4.

Home Office Scottish Home Department, *Report of the Committee on Homosexual Offenses and Prostitution (Wolfenden Report)* (1963).

Hook, Sydney, ed., *Law and Philosophy,* Part I (1964).

Hughes, Graham, "Civil Disobedience and the Political Question Doctrine," 43 *N.Y.U.L. Rev.* 1 (1968).

Hughes, Graham, "Morals and the Criminal Law," 71 *Yale L.J.* 662 (1962).

Kadish, S. H., "The Crisis of Overcriminalization," 374 *Annals* 157 (1957).

Kadish, M. R. and S. H. Kadish, *Discretion to Disobey* (1973).

Kalven, Harry, Jr., "The Metaphysics of the Law of Obscenity," in *The Supreme Court Review,* ed. P. B. Kurland, (1960).

Kaufman, Arnold S. and Felix E. Oppenheim, "Democracy and Disorder, A Symposium," in *Society, Revolution and Reform,* eds. R. H. Grimm and A. F. MacKay. (1971).

Kronhausen, E. and P., *Pornography and the Law,* rev. ed., (1964).

Livermore, J. M., C. P. Malmquist, and P. E. Meehl, "On the Justification for Civil Commitment," 117 *U. Pa. L. Rev.,* 75 (1968).

Louch, A. R., "Sins and Crimes," *Philosophy,* Vol. 43 (1968), pp. 163 ff.

McCloskey, H. J., "Mill's Liberalism," *Philosophical Quarterly,* Vol. XIII (1963).

Mewett, A., "Morality and the Criminal Law," 14 *University of Toronto L.J.* 213 (1962).

Miller, Arthur R., *The Assault on Privacy* (1971).

Morris, Norval and Gordon Hawkins, *The Honest Politician's Guide to Crime Control,* (1969), Chapters 1 and 2.

Note, "Civil Commitment of Narcotic Addicts," 76 *Yale L.J.* 1160 (1967).

Packer, Herbert, *The Limits of the Criminal Sanction* (1968).

Pennock, J. R. and J. W. Chapman, eds., Nomos XII: *Political and Legal Obligation* (1970).

Pennock, J. R. and J. W. Chapman, eds., Nomos XIII: *Privacy* (1971).

Pennock, J. R. and J. W. Chapman, eds., *Nomos XV: Limits of Law* (1974).

Resiman, David, "Democracy and Defamation: Control of Group Libel," 42 *Col. L. Rev.* 751 (1942).

Rostow, Eugene, *The Sovereign Prerogative* (1962), Chap. 2.

Ryan, Alan, *The Philosophy of John Stuart Mill* (1970), Chap. XIII.

Sartorius, Rolf, "The Enforcement of Morality," 81 *Yale L.J.* 891 (1972).

Scanlon, Timothy, "A Theory of Freedom of Expression," *Philosophy and Public Affairs,* Vol. I (1972), pp. 204–26.

Skolnick, Jerome, "Coercion to Virtue," 41 *S. Cal. L. Rev.* 588 (1968).

Stephen, James F., *Liberty, Equality, Fraternity* (1873).

Wasserstrom, Richard A., "The Obligation to Obey the Law," 10 *U.C.L.A. L. Rev.* 780 (1963).

Williams, G., "Authoritarian Morals and the Criminal Law," [1966] *Crim. L. Rev.* 132.

Williams, G., *The Sanctity of Life and the Criminal Law,* (1957) Chapters 7 and 8.

Wollheim, Richard, "Crime, Sin and Mr. Justice Devlin," *Encounter* (1959), pp. 34 ff.

Woozley, A. D., "Socrates on Disobeying the Law," in *The Philosophy of Socrates,* ed. Gregory Vlastos, (1971).

Zinn, Howard, *Disobedience and Democracy* (1968).

PART 3 JUSTICE

One of the very oldest conceptions of justice, which must be close to the original seed of the modern concept, derives from pre-Socratic Greek cosmology and its picture of a morally ordered universe in which everything has its assigned place, or natural role. Justice (*dike*) consisted of everything staying in that assigned place, and not usurping the place of another thereby throwing the whole system out of kilter. Elements of this early notion survive in Plato's theory of justice as a virtue both of men and of states. Social justice, according to Plato, exists when every man performs the function for which he is best fitted by nature (his own proper business) and does not infringe upon the natural role of another. A corollary of this principle is that the rulers of the state should be those best fitted by their natures to rule; hence democracy, or rule by everybody, is inherently unjust.

The reason why men live in political communities in the first place, Plato argues in *The Republic,* is that no mere individual is self-sufficient. For all of us to satisfy our needs, we must divide up our labors, with each person performing the task for which he is best fitted by his natural aptitudes. Instead of every man being his own carpenter, toolmaker, farmer, tailor, soldier, and policeman, each man can work at the one thing he does best, while enjoying the benefits of the full-time labors of other specialists. The principle of cooperation by means of the specialization of labor explains what social organization is *for,* and why it should exist. There is justice in a society when everyone does his proper work: when square pegs are in square holes; when no talent is wasted or misused; when those who are naturally fit to rule do rule, and those who are naturally fit to obey, do obey. The sole criterion, then, for justice in assigning positions in society is *fitness for a function.* This is turn is best promoted, according to Plato, by fair educational and testing procedures that give each child, regardless of his race, or sex, or the social rank of his parents, an equal opportunity to rise to his appropriate slot in the social hierarchy.

Aristotle, in the famous discussion of the virtue of justice which leads off this section, shares Plato's view that only the best should rule and Plato's disdain for perfect equality in the distribution of political burdens and benefits. His analysis of justice, however, is more subtle and more faithful to complexities in the concept's multifaceted employment. He acknowledges at the start that the word for justice is ambiguous, referring both to the whole of social virtue ("virtue in relation to our neighbor") and to one specific type of social virtue. The wider or generic concept Aristotle calls "universal justice"; the narrower he calls "particular justice." Unlike Plato in the *Republic*, Aristotle's chief concern is with the particular virtue that is only a part, not the whole, of social virtue. He does say of universal justice, however, that it coincides with conformity to *law*. What he apparently means by this is that the positive law of the state *should* aim at the enforcement of the social virtues (including not only "particular justice" but also benevolence, charity, fidelity, and so on), and that insofar as a given legal code does support social virtue, violation of "universal justice" will at the same time be violation of positive law.

Particular justice, as Aristotle understands it, is the same as *fairness*. The Greek word for fairness in Aristotle's time also meant *equality*. Thus, Aristotle's initial contention is that there are two concepts of justice: lawfulness and equality. Particular justice (fairness), he tells us, is of two kinds: *distributive and rectificatory justice*. His conviction that most fair distributions are unequal, held at a time when "just" meant or strongly suggested "equal," drove him (as Gregory Vlastos has put it) to "linguistic acrobatics."[1] Distributive justice, he argued ingeniously, does not consist in absolute equality (that is, perfectly equal shares for all those among whom something is to be distributed) but rather a proportionate equality, which is to say an equality of ratios. What justice requires, he insists, is that equal cases be treated alike (equally), and that unequal cases be treated unalike (unequally) in direct proportion to the differences (inequalities) between them, so that between any two persons the ratio between their shares $(S_1:S_2)$ should equal the ratio between their qualifying characteristics $(C_1:C_2)$.

Aristotle concedes that people disagree over which characteristics of persons should be taken into account in assessing their equality or the degree of their inequality, but all parties to these disagreements (except extreme democrats who insist upon absolute equality) employ tacitly the notion of proportionate equality. However "merit" is conceived, for example, those for whom it would be the sole criterion in awarding shares would give one person twice as large a share of some benefit as they would to any other person deemed only half as meritorious. The common object of these distributors, even when they disagree over what merit is, will be to divide shares into a ratio (2:1) equal to the ratio of the merits of the two persons (2:1). Such distributions are sometimes necessarily impressionistic (how can one person's value be seen to be exactly one half another's?), but when the criterion of merit is exactly definable, and the shares themselves can be measured in terms of money, the calculations can sometimes achieve a mathematical precision. Aristotle sometimes seems to have in mind, for example, "the distribution of profits between partners in proportion to what each has put into the business."[2] Such contributions ("merits" in an extended, but properly Aristotelian, sense) as capital, time, and labor are readily measurable.

Since any two persons will be unequal in some respects and equal in others, Aristotle's theory of distributive justice is incomplete until he tells us which personal characteristics are *relevant* factors to be considered in the balancing of ratios. Various criteria of relevance have been proposed by writers of different schools. Some have held that A's share should be to B's share as A's ability is to B's ability, or as A's moral virtue is to B's, or as A's labor is to B's, and so on. All the above maxims could be said to specify different forms of "merit," so that a *meritarian* theorist would be one who held that the only personal characteristics relevant to a just distribution of goods are such forms of personal "merit." Aristotle was undoubtedly a meritarian in this broad sense. Meritarian social philosophers then can disagree among themselves over which forms of merit are relevant and over criteria for assessing a given form of merit, or they might hold that some forms of merit are relevant to some types of distribution, and other merits to other types. A nonmeritarian theory would be one which found exclusive relevance in personal characteristics (for example, needs) that are in no sense "merits," and of course mixed theories too are possible. Even a "democratic" or "equalitarian" theory, one which is wholly nonmeritarian, might plausibly be said to employ tacitly Aristotle's *analysis* of distributive justice as proportionate equality, while rejecting of course Aristotle's suggested criteria of relevance. Even a perfect equalitarian presumably would wish to endorse such maxims as: A's share should be to B's share as A's needs are to B's needs, or as A's "infinite human worth" is to B's "infinite human worth" (that is, the same). It seems likely, therefore, that all complete theories of social justice must contain maxims specifying relevant characteristics, and that all of them presuppose Aristotle's formal analysis of distributive justice as proportionate equality between shares and relevant characteristics.

Distributive justice applies to statesmen distributing honors, rewards, public property (as, for example, land in a new Athenian or Macedonian colony), public assistance to the needy, or to divisions of corporate profits or inheritances. Aristotle does not discuss the distribution of burdens such as taxation and military service, but his principle of proportionate equality presumably applies to them too. The second kind of particular justice, *rectificatory justice,* applies to private transactions or business deals in which some unfair advantage or undeserved harm has occurred and one party sues for a "remedy." (Aristotle's phrase for rectificatory justice is sometimes translated as "remedial," as well as "corrective" or "compensatory" justice). A judge then must assess the damages and order one party to make a payment to the other. These cases, Aristotle says, are of two kinds. In one type the harm to the plaintiff results from a transaction in which he voluntarily participated: buying, selling, loaning, pledging, depositing, hiring out, and the like. The law governing these cases corresponds roughly to our law of contracts. In the other type of case, the harm to the plaintiff results from a "transaction" in which he involuntarily participates as a victim from the start: fraud, theft, adultery, assault, imprisonment, or homicide. The law governing these cases, when the aim is to correct an unfairness by compensating a victim for his loss or injury, corresponds roughly to our law of torts.

Rectificatory justice, too, essentially involves the notion of equality. Its aim, Aristotle says, it to redress the "inequality" that results when one person profits unfairly at the expense of another. If *A* steals one hundred dollars from *B*, for example, he becomes one hundred dollars better off, an amount that is exactly equal to the amount by which *B* becomes worse off. The "equality" between *A* and *B* was their starting position before the "transaction," and that equality is restored by an order that requires *A* to pay to *B* exactly one hundred dollars. It is well to notice that rectificatory justice, as Aristotle understands it, does not apply to the criminal law at all. If there is a justice in punishing *A* for his peculation beyond the penalty that merely restores the *status quo ante,* that must be justice of a different kind. Retributive justice, as such, does not receive a thorough discussion in Aristotle, and does not even receive a separate rubric in his classification of the types of justice.

Neither does Aristotle's analysis of rectificatory justice appear to be an adequate guide through the complexities of the law of torts. More than the restoration of equality by a simple arithmetical formula, at any rate, is involved in all but the simplest cases in deliberations aiming at the determination of compensatory damages. Suppose *A*'s wrongful act makes him $500 better off and *B* (the plaintiff) $200 worse off? What if *A*'s malevolence or spitefulness toward *B* is so great that he is willing to undergo a loss for himself in order to inflict one on *B*? Suppose, in that example, that *A*'s malicious act costs himself $500 and inflicts only a $100 loss on *B*. Or suppose, what is admittedly somewhat fanciful, that *A*'s wrongful act actually creates a $100 windfall for wholly innocent *B* while earning himself $1,000. It will tax the student reader's ingenuity (in itself a good thing) to apply Aristotle's simple formulas for "arithmetical progression" to these hypothetical cases.

Some parts of Aristotle's discussion are primarily of antiquarian interest. His sketchy account in Chapter 5, for example, of "Justice in Exchange" is one of the earliest discussions on record of economic justice. Several other sections of his treatment of justice are important both for their intrinsic interest and their historical influence. Chapter 7 on "Natural and Legal Justice," for instance, is a classical source for the long and still vital tradition of natural law, and the theory of Equity in Chapter 10 (to be discussed below) has had a direct effect on the development of legal institutions that is still felt. In addition to the distinctions between natural and legal justice and between equity and law, there is still another important distinction that Aristotle was the first to treat with great subtlety: that between the just or unjust *quality* of an act and the just or unjust *effect* of an act on others. Injustice is always a violation of someone's rights or deserts, but such an effect can be brought about involuntarily, in which case the action that produced it cannot be unjust in itself, for normally to ascribe an unjust act to a person is to blame him, and involuntary acts are not blameworthy. Moreover, there are occasions, unhappily, in which a person can be fully justified in voluntarily producing an unjust effect on another: when that effect, for example, is the least evil result the actor could produce in the circumstances. *A* may be justified in violating *B*'s rights instead of *C*'s and *D*'s when there is no third alternative open to him, but that justification does not cancel the injustice done to *B*. In that case, we can say that *B* was unjustly *treated* although *A*'s act resulting in that effect was not an instance of unjust *behavior.* For an act to have an unjust quality (whatever its effects) it must be, objectively speaking, the wrong thing to do in the circumstances, unexcused and unjustified, voluntarily undertaken, and deliberately chosen by an unrushed actor who is well aware of the alternatives open to him. Other parties can be injured by unforeseeable accidents (mere mishaps), foreseeable accidents (blunders), by voluntary acts done in a fit of anger (*akrasia*), or by deliberate choice. Only in the last case is there unjust behavior, although there is blameworthiness of other kinds (negligence and hot-tempered impetuousness) in blunders and in angry violence, too.

Equity, Aristotle tells us in Chapter 10, is "a correction of law where it is defective owing to its universality." Richard A. Wasserstrom, in the second essay in this section, criticizes Aristotle's view that the character of law as "universal" *necessarily* leads to injustices in some individual cases. It is always possible in theory, Wasserstrom argues, to reformulate universal laws so that they contain exceptive clauses excluding hardship cases from the scope of their application. In practice, however, this might lead to an unworkable proliferation of very precise rules, each applying to very few cases. Aristotle's account of equity then is an overstatement, but one which suggests to Wasserstrom some important theses about the role of general rules in a just legal system. Wasserstrom's essay is a chapter drawn from his important book, *The Judicial Decision.* His primary concern in that chapter is to evaluate the group of theories about proper courtroom decision procedures which hold that cases can and should be decided "by direct appeal to justice or equity rather than by legal rules," and that the best decision, in some if not all kinds of cases, is the one based on unique features of the particular case before the court. In his vindication of the function of rules, Wasserstrom criticizes not only Aristotle, but also Jerome Frank, for whom rules have little relevance to just decision-making, and Roscoe Pound, who restricts their relevance to a relatively narrow class of cases. (The reader should notice that Wasserstrom, in the chapter included here, like Aristotle, seems to have "controversies between litigants" in civil cases, and not criminal trials, primarily in mind).

The essay by the distinguished contemporary moral philosopher, William K. Frankena, is mainly about distributive justice. Like most other writers, Frankena begins by accepting Aristotle's formal principle of justice, that relevantly similar cases should be treated similarly, but Frankena devotes more attention than Aristotle did to the selection of a material principle of distribution. He agrees with Aristotle that the essence of distributive injustice is arbitrary discrimination between relevantly similar cases, but disagrees over which characteristics are relevantly similar and which discriminations are arbitrary, aligning himself with Aristotle's old adversaries, the equalitarian democrats. The "foundational principle of social justice," Frankena concludes, is that the benefits and burdens of social life should be distributed not with the primary aim of rewarding "merit," but rather to ensure that "everyone has an equal chance of achieving the best life he is capable of." Frankena's recommendations have a direct bearing on the philosophy of law, constituting an ultimate criterion for assessing the justice of laws that affect distributions.

Some of the most important contributions to the theory of justice, especially in Great Britain, have been made by writers in the utilitarian moral tradition. In the eighteenth century, David Hume argued that all rules of justice (thinking primarily of rules pertaining to contracts and property) "owe their origin and existence to that utility which results to the public from their strict and regular observance."[3] Hume admitted that there may sometimes be negative social utility in a particular observance of a rule of justice. For example, restoring a fortune to a miser or a seditious bigot is just, but socially harmful. "But however single acts of justice may be contrary either to public or private interest, 'tis certain that the *whole plan or scheme* is highly conducive, or indeed absolutely requisite to the support of society and the wellbeing of every individual."[4] Hume, in short, is a rule-utilitarian, not an act-utilitarian.

There is some doubt whether John Stuart Mill, the next essayist presented, would make conductibility to the common good the standard of right conduct applying directly to *single acts,* or make it the standard of *good rules* applying to the products of the legislature's work or to the determination of the sound rules of natural morality. The balance of reasons, however, as J. O. Urmson has shown convincingly,[5] favors the interpretation of Mill as a rule-utilitarian whose view is a further elaboration of Hume's. Mill's theory is interesting primarily for the way it accounts for the "distinguishing character of justice" and the way he *argues* that justice is derived from utility rather than being an underivative independent principle in its own right.

What distinguishes injustice from other types of wrongdoing, according to Mill, is that injustice must always be injustice *to* someone or other, the violation of the rights or deserts of some "assignable" person who is thereby entitled to feel aggrieved and righteously indignant on his own behalf. Duties of justice, therefore, are only one subclass of moral duties generally. If I fail to discharge my moral obligation to be generous, or beneficent, I do wrong, but there is no determinate person who can complain of being personally wronged by my omission, for "no one has a moral right to our generosity or beneficence." But it is clearly otherwise when I renege on a promise, a vow, or a loan; when as an authority, I treat my friends or relations more leniently or generously than others; when as a teacher, I give a low grade to an excellent student who deserves better; when as a legislator, I help create a statute that arbitrarily discriminates against a whole class of persons; or when as policeman or judge, I enforce the law irregularly or unequally among those to whom it explicity applies. In all these cases, valid moral claims have been ignored or rejected, and the claimants have at least "a right to complain," and at most, a right to rectification, restitution, or even retribution.

That the standard of justice is independent of social utility is usually supported by an attempt to show that social utility as an ultimate moral principle would in some circumstances justify acts, rules, or practices that are patently unjust. Mill does very little to defend utilitarianism against this charge, which has been debated so thoroughly by twentieth century philosophers. Instead, he takes the offensive as a utilitarian, attacking what he calls "the alternative view of justice as independent of utility, a standard *per se,* which the mind can recognize by simple introspection of itself." The argument is simple enough. If there is an autonomous sense of justice limiting the dictates of utility and guiding us to the right moral decision where utility would lead us astray, how are we to understand "why the internal oracle is so ambiguous?" When people leave off calculating utilities to voice instead their sense of justice, there is nothing but controversy, with no rational resolution of differences possible. "In fact, justice is not some one rule, principle or maxim, but many, which do not always coincide in their dictates, and in choosing between which, one is guided either by some extraneous standard [such as social utility] or by his own personal predilections."

Mill then provides numerous persuasive examples of the conflict between plausible maxims of justice that apply to controversies over punishment, distribution of wealth, and taxation. In each instance justice seems to have "two sides to it." Mill turns from these controversies in bewilderment, concluding that each of the opposed maxims "from its own point of view is unanswerable, and any choice between them on grounds of justice must be perfectly arbitrary. Social utility alone can decide the preference."

Mill's argument is hardly decisive. A defender of "the alternative theory of justice" might well reply: The contention that justice is a principle independent of, and sometimes in conflict with, utility does not imply that the dictates of justice are always perfectly clear and unambiguous, or that there is even one supreme principle of justice harmonizing all the conflicting maxims. That the method of determining justice is distinct from the method of calculating social utility does not imply that one is simple and the other difficult, or even that one has necessary priority over the other. It means simply what it says: that the one is distinct from, and irreducible to, the other.

Moreover, Mill's opponent might argue, the method of utility involves just as many complexities and difficulties as the method of justice. One might even speak of distinct and rival "maxims" of utility. What promotes the greatest good may help the smallest number and what helps the largest number may promote the smallest net good. What creates the most happiness may entail the most blissful ignorance as by-product, and what promotes knowledge may increase despair; and yet both happiness and knowledge are presumably components of "utility." And which should the utilitarian choose when he must choose between irreconcilable goods of separate groups or separate individuals, or when a net gain in pleasure and knowledge is balanced against a net loss in virtue and equality, or when intense pleasure of short duration is the alternative to mild pleasure of long duration? This *tu quoque,* while also undecisive, has considerable punch.

Philosophers often distinguish between the fairness or unfairness of procedures and the justice or injustice of outcomes. Sometimes the labels "procedural" and "substantive" justice are used to mark the distinction, and the student should be wary of confusing these technical terms with the phrases "formal" and "material" which are used to mark the quite different distinction between the "formal" requirement that similar cases be treated similarly, and "material" interpretations of that requirement that provide criteria for the relevance of differences. (To compound the terminological confusion, Brian Barry uses the term "equity," which as we have seen already has the Aristotelian sense of "modification of general rules to meet special situations,"[6] to refer to the basic "formal" requirement that rules should treat like cases alike).

The selection from Barry presupposes the discussion in an earlier part of his important book, *Political Argument,* in which he classifies the various contexts in which the notions of fair procedure and just outcome have application. These contexts all involve the employment of techniques for settling conflicts of wants or opinions. Barry calls these "social decision procedures," and lists the following seven types:

1. *Combat.* The issue is settled directly by force.
2. *Discussion on Merits.* The parties argue the rights and wrongs of the conflict and seek agreement by appealing to jointly accepted standards, ideals, or rules.
3. *Bargaining.* "One party offers another either some advantage or the removal of the threat of disadvantage in return for the other party's performing some specific action."[7] The rights and wrongs of the conflict, or the merits of the opposed positions, are not considered.
4. *Voting* (where more than two parties are involved).
5. *Chance* (for example, by flipping a coin or drawing straws).
6. *Contest* (for example, foot races, boxing matches) for settling the question of which contestant is "best at" some activity requiring skill.
7. *Authoritative Determination.* The issue is settled by the judgment of a party (or parties) whose authority to do so, under the governing rules, is recognized by the disputants, for example, an administrative tribunal, a judge or jury, a labor arbitrator.

A decision procedure (excepting combat, a special case) may itself be fair or unfair, and even a fair procedure may be applied fairly or unfairly in a given case. Taking each type of procedure in turn, Barry tells us what fair application consists in, and what further is required as "background fairness." In the case of authoritative determination, the application of a specified procedure can be appraised as fair or unfair in a distinctively legalistic way (Barry calls this "legal justice"), namely, by determining whether rules requiring certain decisions in cases of a specified kind have been adhered to.

Barry then asks why procedural fairness should be valued as an important thing. He advances both utilitarian and equalitarian considerations (he calls these "aggregative" and "distributive," respectively) for taking "legal justice" seriously. Similarly, in respect to procedural and background fairness, he finds their justifications in their conduciveness to "some more general consideration," namely, their tendency to produce just results. Thus Barry concludes that "the value of [procedural] fairness is subordinate to that of justice," and finds in the opposite view an element of irrational "rule worship."

John Rawls also attaches importance to the distinction between justice (of results) and fairness (of procedures), but as his title, "Justice as Fairness" indicates, fairness is given a certain methodological priority. But that is not to say that Rawls is in serious disagreement with Barry. His essay (the germ of his monumental study, *A Theory of Justice*) is addressed to somewhat different questions. Rawls is almost exclusively concerned with the justice of political, social, and economic institutions, as opposed to the justice of individual actions, persons, or policies. "The primary subject of justice," he wrote in *A Theory of Justice,* "is the basic structure of society."[8] Those basic institutions are just, Rawls maintains, that accord with the principles of justice that would be adopted by reasonable and normally self-interested persons employing an ideally fair selection procedure. Rawls describes that procedure and derives from it two basic principles of justice. These principles, and the method of their derivation, constitute the major alternative to utilitarianism among recent general theories of justice.

Invidiously discriminatory treatment in the distribution of benefits (including opportunities) and burdens is the essential feature of what Aristotle called "distributive injustice." In the United States grossly discriminatory rules and practices have only recently begun to crumble, and for the first time in centuries there is hope that the ideal of equal opportunity will one day be fulfilled. To expect the effects of racial and sexual discrimination to vanish overnight with the abrogation of ancient rules, however, would be exceedingly naive. Many reformers, in fact, have been urging that the elimination of discriminatory practices is not enough, and that a kind of "reverse discrimination," especially in the allocation of educational and professional opportunities for such groups as blacks and women, is required by social justice. Louis Katzner, in his penetrating article, subjects this claim to close philosophical analysis, and concludes with a statement of four conditions which must be satisfied if reverse discrimination is to be justified. It is an interesting apparent consequence of Katzner's view that, while reverse discrimination in favor of blacks might in some circumstances be justified, reverse discrimination in favor of (all) women would not likely pass Katzner's test.

Arbitrary inequalities in the distribution of legal rights among various defined classes of the population is firmly prohibited by the "equal protection" clause of the Fourteenth Amendment, and (indirectly) by the "due process" clause of the Fifth Amendment. More and more, women have been relying on these constitutional grounds to secure judicial overruling of statutes that discriminate against them. In *Reed v. Reed,* included in this section, the United States Supreme Court in a unanimous opinion written by Mr. Chief Justice Burger argues that while it is constitutionally permissible for legislation to distinguish among classes, this must be done in a "reasonable, not arbitrary" way, and "not on the basis of criteria wholly unrelated to the objective of the statute." The language becomes explicitly Aristotelian when the court declares all statutes to be unconstitutional which command "dissimilar treatment for men and women who are . . . similarly situated."

In *Frontiero v. Richardson,* a somewhat more complicated case, another statute which made sex the basis of differences in the assignment of legal rights and duties was overturned, this time on the ground that the Fifth Amendment forbids discrimination that is "so unjustifiable as to be violative of due process." The majority opinion in *Frontiero* declares that sex is a "suspect classification," that is, one whose moral or constitutional relevance is "inherently suspect," and therefore properly "subjected to close judicial scrutiny." Sexual distinctions in the law, in other words, are *prima facie* unjust, and will be declared unconstitutional unless "close judicial scrutiny" uncovers some general causal connection between sex difference and other traits that clearly are relevant to some valid legislative purpose, (presumably) like the strengthening of national security or the protection of individual privacy. Careful notice should be given to four points about the principles applied in the *Reed* and *Frontiero* decisions.

1. Like the Aristotelian "formal principle" that relevantly like cases should be treated in like ways, the Equal Protection clause of the Fourteenth Amendment also needs supplementation by criteria of the relevance or nonarbitrariness of differences between classes of persons.

2. Sex *as such* is not a relevant or nonarbitrary difference. Thus, statutory classifications whose *whole basis* is "the sex of the individuals involved" are "inherently invidious," and proscribed by the Equal Protection clause.

3. The causal connection between sex difference and traits that *are* relevant must be *perfectly* general. It is not sufficient that *most* males have greater physical strength or greater business experience than *most* females. Only if these connections were exceptionless and necessary would a statute permit sex to be a ground, say, for job qualifications, for example, combat duty in the armed forces or administration of a decedent's estate. Otherwise, as Mr. Justice Brennan put it in *Frontiero,* "statutory distinctions between the sexes [would] often have the effect of invidiously relegating the entire class of females to inferior legal status without regard to the actual capabilities of its individual members."

4. Valid legislative purposes to which discrimination between the sexes might be reasonably related do not include "mere administrative convenience," though administrative convenience in the conduct of a war, say, might be so related to national security as to justify sexual distinctions in the assignment of combat duty; and *another* constitutional protection, for example, that said to be provided by the Constitution to personal privacy, might justify sexual distinctions in the rules permitting entry to public rest rooms.

Despite the trend represented by the *Reed* and *Frontiero* decisions, most feminists are not content to rest the moral claim to equality on the Fourteenth Amendment, and have advocated instead a Sexual Equality Amendment to the United States Constitution specifying that "Equality of rights under the law shall not be denied or abridged by the United States or by any State on account of sex." The proposed amendment was quickly approved by the Congress, but by June, 1973, it had run into fierce resistance in many state legislatures. Seldom has a controversial public issue been so ensnared in philosophical subtleties! The proposed new legal equality would make sexual difference an invalid ground for legal classifications, but would that necessarily lead to bisexual rest rooms, female combat troops, the invalidating of statutes creating sex crimes or of those specifying the amount of weight a woman could be required to lift on a job? Even if the answers to these and similar questions are affirmative, would that necessarily be a bad thing? Leading constitutional scholars have differed in their approaches to these partly philosophical problems, and at the time of printing, the fate of the Sexual Equality Amendment is still in doubt. There is no better illustration than this public issue of how the traditional concerns of the philosopher and the lawmaker can come together.

J. F.

NOTES

1. Gregory Vlastos, "Justice and Equality," in *Social Justice,* ed. Richard B. Brandt (Englewood Cliffs, N.J.: Prentice-Hall, Inc., 1962), p. 32.

2. W. D. Ross, *Aristotle* (London: Methuen & Co., 1949), p. 210.

3. David Hume, *An Enquiry Concerning the Principles of Morals* (LaSalle, Illinois: The Open Court Publishing Co., 1947), p. 20.

4. David Hume, *A Treatise of Human Nature* (Oxford: The Clarendon Press, 1888), p. 497.

5. J. O. Urmson, "The Moral Philosophy of J. S. Mill," *The Philosophical Quarterly,* Vol. 3 (1953), pp. 33–39.

6. Brian Barry, *Political Argument* (London: Routledge, Kegan Paul, 1965), p. 96.

7. *Ibid.,* p. 86.

8. John Rawls, *A Theory of Justice* (Cambridge, Mass.: Harvard University Press, 1971), p. 7.

ARISTOTLE

Justice*

JUSTICE: ITS SPHERE AND OUTER NATURE: IN WHAT SENSE IT IS A MEAN

THE JUST AS THE LAWFUL (UNIVERSAL JUSTICE) AND THE JUST AS THE FAIR AND EQUAL (PARTICULAR JUSTICE): THE FORMER CONSIDERED

1. With regard to justice and injustice we must consider (1) what kind of actions they are concerned with, (2) what sort of mean justice is, and (3) between what extremes the just act is intermediate. Our investigation shall follow the same course as the preceding discussions.

We see that all men mean by justice that kind of state of character which makes people disposed to do what is just and makes them act justly and wish for what is just; and similarly by injustice that state which makes them act unjustly and wish for what is unjust. Let us too, then, lay this down as a general basis. For the same is not true of the sciences and the faculties as of states of character. A faculty or a science which is one and the same is held to relate to contrary objects, but a state of character which is one of two contraries does *not* produce the contrary results; for example, as a result of health we do not do what is the opposite of healthy, but only what is healthy; for we say a man walks healthily, when he walks as a healthy man would.

Now often one contrary state is recognized from its contrary, and often states are recognized from the subjects that exhibit them; for (A) if good condition is known, bad condition also becomes known, and (B) good condition is known from the things that are in good condition, and they from it. If good condition is firmness of flesh, it is necessary both that bad condition should be flabbiness of flesh and that the wholesome should be that which causes firmness in flesh. And it follows for the most part that if one contrary is ambiguous the other also will be ambiguous; for example, that if 'just' is so, 'unjust' will be so too.

Now 'justice' and 'injustice' seem to be ambiguous, but because their different meanings approach near to one another the ambiguity escapes notice and is not obvious as it is, comparatively, when the meanings are far apart, for example, (for here the difference in outward form is great) as the ambiguity in the use of κλείς for the collarbone of an animal and for that with which we lock a door. Let us take as a starting-point, then, the various meanings of 'an unjust man'. Both the lawless man and the grasping and unfair man are thought to be unjust, so that evidently both the law-abiding and the fair man will be just. The just, then, is the lawful and the fair, the unjust the unlawful and the unfair.

Since the unjust man is grasping, he must be concerned with goods—not all goods, but those with which prosperity and adversity have to do, which taken absolutely are always good, but for a particular person are not always good. Now men pray for and pursue these things; but they should not, but should pray that the things that are good absolutely may also be good for them, and should choose the things that *are* good for them. The unjust man does not always choose the greater, but also the less—in the case of things bad absolutely; but because the lesser evil is itself thought to be in a sense good, and graspingness is directed at the good, therefore he is thought to be grasping. And he is unfair; for this contains and is common to both.

*Book V (complete) from *The Nicomachean Ethics*, translated by W. D. Ross, from *The Oxford Translation of Aristotle* edited by W. D. Ross, vol. 9 (1925). Reprinted by permission of The Clarendon Press, Oxford. Some footnotes have been deleted. The remainder have been renumbered.

Since the lawless man was seen to be unjust and the law-abiding man just, evidently all lawful acts are in a sense just acts; for the acts laid down by the legislative art are lawful, and each of these, we say, is just. Now the laws in their enactments on all subjects aim at the common advantage either of all or of the best or of those who hold power, or something of the sort; so that in one sense we call those acts just that tend to produce and preserve happiness and its components for the political society. And the law bids us do both the acts of a brave man (for example, not to desert our post nor take to flight nor throw away our arms), and those of a temperate man (for example, not to commit adultery nor to gratify one's lust), and those of a good-tempered man (for example, not to strike another nor to speak evil), and similarly with regard to the other virtues and forms of wickedness, commanding some acts and forbidding others; and the rightly-framed law does this rightly, and the hastily conceived one less well.

This form of justice, then, is complete virtue, but not absolutely, but in relation to our neighbour. And therefore justice is often thought to be the greatest of virtues, and 'neither evening nor morning star' is so wonderful; and proverbially 'in justice is every virtue comprehended'. And it is complete virtue in its fullest sense because it is the actual exercise of complete virtue. It is complete because he who possesses it can exercise his virtue not only in himself but towards his neighbour also; for many men can exercise virtue in their own affairs, but not in their relations to their neighbour. This is why the saying of Bias is thought to be true, that 'rule will show the man'; for a ruler is necessarily in relation to other men, and a member of a society. For this same reason justice, alone of the virtues, is thought to be 'another's good', because it is related to our neighbour; for it does what is advantageous to another, either a ruler or a co-partner. Now the worst man is he who exercises his wickedness both towards himself and towards his friends, and the best man is not he who exercises his virtue towards himself but he who exercises it towards another; for this is a difficult task. Justice in this sense, then, is not part of virtue but virtue entire, nor is the contrary injustice a part of vice but vice entire. What the difference is between virtue and justice in this sense is plain from what we have said; they are the same but their essence is not the same; what,

as a relation to one's neighbour, is justice is, as a certain kind of state without qualification, virtue.

THE JUST AS THE FAIR AND EQUAL: DIVIDED INTO DISTRIBUTIVE AND RECTIFICATORY JUSTICE

2. But at all events what we are investigating is the justice which is a *part* of virtue; for there is a justice of this kind, as we maintain. Similarly it is with injustice in the particular sense that we are concerned.

That there is such a thing is indicated by the fact that while the man who exhibits in action the other forms of wickedness acts wrongly indeed, but not graspingly (for example, the man who throws away his shield through cowardice or speaks harshly through bad temper or fails to help a friend with money through meanness), when a man acts graspingly he often exhibits none of these vices—no, nor all together, but certainly wickedness of some kind (for we blame him) and injustice. There is, then, another kind of injustice which is a part of injustice in the wide sense, and a use of the word 'unjust' which answers to a part of what is unjust in the wide sense of 'contrary to the law'. Again, if one man commits adultery for the sake of gain and makes money by it, while another does so at the bidding of appetite though he loses money and is penalized for it, the latter would be held to be self-indulgent rather than grasping, but the former is unjust, but not self-indulgent; evidently, therefore, he is unjust by reason of his making gain by his act. Again, all other unjust acts are ascribed invariably to some particular kind of wickedness, for example, adultery to self-indulgence, the desertion of a comrade in battle to cowardice, physical violence to anger; but if a man makes gain, his action is ascribed to no form of wickedness but injustice. Evidently, therefore, there is apart from injustice in the wide sense another, 'particular', injustice which shares the name and nature of the first, because its definition falls within the same genus; for the significance of both consists in a relation to one's neighbour, but the one is concerned with honour or money or safety—or that which includes all these, if we had a single name for it—and its motive is the pleasure that arises from gain; while the other is concerned with all the objects with which the good man is concerned.

It is clear, then, that there is more than one kind of justice, and that there is one which is distinct from virtue entire; we must try to grasp its genus and differentia.

The unjust has been divided into the unlawful and the unfair, and the just into the lawful and the fair. To the unlawful answers the aforementioned sense of injustice. But since the unfair and the unlawful are not the same, but are different as a part is from its whole (for all that is unfair is unlawful, but not all that is unlawful is unfair), the unjust and injustice in the sense of the unfair are not the same as but different from the former kind, as part from whole; for injustice in this sense is a part of injustice in the wide sense, and similarly justice in the one sense of justice in the other. Therefore we must speak also about particular justice and particular injustice, and similarly about the just and the unjust. The justice, then, which answers to the whole of virtue, and the corresponding injustice, one being the exercise of virtue as a whole, and the other that of vice as a whole, towards one's neighbour, we may leave on one side. And how the meanings of 'just' and 'unjust' which answer to these are to be distinguished is evident; for practically the majority of the acts commanded by the law are those which are prescribed from the point of view of virtue taken as a whole; for the law bids us practise every virtue and forbids us to practise any vice. And the things that tend to produce virtue taken as a whole are those of the acts prescribed by the law which have been prescribed with a view to education for the common good. But with regard to the education of the individual as such, which makes him without qualification a good *man,* we must determine later whether this is the function of the political art or of another; for perhaps it is not the same to be a good man and a good citizen of any state taken at random.

Of particular justice and that which is just in the corresponding sense, (A) one kind is that which is manifested in distributions of honour or money or the other things that fall to be divided among those who have a share in the constitution (for in these it is possible for one man to have a share either unequal or equal to that of another), and (B) one is that which plays a rectifying part in transactions between man and man. Of this there are two divisions; of transactions (1) some are voluntary and (2) others involuntary—voluntary such transactions as sale, purchase, loan for consumption, pledging, loan for use, depositing, letting (they are called voluntary because the *origin* of these transactions is voluntary), while of the involuntary (*a*) some are clandestine, such as theft, adultery, poisoning, procuring, enticement of slaves, assassination, false witness, and (*b*) others are violent, such as assault, imprisonment, murder, robbery with violence, mutilation, abuse, insult.

DISTRIBUTIVE JUSTICE, IN ACCORDANCE WITH GEOMETRICAL PROPORTION

3. (A) We have shown that both the unjust man and the unjust act are unfair or unequal; now it is clear that there is also an intermediate between the two unequals involved in either case. And this is the equal; for in any kind of action in which there is a more and a less there is also what is equal. If, then, the unjust is unequal, the just is equal, as all men suppose it to be, even apart from argument. And since the equal is intermediate, the just will be an intermediate. Now equality implies at least two things. The just, then, must be both intermediate and equal and relative (for example, for certain persons). And *qua* intermediate it must be between certain things (which are respectively greater and less); *qua* equal, it involves *two* things; *qua* just, it is for certain people. The just, therefore, involves at least four terms; for the persons for whom it is in fact just are two, and the things in which it is manifested, the objects distributed, are two. And the same equality will exist between the persons and between the things concerned; for as the latter—the things concerned—are related, so are the former; if they are not equal, they will not have what is equal, but this is the origin of quarrels and complaints—when either equals have and are awarded unequal shares, or unequals equal shares. Further, this is plain from the fact that awards should be 'according to merit'; for all men agree that what is just in distribution must be according to merit in some sense, though they do not all specify the same sort of merit, but democrats identify it with the status of freemen, supporters of oligarchy with wealth (or with noble birth), and supporters of aristocracy with excellence.

The just, then, is a species of the proportionate

(proportion being not a property only of the kind of number which consists of abstract units, but of number in general). For proportion is equality of ratios, and involves four terms at least (that discrete proportion involves four terms is plain, but so does continuous proportion, for it uses one term as two and mentions it twice; for example, 'as the line A is to the line B, so is the line B to the line C'; the line B, then, has been mentioned twice, so that if the line B be assumed twice, the proportional terms will be four); and the just, too, involves at least four terms, and the ratio between one pair is the same as that between the other pair; for there is a similar distinction between the persons and between the things. As the term A, then, is to B, so will C be to D, and therefore, *alternando*, as A is to C, B will be to D. Therefore also the whole is in the same ratio to the whole;[1] and this coupling the distribution effects, and, if the terms are so combined, effects justly. The conjunction, then, of the term A with C and of B with D is what is just in distribution,[2] and this species of the just is intermediate, and the unjust is what violates the proportion; for the proportional is intermediate, and the just is proportional. (Mathematicians call this kind of proportion geometrical; for it is in geometrical proportion that it follows that the whole is to the whole as either part is to the corresponding part.) This proportion is not continuous; for we cannot get a single term standing for a person and a thing.

This, then, is what the just is—the proportional; the unjust is what violates the proportion. Hence one term becomes too great, the other too small, as indeed happens in practice; for the man who acts unjustly has too much, and the man who is unjustly treated too little, of what is good. In the case of evil the reverse is true; for the lesser evil is reckoned a good in comparison with the greater evil, since the lesser evil is rather to be chosen than the greater, and what is worthy of choice is good, and what is worthier of choice a greater good.

This, then, is one species of the just.

RECTIFICATORY JUSTICE, IN ACCORDANCE WITH ARITHMETICAL PROGRESSION

4. (B) The remaining one is the rectificatory, which arises in connexion with transactions both voluntary and involuntary. This form of the just has a different specific character from the former. For the justice which distributes common possessions is always in accordance with the kind of proportion mentioned above (for in the case also in which the distribution is made from the common funds of a partnership it will be according to the same ratio which the funds put into the business by the partners bear to one another); and the injustice opposed to this kind of justice is that which violates the proportion. But the justice in transactions between man and man is a sort of equality indeed, and the injustice a sort of inequality; not according to that kind of proportion, however, but according to arithmetical proportion. For it makes no difference whether a good man has defrauded a bad man or a bad man a good one, nor whether it is a good or a bad man that has committed adultery; the law looks only to the distinctive character of the injury, and treats the parties as equal, if one is in the wrong and the other is being wronged, and if one inflicted injury and the other has received it. Therefore, this kind of injustice being an inequality, the judge tries to equalize it; for in the case also in which one has received and the other has inflicted a wound, or one has slain and the other been slain, the suffering and the action have been unequally distributed; but the judge tries to equalize things by means of the penalty, taking away from the gain of the assailant. For the term 'gain' is applied generally to such cases—even if it be not a term appropriate to certain cases, for example, to the person who inflicts a wound—and 'loss' to the sufferer; at all events when the suffering has been estimated, the one is called loss and the other gain. Therefore the equal is intermediate between the greater and the less, but the gain and the loss are respectively greater and less in contrary ways; more of the good and less of the evil are gain, and the contrary is loss; intermediate between them is, as we saw, the equal, which we say is just; therefore corrective justice will be the intermediate between loss and gain. This is why, when people dispute, they take refuge in the judge; and to go to the judge is to go to justice; for the nature of the judge is to be a sort of animate justice; and they seek the judge as an intermediate, and in some states they call judges mediators, on the assumption that if they get what is intermediate they will get what is just.

The just, then, is an intermediate, since the judge is so. Now the judge restores equality; it is as though there were a line divided into unequal parts, and he took away that by which the greater segment exceeds the half, and added it to the smaller segment. And when the whole has been equally divided, then they say they have 'their own'—that is, when they have got what is equal. The equal is intermediate between the greater and the lesser line according to arithmetical proportion. It is for this reason also that it is called just (δίκαιον), because it is a division into two equal parts (δίχα), just as if one were to call it δίχαιον; and the judge (δικαστής) is one who bisects (διχαστής). For when something is subtracted from one of two equals and added to the other, the other is in excess by these two; since if what was taken from the one had not been added to the other, the latter would have been in excess by one only. It therefore exceeds the intermediate by one, and the intermediate exceeds by one that from which something was taken. By this, then, we shall recognize both what we must subtract from that which has more, and what we must add to that which has less; we must add to the latter that by which the intermediate exceeds it, and subtract from the greatest that by which it exceeds the intermediate. Let the lines AA', BB', CC' be equal to one another; from the line AA' let the segment AE have been subtracted, and to the line CC' let the segment CD[1] have been added, so that the whole line DCC' exceeds the line EA' by the segment CD and the segment CF; therefore it exceeds the line BB' by the segment CD.

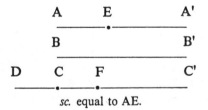

sc. equal to AE.

These names, both loss and gain, have come from voluntary exchange; for to have more than one's own is called gaining, and to have less than one's original share is called losing, for example, in buying and selling and in all other matters in which the law has left people free to make their own terms; but when they get neither more nor less but just what belongs to themselves, they say that they have their own and that they neither lose nor gain.

Therefore the just is intermediate between a sort of gain and a sort of loss, to wit, those which are involuntary;[3] it consists in having an equal amount before and after the transaction.

JUSTICE IN EXCHANGE, RECIPROCITY IN ACCORDANCE WITH PROPORTION

5. Some think that *reciprocity* is without qualification just, as the Pythagoreans said; for they defined justice without qualification as reciprocity. Now 'reciprocity' fits neither distributive nor rectificatory justice—yet people *want* even the justice of Rhadamanthus to mean this:

Should a man suffer what he did, right justice would be done.

—for in many cases reciprocity and rectificatory justice are not in accord; for example, (1) if an official has inflicted a wound, he should not be wounded in return, and if someone has wounded an official, he ought not to be wounded only but punished in addition. Further (2) there is a great difference between a voluntary and an involuntary act. But in associations for exchange this sort of justice does hold men together—reciprocity in accordance with a proportion and not on the basis of precisely equal return. For it is by proportionate requital that the city holds together. Men seek to return either evil for evil—and if they cannot do so, think their position mere slavery—or good for good—and if they cannot do so there is no exchange, but it is by exchange that they hold together. This is why they give a prominent place to the temple of the Graces—to promote the requital of services; for this is characteristic of grace—we should serve in return one who has shown grace to us, and should another time take the initiative in showing it.

Now proportionate return is secured by cross-conjunction.[4] Let A be a builder, B a shoemaker, C a house, D a shoe. The builder, then, must get from the shoemaker the latter's work, and must himself give him in return his own. If, then, first there is proportionate equality of goods, and then reciprocal action takes place, the result we mention will be effected. If not, the bargain is not equal, and does not hold; for there is nothing to prevent the work of the one being better than that of the other; they must therefore be equated. (And this is true of the other arts also; for they would have been destroyed if what the patient suffered had not been just what the agent did, and of the same amount and kind.) For it is not two doctors that associate for exchange, but a doctor and a farmer, or in general people who are different and unequal; but these must be equated. This is why all things that are exchanged must be somehow comparable. It is for this end that money has been introduced, and it becomes in a sense an intermediate; for it measures all things, and therefore the excess and the defect—how many shoes are equal to a house or to a given amount of food. The number of shoes exchanged for a house [or for a given amount of food] must therefore correspond to the ratio of builder to shoemaker. For if this be not so, there will be no exchange and no intercourse. And this proportion will not be effected unless the goods are somehow equal. All goods must therefore be measured by some one thing, as we said before. Now this unit is in truth demand, which holds all things together (for if men did not need one another's goods at all, or did not need them equally, there would be either no exchange or not the same exchange); but money has become by convention a sort of representative of demand; and this is why it has the name 'money' (νόμισμα) —because it exists not by nature but by law (νόμος) and it is in our power to change it and make it useless. There will, then, be reciprocity when the terms have been equated so that as farmer is to shoemaker, the amount of the shoemaker's work is to that of the farmer's work for which it exchanges. But we must not bring them into a figure of proportion when they have already exchanged (otherwise one extreme will have both excesses), but when they still have their own goods. Thus they are equals and associates just because this equality can be effected in their case. Let A be a farmer, C food, B a shoemaker, D his product equated to C. If it had not been possible for reciprocity to be thus effected, there would have been no association of the parties. That demand holds things together as a single unit is shown by the fact that when men do not need one another, that is, when neither needs the other or one does not need the other, they do not exchange, as we do when someone wants what one has oneself, for example, when people

permit the exportation of corn in exchange for wine. This equation therefore must be established. And for the future exchange—that if we do not need a thing now we shall have it if ever we do need it—money is as it were our surety; for it must be possible for us to get what we want by bringing the money. Now the same thing happens to money itself as to goods—it is not always worth the same; yet it tends to be steadier. This is why all goods must have a price set on them for then there will always be exchange, and if so, association of man with man. Money, then, acting as a measure, makes goods commensurate and equates them; for neither would there have been association if there were not exchange, nor exchange if there were not equality, nor equality if there were not commensurability. Now in truth it is impossible that things differing so much should become commensurate, but with reference to demand they may become so sufficiently. There must, then, be a unit, and that fixed by agreement (for which reason it is called money); for it is this that makes all things commensurate, since all things are measured by money. Let A be a house, B ten minae, C a bed. A is half of B, if the house is worth five minae or equal to them; the bed, C, is a tenth of B; it is plain, then, how many beds are equal to a house, to wit, five. That exchange took place thus before there was money is plain; for it makes no difference whether it is five beds that exchange for a house, or the money value of five beds.

We have now defined the unjust and the just. These having been marked off from each other, it is plain that just action is intermediate between acting unjustly and being unjustly treated; for the one is to have too much and the other to have too little. Justice is a kind of mean, but not in the same way as the other virtues, but because it relates to an intermediate amount, while injustice relates to the extremes. And justice is that in virtue of which the just man is said to be a doer, by choice, of that which is just, and one who will distribute either between himself and another or between two others not so as to give more of what is desirable to himself and less to his neighbour (and conversely with what is harmful), but so as to give what is equal in accordance with proportion; and similarly in distributing between two other persons. Injustice on the other hand is similarly related to the unjust, which is excess and defect, contrary to proportion, of the useful or hurtful. For which reason injustice is excess and defect, to wit, because it is productive of excess and defect—in one's own case excess of what is in its own nature useful and defect of what is hurtful, while in the case of others it is a whole like what it is in one's own case, but proportion may be violated in either direction. In the unjust act to have too little is to be unjustly treated; to have too much is to act unjustly.

Let this be taken as our account of the nature of justice and injustice, and similarly of the just and the unjust in general.

POLITICAL JUSTICE AND ANALOGOUS KINDS OF JUSTICE

6. Since acting unjustly does not necessarily imply being unjust, we must ask what sort of unjust acts imply that the doer is unjust with respect to each type of injustice, for example, a thief, an adulterer, or a brigand. Surely the answer does not turn on the difference between these types. For a man might even lie with a woman knowing who she was, but the origin of his act might be not deliberate choice but passion. He acts unjustly, then, but is not unjust; for example, a man is not a thief, yet he stole, nor an adulterer, yet he committed adultery; and similarly in all other cases.

Now we have previously stated how the reciprocal is related to the just, but we must not forget that what we are looking for is not only what is just without qualification but also political justice. This is found among men who share their life with a view to self-sufficiency, men who are free and either proportionately or arithmetically equal, so that between those who do not fulfil this condition there is no political justice but justice in a special sense and by analogy. For justice exists only between men whose mutual relations are governed by law; and law exists for men between whom there is injustice; for legal justice is the discrimination of the just and the unjust. And between men between whom injustice is done there is also unjust action (though there is not injustice between all between whom there is unjust action), and this is assigning too much to oneself of things good in themselves and too little of things evil in themselves. This is why we do not allow a *man* to rule, but *rational principle*, because a man behaves thus in his own interests and becomes a tyrant. The magistrate on the other hand is the guardian of justice, and, if of justice, then of equality also. And since he is assumed to have no more than his share, if he is just (for he does not assign to himself more of what is good in itself, unless such a share is proportional to his merits—so that it is for others that he labours, and it is for this reason that men, as we stated previously, say that justice is 'another's good'), therefore a reward must be given him, and this is honour and privilege; but those for whom such things are not enough become tyrants.

The justice of a master and that of a father are not the same as the justice of citizens, though they are like it; for there can be no injustice in the unqualified sense towards things that are one's own, but a man's chattel,[5] and his child until it reaches a certain age and sets up for itself, are as it were part of himself, and no one chooses to hurt himself (for which reason there can be no injustice towards oneself). Therefore the justice or injustice of citizens is not manifested in these relations; for it was as we saw according to law, and between people naturally subject to law, and these as we saw are people who have an equal share in ruling and being ruled. Hence justice can more truly be manifested towards a wife than towards children and chattels, for the former is household justice; but even this is different from political justice.

NATURAL AND LEGAL JUSTICE

7. Of political justice part is natural, part legal, —natural, that which everywhere has the same force and does not exist by people's thinking this or that; legal, that which is originally indifferent, but when it has been laid down is not indifferent, for example, that a prisoner's ransom shall be a mina, or that a goat and not two sheep shall be sacrificed, and again all the laws that are passed for particular cases, for example, that sacrifice shall be made in honour of Brasidas, and the provisions of decrees. Now some think that all justice is of this sort, because that which is by nature is unchangeable and has everywhere the same force (as fire burns both here and in Persia), while they see change in the things recognized as just. This, however, is not true in this unqualified way, but is true in a sense; or rather, with the gods it is perhaps not true at all, while with us there is something that is just even by nature, yet all of it is changeable; but still some is by nature, some

not by nature. It is evident which sort of thing, among things capable of being otherwise, is by nature; and which is not but is legal and conventional, assuming that both are equally changeable. And in all other things the same distinction will apply; by nature the right hand is stronger, yet it is possible that all men should come to be ambidextrous. The things which are just by virtue of convention and expediency are like measures; for wine and corn measures are not everywhere equal, but larger in wholesale and smaller in retail markets. Similarly, the things which are just not by nature but by human enactment are not everywhere the same, since constitutions also are not the same, though there is but one which is everywhere by nature the best.

Of things just and lawful each is related as the universal to its particulars; for the things that are done are many, but of *them* each is one, since it is universal.

There is a difference between the act of injustice and what is unjust, and between the act of justice and what is just; for a thing is unjust by nature or by enactment; and this very thing, when it has been done, is an act of injustice, but before it is done is not yet that but is unjust. So, too, with an act of justice (though the general term is rather 'just action', and 'act of justice' is applied to the correction of the act of injustice).

Each of these must later be examined separately with regard to the nature and number of its species and the nature of the things with which it is concerned.

JUSTICE: ITS INNER NATURE AS INVOLVING CHOICE

THE SCALE OF DEGREES OF WRONGDOING

8. Acts just and unjust being as we have described them, a man acts unjustly or justly whenever he does such acts voluntarily; when involuntarily, he acts neither unjustly nor justly except in an incidental way; for he does things which happen to be just or unjust. Whether an act is or is not one of injustice (or of justice) is determined by its voluntariness or involuntariness; for when it is voluntary it is blamed, and at the same time is then an act of injustice; so that there will be things that are unjust but not yet acts of injustice, if voluntariness be not present as well. By the

voluntary I mean, as has been said before, any of the things in a man's own power which he does with knowledge, that is, not in ignorance either of the person acted on or of the instrument used or of the end that will be attained (for example, whom he is striking, with what, and to what end), each such act being done not incidentally nor under compulsion (for example, if A takes B's hand and therewith strikes C, B does not act voluntarily; for the act was not in his own power). The person struck may be the striker's father, and the striker may know that it is a man or one of the persons present, but not know that it is his father; a similar distinction may be made in the case of the end, and with regard to the whole action. Therefore that which is done in ignorance, or though not done in ignorance is not in the agent's power, or is done under compulsion, is involuntary (for many natural processes, even, we knowingly both perform and experience, none of which is either voluntary or involuntary; for example, growing old or dying). But in the case of unjust and just acts alike the injustice or justice may be only incidental; for a man might return a deposit unwillingly and from fear, and then he must not be said either to do what is just or to act justly, except in an incidental way. Similarly the man who under compulsion and unwillingly fails to return the deposit must be said to act unjustly, and to do what is unjust, only incidentally. Of voluntary acts we do some by choice, others not by choice; by choice those which we do after deliberation, not by choice those which we do without previous deliberation. Thus there are three kinds of injury in transactions between man and man; those done in ignorance are mistakes when the person acted on, the act, the instrument, or the end that will be attained is other than the agent supposed; the agent thought either that he was not hitting any one or that he was not hitting with this missile or not hitting this person or to this end, but a result followed other than that which he thought likely (for example, he threw not with intent to wound but only to prick), or the person hit or the missile was other than he supposed. Now when (1) the injury takes place contrary to reasonable expectation, it is *misadventure*. When (2) it is not contrary to reasonable expectation, but does not imply vice, it is a *mistake* (for a man makes a mistake when the fault originates in him, but is the victim of accident when the origin lies outside him). When (3) he acts with knowledge but not after deliberation, it is an *act of injustice*—for example, the acts due to anger or to other passions necessary or natural to man; for when men do such harmful and mistaken acts they act unjustly, and the acts are acts of injustice, but this does not imply that the doers are unjust or wicked; for the injury is not due to vice. But when (4) a man acts from choice, he is an *unjust man* and a vicious man.

Hence acts proceeding from anger are rightly judged not to be done of malice aforethought; for it is not the man who acts in anger but he who enraged him that starts the mischief. Again, the matter in dispute is not whether the thing happened or not, but its justice; for it is apparent injustice that occasions rage. For they do not dispute about the occurrence of the act—as in commercial transactions where one of the two parties *must* be vicious[6]—unless they do so owing to forgetfulness; but, agreeing about the fact, they dispute on which side justice lies (whereas a man who has deliberately injured another cannot help knowing that he has done so), so that one thinks he is being treated unjustly and the other disagrees.

But if a man harms another by choice, he acts unjustly; and *these* are the acts of injustice which imply that the doer is an unjust man, provided that the act violates proportion or equality. Similarly, a man *is just* when he acts justly by choice; but he *acts justly* if he merely acts voluntarily.

Of involuntary acts some are excusable, others not. For the mistakes which men make not only in ignorance but also from ignorance are excusable, while those which men do not from ignorance but (though they do them *in* ignorance) owing to a passion which is neither natural nor such as man is liable to, are not excusable.

Can a man be voluntarily treated unjustly? Is it the distributor or the recipient that is guilty of injustice in distribution? Justice is not so easy as it might seem, because it is not a way of acting but an inner disposition

9. Assuming that we have sufficiently defined the suffering and doing of injustice, it may be asked (1) whether the truth is expressed in Euripides' paradoxical words:

'I slew my mother, that's my tale in brief.'
'Were you both willing, or unwilling both?'

Is it truly possible to be willingly treated unjustly, or is all suffering of injustice on the contrary involuntary, as all unjust action is voluntary? And is all suffering of injustice of the latter kind or else all of the former, or is it sometimes voluntary, sometimes involuntary? So, too, with the case of being justly treated; all just action is voluntary, so that it is reasonable that there should be a similar opposition in either case—that both being unjustly and being justly treated should be either alike voluntary or alike involuntary. But it would be thought paradoxical even in the case of being justly treated, if it were always voluntary; for some are unwillingly treated justly. (2) One might raise this question also, whether everyone who has suffered what is unjust is being unjustly treated, or on the other hand it is with suffering as with acting. In action and in passivity alike it is possible for justice to be done incidentally, and similarly (it is plain) injustice; for to do what is unjust is not the same as to act unjustly, nor to suffer what is unjust as to be treated unjustly, and similarly in the case of acting justly and being justly treated; for it is impossible to be unjustly treated if the other does not act unjustly, or justly treated unless he acts justly. Now if to act unjustly is simply to harm someone voluntarily, and 'voluntarily' means 'knowing the person acted on, the instrument, and the manner of one's acting', and the incontinent man voluntarily harms himself, not only will he voluntarily be unjustly treated but it will be possible to treat oneself unjustly. (This also is one of the questions in doubt, whether a man can treat himself unjustly.) Again, a man may voluntarily, owing to incontinence, be harmed by another who acts voluntarily, so that it would be possible to be voluntarily treated unjustly. Or is our definition incorrect; must we to 'harming another, with knowledge both of the person acted on, of the instrument, and of the manner' add 'contrary to the wish of the person acted on'? Then a man may be voluntarily harmed and voluntarily suffer what is unjust, but no one is voluntarily treated unjustly; for no one wishes to be unjustly treated, not even the incontinent man. He acts contrary to his wish; for no one *wishes* for what he does not think to be good, but the incontinent man does *do* things that he does not think he ought to do. Again, one who gives what is his own, as Homer says Glaucus gave Diomede

> Armour of gold for brazen, the price of a hundred
>   beeves for nine,

is not unjustly treated; for though to give is in his power, to be unjustly treated is not, but there must be someone to treat him unjustly. It is plain, then, that being unjustly treated is not voluntary.

Of the questions we intended to discuss two still remain for discussion; (3) whether it is the man who has assigned to another more than his share that acts unjustly, or he who has the excessive share, and (4) whether it is possible to treat oneself unjustly. The questions are connected; for if the former alternative is possible and the distributor acts unjustly and not the man who has the excessive share, then if a man assigns more to another than to himself, knowingly and voluntarily, he treats himself unjustly; which is what modest people seem to do, since the virtuous man tends to take less than his share. Or does this statement too need qualification? For (a) he perhaps gets more than his share of some other good, for example, of honour or of intrinsic nobility. (b) The question is solved by applying the distinction we applied to unjust action, for he suffers nothing contrary to his own wish, so that he is not unjustly treated so far as this goes, but at most only suffers harm.

It is plain too that the distributor acts unjustly, but not always the man who has the excessive share; for it is not he to whom injustice is done that acts unjustly, but he to whom it appertains to do the unjust act voluntarily, that is, the person in whom lies the origin of the action, and this lies in the distributor, not in the receiver. Again, since the word 'do' is ambiguous, and there is a sense in which lifeless things, or a hand, or a servant who obeys an order, may be said to slay, he who gets an excessive share does not act unjustly, though he 'does' what is unjust.

Again, if the distributor gave his judgement in ignorance, he does not act unjustly in respect of legal justice, and his judgement is not unjust in this sense, but in a sense it *is* unjust (for legal justice and primordial justice are different); but if with the knowledge he judged unjustly, he is himself aiming at an excessive share either of gratitude or of revenge. As much, then, as if he were to share in the plunder, the man who has judged unjustly for these reasons has got too much; the fact that what he gets is different from what he distributes makes no difference, for even if he awards land with a view to sharing in the plunder he gets not land but money.

Men think that acting unjustly is in their power, and therefore that being just is easy. But it is not; to lie with one's neighbour's wife, to wound another, to deliver a bribe, is easy and in our power, but to do these things as a result of a certain state of character is neither easy nor in our power. Similarly to know what is just and what is unjust requires, men think, no great wisdom, because it is not hard to understand the matters dealt with by the laws (though these are not the things that are just, except incidentally); but how actions must be done and distributions effected in order to be just, to know *this* is a greater achievement than knowing what is good for the health; though even there, while it is easy to know that honey, wine, hellebore, cautery, and the use of the knife are so, to know how, to whom, and when these should be applied with a view to producing health, is no less an achievement than that of being a physician. Again, for this very reason[7] men think that acting unjustly is characteristic of the just man no less than of the unjust, because he would be not less but even more capable of doing each of these unjust acts, for he could lie with a woman or wound a neighbour; and the brave man could throw away his shield and turn to flight in this direction or in that. But to play the coward or to act unjustly consists not in doing these things, except incidentally, but in doing them as the result of a certain state of character, just as to practise medicine and healing consists not in applying or not applying the knife, in using or not using medicines, but in doing so in a certain way.

Just acts occur between people who participate in things good in themselves and can have too much or too little of them; for some beings (for example, presumably the gods) cannot have too much of them, and to others, those who are incurably bad, not even the smallest share in them is beneficial but all such goods are harmful, while to others they are beneficial up to a point; therefore justice is essentially something human.

EQUITY, A CORRECTIVE
OF LEGAL JUSTICE

10. Our next subject is equity and the equitable and their respective relations to justice and the

just. For on examination they appear to be neither absolutely the same nor generically different; and while we sometimes praise what is equitable and the equitable man, at other times, when we reason it out, it seems strange if the equitable, being something different from the just, is yet praiseworthy; for either the just or the equitable is not good, if they are different; or, if both are good, they are the same.

These, then, are pretty much the considerations that give rise to the problem about the equitable; they are all in a sense correct and not opposed to one another; for the equitable, though it is better than one kind of justice, yet is just, and it is not as being a different class of thing that it is better than the just. The same thing, then, is just and equitable, and while both are good the equitable is superior. What creates the problem is that the equitable is just, but not the legally just but a correction of legal justice. The reason is that all law is universal but about some things it is not possible to make a universal statement which shall be correct. In those cases, then, in which it is necessary to speak universally, but not possible to do so correctly, the law takes the usual case, though it is not ignorant of the possibility of error. And it is none the less correct; for the error is not in the law nor in the legislator but in the nature of the thing, since the matter of practical affairs is of this kind from the start. When the law speaks universally, then, and a case arises on it which is not covered by the universal statement, then it is right, where the legislator fails us and has erred by over-simplicity, to correct the omission—to say what the legislator himself would have said had he been present, and would have put into his law if he had known. Hence the equitable is just, and better than one kind of justice—not better than absolute justice, but better than the error that arises from the absoluteness of the statement. And this is the nature of the equitable, a correction of law where it is defective owing to its universality. In fact this is the reason why all things are not determined by law, to wit, that about some things it is impossible to lay down a law, so that a decree is needed. For when the thing is indefinite the rule also is indefinite, like the leaden rule used in making the Lesbian moulding; the rule adapts itself to the shape of the stone and is not rigid, and so too the decree is adapted to the facts.

It is plain, then, what the equitable is, and that it is just and is better than one kind of justice. It is evident also from this who the equitable man is; the man who chooses and does such acts, and is no stickler for his rights in a bad sense but tends to take less than his share though he has the law on his side, is equitable, and this state of character is equity, which is a sort of justice and not a different state of character.

CAN A MAN TREAT HIMSELF UNJUSTLY?

11. Whether a man can treat himself unjustly or not, is evident from what has been said. For (a) one class of just acts are those acts in accordance with any virtue which are prescribed by the law, for example, the law does not expressly permit suicide, and what it does not expressly permit it forbids. Again, when a man in violation of the law harms another (otherwise than in retaliation) voluntarily, he acts unjustly, and a voluntary agent is one who knows both the person he is affecting by his action and the instrument he is using; and he who through anger voluntarily stabs himself does this contrary to the right rule of life, and this the law does not allow; therefore he is acting unjustly. But towards whom? Surely towards the state, not towards himself. For he suffers voluntarily, but no one is voluntarily treated unjustly. This is also the reason why the state punishes; a certain loss of civil rights attaches to the man who destroys himself, on the ground that he is treating the state unjustly.

Further, (b) in that sense of 'acting unjustly' in which the man who 'acts unjustly' is unjust only and not bad all round, it is not possible to treat oneself unjustly (this is different from the former sense; the unjust man in one sense of the term is wicked in a particularized way just as the coward is, not in the sense of being wicked all round, so that his 'unjust act' does not manifest wickedness in general). For (i) that would imply the possibility of the same thing's having been subtracted from and added to the same thing at the same time; but this is impossible—the just and the unjust always involve more than one person. Further; (ii) unjust action is voluntary and done by choice, and *takes the initiative* (for the man who because he has suffered does the same in return is not thought to act unjustly); but if a man harms himself he suffers and does the same things *at the same time.* Further, (iii) if a man could treat himself unjustly, he could be voluntarily treated unjustly. Besides, (iv) no one acts unjustly without committing particular acts of injustice; but no one can commit adultery with his own wife or housebreaking on his own house or theft on his own property.

In general, the question 'Can a man treat himself unjustly?' is solved also by the distinction we applied to the question 'Can a man be voluntarily treated unjustly?'

(It is evident too that both are bad, being unjustly treated and acting unjustly; for the one means having less and the other having more than the intermediate amount, which plays the part here that the healthy does in the medical art, and the good condition does in the art of bodily training. But still acting unjustly is the worse, for it involves vice and is blameworthy—involves vice which is either of the complete and unqualified kind or almost so (we must admit the latter alternative, because not all voluntary unjust action implies injustice as a state of character), while being unjustly treated does not involve vice and injustice in oneself. In itself, then, being unjustly treated is less bad, but there is nothing to prevent its being incidentally a greater evil. But theory cares nothing for this; it calls pleurisy a more serious mischief than a stumble; yet the latter may become incidentally the more serious, if the fall due to it leads to your being taken prisoner or put to death by the enemy.)

Metaphorically and in virtue of a certain resemblance there is a justice, not indeed between a man and himself, but between certain parts of him; yet not every kind of justice but that of master and servant or that of husband and wife. For these are the ratios in which the part of the soul that has a rational principle stands to the irrational part; and it is with a view to these parts that people also think a man can be unjust to himself, to wit, because these parts are liable to suffer something contrary to their respective desires; there is therefore thought to be a mutual justice between them as between ruler and ruled.

Let this be taken as our account of justice and the other, that is, the other moral, virtues.

NOTES

1. Person A + thing C to person B + thing D.
2. The problem of distributive justice is to divide the distributable honour or reward into parts which are to one another as are the merits of the persons who are to participate. If

A (first person): B (second person) :: C (first portion) : D (second portion),
then (*alternando*) A : C :: B : D,
and therefore (*componendo*) A + C : B + D :: A : B.
In other words the position established answers to the relative merits of the parties.
3. that is, for the loser.
4. The working of 'proportionate reciprocity' is not very clearly described by Aristotle, but seems to be as follows. A and B are workers in different trades, and will normally be of different degrees of 'worth'. Their products, therefore, will also have unequal worth, that is (though Aristotle does not expressly reduce the question to one of time) if A = nB, C (what A makes, say, in an hour) will be worth n times as much as D (what B makes in an hour). A fair exchange will then take place if A gets nD and B gets 1 C; that is if A gives what it takes him an hour to make, in exchange for what it takes B n hours to make.
5. that is, his slave.
6. The plaintiff, if he brings a false accusation; the defendant, if he denies a true one.
7. that is, that stated in 11. 4 f., that acting unjustly is in our own power.

RICHARD A. WASSERSTROM

Equity*

THE CASE FOR AN EQUITABLE DECISION PROCEDURE

A decision procedure based upon precedent, it can be argued, is an anachronism if not an absurdity. For despite the possible benefits of certainty and efficiency that might accrue from its operation, it stands ultimately for the proposition that legal rules are to be applied to particular cases simply because they are the extant legal rules. Even the most uncritical examination of the function of a legal system reveals, however, that rules should never be applied in this manner. Courts of law obviously are created to dispense justice in the cases that come before them for adjudication. The most desirable procedure, therefore, is one that seeks to ensure that all cases and controversies will be decided justly.

Were society so organized that conflicts never arose, the argument might continue, were there never "pathological cases," a legal system might well be a superfluous societal institution. But problems do arise, conflicting interests require accommodation, and as a result of acts both intentional and unintentional, parties find themselves in situations that call for the aid of some disinterested third party before whom they can place their problems and by whose authority compromise and resolution can be effected.

In a society such as ours, the legal system is called upon to resolve a multiplicity of problems and to settle innumerable controversies. It is also its function to ensure that certain standards are given effect in the deliberative dealings of man with man. The judiciary is entrusted with a delicate but almost boundless power over the lives of those persons who have been accused of transgressions against the community; it is also given the authority to decide what shall be done in those cases in which the parties have quite inadvertently worked themselves into a position from which voluntary extrication is impossible. These situations may all involve considerations of the greatest import to the litigants; they all surely demand that the judiciary function in such a way that each case is justly decided.

For this reason it is unnecessary, so the argument continues, for there to be positive, mechanically applied rules of law within the legal system. Not only is it unnecessary, but it is also undesirable. Rules of law are superfluous because it is the justice of the result that counts. Rules of law are undesirable because of the danger that they may be mechanically applied without regard for the justice in the case. The problems with which a judiciary is forced to deal, and the matters with which it should concern itself, lend themselves far better to a direct consideration of the merits of each particular case than to the sterile, unfeeling application of extant laws. Opposed, therefore, to the theory that justice requires the application of fixed rules of law to particular cases is the notion that justice means the "natural," "individualistic," or "discretionary" adjudication of each case as it arises.

This is the position that must now be examined: the view that it is both possible and desirable for cases to be decided by an appeal to considerations of justice or equity rather than by reference to legal rules.

The concept that forms the basis of this decision procedure has enjoyed a long life under a variety of names—"equity," "discretion," "natural justice," "good conscience," "fairness," and "righteousness" are all epithets that have been applied to it. This position, moreover, is one that

*Chapter 5 (complete) of *The Judicial Decision: Toward a Theory of Legal Justification,* by Richard A. Wasserstrom (Stanford, California: Stanford University Press, 1961). Reprinted by permission of the publishers, Stanford University Press, and by permission of the author. © 1961 by the Board of Trustees of the Leland Stanford Junior University.

at first sight is quite attractive, and that has at times been widely accepted and advocated. For it seems to insist from the outset that the legal system must perform precisely those duties for which it most obviously exists.

Proponents of an equitable decision procedure, as we shall see, have been both ambiguous and unspecific in directing their approval toward a process of equitable justification. But there is one characteristic about which they appear to be in accord. In all equitable procedures of justification, the necessary and sufficient justification for any particular decision consists in the fact that the decision is the *most just for the particular case*. That the decision may be deducible from some legal rule is irrelevant; that the decision in itself is just for the case is alone significant.

Examples of what have been considered systems in which justice has been administered by means of an equitable decision process are highly diverse. Roscoe Pound, for instance, suggests the example of Oriental justice. In his discussion of this "lawless" kind of judicial administration, Pound refers to Kipling's description of the court of the Oriental sovereign.

By the custom of the East, any man or woman having a complaint to make, or an enemy against whom to be avenged, has the right of speaking face to face with the king at the daily public audience. . . . The privilege of open speech is of course exercised at certain personal risk. The king may be pleased and raise the speaker to honour for that very bluntness of speech which three minutes later brings a too imitative petitioner to the edge of the ever-ready blade.[1]

Another example offered by Pound, and one much more familiar to the Occidental way of life, is martial law. For here, too, controversies are solved not by an appeal to laws as such, but rather by the direct intervention and application of the general's authority. "Martial law is regulated by no known or established system or code of laws, as it is over and above all of them. The commander is the legislator, judge and executioner."[2] Somehow, both examples miss the main feature of the procedure of equitable adjudication. They are, admittedly, systems in which particular cases are not decided by an appeal to rules of law. But they are also clearly systems in which there is no emphasis upon the desirability of effecting justice between the parties. They impose no re-

quirement that he who pronounces decisions should attempt to do justice. They guarantee only that decisions will be made. The general theory of "natural justice" may have many serious weaknesses, but it surely sets a higher ideal of adjudication than this.

There is, however, one example that embodies many of the characteristics of such a procedure, namely, the system of equitable adjudication, which has played so conspicuous and so controversial a part in the history of Anglo-American law. As a historical proposition it is doubtless incorrect to consider the equity courts as a complete, self-contained institution for the administration of justice. It is surely more accurate to regard the function performed by the equity courts as only one of the several functions that the Anglo-American judicial system has in fact fulfilled.[3] Reference to the courts of equity is useful, nevertheless, because many of the adherents of a decision procedure based upon "doing justice in the particular case" have pointed to the equity courts as exemplifying the kind of procedure that is desirable. And it is a fruitful example, too, because the equity courts have at times spoken of this procedure in an equally approving manner. Thus, although to do so is to be false to the historical meaning or function of the courts of equity, I shall refer to procedures which share this characteristic as "equitable" procedures of justification.

Descriptions of an equitable decision procedure abound in the literature of judicial opinions; typical are the two that follow.

One of the most salutary principles of chancery jurisprudence is that it, strictly speaking, has no immutable rules. It lights its own pathway; it blazes its own trail; it paves its own highway; it is an appeal to the conscience of the chancellor. It had its origin in the breast of the king, who upon complaint of one of the king's subjects who found he had no plain, adequate, and complete remedy at law, appealed to his king, who thereupon instructed an ecclesiastic, the keeper of the king's conscience, to make an investigation, and regardless of the narrow and technical rules of law, mete out equal and exact justice. The Lord Chancellor became the head of these ecclesiastical or chancery courts, and thus the jurisdiction of courts of equity rests upon the fundamental principles of right and fair dealing; its creed is justice between man and man.

A court of equity acts only when and as conscience commands, and if the conduct of the plaintiff be offensive to the dictates of natural justice . . . he will be held remediless. . . . A court of equity has been said to be the forum of conscience, and an appeal directed to it is an appeal to the moral sense of the judge. In a proper case, the court acts upon the conscience of the defendant and compels him to do that which is just and right.[4]

Commentators have furnished (although not always with approval) comparable characterizations. John Pomeroy, for example, speaks of one possible concept of equity—he finds it undesirable—as being that theory which asserts that judges have the power

and even the duty resting upon them—to decide every case according to a high standard of morality and abstract right; that is, the power and duty of the judge to do justice to the individual parties in each case. This conception of equity was known to the Roman jurists, and was described by the phrase, *Arbitrium boni viri,* which may be freely translated as the decision upon the facts and circumstances of a case which would be made by a man of intelligence and of high moral principles . . .

Charles Phelps provides a comparable characterization:

By juridical equity is meant a systematic appeal for relief from a cramped administration of defective laws to the disciplined conscience of a competent magistrate, applying to the special circumstances of defined and limited cases the principles of natural justice, controlled in a measure as much by consideration of public policy as by established precedent and by positive provisions of law.

In describing the ideal function of the judge, Jerome Frank gives a clearly commendatory statement of the same position.

The judge, at his best, is an arbitrator, a "sound man" who strives to do justice to the parties by exercising a wise discretion with reference to the peculiar circumstances of the case. He does not merely "find" or invent some generalized rule which he "applies" to the facts presented to him. He does "equity" in the sense in which Aristotle—when thinking most clearly—described it. . . . The arbitral function is the central fact in the administration of justice.

And Julius Stone provides a more neutral account:

In the last resort what he prescribed was a dictate of his, the Chancellor's, conscience—or at least the King's conscience secreted in the Chancellor's breast.

Although much rhetoric invoking the divine law and universal justice is to be found, equity jurisdiction was based essentially on the appeal to the particular reason or conscience of the King and his Chancellor. Again this jurisdiction was not pursued, ostensibly at any rate, by promulgating rules binding on all men. At first, both in theory and practice, it was enforced by an appeal to the particular defendant's conscience, he being if necessary detained so as to permit his conscience to operate. . . . The main difference between the Chancellor and the natural lawyer was that the former refrained from formulating in advance the assumptions on which he proceeded.[5]

The espousal of a decision procedure which ensures that justice will be done in every case is certainly commendable. Like the commitments to goodness, truth, beauty, and motherhood, devotion to justice is self-evidently praiseworthy. But to insist that justice ought to be done is not to tell us how it can be, and unfortunately, the advocates of an equitable decision procedure have not carried the task of specification very far. They seem rather to have assumed that once the goal of doing justice in the particular case has been postulated, the way in which this goal is to be realized becomes obvious. They have not indicated the nature of the specific decision procedure according to which such justice is best attained.

It would, however, be unfair to assert that nothing in the way of substantive methodology or argumentation has been offered to clarify the form and content of an equitable decision procedure. It has been argued, for example, that there are *certain features* of legal rules and particular cases that make it inappropriate to decide cases by an appeal to legal rules. Concomitantly, many have insisted that for this reason a nonrational, nondeductive method of justification should be employed. Intuition rather than reason, it is urged, should be the means by which *justification* is effected.* It should be noted, however, that

*Throughout this chapter the word "intuition" is used in a special sense, one that admittedly is broader than ordinary philosophical usage. For I employ "intuition" to denote any process by which truth or correctness is *directly apprehended.* In this sense it includes both intuition in the more usual philosophic sense and also such things as *emotional apprehension.* In other words, I do not distinguish between an epistemology based upon an intuition of justice and one based upon knowledge directly acquired by the "sense of justice" or the "sense of injustice." There may be differences between the two approaches, but for my purposes they can be treated as being essentially similar.

reliance upon a nonrational methodology is not characteristic of all equitable procedures, although an appeal to intuition is present in most.

This chapter deals in detail with only two of the above general claims: (1) that the intuition of justice should be the essential attribute of an equitable decision procedure; and (2) that the nature of particular cases and of legal rules makes the application of legal rules to these cases undesirable . . .

As it is usually presented, the first of these claims—that an intuitive approach ought to be employed—is difficult to discuss and evaluate, for the requirement is in itself far from unambiguous, and the proponents of this procedure have provided little in the way of elucidation. Consequently, this chapter is primarily an attempt to explicate various procedures, all of which might be considered intuitive in nature. There are, more specifically, at least two distinct decision procedures that could be called "intuitive procedures" and that must be delineated and analyzed in turn. I cannot confidently assert that either of these procedures has in fact been advocated by anyone. I can only suggest that the description of these variant processes probably includes most or all of the more specific procedures that proponents of the intuitive approach have had in mind.

The first of these intuitive procedures rests upon what I shall call the theory of *particular justice*. In its simplest and most extreme form, it is the view that there is some particular feature or set of features in every case that makes it both possible and desirable to determine directly the justice or injustice of the decision in the instant controversy. The justification of any decision results from a particular intuition that reveals the decision to be just for this particular case. The second decision procedure can be characterized as a modified version of the theory of particular justice. Its basic premise is that some cases, but not all, are to be justified by an appeal to the relevant legal rule and that some cases, but not all, are to be justified by an intuition of the justness of the decision.

The modified version has itself commonly assumed one of two forms. The first of these forms, here termed the *bifurcation theory of justice*, holds that *all* members of *some* classes of cases coming before the legal system for adjudication cannot be properly decided by appealing to the relevant legal rule. The theory holds, too, that intuition must be used for those classes of cases for which rules are inappropriate.

The second form of the modified version, here termed the *Aristotelian theory of equity*, insists that *some* members of *all* classes of cases coming before the legal system for adjudication cannot be properly decided by appeal to the relevant legal rule.

A third, rather different, equitable decision procedure is delineated (but not evaluated) in this chapter. This nonintuitive procedure stipulates that a decision is justifiable if and only if it best takes into account the interests of the litigants before the court. It says nothing about intuition being the criterion for justifying a decision, and it says nothing about the kinds of cases for which this justification ought to be conclusive. It requires only that such things as the satisfactions, pleasure, needs, and aspirations of the two litigants be accorded exclusive consideration in the justification of any decision.

Besides attempting to specify more precisely the nature of these various procedures, this chapter will examine the theoretical assumptions upon which they rest, and assess the degree to which some of them would in fact succeed in realizing the goal of consistently just decisions.

THE THEORY OF PARTICULAR JUSTICE

As we have noted, the advocates of an equitable decision procedure have failed to specify the way in which such a procedure should operate. It is uncertain, therefore, whether anyone has ever urged the desirability of a decision procedure based upon the theory of particular justice. Cryptic statements, which could be interpreted as adopting such a position and as prescribing its implementation, can be located. Oliphant, for example, in a passage cited earlier observed that "courts are dominantly coerced, not by the essays of their predecessors but by a surer thing—*by an intuition of fitness of solution to problem.*"[6] Judge Joseph Hutcheson, Jr., was insistent that the crucial moment in the judicial decision process occurred at the moment when the judge was witness to that "intuitive sense of what is right or wrong for that cause."[7] And Jerome Frank has offered a similar assessment. The judge should have the utmost latitude, Frank insists, if he is to effect real justice between the parties. The judge can and should respond to the unique aspects of each case that comes before him. For it is this "power to individualize and to legislate judically [which] is of the very essence of [his] function."[8]

At a minimum the theory of particular justice as here presented is not inconsistent with these and comparable suggestions. For the theory insists that any judicial decision has been properly justified if and only if the decision has been directly perceived to be the just decision for the particular case. An appeal to a legal rule, a moral principle, or a future consequence is both inconclusive and unresponsive. The justice-creating features of the case are just in and of themselves. Once they are known by direct intuition, inquiry about justification is at an end. Until the features of the case are so grasped by intuition, all other investigation is futile.

It should be evident that what is *not* at issue is whether intuition can or should *suggest* to the judge what decision ought to be rendered. What is *not* relevant is the question of to what degree decisions are initially "hit upon" by intuition. (Or, in other words, what is *not* at issue is the question of discovery.) Rather, the theory of particular justice, as here interpreted, insists that a procedure of justification ought to be employed in which the fact that a judge has had an intuition of some kind is a conclusive justification for making that intuition the binding decision of the case. If a judge has intuited that a particular decision is the just one for this case, then the fact that this intuition was present is what makes the decision justifiable. Whether the judge suddenly "sees" *the decision* which ought to be given or intuits *that a certain decision* ought to be rendered, it is the intuition which provides the justification for the decision.

The significant features of this theory of justification emerge most clearly from an examination of what could count as a valid justification for any particular legal decision. The following imaginary dialogue between a judge and a questioner is admittedly not the kind of justification that any court has ever given for a decision. But if the language of some of the proponents of equity is to be taken seriously, it does indicate accurately the attributes that a procedure based strictly upon intuitions of particular justice would possess. The following discourse is one between a judge who has decided a case in a certain way and

a questioner who is seeking to ascertain the justification for the judge's decision.

Q: "On what grounds do you justify your decision in this case?"

J: "The justification for this decision rests upon the fact that I have intuited this result to be the best possible one for this case."

Q: "Oh, you mean that there is some general moral principle which requires that a case involving this kind of fact situation be decided in this way?"

J: "No, I mean simply that this decision is just *[playing]* because I have intuited it to be just for this case." *[with word]*

Q: "But how can I decide whether or not you *[word]* have intuited correctly?"

J: "Just look at all the facts of this case. Doesn't it seem obvious to you that this is the only just result? Look again and perhaps you will have the same intuition."

Q: "But if I cannot have an intuition of any kind, or if I have a contrary one, then is there nothing else you can tell me in order to persuade me of the justifiability of your decision?"

J: "That is correct. I know that the decision is just, and so does everyone else with the same intuition."

Q: "I suppose it would be fair to say, at least, that you would decide other cases of this kind in the same way?"

J: "No. I cannot commit myself, a priori, to a conclusion of what would be just in any other case. I have to have all of the facts of each particular case before me before I can properly intuit what would be truly just for that case. I can only discover what is the just decision for any case as that case is actually presented for adjudication."

Assuming that this caricature of any actual judicial justification is true to the essential features of the procedure of particular justice, there are several grounds upon which the desirability of such a justificatory procedure may be doubted. The first of these relates to eliminating the probability of bias or prejudice in the judicial decision process.

In Chapter 4 it was assumed that the legal system ought to be free from the biases, partialities, and like peculiarities of the judges who render decisions. It was concluded in that chapter that the precedential decision procedure was a partially ineffective means by which to realize that end. A stronger objection can be made to the

[He is exaggerating the point to make his arg. A judge would be able to explain his intuition]

efficacy of the theory of particular justice in this respect. Roscoe Pound has put the point this way:

Scientific law is a reasoned body of principles for the administration of justice, and its antithesis is a system of enforcing magisterial caprice, however honest, and however much disguised under the name of justice or equity or natural law. . . . Law is scientific in order to eliminate so far as may be the personal equation in judicial administration, to preclude corruption and to limit the dangerous possibilities of magisterial ignorance.[9]

The sentiments expressed by Pound are admirable; but they require further amplification if it is to be shown that the theory of particular justice does not succeed in eliminating this "personal equation."

For the purposes of this inquiry, the assertion that certain procedures are more conducive than others to the achievement of impartiality can be understood to be either an accurate empirical observation or a defensible normative hypothesis. Those procedures, moreover, which can best achieve that end must have at least three characteristics. First, under such procedures there should be certain independent criteria by which the one who makes a decision can evaluate the conclusion reached or the course of action decided upon. This requirement ensures, among other things, that the proponent of any plan of behavior must first persuade himself on "external" grounds of the desirability of his proposal. The second, and perhaps a more significant, requirement is that the justification for any proposal should be submitted to and should be able to withstand public examination. For the prerequisite of publicity provides what has consistently proved to be the most effective means by which the enthusiasms of the advocate and the visions of the would-be seer can be measured against the less personal and more sober and disinterested wisdom of the community. To require that the grounds of a decision be made public is to insist that an avenue of independent verification and criticism be kept open. The third requirement, which is closely related to the first two, stipulates that *all* the grounds or reasons for the decision be both revealed and evaluated. It insists that the processes of argumentation, justification, and enlightened persuasion not be prematurely cut

short. It demands that the process of justification continue until the "ultimate" premise upon which any decision stands and from which it draws its claim for acceptability is fully revealed. For it is only after this point has been reached that it is legitimate—if it is ever legitimate—to conclude that grounds for intelligent discussion no longer in fact exist. To urge that these requirements be present is to insist that men be *rational* —in the best sense of the word—so that the conclusions they have reached may be as accurate as possible, and the conduct undertaken as beneficial as possible.

The central role that rational inquiry and justification should play in the law has been nicely indicated in an essay by John Dewey, entitled "Logical Method and Law."

Courts not only reach decisions; they expound them, and the exposition must state justifying reasons. . . . Exposition implies that a definitive solution is reached, that the situation is now determinate with respect to its legal implication. Its purpose is to set forth grounds for the decision reached so that it will not appear as an arbitrary dictum, and so that it will indicate a rule for dealing with similar cases in the future. It is highly probable that the need of justifying to others conclusions reached and decisions made has been the chief cause of the origin and development of logical operations in the precise sense; of abstraction, generalization, regard for consistency of implications. It is quite conceivable that if no one had ever had to account to others for his decisions, logical operations would never have developed, but men would use exclusively methods of inarticulate intuition and impression, feeling; so that only after considerable experience in accounting for their decisions to others who demanded a reason, or exculpation, and were not satisfied till they got it, did men begin to give an account to themselves of the process of reaching a conclusion in a justified way. However this may be, it is certain that in judicial decisions the only alternative to arbitrary dicta, accepted by the parties to a controversy only because of the authority or prestige of the judge, is a rational statement which formulates grounds and exposes connecting or logical links.[10]

A procedure founded upon intuitions of particular just decisions does not meet these conditions. Intuitions are essentially private affairs. They are difficult to obtain; they are even harder to repeat and thereby verify. The evidence for the correctness of the conclusion reached and advanced must consist in the testimony of the "intuitor" that he has had the proper intuition. Unless one has had a comparable intuition, the word of the "intuitor" must be taken both for the fact that he has had the vision and for the fact that he has interpreted its commands faithfully. The course of human history has revealed the desirability of imposing far more stringent requirements than this in other areas of consequence; it seems strange, therefore, to argue that an institution so vital as the legal system ought to settle for so little.

This is of course not to suggest that what is needed before a good legal system is possible is an "escape from the prison house of the body" into a realm of abstract, nonsensual existences. The requirement that decisions be justifiable on rational grounds imposes no such demand. What is insisted upon, however, is that intuitions, especially if of particular decisions, should not constitute the kind of *ground* which justifies a legal decision. Since they are perforce private in nature, dependence upon them precludes any external evaluation of the judicial command. Being in essence nonrational, they can only blur the divide between fantasy and fact, between wish and ideal. Certainly it may be true that even the rational life, in this sense of the term, has not proved as conducive to happiness and freedom from conflict as some have supposed. But it is just as certainly true that the number and magnitude of undesirable actions performed under the banner of private truth and personal revelation is infinitely greater. It is surely a commonplace to observe that so long as there are men there will be judges who think they have had infallible intuitions of particular justice. But again it is also true that reliance upon the intuitive faculty as the ideal criterion of justification can only be deemed an unwise, ill-conceived, and indefensible normative position.

A related point deserves some mention, if not discussion. It was seen in Chapter 4 that the possibility of antecedent prediction of judicial consequences was a significant and desirable attribute for a legal system to possess. This goal, too, seems singularly unattainable by the kind of intuitive theory of justification presented here. If the judge is to adjudicate cases on the basis of what is just *in the particular case,* and solely in the light of the uniqueness of that case, then three things follow:

first, the task of classification becomes increasingly difficult, if not impossible; second, because the *particularity* of the situation is what is crucial, past decisions are, *ex hypothesi,* extremely unreliable guides for future judicial action; and third, to the extent to which intuitions are apt to be peculiar to a particular judge, the path of adjudication is rendered still more wavering and unpredictable.

It could be argued that the justice-making conditions of particular cases need not be different in every case. But if this is so, it is hard to see why proponents of the theory of particular justice insist that it is the *unique* factors of each case that are truly significant. It is also possible to argue that independent verification might be achievable because other people can have the same intuition of particular justice and thereby test the original conclusion's correctness. But if so, then the empirical thesis upon which this claim rests ought to be demonstrated quite convincingly before it is accepted—particularly in the light of the extensive historical evidence to the contrary.

The failure of the theory of particular justice to provide a means by which a decision can be tested on rational grounds, or sufficient legal data from which rational inferences about the future can successfully be made, constitutes one of the more serious limitations upon the possible value of such a theory of justification. Equally important is the previously postulated inherent unreliability of particular intuitions. If the theory of equity implies the acceptance of a procedure such as this (and of course it need not), there are, it is submitted, reasons more than sufficient to justify its rejection.

MODIFIED THEORIES OF PARTICULAR JUSTICE

That all decisions ought to be fully justified solely by an intuition of the justice of the decision is admittedly an extreme position. It is perhaps inaccurate even to attribute its advocacy to any particular legal philosopher. But there are two restricted or modified versions of the theory of particular justice which have been quite explicitly formulated and widely accepted. On the one hand, the *bifurcation theory of justice,* urged most consistently by Roscoe Pound, insists that there is a fundamental distinction between two kinds of cases, namely those which relate to matters of property and contract, and those which involve conflicts of human conduct and enterprises. The former class of cases should, Pound insists, be decided by appeal to rule; the latter class by appeal to intuition. The *Aristotelian theory of equity*, on the other hand, holds that legal rules ought to be used to decide cases of all kinds, but that within every class of cases there are some particular cases to which legal rules are *necessarily* inapplicable.

Both theories raise two questions: (1) Why should rules of the form of ordinary legal rules not be used to decide all cases coming before the courts for adjudication? and (2) How should those cases which should not be decided by appeal to legal rules be decided? Because neither Pound nor Aristotle has provided a convincing argument in support of the dichotomies proposed, the first question will be the focal point of the discussion. The theories are studied essentially for the arguments offered in support of the thesis that at least some cases ought to be decided by appeal to something other than the relevant legal rule which has been or which could be formulated. However, to the extent to which they suggest a different way in which cases of this kind ought to be decided, these procedures are also analyzed.

THE BIFURCATION THEORY OF JUSTICE

The clearest and most complete statement of the bifurcation theory is found in a lengthy article by Pound, entitled "The Theory of Judicial Decision." Here, relying heavily upon his own interpretation of Henri Bergson's metaphysics, Pound proposes that cases involving contract and property rights be decided by rules and abstract conceptions. And he proposes that cases which are concerned with human conduct ought to be dealt with intuitively.

We should not be ashamed, Pound insists, to admit that intuition should play the decisive role in the adjudication of cases involving human life.

Bergson tells us that intelligence, which frames and applies rules, is more adapted to the inorganic, while intuition is more adapted to life. In the same way rules of law and legal conceptions which are applied mechanically are more adapted to property and to business transactions; standards where application

proceeds upon intuition are more adapted to human conduct and to the conduct of enterprises. Bergson tells us that what characterizes intelligence as opposed to instinct is "its power of grasping the general element in a situation and relating it to past situations." But, he points out, this power is acquired by loss of "that perfect mastery of a special situation in which instinct rules." Standards applied intuitively by court or jury or administrative officer, are devised for situations in which we are compelled to take circumstances into account; for classes of cases in which each case is to a large degree unique. For such cases we must rely on the common sense of the common man as to common things and the trained common sense of the expert as to uncommon things. Nor may this common sense be put in the form of a syllogism. To make use once more of Bergson's discussion of intelligence and instinct, the machine works by repetition; "its use is mechanical and because it works by repetition there is no individuality in its products." The method of intelligence is admirably adapted to the law of property and to commercial law, where one fee simple is like every other and no individuality of judicial product is called for as between one promissory note and another. On the other hand, in the handwrought product the specialized skill of the workman, depending upon familiar acquaintance with particular objects, gives us something infinitely more subtle than can be expressed in rules. In the administration of justice some situations call for the product of hands not of machines. Where the call is for individuality in the product of the legal mill—for example, where we are applying law to human conduct and to the conduct of enterprises—we resort to standards and to intuitive application.[11]

The foundation offered by Pound for the bifurcation of cases is this: One fee simple or one promissory note is like every other one of the same class. Consequently, each can be treated like every other. Any case involving human conduct is essentially different from every other one. Consequently, each must be treated intuitively on its own merits and peculiar facts.[12] The dichotomy, when based upon this rationale, is untenable. In order to demonstrate wherein lies the fallacy of Pound's argument and in order to be certain that he is not being misinterpreted, an acceptable example of each of the two kinds of cases must first be given.

Examples of the first kind of case are plentiful. I assume that Pound would accept the following as an illustration of the kind of property or contract case that should be adjudicated mechan-

Misunderstanding pt. of "equity". Not to be used as a pres.- of rich + poor this judge must not account for; but equity should be used for partic facts of the case; not of status of person.

ically or conceptually. *A,* the owner of Blackacre in fee simple, has leased Blackacre to *B* for one year for a yearly rental of $5,000. At the end of the year, despite *A's* insistent pleas, *B* fails to vacate the premises and remains in possession of Blackacre after the expiration date of the lease. *A* sues *B* for $5,000, claiming that since *B* "held over" beyond the time of the original rental period, *A* can treat *B* as a tenant for another term —in this case one year—and recover the rental for that term.

I am not so confident that I can locate a clear-cut example of the second kind of case. I think, however, that Pound would agree that the following exemplifies the type of case that manifestly called for intuitive adjudication because it had circumstances which required individualized treatment.

On July 8, 1916, Harvey Hynes, a lad of sixteen, swam with two companions from the Manhattan to the Bronx side of the Harlem river or United States Ship Canal, a navigable stream. Along the Bronx side of the river was the right of way of the defendant, the New York Central railroad, which operated its trains at that point by high tension wires, strung on poles and cross-arms. Projecting from the defendant's bulkhead above the waters of the river was a plank or springboard from which the boys of the neighborhood used to dive. One end of the board had been placed under a rock on the defendant's land, and nails had been driven at its point of contact with the bulkhead. ... For more than five years swimmers had used it as a diving board without protest or obstruction.

On this day Hynes and his companions climbed on top of the bulkhead intending to leap into the water. One of them made the plunge in safety. Hynes followed to the front of the springboard, and stood poised for his dive. At that moment a crossarm with electric wires fell from the defendant's pole. The wires struck the diver, flung him from the shattered board, and plunged him to his death below. His mother, suing as administratrix, brings this action for her damages.[13]

Assuming that Pound would accept these as typical of the two kinds of cases distinguished, he might argue by way of clarification that they should be so distinguished on the following grounds. In the case between *A* and *B* there was a perfectly valid written lease between the parties, under which *B* was only entitled to the premises for one year. By refusing to vacate by the termination date of the lease, *B* became a "holdover"

tenant. A holdover in this case is no different from a holdover in any other case. Consequently, *B's* rights should be no different from any other holdover tenant's and *A* should, therefore, be able to recover the rental for the entire term.

The case of poor Harvey Hynes is essentially different. All sorts of imponderables are present in such a case, and because they are imponderables, they cannot be clearly specified. Although only approximations of the nature of *this* case, the fact that Harvey was a poor city boy who had nowhere else to swim, the fact that he and his friends had been swimming there for years, the fact that the defendant was a wealthy railroad, and the fact that it probably knew the boys had been swimming there, all go to make this particular case the kind that should not be decided by the mechanical application of the rules of trespasser-landowner liability.

When stated in this fashion, Pound's bifurcation has ostensive persuasiveness. The comparison of one lease with another lease, one can argue, does not reveal any significant differences between them; the respective positions of Harvey Hynes and the New York Central Railroad, when put in the particular context of Harvey's death, seem to make a special case. The persuasiveness of the dichotomy lies not in any substantial difference between two kinds of cases, however, but rather in the way in which the two cases are described. The superficiality of the supposed essential distinction can be demonstrated most dramatically by reporting the two cases at issue in a quite different fashion. Instead of merely announcing that there was a properly executed lease between two unnamed persons—two letters —*A* and *B,* the so-called "property" kind of case can be described in the following manner. The lessee, Herter by name, admits that he was to vacate the lessor's dwelling house on May 1, 1895. But on May 1, 1895, Herter's mother, who lived in the house with him, was afflicted with a disease which

confined her to her bed so that it would have endangered her life to take her from the house; that for that reason, and no other, of which the plaintiff [lessor] had full knowledge and notice, the defendants were obliged to and did occupy a small portion of the premises until May 15th; that all their property, furniture and belongings and their family were removed from the premises, and every part thereof, on May 1, 1895, except from the sick room in which their mother was confined, and that they were forbidden by the physician in charge to remove her until May 15th, when she was at once removed.[14]

In the same manner, the *Hynes* case can be presented in an impersonal fashion: *A,* a trespasser upon *B's* land, was killed when an electric wire, necessary to the operation of *B's* business, fell from its point of attachment and struck the trespasser. The trespasser's estate sues the landowner, *B,* for damages.

The point of these two restatements is simply this. It seems just as plausible to argue that one trespass is like any other trespass as it does to argue that one lease is like any other lease. If one looks only to the "transaction" and not to the parties to the transaction, a "mechanical" application of rule to transaction seems precisely as sensible in the one case as in the other. Conversely, if one looks to the "special circumstances" of a case, just as many special circumstances may constitute a property case as a tort case.

The conclusion is not that "special circumstances" ought never to be taken into account, nor that all cases ought to be decided "mechanically." Rather, it is simply that the differentiation of cases *on the grounds that all property cases are alike whereas all tort cases are different* cannot be intelligently sustained. There may indeed be good reasons for treating property and contract cases in one way, and cases like the *Hynes* case in a different way. Some of these reasons are discussed in the next chapters. But to assert that the realm of legal cases should be bifurcated for the reason given by Pound just does not make sense. If one should decide not to consider the special circumstances in property cases but to consider them in tort cases, then of course there will be a difference between the two kinds of cases. The fact remains, nevertheless, that special circumstances are present in any property case precisely to the same extent to which they are present in any other case that might require adjudication. A lease is no more and no less unique than a trespass. Circumstances can be taken into account just as sensibly in the one kind of case as in the other. If the two kinds of cases ought to be treated differently, it is not because there is any-

thing *inherently* different about either class. Thus, if the bifurcation is to be allowed to stand, some other substantiation must be forthcoming.

Similarly, there may be nothing objectionable in suggesting, as Pound does, that there are some cases which ought to be decided by an appeal to different kinds of rules than the rules used to justify other decisions. It is probably of considerable significance to observe that there are some kinds of cases that can best be decided by rules which themselves contain reference to some very general standard rather than to some more narrow set of conditions. This appears to be what Pound has in mind when he says:

> Frequently application of the legal precept, as found and interpreted, is intuitive. This is conspicuous when a court of equity judges of the conduct of a fiduciary, or exercises its discretion in enforcing specific performance, or passes upon a hard bargain, or where a court sitting without a jury determines a question of negligence. However repugnant to our nineteenth century notions it may be to think of anything anywhere in the judicial administration of justice as proceeding otherwise than on rule and logic, we cannot conceal from ourselves that in at least three respects the trained intuition of the judge does play an important rôle in the judicial process. One is in the selection of grounds of decision—in finding the legal materials that may be made both to furnish a legal ground of decision and to achieve justice in the concrete case. It is an everyday experience of those who study judicial decisions that the results are usually sound, whether the reasoning from which the results purport to flow is sound or not. The trained intuition of the judge continually leads him to right results for which he is puzzled to give unimpeachable legal reasons. Another place where the judge's intuition comes into play is in development of the grounds of decision, or interpretation. This is especially marked when it becomes necessary to apply the criterion of the intrinsic merit of the possible interpretations. A third is in application of the developed grounds of decision to the facts.[15]

Like so many discussions of the role of intuition, the above quotation is more than a little perplexing. Perhaps Pound is correct in suggesting that tort cases, for instance, are and ought to be decided by an appeal to a standard of reasonableness rather than by reference to particular rules which specify with greater precision what shall and shall not be reasonable conduct. (This is a matter which is discussed in greater detail in

Chapter 7.) But even if this is what Pound means, it does not follow that two different "kinds" of justification ought to be employed *because* there are two fundamentally different kinds of cases, for example, those which are essentially similar one to another and those which are inherently unique.

Furthermore, it is hard to understand what it means to say that the grounds of decision are and ought to be selected intuitively. If this means that the only justification which can be given for supporting a decision on a certain ground is that the judge intuited the ground to be appropriate for the decision, then the intuitive selection of grounds seems open to the same criticism made earlier of the intuitive selection of particular decisions. And in this connection it is even more difficult to comprehend how developed grounds are to be applied intuitively to facts. For if there is one place in which logic—in the narrow or formal sense—seems directly applicable, it is in the application of rules or grounds to the particular fact situations already described.

Again, if it is correct to say that there are cases in which a general standard, rather than a legal rule, ought to be appealed to, it does not follow that the appeal need be intuitive in nature. Even if there are cases in which the crucial question is one of whether conduct was reasonable or unreasonable, it is not obvious that this is the kind of question which cannot be answered "rationally." Pound's remarks are at least open to the interpretation that if a general standard is to be applied to conduct, the only thing which can be said about that conduct is that the activity was intuited to be reasonable or unreasonable. Yet it does seem that reasons of a nonintuitive kind can be given to support a view that conduct was or was not reasonable in the light of a particular standard. Indeed, it is difficult to understand what role the standard is to play in the process of justification if it is to be taken into account only intuitively.

And finally, if Pound is correct in asserting that judges have "reached the right results" even though they have given the wrong reasons, then he seems here to be suggesting that there are "right reasons" which could and should have been given. Now perhaps all he means by a right reason is an intuition of the correctness of the decision. But if he means something else, if he

means that there are other criteria by which the "rightness" of a decision can be evaluated, then it would seem that it is *these* criteria, rather than intuition, which ought to be explicated. The fact that courts have often given "wrong reasons" does not by itself imply that reasons ought not be given. And if it makes sense to talk about the "rightness" or "wrongness" of judicial decisions (in some nonintuitive sense), this would seem to imply that there are reasoned justifications that courts could and should have given for their decisions. It is these reasons that the courts should have given but did not give which ought to count as the proper justification for deciding a case in a certain fashion. And whatever it is that makes these reasons "good" ought to be made the criteria of justification. Thus, although there may be some purpose in retaining Pound's bifurcation, the justification for retaining it remains unstated. And although it may be useful to observe that some cases ought to be decided by appealing to a standard rather than a rule, this does not imply that intuition ought to be the criterion of either their correct selection or their application.

THE ARISTOTELIAN THEORY OF EQUITY

The acceptance of an argument like Pound's is not uncommon. Far more usual, however, is the recourse to an argument based upon the thesis that rules cannot properly be employed to decide *all* cases of any *class*. There will always be, it is insisted, *some* members of any class for which the application of the desirable legal rule is inappropriate. Legal rules simply cannot take an adequate account of all cases of any kind; some cases must be decided by a direct appeal to considerations of justice.

Such a view has been accepted quite uncritically by almost all commentators upon and philosophers of the law as well as by many courts.[16] The *locus classicus* of this position is Chapter 10, Book v, of the *Nicomachean Ethics;* in more recent sources, Aristotle's language is repeated with only a minimum of alteration. As stated by Aristotle and reiterated by subsequent philosophers, the justification for this hypothesis is, I submit, without substantial foundation. But deference to both its author and its widespread acceptance requires that the proposal be given careful consideration.

Aristotle begins by distinguishing between two kinds of justice: legal justice and some other form of justice with which equity is perhaps to be equated. This distinction is necessary because, says Aristotle, there is something about the generality of rules which makes it incorrect to identify completely justice with rules. The reason this is so

is that all law is universal but about some things it is not possible to make a universal statement which shall be correct. In those cases, then, in which it is necessary to speak universally, but not possible to do so correctly, the law takes the usual case, though it is not ignorant of the possibility of error. And it is none the less correct; for the error is not in the law nor in the legislator but in the nature of the thing, since the matter of practical affairs is of this kind from the start . . . Hence the equitable is the just, and better than one kind of justice—not better than absolute justice but better than the error that arises from the absoluteness of the statement. And this is the nature of the equitable, a correction of law where it is defective owing to its universality. In fact this is the reason why all things are not determined by law, to wit, that about some things it is impossible to lay down a law, so that a decree is needed.[17]

It should be evident that this passage reveals a reliance upon some of the theories and problems with which this analysis has already dealt. But Aristotle's statement also presents several new issues; in particular, these conditions under which a relevant rule ought not to be applied to a particular fact situation must be formulated and evaluated more precisely. There appear to be two possible interpretations of what Aristotle has in mind.

On the one hand, the passage might be construed to be merely putting forth the view that there will always be some cases that will not have been envisioned ahead of time by a legislator. This might be what Aristotle means when he says: "When the law speaks universally, then, and a case arises on it which is not covered by the universal statement, then it is right, where the legislator fails us and has erred by oversimplicity, to correct the omission—to say what the legislator himself would have said had he been present, and would have put into his law if he had known."[18] The Swiss Civil Code appears to follow Aristotle's advice here. "The Law must be applied in all cases which come within the letter or the spirit of any of its provisions. Where no provision is applicable, the judge shall decide according to existing Customary Law and, in default thereof, according to the rules which he would lay down if he had himself to act as legislator."[19] If, in other words, a case arises for which there is no relevant legal rule, then the judge clearly must look to something other than the set of positive rules for the justification for his decision.

For example, there is not at present any relevant law on the subject of drivers' licenses for interspace vehicles. The legislator—and here it is immaterial whether he be the legislator *qua* legislator or the judge *qua* legislator—would quite understandably not have enacted such a law simply because there does not, at present, appear to be any need to regulate such a class of occurrences. And there doubtless is a limitless number of classes of cases which at any given time cannot be foreseen and therefore legislated about simply because the existence of any of their members has not yet been envisioned.

On the other hand, it is also apparent that this is not the real import of Aristotle's point. On the contrary, the first passage quoted above rests on quite a different supposition. It seems to depend upon the premise, also crucial to Pound's bifurcation theory and to the theory of particular justice, that there are at least some situations that are *simply not amendable to general rules of any kind.* In at least three different places Aristotle comments on this point: "about some things it is not possible to make a universal statement which shall be correct"; "the error is not in the law nor in the legislator but in the nature of the thing"; "about some things it is impossible to lay down a law."

These passages, in turn, would once again appear to support two different interpretations. (1) Aristotle might mean that there are certain classes of acts or situations about which rules ought not to be laid down at all. The characteristics of some kinds of cases do not justifiably permit of that abstraction and classification necessary for the adjudication of particular cases by means of ordinary legal rules. Aristotle might, that is, be suggesting a theory very much like Pound's: There are fundamentally two different kinds of classes of cases.

(2) There is, however, another more plausible interpretation of these same statements. The passages appear to imply that for any given general rule which prescribes how any member of a class of cases is to be treated, there will always be some particular fact situation which is indisputably a member of that class of situations, but which nevertheless ought not to be treated in accordance with that law. This interpretation has been accepted by modern theorists as the explanation for the so-called hardship case.

In many of the hardship cases some characteristic of the individual claimant's situation which indicates weakness (but which is legally irrelevant in private law under the principle of "equality before the law") arouses sympathy for him or her: The widow who bought from the banker her deceased husband's worthless note, giving her valuable promise; the poor city youth who found his precarious recreation on the springboard projecting over the river from the wealthy railroad's right-of-way; the poor manual worker who loyally crippled himself for life in order to save his employer from injury; a veteran of a recent war, seeking a desperately needed home for his family and himself, [who] made a contract on Sunday for the purchase of a house.[20]

It is this second interpretation of Aristotle which calls for careful analysis.

The most troublesome feature of the theory centers about the claim that the fault lies not in the general laws. Aristotle does not appear to argue that the law was improperly or incorrectly formulated, that, in other words, the legislator failed to take into account certain factors which should have been considered. Nor does he rest his claim upon the premise that there are certain borderline cases in which classification is extremely difficult and in which, therefore, there is always the possibility that an unjust result will be reached because the case was not in fact properly a member of the class controlled by the rule. The problem, in short, is neither one of insufficient legislative competence nor one of incorrect judicial application. Rather, the claim appears to be that regardless of the care with which any law may be drafted, it is not possible that it can adequately take into account all relevant cases.

If the latter interpretation is correct, the theory is bewildering simply because it is so difficult to envision a substantiating example. While one can think, for example, of hundreds of cases in which an "unjust" result might be reached by applying a given rule to a case, one cannot think of a single instance in which a rule could not be formulated that would cover the instant case and all other cases of the same kind in such a way as to produce a just result in all cases. If Aristotle is saying merely that *for any given set of rules,* it will probably happen that some unjust results will occur when these rules are applied in all relevant instances, then the thesis is unobjectionable. But if something more is meant, if it is insisted that the continual revision of the rules would still not alleviate the problem, then the theory is less intelligible. For it seems always theoretically possible to formulate a rule whose classification would be sufficiently restrictive to exclude all cases in which an "unjust" result might be produced. Another way to make the same point is to observe that in theory to make an exception to a rule is simply to introduce two more restrictive rules in place of the original.

Reference to one of the "hardship cases" may help to clarify the issue. The case of Webb, the devoted employee, is typical.[21] Webb was at work on one of the upper floors of the Smith Company Lumber Mill. He was clearing the floor of scrap wood. The usual and accepted way of doing this was by dropping the wood down to the floor below. As he was just about to drop a 75-pound block of pine, Webb saw that his employer, J. Greely McGowin, was standing directly on the spot that would be hit by the block if it were to fall straight down. The only way by which Webb could prevent McGowin from being seriously injured was for him, Webb, to divert the block from its course of fall; and the only way he could reasonably do this was by falling to the ground with the block. This is precisely what he did. He saved McGowin from harm but only at the cost of inflicting serious injury upon himself. He was, in fact, badly crippled for the remainder of his life.

McGowin, understandably grateful, soon entered into an agreement with Webb whereby he promised to pay Webb $15 every two weeks for the remainder of Webb's life in gratitude for Webb's courageous act. McGowin did this up until the time of his death. His estate continued the payments for another three years and then stopped them even though Webb was still alive. The problem confronting the court when Webb brought suit to compel the estate to continue payment was this: There was a rule of long standing which held that a promise is binding upon the promisor if and only if it is given in exchange for services which have yet to be performed or for a promise to perform some act in the future. In other words, the fact that Webb acted with no prior request from McGowin, coupled with McGowin's subsequent promise to pay Webb for his past injuries, amounted to a mere "past" or "moral" consideration, the kind of consideration which could not support a legal action to enforce performance of that promise.

Let it be assumed that Webb ought to be able to enforce McGowin's agreement and that an unjust result would be reached if he were not allowed to do so. Let it also be agreed that to apply the extant rule to this case would produce an unjust result. To grant these two premises is still not to grant Aristotle's point. Why, if it is unjust not to give legal effect to this agreement, is this not a *kind* of case for which a rule could be formulated that would be capable of producing a just result if applied to all cases of this class? For example, a rule such as the following might be introduced: "Whenever an employee engaged in a proper course of conduct finds that the only way he can reasonably prevent serious injury to his employer is by injuring himself, and whenever a promise is made thereafter by the person saved from injury to pay that person for his injury, this promise is enforcible." It is difficult to find anything which *in theory* requires the inference that if this rule were to be applied to all members of the specified class, some unjust results would necessarily be produced. As will become evident in a moment, there may be weaknesses inherent in rules of this specificity; but the difficulties are practical rather than theoretical. The issue here is simply that there is nothing which *in principle* prevents a situation such as the one Webb found himself in from being treated as one of a definite class of situations. And if it can be treated as a member of one or more classes, then, again, there is nothing in principle that precludes the formulation of a rule which could produce just results when applied to every member of that class.

The plausibility of a view such as Aristotle's derives in part perhaps from a confusion between two different concepts—from the failure to distinguish what I shall call a law's *universality* from its *generality*. To say that a law is or should be *universal* is simply to assert that the law applies without exception to all the members of the class included within the scope of the law. To speak of the universality of law is to refer to that feature which renders the law applicable to every member of the specified class. A strong case can be made for the analytic truth of the proposition that all laws are universal in this sense.

The generality of a law is something quite different. To speak of a law's generality is to observe the degree to which the class which is governed by the law is discriminated from all other possible classes. The generality of a law is concerned, therefore, with the particular class which is named and controlled by the law; universality, on the other hand, is concerned with the way in which the law is to be applied to the members of the class. Universality is a formal characteristic; generality is a material one.

An adherence to this distinction permits more meaningful discussion of the Aristotelian thesis and its implications. For it becomes obvious that the most important problems it raises center about the generality rather than the universality of rules. That all laws should be universal seems evident; that all laws should be of *any particular* generality is far less certain. Two competing considerations are relevant to the question of what constitutes the desirable generality of ordinary rules of law.

First, if all rules of law were absolutely general, that is, if they dictated the same result for every member of the class consisting of all persons, the number of substantively unjust results would undoubtedly be very great. For as was observed above, it is only as the generality of the rule is "contracted" that the chance of just results in every case increases. As more conditions are placed upon membership in the class controlled by the rule, it becomes increasingly unlikely that an "exceptional" case will arise.

Second, and serving to support the contrary hypothesis that legal rules should "expand" their generality, is the consideration that as rules become too specific their utility *qua* rules diminishes. That is, although the proposed rule for the Webb type of situation may be sufficiently "narrow" so that injustices will not result, it is also so specific that it enables prediction of very few cases. The issue here is wholly analogous to one raised earlier. Rules are useful because they enable one to predict a legal result in advance. But if the rule applies only to a very limited class, if its generality is minimal, then knowledge of the rule does not permit the accurate prediction of many cases. Concomitantly, a minimal generality requires—if prediction is to be possible—a proliferation of rules. Because each rule controls only a small class, many rules are needed to take account of all cases. A mastery of the content of a great number of rules becomes a precondition of successful prediction.

Thus in a different context, Aristotle's position is not without significance. Theoretically, the thesis is untenable. Given an indefinitely large number of rules there is no reason why all cases could not be decided justly by means of an appeal to rules. But as a practical matter, rules cannot become too specific and still fulfill their most important function as rules. The number of rules cannot be multiplied indefinitely without creating a comparable impairment of function. Thus if the rules of a legal system are to be general enough to function properly as rules, there is good reason to suppose that they might not be able to take an adequate account of all cases controlled by the rules . . .

Before we leave the question of minimal generality one point deserves some mention. It has been argued by Patterson, among others, that the principle of "equality before the law" is at issue here; but it is difficult to see how the introduction of this principle clarifies or solves anything. For this principle, although doubtless commendable in the abstract, proves to have amazingly little content in concrete situations. What does it mean to say that people ought to be treated equally before the law? Does it mean that the only rules of law which are justifiable are those which apply indiscriminately to all persons? If so, then such a law is sufficiently rare as to be a curiosity. For almost every law, either explicitly or implicitly, makes exceptions for children, incompetents, sleepwalkers, and the like. In addition, almost all laws further circumscribe the class of persons who are to be treated in "equal" fashion by specifying the conditions that must be present before the law is to be applied. And here, too, very often these conditions include certain characteristics of possible litigants. For instance, there is generally one property law for good-faith purchasers and another for purchasers with notice; there may be one set of constitutional protections for aliens and another for citizens.

If, on the other hand, the principle of equality before the law imposes a weaker requirement upon justifiable laws—the requirement alluded to earlier that there be some reason for making the distinction made by the law—then appeal to the principle is simply not very helpful in any a priori fashion. Perhaps, for example, there is no good reason for making a rule which expressly recognizes that class of employees who have aided their employer, been injured, and subsequently received a promise of compensation from their grateful employer. Perhaps on balance such a "specialized" classification would be undesirable. But saying this is something quite different from asserting simply that the principle of "equality before the law" is necessarily violated whenever such a classification is made. Unless one is prepared to assert that all classifications, except those which include all human beings without exception, are inherently undesirable, an appeal to the principle of "equality before the law" is not by itself a forceful or convincing criticism of some "less inclusive" law. What must be shown is not the presence of a more selective classification, but rather the undesirability of making this kind of classification in this kind of case.

This does not mean that laws which make distinctions between persons on the basis of race, religion, place of origin, and the like cannot in most circumstances be condemned. This does not mean that laws which treat "equals unequally" are less abhorrent now than before. But it does mean that there may always be good reasons for making certain kinds of distinctions among persons. And it does mean that it is more appropriate to criticize the reasons offered than just to appeal to the principle of "equality before the law." The fact that a law discriminates among persons does not make the law bad; the fact that the law discriminates badly does. A "bad" law should be shown to be "bad" on this latter ground.

NONINTUITIVE EQUITY

In the course of the discussion so far, an equitable procedure has been defined as one that holds an intuition of the justness of a decision to be the necessary and sufficient justification for deciding a case in a certain fashion. It should be apparent, however, that those who have opposed equity to precedent have not limited their proposals solely to a demand for intuitive adjudication. Instead, much of what has been written about the desirability of equity has been written in praise of a procedure of justification in which precedents are not followed *and* in which intuition plays no role. Thus, even if intuition should be rejected as a criterion of justification—either for all cases or only for some—it does not follow that some other form of equitable justification must thereby be dismissed as unsatisfactory. In the remainder of this chapter the character of a nonintuitive equitable procedure will be presented very briefly; in the succeeding chapters it will be evaluated in considerably greater detail.

As has already been observed, the concept of an equitable procedure of justification rests very largely upon the notion that the peculiar or unique facts of each case ought to be taken into express account and given primary significance in order to do justice in the particular case. And there is at least one distinctly nonintuitive equitable procedure that would do just that. This nonintuitive equitable procedure stipulates that the court should concentrate upon the facts of a particular case, and should, after a "rational" consideration of all the facts, decide the case in such a way that justice is done for the litigants. Here, the rule of decision would prescribe that a decision is justifiable if and only if it best takes into account the interests of the litigants who are currently before the court. A decision is not justifiable because it is intuited to be such, or because it accords with some precedent. Rather, it is justifiable because the consequences of that decision are found to be more desirable for the litigants than those of any other possible decision. The interests of the litigants are primary; the consequences to them of deciding the case in one way rather than another are alone relevant to the question of what shall be regarded as a justifiable decision. If the courts consistently focus their attention upon the ways in which the litigants themselves will be affected by various possible decisions, and if the courts justify their decisions accordingly, then, it might be argued, they will render more justifiable decisions than they would were they to employ any other procedure of justification. Thus, this kind of nonintuitive equity would be embodied in a procedure in which

courts justified their decisions solely on the basis of what decision would be best for the litigants.

A decision process such as this has considerable initial appeal. It does not seem to be open to the same criticisms which were made earlier of intuition as a criterion of justification. For under this form of an equitable procedure a judge could give perfectly good, independently verifiable reasons for deciding a case in a certain fashion. He could point to the way in which the decision would produce a minimum of discomfort and a maximum of satisfaction vis-à-vis the two litigants. He could receive evidence and analyze arguments that tended to show that one rather than another decision would be more justifiable on these grounds. Furthermore, such an equitable procedure would be free from many of the defects latent in a precedential procedure. Courts would not be bound by the errors of earlier procedure. They would be unhampered by tradition. They could meet each case as it came along and feel free to decide it and nothing more. This is, therefore, a procedure which surely requires careful study. And it may very well be the procedure which so many proponents of equitable adjudication have been implicitly suggesting all the time. Throughout the remainder of this work, I shall restrict the denotation of "equitable procedure" to a procedure which prescribes that cases ought to be decided in such a way as to bring about the best result as between the parties at present before the court. I shall assume that this is or can be a distinctly nonintuitive procedure.

At this juncture someone might object that, although the possibility of nonintuitive equitable procedures has been recognized, the discussion is still incomplete. For there is, the objection might continue, an additional and perhaps related theme which runs through almost all discussions of equity. It concerns the desirability of adjudicating either some or all cases by an appeal to moral rules or principles. Under this view, an equitable decision procedure is one which courts are instructed to take moral rules or standards expressly into account and to employ these rules, rather than legal rules, as the criteria by which to justify particular decisions. Such a procedure could also be nonintuitive since moral rules can, arguably, be applied in the same fashion in which any other rules are applied. And the procedure could be nonprecedential, since an appeal to moral rules, rather than to already existing legal rules, constitutes the justification for deciding a case in a certain fashion.

This suggestion that cases ought to be decided in accordance with moral rather than legal rules is surely to be found in many of the writings to which reference has already been made. As usually formulated, however, its precise meaning is unclear. More specifically, there are at least two questions which must be resolved before it can even be considered as a possible, independent program of legal justification.

First, the *role* that moral rules or standards are to play in the process of justification must be delineated more precisely. Are the moral principles to function in the same manner in which legal rules function in a precedential decision procedure? If so, they would serve directly as the justification for a particular decision. Or are they to function instead as the criterion by which to evaluate particular legal rules? If so, they would not be the ostensible justification for particular decisions, but rather would be the justification for using a particular legal rule as the justification for a particular decision.

And second, the differences, if any, between moral and legal rules or principles must be examined more closely. Are there any formal differences between the two that would make it possible to say of any rule that if it is clearly a moral rule then it cannot be a legal rule, or if it is clearly a legal rule then it cannot be a moral rule? If a rule is a moral rule, does it follow that it cannot function in a procedure of justification in the same fashion in which a legal rule would function? If there is no inherent difference between the two kinds of rule, then is the suggestion that cases ought to be decided by an appeal to moral rules any different from the proposal that cases ought to be justified by reference to "new" or "alterable" legal rules? Is the suggestion that courts ought to be "equitable" any different from the proposal that courts ought to be free to change existing legal rules? Until these questions are answered, the possible significance of this second kind of nonintuitive equitable procedure cannot be fully understood. And once these questions are answered, as the questions themselves suggest, it may turn out that this is not even a distinctly equitable procedure at all.

Because almost all discussions of equity do invoke reference to adjudication in accordance with moral rules, and because this in turn can mean any one of several things, the following chapter constitutes something of a digression—although a necessary one—from the course of the argument so far. For in recent years, moral philosophers have been concerned with certain issues that have considerable relevance to a resolution of some of the problems just raised. In particular, they have sought to concern themselves with the role that the principle of utility ought to play in the justification of individual moral acts or decisions. The controversy that has been engendered over this point and the solutions that have been proposed are particularly useful in that they furnish instructive analogies to the possible roles which moral rules or principles—such as, for example, the principle of utility—might play in a procedure of legal justification.

NOTES

1. Kipling, "The Ameer's Homily," quoted in Pound, "Justice According to Law," p. 697 n.
2. *In re* Egan, 5 Blatchford 319, 321 (1866), quoted in *ibid.*, p. 697.
3. Cf., for instance, Pound's thesis that there are two fundamental elements present in all mature legal systems, namely, the "legal" and the "discretionary." "Before the law we have justice without law; and after the law and during the evolution of law we still have it under the name of discretion, or natural justice, or equity and good conscience, as an antilegal element." Pound, "The Decadence of Equity," p. 20.
4. *Cobb v. Whitney*, 124 Okla. 188, 192 (1926); *Kenyon v. Weissberg*, 240 F. 536, 537 (1917).
5. Pomeroy, *A Treatise on Equity Jurisprudence*, pp. 46–47; Phelps, *Elements of Juridical Equity*, § 143; Frank, *Law and the Modern Mind*, p. 157; Stone, *The Province and Function of Law*, pp. 228–29.
6. Oliphant, "A Return to Stare Decisis," p. 159. Italics mine.
7. Hutcheson, "The Judgment Intuitive," p. 285. As is characteristic of one who adheres to an intuitive scheme of justification, Hutcheson resorts at times to rather mystical statements of approval. He announces, for example, that: "It is such judicial intuitions, and the opinions lighted and warmed by the feeling which produced them, that not only give justice in the cause, but like a great white way, make plain in the wilderness the way of the Lord for judicial feet to follow" (pp. 287–88).
8. Frank, p. 121. See also Gmelin, "Sociological Method," in *Science of Legal Method*, p. 100, where he seems to be proposing a similar view: "We need a vivid understanding of the facts, a sympathetic treatment of the human destinies that are passing before our eyes. We must strive to penetrate into the needs of the parties who come before the judge as patients come before the physician, so that we may not offer them the stone of bald reasoning but the bread of sympathetic relief."
9. Pound, "Mechanical Jurisprudence," p. 605.

10. Dewey, "Logical Method and Law," p. 24.

11. Pound, "The Theory of Judicial Decision," pp. 951–52.

12. Although giving a somewhat different justification for treating all contract and property cases in a manner different from tort and other analogous kinds of cases, Dickinson seems to adopt Pound's rationale at least in part. For he agrees with Pound that there is a field in which "every case involves a multitude of pertinent elements which vary in importance from case to case, [and therefore] it is practically impossible fairly to select any special factor or factors and apply them as criteria over the whole field. This is true of all ordinary matters of conduct not definitely directed, like business transactions, to the production of a legal result." Dickinson, *Administrative Justice and the Supremacy of Law,* pp. 145–46.

13. *Hynes v. New York Central RR. Co.,* 231 N.Y. 229, 231 (1921).

14. *Herter v. Mullen,* 159 N.Y. 28, 41–42 (1899).

15. Pound, "The Theory of Judicial Decision," p. 951.

16. Cf., for instance, Frank, pp. 118–19, and Patterson, *Jurisprudence,* p. 582. Cf. also Salmond, *Jurisprudence,* p. 83: "For the law lays down general principles, taking of necessity no account of the special circumstances of individual cases in which such generality may work injustice. ... In all such cases, in order to avoid injustice, it may be considered needful to go beyond the law, or even contrary to the law, and to administer justice in accordance with the dictates of natural reason."

For a judicial expression of the same view see *Berkel v. Berwind-White Coal Mining Co.,* 220 Pa. 65 (1908): "The whole system of equity jurisprudence is founded on the theory that the law, by reason of its universality, is unable to do justice between the parties, and equity, not being bound by common-law forms and pleadings, has more elasticity and can better reach this end" (p. 75).

Ehrlich seems to make a still stronger assertion along the same lines: "It is certain that one need not expect better or juster results from such technical decisions than from free ones. Generally speaking, it is undoubtedly much easier to decide a definite case correctly than to establish an abstract rule universally applicable for all imaginable cases; and surely it can hardly be maintained seriously that such a rule will invariably result in the fairest decision, even in those cases which nobody had thought of when the rule was made." (Ehrlich, "Judicial Freedom of Decision," in *Science of Legal Method,* p. 63.)

The dichotomy, as set up by Ehrlich, appears convincing. The difficult problem, however, concerns the ways, if any, in which knowing that a definite case has been decided correctly differs from formulating and applying a rule for that kind of case. If a case cannot be decided correctly without laying down a rule, then the argument advanced by Ehrlich seems less attractive. See Chaps. 6 and 7, in which this point is explored in detail.

17. Aristotle, *Nicomachean Ethics,* 1137b, 12–29.

18. *Ibid.,* 20.

19. Swiss Civil Code, Article I. See also Cardozo, *The Nature of the Judicial Process,* pp. 142–43.

20. Patterson, p. 582.

21. *Webb v. McGowin,* 27 Ala. App. 82 (1935).

WILLIAM K. FRANKENA

Some Beliefs About Justice*

"Masters, give unto your servants that which is just and equal."

St. Paul, *Colossians,* 4:1.

The topic of this lecture is social justice, more specifically, distributive justice. One of the good things about this topic is that one does not have to be kind to it; one has only to be just. Having twice in the past sought to do it justice without success,[1] I now propose to try once more. If I fail to do it justice this time—and I am sure I shall —at least it will not be for lack of trying.

Now, as Aristotle points out, one can conceive of justice as covering the whole area of morality, of moral virtue, or at least of moral rightness; Plato, Kant, and, more recently, C. I. Lewis come close to conceiving it thus. But this seems to be distributing justice a little thin. As J. S. Mill says, we must distinguish between justice and "other obligations of morality" like "charity or beneficence."[2] Even if, like Lewis, we refuse to regard charity or beneficence as obligations of morality, we still cannot identify distributive justice with the whole requirement of the moral. For, as Aristotle also says, the justice we are investigating is only a part of virtue, as is shown by the fact that, if a man throws down his shield in battle, uses abusive language, refuses to assist a friend with money, or commits adultery, we accuse him, not of injustice (certainly not of distributive injustice), but of cowardice, bad temper, meanness, or profligacy.

"Well," it may be said at this point, "this is true of justice as ascribed to *individuals;* there are other things that morality requires of individuals besides justice. However, all that can be required of a *society* or *state* is that it be just—that it

*The Lindley Lecture, 1966. Reprinted with permission of the author and the Department of Philosophy of the University of Kansas.

distribute justly what it is within its power to distribute. That is, in the case of society or the state virtue equals justice, distributive justice." This view has a good deal of plausibility, but it raises the problems of the relation of justice to welfare and of welfare to the state, and we cannot discuss these here. Our concern now is with the question when a society or state is distributively just, not with the question whether this is all it should be.

I.

There is one principle of distributive justice on which there seems to be general agreement, namely, that like cases or individuals are to be dealt with in the same way or treated alike, or that similar cases are to be treated similarly. Chaim Perelman calls this the *formal* principle of justice.[3] Now, it does seem clear that an act of distributing is at least *prima facie* unjust if it involves treating differently, or discriminating between, individuals whose cases are similar in all important respects. If my case is substantially like yours but it is treated differently, one of us has grounds for crying that injustice has been done, as any child seems to see instinctively. In this sense, the formal principle of justice does formulate a *necessary* condition of the existence of distributive justice. For justice to exist there must be regularities or rules that are followed in the distribution of what is distributed. Yet a land may be without justice even if similar cases are always treated similarly, even if it always distributes according to rules which are known. A society may have and act without fail on rules, laws, and conventions, and yet be an epitome of injustice. It depends on what the rules and conventions are. In other words, rules, laws, and conventions may themselves be unjust or incorporate injustice. They all take the form, "Treat every case of kind

X in manner Y," as is required by the formal principle, but the manner specified may in fact be an unjust way of treating things of the kind in question.

Any set of rules that may prevail in a given society is a selection from among all possible rules. They classify people in terms of certain similarities and neglect others; they also neglect certain dissimilarities. They likewise select, from among the possible ways of treating people, certain ones, and they assign these ways of treatment to the different classes they define. But human beings are alike and unlike in all sorts of respects. Not all of their similarities and differences are important or even relevant to the question how they are to be treated, and not just any manner of treatment may be assigned to just any class of cases. Consistency is a requirement of justice, not merely "a hobgoblin of little minds"; but it is not enough, it is not the whole of justice.

In other words, the formal principle of justice does not give us a *sufficient* condition for the existence of justice. As Perelman insists,[4] we must also have some *material* principles of distribution, principles that tell us something more about the content of our rules, more about the similarities and differences that are to be regarded as relevant, more about what Jesus called the measures with which we are to mete and be measured to. This is what we must look for. I shall, however, not seek to give a complete and systematic account of the material principles of justice. I shall limit my discussion almost entirely to a review of some views about the nature of the most *basic* material principle of justice, and to a defense of one of them.

It is sometimes said that, while the formal principle of justice is certain but empty, any material principle must be arbitrary and uncertain. We must choose one, if we are to have any system of justice at all, but our choice cannot have any rational basis, since equally valid reasons can be given for choosing another.[5] I shall not try to take this metaethical position by frontal attack, but, instead, will seek to bypass it by offering, not indeed a "proof" of any material principle of distributive justice, but what Mill calls "considerations determining the intellect to give its assent" to one view of justice and to withhold it from others.[6] That is, I shall simply try to give a rational case for one principle and against others. Af-

ter all, as someone once said, the best way to answer a man who says there are no giraffes is to show him one. The only trouble about that is that one may be caught by a skeptical lion while looking for a giraffe, like the drunk who saw double and tried to climb the wrong tree.

II.

Aristotle's discussion of distributive justice in the *Ethics* and *Politics* will serve as a useful basis for our inquiry.[7] Following his lead we may say that the typical case of distributive justice involves (1) at least two persons, A and B, (2) something to be distributed, P, (3) some basis of distribution, Q, and (4) a geometrical proportion or ratio such that

$$\frac{\text{A's share of P}}{\text{B's share of P}} = \frac{\text{A's share of Q}}{\text{B's share of Q}}$$

Then a society is distributively just or has distributive justice in so far as it distributes P among its members in proportion to their shares of Q. Not all theories of distributive justice accept this model quite literally, as we shall see, but we can nevertheless use it in order to state the problems involved and the main ways in which they may be answered. Clearly, there are two questions:

(a) What is P? That is, what is to be distributed?
(b) What is Q? What is to be taken as the basis of distribution?

Different theories about the material principles of distributive justice give different answers to these two questions, especially to the second.

Actually, P, or what is to be distributed, may be almost anything, and will vary from context to context; but on all theories of social justice it will consist primarily of such things as offices, privileges, tasks, tax burdens, powers, goods, educational opportunities, vocational opportunities, and the conditions of happiness or of the good life. As for Q, or the basis of distribution, one might, of course, have different theories about the nature of Q depending on what P is; for example, if it is musical instruments that are to be distributed one might take musical aptitude or taste as a basis of distribution, but if it is college credits and grades one might, and presumably should, take performance in college courses as a basis.

Even so, we want to know—and this is our main problem—what the most *basic* Q is, if there is one, on the basis of which such P's as have been mentioned are to be distributed.

In his discussion of this question Aristotle indicates that there have been three main theories of social justice: the oligarchical, the aristocratic, and the democratic theories. They agree about what P is: offices, powers, honors, external goods, etcetera; what they differ about is Q, the basis of distribution. The oligarchical theory says that Q is wealth or property, that is, that P is to be distributed to people in proportion to their wealth; the aristocratic theory holds that Q is merit, that is, that P is to be distributed in accordance with merit; and the democratic theory, as Aristotle conceives of it, claims that Q is simply the fact of free birth and that P is to be distributed equally among those who are born free, but, of course, he was making allowance for slavery, and a contemporary democrat would prefer to say that Q is simply the fact of being human.

Revising Aristotle's scheme somewhat, we may classify theories of distributive justice as follows: (1) Inequalitarian theories hold that P is to be distributed in proportion to some Q which people have in different amounts, degrees, or forms, that is, in proportion to some feature in which people are unequal. They are of three sorts: (a) the oligarchical theory, (b) the meritarian or aristocratic theory, (c) other inequalitarian theories, for example, those that identify Q with blood, sex, color, height, or native intelligence. (2) Equalitarian or democratic theories hold that basically P is to be distributed equally. They are of two kinds:[8] (a) Substantive equalitarianism holds that P is to be distributed in proportion to Q; and it identifies Q with some feature in which all men are alike or equal. It is hard to give a good example of such a theory because it is hard to find any feature in which all men are alike and equal. That is one reason why this kind of equalitarianism finds it so difficult to answer the argument that men are not equal since there is no Q, no property, which they all have in the same amount and form. For example, they all have reason, but they have it in different degrees. They all have color, presumably in the same degree, but they have it in different forms. One might reply that all men are alike or equal in being men or in being human, but it is very difficult to make out just what property "being human" is, or whether it is

a property at all, let alone one which everyone has in the same degree and form. (b) Procedural equalitarianism agrees with inequalitarianism in denying that there is any Q which all men have in the same degree and form. But it still maintains a basically equalitarian view of distributive justice. To do this it gives up the Aristotelian model which holds that P is to be distributed in accordance with some Q. There is, it maintains, no Q of the kind required. It therefore regards equalitarianism as a "procedural" principle: Treat people equally unless and until there is a justification for treating them unequally. This is a procedural principle because it says, not that men are equal in a certain respect and therefore should be treated equally, but only that unequal treatment must be justified or defended, whereas equality of treatment needs no justification.

Before going on, I should like to say something here about the question, "Are Men Equal?" All equalitarians answer "Yes" to this in some sense, and all inequalitarians "No." But we must notice that the question has two senses, a factual sense and a normative one. In the factual sense it asks, "Is there any respect in which all men are in fact equal, any Q which they all have in the same degree and form?" In the normative sense it asks something very different, namely, "*Ought* all men to be treated as equals?" Thus there are really two distinct questions, though this is not always noticed. The real issue between equalitarians and inequalitarians is over the normative question whether all men ought to be treated equally; it is to this question that the former must say "Yes" and the latter "No." But the inequalitarians always say "No" to the factual question too, and, in fact, they rest their negative answer to the normative question at least in part on a negative answer to the factual one; they argue that men should be treated differently because they are different. Equalitarians, on the other hand, though they all say "Yes" to the normative questions, may say either "Yes" or "No" to the factual one. Substantive equalitarians say "Yes," and procedural equalitarians say "No." These points are very important to keep in mind in any discussion of distributive justice.

III.

Let us now proceed to a discussion of inequalitarian theories of the basic material principle of distributive justice. The oligarchical theory is perhaps not often espoused in so many words, but it does appear to be acted on to a considerable extent in practice, and, in any case, it is a very instructive theory to study. It maintains, it will be remembered, that the Q in proportion to which P is to be distributed is wealth, material possessions. It takes quite literally at least the first part of the saying of Jesus,

> For whosoever hath, to him shall be given, and he shall have more abundance; but whosoever hath not, from him shall be taken away, even that he hath.[9]

But, with all due respect for Jesus' real meaning, it seems reasonable to say that the oligarchical way of favoring the haves over the have nots is a very paradigm of injustice. Such a theory of distributive justice seems to be mistaken in principle, and it is important to see why. It is mistaken, it seems to me, for this reason: because the Q which it takes as a basis for distribution is itself something that is distributed by human actions and social institutions, and hence something that may itself be or have been distributed justly or unjustly, namely wealth or property. If this point is well taken, then we may argue quite generally that no theory is acceptable which offers as its *basic* principle of distribution the principle that P is to be distributed in proportion to some Q whose distribution is itself dependent on human action and social policy, for example, wealth, power, or social position. It also follows that even the democratic theory, as Aristotle understood it, is mistaken; for its Q was "free birth," and this, in the sense in which the Greeks took it, was something socially determined, not something one had either by nature or by one's own efforts.

It should be added that, in any case, already possessed wealth is plausible as a basis for distributing other things only if it is a reliable index of the presence of some other Q which is more reasonably taken as a basis of distribution, for example, ability, intelligence, or merit. This is shown by the fact that the defenders of oligarchy have usually argued that the possession of wealth actually is an index of something more fundamental, when they have bothered to give any argument at all.

Putting off the meritarian or aristocratic theory for a moment, let us look at inequalitarian views of our third sort, those taking as a basis for distri-bution such Q's as blood, sex, color, height, or native intelligence. These views are right in not choosing as the fundamental basis of distribution anything that is directly distributable by man or society. Instead they take as the basis of distribution some Q whose presence is due to nature (though, indirectly, through eugenics, man can do something even about the distribution of color, etcetera). It seems apparent, however, that this too is a mistake. For it is reasonable to claim that the use of blood, color, height, etcetera, as a fundamental basis of distribution is also unjust in itself. It is fair enough to use them as a basis of distribution in certain contexts, for example, as for basis for distributing costumes or parts in plays. But to take any of them as the most basic Q for the distribution of opportunities, offices, etcetera, is as unjust as taking wealth as one's basic Q, though for a different reason. The reason (the main reason, not the only one) in this case, I think, is that, if we take color, height, etcetera, as a basis for distributing P, then we are basing our distribution on a feature which discriminates [among] between individuals but which the individual has done and can do nothing about; we are treating people differently in ways that profoundly effect their lives because of differences for which they have no responsibility.

The most plausible of the natural Q's just mentioned to take as a basis of distribution is native intelligence. Even native intelligence (to be distinguished here from developed intelligence) will not do, however, as our ultimate basis of distribution, though it is certainly in a better case than height or color of skin. For it is something that can be adequately detected and gauged only in the course of some kind of program of education, formal or informal, so that its use as a basis of distribution presupposes a prior equal distribution of the opportunities for such an education.

In any case, we may also say that blood, sex, color, height, etcetera, cannot reasonably be taken as important bases of distribution unless they serve as reliable signs of some Q, like ability or merit, which is more justly employed as a touchstone for the treatment of individuals. This gain is shown by the fact that when proponents of racial discrimination and slavery have given arguments at all, they have often argued precisely that these features may be taken as signs of such more acceptable Q's.

We have mentioned merit as clearly a more acceptable Q than acquired features like wealth on the one hand or natural ones like color on the other. Shall we then use merit as our most fundamental basis of distribution? That we should is the position of the aristocrats or meritarians, including Aristotle himself and, more recently, Sir David Ross. What do they mean by "merit?" Aristotle meant excellence or virtue, and he distinguished two kinds of excellences or virtues: intellectual ones and moral ones; Sir David, however, means by "merit" simply moral virtue.[10] We may therefore understand the meritarians to hold that, basically at any rate, P is to be distributed to people in proportion to their degree of excellence, intellectual, moral, or both. What shall we say of this conception of social justice?

It certainly has a good deal of plausibility. In particular, its Q does not suffer from the defects of those of the other two kinds of inequalitarianism. For merit or excellence is not something distributed (differentially) by nature without any help from the individual, as color, blood, and height are; nor is it something that can be distributed justly or unjustly by man or his social institutions, as wealth is. Only the potentialities for excellence can be provided by nature, and only the opportunities and accessories for it can be provided by society; excellence or merit itself must be achieved or won by individuals themselves. It looks, therefore, as if merit may be just the Q we are looking for. Nevertheless, I am convinced that it will not do either. I tried to show this once or twice before but now suspect that the argument I then used is fallacious.[11] There is, however, another argument which I hope is better. This argument is that merit cannot be the *basic* Q in matters of distributive justice, since a recognition of merit as the basis of distribution is justified only if every individual has an equal chance of achieving all the merit he is capable of (and it cannot simply be assumed that they have had this chance). If the individuals competing for P have not had an equal chance to achieve all the merit they are capable of, then merit is not a fair basis for distributing shares of P among them. If this is so, then, before merit can reasonably be adopted as a ground of distribution, there must first be a prior *equal* distribution of the conditions for achieving merit, at least so far as this is within the power of human society. This is where

such things as equality of opportunity, equality before the law, and equality of access to the means of education come into the picture. In other words, recognition of merit as a criterion of distribution is reasonable only against the background of a recognition of the principle of equality, the primary basis of distribution is not merit but equality, substantive or procedural.

It is worth mentioning, in view of the many recent discussions of "the distribution of education," first, that, strictly speaking, society cannot distribute education but only the means of and opportunities for education, and, second, that it cannot distribute these in accordance with excellence or merit, since the achievement of excellence or merit presupposes a process of education. To this it may be replied that educational means and opportunities are to be distributed, not equally, but according to capacity. But then we may rejoin by pointing out that people's capacities can be determined only by educating them in some way, and that basic educational means and opportunities must therefore be distributed equally, since all must be given an equal chance to show their capacities if their capacities are to be used as a basis for determining their shares of other things. It follows, of course, from such premises, that a program of merit scholarships is fully just only if all of the candidates have had equal educational opportunities of the relevant kinds, though it may be a good thing anyway, as I believe it is.

None of what I have said is meant to imply that merit is not an acceptable basis of distribution in some contexts. I believe, indeed, that it is just to recognize and reward merit or excellence in certain ways; I have been trying to show only that merit cannot reasonably be regarded as our most *basic* criterion of distribution, as meritarians think.

Excellence is an excellent thing, but, if it is not taken to be its own sole reward, we must all equally be given the chance to attain it so far as we are able.

In this discussion I have been identifying merit with excellence, intellectual or moral; but there are, of course, other things that it may be taken to mean, for example, contribution to society or to the welfare of mankind, and it may be proposed that we should employ one of these things as our basis of distribution. What I have just said applies, however, to these further forms of merit also; they may be acceptable as secondary grounds of distributive policy, but they will not do as primary ones. It should be added that at least one of the reasons for rewarding merit in these and other forms is that doing so is useful, that is, conducive to the public good. But to argue that merit should be rewarded because it is *useful* to do so is not yet to show that *justice* requires us to reward it. What is useful may be right to do, but it is not *ipso facto* a requirement of justice, though it need not be unjust either. This *may* be one of the meanings of the puzzling parable of the workers in the vineyard.

It may be objected that we have been neglecting an important theory of social justice, one which may have more subscribers, if we count both sides of the Iron Curtain, than any other, namely, that the just society is that which takes from each according to his ability and gives to each according to his needs. This theory sounds like a form of inequalitarianism, since it is obvious that people's abilities and needs differ widely. It may, however, be contended that it presupposes a basic equalitarianism, and this contention seems to be supported by the fact that those who accept the theory mean to be equalitarians at least in principle. One of the good things about this ability-need theory, whether one accepts it or not, is its recognition that duties and tasks are to be distributed, as well as opportunities, rights, and goods. But what is involved in the notion that tasks are to be distributed according to ability? Not a belief in inequality, but precisely the reverse. For we do not treat people equally if we ask of them exactly the same performance. To some a given task is easy, to others it is difficult, and hence, to ask the same of everyone is actually to treat them unequally, asking sacrifices from some that others are not required to make. To ask from each according to his ability, then, is to ask the same *proportionate* effort and sacrifice from each, in an effort to leave all as nearly equally well off as possible. In the same way, since needs differ, to give equally to all does not entail giving exactly the same thing to each. Shakespeare is surely unjust when he tells us in *The Merchant of Venice* not to trust

The man that hath no music in himself,
Nor is not moved with concord of sweet sounds,

but it would not be unjust to give such a man a pair of skis when everyone else is being given a violin or a set of the latest Beatles recordings. To give to each according to his need is, again, to make the same *proportionate* contribution to the welfare of each, in an effort to make all as nearly equally well off as possible. The ability-need theory is therefore reasonable only if it presupposes an equalitarian goal or ideal.

IV.

If what has been said is correct, then we may reasonably regard inequalitarian views about the basic material principle of distributive justice as unsatisfactory, even if we cannot claim to have "disproved" them. The basic principle is that of equality, as Aristotle's democrats thought. Merit and other Q's which men have unequally may serve acceptably as secondary criteria of distribution, but the basic framework must be the principle of equality. This we may now state. It is the principle that matters are to be so disposed, that is, P is to be so distributed, that everyone has an equal chance of achieving the best life he is capable of. This is the foundational principle of social justice. Of course, to apply this principle we must have some defensible conception of what the good life is, and which lives are better than others, and these are not easy matters; but they must be left for another occasion.

For what it is worth, it may be pointed out that at least one leading meritarian, Aristotle, sometimes seems to presuppose the principle of equality just stated. For example, he regards slavery as justified because he believes that there are people who can enjoy the best lives they are capable of only if they are slaves of some master. In fact, more generally, he seems at his best to define the ideal state as one in which each member enjoys the highest happiness—the most excellent activity—he is capable of attaining.

To avoid misunderstanding, I should add that I do not mean to suggest that no extra attention should be given either to handicapped persons on the one hand, or to gifted individuals on the other. I have no wish to attack enterprises like Project Head Start, fellowship programs, etcetera. All that the principle of equal justice requires is that everyone be given an equal chance to enjoy the best life he is capable of, but it may be that doing this entails our giving what seems to be extra attention to certain sorts of people. Such attention seems extra only because it involves more effort or money, but it is not really extra (unjust), since it is necessary if we are to make the same *proportionate* contribution to the best of life of everyone. Some people simply are by nature harder to help on their way, and others easier, and we are, therefore, not unjust if we put more effort or money into helping some than we do into helping others, as long as all are enabled to make the same *relative* advance toward the good life.

One might object here that social justice consists, not in making possible the same relative advance for everyone, but rather in bringing everyone up to the same absolute level. One might contend, for example, that it is unjust for society to put anything extra into its gifted individuals until all the others, whether handicapped or not, have been brought up to the highest level possible for them, and that even then it is not unjust if it does not do anything extra for them. To deal with this objection we must distinguish two things a society might do for its members: (1) it might provide them with a certain level of material goods, (2) it might promote a certain level of goodness of life for them. These two things may overlap, but they are not the same. I am somewhat inclined to agree that society should try to make available to everyone the same general level of material possessions, at least up to a certain point. But material possessions are only externally connected with goodness of life, and it is the latter that society should be mainly concerned with. Now, some people just *are* capable of leading better lives than others; these are, in fact, the "gifted" ones. Should not society, in justice, do what it can to help these members achieve the best lives they are capable of (provided it also helps the others), at least after and perhaps even before the others have reached their peaks? A few remarks may perhaps serve to guide further thinking on this matter.

(a) It certainly seems only just that they should be helped if necessary, at least *after* the less gifted have reached their peaks. We must remember, however, that a just society will also be a free one, and that in a free society such individuals can and will do much to help themselves. (b) It is obviously conducive to the good, not only of the gifted individuals, but of others,

if the gifted are aided even *before* the others have gone as high as they can. For, like Plato's rulers, they can then put their gifts to the social use of helping the others. (c) It would seem clear, at any rate, that a just society must at least *permit* exceptional individuals to realize themselves, insofar as this is compatible with others' doing so. (d) Since a just society must provide the utmost freedom for each individual consistent with the freedom and welfare of others, it must even run the *risk* that some, in seeking their own best life, will endanger those of others. (e) In practice, perhaps, any society that seeks to be just must work on two fronts all the time: that of making possible the achievement by the gifted of the best lives they can attain and that of making *sure* that others also are so positioned as to be able to attain the best lives open to them by virtue of their potentialities.

V.

Now, having steered the good ship Justice safely though the straits of inequalitarianism into the haven of equalitarianism, we must ask what side of the harbor we are to anchor on, that of substantive or that of procedural equalitarianism. As was indicated earlier, the difficulty in substantive equalitarianism is that there seems to be no factual respect in which all human beings are equal, no Q which they all have in the same degree and form. (There is the further point that, even if there were such a Q, it still might not follow that all men ought to be treated as equals; but this is balanced by the fact that, if there is no such Q, it also does not follow that men ought not to be treated as equals.) As Benn and Peters put it,[12]

... if we strip away [from human nature] all the qualities in respect of which men differ, what is left? ... we are left with an undifferentiated potentiality ... 'Human nature' implies a varying potentiality for a certain limited range of qualities ...; it is not another quality that all men posses equally, on account of which they should in some positive way be treated alike.

Benn and Peters conclude that equalitarianism must take a procedural form.[13]

... What we really demand, when we say that all men are equal, is that *none shall be held to have a claim to better treatment than another, in advance of good grounds being produced.* ... Understood in this way, the principle of equality does not prescribe positively that all human beings be treated alike; it is a presumption against treating them differently, in any respect, until grounds for distinction have been shewn. It does not assume, therefore, a quality which all men have to the same degree, which is the ground of the presumption, for to say that there is a presumption means that no grounds need be shewn. The onus of justification rests on whoever would make distinctions. To act justly, then, is to treat all men alike except where there are relevant differences between them. ... Presume equality until there is reason to presume otherwise.

With some qualifications, I am inclined to agree with this view of the matter. It still seems reasonable, however, to ask why we should adopt this procedural principle in the case of *all* the beings who are *human,* if they are not equal in any factual sense. The answer, I think, has two parts. (1) One part is that it seems to be a rule of reason to deal with similar things in similar ways. Thus, inductive reasoning may be thought of as depending on a presumption that we are to make similar assertions about similar things, unless we have evidence to the contrary. To quote Perelman:

The fact is, the rule of justice results from a tendency, natural to the human mind, to regard as normal and rational, and so as requiring no supplementary justification, a course of behaviour in conformity with precedent.[14]

This view may be substantiated somewhat by reference to the work of Piaget on the moral judgment of children.[15] But it does not suffice as an answer to our question. For, as we saw, and as Perelman recognizes, this rule of reason—treat similar cases similarly—is purely formal. Besides, even though, in our geological inductions, we must presume that what is true of one rock is true of others unless there is evidence to the contrary, we hardly need draw the conclusion that, in our behavior, we ought to *treat* all rocks in the same way unless we can show good reasons for treating them differently. Why then should we treat all *human* beings equally until we have good reasons for not doing so? (2) The reply, it seems to me, must be that human beings are different from rocks, they have desires, emotions, and minds, and are capable, as rocks are not, of having lives

that are good or bad. It is this fact that all men are similarly capable of experiencing a good or bad life, not the fact that they are equal in some respect (if they are), that justifies the presumption that they are to be treated as equals. With this, somewhat hesitantly, I drop anchor on the procedural equalitarian side.

VI.

Many problems remain, but we can take up only two of them, and then only briefly. (1) An equalitarian might hold, not only that justice requires us to treat all human beings equally (in the sense explained above, in which giving A a violin and B a pair of skis may be treating them equally, not in the sense of treating them exactly alike), but that any departure from equality, any unequal treatment is *ipso facto* unjust and wrong. But few equalitarians have had the temerity to espouse this position, nor have I, though I should point out that it is much more plausible to maintain that it is never just or right to treat people *unequally* than that it is never just or right to treat them differently. If one does not adopt this position, however, one must allow that unequal treatment is sometimes just or right, that the differences among people sometimes justify treating them unequally. And then the question arises: what differences among humans justify treating them unequally? What differences are relevant to questions of distribution? This is not an easy question, and it is sometimes felt that the relevant differences are so many and so various as to render the principle of equality of no effect. An inequalitarian must answer the question, too; but he *could* say that all differences are relevant, if not, prove why not; whereas the equalitarian must claim that the relevant differences can be limited in some way. Now, I have already intimated that in various kinds of context various kinds of considerations are relevant to questions of distribution, for example, that differences in height or color of skin may be relevant to decisions about the distribution of costumes and roles in plays. In a sense, then, if we abstract from context, the variety of relevant considerations, like that of evil spirits, is indeed legion. In another sense, however, each context determines what considerations are relevant and limits them; not all considerations are relevant in all contexts. Differences in sex, color, height, or dramatic ability may be relevant to decisions about casting players, but they are not always relevant; indeed they seem obviously irrelevant to most questions of social policy of the kind that a theory of distributive justice is primarily concerned to provide for. For such questions, I suggest, the relevant features of people are not such things as color, height, and the like, but only those features that bear, directly or indirectly, on the goodness or badness of the lives of which they are capable, for example, differences in ability or need.

(2) The last question is somewhat different, and may be put roughly by asking, "Why should we be just?" More accurately put, it is this: Why is justice, conceived as treating people equally in the sense explained, right?[16] One traditional answer is that of the deontologist in ethics, namely, that justice or equality of treatment is right in itself, as keeping promises is, or telling the truth. Another standard answer is that of the utilitarian, that justice or equal treatment is right because it is necessary for or at least conducive to the greatest general good or the greatest general happiness. As between these two views I should say that the first is essentially correct and the second mistaken. I should like, however, to propose a third mediating possibility. If we ask what the Ideal state of affairs would be, then, as far as I can see, the deontologist and the utilitarian can both accept the following statement:

The Ideal is that state of affairs in which *every person* (or perhaps every sentient being) has the best life he is capable of.

If this formulation of the Ideal is correct, as I believe it is, then we can plausibly argue that justice in the sense of equal treatment is right because it is a constitutive condition of the Ideal. For then, as Bentham declared, it is an essential aspect of the Ideal that everybody be counted as one and nobody as more than one. In the Ideal, as thus formulated, everyone is equally well off in the sense that everyone has the best life he is

capable of, which is all that can reasonably be asked for. An even more ideal equality would be realized, it is true, in a state of affairs in which everyone had the ideally best life or at least the best life that any human being is capable of; but such a state of affairs would be wholly impractical and Utopian as an ideal. It could only be wished, not worked, for. Logically, of course, one could reject even the more practical Ideal sketched in my statement, since "questions of ultimate ends do not admit of proof";[17] but it is hard to believe that anybody would in fact reject it if he were fully informed and completely reasonable,

> ... whose even-balanced soul
> From first youth tested up to extreme old age,
> Business could not make dull, nor passion wild;
> Who saw life steadily, and saw it whole ... [18]

NOTES

1.   See W. K. Frankena, "The Concept of Social Justice," in R. B. Brandt (ed.), *Social Justice* (Englewood Cliffs, N.J., 1962); W. K. Frankena, *Ethics* (Englewood Cliffs, N.J., 1963), ch. 3.
2.   Cf. J. S. Mill, *Utilitarianism,* Ch. V.
3.   *The Idea of Justice and the Problem of Argument* (London, 1963), pp. 15–16.
4.   *Ibid.,* pp. 27–28.
5.   Cf. *ibid.,* p. 11. But see also pp. ix–x.
6.   *Op. cit.,* near end of Ch. I.
7.   See *Nicomachean Ethics,* Bk. V; *Politics,* Bk. III, Ch. IX, XII, XIII.
8.   See S. I. Benn and R. S. Peters, *Social Principles and the Democratic State* (London, 1959), pp. 108–111.
9.   *Matt.* 13:12.
10.   W. D. Ross, *The Right and the Good* (Oxford, 1930), pp. 135–138.
11.   Cf. *Ethics,* p. 40.
12.   *Op. cit.,* p. 109.
13.   *Ibid.,* pp. 110–111; cf. M. Ginsberg, *On Justice in Society* (Pelican Books, 1965), p. 79.
14.   *Op. cit.,* p. 86. For the point I am borrowing, see pp. 79–87. Cf. J. N. Findlay, *Language, Mind and Value* (London, 1963), p. 250.
15.   Jean Piaget, *The Moral Judgment of the Child* (New York, 1948). Perelman refers to Piaget's *Apprentissage et connaissance,* p. 42.
16.   Meritarians have a corresponding question: why is justice, conceived as treating people according to their merits, right? They too can give either deontological or utilitarian answers.
17.   Mill, *op. cit.,* opening sentence of Ch. IV.
18.   Matthew Arnold, "To a Friend."

JOHN STUART MILL

On the Connection Between Justice and Utility*

In all ages of speculation, one of the strongest obstacles to the reception of the doctrine that Utility or Happiness is the criterion of right and wrong, has been drawn from the idea of Justice. The powerful sentiment and apparently clear perception which that word recalls, with a rapidity and certainty resembling an instinct, have seemed to the majority of thinkers to point to an inherent quality in things, to show that the Just must have an existence in nature as something absolute, generically distinct from every variety of the Expedient and, in idea, opposed to it, though (as is commonly acknowledged) never, in the long run, disjoined from it in fact.

In the case of this, as of our other moral sentiments, there is no necessary connection between the question of its origin and that of its binding force. That a feeling is bestowed on us by Nature does not necessarily legitimate all its promptings. The feeling of justice might be a peculiar instinct, and might yet require, like our other instincts, to be controlled and enlightened by a higher reason. If we have intellectual instincts leading us to judge in a particular way, as well as animal instincts that prompt us to act in a particular way, there is no necessity that the former should be more infallible in their sphere than the latter in theirs; it may as well happen that wrong judgments are occasionally suggested by those, as wrong actions by these. But though it is one thing to believe that we have natural feelings of justice and another to acknowledge them as an ultimate criterion of conduct, these two opinions are very closely connected in point of fact. Mankind are always predisposed to believe that any subjective feeling not otherwise accounted for, is a revelation of some objective reality. Our present object is to determine whether the reality to which the feeling of justice corresponds, is one which needs any such special revelation, whether the justice or injustice of an action is a thing intrinsically peculiar, and distinct from all its other qualities, or only a combination of certain of those qualities, presented under a peculiar aspect. For the purpose of this inquiry, it is practically important to consider whether the feeling itself of justice and injustice is *sui generis* like our sensations of color and taste, or a derivative feeling, formed by a combination of others. And this it is the more essential to examine, as people are in general willing enough to allow that, objectively, the dictates of Justice coincide with a part of the field of General Expediency; but inasmuch as the subjective mental feeling of Justice is different from that which commonly attaches to simple expediency and, except in the extreme cases of the latter, is far more imperative in its demands, people find it difficult to see, in Justice, only a particular kind or branch of general utility, and think that its superior binding force requires a totally different origin.

To throw light upon this question, it is necessary to attempt to ascertain what is the distinguishing character of justice or of injustice; what is the quality, or whether there is any quality, attributed in common to all modes of conduct designated as unjust (for justice, like many other moral attributes, is best defined by its opposite), and distinguishing them from such modes of conduct as are disapproved, but without having that particular epithet of disapprobation applied to them. If, in everything which men are accustomed to characterize as just or unjust, some one common attribute or collection of attributes is always present, we may judge whether this particular attribute, or combination of attributes, would be capable of gathering round it a sentiment of that peculiar character and intensity by

*Chapter 5 (complete) of *Utilitarianism*. First published in 1861.

virtue of the general laws of our emotional constitution, or whether the sentiment is inexplicable and requires to be regarded as a special provision of nature. If we find the former to be the case, we shall, in resolving this question, have resolved also the main problem; if the latter, we shall have to seek for some other mode of investigating it.

To find the common attributes of a variety of objects, it is necessary to begin by surveying the objects themselves in the concrete. Let us therefore avert successively to the various modes of action, and arrangements of human affairs, which are classed, by universal or widely spread opinion, as Just or Unjust. The things well known to excite the sentiments associated with those names are of a very multifarious character. I shall pass them rapidly in review, without studying any particular arrangement.

In the first place, it is mostly considered unjust to deprive any one of his personal liberty, his property, or any other thing which belongs to him by law. Here, therefore, is one instance of the application of the terms Just and Unjust in a perfectly definite sense, namely, that it is just to respect, unjust to violate, the *legal rights* of any one. But this judgment admits of several exceptions, arising from the other forms in which the notions of justice and injustice present themselves. For example: The person who suffers the deprivation may (as the phrase is) have *forfeited* the rights which he is so deprived of; a case to which we shall return presently. But also,

Secondly, The legal rights of which he is deprived may be rights which *ought* not to have belonged to him; in other words, the law which confers on him these rights may be a bad law. When it is so, or when (which is the same thing for our purpose) it is supposed to be so, opinions will differ as to the justice or injustice of infringing it. Some maintain that no law, however bad, ought to be disobeyed by an individual citizen, that his opposition to it, if shown at all, should only be shown in endeavoring to get it altered by competent authority. This opinion (which condemns many of the most illustrious benefactors of mankind, and would often protect pernicious institutions against the only weapons which, in the state of things existing at the time, have any chance of succeeding against them) is defended, by those who hold it, on grounds of expediency,

principally on that of the importance, to the common interest of mankind, of maintaining inviolate the sentiment of submission to law. Other persons, again, hold the directly contrary opinion that any law judged to be bad may blamelessly be disobeyed, even though it be not judged to be unjust, but only inexpedient, while others would confine the license of disobedience to the case of unjust laws. But, again, some say that all laws which are inexpedient are unjust, since every law imposes some restriction on the natural liberty of mankind, which restriction is an injustice, unless legitimated by tending to their good. Among these diversities of opinion, it seems to be universally admitted that there may be unjust laws, and that law, consequently, is not the ultimate criterion of justice, but may give to one person a benefit, or impose on another an evil, which justice condemns. When, however, a law is thought to be unjust, it seems always to be regarded as being so in the same way in which a breach of law is unjust —namely, by infringing somebody's right; which, as it cannot in this case be a legal right, receives a different appellation and is called a moral right. We may say, therefore, that a second case of injustice consists in taking or withholding from any person that to which he has a *moral right.*

Thirdly, It is universally considered just that each person should obtain that (whether good or evil) which he *deserves,* and unjust, that he should obtain a good, or be made to undergo an evil, which he does not deserve. This is, perhaps, the clearest and most emphatic form in which the idea of justice is conceived by the general mind. As it involves the notion of desert, the question arises, What constitutes desert? Speaking in a general way, a person is understood to deserve good if he does right, evil, if he does wrong; and, in a more particular sense, to deserve good from those to whom he does or has done good, and evil from those to whom he does or has done evil. The precept of returning good for evil has never been regarded as a case of the fulfilment of justice, but as one in which the claims of justice are waived, in obedience to other considerations.

Fourthly, It is confessedly unjust to *break faith* with any one, to violate an engagement, either express or implied, or disappoint expectations raised by our own conduct, at least if we have raised those expectations knowingly and voluntarily. Like the other obligations of justice already spoken of, this one is not regarded as absolute, but as capable of being overruled by a stronger obligation of justice on the other side, or by such conduct on the part of the person concerned as is deemed to absolve us from our obligation to him and to constitute a *forfeiture* of the benefit which he has been led to expect.

Fifthly, It is, by universal admission, inconsistent with justice to be *partial,* to show favor or preference to one person over another in matters to which favor and preference do not properly apply. Impartiality, however, does not seem to be regarded as a duty in itself, but rather as instrumental to some other duty, for it is admitted that favor and preference are not always censurable, and indeed the cases in which they are condemned are rather the exception than the rule. A person would be more likely to be blamed than applauded for giving his family or friends no superiority in good offices over strangers, when he could do so without violating any other duty, and no one thinks it unjust to seek one person in preference to another as a friend, connection, or companion. Impartiality, where rights are concerned, is of course obligatory, but this is involved in the more general obligation of giving to every one his right. A tribunal, for example, must be impartial, because it is bound to award, without regard to any other consideration, a disputed object to the one of two parties who has the right to it. There are other cases in which impartiality means, being solely influenced by desert, as with those who, in the capacity of judges, preceptors, or parents, administer reward and punishment as such. There are cases, again, in which it means being solely influenced by consideration for the public interest, as in making a selection among candidates for a government employment. Impartiality, in short, as an obligation of justice, may be said to mean being exclusively influenced by the considerations which it is supposed ought to influence the particular case in hand, and resisting the solicitation of any motives which prompt to conduct different from what those considerations would dictate.

Nearly allied to the idea of impartiality is that of *equality,* which often enters as a component part both into the conception of justice and into the practice of it and, in the eyes of many persons, constitutes its essence. But, in this still more than in any other case, the notion of justice varies in different persons, and always conforms in its variations to their notion of utility. Each person maintains that equality is the dictate of justice, except where he thinks that expediency requires inequality. The justice of giving equal protection to the rights of all is maintained by those who support the most outrageous inequality in the rights themselves. Even in slave countries, it is theoretically admitted that the rights of the slave, such as they are, ought to be as sacred as those of the master, and that a tribunal which fails to enforce them with equal strictness is wanting in justice, while, at the same time, institutions which leave to the slave scarcely any rights to enforce are not deemed unjust, because they are not deemed inexpedient. Those who think that utility requires distinctions of rank do not consider it unjust that riches and social privileges should be unequally dispensed, but those who think this inequality inexpedient think it unjust also. Whoever thinks that government is necessary sees no injustice in as much inequality as is constituted by giving to the magistrate powers not granted to other people. Even among those who hold leveling doctrines, there are as many questions of justice as there are differences of opinion about expediency. Some Communists consider it unjust that the produce of the labor of the community should be shared on any other principle than that of exact equality, others think it just that those should receive most whose wants are greatest, while others hold that those who work harder, or who produce more, or whose services are more valuable to the community, may justly claim a larger quota in the division of the produce. And the sense of natural justice may be plausibly appealed to in behalf of every one of these opinions.

Among so many diverse applications of the term Justice, which yet is not regarded as ambiguous, it is a matter of some difficulty to seize the mental link which holds them together, and on which the moral sentiment adhering to the term essentially depends. Perhaps, in this embarrassment, some help may be derived from the history of the word, as indicated by its etymology.

[In most, if not all languages, the etymology of the word which corresponds to Just points distinctly to an origin connected with the ordinance of law. *Justum* is a form of *jussum*—that which has been ordered. Δίκαιον comes directly from δίκη, a suit at law. *Recht,* from which came *right* and *righteous,* is synonymous with law. The courts of justice, the administration of justice, are the courts and administration of law. *La justice,* in French, is the established term for judicature. I am not commiting the fallacy imputed with some show of truth to Horne Tooke, of assuming that a word must still continue to mean what it originally meant. Etymology is slight evidence of what the idea now signified is, but the very best evidence of how it sprang up.] There can, I think, be no doubt that the *idée mère,* the primitive element, in the formation of the notion of justice, was conformity to law. It constituted the entire idea among the Hebrews up to the birth of Christianity, as might be expected in the case of a people whose laws attempted to embrace all subjects on which precepts were required, and who believed those laws to be a direct emanation from the Supreme Being. But other nations, and in particular the Greeks and Romans, who knew that their laws had been made originally, and still continued to be made, by men, were not afraid to admit that those men might make bad laws, might do, by law, the same things, and from the same motives, which, if done by individuals without the sanction of law, would be called unjust. And hence the sentiment of justice came to be attached, not to all violations of law, but only to violations of such laws as *ought* to exist, including such as ought to exist, but do not, and to laws themselves, if supposed to be contrary to what ought to be law. In this manner, the idea of law and of its injunctions was still predominant in the notion of justice, even when the laws actually in force ceased to be accepted as the standard of it.

It is true that mankind consider the idea of justice and its obligations as applicable to many things which neither are, nor is it desired that they should be, regulated by law. Nobody desires that laws should interfere with the whole detail of private life, yet every one allows that, in all daily conduct, a person may and does show himself to be either just or unjust. But even here, the idea of the breach of what ought to be law still lingers in a modified shape. It would always give us pleasure, and chime in with our feelings of fitness, that acts which we deem unjust should be punished, though we do not always think it expedient that this should be done by the tribunals. We forego that gratification on account of incidental inconveniences. We should be glad to see just conduct enforced, and injustice repressed, even in the minutest details, if we were not with reason afraid of trusting the magistrate with so unlimited an amount of power over individuals. When we think that a person is bound in justice to do a thing, it is an ordinary form of language to say that he ought to be compelled to do it. We should be gratified to see the obligation enforced by anybody who had the power. If we see that its enforcement by law would be inexpedient, we lament the impossibility, we consider the impunity given to injustice as an evil, and strive to make amends for it by bringing a strong expression of our own and the public disapprobation to bear upon the offender. Thus the idea of legal constraint is still the generating idea of the notion of justice, though undergoing several transformations before that notion, as it exists in an advanced state of society, becomes complete.

The above is, I think, a true account, as far as it goes, of the origin and progressive growth of the idea of justice. But we must observe that it contains, as yet, nothing to distinguish that obligation from moral obligation in general. For the truth is that the idea of penal sanction, which is the essence of law, enters not only into the conception of injustice, but into that of any kind of wrong. We do not call anything wrong, unless we mean to imply that a person ought to be punished in some way or other for doing it, if not by law, by the opinion of his fellow-creatures, if not by opinion, by the reproaches of his own conscience. This seems the real turning point of the distinction between morality and simple expediency. It is a part of the notion of Duty in every one of its forms that a person may rightfully be compelled to fulfill it. Duty is a thing which may be *exacted* from a person, as one exacts a debt. Unless we think that it may be exacted from him, we do not call it his duty. Reasons of prudence, or the interest of other people, may militate against actually exacting it, but the person himself, it is clearly understood, would not be entitled to complain. There are other things, on the contrary, which we wish that people should do, which we like or admire them for doing, perhaps dislike or despise them for not doing, but yet admit that they are not bound to do; it is not a case of moral obligation; we do not blame them, that is, we do not think that they are proper objects of punishment. How we come by these ideas of deserving and not deserving punishment, will appear, perhaps, in the sequel; but I think there is no doubt that this distinction lies at the bottom of the notions of right and wrong, that we call any conduct wrong, or employ instead some other term of dislike or disparagement, according as we think that the person ought or ought not to be punished for it, and we say it would be right to do so and so, or merely that it would be desirable or laudable, according as we would wish to see the person whom it concerns compelled, or only persuaded and exhorted, to act in that manner.[1]

This, therefore, being the characteristic difference which marks off, not justice but morality in general, from the remaining provinces of Expediency and Worthiness, the character is still to be sought which distinguishes justice from other branches of morality. Now, it is known that ethical writers divide moral duties into two classes, denoted by the ill-chosen expressions, duties of perfect and of imperfect obligation; the latter being those in which, though the act is obligatory, the particular occasions of performing it are left to our choice, as in the case of charity or beneficence, which we are indeed bound to practice, but not towards any definite person, nor at any prescribed time. In the more precise language of philosophic jurists, duties of perfect obligation are those duties in virtue of which a correlative *right* resides in some person or persons; duties of imperfect obligation are those moral obligations which do not give birth to any right. I think it will be found that this distinction exactly coincides with that which exists between justice and the other obligations of morality. In our survey of the various popular acceptations of justice, the term appeared generally to involve the idea of personal right—a claim on the part of one or more individuals, like that which the law gives when it confers a proprietary or other legal right. Whether the injustice consists in depriving a person of a possession, or in breaking faith with him, or in treating him worse than he deserves, or worse than other people who have no greater claims, in each case the supposition implies two things—a wrong done, and some assignable person who is wronged. Injustice may also be done by treating a person better than others, but the wrong in this case is to his competitors, who are also assignable persons. It seems to me that this feature in the case—a right in some person, correlative to the moral obligation—constitutes the specific difference between justice and generosity or beneficence. Justice implies something which it is not only right to do and wrong not to do, but which some individual person can claim from us as his moral right. No one has a moral right to our generosity or beneficence, because we are not morally bound to practice those virtues towards any given individual. And it will be found, with respect to this as to every correct definition, that the instances which seem to conflict with it are those which most confirm it, for if a moralist attempts, as some have done, to make out that mankind generally, though not any given individual, have a right to all the good we can do them, he at once, by that thesis, includes generosity and beneficence within the category of justice. He is obliged to say that our utmost exertions are *due* to our fellow creatures, thus assimilating them to a debt, or that nothing less can be a sufficient *return* for what society does for us, thus classing the case as one of gratitude, both of which are acknowledged cases of justice. Wherever there is a right, the case is one of justice, and not of the virtue of beneficence, and whoever does not place the distinction between justice and morality in general where we have now placed it will be found to make no distinction between them at all, but to merge all morality in justice.

Having thus endeavored to determine the distinctive elements which enter into the composition of the idea of justice, we are ready to enter on the inquiry, whether the feeling which accompanies the idea is attached to it by a special dispensation of nature, or whether it could have grown up by any known laws out of the idea itself, and, in particular, whether it can have originated in considerations of general expediency.

I conceive that the sentiment itself does not arise from anything which would commonly or correctly be termed an idea of expediency, but that, though the sentiment does not, whatever is moral in it does.

We have seen that the two essential ingredients in the sentiment of justice are the desire to punish a person who has done harm, and the knowledge or belief that there is some definite individual or individuals to whom harm has been done.

Now, it appears to me that the desire to punish a person who has done harm to some individual is a spontaneous outgrowth from two sentiments, both in the highest degree natural, and which either are or resemble instincts—the impulse of self-defense, and the feeling of sympathy.

It is natural to resent, and to repel or retaliate, any harm done or attempted against ourselves or against those with whom we sympathize. The origin of this sentiment it is not necessary here to discuss. Whether it be an instinct or a result of intelligence, it is, we know, common to all animal nature, for every animal tries to hurt those who have hurt, or who it thinks are about to hurt, itself or its young. Human beings, on this point, only differ from other animals in two particulars: first, in being capable of sympathizing, not solely with their offspring or, like some of the more noble animals, with some superior animal who is kind to them, but with all human and even with all sentient beings; secondly, in having a more developed intelligence, which gives a wider range to the whole of their sentiments, whether self-regarding or sympathetic. By virtue of his superior intelligence, even apart from his superior range of sympathy, a human being is capable of apprehending a community of interest between himself and the human society of which he forms a part, such that any conduct which threatens the security of the society generally is threatening to his own, and calls forth his instinct (if instinct it be) of self-defense. The same superiority of intelligence, joined to the power of sympathizing with human beings generally, enables him to attach himself to the collective idea of his tribe, his country, or mankind, in such a manner that any act hurtful to them raises his instinct of sympathy, and urges him to resistance.

The sentiment of justice, in that one of its elements which consists of the desire to punish, is thus, I conceive, the natural feeling of retaliation or vengeance, rendered by intellect and sympathy applicable to those injuries—that is, to those hurts—which wound us through, or in common with, society at large. This sentiment in itself has nothing moral in it; what is moral is the exclusive subordination of it to the social sympathies, so as to wait on and obey their call. For the natural feeling would make us resent indiscriminately whatever any one does that is disagreeable to us, but, when moralized by the social feeling, it only acts in the directions conformable to the general good: just persons resenting a hurt to society, though not otherwise a hurt to themselves, and not resenting a hurt to themselves, however painful, unless it be of the kind which society has a common interest with them in the repression of.

It is no objection against this doctrine to say that, when we feel our sentiment of justice outraged, we are not thinking of society at large, or of any collective interest, but only of the individual case. It is common enough, certainly, though the reverse of commendable, to feel resentment merely because we have suffered pain, but a person whose resentment is really a moral feeling—that is, who considers whether an act is blamable before he allows himself to resent it—such a person, though he may not say expressly to himself that he is standing up for the interest of society, certainly does feel that he is asserting a rule which is for the benefit of others as well as for his own. If he is not feeling this, if he is regarding the act solely as it affects him individually—he is not consciously just, he is not concerning himself about the justice of his actions. This is admitted even by anti-utilitarian moralists. When Kant (as before remarked) propounds as the fundamental principle of morals, "So act that thy rule of conduct might be adopted as a law by all rational beings," he virtually acknowledges that the interest of mankind collectively, or at least of mankind indiscriminately, must be in the mind of the agent when conscientiously deciding on the morality of the act. Otherwise he uses words without a meaning, for that a rule even of utter selfishness could not *possibly* be adopted by all rational beings—that there is any insuperable obstacle in the nature of things to its adoption—cannot be even plausibly maintained. To give any meaning to Kant's principle, the sense put upon it must be that we ought to shape our conduct by a rule which all rational beings might adopt *with benefit to their collective interest.*

To recapitulate: The idea of justice supposes two things—a rule of conduct and a sentiment which sanctions the rule. The first must be supposed common to all mankind, and intended for their good; the other (the sentiment) is a desire that punishment may be suffered by those who infringe the rule. There is involved, in addition, the conception of some definite person who suffers by the infringement, whose rights (to use the expression appropriated to the case) are violated by it. And the sentiment of justice appears to me to be the animal desire to repel or retaliate a hurt or damage to one's self or to those with whom one sympathizes, widened so as to include all persons, by the human capacity of enlarged sympathy, and the human conception of intelligent self-interest. From the latter elements, the feeling derives its morality; from the former, its peculiar impressiveness and energy of self-assertion.

I have throughout treated the idea of a *right* residing in the injured person, and violated by the injury, not as a separate element in the composition of the idea and sentiment, but as one of the forms in which the other two elements clothe themselves. These elements are a hurt to some assignable person or persons on the one hand, and a demand for punishment on the other. An examination of our own minds, I think, will show that these two things include all that we mean when we speak of violation of a right. When we call any thing a person's right, we mean that he has a valid claim on society to protect him in the possession of it, either by the force of law, or by that of education and opinion. If he has what we consider a sufficient claim, on whatever account, to have something guaranteed to him by society, we say that he has a right to it. If we desire to prove that anything does not belong to him by right, we think this done as soon as it is admitted that society ought not to take measures for securing it to him, but should leave him to chance or to his own exertions. Thus a person is said to have a right to what he can earn in fair professional competition, because society ought not to allow any other person to hinder him from endeavoring to earn in that manner as much as he can. But he has not a right to three hundred a year, though he may happen to be earning it, because society is not called on to provide that he shall earn that sum. On the contrary, if he owns ten thousand pounds three-per-cent stock, he *has* a right to three hundred a year, because society has come under an obligation to provide him with an income of that amount.

To have a right then is, I conceive, to have something which society ought to defend me in the possession of. If the objector goes on to ask why it ought, I can give him no other reason than general utility. If that expression does not seem to convey a sufficient feeling of the strength of the obligation, nor to account for the peculiar energy of the feeling, it is because there goes to the composition of the sentiment, not a rational only but also an animal element—the thirst for retaliation, and his thirst derives its intensity, as well as its moral justification, from the extraordinarily important and impressive kind of utility which is concerned. The interest involved is that of security, to every one's feelings, the most vital of all interests. All other earthly benefits are needed by one person, not needed by another, and many of them can, if necessary, be cheerfully foregone, or replaced by something else. But security no human being can possibly do without; on it we depend for all our immunity from evil, and for the whole value of all and every good, beyond the passing moment, since nothing but the gratification of the instant could be of any worth to us if we could be deprived of everything the next instant by whoever was momentarily stronger than ourselves. Now, this most indispensable of all necessaries, after physical nutriment, cannot be had, unless the machinery for providing it is kept unintermittedly in active play. Our notion, therefore, of the claim we have on our fellow creatures to join in making safe for us the very groundwork of our existence, gathers feelings around it so much more intense than those concerned in any of the more common cases of utility, that the difference in degree (as is often the case in psychology) becomes a real difference in kind. The claim assumes that character of absoluteness, that apparent infinity and incommensurability with all other considerations, which constitute the distinction between the feeling of right and wrong and that of ordinary expediency and inexpediency. The feelings concerned are so powerful, and we count so positively on finding a responsive feeling in others (all being alike interested), that *ought* and *should* grow into *must,* and recognized indispensability becomes a moral necessity, analogous to physical, and often not inferior to it in binding force.

If the preceding analysis, or something resembling it, be not the correct account of the notion of justice, if justice be totally independent of utility, and be a standard *per se,* which the mind can recognize by simple introspection of itself—it is hard to understand why that internal oracle is so ambiguous, and why so many things appear either just or unjust, according to the light in which they are regarded.

We are continually informed that Utility is an uncertain standard, which every different person interprets differently, and that there is no safety but in the immutable, ineffaceable, and unmistakable dictates of Justice, which carry their evidence in themselves and are independent of the fluctuations of opinion. One would suppose from this that, on questions of justice, there could be no controversy, that, if we take that for our rule, its application to any given case could leave us in as little doubt as a mathematical demonstration. So far is this from being the fact, that there is as much difference of opinion and as much discussion about what is just as about what is useful to society. Not only have different nations and individuals different notions of justice but, in the mind of one and the same individual, justice is not some one rule, principle, or maxim, but many, which do not always coincide in their dictates, and, in choosing between which, he is guided either by some extraneous standard, or by his own personal predilections.

For instance: There are some who say that it is unjust to punish any one for the sake of example to others, that punishment is just, only when intended for the good of the sufferer himself. Others maintain the extreme reverse, contending that to punish persons who have attained years of discretion, for their own benefit, is despotism and injustice, since, if the matter at issue is solely their own good, no one has a right to control their own judgment of it, but that they may justly be punished to prevent evil to others, this being the exercise of the legitimate right of self-defense. Mr. Owen, again, affirms that it is unjust to punish at all, for the criminal did not make his own character; his education, and the circumstances which surrounded him, have made him a criminal, and for these he is not responsible. All these opinions are extremely plausible, and so long as the question is argued as one of justice simply, without going down to the principles which lie under justice, and are the source of its authority, I am unable to see how any of these reasoners can be refuted. For, in truth, every one of the three builds upon rules of justice of singling out an individual, and making him a sacrifice, without his consent, for other people's benefit. The second relies on the acknowledged justice of self-defense,

and the admitted injustice of forcing one person to conform to another's notions of what constitutes his good. The Owenite invokes the admitted principle that it is unjust to punish any one for what he cannot help. Each is triumphant so long as he is not compelled to take into consideration any other maxims of justice than the one he has selected but, as soon as their several maxims are brought face to face, each disputant seems to have exactly as much to say for himself as the others. No one of them can carry out his own notion of justice without trampling upon another equally binding. These are difficulties, they have always been felt to be such, and many devices have been invented to turn rather than to overcome them. As a refuge from the last of the three, men imagined what they called the "freedom of the will," fancying that they could not justify punishing a man whose will is in a thoroughly hateful state, unless it be supposed to have come into that state through no influence of anterior circumstances. To escape from the other difficulties, a favorite contrivance has been the fiction of a contract, whereby, at some unknown period all the members of society engaged to obey the laws, and consented to be punished for any disobedience to them, thereby giving to their legislators the right, which it is assumed they would not otherwise have had, of punishing them, either for their own good or for that of society. This happy thought was considered to get rid of the whole difficulty, and to legitimate the infliction of punishment, in virtue of another received maxim of justice, *volenti non fit injuria,* "That is not unjust which is done with the consent of the person who is supposed to be hurt by it." I need hardly remark that, even if the consent were not a mere fiction, this maxim is not superior in authority to the others which it is brought in to supersede. It is, on the contrary, an instructive specimen of the loose and irregular manner in which supposed principles of justice grow up. This particular one evidently came in use as a help to the coarse exigencies of courts of law, which are sometimes obliged to be content with very uncertain presumptions, on account of the greater evils which would often arise from any attempt on their part to cut finer. But even courts of law are not able to adhere consistently to the maxim, for they allow voluntary engagements to be set aside on the ground of fraud, and sometimes on that of mere mistake or misinformation.

Again: when the legitimacy of inflicting punishment is admitted, how many conflicting conceptions of justice come to light in discussing the proper apportionment of punishments to offenses! No rule on the subject recommends itself so strongly to the primitive and spontaneous sentiment of justice, as the *lex talionis,* "An eye for an eye, and a tooth for a tooth." Though this principle of the Jewish and of the Mohammedan law has been generally abandoned in Europe as a practical maxim, there is, I suspect, in most minds, a secret hankering after it and, when retribution accidentally falls on an offender in that precise shape, the general feeling of satisfaction evinced bears witness how natural is the sentiment to which this repayment in kind is acceptable. With many, the test of justice in penal infliction is that the punishment should be proportioned to the offence; meaning that it should be exactly measured by the moral guilt of the culprit (whatever be their standard for measuring moral guilt): the consideration, what amount of punishment is necessary to deter from the offense, having nothing to do with the question of justice, in their estimation: while there are others to whom that consideration is all in all; who maintain that it is not just, at least for man, to inflict on a fellow-creature, whatever may be his offences, any amount of suffering beyond the least that will suffice to prevent him from repeating, and others from imitating, his misconduct.

To take another example from a subject already once referred to. In a co-operative industrial association, is it just or not that talent or skill should give a title to superior remuneration? On the negative side of the question it is argued, that whoever does the best he can, deserves equally well, and ought not in justice to be put in a position of inferiority for no fault of his own; that superior abilities have already advantages more than enough, in the admiration they excite, the personal influence they command, and the internal sources of satisfaction attending them, without adding to these a superior share of the world's goods; and that society is bound in justice rather to make compensation to the less favoured, for this unmerited inequality of advantages, than to aggravate it. On the contrary side it is contended, that society receives more from the more efficient

labourer; that his services being more useful, society owes him a larger return for them; that a greater share of the joint result is actually his work, and not to allow his claim to it is a kind of robbery; that if he is only to receive as much as others, he can only be justly required to produce as much, and to give a smaller amount of time and exertion, proportioned to his superior efficiency. Who shall decide between these appeals to conflicting principles of justice? Justice has in this case two sides to it, which it is impossible to bring into harmony, and the two disputants have chosen opposite sides; the one looks to what it is just that the individual should receive, the other to what it is just that the community should give. Each, from his own point of view, is unanswerable; and any choice between them, on grounds of justice, must be perfectly arbitrary. Social utility alone can decide the preference.

How many, again, and how irreconcilable, are the standards of justice to which reference is made in discussing the repartition of taxation. One opinion is that payment to the State should be in numerical proportion to pecuniary means. Others think that justice dictates what they term graduated taxation; taking a higher percentage from those who have more to spare. In point of natural justice a strong case might be made for disregarding means altogether, and taking the same absolute sum (whenever it could be got) from every one: as the subscribers to a mess, or to a club, all pay the same sum for the same privileges, whether they can all equally afford it or not. Since the protection (it might be said) of law and government is afforded to, and is equally required by all, there is no injustice in making all buy it at the same price. It is reckoned justice, not injustice, that a dealer should charge to all customers the same price for the same article, not a price varying according to their means of payment. This doctrine, as applied to taxation, finds no advocates because it conflicts so strongly with man's feelings of humanity and of social expediency: but the principle of justice which it invokes is as true and as binding as those which can be appealed to against it. Accordingly it exerts a tacit influence on the line of defence employed for other modes of assessing taxation. People feel obliged to argue that the State does more for the rich than for the poor, as a justification for its taking more from them: though this is in reality not true, for the rich would be far better able to protect themselves, in the absence of law or government, than the poor, and indeed would probably be successful in converting the poor into their slaves. Others again, so far defer to the same conception of justice, as to maintain that all should pay an equal capitation tax for the protection of their persons (these being of equal value to all), and an unequal tax for the protection of their property, which is unequal. To this others reply, that the all of one man is as valuable to him as the all of another. From these confusions there is no other mode of extrication than the utilitarian.

Is, then, the difference between the Just and the Expedient a merely imaginary distinction? Have mankind been under a delusion in thinking that justice is a more sacred thing than policy, and that the latter ought only to be listened to after the former has been satisfied? By no means. The exposition we have given of the nature and origin of the sentiment recognizes a real distinction, and no one of those who profess the most sublime contempt for the consequences of actions as an element in their morality attaches more importance to the distinction than I do. While I dispute the pretensions of any theory which sets up an imaginary standard of justice not grounded on utility, I account the justice which is grounded on utility to be the chief part, and incomparably the most sacred and binding part, of all morality. Justice is a name for certain classes of moral rules which concern the essentials of human well-being more nearly, and are therefore of more absolute obligation, than any other rules for the guidance of life, and the notion which we have found to be of the essence of the idea of justice, that of a right residing in an individual, implies and testifies to this more binding obligation.

The moral rules which forbid mankind to hurt one another (in which we must never forget to include wrongful interference with each other's freedom) are more vital to human well-being than any maxims, however important, which only point out the best mode of managing some department of human affairs. They have also the peculiarity that they are the main element in determining the whole of the social feelings of mankind. It is their observance which alone preserves peace among human beings; if obedience to them were not the rule, and disobedience the exception, every one would see in every one else an enemy, against whom he must be perpetually guarding himself. What is hardly less important, these are the precepts which mankind have the strongest and the most direct inducements for impressing upon one another. By merely giving to each other prudential instruction or exhortation, they may gain, or think they gain, nothing; in inculcating on each other the duty of positive beneficence, they have an unmistakable interest, but far less in degree: a person may possibly not need the benefits of others, but he always needs that they should not do him hurt. Thus the moralities which protect every individual from being harmed by others, either directly or by being hindered in his freedom of pursuing his own good, are at once those which he himself has most at heart, and those which he has the strongest interest in publishing and enforcing by word and deed. It is by a person's observance of these, that his fitness to exist as one of the fellowship of human beings, is tested and decided; for on that depends his being a nuisance or not to those with whom he is in contact. Now it is these moralities primarily, which compose the obligations of justice. The most marked cases of injustice, and those which give the tone to the feeling of repugnance which characterizes the sentiment, are acts of wrongful aggression, or wrongful exercise of power over some one; the next are those which consist in wrongfully witholding from him something which is his due; in both cases, inflicting on him a positive hurt, either in the form of direct suffering, or of the privation of some good which he had reasonable ground either of a physical or of a social kind, for counting upon.

The same powerful motives which command the observance of these primary moralities, enjoin the punishment of those who violate them; and as the impulses of self-defence, of defence of others, and of vengeance, are all called forth against such persons, retribution, or evil for evil, becomes closely connected with the sentiment of justice, and is universally included in the idea. Good for good is also one of the dictates of justice; and this, though its social utility is evident, and though it carries with it a natural human feeling, has not at first sight that obvious connexion with hurt or injury, which, existing in the most elementary cases of just and unjust, and is the source of the characteristic intensity of the sentiment. But the connexion, though less obvious, is not less real. He who accepts benefits, and denies a return of them when needed, inflicts a real hurt, by disappointing one of the most natural and reasonable of expectations, and one which he must at least tacitly have encouraged, otherwise the benefits would seldom have been conferred. The important rank, among human evils and wrongs, of the disappointment of expectation, is shown in the fact that it constitutes the principal criminality of two such highly immoral acts as a breach of friendship and a breach of promise. Few hurts which human beings can sustain are greater, and none wound more, than when that on which they habitually and with full assurance relied, fails them in the hour of need; and few wrongs are greater than this mere witholding of good; none excite more resentment, either in the person suffering, or in a sympathizing spectator. The principle, therefore, of giving to each what they deserve—that is, good for good, as well as evil for evil—is not only included within the idea of Justice as we have defined it, but is a proper object of that intensity of sentiment which places the Just, in human estimation, above the simply Expedient.

Most of the maxims of justice current in the world, and commonly appealed to in its transactions, are simply instrumental to carrying into effect the principles of justice which we have now spoken of. That a person is only responsible for what he has done voluntarily, or could voluntarily have avoided, that it is unjust to condemn any person unheard, that the punishment ought to be proportioned to the offense, and the like—are maxims intended to prevent the just principle of evil for evil from being perverted to the infliction of evil without that justification. The greater part of these common maxims have come into use from the practice of courts of justice, which have been naturally led to a more complete recognition and elaboration than was likely to suggest itself to others, of the rules necessary to enable them to fulfill their double function, of inflicting punishment when due, and of awarding to each person his right.

That first of judicial virtues, impartiality, is an obligation of justice, partly for the reason last mentioned, as being a necessary condition of the fulfillment of the other obligations of justice. But this is not the only source of the exalted rank, among human obligations, of those maxims of equality and impartiality, which, both in popular estimation and in that of the most enlightened, are included among the precepts of justice. In one point of view, they may be considered as corollaries from the principles already laid down. If it is a duty to do to each according to his deserts, returning good for good as well as repressing evil by evil, it necessarily follows that we should treat all equally well (when no higher duty forbids) who have deserved equally well of *us,* and that society should treat all equally well who have deserved equally well of *it*—that is, who have deserved equally well absolutely. This is the highest abstract standard of social and distributive justice, towards which all institutions, and the efforts of all virtuous citizens, should be made in the utmost possible degree to converge. But this great moral duty rests upon a still deeper foundation, being a direct emanation from the first principle of morals, and not a mere logical corollary from secondary or derivative doctrines. It is involved in the very meaning of Utility, or the Greatest-happiness Principle. That principle is a mere form of words without rational signification, unless one person's happiness, supposed equal in degree (with the proper allowance made for kind), is counted for exactly as much as another's. Those conditions being supplied, Bentham's dictum, "Everybody to count for one, nobody for more than one," might be written under the principle of utility as an explanatory commentary.[2] The equal claim of everybody to happiness, in the estimation of the moralist and the legislator, involves an equal claim to all the means of happiness, except in so far as the inevitable conditions of human life, and the general interest, in which that of every individual is included, set limits to the maxim, and those limits ought to be strictly construed. As every other maxim of justice, so this, is by no means applied or held applicable universally; on the contrary, as I have already remarked, it bends to every person's ideas of social expediency. But, in whatever case it is deemed applicable at all, it is held to be the dictate of justice. All persons are deemed to have a *right* to equality of treatment, except when some recognized social expediency requires the reverse. And hence all social inequalities, which have ceased to be considered expedient, assume the character, not of simple inexpediency but of injustice, and appear so tyrannical that people are apt to wonder how they ever could have been tolerated, forgetful that they themselves perhaps tolerate other inequalities under an equally mistaken notion of expediency, the correction of which would make that which they approve seem quite as monstrous as what they have at last learnt to condemn. The entire history of social improvement has been a series of transitions, by which one custom or institution after another, from being a supposed primary necessity of social existence, has passed into the rank of an universally stigmatized injustice and tyranny. So it has been with the distinctions of slaves and freemen, nobles and serfs, patricians and plebeians, and so it will be, and in part already is, with the aristocracies of color, race, and sex.

It appears, from what has been said, that justice is a name for certain moral requirements which, regarded collectively, stand higher in the scale of social utility, and are therefore of more paramount obligation, than any others, though particular cases may occur in which some other social duty is so important as to overrule any one of the general maxims of justice. Thus, to save a life, it may not only be allowable, but a duty, to steal, or take by force, the necessary food or medicine, or to kidnap and compel to officiate, the only qualified medical practitioner. In such cases, we do not call any thing justice which is not a virtue, we usually say, not that justice must give way to some other moral principle, but that what is just in ordinary cases is, by reason of that other principle, not just in the particular case. By this useful accommodation of language, the character of indefeasibility attributed to justice is kept up, and we are saved from the necessity of maintaining that there can be laudable injustice.

The considerations which have now been adduced, resolve, I conceive, the only real difficulty in the utilitarian theory of morals. It has always been evident that all cases of justice are also cases of expediency; the difference is in the peculiar sentiment which attaches to the former, as contradistinguished from the latter. If this characteristic sentiment has been sufficiently accounted for, if there is no necessity to assume for it any peculiarity of origin, if it is simply the natural feeling of resentment, moralized by being made coextensive with the demands of social good, and if this feeling not only does but ought to exist in all the classes of cases to which the idea of justice corresponds—that idea no longer presents itself as a stumbling-block to the utilitarian ethics. Justice remains the appropriate name for certain social utilities which are vastly more important, and therefore more absolute and imperative, than any others are as a class (though not more so than others may be in particular cases), and which therefore ought to be, as well as naturally are, guarded by a sentiment not only different in degree, but also in kind, distinguished from the milder feeling which attaches to the mere idea of promoting human pleasure or convenience, at once by the more definite nature of its commands, and by the sterner character of its sanctions.

NOTES

1. See this point enforced and illustrated by Professor Bain, in an admirable chapter (entitled "The Ethical Emotions, or the Moral Sense") of the second of the two treatises composing his elaborate and profound work on the Mind.

2. This implication, in the first principle of the utilitarian scheme, of perfect impartiality between persons is regarded by Mr. Herbert Spencer (in his *Social Statics*) as a disproof of the pretensions of utility to be a sufficient guide to right, since (he says) the principle of utility presupposes the anterior principle, that everybody has an equal right to happiness. It may be more correctly described as supposing that equal amounts of happiness are equally desirable, whether felt by the same or by different persons. This, however, is not a *pre*-supposition, not a premise needful to support the principle of utility, but the very principle itself; for what is the principle of utility, if it be not that "happiness" and "desirable" are synonymous terms? If there is any anterior principle implied, it can be no other than this—that the truths of arithmetic are applicable to the valuation of happiness, as of all other measurable quantities.

[Mr. Herbert Spencer, in a private communication on the subject of the preceding note, objects to being considered an opponent of Utilitarianism, and states that he regards happiness as the ultimate end of morality, but deems that end only partially attainable by empirical generalizations from the observed results of conduct, and completely attainable only by deducing, from the laws of life and the conditions of existence, what kinds of action necessarily tend to produce happiness, and what kinds to produce unhappiness. With the exception of the word "necessarily," I have no dissent to express from this doctrine, and (omitting that word) I am not aware that any modern advocate of Utilitarianism is of a different opinion. Bentham certainly, to whom, in the *Social Statics*, Mr. Spencer particularly referred, is, least of all writers, chargeable with unwillingness to deduce the effect of actions on happiness from the laws of human nature and the universal conditions of human life. The common charge against him is of relying too exclusively upon such deductions, and declining altogether to be bound by the generalizations from specific experience which Mr. Spencer thinks that utilitarians generally confine themselves to. My own opinion (and, as I collect, Mr. Spencer's) is, that in ethics, as in all other branches of scientific study, the consilience of the results of both these processes, each corroborating and verifying the other, is requisite to give to any general proposition the kind and degree of evidence which constitutes scientific proof.]

BRIAN BARRY

Justice and Fairness*

PROCEDURAL FAIRNESS, BACKGROUND FAIRNESS AND LEGAL JUSTICE

PROCEDURAL FAIRNESS

To say that a procedure is being fairly operated is to say that the formalities which define the procedure have been correctly adhered to. A fair race, for example, is one in which the competitors start together (nobody 'jumps the gun'), do not elbow one another or take short cuts, and in which the first person past the line and not disqualified is recognized as the winner; a fair fight is one in which the contestants are not allowed to get away with fouls; and so on. Fairness in the operation of the authoritative determination procedure has more or less content according to the detail with which the procedure is specified in any given case. A 'fair trial', for example, must satisfy elaborate procedural safeguards, whereas a 'fair administrative decision' need mean only that the official taking it was impartial or 'fair minded'.[1] In terms of formalities an administrative tribunal or an official inquiry occupy an intermediate position.[2] The fair application of a chance procedure requires the procedure to be genuinely random (a true die, for example) so as to give everyone a 'fair chance'. A 'fair election' rules out ballot stuffing, double voting, miscounts, etc.

This leaves the first three procedures. 'Fair war' has no use (though 'just war' has): 'All's fair in love and war.' The explanation is that war does not specify rules to be followed before what is happening can be called 'war'; indeed, it is the negation of orderly procedures.[3] War in its fullest sense is an attempt to impose one's will on another by violence; as soon as conventions come in

(if you capture place A or man B you win) an element of contest enters in. Winning becomes not merely *being in a position* to impose your will but *being allowed* to impose your will in virtue of having satisfied a certain standard.[4] A duel is a contest just as a boxing match is, because if it settles, say, who gets the lady, it does so by convention: 'Let the best man win.'[5]

The notion of 'fair discussion on merits' also has no obvious use, again because there are no prescribed formalities to be observed; nor has 'fair bargaining' in general any use, since if threats are included it is simply the verbal counterpart to combat. Under more restricted conditions, however, considerations of procedural fairness can be invoked. Thus, in a context where threats are supposed to be ruled out it is 'unfair' to make threats. More subtly, in a context which is supposed to be one of 'perfect competition' it is unfair for a rich company to sell below cost in order to drive out its competitors. 'Fair trade', the traditional name for all restrictive practices aimed at protecting the inefficient producer and retailer, in theory usually means this, while in practice it normally degenerates into an attempt to guarantee 'cost plus' all around.[6] It is also used in connection with the closely similar proposal of tariffs against foreign 'dumping', which again generally comes to mean 'effective foreign competition'.

BACKGROUND FAIRNESS

While still concentrating on the way the procedure works, some evaluations in terms of 'fairness' dig a little deeper and ask whether the background conditions are satisfactory. Some examples should make the notion of 'background conditions' clear. Procedural fairness rules out one boxer having a piece of lead inside his gloves, but background fairness would also rule out any

*From *Political Argument* by Brian Barry (London: Routledge & Kegan Paul, 1965), pp. 97–106. Reprinted by permission of the author and the publisher.

undue disparity in the weight of the boxers; similarly background fairness would rule out sailing boats or cars of different sizes being raced against one another unless suitably handicapped. In a court case the fact that one side's counsel showed far greater forensic skill than the other's would be grounds for complaint under the rubric of background fairness but not procedural fairness. Background fairness in voting might be thought to require that the opportunities available to those supporting the different sides should be equal, or roughly proportional to their strength among the voters. On these grounds one might well object to the two-to-one superiority in resources of Republicans and Conservatives or to de Gaulle's use of the government monopoly in radio and television to further his referenda. Chance has no room for background fairness alongside procedural fairness, nor, except in a loose sense, has bargaining. Exactly why this is will be examined in Section 3 when I consider the justification of evaluations in terms of procedural and background fairness.

LEGAL JUSTICE

Procedural fairness and background fairness are concerned respectively with whether the prescribed formalities have been observed and whether the initial position of the parties was right. There is a third type of evaluation which is based on the working of procedures: legal or (more generally) rule-based justice.

Henry Sidgwick noted that one of the clearest and most frequent uses of 'justice' is in a legal context: A verdict is just when it is a correct application of the relevant rule of law. He also noted that it is not the *only* use of 'justice' because we can for example say (Hobbes notwithstanding) that a law is itself unjust.[7] The restriction to legal rules does not correspond to any difference in terms or evaluations; if the rules of the club allow expulsion for cheating and I am expelled without having cheated this is unjust in exactly the same way as a punishment inflicted by a court can be unjust. I shall therefore use the same term 'legal justice' whether the rule in question is a rule of law or not.[8]

The criterion of legal justice can be employed only where a decision is reached in the light of some rule(s), held by those taking the decision to give the answer in cases of that kind. It can there-fore be used only in conjunction with the author-itative determination procedure. There may also perhaps be a marginal application to contest: a bad interpretation of the rules could at a pinch be called unjust; but it is more natural to say that it was unfair. This is closely bound up with a point made in the previous chapter: a referee does not determine the result of a football match in the same way as a judge determines the result of a trial. A bad decision by the referee only gives an 'unfair advantage' to one side; the other side may still win. When I try to think of a referee's decision for which I should feel 'unjust' to be the appropriate epithet, I immediately light on something like sending a man off the field or recommending his suspension, which are of course examples of a direct effect on the player rather than (or at least in addition to) an indirect effect on the result of the game.[9]

JUSTIFICATIONS

LEGAL JUSTICE

So far I have simply presented procedural and background fairness and legal justice. It must now be asked why the honorific names of 'fair' and 'just' should be applied to the correct carrying out of procedures and the correct application of rules. Unless one is a 'rule worshipper' one must presumably ask for a justification of these procedural considerations in terms of conduciveness to some more general consideration, either aggregative or distributive.[10]

I shall begin by advancing three reasons of this more general kind for taking legal justice seriously. One argument is that any consistent application of a rule creates a primitive variety of equity—like cases being treated alike—though this is a rather weak sort of distributive principle because the basis of 'likeness' is stipulated by the rule and it may be outrageous. Another argument is that if known rules are applied, everyone can if he chooses avoid the consequences of infringing them; this applies to any rule, good or bad, unless it prescribes penalties for something nobody can do anything about (such as being a Jew or a Negro) or for past voluntary actions done before the rule was promulgated (such as having joined the Communist Party in the nineteen thirties). Both distributive and aggregative justifications underlie this second argument. Reasoning on aggregative premises one may say that following rules of the required kind prevents insecurity (the knock on the door in the early morning) and allows punishment to be deterrent rather than a dead loss of total want-satisfaction. On distributive premises one may say that if the required kinds of rule are followed then at least nobody will suffer for something he could not have helped doing, and this is at least a *part* of the criteria for 'desert'.

Finally, legal justice tends to reduce the incidence of unfulfilled expectations. The principle that unfulfilled expectations should be avoided if possible can itself be justified on both aggregative and distributive grounds, and then applies to legal justice as a special case.[11] The aggregative argument, for what it is worth, was elaborately worked out by Bentham in his analysis of the competing (utilitarian) claims of security and equality.

... 'the *advantage of gaining* cannot be compared with the *evil of losing.*' This proposition is itself deduced from two others. On the one hand every man naturally expects to preserve what he has; the feeling of expectation is natural to man and is founded on the ordinary course of events, since, taking the whole sum of men, acquired wealth is not only preserved but even increased. All loss is therefore unexpected, and gives rise to deception, which is a pain—the pain of frustrated expectation. On the other hand the deduction (or addition) of a portion of wealth will produce in the sum of happiness of each individual a deduction (or an addition) more or less great according to the portion deducted and the remaining or original proportion.[12]

The distributive argument is of more limited import and refers specifically to cases where people have invested money, changed jobs, moved house, etcetera, in the belief that the state of affairs which induced them to do so would continue indefinitely. If they have, then it is wrong for this state of affairs to be suddenly changed.[13]

When a legislature passes a law, not for any temporary purposes, nor limited as to the time of its operation, and which therefore may be reasonably expected to be permanent,—and persons, confiding in its permanency, embark their capital, bestow their labour, or shape the course of their life, so that their only hope of success is founded on the existence of the law,—the rights which they have acquired in the reliance upon

its continuance are termed '*vested rights*'; and persons in this situation are considered as having a moral claim on the legislature for the maintenance of the law, or at least for the allowance of a sufficient time to withdraw their investments, and to take the measures necessary for guarding against the loss consequent on so large a change.[14]

PROCEDURAL AND BACKGROUND FAIRNESS

Now take procedural and background fairness. What, first of all, is the relation between a fair trial and a just verdict? The answer seems to me to be the empirical one that fair trials tend to produce just verdicts more often than unfair trials and that the more respects in which a trial is fair the more likely it is to eventuate in a just verdict.[15] The value of fairness is thus a subordinate to that of justice: Fair procedures and background conditions are to be valued for their tendency to produce (rule-based) justice. Procedural fairness provides the minimum conditions while background fairness constitutes a refinement.[16]

Now consider contest. Again the criteria of fairness are empirically related to a tendency for fair contests to produce the 'right' results; and it is even clearer than before that the criteria for fairness are drawn with this requirement in mind. In Section 2 and again above, I have used the expression 'the right result', and this bears the same relation to the contest procedure as 'rule-based justice' does to 'rule-based authoritative determination'. But whereas one can define 'justice' as 'conformity with the rule', one cannot give a general characterization of 'the right result' except as 'a result which is an accurate index of the quality which the contest was supposed to be testing'.

Procedural fairness (conformity with the procedural rules) is always more likely than not to produce the 'right results'—whatever they may be—because it merely specifies that everyone does the same thing. Whatever it is that the race is supposed to be testing, it is hard to see how its reliability would be improved if some competitors got away with jumping the gun, except in the perverse case where the race is a blind and the real test is in gun-jumping ability.

The criteria of background fairness, on the other hand, vary according to the 'right result'. If all that is being tested is ability to knock out an opponent, there is no need for any limits on disparity of size between boxers; but if the boxing match is supposed to be a test of skill, 'background fairness' must be brought in to specify the maximum disparity beyond which skill is secondary in determining the result to brute force. Again, if an examination is supposed to be testing *effort,* a different method of marking will be required from that necessary to test *ability.*

As with rule-based authoritative determination, the main justification for procedural and background fairness lies in its tendency to produce certain results. If these results are good then fairness, as a means to them, is also good; if not, not. The results of contest are to match rewards and deprivations (perhaps only immaterial ones such as prestige and chagrin) to performance, and for this to be desirable the scale of rewards and deprivations must be such that when it is adhered to they are appropriate to the performances. 'Equality of opportunity' (the honorific name for background and procedural fairness) is not very important if the achievements which are rewarded are base or trifling.[17] However, as before, we can suggest that there are certain virtues in procedural and background fairness in a contest regardless of the result to which the contest is directed. These are, as before, the minimal equity of like cases being treated alike (even though 'likeness' may be defined in any way) and the fact that contestants at least know what they are supposed to be trying to do. It must be allowed that these general considerations seem to be a good deal weaker than those raised in connection with rule-based authoritative determination.

The link between justifying procedural and background fairness and justifying the use of the procedure itself comes out even more clearly if we look at voting. If we suppose that the object of the voting procedure is to ascertain the opinions of the voters then plainly the formal requirements are a necessary condition of this. If in addition we say that the object is to secure their informed opinions we have to introduce the background conditions as well. If these objects are good then the means to them are good.

I have now covered the three procedures of whose operation both procedural and background fairness can be predicated. Of the rest, chance, I remarked, is liable to procedural fairness (or unfairness) only. This follows from the rather peculiar fact that there is no end in view when a chance procedure is employed beyond settling something on a random basis.[18] Since the end is identified with the actual mechanical procedure there is no room for background fairness. Indeed, procedural and substantive fairness are merged since the distributive value *is* the randomness.

I also suggested that bargaining is in the reverse position. It cannot be procedurally fair (or unfair) but at least in a loose sense background fairness (or unfairness) can sometimes be attributed to it. Indeed, I may add that the same can sometimes be said of combat. This odd state of affairs arises whenever something which those taking part in it define to themselves as combat is at the same time being evaluated by a third party as if it were a contest. This observer, but not the combatants, may then speak of fairness—but only loosely and perhaps one might even say improperly.[19]

So far I have dealt with justifications for fairness taking one procedure at a time; but are there general reasons for following a prescribed form which applies to *any* form? I can suggest two. One is the argument (offered by Rawls) from 'fair play'.[20] This is essentially a distributive argument, which runs as follows: If you have accepted benefits arising from a certain practice then (unless you have given notice to the contrary) it is only fair that you should continue to adhere to it even when in some specific case it would suit you better not to. The other is an aggregative argument to the effect that the more a society is divided on substantive values, the more precious as a means of preserving social peace is any agreement that can be reached on procedure. The connection between liberalism and an emphasis on 'due process' is not fortuitous. Procedures cannot be justified by the results they produce because a result which one approves of another disapproves; the adherence to procedures is justified instead by saying that everyone agrees on them and this is the only thing on which everyone does agree. Whether these considerations are sufficiently universal or compelling to account for the importance which is often attached to a meticulous adherence to prescribed forms I shall not guess. Perhaps there is an element of 'rule worship' which can be supported by neither aggregative nor distributive principles; but the rationality of general adherence to prescribed forms is high on almost any principles.

NOTES

1. 'Impartiality as an obligation of justice may be said to mean being exclusively influenced by considerations which it is supposed ought to influence the particular case in hand, and resisting the solicitation of any motives which prompt to conduct different from what these considerations would dictate.' J. S. Mill, *Utilitarianism,* Chapter V.

2. See the Franks Report (Cmnd 218, 1957), *passim.*

3. It is quite correct for the old saw to include 'love' in the same category, at least if it is taken to mean 'attaining the object of sexual desire'. There are no rules, no formal requirements, to satisfy before you can get your girl (or your man); you may have all the virtues but if you don't happen to have appeal you don't win.

4. I am not saying that war, still less combat in general, cannot be limited in its means (or in its ends) but that there cannot, by my definitions, be a conventional connection between achieving a certain feat and winning; the only connection can be that the other side in fact gives up. A strike or a lockout, for example, can be limited in means (no shooting, no sabotage) and ends (a rise of 5 per cent or a reduction of 5 per cent). But it is still combat and not contest because each is aiming directly at changing the attitude of the other, not at some separate standard of achievement which is then taken as settling the dispute. A contest would occur if the trade union and the employer agreed in advance that whichever side was the first to cost the other a million pounds should get its demand fulfilled.

5. A duel *à l'outrance* of course removes the loser not conventionally but necessarily; but the removal is still in the course of an activity with formal rules. If we have a duel fixed for tomorrow it would still be 'unfair' for me to shoot you in the back today as you walk along the street.

6. E.g., the 'Codes of Fair Practice' produced under the NRA, in the New Deal.

7. H. Sidgwick, *The Methods of Ethics,* Book III, Chapter V.

8. Sidgwick indeed extended the term 'legal justice' to cover promises and similar social obligations.

9. The *result* of a match may be unjust in that it does not reflect the relative merits of the teams, but this is a different use of 'unjust' bound up with desert. An unjust result in this sense may be due equally to a bad decision or an unlucky gust of wind.

10. See J. J. C. Smart, *An Outline of a System of Utilitarian Ethics* (Melbourne, 1961). Smart's 'utilitarianism' appears to be *entirely* made up of a rejection of 'rule worship'. Not only is the position he defends not (necessarily) hedonistic; it is not even aggregative. This—formerly, I should have thought, the sole distinguishing mark of nonhedonistic utilitarianism—is abandoned when Smart admits that different utilitarians may disagree on distributive questions.

11. Sidgwick, in *The Methods of Ethics* sugₕ avoiding of unfulfilled expectations constitutes m Common Sense idea of 'justice' but (at least nowaday tice' does not seem to be used so widely. There still seems be agreement that there *is* a value in not frustrating expectations, however. Consider the contrasting attitudes of many people to death duties on one hand and a capital levy on the other. (I am referring to the opinions of those who are naïve enough to believe that death duties, as currently operated in the UK, are effective in reducing fortunes.)

12. In Halévy, *The Growth of Philosophical Radicalism* (Beacon, 1955), p. 40. Note that the second argument would sometimes *favour* redistribution. Take £10 from a man with £1,000 and give it to one with £100. You decrease the happiness of the former by 1 per cent, but increase the happiness of the latter by 10 per cent. The argument in any case rests on a peculiar assumption about the marginal utility of money —far more questionable than the simple diminishing marginal utility idea.

13. Sidgwick's claim that 'just' is used to refer to fulfilling expectations would be more plausible if restricted to cases which fall under this argument.

14. Sir George Cornewall Lewis, *Remarks on the Use and Abuse of Some Political Terms* (London, 1832), p. 25.

15. When I say that this is a matter of fact I do not mean that the dovetailing of fair procedures and just results is an accident, for the criteria of a fair trial are selected with an eye on this dovetailing. What I am denying is any analytic connection between the two such that a just verdict entails a fair trial or a fair trial entails a just verdict: there can be fair trials which still produce unjust verdicts.

16. Indeed, it is quite plausible to suggest that background fairness is only relevant to trials insofar as they partake of contest, by their use of the adversary system which thus places a premium on equally matched counsel. Courts do not *have* to be so organized. See Sybille Bedford, *The Faces of Justice* (London, 1961).

17. Compare 'equality before the law', the honorific name for procedural fairness in connection with rule-based authoritative determination: 'Equality before the law' does not guarantee that outrageous actions are not rewarded and good ones punished. It should hardly need saying that neither form of procedural 'equality' has anything to do with substantial equality though the possibility of confusion is convenient for those who prefer the rhetoric to the reality of equality. (See, e.g., C. A. R. Crosland, *The Future of Socialism* (London, 1956)). Plato in *The Republic* and Michael Young in *The Rise of the Meritocracy* (Penguin Books, 1961) have both given us pictures of extremely hierarchical societies based on 'equality of opportunity'.

18. An apparent exception would be the use of a random device in the belief that God will arrange for a substantively good result; but then the arrangement is not (in the eyes of the people operating it) to be regarded as invoking a *chance* mechanism.

19. This point is pursued in the context of J. K. Galbraith's 'concept of countervailing power'.

20. John Rawls, 'Justice as Fairness', *Philosophical Review,* LXVII (1958).

I

It might seem at first sight that the concepts of justice and fairness are the same, and that there is no reason to distinguish them, or to say that one is more fundamental than the other. I think that this impression is mistaken. In this paper I wish to show that the fundamental idea in the concept of justice is fairness; and I wish to offer an analysis of the concept of justice from this point of view. To bring out the force of this claim, and the analysis based upon it, I shall then argue that it is this aspect of justice for which utilitarianism, in its classical form, is unable to account, but which is expressed, even if misleadingly, by the idea of the social contract.

To start with I shall develop a particular conception of justice by stating and commenting upon two principles which specify it, and by considering the circumstances and conditions under which they may be thought to arise. The principles defining this conception, and the conception itself, are, of course, familiar. It may be possible, however, by using the notion of fairness as a framework, to assemble and to look at them in a new way. Before stating this conception, however, the following preliminary matters should be kept in mind.

Throughout I consider justice only as a virtue of social institutions, or what I shall call practices.[1] The principles of justice are regarded as formulating restrictions as to how practices may define positions and offices, and assign thereto powers and liabilities, rights, and duties. Justice as a virtue of particular actions or of persons I do not take up at all. It is important to distinguish these various subjects of justice, since the meaning of the concept varies according to whether it is applied to practices, particular actions, or persons. These meanings are, indeed, connected, but they are not identical. I shall confine my discussion to the sense of justice as applied to practices, since this sense is the basic one. Once it is understood, the other senses should go quite easily.

Justice is to be understood in its customary sense as representing but *one* of the many virtues of social institutions, for these may be antiquated, inefficient, degrading, or any number of other things, without being unjust. Justice is not to be confused with an all-inclusive vision of a good society; it is only one part of any such conception. It is important, for example, to distinguish that sense of equality which is an aspect of the concept of justice from that sense of equality which belongs to a more comprehensive social ideal. There may well be inequalities which one concedes are just, or at least not unjust, but which, nevertheless, one wishes, on other grounds, to do away with. I shall focus attention, then, on the usual sense of justice in which it is essentially the elimination of arbitrary distinctions and the establishment, within the structure of a practice, of a proper balance between competing claims.

Finally, there is no need to consider the principles discussed below as *the* principles of justice. For the moment it is sufficient that they are typical of a family of principles normally associated with the concept of justice. The way in which the principles of this family resemble one another, as shown by the background against which they may be thought to arise, will be made clear by the whole of the subsequent argument.

*From *The Philosophical Review,* Vol. 67 (1958), pp. 164–94. Reprinted by permission of the author and the publisher. An abbreviated version of this paper (less than one-half the length) was presented in a symposium with the same title at the American Philosophical Association, Eastern Division, December 28, 1957, and appeared in the *Journal of Philosophy,* LIV, 653–662. Footnotes have been renumbered.

II

The conception of justice which I want to develop may be stated in the form of two principles as follows: First, each person participating in a practice, or affected by it, has an equal right to the most extensive liberty compatible with a like liberty for all; and second, inequalities are arbitrary unless it is reasonable to expect that they will work out for everyone's advantage, and provided the positions and offices to which they attach, or from which they may be gained, are open to all. These principles express justice as a complex of three ideas: liberty, equality, and reward for services contributing to the common good.[2]

The term "person" is to be construed variously depending on the circumstances. On some occasions it will mean human individuals, but in others it may refer to nations, provinces, business firms, churches, teams, and so on. The principles of justice apply in all these instances, although there is a certain logical priority to the case of human individuals. As I shall use the term "person," it will be ambiguous in the manner indicated.

The first principle holds, of course, only if other things are equal: That is, while there must always be a justification for departing from the initial position of equal liberty (which is defined by the pattern of rights and duties, powers and liabilities, established by a practice), and the burden of proof is placed on him who would depart from it, nevertheless, there can be, and often there is, a justification for doing so. Now, that similar particular cases, as defined by a practice, should be treated similarly as they arise, is part of the very concept of a practice; it is involved in the notion of an activity in accordance with rules.[3] The first principle expresses an analogous conception, but as applied to the structure of practices themselves. It holds, for example, that there is a presumption against the distinctions and classifications made by legal systems and other practices to the extent that they infringe on the original and equal liberty of the persons participating them. The second principle defines how this presumption may be rebutted.

It might be argued at this point that justice requires only an equal liberty. If, however, a greater liberty were possible for all without loss or conflict, then it would be irrational to settle on a lesser liberty. There is no reason for circumscribing rights unless their exercise would be incompatible, or would render the practice defining them less effective. Therefore no serious distortion of the concept of justice is likely to follow from including within it the concept of the greatest equal liberty.

The second principle defines what sorts of inequalities are permissible; it specifies how the presumption laid down by the first principle may be put aside. Now by inequalities it is best to understand not *any* differences between offices and positions, but differences in the benefits and burdens attached to them either directly or indirectly, such as prestige and wealth, or liability to taxation and compulsory services. Players in a game do not protest against there being different positions, such as batter, pitcher, catcher, and the like, nor to there being various privileges and powers as specified by the rules; nor do the citizens of a country object to there being the different offices of government such as president, senator, governor, judge, and so on, each with its special rights and duties. It is not differences of this kind that are normally thought of as inequalities, but differences in the resulting distribution established by a practice, or made possible by it, of the things men strive to attain or avoid. Thus they may complain about the pattern of honors and rewards set up by a practice (for example, the privileges and salaries of government officials) or they may object to the distribution of power and wealth which results from the various ways in which men avail themselves of the opportunities allowed by it (for example, the concentration of wealth which may develop in a free price system allowing large entrepreneurial or speculative gains).

It should be noted that the second principle holds that an inequality is allowed only if there is reason to believe that the practice with the inequality, or resulting in it, will work for the advantage of *every* party engaging in it. Here it is important to stress that *every* party must gain from the inequality. Since the principle applies to practices, it implies that the representative man in every office or position defined by a practice, when he views it as a going concern, must find it reasonable to prefer his condition and prospects with the inequality to what they would be under the practice without it. The principle excludes, therefore, the justification of inequalities on the grounds that the disadvantages of those in one position are outweighed by the greater advantages of those in another position. This rather simple restriction is the main modification I wish to make in the utilitarian principle as usually understood. When coupled with the notion of a practice, it is a restriction of consequence[4], and one which some utilitarians, for example, Hume and Mill, have used in their discussions of justice without realizing apparently its significance, or at least without calling attention to it.[5] Why it is a significant modification of principle, changing one's conception of justice entirely, the whole of my argument will show.

Further, it is also necessary that the various offices to which special benefits or burdens attach are open to all. It may be, for example, to the common advantage, as just defined, to attach special benefits to certain offices. Perhaps by doing so the requisite talent can be attracted to them and encouraged to give its best efforts. But any offices having special benefits must be won in a fair competition in which contestants are judged on their merits. If some offices were not open, those excluded would normally be justified in feeling unjustly treated, even if they benefited from the greater efforts of those who were allowed to compete for them. Now if one can assume that offices are open, it is necessary only to consider the design of practices themselves and how they jointly, as a system, work together. It will be a mistake to focus attention on the varying relative positions of particular persons, who may be known to us by their proper names, and to require that each such change, as a once for all transaction viewed in isolation, must be in itself just. It is the system of practices which is to be judged, and judged from a general point of view: Unless one is prepared to criticize it from the standpoint of a representative man holding some particular office, one has no complaint against it.

III

Given these principles one might try to derive them from a priori principles of reason, or claim that they were known by intuition. These are familiar enough steps and, at least in the case of the first principle, might be made with some success. Usually, however, such arguments, made at this point, are unconvincing. They are not likely to lead to an understanding of the basis of the principles of justice, not at least as principles of justice. I wish, therefore, to look at the principles in a different way.

Imagine a society of persons amongst whom a certain system of practices is *already* well established. Now suppose that by and large they are mutually self-interested; their allegiance to their established practices is normally founded on the prospect of self-advantage. One need not assume that, in all senses of the term "person," the persons in this society are mutually self-interested. If the characterization as mutually self-interested applies when the line of division is the family, it may still be true that members of families are bound by ties of sentiment and affection and willingly acknowledge duties in contradiction to self-interest. Mutual self-interestedness in the relations between families, nations, churches, and the like, is commonly associated with intense loyalty and devotion on the part of individual members. Therefore, one can form a more realistic conception of this society if one thinks of it as consisting of mutually self-interested families, or some other association. Further, it is not necessary to suppose that these persons are mutually self-interested under all circumstances, but only in the usual situations in which they participate in their common practices.

Now suppose also that these persons are rational: they know their own interests more or less accurately; they are capable to tracing out the likely consequences of adopting one practice rather than another; they are capable of adhering to a course of action once they have decided upon it; they can resist present temptations and the enticements of immediate gain; and the bare knowledge or perception of the difference between their condition and that of others is not, within certain limits and in itself, a source of great dissatisfaction. Only the last point adds anything to the usual definition of rationality. This defination should allow, I think, for the idea that a rational man would not be greatly downcast from knowing, or seeing, that others are in a better position than himself, unless he thought their being so was the result of injustice, or the consequence of letting chance work itself out for no useful common purpose, and so on. So if these persons strike us as unpleasantly egoistic, they are at least free in some degree from the fault of envy.[6]

Finally, assume that these persons have roughly similar needs and interests, or needs and interests in various ways complementary, so that fruitful cooperation amongst them is possible; and suppose that they are sufficiently equal in power and ability to guarantee that in normal circumstances none is able to dominate the others. This condition (as well as the others) may seem excessively vague; but in view of the conception of justice to which the argument leads, there seems no reason for making it more exact here.

Since these persons are conceived as engaging in their common practices, which are already established, there is no question of our supposing them to come together to deliberate as to how they will set these practices up for the first time. Yet we can imagine that from time to time they discuss with one another whether any of them has a legitimate complaint against their established institutions. Such discussions are perfectly natural in any normal society. Now suppose that they have settled on doing this in the following way. They first try to arrive at the principles by which complaints, and so practices themselves, are to be judged. Their procedure for this is to let each person propose the principles upon which he wishes his complaints to be tried with the understanding that, if acknowledged, the complaints of others will be similarly tried, and that no complaints will be heard at all until everyone is roughly to one mind as to how complaints are to be judged. They each understand further that the principles proposed and acknowledged on this occasion are binding on future occasions. Thus each will be wary of proposing a principle which would give him a peculiar advantage, in his present circumstances, supposing it to be accepted. Each person knows that he will be bound by it in future circumstances the peculiarities of which cannot be known, and which might well be such that the principle is then to his disadvantage. The idea is that everyone should be required to make *in advance* a firm commitment, which others also may reasonably be expected to make, and that no one be given the opportunity to tailor the canons of a legitimate complaint to fit his own special condition, and then to discard them when they no longer suit his purpose. Hence each person will propose principles of a general kind which will, to a large degree, gain their sense from the various applications to be made of them, the particular circumstances of which being as yet unknown. These principles will express the conditions in accordance with which each is the least unwilling to have his interests limited in the design of practices, given the competing interests of the others, on the supposition that the interests of others will be limited likewise. The restrictions which would so arise might be thought of as those a person would keep in mind if he were designing a practice in which his enemy were to assign him his place.

The two main parts of his conjectural account have a definite significance. The character and respective situations of the parties reflect the typical circumstances in which questions of justice arise. The procedure whereby principles are proposed and acknowledged represents constraints, analogous to those of having a morality, whereby rational and mutually self-interested persons are brought to act reasonably. Thus the first part reflects the fact that questions of justice arise when conflicting claims are made upon the design of a practice and where it is taken for granted that each person will insist, as far as possible, on what he considers his rights. It is typical of cases of justice to involve persons who are pressing on one another their claims, between which a fair balance or equilibrium must be found. On the other hand, as expressed by the second part, having a morality must at least imply the acknowledgment of principles as impartially applying to one's own conduct as well as to another's, and moreover principles which may constitute a constraint, or limitation, upon the pursuit of one's own interests. There are, of course, other aspects of having a morality: The acknowledgment of moral principles must show itself in accepting a reference to them as reasons for limiting one's claims, in acknowledging the burden of providing a special explanation, or excuse, when one acts contrary to them, or else in showing shame and remorse and a desire to make amends, and so on. It is sufficient to remark here that having a morality is analogous to having made a firm commitment in advance; for one must acknowledge the principles of morality even when to one's disadvantage.[7] A man whose moral judgments always coincided with his interests could be suspected of having no morality at all.

Thus the two parts of the foregoing account are intended to mirror the kinds of circumstances in which questions of justice arise and the constraints which having a morality would impose upon persons so situated. In this way one can see how the acceptance of the principles of justice might come about, for given all these conditions as described, it would be natural if the two principles of justice were to be acknowledged. Since there is no way of anyone to win special advantages for himself, each might consider it reasonable to acknowledge equality as an initial principle. There is, however, no reason why they should regard this position as final; for if there are inequalities which satisfy the second principle, the immediate gain which equality would allow can be considered as intelligently invested in view of its future return. If, as is quite likely, these inequalities work as incentives to draw out better efforts, the members of this society may look upon them as concessions to human nature: they, like us, may think that people ideally should want to serve one another. But as they are mutually self-interested, their acceptance of these inequalities is merely the acceptance of the relations in which they actually stand, and a recognition of the motives which lead them to engage in their common practices. *They* have no title to complain of one another. And so provided that the conditions of the principle are met, there is no reason why they should not allow such inequalities. Indeed, it would be short-sighted of them to do so, and could result, in most cases, only from their being dejected by the bare knowledge, or perception, that others are better situated. Each person will, however, insist on an advantage to himself, and so on a common advantage, for none is willing to sacrifice anything for the others.

These remarks are not offered as a proof that persons so conceived and circumstanced would settle on the two principles, but only to show that these principles could have such a background, and so can be viewed as those principles which mutually self-interested and rational persons, when similarly situated and required to make in advance a firm commitment, could acknowledge as restrictions governing the assignment of rights and duties in their common practices, and thereby accept as limiting their rights against one another. The principles of justice may, then, be regarded as those principles which arise when the constraints of having a morality are imposed upon parties in the typical circumstances of justice.

IV

These ideas are, of course, connected with a familiar way of thinking about justice which goes back at least to the Greek Sophists, and which regards the acceptance of the principles of justice as a compromise between persons of roughly equal power who would enforce their will on each other if they could, but who, in view of the equality of forces amongst them and for the sake of their own peace and security, acknowledge certain forms of conduct insofar as prudence seems to require. Justice is thought of as a pact between rational egoists the stability of which is dependent on a balance of power and a similarity of circumstances.[8] While the previous account is connected with this tradition, and with its most recent variant, the theory of games,[9] it differs from it in several important respects which, to forestall misinterpretations, I will set out here.

First, I wish to use the previous conjectural account of the background of justice as a way of analyzing the concept. I do not want, therefore, to be interpreted as assuming a general theory of human motivation: When I suppose that the parties are mutually self-interested, and are not willing to have their (substantial) interests sacrificed to others, I am referring to their conduct and motives as they are taken for granted in cases where questions of justice ordinarily arise. Justice is the virtue of practices where there are assumed to be competing interests and conflicting claims, and where it is supposed that persons will press their rights on each other. That persons are mutually self-interested in certain situations and for certain purposes is what gives rise to the question of justice in practices covering those circumstances. Amongst an association of saints, if such a community could really exist, the disputes about justice could hardly occur; for they would all work selflessly together for one end, the glory of God as defined by their common religion, and reference to this end would settle every question of right. The justice of practices does not come up until there are several different parties (whether we think of these as individuals, associations, or nations and so on, is irrelevant) who do press their claims on one another, and who do regard themselves as representatives of interests which deserve to be considered. Thus the previous account involves no general theory of human motivation. Its intent is simply to incorporate into the conception of justice the relations of men to one another which set the stage for questions of justice. It makes no difference how wide or general these relations are, as this matter does not bear on the analysis of the concept.

Again, in contrast to the various conceptions of the social contract, the several parties do not establish any particular society or practice; they do not convenant to obey a particular sovereign body or to accept a given constitution.[10] Nor do they, as in the theory of games (in certain respects a marvelously sophisticated development of this tradition), decide on individual strategies adjusted to their respective circumstances in the game. What the parties do is to *jointly* acknowledge certain *principles* of appraisal relating to their common *practices* either as already established or merely proposed. They accede to standards of judgment, not to a given practice; they do not make any specific agreement, or bargain, or adopt a particular strategy. The subject of their acknowledgment is, therefore, very general indeed; it is simply the acknowledgment of certain principles of judgment, fulfilling certain general conditions, to be used in criticizing the arrangement of their common affairs. The relations of mutual self-interest [among] the parties who are similarly circumstanced mirror the conditions under which questions of justice arise, and the procedure by which the principles of judgment are proposed and acknowledged reflects the constraints of having a morality. Each aspect, then, of preceding hypothetical account serves the purpose of bringing out a feature of the notion of justice. One could, if one liked, view the principles of justice as the "solution" of this highest order "game" of adopting, subject to the procedure described, principles of argument for all coming particular "games" whose peculiarities one can in no way foresee. But this comparison, while no doubt helpful, must not obscure the fact that this highest order "game" is of a special sort.[11] Its significance is that its various pieces represent aspects of the concept of justice.

Finally, I do not, of course, conceive the several parties as necessarily coming together to establish their common practices for the first time. Some institutions may, indeed, be set up *de novo;* but I have framed the preceding account so that it will apply when the full complement of social institutions already exists and represents the result of a long period of development. Nor is the account in any way fictitious. In any society where people reflect on their institutions they will have an idea of what principles of justice would be acknowledged under the conditions described, and there will be occasions when the questions of justice are actually discussed in this way. Therefore if their practices do not accord with these principles, this will affect the quality of their social relations. For in this case there will be some recognized situations wherein the parties are mutually aware that one of them is being forced to accept what the other would concede is injust. The foregoing analysis may then be thought of as representing the actual quality of relations [among] persons as defined by practices accepted as just. In such practices the parties will acknowledge the principles on which it is constructed, and the general recognition of this fact shows itself in the absence of resentment and in the sense of being justly treated. Thus one common objection to the theory of the social contract, its apparently historical and fictitious character, is avoided.

V

That the principles of justice may be regarded as arising in the manner described illustrates an important fact about them. Not only does it bring out the idea that justice is a primitive moral notion in that it arises once the concept of morality is imposed on mutually self-interested agents similarly circumstanced, but it emphasizes that, fundamental to justice, is the concept of fairness which relates to right dealing between persons who are cooperating with or competing against one another, as when one speaks of fair games, fair competition, and fair bargains. The question of fairness arises when free persons, who have no authority over one another, are engaging in a joint activity and amongst themselves settling or acknowledging the rules which define it and which determine the respective shares in its benefits and burdens. A practice will strike the parties as fair if none feels that, by participating in it, they or any of the others are taken advantage of, or forced to give in to claims, which they do not regard as legitimate. This implies that each has a conception of legitimate claims which he thinks it reasonable for others as well as himself to acknowledge. If one thinks of the principles of justice as arising in the manner described, then they do define this sort of conception. A practice is just or fair, then, when it satisfies the principles which those who participate in it could propose to one another for mutual acceptance under the aforementioned circumstances. Persons engaged in a just, or fair, practice can face one another openly and support their respective positions, should they appear questionable, by reference to principles which it is reasonable to expect each to accept.

It is this notion of the possibility of mutual acknowledgment of principles by free persons who have no authority over one another which makes the concept of fairness fundamental to justice. Only if such acknowledgment is possible can there be true community between persons in their common practices; otherwise their relations will appear to them as founded to some extent on force. If, in ordinary speech, fairness applies more particularly to practices in which there is a choice whether to engage or not (for example, in games, business competition), and justice to practices in which there is no choice (for example, in slavery), the element of necessity does not render the conception of mutual acknowledgment inapplicable, although it may make it much more urgent to change unjust than unfair institutions. For one activity in which one can always engage is that of proposing and acknowledging principles to one another supposing each to be similarly circumstanced; and to judge practices by the principles so arrived at is to apply the standard of fairness to them.

Now if the participants in a practice accept its rules as fair, and so have no complaint to lodge against it, there arises a prima facie duty (and a corresponding prima facie right) of the parties to each other to act in accordance with the practice when it falls upon them to comply. When any number of persons engage in a practice, or conduct a joint undertaking according to rules, and thus restrict their liberty, those who have submitted to these restrictions when required have the right to a similar acquiescence on the part of those who have benefited by their submission. These conditions will obtain if a practice is correctly acknowledged to be fair, for in this case all who participate in it will benefit from it. The rights and duties so arising are special rights and duties in that they depend on previous actions voluntarily undertaken, in this case on the parties having engaged in a common practice and knowingly accepted its benefits.[12] It is not, however, an obligation which presupposes a deliberate performative act in the sense of a promise, or contract, and the like.[13] An unfortunate mistake of proponents of the idea of the social contract was to suppose that political obligation does require some such act, or at least to use language which suggests it. It is sufficient that one has knowingly participated in and accepted the benefits of a practice acknowledged to be fair. This prima facie obligation may, of course, be overridden: It may happen, when it comes one's turn to follow a rule, that other considerations will justify not doing so. But one cannot, in general, be released from this obligation by denying the justice of the practice only when it falls on one to obey. If a person rejects a practice, he should, so far as possible, declare his intention in advance, and avoid participating in it or enjoying its benefits.

This duty I have called that of fair play, but it should be admitted that to refer to it in this way is, perhaps, to extend the ordinary notion of fairness. Usually acting unfairly is not so much the breaking of any particular rule, even if the infraction is difficult to detect (cheating), but taking advantage of loopholes or ambiguities in rules, availing oneself of unexpected or special circumstances which make it impossible to enforce them, insisting that rules be enforced to one's advantage when they should be suspended, and more generally, acting contrary to the intention of a practice. It is for this reason that one speaks of the sense of fair play: Acting fairly requires more than simply being able to follow rules; what is fair must often be felt, or perceived, one wants to say. It is not, however, an unnatural extension of the duty of fair play to have it include the obligation which participants who have knowingly accepted the benefits of their common practice owe to each other to act in accordance with it when their performance falls due; for it is usually considered unfair if someone accepts the benefits of a practice but refuses to do his part in maintaining it. Thus one might say of the tax-dodger that he violates the duty of fair play: He accepts the benefits of government but will not do his part in releasing resources to it; and members of labor unions often say that fellow workers who refuse to join are being unfair: They refer to them as "free riders," as persons who enjoy what are the supposed benefits of unionism, higher wages, shorter hours, job security, and the like, but who refuse to share in its burdens in the form of paying dues, and so on.

The duty of fair play stands beside other prima facie duties such as fidelity and gratitude as a basic moral notion; yet it is not to be confused with them.[14] These duties are all clearly distinct, as would be obvious from their definitions. As with any moral duty, that of fair play implies a constraint on self-interest in particular cases; on occasion it enjoins conduct which a rational egoist strictly defined would not decide upon. So while justice does not require of anyone that he sacrifice his interests in that *general position* and procedure whereby the principles of justice are proposed and acknowledged, it may happen that in particular situations, arising in the context of engaging in a practice, the duty of fair play will often cross his interests in the sense that he will be required to forego particular advantages which the peculiarities of his circumstances might permit him to take. There is, of course, nothing surprising in this. It is simply the consequence of the firm commitment which the parties may be supposed to have made, or which they would make, in the general position, together with the fact that they have participated in and accepted the benefits of a practice which they regard as fair.

Now the acknowledgment of this constraint in particular cases, which is manifested in acting fairly or wishing to make amends, feeling ashamed, and the like, when one has evaded it, is one of the forms of conduct by which participants in a common practice exhibit their recognition of each other as persons with similar interests and capacities. In the same way that, failing a special explanation, the criterion for the recognition of suffering is helping one who suffers, acknowledging the duty of fair play is a necessary part of the criterion of recognizing another as a person with similar interests and feelings as oneself.[15] A person who never under any circumstances showed

a wish to help others in pain would show, at the same time, that he did not recognize that they were in pain; nor could he have any feelings of affection or friendship for anyone; for having these feelings implies, failing special circumstances, that he comes to their aid when they are suffering. Recognition that another is a person in pain shows itself in sympathetic action; this primitive natural response of compassion is one of those responses upon which the various forms of moral conduct are built.

Similarly, the acceptance of the duty of fair play by participants in a common practice is a reflection in each person of the recognition of the aspirations and interests of the others to be realized by their joint activity. Failing a special explanation, their acceptance of it is a necessary part of the criterion for their recognizing one another as persons with similar interests and capacities, as the conception of their relations in the general position supposes them to be. Otherwise they would show no recognition of one another as persons with similar capacities and interests, and indeed, in some cases perhaps hypothetical, they would not recognize one another as persons at all, but as complicated objects involved in a complicated activity. To recognize another as a person one must respond to him and act towards him in certain ways; and these ways are intimately connected with the various prima facie duties. Acknowledging these duties in *some* degree, and so having the elements of morality, is not a matter of choice, or of intuiting moral qualities, or a matter of the expression of feelings or attitudes (the three interpretations between which philosophical opinion frequently oscillates); it is simply the possession of one of the forms of conduct in which the recognition of others as persons is manifested.

These remarks are unhappily obscure. Their main purpose here, however, is to forestall, together with the remarks in section IV, the misinterpretation that, on the view presented, the acceptance of justice and the acknowledgment of the duty of fair play depends in every day life solely on their being a *de facto* balance of forces between the parties. It would indeed be foolish to underestimate the importance of such a balance in securing justice; but it is not the only basis thereof. The recognition of one another as persons with similar interests and capacities engaged in a common practice must, failing a special explanation, show itself in the acceptance of the principles of justice and the acknowledgment of the duty of fair play.

The conception at which we have arrived, then, is that the principles of justice may be thought of as arising once the constraints of having a morality are imposed upon rational and mutually self-interested parties who are related and situated in a special way. A practice is just if it is in accordance with the principles which all who participate in it might reasonably be expected to propose or to acknowledge before one another when they are similarly circumstanced and required to make a firm commitment in advance without knowledge of what will be their peculiar condition, and thus when it meets standards which the parties could accept as fair should occasion arise for them to debate its merits. Regarding the participants themselves, once persons knowingly engage in a practice which they acknowledge to be fair and accept the benefits of doing so, they are bound by the duty of fair play to follow the rules when it comes their turn to do so, and this implies a limitation on their pursuit of self-interest in particular cases.

Now one consequence of this conception is that, where it applies, there is no moral value in the satisfaction of a claim incompatible with it. Such a claim violates the conditions of reciprocity and community amongst persons, and he who presses it, not being willing to acknowledge it when pressed by another, has no grounds for complaint when it is denied; whereas he against whom it is pressed can complain. As it cannot be mutually acknowledged it is a resort to coercion; granting the claim is possible only if one party can compel acceptance of what the other will not admit. But it makes no sense to concede claims the denial of which cannot be complained of in preference to claims the denial of which can be objected to. Thus in deciding on the justice of a practice it is not enough to ascertain that it answers to wants and interests in the fullest and most effective manner. For if any of these conflict with justice, they should not be counted, as their satisfaction is no reason at all for having a practice. It would be irrelevant to say, even if true, that it resulted in the greatest satisfaction of desire. In tallying up the merits of a practice one must toss out the satisfaction of interests the claims of which are incompatible with the principles of justice.

VI

The discussion so far has been excessively abstract. While this is perhaps unavoidable, I should now like to bring out some of the features of the conception of justice as fairness by comparing it with the conception of justice in classical utilitarianism as represented by Bentham and Sidgwick, and its counterpart in welfare economics. This conception assimilates justice to benevolence and the latter in turn to the most efficient design of institutions to promote the general welfare. Justice is a kind of efficiency.[16]

Now it is said occasionally that this form of utilitarianism puts no restrictions on what might be a just assignment of rights and duties in that there might be circumstances which, on utilitarian grounds, would justify institutions highly offensive to our ordinary sense of justice. But the classical utilitarian conception is not totally unprepared for this objection. Beginning with the notion that the general happiness can be represented by a social utility function consisting of a sum of individual utility functions with identical weights (this being the meaning of the maxim that each counts for one and no more than one),[17] it is commonly assumed that the utility functions of individuals are similar in all essential respects. Differences [among] individuals are ascribed to accidents of education and upbringing, and they should not be taken into account. This assumption, coupled with that of diminishing marginal utility, results in a prima facie case for equality, for example, of equality in the distribution of income during any given period of time, laying aside indirect effects on the future. But even if utilitarianism is interpreted as having such restrictions built into the utility function, and even if it is supposed that these restrictions have in practice much the same result as the application of the principles of justice (and appear, perhaps, to be ways of expressing these principles in the language of mathematics and psychology), the fundamental idea is very different from the conception of justice as fairness. For one thing, that the principles of justice should be accepted is interpreted as the contingent result of a higher order administrative decision. The form of this decision is regarded as being similar to that of an entrepreneur deciding how much to produce of this or that commodity in view of its marginal revenue, or to that of someone distributing goods to needy persons according to the relative urgency of their wants. The choice between practices is thought of as being made on the basis of the allocation of benefits and burdens to individuals (these being measured by the present capitalized value of their utility over the full period of the practice's existence), which results from the distribution of rights and duties established by a practice.

Moreover, the individuals receiving these benefits are not conceived as being related in any way: They represent so many different directions in which limited resources may be allocated. The value of assigning resources to one direction rather than another depends solely on the preferences and interests of individuals as individuals. The satisfaction of desire has its value irrespective of the moral relations between persons, say as members of a joint undertaking, of the claims which, in the name of these interests, they are prepared to make on one another;[18] and it is this value which is to be taken into account by the (ideal) legislator who is conceived as adjusting the rules of the system from the center so as to maximize the value of the social utility function.

It is thought that the principles of justice will not be violated by a legal system so conceived provided these executive decisions are correctly made. In this fact the principles of justice are said to have their derivation and explanation; they simply express the most important general features of social institutions in which the administrative problem is solved in the best way. These principles have, indeed, a special urgency because, given the facts of human nature, so much depends on them; and this explains the peculiar quality of the moral feelings associated with justice.[19] This assimilation of justice to a higher order executive decision, certainly a striking conception, is central to classical utilitarianism; and it also brings out its profound individualism, in one sense of this ambiguous word. It regards persons as so many *separate* directions in which benefits and burdens may be assigned; and the value of the satisfaction or dissatisfaction of desire is not thought to depend in any way on the moral relations in which individuals stand, or on the

kinds of claims which they are willing, in the pursuit of their interests, to press on each other.

VII

Many social decisions are, of course, of an administrative nature. Certainly this is so when it is a matter of social utility in what one may call its ordinary sense: that is, when it is a question of the efficient design of social institutions for the use of common means to achieve common ends. In this case either the benefits and burdens may be assumed to be impartially distributed, or the question of distribution is misplaced, as in the instance of maintaining public order and security or national defense. But as an interpretation of the basis of the principles of justice, classical utilitarianism is mistaken. It *permits* one to argue, for example, that slavery is unjust on the grounds that the advantages to the slaveholder as slaveholder do not counterbalance the disadvantages to the slave and to society at large burdened by a comparatively inefficient system of labor. Now the conception of justice as fairness, when applied to the practice of slavery with its offices of slaveholder and slave, would not allow one to consider the advantages of the slaveholder in the first place. As that office is not in accordance with principles which could be mutually acknowledged, the gains accruing to the slaveholder, assuming them to exist, cannot be counted as in *any* way mitigating the injustice of the practice. The question whether these gains outweigh the disadvantages to the slave and to society cannot arise, since in considering the justice of slavery these gains have no weight at all which requires that they be overridden. Where the conception of justice as fairness applies, slavery is *always* unjust.

I am not, of course, suggesting the absurdity that the classical utilitarians approved of slavery. I am only rejecting a type of argument which their view allows them to use in support of their disapproval of it. The conception of justice as derivative from efficiency implies that judging the justice of a practice is always, in principle at least, a matter of weighing up advantages and disadvantages, each having an intrinsic value or disvalue as the satisfaction of interests, irrespective of whether or not these interests necessarily involve acquiescence in principles which could not be mutually acknowledged. Utilitarianism cannot account for the fact that slavery is always unjust, nor for the fact that it would be recognized as irrelevant in defeating the accusation of injustice for one person to say to another, engaged with him in a common practice and debating its merits, that nevertheless it allowed of the greatest satisfaction of desire. The charge of injustice cannot be rebutted in this way. If justice were derivative from a higher order executive efficiency, this would not be so.

But now, even if it is taken as established that, so far as the ordinary conception of justice goes, slavery is always unjust (that is, slavery by definition violates commonly recognized principles of justice), the classical utilitarian would surely reply that these principles, as other moral principles subordinate to that of utility, are only generally correct. It is simply for the most part true that slavery is less efficient than other institutions; and while common sense may define the concept of justice so that slavery is unjust, nevertheless, where slavery would lead to the greatest satisfaction of desire, it is not wrong. Indeed, it is then right, and for the very same reason that justice, as ordinarily understood, is usually right. If, as ordinarily understood, slavery is always unjust, to this extent the utilitarian conception of justice might be admitted to differ from that of common moral opinion. Still the utilitarian would want to hold that, as a matter of moral principle, his view is correct in giving no special weight to considerations of justice beyond that allowed for by the general presumption of effectiveness. And this, he claims, is as it should be. The everyday opinion is morally in error, although, indeed, it is a useful error, since it protects rules of generally high utility.

The question, then relates not simply to the analysis of the concept of justice as common sense defines it, but the analysis of it in the wider sense as to how much weight considerations of justice, as defined, are to have when laid against other kinds of moral considerations. Here again I wish to argue that reasons of justice have a *special* weight for which only the conception of justice as fairness can account. Moreover, it belongs to the concept of justice that they do have this special weight. While Mill recognized that this was so, he thought that it could be accounted for by the special urgency of the moral feelings which naturally support principles of such high utility. But it is a mistake to resort to the urgency of feeling;

as with the appeal to intuition, it manifests a failure to pursue the question far enough. The special weight of considerations of justice can be explained from the conception of justice as fairness. It is only necessary to elaborate a bit what has already been said as follows.

If one examines the circumstances in which a certain tolerance of slavery is justified, or perhaps better, excused, it turns out that these are of a rather special sort. Perhaps slavery exists as an inheritance from the past and it proves necessary to dismantle it piece by piece; at times slavery may conceivably be an advance on previous institutions. Now while there may be some excuse for slavery in special conditions, it is never an excuse for it that it is sufficiently advantageous to the slaveholder to outweigh the disadvantages to the slave and to society. A person who argues in this way is not perhaps making a wildly irrelevant remark; but he is guilty of a moral fallacy. There is disorder in his conception of the ranking of moral principles. For the slaveholder, by his own admission, has no moral title to the advantages which he receives as a slaveholder. He is no more prepared than the slave to acknowledge the principle upon which is founded the respective positions in which they both stand. Since slavery does not accord with principles which they could mutually acknowledge, they each may be supposed to agree that it is unjust: it grants claims which it ought not to grant and in doing so denies claims which it ought not to deny. Amongst persons in a general position who are debating the form of their common practices, it cannot, therefore, be offered as a reason for a practice that, in conceding these very claims that ought to be denied, it nevertheless meets existing interests more effectively. By their very nature the satisfaction of these claims is without weight and cannot enter into any tabulation of advantages and disadvantages.

Furthermore, it follows from the concept of morality that, to the extent that the slaveholder recognizes his position vis-à-vis the slave to be unjust, he would not choose to press his claims. His not wanting to receive his special advantages is one of the ways in which he shows that he thinks slavery is unjust. It would be fallacious for the legislator to suppose, then, that it is a ground for having a practice that it brings advantages greater than disadvantages, if those for whom the practice is designed, and to whom the advantages flow, acknowledge that they have no moral title to them and do not wish to receive them.

For these reasons the principles of justice have a special weight; and with respect to the principle of the greatest satisfaction of desire, as cited in the general position amongst those discussing the merits of their common practices, the principles of justice have an absolute weight. In this sense they are not contingent; and this is why their force is greater than can be accounted for by the general presumption (assuming that there is one) of the effectiveness, in the utilitarian sense, of practices which in fact satisfy them.

If one wants to continue using the concepts of classical utilitarianism, one will have to say, to meet this criticism, that at least the individual or social utility functions must be so defined that no value is given to the satisfaction of interests the representative claims of which violate the principles of justice. In this way it is no doubt possible to include these principles within the form of the utilitarian conception; but to do so is, of course, to change its inspiration altogether as a moral conception. For it is to incorporate within it principles which cannot be understood on the basis of a higher order executive decision aiming at the greatest satisfaction of desire.

It is worth remarking, perhaps, that this criticism of utilitarianism does not depend on whether or not the two assumptions, that of individuals having similar utility functions and that of diminishing marginal utility, are interpreted as psychological propositions to be supported or refuted by experience, or as moral and political principles expressed in a somewhat technical language. There are, certainly, several advantages in taking them in the latter fashion.[20] For one thing, one might say that this is what Bentham and others really meant by them, as least as shown by how they were used in arguments for social reform. More importantly, one could hold that the best way to defend the classical utilitarian view is to interpret these assumptions as moral and political principles. It is doubtful whether, taken as psychological propositions, they are true of men in general as we know them under normal conditions. On the other hand, utilitarians would not have wanted to propose them merely as practical working principles of legislation, or as expedient maxims to guide reform, given the egalitarian

sentiments of modern society.[21] When pressed they might well have invoked the idea of a more or less equal capacity of men in relevant respects if given an equal chance in a just society. But if the argument above regarding slavery is correct, then granting these assumptions as moral and political principles makes no difference. To view individuals as equally fruitful lines for the allocation of benefits, even as a matter of moral principle, still leaves the mistaken notion that the satisfaction of desire has value in itself irrespective of the relations between persons as members of a common practice, and irrespective of the claims upon one another which the satisfaction of interests represents. To see the error of this idea one must give up the conception of justice as an executive decision altogether and refer to the notion of justice as fairness: that participants in a common practice be regarded as having an original and equal liberty and that their common practices be considered unjust unless they accord with principles which persons so circumstanced and related could freely acknowledge before one another, and so could accept as fair. Once the emphasis is put upon the concept of the mutual recognition of principles by participants in a common practice the rules of which are to define their several relations and give form to their claims on one another, then it is clear that the granting of a claim the principle of which could not be acknowledged by each in the general position (that is, in the position in which the parties propose and acknowledge principles before one another) is not a reason for adopting a practice. Viewed in this way, the background of the claim is seen to exclude it from consideration; that it can represent a value in itself arises from the conception of individuals as separate lines for the assignment of benefits, as isolated persons who stand as claimants on an administrative or benevolent largesse. Occasionally persons do so stand to one another; but this is not the general case, nor, more importantly, is it the case when it is a matter of the justice of practices themselves in which participants stand in various relations to be appraised in accordance with standards which they may be expected to acknowledge before one another. Thus however mistaken the notion of the social contract may be as history, and however far it may overreach itself as a general theory of social and political obligation, it does express, suitably interpreted, an essential part of the concept of justice.[22]

VIII

By way of conclusion I should like to make two remarks: first, the original modification of the utilitarian principle (that it require of practices that the offices and positions defined by them be equal unless it is reasonable to suppose that the representative man in *every* office would find the inequality to his advantage), slight as it may appear at first sight, actually has a different conception of justice standing behind it. I have tried to show how this is so by developing the concept of justice as fairness and by indicating how this notion involves the mutual acceptance, from a general position, of the principles on which a practice is founded, and how this in turn requires the exclusion from consideration of claims violating the principles of justice. Thus the slight alteration of principle reveals another family of notions, another way of looking at the concept of justice.

Second, I should like to remark also that I have been dealing with the *concept* of justice. I have tried to set out the kinds of principles upon which judgments concerning the justice of practices may be said to stand. The analysis will be successful to the degree that it expresses the principles involved in these judgments when made by competent persons upon deliberation and reflection.[23] Now every people may be supposed to have the concept of justice, since in the life of every society there must be at least some relations in which the parties consider themselves to be circumstanced and related as the concept of justice as fairness requires. Societies will differ from one another not in having or in failing to have this notion but in the range of cases to which they apply it and in the emphasis which they give to it as compared with other moral concepts.

A firm grasp of the concept of justice itself is necessary if these variations, and the reasons for them, are to be understood. No study of the development of moral ideas and of the differences between them is more sound than the analysis of the fundamental moral concepts upon which it must depend. I have tried, therefore, to give an analysis of the concept of justice which should apply generally, however large a part the concept may have in a given morality, and which can be used in explaining the course of men's thoughts about justice and its relations to other moral concepts. How it is to be used for this purpose is a large topic which I cannot, of course, take up here. I mention it only to emphasize that I have been dealing with the concept of justice itself and to indicate what use I consider such an analysis to have.

NOTES

1.   I use the word "practice" throughout as a sort of technical term meaning any form of activity specified by a system of rules which defines offices, roles, moves, penalties, defenses, and so on, and which gives the activity its structure. As examples one may think of games and rituals, trials and parliaments, markets and systems of property. I have attempted a partial analysis of the notion of a practice in a paper "Two Concepts of Rules," *Philosophical Review,* LXIV (1955), 3–32.

2.   These principles are, of course, well known in one form or another and appear in many analyses of justice even where the writers differ widely on other matters. Thus if the principle of equal liberty is commonly associated with Kant (see *The Philosophy of Law,* tr. by W. Hastie, Edinburgh, 1887, pp. 56 f.), it may be claimed that it can also be found in J. S. Mill's *On Liberty* and elsewhere, and in many other liberal writers. Recently H. L. A. Hart has argued for something like it in his paper "Are There Any Natural Rights?" *Philosophical Review,* LXIV (1955), 175–191. The injustice of inequalities which are not won in return for a contribution to the common advantage is, of course, widespread in political writings of all sorts. The conception of justice here discussed is distinctive, if at all, only in selecting these two principles in this form; but for another similar analysis, see the discussion by W. D. Lamont, *The Principles of Moral Judgment* (Oxford, 1946), ch. v.

3.   This point was made by Sidgwick, *Methods of Ethics,* 6th ed. (London, 1901), Bk. III, ch. v, sec. 1. It has recently been emphasized by Sir Isaiah Berlin in a symposium, "Equality," *Proceedings of the Aristotelian Society,* n.s. LVI (1955–56), 305 f.

4.   In the paper referred to above, footnote 1, I have tried to show the importance of taking practices as the proper subject of the utilitarian principle. The criticisms of so-called "restricted utilitarianism" by J. J. C. Smart, "Extreme and Restricted Utilitarianism," *Philosophical Quarterly,* VI (1956), 344–354, and by H. J. McCloskey, "An Examination of Restricted Utilitarianism," *Philosophical Review,* LXVI (1957), 466–485, do not affect my argument. These papers are concerned with the very general proposition, which is attributed (with what justice I shall not consider) to S. E. Toulmin and P. H. Nowell-Smith (and in the case of the latter paper, also, apparently, to me); namely, the proposition that particular moral actions are justified by appealing to moral rules, and moral rules in turn by reference to utility. But clearly I meant to defend no such view. My discussion of the concept of rules as maxims is an explicit rejection of it. What I did argue was that, in the *logically special* case of practices (although actually quite a common case) where the rules have special features and are not moral rules at all but legal rules or rules of games and the like (except, perhaps, in the case of promises), there is a peculiar force to the distinction between justifying particular actions and justifying the system of rules themselves. Even then I claimed only that restricting the

utilitarian principle to practices as defined strengthened it. I did not argue for the position that this amendment alone is sufficient for a complete defense of utilitarianism as a general theory of morals. In this paper I take up the question as to how the utilitarian principle itself must be modified, but here, too, the subject of inquiry is not all of morality at once, but a limited topic, the concept of justice.

5. It might seem as if J. S. Mill, in paragraph 36 of Chapter v of *Utilitarianism*, expressed the utilitarian principle in this modified form, but in the remaining two paragraphs of the chapter, and elsewhere, he would appear not to grasp the significance of the change. Hume often emphasizes that *every* man must benefit. For example, in discussing the utility of general rules, he holds that they are requisite to the "well-being of every individual"; from a stable system of property "every individual person must find himself a gainer in balancing the account. . . . " "Every member of society is sensible of this interest; everyone expresses this sense to his fellows along with the resolution he has taken of squaring his actions by it, on the conditions that others will do the same." *A Treatise of Human Nature,* Bk. III, Pt. II, Section II, paragraph 22.

6. It is not possible to discuss here this addition to the usual conception of rationality. If it seems peculiar, it may be worth remarking that it is analogous to the modification of the utilitarian principle which the argument as a whole is designed to explain and justify. In the same way that the satisfaction of interests, the representative claims of which violate the principles of justice, is not a reason for having a practice (see sec. VII), unfounded envy, within limits, need not to be taken into account.

7. The idea that accepting a principle as a moral principle implies that one generally acts on it, failing a special explanation, has been stressed by R. M. Hare, *The Language of Morals* (Oxford, 1952). His formulation of it needs to be modified, however, along the lines suggested by P. L. Gardiner, "On Assenting to a Moral Principle," *Proceedings of the Aristotelian Society,* n.s. LV (1955), 23–44. See also C. K. Grant, "Akrasia and the Criteria of Assent to Practical Principles," *Mind,* LXV (1956), 400–407, where the complexity of the criteria for assent is discussed.

8. Perhaps the best known statement of this conception is that given by Glaucon at the beginning of Book II of Plato's *Republic.* Presumably it was, in various forms, a common view among the Sophists; but that Plato gives a fair representation of it is doubtful. See K. R. Popper, *The Open Society and Its Enemies,* rev. ed. (Princeton, 1950), pp. 112–118. Certainly Plato usually attributes to it a quality of manic egoism which one feels must be an exaggeration; on the other hand, see the Melian Debate in Thucydides, *The Peloponnesian War,* Book V, ch. vii, although it is impossible to say to what extent the views expressed there reveal any current philosophical opinion. Also in this tradition are the remarks of Epicurus on justice in *Principal Doctrines,* XXXI–XXXVIII. In modern times elements of the conception appear in a more sophisticated form in Hobbes's *The Leviathan* and in Hume's *A Treatise of Human Nature,* Book III, Pt. II, as well as in the writings of the school of natural law such as Pufendorf's *De jure naturae et gentium.* Hobbes and Hume are especially instructive. For Hobbe's argument see Howard Warrender's *The Political Philosophy of Hobbes* (Oxford, 1957). W. J. Baumol's *Welfare Economics and the Theory of the State* (London, 1952), is valuable in showing the wide applicability of Hobbes's fundamental idea (interpreting his natural law as principles of prudence), although in this book it is traced back only to Hume's *Treatise.*

9. See J. von Neumann and O. Morgenstern, *The Theory of Games and Economic Behavior,* 2nd ed. (Princeton, 1947). For a comprehensive and not too technical discussion of the developments since, see R. Duncan Luce and Howard Raiffa, *Games and Decisions: Introduction and Critical Survey* (New York, 1957). Chs. vi and xiv discuss the developments most obviously related to the analysis of justice.

10. For a general survey see J. W. Gough, *The Social Contract,* 2nd ed. (Oxford, 1957), and Otto von Gierke, *The Development of Political Theory,* tr. by B. Freyd (London, 1939), Pt. II, ch. II.

11. The difficulty one gets into by a mechanical application of the theory of games to moral philosophy can be brought out by considering among several possible examples, R. B. Braithwaite's study, *Theory of Games as a Tool for the Moral Philosopher* (Cambridge, 1955). On the analysis there given, it turns out that the fair division of playing time between Matthew and Luke depends on their preferences, and these in turn are connected with the instruments they wish to play. Since Matthew has a threat advantage over Luke, arising purely from the fact that Matthew, the trumpeter, prefers both of them playing at once to neither of them playing, whereas Luke, the pianist, prefers silence to cacophony, Matthew is alloted 26 evenings of play to Luke's 17. If the situation were reversed, the threat advantage would be with Luke. See pp. 36 f. But now we have only to suppose that Matthew is a jazz enthusiast who plays the drums, and Luke a violinist who plays sonatas, in which case it will be fair, on this analysis, for Matthew to play whenever and as often as he likes, assuming, of course, as it is plausible to assume, that he does not care whether Luke plays or not. Certainly something has gone wrong. To each according to his threat advantage is hardly the principle of fairness. What is lacking is the concept of morality, and it must be brought into the conjectural account in some way or other. In the text this is done by the form of the procedure whereby principles are proposed and acknowledged (section III). If one starts directly with the particular case as known, and if one accepts as given and definitive the preferences and relative positions of the parties, whatever they are, it is impossible to give an analysis of the moral concept of fairness. Braithwaite's use of the theory of games, insofar as it is intended to analyze the concept of fairness, is, I think, mistaken. This is not, of course, to criticize in any way the theory of games as a mathematical theory, to which Braithwaite's book certainly contributes, nor as an analysis of how rational (and amoral) egoists might behave (and so as an analysis of how people sometimes actually do behave). But it is to say that if the theory of games is to be used to analyze moral concepts, its formal structure must be interpreted in a special and general manner as indicated in the text. Once we do this, though, we are in touch again with a much older tradition.

12. For the definition of this prima facie duty, and the idea that it is a special duty, I am indebted to H. L. A. Hart. See his paper "Are There Any Natural Rights?" *Philosophical Review,* LXIV (1955), 185 f.

13. The sense of "performative" here is to be derived from J. L. Austin's paper in the symposium, "Other Minds," *Proceedings of the Aristotelian Society,* Supplementary Volume (1946), pp. 170–174.

14. This, however, commonly happens. Hobbes, for example, when invoking the notion of a "tácit covenant," appeals not to the natural law that promises should be kept but to his fourth law of nature, that of gratitude. On Hobbes's shift from fidelity to gratitude, see Warrender, *Political Philosophy of Hobbes* (footnote 8), pp. 51–52, 233–237. While it is not a serious criticism of Hobbes, it would have improved his argument had he appealed to the duty of fair play. On his premises he is perfectly entitled to do so. Similarly Sidgwick

thought that a principle of justice, such as every man ought to receive adequate requital for his labor, is like gratitude universalized. See *Methods of Ethics,* Bk. III, ch. v, Sec. 5. There is a gap in the stock of moral concepts used by philosophers into which the concept of the duty of fair play fits quite naturally.

15.   I am using the concept of criterion here in what I take to be Wittgenstein's sense. See *Philosophical Investigations,* (Oxford, 1953); and Norman Malcolm's review, "Wittgenstein's *Philosophical Investigations,*" *Philosophical Review,* LXIII (1954), 543–547. That the response of compassion, under appropriate circumstances, is part of the criterion for whether or not a person understands what "pain" means, is, I think, in the *Philosophical Investigations.* The view in the text is simply an extension of this idea. I cannot, however, attempt to justify it here. Similar thoughts are to be found, I think, in Max Scheler, *The Nature of Sympathy,* tr. by Peter Heath (New Haven, 1954). His way of writing is often so obscure that I cannot be certain.

16.   While this assimilation is implicit in Bentham's and Sidgwick's moral theory, explicit statements of it as applied to justice are relatively rare. One clear instance in *The Principles of Morals and Legislation* occurs in ch. x, footnote 2 to section XL: ". . . justice, in the only sense in which it has a meaning, is an imaginary personage, feigned for the convenience of discourse, whose dictates are the dictates of utility, applied to certain particular cases. Justice, then, is nothing more than an imaginary instrument, employed to forward on certain occasions, and by certain means, the purposes of benevolence. The dictates of justice are nothing more than a part of the dictates of benevolence, which, on certain occasions, are applied to certain subjects. . . ." Likewise in *The Limits of Jurisprudence Defined,* ed. by C. W. Everett (New York, 1945), pp. 117 f., Bentham criticizes Grotius for denying that justice derives from utility; and in *The Theory of Legislation,* ed. by C. K. Ogden (London, 1931), p. 3, he says that he uses the words "just" and "unjust" along with other words "simply as collective terms including the ideas of certain pains or pleasures." That Sidgwick's conception of justice is similar to Bentham's is admittedly not evident from his discussion of justice in Book III, ch. v of *Methods of Ethics.* But it follows, I think, from the moral theory he accepts. Hence C. D. Broad's criticism of Sidgwick in the matter of distributive justice in *Five Types of Ethical Theory* (London, 1930), pp. 249–253, do not rest on a misinterpretation.

17.   This maxim is attributed to Bentham by J. S. Mill in *Utilitarianism,* ch. v, paragraph 36. I have not found it in Bentham's writings, nor seen such a reference. Similarly James Bonar, *Philosophy and Political Economy* (London, 1893), p. 234 n. But it accords perfectly with Bentham's ideas. See the hitherto unpublished manuscript in David Baumgardt, *Bentham and the Ethics of Today* (Princeton, 1952), Appendix IV. For example, "the total value of the stock of pleasure belonging to the whole community is to be obtained by multiplying the number expressing the value of it as respecting any one person, by the number expressing the multitude of such individuals" (p. 556).

18.   An idea essential to the classical utilitarian conception of justice. Bentham is firm in his statement of it: "It is only upon that principle [the principle of asceticism], and not from the principle of utility, that the most abominable pleasure which the vilest of malefactors ever reaped from his crime would be reprobated, if it stood alone. The case is, that it never does stand alone; but is necessarily followed by such a quantity of pain (or, what comes to the same thing, such a chance

for a certain quantity of pain) that the pleasure in comparison of it, is as nothing: and this is the true and sole, but perfectly sufficient, reason for making it a ground for punishment" (*The Principles of Morals and Legislation,* ch. II, sec. iv. See also ch. x, sec. x, footnote I). The same point is made in *The Limits of Jurisprudence Defined,* pp. 115 f. Although much recent welfare economics, as found in such important works as I. M. D. Little, *A Critique of Welfare Economics,* 2nd ed. (Oxford, 1957) and K. J. Arrow, *Social Choice and Individual Values* (New York, 1951), dispenses with the idea of cardinal utility, and uses instead the theory of ordinal utility as stated by J. R. Hicks, *Value and Capital,* 2nd ed. (Oxford, 1946), Pt. I, it assumes with utilitarianism that individual preferences have value as such, and so accepts the idea being criticized here. I hasten to add, however, that this is no objection to it as a means of analyzing economic policy, and for that purpose it may, indeed, be a necessary simplifying assumption. Nevertheless it is an assumption which cannot be made insofar as one is trying to analyze moral concepts, especially the concept of justice, as economists would, I think, agree. Justice is usually regarded as a separate and distinct part of any comprehensive criterion of economic policy. See, for example, Tibor Scitovsky, *Welfare and Competition* (London, 1952), pp. 59–69, and Little, *Critique of Welfare Economics* (this footnote), ch. VII.

19.   See J. S. Mill's argument in *Utilitarianism,* ch. v, pars. 16–25.

20.   See D. G. Ritchie, *Natural Rights* (London, 1894), pp. 95 ff., 249 ff. Lionel Robbins has insisted on this point on several occasions. See *An Essay on the Nature and Significance of Economic Science,* 2nd ed. (London, 1935), pp. 134–43, "Interpersonal Comparisons of Utility: A Comment," *Economic Journal,* XLVIII (1938), 635–41, and more recently, "Robertson on Utility and Scope," *Economica,* n.s. XX (1953), 108 f.

21.   As Sir Henry Maine suggested Bentham may have regarded them. See *The Early History of Institutions* (London, 1875), pp. 398 ff.

22.   Thus Kant was not far wrong when he interpreted the original contract merely as an "Idea of Reason"; yet he still thought of it as a *general* criterion of right and as providing a general theory of political obligation. See the second part of the essay, "On the Saying 'That may be right in theory but has no value in practice' " (1793), in *Kant's Principles of Politics,* tr. by W. Hastie (Edinburgh, 1891). I have drawn on the contractarian tradition not for a general theory of political obligation but to clarify the concept of justice.

23.   For a further discussion of the idea expressed here, see my paper, "Outline of a Decision Procedure for Ethics," in the *Philosophical Review,* LX (1951), 177–197. For an analysis, similar in many respects but using the notion of the ideal observer instead of that of the considered judgment of a competent person, see Roderick Firth, "Ethical Absolutism and the Ideal Observer," *Philosophy and Phenomenological Research,* XII (1952), 317–345. While the similarities between these two discussions are more important than the differences, an analysis based on the notion of a considered judgment of a competent person, as it is based on a kind of judgment, may prove more helpful in understanding the features of moral judgment than an analysis based on the notion of an ideal observer, although this remains to be shown. A man who rejects the conditions imposed on a considered judgment of a competent person could no longer profess to *judge* at all. This seems more fundamental than his rejecting the conditions of observation, for these do not seem to apply, in an ordinary sense, to making a moral judgment.

LOUIS KATZNER

Is the Favoring of Women and Blacks in Employment and Educational Opportunities Justified?*

There is presently a call to favor blacks and women in employment and educational opportunities because in the past many of them have been discriminated against in these areas. The basic concern of this paper is whether or not reverse discrimination in this sense is justified. Given that, as will be shown, all acts of reverse discrimination involve prejudgment, it is appropriate to scrutinize first the notion of discrimination itself. Next, the idea of reverse discrimination will be explicated by distinguishing among several different forms that it may take; and from this explication the set of conditions under which a bias of redress is justified will emerge. Finally, the situation of blacks and women in the United States will be examined to see what conclusions can be drawn concerning the justification of reverse discrimination for these two classes.

I. DISCRIMINATION

There are certain things that are relevant to the way people should be treated and certain things that are not. The size of one's chest is relevant to the size shirt he should have, but it has nothing to do with the size his shoes should be. The rate of one's metabolism is pertinent to the amount of food she should be served, but not to the color of the napkin she is given. People should be treated on the basis of their attributes and merits that are relevant to the circumstances. When they are, those who are similar are treated similarly and those who are dissimilar are treated differently. Although these distinctions do involve treating people differently (those with larger chests get larger shirts than those with smaller chests), it does not involve discrimination. For discrimination means treating people differently when they are similar in the relevant respects or treating

them similarly when they are different in the relevant respects.

It follows that to determine what constitutes discrimination in vocational and education opportunities, we must first determine what qualities are relevant to a career and the capacity to learn. People today generally seem to accept the principle of meritocracy—that is, that an individual's potential for success, which is a combination of his native and/or developed ability and the amount of effort he can be expected to put forth, is the sole criterion that should be used in hiring and college admissions practices. It may be that until recently many people did not accept this view, and it may be that there are some even today who do not accept it. Nevertheless, this is one of the basic principles of the "American Dream"; it is the foundation of the civil service system; it is a principle to which even the most ardent racists and sexists at least give lipservice; and it is the principle that most people seem to have in mind when they speak of the problem of discrimination in hiring and college admissions practices. And because it is generally agreed that people with the same potential should be treated similarly in employment and college admissions, and that those with more potential should receive preference over those with less, the discussion begins with this assumption.

II. REVERSE DISCRIMINATION

With the notion of discrimination clarified, it is now possible to see what is involved in the idea of reverse discrimination. Reverse discrimination is much more than a call to eliminate bias; it is a call to offset the effects of past acts of bias by skewing opportunity in the opposite direction. This paper will consider only the claims that blacks, women, etcetera, have been discriminated against in the past (that is, they have been

*This essay has not been previously published.

treated as if they have less potential than they actually do); and that the only way to offset their subsequent disadvantages is to discriminate now in their favor (that is, to treat them as if they have more potential than they actually do).

It follows that those who are currently calling for the revision of admission standards at our colleges because they do not accurately reflect a student's chances of success there are not calling for reverse discrimination. They are merely saying that we should find a way of determining precisely who is qualified (that is, who has the potential) to go to college, and then admit the most qualified. On the other hand, those who are calling for us to admit students whom they allow are less qualified than others who are denied admission, and to provide these less qualified students with special tutorial help, are calling for reverse discrimination.

This example clearly illustrates the basic problem that any justification of reverse discrimination must come to grips with—viz., that every act of reverse discrimination is itself discriminatory. For every less qualified person who is admitted to a college, or hired for a job, there is a more qualified person who is being discriminated against, and who has a right to complain. Hence the justification of reverse discrimination must involve not only a justification of *discriminating for* those who are benefiting from it, it must also involve a justification of discriminating *against* those at whose expense the reverse discrimination is being practiced.

III. JUSTIFICATION OF REVERSE DISCRIMINATION: DIRECT

There are at least two significantly different kinds of situations in which reverse discrimination can be called for. On the one hand, a person might argue that he should be favored because he was arbitrarily passed over at some time in the past. Thus, for example, a Chicano might maintain that since he was denied a job for which he was the most qualified candidate simply because of his race, he should now be given one for which he is not the most qualified candidate, simply because he was discriminated against in the past. On the other hand, one might argue that he should be given preference because his ancestors (parents, grandparents, great-grandparents, et cetera) were discriminated against. In this case,

the Chicano would claim that he should be given a job for which he is not the most qualified applicant because his ancestors were denied jobs for which they were the most qualified.

In the former case, that of rectifying bias against an individual by unduly favoring him, there are several interesting points that can be made. First of all, the case for reverse discrimination of this type is strongest when the person to be passed over in the reverse discrimination is the same one who benefited from the initial discriminatory act. Suppose, for example, that when it comes time to appoint the vice-president of a company, the best qualified applicant (that is, the one who has the most potential) is passed over because of his race, and a less qualified applicant is given the job. Suppose that the following year the job of president in the same firm becomes open. At this point, the vice-president, because of the training he had as second in command, is the most qualified applicant for the job. It could be argued, however, that the presidency should go to the person who was passed over for the vice-presidency. For he should have been the vice-president, and if he had been he would probably now be the best-equipped applicant for the top post; it is only because he was passed over that the current vice-president is now the most qualified candidate. In other words, since the current vice-president got ahead at his expense, it is warranted for him to move up at the vice-president's expense. In this way the wrong that was done him will be righted.

There are two main problems with this argument. First of all, certainly to be considered is how well the individual who benefited from the initial act of discrimination exploited his break. If he used this opportunity to work up to his capacity, this would seem to be a good reason for not passing him over for the presidency. If, on the other hand, although performing very adequately as vice-president, he was not working up to the limits of his capacity, then perhaps the job of president should be given to the man who was passed over in the first place—even though the vice-president's experience in his job leads one to think that he is the one most qualified to handle the difficult tasks of the presidency. In other words, how much a person has made of the benefit he has received from an act of discrimination seems to be relevant to the question of whether or not he should be discriminated against so that the victim of that discrimination may now be benefited.

Secondly, there are so few cases of this kind that even if reverse discrimination is justified in such cases, this would not show very much. In most instances of reverse discrimination, the redress is at the expense of someone who did not benefit from the initial act of discrimination rather than someone who did.

One species of this form of reverse discrimination is that in which the victim of the proposed act of reverse discrimination has not benefited from *any* acts of discrimination. In such a case, what is in effect happening is that the burden of discrimination is being transferred from one individual who does not deserve it to another individual who does not deserve it. There is no sense in which "the score is being evened," as in the case above. Because there is no reason for saying that one of the individuals deserves to be penalized by prejudice while the other one does not, it is difficult to see how this kind of reverse discrimination can be justified.

The only argument that comes to mind as a justification for this species of reverse discrimination is the following: The burdens of discrimination should be shared rather than placed on a few. It is better that the liabilities of discrimination be passed from person to person than that they remain the handicap only of those who have been disfavored. It follows that if we find someone who has been discriminated against, we are warranted in rectifying that injustice by an act of reverse discrimination, as long as the victim of the reverse discrimination has not himself been discriminated against in the past.

But this is not a very persuasive argument. For one thing, the claim that discrimination should be shared does not seem a very compelling reason for discriminating against a totally innocent bystander. Secondly, even if this is viewed as a forceful reason, the image of society that emerges is a horrifying one. The moment someone is discriminated against, he seeks out someone who has not been unfairly barred, and asks for reverse discrimination against this person to rectify the wrong he has suffered. Such a procedure would seem to entrench rather than eliminate discrimination, and would produce an incredibly unstable society.

Another species of this form of reverse discrimination is that in which the victim of the proposed reverse bias has benefited from a previous unfair decision, although it is not the particular act that is being rectified. In other words, he did not get ahead at the expense of the individual to whom we are trying to "make things up" by reverse discrimination, but he has benefited from bias against other individuals. In such a case, there is a sense, admittedly extended, in which a score is being evened.

Now it appears that such cases are more like those in which the victim of the proposed act of reverse discrimination benefited from the initial instance of discrimination than those in which he is a completely innocent bystander, and hence in such cases reverse discrimination can be justified. Of course it would be preferable if we could find the beneficiary of the original act of discrimination—but very often this just is not possible. And we must make sure that the reverse discrimination is proportionate to both the liability suffered by the proposed beneficiary and the advantage previously gained by the proposed victim—a very difficult task indeed. But there does not seem to be any reason for saying that reverse discrimination can only be visited upon those who benefited from the particular discriminatory act that is being rectified. It seems more reasonable to say that reverse discrimination can be visited upon those who benefited from either the particular instance of discrimination being rectified or from roughly similar acts.

Although the conclusions drawn from this discussion of the various species of one form of reverse discrimination do not seem conclusive, this discussion has brought to light three conditions which are necessary for the justification of reverse discrimination: First, there must have been an act of discrimination that is being rectified. Second, the initial act of discrimination must have in some way handicapped its victim, for if he has not been handicapped or set back in some way, then there is nothing to "make up to him" through reverse discrimination. And third, the victim of the proposed reverse discrimination must have benefited from an act of discrimination (either the one that is being rectified or a similar one); otherwise it is unacceptable to say that he should now be disfavored.

IV. JUSTIFICATION OF REVERSE DISCRIMINATION: INDIRECT

Not all of the claims that are made for reverse discrimination, however, assume that the individual involved has himself been the victim of bias. In many cases what is being claimed is that an individual is entitled to benefit from a rectifying bias because his ancestors (parents, grandparents, great grandparents, etcetera) were unfairly denied opportunity. Keeping in mind the three conditions necessary for reverse discrimination that we have just developed, this form of reverse discrimination will be examined.

In a society in which wealth could not be accumulated or, even if it could, it did not give one access to a better education and/or job, and a good education did not give one access to a better job and/or greater wealth, it would be hard to see how educational and/or economic discrimination against one's ancestors could be a handicap. That is, if education was not a key to economic success, then the educational discrimination one's ancestors suffered could not handicap one in the search for a job. If wealth did not buy better teachers and better schools, then the fact that one's ancestors have been handicapped economically could not be a reason for his being educationally disadvantaged. If wealth could not start a business, buy into a business, or give one direct access to a good job, then the economic shackling one's ancestors endured could in no way handicap her in the economic realm. But if wealth and education do these things, as in our society they clearly do, and if because of discrimination some people were not allowed to accumulate the wealth that their talents normally would bring, then it is quite clear that their offspring are handicapped by the discrimination they have suffered.

It is important to note that this point in no way turns on the controversy that is currently raging over the relationship between IQ and race. For it is not being claimed that unless there is complete equality there is discrimination. The members of a suppressed group may be above, below, or equal to the other members of society with regard to potential. All that is being claimed is that to the extent that the members of a group have been denied a fair chance to do work commensurate with their capacities, and to the extent that this has handicapped subsequent members of that group, reverse discrimination may be justified to offset this handicap.

But, as we have already seen, for reverse discrimination to be justified, not only must the victims of discrimination be handicapped by the discrimination, those who will suffer from its reversal must have benefited from the original injustice. In this particular case, it may be that they are the children of the beneficiaries of discrimination who have passed these advantages on to them. Or it may be that they benefit in facing reduced competition for schooling and jobs, and hence they are able to get into a better school and land a better job than they would if those suffering the effects of discrimination were not handicapped. Or they may have benefited from discrimination in some other way. But the proposed victims of reverse discrimination must be the beneficiaries of previous discrimination.

In addition to all of this, however, it seems that there is one more condition that must be met for reverse discrimination to be justified. Assuming that if we eliminated all discrimination immediately, the people who have suffered from it could compete on an equal basis with all other members of society, then reverse discrimination would not be justified. This of course is trivially true if it is only being claimed that if the elimination of all discrimination entails the eradication of all the handicaps it creates, then only the elimination of discrimination (and not reverse discrimination) is justified. But the claim involves much more than this. What is being argued is that even if the immediate elimination of all discrimination does not allow all suppressed people to compete equally with other members of society, as long as it allows equal opportunity to all children born subsequent to the end of discrimination, then reverse discrimination is not justified—*not even for those who have been handicapped by discrimination.* In other words, reverse discrimination will not prevent its debilitating effects from being passed on to generations yet unborn.

The justification of this claim is a straightforward utilitarian one (it cannot be a justification in terms of justice since what is being countenanced is blatant injustice). The social cost of implementing a policy of reverse discrimination is very high. The problems in determining who are the victims of discrimination and how great their handicaps, and who are the beneficiaries of discrimination and how great their benefits, as well as the problems in both developing and administering policies that will lead to a proper rectification of discrimination, are not merely enormously complex, they are enormously costly to solve. Moreover, the benefits of ending all discrimination are very great. Not only will many people be hired for jobs and admitted to colleges otherwise barred to them because of discrimination, but many people who have themselves been handicapped by discrimination will take great satisfaction in the knowledge that their offspring will not be held back as they have. This, of course, in no way eliminates the injustice involved in allowing acts of reverse discrimination to go unrectified. All it shows is that given the tremendous cost of implementing a comprehensive program of reverse discrimination, and given the tremendous benefits that would accrue simply from the elimination of all discrimination, it is reasonable to claim that reverse discrimination is justified only if the elimination of discrimination will not prevent its debilitating effects from being passed on to generations yet unborn.

Thus there is a fourth condition that must be added to the list of conditions that are necessary for the justification of reverse discrimination. Moreover, the addition of this condition renders the list jointly sufficient for the justification of reverse discrimination. Thus, reverse discrimination is justified if, and only if, the following conditions are met:

1. There must have been an initial act of discrimination that the reverse discrimination is going to rectify.
2. The beneficiary of the proposed act of reverse discrimination must have been handicapped by the initial act—either directly, if he was the victim of the initial discrimination, or indirectly, if he is the offspring of a victim (and inherited the handicap).
3. The victim of the proposed act of reverse discrimination must have benefited from an act of discrimination—the one that is being rectified or a similar one—and either directly, if he was the beneficiary of an initial act of discrimination or indirectly, if he is the offspring of a beneficiary (and inherited the benefit).
4. It must be the case that even if all discrimination were ended immediately, the debilitating effects of discrimination would be passed on to generations yet unborn.

V. REVERSE DISCRIMINATION FAVORING WOMEN AND BLACKS

A partial answer, at least, to the question of whether or not reverse discrimination is justified in the case of women and blacks is now possible. Let us begin with blacks.

It seems clear that the situation of many blacks in this country meets the four conditions shown to be individually necessary and jointly sufficient for the justification of reverse discrimination. First, there can be no doubt that many blacks have been the victims of educational and vocational discrimination. Second, given the relationships existing between wealth, education, and vocation, there can be no doubt that the discrimination that blacks have met with has handicapped both themselves and their offspring. Third, it also seems clear that within our economic framework, if blacks had not been discriminated against, there are many whites (those who got an education or a job at the expense of a more qualified black or in competition with the handicapped offspring of disadvantaged blacks) who would be in far less advantageous educational and vocational situations than they currently are—that is, there are people who have benefited from discrimination. And finally, again given the relationships existing among wealth, education, and vocation, even if all discrimination against blacks were to cease immediately, many black children born subsequent to this time would not be able to compete for educational and vocational opportunities on the same basis that they would had there been no bias against their ancestors.

Of course this in no way shows that reverse discrimination for all blacks is justified. After all, there are some blacks who have not let themselves be handicapped by discrimination. There are also undoubtedly some whites who have not benefited from the discrimination against blacks. And finally, there are many whites who have endured discrimination in the same way blacks have. In other words, so far it has only been shown that all those who have been discriminated against in a way that meets the conditions established are entitled to reverse discrimination and that some blacks have been discriminated against in this way.

To move from this claim to the conclusion that blacks as a class are entitled to reverse discrimination, several additional things must be shown. First, it must be demonstrated that it is unfeasible to handle reverse discrimination on a case by case basis (for example, it might be argued that such a procedure would be far too costly). Second, it must be proven that the overwhelming percentage of blacks have been victimized by discrimination—that is, the number of blacks who would benefit from reverse discrimination, but who do not deserve to, must be very small. And finally, it must be shown that the overwhelming majority of the potential victims of bias of redress have benefited from the acts of discrimination (or similar acts) that are being rectified—that is, it must be that the number of whites who will suffer the effects of reverse discrimination, without deserving to, must also be very small. If these conditions are met, then although there will be some unwarranted discrimination resulting from the reverse discrimination in favor of blacks (that is, some blacks benefiting who were not victimized and some whites suffering who were not benefited), such cases will be kept to a bare minimum, and hence the basic result will be the offsetting of the handicaps with which blacks have unwarrantedly been saddled.

When it comes to the case of (white) women, however, the situation is quite different. There is little doubt that many women have been denied opportunity, and thus handicapped while many men have benefited from this discrimination (although I believe that discrimination has been far less pervasive in the case of women than it has been for blacks). But women generally do not constitute the kind of class in which the handicaps of discrimination are passed on to one's offspring. This is because, unlike blacks, they are not an isolated social group. Most women are reared in families in which the gains a father makes, even if the mother is limited by society's prejudice, work to the advantage of *all* offspring. (White) women have attended white schools and colleges and, even if they have been discriminated against, their children have attended these same schools and colleges. If all discrimination were ended tomorrow, there would be no external problem at all for most women in competing, commensurate with their potential, with the male population.

Two important things follow from this. First, it is illegitimate for most women to claim that they should be favored because their mothers were disfavored. Second, and most importantly, if all discrimination against women were ended immediately, in most cases none of its debilitating effects would be transmitted to the generations of women yet unborn; hence, for most women, the fourth condition necessary for the justification of reverse discrimination is not satisfied. Thus, reverse discrimination for women as a class cannot be justified, although there are undoubtedly some cases in which, for a particular woman, it can.

One must be careful, however, not to interpret this judgment too broadly. For one thing, the conclusion that reverse discrimination is not warranted for women as a class is contingent upon the immediate elimination of all discrimination. Hence it does not apply if discrimination against women continues. In other words, the conclusion does not show that reverse discrimination for women as a class is unjustified in the face of continuing bias against them. Under these circumstances, reverse discrimination may or may not be justified.

Secondly, as reverse discrimination has been described here, it involves offsetting the impact of a particular kind of discrimination (that is, in educational and job opportunities) by another instance of the same kind of discrimination (that is, preferential treatment in education and job opportunities). All our argument shows is that this is unwarranted for women as a class. One might, however, want to argue in favor of discriminating for women as a class in the area of education and jobs, not to offset previous discrimination in this area, but rather to counter the debilitating effects that institutionalized sexism has had on the female psyche. That is, one might argue that because our society has conditioned women to desire subservient roles (for example, that of a nurse rather than doctor, secretary rather than executive, housewife rather than breadwinner, and so on), even if all forms of discrimination were eliminated tomorrow, very few (or at least not enough) women would take advantage of the opportunities open to them. Hence we need (reverse) discrimination as a means of placing women in visible positions of success, so that other women will have models to emulate and will strive for success in these areas. Now although it is not clear whether or not such a program can legitimately be labelled "reverse discrimination," the important point is that this paper has not been addressed to this kind of problem, and hence has not shown that it is illegitimate to give preferential treatment to women (or blacks) for this reason.

REED v. REED ADMINISTRATOR

United States Supreme Court, 1971*

Mr. Chief Justice Burger delivered the opinion of the Court.

Richard Lynn Reed, a minor, died intestate in Ada County, Idaho, on March 29, 1967. His adoptive parents, who had separated sometime prior to his death, are the parties to this appeal. Approximately seven months after Richard's death, his mother, appellant Sally Reed, filed a petition in the Probate Court of Ada County, seeking appointment as administratrix of her son's estate.[1] Prior to the date set for a hearing on the mother's petition, appellee Cecil Reed, the father of the decedent, filed a competing petition seeking to have himself appointed administrator of the son's estate. The probate court held a joint hearing on the two petitions and thereafter ordered that letters of administration be issued to appellee Cecil Reed upon his taking the oath and filing the bond required by law. The court treated §§ 15–312 and 15–314 of the Idaho Code as the controlling statutes and read those sections as compelling a preference for Cecil Reed because he was a male.

Section 15–312[2] designates the persons who are entitled to administer the estate of one who dies intestate. In making these designations, that section lists 11 classes of persons who are so entitled and provides, in substance, that the order in which those classes are listed in the section shall be determinative of the relative rights of competing applicants for letters of administration. One of the 11 classes so enumerated is "[t]he father or mother" of the person dying intestate. Under this section, then, appellant and appellee, being members of the same entitlement class, would seem to have been equally entitled to administer their son's estate. Section 15–314 provides, however, that

"[o]f several persons claiming and equally entitled [under § 15–312] to administer, males must be preferred to females, and relatives of the whole to those of the half blood."

In issuing its order, the probate court implicitly recognized the equality of entitlement of the two applicants under § 15–312 and noted that neither of the applicants was under any legal disability; the court ruled, however, that appellee, being a male, was to be preferred to the female appellant "by reason of Section 15–314 of the Idaho Code." In stating this conclusion, the probate judge gave no indication that he had attempted to determine the relative capabilities of the competing applicants to perform the functions incident to the administration of an estate. It seems clear the probate judge considered himself bound by statute to give preference to the male candidate over the female, each being otherwise "equally entitled."

Sally Reed appealed from the probate court order, and her appeal was treated by the District Court of the Fourth Judicial District of Idaho as a constitutional attack on § 15–314. In dealing with the attack, that court held that the challenged section violated the Equal Protection Clause of the Fourteenth Amendment[3] and was, therefore, void; the matter was ordered "returned to the Probate Court for its determination of which of the two parties" was better qualified to administer the estate.

This order was never carried out, however, for Cecil Reed took a further appeal to the Idaho Supreme Court, which reversed the District Court and reinstated the original order naming the father administrator of the estate. In reaching this result, the Idaho Supreme Court first dealt with the governing statutory law and held that under § 15–312 "a father and mother are 'equally entitled' to letters of administration," but the preference given to males by § 15–314 is "mandatory" and leaves no room for the exercise of a probate court's discretion in the appointment of administrators. Having thus definitively and authoritatively interpreted the statutory provisions involved, the Idaho Supreme Court then proceeded to examine, and reject, Sally Reed's contention that § 15–314 violates the Equal Protection Clause by giving a mandatory preference to males over females, without regard to their individual qualifications as potential estate administrators.

Sally Reed thereupon appealed for review by this Court . . ., and we noted probable jurisdiction.* Having examined the record and considered the briefs and oral arguments of the parties, we have concluded that the

*Citation omitted [Eds.]

arbitrary preference established in favor of males by § 15–314 of the Idaho Code cannot stand in the face of the Fourteenth Amendment's command that no State deny the equal protection of the laws to any person within its jurisdiction.[4]

Idaho does not, of course, deny letters of administration to women altogether. Indeed, under § 15–312, a woman whose spouse dies intestate has a preference over a son, father, brother, or any other male relative of the decedent. Moreover, we can judicially notice that in this country, presumably due to the greater longevity of women, a large proportion of estates, both intestate and under wills of decedents, are administered by surviving widows.

Section 15–314 is restricted in its operation to those situations where competing applications for letters of administration have been filed by both male and female members of the same entitlement class established by § 15–312. In such situations, § 15–314 provides that different treatment be accorded to the applicants on the basis of their sex; it thus establishes a classification subject to scrutiny under the Equal Protection Clause.

In applying that clause, this Court has consistently recognized that the Fourteenth Amendment does not deny to States the power to treat different classes of persons in different ways. The Equal Protection Clause of that amendment does, however, deny to States the power to legislate that different treatment be accorded to persons placed by a statute into different classes on the basis of criteria wholly unrelated to the objective of that statute. A classification "must be reasonable, not arbitrary, and must rest upon some ground of difference having a fair and substantial relation to the object of the legislation, so that all persons similarly circumstanced shall be treated alike." *Royster Guano Co.* v. *Virginia*, 253 U.S. 412, 415 (1920). The question presented by this case, then, is whether a difference in the sex of competing applicants for letters of administration bears a rational relationship to a state objective that is sought to be advanced by the operation of §§ 15–312 and 15–314.

In upholding the latter section, the Idaho Supreme Court concluded that its objective was to eliminate one area of controversy when two or more persons, equally entitled under § 15–312, seek letters of administration and thereby present the probate court "with the issue of which one should be named." The court also concluded that where such persons are not of the same sex, the elimination of females from consideration "is neither an illogical nor arbitrary method devised by the legislature to resolve an issue that would otherwise require a hearing as to the relative merits . . . of the two or more petitioning relatives. . . ."*

Clearly the objective of reducing the workload on probate courts by eliminating one class of contests is not without some legitimacy. The crucial question, however, in whether § 15–314 advances that objective in a manner consistent with the command of the Equal Protection Clause. We hold that it does not. To give a mandatory preference to members of either sex over members of the other, merely to accomplish the elimination of hearings on the merits, is to make the very kind of arbitrary legislative choice forbidden by the Equal Protection Clause of the Fourteenth Amendment; and whatever may be said as to the positive values of avoiding intrafamily controversy, the choice in this context may not lawfully be mandated solely on the basis of sex.

We note finally that if § 15–314 is viewed merely as a modifying appendage to § 15–312 and as aimed at the same objective, its constitutionality is not thereby saved. The objective of § 15–312 clearly is to establish degrees of entitlement of various classes of persons in accordance with their varying degrees and kinds of relationship to the intestate. Regardless of their sex, persons within any one of the enumerated classes of that section are similarly situated with respect to that objective. By providing dissimilar treatment for men and women who are thus similarly situated, the challenged section violates the Equal Protection Clause.

The judgment of the Idaho Supreme Court is reversed and the case remanded for further proceedings not inconsistent with this opinion.

Reversed and remanded.

NOTES

1. In her petition, Sally Reed alleged that her son's estate, consisting of a few items of personal property and a small savings account, had an aggregate value of less than $1,000.

2. Section 15–312 provides as follows:
"Administration of the estate of a person dying intestate must be granted to some one or more of the persons hereinafter mentioned, and they are respectively entitled thereto in the following order:
"1. The surviving husband or wife or some competent person whom he or she may request to have appointed.
"2. The children.
"3. The father or mother.
"4. The brothers.
"5. The sisters.
"6. The grandchildren.
"7. The next of kin entitled to share in the distribution of the estate.
"8. Any of the kindred.
"9. The public administrator.
"10. The creditors of such person at the time of death.
"11. Any person legally competent.
"If the decedent was a member of a partnership at the time of his decease, the surviving partner must in no case be appointed administrator of his estate."

3. The court also held that the statute violated Art. I, § 1, of the Idaho Constitution.

*Citation omitted [Eds.]

4. We note that § 15–312, set out in n. 2, *supra,* appears to give a superior entitlement to brothers of an intestate (class 4) than is given to sisters (class 5). The parties now before the Court are not affected by the operation of § 15–312 in this respect, however, and appellant has made no challenge to that section.

We further note that on March 12, 1971, the Idaho Legislature adopted the Uniform Probate Code, effective July 1, 1972. Idaho Laws 1971, c. 111, p. 233. On that date, §§ 15–312 and 15–314 of the present code will, then, be effectively repealed, and there is in the new legislation no mandatory preference for males over females as administrators of estates.

FRONTIERO v. RICHARDSON

United States Supreme Court, 1973*

Mr. Justice Brennan announced the judgment of the Court and an opinion in which Mr. Justice Douglas, Mr. Justice White, and Mr. Justice Marshall join.

The question before us concerns the right of a female member of the uniformed services to claim her spouse as a "dependent" for the purposes of obtaining increased quarters allowances and medical and dental benefits under 37 U. S. C. §§ 401, 403, and 10 U. S. C. §§ 1072, 1076, on an equal footing with male members. Under these statutes, a serviceman may claim his wife as a "dependent" without regard to whether she is in fact dependent upon him for any part of her support. A servicewoman, on the other hand, may not claim her husband as a "dependent" under these programs unless he is in fact dependent upon her for over one-half of his support. Thus, the question for decision is whether this difference in treatment constitutes an unconstitutional discrimination against servicewomen in violation of the Due Process Clause of the Fifth Amendment. A three-judge District Court for the Middle District of Alabama, one judge dissenting, rejected this contention and sustained the constitutionality of the provisions of the statutes making this distinction.* We reverse.

I

In an effort to attract career personnel through reenlistment, Congress established a scheme for the provision of fringe benefits to members of the uniformed

services on a competitive basis with business and industry. Thus, under 37 U. S. C. § 403, a member of the uniformed services with dependents is entitled to an increased "basic allowance for quarters" and, under 10 U. S. C. § 1076, a member's dependents are provided comprehensive medical and dental care.

Appellant Sharron Frontiero, a lieutenant in the United States Air Force, sought increased quarters allowances, and housing and medical benefits for her husband, appellant Joseph Frontiero, on the ground that he was her "dependent." Although such benefits would automatically have been granted with respect to the wife of a male member of the uniformed services, appellant's application was denied because she failed to demonstrate that her husband was dependent on her for more than one-half of his support.[1] Appellants then commenced this suit, contending that, by making this distinction, the statutes unreasonably discriminate on the basis of sex in violation of the Due Process Clause of the Fifth Amendment.[2] In essence, appellants asserted that the discriminatory impact of the statutes is two-fold: first, as a procedural matter, a female member is required to demonstrate her spouse's dependency, while no such burden is imposed upon male members; and second, as a substantive matter, a male member who does not provide more than one-half of his wife's support receives benefits, while a similarly situated female member is denied such benefits. Appellants therefore sought a permanent injunction against the continued enforcement of these statutes and an order directing the appellees to provide Lieutenant Frontiero with the same housing and medical benefits that a similarly situated male member would receive.

*93 *S. Ct.* 1764 (1973). Some footnotes omitted, and the remainder renumbered.

Although the legislative history of these statutes sheds virtually no light on the purposes underlying the differential treatment accorded male and female members, a majority of the three-judge District Court surmised that Congress might reasonably have concluded that, since the husband in our society is generally the "breadwinner" in the family—and the wife typically the "dependent" partner—"it would be more economical to require married female members claiming husbands to prove actual dependency than to extend the presumption of dependency to such members."* Indeed, given the fact that approximately 99% of all members of the uniformed services are male, the District Court speculated that such differential treatment might conceivably lead to a "considerable saving of administrative expense and manpower."

II

At the outset, appellants contend that classifications based upon sex, like classifications based upon race, alienage, and national origin, are inherently suspect and must therefore be subjected to close judicial scrutiny. We agree and, indeed, find at least implicit support for such an approach in our unanimous decision only last Term in *Reed* v. *Reed*, 404 U. S. 71 (1971).

In *Reed*, the Court considered the constitutionality of an Idaho statute providing that, when two individuals are otherwise equally entitled to appointment as administrator of an estate, the male applicant must be preferred to the female. Appellant, the mother of the deceased, and appellee, the father, filed competing petitions for appointment as administrator of their son's estate. Since the parties, as parents of the deceased, were members of the same entitlement class, the statutory preference was invoked and the father's petition was therefore granted. Appellant claimed that this statute, by giving a mandatory preference to males over females without regard to their individual qualifications, violated the Equal Protection Clause of the Fourteenth Amendment.

The Court noted that the Idaho statute "provides that different treatment be accorded to the applicants on the basis of their sex; it thus establishes a classification subject to scrutiny under the Equal Protection Clause." Under "traditional" equal protection analysis, a legislative classification must be sustained unless it is "patently arbitrary" and bears no rational relationship to a legitimate governmental interest.*

In an effort to meet this standard, appellee contended that the statutory scheme was a reasonable measure designed to reduce the workload on probate courts by eliminating one class of contests. Moreover,

appellee argued that the mandatory preference for male applicants was in itself reasonable since "men [are] as a rule more conversant with business affairs than . . . women." Indeed, appellee maintained that "it is a matter of common knowledge that women still are not engaged in politics, the professions, business or industry to the extent that men are." And the Idaho Supreme Court, in upholding the constitutionality of this statute, suggested that the Idaho Legislature might reasonably have "concluded that in general men are better qualified to act as an administrator than are women." [*Reed* v. *Reed*]

Despite these contentions, however, the Court held the statutory preference for male applicants unconstitutional. In reaching this result, the Court implicitly rejected appellee's apparently rational explanation of the statutory scheme, and concluded that, by ignoring the individual qualifications of particular applicants, the challenged statute provided "dissimilar treatment for men and women who are . . . similarly situated." *Reed* v. *Reed*, *supra*, at 77. The Court therefore held that, even though the State's interest in achieving administrative efficiency "is not without some legitimacy," "[t]o give a mandatory preference to members of either sex over members of the other, merely to accomplish the elimination of hearings on the merits, is to make the very kind of arbitrary legislative choice forbidden by the [Constitution]. . . ." *Id.*, at 76. This departure from "traditional" rational basis analysis with respect to sex-based classifications is clearly justified.

There can be no doubt that our Nation has had a long and unfortunate history of sex discrimination.[3] Traditionally, such discrimination was rationalized by an attitude of "romantic paternalism" which, in practical effect, put women not on a pedestal, but in a cage. Indeed, this paternalistic attitude became so firmly rooted in our national consciousness that, exactly 100 years ago, a distinguished member of this Court was able to proclaim:

"Man is, or should be, woman's protector and defender. The natural and proper timidity and delicacy which belongs to the female sex evidently unfits it for many of the occupations of civil life. The constitution of the family organization, which is founded in the divine ordinance, as well as in the nature of things, indicates the domestic sphere as that which properly belongs to the domain and functions of womanhood. The harmony, not to say identity, of interests and views which belong, or should belong, to the family institution is repugnant to the ideas of a woman adopting a distinct and independent career from that of her husband. . . .

". . . The paramount destiny and mission of woman are to fulfil the noble and benign offices of wife and mother. This is the law of the Creator." *Bradwell* v. *Illinois*, 83 U. S. [16 Wall.] 130, 141 (1873) (Bradley, J., concurring).

As a result of notions such as these, our statute books gradually became laden with gross, stereotypical

*Citations omitted [Eds.]

distinctions between the sexes and, indeed, throughout much of the 19th century, the position of women in our society was, in many respects, comparable to that of blacks under the pre-Civil War slave codes. Neither slaves nor women could hold office, serve on juries, or bring suit in their own names, and married women traditionally were denied the legal capacity to hold or convey property or to serve as legal guardians of their own children. See generally, L. Kantowitz, Women and the Law: The Unfinished Revolution 5–6 (1969); G. Mydral, An American Dilemma 1073 (2d ed. 1962). And although blacks were guaranteed the right to vote in 1870, women were denied even that right—which is itself "preservative of other basic civil and political rights"[4]—until adoption on the Nineteenth Amendment half a century later.

It is true, of course, that the position of women in America has improved markedly in recent decades.[5] Nevertheless, it can hardly be doubted that, in part because of the high visibility of the sex characteristic, women still face pervasive, although at times more subtle, discrimination in our educational institutions, on the job market and, perhaps most conspicuously, in the political arena.[6] See generally, K. Amundsen, The Silenced Majority: Women and American Democracy (1971).

Moreover, since sex, like race and national origin, is an immutable characteristic determined solely by the accident of birth, the imposition of special disabilities upon the members of a particular sex because of their sex would seem to violate "the basic concept of our system that legal burdens should bear some relationship to individual responsibility. . . ." *Weber* v. *Aetna Casualty & Surety Co.,* 406 U. S. 164, 175 (1972). And what differentiates sex from such nonsuspect statutes as intelligence or physical disability, and aligns it with the recognized suspect criteria, is that the sex characteristic frequently bears no relation to ability to perform or contribute to society. As a result, statutory distinctions between the sexes often have the effect of invidiously relegating the entire class of females to inferior legal status without regard to the actual capabilities of its individual members.

We might also note that, over the past decade, Congress has itself manifested an increasing sensitivity to sex-based classifications. In Tit. VII of the Civil Rights Act of 1964, for example, Congress expressly declared that no employer, labor union, or other organization subject to the provisions of the Act shall discriminate against any individual on the basis of "race, color, religion, *sex,* or national origin." Similarly, the Equal Pay Act of 1963 provides that no employer covered by the Act "shall discriminate . . . between employees on the basis of *sex.*" And §1 of the Equal Rights Amendment, passed by Congress on March 22, 1972, and

submitted to the legislatures of the States for ratification, declares that "[e]quality of rights under the law shall not be denied or abridged by the United States or by any State on account of sex." Thus, Congress·has itself concluded that classifications based upon sex are inherently invidious, and this conclusion of a coequal branch of Government is not without significance to the question presently under consideration.*

With these considerations in mind, we can only conclude that classifications based upon sex, like classifications based upon race, alienage, or national origin, are inherently suspect, and must therefore be subjected to strict judicial scrutiny. Applying the analysis mandated by that stricter standard of review, it is clear that the statutory scheme now before us is constitutionally invalid.

III

The sole basis of the classification established in the challenged statutes is the sex of the individuals involved. Thus, under 37 U. S. C. §§ 401, 403, and 10 U. S. C. §§ 2072, 2076, a female member of the uniformed services seeking to obtain housing and medical benefits for her spouse must prove his dependency in fact, whereas no such burden is imposed upon male members. In addition, the statutes operate so as to deny benefits to a female member, such as appellant Sharron Frontiero, who provides less than one-half of her spouse's support, while at the same time granting such benefits to a male member who likewise provides less than one-half of his spouse's support. Thus, to this extent at least, it may fairly be said that these statutes command "dissimilar treatment for men and women who are . . . similarly situated." *Reed* v. *Reed, supra,* at 77.

Moreover, the Government concedes that the differential treatment accorded men and women under these statutes serves no purpose other than mere "administrative convenience." In essence, the Government maintains that, as an empirical matter, wives in our society frequently are dependent upon their husbands, while husbands rarely are dependent upon their wives. Thus, the Government argues that Congress might reasonably have concluded that it would be both cheaper and easier simply conclusively to presume that wives of male members are financially dependent upon their husbands, while burdening female members with the task of establishing dependency in fact.[7]

The Government offers no concrete evidence, however, tending to support its view that such differential treatment in fact saves the Government any money. In order to satisfy the demands of strict judicial scrutiny, the Government must demonstrate, for example, that

*Citations omitted [Eds.]

it is actually cheaper to grant increased benefits with respect to *all* male members, than it is to determine which male members are in fact entitled to such benefits and to grant increased benefits only to those members whose wives actually meet the dependency requirement. Here, however, there is substantial evidence that, if put to the test, many of the wives of male members would fail to qualify for benefits. And in light of the fact that the dependency determination with respect to the husbands of female members is presently made solely on the basis of affidavits, rather than through the more costly hearing process, the Government's explanation of the statutory scheme is, to say the least, questionable.

In any case, our prior decisions make clear that, although efficacious administration of governmental programs is not without some importance, "the Constitution recognizes higher values than speed and efficiency."* And when we enter the realm of "strict judicial scrutiny," there can be no doubt that "administrative convenience" is not a shibboleth, the mere recitation of which dictates constitutionality.* On the contrary, any statutory scheme which draws a sharp line between the sexes, *solely* for the purpose of achieving administrative convenience, necessarily commands "dissimilar treatment for men and women who are . . . similarly situated," and therefore involves the "very kind of arbitrary legislative choice forbidden by the [Constitution]. . . ." *Reed* v. *Reed, supra,* at 77, 76. We therefore conclude that, by according differential treatment to male and female members of the uniformed services for the sole purpose of achieving administrative convenience, the challenged statutes violate the Due Process Clause of the Fifth Amendment insofar as they require a female member to prove the dependency of her husband.

Reversed.

Mr. Justice Stewart concurs in the judgment, agreeing that the statutes before us work an invidious discrimination in violation of the Constitution. *Reed* v. *Reed,* 404 U. S. 71.

Mr. Justice Rehnquist dissents for the reasons stated by Judge Rives in his opinion for the District Court, *Frontiero* v. *Laird,* 341 F. Supp. 201 (1972).

Mr. Justice Powell, with whom The Chief Justice and Mr. Justice Blackmun join, concurring in the judgment.

I agree that the challenged statutes constitute an unconstitutional discrimination against service women in violation of the Due Process Clause of the Fifth Amendment, but I cannot join the opinion of Mr. Justice Brennan, which would hold that all classifications based upon sex, "like classifications based upon race, alienage, and national origin," are "inherently suspect and must therefore be subjected to close judicial scrutiny." It is unnecessary for the Court in this case to characterize sex as a suspect classification, with all of the far-reaching implications of such a holding. *Reed* v. *Reed,* 404 U. S. 71 (1971), which abundantly supports our decision today, did not add sex to the narrowly limited group of classifications which are inherently suspect. In my view, we can and should decide this case on the authority of *Reed* and reserve for the future any expansion of its rationale.

There is another, and I find compelling, reason for deferring a general categorizing of sex classifications as invoking the strictest test of judicial scrutiny. The Equal Rights Amendment, which if adopted will resolve the substance of this precise question, has been approved by the Congress and submitted for ratification by the States. If this Amendment is duly adopted, it will represent the will of the people accomplished in the manner prescribed by the Constitution. By acting prematurely and unnecessarily, as I view it, the Court has assumed a decisional responsibility at the very time when state legislatures, functioning within the traditional democratic process, are debating the proposed Amendment. It seems to me that this reaching out to pre-empt by judicial action a major political decision which is currently in process of resolution does not reflect appropriate respect for duly prescribed legislative processes.

There are times when this Court, under our system, cannot avoid a constitutional decision on issues which normally should be resolved by the elected representatives of the people. But democratic institutions are weakened, and confidence in the restraint of the Court is impaired, when we appear unnecessarily to decide sensitive issues of broad social and political importance at the very time they are under consideration within the prescribed constitutional processes.

NOTES

1. Appellant Joseph Frontiero is a full-time student at Huntingdon College in Montgomery, Alabama. According to the agreed stipulation of facts, his living expenses, including his share of the household expenses, total approximately $354 per month. Since he receives $205 per month in veterans' benefits, it is clear that he is not dependent upon appellant Sharron Frontiero for more than one-half of his support.
2. "[W]hile the Fifth Amendment contains no equal protection clause, it does forbid discrimination that is 'so unjustifiable as to be violative of due process.' " *Schneider* v. *Rusk,* 377 U. S. 163, 168 (1964).
3. Indeed, the position of women in this country at its inception is reflected in the view expressed by Thomas Jefferson that women should be neither seen nor heard in society's decisionmaking councils. See M. Gruberg, Women in American Politics 4 (1968). See also A. de Tocqueville, Democracy

*Citations omitted [Eds.]

in America, pt. 2 (Reeves tr. 1840), in World's Classic Series 400 (Galaxy ed. 1947).

4. *Reynolds* v. *Sims,* 377 U. S. 533, 562 (1964).

5. See generally, The President's Task Force on Women's Rights and Responsibilities, A Matter of Simple Justice (1970); L. Kantowitz, Women and the Law: The Unfinished Revolution (1969); A. Montague, Man's Most Dangerous Myth (4th ed. 1964); The President's Commission on the Status of Women, American Women (1963).

6. It is true, of course, that when viewed in the abstract, women do not constitute a small and powerless minority. Nevertheless, in part because of past discrimination, women are vastly underrepresented in this Nation's decisionmaking councils. There has never been a female President, nor a female member of this Court. Not a single woman presently sits in the United States Senate, and only 14 women hold seats in the House of Representatives. And, as appellants point out, this underrepresentation is present throughout all levels of our State and Federal Government. See Joint Reply Brief of Appellants and American Civil Liberties Union (*Amicus Curiae*) 9.

7. It should be noted that these statutes are not in any sense designed to rectify the effects of past discrimination against women. On the contrary, these statutes seize upon a group—women—who have historically suffered discrimination in employment, and rely on the effects of this past discrimination as a justification for heaping on additional economic disadvantages.

Suggestions for Further Reading

Baldwin, R. W., *Social Justice* (1966).

Bayles, Michael, "Compensatory Reverse Discrimination in Hiring," in *Social Theory and Practice,* Vol. 2 (1973), pp. 301–12.

Bayles, Michael, "Reparation to Wronged Groups," *Analysis,* Vol. 33 (1973).

Bedau, Hugo A., ed. *Justice and Equality* (1971).

Benn, S. I. and R. S. Peters, *Social Principles and the Democratic State* (1958), Chaps. 5, 6.

Bergler, E. and Meerloo, J. A. M., *Justice and Injustice* (1963).

Bowie, Norman E., *Towards a New Theory of Distributive Justice* (1971).

Brandt, Richard B., *Ethical Theory* (1959), Chap. 16.

Brandt, Richard B., ed., *Social Justice* (1962).

Brown, Emerson, Falk, Freedman, "The Equal Rights Amendment: A Constitutional Basis for Equal Rights for Women," 80 *Yale L.J.* 871, (1971).

Cahn, Edmond, *The Sense of Injustice* (1949).

Feinberg, Joel, "Justice and Personal Desert," reprinted in *Doing and Deserving* (1970), pp. 55–94.

Feinberg, Joel, "Noncomparative Justice," *Philosophical Review,* Vol. LXXXIII (1974), pp. 297–338.

Feinberg, Joel, *Social Philosophy* (1973), Chap. 7.

Frankel, Charles, "The New Egalitarianism and the Old," *Commentary,* Vol. 56 (Sept., 1973).

Freund, Paul A., "The Equal Rights Amendment is Not the Way," 6 *Harv. Civ. Rights—Civ. Lib. L. Rev.* 234 (1971).

Friedrich, C. J. and J. W. Chapman, eds., *Nomos VI: Justice* (1963).

Getman, J. G., "Emerging Constitutional Principle of Sexual Equality," 1972 *Supreme Court Review* 157.

Ginsberg, Morris, *On Justice in Society* (1965).

Godwin, William, *Political Justice* (1890).

Hardie, W. F., *Aristotle's Ethical Theory* (1968), Chap. X.

Hart, H. L. A., *The Concept of Law* (1961), Chaps. 5, 6.

Hobhouse, L. T., *Elements of Social Justice* (1922), Chaps. 5, 6.

Honore, A. M., "Social Justice," 8 *McGill L.J.* 78, (1962).

Hume, David, *An Enquiry Concerning the Principles of Morals* (1777), Chap. III.

Jencks, Christopher, *Inequality* (1972).

Kamenka, Eugene, *The Ethical Foundations of Marxism* (1962).

Katzner, Louis, "Presumptivist and Nonpresumptivist Principles of Formal Justice," *Ethics,* Vol. LXXXI (1971), pp. 253–58.

Kaufman, Walter, *Without Guilt and Justice* (1973), Chaps. 1–3.

Kelsen, Hans, *What is Justice?* (1957).

Kurland, Philip B., "The Equal Rights Amendment: Some Problems of Construction," 6 *Harv. Civ. Rights—Civ. Lib. L. Rev.* 243 (1971).

Lamont, W. D., *The Problems of Moral Judgment* (1946), Chap. 5.

Lewis, Anthony, *Gideon's Trumpet* (1964).

Lucas, J. R., *The Principles of Politics* (1966), Chaps. 28–9, 55–60.

Lyons, David, *The Forms and Limits of Utilitarianism* (1965), Chap. 5.

Nagel, Thomas, "Equal Treatment and Compensatory Discrimination," *Philosophy and Public Affairs,* Vol. 2 (1973), pp. 348–63.

Narveson, Jan, *Morality and Utility* (1967), Chaps. 6, 7.

Note, "Are Sex-Based Classifications Constitutionally Suspect?" 66 *Northwestern U.L. Rev.* 581 (1971).

Note, "Decline and Fall of the New Equal Protection: A Polemical Approach," 58 *Va. L. Rev.* 1489 (1972).

Note, "Legality of Homosexual Marriage," 82 *Yale L. J.* 573 (1973).

Note, "Pregnancy Discharges in the Military: The Air Force Experience," 86 *Harv. L. Rev.* 568 (1973).

Note, "Reverse Discrimination," 41 *U. Cincinatti L. Rev.* 250 (1972).

Olafson, Frederick A., ed., *Justice and Social Policy* (1961).

Pennock, J. R. and Chapman, J. W., eds., Nomos IX: *Equality* (1967).

Perelman, Chaim, *The Idea of Justice and the Problem of Argument* (1963).

Perelman, Chaim, *Justice* (1967).

Piaget, Jean, *The Moral Judgment of the Child* (1932).

Raphael, D. D., *Problems of Political Philosophy* (1970), Chap. 7.

Rashdall, Hastings, *Theory of Good and Evil* (1924), Vol. I, Chap. 8.

Rawls, John, *A Theory of Justice* (1972).

Rescher, Nicholas, *Distributive Justice* (1966).

Scanlon, Timothy M., Jr., "Rawls' Theory of Justice," 121 *U. Pa. L.R.* 1020 (1973).

Sidgwick, Henry, *The Methods of Ethics,* 7th ed. (1874), Book I, Chap. V.

Symposium, "Equal Rights for Women: A Symposium on the Proposed Constitutional Amendment," 6 *Harv. Civ. Rights—Civ. Lib. L. Rev.* 215 (1971).

Tawney, R. H., *Equality* (1929).

Thomson, Judith J., "Preferential Hiring," *Philosophy and Public Affairs,* Vol. 2 (1973), pp. 364–84.

Von Wright, G. H., *The Varieties of Goodness* (1963), Chap. X.

Williams, Bernard, "The Idea of Equality," in *Philosophy, Politics and Society,* 2nd series, ed. P. Laslett and W. G. Runciman (1962).

Wilson, John *Equality* (1966).

Woozley, A. D., "Injustice," *American Philosophical Quarterly,* Monograph No. 7 (1973), pp. 109–22.

Young, Michael, *The Rise of the Meritocracy* (1958).

PART 4 RESPONSIBILITY

Critical judgments about what people do occupy a very large place in our daily life. Philosophers want to make sure that these judgments are valid, and so seek principles under which the judgments may in turn themselves be criticized. There are urgent practical reasons for making sure that our criticism of conduct is sound. We live our lives in a community of persons each of whom pursues his own interests, yet each is required to respect the interests of others in order to make possible the benefits of life in a civilized society. Since disinterested benevolence is not a regular feature of social life, people must be encouraged to avoid harming others as they seek their own ends. When harm is done, it is important that acceptable remedies be applied to undo the harm as much as possible. It is also important to take steps that will reduce the likelihood of harm being done in the future. This requires holding to account those (and only those) who properly are accountable when something untoward occurs. It is a matter of some importance also that those (and only those) who are entitled to recognition for good works receive it, so that encouragement of socially valuable activities is provided. What we need, then, are ways of criticizing conduct that are rational and fair. Theoretical work concerned with responsibility seeks to increase our understanding of our critical practices, and through better understanding to make our critical conclusions more reasonable and just.

Legal theory is nowhere more generously endowed with philosophical substance than in those parts that address questions of responsibility. It is also true that the law offers more promising material than any other human endeavor to the philosopher who seeks to develop a theory of responsibility. This happy coincidence makes the subjects sampled in this part of the volume preeminent among concerns of legal philosophy. It is the criminal law that presents the most philosophically important questions, for a just system of criminal liability requires as a foundation principles of responsibility that are just. Civil liability, and especially the law of torts, also poses many similar questions under such textbook headings as fault, negligence, causation, and strict liability. Regarding criminal liability, we want to know when punishment is warranted. Responsibility of the accused is always the first (and sometimes the only) consideration in deciding that. In considering civil liability, we want to know when a loss suffered by one person is to be made up by another; and that often (though not always) involves issues of responsibility, sometimes to the exclusion of all other questions.

"A Plea for Excuses," which appeared in the 1950s, is one of a small number of pieces by J. L. Austin to be published in his lifetime. A leading figure in modern Oxford philosophy, Professor Austin here not only illuminates the method of linguistic philosophical investigation that is so prominent in much of modern Anglo-American philosophy, but also shows how an understanding of the important questions of responsibility at the intersection of law and moral philosophy is to be advanced by it. The small-scale, low-level questions are the rewarding ones, and one must be prepared, in Austin's work, not for global theories employing the grand concepts but rather for an uncovering of those innumerable and subtle differences in the details that together present a picture of human intelligence at work passing judgment on human actions. Professor Austin makes clear how extensive is the law's involvement in this critical practice—indeed the very lives of accused persons often turn on such judgments. While legal cases provide an endless supply of specimens for philosophical dissection, each in some respect different from any other, there are some caveats which Austin notes. Both philosophers and legal theorists should beware of sterile legal jargon and barren appeals to naked legal authority. The utterances of judges and legislatures not uncommonly contain appalling misuses of crucial terms (which Austin illustrates with the case of *Regina v. Finney*); or even worse, they contain faulty attempts at theory which then serve to mislead those who rely on the authority of what is said in deciding subsequent cases.

Even the little that has been said about responsibility so far will likely have created an impression in the reader's mind that the very subject of the discussion is not entirely clear. Just what is it that those who speak of responsibility are speaking of? H. L. A. Hart distinguishes the separate though related ideas concerning responsibility that are marked by different forms of expression and different contexts. There are four major categories, and within them a considerable number of important distinctions. As this sorting of expressions makes clear, much in critical practice and in its theory depends upon recognizing differences among expressions that on their face appear alike. This reminds us of J. L. Austin's observation that "words are our tools, and, as a minimum, we should use clean tools: we should know what we mean and what we do not, and must forearm ourselves against the traps that language sets us." Even more important, through work like Professor Hart's we become clear about the word and as a result of that learn about responsibility itself. Again Austin put the point sharply. "When we examine what we should say when, what words we should use in what situations, we are looking again not *merely* at words (or 'meanings,' whatever they may be) but also at the realities we use the words to talk about: we are using a sharpened awareness of words to sharpen our perception of, though not as final arbiter of, the phenomena." One may profitably consider here what the "final arbiter" is, with reference to responsibility as it is dealt with in Hart's analysis. If one wishes to understand what responsibility is, is there anything further that must be understood after one has exhaustively analyzed characteristic correct uses of the term? The value of Professor Hart's analysis is apparent to anyone who has experienced the confusion of responsibility and liability that permeates legal literature. Setting inappropriate requirements of responsibility for some legal liability, and imposing legal liability on some inappropriate occasions of responsibility, have both frequently resulted from just such confusion.

In ordinary life or in legal proceedings, whenever we assert that a person is responsible for some harm, we may be challenged on grounds of causation. It often counts conclusively against responsibility that what was done by the accused did not cause the unhappy event for which we wish to hold him liable. Yet clear as that is, there is hardly a more difficult task for the theorist than that of spelling out principles which determine in any given case whether the act was or was not the cause of the harm. At the heart of the difficulty is understanding what we *mean* by a cause when the cause is an act. Formidable difficulties about causation arise when general accounts of the relations among events of the physical world are attempted, and these difficulties are often imported into the special cause accounting that issues of personal responsibility call for. But should they be? Causation in a theory of responsibility may be very different in important respects from causation in a theory of scientific explanation or in metaphysics. Many things which are singled out as counting for or against the causal status of one event in relation to another seem not really to matter, as it turns out, when we are talking about *acts* (as acts) and their consequences. Who can deny that in some sense an ancestor's act of reproduction was a cause of the death of the person that his descendent murdered, yet who would assert that the act of reproduction caused the death? Even more revealing, perhaps, is the fact that *doing* harm and *causing* harm are quite different notions, yet an act which is the *doing* surely is in some other more general sense a cause of the harm, every bit as much a cause as another act which is spoken of as *causing* it. This strongly suggests that there is indeed something special about conceiving acts as causes, quite unlike conceiving viruses or volcanoes as causes.

Professor Hart and his Oxford colleague, A. M. Honoré, undertake to clarify causation as it bears on questions of responsibility in the law. In the first part of this selection from their book *Causation in the Law,* they consider the similarity in the concept of causation to be found in law and in morality. This can be accounted for by the common concern of both law and morality to ascertain responsibility. In this part they also point out certain differences, not in the very concept, but in the rules that are used by both law and morality to decide whether an act truly caused a harm. Considerations of legal policy require that the rules the law adopts be suited to the purposes the law must serve, and it is this that accounts for the difference. In the second and larger portion of this selection, the authors take up the master problem of when (ignoring such special restrictions) the consequences of an act can rightly be said to have been caused by it.

Three sorts of problematic cases are analyzed. All of them deal with intervening or supervening events but for which the harm would not have occurred. If what was done would not have resulted in the harm but for something subsequent which was quite usual, the subsequent event does not deprive the act of its causal status. If, however, there is an intervening voluntary act (subject to two major exceptions and certain qualifications), that deprives the earlier act of its causal status. Finally, in cases in which the harm is a result of mere coincidence of the consequence of the act and something else, the act is deprived of its causal status (though once again there is an important exception). After reading this selection, it seems appropriate to pose again and extend the question raised earlier. Is it the concept of causation one finds useful in explaining the physical world that is really germane to issues of responsibility? Have these authors been unduly influenced at any point by the problem of physical causation? And what, in any case, is it really that makes responsibility depend in part on whether one's act was the cause of the harm?

Robert E. Keeton shifts attention to risks in deciding whether or not an act caused harm. In "The Basic Rule of Legal Cause in Negligence Cases," Professor Keeton expounds a risk rule of causation which draws on the insight that causation issues in the law resolve themselves into issues about whether in acting one ought to have regard for some possible harm. The insight is not without its difficulties, however. One may wonder whether the modest claim that A is the cause of harm B has not been unduly enlarged in risk theory. It is not normally thought to be an objection to such a claim that act A was not negligent, for one who causes harm need not be at fault in doing so. Risk theory, however, seems to suggest the contrary. It suggests that when harm occurs and certain conduct caused it, the conduct is the cause of the harm because it created a risk of the harm and the harm was one that falls within the hazards of what was done. But creating a risk of the sort of harm that falls within the risks of what one is doing is (at the least) negligence. The challenge presented by risk analysis, then, is to separate its insight about risk from unwarranted implications concerning culpability.

The New York Times story reporting the tragedy of the Ault family presents a case in which the parents of the victim cannot be held liable for causing their daughter's death, even though they are the authors of the events that resulted in it. The story provides an opportunity for comparative testing of the voluntary intervention principle of Hart and Honoré, and the risk theory analysis of Keeton to see which provides the more illuminating account.

In the Palsgraf case, the Court's opinion by Judge Cardozo contains the following statement: "The law of causation, remote or proximate, is thus foreign to the case before us." Few on any court in the United States have been Cardozo's equal as a theorist of the law; yet in spite of his statement, this case has enjoyed the greatest popularity in American law schools as a case presenting the causation issue in torts. It therefore is incumbent on one who reads the case to ask first whether causation is indeed the issue. If the answer accords with the prevailing view, the next questions must be (1) what criteria are invoked in the opinions of the two judges to decide that issue (under whatever rubric they may place it); (2) what principle of causation, if any, can be extracted from the opinions; and (3) what could Judge Cardozo have meant?

Issues of causation raise questions about the antecedents of untoward events that occur. Problems of attempts resemble these issues (though the similarity is often not recognized by theorists). In their own way, attempts also raise questions of what harm is expectable. When there is a criminal attempt but not the completed crime, there has been conduct for which criminal liability is prescribed; but the harm which is also required for the completed crime has not occurred. There has been far less philosophical interest in attempts than in causation, the only question at all widely discussed among philosophers being whether (or why) it is just to punish attempts less severely than completed crimes. But legal theorists have been faced with philosophically rich problems of two sorts. One is the matter of distinguishing an attempt from what is usually called "mere preparation," so that activity far enough advanced for criminal liability may be distinguished from something less than that. The other problem, even more perplexing and offering even greater rewards for the theory of responsibility, is whether the impossibility of the harm occurring (whatever that might mean) is a bar to liability for attempt. Both of these issues, like causation questions, really require judgments about whether the harm of the completed crime is expectable given the conduct engaged in by the accused. Graham Hughes, in the selection entitled "Attempting the Impossible," examines the attempt defense that is based on a claim that the completed crime was impossible. His starting point is the orthodox distinction between a valid defense of legal impossibility and an invalid one of factual impossibility. Leading cases in the literature, both actual and imaginary, are analyzed and compared to extract a better principle, and a dialogue is presented that illustrates the difficulties. Professor Hughes's conclusions are based mainly on rather special considerations of legal policy and have not been included in the selection here. Though such policy considerations may ultimately dictate legal rules that are not pure reflections of principles of responsibility, it is always important first to get those principles as clear as one can, and the portions of the article included here provide much material for that endeavor.

"He is to blame" or "it is his fault" are judgments that often express the point of ascertaining responsibility. There is indeed a common emphatic sense of "he is responsible" that is equivalent to "he is to blame," and the subordinate considerations which lead to that are then obscured by an expression of the ultimate conclusion. In the nonlegal affairs of life we often want to fix blame when something bad has happened, either to fix the stigmata and apply for the remedies that social conventions warrant, or at least to set the record straight for future dealings. In legal contexts, both civil and criminal, fixing blame, while far from the whole matter, is nevertheless of the greatest importance in determining liability. In "Sua Culpa" Joel Feinberg separates and examines the different threads which compose a claim that a harm *is his fault*. The claim is first contrasted with two other fault-imputing expressions, *having a fault* and *being at fault.* One's act is at fault when the harm is one's fault; but there are two other conditions that must be satisfied. The act must be the cause of the harm; and the aspect of it that was faulty must be one of the aspects in virtue of which the act was the cause of the harm. The difficulties of the causal requirement again obtrude themselves, and the author endeavors to define the requirement in the face of them. Criteria for a cause are developed, and the reader may wish to consider what reason there is for an act to meet these criteria in order for blame to be fixed for that act. Finally, the suggestion that "his fault" can be dispensed with as a requirement for tort liability is assessed morally.

Professors Robert E. Keeton and Jeffrey O'Connell are the pioneer theorists and architects of no-fault automobile insurance in the United States, and in "Why Shift Loss?," excerpted from their book *Basic Protection for the Traffic Victim,* they consider reasons that justify shifting loss from the victim to someone else. In doing so, they criticize the two most prominent standing objections to no-fault insurance—that it disregards moral considerations by overlooking blameworthiness, and that it removes the deterrent to careless driving. The reader may wish to consider what moral considerations survive when the burden of liability is in any event placed on an insurance company, and whether there is a conflict between principles of responsibility and principles of justice (including principles supporting a socially desirable wide distribution of risk).

So far, criticism of the fault requirement has questioned whether it is needed in order to do justice. Professor Guido Calabresi carries the attack even further by claiming that it interferes with a fairer system and is a positive source of injustice in tort liability. In the selection from his book *The Cost of Accidents* entitled "The Fairness of the Fault System," the victims and those who injure them are conceived not in a bilateral relation defined by single occasions of injury, but rather in a multilateral web of those who cause and those who suffer harm in a world of accidents. Calabresi's points are not fully developed here, but the reader may wish to spell them out himself and to consider whether (or in what ways) the system the author advocates is more just as a system of accident compensation.

There has also been philosophically important debate about *criminal* liability for negligence, though in this situation it is said by critics that (mere) fault, far from being unnecessary, is not enough. Many theorists in England and America (though not on the Continent) have argued that on grounds of expediency and of justice it is wrong to punish those who did not mean to do harm, or at least were not aware of the harm that might result when they acted. In his essay "Negligence, *Mens Rea* and Criminal Responsibility," H. L. A. Hart makes clear what it is that may be said to justify criminal liability for negligence and shows how common misconceptions in theorizing are responsible for a contrary view. In addition to clarifying the notion of negligence, Professor Hart's discussion advances our understanding of how the criminal law is concerned with conduct when responsibility is at issue.

It may seem paradoxical that punishment for the relatively slight fault of negligence (even gross negligence) has excited more concern among lawyers than has punishment for totally faultless acts. This may be because of the relatively mild punishment and absence of criminal stigma that is usual when the offense is one requiring no fault— a sort of publicly accountable tort that hardly touches the perpetrator's respectability, and does not call for the curtailment of his liberty. Sometimes, however, harsher consequences await the blameless, and then instead of a petty though odious penalty in the interest of public welfare, we have (unless there is good reason for it) a cruel injustice. Liability without fault is most often referred to as "strict liability," and discussions of it in criminal law theory are almost always about when and why it is justified, not whether it ever is. In the selection "Strict Liability," excerpted from Professor Herbert Packer's book *The Limits of the Criminal Sanction,* strict liability is regarded as the preclusion of an excuse of mistake when offered as a defense to a criminal accusation. One must consider carefully whether in the cases discussed the accused is indeed without fault. If he turns out not to be without fault in what he did, there is still the important question whether it is *fair* to impose liability, all things considered. (Lawyers and public officials, as well as philosophers, will also want to ask whether it is prudent as a matter of public policy to do so.)

Liability when harm is not really "his fault" (as "his fault" is explicated in "Sua Culpa") is examined by Joel Feinberg in "Collective Responsibility." Strict liability, both civil and criminal, is explained according to the conventional rationale, and the various ways in which vicarious liability may arise are made clear, as are its proper limits. Collective responsibility is the subject that then occupies the remainder of the essay. Consideration is given first to a form of strict liability deriving from group solidarity. Then there is analysis of the several ways that the fault principles may result in liability for individuals and groups through mediating principles of distribution and collection when the party upon whom liability is imposed would not be liable according to fault principles alone.

One variety of collective responsibility discussed by Feinberg is the responsibility borne by all members of a group who could have and should have acted to save someone in distress but failed to do so. This suggests the more basic problem of when anyone is responsible for failing to act as a "volunteer" (as lawyers put it) or as a "Good Samaritan" (as moralists and laymen would characterize it). On one side, against responsibility, there are purported rights to mind one's own business, if one so chooses, and to avoid any risks—whether of legal liability for an unfortunate outcome, or of harm to oneself in the course of the intervention. In favor of some responsibility, it is argued that indifference to the plight of others in some situations is a willful disregard which is of such immoral proportions that the law must take notice. The argument against responsibility, no matter what, is obviously a losing one in a moral forum, for clearly there are sometimes moral duties of rescue. The issue, then, is whether moral duties ought ever to be recognized as legal duties, the breach of which is grounds for civil or even criminal liability. "Law, Morals, and Rescue" by A. M. Honoré takes up that question. There are subsidiary issues here which the author takes up first: What is required for there to be a moral duty of this sort that is recognized generally in the community? How shall we distinguish between moral duties and moral ideals? When is someone truly a "volunteer" rather than a person who has a duty which the law recognizes on other grounds? What are the limits to be imposed on officious intermeddling so that professed Good Samaritanism does not become an excuse for interference with privacy and self–determination? What claims for compensation may the rescuer assert, and against whom? All these are matters preliminary to the major question that the author then addresses: What policy reasons are there for imposing a legal duty of rescue that at bottom is only the enforcement of a moral duty?

The Good Samaritan may act to rescue someone apparently in distress so that he not only discharges a moral duty, but even more, acts beyond the call of duty as a moral hero. If such a person is then punished as a criminal, we might at first suspect the law has gone mad. But in fact the case of such a moral hero can be a close one, as the New York case of *People v. Young* makes clear. Included here in their entirety are the courts' opinions as well as the dissenting opinions in both the Appellate Division of the Supreme Court and then in the state's highest court, the Court of Appeals. The issues are subtle and challenging, and the reader will be well repaid if he pursues them. As it turned out, the defendant in this case was mistaken about the need for rescue when he saw a youth on the street being forced against his will to accompany two older men. Unknown to the defendant, the two men were detectives making an arrest. His attack upon the man in an attempt to aid the youth resulted in his being charged with criminal assault. As the opinions make clear, no outright justification is possible under New York law, since for that the defendant would have to be bound to protect the one he sought to help (which he was not); or—in a more strictly Good Samaritan vein—would have to have been attempting to prevent an offense against the youth (which was not constituted by the force employed in making a lawful arrest). It is the *mistake* which receives the greatest attention in these opinions. If it is reasonable it is an excuse that should exculpate, so runs the argument on one side. But whether that argument prevails depends on just what intent is legally necessary for the assault, for a mistake has relevance only if the law requires for liability that the thing done by mistake be done intentionally. Does the law, then, require that the accused intentionally do wrong, or only that he do intentionally what happens to be wrong? It seems on all sides to be agreed that the defendant here did the latter but not the former. Disagreement in the opinions is about what the law requires for liability. But those who hold that his mistake exonerates the defendant appear at times to go even further. There is some suggestion that even if the law only requires that he do intentionally what happens to be wrong, the attack is not wrong by virtue of the circumstances; the intimation is that there is a kind of subsidiary justification when a reasonable rescue is made, that it is a worthy endeavor which removes the curse of offensiveness from the otherwise offensive physical contacts. At this point a policy decision is called for, and the interest in safeguarding police from the perils of unwarranted interference is weighed against the countervailing interest of citizens being free to rescue each other from harm.

Concern about justice has so far dominated the discussions of responsibility in a criminal context. It is concern that criminal liability be deserved. But there is another perspective that is radically different, one in which the criminal law appears as an instrument of crime prevention. Convictions, in this view, are for the purpose of being able to subject to remedial treatment those who bring about the socially significant harms that concern the criminal law. Whether a person is responsible or not is then irrelevant (at least when "responsible" means "to blame"). Indeed the very issue of responsibility is a hindrance to the proper functioning of the system of correction that the criminal law serves, for it allows those in need of correction to avoid it by showing that with respect to matters that are significant only for moral judgments they are innocent. Lady Barbara Wootton in the excerpts from her book *Crime and the Criminal Law* advocates such a new perspective and declares that "the concept of responsibility should be allowed to wither away." That concept is attacked in the selection on two fronts. First there is the matter of *mens rea,* a term of art in criminal law theory that lends itself all too readily to gross abuse. Literally it means "culprit" or "guilty" mind, but that tells us nothing about its proper use. As Professor Hart's discussion in "Negligence, *Mens Rea,* and Criminal Responsibility" makes clear, it is a compendious expression characteristically used in denials of such excuses as *mistake* or *accident.* Lady Wootton adopts an interpretation suggested by its literal meaning, however, so that questions of *mens rea* become "questions of motivation," and she then proceeds to criticize the requirement of *mens rea* for criminal liability as undesirable moralism that interferes with the objectives of a forward-looking criminal process. In advocating elimination of the requirement of *mens rea* (to what extent exactly is not clear), she proposes very extensive strict criminal liability. And instead of degrees of culpability according to intention which now separate the more and the less serious forms of each kind of crime, she seems to believe that "the criterion of gravity" of an offense is "the amount of social damage which a crime causes."

Mental abnormality is the second front on which Lady Wootton attacks responsibility. Her discussion points out that unfortunate, even absurd, results may be expected from the way existing defenses of mental abnormality are given effect, and this is especially so in view of present institutional arrangements. Several considerations do indeed argue for reform. One is that there be deprivation of liberty (in whatever form) only when either criminal liability or dangerousness of the person warrants it. Another is that those who are sick (whether criminals or not) be given the care and treatment that humanity requires. Finally, when a person is truly dangerous and without ability to control himself, whether subject to criminal liability for his conduct or not, he is not to be left free to harm others. One may recognize that reform is urgently needed since, as things now stand, these considerations are often not respected. But the elimination from proceedings of concern about whether the accused had capacity to conform his conduct to law may seem to many not only an unnecessary encroachment on justice, but an encouragement of opportunities for violation of rights that are among the most basic a person has. Indeed, the concluding sentence of this selection in which Lady Wootton speaks of "places of safety" for offenders cannot help but sound ominous in view of what has more recently come to be known as "Clockwork Orange" correctional regimes. Further discussion of these matters is to be found in selections in the latter portion of Part Five of this volume.

Professor Hart in "Changing Conceptions of Responsibility" takes up the challenge Lady Wootton has presented. He scrutinizes the consequences of eliminating responsibility from the requirements for criminal conviction, particularly with reference to mental abnormality. Little need be said by way of introduction, for the issue is joined perfectly and the argument pursued with exemplary clarity and order. It does seem desirable, however, to note one point concerning Professor Hart's use here of the troublesome expression *mens rea.* It is a matter of some dispute among theorists whether there is *mens rea* in crimes of negligence, and also whether there can be *mens rea* when there is mental abnormality sufficient to exonerate. The first question is really about what conventions govern the use of a jargon term in criminal law theory. The second question, while it might also be construed that way, is better understood as an inquiry concerning certain matters of fact. As Professor Hart has made abundantly clear in other writings, in its characteristic employment the term is used to preclude excuses claiming that an act was done unintentionally, through assertions that there was *mens rea.* But many persons (though indeed not all) who are legally insane can act fully as intentionally as perfectly normal persons. The relevant abnormality of such a person would, for example, consist of psychotic notions of danger to himself or psychotic misconceptions of the justifiability of the harm he does. It would seem then that while *mens rea* requirements are fully satisfied, there is still a mental abnormality defense available quite independently based on a lack of capacity to choose to do otherwise. In Professor Hart's discussion here, however, this distinction among excuses seems not to be observed.

In "Mental Abnormality as a Criminal Excuse," Hyman Gross has endeavored to make clear the full range of exculpatory claims that look to mental abnormality and to discover what good reasons there are in principle for recognizing them as defenses in a criminal prosecution. Particular attention is given to the defense of insanity in the various versions in which that defense has been developed, and there is an assessment of each version in the light of more general concerns about responsibility as a condition of criminal liability.

The most controversial among the varieties of insanity defense in the United States has been the so-called Durham rule. In 1954, in the case of *Durham v. United States,* the Federal Court of Appeals for the District of Columbia adopted as a new insanity defense for that jurisdiction the rule that an unlawful act that was the product of mental disease or defect does not subject the perpetrator to criminal liability. Such a defense had in essence first been recognized in 1870 in New Hampshire, and two American jurisdictions other than the District of Columbia have also adopted it. In using it, two principal difficulties arise. The more obvious one is how to tell when conduct is the "product" of the abnormal condition. This raises both conceptual issues about just what it takes to be a "product" in the relevant sense, and factual questions about whether what the accused did was or was not a product (in the relevant sense) of his abnormal state. A less obvious but even more basic question is why the product of any mental disease or defect should not be a basis of criminal liability. No hint is given about what grounds there are in considerations of legal policy, justice, humanity, or anything else that might justify an excuse each and every time mental abnormality "produces" the criminal product.

In 1972, the *Durham* rule was overruled in *United States v. Brawner.* The Court's opinion is an ambitious attempt to consider the problems of practice and theory in light of the experience of the intervening years, and to provide instructions for properly implementing the new rule of the Model Penal Code (the ALI rule). The excerpts from the Court's opinion that are included here put the recurring issues in sharp focus. The last portion of these excerpts deals with questions of how culpability may be affected by mental abnormality other than by ways recognized in an insanity defense.

H. G.

J. L. A U S T I N

A Plea for Excuses*

The subject of this paper, *Excuses,* is one not to be treated, but only to be introduced, within such limits. It is, or might be, the name of a whole branch, even a ramiculated branch, of philosophy, or at least of one fashion of philosophy. I shall try, therefore, first to state *what* the subject is, *why* it is worth studying, and *how* it may be studied, all this at a regrettably lofty level: and then I shall illustrate, in more congenial but desultory detail, some of the methods to be used, together with their limitations, and some of the unexpected results to be expected and lessons to be learned. Much, of course, of the amusement, and of the instruction, comes in drawing the coverts of the microglot, in hounding down the minutiae, and to this I can do no more here than incite you. But I owe it to the subject to say, that it has long afforded me what philosophy is so often thought, and made, barren of—the fun of discovery, the pleasures of cooperation, and the satisfaction of reaching agreement.

What, then, is the subject? I am here using the word 'excuses' *for a title,* but it would be unwise to freeze too fast to this one noun and its partner verb: indeed for some time I used to use 'extenuation' instead. Still, on the whole 'excuses' is probably the most central and embracing term in the field, although this includes others of importance —'plea', 'defence', 'justification', and so on. When, then, do we 'excuse' conduct, our own or somebody else's? When are 'excuses' proffered?

In general, the situation is one where someone is *accused* of having done something, or (if that will keep it any cleaner) where someone is *said* to have done something which is bad, wrong, inept, unwelcome, or in some other of the numerous possible ways untoward. Thereupon he, or someone on his behalf, will try to defend his conduct or to get him out of it.

One way of going about this is to admit flatly that he, X, did do that very thing, A, but to argue that it was a good thing, or the right or sensible thing, or a permissible thing to do, either in general or at least in the special circumstances of the occasion. To take this line is to *justify* the action, to give reasons for doing it: not to say, to brazen it out, to glory in it, or the like.

A different way of going about it is to admit that it wasn't a good thing to have done, but to argue that it is not quite fair or correct to say *baldly* 'X did A'. We may say it isn't fair just to say X did it; perhaps he was under somebody's influence, or was nudged. Or, it isn't fair to say baldly he *did* A; it may have been partly accidental, or an unintentional slip. Or, it isn't fair to say he did simply A—he was really doing something quite different and A was only incidental, or he was looking at the whole thing quite differently. Naturally these arguments can be combined or overlap or run into each other.

In the one defence, briefly, we accept responsibility but deny that it was bad; in the other, we admit that it was bad but don't accept full, or even any, responsibility.

By and large, justifications can be kept distinct from excuses, and I shall not be so anxious to talk about them because they have enjoyed more than their fair share of philosophical attention. But the two certainly can be confused, and can *seem* to go very near to each other, even if they do not perhaps actually do so. You dropped the tea-tray: Certainly, but an emotional storm was about to break out: or, Yes, but there was a wasp. In each case the defence, very soundly, insists on a fuller description of the event in its context; but the first is a justification, the second an excuse. Again, if

*From *Aristotelian Society Proceedings,* LVII (1956–57), pp. 1–30. Reprinted by courtesy of the Editor of the Aristotelian Society, © 1957, The Aristotelian Society. Footnotes have been renumbered.

the objection is to the use of such a dyslogistic verb as 'murdered', this may be on the ground that the killing was done in battle (justification) or on the ground that it was only accidental if reckless (excuse). It is arguable that we do not use the terms justification and excuse as carefully as we might; a miscellany of even less clear terms, such as 'extenuation', 'palliation', 'mitigation', hovers uneasily between partial justification and partial excuse; and when we plead, say, provocation, there is genuine uncertainty or ambiguity as to what we mean—is he partly responsible, because he roused a violent impulse or passion in me, so that it wasn't truly or merely me acting 'of my own accord' (excuse)? Or is it rather that, he having done me such injury, I was entitled to retaliate (justification)? Such doubts merely make it the more urgent to clear up the usage of these various terms. But that the defences I have for convenience labelled 'justification' and 'excuse' are in principle distinct can scarcely be doubted.

This then is the sort of situation we have to consider under 'excuses'. I will only further point out how very wide a field it covers. We have, of course, to bring in the opposite numbers of excuses—the expressions that *aggravate*, such as 'deliberately', 'on purpose' and so on, if only for the reason that an excuse often takes the form of a rebuttal of one of these. But we have also to bring in a large number of expressions which at first blush look not so much like excuses as like accusations—'clumsiness', 'tactlessness', 'thoughtlessness', and the like. Because it has always to be remembered that few excuses get us out of it *completely:* the average excuse, in a poor situation, gets us only out of the fire into the frying pan—but still, of course, any frying pan in a fire. If I have broken your dish or your romance, maybe the best defence I can find will be clumsiness.

Why, if this is what 'excuses' are, should we trouble to investigate them? It might be thought reason enough that their production has always bulked so large among human activities. But to moral philosophy in particular, a study of them will contribute in special ways, both positively towards the development of a cautious, latter-day version of conduct, and negatively towards the correction of older and hastier theories.

In ethics we study, I suppose, the good and the bad, the right and the wrong, and this must be for the most part in some connexion with conduct or the doing of actions. Yet before we consider what actions are good or bad, right or wrong, it is proper to consider first what is meant by, and what not, and what is included under, and what not, the expression 'doing an action' or 'doing something'. These are expressions still too little examined on their own account and merits, just as the general notion of 'saying something' is still too lightly passed over in logic. There is indeed a vague and comforting idea in the background that, after all, in the last analysis, doing an action must come down to the making of physical movements with parts of the body; but this is about as true as that saying something must, in the last analysis, come down to making movements of the tongue.

The beginning of sense, not to say wisdom, is to realize that 'doing an action', as used in philosophy,[1] is a highly abstract expression—it is a stand-in used in the place of any (or almost any?) verb with a personal subject, in the same sort of way that 'thing' is a stand-in for any (or when we remember, almost any) noun substantive, and 'quality' a stand-in for the adjective. Nobody, to be sure, relies on such dummies quite implicitly quite indefinitely. Yet notoriously it is possible to arrive at, or to derive the idea for, an over-simplified metaphysics from the obsession with 'things' and their 'qualities.' In a similar way, less commonly recognized even in these semisophisticated times, we fall for the myth of the verb. We treat the expression 'doing an action' no longer as a stand-in for a verb with a personal subject, as which it has no doubt some uses, and might have more if the range of verbs were not left unspecified, but as a self-explanatory, ground-level description, one which brings adequately into the open the essential features of everything that comes, by simple inspection, under it. We scarcely notice even the most patent exceptions or difficulties (is to think something, or to say something, or to try to do something, to do an action?), any more than we fret, in the *ivresse des grandes profondeurs,* as to whether flames are things or events. So we come easily to think of our behaviour over any time, and of a life as a whole, as consisting in doing now action A, next action B, then action C, and so on, just as elsewhere we come to think of the world as consisting of this, that and the other substance or material thing, each with its properties. All 'actions' are, as actions (meaning what?), equal, composing a quarrel with striking a match, winning a war with sneezing: worse still, we assimilate them one and all to the supposedly most obvious and easy cases, such as posting letters or moving fingers, just as we assimilate all 'things' to horses or beds.

If we are to continue to use this expression in sober philosophy, we need to ask such questions as: Is to sneeze to do an action? Or is to breathe, or to see, or to checkmate, or each one of countless others? In short, for what range of verbs, as used on what occasions, is 'doing an action' a stand-in? What have they in common, and what do those excluded severally lack? Again we need to ask how we decide what is the correct name for 'the' action that somebody did—and what, indeed, are the rules for the use of 'the' action, 'an' action, 'one' action, a 'part' or 'phase' of an action and the like. Further, we need to realize that even the 'simplest' named actions are not so simple—certainly are not the mere makings of physical movements, and to ask what more, then, comes in (intentions? conventions?) and what does not (motives?), and what is the detail of the complicated internal machinery we use in 'acting'—the receipt of intelligence, the appreciation of the situation, the invocation of principles, the planning, the control of execution and the rest.

In two main ways the study of excuses can throw light on these fundamental matters. First, to examine excuses is to examine cases where there has been some abnormality or failure: and as so often, the abnormal will throw light on the normal, will help us to penetrate the blinding veil of case and obviousness that hides the mechanisms of the natural successful act. It rapidly becomes plain that the breakdowns signalized by the various excuses are of radically different kinds, affecting different parts or stages of the machinery, which the excuses consequently pick out and sort out for us. Further, it emerges that not *every* slip-up occurs in connexion with *everything* that could be called an 'action', that not every excuse is apt with every verb—far indeed from it: and this provides us with one means of introducing some classification into the vast miscellany of 'actions'. If we classify them according to the particular selection of breakdowns to which each is liable, this should assign them their places in some family group or groups of actions,

or in some model of the machinery of acting.

In this sort of way, the philosophical study of conduct can get off to a positive fresh start. But by the way, and more negatively, a number of traditional cruces or mistakes in this field can be resolved or removed. First among these comes the problem of freedom. While it has been the tradition to present this as the 'positive' term requiring elucidation, there is little doubt that to say we acted 'freely' (in the philosopher's use, which is only faintly related to the everyday use) is to say only that we acted *not* unfreely, in one or another of the many heterogeneous ways of so acting (under duress, or what not). Like 'real', 'free' is only used to rule out the suggestion of some or all of its recognized antitheses. As 'truth' is not a name for a characteristic of assertions, so 'freedom' is not a name for a characteristic of actions, but the name of a dimension in which actions are assessed. In examining all the ways in which each action may not be free, that is, the cases in which it will not do to say simply 'X did A', we may hope to dispose of the problem of freedom. Aristotle has often been chidden for talking about excuses or pleas and overlooking 'the real problem'; in my own case, it was when I began to see the injustice of this charge that I first became interested in excuses.

There is much to be said for the view that, philosophical tradition apart, responsibility would be a better candidate for the role here assigned to freedom. If ordinary language is to be our guide, it is to evade responsibility, or full responsibility, that we most often make excuses, and I have used the word myself in this way above. But in fact 'responsibility' too seems not really apt in all cases: I do not exactly evade responsibility when I plead clumsiness or tactlessness, nor, often, when I plead that I only did it unwillingly or reluctantly, and still less if I plead that I had in the circumstances no choice: here I was constrained and have an excuse (or justification), yet may accept responsibility. It may be, then, that at least two key terms, freedom and responsibility, are needed: the relation between them is not clear, and it may be hoped that the investigation of excuses will contribute towards its clarification.[2]

So much, then, for ways in which the study of excuses may throw light on ethics. But there are also reasons why it is an attractive subject methodologically, at least if we are to proceed from 'ordinary language', that is, by examining *what we should say when,* and so why and what we should mean by it. Perhaps this method, at least as *one* philosophical method, scarcely requires justification at present—too evidently, there is gold in them thar hills: more opportune would be a warning about the care and thoroughness needed if it is not to fall into disrepute. I will, however, justify it very briefly.

First, words are our tools, and, as a minimum, we should use clean tools: we should know what we mean and what we do not, and we must forearm ourselves against the traps that language sets us. Secondly, words are not (except in their own little corner) facts or things: we need therefore to prise them off the world, to hold them apart from and against it, so that we can realize their inadequacies and arbitrariness, and can relook at the world without blinkers. Thirdly, and more hopefully, our common stock of words embodies all the distinctions men have found worth drawing, and the connexions they have found worth marking, in the lifetimes of many generations: these surely are likely to be more numerous, more sound, since they have stood up to the long test of the survival of the fittest, and more subtle, at least in all ordinary and reasonably practical matters, than any that you or I are likely to think up in our armchairs of an afternoon—the most favoured alternative method.

In view of the prevalence of the slogan 'ordinary language', and of such names as 'linguistic' or 'analytic' philosophy or 'the analysis of language', one thing needs specially emphasizing to counter misunderstandings. When we examine what we should say when, what words we should use in what situations, we are looking again not *merely* at words (or 'meanings', whatever they may be) but also at the realities we use the words to talk about: we are using a sharpened awareness of words to sharpen our perception of, though not as the final arbiter of, the phenomena. For this reason I think it might be better to use, for this way of doing philosophy, some less misleading name than those given above—for instance, 'linguistic phenomenology', only that is rather a mouthful.

Using, then, such a method, it is plainly preferable to investigate a field where ordinary language is rich and subtle, as it is in the pressingly practical matter of excuses, but certainly is not in the matter, say, of time. At the same time we should prefer a field which is not too much trodden into bogs or tracks by traditional philosophy, for in that case even 'ordinary' language will often have become infected with the jargon of extinct theories, and our own prejudices too, as the upholders or imbibers of theoretical views, will too readily, and often insensibly, engaged. Here too, excuses form an admirable topic; we can discuss at least clumsiness, or absence of mind, or inconsiderateness, even spontaneousness, without remembering what Kant thought, and so progress by degrees even to discussing deliberation without for once remembering Aristotle or self-control without Plato. Granted that our subject is, as already claimed for it, neighbouring, analogous or germane in some way to some notorious centre of philosophical trouble, then, with these two further requirements satisfied, we should be certain of what we are after: a good site for *field work* in philosophy. Here at last we should be able to unfreeze, to loosen up and get going on agreeing about discoveries, however small, and on agreeing about how to reach agreement.[3] How much it is to be wished that similar field work will soon be undertaken in, say, aesthetics; if only we could forget for a while about the beautiful and get down instead to the dainty and the dumpy.

There are, I know, or are supposed to be, snags in 'linguistic' philosophy, which those not very familiar with it find, sometimes not without glee or relief, daunting. But with snags as with nettles, the thing to do is to grasp them—and to climb above them. I will mention two in particular, over which the study of excuses may help to encourage us. The first is the snag of loose (or divergent or alternative) usage; and the second the crux of the last word. Do we all say the same, and only the same, things in the same situations? Don't usages differ? And, Why should what we all ordinarily say be the only or best or final way of putting it? Why should it even be true?

Well, people's usages do vary, and we do talk loosely, and we do say different things apparently indifferently. But first, not nearly as much as one would think. When we come down to cases, it transpires in the very great majority that what we had thought was our wanting to say different things of and in *the same* situation was really not so—we had simply imagined the situation *slightly* differently: which is all too easy to do, because of course no situation (and we are dealing with *imagined* situations) is ever 'completely' described. The more we imagine the situation in detail, with a background of story—and it is worth employing the most idiosyncratic or, sometimes, boring means to stimulate and to discipline our wretched imaginations—the less we find we disagree about what we should say. Nevertheless, *sometimes* we do ultimately disagree: sometimes we must allow a usage to be, though appalling, yet actual; sometimes we should genuinely use either or both of two different descriptions. But why should this daunt us? All that is happening is entirely explicable. If our usages disagree, then you use 'X' where I use 'Y', or more probably (and more intriguingly) your conceptual system is different from mine, though very likely it is at least equally consistent and serviceable: in short, we can find *why* we disagree —you choose to classify in one way, I in another. If the usage is loose, we can understand the temptation that leads to it, and the distinctions that it blurs: if there are 'alternative' descriptions, then the situation can be described or can be 'structured' in two ways, or perhaps it is one where, for current purposes, the two alternatives come down to the same. A disagreement as to what we should say is not to be shied off, but to be pounced upon; for the explanation of it can hardly fail to be illuminating. If we light on an electron that rotates the wrong way, that is a discovery, a portent to be followed up, not a reason for chucking physics; and by the same token, a genuinely loose or eccentric talker is a rare specimen to be prized.

As practice in learning to handle this bogey, in learning the essential *rubrics,* we could scarcely hope for a more promising exercise than the study of excuses. Here, surely, is just the sort of situation where people will say 'almost anything', because they are so flurried, or so anxious to get off. 'It was a mistake', 'It was an accident'—how readily these can *appear* indifferent, and even be used together. Yet, a story or two, and everybody will not merely agree that they are completely different, but even discover for himself what the difference is and what each means.[4]

Then, for the Last Word. Certainly ordinary language has no claim to be the last word, if there is such a thing. It embodies, indeed, something better than the metaphysics of the Stone Age, namely, as was said, the inherited experience and acumen of many generations of men. But then, that acumen has been concentrated primarily upon the practical business of life. If a distinction works well for practical purposes in ordinary life (no mean feat, for even ordinary life is full of hard cases), then there is sure to be something in it, it will not mark nothing; yet this is likely enough to be not the best way of arranging things if our interests are more extensive or intellectual than the ordinary. And again, that experience has been derived only from the sources available to ordinary men throughout most of civilized history: it has not been fed from the resources of the microscope and its successors. And it must be added too, that superstitition and error and fantasy of all kinds do become incorporated in ordinary language and even sometimes stand up to the survival test (only, when they do, why should we not detect it?). Certainly, then, ordinary language is *not* the last word: in principle it can everywhere be supplemented and improved upon and superseded. Only remember, it *is* the *first* word.[5]

For this problem too the field of excuses is a fruitful one. Here is matter both contentious and practically important for everybody, so that ordinary language is on its toes: yet also, on its back it long had a bigger flea to bite it, in the shape of the law, and both again have lately attracted the attentions of yet another, and at last a healthily growing, flea, in the shape of psychology. In the law a constant stream of actual cases, more novel and more tortuous than the mere imagination could contrive, are brought up *for decision*— that is, formulae for docketing them must somehow be found. Hence it is necessary first to be careful with, but also to be brutal with, to torture, to fake and to override, ordinary language: we cannot here evade or forget the whole affair. (In ordinary life we dismiss the puzzles that crop up about time, but we cannot do that indefinitely in physics). Psychology likewise produces novel cases, but it also produces new methods for bringing phenomena under observation and study; moreover, unlike the law, it has an unbiased interest in the totality of them and is unpressed for decision. Hence its own special and constant need to supplement, to revise and to supersede the classifications of both ordinary life and the law. We have, then, ample material for practice in learning to handle the bogey of the last word, however it should be handled.

Suppose, then, that we set out to investigate excuses, what are the methods and resources initially available? Our object is to imagine the varieties of situation in which we make excuses, and to examine the expressions used in making them. If we have a lively imagination, together perhaps with an ample experience of dereliction, we shall go far, only we need system: I do not know how many of you keep a list of the kinds of fool you make of yourselves. It is advisable to use systematic aids, of which there would appear to be three at least. I list them here in order of availability to the layman.

First we may use the dictionary—quite a concise one will do, but the use must be *thorough*. Two methods suggest themselves, both a little tedious, but repaying. One is to read the book through, listing all the words that seem relevant; this does not take as long as many suppose. The other is to start with a widish selection of obviously relevant terms, and to consult the dictionary under each; it will be found that, in the explanations of the various meanings of each, a surprising number of other terms occur, which are germane though of course not often synonymous. We then look up each of *these,* bringing in more for our bag from the 'definitions' given in each case; and when we have continued for a little, it will generally be found that the family circle begins to close, until ultimately it is complete and we come only upon repetitions. This method has the advantage of grouping the terms into convenient clusters—but of course a good deal will depend upon the comprehensiveness of our initial selection.

Working the dictionary, it is interesting to find that a high percentage of the terms connected with excuses prove to be *adverbs,* a type of word which has not enjoyed so large a share of the philosophical limelight as the noun, substantive or adjective, and the verb: this is natural because, as was said, the tenor of so many excuses is that I did it but only *in a way,* not just flatly like that —that is, the verb needs modifying. Besides adverbs, however, there are other words of all kinds, including numerous abstract nouns, 'misconception', 'accident', 'purpose', and the like, and a few verbs too, which often hold key positions for the grouping of excuses into classes at a high level

('couldn't help', 'didn't mean to', 'didn't realize', or again 'intend', and 'attempt'). In connexion with the nouns another neglected class of words is prominent, namely, prepositions. Not merely does it matter considerably which preposition, often of several, is being used with a given substantive, but further the prepositions deserve study on their own account. For the question suggests itself, Why are the nouns in one group governed by 'under', in another by 'on', in yet another by 'by', or 'through' or 'from' or 'for' or 'with', and so on? It will be disappointing if there prove to be no good reasons for such groupings.

Our second source book will naturally be the law. This will provide us with an immense miscellany of untoward cases, and also with a useful list of recognized pleas, together with a good deal of acute analysis of both. No one who tries this resource will long be in doubt, I think, that the common law, and in particular the law of tort, is the richest storehouse; crime and contract contribute some special additions of their own, but tort is altogether more comprehensive and more flexible. But even here, and still more with so old and hardened a branch of the law as crime, much caution is needed with the arguments of counsel and the dicta or decisions of judges: acute though these are, it has always to be remembered that, in legal cases—

(1) there is the overriding requirement that a decision be reached, and a relatively black or white decision—guilty or not guilty—for the plaintiff or for the defendant;

(2) there is the general requirement that the charge or action and the pleadings be brought under one or another of the heads and procedures that have come in the course of history to be accepted by the courts. These, though fairly numerous, are still few and stereotyped in comparison with the accusations and defences of daily life. Moreover contentions of many kinds are beneath the law, as too trivial, or outside it, as too purely moral—for example, inconsiderateness;

(3) there is the general requirement that we argue from and abide by precedents. The value of this in the law is unquestionable, but it can certainly lead to distortions of ordinary beliefs and expressions.

For such reasons as these, obviously closely connected and stemming from the nature and function of the law, practising lawyers and jurists are by no means so careful as they might be to give to our ordinary expressions their ordinary meanings and applications. There is special pleading and evasion, stretching and strait-jacketing, besides the invention of technical terms, or technical senses for common terms. Nevertheless, it is a perpetual and salutary surprise to discover how much is to be learned from the law; and it is to be added that if a distinction drawn is a sound one, even though not yet recognized in law, a lawyer can be relied upon to take note of it, for it may be dangerous not to—if he does not, his opponent may.

Finally, the third source book is psychology, with which I include such studies as anthropology and animal behaviour. Here I speak with even more trepidation than about the law. But this at least is clear, that some varieties of behaviour, some ways of acting or explanations of the doing of actions, are here noticed and classified which have not been observed or named by ordinary men and hallowed by ordinary language, though perhaps they often might have been so if they had been of more practical importance. There is real danger in contempt for the 'jargon' of psychology, at least when it sets out to supplement, and at least sometimes when it sets out to supplant, the language of ordinary life.

With these sources, and with the aid of the imagination, it will go hard if we cannot arrive at the meanings of large numbers of expressions and at the understanding and classification of large numbers of 'actions'. Then we shall comprehend clearly much that, before, we only made use of *ad hoc*. Definition, I would add, explanatory definition, should stand high among our aims: it is not enough to show how clever we are by showing how obscure everything is. Clarity, too, I know, has been said to be not enough; but perhaps it will be time to go into that when we are within measurable distance of achieving clarity on some matter.

So much for the cackle. It remains to make a few remarks, not, I am afraid, in any very coherent order, about the types of significant result to be obtained and the more general lessons to be learned from the study of excuses.

1. *No modification without aberration.* When it is stated that X did A, there is a temptation to suppose that given some, indeed perhaps *any*, expression modifying the verb we shall be entitled to insert either it or its opposite or negation in our statement: that is, we shall be entitled to ask, typically, 'Did X do A Mly or not Mly? (for example, 'Did X murder Y voluntarily or involuntarily?'), and to answer one or the other. Or as a minimum it is supposed that if X did A there must be at *least one* modifying expression that we could, justifiably and informatively, insert with the verb. In the great majority of cases of the use of the great majority of verbs ('murder' perhaps is not one of the majority) such suppositions are quite unjustified. The natural economy of language dictates that for the *standard* case covered by any normal verb—not, perhaps, a verb of omen such as 'murder', but a verb like 'eat' or 'kick' or 'croquet'—no modifying expression is required or even permissible. Only if we do the action named in some *special* way or circumstances, different from those in which such an act is naturally done (and of course both the normal and the abnormal differ according to what verb in particular is in question) is a modifying expression called for, or even in order. I sit in my chair, in the usual way—I am not in a daze or influenced by threats or the like; here, it will not do to say either that I sat in it intentionally or that I did not sit in it intentionally,[6] nor yet that I sat in it automatically or from habit or what you will. It is bedtime, I am alone, I yawn: but I do not yawn involuntarily (or voluntarily!), nor yet deliberately. To yawn in any such peculiar way is just not to just yawn.

2. *Limitation of application.* Expressions modifying verbs, typically adverbs, have limited ranges of application. That is, given any adverb of excuse, such as 'unwittingly' or 'spontaneously' or 'impulsively', it will not be found that it makes good sense to attach it to any and every verb of 'action' in any and every context: indeed, it will often apply only to a comparatively narrow range of such verbs. Something in the lad's upturned face appealed to him, he threw a brick at it—'spontaneously'? The interest then is to discover why some actions can be excused in a particular way but not others, particularly perhaps the latter.[7] This will largely elucidate the meaning of the excuse, and at the same time will illuminate the characteristics typical of the group of 'actions' it picks out: very often too it will throw light on some detail of the machinery of 'action' in general (see 4), or on our standards of accept-

able conduct (see 5). It is specially important in the case of some of the terms most favoured by philosophers or jurists to realize that at least in ordinary speech (disregarding back-seepage of jargon) they are not used so universally or so dichotomistically. For example, take 'voluntarily' and 'involuntarily': we may join the army or make a gift voluntarily, we may hiccough or make a small gesture involuntarily, and the more we consider further actions which we might naturally be said to do in either of these ways, the more circumscribed and unlike each other do the two classes become, until we even doubt whether there is *any* verb with which both adverbs are equally in place. Perhaps there are some such; but at least sometimes when we may think we have found one it is an illusion, an apparent exception that really does prove the rule. I can perhaps 'break a cup' voluntarily, *if* that is done, say, as an act of self-impoverishment: and I can perhaps break another involuntarily, *if*, say, I make an involuntary movement which breaks it. Here, plainly, the two acts described each as 'breaking a cup' are really very different, and the one is similar to acts typical of the 'voluntary' class, the other to acts typical of the 'involuntary' class.

3. *The importance of Negations and Opposites.* 'Voluntarily' and 'involuntarily', then, are not opposed in the obvious sort of way that they are made to be in philosophy or jurisprudence. The 'opposite', or rather 'opposites', of 'voluntarily' might be 'under constraint' of some sort, duress or obligation or influence:[8] the opposite of 'involuntarily' might be 'deliberately' or 'on purpose' or the like. Such divergences in opposites indicate that 'voluntarily' and 'involuntarily', in spite of their apparent connexion, are fish from very different kettles. In general, it will pay us to take nothing for granted or as obvious about negations and opposites. It does not pay to assume that a word must have an opposite, or one opposite, whether it is a 'positive' word like 'wilfully' or a 'negative' word like 'inadvertently'. Rather, we should be asking ourselves such questions as why there is no use for the adverb 'advertently'. For above all it will not do to assume that the 'positive' word must be around to wear the trousers; commonly enough the 'negative' (looking) word marks the (positive) abnormality, while the 'positive' word, *if* it exists, merely serves to rule out the suggestion of that abnormality. It is natural

enough, in view of what was said in (1) above, for the 'positive' word not to be found at all in some cases. I do an act A_1 (say, crush a snail) *inadvertently* if, in the course of executing by means of movements of my bodily parts some other act A_2 (say, in walking down the public path) I fail to exercise such meticulous supervision over the courses of those movements as would have been needed to ensure that they did not bring about the untoward event (here, the impact on the snail).[9] By claiming that A_1 was inadvertent we place it, where we imply it belongs, on this special level, in a class of incidental happenings which must occur in the doing of any physical act. To lift the act out of this class, we need and possess the expression 'not ... inadvertently': 'advertently', if used for this purpose, would suggest that, if the act was not done inadvertently, then it must have been done noticing what I was doing, which is far from necessarily the case (for example, if I did it absent-mindedly), or at least that there is *something* in common to the ways of doing all acts not done inadvertently, which is not the case. Again, there is no use for 'advertently' at the *same* level as 'inadvertently': in passing the butter I do not knock over the cream-jug, though I do (inadvertently) knock over the teacup—yet I do not by-pass the cream-jug *advertently:* for at this level, below supervision in detail, *anything* that we do is, if you like, inadvertent, though we only call it so, and indeed only call it something we have done, if there is something untoward about it.

A further point of interest in studying so-called 'negative' terms is the manner of their formation. Why are the words in one group formed with *un-* or *in-*, those in another with *-less* ('aimless', 'reckless', 'heedless', et cetera), and those in another with *mis-* ('mistake', 'misconception', 'misjudgment', et cetera)? Why carelessly but *in-*attentively? Perhaps care and attention, so often linked, are rather different. Here are remunerative exercises.

4. *The machinery of action.* Not merely do adverbial expressions pick out classes of actions, they also pick out the internal detail of the machinery of doing actions, or the departments into which the business of actions is organized. There is for example the stage at which we have actually to *carry out* some action upon which we embark —perhaps we have to make certain bodily movements or to make a speech. In the course of actu-

ally *doing* these things (getting weaving) we have to pay (some) attention to what we are doing and to take (some) care to guard against (likely) dangers: we may need to use judgment or tact; we must exercise sufficient control over our bodily parts, and so on. Inattention, carelessness, errors of judgment, tactlessness, clumsiness, all these and others are ills (with attendant excuses) which affect one specific stage in the machinery of action, the *executive* stage, the stage where we *muff* it. But there are many other departments in the business too, each of which is to be traced and mapped through its cluster of appropriate verbs and adverbs. Obviously there are departments of intelligence and planning, of decision and resolve, and so on, but I shall mention one in particular, too often overlooked, where troubles and excuses abound. It happens to us, in military life, to be in receipt of excellent intelligence, to be also in self-conscious possession of excellent principles (the five golden rules for winning victories), and yet to hit upon a plan of action which leads to disaster. One way in which this can happen is through failure at the stage of *appreciation* of the situation, that is at the stage where we are required to cast our excellent intelligence into such a form, under such heads and with such weights attached, that our equally excellent principles can be brought to bear on it properly, in a way to yield the right answer.[10] So too in real, or rather civilian, life, in moral or practical affairs, we can know the facts and yet look at them mistakenly or perversely, or not fully realize or appreciate something, or even be under a total misconception. Many expressions of excuse indicate failure at this particularly tricky stage: even thoughtlessness, inconsiderateness, lack of imagination, are perhaps less matters of failure in intelligence or planning than might be supposed, and more matters of failure to appreciate the situation. A course of E. M. Forster and we see things differently: yet perhaps we know no more and are no cleverer.

5. *Standards of the unacceptable.* It is characteristic of excuses to be 'unacceptable': given, I suppose, almost any excuse, there will be cases of such a kind or of such gravity that 'we will not accept' it. It is interesting to detect the standards and codes we thus invoke. The extent of the supervision we exercise over the execution of any act can never be quite unlimited, and usually is expected to fall within fairly definite limits ('due care and attention') in the case of acts of some general kind, though of course we set very different limits in different cases. We may plead that we trod on the snail inadvertently: but not on a baby —you ought to look where you are putting your great feet. Of course it *was* (*really*), if you like, inadvertence; but that word constitutes a plea, which is not going to be allowed, because of standards. And if you try it on, you will be subscribing to such dreadful standards that your last state will be worse than your first. Or again, we set different standards, and will accept different excuses, in the case of acts which are rule-governed, like spelling, and which we are expected absolutely to get right, from those we set and accept for less stereotyped actions: a wrong spelling may be a slip, but hardly an accident, a winged beater may be an accident, but hardly a slip.

6. *Combination, dissociation and complication.* A belief in opposites and dichotomies encourages, among other things, a blindness to the combinations and dissociations of adverbs that are possible, even to such obvious facts as that we can act at once on impulse and intentionally, or that we can do an action intentionally yet for all that not deliberately, still less on purpose. We walk along the cliff, and I feel a sudden impulse to push you over, which I promptly do: I acted on impulse, yet I certainly intended to push you over, and may even have devised a little ruse to achieve it: yet even then I did not act deliberately, for I did not (stop to) ask myself whether to do it or not.

It is worth bearing in mind, too, the general rule that we must not expect to find simple labels for complicated cases. If a mistake results in an accident, it will not do to ask whether 'it' was an accident or a mistake, or to demand some briefer description of 'it'. Here the natural economy of language operates: if the words already available for simple cases suffice in combination to describe a complicated case, there will be need for special reasons before a special new word is invented for the complication. Besides, however well-equipped our language, it can never be forearmed against all possible cases that may arise and call for description: fact is richer than diction.

7. *Regina v. Finney.* Often the complexity and difficulty of a case is considerable. I will quote the case of *Regina v. Finney*:[11]

Shrewsbury Assizes. 1874.   12 Cox 625.

Prisoner was indicted for the manslaughter of Thomas Watkins.

The Prisoner was an attendant at a lunatic asylum. Being in charge of a lunatic, who was bathing, he turned on hot water into the bath, and thereby scalded him to death. The facts appeared to be truly set forth in the statement of the prisoner made before the committing magistrate, as follows: 'I had bathed Watkins, and had loosed the bath out. I *intended putting in a clean bath,* and asked Watkins if he would get out. At this time *my attention was drawn* to the next bath by the new attendant, who was asking me a question; and *my attention was taken from the bath* where Watkins was. I put my hand down to turn water on in the bath where Thomas Watkins was. *I did not intend to turn the hot water,* and *I made a mistake in the tap. I did not know what I had done until* I heard Thomas Watkins shout out; and *I did not find my mistake out till* I saw the steam from the water. You cannot get water in this bath when they are drawing water at the other bath; but at other times it shoots out like a water gun when the other baths are not is use. . . .'

(It was proved that the lunatic had such possession of his faculties as would enable him to understand what was said to him, and to get out of the bath.)

A. *Young* (for Prisoner). The death *resulted from accident.* There was no such *culpable negligence* on the part of the prisoner as will support this indictment. A *culpable mistake,* or some degree of *culpable negligence,* causing death, will not support a charge of manslaughter; unless the *negligence* be so gross as to be *reckless. (R. v. Noakes).*

Lush, J. To render a person liable for *neglect of duty* there must be such a degree of culpability as to amount to *gross negligence* on his part. If you accept the prisoner's own statement, you find no such amount of *negligence* as would come within this definition. It is not every little *trip or mistake* that will make a man so liable. It was the duty of the attendant not to let hot water into the bath while the patient was therein. According to the prisoner's own account, *he did not believe that* he was letting the hot water in while the deceased remained there. The lunatic was, we have heard, a man capable of getting out by himself and of understanding what was said to him. He was told to get out. A new attendant who had come on this day, was at an adjoining bath and he *took off the prisoner's attention.* Now, if the prisoner, knowing that the man was in the bath, had turned on the tap, and turned on the hot instead of the cold water, I should have said there was gross negligence; for he ought to have looked to see. But from his own account he had told the deceased to get out, and *thought he had got out.* If you think that

indicates gross *carelessness,* then you should find the prisoner guilty of manslaughter. But if you think it *inadvertence* not amounting to culpability—that is, what is properly termed an *accident*—then the prisoner is not liable.

Verdict, Not guilty.

In the case there are two morals that I will point:

(i) Both counsel and judge make very free use of a large number of terms of excuse, using several as though they were, and even stating them to be, indifferent or equivalent when they are not, and presenting as alternatives those that are not.

(ii) It is constantly difficult to be sure *what* act it is that counsel or judge is suggesting might be qualified by what expression of excuse.

The learned judge's concluding direction is a paradigm of these faults.[12] Finney, by contrast, stands out as an evident master of the Queen's English. He is explicit as to each of his acts and states, mental and physical: he uses different, and the correct, adverbs in connexion with each: and he makes no attempt to boil down.

8. *Small distinctions, and big too.* It should go without saying that terms of excuse are not equivalent, and that it matters which we use: we need to distinguish inadvertence not merely from (save the mark) such things as mistake and accident, but from such nearer neighbours as, say, aberration and absence of mind. By imagining cases with vividness and fullness we should be able to decide in which precise terms to describe, say, Miss Plimsoll's action in writing, so carefully, 'DAIRY' on her fine new book: We should be able to distinguish between sheer, mere, pure, and simple mistake or inadvertence. Yet unfortunately, at least when in the grip of thought, we fail not merely at these stiffer hurdles. We equate even—I have seen it done—'inadvertently' with 'automatically': as though to say I trod on your toe inadvertently means to say I trod on it automatically. Or we collapse succumbing to temptation into losing control of ourselves—a bad patch, this, for telescoping.[13]

All this is not so much a *lesson* from the study of excuses as the very object of it.

9. *The exact phrase and its place in the sentence.* It is not enough, either, to attend simply to the 'key' word: notice must also be taken of the

full and exact form of the expression used. In considering mistakes, we have to consider seriatim 'by mistake', 'owning to a mistake', 'mistakenly', 'it was a mistake to', 'to make a mistake in or over or about,' 'to be mistaken about', and so on: in considering purpose, we have to consider 'on', 'with the', 'for the', et cetera, besides 'purposeful', 'purposeless', and the like. These varying expressions may function quite differently—and usually do, or why should we burden ourselves with more than one of them?

Care must be taken too to observe the precise position of an adverbial expression in the sentence. This should of course indicate what verb it is being used to modify: but more than that, the position can also affect the *sense* of the expression, that is, the way in which it modifies that verb. Compare, for example:

a₁ He clumsily trod on the snail.
a₂ Clumsily he trod on the snail.
b₁ He trod clumsily on the snail.
b₂ He trod on the snail clumsily.

Here, in a₁ and a₂, we describe his treading on the creature at all as a piece of clumsiness, incidental, we imply, to his performance of some other action: but with b₁ and b₂ to tread on it is, very likely, his aim or policy, what we criticize is his execution of the feat.[14] Many adverbs, though far from all (not, for example, 'purposely') are used in these two typically different ways.

10. *The style of performance.* With some adverbs the distinction between the two senses referred to in the last paragraph is carried a stage further. 'He ate his soup deliberately' may mean, like 'He deliberately ate his soup', that his eating his soup was a deliberate act, one perhaps that he thought would annoy somebody, as it would more commonly if he deliberately *ate my* soup, and which he decided to do; but it will often mean that he went through the performance of eating his soup in a noteworthy manner or *style*—pause after each mouthful, careful choice of point of entry for the spoon, sucking of moustaches, and so on. That is, it will mean that he ate *with* deliberation rather than *after* deliberation. The style of the performance, show and unhurried, is understandably called 'deliberate' because each movement *has the typical look* of a deliberate act;

but it is scarcely being said that the making of each motion *is* a deliberate act or that he is 'literally' deliberating. This case, then, is more extreme than that of 'clumsily', which does in both uses describe literally a manner of performing.

It is worth watching out for this secondary use when scrutinizing any particular adverbial expression: when it definitely does not exist, the reason is worth inquiring into. Sometimes it is very hard to be sure whether it does exist or does not: it does, one would think, with 'carelessly', it does not with 'inadvertently', but does it or does in not with 'absent-mindedly' or 'aimlessly'? In some cases a word akin to but distinct from the primary adverb is used for this special role of describing a style of performance: we use 'purposefully' in this way, but never 'purposely'.

11. *What modifies what?* The judge in *Regina v. Finney* does not make clear what event is being excused in what way. 'If you think that indicates gross carelessness, then. . . . But if you think it inadvertence not amounting to culpability—that is, what is properly called an accident—then. . . .' Apparently he means that Finney may have *turned on the hot tap* inadvertently:[15] does he mean also that the tap may have been turned accidentally, or rather that *Watkins may have been scalded* and killed accidentally? And was the carelessness in turning the tap or in thinking Watkins had got out? Many disputes as to what excuse we should properly use arise because we will not trouble to state explicitly *what* is being excused.

To do so is all the more vital because it is in principle always open to us, along various lines, to describe or refer to 'what I did' in so many different ways. This is altogether too large a theme to elaborate here. Apart from the more general and obvious problems of the use of 'tendentious' descriptive terms, there are many special problems in the particular case of 'actions'. Should we say, are we saying, that he took her money, or that he robbed her? That he knocked a ball into a hole, or that he sank a putt? That he said 'Done', or that he accepted an offer? How far, that is, are motives, intentions and conventions to be part of the description of actions? And more especially here, what is *an* or *one* or *the* action? For we can generally split up what might be named as one action in several distinct ways, into different *stretches* or *phrases* or *stages.*

Stages have already been mentioned: We can dismantle the machinery of the act, and describe (and excuse) separately the intelligence, the appreciation, the planning, the decision, the execution and so forth. Phases are rather different: we can say that he painted a picture or fought a campaign, or else we can say that first he laid on this stroke of paint and then that, first he fought this action and then that. Stretches are different again: a single term descriptive of what he did may be made to cover either a smaller or a larger stretch of events, those excluded by the narrower description being then called 'consequences' or 'results' or 'effects' or the like of his act. so here we can describe Finney's act *either* as turning on the hot tap, which he did by mistake, with the result that Watkins was scalded, or as scalding Watkins which he did *not* do by mistake.

It is very evident that the problems of excuses and those of the different descriptions of actions are throughout bound up with each other.

12. *Trailing clouds of etymology.* It is these considerations that bring us up so forcibly against some of the most difficult words in the whole story of excuses, such words as 'result', 'effect', and 'consequence', or again as 'intention', 'purpose', and 'motive'. I will mention two points of method which are, experience has convinced me, indispensable aids at these levels.

One is that a word never—well, hardly ever—shakes off its etymology and its formation. In spite of all changes in and extensions of and additions to its meanings and indeed rather pervading and governing these, there will still persist the old idea. In an *accident* something befalls: by *mistake* you take the wrong one: in *error* you stray: when you act *deliberately* you act after weighing it up (*not* after thinking out ways and means). It is worth asking ourselves whether we know the etymology of 'result' or of 'spontaneously', and worth remembering that 'unwillingly' and 'involuntarily' come from very different sources.

And the second point is connected with this. Going back into the history of a word, very often into Latin, we come back pretty commonly to pictures of *models* of how things happen or are done. These models may be fairly sophisticated and recent, as is perhaps the case with 'motive' or 'impulse', but one of the commonest and most primitive types of model is one which is apt to baffle us through its very naturalness and simplicity. We take *some very simple action,* like shoving a stone, usually as done by and viewed by oneself, and use *this,* with the features distinguishable in it, as our model in terms of which to talk about other actions and events: and we continue to do so, scarcely realizing it, even when these other actions are pretty remote and perhaps much more interesting to us in their own right than the acts originally used in constructing the model ever were, and even when the model is really distorting the racts rather than helping us to observe them. In primitive cases we may get to see clearly the differences between, say, 'results', 'effects', and 'consequences', and yet discover that these differences are no longer clear, and the terms themselves no longer of real service to us, in the more complicated cases where we had been bandying them about most freely. A model must be recognized for what it is. 'Causing', I suppose, was a notion taken from a man's own experience of doing simple actions, and by primitive man every event was construed in terms of this model: every event has a cause, that is, every event is an action done by somebody—if not by a man, then by a quasiman, a spirit. When, later, events which are *not* actions are realized to be such, we still say that they must be 'caused', and the word snares us: we are struggling to ascribe to it a new, unanthropomorphic meaning, yet constantly, in searching for its analysis, we unearth and incorporate the lineaments of the ancient model. As happened even to Hume, and consequently to Kant. Examining such a word historically, we may well find that it has been extended to cases that have by now too tenuous a relation to the model case, that it is a source of confusion and superstition.

There is too another danger in words that invoke models, half-forgotten or not. It must be remembered that there is no necessity whatsoever that the various models used in creating our vocabulary, primitive or recent, should all fit together neatly as parts into one single, total model or scheme of, for instance, the doing of actions. It is possible, and indeed highly likely, that our assortment of models will include some, or many, that are overlapping, conflicting, or more generally simply *disparate.* [16]

13. In spite of the wide and acute observation of the phenomena of action embodied in ordinary speech, modern scientists have been able, it seems

to me, to reveal its inadequacy at numerous points, if only because they have had access to more comprehensive data and have studied them with more catholic and dispassionate interest than the ordinary man, or even the lawyer, has had occasion to do. I will conclude with two examples.

Observation of animal behaviour shows that regularly, when an animal is embarked on some recognizable pattern of behaviour but meets in the course of it with an insuperable obstacle, it will betake itself to energetic, but quite unrelated, activity of some wild kind, such as standing on its head. This phenomenon is called 'displacement behaviour' and is well identifiable. If now, in the light of this, we look back at ordinary human life, we see that displacement behaviour bulks quite large in it: yet we have apparently no word, or at least no clear and simple word, for it. If, when thwarted, we stand on our heads or wiggle our toes, then we are not exactly *just* standing on our heads, don't you know, in the ordinary way, yet is there any convenient adverbial expression we can insert to do the trick? 'In desperation'?

Take, again, 'compulsive' behaviour, however exactly psychologists define it, compulsive washing for example. There are of course hints in ordinary speech that we do things in this way—'just feel I have to', 'shouldn't feel comfortable unless I did', and the like: but there is no adverbial expression satisfactorily preempted for it, as 'compulsively' is. This is understandable enough, since compulsive behaviour, like displacement behaviour, is not in general going to be of great practical importance.

Here I leave and commend the subject to you.

NOTES

1. This use has little to do with the more down-to-earth occurrences of 'action' in ordinary speech.

2. Another well-flogged horse in these same stakes is blame. At least two things seem confused together under this term. Sometimes when I blame X for doing A, say for breaking the vase, it is a question simply or mainly of my disapproval of A, breaking the vase, which unquestionably X did: but sometimes it is, rather, a question simply or mainly of how far I think X responsible for A, which unquestionably was bad. Hence if somebody says he blames me for something, I may answer by giving a *justification,* so that he will cease to disapprove of what I did, or else by giving an *excuse,* so that he will cease to hold me, at least entirely and in every way, responsible for doing it.

3. All of which was seen and claimed by Socrates, when he first betook himself to the way of Words.

4. You have a donkey, so have I, and they graze in the same field. The day comes when I conceive a dislike for mine. I go to shoot it, draw a bead on it, fire: the brute falls in its tracks. I inspect the victim, and find to my horror that it is *your* donkey. I appear on your doorstep with the remains and say—what? 'I say, old sport, I'm awfully sorry, et cetera, I've shot your donkey by *accident?* Or *'by mistake'?* Then again, I go to shoot my donkey as before, draw a bead on it, fire— but as I do so, the beasts move, and to my horror yours falls. Again the scene on the doorstep—what do I say? 'By mistake'? Or 'by accident'?

5. And forget, for once and for a while, that other curious question 'Is it true?' May we?

6. Caveat or hedge: of course we can say 'I did *not* sit in it "intentionally" ' as a way simply of repudiating the suggestion that I sat in it intentionally.

7. For we are sometimes not so good at observing what we *can't* say as what we can, yet the first is pretty regularly the more revealing.

8. But remember, when I sign a cheque in the normal way, I do *not* do so *either* 'voluntarily' or 'under constraint'.

9. Or analogously: I do an act A¹ (say, divulge my age, or imply you are a liar), *inadvertently* if, in the course of executing by the use of some medium of communication some other act. A² (say, reminiscing about my war service) I fail to exercise such meticulous supervision over the choice and arrangement of the signs as would have been needed to ensure that. . . . It is interesting to note how such adverbs lead parallel lives, one in connexion with physical actions ('doing') and the other in connexion with acts of communication ('saying'), or sometimes also in connexion with acts of 'thinking' ('inadvertently assumed').

10. We know all about how to do quadratics: we know all the needful facts about pipes, cisterns, hours and plumbers: yet we reach the answer '3¾ men'. We have failed to cast our facts correctly into mathematical form.

11. A somewhat distressing favourite in the class that Hart used to conduct with me in the years soon after the war. The italics are mine.

12. Not but what he probably manages to convey his meaning somehow or other. Judges seem to acquire a knack of conveying meaning, and even carrying conviction, through the use of a pithy Anglo-Saxon which sometimes has literally no meaning at all. Wishing to distinguish the case of shooting at a post in the belief that it was an enemy, as *not* an 'attempt', from the case of picking an empty pocket in the belief that money was in it, which *is* an 'attempt', the judge explains that in shooting at the post 'the man is never on the thing at all'.

13. Plato, I suppose, and after him Aristotle, fastened this confusion upon us, as bad in its day and way as the later, grotesque, confusion of moral weakness with weakness of will. I am very partial to ice cream, and a bombe is served divided into segments corresponding one to one with the persons at High Table: I am tempted to help myself to two segments and do so, thus succumbing to temptation and even conceivably (but why necessarily?) going against my principles. But do I lose control of myself? Do I raven, do I snatch the morsels from the dish and wolf them down, impervious to the consternation of my colleagues? Not a bit of it. We often succumb to temptation with calm and even with finesse.

14. As a matter of fact, most of these examples *can* be understood the other way, especially if we allow ourselves inflexions of the voice, or commas, or contexts. a₂ might be a poetic inversion for b₂: b₁, perhaps with commas round the 'clumsily', might be used for a₁: and so on. Still, the two senses are clearly enough distinguishable.

15. What Finney says is different: he says he 'made a mistake in the tap'. This is the basic use of 'mistake', where we simply, and not necessarily accountably, take the wrong one. Finney here attempts to account for his mistake, by saying that his attention was distracted. But suppose the order is 'Right turn' and I turn left: No doubt the sergeant will insinuate that my attention was distracted, or that I cannot distinguish my right from my left—but it was not and I can, this was a simple, pure mistake. As often happens. Neither I nor the sergeant will suggest that there was any accident, or any inadvertence either. If Finney had turned the hot tap inadvertently, then it would have been knocked, say, in reaching for the cold tap: a different story.

16. This is by way of a general warning in philosophy. It seems to be too readily assumed that if we can only discover the true meanings of each of a cluster of key terms, usually historic terms, that we use in some particular field (as, for example, 'right', 'good' and the rest in morals), then it must without question transpire that each will fit into place in some single, interlocking, consistent, conceptual scheme. Not only is there no reason to assume this, but all historical probability is against it, especially in the case of a language derived from such various civilizations as ours is. We may cheerfully use, and with weight, terms which are not so much head-on incompatible as simply disparate, which just do not fit in or even on. Just as we cheerfully subscribe to, or have the grace to be torn between, simply disparate ideals—why *must* there be a conceivable amalgam, the Good Life for Man?

H. L. A. HART

Responsibility*

A wide range of different, though connected, ideas is covered by the expressions 'responsibility', 'responsible', and 'responsible for', as these are standardly used in and out of the law. Though connections exist among these different ideas, they are often very indirect, and it seems appropriate to speak of different *senses* of these expressions. The following simple story of a drunken sea captain who lost his ship at sea can be told in the terminology of responsibility to illustrate, with stylistically horrible clarity, these differences of sense.

'As a captain of the ship, X was responsible for the safety of his passengers and crew. But on his last voyage he got drunk every night and was responsible for the loss of the ship with all aboard. It was rumoured that he was insane, but the doctors considered that he was responsible for his actions. Throughout the voyage he behaved quite irresponsibly, and various incidents in his career showed that he was not a responsible person. He always maintained that the exceptional winter storms were responsible for the loss of the ship, but in the legal proceedings brought against him he was found criminally responsible for his negligent conduct, and in separate civil proceedings he was held legally responsible for the loss of life and property. He is still alive and he is morally responsible for the deaths of many women and children.'

This welter of distinguishable senses of the word 'responsibility' and its grammatical cognates can, I think, be profitably reduced by division and classification. I shall distinguish four heads of classification to which I shall assign the following names:

   (a) Role-Responsibility
   (b) Causal-Responsibility
   (c) Liability-Responsibility
   (d) Capacity-Responsibility.

I hope that in drawing these dividing lines, and in the exposition which follows, I have avoided

*From the *Law Quarterly Review* (1967), Vol. 83. Reprinted by permission of the Editor. This selection was reprinted as the first part of an essay entitled "Postscript: Responsibility and Retribution" in H. L. A. Hart, *Punishment and Responsibility* (New York and Oxford: Oxford University Press, 1968), pp. 211–30.

the arbitrary pedantries of classificatory systematics, and that my divisions pick out and clarify the main, though not all, varieties of responsibility to which reference is constantly made, explicitly or implicitly, by moralists, lawyers, historians, and ordinary men. I relegate to the notes[1] discussion of what unifies these varieties and explains the extension of the terminology of responsibility.

ROLE-RESPONSIBILITY

A sea captain is responsible for the safety of his ship, and that is his responsibility, or one of his responsibilities. A husband is responsible for the maintenance of his wife; parents for the upbringing of their children; a sentry for alerting the guard at the enemy's approach; a clerk for keeping the accounts of his firm. These examples of a person's responsibilities suggest the generalization that, whenever a person occupies a distinctive place or office in a social organization, to which specific duties are attached to provide for the welfare of others or to advance in some specific way the aims or purposes of the organization, he is properly said to be responsible for the performance of these duties, or for doing what is necessary to fulfil them. Such duties are a person's responsibilities. As a guide to this sense of responsibility this generalization is, I think, adequate, but the idea of a distinct role or place or office is, of course, a vague one, and I cannot undertake to make it very precise. Doubts about its extension to marginal cases will always arise. If two friends, out on a mountaineering expedition, agree that the one shall look after the food and the other the maps, then the one is correctly said to be responsible for the food, and the other for the maps, and I would classify this as a case of role-responsibility. Yet such fugitive or temporary assignments with specific duties would not usually be considered by sociologists, who mainly use the word, as an example of a 'role'. So 'role' in my classification is extended to include a task assigned to any person by agreement or otherwise. But it is also important to notice that not all the duties which a man has in virtue of occupying what in a quite strict sense of role is a distinct role, are thought or spoken of as 'responsibilities'. A private soldier has a duty to obey his superior officer and, if commanded by him to form fours or present arms on a given occasion, has a duty

to do so. But to form fours or present arms would scarcely be said to be the private's responsibility; nor would he be said to be responsible for doing it. If on the other hand a soldier was ordered to deliver a message to H.Q. or to conduct prisoners to a base camp, he might well be said to be responsible for doing these things, and these things to be his responsibility. I think, though I confess to not being sure, that what distinguishes those duties of a role which are singled out as responsibilities is that they are duties of a relatively complex or extensive kind, defining a 'sphere of responsibility' requiring care and attention over a protracted period of time, while short-lived duties of a very simple kind, to do or not do some specific act on a particular occasion, are not termed responsibilities. Thus a soldier detailed off to keep the camp clean and tidy for the general's visit of inspection has this as his sphere of responsibility and is responsible for it. But if merely told to remove a piece of paper from the approaching general's path, this would be at most his duty.

A 'responsible person', 'behaving responsibly' (not 'irresponsibly'), require for their elucidation a reference to role-responsibility. A responsible person is one who is disposed to take his duties seriously; to think about them, and to make serious efforts to fulfil them. To behave responsibly is to behave as a man would who took his duties in this serious way. Responsibilities in this sense may be either legal or moral, or fall outside this dichotomy. Thus a man may be morally as well as legally responsible for the maintenance of his wife and children, but a host's responsibility for the comfort of his guests, and a referee's responsibility for the control of the players is neither legal nor moral, unless the word 'moral' is unilluminatingly used simply to exclude legal responsibility.

CAUSAL RESPONSIBILITY

'The long drought was responsible for the famine in India'. In many contexts, as in this one, it is possible to substitute for the expression 'was responsible for' the words 'caused' or 'produced' or some other causal expression in referring to consequences, results, or outcomes. The converse, however, is not always true. Examples of this causal sense of responsibility are legion. 'His neglect was responsible for her distress.' 'The Prime Minister's speech was responsible for the panic.' 'Disraeli was responsible for the defeat of the Government.' 'The icy condition of the road was responsible for the accident.' The past tense of the verb used in this causal sense of the expression 'responsible for' should be noticed. If it is said of a living person, who has in fact caused some disaster, that he *is* responsible for it, this is not, or not merely, an example of causal responsibility, but of what I term 'liability-responsibility'; it asserts his liability on account of the disaster, even though it is also true that he is responsible in that sense *because* he caused the disaster, and that he caused the disaster may be expressed by saying that he was responsible for it. On the other hand, if it is said of a person no longer living that he was responsible for some disaster, this may be either a simple causal statement or a statement of liability-responsibility, or both.

From the above examples it is clear that in this causal sense not only human beings but also their actions or omissions, and things, conditions, and events, may be said to be responsible for outcomes. It is perhaps true that only where an outcome is thought unfortunate or felicitous is its cause commonly spoken of as responsible for it. But this may not reflect any aspect of the meaning of the expression 'responsible for'; it may only reflect the fact that, except in such cases, it may be pointless and hence rare to pick out the causes of events. It is sometimes suggested that, though we may speak of a human being's action as responsible for some outcome in a purely causal sense, we do not speak of a person, as distinct from his actions, as responsible for an outcome, unless he is felt to deserve censure or praise. This is, I think, a mistake. History books are full of examples to the contrary. 'Disraeli was responsible for the defeat of the Government' need not carry even an implication that he was deserving of censure or praise; it may be purely a statement concerned with the contribution made by one human being to an outcome of importance, and be entirely neutral as to its moral or other merits. The contrary view depends, I think, on the failure to appreciate sufficiently the ambiguity of statements of the form 'X *was* responsible for Y' as distinct from 'X *is* responsible for Y' to which I have drawn attention above. The former expression in the case of a person no longer living may be (though it *need* not be) a statement of liability-responsibility.

LEGAL LIABILITY-RESPONSIBILITY

Though it was noted that role-responsibility might take either legal or moral form, it was not found necessary to treat these separately. But in the case of the present topic of liability-responsibility, separate treatment seems advisable. For responsibility seems to have a wider extension in relation to the law than it does in relation to morals, and it is a question to be considered whether this is due merely to the general differences between law and morality, or to some differences in the sense of responsibility involved.

When legal rules require men to act or abstain from action, one who breaks the law is usually liable, according to other legal rules, to punishment for his misdeeds, or to make compensation to persons injured thereby, and very often he is liable to both punishment and enforced compensation. He is thus liable to be 'made to pay' for what he has done in either or both of the senses which the expression 'He'll pay for it' may bear in ordinary usage. But most legal systems go much further than this. A man may be legally punished on account of what his servant has done, even if he in no way caused or instigated or even knew of the servant's action, or knew of the likelihood of his servant so acting. Liability in such circumstances is rare in modern systems of criminal law; but it is common in all systems of civil law for men to be made to pay compensation for injuries caused by others, generally their servants or employees. The law of most countries goes further still. A man may·be liable to pay compensation for harm suffered by others, though neither he nor his servants have caused it. This is so, for example, in Anglo-American law when the harm is caused by dangerous things which escape from a man's possession, even if their escape is not due to any act or omission of his or his servants, or if harm is caused to a man's employees by defective machinery whose defective condition he could not have discovered.

It will be observed that the facts referred to in the last paragraph are expressed in terms of 'liability' and not 'responsibility'. In the preceding essay in this volume I ventured the general statement that to say that someone is legally responsible for something often means that under legal rules he is liable to be made either to suffer or to pay compensation in certain eventualities. But I now think that this simple account of liability-responsibility is in need of some considerable modification. Undoubtedly, expressions of the form 'he is legally responsible for Y' (where Y is some action or harm) and 'he is legally liable to be punished or to be made to pay compensation for Y' are very closely connected, and sometimes they are used as if they were identical in meaning. Thus, where one legal writer speaks of 'strict responsibility' and 'vicarious responsibility', another speaks of 'strict liability' and 'vicarious liability'; and even in the work of a single writer the expressions 'vicarious responsibility' and 'vicarious liability' are to be found used without any apparent difference in meaning, implication, or emphasis. Hence, in arguing that it was for the law to determine the mental conditions of responsibility, Fitzjames Stephen claimed that this must be so because 'the meaning of responsibility is liability to punishment'.[2]

But though the abstract expressions 'responsibility' and 'liability' are virtually equivalent in many contexts, the statement that a man is responsible for his actions, or for some act or some harm, is usually not identical in meaning with the statement that he is liable to be punished or to be made to pay compensation for the act or the harm, but is directed to a narrower and more specific issue. It is in this respect that my previous account of liability-responsibility needs qualification.

The question whether a man is or is not legally liable to be punished for some action that he has done opens up the quite general issue whether all of the various requirements for criminal liability have been satisfied, and so will include the question whether the kind of action done, whatever mental element accompanied it, was ever punishable by law. But the question whether he is or is not legally responsible for some action or some harm is usually not concerned with this general issue, but with the narrower issue whether any of a certain range of conditions (mainly, but not exclusively, psychological) are satisfied, it being assumed that all other conditions are satisfied. Because of this difference in scope between questions of liability to punishment and questions of responsibility, it would be somewhat misleading, though not unintelligible, to say of a man who had refused to rescue a baby drowning in a foot of water, that he was not, according to English law, legally responsible for leaving the baby to drown or for the baby's death, if all that is meant is that he was not liable to punishment because refusing aid to those in danger is not generally a crime in English law. Similarly, a book or article entitled 'Criminal Responsibility' would not be expected to contain the whole of the substantive criminal law determining the conditions of liability, but only to be concerned with a specialized range of topics such as mental abnormality, immaturity, *mens rea,* strict and vicarious liability, proximate cause, or other general forms of connection between acts and harm sufficient for liability. These are the specialized topics which are, in general, thought and spoken of as 'criteria' of responsibility. They may be divided into three classes: (i) mental or psychological conditions; (ii) causal or other forms of connection between act and harm; (iii) personal relationships rendering one man liable to be punished or to pay for the acts of another. Each of these three classes requires some separate discussion.

(i) *Mental or psychological criteria of responsibility.* In the criminal law the most frequent issue raised by questions of responsibility, as distinct from the wider question of liability, is whether or not an accused person satisfied some mental or psychological conditions required for liability, or whether liability was strict or absolute, so that the usual mental or psychological conditions were not required. It is, however, important to notice that these psychological conditions are of two sorts, of which the first is far more closely associated with the use of the word responsibility than the second. On the one hand, the law of most countries requires that the person liable to be punished should at the time of his crime have had the capacity to understand what he is required by law to do or not to do, to deliberate and to decide what to do, and to control his conduct in the light of such decisions. Normal adults are generally assumed to have these capacities, but they may be lacking where there is mental disorder or immaturity, and the possession of these normal capacities is very often signified by the expression 'responsible for his actions'. This is the fourth sense of responsibility which I discuss below under the heading of 'Capacity-Responsibility'. On the other hand, except where responsibility is strict, the law may excuse from punishment persons of normal capacity if, on particular occasions where their outward conduct fits the definition of the crime, some element of intention or knowledge, or some other of the familiar constituents of *mens rea,* was absent, so that the particular action done was defective, though the agent had the normal capacity of understanding and control. Continental codes usually make a firm distinction between these two main types of psychological conditions: Questions concerning general capacity are described as matters of responsibility or 'imputability', whereas questions concerning the presence or absence of knowledge or intention on particular occasions are not described as matters of 'imputability', but are referred to the topic of 'fault' (*schuld, faute, dolo,* et cetera).

English law and English legal writers do not mark quite so firmly this contrast between general capacity and the knowledge or intention accompanying a particular action; for the expression *mens rea* is now often used to cover all the variety of psychological conditions required for liability by the law, so that both the person who is excused from punishment because of lack of intention or some ordinary accident or mistake on a particular occasion and the person held not to be criminally responsible on account of immaturity or insanity are said not to have the requisite *mens rea.* Yet the distinction thus blurred by the extensive use of the expression *mens rea* between a persistent incapacity and a particular defective action is indirectly marked in terms of responsibility in most Anglo-American legal writing, in the following way. When a person is said to be not responsible for a particular act or crime, or when (as in the formulation of the M'Naghten Rules and s. 2 of the Homicide Act, 1957) he is said not to be responsible for his 'acts and omissions in doing' some action on a particular occasion, the reason for saying this is usually some mental abnormality or disorder. I have not succeeded in finding cases where a normal person, merely lacking some ordinary element of knowledge or intention on a particular occasion, is said for that reason not to be responsible for that particular action, even though he is for that reason not liable to punishment. But though there is this tendency in statements of liability-responsibility to confine the use of the expression 'responsible' and 'not responsible' to questions of mental abnormality or general incapacity, yet all the psychological conditions of liability are to be

found discussed by legal writers under such headings as 'Criminal Responsibility' or 'Principles of Criminal Responsibility'. Accordingly I classify them here as criteria of responsibility. I do so with a clear conscience, since little is to be gained in clarity by a rigid division which the contemporary use of the expression *mens rea* often ignores.

The situation is, however, complicated by a further feature of English legal and non-legal usage. The phrase 'responsible for his actions' is, as I have observed, frequently used to refer to the capacity-responsibility of the normal person, and, so used, refers to one of the major criteria of liability-responsibility. It is so used in s. 2 of the Homicide Act 1957, which speaks of a person's mental 'responsibility' for his actions being *impaired,* and in the rubric to the section, which speaks of persons 'suffering from diminished responsibility'. In this sense the expression is the name or description of a psychological condition. But the expression is also used to signify liability-responsibility itself, that is, liability to punishment so far as such liability depends on psychological conditions, and is so used when the law is said to 'relieve insane persons of responsibility for their actions'. It was probably also so used in the form of verdict returned in cases of successful pleas of insanity under English law until this was altered by the Insanity Act 1964: the verdict was 'guilty but insane so as not to be responsible according to law for his actions'.

(ii) *Causal or other forms of connection with harm.* Questions of legal liability-responsibility are not limited in their scope to psychological conditions of either of the two sorts distinguished above. Such questions are also (though more frequently in the law of tort than in the criminal law) concerned with the issue whether some form of connection between a person's act and some harmful outcome is sufficient according to law to make him liable; so if a person is accused of murder the question whether he was or was not legally responsible for the death may be intended to raise the issue whether the death was too remote a consequence of his acts for them to count as its cause. If the law, as frequently in tort, is not that the defendant's action should have caused the harm, but that there be some other form of connection or relationship between the defendant and the harm, for example, that it should have been caused by some dangerous thing escaping from the defendant's land, this connection or relationship is a condition of civil responsibility for harm, and, where it holds, the defendant is said to be legally responsible for the harm. No doubt such questions of connection with harm are also frequently phrased in terms of liability.

(iii) *Relationship with the agent.* Normally in criminal law the minimum condition required for liability for punishment is that the person to be punished should himself have done what the law forbids, at least so far as outward conduct is concerned; even if liability is 'strict', it is not enough to render him liable for punishment that someone else should have done it. This is often expressed in the terminology of responsibility (though here, too, 'liability' is frequently used instead of 'responsibility') by saying that, generally, vicarious responsibility is not known to the criminal law. But there are exceptional cases; an innkeeper is liable to punishment if his servants, without his knowledge and against his orders, sell liquor on his premises after hours. In this case he is vicariously responsible for the sale, and of course, in the civil law of tort there are many situations in which a master or employer is liable to pay compensation for the torts of his servant or employee, and is said to be vicariously responsible.

It appears, therefore, that there are diverse types of criteria of legal liability-responsibility: The most prominent consist of certain mental elements, but there are also causal or other connections between a person and harm, or the presence of some relationship, such as that of master and servant, between different persons. It is natural to ask why these very diverse conditions are singled out as criteria of responsibility, and so are within the scope of questions about responsibility, as distinct from the wider question concerning liability for punishment. I think that the following somewhat Cartesian figure may explain this fact. If we conceive of a person as an embodied mind and will, we may draw a distinction between two questions concerning the conditions of liability and punishment. The first question is what general types of outer conduct *(actus reus)* or what sorts of harm are required for liability? The second question is how closely connected with such conduct or such harm must the embodied mind or will of an individual person be to render him liable to punishment? Or, as some would put it, to what extent must the embodied mind or will be the author of the conduct or the harm in order to render him liable? Is it enough that the person made the appropriate bodily movements? Or is it required that he did so when possessed of a certain capacity of control and with a certain knowledge or intention? Or that he caused the harm or stood in some other relationship to it, or to the actual doer of the deed? The legal rules, or parts of legal rules, that answer these various questions define the various forms of connection which are adequate for liability, and these constitute conditions of legal responsibility which form only a part of the total conditions of liability for punishment, which also include the definitions of the *actus reus* of the various crimes.

We may therefore summarize this long discussion of legal liability-responsibility by saying that, though in certain general contexts legal responsibility and legal liability have the same meaning, to say that a man is legally responsible for some act or harm is to state that his connection with the act or harm is sufficient according to law for liability. Because responsibility and liability are distinguishable in this way, it will make sense to say that because a person is legally responsible for some action he is liable to be punished for it.

LEGAL LIABILITY-RESPONSIBILITY AND MORAL BLAME

My previous account of legal liability-responsibility, in which I claimed that in one important sense to say that a person is legally responsible meant that he was legally liable for punishment or could be made to pay compensation, has been criticized on two scores. Since these criticisms apply equally to the above amended version of my original account, in which I distinguish the general issue of liability from the narrower issue of responsibility, I shall consider these criticisms here. The first criticism, made by Mr. A. W. B. Simpson,[3] insists on the strong connection between statements of legal responsibility and moral judgment, and claims that even lawyers tend to confine statements that a person is legally responsible for something to cases where he is considered morally blameworthy, and, where this is not so, tend to use the expression 'liability' rather than 'responsibility'. But, though moral blame and legal responsibility may be connected in some ways, it is surely not in this simple way.

Against any such view not only is there the frequent use already mentioned of the expressions 'strict responsibility' and 'vicarious responsibility', which are obviously independent of moral blameworthiness, but there is the more important fact that we can, and frequently do, intelligibly debate the question whether a mentally disordered or very young person who has been held legally responsible for a crime is morally blameworthy. The coincidence of legal responsibility with moral blameworthiness may be a laudable ideal, but it is not a necessary truth nor even an accomplished fact.

The suggestion that the statement that a man is responsible generally means that he is blameworthy and not that he is liable to punishment is said to be supported by the fact that it is possible to cite, without redundancy, the fact that a person is responsible as a ground or reason for saying that he is liable to punishment. But, if the various kinds or senses of responsibility are distinguished, it is plain that there are many explanations of this last mentioned fact, which are quite independent of any essential connection between legal responsibility and moral blameworthiness. Thus cases where the statement that the man is responsible constitutes a reason for saying that he is liable to punishment may be cases of role-responsibility (the master is legally responsible for the safety of his ship, therefore he is liable to punishment if he loses it) or capacity-responsibility (he was responsible for his actions therefore he is liable to punishment for his crimes); or they may even be statements of liability-responsibility, since such statements refer to part only of the conditions of liability and may therefore be given, without redundancy, as a reason for liability to punishment. In any case this criticism may be turned against the suggestion that responsibility is to be equated with moral blameworthiness; for plainly the statement that someone is responsible may be given as part of the reason for saying that he is morally blameworthy.

LIABILITY-RESPONSIBILITY FOR PARTICULAR ACTIONS

An independent objection is the following, made by Mr. George Pitcher.[4] The wide extension I have claimed for the notion of liability-responsibility permits us to say not only that a man is legally responsible in this sense for the consequences of his action, but also for his action or actions. According to Mr. Pitcher 'this is an improper way of talking', though common amongst philosophers. Mr. Pitcher is concerned primarily with moral, not legal, responsibility, but even in a moral context it is plain that there is a very well established use of the expression 'responsible for his actions' to refer to capacity-responsibility for which Mr. Pitcher makes no allowance. As far as the law is concerned, many examples may be cited from both sides of the Atlantic where a person may be said to be responsible for his actions, or for his act, or for his crime, or for his conduct. Mr. Pitcher gives, as a reason for saying that it is improper to speak of a man being responsible for his own actions, the fact that a man does not produce or cause his own actions. But this argument would prove far too much. It would rule out as improper not only the expression 'responsible for his actions', but also our saying that a man was responsible vicariously or otherwise for harmful outcomes which he had not caused, which is a perfectly well established legal usage.

None the less, there are elements of truth in Mr. Pitcher's objection. First, it seems to be the case that even where a man is said to be legally responsible for what he has done, it is rare to find this expressed by a phrase conjoining the verb of action with the expression 'responsible for'. Hence, 'he is legally responsible for killing her' is not usually found, whereas 'he is legally responsible for her death' is common, as are the expressions 'legally responsible for his act (in killing her)'; 'legally responsible for his crime'; or, as in the official formulation of the M'Naghten Rules, 'responsible for his actions or omissions in doing or being a party to the killing'. These common expressions in which a noun, not a verb, follows the phrase 'responsible for' are grammatically similar to statements of causal responsibility, and the tendency to use the same form no doubt shows how strongly the overtones of causal responsibility influence the terminology ordinarily used to make statements of liability-responsibility. There is, however, also in support of Mr. Pitcher's view, the point already cited that, even in legal writing, where a person is said to be responsible for his act or his conduct, the relevant mental element is usually the question of insanity or immaturity, so that the ground in such cases for the assertion that the person is responsible or is not responsible for his act is the presence or absence of 'responsibility for actions' in the sense of capacity-responsibility, and not merely the presence or absence of knowledge or intention in relation to the particular act.

MORAL LIABILITY-RESPONSIBILITY

How far can the account given above of legal liability-responsibility be applied *mutatis mutandis* to moral responsibility? The *mutanda* seem to be the following: 'deserving blame' or 'blameworthy' will have to be substituted for 'liable to punishment', and 'morally bound to make amends or pay compensation' for 'liable to be made to pay compensation'. Then the moral counterpart to the account given of legal liability-responsibility would be the following: To say that a person is morally responsible for something he has done or for some harmful outcome of his own or others' conduct, is to say that he is morally blameworthy, or morally obliged to make amends for the harm, so far as this depends on certain conditions. These conditions relate to the character or extent of a man's control over his own conduct, or to the causal or other connection between his action and harmful occurrences, or to his relationship with the person who actually did the harm.

In general, such an account of the meaning of 'morally responsible' seems correct, and the striking differences between legal and moral responsibility are due to substantive differences between the content of legal and moral rules and principles rather than to any variation in meaning of responsibility when conjoined with the word 'moral' rather than 'legal'. Thus, both in the legal and the moral case, the criteria of responsibility seem to be restricted to the psychological elements involved in the control of conduct, to causal or other connections between acts and harm, and to the relationships with the actual doer of misdeeds. The interesting differences between legal and moral responsibility arise from the differences in the particular criteria falling under these general heads. Thus a system of criminal law may make responsibility strict, or even absolute, not even exempting very young children or the grossly insane from punishment; or it may vicariously punish one man for what another has done, even though the former had no control of

the latter; or it may punish an individual or make him compensate another for harm which he neither intended nor could have foreseen as likely to arise from his conduct. We may condemn such a legal system which extends strict or vicarious responsibility in these ways as barbarous or unjust, but there are no conceptual barriers to be overcome in speaking of such a system as a legal system, though it is certainly arguable that we should not speak of 'punishment' where liability is vicarious or strict. In the moral case, however, greater conceptual barriers exist: The hypothesis that we might hold individuals morally blameworthy for doing things which they could not have avoided doing, or for things done by others over whom they had no control, conflicts with too many of the central features of the idea of morality to be treated merely as speculation about a rare or inferior kind of moral system. It may be an exaggeration to say that there could not logically be such a morality or that blame administered according to principles of strict or vicarious responsibility, even in a minority of cases, could not logically be moral blame; none the less, admission of such a system as a morality would require a profound modification in our present concept of morality, and there is no similar requirement in the case of law.

Some of the most familiar contexts in which the expression 'responsibility' appears confirm these general parallels between legal and moral liability-responsibility. Thus in the famous question 'Is moral responsibility compatible with determinism?' the expression 'moral responsibility' is apt just because the bogey raised by determinism specifically relates to the usual criteria of responsibility; for it opens the question whether, if 'determinism' were true, the capacities of human beings to control their conduct would still exist or could be regarded as adequate to justify moral blame.

In less abstract or philosophical contexts, where there is a present question of blaming someone for some particular act, the assertion or denial that a person is morally responsible for his actions is common. But this expression is as ambiguous in the moral as in the legal case: It is most frequently used to refer to what I have termed 'capacity-responsibility', which is the most important criterion of moral liability-responsibility; but in some contexts it may also refer to moral liability-responsibility itself. Perhaps the most frequent use in moral contexts of the expression 'responsible for' is in cases where persons are said to be morally responsible for the outcomes or results of morally wrong conduct, although Mr. Pitcher's claim that men are never said in ordinary usage to be responsible for their actions is, as I have attempted to demonstrate above with counter-examples, an exaggerated claim.

CAPACITY-RESPONSIBILITY

In most contexts, as I have already stressed, the expression 'he is responsible for his actions' is used to assert that a person has certain normal capacities. These constitute the most important criteria of moral liability-responsibility, though it is characteristic of most legal systems that they have given only a partial or tardy recognition to all these capacities as general criteria of legal responsibility. The capacities in question are those of understanding, reasoning, and control of conduct: the ability to understand what conduct legal rules or morality require, to deliberate and reach decisions concerning these requirements, and to conform to decisions when made. Because 're-sponsible for his actions' in this sense refers not to a legal status but to certain complex psychological characteristics of persons, a person's responsibility for his actions may intelligibly be said to be 'diminished' or 'impaired' as well as altogether absent, and persons may be said to be 'suffering from diminished responsibility' much as a wounded man may be said to be suffering from a diminished capacity to control the movements of his limbs.

No doubt the most frequent occasions for asserting or denying that a person is 'responsible for his actions' are cases where questions of blame or punishment for particular actions are in issue. But, as with other expressions used to denote criteria of responsibility, this one also may be used where no particular question of blame or punishment is in issue, and it is then used simply to describe a person's psychological condition. Hence it may be said purely by way of description of some harmless inmate of a mental institution, even though there is no present question of his misconduct, that he is a person who is not responsible for his actions. No doubt if there were no social practice of blaming and punishing people for their misdeeds, and excusing them from pun-ishment because they lack the normal capacities of understanding and control, we should lack this shorthand description for describing their condition which we now derive from these social practices. In that case we should have to describe the condition of the inmate directly, by saying that he could not understand what people told him to do, or could not reason about it, or come to, or adhere to any decisions about his conduct.

Legal systems left to themselves may be very niggardly in their admission of the relevance of liability to legal punishment of the several capacities, possession of which are necessary to render a man morally responsible for his actions. So much is evident from the history sketched in the preceding chapter of the painfully slow emancipation of English criminal law from the narrow, cognitive criteria of responsibility formulated in the M'Naghten Rules. Though some Continental legal systems have been willing to confront squarely the question whether the accused 'lacked the ability to recognize the wrongness of his conduct and to act in accordance with that recognition,'[5] such an issue, if taken seriously, raises formidable difficulties of proof, especially before juries. For this reason I think that, instead of a close determination of such questions of capacity, the apparently coarser-grained technique of exempting persons from liability to punishment if they fall into certain recognized categories of mental disorder is likely to be increasingly used. Such exemption by general category is a technique long known to English law; for in the case of very young children it has made no attempt to determine, as a condition of liability, the question whether on account of their immaturity they could have understood what the law required and could have conformed to its requirements, or whether their responsibility on account of their immaturity was 'substantially impaired', but exempts them from liability for punishment if under a specified age. It seems likely that exemption by medical category rather than by individualized findings of absent or diminished capacity will be found more likely to lead in practice to satisfactory results, in spite of the difficulties pointed out in the last essay in the discussion of s. 60 of the Mental Health Act, 1959.

Though a legal system may fail to incorporate in its rules any psychological criteria of responsibility, and so may apply its sanction to those who are not morally blameworthy, it is none the less dependent for its efficacy on the possession by a sufficient number of those whose conduct it seeks to control of the capacities of understanding and control of conduct which constitute capacity-responsibility. For if a large proportion of those concerned could not understand what the law required them to do or could not form and keep a decision to obey, no legal system could come into existence or continue to exist. The general possession of such capacities is therefore a condition of the *efficacy* of law, even though it is not made a condition of liability to legal sanctions. The same condition of efficacy attaches to all attempts to regulate or control human conduct by forms of *communication:* such as orders, commands, the invocation of moral or other rules or principles, arguments, and advice.

'The notion of prevention through the medium of the mind assumes mental ability adequate to restraint'. This was clearly seen by Bentham and by Austin, who perhaps influenced the seventh report of the Criminal Law Commissioners of 1833 containing this sentence. But they overstressed the point; for they wrongly assumed that this condition of efficacy must also be incorporated in legal rules as a condition of liability. This mistaken assumption is to be found not only in the explanation of the doctrine of *mens rea* given in Bentham's and Austin's works, but is explicit in the Commissioners' statement preceding the sentence quoted above that 'the object of penal law being the prevention of wrong, the principle does not extend to mere involuntary acts or even to harmful consequences the result of inevitable accident'. The case of morality is however different in precisely this respect: the possession by those to whom its injunctions are addressed of 'mental ability adequate to restraint' (capacity-responsibility) has there a double status and importance. It is not only a condition of the efficacy of morality; but a system or practice which did not regard the possession of these capacities as a necessary condition of liability, and so treated blame as appropriate even in the case of those who lacked them, would not, as morality is at present understood, be a morality.

NOTES

1. The author's discussion of this appears at pp. 264–65 of *Punishment and Responsibility* [editors].
2. *A History of The Criminal Law,* Vol. II, p. 183.
3. In a review of 'Changing Conceptions & Responsibility', in *Crim. L. R.* (1966) 124.
4. In 'Hart on Action and Responsibility', *The Philosophical Review* (1960), p. 266.
5. German Criminal Code, Art. 51.

H. L. A. HART AND
A. M. HONORÉ

Causation and Responsibility*

I. RESPONSIBILITY IN LAW AND MORALS

... In the moral judgments of ordinary life, we have occasion to blame people because they have caused harm to others, and also, if less frequently, to insist that morally they are bound to compensate those to whom they have caused harm. These are the moral analogues of more precise legal conceptions; for, in all legal systems, liability to be punished or to make compensation frequently depends on whether actions (or omissions) have caused harm. Moral blame is not of course confined to such cases of causing harm. We blame a man who cheats or lies or breaks promises, even if one one has suffered in the particular case: This has its legal counterpart in the punishment of abortive attempts to commit crimes, and of offences constituted by the unlawful possession of certain kinds of weapons, drugs, or materials, for example, for counterfeiting currency. When the occurrence of harm is an essential part of the ground for blame the connection of the person blamed with the harm may take any of the forms of causal connection we have examined. His action may have initiated a series of physical events dependent on each other and culminating in injury to persons or property, as in wounding and killing. These simple forms are the paradigms for the lawyer's talk of harm 'directly' caused. But we blame people also for harm which arises from or is the consequence of their neglect of common precautions; we do this even if harm would not have come about without the intervention of an-

other human being deliberately exploiting the opportunities provided by neglect. The main legal analogue here is liability for 'negligence'. The wish of many lawyers to talk in this branch of the law of harm being 'within the risk' rather than 'caused by' the negligent conduct manifests appreciation of the fact that a different form of relationship is involved in saying that harm is the consequence, on the one hand, of an explosion and, on the other, of a failure to lock the door by which a thief has entered. Again, we blame people for the harm which we say is the consequence of their influence over others, either exerted by nonrational means or in one of the ways we have designated 'interpersonal transactions'. To such grounds for responsibility there correspond many important legal conceptions: The instigation of crimes ('commanding' or 'procuring') constitutes an important ground of criminal responsibility and the concepts of enticement and of inducement (by threats or misrepresentation) are an element in many civil wrongs as well as in criminal offences.

The law, however, especially in matters of compensation, goes far beyond these causal grounds for responsibility in such doctrines as the vicarious responsibility of a master for his servant's civil wrongs and that of the responsibility of an occupier of property for injuries suffered by passersby from defects of which the occupier had no knowledge and which he had no opportunity to repair. There is a recognition, perhaps diminishing, of this noncausal ground of responsibility outside the law; responsibility is sometimes admitted by one person or group of persons, even if no precaution has been neglected by them, for harm done by persons related to them in a special way, either by family ties or as members of the

*From *Causation in the Law* by H. L. A. Hart and A. M. Honoré (Oxford: The Oxford University Press, 1959), pp. 59–78, © 1959 Oxford University Press. Reprinted by permission of The Clarendon Press, Oxford. Footnotes have been renumbered.

same social or political association. Responsibility may be simply 'placed' by moral opinion on one person for what others do. The simplest case of such vicarious moral responsibility is that of a parent for damage done by a child; its more complex (and more debatable) form is the moral responsibility of one generation of a nation to make compensation for their predecessors' wrong, such as the Germans admitted in payment of compensation to Israel.

At this point it is necessary to issue a *caveat* about the meaning of the expression 'responsible' if only to avoid prejudicing a question about the character of *legal* determinations of causal connection with which we shall be much concerned in later chapters. Usually in discussion of the law and occasionally in morals, to say that someone is responsible for some harm means that in accordance with legal rules or moral principles it is at least permissible, if not mandatory, to blame or punish or exact compensation from him. In this use[1] the expression 'responsible for' does not refer to a factual connection between the person held responsible and the harm but simply to his liability under the rules to be blamed, punished, or made to pay. The expressions 'answerable for' or 'liable for' are practically synonymous with 'responsible for' in *this* use, in which there is no implication that the person held responsible actually *did* or *caused* the harm. In this sense a master is (in English law) responsible for the damage done by his servants acting within the scope of their authority and a parent (in French and German law) for that done by his children; it is in this sense that a guarantor or surety is responsible for the debts or the good behaviour of other persons. Very often, however, especially in discussion of morals, to say that someone is responsible for some harm is to assert (*inter alia*) that he *did* the harm or *caused* it though such a statement is perhaps rarely confined to this for it usually also carries with it the implication that it is at least permissible to blame or punish. This double use of the expression no doubt arises from the important fact that doing or causing harm constitutes not only the most usual but the primary type of ground for holding persons responsible in the first sense. We still speak of inanimate or natural causes such as storms, floods, germs, or the failure of electricity supply as 'responsible for' disasters; this mode of expression, now taken only to

mean that they caused the disasters, no doubt originated in the belief that all that happens is the work of spirits when it is not that of men. Its survival in the modern world is perhaps some testimony to the primacy of causal connection as an element in responsibility and to the intimate connection between the two notions.

We shall consider later an apparent paradox which interprets in a different way the relationship between cause and responsibility. Much modern thought on causation in the law rests on the contention that the statement that someone has caused harm either means no more than that the harm would not have happened without ('but for') his action or where (as in normal legal usage and in all ordinary speech), it apparently means more than this, it is a disguised way of asserting the 'normative' judgment that he is responsible in the first sense, that is, that it is proper or just to blame or punish him or make him pay. On this view to say that a person caused harm is not really, though ostensibly it is, to give a *ground or reason* for holding him responsible in the first sense; for we are only in a position to say that he has caused harm when we have decided that he is responsible. Pending consideration of the theories of legal causation which exploit this point of view we shall use the expression 'responsible for' only in the first of the two ways explained, that is, without any implication as to the type of factual connection between the person held responsible and the harm; and we shall provisionally, though without prejudicing the issue, treat statements that a person caused harm as one sort of nontautologous ground or reason for saying that he is responsible in this sense.

If we may provisionally take what in ordinary life we say and do at its face value, it seems that there coexist in ordinary thought, apart from the law though mirrored in it, several different types of connection between a person's action and eventual harm which render him responsible for it; and in both law and morals the various forms of causal connection between act or omission and harm are the most obvious and least disputable reasons for holding anyone responsible. Yet, in order to understand the extent to which the causal notions of ordinary thought are used in the law, we must bear in mind the many factors which must differentiate moral from legal responsibility in spite of their partial correspondence:

the law is not only not bound to follow the moral patterns of attribution of responsibility but, even when it does, it must take into account, in a way which the private moral judgment need not and does not, the general social consequences which are attached to its judgments of responsibility; for they are of a gravity quite different from those attached to moral censure. The use of the legal sanctions of imprisonment, or enforced monetary compensation against individuals, has such formidable repercussions on the general life of society that the fact that individuals have a type of connection with harm which is adequate for moral censure or claims for compensation is only *one* of the factors which the law most consider, in defining the kinds of connection between actions and harm for which it will hold individuals legally responsible. Always to follow the private moral judgment here would be far too expensive for the law: not only in the crude sense that it would entail a vast machinery of courts and officials, but in the more important sense that it would inhibit or discourage too many other valuable activities of society. To limit the *types* of harm which the law will recognize is not enough; even if the types of harm are limited it would still be too much for any society to punish or exact compensation from individuals whenever their connection with harm of such types would justify moral censure. Conversely, social needs may require that compensation should be paid and even (though less obviously) that punishment be inflicted where no such connection between the person held responsible and the harm exists.

So causing harm of a legally recognized sort or being connected with such harm in any of the ways that justify moral blame, though vitally important and perhaps basic in a legal system, is not and should not be either always necessary or always sufficient for legal responsibility. All legal systems in response either to tradition or to social needs both extend responsibility and cut it off in ways which diverge from the simpler principles of moral blame. In England a man is not guilty of murder if the victim of his attack does not die within a year and day. In New York a person who negligently starts a fire is liable to pay only for the first of several houses which it destroys. These limitations imposed by legal policy are *prima facie* distinguishable from limitations due to the frequent requirement of legal rules that responsi-

bility be limited to harm caused by wrongdoing. Yet a whole school of thought maintains that this distinction does not exist or is not worth drawing.

Apart from this, morality can properly leave certain things vague into which a legal system must attempt to import some degree of precision. Outside the law nothing requires us, when we find the case too complex or too strange, to say whether any and, if so, which of the morally significant types of connection between a person's action and harm exists; we can simply say the case is too difficult for us to pass judgment, at least where moral condemnation of others is concerned. No doubt we evade less easily our questions about our own connection with harm, and the great novelists have often described, sometimes in language very like the lawyers, how the conscience may be still tortured by uncertainties as to the *character* of a part in the production of harm, even when all the facts are known.[2] The fact that there is no precise system of punishments or rewards for common sense to administer, and so there are no 'forms of action' or 'pleadings' to define precise heads of responsibility for harm, means that the principles which guide common-sense attributions of responsibility give precise answers only in relatively simple types of case.

II. TRACING CONSEQUENCES

'To consequences no limit can be set': 'Every event which would not have happened if an earlier event had not happened is the consequence of that earlier event.' These two propositions are not equivalent in meaning and are not equally or in the same way at variance with ordinary thought. They have, however, both been urged sometimes in the same breath by the legal theorist[3] and the philosopher: They are indeed sometimes said by lawyers to be 'the philosophical doctrine' of causation. It is perhaps not difficult even for the layman to accept the first proposition as a truth about certain physical events; an explosion may cause a flash of light which will be propagated as far as the outer nebulae; its effects or consequences continue indefinitely. It is, however, a different matter to accept the view that whenever a man is murdered with a gun his death was the consequence of (still less an 'effect' of or 'caused by') the manufacture of the bullet. The first tells a perhaps unfamiliar tale about unfamiliar events;

the second introduces an unfamiliar, though, of course, a possible way of speaking about familiar events. It is not that this unrestricted use of 'consequence' is unintelligible or never found; it is indeed used to refer to bizarre or fortuitous connections or coincidences: but the point is that the various causal notions employed for the purposes of explanation, attribution of responsibility or the assessment of contributions to the course of history carry with them implicit limits which are similar in these different employments.

It is, then, the second proposition, defining consequence in terms of 'necessary condition', with which theorists are really concerned. This proposition is the corollary of the view that, if we look into the past of any given event, there is an infinite number of events, each of which is a necessary condition of the given event and so, as much as any other, is its cause. This is the 'cone'[4] of causation, so-called because, since any event has a number of simultaneous conditions, the series fans out as we go back in time. The justification, indeed only partial, for calling this 'the philosophical doctrine' of causation is that it resembles Mill's doctrine that 'we have no right to give the name of cause to one of the conditions exclusive of the others of them'. It differs from Mill's view in taking the essence of causation to be 'necessary condition' and not 'the sum total'[5] of the sufficient conditions of an event.

Legal theorists have developed this account of cause and consequence to show what is 'factual', 'objective', or 'scientific' in these notions: this they call 'cause in fact' and it is usually stressed as a preliminary to the doctrine that any more restricted application of these terms in the law represents nothing in the facts or in the meaning of causation, but expresses fluctuating legal policy or sentiments of what is just or convenient. Moral philosophers have insisted in somewhat similar terms that the consequences of human action are 'infinite': this they have urged as an objection against the utilitarian doctrine that the rightness of a morally right action depends on whether its consequences are better than those of any alternative action in the circumstances. 'We should have to trace as far as possible the consequences not only for the persons affected directly but also for those indirectly affected and to these no limit can be set.'[6] Hence, so the argument runs, we cannot either inductively establish the

utilitarian doctrine that right acts are 'optimific' or use it in particular cases to discover what is right. Yet, however vulnerable at other points utilitarianism may be as an account of moral judgment, this objection seems to rest on a mistake as to the sense of 'consequence'. The utilitarian assertion that the rightness of an action depends on its consequences is not the same as the assertion that it depends on all those later occurrences which would not have happened had the action not been done, to which indeed 'no limit can be set'. It is important to see that the issue here is not the linguistic one whether the word 'consequence' would be understood if used in this way. The point is that, though we could, we do not think in this way in tracing connections between human actions and events. Instead, whenever we are concerned with such connections, whether for the purpose of explaining a puzzling occurrence, assessing responsibility, or giving an intelligible historical narrative, we employ a set of concepts restricting in various ways what counts as a consequence. These restrictions colour *all* our thinking in causal terms; when we find them in the law we are not finding something invented by or peculiar to the law, though of course it is for the law to say when and how far it will use them and, where they are vague, to supplement them.

No short account can be given of the limits thus placed on 'consequences' because these limits vary, intelligibly, with the variety of causal connection asserted. Thus we may be tempted by the generalization that consequences must always be something intended or foreseen or at least foreseeable with ordinary care: but counter-examples spring up from many types of context where causal statements are made. If smoking is shown to cause lung cancer, this discovery will permit us to describe past as well as future cases of cancer as the effect or consequence of smoking even though no one foresaw or had reasonable grounds to suspect this in the past. What is common and commonly appreciated and hence foreseeable certainly controls the scope of consequences in certain varieties of causal statement but not in all. Again the voluntary intervention of a second person very often constitutes the limit. If a guest sits down with a table laid with knife and fork and plunges the knife into his hostess's breast, her death is not in any context thought of as caused by, or the effect or result of the waiter's action in laying the table; nor would it be linked with this action as its consequence for any of the purposes, explanatory or attributive, for which we employ causal notions. Yet as we have seen there are many other types of case where a voluntary action or the harm it does are naturally attributed to some prior neglect of precaution as its consequence. Finally, we may think that a simple answer is already supplied by Hume and Mill's doctrine that causal connection rests on general laws asserting regular connection; yet, even in the type of case to which this important doctrine applies, reference to it alone will not solve our problem. For we often trace a causal connection between an antecedent and a consequent which themselves very rarely go together: we do this when the case can be broken down into intermediate stages, which themselves exemplify different generalizations, as when we find that the fall of a tile was the cause of someone's death, rare though this be. Here our problem reappears in the form of the question: When can generalizations be combined in this way?

We shall examine first the central type of case where the problem is of this last-mentioned form. Here the gist of the causal connection lies in the general connection with each other of the successive stages; and is not dependent on the special notions of one person providing another with reasons or exceptional opportunities for actions. This form of causal connection may exist between actions and events, and between purely physical events, and it is in such cases that the words 'cause' and 'causing' used of the antecedent action or event have their most obvious application. It is convenient to refer to cases of the first type where the consequence is harm as cases of 'causing harm', and to refer to cases where harm is the consequence of one person providing another with reasons or opportunities for doing harm as cases of 'inducing', 'advising', or 'occasioning' harmful acts. In cases of the first type a voluntary act, or a conjunction of events amounting to a coincidence, operates as a limit in the sense that events subsequent to these are not attributed to the antecedent action or event as its consequence even though they would not have happened without it. Often such a limiting action or coincidence is thought of and described as 'intervening': and lawyers speak of them as 'superseding' or 'extra-

neous' causes 'breaking the chain of causation'. To see what these metaphors rest on (and in part obscure) and how such factors operate as a limit we shall consider the detail of three simple cases.

(i) A forest fire breaks out, and later investigation shows that shortly before the outbreak A had flung away a lighted cigarette into the bracken at the edge of the forest, the bracken caught fire, a light breeze got up, and fanned the flames in the direction of the forest. If, on discovering these facts, we hesitate before saying that A's action caused the forest fire this would be to consider the alternative hypothesis that in spite of appearances the fire only succeeded A's action in point of time, that the bracken flickered out harmlessly and the forest fire was caused by something else. To dispose of this it may be necessary to examine in further detail the process of events between the ignition of the bracken and the outbreak of fire in the forest and to show that these exemplified certain types of continuous change. If this is shown, there is no longer any room for doubt: A's action *was* the cause of the fire, whether he intended it or not. This seems and is the simplest of cases. Yet it is important to notice that even in applying our general knowledge to a case as simple as this, indeed in regarding it as simple, we make an implicit use of a distinction between types of factor which constitute a limit in tracing consequences and those which we regard as mere circumstances 'through' which we trace them. For the breeze which sprang up after A dropped the cigarette, and without which the fire would not have spread to the forest, was not only subsequent to his action but entirely independent of it: It was, however, a common recurrent feature of the environment, and, as such, it is thought of not as an 'intervening' force but as merely part of the circumstances in which the cause 'operates'. The decision so to regard it is implicitly taken when we combine our knowledge of the successive stages of the process and assert the connection.

It is easy here to be misled by the natural metaphor of a causal 'chain', which may lead us to think that the causal process consists of a series of single events each of which is dependent upon (would not have occurred without) its predecessor in the 'chain' and so is dependent upon the initiating action or event. In truth in any causal process we have at each phase not single events but complex sets of conditions, and among these conditions are some which are not only subsequent to, but independent of, the initiating action or event. Some of these independent conditions such as the evening breeze in the example chosen, we classify as mere conditions in or on which the cause operates; others we speak of as 'interventions' or 'causes'. To decide how such independent elements shall be classified is also to decide how we shall combine our knowledge of the different general connections which the successive stages exemplify, and it is important to see that nothing *in* this knowledge itself can resolve this point. We may have to go to science for the relevant general knowledge before we can assert with proper confidence that A's action did cause the fire, but science, though it tells us that an air current was required, is silent on the difference between a current in the form of an evening breeze and one produced by someone who deliberately fanned the flames as they were flickering out in the bracken. Yet an air current in this form is not a 'condition' or 'mere circumstance' through which we can trace the consequence; its presence would force us to revise the assertion that A caused the fire. Conversely if science helped us to identify as a necessary factor in producing the fire some condition or element of which we had previously been totally ignorant, for example the persistence of oxygen, this would leave our original judgment undisturbed if this factor were a common or pervasive feature of the environment or of the thing in question. There is thus indeed an important sense in which it is true that the distinction between cause and conditions is not a 'scientific' one. It is not determined by laws or generalizations concerning connections between events.

When we have assembled all our knowledge of the factors involved in the fire, the residual question which we then confront (the attributive question) may be typified as follows: Here is A's action, here is the fire. Can the fire be attributed to A's action as its consequence given that there is also this third factor (the breeze or B's intervention) without which the fire would not have happened? It is plain that, both in raising questions of this kind and in answering them, ordinary thought is powerfully influenced by the analogy between the straightforward cases of causal attribution (where the elements required for the production of harm in addition to the initiating action are all 'normal' conditions) and even simpler cases of responsibility which we do not ordinarily describe in causal language at all but by the simple transitive verbs of action. These are the cases of the direct manipulation of objects involving changes in them or their position: cases where we say 'He pushed it', 'He broke it,' 'He bent it.' The cases which we do confidently describe in causal language ('The fire was caused by his carelessness,' 'He caused a fire') are cases where no other human action or abnormal occurrence is required for the production of the effect, but only normal conditions. Such cases appear as mere long range or less direct versions or extensions of the most obvious and fundamental case of all for the attribution of responsibility: the case where we can simply say 'He did it.' Conversely in attaching importance to thus causing harm as a distinct ground of responsibility and in taking certain kinds of factor (whether human interventions or abnormal occurrences), without which the initiating action would not have led to harm, to preclude the description of the case in simple causal terms, common sense is affected by the fact that here, because of the manner in which the harm eventuates, the outcome cannot be represented as a mere extension of the initiating action; the analogy with the fundamental case for responsibility ('He did it') has broken down.

When we understand the power exerted over our ordinary thought by the conception that causing harm is a mere extension of the primary case of doing harm, the interrelated metaphors which seem natural to lawyers and laymen, in describing various aspects of causal connection, fall into place and we can discuss their factual basis. The persistent notion that some kinds of event required in addition to the initiating action for the production of harm 'break the chain of causation' is intelligible, if we remember that though such events actually complete the *explanation* of the harm (and so *make* rather than *break* the causal explanation) they do, unlike mere normal conditions, break the *analogy* with cases of simple actions. The same analogy accounts for the description of these factors as 'new actions' (*novus actus*) or 'new causes', 'superseding', 'extraneous', 'intervening forces': and for the description of the initiating action when 'the chain of causation' is broken as 'no longer operative', 'having worn out', *functus officio.*[7] So too when the 'chain' is held not to be 'broken' the initiating action is said to be still 'potent',[8] 'continuing', 'contributing', 'operative', and the mere conditions held insufficient to break the chain are 'part of the background',[9] 'circumstances in which the cause operates',[10] 'the stage set', 'part of the history'.

(ii) A throws a lighted cigarette into the bracken which catches fire. B, just as the flames are about to flicker out, deliberately pours petrol on them. The fire spreads and burns down the forest. A's action, whether or not he intended the forest fire, was not the cause of the fire: B's was.

The voluntary intervention of a second human agent, as in this case, is a paradigm among those factors which preclude the assimilation in causal judgments of the first agent's connection with the eventual harm to the case of simple direct manipulation. Such an intervention displaces the prior action's title to be called the cause and, in the persistent metaphors found in the law, it 'reduces' the earlier action and its immediate effects to the level of 'mere circumstances' or 'part of the history.' B in this case was not an 'instrument' through which A worked or a victim of the circumstances A has created. He has, on the contrary, freely exploited the circumstances and brought about the fire without the cooperation of any further agent or any chance coincidence. Compared with this the claim of A's action to be ranked the cause of the fire fails. That this and not the moral appraisal of the two actions is the point of comparison seems clear. If A and B both intended to set the forest on fire, and this destruction is accepted as something wrong or wicked, their moral wickedness, judged by the criterion of intention, is the same. Yet the causal judgment differentiates between them. If their moral guilt is judged by the outcome, this judgment though it would differentiate between them cannot be the source of the causal judgment; for it presupposes it. The difference just is that B has caused the harm and A has not. Again, if we appraise these actions as good or bad from different points of view, this leaves the causal judgments unchanged. A may be a soldier of one side anxious to burn down the enemy's hideout: B may be an enemy soldier who has decided that his side is too iniquitous to defend. Whatever is the moral judgment passed on these actions by different speakers it would remain true that A had not caused the fire and B had.

There are, as we have said, situations in which a voluntary action would not be thought of as an intervention precluding causal connection in this way. These are the cases discussed further below where an opportunity commonly exploited for harmful actions is negligently provided, or one person intentionally provides another with a certain type of reason for wrongdoing. Except in such cases a voluntary intervention is a limit past which consequences are not traced. By contrast, actions which in any of a variety of different ways are less than fully voluntary are assimilated to the means by which or the circumstances in which the earlier action brings about the consequences. Such actions are not the outcome of an informed choice made without pressure from others, and the different ways in which human action may fall short in this respect range from defective muscular control, through lack of consciousness or knowledge, to the vaguer notions of duress and of predicaments, created by the first agent for the second, in which there is no 'fair' choice.

In considering examples of such actions and their bearing on causal judgments there are three dangers to avoid. It would be folly to think that in tracing connections through such actions instead of regarding them, like voluntary interventions, as a limit, ordinary thought has clearly separated out their nonvoluntary aspect from others by which they are often accompanied. Thus even in the crude case where A lets off a gun (intentionally or not) and startles B, so that he makes an involuntary movement of his arm which breaks a glass, the commonness of such a reaction as much as its compulsive character may influence the judgment that A's action was the cause of the damage.

Secondly we must not impute to ordinary thought all the fine discriminations that could be made and in fact are to be found in a legal system, or an equal willingness to supply answers to complex questions in causal terms. Where there is no precise system of punishment, compensation or reward to administer, ordinary men will not often have faced such questions as whether the injuries suffered by a motorist who collides with another in swerving to avoid a child are consequences attributable to the neglect of the child's parents in allowing it to wander on to the road. Such questions courts have to answer and in such cases common judgments provide only a general, though still an important indication of what are the relevant factors.

Thirdly, though very frequently nonvoluntary actions are assimilated to mere conditions or means by which the first agent brings about the consequences, the assimilation is never quite complete. This is manifested by the general avoidance of many causal locutions which are appropriate when the consequences are traced (as in the first case) through purely physical events. Thus even in the case in which the second agent's rôle is hardly an 'action' at all, for example, where A hits B, who staggers against a glass window and breaks it, we should say that A's blow made B stagger and break the glass, rather than that A's blow caused the glass to break, though in any explanatory or attributive context the case would be *summarized* by saying that A's action was the cause of the *damage* or that A had caused it.

In the last two cases where B's movements are involuntary in the sense that they are not part of any action which he chose or intended to do, their connection with A's action would be described by saying that A's blow *made* B stagger or *caused* him to stagger or that the noise of A's shot *made* him jump or *caused* him to jump. This would be true, whether A intended or expected B to react in this way or not, and the naturalness of treating A's action as the cause of the ultimate damage is due to the causal character of this part of the process involving B's action. The same is however true where B's actions are not involuntary movements but A is considered to have made or caused B to do them by less crude means. This is the case if, for example, A uses treats or exploits his authority over B to make B do something, for example, knock down a door. At least where A's threats are of serious harm, or B's act was unquestionably within A's authority to order, he too has made or forced or (in formal quasi-legal parlance) 'caused' B to act.

Outside the area of such cases, where B's will would be either said not to be involved at all, or to be overborne by A, are cases where A's act creates a predicament for B *narrowing* the area of choice so that he has either to inflict some harm on himself or others, or sacrifice some important interest or duty. Such cases resemble coercion in

that A narrows the area of B's choice but differ from it in that this predicament need not be intentionally created. A sets a house on fire (intentionally or unintentionally): B to save himself has to jump from a height involving certain injury, or to save a child rushes in and is seriously burned. Here of course B's movements are not involuntary; the 'necessity' of his action is here of a different order. His action is the outcome of a choice between two evils forced on him by A's action. In such cases, when B's injuries are thought of as the consequence of the fire, the implicit judgment is made that his action was the lesser of two evils and in this sense a 'reasonable' one which he was obliged to make to avoid the greater evil. This is often paradoxically, though understandably, described by saying that here the agent 'had no choice' but to do what he did. Such judgments involve a comparison of the importance of the respective interests sacrificed and preserved, and the final assertion that A's action was the cause of the injuries rests on evaluations about which men may differ.

Finally, ground for treating some harm which would not have occurred without B's action as the consequence of A's action may be that B acted in ignorance of, or under a mistake as to some feature of, the situation created by A. Poisoning offers perhaps the simplest example of the bearing on causal judgments of actions which are less than voluntary in this Aristotelian sense. If A intending B's death deliberately poisons B's food and B, knowing this, deliberately takes the poison and dies, A has not caused B's death: if however B does not know the food to be poisoned, eats it and dies A has caused his death, even if he put the poison in unwittingly. Of course only the roughest judgments are passed in causal terms in such cases outside law courts, where fine degrees of 'appreciation' or reckless shutting of the eyes, may have to be discriminated from 'full knowledge'. Yet, rough as these are, they indicate clearly enough the controlling principles.

Though in the foregoing cases A's initiating action might often be described as 'the cause' of the ultimate harm, this linguistic fact is of subordinate importance to the fact that, for whatever purpose, explanatory, descriptive or evaluative, consequences of an action are traced, discriminations are made (except in the cases discussed later) between free voluntary interventions and less than voluntary reactions to the first action or the circumstances created by it.

(iii) The analogy with single simple actions which guides the tracing of consequences may be broken by certain kinds of conjunctions of physical events. A hits B who falls to the ground stunned and bruised by the blow; at that moment a tree crashes to the ground and kills B. A has certainly caused B's bruises but not his death: for though the fall of the tree was, like the evening breeze, in our earlier example, independent of and subsequent to the initiating action, it would be differentiated from the breeze in any description in causal terms of the connection of B's death with A's action. It is to be noticed that this is not a matter which turns on the intention with which A struck B. Even if A hit B inadvertently or accidentally his blow would still be the cause of B's bruises: he would have caused them though unintentionally. Conversely even if A had intended his blow to kill, this would have been an attempt to kill but still not the cause of B's death. On this legal and ordinary judgments would be found to agree; and most legal systems would distinguish for the purposes of punishment an attempt with a fatal upshot, issuing by such chance or anomalous events, from 'causing death' —the terms in which the offences of murder and manslaughter are usually defined.

Similarly the causal description of the case does not turn on the moral appraisal of A's action or the wish to punish it. A may be a robber and a murderer and B a saint guarding the place A hoped to plunder. Or B may be a murderer and A a hero who has forced his way into B's retreat. In both cases the causal judgment is the same. A had caused the minor injuries but not B's death, though he tried to kill him. A may indeed be praised or blamed but not for causing B's death. However intimate the connection between causation and responsibility, it does not determine causal judgments in this simple way. Nor does the causal judgment turn on a refusal to attribute grave consequences to actions which normally have less serious results. Had A's blow killed B outright and the tree, falling on his body, merely smashed his watch we should still treat the coincidental character of the fall of the tree as determining the form of causal statement. We should then recognize A's blow as the cause of B's death but not of the breaking of the watch.

The connection between A's action and B's death in the first case would naturally be described in the language of *coincidence*. 'It was a coincidence: it just happened that, at the very moment when A knocked B down, a tree crashed at the very place where he fell and killed him.' The common legal metaphor would describe the fall of the tree as an 'extraneous' cause. This, however, is dangerously misleading, as an analysis of the notion of coincidence will show. It suggests merely an event which is subsequent to and independent of some other contingency, and of course the fall of the tree has both these features in relation to A's blow. Yet in these respects the fall of the tree does not differ from the evening breeze in the earlier case where we found no difficulty in tracing causal connection. The full elucidation of the notion of a coincidence is a complex matter for, though it is very important as a limit in tracing consequences, causal questions are not the only ones to which the notion is relevant. The following are its most general characteristics. We speak of a coincidence whenever (1) the conjunction of two or more events in certain spatial or temporal relations is very unlikely by ordinary standards and (2) is for some reason significant or important, provided (3) that they occur without human contrivance and (4) are independent of each other. It is therefore a coincidence if two persons known to each other in London meet without design in Paris on their way to separate independently chosen destinations; or if two persons living in different places independently decide to write a book on the same subject. The first is a coincidence of time and place ('It just happened that we were at the same place at the same time'), and the second a coincidence of time only ('It just happened that they both decided to write on the subject at the same time').

Use of this general notion is made in the special case when the conjunction of two or more events occurs in temporal and/or spatial relationships which are significant, because, as our general knowledge of causal processes shows, this conjunction is required for the production of some given further event. In the language of Mill's idealized model, they form a necessary part of a complex set of jointly sufficient conditions. In the present case the fall of the tree just as B was struck down within its range satisfies the four criteria for a coincidence which we have enumerated. First, though neither event was of a very rare or exceptional kind, their conjunction would be rated very unlikely judged by the standards of ordinary experience. Secondly, this conjunction was causally significant for it was a necessary part of the process terminating in B's death. Thirdly, this conjunction was not consciously designed by A: had he known of the impending fall of the tree and hit B with the intention that he should fall within its range B's death would not have been the result of any coincidence. A would certainly have caused it. The common-sense principle that a contrived conjunction cannot be a coincidence is the element of truth in the legal maxim (too broadly stated even for legal purposes) that an intended consequence cannot be too 'remote'. Fourthly, each member of the conjunction in this case was independent of the other; whereas if B had fallen against the tree with an impact sufficient to bring it down on him, this sequence of physical events, though freakish in its way, would not be a coincidence and in most contexts of ordinary life, as in the law, the course of events would be summarized by saying that in this case, unlike that of the coincidence, A's act was the cause of B's death, since each stage is the effect of the preceding stage. Thus, the blow forced the victim against the tree, the effect of this was to make the tree fall and the fall of the tree killed the victim.

One further criterion in addition to these four must be satisfied if a conjunction of events is to rank as a coincidence and as a limit when the consequences of the action are traced. This further criterion again shows the strength of the influence which the analogy with the case of the simple manipulation of things exerts over thought in causal terms. An abnormal *condition* existing at the time of a human intervention is distinguished both by ordinary thought and, with a striking consistency, by most legal systems from an abnormal event or conjunction of events subsequent to that intervention; the former, unlike the latter, are not ranked as coincidences or 'extraneous' causes when the consequences of the intervention come to be traced. Thus A innocently gives B a tap over the head of a normally quite harmless character, but because B is then suffering from some rare disease the tap has, as we say, 'fatal results'. In this case A has caused B's death though unintentionally. The scope of the principle which thus distinguishes contempo-

raneous abnormal conditions from subsequent events is unclear; but at least where a human being initiates some physical change in a thing, animal, or person, abnormal physical states of the object affected, existing at the time, are ranked as part of the circumstances in which the cause 'operates'. In the familiar controlling imagery these are part of 'the stage already set' before the 'intervention'.

Judgments about coincidences, though we often agree in making them, depend on two related ways on issues incapable of precise formulation. One of these is patent, the other latent but equally important. Just how unlikely must a conjunction be to rank as a coincidence, and in the light of what knowledge is likelihood to be assessed? The only answer is: 'very unlikely in the light of the knowledge available to ordinary men.' It is of course the indeterminacies of such standards, implicit in causal judgments, that make them inveterately disputable, and call for the exercise of discretion or choice by courts. The second and latent indeterminacy of these judgments depends on the fact that the things or events which they relate do not have pinned to them some uniquely correct description always to be used in assessing likelihood. It is an important pervasive feature of all our empirical judgments that there is a constant possibility of more or less specific description of any event or thing with which they are concerned. The tree might be described not simply as 'a tree' but as a 'rotten tree' or as a 'fir tree' or a 'tree sixty feet tall'. So too its fall might be described not as a 'fall' but as a fall of a specified distance at a specified velocity. The likelihood of conjunctions framed in these different terms would be differently assessed. The criteria of appropriate description like the standard of likelihood are supplied by consideration of common knowledge. Even if the scientist knew the tree to be rotten and could have predicted its fall with accuracy, this would not change the judgment that its fall at the time when B was struck down within its range was a coincidence; nor would it make the description 'rotten tree' appropriate for the assessment of the chances involved in this judgment. There are other controls over the choice of description derived from the degree of specificity of our interests in the final outcome of the causal process. We are concerned with the fall of an object sufficient to cause 'death' by impact and the precise force or direction which may account for the detail of the wounds is irrelevant here.

OPPORTUNITIES AND REASONS

Opportunities. The discrimination of voluntary interventions as a limit is no longer made when the case, owing to the commonness or appreciable risk of such harmful intervention, can be brought within the scope of the notion of providing an opportunity, known to be commonly exploited for doing harm. Here the limiting principles are different. When A leaves the house unlocked the range of consequences to be attributed to this neglect, as in any other case where precautions are omitted, depends primarily on the way in which such opportunities are commonly exploited. An alternative formulation of this idea is that a subsequent intervention would fall within the scope of consequences if the likelihood of its occurring is one of the reasons for holding A's omission to be negligent.

It is on these lines that we would distinguish between the entry of a thief and of a murderer; the opportunity provided is believed to be sufficiently commonly exploited by thieves to make it usual and often morally or legally obligatory not to provide it. Here, in attributing consequences to prior actions, causal judgments are directly controlled by the notion of the risk created by them. Neglect of such precautions is both unusual and reprehensible. For these reasons it would be hard to separate the two ways in which such neglect deviates from the 'norm'. Despite this, no simple identification can be made of the notion of responsibility with the causal connection which is a ground for it. This is so because the provision of an opportunity commonly taken by others is ranked as the cause of the outcome independently of the wish to praise or blame. The causal judgment may be made simply to assess a contribution to some outcome. Thus, whether we think well or ill of the use made of railways, we would still claim that the greater mobility of the population in the nineteenth century was a consequence of their introduction.

It is obvious that the question whether any given intervention is a sufficiently common exploitation of the opportunity provided to come within the risk is again a matter on which judgments may differ though they often agree. The courts, and perhaps ordinary thought also, often describe those that are sufficiently common as 'natural' consequences of the neglect. They have in these terms discriminated the entry of a thief from the entry of a man who burnt the house down, and refused to treat the destruction of the house as a 'natural' consequence of the neglect. . . .[11]

Reasons. In certain varieties of interpersonal transactions, unlike the case of coercion, the second action is quite voluntary. A may not threaten B but may bribe or advise or persuade him to do something. Here, A does not 'cause' or 'make' B do anything: the strongest words we should use are perhaps that he 'induced' or 'procured' B's act. Yet the law and moral principles alike may treat one person as responsible for the harm which another free agent has done 'in consequence' of the advice or the inducements which the first has offered. In such cases the limits concern the range of those actions done by B which are to rank as the consequence of A's words or deeds. In general this question depends on A's intentions or on the 'plan of action' he puts before B. If A advises or bribes B to break in and steal from an empty house and B does so, he acts in consequence of A's advice or bribe. If he deliberately burns down the house this would not be treated as the consequence of A's bribe or advice, legally or otherwise, though it may in some sense be true that the burning would not have taken place without the advice or bribe. Nice questions may arise, which the courts have to settle, where B diverges from the detail of the plan of action put before him by A.

NOTES

1. Cf. *O.E.D. sub tit.* Responsible: Answerable, Accountable (*to* another *for* something); liable to be called to account 'being responsible to the King for what might happen to us', 1662.

2. See the following passage from *The Golden Bowl* by Henry James. (Mrs. Assingham whose uncertain self-accusation is described here, had, on the eve of the Prince's marriage, encouraged him to resume an old friendship with Charlotte Stant. The relationship which developed came to threaten the marriage with disaster.) 'She had stood for the previous hour in a merciless glare, beaten upon, stared out of countenance, it fairly seemed to her, by intimations of her mistake. For what she was most immediately feeling was that she had in the past been active for these people to ends that were now bearing fruit and that might yet bear a greater crop. She but brooded at first in her corner of the carriage: it was like burying her exposed face, a face too helplessly exposed in the

cool lap of the common indifference ... a world mercifully unconscious and unreproachful. It wouldn't like the world she had just left know sooner or later what she had done or would know it only if the final consequence should be some quite overwhelming publicity. ... The sense of seeing was strong in her, but she clutched at the comfort of not being sure of what she saw. Not to know what it would represent on a longer view was a help in turn to not making out that her hands were embrued; since if she had stood in the position of a producing cause she should surely be less vague about what she had produced. This, further, in its way, was a step toward reflecting that when one's connection with any matter was too indirect to be traced, it might be described also as too slight to be deplored' (*The Golden Bowl*, Book 3, chap. 3). We are much indebted to Mrs. H. M. Warnock for this quotation.

3. Lawson, *Negligence in the Civil Law*, p. 53.
4. Glanville Williams, *Joint Torts and Contributory Negligence*, p. 239.
5. Mill, Book III, chap. v, s. 2.
6. Ross, *The Right and the Good*, p. 36.
7. *Davies v. Swan Motor Co.*, [1947] 2 K.B. 291, 318.
8. *Minister of Pensions v. Chennell*, [1947] K.B. 250, 256. Lord Wright (1950), 13 *Mod. L.R.* 3.
9. *Norris v. William Moss & Son Ltd.*, [1954] 1 W.L.R. 46, 351.
10. *Minister of Pensions v. Chennell*, [1947] K.B. 250, 256.
11. *Bellows v. Worcester Storage Co.* (1937), 297 Mass 188, 7 N.E. 2d 588.

ROBERT E. KEETON

The Basic Rule of Legal Cause in Negligence Cases*

DIVERSE FORMULATIONS OF THE RISK RULE

STATEMENT AND ILLUSTRATION OF THREE FORMULATIONS

The defendant, proprietor of a restaurant, placed a large, unlabeled can of rat poison beside cans of flour on a shelf near a stove in a restaurant kitchen. The victim, while in the kitchen making a delivery to the restaurant, was killed by an explosion of the poison. Assume that the defendant's handling of the rat poison was negligent because of the risk that someone would be poisoned but that defendant had no reason to know of the risk that the poison would explode if left in a hot place. Is the defendant liable for the death of the victim?[1]

This question illustrates the central problem of scope of liability for negligence. The problem is commonly subdivided into issues associated with, first, the foreseeability of any kind of harm to the

victim who, in fact, was harmed and, second, the foreseeability of the particular harm or kind of harm that occurred.

The predominant theme in judicial utterances on the scope of liability in negligence cases is expressed in a proposition that, for convenience, will be referred to as the Risk Rule. This rule, quite commonly expressed in substance both in charges to the jury and in appellate opinions, is as follows:

A negligent actor is legally responsible for that harm, and only that harm, of which *negligence* is a cause in fact.

Some explanatory comments are in order. First, this rule is addressed not only to matters uniformly classified as problems of legal cause but also to other matters sometimes classified as problems of duty. Comments directed specifically to this choice of terminology are reserved for the second and third chapters.[2]

Other explanatory comments that seem necessary at the outset are concerned with the meaning

*Reprinted from *Legal Cause in the Law of Torts* by Robert E. Keeton, Copyright © 1963 by the Ohio State University Press, by permission of the author and the publisher.

of the words "actor" and "negligence." "Actor" is used here to signify the person whose "conduct" is being judged, whether plaintiff or defendant, and whether charged with acting negligently or with negligently failing to act. "Conduct" is used in a sense that includes both "acting" and "failing to act." "Negligence," in the context of this rule, must be understood in a more precise sense than merely "the negligent actor's conduct." This statement of the Risk Rule makes no sense unless interpreted as meaning that the actor's *conduct* during the period of his negligence may be a cause of harm of which his *negligence* is not a cause. For example, in the case of the explosive rat poison, it is not enough to ask whether the defendant's conduct in placing the poison where he did was a cause of the death of the victim. We should, as well, ask whether the defendant's negligence was a cause of the death. As a means of arriving at a satisfactory answer to that question, it will be useful to consider another.

What was that aspect of the conduct of the defendant that caused it to be characterized as negligence? Placing rat poison on a shelf may or may not be negligence. The negligence here consisted of placing the poison where it was likely to be mistaken for something intended for human consumption. This description says nothing about the proximity of the shelf to heat. That circumstance is omitted because of the assumption that the defendant had no reason to know of the explosive character of the poison; in such a situation it would not have been negligent to put the poison in a place that happened to be near heat, provided it was not a place where the poison was likely to be mistaken as something intended for human consumption. Thus, the defendant's *negligence* (his placing the poison where it was likely to be mistaken for something intended for human consumption) was not a *sine qua non* of the harm. For present purposes I draw no distinction between the several expressions "but-for cause," "necessary antecedent," and "*sine qua non*."[3] That is, I am speaking simply of the concept that it cannot be said that the harm of death from explosion would not have occurred but for defendant's placing the poison where it was likely to be mistaken for something intended for human consumption. Defendant's negligence was not in this sense a but-for cause, or a necessary anteced-

ent, or a *sine qua non* of the death. But his conduct (placing the poison near heat) was, at least in a qualified sense, a *sine qua non*.

The qualification is concerned with the hypothetical character of the assertion. That is, the assertion that the harm would not have occurred but for the defendant's conduct is a hypothetical assertion the accuracy of which is not subject to demonstration. For example, how are we to know that, had the poison been placed elsewhere than near a hot stove, it would not have been exploded by some other source of heat that might have happened to be applied to the poison while the victim was present? Also, imbedded in the hypothetical assertion of what would not have happened are ambiguities in the meaning of "conduct" and "harm." Does "conduct" refer to placing the poison in the exact spot where it was placed? If so, might it not be said that the conduct was not a *sine qua non* since death at the same time and place might have occurred if the poison had been placed near a hot radiator rather than the stove? Does "the harm" refer merely to death of the victim, or to the time, place, and manner of death in all their detail, or to something between these extremes? In some instances, the ambiguity and hypothetical character of the assertion will present serious difficulty.[4] But, in the case of the explosive rat poison, we can readily understand and accept, in at least a rough sense, the assertion that the defendant's conduct was a *sine qua non* of the harm because there appears to have been no substantial possibility either that the harm in all its details would have occurred or that something generally resembling it would have occurred in the absence of defendant's conduct of placing the rat poison near heat. Also, no doubt, we can agree that if defendant's negligence is defined in the limited sense of that quality of his conduct consisting of his placing the poison where it was likely to be mistaken for something intended for human consumption, his negligence was not a *sine qua non*.

There is yet another difficulty, however, in the assertion that one aspect of his conduct was a cause of harm and another aspect of the same conduct, the same single action of putting down a can of poison, was not a cause of the harm. It is more normal, perhaps, to think of the conduct as indivisible and to reject the suggestion that the negligent aspect can be separated from other aspects for an inquiry into causal relation. Perhaps it will be helpful in this respect to think of negligence as the creation of unreasonable risks[5] and, rather than thinking of harm itself as the focus of the concept of risk, to think of a risk as a set of forces and conditions and circumstances that might foreseeably bring about harm.[6] No special point is made here regarding the choice among the terms "force," "condition," and "circumstance" to convey the intended idea, though the word "circumstance" seems the most congenial to the separation of aspects of a single state of affairs. Negligence, then, consists of creating a set of unduly risky forces or conditions or circumstances, and the negligence is a *sine qua non* of subsequent harm only if some force or condition or circumstance within this set is a *sine qua non*. In the case of the rat poison, the negligence consisted of creating a force or condition or circumstance of having a poisonous substance where it might be mistaken as something intended for human consumption. That circumstance was not a cause of the harm, though the coexisting circumstance of having an explosive substance near heat was a cause.

This focus upon the negligent aspect of conduct as the meaning of the unqualified word "negligence" in the statement of the Risk Rule presented above suggests a second, perhaps less ambiguous, formulation of exactly the same meaning:

A negligent actor is legally responsible for that harm, and only that harm, of which the *negligent aspect of his conduct* is a cause in fact.

In many cases it is less easy than in the case of the explosive rat poison to extract the negligent aspect from the total conduct. To meet this difficulty, still another formulation of the Risk Rule is helpful. A moment ago, we were thinking of risk with a focus upon the forces or conditions or circumstances that might produce harm. Shift the focus now to the harm that might be produced. With this focus, in order to find that the negligence (that is, the negligent aspect of the conduct) bears a causal relation to the harm, we must find that the harm that came about was one of the things that was risked. Another way of expressing the same idea is to say that the harm must be a result within the scope of at least one of the risks on the basis of which the actor is found to be negligent. Thus the Risk Rule of legal cause as stated in the first and second formulations above may be restated in a third formulation without change of meaning:

A negligent actor is legally responsible for the harm, and only the harm, that not only (1) is caused in fact by his conduct but also (2) is a result within the scope of the risks by reason of which the actor is found to be negligent.

In the case of the explosive rat poison, injury by explosion was not a result within the scope of the risks by reason of which the defendant was found to be negligent, though injury by poisoning would have been.

The third formulation of the rule is often expressed in the statement that the actor is responsible only for "results within the risk." Among those who remain constantly alert to its meaning, there is no objection to use of such a shorthand expression. But this cryptic phrase is apt to be misleading to the unsophisticated because it does not designate the point of view from which the composite of risks is defined. The concept of "risk" and the cognate concept of "probability" are founded on prediction from some selected point of view. But they do not necessarily imply any particular point of view, such as that of a reasonable man in the position of the actor. Thus, results that in the wisdom of hindsight are said to have been "probable" may yet have been beyond the scope of those risks by reason of which the actor's conduct is found to have been negligence. Also, such concepts as "risk," "probability," and "foreseeability" imply a point of view involving a degree of ignorance about the factors at work in a situation. To one who knows all, a future event is not "probable" or merely "foreseeable" but either certain to occur or certain not to occur. When we say a result was "probable" as a matter of hindsight, we are using a point of view that is neither that of a reasonable person in the actor's position nor that of an omniscient observer after the fact. It is a point of view based on foresight in the face of incomplete knowledge, but with greater knowledge or greater mental capacity than that of the actor or that of the standard man in the actor's circumstances. As used in the Risk Rule, on the other hand, "risk" implies a standard based on foresight from the point of view of the standard man in the actor's circumstances at the time of the conduct that is being judged.

As we examine the policy foundation of the Risk Rule, reasons will appear for using, in relation to problems of legal cause, this standard of foresight that is also used in determining whether the actor was negligent. But, first, we digress for further explanation of the use of three formulations of the Risk Rule.

WHY THREE FORMULATIONS?

The first formulation of the Risk Rule tracks language found in many jury charges today, as well as in appellate opinions, though supplemented usually by elaborations upon the theme and occasionally by qualifications. The third formulation tracks the rationale of exponents of what has come to be known as the risk theory of legal cause, and of Professor Seavey in particular.[7] Professors Harper and James also recommended an inquiry in terms generally consistent with the rationale expressed in the third formulation,[8] though they appear less happy than Professor Seavey with adherence to the limitation on scope of liability implicit in accepting this as the basic rule of legal cause. They also observed that in essence this is the same inquiry as the question whether there is causal relation "between *that aspect of the defendant's conduct which is wrongful* and the injury."[9] Thus, the second formulation offered here is supported by their analysis. This formulation is offered as a transitional bond between the first and the third, in the belief that the intended substance of these different expressions is the same. Candor requires disclosure that Professor Seavey dislikes both the first and the second formulations because of a concern, as I understand him, that they are more likely to mislead than to clarify. His disfavor is firm, though expressed in the warmhearted spirit that has characterized his rigorous intellectual assaults upon the ideas of generations of students, colleagues, and judges. At the risk of suffering an intermeddler's unhappy fate, I persist in offering the second formulation and in marshaling the three together in the hope of improving relations between adherents of two ways of thought that I believe to be compatibly directed toward the same goal.

THE RISK RULE AS A RULE OF CAUSATION

Perhaps a secondary benefit of this focus on three formulations of one rule is to expose rather persuasive evidence that the Risk Rule is indeed a rule of causation in a cause-in-fact sense. There are various deviations from the Risk Rule—some toward greater liability, some toward less—that are founded in notions beyond causation. But the predominant theme represented by the Risk Rule is a theme of causation. It concerns cause-in-fact relation between the negligent aspect of the conduct and the harm.

This conclusion is supported by only a few of the multitude of authors on legal cause—among them Professor Carpenter,[10] and, more recently, Professors Harper and James.[11] Even these three appear not willing to carry the separation of aspects of the conduct as far as is suggested here. The following passage from Harper and James is relevant:

> But there are cases where causal relation exists between defendant's fault and the injury, yet where liability will not be imposed. Thus in Gorris v. Scott, L.R. 9 Ex. 125 (1874), defendants' wrongful failure to have pens for cattle on shipboard was the cause in fact of their being washed overboard in a heavy sea. There was no liability, however, since the statutory requirement was designed to protect the cattle only from perils from contagious disease, a hazard which was not encountered and from which their loss did not result. See Carpenter, Workable Rules for Determining Proximate Cause, 20 Calif. L. Rev. 396, 408 (1932).[12]

The claim of negligence in *Gorris* v. *Scott* was violation of orders issued pursuant to the Contagious Diseases (Animals) Act of 1869, the violation being failure to provide battens or foot-holds for the animals and failure to provide pens not larger than 9 by 15 feet each. Under the analysis suggested in this chapter, the negligent aspect of the conduct was not the circumstance that absence of such pens and foot-holds placed the cattle in position to be washed overboard. No doubt, reluctance to declare that there is no causal connection between the the negligent aspect of the conduct and the result in these circumstances arises from the difficulty of imagining facts in which compliance with the required safeguards against disease would not also protect the cattle against being washed overboard. The case is thus unlike that of the speeding automobile that strikes a child who could not have been avoided by a driver proceeding at a reasonable speed; in that situation, speed causes the automobile to be at the scene at the critical time, but we can imagine the defendant's starting sooner and arriving in time to strike the child though he drives at a reasonable speed throughout the journey. Perhaps the converse point of view is also relevant, however. That is, perhaps we should consider not only whether situations can be imagined in which the required safeguard would have been ineffectual to prevent the particular kind of harm of which plaintiff is complaining but also whether situations can be imagined in which despite absence of the required safeguards the plaintiff would have been fully protected against this kind of harm. This is not to say that a required safeguard is intended to be an exclusive safeguard against the dangers to which it is directed. But this point of view does suggest that, when we treat one circumstance (that absence of pens placed the cattle in position to be washed overboard) as an aspect of the conduct separate from another circumstance (that absence of pens placed the cattle in position to be subject to an increased risk of contagious disease), we are no more attempting to separate inseparable aspects of a single faulty course of conduct than in the converse situation illustrated by the case of excessive speed. Pursuing this line of thought, we may observe that it would have been possible in *Gorris v. Scott* to have larger pens and no footholds and yet have the cattle protected against the risk of being washed overboard. In any event, the negligence was concerned with the circumstance that absence of the required safeguards increased the risks of disease, including the risk that affected cattle would communicate the disease widely among animals not separated into small groups by use of small enclosures. It was not concerned with the circumstance that the cattle were in position to be washed overboard. Thus, there was no causal relation between the negligent aspect of the conduct and the harm.

Possibly some passages in the recent broad study of causation by a distinguished pair of English scholars, Hart and Honoré, can also be fairly interpreted as supporting the assertion that the Risk Rule is concerned with causal relation between the negligent aspect of conduct and the harm of which plaintiff complains.[13] Yet, elsewhere they may be thought to be saying that foreseeability is a policy factor, that causal principles are policy neutral, and that use of foreseeability as a test for scope of liability is a departure from use of causal criteria.[14] They argue that the foreseeability test breaks down, especially in cases of what they call "ulterior" harm (e.g., harm following a foreseeable impact on an unforeseeably thin skull), and that causal criteria must be used instead.[15] Perhaps these several passages can be reconciled on the basis that Hart and Honoré mean not to declare that the foreseeability test is unconcerned with causal relation between the negligent aspect of the conduct and the harm but only that in some situations, especially those of "ulterior" harm, the scope of liability is fixed by a test of causal relation between conduct and harm rather than between negligent aspect of conduct and harm. If this reading of their book is proper, then the views of Hart and Honoré tend to support the assertion that the three separate formulations of the Risk Rule are in essence expressions of one idea and that this idea is concerned with cause-in-fact relation between the negligent aspect of the conduct and the harm.

To the contrary, other writers, probably a majority, have insisted that doctrines of legal cause generally, and the result-within-the-risk formulation in particular, are based on policy considerations having nothing to do with cause in fact.[16] The insight produced by a focus upon the relation between the negligent aspect of conduct and the ensuing harm is nevertheless persuasive. The persistence of courts in dealing with this problem under the rubric of causation is perhaps more than evidence of a judicial instinct for right results; perhaps it is also evidence that on occasion judicial perception surpasses that of the majority of reflective critics. This accolade to the courts is not intended to imply a preference for the first or the second formulation of the Risk Rule over the third. It does, however, express a conviction that the first and second formulations offer added illumination on the problem though the third is generally the more manageable in difficult applications. Inevitably, different formulations are likely to produce different nuances and connotations. Since all three formulations are expressions of a single theme, it will often be an aid to deliberate and rational choice to examine the implications of the Risk Rule from the several points of view of all three formulations.

THE POLICY FOUNDATION OF THE RISK RULE

SCOPE OF LIABILITY COMMENSURATE WITH THE BASIS OF LIABILITY

The policy foundation of the Risk Rule can be summarized in this way: The factors determining that the actor is liable for unintended harm caused by his conduct should also determine the scope of his liability. There is surely an interest of public policy in formulating rules that do not impose crushing liability.[17] Since the unintended consequences of one's conduct go on indefinitely, some limit of responsibility is a practical necessity. The theory of the Risk Rule is that the scope of liability should be commensurate with the basis of liability. "Prima facie at least, the reasons for creating liability should limit it."[18]

Opponents of the Risk Rule have argued that in applying the risk concept first to the issue of liability and again to the issue of scope of liability a court gives the defendant an unwarranted advantage by applying twice a restrictive test of foreseeability of harm.[19] The argument is not persuasive. In the first place, the test is expansive rather than restrictive if we start with the assumption that the burden is on the plaintiff to prove some good reason for entering a loss-shifting judgment. That is, when the test for negligence is found to have been fulfilled, liability is expanded in the sense of establishment of an obligation not previously acknowledged. Only if we make a comparison with an assumed state of broader liability, or if we start with the assumption that there is a burden on the defendant to prove nonliability, can we think of an application of the test of foreseeability of harm as restrictive rather than expansive. This is true whether it be applied to the liability issue alone, to the scope of liability issue as well, or to the combination as a unit. In the second place, separating the issues of liability and scope of liability is simply a means of organizing thought. There is no more reason for characterizing the process as a double application of a standard, either restrictive or expansive, when the issues are separated than when they are merged into one issue of liability for how much

—none, all, or something between. This double-advantage argument is a conclusion derived from the premise that the scope of liability *should be* governed by a separate test. The opposing premise on which the Risk Rule is founded—the premise that the scope of liability should be limited by the factors accounting for liability—has been described as the view that there is only one question in negligence cases, not two.[20]

RELATION TO THE PRINCIPLE THAT LIABILITY IS BASED ON FAULT

The policy argument underlying use of the Risk Rule in negligence cases is a corollary of the foundation of tort law on fault. Generally one is not liable for an unintended harm caused by his nonnegligent conduct. If negligence in one respect were to make the actor liable for all unintended harms to follow, the legal consequences would be disproportionate to the fault. For example, suppose the defendant's negligence consisted of his transporting dynamite in an unmarked truck, otherwise carefully operated, and the only harm caused was injury to one who, without negligence, fainted, fell into the path of the truck, and was run down. Defendant was negligent with respect to risks of explosion but not with respect to risks of an injury of the kind that occurred. The policy judgment underlying the Risk Rule is that with respect to the kind of injury that occurred, the defendant was not at fault.

It may be argued that, as between a negligent defendant and a nonnegligent plaintiff, a loss of which defendant's conduct was a cause in fact ought to be imposed upon the defendant irrespective of whether it was a kind of loss within the risks by reason of which his conduct is characterized as negligence. But if it is relevant to take into account defendant's fault with respect to a risk different from any that would include the harm plaintiff has suffered, then would it not also be relevant to take into account his other faults as well? And would it not seem equally relevant to consider plaintiff's shortcomings? Shall we fix legal responsibility by deciding who is the better and who the worse person? An affirmative answer might involve us, and quickly too, in the morality of run-of-the-ranch TV drama, where the good guys always win.

If we reject this standard of judgment, then so long as liability is to be based on fault, should we not limit the scope of legal responsibility to those consequences with respect to which the actor was negligent—to those consequences of which the negligent aspect of his conduct was a cause? An affirmative answer implies, in relation to the hypothetical case of the transportation of explosives, that legal responsibility should be limited to damages caused by explosion or by conduct responsive to the explosion risk, rather than being extended to injuries that would have occurred even if the driver had used warning signs or had transported no explosives, while acting in other respects exactly as he did.

The policy foundation for the Risk Rule, though applicable more broadly to all problems of results outside the risk, is seen in its most persuasive context in relation to *persons outside the risk*. In this context Judge Learned Hand expressed the philosophy of the rule in an opinion that is especially illuminating on matters of legal cause. After noting that there are in tort law some instances of strict liability, he said:

But so long as it is an element of imposed liability that the wrongdoer shall in some degree disregard the sufferer's interests, it can only be an anomaly, and indeed vindictive, to make him responsible to those whose interests he has not disregarded.[21]

Perhaps this is as forcefully as one can fairly state the policy justification for the Risk Rule. Indeed, it is easy to exaggerate the weight of this argument as brought to bear upon one of those close cases about which dispute is likely. In the first place, this policy argument is essentially one of blameworthiness, resting distinctly on moral judgment. The twilight zones of disputed legal judgment are also zones of disputed moral judgment, not alone in the minds of judges, but as well in the views of the community at large.[22] Uncertainty is increased by the multiplicity of influences that bear on judgments of blameworthiness. Moreover, even aside from this element of uncertainty about which way underlying moral justifications point for a particular case in the twilight zone, the very fact that the policy is one based on a moral judgment exerts a restraint upon its influence, because we are less content today with moral justifications for our legal rules than with

political, economic, and social justifications. It is characteristic of our time to be discomfited about the imposition of our moral judgments on others, especially judgments concerning individual rather than group morality.

One may disagree with the policy argument underlying the Risk Rule, or he may believe that it has been too widely influential, or he may believe that we should now move beyond the Risk Rule in sympathetic conformity with a trend away from liability based on fault and toward strict liability. But to believe that the Risk Rule is without rational, policy foundation is to misunderstand, and to deny the existence of that foundation because of aversion to its moralizing quality is to misrepresent. Its force may be doubtful in a range of close cases; and, like most policy arguments, it falls short of providing a firm guide to decision in close cases. But demonstration of these uncertainties on the fringe leaves the hard core of the policy argument intact. This hard core continues to serve as the basic theme of decisions on legal cause.

NOTES

1. Cf. Larrimore v. American Nat'l Ins. Co., 184 Okla. 614, 89 P.2d 340 (1939). This hypothetical variation upon the facts of that case is chosen for the purpose of eliminating possible grounds of decision other than those to which attention is directed here.

2. The author's reference is to his discussion of the *Palsgraf* case—Eds.

3. Challenges to some of the common assumptions about these expressions appear in Hart & Honoré, Causation in the Law 19 n.1, 84 n.2, 103–22 (1959); and in Becht & Miller, The Test of Factual Causation in Negligence and Strict Liability Cases 13–21 (1961). See also Williams, *Causation in the Law*, 1961 Camb. L. J. 62, 63–79, for comments evoked by the Hart & Honoré book.

4. See, *e.g.*, Hart & Honoré, Causation in the Law 95–96 (1959); 2 Harper & James, Torts 1138 (1956). Compare Becht & Miller, The Test of Factual Causation in Negligence and Strict Liability Cases 21–25 (1961), discussing the hypothetical character of any assertion that an omission was a cause of a subsequent occurrence. Their discussion is addressed to what might be thought of as the converse of the problem referred to here. Here the issue is, Would the same thing have happened if the actor had not engaged in the conduct (whether described as an act, an omission, or a combination) alleged to be negligent? The issue they discuss is, Would the same thing have happened if the actor had done a particular thing he omitted doing? Both inquiries are hypothetical.

5. In the context of this discussion of legal cause, the plural, "risks," is chosen in preference to the more commonly used singular form as a means of avoiding the confusion that the risk within which the result falls must be such that, standing alone, it would make the conduct unreasonable. A composite of substantial, foreseeable risks is weighed against utility in judging whether the conduct is unreasonable.

6. Cf. P. Keeton, *Negligence, Duty, and Causation in Texas,* 16 Texas L. Rev. 1, 11–12 (1937). Though the idea expressed in the text above was suggested to me by the cited passage, the subsequent development in that article of the meaning of "force" (*id.* at 12–14) indicates that its author might not regard the present idea as one of the legitimate progeny of his teaching.

7. E.g., see Seavey, Cogitations on Torts 31–36 (1954); Seavey *Principles of Torts,* 56 Harv. L. Rev. 72, 90–93 (1942); Seavey, *Mr. Justice Cardozo and the Law of Torts,* 39 Colum. L. Rev. 20, 29–39; 52 Harv. L. Rev. 372, 381–91; 48 Yale L.J. 390, 399–409 (1939). For expressions of generally compatible points of view from the other side of the Atlantic, see Goodhart, *Liability and Compensation,* 76 L.Q. Rev. 567 (1960) and Williams, *The Risk Principle,* 77 L.Q. Rev. 179 (1961).

8. 2 Harper & James, Torts 1138 (1956).

9. *Ibid.* (emphasis in original).

10. Carpenter, *Workable Rules for Determining Proximate Cause,* 20 Calif. L. Rev. 229, 231, 408–19 (1932).

11. 2 Harper & James, Torts 1138 (1956). Perhaps some degree of support for this thesis can be found in the analysis of Becht and Miller, which, for the purpose of inquiries into "factual causation," distinguishes between conduct and the "negligent segment" of it. See Becht & Miller, The Test of Causation in Negligence and Strict Liability Cases 25–28 (1961). But both the explanation of their distinction and the applications of it in their book indicate that it is a physical, rather than a qualitative, distinction. That is, a segment of conduct is an act or an omission among the many acts and omissions that make up the conduct, rather than an unreasonably risky quality of either the total conduct or some part of it. Thus, their distinction is not directed to the question whether the Risk Rule concerns cause-in-fact relation between the harm and the negligent *aspect* of conduct, as that concept is developed here. Moreover, in some situations where their thesis produces a finding of causal relation between the negligent *segment* of the conduct and the harm (and either supports liability or else explains nonliability on the "policy" ground that the harm is not within the type against which the rule of conduct is directed), the present thesis produces a finding of no causal relation between the negligent *aspect* of the conduct and the harm. *E.g.,* they find that the negligent segment of a plaintiff's conduct in sitting on an unsafe wall was a cause of the injury he suffered when the wall was knocked down by a careless motorist whose conduct would have caused the same injuries if the wall had been safe. See *id.* at 182–84, where they criticize the view of Hart and Honoré that the plaintiff's negligence in this situation was causally irrelevant. Under the thesis presented here, as under the thesis of Hart and Honoré apparently, the plaintiff's negligence consisted of placing himself where he was likely to be injured by the collapse of the wall, either without an external impact or under an external impact insufficient to cause the collapse of a safe wall. This aspect of his conduct was not a *sine qua non* of the injury he suffered.

12. 2 Harper & James, Torts 1138 n. 15 (1956).

13. Hart & Honoré, Causation in the Law 110–12, 192–93 (1959).

14. See, *e.g., id.* at 231–38, 259, and 266.

15. See *id.* at 259.

16. E.g., Green, *The Causal Relation Issue in Negligence Law,* 60 Mich. L. Rev. 543, 576 (1962) ("the *only cause issue* is the connection between the defendant's conduct and the victim's injury"; the issue of causal relation should be unloaded of other considerations [emphasis in the original]); Prosser, Torts 252, 258, 266 (2d ed. 1955), (proximate cause "is nearly always a matter of various considerations of policy which have nothing to do with the fact of causation"; the problem of scope of liability for unforeseeable consequences "is in no way one of causation, and it does not arise until causation has been established"; the problem of intervening causes is one of policy, not causation); Restatement, Torts § 433, Reason for Changes (1948 Supp.), (Legal cause consists of two elements: 'the substantial factor' element deals with causation in fact"; the second element is concerned with whether there is a rule of law restricting "liability for harm occurring in the particular manner" at issue, and "deals with a legal policy relieving the actor of liability for harm he has, as a matter of fact, caused"; "[i]t is completely faulty analysis" to confuse "the question of policy with the question of fact"). Insistence that the result-within-the-risk problem is not one of causation is found even among advocates of the principle expressed in the several formulations of the Risk Rule. For example, Professor Goodhart declares: "But consequences cannot 'flow' from negligence. Consequences 'flow' from an act or an omission." Goodhart, *Liability for the Consequences of a "Negligent Act,"* in Cambridge Legal Essays 101, 105–6 (1926), reprinted in Goodhart, Essays in Jurisprudence and the Common Law 110, 114 (1931). See also Foster, Grant & Green, *The Risk Theory and Proximate Cause—A Comparative Study,* 32 Neb. L. Rev. 72, 79–80 (1952) (advocating the risk theory and the "relational" quality of negligence, but declaring that "proximate cause often has little if anything to do with causation in fact, except that no issue of proximate cause arises unless actual causation is present," and observing of a typical case that if defendant is held not liable "it is not because its fault was not a cause of the disaster").

17. Cf. 2 Harper & James, Torts 1132–33 (1956).

18. Seavey, *Mr. Justice Cardozo and the Law of Torts,* 39 Colum. L. Rev. 20, 34; 52 Harv. L. Rev. 372, 386; 48 Yale L. J. 390, 404 (1939).

19. E. g., Smith, *Legal Cause in Actions of Tort,* 25 Harv. L. Rev. 103, 223, 245 (1912). Cf. Green, *Foreseeability in Negligence Law,* 61 Colum. L. Rev. 1401, 1408 (1961), noting that there are numerous devices for controlling decisions of both liability and damages, and asserting that "the foreseeability formula" need not "reach beyond the negligence issue" into the area of other limitations on scope of liability.

20. See Pound, *Causation,* 67 Yale L. J. 1, 10 (1957), referring to Pollock's view. Pollock stated the question as one "whether the accepted test of liability for negligence in the first instance is or not also the proper measure of liability for the consequences of proved or admitted default." Pollock, *Liability for Consequences,* 38 L.Q. Rev. 165 (1922).

21. Sinram v. Pennsylvania R.R., 61 F.2d 767, 770 (2d Cir. 1932).

22. Cf. Morris, *Proximate Cause in Minnesota,* 34 Minn L. Rev. 185, 207 (1950).

THE AMBIGUOUS SUICIDE CASE

N.Y. Times, February 7, 1968: "Phoenix, Ariz., Feb. 6 (AP)—Linda Marie Ault killed herself, policemen said today, rather than make her dog Beauty pay for her night with a married man.

" 'I killed her. I killed her. It's just like I killed her myself,' a detective quoted her grief-stricken father as saying.

" 'I handed her the gun. I didn't think she would do anything like that.'

"The 21-year-old Arizona State University coed died in a hospital yesterday of a gunshot wound in the head.

"The police quoted her parents, Mr. and Mrs. Joseph Ault, as giving this account:

"Linda failed to return home from a dance in Tempe Friday night. On Saturday she admitted she had spent the night with an Air Force lieutenant.

"The Aults decided on a punishment that would 'wake Linda up.' They ordered her to shoot the dog she had owned about two years.

"On Sunday, the Aults and Linda took the dog into the desert near their home. They had the girl dig a shallow grave. Then Mrs. Ault grasped the dog between her hands, and Mr. Ault gave his daughter a .22-caliber pistol and told her to shoot the dog.

"Instead, the girl put the pistol to her right temple and shot herself.

"The police said there were no charges that could be filed against the parents except possibly cruelty to animals."

PALSGRAF v. THE LONG ISLAND RAILROAD CO.

New York Court of Appeals, 1928*

CARDOZO, Ch. J. Plaintiff was standing on a platform of defendant's railroad after buying a ticket to go to Rockaway Beach. A train stopped at the station, bound for another place. Two men ran forward to catch it. One of the men reached the platform of the car without mishap, though the train was already moving. The other man, carrying a package, jumped aboard the car, but seemed unsteady as if about to fall. A guard on the car, who had held the door open, reached forward to help him in, and another guard on the platform pushed him from behind. In this act, the package was dislodged, and fell upon the rails. It was a package of small size, about fifteen inches long, and was covered by a newspaper. In fact it contained fireworks, but there was nothing in its appearance to give notice of its contents. The fireworks when they fell exploded. The shock of the explosion threw down some scales at the other end of the platform, many feet away. The scales struck the plaintiff, causing injuries for which she sues.

The conduct of the defendant's guard, if a wrong in its relation to the holder of the package, was not a wrong in its relation to the plaintiff, standing far away.

*248 N.Y. 339 (1928).

Relatively to her it was not negligence at all. Nothing in the situation gave notice that the falling package had in it the potency of peril to persons thus removed. Negligence is not actionable unless it involves the invasion of a legally protected interest, the violation of a right. "Proof of negligence in the air, so to speak, will not do."* "Negligence is the absence of care, according to the circumstances."* The plaintiff as she stood upon the platform of the station might claim to be protected against intentional invasion of her bodily security. Such invasion is not charged. She might claim to be protected against unintentional invasion by conduct involving in the thought of reasonable men an unreasonable hazard that such invasion would ensue. These, from the point of view of the law, were the bounds of her immunity, with perhaps some rare exceptions, survivals for the most part of ancient forms of liability, where conduct is held to be at the peril of the actor (*Sullivan* v. *Dunham,* 161 N.Y. 290). If no hazard was apparent to the eye of ordinary vigilance, an act innocent and harmless, at least to outward seeming, with reference to her, did not take to itself the quality of a tort because it happened to be a wrong, though apparently not one involving the risk of bodily insecurity, with reference to some one else. "In every instance, before negligence can be predicated of a given act, back of the act must be sought and found a duty to the individual complaining, the observance of which would have averted or avoided the injury."* "The ideas of negligence and duty are strictly correlative."* (BOWEN, L. J., in *Thomas* v. *Quartermaine,* 18 Q. B. D. 685, 694). The plaintiff sues in her own right for a wrong personal to her, and not as the vicarious beneficiary of a breach of duty to another.

A different conclusion will involve us, and swiftly too, in a maze of contradictions. A guard stumbles over a package which has been left upon a platform. It seems to be a bundle of newspapers. It turns out to be a can of dynamite. To the eye of ordinary vigilance, the bundle is abandoned waste, which may be kicked or trod on with impunity. Is a passenger at the other end of the platform protected by the law against the unsuspected hazard concealed beneath the waste? If not, is the result to be any different, so far as the distant passenger is concerned, when the guard stumbles over a valise which a truckman or a porter has left upon the walk? The passenger far away, if the victim of a wrong at all, has a cause of action, not derivative, but original and primary. His claim to be protected against invasion of his bodily security is neither greater nor less because the act resulting in the invasion is a wrong to another far removed. In this case, the rights that are said to have been violated, the interests said to have

been invaded, are not even of the same order. The man was not injured in his person nor even put in danger. The purpose of the act, as well as its effect, was to make his person safe. If there was a wrong to him at all, which may very well be doubted, it was a wrong to a property interest only, the safety of his package. Out of this wrong to property, which threatened injury to nothing else, there has passed, we are told, to the plaintiff by derivation or succession a right of action for the invasion of an interest of another order, the right to bodily security. The diversity of interests emphasizes the futility of the effort to build the plaintiff's right upon the basis of a wrong to some one else. The gain is one of emphasis, for a like result would follow if the interests were the same. Even then, the orbit of the danger as disclosed to the eye of reasonable vigilance would be the orbit of the duty. One who jostles one's neighbor in a crowd does not invade the rights of others standing at the outer fringe when the unintended contact casts a bomb upon the ground. The wrongdoer, as to them is the man who carries the bomb, not the one who explodes it without suspicion of the danger. Life will have to be made over, and human nature transformed, before prevision so extravagant can be accepted as the norm of conduct, the customary standard to which behavior must conform.

The argument for the plaintiff is built upon the shifting meanings of such words as "wrong" and "wrongful," and shares their instability. What the plaintiff must show is "a wrong" to herself, *i. e.,* a violation of her own right, and not merely a wrong to some one else, nor conduct "wrongful" because unsocial, but not "a wrong" to any one. We are told that one who drives at reckless speed through a crowded city street is guilty of a negligent act and, therefore, of a wrongful one irrespective of the consequences. Negligent the act is, and wrongful in the sense that it is unsocial, but wrongful and unsocial in relation to other travelers, only because the eye of vigilance perceives the risk of damage. If the same act were to be committed on a speedway or a race course, it would lose its wrongful quality. The risk reasonably to be perceived defines the duty to be obeyed, and risk imports relation; it is risk to another or to others within the range of apprehension (Seavey, Negligence, Subjective or Objective, 41 H. L. Rv. 6; *Boronkay* v. *Robinson & Carpenter,* 247 N.Y. 365). This does not mean, of course, that one who launches a destructive force is always relieved of liability if the force, though known to be destructive, pursues an unexpected path. It was not necessary that the defendant should have had notice of the particular method in which an accident would occur, if the possibility of an accident was clear to the ordinarily prudent eye" (*Munsey* v. *Webb,* 231 U.S. 150, 156; *Condran* v. *Park & Tilford,* 213 N.Y. 341, 345; *Robert* v. *U.S.E.F.*

*Citations omitted [Ed.].

Corp., 240 N.Y. 474, 477). Some acts, such as shooting, are so imminently dangerous to any one who may come within reach of the missile, however unexpectedly, as to impose a duty of prevision not far from that of an insurer. Even today, and much oftener in earlier stages of the law, one acts sometimes at one's peril.* Under this head, it may be, fall certain cases of what is known as transferred intent, an act willfully dangerous to A resulting by misadventure in injury to B.* These cases aside, wrong is defined in terms of the natural or probable, at least when unintentional.* The range of reasonable apprehension is at times a question for the court, and at times, if varying inferences are possible, a question for the jury. Here, by concession, there was nothing in the situation to suggest to the most cautious mind that the parcel wrapped in newspaper would spread wreckage through the station. If the guard had thrown it down knowingly and willfully, he would not have threatened the plaintiff's safety, so far as appearances could warn him. His conduct would not have involved, even then, an unreasonable probability of invasion of her bodily security. Liability can be no greater where the act is inadvertent.

Negligence, like risk, is thus a term of relation. Negligence in the abstract, apart from things related, is surely not a tort, if indeed it is understandable at all.* Negligence is not a tort unless it results in the commission of a wrong, and the commission of a wrong imports the violation of a right, in this case, we are told, the right to be protected against interference with one's bodily security. But bodily security is protected, not against all forms of interference or aggression, but only against some. One who seeks redress at law does not make out a cause of action by showing without more that there has been damage to his person. If the harm was not willful, he must show that the act as to him had possibilities of danger so many and apparent as to entitle him to be protected against the doing of it though the harm was unintended. Affront to personality is still the keynote of the wrong. Confirmation of this view will be found in the history and development of the action on the case. Negligence as a basis of civil liability was unknown to mediaeval law.* For damage to the person, the sole remedy was trespass, and trespass did not lie in the absence of aggression, and that direct and personal.* Liability for other damage, as where a servant without orders from the master does or omits something to the damage of another, is a plant of later growth.* When it emerged out of the legal soil, it was thought of as a variant of trespass, an offshoot of the parent stock. This appears in the form of action, which was known as trespass on the case.* The victim does not sue derivatively, or by right of subrogation, to vindicate an interest invaded in the person of another. Thus to view his cause of action is to ignore the fundamental difference between tort and crime.* He sues for breach of a duty owing to himself.

The law of causation, remote or proximate, is thus foreign to the case before us. The question of liability is always anterior to the question of the measure of the consequences that go with liability. If there is no tort to be redressed, there is no occasion to consider what damage might be recovered if there were a finding of a tort. We may assume, without deciding, that negligence, not at large or in the abstract, but in relation to the plaintiff, would entail liability for any and all consequences, however novel or extraordinary.* There is room for argument that a distinction is to be drawn according to the diversity of interests invaded by the act, as where conduct negligent in that it threatens an insignificant invasion of an interest in property results in an unforeseeable invasion of an interest of another order, as *e. g.*, one of bodily security. Perhaps other distinctions may be necessary. We do not go into the question now. The consequences to be followed must first be rooted in a wrong.

The judgment of the Appellate Division and that of the Trial Term should be reversed, and the complaint dismissed, with costs in all courts.

ANDREWS, J. (dissenting). Assisting a passenger to board a train, the defendant's servant negligently knocked a package from his arms. It fell between the platform and the cars. Of its contents the servant knew and could know nothing. A violent explosion followed. The concussion broke some scales standing a considerable distance away. In falling they injured the plaintiff, an intending passenger.

Upon these facts may she recover the damages she has suffered in an action brought against the master? The result we shall reach depends upon our theory as to the nature of negligence. Is it a relative concept—the breach of some duty owing to a particular person or to particular persons? Or where there is an act which unreasonably threatens the safety of others, is the doer liable for all its proximate consequences, even where they result in injury to one who would generally be thought to be outside the radius of danger? This is not a mere dispute as to words. We might not believe that to the average mind the dropping of the bundle would seem to involve the probability of harm to the plaintiff standing many feet away whatever might be the case as to the owner or to one so near as to be likely to be struck by its fall. If, however, we adopt the second hypothesis we have to inquire only as to the relation between cause and effect. We deal in terms of proximate cause, not of negligence.

Negligence may be defined roughly as an act or omission which unreasonably does or may affect the rights of others, or which unreasonably fails to protect oneself from the dangers resulting from such acts. Here I confine myself to the first branch of the definition. Nor do I comment on the word "unreasonable." For present purposes it sufficiently describes that average of conduct that society requires of its members.

There must be both the act or the omission, and the right. It is the act itself, not the intent of the actor, that is important.* In criminal law both the intent and the result are to be considered. Intent again is material in tort actions, where punitive damages are sought, dependent on actual malice—not on merely reckless conduct. But here neither insanity nor infancy lessens responsibility.

As has been said, except in cases of contributory negligence, there must be rights which are or may be affected. Often though injury has occurred, no rights of him who suffers have been touched. A licensee or trespasser upon my land has no claim to affirmative care on my part that the land be made safe.* Where a railroad is required to fence its tracks against cattle, no man's rights are injured should he wander upon the road because such fence is absent.* An unborn child may not demand immunity from personal harm.*

But we are told that "there is no negligence unless there is in the particular case a legal duty to take care, and this duty must be one which is owed to the plaintiff himself and not merely to others."* This, I think too narrow a conception. Where there is the unreasonable act, and some right that may be affected there is negligence whether damage does or does not result. That is immaterial. Should we drive down Broadway at a reckless speed, we are negligent whether we strike an approaching car or miss it by an inch. The act itself is wrongful. It is a wrong not only to those who happen to be within the radius of danger but to all who might have been there—a wrong to the public at large. Such is the language of the street. Such the language of the courts when speaking of contributory negligence. Such again and again their language in speaking of the duty of some defendant and discussing proximate cause in cases where such a discussion is wholly irrelevant on any other theory.* As was said by Mr. Justice HOLMES many years ago, "the measure of the defendant's duty in determining whether a wrong has been committed is one thing, the measure of liability when a wrong has been committed is another."* Due care is a duty imposed on each one of us to protect society from unnecessary danger, not to protect A, B or C alone.

It may well be that there is no such thing as negligence in the abstract. "Proof of negligence in the air, so to speak, will not do." In an empty world negligence would not exist. It does involve a relationship between man and his fellows. But not merely a relationship between man and those whom he might reasonably expect his act would injure. Rather, a relationship between him and those whom he does in fact injure. If his act has a tendency to harm some one, it harms him a mile away as surely as it does those on the scene. We now permit children to recover for the negligent killing of the father. It was never prevented on the theory that no duty was owing to them. A husband may be compensated for the loss of his wife's services. To say that the wrongdoer was negligent as to the husband as well as to the wife is merely an attempt to fit facts to theory. An insurance company paying a fire loss recovers its payment of the negligent incendiary. We speak of subrogation—of suing in the right of the insured. Behind the cloud of words is the fact they hide, that the act, wrongful as to the insured, has also injured the company. Even if it be true that the fault of father, wife or insured will prevent recovery, it is because we consider the original negligence not the proximate cause of the injury.*

In the well-known *Polemis Case* (1921, 3 K. B. 560), SCRUTTON, L. J., said that the dropping of a plank was negligent for it might injure "workman or cargo or ship." Because of either possibility the owner of the vessel was to be made good for his loss. The act being wrongful the doer was liable for its proximate results. Criticized and explained as this statement may have been, I think it states the law as it should be and as it is.*

The proposition is this. Every one owes to the world at large the duty of refraining from those acts that may unreasonably threaten the safety of others. Such an act occurs. Not only is he wronged to whom harm might reasonably be expected to result, but he also who is in fact injured, even if he be outside what would generally be thought the danger zone. There needs be duty due the one complaining but this is not a duty to a particular individual because as to him harm might be expected. Harm to some one being the natural result of the act, not only that one alone, but all those in fact injured may complain. We have never, I think, held otherwise. Indeed in the *Di Caprio* case we said that a breach of a general ordinance defining the degree of care to be exercised in one's calling is evidence of negligence as to every one. We did not limit this statement to those who might be expected to be exposed to danger. Unreasonable risk being taken, its consequences are not confined to those who might probably be hurt.

If this be so, we do not have a plaintiff suing by "derivation or succession." Her action is original and primary. Her claim is for a breach of duty to herself— not that she is subrogated to any right of action of the owner of the parcel or of a passenger standing at the scene of the explosion.

*Citations omitted [Eds.].

The right to recover damages rests on additional considerations. The plaintiff's rights must be injured, and this injury must be caused by the negligence. We build a dam, but are negligent as to its foundations. Breaking, it injures property down stream. We are not liable if all this happened because of some reason other than the insecure foundation. But when injuries do result from our unlawful act we are liable for the consequences. It does not matter that they are unusual, unexpected, unforeseen and unforeseeable. But there is one limitation. The damages must be so connected with the negligence that the latter may be said to be the proximate cause of the former.

These two words have never been given an inclusive definition. What is a cause in a legal sense, still more what is a proximate cause, depend in each case upon many considerations, as does the existence of negligence itself. Any philosophical doctrine of causation does not help us. A boy throws a stone into a pond. The ripples spread. The water level rises. The history of that pond is altered to all eternity. It will be altered by other causes also. Yet it will be forever the resultant of all causes combined. Each one will have an influence. How great only omniscience can say. You may speak of a chain, or if you please, a net. An analogy is of little aid. Each cause brings about future events. Without each the future would not be the same. Each is proximate in the sense it is essential. But that is not what we mean by the word. Nor on the other hand do we mean sole cause. There is no such thing.

Should analogy be thought helpful, however, I prefer that of a stream. The spring, starting on its journey, is joined by tributary after tributary. The river, reaching the ocean, comes from a hundred sources. No man may say whence any drop of water is derived. Yet for a time distinction may be possible. Into the clear creek, brown swamp water flows from the left. Later, from the right comes water stained by its clay bed. The three may remain for a space, sharply divided. But at last, inevitably no trace of separation remains. They are so commingled that all distinction is lost.

As we have said, we cannot trace the effect of an act to the end, if end there is. Again, however, we may trace it part of the way. A murder at Serajevo may be the necessary antecedent to an assassination in London twenty years hence. An overturned lantern may burn all Chicago. We may follow the fire from the shed to the last building. We rightly say the fire started by the lantern caused its destruction.

A cause, but not the proximate cause. What we do mean by the word "proximate" is, that because of convenience, of public policy, of a rough sense of justice, the law arbitrarily declines to trace a series of events beyond a certain point. This is not logic, it is practical politics. Take our rule as to fires. Sparks from my burning haystack set on fire my house and my neighbor's. I may recover from a negligent railroad. He may not. Yet the wrongful act as directly harmed the one as the other. We may regret that the line was drawn just where it was, but drawn somewhere it had to be. We said the act of the railroad was not the proximate cause of our neighbor's fire. Cause it surely was. The words we used were simply indicative of our notions of public policy. Other courts think differently. But somewhere they reach the point where they cannot say the stream comes from any one source.

Take the illustration given in an unpublished manuscript by a distinguished and helpful writer on the law of torts. A chauffeur negligently collides with another car which is filled with dynamite, although he could not know it. An explosion follows. A, walking on the sidewalk nearby, is killed. B, sitting in a window of a building opposite, is cut by flying glass. C, likewise sitting in a window a block away, is similarly injured. And a further illustration. A nursemaid, ten blocks away, startled by the noise, involuntarily drops a baby from her arms to the walk. We are told that C may not recover while A may. As to B it is a question for court or jury. We will all agree that the baby might not. Because, we are again told, the chauffeur had no reason to believe his conduct involved any risk of injuring either C or the baby. As to them he was not negligent.

But the chauffeur, being negligent in risking the collision, his belief that the scope of the harm he might do would be limited is immaterial. His act unreasonably jeopardized the safety of any one who might be affected by it. C's injury and that of the baby were directly traceable to the collision. Without that, the injury would not have happened. C had the right to sit in his office, secure from such dangers. The baby was entitled to use the sidewalk with reasonable safety.

The true theory is, it seems to me, that the injury to C, if in truth he is to be denied recovery, and the injury to the baby is that their several injuries were not the proximate result of the negligence. And here not what the chauffeur had reason to believe would be the result of his conduct, but what the prudent would foresee, may have a bearing. May have some bearing, for the problem of proximate cause is not to be solved by any one consideration.

It is all a question of expediency. There are no fixed rules to govern our judgment. There are simply matters of which we may take account. We have in a somewhat different connection spoken of "the stream of events." We have asked whether that stream was deflected— whether it was forced into new and unexpected channels.[*] This is rather rhetoric than law. There is in truth little to guide us other than common sense.

*Citations omitted [Eds.].

There are some hints that may help us. The proximate cause, involved as it may be with many other causes, must be, at the least, something without which the event would not happen. The court must ask itself whether there was a natural and continuous sequence between cause and effect. Was the one a substantial factor in producing the other? Was there a direct connection between them, without too many intervening causes? Is the effect of cause on result not too attentuated? Is the cause likely, in the usual judgment of mankind, to produce the result? Or by the exercise of prudent foresight could the result be foreseen? Is the result too remote from the cause, and here we consider remoteness in time and space,* where we passed upon the construction of a contract—but something was also said on this subject. Clearly we must so consider, for the greater the distance either in time or space, the more surely do other causes intervene to affect the result. When a lantern is overturned the firing of a shed is a fairly direct consequence. Many things contribute to the spread of the conflagration—the force of the wind, the direction and width of streets, the character of intervening structures, other factors. We draw an uncertain and wavering line, but draw it we must as best we can.

Once again, it is all a question of fair judgment, always keeping in mind the fact that we endeavor to make a rule in each case that will be practical and in keeping with the general understanding of mankind.

Here another question must be answered. In the case supposed it is said, and said correctly, that the chauffeur is liable for the direct effect of the explosion although he had no reason to suppose it would follow a collision. "The fact that the injury occurred in a different manner than that which might have been expected does not prevent the chauffeur's negligence from being in law the cause of the injury." But the natural results of a negligent act—the results which a prudent man would or should foresee—do have a bearing upon the decision as to proximate cause. We have said so repeatedly. What should be foreseen? No human foresight would suggest that a collision itself might injure one a block away. On the contrary, given an explosion, such a possibility might be reasonably expected. I think the direct connection, the foresight of which the courts speak, assumes prevision of the explosion, for the immediate results of which, at least, the chauffeur is responsible.

*Citations omitted [Eds.].

It may be said this is unjust. Why? In fairness he should make good every injury flowing from his negligence. Not because of tenderness toward him we say he need not answer for all that follows his wrong. We look back to the catastrophe, the fire kindled by the spark, or the explosion. We trace the consequences—not indefinitely, but to a certian point. And to aid us in fixing that point we ask what might ordinarily be expected to follow the fire or the explosion.

This last suggestion is the factor which must determine the case before us. The act upon which defendant's liability rests is knocking an apparently harmless package onto the platform. The act was negligent. For its proximate consequences the defendant is liable. If its contents were broken, to the owner; if it fell upon and crushed a passenger's foot, then to him. If it exploded and injured one in the immediate vicinity, to him also as to A in the illustration. Mrs. Palsgraf was standing some distance away. How far cannot be told from the record—apparently twenty-five or thirty feet. Perhaps less. Except for the explosion, she would not have been injured. We are told by the appellant in his brief "it cannot be denied that the explosion was the direct cause of the plaintiff's injuries." So it was a substantial factor in producing the result—there was here a natural and continuous sequence—direct connection. The only intervening cause was that instead of blowing her to the ground the concussion smashed the weighing machine which in turn fell upon her. There was no remoteness in time, little in space. And surely, given such an explosion as here it needed no great foresight to predict that the natural result would be to injure one on the platform at no greater distance from its scene than was the plaintiff. Just how no one might be able to predict. Whether by flying fragments, by broken glass, by wreckage of machines or structures no one could say. But injury in some form was most probable.

Under these circumstances I cannot say as a matter of law that the plaintiff's injuries were not the proximate result of the negligence. That is all we have before us. The court refused to so charge. No request was made to submit the matter to the jury as a question of fact, even would that have been proper upon the record before us.

The judgment appealed from should be affirmed, with costs.

POUND, LEHMAN and KELLOGG, JJ., concur with CARDOZO, Ch. J.; ANDREWS, J., dissents in opinion in which CRANE and O'BRIEN, JJ., concur.

Judgment reversed, etc.

GRAHAM HUGHES

Attempting the Impossible*

The relevance on a charge of criminal attempt of the impossibility of the accused's attaining his objective has for some time been a subject of sharp dispute among jurists of the criminal law, although it has not received a great deal of attention in the courts. That teachers of criminal law and writers in the field should devote time and energy to this question is perfectly proper, for it is an important question in a number of ways. It raises very basic interrogatories concerning the aims and purposes of the criminal law; it compels us to focus attention on concepts such as "intention" and "purpose," an analysis of which is indispensable to criminal law scholarship; and it provides an excellent opportunity for reflecting on the pervasive and difficult distinction between mistake of fact and mistake of law. For these reasons the problem is a splendid set-piece which exhibits in a short space some of the most difficult issues of criminal law analysis. Before offering any new comment it will be necessary to sketch the apparent state of the law and the divergent opinions of the commentators.

I

It has long been agreed that impossibility is not a general defense to a charge of attempt.[1] But it is just as generally agreed that in some circumstances impossibility may be a defense, and we are therefore faced initially with the task of discriminating between two senses of the concept of impossibility. This has been done conventionally by distinguishing between legal impossibility and factual impossibility.[2]

Legal impossibility describes a situation in which the objective of the accused (an admittedly

ambiguous phrase to which we shall return later) does not constitute an offense known to the law, even though the accused may mistakenly believe the law to be other than it is. Mistake of law may not generally excuse, but neither can it in itself be a sufficient ground for indictment. So an American on a visit to England might quite reasonably have the mistaken belief that fornication is a crime in England since it is one in the American jurisdiction in which he resides. Such a mistaken belief clearly cannot subject him to prosecution for a nonexistent crime of committing the sexual act, and it would be a strange notion to talk of a prosecution for attempting to commit a crime which is not on the statute book. How after all could the indictment be drafted, unless we recognized the existence of a general offense of doing what one mistakenly believed to be a crime? It will be noticed that the argument here does not essentially depend on the concept of attempt in the usual sense of that word, for it is not necessarily a case of trying and failing. The inappropriateness of convicting such a person remains whether he has committed sexual intercourse or only attempted it. The reason for not convicting him has nothing to do with the failure of the enterprise, but rather with the absence of any prohibition of the conduct whether completed or not.

Factual impossibility, by contrast, is thought of as a situation in which the objective of the accused, if achieved, would amount to an offense known to the law, but where the achievement is frustrated by some circumstance such as the inadequacy of the instrument, the intervention of some third person, or the misapprehension of some material matter by the accused. Picking the empty pocket is a classic example of this; others would be attempting to open a safe with instruments which turn out to be inadequate for the job,

*From Graham Hughes, "One Further Footnote on Attempting the Impossible," *New York University Law Review,* Vol. 42, No. 6 (1967); pp. 1005–1020. Reprinted by permission of the author and the publisher.

or shooting a bullet into the head of a dummy which is arranged in a bed in which the intended victim habitually sleeps, the accused believing that he was shooting into the head of his victim. Here there is thought to be no barrier to conviction if the acts done go beyond mere preparation and are accompanied by the accused's intention to achieve the objective which, if achieved, would constitute an offense known to the law. Here, unlike the case of legal impossibility, we are dealing with the failure of an endeavor which, if successful, would have amounted to a known offense.

This distinction between legal and factual impossibility has been crystallized in the famous hypotheticals concerning Lady Eldon and her, by now surely bedraggled, French lace.

Lady Eldon, when traveling with her husband on the Continent, bought what she supposed to be a quantity of French lace, which she hid, concealing it from Lord Eldon in one of the pockets of the coach. The package was brought to light by a customs officer at Dover. The lace turned out to be an English manufactured article of little value and, of course, not subject to duty. Lady Eldon had bought it at a price vastly above its value, believing it to be genuine, intending to smuggle it into England.[3]

The majority opinion among the writers is that Lady Eldon might properly be convicted of an attempt to smuggle dutiable lace into England, the facts being treated as amounting to an attempt to commit an offense known to the law and being thus diagnosed as factual rather than legal impossibility.[4]

The contrast with legal impossibility is underlined by the variation on the Lady Eldon hypothetical devised by Professors Paulsen and Kadish.

Suppose the lace which Lady Eldon had purchased was in fact the expensive French lace she meant to buy. The customs officer at Dover brings it to light. He then says to Lady Eldon: "Lucky for you you returned to England today rather than yesterday. I just received word this morning that the Government has removed French lace from the duty list." Could Lady Eldon be held for attempt to smuggle in these circumstances?[5]

The answer must be negative, for there is no offense known to the law which can be said to be Lady Eldon's objective. (It will be suggested later

that this is very questionable, but at this point I am interested only in expounding the current orthodox view.) It is true that Lady Eldon had an intent to do what she believed to be criminal, but the law can only concern itself with intents that go to objectives which as a matter of fact have been declared to be criminal objectives by the law of the land. "Criminal intent" in this connection must be taken to mean an intent to do that which is a crime, and not that which the party thinks is a crime. A broader view would involve the law in punishment for thoughts unexpressed in significant behavior. If a man does his best to kill a victim who fortunately survives, we do not punish him for murder. He gets the benefit of the lucky circumstance, quite undesired by him, that the victim survived. Similarly Lady Eldon must get the benefit of the lucky circumstance, quite unknown to her, that the duty on French lace had been repealed.

This distinction between legal and factual impossibility now seems to be the dominant orthodox position. It has been reinforced by an opinion of the United States Court of Military Appeals in 1962, where a majority of the court restored a conviction of the defendants for attempted rape although the victim, unknown to the accused, was dead at the time of the assault.[6] There is some disagreement about the use of the labels "legal" and "factual" impossibility, but there is no doubt that the way in which the distinction has been set out above represents majority opinion.

But many dissident voices have been raised from time to time both in the courts and in academic commentaries. Some of the major dissents from current orthodoxy in this area will now be examined, in the hope of assessing the sense and utility of the principal distinction between legal and factual impossibility. It will be suggested that though there is some validity and cogency in some of the criticisms that have been made, there has not yet been any full articulation or exploration of the most important weaknesses and difficulties that attend the prevalent doctrine.

A leading case which obtrudes irritatingly in defiance of majority opinion is the 1906 decision of the New York Court of Appeals in *People v. Jaffe.*[7] The accused had been charged with receiving stolen goods. The evidence disclosed that though the accused believed the goods to have a stolen character at the time of his receipt, they had in fact by that time lost such a character since, between the original theft and the receipt, the true owner had re-acquired possession. The defendant was convicted of an attempt to receive stolen goods, and this conviction was affirmed by the appellate division. In quashing the conviction, the court of appeals offered the following analysis:

[I]t is important to bear in mind precisely what it was that the defendant attempted to do. He simply made an effort to purchase certain specific pieces of cloth. He believed the cloth to be stolen property, but it was not such in fact. The purchase, therefore, if it had been completely effected, could not constitute the crime of receiving stolen property. . . .

[T]he act, which it was doubtless the intent of the defendant to commit, would not have been a crime if it had been consummated. . . .

. . . .

If all which an accused person intends to do would if done constitute no crime, it cannot be a crime to attempt to do with the same purpose a part of the thing intended.[8]

The critics of *Jaffe* have not found much difficulty in demolishing the analysis contained in this passage. It has been pointed out that the *Jaffe* court's statement that "the act, which it was doubtless the intent of the defendant to commit would not have been a crime if it had been consummated" is very questionable and turns upon a choice of what is relevant in establishing what his intention was.[9] It certainly seems no defiance of ordinary language to say that Jaffe intended to receive stolen goods, for, in speaking of a person's intention, we frequently incorporate his mistaken view of a situation, since belief and intent cannot be neatly separated. So, if I am sitting in a plane flying from New York to Los Angeles, which I mistakenly think is flying to London—my desired destination—it would be a perfectly reasonable statement to say that, at least until the mistake is pointed out to me, it was my intention to reach London on that plane. The rejection of *Jaffe*, so Professor Glanville Williams contends, is not only supported by such a view of intent but also by the policy underlying the law of attempts. Jaffe, in this way of looking at the facts, intended to commit an offense known to the law, so this is not a case of legal impossibility.[10] Where the prosecution can discharge its burden of proof by

showing beyond a reasonable doubt that an accused had such an intent, expressed in a sufficient overt act, then in terms of the prohibitions of the criminal law such a person is socially dangerous and deserves punishment.

This certainly has a superficial appearance of being an adequate demolition of the *Jaffe* opinion. Later I shall suggest that there are arguments in favor of the outcome in the *Jaffe* case which are not so easily met by the conventional refutation of the opinion.

Another well known judicial calling in question of the majority view is to be found in the English case of *Rex v. Osborn*.[11] The accused was charged with the statutory offense of attempting to administer a noxious thing to a woman, in that he had given to a pregnant woman some pills with the belief that they would induce an abortion. At the trial the questions were raised of whether the pills were in fact an effective abortifacient and, if not, whether the accused mistakenly believed them to be effective. In directing the jury on the latter question, Mr. Justice Rowlatt said:

[S]uppose it was innoxious but he thought it was noxious. . . . [I]f he does not begin to do the very thing, however morally culpable he may be, he does not attempt. . . . It is well known that the impossibility of the thing does not prevent an attempt being made. If you try to burst open the very best kind of steel safe with a wholly insufficient instrument, . . . still you are guilty of the attempt although you never could have completed it, because you are at it, you are at the very thing and trying to do it. . . . But . . . where the man is never on the thing itself at all—it is not a question of the impossibility—he is not on the job although he thinks he is; if he fires a gun at a stump of a tree thinking it is his enemy and his enemy is miles away, and there is nobody in the field at all, he is not near enough to the job to attempt it; he has not begun it; he has done it all under a misapprehension. . . . [I]f the thing was not noxious though he thought it was, he did not attempt to administer a noxious thing by administering the innoxious thing. . . .

[T]he real question . . . is whether it was noxious.[12]

This "on the job" test, as Glanville Williams has styled it,[13] is clearly difficult of application in its invitation to distinguish between doing a thing with inadequate means and not doing a thing at all. In the first place, as put by Mr. Justice Rowlatt, it comes close to a demand that the "victim" of the crime at least be physically present, but this is clearly an unnecessary condition in many situations. If I plant a bomb in my victim's house set to explode at night when he is asleep, am I not guilty of attempted murder because he does not sleep at home that night? There may be thought to be a difference between such a case and shooting at the stump of a tree believing it to be a man, in that when I put a bomb in the house I am quite overtly, and apart from any question of mistake, planting a lethal device in a place where a person habitually sleeps. This may indeed be a significant difference but it has nothing to do with the actual presence of the victim or the question of inadequate means. At the risk of being facetious, one might ask whether the impotent man who makes a sexual attack on a woman should be thought of, in the context of rape, as attempting to attain his objective with inadequate means or as never being on the job at all. (The conventional mistake test is not so easy here either. Should it depend on whether he mistakenly believed himself to be potent or had a mere, as it were, *spes successionis?*) As Glanville Williams points out, it has been held that to administer an inadequate dose of poison under the mistaken belief that the dose is lethal is generally treated as attempted murder. Should it make a difference if the mistake is more radical in that the accused mistakes water for poison?[14] Or what if the intended victim is already dead, unknown to the accused? Here again conviction is generally thought to be possible, as in the recent court martial case of *United States v. Thomas,*[15] though this was a case of rape and not murder. The distinction between inadequate means and not being on the job is much too imprecise to be of help as an explanation of such cases. While a proper uneasiness lies behind Mr. Justice Rowlatt's remarks in *Osborn,* his formulation of it was very defective and therefore fairly easily disposed of by the champions of the current position.

In the academic literature, several forceful dissenting opinions have been expressed, notably by Professor Keedy and Professor Perkins in the United States and by Professor Smith in England. Professor Keedy writes:

The first requisite of a criminal attempt is the intent to commit a specific crime. . . .
Intent as used in this connection must be distin-

guished from motive, desire, and expectation. If C by reason of his hatred of A plans to kill him, but mistaking B for A shoots B, his motive, desire and expectation are to Kill A but his intent is to kill B. If a married man forcibly has intercourse with a woman whom he believes to be his wife's twin sister, but who in fact is his wife, he is not guilty of rape because his intent was to have intercourse with the woman he attacked, who was in fact his wife. If A takes an umbrella which he believes to belong to B, but which is in fact his own, he does not have the intent to steal, his intent being to take the umbrella he grasps in his hand, which is his own umbrella. If a man mistaking a dummy in female dress for a woman, tries to ravish it he does not have the intent to commit rape since the ravishment of an inanimate object cannot be rape. If a man mistakes a stump for his enemy and shoots at it, notwithstanding his desire and expectation to shoot his enemy, his intent is to shoot the object aimed at, which is the stump.[16]

In a similar vein Professor Perkins distinguishes between "primary" and "secondary" intent to argue for an absence of liability in this type of case.[17] Such distinctions might be acceptable if they fulfilled the requirements of being intelligible, workable, and compliant with sensible policy justifications. They are in essence once more an invitation to confine the concept of an intent to the circumstances which in fact exist and to dub the accused's mistaken view of the situation as being a matter of "motive" or "secondary intent." Such an invitation must at the least be supported by argument before we can accept it, for it certainly is not supported by the conventions of ordinary language, which would not in the least be strained by saying, for example, that a man who forcibly has intercourse with his wife believing her to be her own twin sister intends to commit rape. Professors Keedy and Perkins offer no reasons founded either in morality or policy why we should depart from such ordinary usage. If a man forcibly has intercourse with his wife's sister, mistakenly believing her to be his wife, he may have an excuse in that there is an absence of mens rea, that is, he did not intent to rape a woman other than his wife. But if he believed the woman to be his wife's sister when in fact she was his wife, then lack of intent is a strange ground for refusing to convict him. If we come to the conclusion that a conviction is for some reason unjustified here, lack of intent is surely not the appropriate justification.

Professors Paulsen and Kadish raise an interesting hypothetical calculated to expose an alleged anomaly raised by the orthodox analysis:

Consider the following case. Two friends, Mr. Fact and Mr. Law, go hunting in the morning of October 15 in the fields of the state of Dakota, whose law makes it a misdemeanor to hunt any time other than from October 1 to November 30. Both kill deer on the first day out, October 15. Mr. Fact, however, was under the erroneous belief that the date was September 15; and Mr. Law was under the erroneous belief that the hunting season was confined to the month of November, as it was the previous year. Under the Lady Eldon formulation Mr. Fact could be convicted of an attempt to hunt out of season; but Mr. Law could not be. We fail to see how any rational system of criminal law could justify convicting one and acquitting the other on so fragile and unpersuasive a distinction that one was suffering under a mistake of fact, and the other under a mistake of law. Certainly if the ultimate test is the dangerousness of the actor (that is, readiness to violate the law), as Lady Eldon would have it, no distinction is warranted—Mr. Law has indicated himself to be no less "dangerous" than Mr. Fact.[18]

This doubt about the way in which the conventional position works out has in principle already been answered when it was pointed out earlier that the only intents which it is proper for the law to notice are those which relate to behavior or consequences which as a matter of fact have been declared criminal. But it is true that an uneasiness remains about the conviction of Mr. Fact and the acquittal of Mr. Law, if that should be the stipulated outcome of the hypothetical. This uneasiness is difficult to dispel within the confines of the orthodox position. Perhaps the defenders of orthodoxy could point to the comparatively innocuous character of the crime in question. The concept of attempt is in practice seldom invoked outside crimes of some gravity, and in England the better opinion seems to be that it relates only to indictable offenses and that a charge of attempting to commit a summary offense will not lie.[19] A second comment might relate to the regulatory nature of the offense in question and what might be a relative indifference about the dates on which hunting is permitted as long as it is only permitted for a portion of the year. Given such a relative indifference and the concomitant somewhat arbitrary selection of permitted and forbidden periods, Mr. Fact and Mr. Law certainly appear to differ little in their dangerousness. The lesson of this is perhaps that as either a matter of law or prosecutorial discretion, it is better to confine prosecutions for attempts to offenses of some gravity.

A fresh attack on the legal impossibility-factual impossibility division has been made by an English criminal lawyer, Professor J. C. Smith.[20] Professor Smith introduces a distinction between those who have failed in their purpose (perhaps because of inadequate means) and those who have succeeded in their purpose which turns out not to be a completed crime at all. The former, he suggests, may properly be convicted but not the latter, for in the second group of cases the activities of the defendants "do not look like attempts." "One reason [why they do not look like attempts] appears to be that, while there was a failure of *intention* in each of these cases, D succeeded in his *purpose*. Purpose and intention may be the same thing, but they are by no means necessarily so; and attempt, as we have seen, is essentially concerned with purpose."[21]

Professor Smith has certainly got hold of a perceptible difference here between two kinds of cases, but the conclusion he bases upon it is questionable. He is correct in drawing our attention to the circumstance that in some of these cases the defendant is thwarted because of his mistake (for example, finding a pocket empty), while in others his mistake does not seem to detract in any substantial sense from the successful outcome of his project (for example, buying at a very low price goods that one wishes to acquire, believing them to be stolen when in fact they are not). But it is not easy to see how this could be a workable test nor why it should be thought to be very relevant. As Professor Williams has pointed out, the test would involve us in a very curious inquiry into whether the defendant felt himself to be disappointed or not.[22] It may be that for special reasons it is important to the defendant that the goods he is receiving should be stolen quite apart from the low price he is paying. Are we to convict him only if their stolen character was an important part of his motivation and acquit him if he was indifferent to this although he believed them to be stolen? The difficulty of the test is apparent in the way in which Smith himself classifies some of the cases he examines. Thus he seems to regard *Jaffe* as a case where the defendant succeeded in his purpose, but he regards *Regina v. Hensler*[23] as one where the defendant failed to achieve his purpose.[24] In *Hensler,* the defendant made a false representation in a begging letter; the recipient of the letter, aware that the representation was false, nevertheless sent the money. If Jaffe did not really care whether the goods were stolen as long as he got them at a low price, it seems equally likely that Hensler cared little about whether his representation was believed or not as long as he got the money.

Professor Smith does not assert that failure is an essential element in the concept of attempt, but he does argue that where the defendant succeeds in his purpose and that successful venture turns out to be no complete crime, then a conviction for attempt is improper. Glanville Williams comments: "Consider the situation where D takes his own umbrella, mistakenly thinking that he is stealing P's. Professor Smith assumes that this is not attempted larceny, because D has achieved his purpose. But has he? Since his purpose was to steal, he evidently intended to enrich himself by the acquisition of an umbrella, and this he has not succeeded in doing."[25]

In the umbrella controversy, Professor Smith seems to have refined his position somewhat in his later writings. He now offers two versions of the umbrella hypothetical:

D finds an umbrella left in his house after a party. He hides it, intending to steal it. It has been left by P and there is a note inside it saying that it is a present to D. D is not guilty of an attempt.

D sees P, a celebrity, put his umbrella in a stand at D's club. D resolves to steal it. When no one is looking, he goes to the stand and takes the umbrella in the place where P's was. But, someone has moved the umbrella and D has taken his own. He is guilty of an attempt.[26]

Presumably the conclusion is thought to differ in the two examples because in the first D has achieved his objective or purpose of acquiring an umbrella that was not his own and in the circumstances this turns out to be no completed crime, while in the second D has failed in his purpose of acquiring an umbrella not his own, a purpose which if achieved would in the circumstances have constituted a completed crime. There are certainly real differences in the two hypotheticals. In the first only one umbrella is involved; in the second there are two umbrellas, and D does not get the particular umbrella he intended to get. In the first example D might be said to be proceeding under ignorance of the exercise of a legal power by P, while in the second D is ignorant of or mistaken about the physical location of a particular umbrella at a particular time. We may wish to decide on further reflection that these are indeed significant differences, but the point to be made now is that they are not happily expressed in Professor Smith's emphasis on the notion of purpose as the relevant issue. It may well be that in the first example D is not at all interested in acquiring an umbrella for himself but only in doing P an injury. He may mean to destroy the umbrella. If such were the case, it would make no sense to say that D has succeeded in his objective or purpose. He has failed just as much as in the second hypothetical. But can we then say that D is to be convicted if his motive was to injure P but acquitted if his motive was the acquisition of someone else's umbrella? The fundamental weakness in Professor Smith's formulation is that, although he steers away from the word, his test really turns on an inquiry into the motive of the accused which, for evident and excellent reasons, is generally dismissed in the criminal law as being irrelevant to culpability, though it may be relevant to severity of punishment.

II

From the above it can be seen that there has been a constant current of unease about the dominant juristic position with regard to attempting the impossible. The real difficulties with the orthodox view have not been fully articulated. In this connection it is first necessary to demonstrate the full complexity of the orthodox position by tracking down the rather fine distinctions that it forces one to draw. An attempt will now be made to do this, by conducting a running dialogue about ways of applying the legal impossibility-factual impossibility distinction. A good starting point will be the second Lady Eldon hypothetical and we will cast A in the role of the defender of orthodoxy and B as the gadfly:

A. "The correctness of the contention that Lady Eldon must be acquitted in the second French lace hypothetical is demonstrated by the impossibility of drafting an acceptable indictment. To speak of 'attempting to import a dutiable article, to wit French lace' will not do because French lace simply is not a dutiable article."

B. "That may be so but then you must admit that it is equally difficult to argue for the propriety of convicting Jaffe whom it seems you want to convict. For how could the indictment speak of 'attempting to receive certain stolen goods, to wit certain rolls of cloth' when in fact the cloth simply was not stolen at the time of the receipt?[27] And this would apply also to the hypothetical of attempting to steal an umbrella which turns out to be one's own. For what would the indictment say? 'Attempting to take an umbrella the property of ? ? ?' It was the property of the defendant all the time and the indictment simply would not on its face allege an essential ingredient of the crime of larceny as set out in the general definitions of larceny, that the article should be the property of another."

A. "In *Jaffe* I think the answer would be this. The completed crime of receiving requires knowledge that the goods are stolen. In a crime of attempting to receive, why should it not be enough to allege in the indictment that the accused believed the goods to be stolen?[28] After all everyone seems to agree that it is proper to convict a person of attempting to pick an empty pocket and yet in such a case there is also no specific property of another which can be named in the indictment. Again, in the umbrella case, why should the indictment not say that the accused took an umbrella which he believed to be the property of another? The attempt notion in such a case does not consist in the failure to take an umbrella at all but in the failure to take the umbrella of another."

B. "But if you want to put it that way, I don't see now why you want to argue for the acquittal of Lady Eldon in the second French lace case. Can't you say that the complete crime there consists of failing to pay duty on a dutiable article, and Lady Eldon did believe the article to be dutiable? So, according to the position you now seem to be adopting, we could draft an indictment for Lady Eldon that would allege her attempt to import an article that she believed to be dutiable, to wit French lace. This seems to go back on the proposition with which you began."

A. "I think that to answer the point you have just made the argument will have to become rather subtle. It depends, I think, on exactly what

the actus reus of the offense is under the wording of the statute. If the offense in Lady Eldon's case were phrased in terms of 'importing a dutiable article,' I agree that at first sight it seems difficult to distinguish the Lady Eldon case from *Jaffe*. But we have to look further and inquire how the concept of 'dutiable article' is amplified in the law. We shall probably find that there is a schedule (amended from time to time) of articles on which varying customs duties must be paid and that there is then a general criminal provision which makes it an offense to import any article named in the schedule without paying the duty. The concept of 'stolen goods' is rather different. It is not amplified by a detailed catalogue or listing of individual items of merchandise but is amplified rather by reference to a generic description contained in other rules of law. Thus the statute might say that for the purposes of the crime of receiving, the term "stolen goods" shall mean any goods acquired in a way that constitutes one of the offenses of larceny, embezzlement, or obtaining by false pretenses. Now Jaffe was not under any mistake about the general circumstances in which according to law goods are stolen. But Lady Eldon was under a mistake about the legal amplification of the notion of a dutiable article. And that is why it is proper to convict Jaffe but not Lady Eldon."

B. "It sounds to me as if you are making everything turn on a distinction between a mistake of fact and a mistake of law. That distinction has always been an obscure one to make in theory and practice, and it seems to present particular difficulties in this area. Let me give you a few hypotheticals around the facts of *Jaffe* to see how you would deal with them. It seems from what you have just said that you look upon a conviction as proper in *Jaffe* by taking the view that Jaffe made a mistake of fact. He was not mistaken about the legal definition of circumstances in which goods are stolen but only ignorant of the factual circumstance that the goods had come back into the control of the true owner or the police acting as the owner's agents. So his mistake was not about what makes goods stolen goods but about whether the particular goods had those qualities at that time. Suppose then that D receives goods from X which X has obtained from Y by false promises which X never intended to perform. Suppose further that in the particular jurisdiction, obtaining goods in this way by making false promises *de futuro* is not a crime, but that D, not being a good scholar of the criminal law, believed that X's mode of obtaining the goods amounted to a crime. Would you have to say that D should be acquitted since he is making a mistake of law? And let me give you a second hypothetical, closer to the facts of *Jaffe*. Suppose that Jaffe did know that the goods which had been initially stolen had come back fleetingly into the control of the true owner. Jaffe believed that this contact was insufficient in law to restore the possession of the owner and therefore concluded that the goods were still stolen. His view of the law is wrong, and it is held that the goods had come back into the possession of the owner and were therefore not stolen goods at the time of D's receipt. That looks to me like a mistake of law, so I imagine that you would have to say that Jaffe should be acquitted."

A. "Certainly that conclusion would be correct in your first hypothetical. We can't convict people for attempting to receive stolen goods when the goods never were stolen, even under the circumstances as the accused believed them to be. Your variation on *Jaffe* is a bit different because the goods were initially stolen there, but again I think the conclusion is correct that we cannot convict because here too the elements of the actus reus of the completed crime are present neither in fact nor in the mind of the accused. After all a full statement of the concept of stolen goods in law would require one not only to state that the goods were acquired in circumstances amounting to theft, but also to state the negative condition, that circumstances had not occurred after the theft which would amount to recaption by the owner. Jaffe in the case of that name was mistaken about whether such circumstances had occurred and was thus making a mistake of fact about the actus reus. But the defendant in your hypothetical is well aware of the circumstances that have occurred but is mistaken about their legal import. He therefore should be acquitted. Curiously here the usual position is reversed, for we are saying that mistake of fact will not be a defense while mistake of law will be. The apparent paradox of saying that is of course really quite sensible since the mistake is an inculpating one and not an exculpating one in the sense that, but for proof of the mistake, there would be no other demonstration of liability."

B. "Aren't you now admitting that the line between guilt and innocence here is a very obscure one? It seems to me that in practice it would be enormously difficult to prove what kind of mistake the defendant had made. Let me inflict one or two more hypotheticals on you. Suppose someone in an eccentric whim builds a small office building which looks exactly like a dwelling-house. D comes along at night and believing it to be a dwelling-house breaks and enters with intent to steal. He is clearly guilty of some degree of the offense of burglary. But what if the jurisdiction confines first-degree burglary to breaking and entering dwelling-houses? Is D guilty of an attempt to commit burglary in the first degree? To convict him under your approach, I suppose, we would have to show that his mistake related to the existence of one of those elements which in law go to make up the concept of a dwelling-house—that somebody habitually slept there *animo revertendi,* and otherwise treated it as a home, etcetera. If he thought that first-degree burglary covered office buildings as well as dwelling-houses, he could not be convicted; at least not for that reason alone, unless he also believed this structure to be a dwelling-house."

A. "I think that analysis is quite correct."

B. "Well, suppose D comes along in the night and finds a converted bus or railroad coach in which a family is living. He breaks and enters with intent to steal. Let us assume that in this jurisdiction the courts have held that such a structure is not a dwelling-house if it remains in a readily mobile condition, but may be classified as a dwelling-house if it has lost its mobility by becoming attached to the realty. Do you really want to say that D is guilty of attempted burglary in the first degree if he thought the structure was embedded in concrete when in fact it had wheels, but not guilty if he knew very well that it had wheels but believed that the law on first degree burglary included such structures?"

A. "Yes, indeed, and I can't see what is objectionable about saying that. After all the burden of proof here is on the prosecution. If they want to get a conviction, they will have to prove beyond a reasonable doubt that the kind of mistake D was making was such that if his mistaken belief had been true all the elements of the actus reus would have been present. It may well be that in the kind of ingenious hypothetical you are constructing such proof would be very difficult to furnish. But in that case there probably will be no prosecution on such a count, which no doubt explains the dearth of cases of this kind in the reports. But I must still insist that where the prosecution is able to make such proof then a conviction would be perfectly proper."

B. "I think the position with which you began has now become rather tortuously convoluted."

A. "I would prefer to say I have refined it."

NOTES

1.   The English courts held in 1892 that the accused could be convicted of attempting to pick an empty pocket, Regina v. Ring, 17 Cox Crim. Cas. 491 (1892), and had earlier held that the accused could be convicted of attempting to obtain money by false pretenses even though the recipient of his "begging" letter well knew the pretense to be false. Regina v. Hensler, 11 Cox Crim. Cas. 570 (1870). In 1897, Mr. Justice Holmes, then of the Massachusetts court, was firmly of the opinion that impossibility was not a general defense. Commonwealth v. Kennedy, 170 Mass. 18, 48 N.E. 770 (1897). For a good review of the American cases, see United States v. Thomas, 13 U.S.C.M.A. 278, 32 C.M.R. 278 (1962).

2.   The leading exponents of this view are, perhaps, Glanville Williams and Jerome Hall. See G. Williams, Criminal Law: The General Part 633–37 (2d ed. 1961) [hereinafter Williams]; J. Hall, General Principles of Criminal Law 586 (2d ed. 1960).

3.   1 F. Wharton, Criminal Law 304 n.9 (12th ed. 1932).

4.   Id.; see Sayre, Criminal Attempts, 41 Harv. L. Rev. 821, 852 (1928).

5.   M. Paulsen & S. Kadish, Criminal Law and Its Processes 484 (1962).

6.   United States v. Thomas, 13 U.S.C.M.A. 278, 32 C.M.R. 278 (1962).

7.   185 N.Y. 497, 78 N.E. 169 (1906).

8.   Id. at 500–01, 78 N.E. at 169–70.

9.   Williams 650.

10.   Id.

11.   84 J.P. 63 (1919).

12.   Id. at 63–64.

13.   Williams 638.

14.   Williams thinks not. Id. at 643–44.

15.   13 U.S.C.M.A. 278, 32 C.M.R. 278 (1962).

16.   Keedy, Criminal Attempts at Common Law, 102 U. Pa. L. Rev. 464, 466–67 (1954).

17.   Perkins, Criminal Attempts and Related Problems, 2 U.C.L.A.L. Rev. 319, 330–32 (1955).

18.   M. Paulsen & S. Kadish, supra note 5, at 485–86.

19.   Williams 614.

20.   Smith, Two Problems in Criminal Attempts Re-Examined, [1962] Crim. L. Rev. 212.

21.   Id. Criminal Attempts, at 217.

22.   Williams, Criminal Attempts—A Reply, [1962] Crim. L. Rev. 300.

23.   11 Cox Crim. Cas. 570 (1870).

24.   Smith, Criminal Attempts, supra note 20, at 215.

25.   Williams, Criminal Attempts, supra note 22, at 301.

26.   J. C. Smith & B. Hogan, Criminal Law 157–58 (1965).

27.   This difficulty of drafting the indictment in such cases is raised by Smith, Criminal Attempts, supra note 20, at 218.

28.   This point is convincingly made by Williams. Williams 650–51.

JOEL FEINBERG

Sua Culpa*

I

It is common enough for philosophers to analyze moral judgments and for philosophers—usually other philosophers—to analyze causal judg-

*From *Doing and Deserving: Essays in the Theory of Responsibility* (Princeton, N.J.: Princeton University Press, 1970), pp. 187–221. Copyright © 1970 by Princeton University Press. Reprinted by permission of the Princeton University Press.

ments. But statements to the effect that a given harm is some assignable person's fault, having both moral and causal components, import the complexities of judgments of the other two kinds. They are, therefore, especially challenging. Yet they are rarely considered by analytical philosophers. This neglect is to be regretted, because "his fault" judgments (as I shall call them) are important and ubiquitous in ordinary life. Historians employ them to assign blame for wars and depressions; politicians, sportswriters, and litigants use them to assign blame for losses. The disagreements they occasion are among the most common and intensely disputed in all "ethical discourse."

It may seem that most of those who quibble and quarrel about "his fault" are either children or lawyers; and even lawyers, therefore, can seem childish when they are preoccupied with the question. But investigators, editorialists, and executives must assign blame for failures and thereby judge the faults of their fellows. (Indeed, their inquiries and debates are most childish when they do *not* carefully consider fault and instead go scapegoat-hunting.) My assumption in what follows is that the faults that concern non-lawyers, both children and adults, are faults in the same sense of the word as those that concern the lawyer, that the concept of "his fault" is imported into the law from the world of everyday affairs. On the other hand, "proximate cause" (to pick just one of a thousand examples) is a technical term of law invented by lawyers to do a special legal job and subject to continual refashioning in the interests of greater efficiency in the performance of its assigned legal task. To explain this term to a layman is precisely to explain what *lawyers* do with it; if it should ever happen that a child, or a sportswriter, or an historian should use the expression, that fact would be of no relevance to its proper analysis. But to explain the concept of "his fault," we must give an account that explains what both lawyers and laymen do with it and how it is possible for each to understand and to communicate with the other by means of it.

An equivalent way of saying that some result is a man's fault is to say that he is to *blame* for it. Precisely the same thing can also be said in the language of *responsibility*. Of course, to be responsible for something (after the fact) may also mean that one did it, or caused it, or now stands answerable, or accountable, or liable to unfavorable responses from others for it. One can be responsible for a result in all those senses without being to blame for it. One can be held liable for a result either because it is one's fault or for some quite different kind of reason; and one can be to blame for an occurrence and yet escape all liability for it. Still, when one is to blame for harm, one can properly be said to be "responsible for it *re-*

ally"; that is, there is a sense of "responsible for" that simply means "chargeable to one as one's fault." One of the commonest uses of the expression "*morally* responsible for" is for being responsible for something in this sense. (Another is for chargeability to a fault of a distinctively moral kind. Still another is for being *liable* to responses of a distinctively moral kind.)

II

The word "fault" occurs in three distinct idioms. We can say of a man that he *has a fault,* or that he is (or was) *at fault,* or that he is "to blame" for a given harm, which is to say that the harm is (or was) *his fault.* In this essay I shall be directly concerned only with the last of these idioms, except to make some necessary preliminary remarks about the other two.

TO HAVE A FAULT

A fault is a shortcoming, that is, a failure to conform to some norm or standard. Originally, perhaps, the word "fault" gave emphasis to failures through deficiency; but now any sort of failure to "measure up" is a fault, and we find no paradox in "falling short through excess." Not all defective human properties are faults. Evanescent qualities are hardly around long enough to qualify. To be a fault, a defective property must be sufficiently durable, visible, and potent to tell us something interesting about its possessor. A fault can be a durable manifestation almost constantly before the eye; but, more typically, human faults are latencies that manifest themselves only under special circumstances. Flaws of character are tendencies to act or feel in subpar ways, which, as tendencies, are *characteristic* of their possessor, that is, genuinely representative of him. Moreover, faults, like virtues, are commonly understood as comparative notions. An irascible man, for example, is not merely one who can become angry, for on that interpretation we may all be considered irascible. Rather, he is one who is more prone than most to become angry, either in the sense that he becomes angry on occasions when most men would not or in the sense that he gets angrier than most men on those occasions when most men would be angry. Equally commonly, however, we interpret a tendency-fault as a failure to satisfy not merely a statistical norm, but a norm of propriety; an irascible man has a tendency to get angry on occasions when he *ought* not to. And even when the implied norm is a statistical one, the fault predicate does more than describe neutrally. A fault word always expresses derogation.

The concept of fault has a close relation to that of harm, but it would be an overstatement to claim that all human faults create the risk of harm. David Hume was closer to the mark when he divided faults into four categories: those that cause displeasure or harm to self or others. Immediate displeasure, however, is only one of the diverse negative reactions that, quite apart from harmfulness, can be the sign of a fault. I would also include, for example, offense, wounded feelings, disaffection, aversion, disgust, shock, annoyance, and "uneasy sensations"—reactions either of the faulty self or of others. If we use the word "offensiveness" to cover the provoking of this whole class of negative responses, and if we assume that everything that is offensive to self, in this broad sense, is likely also to be offensive to others, we can summarize Hume's view by saying that it is either harmfulness or social offensiveness that makes some characteristics faults. Hume notwithstanding, there are some (though perhaps not many) faults that neither harm nor offend but simply fail to benefit, such as unimaginativeness and various minor intellectual flaws. We can modify Hume's account of the offensive faults further, perhaps in a way Hume would not have welcomed, by adding that it is not the mere *de facto* tendency of a trait to offend that renders it a fault. Normally when we attach the fault label to personal characteristics—that is, when we speak as moralists expressing our own judgments, and not merely as sociologists describing the prevailing sentiments of our communities—we are not simply predicting that the characteristics will offend; we are instead (or also) endorsing offense as an appropriate reaction to them. Most of those faults that do not harm, we think, are traits that naturally, or properly, or understandably offend (in the widest sense of "offend").

Often we speak as if a man's fault can enter into causal relations with various outcomes external to him. These assertions, when sensible, must be taken as elliptical forms of more complex statements. To say that a man's faulty disposition, his carelessness or greed, caused some harm is to say

that the man's action or omission that did the causing was of the type that he characteristically does (or would do) in circumstances of the kind that in fact were present, or that the act or omission was of the sort he has a predominant tendency to do in circumstances of that kind. (He may, of course, also have a countertendency to restrain himself by an act of will, or the like.) To cite a man's character flaw as a cause of a harm, in short, is to *ascribe* the cause to an act or omission and then to *classify* that act or omission in a certain way—as characteristic of the actor. (It is just the sort of thing he *would* do, as we say.) It is also, finally, to *judge* the manifested characteristic as substandard and thereby to derogate it.

One can be *at fault* on a given occasion, however, even though one does not act in a characteristic way. Even very careful men sometimes slip up; even the most talented make mistakes; even the very calm sometimes lose their tempers. When these uncharacteristic failures cause harm, it is correct to say that a *faulty aspect* of some act or omission did the causing, but incorrect to ascribe the cause to some faulty characteristic of the actor, for that would be to imply, contrary to the hypothesis, that he is a generally careless, irascible, or inept person. This is the kind of faulty doing (as opposed to "faulty being") that could happen, as we say, to anyone; but in the long run it will be done more often to those who have serious character faults than by those who do not.

"Being at fault," even in one's perfectly voluntary and representative conduct, is in a sense partly a matter of luck. No one has complete control over what circumstances he finds himself in—whether, for example, he lives in times of war or peace, prosperity or depression, under democratic or autocratic government, in sickness or health, and so on. Consequently, a man may, by luck merely, escape those circumstances that would actualize some dreadful latency in him of which he is wholly unaware. It may even be true of *most* of us virtuous persons that we are to some small degree, at least, "lucky" in this sense. (We do not, however, normally refer to the mere absence of very bad luck as "good luck.") Not only can one *have a fault*; and "luckily" escape *being at fault* in one's actions (on analogy with the hemophiliac who never in fact gets cut); one can also have a small fault (that is, a disposition very difficult to actualize) and unluckily stumble into those very rare circumstances that can actualize it. (The latter is "bad luck" in a proper sense.) Both of these possibilities—the luckily unactualized and the unluckily actualized latencies—follow from the analysis of faults as dispositions and, if that analysis is correct, should be sufficient at least to temper anyone's self-righteousness about the faulty actions of others.

TO BE AT FAULT

When a man is "at fault" on a given occasion, the fault characterizes his action itself and not necessarily the actor, except as he was during the performance of the action. There is no necessary relation between this kind of fault and general dispositions of the actor—though, for all we know, every faultily undertaken or executed action *may* exemplify extremely complicated dispositions. When we say that a man is at fault, we usually mean only to refer to occurrent defects of acts or omissions, and only derivatively to the *actor's* flaw as the doer of the defective deed. Such judgments are at best presumptive evidence about the man's general character. An act can be faulty even when not characteristic of the actor, and the actor may be properly "to blame" for it anyway; for if the action is faulty and it is also *his* action (characteristic or not), then he must answer for it. The faultiness of an action always reflects *some* discredit upon its doer, providing the doing is voluntary.

One standard legal classification divides all ways of being at fault into three categories: intentional wrongdoing, recklessness, and negligence. The traditional legal test of intentional doing has been a disjunctive one: There is intentional wrongdoing if either one acts with a wrongful conscious objective or one knowingly produces a forbidden result even incidentally as a kind of side-effect of his effort to achieve his objective. When the occurrence of the forbidden or undesirable side-effect is not certain, but nevertheless there is a known substantial likelihood of its coming about as an incidental byproduct of one's action, its subsequent production cannot be called "intentional" or "knowing" but verges into *recklessness.* What is known in recklessness is the existence of a *risk.* When the actor knowingly runs the risk, when he is willing to gamble with his own interests or the interests of others, then,

providing the risk itself is unreasonable, his act is reckless.[1]

One can hardly escape the impression that what is called "negligence" in the law is simply the miscellaneous class of faulty actions that are not intentional (done purposely or knowingly) or reckless; that in this classification of faults, once wrongful intentions and reckless quasi-intentions have been mentioned, "negligence" stands for everything else. This would leave a class of faults, however, that is *too* wide and miscellaneous. Humorlessness (to take just one example) is a kind of fault that is not intentional; yet we would hardly accuse a man of being "negligent" in failing to be amused or to show amusement at what is truly amusing. The point, I think, is that inappropriate failures to be amused are not the sorts of faults likely to cause *harm.* There is no great risk in a blank stare or a suppressed giggle. Negligence is the name of a heterogeneous class of acts and omissions that are unreasonably *dangerous.* Creation of risk is absolutely essential to the concept, and so is fault. But the fault is not merely conjoined coincidentally to the risk; rather, the fault consists in creating the risk, however unintentionally. When one knowingly creates an unreasonable risk to self or others, one is reckless; when one unknowingly but faultily creates such a risk, one is negligent.

There are a large number of ways of "unintentionally but faultily" creating an unreasonable risk. One can consciously weigh the risk but misassess it, either because of hasty or otherwise insufficient scrutiny (rashness), or through willful blindness to the magnitude of the risk, or through the conscientious exercise of inherently bad judgment. Or one can unintentionally create an unreasonable risk by failing altogether to attend either to what one is doing (the manner of execution) or to the very possibility that harmful consequences might ensue. In the former case, best called *carelessness* or *clumsiness* (in execution), one creates a risk precisely in virtue of not paying sufficient attention to what one is doing; in the latter case, which we can call *heedlessness* (in the very undertaking of the action), the risk is already there in the objective circumstances, but unperceived or mindlessly ignored.

There are still other faults that can render a given act or omission, unknown to its doer, unreasonably dangerous. Overly attentive drivers with the strongest scruples and the best intentions can drive as negligently as inattentive drivers and, indeed, a good deal more negligently than experienced drivers of strong and reliable habits who rely on those habits while daydreaming, their car being operated in effect by a kind of psychic "automatic pilot." Timidity, excitability, organic awkwardness, and slow reflexes can create unreasonable risks too, even when accompanied by attentive and conscientious advertence; and so can normal virtues like gallantry when conjoined with inexperience or poor judgment. (Imagine stopping one's car and waving a pretty pedestrian across the street right into the path of a speeding car passing on the right, unseen because momentarily in the "blind spot" of one's rear view mirror.) Almost any defect of conduct, except the likes of humorlessness, can be the *basis* of negligence, that is, the fault in virtue of which a given act or omission becomes, unknown to its actor, unreasonably dangerous. "Negligence" in the present sense is the name of a category of faulty acts. The negligence of any particular act or kind of act in the general category is always a consequential fault, a fault supervenient upon a fault of another kind that leads to an unreasonable risk in the circumstances.

It is worth emphasizing that this analysis applies to *legal negligence* only, which is negligence in a quite special sense. In ordinary nontechnical discourse, the word "negligence" is often a rough synonym for "carelessness" and as such refers to only one of the numerous possible faults that can, in a given set of circumstances, be the faulty basis of negligent conduct in the legal sense.

III

We come now to the main business at hand: the analysis of the concept of "his fault." It should be clear at the outset that, in order for a given harm to be someone's fault, he must have been somehow "at fault" in what he did or omitted to do, and also that there must have been some sort of causal connection between his action or omission and the harm. It is equally obvious that neither of these conditions by itself can be sufficient. Thus a motorist may be at fault in driving with an expired license or in exceeding the speed limit by five miles per hour, but unless his faulty act is a cause of the collision that ensues, the accident can hardly be his fault. Fault without causally determining action, then, is not sufficient. Similarly, causation without fault is not sufficient for the caused harm to be the causer's fault. It is no logical contradiction to say that a person's action caused the harm yet the harm was not his fault.

THE TRICONDITIONAL ANALYSIS

It is natural at this point to conclude that a harm is "his fault" if and only if (1) he was at fault in acting (or omitting) and (2) his faulty act (or omission) caused the harm. This analysis, however, is incomplete, being still vulnerable to counterexamples of faulty actions causing harm that is nevertheless not the actor's fault. Suppose that *A* is unlicensed to drive an automobile but drives anyway, thereby "being at fault." The appearance of him driving in an (otherwise) faultless manner causes an edgy horse to panic and throw his rider. His faultily undertaken act caused a harm that cannot be imputed to him because the respect in which his act was faulty was causally irrelevant to the production of the harm. (When we come to give a causal explanation of the harm, we will not mention the fact that the driver had no license in his pocket. *That* is not what scared the horse.) This example suggests that a further condition is required to complete the analysis: (3) the aspect of the act that was faulty was also one of the aspects in virtue of which the act was a cause of the harm.

The third condition in the analysis is especially important when the fault in question falls under the general heading of negligence. Robert Keeton in effect devotes most of a book to commentary on a hypothetical example which illustrates this point:

The defendant, proprietor of a restaurant, placed a large unlabelled can of rat poison beside cans of flour on a shelf near a stove in a restaurant kitchen. The victim, while in the kitchen making a delivery to the restaurant, was killed by an explosion of the poison. Assume that the defendant's handling of the rat poison was negligent because of the risk that someone would be poisoned but that the defendant had no reason to know of the risk that the poison would explode if left in a hot place.[2]

The defendant's action, in Keeton's example, was faulty, and it was also the cause of the victim's death; but, on the analysis I have suggested, the death was nevertheless not his fault. The defendant's conduct was negligent because it created a risk of *poisoning*, but the harm it caused was not within the ambit of *that* risk. The risk of *explosion* was not negligently created. Hence the aspect of the act in virtue of which it was faulty was not the cause of the harm. Keeton puts the point more exactly: the harm was not "a result within the scope of the risks by reason of which the actor is found to be negligent."[3] Keeton's concern is with a theory of liability for negligence, not with an analysis of the nontechnical concept of "his fault"; but, liability aside, the analysis I have given entails that the death, in Keeton's example, was *not* the defendant's fault.

We can refer to this account as "the triconditional analysis" and to its three conditions as (in order) "the fault condition," "the causal condition" (that the act was a cause of the harm), and "the causal relevance condition" (that the faulty aspect of the act was its causal link to the harm). I shall conclude that the triconditional analysis goes a long way toward providing a correct account of the commonsense notion of "his fault" and that its three conditions are indeed necessary to such an account even if, in the end, they must be formulated much more carefully and even supplemented by other conditions in an inevitably more complicated analysis. The remainder of this section discusses difficulties for the analysis as it stands which, I think, it can survive (at least after some tinkering, modifying, and disclaiming). One of these difficulties stems from a heterogeneous group of examples of persons who, on our analysis, would be blamed for harms that are clearly not their fault. I try to sidestep these counterexamples by affixing a restriction to the fault condition and making corresponding adjustments in the formulation of the relevance condition. The other difficulties directly concern the causal condition and the relevance condition. Both of these can involve us quickly in some fundamental philosophical problems.

RESTRICTIONS ON THE FAULT CONDITION

There are some exceptional cases (but readily accessible to the philosophical imagination) in which a person who is clearly not to blame for a given harm nevertheless is the sole person who satisfies the conditions of the tripartite analysis.

These cases, therefore, constitute counterexamples to that analysis if it is taken to state not only necessary but sufficient conditions for blame. Nicholas Sturgeon has suggested an especially ingenious case:

A has made a large bet that no infractions of the law will occur at a certain place in a certain period of time; but *B*, at that place and time, opens a pack of cigarettes and fails to destroy the federal tax seal thereby breaking the law. *A*, seeing *B's* omission, is so frustrated that he suffers a fatal heart attack on the spot. (To simplify matters, we may suppose that no one has any reason to suppose *A* is endangering his health by gambling in this way.)[4]

Clearly, *A's* death is not *B's* fault. Yet (1) *B* was at fault in acting contrary to law; (2) his faulty act frustrated *A*, causing the heart attack; and (3) the aspects of *B's* act (omission) that were faulty (the illegality of his omission to destroy the tax stamps) were also among the aspects of it in virtue of which there was a causal connection between it and the harm. A similar example is provided by John Taurek:

C is so programmed (by hypnosis, perhaps *C* is a clever robot, whatever) that if *A* lies in answering *B's* question, *C* will harm *D*. *B* asks *A* her age and she lies. *C* harms *D*. *A's* action seems to be a causal factor in the production of harm to *D*, and just in virtue of his faulty aspect. Yet who would hold that *D's* harm was *A's* fault?[5]

Perhaps it is possible to add further conditions to the analysis to obviate this kind of counterexample, but a more likely remedy would be to restrict the kinds of faults that can be elements of "his fault" judgments. Sometimes a man can be said to be at fault in acting (or omitting to act) precisely because his action or omission will offend or fail to benefit himself or others, or because it is a violation of faith (even a *harmless* instance of promise-breaking, such as a secret breaking of faith to a person now dead), or simply and precisely because it breaks an authoritative legal rule. Most intentional wrongdoing, on the other hand, and all recklessness and negligence are instances of being at fault for another (perhaps additional) reason—either because "they make a certain kind of harm or injury inevitable, or because they create an unreasonable risk of a certain kind of harm."[6] We can attempt to avoid counterexamples of the sort Sturgeon and Taurek suggested by tampering with the first condition (the fault condition). We can say now (of course, only tentatively and not without misgiving) that, for the purpose of this analysis, the way of being at fault required by the fault condition is to be understood as the harm-threatening way, not the nonbenefiting, offense-threatening, harmless faith-breaking, or law-violating ways. The fault condition then can be reformulated as follows (in words suggested by Sturgeon): a given harm is *A's* fault only if (1) *A* was at fault in acting or omitting to act and "the faultiness of his act or omission consisted, at least in part, in the creation of either a certainty or an unreasonable risk of harm. . . ."[7] Now the faulty smoker in Sturgeon's example and the liar in Taurek's example are no longer "at fault" in the requisite way, and the revised analysis no longer pins the blame for coincidental harms on them. To open a cigarette package in an overly fastidious fashion is not to endanger unduly the health of others; nor is lying about one's age (except in very special contexts) to threaten others with harm.

In the light of this new restriction on the fault condition, we can formulate the causal relevance condition in an alternative way, along the lines suggested by Keeton's account of harm caused by negligence. We can now say that the (harm-threatening) "faulty aspect" of an act is a cause of subsequent harm when the risk or certainty of harm in virtue of which the act was at fault was a risk or certainty of "just the sort of harm that was in fact caused,"[8] and not harm of some other sort. The resultant harm, in other words, must be within the scope of the risk (or certainty) in virtue of which the act is properly characterized as faulty. This is more than a mere explication of the original way of putting the third condition. It is a definite modification designed to rule out cases of *coincidence* where the faulty aspect of an act, even when it is of the harm-threatening sort, may be causally linked to a subsequent harm via such adventitious conditions as standing wagers and programmed robots. Under the revised formulation, the very same considerations involved in the explanation of *why* the act is faulty are also involved, esentially and sufficiently, in the explanation of *how* the harm was caused.

We have not even considered, of course, the crucial question of how reasonable risks are to be distinguished from unreasonable ones; and there are still other problems resulting from the fact that a "sort of harm" (crucial phrase) can be described in either more or less full and determinate ways. These problems, like several other closely related ones, are too complicated to be tackled here.

FAULT AND CAUSE: DEPENDENT AND INDEPENDENT DETERMINATIONS

Can we tell whether an act caused a given harm independently of knowing whether the actor was at fault in acting? The answer seems to be that we can determine the causal question independently of the fault question in some cases but not in others. Part of our problem is to explain his variation. Consider first some examples. A blaster takes every reasonable precaution, and yet by a wildly improbable fluke his explosion of dynamite sends a disjarred rock flying through the window of a distant isolated cabin. He was not at fault, but whether he was or not, we are able to say independently that his setting off the blast was the cause of the broken window. Similarly, the motorist in our earlier example, by driving (whether with or without fault is immaterial to this point) along a rarely traveled stretch of country road, caused a nervous horse to bolt. That is, it was his activity as he conducted it then and there, with its attendant noise and dust, that caused the horse to bolt; and we can know this independently of any determination of fault.

Examples provided by J. L. Mackie and William Dray, however, seem to cut the other way. Mackie[9] describes an episode in which a motorcyclist exceeded a speed limit and was chased by a policeman, also on a motorcycle, at speeds up to seventy miles per hour. An absentminded pedestrian stepped off a bus into the policeman's path and was killed instantly. The newspapers for the next few days were full of debates over the questions of whose conduct was the "real cause" of the death, debates that seemed to center on the question of whose conduct was the least *reasonable* intrusion into the normal course of events. To express an opinion at all on the causal question seemed to be to take a stand, plain and simple, about the *propriety* of pursuits by police in heavily populated areas.

Dray discusses a hypothetical debate between two historians who argue "whether it was Hitler's invasion of Poland or Chamberlain's pledge to defend it which caused the outbreak of the Second World War." The question they *must* be taken to be trying to settle, he avers, is "who was to blame." "The point," he says, "is not that we cannot hold an agent responsible for a certain happening unless his action can be said to have caused it. It is rather that, unless we are prepared to hold the agent responsible for what happened, we cannot say that his action *was* the cause."[10] Mackie comes to a similar conclusion, embracing what he calls a "curious inversion of utilitarianism," namely, that one often cannot tell whether a given harm is a causal consequence of a given act without first deciding whether the actor was *at fault* in acting the way he did.

To clarify the relations between cause and fault, it will be necessary to digress briefly and remind ourselves of certain features of causal judgments as they are made in ordinary life. That one condition is causally necessary or, in a given context, sufficient for the occurrence of a given event is normally a question simply for empirical investigation and the application of a scientific theory. Normally, however, there will be a plurality of distinguishable causal conditions (often called "causal factors") for any given event, and the aim of a causal inquiry will be to single out one[11] of these to be denominated "the cause" of the event in question.[12] A judgment that cites one of the numerous eligible causal conditions for an event as "the cause" I call a *causal citation*. The eligibility of an event or state as a causal factor is determined empirically via the application of inductive criteria.[13] On the other hand, the citation of one of the eligible candidates as "the cause" is normally made, as we shall see, via the application of what Dray calls "pragmatic criteria." In Dray's convenient phrase, the inductive inquiry establishes the "importance of a condition to the event," whereas the causal citation indicates its "importance to the inquirer."

The point of a causal citation is to single out one of the certified causal candidates that is especially *interesting* to us, given our various practical purposes and cognitive concerns. These purposes and concerns provide a convenient way of classifying the "contexts of inquiry" in which causal citations are made. The primary division is between explanatory and nonexplanatory contexts. The occasion for an explanatory citation is one in which there is intellectual puzzlement of a quite specific kind. A suprising or unusual event has occurred which is a deviation from what is understood to be the normal course of things. A teetotaler is drunk, or an alcoholic sober; a punctual man is tardy, or a dilatory man early; it rains in the dry season, or it fails to rain in the wet season. Sometimes the breach of routine is disappointing, and we wish to know what went wrong this time. But sometimes the surprise is pleasant or, more commonly, simply stimulating to one's curiosity. We ask what caused the surprising event and expect an explanation that will cite a factor normally present but absent this time, or normally absent but present this time, that made the difference. The occasion for explanation is a breach of routine; the explanatory judgment cites another deviation from routine to correlate with it.

Very often one of the causal conditions for a given upshot is a faulty human action. Human failings tend to be more "interesting" factors than events of other kinds, even for purely explanatory purposes; but it is important to notice that this need not always be the case. Faulty human actions usually do *not* fall within the normal course of events, so that a dereliction of duty, for example, when it is a causally necessary condition for some puzzling breach of routine, being itself a departure from the normal course of things, is a prime candidate for causal citation. But when the faulty conduct of Flavius is constant and unrelieved and known to be such to Titus, it will not relieve Titus's perplexity over how a given unhappy event came about simply to cite Flavius's habitual negligence or customary dereliction of duty as "the cause." What Titus wishes to know is what new intrusive event made the difference *this* time; and it won't help *him* to mention a causal factor that has always been present even on those occasions when no unhappy result ensued.

Not all causal explanations by any means employ causal citations. Especially when we are puzzled about the "normal course of events" itself and wish explanations for standardly recurring regularities (Why do the tides come in? Why do released objects fall? Why do flowers bloom in the spring?), mere brief citations will not do. In such cases we require long stories involving the descriptions of diverse states of affairs and the invocation of various laws of nature. Similarly, not all causal citations are explanatory. Sometimes there is no gap in a person's understanding of how a given interesting event came about, and yet he may seek nevertheless to learn its "real" or "most important" cause. Nonexplanatory citations are those made for some purpose other than the desire simply to put one's curiosity to rest. Most frequently they cite the causal factor that is of a kind that is easiest to manipulate or control. Engineers and other practical men may be concerned to eliminate events of the kind that occasioned the inquiry if they are harmful or to produce more of them if they are beneficial. In either case, when they seek "the cause," they seek the causal factor that has a handle on it (in Collingwood's phrase) that they can get hold of and manipulate. Another of our practical purposes in making causal citations is to *fix the blame,* a purpose which introduces considerations not present when all the leading causal factors are things other than human actions (as they often are in agricultural, medical, or engineering inquiries). Insects, viruses, and mechanical stresses and strains are often "blamed" for harms, but the word "blame" in these uses, of course, has a metaphorical sense.

In summary, causal citations can be divided into those made from explanatory and those made from nonexplanatory standpoints, and the latter group into those made from the "engineering" and those made from the "blaming" standpoints. Explanatory citations single out abnormal interferences with the normal course of events or hitherto unknown missing links in a person's understanding. They are designed simply to remove puzzlement by citing the causal factor that can shed the most light. Hence we can refer to the criterion of selection in explanatory contexts (for short) as *the lantern criterion.* Causal citations made from the "engineering standpoint" are made with a view to facilitating control over future events by citing the most efficiently and economically manipulable causal factor. The criterion for selection in engineering contexts can thus be called (for short) *the handle criterion.* The point of causal citations in purely blaming

contexts is simply to pin the label of blame on the appropriate causal factor for further notice and practical use. These judgments cite a causal factor that is a human act or omission "stained" (as an ancient figure of speech would have it) with fault. The criterion in blaming contexts can be called (for short) *the stain criterion.* When we look for "the cause," then, we may be looking for the causal factor that has either a lantern, a handle, or a stain on it.

Purely blaming citations can be interpreted in two different ways. On the first model, to say that a person's act was the cause of the harm is precisely equivalent to saying that he is to blame for the harm, that is, that the harm is his fault. The causal inquiry undertaken from the purely blaming perspective, according to this view, is one and the same as the inquiry into the question of who was to blame or of whose fault it was. On this model, then, causal citation is not a condition for the fixing of blame; it is, rather, precisely the same thing. It is simply a fact of usage, which the examples of Dray and Mackie illustrate, that questions of blame often get posed and answered in wholly causal language. Historians, for example, are said by Dray often to "use expressions like 'was responsible for' [or 'was to blame for'] when they want to put into other words conclusions which they would also be prepared to frame in causal language."[14]

On the second model of interpretation, which is also sometimes *a propos,* the truth of the causal citation "His act was the cause of the harm" is only one of the *conditions* for the judgment that "The harm was his fault." Here we separate cause and fault before bringing them together again in a "his fault" judgment, insisting that the harm was his fault *only if* his action caused it. The causal inquiry, so conceived, is undertaken for the sake of the blame inquiry, but its results are established independently.

Now how do we establish a causal citation on the first model (or, what is the same thing, a "his fault" citation on the second)? Again, we have two alternatives: Either we can hold that the person (or his act) was *the cause* of the harm (meaning that he was to blame for it) only if his act was a genuine causal factor in the production of the harm; or we can require that his act be *the cause* of the harm, and not merely a "causal factor." But then we must find a way of avoiding a vitiating circularity. If we mean "the cause" as selected by *the stain criterion,* we have made a full circle; for, on this first model, our *original inquiry* is aimed at citing the cause by a stain criterion, and now we say that the achievement of this goal is a condition of itself. Clearly, if we are going to insist that his act be "the cause" as a condition of its being "the cause for purposes of fixing blame," we have to mean that it must be the cause *as determined by either the lantern or the handle criteria.* A quick examination of cases will show that this is just what we do mean.

When a man sets off a charge of dynamite and the earth shifts, dust rises, and rocks fly, the blasting is conspicuously the cause of these results by the lantern criterion (since it is the abnormal intervention) and equally clearly by the handle criterion (since it is part of the handiest causal recipe for producing results of precisely that kind). We can know, therefore, that the blasting caused the results by these commonsense criteria before we know anything at all about fault. Then we can go on to say, without circularity, that one or another of these causal criteria must be satisfied if those of the results that are harmful are to be charged to the blaster as his fault, but that further conditions of faultiness must also be satisfied.

Should we say that being "the cause" by the other commonsense criteria is *always* a necessary condition of being the cause by the stain criterion? I think this specification would prove to be artificially restrictive, for we sometimes (though perhaps not often) wish to ascribe blame whether or not the blamed action satisfies the lantern and handle criteria, and even in some instances where (allowing for the usual relativity of context) it appears not to. Suppose *A,* an impressive adult figure, offers a cigarette to *B,* an impressionable teenager. *A* is *B's* original attractive model of a smoker and also one who deliberately seduces him into the habit. Much later, after thirty years of continuous heavy smoking, *B* begins to suffer from lung cancer. Neither the lantern nor the handle criteria in most contexts are likely to lead one to cite *A's* earlier act as the cause of *B's* cancer, for *A's* act is not conspicuously "the cause" of the harm by these criteria (as the blasting was, in the earlier example). Yet we may wish to say that *A's* seduction of *B* was the cause of his eventual cancer for purposes of fixing blame or as a mode of expressing that blame. Such a

judgment may not be morally felicitous, but it can be made without committing some sort of conceptual solecism.

The best way of avoiding both circularity and artificial restriction of expression in our account of blame-fixing citations is to require not that the blamed action be citable as "the cause" (by *any* criteria), but only that it be a genuine causal factor, in the circumstances that obtained, and then to add fault and relevance conditions to the analysis. Most of the time, perhaps, being "the cause" by the lantern or handle criteria will also be required; but being a *causal factor merely* will be required always.

THE CAUSAL RELEVANCE CONDITION: IS IT ALWAYS NECESSARY?

Does the analysis of commonsense "his fault" judgments really require a causal relevance condition? Many people, I suspect, are prepared to make "his fault" judgments in particular cases even when they know that a causal relevance condition has not been satisfied; and many puzzling cases are such as to make even most of us hesitate about the matter. Consider, for example, the case of the calamitous soup-spilling at Lady Mary's formal dinner party. Sir John Stuffgut so liked his first and second bowls of soup that he demanded a third just as Lady Mary was prepared to announce with pride to the hungry and restless guests the arrival of the next course. Sir John's tone was so gruff and peremptory that Lady Mary quite lost her composure. She lifted the heavy tureen with shaking arms and, in attempting to pass it to her intemperate guest, spilled it unceremoniously in the lap of the Reverend Mr. Straightlace. Now both Sir John and Lady Mary were at fault in this episode. Sir John was thoughtless, gluttonous, and, especially, *rude* in demanding another bowl in an unsettling tone of voice. Lady Mary was (perháps forgivably) negligent in the way she executed her action, and, besides she should have known that the tureen was too heavy for her to lift. Furthermore, both Lady Mary's faulty action and Sir John's faulty action were necessary conditions for the ensuing harm. Assuming that we must fix the blame for what happened, whose fault, should we say, was the harm?

Most of us would be inclined to single out Sir John's rudeness as "the cause" for purposes of blaming, partly because it was the most striking deviation from routine, perhaps, but mainly because, of the causal factors with stains on them, his action was the most at fault. Moreover, his action was a causal factor in the production of the harm precisely in virtue of that aspect which was faulty, namely, its unsettling rudeness, which created an unreasonable risk of upsetting the hostess, the very result that in fact ensued. Thus the causal relevance condition is satisfied in this example.

Suppose, however, that the facts had been somewhat different. Sir John, at just the wrong moment (as before), requested his third bowl, but in a quiet and gentle manner, and in a soft and mellifluous tone of voice, perfectly designed to calm its auditor. Sir John this time was not being rude, though he was still at fault in succumbing to his excessive appetites and indulging them in an unseemly public way to the inconvenience of others. In short, his primary fault in this new example was not rudeness, but plain gluttony; and (as before), but for his act which was at fault, the harm would not have occurred. Likewise (as before) the clumsiness of Lady Mary was a causal factor in the absence of which the harm would not have resulted. This case differs from the earlier one in that the causal relevance condition is not satisfied, for gluttony normally creates a risk to the glutton's own health and comfort, not to the interests of others. Unlike rudeness, it is a primary self-regarding fault. Thus that aspect of Sir John's request for more soup that was faulty was an irrelevant accompaniment of the aspects that contributed to the accident. Hence we could conclude that, although Sir John was *at fault* in what he did, the resulting harm was not *his fault.* [15]

It would be sanguine, however, to expect everybody to agree with this judgment. Mr. Straightlace, for example, might be altogether indisposed to let Sir John escape the blame so easily. He and others might prefer to reject the causal relevance condition out of hand as too restrictive and urge instead that the blame always be placed on the person *most at fault,* whether the fault is causally relevant or not, providing his faulty action was a genuine causal factor. This alternative would enable one to pin the blame on Sir John in both versions of the soup-spilling story. It does not commend itself to the intuitive understanding in

a quiet reflective hour, however, and seems to me to have no other merit than that of letting the indignation and vindictiveness occasioned by harm have a respectable outlet in our moral judgments. If we really want to keep Sir John on the hook, *we do not have to say* that the harm was "really his fault" and thereby abuse a useful and reasonably precise concept. Rather, if we are vindictively inclined, we can say that to impose liability on a person to enforced compensation or other harsh treatment for some harm does not always require that the harm be his fault. This would be the moral equivalent of a departure from what is called "the fault principle" in the law of torts. It is an attempt to do justice to our spontaneous feelings, without confusing our concepts, and has the merits at least of openness and honesty.

Disinterested parties might reject causal relevance as a condition for being to blame in a skeptical way, offering as an alternative to it a radical contextual relativism. One might profess genuine bafflement when asked whose fault was the second soup-spilling, on the grounds that the question cannot be answered until it is known for what purpose it is asked. Is the person singled out for blame the one to be punished, forced to make compensation, expected to apologize? What is the point of narrowly pinning blame? We could, after all, simply tell the narrative as accurately as possible and decline to say whose fault, on balance, the harm was, although that evasive tactic might not be open to, say, an insurance investigator. The point, according to this skeptical theory, is that, after all the facts are in, we are still not committed by "the very logic of the everyday concept" to saying anything at all about whose fault it was. The blame-fixing decision is still logically open and will be determined in part by our practical purposes in raising the question. This skeptical theory, however, strikes me as a combined insight and *non sequitur.* The insight is that we are not *forced* to pinpoint blame unless some practical question like liability hinges on it and that is often the better part of wisdom to decline to do so when one can. But it does not follow from the fact that "his fault" judgments can sometimes be avoided that it is logically open to us to make them in any way we wish when we do make them. I hold, therefore, to the conclusion that, in fixing the blame for harm, we are restricted by our very concepts to the person(s) whose faulty act was a causal factor in the production of the harm in virtue of its causally relevant faulty aspect.

There often is room for discretion in the making of "his fault" judgments, but it comes at a different place and is subject to strict limitations. The person whose fault the harm is said to be *must* satisfy the conditions of the triconditional analysis (and perhaps others as well); but when more than one person is so qualified, the judgment-maker may sometimes choose between them on "pragmatic grounds," letting some of them off the hook. When this discretion is proper, the three conditions of our analysis must be honored as necessary, but they are no longer taken to be sufficient. Suppose one thousand persons satisfy the three conditions of our analysis in respect to harm *X,* and they acted independently (not in concert) over a period of many years. To say simply that the harm is (all) *their* fault, or part his, and part his, and part his, and so on, would be to defeat altogether the usual point of a "his fault" judgment, namely, to fix more narrowly, to single out, to focus upon. When fixings of blame become too diffuse, they can no longer perform this function. They might still, of course, be *true,* but just not very useful. It is not exactly false to say of the first soup-spilling example that it was the fault of *both* Lady Mary and Sir John; but "practical purposes" may dictate instead that we ignore minor or expectable faults and confer all the blame on the chief culprit. At any rate, if it is given that we must, for some practical purpose, single out a wrongdoer more narrowly, then we have discretion to choose among those (but only those) who satisfy the necessary conditions of the tripartite analysis.[16]

FAULT AND TORT LIABILITY

Suppose we accept the revised triconditional analysis of "his fault" but jettison the causal relevance condition as a requisite for tort *liability,* so that we can get the likes of Sir John on the hook after all, even though we admit he is not *to blame* for the harm. The prime consequence of dropping the causal relevance condition is to downgrade the role of causation as a ground for liability and to increase the importance of simply being at fault. If causal relevance is not required, it would seem that being at fault is the one centrally im-

portant necessary condition for liability, and indeed so important as to render the causal condition itself a mere dispensable formality. To upgrade the fault condition to that extent is most likely to seem reasonable when the fault is disproportionately greater than the harm it occasions. Imagine a heinously faulty act that is a necessary causal condition for a relatively minor harm. Suppose that *A,* a matricidal fiend, in the cruelest way possible sets himself to shoot his mother dead just as *B,* the lady across the street, is fondling a delicate and fragile art object. The sound of the revolver shot startles *B,* causing her to drop the art object which shatters beyond repair. Is its loss *A's* fault? Let us assume (for the sake of the argument) that the murderous act was at fault in at least two ways: (1) it created a certainty of death or severe injury to the actor's mother (the primary way it was at fault); and (2), in making a loud report, it created an unreasonable risk to (among other things) the art objects of neighbors. Thus, in virtue of (2), *A* is at fault in the manner required for his being to blame for breaking the neighbor's glass vase. His act caused the breaking and did so in virtue of its faulty aspect (2); hence it was his fault. But even if he had (thoughtfully) used a silencer on the gun, and nevertheless the very slight noise caused by his act had startled a supernervous vase-fondling neighbor, causing the dropping and breaking, we might find it proper to charge him for the damage *even though the loss was not his fault.* (The "faulty aspect" of his act—its heinousness—was causally irrelevant to that loss.) It is precisely this kind of case where common sense seems most at home without the causal relevance condition; for no question of "fairness" to the faulty one is likely to trouble us when his fault is so great. Any number of minor harms of which his act was a necessary condition can be charged to his moral bill without disturbing us—at least so long as we remain "spontaneous" and unreflective.

It is another matter, however, when the harm is disproportionately greater than the fault, when a mere slap causes an unsuspected hemophiliac to bleed to death, or a clumsy slip on the sidewalk leads one to bump an "old soldier with an egg shell skull," causing his death. Hart and Honoré suggest that even here commonsense considerations can help justify abandonment, in some cases at least, of the causal relevance condition by mitigating its apparent harshness:

The apparent unfairness of holding a defendant liable for a loss much greater than he could foresee to some extent diappears when we consider that a defendant is often negligent without suffering punishment or having to pay compensation. I may drive at an excessive speed a hundred times before the one occasion on which my speeding causes harm. The justice of holding me liable, should the harm on that occasion turn out to be extraordinarily grave, must be judged in the light of the hundred other occasions on which, without deserving such luck, I have incurred no liability.[17]

This argument is reminiscent of the Augustinian theory of salvation. We are all sinners; therefore, no one really deserves to be saved. Hence if anyone at all is saved, it can only be through God's supererogatory grace. The others are (relatively) unlucky; but, being undeserving sinners, they can have no just complaint. All of us are negligent, goes the parallel argument; so none of us really deserves to escape liability for great harm. That majority of us who do escape are lucky, but the others who fall into liability in excess of their fault on the occasion have no just complaint, since they have accumulated enough fault on other occasions to redress the disproportion.

If justice truly requires (as the Hart-Honoré argument suggests) that blame and liability be properly apportioned to *all* a person's faults as accumulated in the long run, causal linkage to harm aside, why not go all the way in this direction and drop the "causal factor" condition altogether in the interest of Aristotelian "due proportion" and fairness? To say that we are all negligent is to say that on other occasions, at least, we have all created unreasonable risk of harms, sometimes great harms of one kind or another, to other persons. Even in circumstances where excessive harm actually results, we may have created other risks of a different kind to other individuals, risks which luckily failed to eventuate in harm. Robert Keeton foresees the consequences for the law of torts of taking all such faults seriously in the assignment of liability for particular harms:

... if it is relevant to take into account defendant's fault with respect to a risk different from any that would include the harm plaintiff has suffered, then would it not also be relevant to take into account his other faults as well? And would it not seem equally relevant to consider plaintiff's shortcomings? Shall we fix legal responsibility by deciding who is the better and who the worse person? An affirmative answer might involve us, and quickly too, in the morality of run-of-the-ranch TV drama, where the good guys always win.[18]

In effect Keeton challenges those who would drop the causal relevance condition to explain why they would maintain any causal condition at all. If the existence of fault of one kind or another, on one occasion or another, is the controlling consideration, why do we not simply tally up merits and demerits and distribute our collective compensation expenses in proportion to each person's moral score?

Why not indeed? This is not an unthinkable alternative system. We could, in principle, begin with the notion of a "compensable harm" as one caused by fault. (Other harms could be paid for out of tax funds or voluntary insurance.) Then we could estimate the total cost of compensable harms throughout the country for a one-year period. We would have to acquire funds equal to that amount by assigning demerits throughout the year to persons discovered to be "at fault" in appropriate ways in their conduct. Those who fail to clear their sidewalks of ice and snow within a reasonable period after the finish of a storm would be given so many demerits per square foot of pavement. Those convicted of traffic offenses would be assigned demerits on a graduated scale corresponding to the seriousness (as compounded out of unreasonableness and dangerousness) of their offense. Then, at the end of the year, the total cost of compensable harms would be divided by the total number of assigned demerits to yield the dollar value per demerit. and each person would be fined the dollar equivalent of the sum of his demerits. These fines would all go into a central fund used to compensate all victims of faulty accidents and crimes. Such a system would impose on some persons penalties disproportionately greater than the harm they actually caused; others would pay less than the harm they caused; but as far as is practically possible, everyone would be fined in exact proportion to the unreasonable risks he created (as well as certain and deliberate harms) to others.[19]

The system just described could be called a system of "liability without *contributory* fault," since it bypasses a causation requirement. It is a system of liability based on fault simply, whether or not the fault contributes to harm. It thus differs sharply from the traditional system of liability based in part upon what is called *the fault principle,* which requires that accidental losses be borne by the party whose fault the accident was. This is liability based on "his fault" ascriptions, rather than "at fault" imputations. In contrast, the principle underlying a system of liability based on fault without causation might well be called the *retributive theory of torts.* It surely deserves this name drawn from the criminal law more than the so-called fault principle does since it bases liability *entirely* upon fault purged of all extraneous and fortuitous elements. To be sure, what is called retributivism in the criminal law[20] is a principle that would base (criminal) liability entirely on *moral* fault, and most retributivists would oppose punishing nonmoral faults, including much negligence, as ardently as they would oppose punishing the wholly faultless. A retributive principle of reparation *could* take this very moralistic form. As we have seen, legal negligence is always supervenient upon a fault of some other kind, sometimes "moral" (callousness, inconsiderateness, self-centeredness), sometimes not (timidity, excitability, awkwardness). A moralistic principle would issue demerits to negligence only when it is supervenient upon a fault judged to be a *moral* failing. In a sense, the more inclusive version of the theory is more "moralistic" still, since it treats even nonmoral failings as essentially deserving of penalty, that is, just *as if* they were moral failings. We can safely avoid these complications here.

One way to understand the retributive theory of torts is to relate it to, or derive it from, a general moral theory that bears the name of retributivism. In treating of this more general theory, it is very important to distinguish a strong from a weak version, for failure to do so has muddled discussions of retributivism in criminal law and would very likely do the same in discussion of principles of tort liability. According to the strong version of the general retributive principle, *all* evil or, more generally still, all *fault* deserves its comeuppance; it is an end in itself, quite apart from other consequences, that all wrongdoers (or faulty doers) be made to suffer some penalty, handicap, or forfeiture as a requital for their wrongdoing. Similarly, it is an end in itself, morally fitting and proper irrespective of other consequences, that the meritorious be rewarded with the means to happiness. Thus the best conceivable world would be that in which the virtuous (or faultless) flourish, the wicked (or, more generally, the faulty) suffer, and those in between perfect virtue and perfect wickedness enjoy happiness or suffer unhappiness in exact proportion to their virtuous and faulty conduct. Both a world in which everyone suffers regardless of moral condition and a world in which everyone flourishes regardless of moral condition would be intrinsically inferior morally to a world in which all and only the good flourish and all and only the bad suffer. If everyone without exception is a miserable sinner, then it is intrinsically better that everybody suffer than that everybody, or even anybody, be happy. There may be intrinsic goods other than the just apportionment of reward and penalty to the virtuous and the faulty respectively; but insofar as a state of affairs deviates from such apportionment, it is intrinsically defective.

Note that this way of putting retributivism makes it apply only to apportionments of a noncomparative kind, where to give to one is not necessarily to take from another and where to take from one is not necessarily to give to another. It is not, therefore, a principle of distributive justice, telling us in the abstract how all pies are to be cut up or how all necessary burdens are to be divided. Indeed, for some situations it would decree that no one get any pie, and in others that no one should suffer any burdens. It is concerned with deserving good or deserving ill, not with deserving one's fair share relative to others. To be sure, the world in which the good suffer and the evil are happy it calls a moral abomination, but not because of the conditions of the parties relative to one another, but rather because the condition of each party is the opposite of what *he* deserves, quite independently of the condition of the others. A world in which every person is equally a sinner and equally very happy would also be moral abomination, on this view, even though it involves no social inequality.

The weaker version of general retributivism, on

the other hand, is essentially a comparative principle, applying to situations in which it is given that someone or other must do without, make a sacrifice, or forfeit his interest. The principle simply asserts the moral priority, *ceteris paribus,* of the innocent party. Put most pithily, it is the principle that *fault forfeits first,* if forfeit there must be. If someone must suffer, it is better, *ceteris paribus,* that it be the faulty than the meritorious. This weaker version of retributivism, which permeates the law, especially the criminal law, has strong support in common sense. It commonly governs the distribution of that special kind of benefit called "the benefit of the doubt," so that, where there is doubt, for example, about the deterrent efficacy of a particular mode of punishment for a certain class of crimes, the benefit of that doubt is given to potential victims instead of convicted criminals.

I find the weaker version of retributivism much more plausible intuitively than the stronger, though even it is limited—for example, by the values of intimacy and friendship. (If I negligently spill your coffee cup at lunch, will you insist that I pay for a new cup, or will you prefer to demonstrate how much more important my friendship is to you than the forfeiture of a dime?) The weaker principle allows us to say, if we wish, though it does not require us to say, that universal happiness, if it were possible, would be intrinsically better than happiness for the good only, with the wicked all miserable. (Indeed, what would wickedness come to if its usually negative effect on the happiness of others was universally mitigated or nullified?) The weak principle also permits but does not require us to say that, even though it is better that the faulty forfeit first where there is no alternative to *someone's* forfeiting, it is better still that some other alternative be found.

Now let us return to our tort principles. What is called the "fault principle" (or, better, the "his fault" principle) does not derive from, and indeed is not even compatible with, the strong version of general retributivism. As we have seen, the causal component of "his fault" ascriptions introduces a fortuitous element, repugnant to pure retributivism. People who are very much at fault may luckily avoid causing proportionate harm, and unlucky persons may cause harm in excess of their minor faults. In the former case, little or no

harm may be a person's fault even though he is greatly at fault; hence his liability, based on "his fault," will not be the burden he deserves, and the moral universe will be out of joint. In the latter case, unhappily coexistent circumstances may step up the normal magnitude of harm resulting from a minor fault, and again the defendant's liability will not do proper justice to his actual fault.

The tort principle that is called for by strong retributivism is that which I have called "the retributive theory of torts." Being at fault gets its proper comeuppance from this principle, whether or not it leads directly to harm; and the element of luck— except for luck in escaping detection— is largely eliminated. Hence fault suffers its due penalty, and if that is an end in itself, as strong retributivism maintains, then the retributive theory of torts is well recommended indeed. But the lack of intuitive persuasiveness of the general theory, I think, diminishes the plausibility of its offshoot in torts. Weak retributivism, which is generally more plausible, in my opinion, than its strong counterpart, does not uniquely favor either the retributive theory of torts or the "his fault" principle. Except in straightforwardly comparative contexts where the necessity of forfeiture is given, it takes no stand whatever about principles of tort liability. If *A* and *B* are involved in an accident causing a loss to *B* only, which is wholly *A's* fault, and it is given that either *A* or *B* must pay for the loss, no other source of compensation being available, then the weak principle says that *A* should be made to pay, or rather (put even more weakly in virtue of the *ceteris paribus* clause) it holds that, insofar as the loss was *A's* fault, that is a good and relevant reason why *A* should pay and, in the absence of other relevant considerations, a sufficient reason. In short, if someone has got to be hurt in this affair, let it be the wrongdoer (other things being equal). But where there is no necessity that the burden of payment be restricted to the two parties involved, weak retributivism has no application and, indeed, is quite compatible with a whole range of nonfault principles.

One final point remains to be made. If we hold that we are all more or less equally sinners in respect to a certain area of conduct or a certain type of fault—if, for example, we are all as likely, more or less, to be erring defendants as wronged plaintiffs in driving accident suits—then the principle of strong retributivism itself would call for the jettisoning of the "his fault" principle in that area of activity. If fault is distributed equally, the "his fault" principle, in distributing liability *unequally* among a group, will cause a lack of correspondence between fault and penalty. On the assumption of equal distribution of fault, the use of the "his fault" principle would lead to *less* correspondence, *less* exact proportioning of penalty to fault, even than various principles of social insurance that have the effect of spreading the losses as widely as possible among a whole community of persons presumed to be equally faulty. But then these schemes of nonfault liability are supported by strong reasons of their own, principles both of justice and economy,[21] and hardly need this bit of surprising added support from the principle of strong retributivism.

NOTES

1. I intend here no more than what is in the Model Penal Code definition: "A person acts recklessly with respect to a material element of an offense when he consciously disregards a substantial and unjustifiable risk that the material element exists or will result from his conduct. . . . Recklessness involves conscious risk creation."

2. *Legal Cause in the Law of Torts* (Columbus: Ohio State University Press, 1963), 3. The facts in Keeton's fictitious case are closely similar to those in the actual case of *Larrimore v. American Nat. Ins. Co.,* 184 Okl. 614 (1930).

3. *Ibid.,* 10 and *passim.*

4. The example is from a very helpful letter sent to me by Professor Sturgeon after I read an earlier version of this paper at Cornell in May 1969.

5. The example is just one of many in an extremely thorough criticism of an earlier version of this paper made by Professor Taurek, who was my official commentator at the Chapel Hill Colloquium in Philosophy, Oct. 17–19, 1969.

6. Sturgeon, letter, note 4.

7. *Ibid.*

8. *Ibid.*

9. "Responsibility and Language," *Australasian Journal of Philosophy, 33* (1955), 145.

10. *Laws and Explanation in History* (London: Oxford University Press, 1957), 100.

11. In unusual cases, two or three.

12. The distinction in common sense between a "causal factor" and "the cause" corresponds roughly—very roughly—to the technical legal distinction between "cause in fact" and "proximate cause."

13. A causal factor is an earlier necessary condition in at least the weaker sense of "necessary condition," *viz.,* a member of a set of jointly sufficient conditions whose presence was necessary to the sufficiency of the set; but it need not be necessary in the stronger sense, *viz.,* a necessary element in every set of conditions that would be jointly sufficient, as oxygen is necessary to every instance of combustion. Not all prior necessary conditions, of course, are genuine causal fac-

tors. Analytic connections ("But for his having been born, the accident would not have happened") are ruled out, and so are "incidental connections" (earlier speeding bringing one to a given point just at the moment a tree falls on the road). Unlike necessary conditions connected in a merely incidental way to results, causal factors are "necessary elements in a set of conditions generally connected through intermediate stages with it." See H. L. A. Hart and A. M. Honoré, *Causation in the Law* (Oxford: Clarendon Press, 1959), 114. See also Keeton, *Legal Cause,* footnote 2, 62.

14. Dray, *Laws and Explanation in History,* footnote 10, 99–100.

15. Perhaps a better example to illustrate this condition would be the following: Sir John is not a glutton. He has requested only one bowl of soup, but it is spilled by the hostess. But Sir John is at fault in agreeing to have even one bowl passed his way, since he knows, or ought to know, that this kind of soup always gives him indigestion, insomnia, allergic reactions, and hiccups. It is not only imprudent for him to taste it; it is also inconsiderate to his wife, who is usually kept awake all night by his restlessness. When his wife is kept awake after this party, *that* is his fault; but when the hostess spills the soup (which she should not have had to pass his way in the first place), that is *not* his fault.

16. If it is given that a particular "his fault" judgment on a particular occasion must single out one or a small number to be assigned the blame, then the concept of "his fault" can perhaps be understood to limit discretion by providing two additional necessary conditions to the triconditional analysis: (4) there is no other person to whom conditions (1)–(3) apply who was substantially more at fault than the present assignee(s); and (5) there is no other person to whom conditions (1)–(3) apply whose act was a more striking deviation from routine, or of a kind patently more manipulable, or otherwise a more "direct" or "substantial" cause. In the first soup-spilling example, Lady Mary satisfies conditions (1)–(3), but certainly not condition (4) and possibly not condition (5).

17. Hart and Honoré, *Causation in the Law,* footnote 13, 243.

18. Keeton, *Legal Cause in the Law of Torts,* footnote 2, 21.

19. This is not quite true of the system as described in the text, for a man's penalty in that system is determined in part by the number of demerits others incur and the total amount of compensable harm caused, both factors over which he has no control. Thus a man who accumulates one hundred demerits in 1970 might pay a smaller fine than he does in 1971 when he accumulates only seventy five. Instead of assigning demerits, therefore, the system would have to impose penalties directly, according to a fixed and invariant retributive scale. These funds could then go into a pool to compensate victims; and if, in a given year, they prove to be insufficient, they could be supplemented, say, by tax funds instead of stepped-up fines; for, on a purely retributive theory, there is one "fitting" penalty for a given degree of fault, and that uniquely correct quantum should be independent of the fluctuations of the marketplace.

20. "Retributivism" has served as the name of the large number of distinct theories of the grounds for justifiable punishment having little in common except that they are all nonutilitarian. The theories referred to in the text are those that hold that a certain degree of pain or deprivation is *deserved* by, or matches, fits, or suits, a certain magnitude of evil, quite apart from consequences. The emphasis is on fitness or proportion; and often the theorists invokes aesthetic analogies. Cf. the definitions of A. C. Ewing in *The Morality of Punishment* (London: Kegan Paul, Trench, Trubner & Co.,

1929), 13, and John Rawls, "Two Concepts of Rules," *The Philosophical Review,* 64 (1955), 4–5. G. E. Morre's "theory of organic unities" also suggests this kind of retributivism. But there are many other theories that have borne the retributive label which I do not refer to here—e.g., Hegel's theory of annulment; theories of punishment as putting the universe back in joint, or wiping clean the criminal's slate, or paying a debt to society, or expiating a sin, or expressing social denunciation, or demonstrating to the criminal the logical consequences of the universalization of his maxim, or satisfying the natural instinct for vengeance, or preventing the criminal from prospering while his victim suffers, or restoring a moral equilibrium between the "burdens" of conformity to law as against the "benefits" of disobedience; and even the "logical truism" of A. M. Quinton (*Analysis,* 14 [1954]).

21. E.g., the *benefit principle* (of commutative justice) that accidental losses should be borne according to the degree to which people benefit from an enterprise or form of activity; the *deep pocket principle* (of distributive justice) that the burden of accidental losses should be borne by those most able to pay in direct proportion to that ability; the *spread-it-out principle* that the cost of accidental losses should be spread as widely as possible "both interpersonally and intertemporally"; the *safety* or *loss-diminution principle* that the method of distributing losses that leads to the smallest net amount of loss to be distributed is the best one.

ROBERT E. KEETON and JEFFREY O'CONNELL

Why Shift Loss?*

Tort law is in one sense public law. It concerns public interest, its impact extends into the lives of all people in the community, and it reflects as faithfully as any branch of law—and more pervasively than most—fundamental assumptions of the social order it serves. Yet in another sense, tort law is distinctly private law. It focuses on private interests, and it concerns the rights and duties of private individuals toward each other. This two-party, plaintiff-defendant focus of tort law contrasts, for example, with labor law and business regulatory law, in which a special focus upon the public interest occurs through the involvement of governmental agencies such as the National Labor Relations Board and the Federal Trade Commission.

The question whether a money judgment should be awarded can be approached from the point of view of the public interest in the effect of awards generally. We shall consider that perspective in due course.[1] First we shall consider reasons for awards through a more limited focus on the reasons for shifting loss from one party to another. This approach emphasizes a comparison of the conduct and circumstances of a plaintiff and defendant in a particular case. What reasons for shifting loss between a plaintiff and a defendant might serve as guiding principles for an automobile claims system? What arguments, beyond simply a need for compensation, might be advanced for a decision that a defendant pay money damages to a plaintiff injured in a traffic accident?

*See Keeton and O'Connell, *Basic Protection for the Traffic Victim: A Blueprint for Reforming Automobile Insurance* (Boston: Little, Brown and Company, 1966), pp. 243–50. Reprinted by permission of the authors and the publisher. Footnotes have been renumbered.

1. FAULT

Fault is the justification most often given for shifting loss in automobile cases. Liability in such cases is ordinarily dependent upon proof of negligence of the defendant or someone for whose conduct he is accountable. A prima facie case of liability is ordinarily subject to defeat by proof of contributory negligence of the plaintiff or someone for whose conduct he is accountable. Thus it has been a commonly accepted principle that the loss is to be shifted from one who has innocently suffered it to another whose fault has caused it. Disagreement emerges, however, about the meaning of fault and the effect that should be given to different degrees of fault. Two questions about the principles of basing awards on fault point up this disagreement.

1. *Subjective or objective standards.* Should the minimum fault required for liability be conduct that is morally blameworthy, or is it enough that the conduct violates some objective standard of judgment that one cannot always be blamed for failing to meet? For example, should it be enough to impose liability that an elderly driver doing his best simply failed to respond as a younger and more nearly "normal" driver would have responded? Or must the elderly driver be personally culpable—for example, because he knew his responses were too slow for driving but drove anyway?

In the early development of the common law, in the view of many historians, objective standards of judgment regarding the causation of injury were preferred over standards that subjectively evaluated the culpability of an individual defendant in the light of his personal traits and the circumstances in which he acted.[2] According to one view of the matter, this penchant for objective standards continued even during the nineteenth century,[3] when the influence of personal culpability as a factor in tort law was most apparent. In twentieth century negligence law, increased reliance plainly has been placed on objective standards that impose liability on some whose conduct does not deserve moral censure. One might justify this use of objective standards on the basis of practicalities of administration.[4] It is after all much simpler to administer a hard-and-fast objective rule applicable to everyone in the same way than a rule subject to all the vicissitudes—both physical and psychological—of infinitely variable human beings. In addition, objective rules need not often in fact punish those who are not morally blameworthy since an objec-

tive standard, which is based on a norm, can be designed to approximate the capabilities of most.

Current use of objective standards cannot be justified, however, on the ground that in most cases only the morally blameworthy are punished. Some applications of modern negligence law quite regularly, rather than only occasionally, produce findings of negligence against defendants whom we would be unwilling to censure as morally blameworthy. A striking example of this is the liability of a mentally incompetent adult for harm caused by conduct falling below the standard of ordinary prudence. Whether such liability would be imposed was still a sharply disputed issue when the first two volumes of the *Restatement of Torts* were published in 1934.[5] Today it is clear that a mentally incompetent adult can be held liable for harm he causes accidentally and nonculpably.[6] A second instance in which negligence law deviates from a basis in moral fault was established at an earlier date. The standard of ordinary prudence has traditionally been applied to the adult below normal capacity but not so far below as to be considered incompetent. While disputes were being waged about the liability of the mentally incompetent, the liability of the barely competent for failure to measure up to ordinary prudence, in motoring cases as well as others, was generally accepted without question. These two examples, along with the widespread use of objective standards generally, demonstrate that tort law, including that segment of it applied in automobile cases, has by no means adhered rigidly to a principle of basing awards on moral fault.

b. *Contributory fault.* A second area of disagreement about basing awards on fault concerns the effect given to contributory fault. The common law rule is clear: Contributory fault is a complete bar to recovery. Latter-day developments working toward apportionment of damages on the basis of respective degrees of fault are commonly regarded as dubious departures from fault principles. The most obvious of these developments is the doctrine of comparative negligence. If, for instance, the defendant's fault is determined to be twice as great as that of the plaintiff, the plaintiff under this doctrine recovers two thirds of his losses and bears the remainder himself. A less obvious example of apportionment is an improper but prevalent practice of juries and some judges in states where contributory negligence is by law a complete bar to recovery. They often find for the plaintiff, despite strong evidence of contributory negligence, and then scale down the damages below the actual loss. Such developments toward apportionment, however, are arguably more consistent with the notion of basing awards on fault than is the doctrine that contributory negligence is a complete bar. They tend toward distributing the loss according to fault rather than placing all the loss on one of two negligent parties. One can consistently embrace such rules of apportionment while adhering tenaciously to fault as the central theme of his favored system.

Despite such disagreements, the principle of basing awards on fault was long so generally accepted as the essence of justice in tort cases that little was to be gained by asking why. Perhaps the only real justification for this principle is that most people believe fairness requires one who causes harm intentionally or carelessly to pay for it. It is important to note, however, that few automobile cases raise issues of intentional tort. Thus the consensus that it is fair to base awards on fault has been virtually a consensus on the desirability of basing awards on negligence. Negligence law, however, has never adhered rigidly to a principle of awards based on fault in the sense of morally blameworthy conduct. Moreover, further inroads upon the role of fault in automobile law have occurred in recent times, particularly as a consequence of the increasing use of liability insurance.

Thus, though "fault" is the explanation most frequently given for shifting losses in automobile cases, this explanation is acceptable only if it is understood that the word is used in a technical sense that does not imply culpability. Despite frequent statements that our lawmaking institutions are committed to a "fault" principle, it has become increasingly clear that culpability has by no means been an exclusive guide in formulating rules for automobile cases.

2. PUNISHMENT AND DETERRENCE

Closely related to fault as a reason for shifting loss are objectives associated with punishment—retribution, reformation, and deterrence. Retribution connotes an avenging condemnation that contributes to keeping the peace by appeasing the victim and reducing the likelihood that he or another acting on his behalf will resort to self-help. This is an objective of little significance in automobile cases. Reformation is concerned with improving the qualities of the individual whose substandard conduct has singled him out for attention. It is an objective of tort law in automobile cases only insofar as the deterrent effects of judgments of liability or denials of recovery work this result.

One way of serving the objective of deterrence is to award punitive damages. Such awards are common in cases of intentional torts and also are given occasionally in instances of risky conduct that is especially blameworthy though falling short of supporting a claim for intentional injury. Thus, in many jurisdictions punitive damages are allowed in cases involving injuries caused by the reckless conduct of the defendant—including reckless driving. In practice, however, the automobile cases in which punitive damages are awarded are relatively few.

Compensatory damages, as well as punitive damages, may have a deterrent effect by imposing economic burdens upon negligent drivers. Similarly, barring an injured person's claim because of his contributory negligence imposes an economic burden on him; the deterrent effect of this doctrine upon drivers as potential victims is, however, countered by withdrawal of the threat of liability to other victims who are also negligent. Deterrence is also served to some extent by the psychological and educational effect of adjudications of fault. Placing the stamp of fault on identifiable aspects of a driver's conduct is likely to influence significantly his future conduct, and that of others as well, if knowledge and understanding of the adjudication is spread through the community. To be effective in this way, however, the standard of adjudication must be one that can be understood and applied by drivers generally. Adjudications cannot serve to educate drivers about dangerous driving practices and to deter them from such conduct unless it is made clear exactly what practices are being condemned. Moreover, the condemned practices must be ones that a driver can avoid if he tries. In fact, however, the meaning of the negligence standard for particular fact situations in traffic cases is uncertain, and there has been a continuing tendency to brand as negligent more and more conduct that is neither avoidable nor morally culpable. These factors sharply reduce the educational and psychological effect of adjudications of negligence, which might otherwise deter dangerous driving. Under these circumstances, the deterrent effect of adjudications of negligence is a matter of speculation. It is our belief that the effect is rather limited and that the objective of deterrence has played a relatively small role in shaping rules of automobile tort law.

At first thought it might seem anomalous that deterrence has played such a minor role in automobile law, especially in view of the great number of motor vehicle accidents and the obvious desirability of reducing this toll. This circumstance, however, is easily explained. In the first place, deterrence looks more to the public interest in the effect of awards than to the private interest of parties to particular cases, and focusing on the contest between two parties after the accident tends to bring private interests rather than public interests into the foreground.[7] A second, more significant reason for the limited role deterrence has played in shaping automobile law is doubt about the effectiveness of personal liability, or the threat of personal liability, as a deterrent influence on drivers. Some observers have taken the view that most accidents are products of personal traits that cannot be controlled by threat of personal liability.[8] In addition, whatever the percentage of accidents attributable to accident-prone individuals may be, many other accidents, involving only normal drivers, are caused by circumstances that cannot be altered by deterrent influences on the driver. This is a consequence of rapidly changing traffic conditions and the quick responses that driving entails. Finally, it seems clear that the deterrent effect of possible liability is minimal compared to other deterrent influences such as fear of injury to oneself and fear of criminal sanctions. A driver who is not deterred from dangerous driving by such possibilities is not likely to be deterred by the added threat of liability for harm resulting to someone else.

3. BEARING AND DISTRIBUTING RISK

As we have seen, neither fault nor deterrence is a wholly adequate answer to the question: Why shift loss? What other answer is there? Implicit in relatively recent writings is the suggestion that the decision to award or deny compensation might be made to turn on one's capacity to bear or distribute the risks of loss. This suggestion takes a wide variety of forms.

Few, if any, advocates of the view that risk-bearing capacity should affect liability would suggest focusing sharply on a comparison between the two parties to a particular case, asking: Which of these two individuals is better able to bear the loss? If that question were asked, one apparent basis for selecting the party better able to bear the loss would be that the wealthier should be chosen. The trouble with this criterion, of course, is that it offends us to hold a man liable for no other reason than his wealth or "deep pocket." This is "one law for the rich and one for the poor," though with a reverse twist in that it favors the latter.

A more appealing variant of the notion that liability should be based on capacity to bear or distribute risk de-emphasizes such capacity of the plaintiff and the defendant considered individually. Instead, this more sophisticated view compares two classes of persons, one including the defendant and the other the plaintiff. This view centers attention, first, on the capacity of a group of similarly circumstanced individuals, engaging in the type of risky activity responsible for a loss, to distribute the risk among themselves and, second, on the fairness of requiring that each bear a share of the losses caused by such activity. This approach can serve, for example, to justify the liability without negligence imposed on those engaged in blasting or other especially dangerous activities. Those persons as a class are better able than victims as a class to make provision for distributing and bearing losses either by purchasing insurance or by self-insuring. This is not to say, of course, that an individual victim will never be better able than an individual dynamiter to provide for distributing and bearing losses. Nonetheless, the generality remains true for the two classes of persons.

This focus on classes and distribution is the only form in which a principle of awards based on capacity to bear or distribute risk is likely to gain acceptance in the foreseeable future. In this form the principle has in fact made very considerable headway already. It is particularly significant that tort liability insurance distributes losses of a prescribed type among the members of a large class of persons whose conduct creates risks of such losses. Thus, to recognize the legitimacy of tort liability insurance is implicitly to approve this principle of distributing losses among a class. The extent to which this principle is operative in present automobile claims systems becomes apparent with awareness of the large number of injured persons who are now compensated by tort liability insurance.

NOTES

1. See pp. 248–249, 259–272 in Keeton and O'Connell, *Basic Protection for the Traffic Victim.*
2. See 3 Holdsworth, A History of English Law 375 (5th ed. 1942); Plucknett, A Concise History of the Common Law 409–411 (2d ed. 1936) (reporting this view and challenging at least its more extreme expressions).
3. Holmes, The Common Law 107–111 (1881). See generally 2 Howe, Justice Oliver Wendell Holmes, The Proving Years 1870–1882, at 184–194 (1963).
4. Cf. Holmes, *supra* at 111.
5. Restatement of Torts § 283, caveat (1934).
6. Id. § 283 (Supp. 1948); 2 Restatement of Torts Second § 283B (1965).
7. See pp. 243–244 in Keeton and O'Connell, *Basic Protection for the Traffic Victim.*
8. See James & Dickinson, Accident Proneness and Accident Law, 63 Harv. L. Rev. 769, 779–789 (1950). Messrs. James and Dickinson believe, however, that large units such as trucking concerns are in a better position than the individual driver to reduce accidents. Threatening such units with liability will have a deterrent effect. Id. at 780.

GUIDO CALABRESI

The Fairness of the Fault System*

There is no doubt that some possible justifications for the fault system can be found in rather undifferentiated notions of justice. It strikes critic and community as unfair if a person injured by someone who has violated a moral code is not compensated, or if someone who violates a moral code and is hurt is compensated at the expense of an innocent party. It also strikes us as unfair if acts that we deem wrong and immoral go unpunished, quite apart from any issue of compensation of the possible victims of such acts. Such sentiments are often said to be the principal mainstays of the fault system.

From the critic's point of view, though these sentiments are valid they do not in reality support the fault system. They would only do so if the choice society faced was which of two or more parties directly involved in each accident should ultimately bear its costs. Then it would be true that if an injured party were not compensated by his faulty injurer, he would go uncompensated. It would also be true that any compensation of a faulty victim would in many cases have to come from the pocket of an innocent party. Such results would, of course, violate the critic's sense of justice. Similarly, it would seem unfair if in the absence of a fault system wrongdoers went unpunished. But to say that to avoid such results we must use the fault system is patent nonsense based on a simplistic bilateral view of the accident problem.

In reality, we live in a multilateral world with a whole population of injurers and victims. The degree of wrongdoing and the amount of damages vary throughout the population. In such a world, the question need not be whether it seems fair for an individual injurer to compensate an

*From *The Cost of Accidents* (New Haven: Yale University Press, 1970), pp. 301–08. Copyright © 1970 by Yale University. Reprinted by permission of the publisher. Footnotes have been renumbered.

individual victim; in our society it can be how much all injurers should pay, in relation to their individual wrongdoing, into a fund to compensate all victims in relation to their injuries and *their* wrongdoing. It is difficult to see why payments based on how faulty a particular injurer is in relation to *all* injurers would not seem fairer than payments depending only on his fault in relation to his victim's fault and to injuries suffered by that particular victim.[1] It is equally difficult to see why recoveries by a victim should depend on how his conduct compares with that of the individual who injured him, rather than how it compares with that of all individuals involved in accidents. Certainly the broader comparison is much more consistent with how we treat wrongdoing in areas other than accident law. Indeed, one could go even further and suggest that the fortuity of involvement in an accident is not a fair manner of determining payments. Would it not seem fairer for compensation of relatively worthy victims to come from a fund made up of payments by all who are at fault that is, who violate society's code) according to their faultiness, whether they are involved in an accident or not? This may not be feasible. But if it were, would it not be more just?[2]

The moment one accepts the notion that justice does not require that an individual injurer compensate his individual victim—and the allowance of insurance for faulty parties is clear indication that this notion is accepted—and the moment one realizes that wrongdoers can be punished for wrongful acts quite apart from whether they must compensate victims, it becomes very hard to see how the fault system can be supported on grounds of justice. Nevertheless, in a world that has abandoned the necessity of a one-to-one relationship between injurer and victim, attempts to support fault on grounds of justice have been made. They usually take the form of suggesting that individual determinations of fault in each accident situation result in the creation of actuarial insurance categories which reflect the risk of faulty conduct being undertaken by its members. This, it is argued, amounts to the same thing as making the least worthy pay for accident costs in relation to their blameworthiness.[3] Passing over the question of whether the fault system with all its defects actually gives rise to such fair insurance categories, one must still ask whether the

categories it creates are the best possible ones in this sense, and whether the fault system is the best way of creating these categories.

I shall not spend much time on these questions; they have been answered earlier. Where conduct can be defined as undesirable with sufficient precision, the best way to make those who engage in it pay (and the way that is most consistent with other areas of law) is to assess them directly and individually—through noninsurable fines if they can be caught regardless of accidents, and through noninsurable tort fines if they cannot. Where conduct cannot be defined with sufficient precision before an accident (if it makes sense to speak of fault at all in this area), our moral imperatives can be worked into actuarial categories— that is, we can charge different groups different amounts in relation to the relative desirability or blameworthiness of the activities in which they are engaged—and more efficiently and effectively through means other than the case-by-case adversary determinations of fault. What I said before still holds: Unless one considers the purpose of creating fair insurance categories to be not the deterrence of wrongful acts, nor the deterrence of accident costs, nor even the deterrence of both, but rather the deterrence of those accidents in which wrongful acts are involved, the insurance categories the fault system creates cannot be thought of as required by fairness.

It may be argued, however, that I have been too quick to suggest that our sense of justice does not require payments by each individual injurer to his victim on the basis of their relative faultiness and the injuries that resulted. Logic is all very well, and it may affect the critic's sense of justice, it may be said, but the community's sense of justice depends on other things. People may require a one-to-one world of payment and compensation even if logic and economics make it unnecessary and even, in some sense, unjust. And it is not enough to point out what ought to satisfy the public's sense of justice if people simply do not view it that way. I would argue, however, that as a practical matter our society is quite ready to abandon the view that justice requires individual injurers to pay their victims on the basis of fault and that moreover, wherever an adequate alternative has been presented, people have tended to prefer it to the traditional fault system.[4]

One need only look at the general acceptance of workmen's compensation and at jury verdicts that seem to ignore negligence on the plaintiff's part and lack of negligence on the defendant's to get some sense of this.[5] Similarly, the general acceptance of insurance strongly suggests that we do not worry too much about whether the individual faulty party pays his victim, so long as the victim is paid. Of course, we have not yet reached a point where we are willing lightheartedly to compensate a victim who is *really* faulty (that is, "wanton and willful"), though we do—with some misgivings—generally allow insurance against liability for wanton and willful misconduct, which is close to the same thing. The source of our misgivings is that we sometimes fear that noninsurable fines proportionate to the wrongdoing and adequate to achieve deterrence will not in fact be placed on wanton and willful wrongdoers. If they were, we would not be troubled by the fact that liability beyond such fines could be insured against. Analogously, were a wanton and willful victim jailed or made to pay a noninsurable fine that was in some way commensurate with his wrongdoing and with the specific deterrence we wished to obtain, we would hardly be troubled if the excess of the damages to him (and inevitably to his family) were compensated, so long as it did not appear that the burden ultimately fell on individual innocent parties. (Such punishment would be totally in keeping with what was needed to destroy a one-to-one, victim-injurer combat right in criminal law.)

I think one can fairly conclude that the traditional defense of the fault system based on the notion that justice requires that the costs of a particular accident be divided according to the relative faultiness of the parties involved has been given more importance in scholarly writings than it deserves. The critic and the public have been concerned, and rightly so, that burdens should not rest heavily on the relatively innocent while the relatively guilty go unpunished. But both the logical and practical indications are that this concern does not necessitate the fault system. It requires only that all parties involved in similar accidents divide all the injury costs according to a scale of relative guilt.

We could go further and perhaps do still better by fining wrongdoers, whether or not an accident occurs, to help pay for compensation of those who are injured, and even by taxing activities and people according to the likelihood of their involvement in accidents in which their conduct would be deemed blameworthy. The burden, whether called fine, tax, or insurance, would depend on the general wrongdoing or undesirability of the activity, not on the fortuity of an accident occurring to the particular parties. Once again, therefore, we return to the fact that the issue does not simply involve two parties to an accident, but involves, instead how we establish insurance categories fairly and how we punish individual wrongdoers justly and effectively. And the fault system cannot deal with that issue as well as a system that mixes noninsurable fines and limitations on undesirable activities with market deterrence in a way that is consistent with our spreading demands.

The basic difficulty with supporting the fault system on grounds of justice can be stated simply. Our sense of justice is made up of history and tradition, but it is also highly dependent on consistency within a moral context. While the fault system may be consistent with our moral history in blaming the relatively guilty party in any given accident situation, it leads to results that are totally inconsistent with other existing penalties because it imposes a burden that is substantially unrelated to wrongdoing or to penalties inflicted on similar wrongdoing in other areas of law. It also leads to results that are totally inconsistent with what occurs in many situations within accident law. Workmen's compensation is the prime example of this inconsistency, but the fact that the fault system allows insurance, and therefore in practice allows faulty injurers to spread the burden more easily than faulty victims, is an equally good instance. Indeed, these basic inconsistencies are additional reasons for the fault system's current instability, since even if the fault system meets some requirements of our sense of justice, its inconsistencies violate still more pressing requirements of that goal.

In the end, justice will support the fault system only if there is no sensible alternative system presented, only if the choice is solely between crushing one relatively wrongful and one relatively innocent party. It will not support the fault system in a world where faulty or undesirable acts, activities, and actors (whether victims or injurers) can be penalized according to their unde-sirability, and injured parties can be compensated according to their injury. I do not suggest for a moment by this that compensation should pre-dominate over deterrence, general or specific. I only suggest that the moral aims of our society, and even our undifferentiated sense of justice, can be better met through systems that concentrate on the deterrence and compensation we want than through an archaic system of liability that presumes an organization of society in which the best that can be done is to treat each accident instance as a universe unto itself.

The fault system may have arisen in a world where one injurer and one victim were the most that society could handle adequately, and in such a world it probably was a fairly good mixed sys-tem. It did a good job of meeting our combination of goals: general and specific deterrence, spread-ing, justice, and even efficiency.[6] But even assum-ing that such was the world in which the fault system grew, it is not today's world. Today acci-dents must be viewed not as incidental events linking one victim with one injurer, but as a more general societal problem. That is why the fault system has become totally inadequate for *any* of our mixed goals, even justice. It has become so inadequate, in fact, that other mixed systems can improve our record as far as *each* of these goals is concerned, even though at their extremes some of the goals are inconsistent with one another.

NOTES

1. This comparison assumes at least a comparative negli-gence system and therefore gives the devil more than his due by considering the fault system as though it were modified in ways that would make it fairer than the present all-or-nothing system.

2. Once again, this would not rule out making a differen-tiation between wrongdoing that resulted in serious harm and wrongdoing that did not, where the fact of serious harm could be taken to be an indication that the injurer was particularly faulty. It should be obvious, however, that in gauging faulti-ness the fact of serious harm is at most one of many factors. See generally supra notes 22, Chapter 6 and 5, Chapter II.

3. Compare and contrast Blum and Kalven, *Public Law Perspectives,* at 14, 66–67. Even if the fault system could be viewed as creating optimal insurance categories for injurers, it does not even pretend to do so for victims.

4. Whether prople say they prefer fault may depend on what question is put to them, of course. When asked: "It has been suggested, when there is an accident involving two cars, that each driver be paid damages by his own insurance com-pany without trying to determine if one driver was at fault. Does that sound like a good idea or a poor idea to you?" only 34% of those questioned in a Minnesota poll said the sugges-tion sounded like a good idea. "Minnesotans Reject Premises of Keeton-O'Connell Plan," 9 *For the Defense* 65 (November 1968).

5. See, e.g., Wilkerson v. McCarthy, 336 U.S. 53 (1949) and the Utah Supreme Court opinion it reversed, 112 Utah 300, 187 P.2d 188 (1947). Said Mr. Justice Jackson in dissent: "I am not unaware that even in this opinion the Court contin-ues to pay lip service to the doctrine that liability in these cases is to be based only upon fault,. But its standard of fault is such in this case as to indicate that the principle is without much practical meaning." 336 U.S. at 76. It is, of course, often difficult to say whether public acceptance of a new approach such as workmen's compensation precedes or results from its institution.

6. If there are only the two parties to choose from, fault can be defended as a fair mixture of such relevant consider-ations as allotting costs to the activities causing them, spread-ing, and providing a just standard of foreseeability. Even in their earliest days juries may well have tempered, somewhat clumsily, the worst evils of fault by modifying the verdict called for under the premises of fault if it resulted in extreme visible hardship or social dislocation. Also, Holmes' argument that efficiency dictates letting costs lie where they fall in the absence of fault may make sense when only the two "in-volved" parties are considered.

An interesting view of the historical development of the law of torts is presented in Jorgensen, "The Decline and Fall of the Law of Torts," soon to be published in the *American Journal of Comparative Law.*

H. L. A. HART

Negligence, Mens Rea and Criminal Responsibility*

'I didn't *mean* to do it: I just didn't think.' 'But you should have thought.' Such an exchange, perhaps over the fragments of a broken vase destroyed by some careless action, is not uncommon; and most people would think that, in ordinary circumstances, such a rejection of 'I didn't think' as an excuse is quite justified. No doubt many of us have our moments of scepticism about both the justice and the efficacy of the whole business of blaming and punishment; but, if we are going in for the business at all, it does not appear unduly harsh, or a sign of archaic of unenlightened conceptions of responsibility, to include gross, unthinking carelessness among the things for which we blame and punish. This does not seem like the 'strict liability' which has acquired such odium among Anglo-American lawyers. There seems a world of difference between punishing people for the harm they unintentionally but carelessly cause, and punishing them for the harm which no exercise of reasonable care on their part could have avoided.

So 'I just didn't think' is not in ordinary life, in ordinary circumstances, an excuse; nonetheless it has its place in the rough assessments which we make, outside the law, of the gravity of different offences which cause the same harm. To break your Ming china, deliberately or intentionally, is worse than to knock it over while waltzing wildly round the room and not thinking of what might get knocked over. Hence, showing that the damage was not intentional, but the upshot of thoughtlessness or carelessness, has its relevance as a mitigating factor affecting the quantum of blame or punishment.

*From *Oxford Essays in Jurisprudence*, ed. by A. G. Guest (Oxford: Oxford University Press, 1961), pp. 29–49, © 1961 Oxford University Press. Reprinted by permission of The Clarendon Press, Oxford. Reprinted in *Punishment and Responsibility: Essays in the Philosophy of Law* (New York and Oxford: Oxford University Press, 1968), pp. 136–57.

1. THE CRIMINAL LAW

These rough discriminations of ordinary life are worked out with more precision in the criminal law, and most modern writers would agree with the following distinctions and terminology. 'Inadvertent negligence' is to be discriminated not only from deliberately and intentionally doing harm but also from 'recklessness', that is, wittingly flying in the face of a substantial, unjustified risk, or the conscious creation of such a risk. The force of the word 'inadvertent' is to emphasize the exclusion both of intention to do harm and of the appreciation of the risk; most writers after stressing this point, then use 'negligence' simply for inadvertent negligence.[1] Further, within the sphere of inadvertent negligence, different degrees are discriminated: 'gross negligence' is usually said to be required for criminal liability in contrast with something less ('ordinary' or 'civil' negligence) which is enough for civil liability.

In Anglo-American law there are a number of statutory offences in which negligence, in the sense of a failure to take reasonable precautions against harm, unaccompanied either by intention to do harm or an appreciation of the risk of harm, is made punishable. In England, the Road Traffic Act, 1960, affords the best known illustration: Under section 10 driving without due care and attention is a summary offence even though no harm ensues. In other jurisdictions, criminal codes often contain quite general provisions penalizing those who 'negligently hurt' or cause bodily harm by negligence.[2] With due respect to one English authority, Dr. Turner (whose views are examined in detail below), the common law as distinct from statute also admits a few crimes,[3] including manslaughter, which can be committed by inadvertent negligence if the negligence is sufficiently 'gross'.[4] It is, however, the case that a number of English and American writers on criminal law feel uneasy about different aspects of negligence. Dr. Glanville Williams[5] thinks that its punishment cannot be justified on either a retributive or a deterrent basis. Professor Jerome Hall[6], who thinks that moral culpability is the basis of criminal responsibility and that punishment should be confined to 'intentional or reckless doing of a morally wrong act', disputes both the efficacy and justice of the punishment of negligence.

In this essay I shall consider a far more thoroughgoing form of scepticism. It is to be found in Dr. Turner's famous essay *The Mental Element in Crimes at Common Law*.[7] There he makes three claims; first, that negligence has no place in the Common Law as a basis of criminal responsibility, and so none in the law of manslaughter; secondly, the idea of degrees of negligence and so of gross negligence is nonsensical; thirdly (and most important), that to detach criminal responsibility from what he terms 'foresight of consequences', in order to admit negligence as a sufficient basis of such responsibility is necessarily to revert to a system of 'absolute' or strict liability in which no 'subjective element' is required.

Dr. Turner's essay has of course been very influential; he has reaffirmed the substance of its doctrines in his editions of both Kenny[8] and Russell.[9] This, however, is not my reason for submitting his essay to a fresh scrutiny so long after its publication. My reason is that his arguments have a general interest and importance quite independent of his conclusions about the place of negligence in the common law. I shall argue that they rest on a mistaken conception both of the way in which mental or 'subjective' elements are involved in human action, and of the reasons why we attach the great importance which we do to the principle that liability to criminal punishment should be conditional on the presence of a mental element. These misconceptions have not been sufficiently examined: yet they are I think widely shared and much encouraged by our traditional legal ways of talking about the relevance of the mind to responsibility. Dr. Turner's arguments are singularly clear and uncompromising; even if I am right in thinking them mistaken, his mistakes are illuminating ones. So much cannot always be said for the truths uttered by other men.

Before we reach the substance of the matter one tiresome question of nomenclature must be got out of the way. This concerns the meaning of the phrase *'mens rea'*. Dr. Turner, as we shall see, confines this expression to a combination of two elements, one of which is the element required if the accused's conduct is to be 'voluntary,' the other is 'foresight' of the consequences of conduct. Dr. Glanville Williams, although he deprecates the imposition of criminal punishment for negligence, does not describe it or (apparently) think of it, as Dr. Turner does, as a form of 'strict' or 'absolute' liability; nonetheless, though not including it under the expression 'strict liability', he excludes it from the scope of the term *'mens rea'*, which he confines to intention and recklessness. Judicial pronouncements, though no very careful ones, can be cited on either side.[10]

There is, I think, much to be said in mid-twentieth century in favour of extending the notion of *'mens'* beyond the 'cognitive' element of knowledge or foresight, so as to include the capacities and powers of normal persons to think about and control their conduct: I would therefore certainly follow Stephen and others and include negligence in *'mens rea'* because, as I shall argue later, it is essentially a failure to exercise such capacities. But this question of nomenclature is not important so long as it is seen for what it is, and not allowed either to obscure or prejudge the issue of substance. For the substantial issue is not whether negligence should be called *'mens rea'*; the issue is whether it is true that to admit negligence as a basis of criminal responsibility is *eo ipso* to eliminate from the conditions of criminal responsibility the subjective element which, according to modern conceptions of justice, the law should require. Is its admission tantamount to that 'strict' liability which we now generally hold odious and tolerate with reluctance?

2. VOLUNTARY CONDUCT AND FORESIGHT OF CONSEQUENCES

According to Dr. Turner, the subjective element required for responsibility for common law crimes consists of two distinct items specified in the second and third of three general rules which he formulates.

'Rule I—It must be proved that the conduct of the accused person caused the *actus reus*.

Rule II—It must be proved that this conduct was *voluntary.*

Rule III—It must be proved that the accused person *realised at the time* that his conduct would, or might *produce results of a certain kind,* in other words that he must have foreseen that certain consequences were likely to follow on his acts or omissions. The extent to which this foresight of the consequences must have extended is fixed by law and differs in the case of each specific crime. . . .'[11]

We shall be mainly concerned with Rule III—as is Dr. Turner's essay. But something must be said about the stipulation in Rule II that the accused's 'conduct' must be 'voluntary'. Dr. Turner himself considers that the truth contained in his Rule III has been obscured because the mental element requried to make conduct voluntary has not been discriminated as a separate item in *mens rea.* I, on the other hand, harbour the suspicion that a failure on Dr. Turner's part to explore properly what is involved in the notion of 'voluntary conduct' is responsible for much that seems to me mistaken in his further argument.

Certainly it is not easy to extract either from this essay or from Dr. Turner's editions of Kenny or Russell what is meant by 'conduct', and what the mental element is which makes conduct 'voluntary'. At first sight Dr. Turner's doctrine on this matter looks very like the old simple Austinian[12] theory that what we normally speak of and think of as actions (killing, hitting, et cetera) must be divided into two parts (*a*) the 'act' or initiating movement of the actor's body or (in more extreme versions) a muscular contraction, (*b*) the consequences of the 'act'; so that an 'act' is voluntary when and only when it is caused by a 'volition' which is a desire for the movement (or muscular contraction). But such an identification of Dr. Turner's 'conduct' with the Austinian 'act' (or movement of the body), and the mental element which makes it voluntary, with the Austinian volition or desire for movement, is precluded by two things. First, Dr. Turner says conduct includes not only physical acts but omissions. Secondly, though 'conduct' is always something less than the *actus reus* which is its 'result' (for example killing in murder) it is by no means confined by him as 'act' is by Austin to the mere initiating movement of the actor's body. Dr. Turner tells us that 'by definition *conduct,* as

such, cannot be criminal'.[13] He also explains that 'conduct is of course itself a series of deeds, each of which is the result of those which have come before it; but at some stage in this series a position of affairs may be brought into existence which the governing power in the state regards as so harmful as to call for repression by the criminal law. It is this point of selection by the law, this designation of an event as an *actus reus,* which for the purposes of our jurisprudence marks the distinction between *conduct* and *deed.* '[14]

About the mental element required to make conduct voluntary, Dr. Turner tells us[15] only that it is a 'mental attitude to [his] conduct' (as distinct from the consequences of conduct) and that if conduct is to be voluntary 'it is essential that the conduct should have been the result of the exercise of the will'. He does however give us examples of involuntary conduct in a list not meant to be exhaustive: 'For example, if *B* holds a weapon and *A,* against *B*'s will, seizes his hand and the weapon, and therewith stabs *C;* and possibly an act done under hypnotic suggestion or when sleep-walking or by pure accident. In certain cases of insanity, infancy and drunkenness the same defence may be successfully raised.'[16]

This account of voluntary conduct presents many difficulties. What is it for conduct to be 'the result of the exercise of the will'? Must the actor desire or will only the initiating movement of his body or the whole course of 'conduct' short of the point when it becomes an *actus reus?* And how does this account of the distinction between the course of conduct and the *actus reus* which is said to be its 'result' apply to omissions? The examples given suggest that Dr. Turner is here grossly hampered by traces of the old psychology of 'act' and 'volition', and no satisfactory account of what it is which makes 'conduct' voluntary or involuntary, capable of covering both acts and omissions can be given in his terminology of 'states of mind', or 'mental attitude'. What is required (as a minimum) is the notion of a general *ability* or *capacity* to control bodily movements, which is usually present but may be absent or impaired.

But even if we waive these difficulties, Dr. Turner's twofold account of *mens rea* in terms of 'voluntary conduct' and 'foresight of consequences' is at points plainly inadequate. It does not fit certain quite straightforward, familiar, cases where criminal responsibility is excluded because of the lack of the appropriate subjective element. Thus it does not, as it stands, accommodate the case of mistake; for a mistaken belief sufficient to exclude liability need not necessarily relate to *consequences;* it may relate to *circumstances* in which the action is done, or to the character or identity of the thing or person affected. Of course, Dr. Turner in his edition of Kenny, under the title of 'Mistake as a Defence at Common Law', discusses well-known cases of mistake such as *Levett's case,*[17] where the innocent victim was killed in mistake for a burglar, and says (in a footnote) that the subjective element in such cases relates to the agent's belief in the facts upon which he takes action.[18] He does not think this calls for a modification in his two-limbed general theory of *mens rea;* instead he adopts the view that such mistakes, since they do not relate to consequences, negative an element in the *actus reus* but do not negative *mens rea.* Besides this curious treatment of mistake, there is also the group of defences which Dr. Turner discusses in the same work under the heading of Compulsion,[19] which include marital coercion and duress *per minas.* Here, as the author rightly says, English law is 'both meagre and vague'; nonetheless, confidence in his general definition as an exhaustive account of *mens rea,* has led him into a curious explanation of the theoretical basis of the relevance to responsibility of such matters of coercion or duress. He cites first an example of compulsion in the case of 'a powerful man who, seizing the hand of one much weaker than himself and overcoming his resistance by sheer strength, forces the hand to strike someone else'.[20] Of this case he says, 'the defence ... must be that the mental element of volition is absent—the accused, in other words, pleads that his conduct was not voluntary'[21] and to explain this he refers back to the earlier account of voluntary conduct which we have discussed. The author then says that compulsion can take other forms than physical force,[22] and he proceeds to discuss under this head obedience to orders, marital coercion, duress, and necessity. It is, however, clear that such defences as coercion or duress (where they are admitted) lie quite outside the ambit of the definition of voluntary *conduct* given by Dr. Turner: they are not just different instances of *movement* which is not voluntary because, like

the case of physical compulsion or that of epilepsy cited earlier, the agent has no control over his bodily movements. Defences like duress or coercion refer not to involuntary *movements,* but, as Austin[23] himself emphasized, to other, quite different ways in which an *action* may fail to be voluntary; here the *action* may not be the outcome of the agent's free choice, though the *movements* of the body are not in any way involuntary.

So far, my objection is that Dr. Turner's formulation of the subjective element in terms of the two elements of voluntary conduct and foresight of consequences leads to a mis-assimilation of different cases; as if the difference between an action under duress and involuntary *conduct* lay merely in the kind of compulsion used. But in fact the definition of *mens rea* in terms of voluntary conduct *plus* foresight of consequences, leads Dr. Turner to great incoherence in the division of the ingredients of a crime between *mens rea* and *actus reus.* Thus in discussing the well-known case of *R.* v. *Prince*[24] (where the accused was found guilty of the statutory offence of taking a girl under 16 out of the possession of her father notwithstanding that he believed on reasonable grounds that she was over 16) Dr. Turner examines the argument that the word 'knowingly' might have been read into the section creating the offence (in which case the offence would not have been committed by the prisoner) and says "this change would merely not affect the *mens rea* of the accused person, but it would add another necessary fact to the *actus reus,* namely the offender's knowledge of the girl's age'.[25] But there is nothing to support[26] this startling view that where knowledge is required as an ingredient of an offence this may be part of the *actus reus,* not of the *mens rea,* except the author's definition of *mens rea* exclusively in terms of the two elements of 'voluntary conduct' and foresight of consequences'. If knowledge (the constituent *par excellence* of *mens rea*) may be counted as part of the *actus reus,* it seems quite senseless to insist on any distinction at all between the *actus reus* and the *mens rea,* or to develop a doctrine of criminal responsibility in terms of this distinction.

3. NEGLIGENCE AND INADVERTENCE

So far it is plain that, quite apart from its exclusion of negligence, the account of the subjective element required for criminal responsibility in terms of the two elements 'voluntary conduct' and 'foresight of consequences' is, at certain points, inadequate. Dr. Turner's arguments against the inclusion of negligence must now be examined. They are most clearly presented by him in connection with manslaughter. Of this, Dr. Turner says[27] 'a man, to be guilty of manslaughter, must have had in his mind the idea of bodily harm to someone'. On this view, what is known to English law as 'manslaughter by negligence' is misdescribed by the words; and Dr. Turner expressly says that judges in trying cases of manslaughter should avoid all reference to 'negligence' and so far as *mens rea* is concerned should direct the jury to two questions:

(i) Whether the accused's conduct was voluntary;
(ii) Whether at the time he either intended to inflict on someone a physical harm, or foresaw the possibility of inflicting a physical harm and took the risk of it.[28]

To treat these cases otherwise would, it is suggested, be to eliminate the element of *mens rea* as an element in criminal liability and to return to the old rule of strict or absolute liability.

In developing his argument Dr. Turner roundly asserts that negligence is a state of mind. It is 'the state of mind of a man who pursues a course of conduct *without adverting at all* to the consequences'.[29] Dr. Turner admits that this state of mind may be 'blameworthy'[30] and ground *civil* liability. Here it is important to pause and note that if anything is 'blameworthy', it is not the 'state of mind' but the agent's failure to inform himself of the facts and so *getting into* this 'state of mind'. But, says Dr. Turner, 'negligence, in its proper meaning of inadvertence cannot at Common Law amount to *mens rea*',[31] for 'no one could reasonably contend that a man, in a fit of inadvertence, could make himself guilty of the following crimes, "arson", "burglary", "larceny," "rape," "robbery" . . .'[32] This of course is quite true; but proves nothing at all, until it is independently shown that to act negligently is the same as to act in 'a fit of inadvertence'. Precisely the same comment applies to the use made by Dr. Turner of many cases[33] where the judges have insisted that for criminal responsibility 'mere inadvertence' is not enough.

It is of course most important at this point to realize that the issue here is *not* merely a verbal one which the dictionary might settle. Much more is at stake; for Dr. Turner is really attempting by the use of his definitions to establish his general doctrine that if a man is to be held criminally responsible he must 'have in his mind the idea of bodily harm to someone', by suggesting that the only alternative to this is the quite repugnant doctrine that a man may be criminally liable for mere inadvertence when, through no failure of his to which the criminal law could attach importance, his mind is a mere blank. This alternative indeed would threaten to eliminate the doctrine of *mens rea*. But we must not be stampeded into the belief that we are faced with this dilemma. For there are not just two alternatives; we can perfectly well both deny that a 'mere inadvertence' and also deny that he is only responsible if 'he has an idea in his mind of harm to someone'. Thus, to take the familiar example, a workman who is mending a roof in a busy town starts to throw down into the street building materials without first bothering to take the elementary precaution of looking to see that no one is passing at the time. We are surely not forced to choose, as Dr. Turner's argument suggests, between two alternatives: (1) Did he have the idea of harm in his mind? (2) Did he merely act in a fit of inadvertence? Why should we not say that he has been grossly negligent because he has failed, though not deliberately, to take the most elementary of the precautions that the law requires him to take in order to avoid harm to others?

At this point, a careful consideration is needed of the differences between the meaning of expressions like 'inadvertently' and 'while his mind was a blank' on the one hand, and 'negligently' on the other. In ordinary English, and also in lawyers' English, when harm has resulted from someone's negligence, if we say of that person that he has acted negligently we are not thereby *merely* describing the frame of mind in which he acted. 'He negligently broke a saucer' is not the same *kind* of expression as 'He inadvertently broke a saucer'. The point of the adverb 'inadvertently' *is* merely to inform us of the agent's psychological state, whereas if we say 'He broke it negligently' we are not merely adding to this an element of blame or reproach, but something quite specific, to wit, we are referring to the fact that the agent failed to comply with a standard of conduct with which any ordinary reasonable man *could* and *would* have complied: a standard requiring him to take precautions against harm. The word 'negligently', both in legal and in nonlegal contexts, makes an essential reference to an omission to do what is thus required: It is not a flatly descriptive psychological expression like 'his mind was a blank'.

By contrast, if we say of an agent 'He acted inadvertently', this contains no implications that the agent fell below any standard of conduct. Indeed it is most often proffered as an excuse. 'X hit Smith inadvertently' means that X, in the course of doing some other action (for example, sweeping the floor) through failing to attend to his bodily movements (for example, his attention being distracted) and, more strongly, not foreseeing the consequences, hit Smith.

There is of course a *connection,* and an important one, between inadvertence and negligence, and it is this. Very often if we are to comply with a rule or standard requiring us to take precautions against harm we must, before we act, acquire certain information: We must examine or *advert* to the situation and its possible dangers (for example, see if the gun we are playing with is loaded) and watch our bodily movements (handle the gun carefully if it is loaded). But this connection far from identifying the concepts of negligence and inadvertence shows them to be different. *Through* our negligence in not examining the situation before acting or in attending to it as we act, we may fail to realise the possibly harmful consequences of what we are doing and as to these our mind is in a sense a 'blank'; but the negligence does not, of course, consist in this blank state of mind but in our failure to take precautions against harm by examining the situation. Crudely put, 'negligence' is not the name of 'a state of mind' while 'inadvertence' is.

We must now confront the claim made by Dr. Turner that there is an absurdity in stipulating that a special (gross) degree of negligence is required. 'There can be no different degrees of inadvertence as indicating a state of mind. The man's mind is a blank as to the consequences in question; his realization of their possibility is nothing and there are no different degrees of nothing'.[34] This *reductio ad absurdum* of the notion of gross negligence depends entirely on the view that negligence is merely a name for a state of mind consisting in the absence of foresight of consequences. Surely we should require some-

thing more to persuade us to drop notions so firmly embedded, not only in the law, but in common speech, as 'very negligent', 'gross carelessness', a 'minor form of negligence'. Negligence is gross if the precautions to be taken against harm are very simple, such as persons who are but poorly endowed with physical and mental capacities can easily take.[35] So, in the workman's case, it was gross negligence not to look and see before throwing off the slates; perhaps it was somewhat less gross (because it required more exertion and thought) to have failed to shout a warning for those not yet in view; it was less gross still to have failed to have put up some warning notice in the street below.

4. NEGLIGENCE AND NORMAL CAPACITIES

At the root of Dr. Turner's arguments there lie, I think, certain unexamined assumptions as to what the mind is and why its 'states' are relevant to responsibility. Dr. Turner obviously thinks that unless a man 'has in his mind the idea of harm to someone' it is not only bad law, but morally objectionable, as a recourse to strict or absolute liability, to punish him. But here we should ask why, in or out of law courts, we should attach this crucial importance to foresight of consequences, to the 'having of an idea in the mind of harm to someone'. On what theory of responsibility is it that the presence of this particular item of mental furniture is taken to be something which makes it perfectly satisfactory to hold that the agent is responsible for what he did? And why should we necessarily conclude that in its absence an agent cannot be decently held responsible? I suspect, in Dr. Turner's doctrine, a form of the ancient belief that possession of knowledge of consequences is a sufficient and necessary condition of the capacity for self-control, so that if the agent knows the consequences of his action we are bound to say 'he could have helped it'; and, by parity of reasoning, if he does not know the consequences of his action, even though he failed to examine or think about the situation before acting, we are bound to say that he could not have helped it.

Neither of these views is acceptable. The first is not only incompatible with what large numbers of scientists and lawyers and plain men now believe about the capacity of human beings for self-control. But it is also true that there is nothing to compel us to say 'He could not have helped it' in *all* cases where a man omits to think about or examine the situation in which he acts and harm results which he has not foreseen. Sometimes we do say this and should say it; this is so when we have evidence, from the personal history of the agent or other sources, that his memory or other faculties were defective, or that he could not distinguish a dangerous situation from a harmless one, or where we know that repeated instructions and punishment have been of no avail. From such evidence we may conclude that he was unable to attend to, or examine the situation, or to assess its risks; often we find this so in the case of a child or a lunatic. We should wish to distinguish from such cases the case of a signalman whose duty it is to signal a train, if the evidence clearly shows that he has the normal capacities of memory and observation and intelligence. He may say after the disaster, 'Yes, I went off to play a game of cards. I just didn't stop to think about the 10.15 when I was asked to play'. Why, in such a case, should we say 'He could not help it—because his mind was a blank as to the consequences'? The kind of evidence we have to go upon in distinguishing those omissions to attend to, or examine, or think about the situation, and to assess its risks before acting, which we treat as culpable, from those omissions (for example, on the part of infants or mentally deficient persons) for which we do not hold the agent responsible, is not different from the evidence we have to use whenever we say of anybody who has failed to do something 'He could not have done it' or 'He could have done it'. The evidence in such cases relates to the general capacities of the agent; it is drawn, not only from the facts of the instant case, but from many sources, such as his previous behaviour, the known effect upon him of instruction or punishment, et cetera. Only a theory that mental operations like attending to, or thinking about, or examining a situation are somehow 'either there or not there', and so utterly outside our control, can lead to the theory that we are *never* responsible if, like the signalman who forgets to pull the signal, we fail to think or remember. And this theory of the uncontrollable character of mental operations would, of course, be fatal to responsibility for even the most cold-blooded, deliberate action performed by an agent with the maximum 'foresight'. For just as the signalman, inspired by Dr. Turner's argument, might say 'My mind was a blank' or 'I just forgot' or 'I just didn't think, I could not help not thinking' so the cold-blooded murderer might say 'I just decided to kill; I couldn't help deciding'. In the latter case we do not normally allow this plea because we know from the general history of the agent, and others like him, that he could have acted differently. This general evidence is what is relevant to the question of responsibility, not the mere presence or absence of foresight. We should have doubts, which now find legal expression in the category of diminished responsibility, even in the case of deliberate murder, if it were shown that in spite of every warning and every danger and without a comprehensible motive the agent had deliberately and repeatedly planned and committed murder. After all, a hundred times a day persons are blamed outside the law courts for not being more careful, for being inattentive and not stopping to think; in particular cases, their history or mental or physical examination may show that they could not have done what they omitted to do. In such cases they are not responsible; but *if* anyone is *ever* responsible for *anything,* there is no general reason why men should not be responsible for such omissions to think, or to consider the situation and its dangers before acting.

5. SUBJECTIVE AND OBJECTIVE

Excessive distrust of negligence and excessive confidence in the respectability of 'foresight of harm' or 'having the thought of harm in the mind' as a ground of responsibility have their roots in a common misunderstanding. Both oversimplify the character of the subjective element required in those whom we punish, if it is to be morally tolerable, according to common notions of justice, to punish them. The reason why, according to modern ideas, strict liability is odious, and appears as a sacrifice of a valued principle which we should make, if at all, only for some overriding social good, is not merely because it amounts, as it does, to punishing those who did not at the time of acting 'have in their minds' the elements of foresight or desire for muscular movement. These psychological elements are not *in themselves* crucial though they are important as aspects of responsibility. What is crucial is that those whom we punish should have had, when they acted, the normal capacities, physical and mental, for doing what the law requires and abstaining from what it forbids, and a fair opportunity to exercise these capacities. Where these capacities and opportunities are absent, as they are in different ways in the varied cases of accident, mistake, paralysis, reflex action, coercion, insanity, et cetera, the moral protest is that it is morally wrong to punish because 'he could not have helped it' or 'he could not have done otherwise' or 'he had no real choice'. But, as we have seen, there is no reason (unless we are to reject the whole business of responsibility and punishment) *always* to make this protest when someone who 'just didn't think' is punished for carelessness. For in some cases at least we may say 'he could have thought about what he was doing' with just as much rational confidence as one can say of any intentional wrongdoing 'he could have done otherwise'.

Of course, the law compromises with competing values over this matter of the subjective element in responsibility as it does over other matters. All legal systems temper their respect for the principle that persons should not be punished if they could not have done otherwise, that is, had neither the capacity nor a fair opportunity to act otherwise. Sometimes this is done in deference to genuine practical difficulties of proof; sometimes it represents an obstinate refusal to recognize that human beings may not be able to control their conduct though they know what they are doing. Difficulties of proof may lead one system to limit consideration of the subjective element to the question whether a person acted intentionally and had volitional control of his muscular movements; other systems may let the inquiry go further and, in relation to some offences, consider whether the accused had, owing to some external cause, lost the power of such control, or whether his capacity to control was 'diminished' by mental abnormality or disease. In these last cases, exemplified in 'provocation' and 'diminished responsibility', if we punish at all we punish *less,* on the footing that, though the accused's capacity for self-control was not absent its exercise was a matter of abnormal difficulty. He is punished in effect for a failure to exercise control; and this is also involved when punishment for negligence is morally justifiable.

The most important compromise which legal systems make over the subjective element consists in its adoption of what has been unhappily termed the 'objective standard'. This may lead to an individual being treated for the purposes of conviction and punishment as if he possessed capacities for control of his conduct which he did not possess, but which an ordinary or reasonable man possesses and would have exercised. The expression 'objective' and its partner 'subjective' are unhappy because, as far as negligence is concerned, they obscure the real issue. We may be tempted to say with Dr. Turner that just because the negligent man does not have 'the thought of harm in his mind', to hold him responsible for negligence is *necessarily* to adopt an objective standard and to abandon the 'subjective' element in responsibility. It then becomes vital to distinguish this (mistaken) thesis from the position brought about by the use of objective standards in the application of laws which make negligence criminally punishable. For, when negligence is made criminally punishable, this itself leaves open the question: whether, before we punish, both or only the first of the following two questions must be answered affirmatively:

(i) Did the accused fail to take those precautions which any reasonable man with normal capacities would in the circumstances have taken?

(ii) Could the accused, given his mental and physical capacities, have taken those precautions?

One use of the dangerous expressions 'objective' and 'subjective' is to make the distinction between these two questions; given the ambiguities of those expressions, this distinction would have been more happily expressed by the expressions 'invariant' standard of care, and 'individualised conditions of liability'. It may well be that, even if the 'standard of care' is pitched very low so that individuals are held liable only if they fail to take very elementary precautions against harm, there will still be some unfortunate individuals who, through lack of intelligence, powers of concentration or memory, or through clumsiness, could not attain even this low standard. If our conditions of liability are invariant and not flexible, that is, if they are not adjusted to the capacities of the accused, then some individuals will be held liable for negligence though they could not have helped their failure to comply with the standard. In *such* cases, indeed, criminal responsibility will be made independent of any 'subjective element', since the accused could not have conformed to the required standard. But this result is nothing to do with negligence being taken as a basis for criminal liability; precisely the same result will be reached if, in considering whether a person acted intentionally, we were to attribute to him foresight of consequences which a reasonable man would have foreseen but which he did not. 'Absolute liability' results, not from the admission of the principle that one who has been grossly negligent is criminally responsible for the consequent harm even if 'he had no idea in his mind of harm to anyone', but from the refusal in the application of this principle to consider the capacities of an individual who has fallen below the standard of care.

It is of course quite arguable that no legal system could afford to individualize the conditions of liability so far as to discover and excuse all those who could not attain the average or reasonable man's standard. It may, in practice, be impossible to do more than excuse those who suffer from gross forms of incapacity, to wit, infants, or the insane, or those afflicted with recognizably inadequate powers of control over their movements, or who are clearly unable to detect, or extricate themselves, from situations in which their disability may work harm. Some confusion is, however, engendered by certain inappropriate ways of describing these excusable cases, which we are tempted to use in a system which, like our own, defines negligence in terms of what the reasonable man would do. We may find ourselves asking whether the infant, the insane, or those suffering from paralysis did all that a reasonable man would *in the circumstances* do, taking 'circumstances' (most queerly) to include personal qualities like being an infant, insane or paralyzed. This paradoxical approach leads to many difficulties. To avoid them we need to hold apart the primary question (1) What *would* the reasonable man with ordinary capacities have done in these circumstances? from the second question (2), *Could* the accused with *his* capacities have done that? Reference to such factors as lunacy or disease would be made in answering only the second of these questions. This simple, and surely realistic, approach avoids difficulties which the notion of individualizing the standard of care has presented for certain writers; for these difficulties are usually created by the mistaken assumption that the only way of allowing for individual incapacities is to treat them as part of the 'circumstances' in which the reasonable man is supposed to be acting. Thus Dr. Glanville Williams said that if 'regard must be had to the make-up and circum-

stances of the particular offender, one would seem on a determinist view of conduct to be pushed to the conclusion that there is no standard of conduct at all. For if every characteristic of the individual is taken into account, including his heredity the conclusion is that he could not help doing as he did.'[36]

But 'determinism' presents no special difficulty here. The question is whether the individual had the capacity (inherited or not) to act otherwise than he did, and 'determinism' has no relevance to the case of one who is accused of negligence which it does not have to one accused of intentionally killing. Dr. Williams supports his arguments by discussion of the case of a motorist whom a blow or illness has rendered incapable of driving properly. His conclusion, tentatively expressed, is that if the blow or illness occurred long ago or in infancy he should not be excused, but if it occurred shortly before the driving in respect of which he is charged he should. Only thus, it seems to him, can any standard of conduct be preserved.[37] But there seems no need to make this extraordinary distinction. Again, the first question which we should ask is: What *would* a reasonable driver with normal capacities have done? The second question is whether or not the accused driver had at the time he drove the normal capacity of control (either in the actual conduct of the vehicle in driving or in the decision to engage in driving). If he was incapable, the date recent or otherwise of the causal origin of the incapacity is surely beside the point, except that if it was of long standing, this would suggest that he knew of it and was negligent in driving with that knowledge.

Equally obscure to me are the reasons given by Dr. Williams for doubting the efficacy of punishment for negligence. He asks, 'Even if a person admits that he occasionally makes a negligent mistake, how, in the nature of things, can punishment for inadvertence serve to deter?[38] But if this question is meant as an argument, it rests on the old, mistaken identification of the 'subjective element' involved in negligence with 'a blank mind', whereas it is in fact a failure to exercise the capacity to advert to, and to think about and control, conduct and its risks. Surely we have plenty of empirical evidence to show that, as Professor Wechsler has said, 'punishment supplies men with an additional motive to take care before acting, to use their faculties, and to draw upon their experience.'[39] Again there is no difficulty here peculiar to negligence, though of course we can doubt the efficacy of any punishment to deter any kind of offence.

I should add (out of abundant caution) that I have not been concerned here to advocate punishing negligence, though perhaps better acquaintance with motoring offences would convert me into a passionate advocate. My concern has been to show only that the belief that criminal responsiblity for negligence is a form of strict or absolute liability, rests on a confused conception of the 'subjective element' and its relation to responsibility.

NOTES

1. This terminology is used by Glanville Williams, *Criminal Law, The General Part* (2nd edn.), Ch. III, p. 100 et seq., and also by the American Law Institute Draft Model Penal Code s. 2.0.2 (Tentative Draft 4, p. 26 and Comment, ibid., pp. 126–7). So, too, Cross and Jones, *Introduction to Criminal Law* (5th edn.). pp. 42–45.

2. See for these and other cases Glanville Williams op. cit., p. 120 n. 22.

3. Other common law crimes commonly cited are non-repair of a highway and public nuisance. Besides these there are controversial cases including certain forms of murder (*R. v. Ward*(1956) 1 Q.B. 351, Cross and Jones, op. cit., pp. 48–52 and *D. P. P. v. Smith* (1961), A.C. 290. These cases some writers consider as authorities for the proposition that criminal negligence is sufficient malice for the crime of murder. There are, however, reasons for doubting this interpretation of these cases.

4. See Cross and Jones, *Introduction to Criminal Law*, pp. 152–5. The American Law Institute accepts this view of the English law of manslaughter (Tentative Draft 9, p. 50) but advocates treatment of negligent homicide as an offence of lower degree than manslaughter. Glanville Williams, *Criminal Law*, p. 106 (s. 39) after stating that manslaughter can be committed by inadvertent negligence 'for the accused need not have foreseen the likelihood of *death*' says that the 'ordinary formulations' leave in doubt the question whether foresight of some bodily harm (not necessarily serious injury or death) is required for manslaughter. He describes (op. cit., p. 108) as 'not altogether satisfactory' the cases usually taken to establish that no such foresight is required viz. *Burdee* (1916), 86 L. J. K. B. 871, 12 Cr. App. Rep. 153; *Pittwood* (1902), 19 T. L. R. 37; *Benge* (1865), 4 F. & F. 504; *John Jones* (1874), 12 Cox 628. Of *Bateman* (1925), 28 Cox 33; 19 Cr. App. Rep. 8 he says 'it may be questioned whether this does not extend the law of manslaughter too widely' and thinks in spite of *Andrews* v. *D. P. P.* (1937), A.C. 576 that the issue is still open for the House of Lords. (op. cit., pp. 107, 110).

5. *Criminal Law*, pp. 122–3.

6. *Principles of Criminal Law*, pp. 366–7, and *43 C. L. R.*, p. 775. Professor Herbert Wechsler (Reporter in the A. L. I. Draft Model Penal Code) rejects this criticism and holds that punishment for conduct which inadvertently creates improper risks 'supplies men with an additional motive to take care before acting, to use their faculties and to draw on their experience in gauging the potentialities of contemplated conduct', Tentative Draft 4, pp. 126–7, and Tentative Draft 9, pp. 52–53.

7. *The Modern Approach to Criminal Law* (1945), p. 195.

8. Kenny's *Outlines of Criminal Law* (19th edn.), pp. 37–40.

9. Russell on Crime (12 edn.), pp. 43–44, 52, 62–66.

10. See Glanville Williams, *Criminal Law*, p. 102, n. 8. Examples on each side are Shearman J. in *Allard* v. *Selfridge*, (1925) 1 K. B. 129, at p. 137. ('The true translation of that phrase is criminal intention, or an intention to do the act which is made penal by statute or by the common law') and Fry L. J. in *Lee* v. *Dangar, Grant & Co.,* (1892) 2 Q. B. 337, at p. 350. 'A criminal mind or that negligence which is itself criminal'. See also for a more discursive statement *R. v. Bateman* (1925), 19 Cr. App. Rep. 8 *per* Hewart C. J.

11. *The Modern Approach to Criminal Law* (1945), p. 199.

12. Austin, *Lectures on Jurisprudence* (5th edn.), Lecture XVIII.

13. *Modern Approach to Criminal Law*, p. 240.

14. Ibid., p. 239.

15. Kenny (19th edn.), p. 30.

16. *The Modern Approach to Criminal Law* (1945), p. 204. See the further examples suggested in Kenny (19th edn.), p. 29: viz., when harm 'results from a man's movements in an epileptic seizure, or while suffering from St. Vitus's Dance'.

17. (1638), Cro. Car. 538.

18. Kenny, *Outlines of Criminal Law*, (19th edn.), p. 58 n. 3.

19. Ibid., p. 66.

20. Kenny, *Outlines of Criminal Law*.

21. Ibid.

22. Ibid.

23. Lectures on Jurisprudence, p. 417. Notes to Lecture XVIII, 'Voluntary—Double Meaning of the word Voluntary'.

24. (1875), L. R. 2 C. C. R. 154.

25. In 'The Mental Element in Crimes at Common Law': *The Modern Approach to Criminal Law* (1945), op. 219.

26. There is plain authority against it: see *R. v. Tolson* (1889), 23Q.B.D. 168 *per* Stephen J. 'The mental element of most crimes is marked by one of the words "maliciously", "fraudulently", "negligently", or "knowingly".'

27. *The Modern Approach to Criminal Law* (1945), p. 228.

28. Ibid., p. 231.

29. Ibid., p. 207.

30. Ibid., p. 208.

31. Ibid., p. 209.

32. Ibid.

33. E.g., *R. v. Finney* (1874), 12 Cox 625. See also *R. v. Bateman, Andrews* v. *D. P. P.,* and others discussed op. cit., pp. 216–17.

34. *The Modern Approach to Criminal Law*, p. 211.

35. 'It is such a degree of negligence as exludes the loosest degree of care' quoted by Hewart C. J. in *R. v. Bateman* (1925), 19 Cr. App. Rep. 8.

36. *Criminal Law: The General Part* (1st edn.), p. 82. In the second edition (p. 101) this passage is replaced by the following: 'But if the notional person by whom the defendant is judged is invested with every characteristic of the defendant, the standard disappears. For, in that case, the notional person would have acted in the same way as the defendant acted."

37. op. cit. (1st edn.), p. 84. This passage is omitted from the second edition.

38. op. cit. (2nd edn.), p. 123.

39. loc. cit. *supra* p. 138, 6.

HERBERT PACKER

Strict Liability*

When we leave the area of the dilemmatic choice, which comprises what is technically known as the law of justification and excuse, "mistake" becomes the operational signal for invoking a vast range of excuses. Indeed, the idea of mistake underlies the whole question of *mens rea* or the mental element, with the dubious exception of the insanity defense (which, as I shall argue subsequently, is most usefully viewed as something other than a problem of *mens rea*). When we say that a person, whose conduct in other respects fits the definition of a criminal offense, lacked the requisite *mens rea,* what we mean is that he made a mistake about some matter of fact or value that constitutes a material element of the offense.

A few examples will show that the question of mistake pervades the entire criminal law. Arthur is charged with homicide and claims that he thought the man he shot at was really a deer. Barry is charged with stealing a raincoat that he claims he thought was really abandoned property. Charlie is charged with possessing heroin; he says he thought the white powder in the packet was talcum powder. Dan is charged with bigamy; he says that he thought his first wife had divorced him. Evan is charged with statutory rape; he claims the girl told him she was over the age of consent. Frank is charged with selling adulterated drugs; he says that so far as he knew the drugs conformed to requirements. George is charged with failing to file his income tax return; he says that he didn't know about the income tax. Harry is charged with carrying a concealed weapon; he claims he didn't know it was against the law to do so.

*Reprinted from *The Limits of the Criminal Sanction* by Herbert L. Packer, with the permission of the publishers, Stanford University Press. © 1968 by Herbert L. Packer. This section of Chapter Six appears at pp. 121–31. Footnotes have been renumbered.

Under existing law Arthur, Barry, and probably Charlie will be listened to. That is, the trier of fact will decide whether each of them really did make the mistake he claims to have made. If it is believed that he did and (ordinarily) if the mistake is thought to be "reasonable," no crime has been committed. As recently as fifteen years ago Dan's mistake was simply ignored; however, he might be excused in some jurisdictions today if his claim is believed. Evan is probably out of luck, although there is a developing trend in his favor. Frank, George, and Harry might just as well save their breath; their exulpatory claim of mistake will not be listened to.

If all this seems confusing and arbitrary, that is only because it is confusing and arbitrary. Traditional criminal law has fallen into the deliberate, and on occasion inadvertent, use of strict liability or liability without fault. For our purposes strict liability can be defined as the refusal to pay attention to a claim of mistake. In a behavioral-utilitarian view of the criminal law there is, as we have seen, good reason to ignore the defense of mistake. But if the preventive goal of criminal law is to be limited by the negative implication of the retributive position, as we have concluded it should, then mistakes must be considered and, if found relevant and believable, accepted as excuses.

The story of how traditional law slipped into an easy reliance on strict liability, to the detriment of its essential doctrinal content, need not concern us here. However, it may be instructive to consider one famous case in which the Supreme Court of the United States contributed to the erosion of *mens rea,* because it shows that important values may be sacrificed as easily through inadvertence as through design. The narrow issue in *United States* v. *Dotterweich*[1] was whether the president of a company that shipped misbranded or adulterated products in interstate commerce was a "person" who had done so under the Food, Drug, and Cosmetic Act, notwithstanding the fact that he had nothing to do with the shipment. Buffalo Pharmacal Company, a drug wholesaler, purchased drugs from manufacturers, repackaged them under its own label, and shipped them on order to physicians. Dotterweich and the company were prosecuted for two interstate shipments alleged to be adulterated or misbranded. The first consisted of a cascara compound that conformed to specifications but whose label included reference to an ingredient that had, a short time before, been dropped from the National Formulary. One infers that the old labels were still being used. The other shipment was of digitalis tablets that were less potent than their label indicated. The company did not manufacture these tablets, but merely repackaged them under its own label. So far as appears, there was no way short of conducting a chemical analysis of the tablets for their seller to know that they were not what their label declared them to be. The jury found Dotterweich guilty but for "some unexplainable reason" disagreed as to the company's guilt. Dotterweich was sentenced to pay a fine and to "probation for 60 days." Under the statute he could have been sentenced to a year's imprisonment. The court of appeals reversed, on the ground that the statute should not be read as applying to an individual agent of the principal (here the company), since only the principal was in a position to exculpate itself by obtaining a guaranty of nonadulteration from its supplier. Since there appeared to be no statutory basis for distinguishing between a high corporate agent, like Dotterweich, who might have obtained such a guaranty, and a shipping clerk or other menial employee who might have actually made the forbidden shipment and who would not necessarily be covered by the statutory provision protecting people who obtained a guaranty, a divided court of appeals concluded that Dotterweich's conviction could not stand.[2]

It will be noticed that the answer to the question whether this was indeed a "forbidden shipment" was dealt with rather cursorily. The court of appeals held merely that "intention to violate the statute" was not an element of the offense. The shipments in question were illegal under the statute, and that was that. Whether Dotterweich (or anyone else) had failed to take reasonable precautions was not put to the jury. Negligence as a possible mode of culpability was overlooked.

The court of appeals opinion had at least the merit of keeping separate two questions that it would confound analysis to blur: first, whether whoever was responsible for the shipment could be held criminally liable, notwithstanding the absence of culpability on his part (the issue of "strict liability"); and second, whether Dotterweich could be held criminally liable, notwithstanding his own lack of connection with the shipment (the issue of "vicarious liability"). It is obvious that the second issue is dependent on the first; if no one committed a crime, there was no crime for which Dotterweich could have been held vicariously liable. The underlying issue was whether the statute imposed strict liability.

The opinion for the Court, by Mr. Justice Frankfurter, did not make the essential distinction between the issues of strict and vicarious liability. It is not paraphrasing unfairly to say that the Court held that since the liability was strict it was also vicarious. But the premise that the Act dispensed with *mens rea* and imposed strictly liability was assumed rather than examined:

The prosecution to which Dotterweich was subjected is based on a now familiar type of legislation whereby penalties serve as effective means of regulation. Such legislation dispenses with the conventional requirement for criminal conduct—awareness of some wrongdoing. In the interest of the larger good it puts the burden of acting at hazard upon a person otherwise innocent but standing in responsible relations to a public danger. *United States* v. *Balint*, 258 U.S. 250. And so it is clear that shipments like those now in issue are "punished by the statute if the article is misbranded [or adulterated], and that the article may be misbranded [or adulterated] without any conscious fraud at all. It was natural enough to throw this risk on shippers with regard to the identity of their wares. . . ."[3]

It is well to note that this offhand passage is precisely all that the opinion had to say on the *mens rea* issue, despite the fact that this was the first time the Supreme Court had before it the construction of the mental element in this important federal criminal statute. It is also well to note the primitive and rigid view of *mens rea* that the quoted passage reflects. "Conscious fraud" and "awareness of some wrongdoing" are impossibly high standards, the opinion seems to say, and that leaves only strict liability. Did the company or its responsible agents behave recklessly or negligently with respect to the possibility that these shipments were not up to standard? Perhaps it was inexcusably careless not to have destroyed the old cascara labels and prepared new ones. Perhaps not. But could not the lower courts have been told that this question should be submitted to the jury? The case posed an obvious opportunity for framing a more discriminating set of standards for the mental element, but the opportunity was forgone.

Next, let us consider the areas in which the minimal doctrinal content of the criminal law has been eroded. There are four categories to be considered in determining how responsive the traditional common law has been to the notion of *mens rea*. These may be characterized as:

(1) Basic offenses dispensing in whole or in part with *mens rea*.
(2) Negligence as a mode of culpability.
(3) The barrier of *ignorantia legis*.
(4) Public welfare offenses.

Basic Offenses. The usual examples are sexual offenses, notably "statutory rape" and bigamy. These are universally regarded, in their traditional manifestations, as examples of strict liability in the criminal law. They serve as the basis for an assertion that might otherwise seem surprising, that there is no adequate operational distinction between offenses that dispense entirely with *mens rea* and offenses that dispense with *mens rea* only partially, or with respect to only one material element of the offense. Indeed, there is no such thing as a "strict liability" offense except as a partial rather than a complete discarding of *mens rea,* for there is always some element of any offense with respect to which a mental element is attached. In both the statutory rape and bigamy situations, it is the exclusion of *mens rea* with respect to the "circumstance" element of the offense that results in the imposition of strict liability: in the case of statutory rape, the circumstance that the girl is under the age of consent; in the case of bigamy, the circumstance that one or both of the parties is not legally free to remarry. Although there is an encouraging trend of contrary decisions in the bigamy field, it probably remains the majority rule in this country that a

good-faith belief that one is legally free to remarry is not a defense to a charge of bigamy. Indeed, this view apparently has constitutional sanction. In the area of statutory rape, the strength of the traditional strict liability view has not been appreciably diminished.

These examples are familiar ones. It might perhaps be thought that they represent rather unusual exceptions to a generally pervasive principle of applicability of *mens rea.* Actually, the contrary is true. Two conspicuous examples arise in the area of homicide. Both the felony-murder and the misdemeanor-manslaughter rules, insofar as they have independent force and are not simply instances of the more general operation of homicide doctrines, reflect the imposition of strict liability as to the homicidal result. If a robber is automatically to be held for the death of an accomplice who is shot by their intended victim, or if a person commits a battery that leads to the unforeseen and reasonably unforeseeable result of the victim's death, liability for the homicide rests upon the refusal to consider *mens rea* as to the result.

The standard rejoinder to the argument that strict liability is being imposed in such a situation is that habitually given in the sex-offense cases. It comes down to the assertion that, since the underlying conduct is "wrongful," the actor must take all the consequences of that conduct, whether or not he foresaw or desired them. But it begs the question to assert that one who has intercourse with an underage girl, even though he is ignorant of her age, is to be held for statutory rape because his underlying conduct is "wrongful." The question is whether he should be held for an offense to whose elements he did not advert as well as for an offense to whose elements he did advert. The fact that various limitations have been worked out to prevent some of the most absurd consequences of rigid adherence to this "at peril" notion should not distract attention from its incompatibility with the spirit of *mens rea.*

NEGLIGENCE

If a man purposely or recklessly brings about a forbidden harm, we have no hesitation in saying that he had the requisite *mens rea* with respect to his conduct. But if he negligently brings about the forbidden harm, a different problem is presented.

Negligence is not readily transformable into a state of mind. It is, by definition, the absence of a state of mind. Negligence is, in short, an extension rather than an example of the idea of *mens rea* in the traditional sense.

There are those who argue that negligence as a mode of culpability has no place in the criminal law, because the threat of punishment for causing harms inadvertently must be either inefficacious or unjust or both.[4] Whatever the merits of this philosophic position, it is plain that negligence has a very strong foothold in the criminal law. It finds its most explicit formulation in the statutes penalizing negligent homicide in the driving of an automobile. But its hold on the criminal law is far more pervasive than this. Negligence suffices as a mode of culpability whenever the question asked with respect to the actor's perception is not whether he knew but whether he should have known. In the case of homicide, the difference between negligent inadvertence to the risk of death and conscious advertence to that risk is, very roughly speaking, the dividing line between manslaughter and murder. But beyond this, murder itself is sometimes treated as an offense that may be committed negligently, either by applying an external standard to the actor's perception of the risk or by applying an external standard to his perception of the basis for some excuse, such as self-defense. To the extent that we subject persons to liability for this most serious of offenses on the basis of an external standard, we are retreating very far from a doctrinal purist's stance. But even if murder by negligence is rejected as anomalous, we must face the challenge that negligence as a mode of culpability cannot be reconciled with the principle of *mens rea*.

It has been suggested that negligence has closer affinities with strict liability than it has with those modes of culpability that reflect subjective awareness on the part of the actor.[5] However, there are important differences between a legislative determination that all instances of a certain kind of conduct are unacceptable and a jury's determination that a particular instance of such conduct falls below a previously established community standard. The decisive difference is that the legislature cannot and does not foresee the infinite variation of circumstance that may affect the jury's view of a particular case. If there is an issue of fault for the jury to adjudicate, the line between

subjective and objective fault—between "he knew" and "he should have known"—is a very shadowy one. Often, a judgment that "he knew" will simply reflect an inference from "he should have known." Conversely, a judgment that "he should have known" may contain the further unarticulated statement: "and we think he probably did know but we aren't sure enough to say so." There simply isn't a definite line between imputations of subjective awareness and those of objective fault: They are points on a continuum. The jury's opportunity to make an individualized determination of fault may focus indifferently upon one or the other. Putting the issue in this light, it seems plausible for the criminal law to employ a negligence standard on occasion, although not as a matter of course, without being charged with having abandoned the substance of *mens rea*. To put it another way, it seems to me proper to view negligence as an extension of rather than a departure from the values associated with the *mens rea* concept.

IGNORANTIA LEGIS

The principle that ignorance of the law is no excuse is deeply embedded in our criminal law. If the criminal law faithfully reflected prevalent community standards of minimally acceptable conduct, there would be no difficulty in reconciling the principle *ignorantia legis* with the requirements of *mens rea*. Yet, the proliferation of minor sumptuary and regulatory offenses, many of them penalizing conduct under circumstances in which the fact of illegality can scarcely be known to a first offender, creates a sharp problem. Sometimes a legislature specifies that awareness of the law's requirement is a necessary ingredient of guilt. More often it does not. Courts rarely remedy the deficiency by fashioning a doctrine that distinguishes sensibly between innocent and guilty conduct in contravention of an esoteric legal proscription.

It has been suggested by the framers of the Model Penal Code that a limited defense should be available to persons accused of crime if they can show a good-faith belief that their conduct does not legally constitute an offense, owing to lack of publication or reasonable availability of the enactment.[6] It is not entirely clear how broad this defense is meant to be. I should like to read it as establishing a negligence standard for the defense of ignorance or mistake of law. If read (or expanded) in this way, the proposal would go a long way toward resolving the *ignorantia legis* paradox. If we assume that an actor is unblameworthy in failing to know that his conduct violates a particular enactment (a condition that will ordinarily obtain only if either he or the enactment is a stranger to prevailing standards in the relevant community), then criminal punishment is objectionable for precisely those reasons that obtain in respect to strict liability.

PUBLIC WELFARE OFFENSES

Ever since Francis B. Sayre gave the phrase currency, this category of offenses has been treated by commentators as the main "exception" to the principle of *mens rea* and by courts as a convenient pigeonhole for any crime construed to dispense with *mens rea*. Perhaps the principal significance of the public welfare offenses lies in their open flouting of *mens rea*, as opposed to the more covert erosions that have gone on in the main body of the criminal law. Despite the enormous body of judge-made law that affirms dispensing with the mental element in violations of food and drug regulations, liquor regulations, traffic rules, and the like, few courts have explicitly considered and avowed the propriety of applying distinctively "criminal" sanctions to minor infractions. On the contrary, these offenses have been treated as something different from traditional criminal law, as a kind of hybrid category to which the odium and hence the safeguards of the criminal process do not attach. However limited in application the departure from *mens rea* may be in this category of offenses, it cannot be doubted that acceptance of this departure has been a powerful brake on the development of a general theory of *mens rea* in the criminal law.

This discussion of the "exceptions" to *mens rea* is intended to suggest that in every one of the cases enumerated at the beginning of this section

the defense of "mistake" should be entertained and, if found warranted by the facts, accepted. This conclusion follows, however, only if what we are confronted with is a case in which the criminal sanction is fully appropriate. Here we are touching on a major thesis of this book, namely, that the criminal sanction should not be applied to trivial infractions such as minor traffic offenses, to cite perhaps the most conspicuous example of current misuse. The culpability issue highlights this point. Treating every kind of conduct that the legislature unthinkingly labels as criminal with the full doctrinal apparatus of culpability would place an intolerable burden on the courts. Yet our principles compel us to entertain *mens rea* defenses whenever the consequences of a criminal conviction are severe, whenever we are using the full force of the criminal sanction. A line must be drawn that does not depend simply upon the fortuitous use of the label "criminal." Labels aside, the combination of stigma and loss of liberty involved in a conditional or absolute sentence of imprisonment sets that sanction apart from anything else the law imposes. When the law permits that degree of severity, the defendant should be entitled to litigate the issue of culpability by raising the kinds of defenses we have been considering. If the burden on the courts is thought to be too great, a less severe sanction than imprisonment should be the maximum provided for. The legislature ought not to be allowed to have it both ways.

NOTES

1. 320 U.S. 277 (1943).
2. United States v. Buffalo Pharmacal Co., 131 F. 2d 500 (2d Cir. 1942).
3. 320 U.S. at 280–81.
4. E.g., Jerome Hall, *General Principles of Criminal Law*, 2d ed. (Indianapolis, 1960), pp. 135–41.
5. Richard Wasserstrom, *Strict Liability in Criminal Law*, 12 Stan. L. Rev. 731, 741–45 (1960).
6. American Law Institute, MODEL PENAL CODE § 2.04 (3), and Comment, pp. 138–39 (Tent. Draft No. 4, 1955).

JOEL FEINBERG

Collective Responsibility*

When we state that a person is responsible for some harm, we sometimes mean to ascribe to him *liability* to certain responsive attitudes, judgments, or actions. Some responsive actions require authority; of these some are punitive, and others force compensation of a harmed victim. In the typical case of individual liability to unfavorable responses from others, three preconditions must be satisfied. First, it must be true that the responsible individual did the harmful thing in question, or at least that his action or omission made a substantial causal contribution to it. Second, the causally contributory conduct must have been in some way *faulty*. Finally, if the harmful outcome was truly "his fault," the requisite causal connection must have been directly between the faulty aspect of his conduct and the outcome. It is not sufficient to have caused harm *and* to have been at fault if the fault was irrelevant to the causing. We can use the expression "contributory fault" to refer compendiously to these three conditions. Thus, in the standard case of responsibility for harm, there can be no liability without contributory fault.

Certain familiar deviations from the standard case, however, give rise to confusion and misgiving. All primitive legal systems, and our own common law until about the fifteenth century, abound with examples of liability without contributory fault. For three centuries or so these examples were gradually eliminated from the common law, but they have returned in somewhat different form, often via statutes, in the last century, to the great alarm of many critics. Some of this alarm, I think, is justified; but there is little ground for fearing a recrudescence of primitive tribalism. Much legal liability without fault rests on very solid rationales, which are quite another thing than primitive supersition. The cases I have in mind can be discussed under three headings.

STRICT LIABILITY

What is called "strict liability" in the law is simply any liability for which the contributory fault condition is weakened or absent. This is the most general category; vicarious and collective liability are among its more interesting subspecies. For the most part, contractual liability has always tended to be "strict." Since this is liability that one imposes on oneself voluntarily, there is rarely any doubt expressed about its propriety. And no doubt can be expressed about its utility. Manufacturers brag about their warrantees and unconditional guarantees; and private bargainers quite often find it to their mutual advantage when one promises that, "if anything goes wrong, I'll bear the loss, no matter whose fault it is." In the law of torts, certain classes of persons are put on warning that, if they engage in certain ultra-hazardous activities, then they must be prepared to compensate any innocent parties who may incidentally be harmed, no matter how carefully and faultlessly the activities are carried out. There is always a risk of harm to others when one starts fires even on his own land, or keeps wild animals, or engages in blasting with high explosives. The law, of course, permits such activities, but it assigns the risk in advance to those who engage in them. This may seem to be a hard arrangement, since even if a construction company, for example, takes every reasonable precaution before dynamiting, it nevertheless can be found liable, if through some freakish chance a person at a great distance is injured by a flying rock set in motion by the blast, and can be forced to compensate the injured party for his losses. That the company

*From the *Journal of Philosophy*, Vol. LXV No. 21, (November 7, 1968), pp. 674–88. Reprinted by permission of the publisher. Reprinted in *Doing and Deserving: Essays in the Theory of Responsibility* (Princeton, N.J.: Princeton University Press, 1970) pp. 222–51.

was faultlessly careful in its operations is no defense. Still, this rule is by no means an arbitrary harassment, and its rigors are easily mitigated. The prospective responsibility imposed on blasters by law applies even to events beyond their control, but, *knowing this in advance* (an all-important consideration), they will be more careful than ever; and, further, they can guard against disastrous expenses by adjusting their prices and figuring compensation costs among their normal business expenses.

Strict liability in the criminal law is much less likely to accord with reasonable standards of justice than in contracts and torts; but even penalties and punishments may, in certain circumstances, dispense with the requirement of fault, provided that prior assignments of risks are clear and that some degree of prior control is possible. Perhaps the best known strict liability statutes in the criminal law are those creating "public welfare offenses." Here the rationale for disregarding actual fault is similar, in part, to that supporting strict liability for ultra-hazardous activities in torts. All milk producers, for example, are put on notice by one statute that, if any of their marketed product is found to be adulterated, they will be subject to stiff penalty. The producers have the power and authority to regulate their own facilities, procedures, and employees. The law in effect tells them that, since there is such a paramount public interest in pure foods, they must give the public an unconditional guarantee of the purity of their product. If the guarantee fails, no questions will be asked about fault; the fine will be imposed automatically. Then it will be up to the company to exercise its control by locating and eliminating the fault. If this arrangement seems unfair, the company can be reminded that the risk is well known and is in fact the price producers pay for the privilege of serving the public for their own profit—a price they presumably have been quite willing to pay. Moreover, it really does protect the public by providing incentive to vigilant safety measures; and the penalties, in any case, are only fines. No perfectly innocent persons are sent to prison.

When criminal punishment involving imprisonment is involved, the case for strict liability, of course, is much weaker; but even here, in certain circumstances, the conviction of the "faultless" can sometimes be supported. Among serious

crimes for which faultless ignorance ("reasonable mistake") is no excuse, the most celebrated example is the old English offense of taking an unmarried girl, under sixteen, from the possession of her father (for illicit purposes) without his consent. The rationale here, apparently, was that the harm done is so serious, and the opportunity and temptation so great, that any philanderer should be put on warning that, even if he has very good reason to believe his prey to be a thirty-year-old woman, he and he alone assumes the risk that she may be only fifteen—and a serious risk it is! The policy underlying the law was that philandery is a socially undesirable activity which it is the business of the law to discourage, but not the kind of moral offense that can properly (or practically) be prohibited absolutely. Hence young men are permitted to engage in it, but at their own peril. Understanding in advance where the risks lie, they will presumably be far more careful than they might otherwise be. The law here gives young sports a sporting chance. If they gamble and lose, even with the best of odds, they can blame no one but themselves. So interpreted, strict liability seems a relatively libertarian and humane means of social control.

In all the examples of plausibly just strict liability, the liable party must have had some control over his own destiny—some choice whether to take the risk assigned him by the law and some power to diminish the risk by his own care. When liability may be imposed even without such control, however, then it can "fall from the sky," like a plague, and land senselessly on complete strangers. Strict liability, when rational, is never totally unconditional or random.

VICARIOUS LIABILITY

Much, but by no means all, strict liability is also vicarious liability. There can be strict liability when *no one* is at fault, or where the question of contributory fault cannot be settled. There is vicarious liability, on the other hand, when the contributory fault, or some element of it, is properly ascribed to one party (or group of parties), but the liability is ascribed to a different party (or parties). In such cases we say that the latter party is responsible for the harmful consequences of a faulty action or omission of the former party. The person who did or caused the harm is not the one who is called upon to answer for it.

One familiar and surely unobjectionable type of vicarious liability is that which derives from the process of *authorization*. One party, called a "principal," authorizes another party, called the "agent," to act, within a certain range, for him. "He that acteth for another," wrote Hobbes, is said to bear his person, or act in his name."[1] Acting in another's name is quite another thing than merely acting in his interests (also called "acting for him") or merely substituting for him, as an understudy, for example, replaces an indisposed actor (also called "acting in place of him"). An agent acts "for" or "in place of" his principal in a different sense. The agent is often given the right to act, speak, sign contracts, make appointments, or the like, and these acts are as binding on the principal as if he had done them himself. The relation of authorization, as Hanna Pitkin points out,[2] is lopsided: The rights go to the agent, and the responsibilities to the principal.

The relation of authorization can take two very different forms, depending on the degree of discretion granted to the agent, and there is a continuum of combinations between the extremes. On the one hand, there is the agent who is the mere "mouthpiece" of his principal. He is a "tool" in much the same sense as is a typewriter or telephone: He simply transmits the instructions of his principal. Thus messengers, delegates, spokesmen, typists, and amanuenses are sometimes called agents. Miss Pitkin points out that such persons are often called "mere agents," or (I might add) "bound agents" as opposed to "free agents."[3] The principal acts *through* his agent much as he might act through some mechanical medium. On the other hand, an agent may be some sort of expert hired to exercise his professional judgment on behalf of, and in the name of, the principal. He may be given, within some limited area of expertise, complete independence to act as he deems best, binding his principal to all the beneficial or detrimental consequences. This is the role played by trustees and some other investment managers, some lawyers, buyers, and ghost-writers. At the extreme of "free agency" is the Hobbesian sovereign; for each of his subjects has in effect authorized in advance *all* of his "actions and judgments . . . in the same manner, as if they were his own."[4]

It is often said that the very actions of agents themselves, and not merely their normative consequences, are directly ascribable to their principals, through "a kind of fiction";[5] but this, I submit, is a dangerously misleading way of talking. If *A* has *B*'s power of attorney, he may have the right to sign *B*'s signature; and if he signs it on a contract or a check, the pecuniary consequences may be exactly as they would be had *B* himself signed his name. The results are *as if B* had himself acted; but it is nevertheless true that *he* did not act—*A* acted for him. Even the Old Testament, which finds nothing objectionable in the vicarious criminal liability of children for the sins of their fathers, balks at the doctrine of literally transferred agency and causality. In Deuteronomy 24:16, Jeremiah and Ezekiel repeat that, if the fathers had eaten sour grapes, the children's teeth would not be set on edge (though if the fathers had *stolen* the grapes, the children, perhaps, would be punishable).

Another form of vicarious liability derives from the relation between superior and subordinate in hierarchical institutions, of which military organizations are perhaps the clearest model. At the lowest rank persons have no authority to command others and are responsible only for their own performances. Officers of the higher ranks have greater authority—that is, the right to command larger numbers of persons and make them "tools"—and correspondingly greater answerability for failures. A superior's failure may be the fault of some of his subordinates, but he must nevertheless answer for it to *his* superiors. Subordinates, on the other hand, are not liable for the foolish or wicked commands of their superiors, since they are not "to reason why" but just to obey. In a way, a military hierarchy, then, can be viewed as a system of unidirectional vicarious liability. Something like it often exists in a less clear-cut form outside of military organizations. A recent press dispatch, for example, reports that there will no longer be automatic promotions of teachers in the Detroit public high schools and that teachers and principals will be held responsible for the academic performance of their students. Thus if students do poorly, their teachers will be "punished," and if they do well, their teachers will be rewarded. This liability is not entirely vicarious, of course, since there is presumably some causal connection between the teacher's performance and the student's; but it can approach pure vicarious liability when classes of students differ widely in ability. Its point, I think, is an interesting one, namely, to bolster the motivation of the *teachers.* (The students presumably do not care enough about the welfare of their teachers to be affected directly by the arrangement). In this respect, it is the very opposite of most forms of vicarious punishment (such as holding hostages, massive reprisals, family liability, blood feuds) whose point is to affect the motivation of the primary wrongdoers, not those who stand to be punished vicariously.

Another form of vicarious liability is the responsibility of employers ("masters") to compensate victims of the negligence or even, in some cases, the deliberate wrongdoing of their employees ("servants"), even when the employee is acting without, or in direct defiance of, the explicit orders of his boss, and the boss committed no negligence in hiring the employee in the first place, or in supervising, instructing, or outfitting him. Here, indeed, "the sins of the servant are visited upon the master." If my dog bites you, the biting is imputed to him, the liability to me.[6] Similarly, if the driver of my delivery truck, while doing his job, puts a dent in your fender or a crease in your skull, the liability to enforced compensation is mine, not his. (*His* liability is to *me;* he is now subject to being fired.) The rationale of this universal but once highly controverted practice is clear enough. If an accident victim has only a truck driver to sue, he may end up paying most of his disastrous medical expenses himself. The employer, having a "deeper pocket," is a more competent compensator; and, moreover, since he has *control* over the selection of employees for dangerous work, the rule will make him more careful in his assignment of tasks. It may be unfair to him to make him pay for an accident that was not his fault, but it would impose an even greater hardship and injustice to put the burden mainly on the shoulders of the equally faultless accident victim. And, again, there are means open to employers of anticipating and redistributing losses caused by their employees' negligence.

Still another form of vicarious liability derives from the relation of *suretyship.* A bonding company may insure an employer against the dishonesty of a new employee for a fee that may be paid by either employer or employee. If the employee commits embezzlement and makes his escape, the fault, guilt, agency, and causation all belong to the employee, but the liability to make good the losses is the innocent surety's. Similarly, the guarantor of another's debt pays if the other fails; and the poster of bail forfeits, if the bailed prisoner fails to make appearance.

Vicarious liability through authorization, hierarchy, mastership, and suretyship can thus be rational, in the sense that they rest on intellectually respectable, if not always convincing, rationales. Most of what has passed as vicarious criminal liability in human history is otherwise. Holmes traced the origin of both civil and criminal liability to certain animistic conceptions common to the Hebrews, Greeks, Romans, and Germans, and apparently to all human cultures at a certain stage in their development. The instrument of harm, whether it were a tool, a weapon, a tree, an ox, a slave, or a child, was regarded as the immediate and "natural" object of vengeance. It was "noxal," that is, accursed, and had to be forfeited to the victim, or his family, to be torn apart and annihilated. Later the principle of composition was adopted, and the owner of the noxal instrument could buy off its victim as an alternative to forfeiture. Nevertheless, in the early centuries of all major legal systems, inanimate objects and animals were "punished"; and the related practices of blood feud, noxal surrender, and substitute sacrifice flourished.

There are more refined forms of vicarious criminal liability for which a more plausible case can be made, although even these "rational" forms are rarely defensible as just. The imposition of punitive vicarious liability arrangements upon a community is always a desperate measure, justifiable at best only in extreme circumstances. I have in mind the taking of hostages by a wartime army of occupation (condemned by The Hague Convention of 1907 but practiced by Germans in two world wars) and stepped-up military reprisals for terrorism or atrocity directed at populations that surely include the innocent as well as the guilty. These cruel practices arouse angry resistance and thus tend to be self-defeating; and, in any case, they are examples of acts of war, rather than rules of a system of criminal law.

Could there be circumstances, in less desperate times, in which authorization, hierarchy, mastership, or suretyship, admittedly plausible bases for noncriminal liabilities, could also be the ground for criminal punishment? Under our present law, a principal will be coresponsible with his agent when the latter commits a criminal act at the former's direction or with his advance knowledge or subsequent ratification. The criminal punishment of superiors for actions done *entirely* on their own by subordinates, however, would be a barbarous regression in normal times. Criminal suretyship is a more difficult matter. I can imagine a voluntary system of suretyship that would permit fathers to arrange in advance to undergo punishment instead of their sons in case the latter committed crimes. Such a system could have some incidental merits among its preponderant disadvantages: deterrence and development of family solidarity. And it makes more sense than certain cosmic systems of criminal law in which the children answer for the sins of their fathers instead of the other way round.

There is an important point about all vicarious punishment: Even when it is reasonable to separate liability from fault, it is only the liability that can be passed from one party to another. In particular, *there can be no such thing as vicarious guilt.* Guilt consists in the intentional transgression of prohibition, "a violation of a specific taboo, boundary, or legal code, by a definite voluntary act." [7] In addition, the notion of guilt has always been essentially connected with the idea of "owing payment." The guilty party must "pay" for his sins, just as a debtor is one who must correct his moral imbalance by repayment. To be guilty is to be out of balance, or unredeemed, stained or impure. The root idea in guilt, then, is to be an appropriate person to make atonement, penance, or self-reproach, in virtue of having intentionally violated a commandment or prohibition. There have been extensions of this idea both through morbid superstition and natural analogy, but flawed intention, transgression, and needed atonement are still its central components. [8]

Now when an innocent man is punished for what a guilty man has done, he is treated *as if* he were himself guilty. There may be a rational point, and perhaps even justice, in certain circumstances, in doing this. Yet even though criminal liability can transfer or extend vicariously from a guilty to an innocent party, it obviously cannot be literally true that the guilt transfers as well. For guilt to transfer literally, action and intention too must transfer literally. But to say of an innocent man that he bears another's guilt is to say that he had one (innocent) intention and yet another (guilty) one, a claim which upon analysis turns out to be contradictory. I think that theologians and others have found it easy to talk of vicarious guilt only because the concept of guilt has always had the double sense of actual sin, on the one hand, and payment, atonement, redemption, and such, on the other; and of course it is at least logically intelligible for concepts of the latter kind to transfer. In short, liability can transfer, but not agency, causation, or fault (the components of "contributory fault"), and certainly not guilt.

COLLECTIVE LIABILITY

In the remainder of this essay, we shall focus our attention on collective-responsibility arrangements. In principle, these can be justified in four logically distinct ways. Whole groups can be held liable even though not all of their members are at fault, in which case collective responsibility is still another form of liability without contributory fault similar to those discussed above; or, second, a group can be held collectively responsible through the fault, contributory or *noncontributory,* of each member; or, third, through the contributory fault of each and every member; or, finally, through the collective but *nondistributive* fault of the group itself. This section will be concerned only with the first of these forms, the collective liability that is one interesting subspecies of that vicarious liability which in turn is one interesting subspecies of strict liability.

Collective liability, as I shall use the term, is the vicarious liability of an organized group (either a loosely organized, impermanent collection or a corporate institution) for the actions of its constituent members. When the whole group as such is held responsible for the actions of one or some of its members, then, from the point of view of any given "responsible" individual, *his* liability in most cases will be vicarious.

Under certain circumstances, collective liability is a natural and prudent way of arranging the affairs of an organization, which the members might well be expected to undertake themselves, quite voluntarily. This expectation applies only to those organizations (usually small ones) where there is already a high degree of *de facto* solidarity. Collective responsibility not only expresses the solidarity but also strengthens it; thus it is a good thing to whatever extent the preexistent solidarity was a good thing. Where prior solidarity is absent, collective liability arrangements may seek their justification through the desperate prior *need* for solidarity.

When does a group have "solidarity"? Three intertwined conditions, I think, must be satisfied to some degree. There has to be first of all, a large *community of interest* among all the members, not merely a specific overlap of shared specialized interests, of the sort that unite the members of a corporation's board of directors, for example, no matter how strong. A community of interest exists between two parties to the extent that each party's integrated set of interests contains as one of its components the integrated interest-set of the other. Obviously, this will be difficult to arrange in large and diverse groups. A husband, for example, might have as his main interests (whose fulfillment as a harmonious set constitutes his *well-being*) his health, his material possessions, his professional reputation, his professional achievement, *and* the well-being (also defined in terms of an integrated set of interests) of his wife and his children. His interests would thus include or contain the interests of several other people. If those other persons' interests, in a precisely similar way, were to embrace his, then there would be between them a perfect community of interest. Secondly, such "community" is often associated with bonds of sentiment directed toward common objects, or of reciprocal affection between the parties. (R. B. Perry defined "love" as an interest in the interests of someone else). Thirdly, solidarity is ordinarily a function of the degree to which the parties share a common lot, the extent to which their goods and harms are necessarily collective and indivisible. When a father is jailed, his whole family shares the disgrace and the loss of his provisions. There is no hurting one member without hurting them all; and because of the way their interests are related, the successes and satisfactions of one radiate their benefits to the others.

Individuals normally pool their liabilities when they share a common cooperative purpose, and each recognizes in the others complementary abilities of a useful or necessary kind. Thus salesmen combine with administrators to become business partners, pooling their talents and sharing their risks. Joint authorships are often cases of mutual ghost-writing, where each party stands answerable for the joint product of their several labors. Athletic team members must all win or all lose together: Victory is not the prize of individual merit alone, nor is defeat linked to "contributory fault." Similarly, in underground conspiracies and desperate dangerous undertakings, the spirit of "all for one and one for all" is not merely a useful device; it is imposed by the very nature of the enterprise. What makes collective liability natural in such cases is that parties who are largely of one mind to begin with are led (or forced) by circumstances to act in concert and share the risk of common failure or the fruits of an indivisible success.

There have been times in the history of civilization when group solidarity was a more common thing, and more easily arranged, than today. In many places, including Northern Europe, the ultimate unit of legal responsibility has been not the individual, but the clan, the kinship group, or the immediate family; and only a couple of centuries ago the English common law still applied to married couples the "fiction of conjugal unity." Only since the passage of Married Women's Acts in the 1840's have married women in America had a legal identity separate, in many kinds of legal situations, from that of their husbands. The world has without a doubt been getting steadily more individualistic in this respect, and it is no wonder. Change is faster, leading at any given time to more continual novelty and consequent greater diversity. Political parties, religious groups, and fraternal associations can no longer count on perfect uniformity and general solidarity across a whole spectrum of attitudes and convictions. And how much harder it is today to be a marriage broker (even with computers) than in other more static ages, when persons were more easily interchangeable and common values could be taken for granted!

De facto solidarity, then, is less easily come by today, even within small family groups. And because it is, there is no longer much point in treating a wife, for example, as part of a single corporate person with her husband. Wives today can own their own property, bargain and trade with their husbands, sign contracts on their own, and sue and be sued in their own names. Still, some of the conditions making for *de facto* solidarity (such as the common lot, and indivisible goods and evils) are necessarily present in every marriage; and when these are reinforced by shared or contained interests and mutual affection, the solidarity that renders joint liabilities reasonable will also be present. When fates are shared, they must be pooled in any case. Where the plural possessive "our" more naturally comes to the lips than the singular "mine," then to enter joint bank accounts and other forms of collective liability is only to certify the given and destroy artificial inconvenience.

There is perhaps no better index to solidarity than vicarious pride and shame. These attitudes occur most frequently in group members on behalf of the larger group, or of some other member(s) of the larger group, of which they are a part. Individuals sometimes feel proud of ashamed of their families, ancestors, countries, or races; and all or most of those who belong to groups may feel pride or shame over the achievements or failures of single members of their groups. Some writers have in effect denied that pride (and presumably shame) can ever be authentically vicarious; and there is no doubt that the appearance of vicariousness can often be explained away. Parental pride in the achievements of a son may be the consequence of a belief that those achievements reflect the influence of the parent, so that it is really pride at "what I have created in my son." This sort of interpretation may be possible in some cases, but it obviously cannot explain the son's filial pride in the achievements of his parents or grandparents. In this connection, H. D. Lewis speaks of "the presumption that we ourselves, having been subject to the same influences, are not without a measure of the qualities for which others of our group are noted." [9] No doubt many occurrences of filial pride and shame can be traced to this source, but clearly it cannot account for the immigrant's pride in the "American way of life" or the war opponent's feeling ashamed "to wear the same uniform" as those he believes have committed atrocities. Of course, the latter may be something different from shame, namely, mortification at being associated by others with actions of which one disapproves and of which one is totally innocent. Normal embarrassment, like pride at what one has helped others to do or be and pride over one's qualities presumptively shared with conspicuously worthy other persons, is a self-centered atti-

tude; an authentically vicarious feeling, if there can be such a thing, must be based on the doings or qualities of others considered entirely on their own account, unrelated to any doings or qualities of the principal.

H. D. Lewis provides a clue when he speaks of the phenomenon of sympathetic identification: "Our interest in those with whom we have special ties of affection will enable us to follow their success with a glow of satisfaction as if it were our own." [10] If this is what authentically vicarious pride is like, it is a phenomenon of the same order as sympathetic pain or compassion. Indeed, any feeling one person can experience can be experienced vicariously by some other imaginatively sensitive person. What we want, however, is not so much an account of vicarious or imaginative *sharing* alone as an account that will also apply to vicarious unshared or substitute feeling. Here too sympathy, I think, is the key. When someone near to me, about whom I care, makes a fool of himself before others, I can feel embarrassed for him, even though he feels no such thing himself. Yet when some total stranger or some person I despise behaves similarly, my reaction will be indifference or pity or contempt—reactions that are not vicarious. Compare "I am proud (or ashamed) because of you" with "I am proud (or ashamed) for you." The former is like taking partial credit (or blame); the latter is like congratulating (or condemning from an internal or sympathetic judgment point). We are inclined to congratulate (or "condemn fraternally") only when we feel some degree of solidarity with the other parties. The solidarity is a necessary condition of the vicarious emotion, which is in turn an index to the solidarity.

I think this account helps explain some puzzling variations. It is natural, for example, that an American Negro should feel solidarity with all other Negroes and speak of what has been done to "the black man" by "the white man" and what the moral relations between "the" black man (all black men) and "the" white man (all white men) ought to be. But I, for one, am quite incapable of feeling the same kind of solidarity with all white men, a motley group of one billion persons who are, in my mind, no more an "organization" than is the entire human race as such. I certainly feel no bonds to seventeenth-century slave traders analogous to those ties of identification an American Negro must naturally feel with the captured slaves. Precisely because of this failure of imagination, I can feel no shame on *their* behalf. Similarly, a European, appalled by American foreign policy, will feel anger or despair, but not vicarious shame unless he has some sentimental attachment to the United States. An American with like views will be ashamed of his country. Indeed, one cannot be intensely ashamed of one's country unless one also loves it.

Collective-responsibility arrangements are most likely to offend our modern sensibilities when the liabilities are to criminal punishment. Yet there was a time when primitive conditions required that the policing function be imposed on local groups themselves through a system of *compulsory universal suretyship.* Among the early Anglo-Saxons, the perfectly trustworthy man was he who did not stray from the village where his many kin resided, for they were his sureties who could guarantee his good conduct. In contrast, the stranger far from his kindred had nothing to restrain him, and since his death would excite no blood feud, he had no legal protection against the assaults of other.[11] With the development of Christian feudalism, the ancient system of kindred liability broke down, for churchmen without kin or local tie began to appear among suspicious villagers, and "as time went on, many men who for one reason or another moved away from their original environments and sought their fortunes elsewhere . . . could not depend on ties of kindred to make them law-worthy and reputable."[12] Hence a new system of compulsory suretyship, based on neighborhood rather than kin was developed. Everyone was *made* "law-worthy and reputable" by being assigned to a neighborhood group every member of which was an insurer of his conduct. If an offender was not produced by his surety group to answer criminal charges, a fine was levied on each member of the group, and sometimes liability to make compensation as well.

Now this may strike us as a barbarous expedient of a primitive people who had no conception of individual justice; but I think that is too severe a judgment. The frankpledge system was a genuine system of criminal law: There was nothing arbitrary, *ad hoc,* or *ex post facto* about it. It was also a system of compulsory group self-policing in an age when there were no professional police.

Moreover, it reinforced a preexisting group solidarity the like of which cannot occur in an era of rapid movement like our own. And most important, the system worked; it prevented violence and became generally accepted as part of the expected natural order of things.

Yet surely there is no going back to this kind of collective responsibility. H. Gomperz concluded an essay by claiming: "That men can be held responsible solely for individual conduct freely willed is certainly wrong; it mistakes a principle characteristic of individualistic ages for an eternal law of human nature."[13] I agree that the principle of individual responsibility is not an "external law"; but Gomperz misleadingly suggests a kind of historical relativism according to which individualistic and collectivistic ages alternate like styles in ladies' skirts. On the contrary, the changes that have come with modern times have dictated quite inevitably that the one principle replace the other, and no "alternation" is remotely foreseeable, unless massive destruction forces the human race to start all over again in tiny isolated farming settlements. Under modern conditions the surety system would not work in the intended way, for the surety groups, being subject to rapid turnover, would lack the necessary cohesion and solidarity to exert much influence or control over their members. It is more difficult now to keep a watchful eye on our neighbors, since we no longer spend the better part of every day working in adjacent fields with them. Moreover, we no longer impose a duty on all citizens to raise the hue and cry upon discovery of a crime, drop their work, arm themselves, and join the hunt, on pain of penalty to their whole surety group. Now we say that detection and pursuit of criminals is the policeman's job. He gets paid for it, not us; and he is much more able to do it well. Besides, we all have other things to do.

But we have paid a price in privacy, which will get steadily stiffer, for the principle of individual criminal responsibility. The technical devices that make modern police work possible are reaching the point where they will make inspection of every person's life and history possible only minutes after a police official desires it. In olden times a man could not wonder for long whether he was his neighbor's keeper, for the voice of authority would instruct him unmistakably that he'd damn well better be. Today we prefer not to become involved in the control of crime, with the result that those who are charged with the control of crime become more and more involved with us.

In summary, collective criminal liability imposed on groups as a mandatory self-policing device is reasonable only when there is a very high degree of antecedent group solidarity and where efficient professional policing is unfeasible. Furthermore, justice requires that the system be part of the expected background of the group's way of life and that those held vicariously liable have some reasonable degree of *control* over those for whom they are made sureties. It is because these conditions are hardly ever satisfied in modern life, and not because individual liability is an eternal law of reason, that collective criminal responsibility is no longer an acceptable form of social organization.

So much for collective responsibility as a form of *liability without fault.* People often have other models in mind, however, when they speak of "collective responsibility."

LIABILITY WITH NONCONTRIBUTORY FAULT

Various faults can exist in the absence of any causal linkage to harm, where that absence is only a lucky accident reflecting no credit on the person who is at fault. Where every member of a group shares the same fault, but only one member's fault leads to any harm, and that not because it was more of a fault than that of the others, but only because of independent fortuities, many outsiders will be inclined to ascribe collective liability to the whole group. Other outsiders may deny the propriety of holding even a faulty or guilty person liable for harm that was not "his fault"; but for a group member himself to take this public stand would be an unattractive piece of self-righteousness. It would be more appropriate for him to grieve, and voluntarily make what amends he can, than to insist stubbornly on the noncontributory character of his fault, which was a matter of pure lucky chance.

In this kind of situation we have a handy model for the interpretation of extravagant hyperboles about universal responsibility. One man drinks heavily at a party and then drives home at normal (high) speeds, injuring a pedestrian along the way. The claim that we are all guilty of this crime, interpreted in a certain way, is only a small exaggeration, for it is a very common practice, in which perhaps *most* of us participate, to drive above posted speed limits at night and also to drive in our usual fashion to and from parties at which we drink. Most of us are "guilty" of this practice, although only the motorist actually involved in the accident is guilty of the resultant injury. He is guilty *of* or *for* more than we are, and more harm is his fault; but it does not necessarily follow that he is more guilty or more at fault than the rest of us.

Now there are some character faults that are present to some, though not the same, degree in almost everyone. These flaws sometimes cause enormous amounts of harm. There is some point in saying that all those who share the flaws, even those who have had no opportunity to do mischief by them, are "responsible" when harm results, in the sense that they are morally no better than those whose fault contributed to the harm and are, therefore, properly answerable for the way they are, if only to their own consciences. There is even a point in the exaggeration that ascribes the common fault to everyone without exception, when in fact there are exceptions; for this may serve to indicate that serious and dangerous faults are far more common than is generally believed and may exist in the least suspected places. Since character flaws are dispositions to act or feel in improper ways in circumstances of various kinds, we may never know of a given man that he has the fault in question until circumstances of the appropriate kind arise; and they may never arise.

Can liability of the noncontributorily faulty be morally palatable? Criminal punishment of whole groups of fault-sharers would for a dozen reasons be impracticable. We have no way of confirming statements about what a man with a given character structure would do if the circumstances were different; so if we are determined to avoid punishing the genuinely faultless, we had better wait until the circumstances *are* different. In any case, the larger and more diverse the group of alleged fault-sharers, the less likely it is that they all share—or share to anything like the same degree—the fault in question. If, nevertheless, the fault is properly ascribed distributively to a group of great size, the probability increases that the fault is common also to judge, jury, and prosecutor. Moral uncertainties of this kind are not likely to be present when we have evidence linking the fault of an individual to some harmful upshot. Those luckier ones who share the fault but escape the causal link to harm must, from the point of view of criminal justice, simply be left to profit from their luck. But when we leave political-legal contexts, the case for causation as a necessary condition of liability weakens considerably. The law will neither punish *B* nor force him to compensate *C* for the harm caused by *A*'s fault, when *B* is as prone as *A* to the fault in question; but that is no reason why private individuals should refrain from censuring or snubbing *B* to the same extent as *A,* or why *B* should not hold himself to account.

CONTRIBUTORY GROUP FAULT: COLLECTIVE AND DISTRIBUTIVE

Sometimes we attribute liability to a whole group because of the contributory fault of each and every member. Group responsibility, so conceived, is simply the sum of all the individual responsibility. Since each individual is coresponsible for the harm in question, no one's responsibility is vicarious. Nevertheless, problems are raised by three kinds of situations: first, where large numbers of people are independently at fault without any concert or communication between them; second, where the harm is caused by a joint undertaking of numerous persons acting cooperatively; and, third, where the harm is to be ascribed to some feature of the common culture consciously endorsed and participated in by every member of the group.

Suppose a man swimming off a public beach that lacks a professional lifeguard shouts for help in a voice audible to a group of one thousand accomplished swimmers lolling on the beach; and yet no one moves to help him, and he is left to drown. The traditional common law imposes no liability, criminal or civil, for the harm in this kind of case. Among the reasons often given are that, if liability were imposed on one, it would, in all consistency, have to be imposed on the whole vast group and that, if a duty to rescue drowning swimmers were imposed on every accomplished swimmer in a position to help, the results would be confusing and chaotic, with hoards of rescuers getting in each other's way and no one quite sure he is not violating the law by not entering the struggle quickly and ardently enough. On the other hand, so the argument goes, if each feels a duty to mitigate the dangerous confusion, there could be an Alphonse-Gaston exchange of courteous omissions on a large and tragic scale. This rationale has always seemed disingenuous to me. I see no reason why legal duties should not correspond here with moral ones: Each has a duty to attempt rescue so long as no more than a few others have already begun their efforts. In short, everyone should use his eyes and his common sense and cooperate as best he can. If no one makes any motion at all, it follows that no one has done his best within the limits imposed by the situation, and *all* are subject at least to blame. Since all could have rescued the swimmer, it is true of each of them that, but for *his* failure to attempt rescue in the circumstances that in fact obtained, the harm would not have occurred. It may be awkward to charge all one thousand persons with criminal responsibility, but the difficulties would be no greater than those involved in prosecuting a conspiracy of equal size. As for civil liability, the problems are even less impressive: The plaintiff (widow) should simply be allowed to choose her own defendants from among the multitudes who were at fault—those, no doubt, with the "deepest pockets."

The second kind of case exemplifying group fault distributable to each member is that where the members are all privy to a crime or tort as conspirators or accomplices or joint tortfeasors. In complicated crimes, *complicity* is ascribed unavoidably to persons whose degree of participation in the crime is unequal. The common law, therefore, divides guilty felons into four categories, namely, "perpetrators," "abettors," "inciters" (all three of these are "accomplices"), and "criminal protectors," so that one may be guilty of a given crime either as its principal perpetrator (and even perpetration is a matter of degree, abettors counting as "principals in the second degree") or as accessories, that is, inciters or protectors. Thus one can be guilty, as an accessory, even of crimes that one is not competent to perpetrate. A woman, for example, may be found guilty of rape, as an abettor or inciter to the man, who must, of course, be the principal perpetrator of the crime on some other woman.

Suppose C and D plan a bank robbery, present their plan to a respected friend A, receive his encouragement, borrow weapons from B for the purpose, hire E as getaway driver, and then execute the plan. Pursued by the police, they are forced to leave their escape route and take refuge at the farm of E's kindly uncle F. F congratulates them, entertains them hospitably, and sends them on their way with his blessing. F's neighbor, G, learns of all that has happened, disapproves, but does nothing. Another neighbor, H, learns of it but is bribed into silence. On these facts, A, B, C, D, E, and F are all guilty of the bank robbery— C and D as perpetrators, A and B as inciters,[14] E as an abettor, and F as a protector. G is guilty of the misdemeanor called "misprision of felony," and H of the misdemeanor called "compounding a felony." On the other hand, if J, an old acquaintance of C and D, sees them about to enter the bank, notices suspicious bulges in their pockets, surmises that they are up to no good, yet does nothing out of simple reluctance to "get involved," he is not legally guilty. Yet he is certainly subject to blame; and, as moralists, we might decide this marginal case differently than the lawyers and brand him a kind of "moral accessory" before the fact, "morally guilty," though to a lesser degree than the others. We can afford to have stricter standards of culpability than the lawyers, since no formal punishment will follow as a result of *our* verdicts and we do not have to worry about procedural complexities.

Part of the problem of determining degrees of responsibility of individuals in joint undertakings, where the responsibility is not vicarious, is assessing the extent of each individual's *contribution* to the undertaking. This involves assessment of various incommensurable dimensions of contribution—degrees of initiative, difficulty or causal crucialness of assigned subtasks, degrees of authority, percentage of derived profit, and so on. Although these matters cannot be settled in any mathematical way, rough and ready answers suggest themselves to common sense, and the legal categories of complicity have proved quite workable. The more difficult problems require estimates of *voluntariness.* Do I carry my own share of "moral guilt" for the Vietnamese abomination as a consequence of my payment of war taxes? Is my position morally analogous to that of B, the "inciter" in the bank robbery example? In avoid-

ing protest demonstrations, am I guilty of "cooperating" with evil, perhaps on the model of J, F, G, or H? The answers to those questions are difficult, I think, not because the (minute) extent of my causal contribution is not easily measurable, but because it is difficult to know how strict should be the standards of voluntariness for cases like this. Since nonpayment of taxes is a crime, the payment of war taxes is less than fully voluntary. To go to prison merely to avoid being associated, however indirectly, with some evil is to adopt the heroic path. The man who "cooperates" with crime under duress is surely in a different position from the man who cooperates, like H, as a result of a bribe, or, like J, out of sloth or cowardice. Yet whether the threat of legal punishment is sufficient duress to excuse "cooperation" with authorities again depends on numerous factors, including the degree of the evil and the probabilities of its alleviation with and without the contemplated resistance. In any case, mere nonresistance does not count as "cooperation" unless various other conditions are fulfilled. Where those conditions are conspicuously unfulfilled, as in Nazi Germany, then nonresistance is entirely involuntary, since its only alternative is pointless self-sacrifice.

The third interesting case of distributive group fault is that which adheres to a group's folkways yet somehow reflects upon every member of the group. Even Dwight Macdonald concedes that there are "folk activities" that a group "takes spontaneously and as a whole ... which are approved by the popular mores" and which are not merely "things done by sharply differentiated sub-groups."[15] Nazi acts of violence against Jews, Macdonald argued, were not genuine folk activities in this sense. In contrast, the constant and widespread acts of violence "against Negroes throughout the South, culminating in lynchings, may be considered real "people's actions," for which the Southern whites bear collective responsibility [because] the brutality ... is participated in, actively or with passive sympathy, by the entire white community."[16] The postbellum Southern social system, now beginning to crumble, was contrived outside of political institutions and only winked at by the law. Its brutalities were "instrumentalities for keeping the Negro in his place and maintaining the supraordinate position of the white caste."[17] Does it follow from this charge, however, that "Southern whites [*all* Southern whites] bear collective responsibility?" I assume that ninety-nine percent of them, having been shaped by the prevailing mores, wholeheartedly approved of these brutalities. But what of the remaining tiny fraction? If they are to be held responsible, they must be so vicariously, on the ground of their strong (and hardly avoidable) solidarity with the majority. But suppose a few hated their Southern tradition, despised their neighbors, and did not think of themselves as Southerners at all? Then perhaps Macdonald's point can be saved by excluding these totally alienated souls altogether from the white Southern community to which Macdonald ascribes collective responsibility. But total alienation is not likely to be widely found in a community that leaves its exit doors open; and, in a community with as powerful social enforcement of mores as the traditional Southern one, the alienated resident would be in no happier a position than the Negro. Collective responsibility, therefore, might be ascribed to all those whites who were not outcasts, taking respectability and material comfort as evidence that a given person did not qualify for the exemption.

CONTRIBUTORY GROUP FAULT: COLLECTIVE BUT NOT DISTRIBUTIVE

There are some harms that are ascribable to group faults but not to the fault of every, or even *any*, individual member. Consider the case of the Jesse James train robbery. One armed man holds up an entire car full of passengers. If the passengers had risen up as one man and rushed at the robber, one or two of them, perhaps, would have been shot; but collectively they would have overwhelmed him, disarmed him, and saved their property. Yet they all meekly submitted. How responsible were they for their own losses? Not very. In a situation like this, only *heroes* could be expected to lead the self-sacrificial charge, so no individual in the group was at fault for not resisting. The whole group, however, had it within its power to resist successfully. Shall we say, then, that the group was collectively but not distributively at fault? Can the responsibility of a group be more than the sum of the responsibility of its members? There is surely a point in affirming so. There was, after all, a flaw in the way the group

of passengers was organized (or unorganized) that made the robbery possible. And the train robbery situation is a model for a thousand crises in the history of our corporate lives. No individual person can be blamed for not being a hero or a saint (what a strange "fault" that would be!), but a whole people can be blamed for not producing a hero when the times require it, especially when the failure can be charged to some discernible element in the group's "way of life" that militates against heroism.

One would think that, where group fault is nondistributive, group liability must be so too, lest it fall vicariously on individual members who are faultless. But, for all overt unfavorable responses, group liability is inevitably distributive: What harms the group as a whole necessarily harms its members. Hence if the conditions of justifiable collective liability—group solidarity, prior notice, opportunity for control, and so on—are not satisfied, group liability would seem unjustified.

An exception, however, is suggested by the case where an institutional group persists through changes of membership and faultless members must answer for harms caused, or commitments made, by an earlier generation of members. Commitments made in the name of an organized group may persist even after the composition of the group and its "will" change. When, nevertheless, the group reneges on a promise, the fault may be that of no individual member, yet the liability for breach of contract, falling on the group as a whole, will distribute burdens quite unavoidably on faultless members. Consider the philosophy department which debated whether to pass a graduate student on his preliminary examinations. The main argument against doing so was that passing him would commit the department to the supervision of the student's dissertation, and no one who knew this particular student was willing to read his thesis. The affirmative carried when two members volunteered to direct the dissertation themselves. One year later, however, one of these sponsors died, and the other took employment elsewhere. Thus *no member* was willing to supervise this student, and the department as a whole had to renege on its promise. No member felt personally bound by the promises of his departed colleagues, which had been made to the student in no one's name but the department's. No legal action, of course, was possible; but if the department had been *forced* to honor its word, this would have been an excellent example of nondistributive group fault (the departmental reneging) and consequent group liability of a necessarily distributive kind.

There is a different sense of "responsibility," and an important one, in which groups can be responsible collectively and distributively for traits (including faulty traits) in the group structure and history that can be ascribed to no given individual as their cause. Sigmund Freud[18] once raised the question whether individuals are "responsible" for their dreams and then astonishingly answered the question in the affirmative. Freud did not mean, however, that dreams are intentionally *acted out* or *caused* by the dreamer, or that they are, in any sense, the dreamer's *fault,* or that the dreamer is *liable* to censure or punishment or to self-directed remorse or guilt for them. What he did mean was that a person's dreams represent him faithfully in that they reveal in some fundamental way what sort of person he is. Freud was denying that dreams are "the meaningless product of disordered mental activity" or the work of "alien spirits." Rather, they have genuine psychological significance. Hence everyone must "take responsibility" for his dreams and not disown or repudiate them; and this is simply to "own up" to even the unpretty aspects of one's self as truly one's own.

Those who have read such works as Richard Hofstadter's *Paranoid Style in American Politics*[19] can hardly fail to be struck by the similarity between the social historian's revelations about the nation and the psychoanalyst's revelations about the individual. Both dredge up experiences from the past that are held to reveal persisting dispositions, trends, and "styles" of response that might otherwise be unknown to the subject. To deny the reality or significance of the child that still lives in the man, or of the early settlers whose imprint is still upon the nation, is to "deny responsibility" for traits that are truly one's own. When a nation's voices fail to acknowledge its own inherited character, the possibilities of understanding and rational control are just so far diminished, and the consequences for faultless individual citizens (as for the neurotically benighted individual in the other case) can be

devastating. But the responsibility I mention here is no kind of agency, causation, fault, or liability; it would less misleadingly, though somewhat awkwardly, be called "representational attributability."

NOTES

1. *Leviathan,* ed. Michael Oakeshott (Oxford: Basil Blackwell, 1946), Part 1, Ch. 16, 105.

2. *The Concept of Representation* (Berkeley and Los Angeles: University of California Press, 1967), 19.

3. *Ibid.,* 122.

4. *Leviathan,* Part 2, Ch. 18, 113.

5. The limits of "fictitious attribution" (the phrase is from Hobbes) are clearly marked out by A. Phillips Griffiths in "How Can One Person Represent Another?", *Proceedings of the Aristotelian Society,* Supp. 34 (1960), 187–224, and by Pitkin, *The Concept of Representation,* 49–54.

6. W. D. Falk, "Intention, Motive and Responsibility," *Proceedings of the Aristotelian Society,* Supp. 19 (1945), 249.

7. H. M. Lynd, *On Shame and the Search for Identity* (New York: Science Editions, 1961), 23.

8. I have been discussing guilt in the sense of one very special way of being *at fault.* Guilt, in this sense, is usually a necessary condition for guilt in a different sense, namely, that of "criminal liability." The model of guilt in the latter sense is the legal condition brought into existence by an authoritatively pronounced verdict in a criminal court. Guilt in this sense is analogous to the state of civil liability also created by authoritative judicial pronouncement as the end product of a civil suit. To be guilty in the sense of criminally liable is to be properly subject to the imposition of punitive sanctions, just as to be civilly liable is to be properly subject to legal pressure to make pecuniary compensation for harm. To call a man guilty of a crime is either to report that he has been authoritatively pronounced guilty or else to express one's own quite unofficial opinion that the conditions of criminal liability have in fact been satisfied so that an official verdict of "guilty" is or was called for.

Almost always in criminal law the *conditions* of criminal liability (that is, of "guilt" in one sense) include the requirement that the defendant intentionally acted (or omitted to act) in a way proscribed (or enjoined) by law (that is, that he was guilty in the other, "at fault" sense of "guilt"). But there is no conceptual necessity that intentional transgression be a condition of guilt (liability). There is no logical contradiction in the rule that permitted German citizens to be found "guilty" of having a Jewish grandparent, or in the rule that makes even bellhops guilty of "possessing" drugs when they carry a hotel guest's bags to his room, or in rules permitting the punishment of "criminal negligence," or in rules creating "strict liability" in criminal law. In Shirley Jackson's famous short story "The Lottery," the "winner" of an annual lottery is customarily stoned to death by his neighbors. The absurdity of calling the randomly selected sacrificial victim "guilty," I submit, is a moral, not a logical or conceptual, absurdity. The condition of criminal liability in this case is not so much being at fault as being unlucky; but, in the sense of "guilt" under consideration, there is no contradiction in saying that a defendant was faultless but guilty nevertheless, providing he satisfied the conditions for liability specified by some rule. The only limit to the possibility of guilt in this sense is the requirement that there be *some conditions or other* for guilt; but the conditions need not include any kind of fault.

9. "Collective Responsibility," *Philosophy,* 23 (1948), 7.

10. *Ibid.*, 8.

11. L. T. Hobhouse, *Morals in Evolution* (London: Chapman & Hall, 1951), 81.

12. S. B. Chrimes, *English Constitutional History* (London: Oxford University Press, 1953), 77.

13. "Individual, Collective, and Social Responsibility," *Ethics,* 69 (1943), 342.

14. "An inciter . . . is one who, with *mens rea,* aids, counsels, commands, procures, or encourages another to commit a crime, or with *mens rea,* supplies him with the weapons, tools, or information needed for his criminal purpose." Rollin

M. Perkins, *Criminal Law* (Brooklyn: The Foundation Press, 1957), 558.

15. *Memoirs of a Revolutionist* (New York: Meridian, 1958), 45.

16. *Loc.cit.* (written in 1945).

17. John Dollard, *Caste and Class in a Southern Town,* as quoted *ibid.,* 45.

18. See *The Collected Papers of Sigmund Freud,* ed. Philip Rieff, BS 189 V, *Therapy and Technique* (New York: Collier Books, 1963), 223–226.

19. (New York: Alfred A. Knopf, 1965.)

A. M. HONORÉ

Law, Morals and Rescue*

A woman, viciously attacked, lies bleeding in the street. Fifty people pass by on the other side. A man destroys his barn to prevent a fire spreading to his neighbor's property. The neighbor refuses to compensate him. A young potholer foolishly becomes trapped below ground. A more experienced man, coming to his aid, breaks a leg. When we contemplate facts such as these, three questions seem to confront us concerning law, morals, and their interrelation. The first is about the shared morality of our society. Is there in modern industrial society, which is the only one most of us know, a shared attitude of praise or condemnation, encouragement, or dissuasion about helping those in peril? If so, two further points arise. Should the law, with its mechanisms of inducement, rewards, and compensation, be used to encourage what the shared morality treats as laudable and discourage what it reprobates? Should the law, thirdly, go further and, by the use of threats and penalties, "enforce" morality, as

the saying goes? These, it seems, are the main issues. In part they concern matters which, in England at least, have lately stirred up a passionate debate.[1] is it justifiable to use the mechanism of criminal law to "enforce" the shared morality, for instance in matters of sex? Greeks and Trojans have sallied forth and the clash of arms has rung out. Our concern, however, is with something wider and different: not sex, not only "enforcement," not only crime. I shall have a word, later on, to say in criticism of the use of the word "enforce" in this context. If we pass it for the moment, it yet remains true that "enforcement" is only part of what the law can do in the Good Samaritan situation. Apart from criminal sanctions, the law can encourage or discourage compliance with the shared morality by the use of techniques drawn from tort, contract, and restitution. Even "enforcement" is not confined to criminal law, because tort law, too, can be used to impose an obligation to aid others.

Our concern is not only wider but different from that of the jurists by whose brilliant and elevated jousting we have been entertained. They have debated whether some parts of the law which coincide with common morality should be

*Law, Morals and Rescue," by Antony M. Honoré, from the book *The Good Samaritan and The Law,* ed. by James M. Ratcliffe (New York: Doubleday & Co., Inc., 1966), pp. 225–42, copyright © 1966 by James M. Ratcliffe. Reprinted by permission of Doubleday & Company, Inc.

scrapped. We, on the other hand, wish to know whether parts of morality, at present outside the law, should be incorporated in it. (I mean here Anglo-American law and not those systems in which this has already come about.) Some people feel that the intrusion of law into the private sphere of sex is indecent and outrageous. Others feel outraged by the failure of the law to intrude in relation to rescue and rescuers. Is the refusal to "enforce" the moral obligation to help others itself a moral offense, of which lawyers and legislators have been guilty in the English-speaking world this hundred years? Does the affront of this refusal bring the law and lawyers into disrepute? Should the law encourage or even insist on Do-Goodery? Or would this be an intrusion into yet another private sphere, not of sex, but of conscience?

Clearly we have a moral issue on our hands, and one which is concerned not with the "enforcement" of morals but with its nonenforcement. A number of writers, following Bentham[2] and Mill,[3] have advocated a legal obligation to rescue. Ames[4] and Bohlen[5] put forward an earnest plea to the same effect. But, though they mentioned, they did not closely analyze the moral issues. It is with these that I shall be principally concerned.

I THE SHARED MORALITY IN MATTERS OF RESCUE

An essential preliminary to the survey of the larger vistas of law and morals is to clear our minds about our moral views in the matter of aid to those in peril. By "our moral views" I mean the shared or common morality. Obviously this is not the same as the statement of what people actually do in a given society—the common practice of mankind. Their actions may fall short of their moral ideals and pretensions. Nor is it the same as that which an individual may accept for himself as morally obligatory. There is a distinction between that which the individual accepts for himself and that which he regards as being of general application. A man may think he has higher ideals, a stricter sense of obligation or duty, than the ordinary run of men could well be expected to entertain. This cherished personal morality, it seems to me, is no part or ingredient of the shared morality, though it may come, in

time, to spread to others and so to influence the shared morality.

The shared morality consists, rather, of those moral ideals and duties or obligations which the bulk of the community regard as applying to persons generally. But is the notion, defined, anything more than a figment? Ought we to refrain from speculating about its content until social surveys have determined whether it really exists? I think one must frankly concede that the results of properly conducted surveys would be far more authoritative than the guesses of moralists or lawyers. The survey which Messrs. Cohen, Robson, and Bates sought to ascertain the moral sense of the Nebraska community on parent-child relations[6] is, no doubt, a forerunner of what will, in time, become common practice. The shared morality of which I am speaking is not, however, quite what the Nebraska inquiry was attempting to ascertain. In that inquiry "community values" were defined as the "choices, expressed verbally, which members of the community feel the law-making authorities ought to make if confronted with alternative courses of action in specified circumstances."[7] These choices surely represent opinion as to legislation on moral issues rather than the shared morality itself. They tell us what people think legislators should do, not what they think ordinary citizens should do. No doubt there is a close, even a very close, connection between the two. Our view of what the law should be will be powerfully shaped by our notions of right and wrong, of what is desirable and what objectionable, but surely the two cannot without more be identified? It must a priori be an open question whether people who share moral ideas also think that these should be mirrored in the law. If they do, that is also a fact susceptible of and demanding confirmation by a properly conducted survey.

It remains doubtful, therefore, whether a suitable technique has yet been evolved for testing the existence and content of the shared morality of a community. Certainly the results are not yet to hand in a usable form. In the meantime, life does not stand still. Decisions must be reached with the aid of such information and intuition as we may possess. We cannot shirk the question of what our shared morality says about rescues and rescuers on the excuse that one day, we hope, a truly reliable answer will be available.

It is unwise in thinking about the shared morality to treat morality as an undifferentiated mass. For instance, there is a distinction between moral ideals and moral duties.[8] This is not the same as the previous distinction between a man's personal morality and the morality which he regards as of general application. Of course, a connection exists. A person may accept as an obligation for himself what he thinks of merely as an ideal for others. Broadly speaking, moral ideals concern patterns of conduct which are admired but not required. To live up to them is praiseworthy but not exigible. Moral duties, on the other hand, concern conduct which is required but not admired. With an important exception, to which I shall come, merely to do one's duty evokes no comment. Moral duties are pitched at a point where the conformity of the ordinary man can reasonably be expected. As a corollary, while it is tolerable, if deplorable, to fall short of the highest ideals, it is not permissible to neglect one's duties.

Certain virtues, notably altruism and generosity, depend on absence of obligation. It is not altruistic to pay one's debts, or generous to support one's parents (in the latter case the duty may in Anglo-American law be merely moral, but this makes no difference). Other virtues seem to hover between the status of ideals and duties. Is this, perhaps, true of the "neighborliness" which the parable of the Good Samaritan is meant both to illustrate and to inculcate? According to Matthew[9] and Mark,[10] the precept "love your neighbor as yourself" expresses a "commandment" and presumably imposes an obligation. Luke,[11] in contrast, treats it as pointing the way to perfection or "eternal life," a moral ideal. It may be that giving aid to those in peril is sometimes an ideal, sometimes a duty. At least three situations demand separate treatment:

1   The first is the rescue undertaken by one who has a professional or quasi-professional duty to undertake rescues. A fireman or life-saver is a professional rescuer. Doctors, nurses, and other members of the medical profession have a duty to save life, which, at times, demands that they should give help in an emergency. A priest must comfort the dying, a policeman must stop acts of violence. Besides these true professionals, there are what one may call devoted amateurs; for instance, experienced mountaineers or potholers, who hold themselves out as ready to effect rescues and, I am told, often welcome the chance to display their skills. Strictly speaking, none of these are "volunteers." They are only doing what they are bound by their calling or public profession to do. A doctor is not praised for coming promptly to the scene of an accident; that is only what we expect. He would be blamed if he delayed or refused to come. But this morally neutral reaction is appropriate only when the rescuer acts without risk or serious inconvenience to himself. If the fireman, policeman, or life-saver risks life or limb to help the imperiled, he deserves and receives praise, because there is an element of self-sacrifice or even heroism in his conduct, though what he does is clearly his duty. Heroism and self-sacrifice, unlike altruism, can be evinced both by those who do their duty and those who have no duty to do.

2   The second is the rescue undertaken by one who has special ties with the person imperiled. Family links, employment, and other associative ties may generate a duty to come to the help of a class of persons more limited than those whom the professional or professed rescuer is bound to assist. It is a parent's duty to snatch his child from the path of an oncoming automobile, an employer's to rescue the workman who has been trapped in the factory machine. It may well be their duty to risk their own safety should that prove necessary. Like the professional rescuer, they can expect no encomium merely for helping, but if they risk themselves they merit commendation.

3   The third situation is that of a person not bound by his profession or by special links with the person imperiled to come to his aid. Even in this case, common opinion would, perhaps, see a limited duty to assist when this is possible without risk or grave inconvenience to the rescuer. "It is undoubtedly the moral duty," an American judge has said, "of every person to extend to others assistance when in danger, to throw, for instance, a plank or rope to the drowning man or make other efforts for his rescue, and if such efforts should be omitted by anyone when they could be made without imperilling his own life, he would, by his conduct, draw upon himself the censure and reproach of good men."[12] Common humanity, then, forges between us a link, but a weak one. The duty stops short at the brink of

danger. Samaritans, it is held, must be good, but need not be moral athletes.

It is in this third situation alone, when the rescuer, bound by no professional duty or special tie to the person imperiled, exposes himself to danger, that we really call him a "volunteer." I appreciate that in Anglo-American law the notion of the "volunteer" has been at times twisted beyond recall. In order to deny the rescuer a remedy, the doctrine of voluntary assumption of risk has sometimes been extended to bar those who were merely doing their duty or responding to an appeal for help.[13] Conversely, in order to afford the rescuer a remedy, courts have at other times treated the altruist as if he were simply doing his plain duty and concluded that his action was a necessary consequence of the hazard and so of the fault of the person who created it.[14] But this is just legal fiction.

If this moral morphology is reasonably accurate, we have four types of rescuer and nonrescuer to contend with. The first is the priest or Levite who passes by on the other side. The second, in ascending order of excellence, is the man who does no more than he is bound to do, whether his duty arises from his profession, from some special link with the person imperiled, or from common humanity. The third is he who, in doing his duty, exposes himself to risk: possibly a hero. The fourth is the true volunteer altruistically exposing himself to danger to help those to whom he is bound by no special tie: perhaps a hero, too.

What should the law have to say to them?

II   THE MYTH OF NONINTERVENTION

First, should the law encourage or discourage the rescuer, or should it remain neutral? Members of my generation remember nonintervention as the name of a policy which, during the Spanish Civil War, ensured the victory of the side which cheated most. It was called by Talleyrand a metaphysical conception, which means very much the same thing as intervention. So with the intervention of law in the sphere of morals. There is no neutrality. If the law does not encourage rescue, it is sure to discourage it. If it does not compensate, it will indirectly penalize. If the rescuer who suffers injury or incurs expense or simply expends his skill goes without compensation, the law, so far as it influences conduct at all, is discouraging rescue.

Perhaps one day sociology will devise means of discovering whether people are really influenced in what they do by the thought of legal remedies. In the meantime, it would be altogether too facile to assume that they are not. A doctor living near a dangerous crossroads is continually called to minister to the victims of the road. The injured are unconscious or, if conscious, are in no mood to contract or to fill in National Health cards. Will the doctor come more readily and care for them more thoroughly if he knows he will be paid? If so, he is a man, not an angel. A mountain guide with a hungry family is called to rescue a foolish climber trapped on the north face of the Eiger. Does anyone imagine him to be indifferent to the question how his family will be kept if he is killed?

The law cannot stay out of the fight and, if it cannot, there is surely a strong case for compensating the rescuer. To do so will be in the interests of those who might be saved. The community applauds the Good Samaritan. So the law, if it encourages rescue, is helping to satisfy the interests of individuals and the wants of the community. If we think of law as being, among other things, a social service designed to maximize welfare and happiness, this is exactly what the law ought to do. One department of the law's service to society will be its moral service, which it performs by encouraging with the appropriate technical remedies whatever is morally approved and discouraging what is condemned.

Unquestionably there are limits to this function of the law. I will deal with only three. The most obvious is the limit set by oppression. If the encouragement of the shared morality and the discouragement of its breach would be a hardship to some without sufficient corresponding benefit to them or to others, the law should not endorse it. The fact that racial prejudice is approved in a given community does not mean that the courts must hold leases to Negroes in white residential areas void. But the encouragement of rescue will oppress neither rescuer nor rescued. The rescued benefits from being saved, and even if he is compelled to compensate the rescuer he will be, by and large, better off. It is true that compensation may be burdensome and I should not care to argue that civil remedies are necessarily less harsh than punishment. If an uninsured person has to pay heavy damages, he is worse off than if he were fined, for the fine, unlike the damages, is geared to his means. But this fact depends on the rules about assessment of damages in Anglo-American law, and these might be changed. It would be no hardship to suggest that the rescuer should receive compensation, if necessary, from the person imperiled, in accordance with the latter's means: *in id quod facere potest,* as the Roman formula ran.

Another limit or supposed limit may be set by the principle that virtue should be its own reward. Strictly speaking, I doubt if this applies to proposals for compensation as opposed to rewards. Still, the doctor's claim to be paid for his ministrations to the unconscious victim of a road accident may be called a claim for reward. Would it be an inroad on his virtue that he was entitled to be paid? Surely the argument is obtuse. No one is compelled to claim a reward he does not want. The doctor, like the finder of lost property, can preserve immaculate his moral idealism if he wishes. No one can be compelled to be compensated.

A third limit concerns the border line between altruism and meddling. Of course we do not want our next-door neighbor to rescue the baby every time he screams or to interrupt our family quarrels. But this merely shows that the received morality draws the line at officiousness. The test of what is officious will usually be whether the intending rescuer would reasonably suppose that his help will be welcome. If the victim objects or would be expected to object, the rescuer should abstain. But this can hardly apply to those victims who are too young or too deranged to know their own interests, and one might justify the rescue of a person attempting suicide (in a jurisdiction in which suicide is not a crime) on the ground that those who attempt it often lack a settled determination in the matter.

The line will be difficult to draw exactly, but lawyers are professional line-drawers. The relevant factors are easy enough to list: the gravity of the peril, the chances of successful intervention, the attitude of the victim, and the likelihood that another better-qualified rescuer will act.

None of the three limits mentioned seems to alter the proposition that the law would be a poor thing if it did not in general encourage rescue.

The means available to do this are essentially the compensation of the rescuer for expenses and injury and the rewarding of his services. It is convenient to take these separately.

1   *Injury.* No immediate difficulty is felt if the rescuer is covered by a personal accident policy or an insurance scheme connected with his employment, as would usually be true of firemen and other professional rescuers. There will still remain the question whether the insurer should be entitled to shift the loss to the person responsible for the peril. Certainly it makes for simplicity if he cannot.

When there is no insurance cover the problem is: Where should the compensation come from? Most people would be inclined to place it in the first instance on the person through whose fault the peril arose, whether the person imperiled or another. In order to justify making the person imperiled liable when he had been at fault, Bohlen argued that the basis of liability was the tendency of the defendant's conduct to cause the rescuer to take the risk involved in the attempted rescue.[15] If "cause" is to be taken seriously, this suggests that the rescuer who acts under a sense of obligation would recover for his injury, while the pure altruist would not, because the latter's act is a fresh cause. Yet altruism is not less but more worthy of the law's encouragement than the conscientious performance of one's duty. If in *Carnea v. Buyea*[16] the plaintiff who snatched the defendant from the path of the runaway automobile had been unrelated to the defendant, could that reasonably have been a ground for denying him a recovery? Surely the remedy should not be confined to cases where the peril "causes" the rescue, but should extend to those in which it merely prompts the rescuer.

Other writers and courts rely on foreseeability as the ground of liability. This, too, is open to objection. Suppose an intrepid but foolhardy explorer is stranded in an area where rescue is atrociously difficult and rescuers scarce. By the heroism of a James Bond he is saved. Surely the fact that rescue could not be foreseen makes no difference to Bond's claim for compensation? Is not the real basis of liability the twofold fact that the person imperiled has created a risk from which he wishes to be saved (whether he thinks rescue likely or not) and that his peril has prompted another to come to his aid (whether it has "caused" him to do so or not).

I have been dealing with the rationale of the imperiled person's duty to compensate the rescuer when the former is at fault. Legally speaking, this is the case that has evoked discussion, because it said that the person in peril owes himself no duty. When the peril is created by a third person, the objection is inapplicable. If the third person is at fault, he should be liable to compensate the rescuer for the reasons already given. If no one is at fault, it still remains a question whether compensation should be payable by either the person imperiled or the state. A remedy against the innocent person in peril can be justified either, if he is saved, on the ground that he has benefited at the rescuer's expense and should not take the benefit without paying the cost of its procurement or (whether he is saved or not) on the ground of unauthorized agency. The guiding notion of this (the Roman *negotiorum gestio* and the French *gestion d'affaire*) is that the agent, acting without the principal's authority, nevertheless does what the principal might be presumed to want done, when it is impracticable to obtain his consent. (If there is actual consent, for instance, if the person in peril calls for help, so much the easier, legally speaking, to justify giving a remedy.)[17]

Anglo-American law, in contrast with civil systems, is impregnated with the maxim, "Mind your own business," though recently there have been signs of a change. If we outflank the maxim by asserting that, to a limited extent, the peril of one is the business of all, it seems fair to make the person imperiled, though free from fault, indemnify the rescuer albeit only so far as his means reasonably permit.

None of the headings so far mentioned may afford an adequate remedy to the rescuer. In that case a state compensation scheme might well fill the gap. If the state is to compensate the victims of crimes of violence, as is now done in England,[18] why not compensate the equal heroism of those who suffer injury in effecting rescues?

2 *Expenses.* In principle the same rules should apply to expenses incurred by the rescuer as to injuries received by him. Two points may be noted. One is that the expense of organizing a rescue may nowadays be enormous. Suppose the Air Force presents the lost mariner with a bill for gasoline, maintenance of aircraft, wages of crew, and so on, perhaps incurred over several days of search. The crushing liability must be mitigated by having regard for the mariner's probably slender means. The other point is that in Anglo-American law there is a traditional reluctance to grant tort actions for negligence when the loss suffered is merely pecuniary. The rescuer who incurs expense but suffers no physical injury may thus find the way barred. It seems that courts will have to extend the bounds of the tort of negligence and the law of restitution if adequate remedies are to be supplied without legislative intervention. These are already some signs that this is happening.[19]

3 *Rewards.* The moral objections to rewarding altruism, we saw, are misconceived. But is there a positive case to be made in favor of rewarding rescuers? In practice, outstanding acts of courage in effecting rescue are marked by the award of medals and decorations. Many persons saved from danger would think themselves morally bound to offer something to their rescuers. But a legal claim to be paid is usually voiced only by the professional rescuer, especially the self-employed, who may spend much time and energy in this way. Take our friend the doctor who lives near an accident black spot. It is mere fiction to say that the unconscious victim impliedly contracts to pay for treatment.[20] Two other theories are possible: one, that payment is less a true reward than compensation for loss of profitable time; the other, that the person in peril, if he could have been consulted, would have agreed to pay for the treatment because medical services are normally paid for. The second theory, unlike the first, has a narrow range, because it does not extend to a rescuer whose services are normally given free.

III   A LEGAL DUTY TO AID THOSE IN PERIL?

My third question raises an issue concerning what is usually called the "enforcement" of morals. The use of this word is, I think, apt to mislead. Literally speaking, the law cannot force citizens to do anything, but only to submit to deprivation of freedom, or to having their money taken from them. Even if "enforcement" is taken, as it normally is, in an extended sense, the notion that morality is enforced by law carries with it the false implication that it is not enforced apart from law. Yet the chief agent for enforcing morality is public opinion. If the approval or disapproval of family and friends is not visited on those who conform or rebel, the conduct in question is not part of the shared morality. Few people, I imagine, would rather incur the censure of family and friends than pay a sum of damages or a fine. This should lead us to suspect that the law, when it imposes a duty to do what the shared morality already requires, is not enforcing but *reflecting, reinforcing,* and *specifying* morality.

There are strong reasons, I think, why the law should reflect, reinforce, and specify, at least that segment of the shared morality which consists in moral duties owed to others. The first is the advantage to those who stand to benefit. It is true that legal incentives probably influence no more than a tiny minority, but they certainly influence some. A driver sees the victim of a highway accident bleeding by the roadside. He knows he ought to stop, but is tempted to drive on in order to keep an assignment. The thought that there is a law requiring him to stop may pull him up short.

Even if the impact of the law is confined to a few, there is a special reason for reinforcing the duty to aid persons in peril. Peril means danger of death or serious injury or, at the least, of grave damage to property. The more serious the harm to be averted, the more worthwhile it is to save even a handful of those who would otherwise suffer irretrievable injury or death.

Secondly, there are some reasons for holding that the law ought in general to mirror moral obligations. In doing so, it ministers to an expectation entertained by the majority of citizens. The lawyer is, perhaps, so used to rules which permit men to flout their moral duties that he is at times benumbed. Promises made without consideration are not binding. A promisor can normally not be compelled to perform his promise but only to pay damage. Children need not support their parents. Samaritans need not be good. When we first learned these rules in law school, I daresay we were a little shocked, but the shock has worn off. It has not worn off the layman.

There are several elements in the sense of shock which laymen feel at the permissive state of the law in regard to moral duties. First, there is the "sense of injustice" of which Edmund Cahn has spoken.[21] If the law permits others to do with impunity that which I am tempted to do, but resist, what is the point of my resistance to temptation? The moral-breaker, like the unpunished lawbreaker, secures an unjust advantage at my expense.

A second element in the layman's sense of shock is the feeling that the law, like an overpermissive father, has set its standard too low. Just as a child loses respect for a father who allows him to back out of his promises, so the community will fail to respect the law which does likewise. It is, I imagine, another of those indubitable and unprovable commonplaces which are the very meat of jurisprudence that people's attitudes to particular laws often depend on their reverence for the law as a whole. If so, the failure of the law to reflect and reinforce moral duties undermines other, quite distinct laws. It may not be sensible for people to think of law in this way as a single, personified whole, but apparently they do.

A third element in the layman's sense of shock is the feeling that the guiding hand has failed. People to some degree expect a lead from the law, not merely threats and incentives. Rules of law which mirror moral duties have, among other things, an educative function. They formulate, in a way which, though not infallible, is yet in a sense authoritative, the content of the shared morality. They specify morality by marking, with more precision than the diffused sense of the people can manage, the minimum that can be tolerated.

The law cannot make men good, but it can, in the sphere of duty at least, encourage and help them to do good. It not only can but should reinforce the sanctions of public opinion, for the reasons given, unless it would be oppressive or impracticable to do so. I need say little of the practicability of imposing a duty to aid those in peril. France, Germany, and other countries have tried it out and found that it works reasonably well. But would it be oppressive? The mere fact that the majority is shocked at certain conduct does not, in my view, justify them in imposing civil or criminal liability unless there is also a balance of advantage in doing so. Difficult as it may be to strike a balance, we have in the case of rescue to add to the evils of injustice, disrespect, and want of guidance (should the law impose no duty to act) the possible benefit of those in peril if such duty is imposed. Then we must subtract the hardship of making people conform to accepted standards of neighborliness or suffer penalties. If the balance is positive, the law not merely may, but should, intervene. It has been urged that there is something peculiarly irksome in requiring people to take positive action as opposed to subjecting them to mere prohibitions. Why this should be so is a mystery. Perhaps we have a picture of Joe lounging in an armchair. It is more effort for him to get up than to stay where he is. But this is not how the law operates. Prohibitions are usually imposed because there is a strong urge or temptation to disregard them. To control the violent impulses of our nature is surely more arduous than to overcome the temptation selfishly to leave others in the lurch. Certainly there are important spheres, for instance, taxation and military service, where the law does not shrink from demanding positive action. Why should it do so in the law of rescue?

If it is argued that to require aid to be given to those in peril saps the roots of altruism by diminishing the opportunities for its exercise, the reply would be that the proposal is merely to impose a legal duty in situations where morality already sees one. Those who go beyond their moral duty will also be going beyond their legal duty. They lose no occasion for displaying altruism, merely because the law reflects a situation which *de facto* already exists.

The apparent objections to the introduction of a legal duty to rescue hardly withstand scrutiny. Perhaps the most substantial of them, in Anglo-American law, is simply tradition. Self-reliance, the outlook epitomized in the words, "Thank you, Jack, I'm all right," an irrational conviction that because law and morals do not always coincide there is some virtue in their being different,[22] all combine to frustrate the promptings of moral sensibility. One cannot but sense in some judicial utterances a certain pride in the irrational, incalculable depravity of the law, as if this demonstrated its status as an esoteric science, inaccessible to the common run of mankind. As the Russians said of Stalin: a monster, but ours. I will quote one or two.

"The only duty arising under such circumstance [that is, when one's employee catches her hand and wrist in a mangle] is one of humanity and for a breach thereof the law does not, so far as we are informed, impose any liability."[23]

Hence, there is no need to help her to free her hand. "With purely moral obligations the law does not deal. For example, the priest and the Levite who passed by on the other side were not, it is supposed, liable at law for the continued suffering of the man who fell among thieves, which they might and morally ought to have prevented or relieved."[24] In the case from which the quotation is taken, it was held to be no legal wrong for a mill owner to allow a boy of eight to meddle with dangerous machinery, in which his hand was crushed. Indeed, the boy was guilty of committing a trespass when he touched the machinery.

Two thousand years ago a Jewish lawyer demanded a definition of the term "neighbor." This makes him, I suppose, an analytical jurist. Whether the tale of the Samaritan answered his perplexities we cannot say. But he would surely have been astonished had he been informed that there were two answers to his question, one if he was asking as a lawyer, another if he was asking as a layman. To him, neighbor was neighbor and duty, duty. Perhaps this ancient lawyer's tale has a moral for law and lawyers today.

NOTES

1. P. Devlin, *The Enforcement of Morals* (Maccabaean Lecture, 1958), reprinted in *The Enforcement of Morals* (Oxford U. P., 1965); W. Friedmann in 4 *Natural Law Forum* (1964), 151; H. L. A. Hart, *Law, Liberty and Morality* (Oxford U. P., 1963); L. Henkin in 63 *Col. L. Rev.* (1963) 393; G. Hughes in 71 *Yale L. J.* (1961) 622; M. Ginsberg in 1964 *British Journal of Criminology,* 283; A. W. Mewett in 14 *Toronto L. J.* (1962) 213; E. Rostow in 1960 *Cambridge L. J.* 174 reprinted in *The Sovereign Prerogative* (Yale U. P., 1962); N. St. John-Stevas, *Life, Death and the Law* (1961); R. S. Summers in 38 *New York U. L. Rev.* (1963), 1201; B. Wootton, *Crime and the Criminal Law* (Stevens, 1963), 41.
2. J. Bentham, *Principles of Morals and Legislation,* 323 ("Who is there that in any of these cases would think punishment misapplied?").
3. J. S. Mill, *On Liberty,* Introduction ("There are also many positive acts for the benefit of others, which he may rightfully be compelled to perform . . . such as saving a fellow-creature's life").
4. J. B. Ames, *Law and Morals, supra,* pp. 1–21.
5. F. Bohlen, *The Moral Duty to Aid Others As a Basis of Liability,* 56 *U. Pa. L. Rev.* (1908) 215, 316.
6. J. Cohen, R. A. H. Robson, and A. Bates, *Ascertaining the Moral Sense of the Community,* 8 *Journal of Legal Education* (1955–56) 137.
7. *Ibid.*
8. E. Cahn, *The Moral Decision* (1956), 39.
9. Matthew 22:34.
10. Mark 12:28.
11. Luke 10:25.

12. U.S. v. Knowles (1864) 26 Fed. Cas. 801.
13. Cutler v. United Dairies (1933) 2 K.B. 297.
14. Pollock, *Torts* (15th ed.), 370; Haynes v. Harwood (1953) 1 K.B. at 163; Morgan v. Aylen (1942)1 All E.R. 489; Baker v. Hopkins (1959) 1 W.L.R. 966.
15. F. Bohlen, *Studies in the Law of Tort*, 569 n. 33.
16. 271 App. Div. 338. 65 N.Y.S. 2d 902 (1946).
17. Brugh v. Bigelow (1944) 16 N.Y.S. 2d 902 (1946).
18. Assessed by the Criminal Injuries Compensation Board (1964).
19. Hadley Byrne v. Heller (1964) A.C. 465.
20. Cotnam v. Wisdom 83 Ark. 601, 104 S.W. 164. 119

Am. St. R. 157 (1907); Greenspan v. Slate 12 N.J. 426, 97 Atl. 2d 390 (1953).
21. E. Cahn, *The Sense of Injustice* (1949); *The Moral Decision* (1956).
22. Historicus (Sir W. Harcourt), *Some Questions of International Law* (1863), 76, cited in R. Pound, *Law and Morals* (1924), 40. The argument that there is value in moral experiments does not apply to experiments in leaving others in the lurch.
23. Allen v. Hixson 36 S.E. 810 (1900).
24. Buch v. Amory Manufacturing Co. 69 N.H. 247; 44 Atl. 809 (1897).

PEOPLE v. YOUNG

Appellate Division, New York Supreme Court, 1961*

BREITEL, Justice.

The question is whether one is criminally liable for assault in the third degree if he goes to the aid of another who he mistakenly, but reasonably, believes is being unlawfully beaten, and thereby injures one of the apparent assaulters. In truth, the seeming victim was being lawfully arrested by two police officers in plain clothes. Defendant stands convicted of such a criminal assault, for which he received a sentence of 60 days in the workhouse, the execution of such sentence being suspended.

Defendant, aged 40, regularly employed, and with a clean record except for an $8 fine in connection with a disorderly conduct charge 19 years before in Birmingham, Alabama, observed two middle-aged men beating and struggling with a youth of 18. This was at 3:40 P.M. on October 17, 1958 in front of 64 West 64th Street in Manhattan. Defendant was acquainted with none of the persons involved; but believing that the youth was being unlawfully assaulted, and this is not disputed by the other participants, defendant went to his rescue, pulling on or punching at the seeming assailants. In the ensuing affray one of the older men got his leg locked with that of defendant and when defendant fell the man's leg was broken at the kneecap. The injured man then pulled out a revolver, announced to

the defendant that he was a police officer, and that defendant was under arrest. It appears that the youth in question had played some part in a street incident which resulted in the two men, who were detectives in plain clothes, seeking to arrest him for disorderly conduct. The youth had resisted, and it was in the midst of this resistance that defendant came upon the scene.

At the trial the defendant testified that he had known nothing about what had happened before he came upon the scene; that he had gone to his aid because the youth was crying and trying to pull away from the middle-aged men; and that the older men had almost pulled the trousers off the youth. The only detective who testified states, in response to a question from the court, that defendant did not know and had no way of knowing, so far as he knew, that they were police officers or that they were making an arrest.

Two things are to be kept sharply in mind in considering the problem at hand. The first is that all that is involved here is a criminal prosecution for simple assault (Penal Law, § 244), and that the court is not concerned with the incidence of civil liability in the law of torts as a result of what happened on the street. Second, there is not here involved any question of criminal responsibility for interfering with an arrest where it is known to the actor that police officers are making an arrest, but he mistakenly believes that the arrest is unlawful.

Assault and battery is an ancient crime cognizable at the common law. It is a crime in which an essential element is intent (1 Wharton's Crim.Law and Proc. [Anderson Ed. 1957] § 329 et seq.; 1 Russell on Crime [11th Ed.] p. 724). Of course, in this state the criminal law is entirely statutory. But, because assault and battery is a "common-law" crime, the statutory provisions, as in the case of most of the common-law crimes, do not purport to define the crime with the same particularity as those crimes which have a statutory origin initially (Penal Law, § 240 et seq.). One of the consequences, therefore, is that while the provisions governing assault, contained in the Penal Law, refer to various kinds of intent, in most instances the intent is related to a supplemental intent, in addition to the unspecified general intent to commit an assault, in order to impose more serious consequences upon the actor (for example, Penal Law § 240). In some instances, of course, the intent is spelled out to distinguish the prohibited activity from what might otherwise be an innocent act or merely an accidental wrong (for example, Penal Law § 242, subds. 1 and 2).

It is in this statutory context that it was held in People v. Katz, 290 N.Y. 361, 49 N.E.2d 482, that in order to sustain a charge of assault in the second degree, based upon the infliction of grievous bodily harm, not only must there be a general intent to commit unlawful bodily harm but there must be a ['specific intent", that is, a supplemental intent to inflict grievous bodily harm. The case therefore does provide an interesting parallel analysis forwarding the idea that assault is always an intent crime even when the statute omits to provide expressly for such general intent, as is the case with regard to assault in the third degree (Penal Law, § 244). Even Russell notes that, "It has been the general practice of the legislature to leave unexpressed some of the mental elements of crime" (op. cit., p. 74).

With respect to intent crimes, under general principles, a mistake of fact relates as a defense to an essential element of the crime, namely, to the mens rea (1 Wharton, op. cit., § 157; 1 Russell, op. cit., pp. 75–85). The development of the excuse of mistake is a relatively modern one and is of expanding growth (1 Bishop on Criminal Law [9th Ed.] p. 202, et seq., esp. the exhaustive and impassioned footnote which commences at p. 206 and continues through to p. 214; see, Shorter v. People, 2 N.Y. 193). But the defense was already on the march at the time of Blackstone (4 Blackstone, Comm. § 27, see esp. the footnote discussion to that section in the Jones Ed. [1916]). Russell, supra, details the tortuous development of the defense and the long road travelled between treating it as a species of involuntary conduct until it was finally recognized as a negation of criminal intent, thus ranging from the older view that criminal liability should depend upon "objective moral guilt", rather than, as in the modern thinking, upon subjective intent, that is, mens rea.

Mistake of fact, under our statutes, is a species of excuse rather than a matter of justification. Consequently, reliance on section 42[1] of the Penal Law which relates exclusively to justification is misplaced. Section 42 would be applicable only to justify a third party's intervention on behalf of a victim of an unlawful assault, but this does not preclude the defense of mistake which is related to subjective intent rather than to the objective ground for action. It is interesting that in tort at the common law excuse was provable under the general issue while justification must have been specially pleaded (1 Bacon, Abr. [1868] tit. Assault and Battery [C] p. 374). While the distinctions between excuse and justification are often fuzzy, and more often fudged, in the instance of section 42 its limited application is clear from its language.

It is in the homicide statutes in which the occasions for excuse or justification are made somewhat clearer (see Penal Law, §§ 1054, 1055); but the distinction is still relevant with respect to most crimes. In homicide it is made explicitly plain that the actor's state of mind, if reasonable, is material and controlling (id. § 1055, penult. par. 1). It does not seem rational that the same reasonable misapprehension of fact should excuse a killing in seeming proper defense of a third person in one's presence but that it should not excuse a lesser personal injury.

In this State there are no discoverable precedents involving mistake of fact when one intervenes on behalf of another person and the prosecution has been for assault, rather than homicide. (The absence of precedents in this state and many others may simply mean that no enforcement agency would prosecute in the situations that must have occurred.) No one would dispute, however, that a mistake of fact would provide a defense if the prosecution were for homicide. This divided approach is sometimes based on the untenable distinction that mistake of fact may negative a "specific" intent required in the degrees of homicide but is irrelevant to the general intent required in simple assault, or, on the even less likely distinction, that the only intent involved in assault is the intent to touch without consent or legal justification (omitting the qualification of unlawfulness). The last, of course, is a partial confusion of tort law with criminal law, and even then is not quite correct (Restatement, Torts, §§ 63–75).

There have been precedents elsewhere among the states (6 C.J.S. Assault and Battery § 93; Am.Dig. System: Assault and Battery [Century Ed.], § 98 [Dec. Dig.] § 68). There is a split among the cases and in the jurisdictions. Most hold that the rescuer intervenes at his own peril (for example, State v. Ronnie, 41 N.J.Super. 339, 125 A.2d 163; Commonwealth v. Hounchell, 280 Ky. 217, 132 S.W.2d 921), but others hold that he is excused if he acts under mistaken but reasonable belief that he is protecting a victim from unlawful attack (for example, Kees v. State, 44 Tex.Cr.R. 543, 72 S.W. 855; Little v. State, 61 Tex.Cr.R. 197, 135 S.W. 119; Brannin v. State, 221 Ind. 123, 46 N.E.2d 599; State v. Mounkes, 88 Kan. 193, 127 P. 637). Many of the cases which hold that the actor proceeds at his peril involve situations where the actor was present throughout, or through most, or through enough of the transaction and, therefore, was in no position to claim a mistake of fact. Others arise in rough situations in which the feud or enmity generally to the peace officer is a significant factor. Almost all apply unanalytically the rubric that the right to intervene on behalf of another is no greater than the other's right to self-defense, a phrasing of ancient but questionable lineage going back to when crime and tort were not yet divided in the common law—indeed, when the right to private redress was not easily distinguishable from the sanction for the public wrong (Russell, op. cit., p. 20, et seq.).

It would protract the discussion and be bootless to detail all the cases, or even to make further illustrative selection. In England, however, it is interesting to observe, a defendant who intervened mistakenly in a proper arrest by peace officers has been held liable, not for assault, but under a specific statute related to police officers acting in the execution of their duty, and which, the courts construed, did not require knowledge on the part of the third party in order to make him responsible (Regina v. Forbes and Webb [1865] 10 Cox C.C. 362; Rex v. Maxwell and Clinchy [1909] 73 J.P. 77, 2 C.R.App. Rep.26 C.C.A.; 1 Russell, op. cit., pp. 764–766). Of course, in this state, too, there is an express crime for interfering with a lawful arrest (Penal Law, § 242, subd. 5). It is a felony and requires a "specific" intent to resist the lawful apprehension. So that here we have rejected the policy adopted in England expressly making innocent interference with a lawful arrest a crime.

The modern view, as already noted, is not to impose criminal responsibility in connection with intent crimes for those who act with good motivation, in mistaken but reasonable misapprehension of the facts. Indeed, Prosser would not even hold such a person responsible in tort (Torts [2d Ed.] pp. 91–92). He makes the added argument that "if an honest mistake is to relieve the defendant of liability when he thinks that he must defend himself, his meritorious defense of another should receive the same consideration." (Restatement, Torts, supra, § 76, also exculpates an actor for intervention on behalf of a third person where the actor has a reasonable belief that the third person is privileged and that such intervention is necessary. No-

tably, the Restatement sharply limits the persons on whose behalf the actor may intervene, but this, of course, is in the area of civil liability and, as already noted, there are those who would extend the privilege.)[2]

More recently in the field of criminal law the American Law Institute in drafting a model penal code has concerned itself with the question in this case. Under section 3.05 of the Model Penal Code the use of force for the protection of others is excused if the actor behaves under a mistaken belief (Model Penal Code, Tent.Draft No. 8, May 9, 1958.)[3]

The comments by the reporters on the Model Penal Code are quite appropriate. After stating that the defense of strangers should be assimilated to the defense of oneself vide the following is said:

"In support of such a ruling, it may perhaps be said that the potentiality for deterring the actor from the use of force is greater where he is protecting a stranger than where he is protecting himself or a loved one, because in the former case the interest protected is of relatively less importance to him; moreover the potential incidence of mistake in estimating fault or the need for action on his part is increased where the defendant is protecting a stranger, because in such circumstances he is less likely to know which party to the quarrel is in the right. These arguments may be said to lead to the conclusion that, in order to minimize the area for error or mistake, the defendant should act at his peril when he is protecting a stranger. This emasculates the privilege of protection of much of its content, introducing a liability without fault which is indefensible in principle. The cautious potential actor who knows the law will, in the vast majority of cases, refrain from acting at all. The result may well be that an innocent person is injured without receiving assistance from bystanders. It seems far preferable, therefore, to predicate the justification upon the actor's belief, safeguarding if thought necessary against abuse of the privilege by the imposition of a requirement of proper care in evolving the belief. Here, as elsewhere, the latter problem is dealt with by the general provision in Section 3.09." (Model Penal Code, Tent.Draft No. 8, supra, at p. 32.)[4]

Apart from history, precedents, and the language distinctions that may be found in the statutes, it stands to reason that a man should not be punished criminally for an intent crime unless he, indeed, has the intent. Where a mistake of relevant facts is involved the premises for such intent are absent. True, there are occasions in public policy and its implementation for dispensing with intent and making one responsible for one's act even without immediate or intentional fault. This is generally accomplished by statute, and generally by statute which expressly dispenses with the presence of intent. Thus, it may well be that a Legislature determine that in order to protect the police in their activities and to make it difficult to promote false defenses one may proceed against a police officer while acting in the line of duty only at one's peril, as do the English, vide supra. But this is not a part of the intent crime of assault as it existed under common law or as it exists today under the statutes.

Indeed, if the analysis were otherwise, then the conductor who mistakenly ejects a passenger for not having paid his fare would be guilty of assault, which is hardly the case (1 Bishop, op. cit., pp. 202–203). So, too, a police officer who came to the assistance of a brother police officer would be guilty of assault if it should turn out that the brother police officer was engaged in making an unlawful arrest or was embarked upon an assault of his own private motivation (cf. Reeves v. State, Tex.Cr. App., 217 S.W. 2d 19).

It is a sterile and desolate legal system that would exact punishment for an intentional assault from one like this defendant, who acted from the most commendable motives and without excessive force. Had the facts been as he thought them, he would have been a hero and not condemned as a criminal actor. The dearth of applicable precedents—as distinguished from theoretical generalizations never, or rarely, applied—in England and in most of the states demonstrates that the benevolent intervenor has not been cast as a pariah. It is no answer to say that the policeman should be called when one sees an injustice. Even in the most populous centers, policemen are not that common or that available. Also, it ignores the peremptory response to injustice that the good man has ingrained. Again, it is to be noted, in a criminal proceeding one is concerned with the act against society, not with the wrong between individuals and the right to reparation, which is the province of tort.

Accordingly, the judgment of conviction should be reversed, on the law, and the information dismissed.

Judgment of conviction reversed upon the law and the information dismissed. All concur except VALENTE and EAGER, JJ., who dissent and vote to affirm in a dissenting opinion by VALENTE, J. Order filed.

VALENTE, Justice (dissenting).

We are concerned on this appeal with a judgment convicting defendant of the crime of assault in the third degree in violation of Section 244, subd. 1, of the Penal Law. The defendant assaulted a plain-clothes police officer, while the latter was attempting to effect a lawful and proper arrest of another. We are to determine whether the defendant's ignorance of the officer's police status and his erroneous belief that the detective was a civilian committing an unjustified assault upon the other person—who was a complete stranger to the defendant—excuses the crime. The majority of the Court, in reversing the judgment of conviction, holds that defendant's mistake removes the element of intent necessary for a criminal act.

I dissent and would affirm the conviction because the intent to commit a battery was unquestionably proven;

and, since there was no relationship between defendant and the person whom the police officers were arresting, defendant acted at his peril in intervening and striking the officer. Under well-established law, defendant's rights were no greater than those of the person whom he sought to protect; and since the arrest was lawful, defendant was no more privileged to assault the police officer than the person being arrested.

Under our statutes a *specific* intent is necessary for the crimes of assault in the first and second degrees (Sections 240 and 242 of the Penal Law). See People v. Katz, 290 N.Y. 361, 49 N.E. 2d 482. Generally, the assaults contemplated by those sections were known as "aggravated" assaults under the common law. (1 Wharton's Crim.Law & Prac. [Anderson Ed. 1957] § 358.) However, assault in the third degree is defined by Section 244, subd. 1, of the Penal Law as an assault and battery not such as is specified in Sections 240 and 242. No specific intent is required under Section 244. All that is required is the knowledgeable doing of the act. "It is sufficient that the defendant voluntarily intended to commit the unlawful act of touching" (1 Wharton's op. cit. § 338, p. 685).

In the instant case, had the defendant assaulted the officer with the specific intent of preventing the lawful apprehension of the other person he would have been subject to indictment under the provisions of subdivision 5 of Section 242 of the Penal Law, which constitutes such an act assault in the second degree. But the inability to prove a specific intent does not preclude the People from establishing the lesser crime of assault in the third degree which requires proof only of the general intent "to commit the unlawful act of touching", if such exists.

There is evidently no New York law on the precise issue on this appeal. However, certain of our statutes point to the proper direction for solution of the problem. Section 42 of the Penal Law provides:

"An act, otherwise criminal, is justifiable when it is done to protect the person committing it, or another whom he is bound to protect, from inevitable and irreparable personal injury. . . ."

Similarly, Section 246, so far as here pertinent, provides:

"To use or attempt, or offer to use, force or violence upon or towards the person of another is not unlawful in the following cases:
. . . .
"3. When committed either by the party about to be injured or by another person in his aid or defense, in preventing or attempting to prevent an offense against his person, or a trespass or other unlawful interference with real or personal property in his lawful possession, if the force or violence used is not more than sufficient to prevent such offense".

These statutes represent the public policy of this State regarding the areas in which an assault will be excused or rendered "not unlawful" where one goes to the assistance of another. They include only those cases in which the other person is one whom the defendant "is bound to protect" (Sec. 42) or where the defendant is "preventing or attempting to prevent an offense against" such other person (Sec. 246). Neither statute applies to the instant case since the other person herein was one unlawfully resisting a legal arrest—and hence no offense was being committed against his person by the officer—and he was not an individual whom defendant was "bound to protect".

It has been held in other states that one who goes to the aid of a third person acts at his peril, and his rights to interfere do not exceed the rights of the person whom he seeks to protect. State v. Ronnie, 41 N.J. Super. 339, 125 A.2d 163; Griffin v. State, 229 Ala. 482, 158 So. 316; Commonwealth v. Hounchell, 280 Ky. 217, 132 S.W.2d 921; 6 C.J.S. Assault and Battery, § 93, p. 950; 1 Wharton's op. cit., § 352; 4 Am. Jur. Assault and Battery, § 54, p. 155. We need not consider to what extent that rule is modified by Section 42 of the Penal Law since there is no question here but that the person being arrested was not in any special relation to defendant so that he was a person whom defendant was "bound to protect". It follows then that there being no right on the part of the person, to whose aid defendant came, to assault the officer—the arrest being legal—defendant had no greater right or privilege to assault the officer.

The conclusion that defendant was properly convicted in this case comports with sound public policy. It would be a dangerous precedent for courts to announce that plain-clothes police officers attempting lawful arrests over wrongful resistance are subject to violent interference by strangers ignorant of the facts, who may attack the officers with impunity so long as their ignorance forms a reasonable basis for a snap judgment of the situation unfavorable to the officers. Although the actions of such a defendant, who acts on appearances, may eliminate the specific intent required to convict him of a felony assault, it should not exculpate him from the act of aggressive assistance to a law breaker in the process of wrongfully resisting a proper arrest.

I do not detract from the majority's views regarding commendation of the acts of a good Samaritan, although it may be difficult in some cases to distinguish such activities from those of an officious intermeddler. But opposed to the encouragement of the "benevolent intervenor" is the conflicting and more compelling interest of protection of police officers. In a city like New York, where it becomes necessary to utilize the services of a great number of plain-clothes officers, the efficacy of their continuing struggle against crime should not be impaired by the possibility of interference by citizens who may be acting from commendable motives. It is more desirable—and evidently up to this point the Legislature has so deemed it—that in such cases the intervening citizen be held to act at his peril when he assaults a stranger, who unknown to him is a police officer legally performing his duty. In this conflict of interests, the balance preponderates in favor of the protection of the police rather than the misguided intervenor.

The majority points to the recommendations of the American Law Institute in drafting a Model Penal Code which makes the use of force justifiable to protect a third person when the actor believes his intervention is necessary for the protection of such third person (Model Penal Code, Tent. Draft No. 8, § 3.05 [1(c)], p. 30). Obviously these are recommendations which properly are to be addressed to a legislature and not to courts. The comments of the reporters on the Model Penal Code, from which the majority quotes, indicate (p. 31) that in the United States the view is preserved in much state legislation that force may not be used to defend others unless they stand in a special relationship to their protector. The reporters state: "The simple solution of the whole problem is to assimilate the defense of strangers to the defense of oneself, and this the present section does". If this be so, then even under the Model Penal Code, since the stranger, who is being lawfully arrested, may not assault the officers a third person coming to his defense may not do so. In any event, the Model Penal Code recognizes that the law as it now stands requires the conviction of the defendant herein. Until the Legislature acts, the courts should adhere to the well-established rules applicable in such cases. Such adherence demands the affirmance of the conviction herein.

NOTES

1. The section reads as follows:
"§ 42. Rule when act done in defense of self or another
"An act, otherwise criminal, is justifiable when it is done to protect the person committing it, or another whom he is bound to protect, from inevitable and irreparable personal injury, and the injury could only be prevented by the act, nothing more being done than is necessary to prevent the injury."
2. It is interesting that Dean Prosser is now the Chief Reporter for the American Law Institute in the draft of Restatement, Torts, Second. Tentative Draft No. 1 [April 5, 1957] of Restatement, Torts, Second, deletes the limitations to section 76 restricting intervention on behalf of strangers. And in the comments it is stated, "There is no modern case holding that there is no privilege to defend a stranger."
3. The full text of subdivision 1 of section 3.05 reads as follows:
"Section 3.05. Use of Force for the Protection of Other Persons.

"(1) The use of force upon or toward the person of another is justifiable to protect a third person when:

"(a) the actor would be justified under Section 3.04 in using such force to protect himself against the injury he believes to be threatened to the person whom he seeks to protect; and

"(b) under the circumstances as the actor believes them to be, the person whom he seeks to protect would be justified in using such protective force; and

"(c) The actor believes that his intervention is necessary for the protection of such other person."

4. Equally valuable comments may be found at p. 17 of the same draft, and at p. 140 of Tent. Draft No. 4.

P E O P L E v. Y O U N G

New York Court of Appeals, 1962*

Per Curiam. Whether one, who in good faith aggressively intervenes in a struggle between another person and a police officer in civilian dress attempting to effect the lawful arrest of the third person, may be properly convicted of assault in the third degree is a question of law of first impression here.

The opinions in the court below in the absence of precedents in this State carefully expound the opposing views found in other jurisdictions. The majority in the Appellate Division have adopted the minority rule in the other States that one who intervenes in a struggle between strangers under the mistaken but reasonable belief that he is protecting another who he assumes is being unlawfully beaten is thereby exonerated from criminal liability.* The weight of authority holds with the dissenters below that one who goes to the aid of a third person does so at his peril.*

While the doctrine espoused by the majority of the court below may have support in some States, we feel that such a policy would not be conducive to an orderly society. We agree with the settled policy of law in most jurisdictions that the right of a person to defend another ordinarily should not be greater than such person's right to defend himself. Subdivision 3 of section 246 of the Penal Law does not apply as no offense was being committed on the person of the one resisting the lawful arrest. Whatever may be the public policy where the felony charged requires proof of a specific intent and the issue is justifiable homicide, it is not relevant in a prosecution for assault in the third degree where it is only necessary to show that the defendant knowingly struck a blow.

In this case there can be no doubt that the defendant intended to assault the police officer in civilian dress. The resulting assault was forceful. Hence motive or mistake of fact is of no significance as the defendant was not charged with a crime requiring such intent or knowledge. To be guilty of third degree assault "It is sufficient that the defendant voluntarily intended to commit the unlawful act of touching" (1 Wharton's Criminal Law and Procedure [1957], § 338, p. 685). Since in these circumstances the aggression was inexcusable the defendant was properly convicted.

Accordingly, the order of the Appellate Division should be reversed and the information reinstated.

Froessel, J. (dissenting). The law is clear that one may kill in defense of another when there is reasonable, though mistaken, ground for believing that the person slain is about to commit a felony or to do some great personal injury to the apparent victim (Penal Law, § 1055); yet the majority now hold, for the first time, that in the event of a simple assault under similar circumstances, the mistaken belief, no matter how reasonable, is no defense.

Briefly, the relevant facts are these: On a Friday afternoon at about 3:40, Detectives Driscoll and Murphy, not in uniform, observed an argument taking place between a motorist and one McGriff in the street in front of premises 64 West 54th Street, in midtown Manhattan. Driscoll attempted to chase McGriff out of the roadway in order to allow traffic to pass, but McGriff refused to move back; his actions caused a

*11 N. Y. 2d 274 (1962)
*Citations omitted [Eds.].

crowd to collect. After identifying himself to McGriff, Driscoll placed him under arrest. As McGriff resisted, defendant "came out of the crowd" from Driscoll's rear and struck Murphy about the head with his fist. In the ensuing struggle Driscoll's right kneecap was injured when defendant fell on top of him. At the station house, defendant said he had not known or thought Driscoll and Murphy were police officers.

Defendant testified that while he was proceeding on 54th Street he observed two white men, who appeared to be 45 or 50 years old, pulling on a "colored boy" (McGriff), who appeared to be a lad about 18, whom he did not know. The men had nearly pulled McGriff's pants off, and he was crying. Defendant admitted he knew nothing of what had transpired between the officers and McGriff, and made no inquiry of anyone; he just came there and pulled the officer away from McGriff.

Defendant was convicted of assault third degree. In reversing upon the law and dismissing the information, the Appellate Division held that one is not "criminally liable for assault in the third degree if he goes to the aid of another whom he mistakenly, but *reasonably,* believes is being unlawfully beaten, and thereby injures one of the apparent assaulters" (emphasis supplied). While in my opinion the majority below correctly stated the law, I would reverse here and remit so that the Appellate Division may pass on the question of whether or not defendant's conduct was reasonable in light of the circumstances presented at the trial (Code Crim. Pro., §§ 543-a, 543-b).

As the majority below pointed out, assault is a crime derived from the common law (*People v. Katz,* 290 N. Y. 361, 365). Basic to the imposition of criminal liability both at common law and under our statutory law is the existence in the one who committed the prohibited act of what has been variously termed a guilty mind, a *mens rea* or a criminal intent.*

Criminal intent requires an awareness of wrongdoing. When conduct is based upon mistake of fact reasonably entertained, there can be no such awareness and, therefore, no criminal culpability. In *People ex rel. Hegeman v. Corrigan* (195 N. Y. 1, 12) we stated: "it is very apparent that the innocence or criminality of the intent in a particular act generally depends on the knowledge or belief of the actor at the time. An honest and *reasonable* belief in the existence of circumstances which, if true, would make the act for which the defendant is prosecuted innocent, would be a good defense." (Emphasis supplied.)

It is undisputed that defendant did not know that Driscoll and Murphy were detectives in plain clothes engaged in lawfully apprehending an alleged disorderly person. If, therefore, defendant *reasonably* believed he was lawfully assisting another, he would not have been guilty of a crime. Subdivision 3 of section 246 of the Penal Law provides that it is not unlawful to use force "When committed either by the party about to be injured or *by another person in his aid or defense, in preventing or attempting to prevent an offense against his person,* * * * if the force or violence used is not more than sufficient to prevent such offense" (emphasis supplied). The law is thus clear that if defendant entertained an "honest and reasonable belief" (*People ex rel. Hegeman v. Corrigan,* 195 N. Y. 1, 12 *supra*) that the facts were as he perceived them to be, he would be exonerated from criminal liability.

By ignoring one of the most basic principles of criminal law—that crimes *mala in se* require proof of at least general criminal intent—the majority now hold that the defense of mistake of fact is "of no significance." We are not here dealing with one of "a narrow class of exceptions" (*People v. Katz,* 290 N. Y. 361, 365, *supra*) where the Legislature has created crimes which do not depend on *criminal* intent but which are complete on the mere intentional doing of an act *malum prohibitum.** (9 N Y 2d 51, 58; *People v. Werner,* 174 N. Y. 132, *supra*).

There is no need, in my opinion, to consider the law of other States, for New York policy clearly supports the view that one may act on appearances reasonably ascertained, as does New Jersey.* Our Penal Law (§ 1055), to which I have already alluded, is a statement of that policy. The same policy was expressed by this court in *People v. Maine* (166 N. Y. 50). There, the defendant observed his brother fighting in the street with two other men; he stepped in and stabbed to death one of the latter. The defense was justifiable homicide under the predecessor of section 1055. The court held it reversible error to admit into evidence the declarations of the defendant's brother, made before defendant happened upon the scene, which tended to show that the brother was the aggressor. We said (p. 52): "Of course the acts and conduct of the defendant must be judged solely with reference to the situation as it was when he first and afterwards saw it." Mistake of relevant fact, reasonably entertained, is thus a defense to homicide under section 1055 (*People v. Governale,* 193 N. Y. 581, 588), and one who kills in defense of another and proffers this defense of justification is to be judged according to the circumstances as they appeared to him.*

The mistaken belief, however, must be one which is reasonably entertained, and the question of reasonableness is for the trier of the facts.* "The question is not merely what did the accused believe, but also, what did he have the right to believe?" (*People v. Rodawald,* 177 N. Y. 408, 427.) Without passing on the facts of the instant case, the Appellate Division had no right to assume that defendant's conduct was reasonable, and to dismiss the information as a matter of law. Nor do we have the right to reinstate the verdict without giving the Appellate Division the opportunity to pass upon the facts (Code Crim. Pro., § 543-b).

Although the majority of our court are now purporting to fashion a policy "conducive to an orderly society", by their decision they have defeated their avowed purpose. What public interest is promoted by a principle which would deter one from coming to the aid of a fellow citizen who he has reasonable ground to apprehend is in imminent danger of personal injury at the hands of assailants? Is it reasonable to denominate, as justifiable homicide, a slaying committed under a mistaken but reasonably held belief, and deny this same defense of justification to one using less force? Logic, as well as historical background and related precedent, dictates that the rule and policy expressed by our Legislature in the case of homicide, which is an assault resulting in death, should likewise be applicable to a much less serious assault not resulting in death.

I would reverse the order appealed from and remit the case to the Appellate Division pursuant to section 543-b of the Code of Criminal Procedure "for determination upon the questions of fact raised in that court."

Chief Judge Desmond and Judges Dye, Fuld, Burke and Foster concur in Per Curiam opinion; Judge Froessel dissents in an opinion in which Judge Van Voorhis concurs.

Order reversed, etc.

BARBARA WOOTTON

Eliminating Responsibility*

THE FUNCTION OF THE COURTS: PENAL OR PREVENTIVE?

... Proposals for the modernisation of the methods by which the criminal courts arrive at their verdicts do not, however, raise any question as to the object of the whole exercise. Much more fundamental are the issues which arise after conviction, when many a judge or magistrate must from time to time have asked himself just what it is that he is trying to achieve. Is he trying to punish the wicked, or to prevent the recurrence of forbidden acts? The former is certainly the traditional answer and is still deeply entrenched both in the legal profession and in the minds of much of the public at large; and it has lately been reasserted in uncompromising terms by a former Lord Chief Justice. At a meeting of magistrates earlier this year Lord Goddard is reported to have said that the duty of the criminal law was to punish—and that reformation of the prisoner was not the courts' business.[1] Those who take this view doubtless comfort themselves with the belief that the two objectives are nearly identical: that the punishment of the wicked is also the best way to prevent the occurrence of prohibited acts. Yet the continual failure of a mainly punitive system to diminish the volume of crime strongly suggests that such comfort is illusory; and it will indeed be a principal theme of these lectures that the choice between the punitive and the preventive[2] concept of the criminal process is a real one; and that, according as that choice is made, radical differences must follow in the courts' approach to their task. I shall, moreover, argue that in recent years

*From Crime and the Criminal Law by Barbara Wootton (London: Sweet & Maxwell, Ltd., 1963), pp. 40–57 and 58–84. Reprinted by permission of the author and the publisher.

a perceptible shift has occurred away from the first and towards the second of these two conceptions of the function of the criminal law; and that this movement is greatly to be welcomed and might with advantage be both more openly acknowledged and also accelerated.

First, however, let us examine the implications of the traditional view. Presumably the wickedness which renders a criminal liable to punishment must be inherent either in the actions which he has committed or in the state of mind in which he has committed them. Can we then in the modern world identify a class of inherently wicked actions? Lord Devlin, who has returned more than once to this theme, holds that we still can, by drawing a sharp distinction between what he calls the criminal and the quasi-criminal law. The distinguishing mark of the latter, in his view, is that a breach of it does not mean that the offender has done anything morally wrong. "Real" crimes, on the other hand, he describes as "sins with legal definitions"; and he adds that "It is a pity that this distinction, which I believe the ordinary man readily recognises, is not acknowledged in the administration of justice." "The sense of obligation which leads the citizen to obey a law that is good in itself is," he says, "different in quality from that which leads to obedience to a regulation designed to secure a good end." Nor does his Lordship see any reason "why the quasi-criminal should be treated with any more ignominy than a man who has incurred a penalty for failing to return a library book in time."[2a] And in a personal communication he has further defined the "real" criminal law as any part of the criminal law, new or old, which the good citizen does not break without a sense of guilt.

Nevertheless this attempt to revive the lawyer's distinction between *mala in se* and *mala prohibita*—things which are bad in themselves and things which are merely prohibited—cannot, I think, succeed. In the first place the statement that a real crime is one about which the good citizen would feel guilty is surely circular. For how is the good citizen to be defined in this context unless as one who feels guilty about committing the crimes that Lord Devlin classifies as "real"? And in the second place the badness even of those actions which would most generally be regarded as *mala in se* is inherent, not in the physical acts themselves, but in the circum-

stances in which they are performed. Indeed it is hard to think of any examples of actions which could, in a strictly physical sense, be said to be bad in themselves. The physical act of stealing merely involves moving a piece of matter from one place to another: what gives it its immoral character is the framework of property rights in which it occurs. Only the violation of these rights transforms an inherently harmless movement into the iniquitous act of stealing. Nor can bodily assaults be unequivocally classified as *mala in se;* for actions which in other circumstances would amount to grievous bodily harm may be not only legal, but highly beneficial, when performed by competent surgeons; and there are those who see no wrong in killing in the form of judicial hanging or in war.

One is indeed tempted to suspect that actions classified as *mala in se* are really only *mala antiqua*—actions, that is to say, which have been recognised as criminal for a very long time; and that the tendency to dismiss sundry modern offences as "merely quasi-crimes" is simply a mark of not having caught up with the realities of the contemporary world. The criminal calendar is always the expression of a particular social and moral climate, and from one generation to another it is modified by two sets of influences. On the one hand ideas about what is thought to be right or wrong are themselves subject to change; and on the other hand new technical developments constantly create new opportunities for antisocial actions which the criminal code must be extended to include. To a thoroughgoing Marxist these two types of change would not, presumably, be regarded as mutually independent: to the Marxist it is technical innovations which cause moral judgments to be revised. But for present purposes it does not greatly matter whether the one is, or is not, the cause of the other. In either case the technical and the moral are distinguishable. The fact that there is nothing in the Ten Commandments about the iniquity of driving a motor vehicle under the influence of drink cannot be read as evidence that the ancient Israelites regarded this offence more leniently than the contemporary British. On the other hand the divergent attitudes of our own criminal law and that of most European countries to homosexual practices has no obvious relation to technical development, and is clearly the expression of differing moral judgments, or at the least to different conceptions of the proper relation between morality and the criminal law.

One has only to glance, too, at the maximum penalties which the law attaches to various offences to realise how profoundly attitudes change in course of time. Life imprisonment, for example, is not only the obligatory sentence for noncapital murder and the maximum permissible for manslaughter. It may also be imposed for blasphemy or for the destruction of registers of births or baptisms. Again, the crime of abducting an heiress carries a potential sentence of fourteen years, while that for the abduction of a child under fourteen years is only half as long. For administering a drug to a female with a view to carnal knowledge a maximum of two years is provided, but for damage to cattle you are liable to fourteen years' imprisonment. For using unlawful oaths the maximum is seven years, but for keeping a child in a brothel it is a mere six months. Such sentences strike us today as quite fantastic; but they cannot have seemed fantastic to those who devised them.

For the origins of the supposed dichotomy between real crimes and quasi-crimes we must undoubtedly look to theology, as Lord Devlin's use of the term "sins with legal definitions" itself implies. The links between law and religion are both strong and ancient. Indeed, as Lord Radcliffe has lately reminded us, it has taken centuries for "English judges to realise that the tenets and injunctions of the Christian religion were not part of the common law of England";[3] and even today such realisation does not seem to be complete. As recently as 1961, in the "Ladies Directory" case, the defendant Shaw, you may remember, was convicted of conspiring to corrupt public morals, as well as of offences against the Sexual Offences Act of 1956 and the Obscene Publications Act of 1959, on account of his publication of a directory in which the ladies of the town advertised their services, sometimes, it would seem, in considerable detail. In rejecting Shaw's appeal to the House of Lords on the charge of conspiracy, Lord Simonds delivered himself of the opinion that without doubt "there remains in the courts a residual power to . . . conserve not only the safety but also the moral welfare of the state"; and Lord Hodson, concurring, added that "even if Chris-

tianity be not part of the law of England, yet the common law has its roots in Christianity."[4]

In the secular climate of the present age, however, the appeal to religious doctrine is unconvincing, and unlikely to be generally acceptable. Instead we must recognise a range of actions, the badness of which is inherent not in themselves, but in the circumstances in which they are performed, and which stretches in a continuous scale from wilful murder at one end to failure to observe a no-parking rule or to return on time a library book (which someone else may be urgently wanting) at the other. (Incidentally a certain poignancy is given to Lord Devlin's choice of this last example by a subsequent newspaper report that a book borrower in Frankfurt who omitted, in spite of repeated requests, to return a book which he had borrowed two years previously was brought before a local magistrate actually— though apparently by mistake—in handcuffs.[5]) But however great the range from the heinous to the trivial, the important point is that the gradation is continuous; and in the complexities of modern society a vast range of actions, in themselves apparently morally neutral, must be regarded as in varying degrees antisocial, and therefore in their contemporary settings as no less objectionable than actions whose criminal status is of greater antiquity. The good citizen will doubtless experience different degrees of guilt according as he may have stabbed his wife, engaged in homosexual intercourse, omitted to return his library book or failed to prevent one of his employees from watering the milk sold by his firm. Technically these are all crimes; whether or not they are also sins in a purely theological matter with which the law has no concern. If the function of the criminal law is to punish the wicked, then everything which the law forbids must in the circumstances in which it is forbidden be regarded as in its appropriate measure wicked.

Although this is, I think, the inevitable conclusion of any argument which finds wickedness inherent in particular classes of action, it seems to be unpalatable to Lord Devlin and others who conceive the function of the criminal law in punitive terms. It opens the door too wide. Still the door can be closed again by resort to the alternative theory that the wickedness of an action is inherent not in the action itself, but in the state of mind of the person who performs it. To punish people merely for what they have done, it is argued, would be unjust, for the forbidden act might have been an accident for which the person who did it cannot be held to blame. Hence the requirement, to which traditionally the law attaches so much importance, that a crime is not, so to speak, a crime in the absence of *mens rea*.

Today, however, over a wide front even this requirement has in fact been abandoned. Today many, indeed almost certainly the majority, of the cases dealt with by the criminal courts are cases of strict liability in which proof of a guilty mind is no longer necessary for conviction. A new dichotomy is thus created, and one which in this instance exists not merely in the minds of the judges but is actually enshrined in the law itself —that is to say, the dichotomy between those offences in which the guilty mind is, and those in which it is not, an essential ingredient. In large measure, no doubt, this classification coincides with Lord Devlin's division into real and quasi-crimes; but whether or not this coincidence is exact must be a question of personal judgment. To drive a car when your driving ability is impaired through drink or drugs is an offence of strict liability: It is no defence to say that you had no idea that the drink would affect you as it did, or to produce evidence that you were such a seasoned drinker that any such result was, objectively, not to be expected. These might be mitigating circumstances after conviction, but are no bar to the conviction itself. Yet some at least of those who distinguish between real and quasi-crimes would put drunken driving in the former category, even though it involves no question of *mens rea*. In the passage that I quoted earlier Lord Devlin, it will be remembered, was careful to include new as well as old offences in his category of "real" crimes; but generally speaking it is the *mala antiqua* which are held to be both *mala in se* and contingent upon *mens rea*.

Nothing has dealt so devastating a blow at the punitive conception of the criminal process as the proliferation of offences of strict liability; and the alarm has forthwith been raised. Thus Dr. J. Ll. J. Edwards has expressed the fear that there is a real danger that the "widespread practice of imposing criminal liability independent of any moral fault" will result in the criminal law being regarded with contempt. "The process of basing criminal liability upon a theory of absolute prohi-

bition," he writes, "may well have the opposite effect to that intended and lead to a weakening of respect for the law."[6] Nor, in his view, is it an adequate answer to say that absolute liability can be tolerated because of the comparative unimportance of the offences to which it is applied and because, as a rule, only a monetary penalty is involved; for, in the first place, there are a number of important exceptions to this rule (drunken driving for example); and, secondly, as Dr. Edwards himself point out, in certain cases the penalty imposed by the court may be the least part of the punishment. A merchant's conviction for a minor trading offence may have a disastrous effect upon his business.

Such dislike of strict liability is not by any means confined to academic lawyers. In the courts, too, various devices have been used to smuggle *mens rea* back into offences from which, on the face of it, it would appear to be excluded. To the lawyer's ingenious mind the invention of such devices naturally presents no difficulty. Criminal liability, for instance, can attach only to voluntary acts. If a driver is struck unconscious with an epileptic seizure, it can be argued that he is not responsible for any consequences because his driving thereafter is involuntary: indeed he has been said not to be driving at all. If on the other hand he falls asleep, this defence will not serve since sleep is a condition that comes on gradually, and a driver has an opportunity and a duty to stop before it overpowers him. Alternatively, recourse can be had to the circular argument that anyone who commits a forbidden act must have intended to commit it and must, therefore, have formed a guilty intention. As Lord Devlin puts it, the word "knowingly" or "wilfully" can be read into acts in which it is not present; although as his Lordship points out this subterfuge is open to the criticism that it fails to distinguish between the physical act itself and the circumstances in which this becomes a crime.[7] All that the accused may have intended was to perform an action (such as firing a gun or driving a car) which is not in itself criminal. Again, in yet other cases such as those in which it is forbidden to permit or to allow something to be done the concept of negligence can do duty as a watered down version of *mens rea:* for how can anyone be blamed for permitting something about which he could not have known?

All these devices, it cannot be too strongly emphasised, are necessitated by the need to preserve the essentially punitive function of the criminal law. For it is not, as Dr. Edwards fears, the criminal law which will be brought into contempt by the multiplication of offences of strict liability, so much as this particular conception of the law's function. If that function is conceived less in terms of punishment than as a mechanism of prevention these fears become irrelevant. Such a conception, however, apparently sticks in the throat of even the most progressive lawyers. Even Professor Hart, in his Hobhouse lecture on *Punishment and the Elimination of Responsibility*,[8] seems to be incurably obsessed with the notion of punishment, which haunts his text as well as figuring in his title. Although rejecting many traditional theories, such as that punishment should be "retributive" or "denunciatory," he nevertheless seems wholly unable to envisage a system in which sentence is not automatically equated with "punishment." Thus he writes of "values quite distinct from those of retributive punishment which the system of responsibility does maintain, and which remain of great importance even if our aims in *punishing* are the forward-looking aims of social protection"; and again "even if we *punish* men not as wicked but as nuisances . . ." while he makes many references to the principle that liability to punishment must depend on a voluntary act. Perhaps it requires the naïveté of an amateur to suggest that the forward-looking aims of social protection might, on occasion, have absolutely no connection with punishment.

If, however, the primary function of the courts is conceived as the prevention of forbidden acts, there is little cause to be disturbed by the multiplication of offences of strict liability. If the law says that certain things are not to be done, it is illogical to confine this prohibition to occasions on which they are done from malice aforethought; for at least the material consequences of an action, and the reasons for prohibiting it, are the same whether it is the result of sinister malicious plotting, of negligence or of sheer accident. A man is equally dead and his relatives equally bereaved whether he was stabbed or run over by a drunken motorist or by an incompetent one; and the inconvenience caused by the loss of your bicycle is unaffected by the question whether or not the youth who removed it had the intention

of putting it back, if in fact he had not done so at the time of his arrest. It is true, of course, as Professor Hart has argued,[9] that the material consequences of an action by no means exhaust its effects. "If one person hits another, the person struck does not think of the other as *just* a cause of pain to him. . . . If the blow was light but deliberate, it has a significance for the person struck quite different from an accidental much heavier blow." To ignore this difference, he argues, is to outrage "distinctions which not only underlie morality, but pervade the whole of our social life." That these distinctions are widely appreciated and keenly felt no one would deny. Often perhaps they derive their force from a purely punitive or retributive attitude; but alternatively they may be held to be relevant to an assessment of the social damage that results from a criminal act. Just as a heavy blow does more damage than a light one, so also perhaps does a blow which involves psychological injury do more damage than one in which the hurt is purely physical.

The conclusion to which this argument leads is, I think, not that the presence or absence of the guilty mind is unimportant, but that *mens rea* has, so to speak—and this is the crux of the matter—*got into the wrong place*. Traditionally, the requirement of the guilty mind is written into the actual definition of a crime. No guilty intention, no crime, is the rule. Obviously this makes sense if the law's concern is with wickedness: where there is no guilty intention, there can be no wickedness. But it is equally obvious, on the other hand, that an action does not become innocuous merely because whoever performed it meant no harm. If the object of the criminal law is to prevent the occurrence of socially damaging actions, it would be absurd to turn a blind eye to those which were due to carelessness, negligence or even accident. The question of motivation is *in the first instance* irrelevant.

But only in the first instance. At a later stage, that is to say, after what is now known as a conviction, the presence or absence of guilty intention is all-important for its effect on the appropriate measures to be taken to prevent a recurrence of the forbidden act. The prevention of accidental deaths presents different problems from those involved in the prevention of wilful murders. The results of the actions of the careless, the mistaken, the wicked and the merely unfortunate may be indistinguishable from one another, but each case calls for a different treatment. Tradition, however, is very strong, and the notion that these differences are relevant only after the fact has been established that the accused committed the forbidden act seems still to be deeply abhorrent to the legal mind. Thus Lord Devlin, discussing the possibility that judges might have taken the line that all "unintentional" criminals might be dealt with simply by the imposition of a nominal penalty, regards this as the "negation of law." "It would,"[10] he says, "confuse the function of mercy which the judge is dispensing when imposing the penalty with the function of justice. It would have been to deny to the citizen due process of law because it would have been to say to him, in effect: 'Although we cannot think that Parliament intended you to be punished in this case because you have really done nothing wrong, come to us, ask for mercy, and we shall grant mercy.' . . . In all criminal matters the citizen is entitled to the protection of the law . . . and the mitigation of penalty should not be adopted as the prime method of dealing with accidental offenders."

Within its own implied terms of reference the logic is unexceptionable. If the purpose of the law is to dispense punishment tempered with mercy, then to use mercy as a consolation for unjust punishment is certainly to give a stone for bread. But these are not the implied terms of reference of strict liability. In the case of offences of strict liability the presumption is not that those who have committed forbidden actions must be punished, but that appropriate steps must be taken to prevent the occurrence of such actions.

Here, as often in other contexts also, the principles involved are admirably illustrated by the many driving offences in which conviction does not involve proof of *mens rea*. If, for instance, the criterion of gravity is the amount of social damage which a crime causes, many of these offences must be judged extremely grave. In 1961, 299 persons were convicted on charges of causing death by dangerous driving, that is to say more than five times as many as were convicted of murder (including those found guilty but insane) and 85 per cent more than the total of convictions for all other forms of homicide (namely murder, manslaughter and infanticide) put together. It is,

moreover, a peculiarity of many driving offences that the offender seldom intends the actual damage which he causes. He may be to blame in that he takes a risk which he knows may result in injury to other people or to their property, but such injury is neither an inevitable nor an intended consequence of the commission of the offence: which is not true of, for example, burglary. Dangerous or careless driving ranges in a continuous series from the almost wholly accidental, through the incompetent and the negligent to the positively and grossly culpable; and it is quite exceptionally difficult in many of these cases to establish just what point along this scale any particular instance should be assigned. In consequence the gravity of any offence tends to be estimated by its consequences rather than by the state of mind of the perpetrator—which is less usual (although attempted murder or grievous bodily harm may turn into murder, if the victim dies) in the case of other crimes. In my experience it is exceptional (though not unknown) for a driving charge to be made unless an accident actually occurs, and the nature of the charge is apt to be determined by the severity of the accident. I recall, for example, a case in which a car driver knocked down an elderly man on a pedestrian crossing, and a month later the victim died in hospital after an operation, his death being, one must suppose, in spite, rather than because, of this. Thereupon the charge, which had originally been booked by the police as careless, not even dangerous, driving was upgraded to causing death by dangerous driving.

For all these reasons it is recognised that if offences in this category are to be dealt with by the criminal courts at all, this can only be on a basis of strict liability. This particular category of offences thus illustrates all too vividly the fact that in the modern world in one way or another, as much and more damage is done by negligence, or by indifference to the welfare or safety of others, as by deliberate wickedness. In technically simpler societies this is less likely to be so, for the points of exposure to the follies of others are less numerous, and the daily chances of being run over, or burnt or infected or drowned because someone has left undone something that he ought to have done are less ominous. These new complexities were never envisaged by the founders of our legal traditions, and it is hardly to be wondered at if the law itself is not yet fully adapted to them. Yet it is by no means certain that the last chapter in the long and chequered history of the concept of guilt, which is so deeply rooted in our traditions, has yet been written. Time was when inanimate objects—the rock that fell on you, the tree that attracted the lightning that killed you— were held to share the blame for the disasters in which they were instrumental; and it was properly regarded as a great step forward when the capacity to acquire a guilty mind was deemed to be one of the distinctive capacities of human' beings.[11] But now, perhaps, the time has come for the concept of legal guilt to be dissolved into a wider concept of responsibility or at least accountability, in which there is room for negligence as well as purposeful wrongdoing; and for the significance of a conviction to be reinterpreted merely as evidence that a prohibited act has been committed, questions of motivation being relevant only insofar as they bear upon the probability of such acts being repeated.

I am not, of course, arguing that all crimes should immediately be transferred into the strict liability category. To do so would in some cases involve formidable problems of definition—as, for instance, in that of larceny. But I do suggest that the contemporary extension of strict liability is not the nightmare that it is often made out to be, that it does not promise the decline and fall of the criminal law, and that it is, on the contrary, a sensible and indeed inevitable measure of adaptation to the requirements of the modern world; and above all I suggest that its supposedly nightmarish quality disappears once it is accepted that the primary objective of the criminal courts is preventive rather than punitive. Certainly we need to pay heed to Mr. Nigel Walker's reminder[12] that "under our present law it is possible for a person to do great harm in circumstances which suggest that there is a risk of his repeating it, and yet to secure an acquittal." In two types of case, in both of which such harm can result, the concept of the guilty mind has become both irrelevant and obstructive. In this lecture I have been chiefly concerned with the first of these categories—that of cases of negligence. The second category—that of mental abnormality—will be the theme of that which follows.

THE PROBLEM OF THE MENTALLY ABNORMAL OFFENDER

The problem of the mentally abnormal offender raises in a particularly acute form the question of the primary function of the courts. If that function is conceived as punitive, mental abnormality must be related to guilt; for a severely subnormal offender must be less blameworthy, and ought therefore to incur a less severe punishment, than one of greater intelligence who has committed an otherwise similar crime, even though he may well be a worse risk for the future. But from the preventive standpoint it is this future risk which matters, and the important question to be asked is not: Does his abnormality mitigate or even obliterate his guilt? but, rather, is he a suitable subject for medical, in preference to any other, type of treatment? In short, the punitive and the preventive are respectively concerned the one with culpability and the other with treatability.

In keeping with its traditional obsession with the concept of guilt, English criminal law has, at least until lately, been chiefly concerned with the effect of mental disorder upon culpability. In recent years, however, the idea that an offender's mental state might also have a bearing on his treatability has begun to creep into the picture— with the result that the two concepts now lie somewhat uneasily side by side in what has become a very complex pattern.

Under the present law there are at least six distinct legal formulae under which an accused person's mental state may be put in issue in a criminal case. First, he may be found unfit to plead, in which case of course no trial takes place at all, unless and until he is thought to have sufficiently recovered. Second, on a charge of murder (and theoretically in other cases also) a defendant may be found to be insane within the terms of the M'Naughten Rules, by the illogical verdict of guilty but insane which, to be consistent with the normal use of the term guilt, ought to be revised to read—as it once did—"not guilty on the ground of insanity." Third, a person accused of murder can plead diminished responsibility under section 2 of the Homicide Act, in which case, if this defence succeeds, a verdict of manslaughter will be substituted for one of murder.

Up to this point it is, I think, indisputable that it is the relation between the accused's mental state and his culpability or punishability which is in issue. Obviously a man who cannot be tried cannot be punished. Again, one who is insane may have to be deprived of his liberty in the interests of the public safety, but, since an insane person is not held to be blameworthy in the same way as one who is in full possession of his faculties, the institution to which he is committed must be of a medical not a penal character; and for the same reason, he must not be hanged if found guilty on a capital charge. So also under the Homicide Act a defence of diminished responsibility opens the door to milder punishments than the sentences of death and life imprisonment which automatically follow the respective verdicts of capital and noncapital murder; and the fact that diminished responsibility is conceived in terms of reduced culpability, and not as indicative of the need for medical treatment, is further illustrated by the fact that in less than half the cases in which this defence has succeeded since the courts have had power to make hospital orders under the Mental Health Act, have such orders actually been made.[13] In the great majority of all the successful cases under section 2 of the Homicide Act a sentence of imprisonment has been imposed, the duration of this ranging from life to a matter of not more than a few months. Moreover, the Court of Criminal Appeal has indicated[14] approval of such sentences on the ground that a verdict of manslaughter based on diminished responsibility implies that a "residue of responsibility" rests on the accused person and that this "residue of criminal intent" may be such as to deserve punishment—a judgment which surely presents a sentencing judge with a problem of nice mathematical calculation as to the appropriate measure of punishment.

Under the Mental Health Act of 1959, however, the notion of reduced culpability begins to be complicated by the alternative criterion of treatability. Section 60 of that Act provides the fourth and fifth of my six formulae. Under the first subsection of this section, an offender who is convicted at a higher court (or at a magistrates' court if his offence is one which carries liability to imprisonment) may be compulsorily detained in hospital, or made subject to a guardianship order, if the court is satisfied, on the evidence of two doctors (one of whom must have special experience in the diagnosis or treatment of mental disorders) that this is in all the circumstances the

most appropriate way of dealing with him. In the making of such orders emphasis is clearly on the future, not on the past: The governing consideration is not whether the offender deserves to be punished, but whether in fact medical treatment is likely to succeed. No sooner have we said this, however, than the old concept of culpability rears its head again. For a hospital order made by a higher court may be accompanied by a restriction order of either specified or indefinite duration, during the currency of which the patient may only be discharged on the order of the Home Secretary; and a magistrates' court also, although it has no similar power itself to make a restriction order, may commit an offender to sessions to be dealt with, if it is of the opinion that, having regard to the nature of the offence, the antecedents of the offender and the risk of his committing further offences if set at liberty, a hospital order should be accompanied by a restriction order.

The restriction order is thus professedly designed as a protection to the public; but a punitive element also, I think, still lingers in it. For if the sole object was the protection of the public against the premature discharge of a mentally disordered dangerous offender, it could hardly be argued that the court's prediction of the safe moment for release, perhaps years ahead, is likely to be more reliable than the judgment at the appropriate time of the hospital authorities who will have had the patient continuously under their surveillance.[15] If their purpose is purely protective all orders ought surely to be of indefinite duration, and the fact that this is not so suggests that they are still tainted with the tariff notion of sentencing—that is to say, with the idea that a given offence "rates" a certain period of loss of liberty. Certainly, on any other interpretation, the judges who have imposed restriction orders on offenders to run for ten or more years must credit themselves with truly remarkable powers of medical prognosis. In fairness, however, it should be said that the practice of imposing indefinite rather than fixed term orders now seems to be growing.

So, too, with the fifth of my formulae, which is to be found in a later subsection of section 60 of the same Act. Under this, an offender who is charged before a magistrates' court with an offence for which he could be imprisoned, may be made the subject of a hospital or guardianship order *without being convicted,* provided that the court is satisfied that he did the act or made the omission of which he is accused. This power, however (which is itself an extended version of section 24 of the Criminal Justice Act, 1948, and has indeed a longer statutory history), may only be exercised if the accused is diagnosed as suffering from either mental illness or severe subnormality. It is not available in the case of persons suffering from either of the two other forms of mental disorder recognised by the Act, namely psychopathy, or simple, as distinct from severe, subnormality. And why not? One can only presume that the reason for this restriction is the fear that in cases in which only moderate mental disorder is diagnosed, or in which the diagnosis is particularly difficult and a mistake might easily be made, an offender might escape the punishment that he deserved. Even though no hospital or guardianship order can be made unless the court is of opinion that this is the "most suitable" method of disposing of the case, safeguards against the risk that this method might be used for the offender who really deserved to be punished are still written into the law.

One curious ambiguity in this provision, however, deserves notice at this stage. Before a hospital order is made, the court must be satisfied that the accused "did the act, or made the omission with which he is charged." Yet what, one may ask, is the meaning, in this context, of "the act"? Except in the case of crimes of absolute liability, a criminal charge does not relate to a purely physical action. It relates to a physical action accompanied by a guilty mind or malicious intention. If then a person is so mentally disordered as to be incapable of forming such an intention, is he not strictly incapable of performing the act with which he is charged? The point seems to have been raised when the 1948 Criminal Justice Bill was in Committee in the House of Commons, but it was not pursued.[16] Such an interpretation would, of course, make nonsense of the section, and one must presume, therefore, that the words "the act" must be construed to refer solely to the prohibited physical action, irrespective of the actor's state of mind. But in that case the effect of this subsection would seem to be to transfer every type of crime, in the case of persons of severely disordered mentality, to the category of offences of absolute liability. In practice little use appears to be made of this provision (and in my experience few magistrates are aware of its existence); but there would seem to be an important principle here, potentially capable, as I hope to suggest later, of wider application.

The last of my six formulae, which, however, antedates all the others, stands in a category by itself. It is to be found in section 4 of the Criminal Justice Act of 1948, under which a court may make mental treatment (residential or nonresidential) a condition of a probation order, provided that the offender's mental condition is "such as requires and as may be susceptible to treatment," but is not such as to justify his being in the language of that day certified as "of unsound mind" or "mentally defective." Such a provision represents a very wholehearted step in the direction of accepting the criterion of treatability. For, although those to whom this section may be applied must be deemed to be guilty—in the sense that they have been convicted of offences involving *mens rea*—the only question to be decided is that of their likely response to medical or other treatment. Moreover, apart from the exclusion of insanity or mental defect, no restriction is placed on the range of diagnostic categories who may be required to submit to mental treatment under this section, although as always in the case of a probation order imposed on adults, the order cannot be made without the probationer's own consent. Nor is any reference anywhere made or even implied as to the effect of their mental condition upon their culpability. It is of interest, too, that, in practice, the use of these provisions has not been confined to what are often regarded as "pathological" crimes. Dr. Grünhut who made a study of cases to which the section was applied in 1953[17] found that out of a total of 636 probationers, 275 had committed offences against property, 216 sexual offences, ninety-seven offences of violence (other than sexual) and forty-eight other types of offence. Some of the property crimes had, it is true, "an apparently pathological background," but no less than 48 per cent were classified as "normal" acquisitive thefts.

All these modifications in the criminal process in the case of the mentally abnormal offender thus tend (with the possible exception of the 1948 Act) to treat such abnormality as in greater or less degree exculpatory. Their purpose is not just to secure that medical treatment should be provided for any offender likely to benefit from this, but rather to guard against the risk that the mentally disordered will be unjustly punished. Their concern with treatability, where it occurs, is in effect consequential rather than primary: The question—can the doctors help him? follows, if at all, upon a negative answer to the question: Is he really to blame?

Nowhere is this more conspicuous than in section 2 of the Homicide Act; and it was indeed from a study of the operation of that section that I was led nearly four years ago to the conclusion that this was the wrong approach; that any attempt to distinguish between wickedness and mental abnormality was doomed to failure; and that the only solution for the future was to allow the concept of responsibility to "wither away" and to concentrate instead on the problem of the choice of treatment, without attempting to assess the effect of mental peculiarities on degrees of culpability. That opinion was based on a study of the files of some seventy-three cases in which a defence of diminished responsibility had been raised,[18] which were kindly made available by the Home Office. To these have since been added the records of another 126 cases, the two series together covering the five and a half years from the time that the Act came into force down to mid-September 1962.

Before I pursue the implications of the suggestion that the concept of responsibility should be allowed to wither away, it may be well to ask whether anything in this later material calls for any modification of my earlier conclusion. I do not think it does. Indeed the experience of the past three and a half years seems to have highlighted both the practical and the philosophical difficulty—or as I would prefer to say the impossibility—of assessing other people's responsibility for their actions.

Some new issues have, however, arisen in the struggle to interpret the relevant section of the Act. Much legal argument has, for example, been devoted to the effect of drink upon responsibility. The Act, as you may remember, provides that a charge of murder may result in a conviction for manslaughter if the accused was suffering from "such abnormality of mind (whether arising from a condition of arrested or retarded development of mind or any inherent causes or induced by disease or injury) as substantially impaired his responsibility for his acts." Accordingly, it has been suggested that the transient effect of drink, if sufficient to produce a toxic effect upon the brain, might amount to an "injury" within the meaning of the Act. Alternatively (in the picturesque phrase of one defence counsel) drink might "make up the deficit" necessary to convert a preexistent minor abnormality into a substantial impairment of responsibility. None of these issues has yet been authoritatively decided. Sometimes the court has been able to wriggle out of a decision, as the Court of Criminal Appeal did when the "injury" argument was used on behalf of Di Duca,[19] on the ground that the particular offender concerned, whether drunk or sober, showed insufficient evidence of abnormality. Sometimes the opposite escape route has been available, as when the trial judge in the case of Dowdall,[20] while careful to emphasise that the section was not to be regarded as "a drunkard's charter," reminded the jury that two doctors had testified to the defendant's gross abnormality even apart from his admitted addiction to liquor. In Samuel's[21] case, on the other hand, in which the "deficit" theory was strongly argued in the absence of the jury, the judge clearly regarded it as inadmissible and made no reference to it in his summing up. But nearly two years later the Court of Criminal Appeal[22] concluded its judgment in Clarke's appeal with a statement that "the court wished to make it clear that it had not considered the effect of drink on a mind suffering from diminished responsibility. The court had not considered whether any abnormality of mind, however slight, would constitute a defence when substantially impaired by drink. That matter would have to be considered on another occasion."

After drink, insanity. A second complication has arisen in the problem of distinguishing between persons whose responsibility is merely diminished, and those who are deemed to be insane within the meaning of the M'Naughten Rules. Here there appears to be a division of opinion among the judges as to the right of the Crown to seek to establish insanity in cases in which the defence pleads only diminished responsibility. In two out of my earlier series of seventy-three cases in which this defence was raised, and in four of the later series of 126 cases, a verdict of guilty but insane was actually returned; and in at least half a dozen others in which this defence did succeed, the witnesses called by the Crown to rebut evidence of diminished responsibility sought to establish that the accused was in fact insane. Such a procedure was in keeping with the forecast of the Attorney-General in his speech on the Second Reading of the Homicide Bill.[23] "If," he said, "the defence raise any question as to the accused's mental capacity, and evidence is called to show that he is suffering from a serious abnormality of mind, then, if the evidence goes beyond a diminution of responsibility and really shows that the accused was within the M'Naughten Rules, it would be right for the judge to leave it to the jury to determine whether the accused was, to use the old phrase, 'guilty but insane,' or to return a verdict of manslaughter on the basis that, although not insane, he suffered from diminished responsibility. ..." Nevertheless in the case of *Price* in 1962[24] the trial judge ruled that "if the Crown raises the issue of insanity and the jury find the accused guilty but insane, he cannot challenge the verdict in any higher court. ... It seems to me," he said, "having regard to the serious consequences which would follow to a man if the Crown does succeed in raising the issue of insanity that the law cannot be, without an Act of Parliament, that a man should lose his right of appeal. In these circumstances I rule that the Crown is not entitled to invite the jury to consider the issue of insanity."

If this ruling is upheld, the result will be that the—at the best of times exceptionally difficult—distinction between insanity and diminished responsibility will be unlikely to be drawn on the merits of the case. For, except in extreme cases, the defence is always likely to prefer a plea of diminished responsibility to one of insanity, since if the latter succeeds indefinite detention necessarily follows, whereas on a conviction for manslaughter, which is the outcome of a successful defence of diminished responsibility, the court has complete discretion to pass whatever sentence it thinks fit. Persons who may be insane within the meaning of the M'Naughten Rules are therefore always likely to be tempted to plead diminished responsibility. Yet if they do, the jury will, if the analogy of the judgment in *Price's* case is followed, be precluded from hearing evidence as to their possible insanity and so arriving at an informed judgment on the issue of diminished responsibility versus insanity.

These developments can only be said to have added to the prevailing confusion. One other step has, however, been taken, which does at least aim at clarification. In the early days of the Act's operation juries were generally given little guidance as to the meaning of diminished responsibility. Judges did not ordinarily go beyond making sure that the members of the jury were familiar with the actual words of the section, which they were then expected to interpret for themselves. In 1960, however, in allowing the appeal of Patrick Byrne, the Birmingham Y.W.C.A. murderer, the Court of Criminal Appeal[25] attempted a formulation of the meaning of diminished responsibility on which judges have subsequently been able to draw in their directions to juries. In the words used by the Lord Chief Justice in this judgment "abnormality of mind" must be defined widely enough "to cover the mind's activities in all its aspects, not only the perception of physical acts and matters, and the ability to form a rational judgment as to whether an act is right or wrong, but also the ability to exercise willpower to control physical acts in accordance with that rational judgment." Furthermore, while medical evidence on this issue was said to be "no doubt of importance," it was not necessarily conclusive and might be outweighed by other material. Juries might also legitimately differ from doctors in assessing whether any impairment of responsibility could properly be regarded as "substantial"; and to guide them on this last point it was suggested that such phrases as "partial insanity" or on "the borderline of insanity" might be possible interpretations of the kind of abnormality which would substantially impair responsibility.

How far this helps may be a matter for argument. In the following year, in the case of Victor Terry, the Worthing bank murderer, Mr. Justice Stable adopted the original course of handing the jury a transcript of the (exceptionally voluminous) medical evidence instead of attempting to sum this up himself; but this procedure did not commend itself to the Court of Criminal Appeal,[26] although the court's disapproval did not go so far as to result in the condemned man's appeal being allowed or save him from being hanged. Certainly for my part I cannot think that anyone can listen to, or read, the sophisticated subtleties in which legal disputations about de-grees of responsibility persistently flounder and founder without reaching the paradoxical conclu-sion that the harder we try to recognise the com-plexity of reality, the greater the unreality of the whole discussion. Indeed it is hardly surprising that in practice most of these subtleties probably pass over the heads of juries, whose conclusions appear to be reached on simpler grounds. At least two-thirds of those persons in whose cases a de-fence of diminished responsibility has succeeded have produced some serious evidence of previous mental instability such as a history of previous attempts at suicide, or of discharge from the Forces on psychiatric grounds, or of some trouble for which psychiatric advice has been sought, while a much higher proportion, though not med-ically diagnosed, are thought by relatives to be in some way peculiar. On the other hand, well under half of those in whose case a defence of dimin-ished responsibility was not successful appear to have had any history of mental instability. It would seem that juries, clutching perhaps at straws, are disposed to take the view that a previ-ous history of mental disturbance indicates (on the balance of probability, which is all that they have to establish) subsequent impairment of re-sponsibility. And in the remaining cases, in which there is no such history, the concept of dimin-ished responsibility seems to be dissolving into what is virtually the equivalent of a mitigating circumstance. Certainly in many of the more re-cent cases it is difficult to establish the presence of mental abnormality unless by the circular ar-gument that anybody who commits homicide must, by definition, be unbalanced. It was surely compassion rather than evidence of mental ab-normality which accounted for the success of a defence of diminished responsibility in the case of the major who found himself the father of a Mon-gol baby and, after reading up the subject of Mon-golism in his public library, decided that the best course for everybody concerned would be to smother the child. And in the not infrequent cases in which a defence of diminished responsi-bility has succeeded, when homicide has resulted from such common human motives as sexual jeal-ousy or the desire to escape from pecuniary em-barrassment, it is hard not to believe that juries were moved more by the familiarity, than by the abnormality, of the offender's mental processes.

The most important development of the past few years lies, however, in the fact that the impos-sibility of keeping a clear line between the wicked and the weak-minded seems now to be officially admitted. In the judgment of the Court of Crimi-nal Appeal on Byrne's appeal, from which I have already quoted, the Lord Chief Justice frankly admitted that "the step between 'he did not resist his impulse,' and 'he could not resist his im-pulse' " was one which was "incapable of scien-tific proof. A fortiori," the judgment continues, "there is no scientific measurement of the degree of difficulty which an abnormal person finds in controlling his impulses. These problems which in the present state of medical knowledge are scientifically insoluble the jury can only approach in a broad commonsense way."

Apart from admiration of the optimism which expects common sense to make good the deficien-cies of science, it is only necessary to add that the problem would seem to be insoluble, not merely in the present, but indeed in any, state of medical knowledge. Improved medical knowledge may certainly be expected to give better insight into the origins of mental abnormalities, and better predictions as to the probability that particular types of individuals will in fact "control their physical acts" or make "rational judgments"; but neither medical nor any other science can ever hope to prove whether a man who does not resist his impulses does not do so because he cannot or because he will not. The propositions of science are by definition subject to empirical validation; but since it is not possible to get inside another man's skin, no objective criterion which can dis-tinguish between "he did not" and "he could not" is conceivable.

Logic, experience and the Lord Chief Justice thus all appear to lead to the same conclusion—that is to say, to the impossibility of establishing any reliable measure of responsibility in the sense of a man's ability to have acted otherwise than as he did. After all, every one of us can say with St. Paul (who, as far as I am aware, is not generally suspected of diminished responsibility) "the good that I would I do not: but the evil which I would not, that I do."

I have dealt at some length with our experience of diminished responsibility cases under the Homicide Act because taken together, the three facts, first, that under this Act questions of responsibility have to be decided before and not after conviction; second, that these questions fall to be decided by juries; and, third, that the charges involved are of the utmost gravity, have caused the relationship of responsibility to culpability to be explored with exceptional thoroughness in this particular context. But the principles involved are by no means restricted to the narrow field of charges of homicide. They have a far wider applicability, and are indeed implicit also in section 60 of the Mental Health Act. Unfortunately, up till now, and pending completion of the researches upon which I understand that Mr. Nigel Walker and his colleagues at Oxford are engaged, little is known of the working of this section. But it seems inevitable that if in any case a convicted person wished (as might well happen) to challenge the diagnosis of mental disorder which must precede the making of a hospital order, he would quickly be plunged into arguments about subnormality and psychopathy closely parallel to those which occupy so many hours of diminished responsibility trials.

At the same time the proposal that we should bypass, or disregard, the concept of responsibility is only too easily misunderstood; and I propose, therefore, to devote the remainder of this lecture to an attempt to meet some of the criticisms which have been brought against this proposal, to clarify just what it does or does not mean in the present context and to examine its likely implications.

First, it is to be observed that the term "responsibility" is here used in a restricted sense, much narrower than that which it often carries in ordinary speech. The measure of a person's responsibility for his actions is perhaps best defined in the words that I used earlier in terms of his capacity to act otherwise than as he did. A person may be described as totally irresponsible if he is wholly incapable of controlling his actions, and as being in a state of diminished responsibility if it is abnormally difficult for him to control them. Responsibility in this restricted sense is not to be confused with the sense in which a man is often said to be responsible for an action if he has in fact committed it. The questions: Who broke the window? and could the man who broke the window have prevented himself from doing so? are obviously quite distinct. To dismiss the second as unanswerable in no way diminishes the impor-

tance of finding an answer to the first. Hence the primary job of the courts in determining by whom a forbidden act has actually been committed is wholly unaffected by any proposal to disregard the question of responsibility in the narrower sense. Indeed the only problem that arises here is linguistic, inasmuch as one is accustomed to say that X was "responsible" for breaking the window when the intention is to convey no more than that he did actually break it. Another word is needed here (and I confess that I have not succeeded in finding one) to describe "responsibility" for doing an action as distinct from the capacity to refrain from doing it. "Accountable" has sometimes been suggested, but its usage in this sense is often awkward. "Instrumental" is perhaps better, though one could still wish for an adjective such perhaps as "agential" derived from the word "agent." However, all that matters is to keep firmly in mind that responsibility in the present context has nothing to do with the authorship of an act, only with the state of mind of its author.

In the second place, to discard the notion of responsibility does not mean that the mental condition of an offender ceases to have any importance, or that psychiatric considerations become irrelevant. The difference is that they become relevant, not to the question of determining the measure of his culpability, but to the choice of the treatment most likely to be effective in discouraging him from offending again; and even if these two aspects of the matter may be related, this is not to be dismissed as a distinction without a difference. The psychiatrist to whom it falls to advise as to the probable response of an offender to medical treatment no doubt has his own opinion as to the man's responsibility or capacity for self-control; and doubtless also those opinions are a factor in his judgment as to the outlook for medical treatment, or as to the probability that the offence will be repeated. But these are, and must remain, matters of opinion, "incapable," in Lord Parker's words, "of scientific proof." Opinions as to treatability, on the other hand, as well as predictions as to the likelihood of further offences can be put to the test of experience and so proved right or wrong. And by systematic observation of that experience, it is reasonable to expect that a body of knowledge will in time be built up, upon which it will be possible to draw, in the attempt to choose the most promising treatment in future cases.

Next, it must be emphasised that nothing in what has been said involves acceptance of a deterministic view of human behaviour. It is an indisputable fact of experience that human beings do respond predictably to various stimuli—whether because they choose to or because they can do no other it is not necessary to inquire. There are cases in which medical treatment works: there are cases in which it fails. Equally there are cases in which deterrent penalties appear to deter those upon whom they are imposed from committing further offences; and there are cases in which they do not. Once the criminal law is conceived as an instrument of crime prevention, it is these facts which demand attention, and from which we can learn to improve the efficiency of that instrument; and the question whether on any occasion a man could or could not have acted otherwise than as he did can be left on one side or answered either way, as may be preferred. It is no longer relevant.

Failure to appreciate this has, I think, led to conflicts between psychiatry and the law being often fought on the wrong ground. Even so radical a criminologist as Dr. Sheldon Glueck seems to see the issue as one between "those who stress the prime social need of blameworthiness and retributive punishment as the core-concept in crime and justice and those who, under the impact of psychiatric, psychoanalytic, sociological, and anthropological views insist that man's choices are the product of forces largely beyond his conscious control . . ."[27] Indeed Dr. Glueck's discussion of the relation of psychiatry to law is chiefly devoted to an analysis of the exculpatory effect of psychiatric knowledge, and to the changes that have been, or should be, made in the assessment of guilt as the result of the growth of this knowledge. In consequence much intellectual ingenuity is wasted in refining the criteria by which the wicked may be distinguished from the weak-minded. For surely to argue thus is to argue from the wrong premises: The real difference between the psychiatric and the legal approach has nothing to do with free will and determinism. It has to do with their conceptions of the objectives of the criminal process, with the question whether the aim of that process is punitive or preventive, whether what matters is to punish the wrongdoer or to set him on the road to virtue;

and, in order to take a stand on that issue, neither party need be a determinist.

So much for what disregard of responsibility does not mean. What, in a more positive sense, is it likely to involve? Here, I think, one of the most important consequences must be to obscure the present rigid distinction between the penal and the medical institution. As things are, the supposedly fully responsible are consigned to the former: Only the wholly or partially irresponsible are eligible for the latter. Once it is admitted that we have no reliable criterion by which to distinguish between those two categories, strict segregation of each into a distinct set of institutions becomes absurd and impracticable. For purposes of convenience offenders for whom medical treatment is indicated will doubtless tend to be allocated to one building, and those for whom medicine has nothing to offer to another; but the formal distinction between prison and hospital will become blurred, and, one may reasonably expect, eventually obliterated altogether. Both will be simply "places of safety" in which offenders receive the treatment which experience suggests is most likely to evoke the desired response.

Does this mean that the distinction between doctors and prison officers must also become blurred? Up to a point it clearly does. At the very least it would seem that some fundamental implications for the medical profession must be involved when the doctor becomes part of the machinery of law enforcement. Not only is the normal doctor-patient relationship profoundly disturbed, but far-reaching questions also arise as to the nature of the condition which the doctor is called upon to treat. If a tendency to break the law is not in itself to be classified as a disease, which does he seek to cure—the criminality or the illness? To the medical profession these questions, which I have discussed at length elsewhere,[28] must be of primary concern. But for present purposes it may be more relevant to notice how, as so often happens in this country, changes not yet officially recognised in theory are already creeping in by the back door. Already the long-awaited institution at Grendon Underwood is administered as an integral part of the prison system; yet the régime is frankly medical. Its purpose has been described by the Prison Commission's Director of Medical Services as the investigation and treatment of mental disorder generally recognised as calling for a psychiatric approach; the investigation of the mental condition of offenders whose offences in themselves suggest mental instability; and an exploration of the problem of the treatment of the psychopath. Recommendations for admission are to come from prison medical officers, and the prison itself is under the charge of a medical superintendent with wide experience in psychiatry.[29]

Grendon Underwood is (unless one should include Broadmoor which has, of course, a much narrower scope) the first genuinely hybrid institution. Interchange between medical and penal institutions is, however, further facilitated by the power of the Home Secretary to transfer to hospital persons whom, on appropriate medical evidence, he finds to be suffering from mental disorder of a nature or degree to warrant their detention in a hospital for medical treatment. Such transfers have the same effect as does a hospital order, and they may be (and usually are) also accompanied by an order restricting discharge. It is, moreover, of some interest that transfers are sometimes made quite soon after the court has passed sentence. Out of six cases convicted under section 2 of the Homicide Act in which transfers under section 72 were effected, three were removed to hospital less than three months after sentence. Although it is, of course, always possible that the prisoner has been mentally normal at the time of his offence and had only suffered a mental breakdown later, transfer after a relatively short period does indicate at least a possibility that in the judgment of the Home Secretary some mental abnormality may have been already present either at the time of sentence or even when the crime was committed.

The courts, however, seem to be somewhat jealous of the exercise of this power, which virtually allows the Home Secretary to treat as sick persons whom they have sentenced to imprisonment and presumably regard as wicked. Indeed it seems that, if a diagnosis of mental disorder is to be made, the courts hold that it is, generally speaking, their business, and not the Home Secretary's, to make it. So at least it would appear from the judgments of the Court of Criminal Appeal in the cases of Constance Ann James[30] and Philip Morris,[31] both of whom had been found guilty of manslaughter on grounds of diminished responsibility and had been sentenced to imprisonment.

In the former case, in which the evidence as to the accused's mental condition was unchallenged, the trial judge apparently had misgivings about the public safety and in particular the safety of the convicted woman's younger child whose brother she had killed. He therefore passed a sentence of three years' imprisonment, leaving it, as he said, to the appropriate authorities to make further inquiries so that the Secretary of State might, if he thought fit, transfer the prisoner to hospital under section 72 of the Mental Health Act. The appeal was allowed, on the ground that there was obviously no need for punishment, and that there were reasonable hopes that the disorder from which the woman suffered would prove curable. In the circumstances, though reluctant to interfere with the discretion of the sentencing court, the Court of Criminal Appeal substituted a hospital order accompanied by an indefinite restriction.

In Philip Morris' case, in which, however, the appellant was unsuccessful, the matter was put even more clearly. Again the trial judge had refused to make a hospital order on grounds of the public safety and, failing any vacancy in a secure hospital, had passed a sentence of life imprisonment. But on this the Court of Criminal Appeal commented as follows: "Although the discretion ... is very wide indeed, the basic principle must be that in the ordinary case where punishment as such is not intended, and where the sole object of the sentence is that a man should receive mental treatment, and be at large as soon as he can safely be discharged, a proper exercise of the discretion demands that steps should be taken to exercise the powers under section 60 and that the matter should not be left to be dealt with by the Secretary of State under section 72."

These difficulties are, one may hope, of a transitional nature. They would certainly not arise if all sentences involving loss of liberty were indeterminate in respect of the type of institution in which the offender is to be detained: still less if rigid distinctions between medical and penal institutions were no longer maintained. The elimination of those distinctions, moreover, though unthinkable in a primary punitive system which must at all times segregate the blameworthy from the blameless, is wholly in keeping with a criminal law which is preventive rather than punitive in intention.

In this lecture and in that which preceded it I have tried to signpost the road towards such a conception of the law, and to indicate certain landmarks which suggest that this is the road along which we are, if hesitantly, already treading. At first blush it might seem that strict liability and mental abnormality have not much in common; but both present a challenge to traditional views as to the point at which, and the purpose for which, considerations of guilty intent become relevant; and both illustrate the contemporary tendency to use the criminal law to protect the community against damage, no matter what might be the state of mind of those by whom that damage is done. In this context, perhaps, the little-noticed provisions of section 60 (2) of the Mental Health Act, with its distinction between the forbidden act and the conviction, along with the liberal implications of section 4 of the Criminal Justice Act, with its emphasis on treatability rather than culpability, are to be seen as the writing on the wall. And perhaps, too, it is significant that Dr. Glueck, notwithstanding his immediate preoccupation with definitions of responsibility, lets fall, almost as if with a sign, the forecast that some day it may be possible "to limit criminal law to matters of behavior alone," and that in his concluding lecture he foresees the "twilight of futile blameworthiness."[32] That day may be still a long way off: but at least it seems to be nearer than it was.

NOTES

1. *The Observer,* May 5, 1963.
2. I use this word throughout to describe a system the primary purpose of which is to prevent the occurrence of offences, whether committed by persons already convicted or by other people . . .
2a. Devlin, Sir Patrick (now Lord), *Law and Morals* (University of Birmingham) 1961, pp. 3, 7, 8, 9.
3. Radcliffe, Lord, *The Law and Its Compass* (Faber) 1961, p. 12.
4. *Shaw* v. *Director of Public Prosecutions* [1961] 2 W.L.R. 897.
5. *The Times,* November 11, 1961.
6. Edwards, J. Ll. J., *Mens Rea in Statutory Offences* (Macmillan) 1955, p. 247.
7. Devlin, Lord, *Samples of Law Making* (O.U.P.) 1962, pp. 71–80.
8. Hart, H. L. A., *Punishment and the Elimination of Responsibility* (Athlone Press) 1962, pp. 27, 28. Italics mine.
9. *Op. cit.,* pp. 29, 30.
10. Devlin, Lord, *Samples of Law Making* (O.U.P.) 1962, p. 73.
11. There could be an argument here, into which I do not propose to enter, as to whether this capacity is not shared by some of the higher animals.
12. Walker, N., "Queen Victoria Was Right," *New Society,* June 27, 1963.
13. House of Lords Debates, May 1, 1963, col. 174.
14. *R.* v. *James* [1961] Crim.L.R. 842.
15. One curious feature of this provision is the fact that a hospital order can apparently be made on a diagnosis of mental disorder, even if the disorder has no connection with the offence. See the Court of Criminal Appeal's judgment in the unsuccessful appeal of *R.* v. *Hatt* ([1962] Crim.L.R. 647) in which the appellant claimed that his predilection for unnecessary surgical operations had no connection with his no less fervent passion for making off with other people's cars.
16. House of Commons Standing Committee A, February 12, 1948, col. 1054.
17. Grünhut, M., *Probation and Mental Treatment* (to be published in the Library of Criminology).
18. Wootton, Barbara, "Diminished Responsibility: A Layman's View" (1960) 76 *Law Quarterly Review* 224.
19. *R.* v. *Di Duca* [1959] 43 Cr.App.R. 167.
20. Unpublished transcript.
21. Unpublished transcript.
22. *R.* v. *Clarke* [1962] Crim.L.R.836.
23. House of Commons Debates, Vol. 560 (November 15, 1956), col. 1252.
24. *R.* v. *Price* [1962] 3 All E.R. 960.
25. *R.* v. *Byrne* (1960) 44 Cr.App.R. 246.
26. *R.* v. *Terry* (1961) 45 Cr.App.R. 180.
27. Glueck, Sheldon, *Law and Psychiatry* (Tavistock Publications) 1962, p. 6.
28. Wootton, Barbara, "The Law, The Doctor and The Deviant," *British Medical Journal,* July 27, 1963.
29. Snell, H. K. (Director of Medical Services, Prison Commission), "H. M. Prison Grendon," *British Medical Journal,* September 22, 1962.
30. *R.* v. *James* [1961] Crim.L.R. 842.
31. *R.* v. *Morris* (1961) 45 Cr.App.R. 233.
32. Glueck, Sheldon, *Law and Psychiatry* (Tavistock Publications) 1962, pp. 33, 147.

H. L. A. HART

Changing Conceptions of Responsibility*

I

This lecture is concerned wholly with criminal responsibility and I have chosen to lecture on this subject here because both English and Israeli law have inherited from the past virtually the same doctrine concerning the criminal responsibility of the mentally abnormal and both have found this inheritance embarrassing. I refer of course to the M'Naghten rules of 1843. In Israel the Supreme Court has found it possible to supplement these exceedingly narrow rules by use of the doctrine incorporated in s. 11 of the Criminal Code Ordinance of 1936 that an 'exercise of will' is necessary for responsibility. This is the effect of the famous case of *Mandelbrot* v. *Attorney General* [1] and the subsequent cases which have embedded Agranat J's construction of s. 11 in Israeli law. English lawyers, though they may admire this bold step, cannot use as an escape route from the confines of the M'Naghten rules the similar doctrine that for any criminal liability there must be a 'voluntary act' which many authorities have said is a fundamental requirement of English criminal law. For this doctrine has always been understood merely to exclude cases where the muscular movements are involuntary as in sleepwalking or 'automatism' or reflex action.[2] Nonetheless there have been changes in England; after a period of frozen immobility the hardened mass of our substantive criminal law is at points softening and yielding to its critics. But both the recent changes and the current criticisms of the law in this matter of criminal responsibility have taken a different direction from development in Israel and for this reason may be of some interest to Israeli lawyers.

*From *The Morality of the Criminal Law* by H. L. A. Hart (Jerusalem: Magnes Press, 1965). Reprinted as Chapter VIII of *Punishment and Responsibility: Essays in the Philosophy of Law* by H. L. A. Hart (New York and Oxford: Oxford University Press, 1967), pp. 186–209.

Let me first say something quite general and very elementary about the historical background to these recent changes. In all advanced legal systems, liability to conviction for serious crimes is made dependent, not only on the offender having done those outward acts which the law forbids, but on his having done them in a certain frame of mind or with a certain will. These are the mental conditions or 'mental elements' in criminal responsibility and, in spite of much variation in detail and terminology, they are broadly similar in most legal systems. Even if you kill a man, this is not punishable as murder in most civilised jurisdictions if you do it unintentionally, accidentally or by mistake, or while suffering from certain forms of mental abnormality. Lawyers of the Anglo-American tradition use the Latin phrase *mens rea* (a guilty mind) as a comprehensive name for these necessary mental elements; and according to conventional ideas *mens rea* is a necessary element in liability to be established *before* a verdict. It is not something which is merely to be taken into consideration in determining the sentence or disposal of the convicted person, though it may also be considered for that purpose as well.

I have said that my topic in this lecture is the recent changes in England on this matter, but I shall be concerned less with changes in the law itself than with changes among critics of the law towards the whole doctrine of the mental element in responsibility. This change in critical attitude is, I believe, more important than any particular change in the detail of the doctrine of *mens rea*. I say this because for a century at least most liberal minded people have agreed in treating respect for the doctrine of *mens rea* as a hallmark of a civilised legal system. Until recently the great aim of most critics of the criminal law has been to secure that the law should take this doctrine very seriously and wholeheartedly. Critics have sought its expansion, and urged that the courts should be required always to make genuine efforts, when a person is accused of crime, to determine before convicting him whether that person actually did have the knowledge or intention or the sanity or any other mental element which the law, in its definition of crimes, makes a necessary condition of criminal liability. It is true that English law has often wavered on this matter and has even quite recently flirted with the idea that it cannot really afford to inquire into an individual's actual mental state before punishing him. There have always been English judges in whom a remark made in 1477 by Chief Justice Brian of the Common Pleas strikes a sympathetic chord. He said 'The thought of man is not triable; the devil alone knoweth the thought of man.'[3] So there are in English law many compromises on this matter of the relevance of a man's mind to the criminality of his deeds. Not only are there certain crimes of 'strict' liability where neither knowledge, nor negligence is required for conviction, but there are also certain doctrines of 'objective' liability such as was endorsed by the House of Lords in the much criticized case of *The Director of Public Prosecutions* v. *Smith*[4] on which Lord Denning lectured to you three years ago.[5] This doctrine enables a court to impute to an accused person knowledge or an intention which he may not really have had, but which an average man would have had. Theories have been developed in support of this doctrine of 'objective liability' of which the most famous is that expounded by the great American judge, Oliver Wendell Holmes in his book *The Common Law.* Nonetheless generations of progressive minded lawyers and liberal critics of the law have thought of the doctrine of *mens rea* as something to be cherished and extended, and against the scepticism of Chief Justice Brian they could quote the robust assertion of the nineteenth-century Lord Justice Bowen that 'the state of a man's mind is as much a fact as the state of his digestion.'[6] And they would have added that for the criminal law the former was a good deal more important than the latter.

But recently in England progressive and liberal criticism of the law has changed its direction. Though I think this change must in the end involve the whole doctrine of *mens rea,* it at present mainly concerns the criminal responsibility of mentally abnormal persons, and I can best convey its character by sketching the course taken in the criticism of the law in this matter. The main doctrine of English law until recently was of course the famous M'Naghten Rules formulated by the Judges of the House of Lords in 1843. As everybody knows, according to this doctrine, mental abnormality sufficient to constitute a defence to a criminal charge must consist of three elements: First, the accused, at the time of his act, must have suffered from a defect of reason; secondly, this must have arisen from disease of the mind; thirdly, the result of it must have been that the accused did not know the nature of his act or that it was illegal. From the start English critics denounced these rules because their effect is to excuse from criminal responsibility only those whose mental abnormality resulted in lack of knowledge: in the eyes of these critics this amounted to a dogmatic refusal to acknowledge the fact that a man might know what he was doing and that it was wrong or illegal and yet because of his normal mental state might lack the capacity to control his action. This lack of capacity, the critics urged, must be the fundamental point in any intelligible doctrine of responsibility. The point just is that in a civilized system only those who *could have* kept the law should be punished. Why else should we bother about a man's knowledge or intention or other mental element except as throwing light on this?

Angrily and enviously, many of the critics pointed to foreign legal systems which were free of the English obsession with this single element of knowledge as the sole constituent of responsibility. As far back as 1810, the French Code simply excused those suffering from madness (démence) without specifying any particular connection between this and the particular act done. The German Code of 1871 spoke of inability or impaired ability to recognize the wrongness of conduct or to act in accordance with this recognition. It thus, correctly, according to the critics, treated as crucial to the issue of responsibility not knowledge but the capacity to conform to law. The Belgian Loi de Défence Sociale of 1930 makes no reference to knowledge or intelligence but speaks simply of a person's lack of ability as a consequence of mental abnormality to control his action. So till recently the great aim of the critics inspired by these foreign models was essentially to secure an amendment of the English doctrine of *mens rea* on this point: to supplement its purely cognitive test by a volitional one, admitting that a man might, while knowing that he was breaking the law, be unable to conform to it.

This dispute raged through the nineteenth century and was certainly marked by some curious features. In James Fitzjames Stephen's great *History of the Criminal Law*[7] the dispute is vividly presented as one between doctors and lawyers. The doctors are pictured as accusing the lawyers of claiming to decide a medical or scientific issue about responsibility by out-of-date criteria when they limited legal inquiry to the question of knowledge. The lawyers replied that the doctors, in seeking to give evidence about other matters, were attempting illicitly to thrust upon juries their views on what should excuse a man when charged with a crime: illicitly, because responsibility is a question not of science but of law. Plainly, the argument was here entrapped in the ambiguities of the word 'responsibility' about which more should have been said. But it is also remarkable that in the course of this long dispute no clear statements were made of the reason why the law should recognise any form of insanity as an excuse. The basic question as to what was at stake in the doctrine of *mens rea* was hardly faced. Is it necessary because punishment is conceived of as paying back moral evil done with some essentially retributive 'fitting' equivalent in pain? If so, what state of mind does a theory of retribution require a person punished to have had? Or is a doctrine of *mens rea* necessary because punishment is conceived as primarily a deterrent and this purpose would be frustrated or useless if persons were punished who at the time of their crime lacked certain knowledge or ability? Or is the doctrine to give effect not to a retributive theory but to principles of fairness or justice which require that a man should not be punished and so be used for the ends of others unless he had the capacity and a fair opportunity to avoid doing the thing for which he is punished? Certainly Bentham and Blackstone had something to say on these matters of fundamental principle, but they do not figure much in the century-long war which was waged by English reformers, sometimes in a fog, against the M'Naghten Rules. But what was clear in the fog was that neither party thought of calling the whole doctrine of *mens rea* in question. What was sought was merely amendments or additions to it.

Assault after assault on the M'Naghten Rules were beaten off until 1957. It cannot be said that the defenders of the doctrine used any very sharp rapiers in their defence. The good old English bludgeon which has beaten off so many reforms of English criminal law was enough. When Lord Atkin's Committee recommended in 1923 an addition to the M'Naghten Rules to cater for what it termed "irresistible impulse,' it was enough in the debate in the House of Lords[8] for judicial members to prophesy the harm to society which would inevitably flow from the amendment. Not a word was said to meet the point that the laws of many other countries already conformed to the proposal: nothing was said about the United States where a similar modification of the M'Naghten Rules providing for inability to conform to the law's requirement as well as defects in knowledge had been long accepted in several States without disastrous results. But in 1957, largely as a result of the immensely valuable examination of the whole topic by the Royal Commission on Capital Punishment[9] the law was amended, not as recommended by the Commission, but in the form of a curious compromise. This was the introduction of the idea borrowed from Scots law of a plea of diminished responsibility. S. 2 of the Homicide Act of 1957 provides that, on a murder charge, if what it most curiously calls the accused's 'mental responsibility' was 'substantially' impaired by mental abnormality, he could be convicted, not of murder, but only of manslaughter, carrying a maximum sentence of imprisonment for life. This change in the law was indeed meagre since it concerned only murder; and even here it was but a halfway house, since the accused was not excused from punishment but was to be punished less than the maximum. The change does not excuse from responsibility but mitigates the penalty.

A word or two about the operation of the new plea of diminished responsibility during the last six years is necessary. The judges at first tended to treat it merely as catering for certain cases on the borderlines of the M'Naghten Rules, not as making a major change. Thus Lord Goddard refused to direct the jury that under the new plea the question of capacity to conform to law and not merely the accused's knowledge was relevant.[10] But the present Lord Chief Justice in a remarkable judgment expressly stated that this was so, and a generous interpretation was given to the section so as to include in the phrase 'abnormality of mind' the condition of the psychopath. He said that it was important to consider not only the accused's knowledge but also his ability 'to exercise will power to control physical acts in accordance with rational judgment.'[11] However, the most remarkable feature of six year's experience of this plea is made evident by the statistics: Apprehensions that it might lead to large-scale evasions of punishment have been shown to be quite baseless. For since the Homicide Act almost precisely the same percentage—about 47 per cent —of persons charged with murder escaped conviction on the ground of mental abnormality as before. What has happened is that the plea of insanity under the old M'Naghten Rules has virtually been displaced in murder cases by the new plea.[12] Though satisfactory, in that the old fears of reform have not been realized, the plea certainly has its critics and in part the general change in attitude of which I shall speak has been accelerated by it.

II

I have said that the change made by the introduction of diminished responsibility was both meagre and half-hearted. Nonetheless it marked the end of an era in the criticism of the law concerning the criminal responsibility of the mentally abnormal. From this point on criticism has largely changed its character. Instead of demanding that the court should take more seriously the task of dividing lawbreakers into two classes— those fully responsible and justly punishable because they had an unimpaired capacity to conform to the law, and those who were to be excused for lack of this—critics have come to think this a mistaken approach. Instead of seeking an expansion of the doctrine of *mens rea* they have argued that it should be eliminated and have welcomed the proliferation of offences of strict liability as a step in the right direction and a model for the future. The bolder of them have talked of the need to 'bypass' or 'dispense with' questions of responsibility and have condemned the old efforts to widen the scope of the M'Naghten Rules as waste of time or worse. In-

deed, their attitude to such reforms is like that of the Communist who condemns private charity in a capitalist system because it tends to hide the radical errors of the system and thus preserve it. By far the best informed, most trenchant and influential advocate of these new ideas is Lady Wootton whose powerful work on the subject of criminal responsibility has done much to change and, in my opinion, to raise, the whole level of discussion.[13]

Hence, since 1957 a new skepticism going far beyond the old criticisms has developed. It is indeed a skepticism of the whole institution of criminal punishment so far as it contains elements which differentiate it from a system of purely forward-looking social hygiene in which our only concern, when we have an offender to deal with, is with the future and the rational aims of the prevention of further crime, the protection of society and the care and if possible the cure of the offender. For criminal punishment, as even the most progressive older critics of the M'Naghten Rules conceived of it, is *not* mere social hygiene. It differs from such a purely forward-looking system in the stress that it places on something in the past: the state of mind of the accused as the time, not of his trial, but when he broke the law.

To many modern critics this backward-looking reference to the accused's past state of mind as a condition of his liability to compulsory measures seems a useless deflection from the proper forward-looking aims of a rational system of social control. The past they urge is over and done with, and the offender's past state of mind is only important as a diagnosis of the causes of his offence and a prognosis of what can be done now to counter these causes. Nothing in the past, according to this newer outlook, can in itself justify or be required to license what we do to the offender now; that is something to be determined exclusively by reference to the consequences to society and to him. Lady Wootton argues that if the aim of the criminal law is to be the prevention of 'socially damaging actions' not retribution for past wickedness, the conventional doctrine puts *mens rea* 'into the wrong place.'[14] *Mens rea* is on her view relevant only *after* conviction as a guide to what measures should be taken to prevent a recurrence of the forbidden act. She considers it 'illogical,' if the aim of the criminal law is prevention, to make *mens rea* part of the definition of a crime and a necessary condition of the offender's liability to compulsory measures.[15]

This way of thinking leads to a radical revision of the penal system which in crude outline and in its most extreme form is as follows: Once it has been proved in a court that a person's outward conduct fits the legal definition of some crime, this without proof or any *mens rea,* is sufficient to bring him within the scope of compulsory measures. These may be either of a penal or therapeutic kind or both; or it may be found that no measures are necessary in a particular case and the offender may be discharged. But the choice between these alternatives is not to be made by reference to the offender's past mental state—his culpability—but by consideration of what steps, in view of his present mental state and his general situation, are likely to have the best consequences for him and for society.

I have called this the extreme form of the new approach because as I have formulated it is generally applicable to all offenders alike. It is not a system reserved solely for those who could be classed as mentally abnormal. The whole doctrine of *mens rea* would on this extreme version of the theory be dropped from the law; so that the distinctions which at present we draw and think vital to draw before convicting an offender, between, for example, intentional and unintentional wrongdoing, would no longer be relevant at this stage. To show that you have struck or wounded another unintentionally or without negligence would not save you from conviction and liability to such treatment, penal or therapeutic, as the court might deem advisable on evidence of your mental state and character.

This is, as I say, the extreme form of the theory, and it is the form that Lady Wootton now advances.[16] But certainly a less extreme though more complex form is conceivable which would replace, not the whole doctrine of *mens rea,* but only that part of it which concerns the legal responsibility of the mentally abnormal. In this more moderate form of the theory, a mentally normal person would still escape conviction if he acted unintentionally or without some other requisite mental element forming part of the definition of the crime charged. The innovation would be that no form of insanity or mental abnormality would bar a conviction, and this would no longer

be investigated before conviction.[17] It would be something to be investigated only after conviction to determine what measures of punishment or treatment would be most efficacious in the particular case. It is important to observe that most advocates of the elimination of responsibility have been mainly concerned with the inadequacies or absurdities of the existing law in relation to mentally abnormal offenders, and some of these advocates may have intended only the more moderate form of the theory which is limited to such offenders. But I doubt if this is at all representative, for many, including Lady Wootton, have said that no satisfactory line can be drawn between the mentally normal and abnormal offenders: There simply are no clear or reliable criteria. They insist that general definitions of mental health are too vague and too conflicting; we should be freed from all such illusory classifications to treat, in the most appropriate way from the point of view of society, all persons who have actually manifested the behaviour which is the *actus reus* of a crime.[18] The fact that harm was done unintentionally should not preclude an investigation of what steps if any are desirable to prevent a repetition. This skepticism of the possibility of drawing lines between the normal and abnormal offenders commits advocates of the elimination of responsibility to the extreme form of the theory.

Such then are the essentials of the new idea. Of course the phrase 'eliminating responsibility' does sound very alarming and when Lady Wootton's work first made it a centre of discussion the columns of *The Times* newspaper showed how fluttered legal and other dovecotes were. But part at least of the alarm was unnecessary because it arose from the ambiguities of the word 'responsibility'; and it is, I think, still important to distinguish two of the very different things this difficult word may mean. To say that someone is legally responsible for something often means only that under legal rules he is liable to be made either to suffer or to pay compensation in certain eventualities. The expression 'he'll pay for it' covers both these things. In this the primary sense of the word, though a man is normally only responsible for his own actions or the harm he has done, he may be also responsible for the actions of other persons if legal rules so provide. Indeed in this sense a baby in arms or a totally insane person might be legally responsible—again, if the rules so provide; for the word simply means liable to be made to account or pay and we might call this sense of the word 'legal accountability.' But the new idea—the programme of eliminating responsibility—is not, as some have feared, meant to eliminate legal accountability: Persons who break the law are not just to be left free. What is to be eliminated are enquiries as to whether a person who has done what the law forbids was responsible at the time he did it and responsible in this sense does not refer to the legal status of accountability. It means the capacity, so far as this is a matter of a man's mind or will, which normal people have to control their actions and conform to law. In this sense of responsibility a man's responsibility can be said to be 'impaired.' That is indeed the language of s. 2 of the Homicide Act 1957 which introduced into English law the idea of diminished responsibility: it speaks of a person's 'mental' responsibility and in the rubric to s. 2 even of persons 'suffering from' diminished responsibility. It is of course easy to see why this second sense of responsibility (which might be called 'personal responsibility') has grown up alongside the primary idea of legal accountability. It is no doubt because the law normally, though not always, confines legal accountability to persons who are believed to have normal capacities of control.

So perhaps the new ideas are less alarming than they seem at first. They are also less new, and those who advocate them have always been able to point to earlier developments within English law which seem to foreshadow these apparently revolutionary ideas. Lady Wootton herself makes much of the fact that the doctrine of mens rea in the case of normal offenders has been watered down by the introduction of strict liability and she deprecates the alarm this has raised. But apart from this, the courts have often been able to deal with mentally abnormal persons accused of crime without confronting the issue of their personal responsibility at the time of their offence. There are in fact several different ways in which this question may be avoided. A man may be held on account of his mental state to be unfit to plead when brought to trial; or he may be certified insane before trial; or, except on a charge of murder, an accused person might enter a plea of guilty with the suggestion that he should be put on probation with a condition of mental treatment.[19] In fact, only a very small percentage of the mentally abnormal have been dealt with under the M'Naghten Rules, a fact which is understandable since a successful plea under those Rules means detention in Broadmoor for an indefinite period and many would rather face conviction and imprisonment and so may not raise the question of mental abnormality at all. So the old idea of treating mental abnormality as bearing on the question of the accused's responsibility and to be settled before conviction, has with few exceptions only been a reality in murder cases to which alone is the plea of diminished responsibility applicable.

But the most important departure from received ideas incorporated in the doctrine of mens rea is the Mental Health Act, 1959, which expands certain principles of older legislation. S. 60 of this Act provides that in any case, except where the crime is not punishable by imprisonment or the sentence is fixed by the law (and this latter exception virtually excludes only murder), the courts may, after conviction of the offender, if two doctors agree that the accused falls into any of four specified categories of mental disorder, order his detention for medical treatment instead of passing a penal sentence, though it requires evidence that such detention is warranted. The four categories of mental disorder are very wide and include even psychopathic disorder in spite of the general lack of clear or agreed criteria of this condition. The courts are told by the statute that in exercising their choice between penal or medical measures to have regard to the nature of the offence and the character and antecedents of the offender. These powers have come to be widely used[20] and are available even in cases where a murder charge has been reduced to manslaughter on a plea of provocation or diminished responsibility.

Advocates of the programme of eliminating responsibility welcome the powers given by the Mental Health Act to substitute compulsory treatment for punishment, but necessarily they view it as a compromise falling short of what is required, and we shall understand their own views better if we see why they think so. It falls short in four respects. First the power given to courts to order compulsory treatment instead of punishment is discretionary, and even if the appropriate medical evidence is forthcoming the courts may still administer conventional punishment if they choose. The judges *may* still think in terms of responsibility, and it is plain that they occasionally do so in these cases. Thus in the majority of cases of conviction for manslaughter following on a successful plea of diminished responsibility, the courts have imposed sentences of imprisonment notwithstanding their powers under s. 60 of the Mental Health Act, and the Lord Chief Justice has said that in such cases the prisoner may on the facts be shown to have *some* responsibility for which he must be punished.[21] Secondly, the law itself still preserves a conception of penal methods, such as imprisonment, coloured by the idea that it is a payment for past wickedness and not just an alternative to medical treatment; for though the courts may order medical treatment or punish, they cannot combine these. This of course is a refusal to think, as the new critics demand we should think,[22] of punitive and medical measures as merely different forms of social hygiene to be used according to a prognosis of their effects on the convicted person. Thirdly, as it stands at present, the scheme presupposes that a satisfactory distinction can be drawn on the basis of its four categories of mental disorder between those who are mentally abnormal and those who are not. But the more radical reformers are not merely sceptical about the adequacy of the criteria which distinguish, for example, the psychopath from the normal offender: They would contend that there may exist propensities to certain types of socially harmful behaviour in people who are in other ways not abnormal and that a rational system should attend to these cases.

But fourthly, and this is most important, the scheme is vitiated for these critics because the courts' powers are only exercisable after the conviction of an offender and, for this conviction, proof of *mens rea* at the time of his offence is still required: The question of the accused's mental abnormality may still be raised before conviction as a defence if the accused so wishes. So the Mental Health Act does not 'bypass' the whole question of responsibility: It does not eliminate the doctrine of *mens rea*. It expands the courts' discretion in dealing with a convicted person, enabling them to choose between penal and therapeutic measures and making this choice in practice largely independent of the offender's state of mind at the time of his offence. Its great merit is that the mentally abnormal offender who would before have submitted to a sentence of imprisonment rather than raise a plea of insanity under the M'Naghten Rules (because success would mean indeterminate detention in Broadmoor) may now be encouraged to bring forward his mental condition after conviction, in the hope of obtaining a hospital order rather than a sentence of imprisonment.

The question which now awaits our consideration is the merits of the claim that we should proceed from such a system as we now have under the Mental Health Act to one in which the criminal courts were freed altogether from the doctrine of *mens rea* and could proceed to the use of either penal or medical measures at discretion simply on proof that the accused had done the outward acts of a crime. Prisons and hospitals under such a scheme will alike 'be simply "places of safety" in which offenders receive the treatment which experience suggests is most likely to evoke the desired response.'[23]

The case for adopting these new ideas in their entirety has been supposed by arguments of varying kinds and quality, and it is very necessary to sift the wheat from the chaff. The weakest of the arguments is perhaps the one most frequently heard, namely, that our concern with personal responsibility incorporated in the doctrine of *mens rea* only makes sense if we subscribe to a retributive theory of punishment according to which punishment is used and justified as an 'appropriate' or 'fitting' return for past wickedness and not merely as a preventive of antisocial conduct. This, as I have argued elsewhere,[24] is a philosophical confusion and Lady Wootton falls a victim to it because she makes too crude a dichotomy between 'punishment' and 'prevention.' She does not even mention a moral outlook on punishment which is surely very common, very simple and, except perhaps for the determinist, perfectly defensible. This is the view that out of considerations of fairness or justice to individuals we should restrict even punishment designed as a 'preventive' to those who had a normal capacity and a fair opportunity to obey. This is still an intelligible ideal of justice to the individuals whom we punish even if we punish them to protect society from the harm that crime does and not to pay back the harm that they have done. And it remains intelligible even if in securing this form of fairness to those whom we punish we secure a lesser measure of conformity to law than a system of total strict liability which repudiated the doctrine of *mens rea.*

But of course it is certainly arguable that, at present, in certain cases, in the application of the doctrine of *mens rea,* we recognize this principle of justice in a way which plays too high a price in terms of social security. For there are indeed cases where the application of *mens rea* operates in surprising and possibly dangerous ways. A man may cause very great harm, may even kill another person, and under the present law neither be punished for it nor subjected to any compulsory medical treatment or supervision. This happened, for example, in February 1961 when a United States Air Force sergeant,[25] after a drunken party, killed a girl, according to his own story, in his sleep. He was tried for murder but the jury were not persuaded by the prosecution, on whom the legal burden of proof rests, that the sergeant's story was false and he was accordingly acquitted and discharged altogether. It is worth observing that in recent years in cases of dangerous driving where the accused claims that he suffered from 'automatism' or a sudden lapse of consciousness, the courts have striven very hard to narrow the scope of this defence because of the obvious social dangers of an acquittal of such persons, unaccompanied by any order for compulsory treatment. They have produced a most complex body of law distinguishing between 'sane' and 'insane' automatism each with their special burdens of proof.[26] No doubt such dangerous cases are not very numerous and the risk of their occurrence is one which many people might prefer to run rather than introduce a new system dispensing altogether with proof of *mens rea.* In any case something less extreme than the new system might deal with such cases; for the courts could be given powers in the case of such physically harmful offences to order, notwithstanding an acquittal, any kind of medical treatment or supervision that seemed appropriate.

But the most important arguments in favour of the more radical system in which proof of the outward act alone is enough to make the accused liable to compulsory measures of treatment or punishment, comes from those who, like Lady Wootton, have closely scrutinized the actual working of the old plea of insanity and the plea of diminished responsibility introduced in 1957 by the Homicide Act into cases of homicide. The latter treats mental abnormality as an aspect of *mens rea* and forces the courts before the verdict to decide the question whether the accused's 'mental responsibility,' that is, his capacity to control his actions was 'substantially impaired' at the time of his offence when he killed another person. The conclusion drawn by Lady Wootton from her impressive and detailed study of all the cases (199 in number) in which this plea was raised down to mid-September of 1962, is that this question which is thus forced upon the courts should be discarded as unanswerable. Here indeed she echoes the cry, often in earlier years thundered from the Bench, that it is impossible to distinguish between an irresistable impulse and an impulse which was merely not resisted by the accused.

But here too if we are to form a balanced view we must distinguish between dubious philosophical contentions and some very good sense. The philosophical arguments (which I will not discuss here in detail) pitch the case altogether too high: They are supposed to show that the question whether a man could have acted differently is *in principle unanswerable* and not merely that in Law Courts we do not usually have clear enough evidence to answer it. Lady Wootton says that a man's responsibility or capacity to resist temptation is something 'buried in [his] consciousness, into which no human being can enter,'[27] known if at all only to him and to God: it is not something which other men may never know; and since 'it is not possible to get inside another man's skin'[28] it is not something of which they can ever form even a reasonable estimate as a matter of probability. Yet strangely enough she does not take the same view of the question which arises under the M'Naghten Rules whether a man knew what he was doing or that it was illegal, although a man's knowledge is surely as much, or as little, locked in his breast as his capacity for self control. Questions about the latter indeed may often be more difficult to answer than questions about a man's knowledge; yet in favourable circumstances if we know a man well and can trust what he says about his efforts or struggles to control himself we may have as good ground for saying

'Well he just could not do it though he tried' as we have for saying 'He didn't know that the pistol was loaded.' And we sometimes may have good general evidence that in certain conditions, for example infancy or a clinically definable state, such as depression after childbirth, human beings are unable or less able than the normal adult to master certain impulses. We are not forced by the facts to say of a child or mental defective, who has struggled vainly with tears, merely 'he usually cries when that happens.' We say—and why not? —'he could not stop himself crying though he tried as hard as he could.'

It must however be conceded that such clear cases are very untypical of those that face the Courts where an accused person is often fighting for his life or freedom. Lady Wootton's best arguments are certainly independent of her more debatable philosophical points about our ability to know what is locked in another's mind or breast. Her central point is that the evidence put before Courts on the question whether the accused lacked the capacity to conform to the law, or whether it was substantially impaired, at the best only shows the *propensity* of the accused to commit crimes of certain sorts. From this, she claims, it is a fallacy to infer that he could not have done otherwise than commit the crime of which he is accused. She calls this fallacious argument 'circular': We infer the accused's lack of capacity to control his actions from his propensity to commit crimes and then both explain this propensity and excuse his crimes by his lack of capacity. Lady Wootton's critics have challenged this view of the medical and other evidence on which the courts act in these cases.[29] They would admit that it is at any rate in part through studying a man's crimes that we may discern his incapacity to control his actions. Nonetheless the evidence for this conclusion is not merely the bare fact that he committed these crimes repeatedly, but the manner and the circumstances and the psychological state in which he did this. Secondly in forming any conclusion about a man's ability to control his action much more than his repeated crimes are taken into account. Antisocial behaviour is not just used to explain and excuse itself, even in the case of the psychopath, the definition of whose disorder presents great problems. I think there is much in these criticisms. Nonetheless the forensic debate before judge and jury of the ques-

tion whether a mentally disordered person could have controlled his action or whether his capacity to do this was or was not 'substantially impaired' seems to me very often very unreal. The evidence tendered is not only often conflicting, but seems to relate to the specific issue of the accused's power or capacity for control on a specific past occasion only very remotely. I can scarcely believe that on this, the supposed issue, anything coherent penetrates to the minds of the jury after they have heard the difficult expert evidence and heard the judge's warning that these matters are 'incapable of scientific proof.'[30] And I sympathize with the judges in their difficult task of instructing juries on this plea. In Israel there are no juries to be instructed and the judges themselves must confront these same difficulties in deciding in accordance with the principle of the *Mandelbrot* case whether or not the action of a mentally abnormal person who knew what he was doing occurred 'independently of the exercise of his will.'

Because of these difficulties I would prefer to the present law the scheme which I have termed the 'moderate' form of the new doctrine. Under this scheme *mens rea* would continue to be a necessary condition of liability to be investigated and settled before conviction except so far as it relates to mental abnormality. The innovation would be that an accused person would no longer be able to adduce any form of mental abnormality as a bar to conviction. The question of his mental abnormality would under this scheme be investigated only after conviction and would be primarily concerned with his present rather than his past mental state. His past mental state at the time of his crime would only be relevant so far as it provided ancillary evidence of the nature of his abnormality and indicated the appropriate treatment. This position could perhaps be fairly easily reached by eliminating the pleas of insanity and diminished responsibility and extending the provisions of the Mental Health Act, 1959 to all offences including murder. But I would further provide that, in cases where the appropriate direct evidence of mental disorder was forthcoming, the courts should no longer be permitted to think in terms of responsibility and mete out penal sentences instead of compulsory medical treatment. Yet even this moderate reform certainly raises some difficult questions requiring careful consideration.[31]

Many I think would wish to go further than this 'moderate' scheme and would join Lady Wootton in a demand for the elimination of the whole doctrine of *mens rea* or at least in the hope that it will 'wither away.' My reasons for not joining them consist of misgivings on three principal points. The first concerns individual freedom. In a system in which proof of *mens rea* is no longer a necessary condition for conviction, the occasions for official interferences with our lives and for compulsion will be vastly increased. Take, for example, the notion of a criminal assault. If the doctrine of *mens rea* were swept away, every blow, even if it was apparent to a policeman that it was purely accidental or merely careless and therefore not, according to the present law, a criminal assault, would be a matter for investigaion under the new scheme, since the possibilities of a curable or treatable condition would have to be investigated and the condition if serious treated by medical or penal methods. No doubt under the new dispensation, as at present, prosecuting authorities would use their common sense; but every considerable discretionary powers would have to be entrusted to them to sift from the mass the cases worth investigation as possible candidates for therapeutic or penal treatment. No one could view this kind of expansion of police powers with equanimity, for with it will come great uncertainty for the individual: Official interferences with his life will be more frequent but he will be less able to predict their incidence if any accidental or careless blow may be an occasion for them.

My second misgiving concerns the idea to which Lady Wootton attaches great importance: that what we now call punishment (imprisonment and the like) and compulsory medical treatment should be regarded just as alternative forms of social hygiene to be used according to the best estimate of their future effects and no judgment of responsibility should be required before we apply to a convicted person those measures, such as imprisonment, which we now think of as penal. Lady Wootton thinks this will present no difficulty as long as we take a firm hold of the idea that the purpose and justification of the criminal law is to prevent crime and not to pay back criminals for their wickedness. But I do not think ob-

jections to detaching the use of penal methods from judgments of responsibility can be disposed of so easily. Though Lady Wootton looks forward to the day when the 'formal distinction' between hospitals and prisons will have disappeared, she does not suggest that we should give up the use of measures such as imprisonment. She contemplates that 'those for whom medicine has nothing to offer'[32] may be sentenced to 'places of safety' to receive 'the treatment which experience suggests is most likely to evoke the desired responses,' and though it will only be for the purpose of convenience that their 'places of safety' will be separate from those for whom medicine has something to offer, she certainly accepts the idea that imprisonment may be used for its deterrent effect on the person sentenced to it.

This vision of the future evokes from me two different responses: One is a moral objection and the other a sociological or criminological doubt. The moral objection is this: If we imprison a man who has broken the law in order to deter him and by his example others, we are using him for the benefit of society, and for many people, including myself, this is a step which requires to be justified by (*inter alia*) the demonstration that the person so treated could have helped doing what he did. The individual according to this outlook, which is surely neither esoteric nor confused, has a right not to be used in this way unless he could have avoided doing what he did. Lady Wootton would perhaps dismiss this outlook as a disguised form of a retributive conception of punishment. But it is in fact independent of it as I have attempted to show: for though we must seek a moral licence for punishing a man in his voluntary conduct in breaking the law, the punishment we are then licensed to use may still be directed solely to preventing future crimes on his part or on others' and not to 'retribution.'

To this moral objection it may be replied that it depends wholly on the assumption that imprisonment for deterrent purposes will, under the new scheme, continue to be regarded by people generally as radically distinct from medical treatment and still requiring justification in terms of responsibility. It may be said that this assumption should not be made; for the operation of the system itself will in time cause this distinction to fade, and conviction by a court, followed by a sentence of imprisonment, will in time be assimilated to such experiences as a compulsory medical inspection followed by detention in an isolation hospital. But here my sociological or criminological doubts begin. Surely there are two features which, at present, are among those distinguishing punishment from medical treatment and will have to be stripped away before this assimilation can take place, and the moral objection silenced. One of these is that, unlike medical treatment, we use deterrent punishment to deter not only the individual punished but others by the example of his punishment and the severity of the sentence may be adjusted accordingly. Lady Wootton is very skeptical of the whole notion that we can deter in this way potential offenders and therefore she may be prepared to forego this aspect of punishment altogether. But can we on the present available evidence safely adopt this course for all crime? The second feature distinguishing punishment from treatment is that unlike a medical inspection followed by detention in hospital, conviction by a court followed by a sentence of imprisonment is a public act expressing the odium, if not the hostility, of society for those who break the law. As long as these features attach to conviction and a sentence of imprisonment, the moral objection to their use on those who could not have helped doing what they did will remain. On the other hand, if they cease to attach, will not the law have lost an important element in its authority and deterrent force—as important perhaps for some convicted persons as the deterrent force of the actual measures which it administers.

My third misgiving is this. According to Lady Wootton's argument it is a mistake, indeed 'illogical,' to introduce a reference to *mens rea* into the definition of an offence. But it seems that a code of criminal law which omitted any reference in the definition of its offences to mental elements could not possibly be satisfactory. For there are some socially harmful activities which are now and should always be treated as criminal offences which can only be identified by reference to intention or some other mental element. Consider the idea of an attempt to commit a crime. It is obviously desirable that persons who attempt to kill or injure or steal, even if they fail, should be brought before courts for punishment or treatment; yet what distinguishes an attempt which fails from an innocent activity is just the fact that

it is a step taken with the intention of bringing about some harmful consequence.

I do not consider my misgivings on these three points as necessarily insuperable objections to the programme of eliminating responsibility. For the first of them rests on a judgment of the value of individual liberty as compared with an increase in social security from harmful activities, and with this comparative judgment others may disagree. The second misgiving in part involves a belief about the dependence of the efficacy of the criminal law on the publicity and odium at present attached to conviction and sentence and on deterrence by example; psychological and sociological researches may one day show that this belief is false. The third objection may perhaps be surmounted by some ingenuity or compromise, since there are many important offences to which it does not apply. Nonetheless I am certain that the questions I have raised here should worry advocates of the elimination of responsibility more than they do; and until they have been satisfactorily answered I do not think we should move the whole way into this part of the Brave New World.

NOTES

1. (1956) 10 P.D. 281.
2. See Edwards, 'Automatism and Criminal Responsibility' 21 M. L. R. (1958), p. 375, and Acts of Will and Responsibility. Chap. IV, *supra*. The doctrine as now formulated descends from Austin, *Lectures in Jurisprudence*, Lectures XVIII and XIX.
3. *Year Book*, 17 Pasch Ed. IV. f. 1. pl. 2.
4. (1961) A. C. 290.
5. Denning, *Responsibility before the Law*, Jerusalem, 1961.
6. *Edgington* v. *Fitzmaurice* (1885), 29 Ch. D. 459.
7. Chap. XIX, Vol. II, 'On the Relation of Madness to Crime.'
8. 57 H. L. Deb. 443–76 (1924), 'if this Bill were passed very grave results would follow' (Lord Sumner, p. 459). 'What a door is being opened!' (Lord Hewart, p. 467). 'This would be a very dangerous change to make' (Lord Cave, p. 475).
9. Cmd. 8932 (1953).
10. *R.* v. *Spriggs* (1958), 1 Q. B. 270.
11. *R.* v. *Byrne* (1960), 44 Cr. App. Rep. 246.
12. For the statistics see *Murder: Home Office Research Unit Report*, H.M.S.O. 1961, Table 7, p. 10.
13. See her *Social Science and Social Pathology* (1959) esp. Chapter VIII on 'Mental Disorder and the Problem of Moral and Criminal Responsibility;' 'Diminished Responsibility: A Layman's View' 76 *L.Q.R.* (1960), p. 224; *Crime and the Criminal Law* (1963).
14. See *Crime and the Criminal Law*, p. 52. But she does not consider explicitly whether, even if the aim of the criminal law is to prevent crime, there are not moral objections to applying its sanctions even as preventives to those who lacked the capacity to conform to the Law. See *infra*, pp. 207–8.

15. Op. cit., p. 51.

16. In *Crime and the Criminal Law* she makes it clear that the elimination or 'withering away' of *mens rea* as a condition of liability is to apply to all its elements not merely to its provisions for mental abnormality. Hence strict liability is welcomed as the model for the future (op. cit., pp. 46–57).

17. Save as indicated *infra* p. 205, n. 31.

18. See Wootton, op. cit., p. 51.

19. In 1962 the number of persons over 17 treated in these ways were respectively 36 (unfit to plead), 5 (insane before trial), and 836 (probation with mental treatment). See *Criminal Statistics* 1962.

20. In 1962 hospital orders under this section were made in respect of 1187 convicted persons (*Criminal Statistics* 1962).

21. *R.* v. *Morris* (1961) 45 Cr. App. Rep. 185.

22. See Wootton, op. cit., pp. 79–80.

23. Wootton, op. cit., pp. 79–80.

24. 'Punishment and the Elimination of Responsibility,' Chap. VII, *supra*.

25. *The Times,* 18 February 1961 (Staff Sergeant Boshears).

26. See *Bratty* v. *Att. Gen. For Northern Ireland* (1961), 3 All E.R., 523 and Cross, 'Reflections on Bratty's Case' 78 *L.Q.R.* (1962), p. 236.

27. See 'Diminished Responsibility: A Layman's View' 76 *L.Q.R.* (1960), p. 232.

28. See *Crime and the Criminal Law*, p. 74.

29. See N. Walker, 'M'Naghten's Ghost,' *The Listener,* 29 Aug. 1963, p. 303.

30. Per Parker C. J. in *R.* v. *Byrne* (1960) 44 Cr. App. 246 at 258.

31. Of these difficult questions the following seem the most important.

(1) If the post-conviction inquiry into the convicted person's mental abnormality is to focus on his present state, what should a court do with an offender (a) who suffered some mental disorder at the time of his crime but has since recovered? (b) who was 'normal' at the time of the crime but at the time of his conviction suffers from mental disorder?

(2) The Mental Health Act does not by its terms require the court to be satisfied before making a hospital order that there was any causal connection between the accused's disorder and his offence, but only provides that the court in the exercise of its discretion shall have regard to the nature of the offence. Would this still be satisfactory if the courts were bound to make a hospital order if the medical evidence of abnormality is forthcoming?

(3) The various elements of *mens rea* (knowledge, intention, and the minimum control of muscular movements required for an act) may be absent either in a person otherwise normal or may be absent because of some mental disorder (compare the distinctions now drawn between 'sane' and 'insane' automatism). (See *supra*, p. 202). Presumably it would be desirable that in the latter case there should not be an acquittal; but to identify such cases where there were grounds for suspecting mental abnormality, some investigation of mental abnormality would be necessary before the verdict.

32. Op. cit., p. 79–80 ('places of safety' are in quotation markes in her text).

HYMAN GROSS

Mental Abnormality as a Criminal Excuse*

I

A person's mental condition at the time he engages in criminal conduct may relieve him from criminal liability. When this is the case, we say that he is not criminally liable because he was not a responsible person at the time of the offense. To say that one was not responsible in this sense is to assert the most personal of all excuses. What interests us is not something about the perfor-

mance but something about the actor. The actor is said not to have had available those personal resources that are necessary to qualify him as accountable for his conduct. Since he is not accountable he cannot be faulted for his conduct and so enjoys exemption from judgments of culpability.

Mental abnormality of a sort relevant to excusing exists, then, when mental resources necessary for accountability are lacking. There are four varieties of relevant abnormality: One is mental illness that, formerly in medical literature

---

*This essay has not been previously published. It is a section of a forthcoming book by the author.

and still in legal literature, would be characterized as a *disease* of the mind, by virtue of a sufficiently definite pathology and sufficiently pronounced morbidity. Intoxication, whatever its source, is another variety. Mental defectiveness is a third sort of relevant abnormality, encompassing cases of serious deficiency mainly in intelligence but including deficiency of any mental capacity necessary to control behavior. Finally, there is a variety of abnormality that may be conveniently referred to as automatism, which includes behavioral phenomena diverse in origin but which all are instances of a gross separation of consciousness and action such as exists during hypnosis, somnambulism, and epileptic seizures.

Relevant impairments of mental capacity may have an orgin which is extrapsychic or intrapsychic. Drugs, alcohol, hypnotic suggestion, a blow on the head, emotional shock, an extra chromosome, or a brain tumor are all ways in which incapacitation may be produced by external interventions upon normal mental functioning. It is clear that a person may himself be responsible for some of these interventions by doing something to himself or allowing others to. When this is the case, he is deemed responsible for the resulting condition he is in, though not otherwise. Still, one's being responsible for his condition does not always entail being criminally liable for what he does while in that condition. If he suffers mental incapacitation sufficient for him not to be responsible, he is then treated as one who is not, regardless of his having been a responsible person with reference to putting himself in that condition. A person may ultimately cause himself to suffer sieges of delirium tremens by the gradual effects of his own alcoholic indulgence. Yet he is entitled to be treated as not responsible regarding acts done during those sieges no less than a person whose delusions have an origin utterly beyond his control. But if a person while responsible does things to put himself in a state of incapacitation in which harmful conduct is expectable—he intoxicates himself to a dangerous degree—he may be liable for that when the harm occurs or, even without it occurring, when he engages in conduct that threatens the harm. The reason is that incapacitating himself while still a responsible person is itself a dangerous act, and so may be regarded as culpable. Other examples would be persons who willingly submit to drugs or hypnosis under circumstances portending harm, or who place themselves in dangerous situations knowing they are epileptics or sleepwalkers prone to violence. Culpability in such cases properly extends only to conduct that produces the loss of capacity and not the further conduct that is engaged in while the person is not responsible. One person may kill another quite deliberately under delusions produced by drugs taken quite deliberately, yet culpability is not for deliberate killing because the accused is not responsible at all for his homicidal conduct but only for the act of taking the drugs. Not without some awkwardness in principle, the lesser culpability is usually reflected in the criminal law by liability for homicide of a lesser degree.

When mental impairment is intrapsychic in origin, the excuse based on it is received more charily. The same debilitation which would easily pass muster for an excuse if externally induced is regarded with skepticism when its origin is not palpably outside the mind of the actor. Initial suspicion is indeed warranted because of increased opportunity for deception. But even after genuineness of the psychopathology is established, there is often lingering skepticism regarding its significance for judgments of responsibility. This skepticism is justified to the extent that it reflects sound opinion that the actor was quite capable of doing otherwise in spite of his illness. But it is not justified when it reflects the belief that a person is in some measure responsible for his mental illness since its origins are within him and, unlike the case of mental abnormalities having identifiable physical causes, it pertains to him in an especially intimate way because of its purely psychic character. Holding a person responsible for his mental illness is in general even more unjust than holding him responsible for his physical illness. Such medical knowledge as we have bearing on the etiology of serious mental illness makes it quite clear that in most cases the sick person could not reasonably be expected to do such things as would probably have prevented the onset of his illness, while in the case of physical illness effective precautions often might quite easily have been taken.

II

It is not any mental abnormality that excuses. Even when the abnormality is of a kind that is relevant to responsibility, certain conditions of incapacitation must be met if there is to be an excuse. In the criminal law these conditions have been formulated as rules which govern the insanity defense. These rules look mainly to mental illness and defectiveness, but the conditions for excusing under them have a rationale which extends to mental abnormality of whatever variety. Four basic versions of this defense have developed in the criminal law and, as shall be shown, the conditions required by each are less dissimilar from those required by the others than would appear from the terms used in formulating each. The first version, which dominates among Anglo-American jurisdictions, turns out to be too meager. The second of these versions (which in some form is now the law in a third of the American jurisdictions and under the Model Penal Code) represents the most satisfactory statement. The third and fourth versions, though lending themselves to suitably restrictive interpretation, as they stand offer too great opportunity for unwarranted excuses and in fact are the versions most often preferred by those advocating unsound excuses. First, each version will be briefly scanned and then good reasons will be distinguished from bad among excuses of this sort. The concern here is only with why a person is not responsible, and so the very difficult medical questions having to do with exactly what states of abnormality leave a person in a condition in which he is not responsible will remain unexplored. Only the more basic question of what it means not to be responsible is taken up here. But without answers to that, one does not know what exculpatory significance, if any, to attach ultimately to the medical facts.

The first version of the insanity defense is represented by the M'Naghten rules. Stated in their original terms, these rules provide that a person has a defense of insanity if he did not know the nature and quality of the act he was doing, or did not know that it was wrong, because laboring under a defect of reason from disease of the mind. There was in the original M'Naghten rules a further proviso that, even if not so afflicted, a person would have a defense if at the time of his act he was suffering from an insane delusion about something such that if—but only if—it were in fact the case, it would furnish a defense. This part of the M'Naghten rules has been generally disregarded because of the limitation it places on delusions which may excuse, though as we shall see

the right reason for ignoring the rule on these grounds has not been generally apprehended. There has been a continuing need for a rule extending the defense generally to all those who have insane delusions about the circumstances under which they act, and this requirement has encouraged strained applications of the remainder of the M'Naghten doctrine to cover such cases.

Despite variations in language and differences in fine points of interpretation, the gist of the M'Naghten formula has remained unchanged in the many jurisdictions that have adopted it since its introduction in England well over a century ago. Serious incapacitation may make it impossible for the actor to be sufficiently aware of what he is doing so that he could choose to do otherwise. It may deprive him of appreciation of the harmfulness of his conduct, or of appreciation of the harm itself, so that a normal disposition to restrain harmful conduct is not aroused. It may deprive him of the ability to comprehend the circumstances in which he acts and so make it impossible for him to choose not to do what under the circumstances is not justifiable. It may make him incapable of knowing that the law prohibits what he does, when only the fact of legal prohibition is a reason for not doing it. In any of these cases, because of a failure of personal resources he cannot help what he does.

The second version of the insanity defense consists of some form of M'Naghten to which is added an excuse based on grossly deficient inhibitory capacity. This additional part is usually referred to as the irresistible impulse rule, though any suggestion that the act need be impulsive to qualify would be seriously misleading. Under this provision, if the accused was incapable of restraining himself from doing what he knew he was doing and knew he ought not to be doing, he may invoke as an excuse his inability to exercise self-control.

The gravamen of this excuse is again the actor's helplessness in being unable to avoid doing or causing harm. The excuse is even stronger than the claim of compulsion that is asserted when one has been forced to do something harmful. Instead of succumbing to pressures which one is nevertheless able to resist, the person without significant capacity for inhibition is simply unable to resist. The excuse is sometimes misconceived, however, so that it is the untoward urge rather than the inhibitory failure which receives primary attention. This distorts the rationale of the excuse. We do not excuse because the actor wanted very desperately to do what he did. By itself powerful determination to do harm is not grounds for exemption from judgments of culpability. On the contrary, it is grounds for a judgment of greater culpability.

The third version of the insanity defense makes mental disease or defect, *when it produces criminal conduct,* the basis of an excuse for that conduct. This version has been adopted in four American jurisdictions (though recently discarded in the one that gave it the name by which it is best known), enjoys considerable psychiatric advocacy, and is generally referred to as the Durham rule. It relies heavily in practice on the same rationale of excuse as the previous version, but offers opportunities for the troublesome departures that will be discussed shortly.

A final version is constituted by those criminal insanity provisions in which mental derangement or deficiency at the time of the act is itself an excuse. The actor need only be seriously defective or not in possession of his faculties in order for his conduct in such a state to be excusable. Unlike the previous version, the relation between the abnormality and the criminal conduct is not of concern here so long as the two are contemporaneous. This version has in somewhat primitive forms preceded M'Naghten in the commom law and now appears in the criminal law of some civil law jurisdictions. It enjoys strong support among those of the medical profession who are interested in these forensic matters and is probably even more congenial to psychiatric views of the insanity defense than is the Durham version. As with Durham there is heavy reliance in practice on the same rationale of excuse that support M'Naghten and irresistible impulse; but again, as with Durham, opportunities for excusing on other grounds are made possible, and these call for careful investigation.

III

The preceding discussion has shown what grounds the law has recognized for an excuse of mental abnormality when the excuse is presented in its most dramatic form as the insanity defense. Many of those who favor the third or fourth version of the insanity defense think it a good defense simply that a person was mentally ill at the time of his criminal act, or that his criminal conduct was a result of the mental illness he suffered at the time. There are three important arguments here, one grounded in moral considerations regarding avoidance of cruelty, and the other two in exculpatory considerations thought to apply to sick persons.

The first contention is that it is wrong to punish a person *when he is sick.* It is generally regarded as inhumane to neglect the suffering of those who are in a debilitated condition and even more inhumane to inflict further suffering on them. It would therefore be barbarous if the criminal law not only withheld comfort and cure from the sick who are subject to its processes but imposed upon such persons a penal regime. Directed to present concerns, this principle of humane treatment clearly requires that a person mentally abnormal at the time of his crime not be subjected to punitive treatment while he continues to be in such a state, but that instead he receive medical treatment.

The principle of humane treatment is unquestionably sound and must be given full effect at all times. It does not, however, confer a cloak of immunity on persons who are sick when committing a crime. Conduct may be culpable even though the actor had chicken pox, pneumonia or multiple sclerosis. It may be culpable when the disorder is mental rather than physical. When a sick person's conduct is culpable, he is to be treated for his illness so long as it lasts by those in whose hands he is placed by virtue of liability for such culpable conduct. But liability for culpable conduct is not avoided by the mere fact of sickness. It is also true that even determination of liability to punishment must be postponed if the continuing illness of the accused makes impossible the proceedings necessary for a just determination of liability, and that those having custody of him must during this time abide by the imperatives of humane treatment. But again there is nothing in this to entitle the accused to exemption from liability.

A second argument derives from general requirements for culpability. It is wrong to punish someone *for being sick.* The reason is that in being sick a person has not done anything blameworthy. Since merely falling ill does not constitute culpable conduct, it may not be punished. (A person might indeed be rightly blamed for making himself sick, or allowing himself to become or to be made sick, and we might well decide that such conduct then deserves punishment when it was understood that the well-being of others depended upon the fitness of the one who became sick. In such a case there is culpability because the accused could have acted to prevent his illness.)

But insofar as a person is being punished for his conduct and not for his disorder, the requirement of culpability is not transgressed. Nevertheless, it is sometimes claimed that when a mentally disordered person is punished for his conduct, he is being punished for his disorder since the conduct is a symptom of it. Such claims are especially prominent in arguments advocating extension of a mental abnormality defense to those persons, often characterized as psychopaths or sociopaths, whose dedication to wrongdoing is especially strong and free of internal conflicts. This claim rests on a misunderstanding of what it means to be punished for something. A person may be punished for a criminal act and that act may in various other perspectives be viewed quite accurately as a symptom of his illness, or indeed of society's illness, as an act of dedicated self-sacrifice, or as an act to advance a socially worthwhile cause. Still in all these cases we are punishing him only for his culpable conduct. We may punish in spite of causes, motives, or intentions, so long as they do not furnish an excuse or other reason for not punishing.

The third argument is that it is wrong to punish someone for what he does *as a result of being mentally sick*. Unlike the previous argument, the position here is not that it is wrong to punish someone for the illness evidenced by criminal conduct, but rather that it is wrong to punish someone for his conduct when it is *produced* by the disorder. The criminal conduct is not viewed as part of a pattern of behavior such that if one so behaves one must by that very fact be judged to be abnormal. Rather the conduct is viewed as determined by the abnormality in the sense that but for the abnormality there would have been no warrant for expecting such conduct.

Treating the fact that conduct resulted from mental abnormality as a reason to excuse the conduct leaves us with no principle on which to rest the excuse. Exculpation by way of justification would indeed be warranted by a principle that what is morbidly determined is not wrong, but there are no good reasons for recognizing as a justifying principle the proposition that condemnation ought to be restricted to healthy determinations to act harmfully. It is true that a person's mental abnormality, if it is to excuse his criminal conduct, must in some significant way be related to that conduct as its cause. This may be put in an even stronger form by saying that we ought to excuse when, but only when, conduct is the "product" of abnormality in the sense that the abnormality is a sufficient condition for the conduct. In that case, but only in that case, the accused was unable to do otherwise because of the abnormality and so is entitled to be excused. It is not true that we ought to excuse simply because the wrong thing that was done would likely not have been done but for the abnormality. Otherwise we should have to excuse anyone who acted from some untoward tendency attributable to a mental abnormality whenever it is unlikely that he would have done the act if he were normal, even in cases where he was quite as capable of acting otherwise as is a normal person subject to the same tendency. This would mean that a bank employee ought to be excused when he embezzles money only because of powerful unconscious wishes to be caught which he could effectively have chosen not to succumb to, although another employee who embezzles only because tempted by healthy fantasies of a life of leisure ought not to be excused.

There is a fourth argument for not punishing wrongdoers who suffered from mental abnormality that in effect requires for an excuse too much rather than too little. It has eminent philosophical credentials and is to be found in the best legal circles as well. The argument derives from general considerations bearing on justification of punishment.

It is pointed out that prescribing punishment for what the insane do is futile since the threat of punishment can have no deterrent effect on such persons. Anyone, therefore, who considers the practice of punishment to be justified by its deterrent effect must hold punishment of the insane to be unjustified and, in fact, a purposeless infliction of suffering. It has been argued in reply that punishment of the insane may still have a deterrent effect on sane persons since it deprives them of hope of escaping punishment by successfully advancing fraudulent claims of having been insane at the time of their offense. That answer is good only to the extent that crimes are committed after decisions to commit them which include deliberation on possible legal tactics to avoid conviction. But since most crimes are committed without decisions of this sort, the deterrent effect of a threat of punishment that makes no allowance for insanity is in any event largely otiose.

There are, however, other answers to the "no deterrence" objection to punishing the insane that do not require belief in such fictitious deliberations by would-be criminals.

If it is being suggested that nondeterribility has been the rationale for the insanity defense in the law as it has developed, we may ask why the law does not refuse by the same rationale to punish those who were genuinely and blamelessly ignorant of the law they broke. Such persons were in a position indistinguishable from the insane with respect to the futility of prospective punishment, and so to punish them is equally a purposeless infliction of suffering. Yet, as we know, in the law as it stands such innocent ignorance does not excuse, and this inconsistency must raise doubts about this rationale for the insanity defense.

But there is a more cogent objection than one based on inconsistency. It is not the case that all, or perhaps even most, insane persons are incapable of being deterred by threat of punishment. Under the prevailing Anglo-American insanity defense, the M'Naghten rules, there is an excuse if the accused by virtue of a defect of reason from disease of the mind did not know he was doing what was wrong. The Model Penal Code similarly establishes as a defense a person's lack of substantial capacity to appreciate the criminality of his conduct (which means more than mere knowledge that it is criminally prohibited) as a result of mental disease or defect. There are many persons who fit these specifications in being unable to appreciate that what they do is wrong and in fact think it for some reason justified, yet are aware and in awe of the threat of punishment quite as much as normal persons. In some of the most notable cases of the insanity defense, the defendant committed murder under the delusion that he was carrying out a divine command, or was giving his due to a man believed to be very wicked, or was killing someone who was bent on harming him. Less dramatic but far more frequent are the family and sex intrigue homicides where the killing was done in a suitably extreme abnormal mental state—usually spoken of as temporary insanity—in which the accused was likewise at the time convinced that he was justified. There is no reason to believe that in general their abnormality rendered the accused in these insanity cases incapable of being deterred by the threat of punishment, though of course like many normal defendants they were not in fact deterred by it. There is, further, every reason to believe that certain abnormal persons who would be entitled to exoneration on grounds of insanity were in fact deterred, just as normal persons would be because the law has made the conduct they contemplated punishable. If these things were not so, the insanity defense could consist simply in establishing the one point that by reason of mental abnormality the accused could not at the time of his crime be deterred by the threat of punishment. In fact what distinguishes the sane from the insane under criminal law standards is the inability of the insane to appreciate the *culpability,* not the punishability, of their conduct. Because of their abnormality the insane cannot at the time apprehend what justifies condemnation of their conduct. Even though amenable to threats of punishment, they lack a resource of appreciation that is necessary if one is to have a reason apart from avoidance of punishment for not doing what the law prohibits. Punishing such persons is indeed a useless infliction of suffering, for it can not serve to uphold the standards that the criminal law exists to preserve.

There is one other argument against mental abnormality defenses that should be noted here. Again it is an argument that by implication requires too much rather than too little for excuse. Many persons who are mentally ill and have committed crimes are dangerous, yet the very abnormality that is evidence of his being dangerous serves to shield the accused from liability. Those who see confinement of dangerous persons as a principal purpose of the criminal law are particularly distressed by this, for in effect just those who are thought to be most properly the concern of the criminal law are allowed to escape its restraints.

The answer to this argument is that not all restraint by the state need be based on criminal liability. If a person is dangerous because of mental abnormality, he may be prevented from doing harm by noncriminal commitment regardless of whether his conduct provided a basis for criminal liability. It is true that persons usually are not found to be a menace for purposes of commitment unless they have done something which would at least provide the substance of a criminal charge. But it is still dangerousness of the person and not criminality of his conduct that warrants deprivation of liberty. Since determinations of dangerousness and determinations of criminal liability are independent matters, a defense of insanity to a criminal charge does not weigh against the accused's subsequent liability to commitment because he is dangerous. Conversely, elimination or postponement of the question of insanity when determining liability would result in branding as criminals persons, whether dangerous or not, who are not to blame for what they did.

IV

The rationale of excusing for mental abnormality may be summarized in this way. Certain forms of mental incapacity deprive a person of ability to act other than the way he does because resources for an effective choice are lacking. When a person lacks capacity to tell what he is doing, whether it is offensive, or what is likely to happen; or lacks capacity to appreciate its harmful significance, or to restrain himself, he is in such a condition. It is apparent that a person incapacitated in any of these ways lacks a resource necessary for control and so necessary for culpable conduct. It is for this reason that an excuse of mental abnormality preempts the field of excuse and makes excuses going directly to culpability inappropriate. There is no point in being concerned about whether something was intentional, when whether it is intentional or not the actor was not a responsible agent. And conversely, when there is a complement of those personal resources that are necessary for responsible conduct, there is a duty to draw upon such resources to avoid harmful conduct. It follows that when a normal person claims he did not at the time appreciate the significance of sticking a knife into another person—his mind was elsewhere—he offers a different kind of excuse than the mentally abnormal man who makes

the same claim. The normal man can only expect by showing less culpability to blunt an accusation of conduct of a higher degree of culpability—he didn't harm the victim knowingly, but only negligently through absent-mindedness in failing to pay attention to the dangers of what he was occupied in doing. But the man who establishes that his failure of appreciation was due to a lack of necessary mental resources exempts himself from any judgment of culpability.

The distinction and connections between lack of responsibility and mere lack of culpability are important with regard to several difficulties surrounding the insanity defense.

We have already mentioned the usually discarded third part of the original M'Naghten rule. It provided that even if the accused person who suffered a defect of reason from disease of the mind could know the nature and quality of his act, and even if he could know that what he was doing was wrong, he still might have a defense if at the time of his act he suffered from a delusion such that had it been a correct belief it would have afforded a defense. This part of the rule has been dropped, but not in order to exclude insanity defenses based on delusion; in fact, delusion cases have always been recognized as paradigms of criminal insanity and are allowed in all M'Naghten rule jurisdictions by strained interpretations of the other parts. It is the limitation upon the kinds of delusion which are acceptable that has been found objectionable. The usual argument is that the limitation leads to absurd results. For example, in accordance with conventional legal rules that preclude criminal jurisdiction for crimes of foreign nationals committed in foreign countries, a homicide defendant in England who in a delusion at the time of his crime believed himself to be Bluebeard reenacting one of his murders in France would have a good defense. But a homicide defendant also in England who in his similar delusion believed himself to be Jack the Ripper would not. Even when the rule has been confined to delusions which bear on exculpatory claims (typically provocation and self-defense), as undoubtedly it was intended to be by its original proponents, criticism has not abated though the reason for rejecting the rule is less clear.

It seems, in fact, that the original rule was a sound one based on the premises concerning the facts of mental abnormality which the M'Naghten judges accepted, but that these premises are incorrect. The mistake from which the rule proceeded has been characterized as the doctrine of partial insanity. It holds that a person whose insanity consists merely in delusions is still capable of choosing to act in conformity with the law that governed the situation as he perceived it. He therefore is to be held accountable for not acting in conformity with law as it would apply to the situation he perceived, though by virtue of his inability to perceive the situation correctly he could not be held accountable for breaking the law with respect to the situation as it actually was. However, according to better medical knowledge, the fact of the matter is that such persons in the grip of their delusions are normally so severely incapacitated that they cannot even choose to act otherwise. We therefore cannot hold them responsible when they act as their delusion dictates and so must consider them ineligible for blame. Questions about matters of culpability (usually matters of justification) which the original rule raises are for this reason superfluous.

A second problem concerns what is meant by "wrong" under the terms of the M'Naghten rule. If the accused, because of a defect of reason from disease of the mind, did not know that what he was doing was wrong he has a defense on grounds of insanity. The question which has persistently troubled courts both in England and the United States is whether the failure of knowledge required is of legal or of moral wrong. Does a psychotic person who knows murder is a crime but believes he may nevertheless commit it because divinely commanded have a defense? What about a mental defective who knows he is not supposed to hurt other people but cannot even comprehend what a criminal law is? The Model Penal Code speaks of the accused's lack of capacity to appreciate the criminality of his conduct, but the difficulty remains, for appreciating the criminality of conduct is not the equivalent of knowing that it has been made a crime. Indeed the final draft of the Code provision offers "wrongfulness" as an optional substitute for "criminality".

The difficulty is removed by recognizing that what is crucial is capacity to know, rather than knowledge; and that it is a capacity to know something that is necessary for culpability. In a just legal system conduct ought not to be treated as legally culpable unless reasonable opportunity exists to become aware of its legal interdiction. Such opportunity for awareness has significance only if there also is ability to take advantage of it. That in turn depends on ability to appreciate the untowardness of conduct, ability to be aware of the range of normal concerns of the law, as well as the ability to become acquainted with the law itself. If there is disabling incapacity with respect to any of these necessary conditions the person incapacitated is not responsible, for to that degree he lacks ability to take advantage of the opportunity to become aware of criminal liabilities and so his conduct cannot be deemed culpable. It turns out, then, that it is misleading to ask whether legal or moral wrong is meant. The question to be answered is whether the accused was deprived of any abilities that are necessary to take advantage of the opportunity of becoming aware of criminal liability.

Another difficulty concerns the irresistible impulse defense. There has been great hesitation in legal circles in admitting as an excuse an inability to exercise self-restraint. It challenges common sense appreciation of behavior to assert that a person possessed of all the abilities necessary to control what he is doing, nevertheless does not have the self-control to choose effectively not to do it. The excuse is therefore often construed as a direct denial of culpability analoguous to external compulsion—he didn't mean to do that, he was forced to—rather than as a denial of responsibility by virtue of incapacity. The excuse so construed is then rejected as being too easy a way out for persons who either have not chosen to resist with sufficient determination powerful untoward urges or have failed to take precaution against succumbing to the urge and are therefore no less culpable than persons who lose their temper and, while in the grip of their rage, commit crimes.

But this excuse of no responsibility becomes plausible as understanding of human pathology advances, and it becomes increasingly clear that there are serious mental abnormalities which consist in inability either by repression or precaution to inhibit acting on certain urges. The claim of irresistible impulse is then no longer construed as one simply of not having effectively chosen to do otherwise, but rather more, as not having the personal resources that are necessary to choose effectively.

V

A stark separation according to mental abnormality of those who are responsible from those who are not seems at times unsatisfactory. We are bound to recognize that sometimes there is not sheer incapacity with regard to elements of control, yet there is deviation from normal capacities great enough to make desirable a limitation on accountability. Accordingly, there has developed in the law a doctrine of diminished (or partial) responsibility which, though still only little and narrowly accepted, offers a path for receiving into the law continuing insights respecting varieties of limited impairment bearing on control of conduct. The most notable legal recognition so far has been in the English Homicide Act of 1957, which reduces what otherwise would be murder to culpable homicide when the accused suffered from such abnormality of mind as "substantially impaired his mental responsibility" for his acts. The rationale for diminished responsibility is simple. If a person who is incapacitated is ineligible for blame, a person who is seriously impaired though not incapacitated is eligible to be blamed only within limits. While not utterly bereft of resources required for accountability, his resources of control are dimished to a point where full faulting according to the tenor of the conduct is inappropriate. But for reasons previously given, it would be a serious mistake to construe the defense of diminished responsibility as a declaration that the somewhat sick, simply because they are sick, ought not to be held to a liability as great as that of the healthy person. Indeed, perfectly healthy persons who have perfectly natural reactions that put them in an abnormal emotional state may rightly claim diminished responsibility. Typically, this is the case when a person acts under the influence of extreme anger or fear because provoked or threatened.

Mental abnormality may affect culpability in a more direct way, however, and some confusion about this has arisen in discussions of diminished responsibility. By virtue of his abnormality, a person may be unable to act in a way that is criminally culpable, or at least not as culpable as the conduct charged. Or, though capable of such conduct, he may simply not have been acting in the way charged but rather was acting in some other way dictated by his abnormal processes. In either case he may lodge an exculpatory claim that his conduct is different than alleged with respect to elements bearing on culpability, and he would rely on the evidence of his mental abnormality to establish this. Such an exculpatory claim in essence is no different from the sort that is appropriate when a normal person has not acted culpably, but the kind of argument which supports the claim is different. Instead of evidence indicating simply that the accused was engaged in a somewhat different enterprise than alleged, the evidence indicates that by virtue of his abnormal mental condition at the time, the accused could not or simply did not engage in the enterprise alleged. Two exculpatory claims are made in this way. Both of them have as their point what in the language of traditional criminal law theory would be called a lack of *mens rea*.

Suppose a prisoner attacks a guard with a knife and inflicts serious wounds. The prisoner is charged with first degree assault, an element of which is intent to cause serious physical injury. It is claimed on his behalf that he was at the time suffering severe paranoid anxieties which led him to misinterpret a routine warning as a sign that he was about to be attacked by the guard, and that he slashed at the guard only to fend off what he believed to be imminent blows. Evidence of his abnormal state would tend to show that he did not have the specific intent to cause serious physical injury. This would mean that while admittedly he exercised control in conducting an assault, he did not exercise control with regard to those features of it that produced the serious injury. The act done, therefore, was something less culpable than the act charged. The same would hold true for a person accused of burglary, which requires an intent to commit a felony, and who at the time of breaking and entering a home was in such a mental condition as to be incapable of having any definite further purpose.

The other challenge to culpability by way of abnormality does not concern the purpose which informs the act, but rather the earlier stages of planning the accomplishment of objectives and attending to the course of conduct while it is in progress. Such operational design and supervision as is referred to by "malice aforethought," "premeditation," "deliberation," "willfully," and "knowingly" may be beyond the accused's capacities or may simply be nonexistent by virtue of his abnormality. Powerful effects of intoxication or of lingering mental illness may render a person unable or unconcerned to form the plan or to remain in control of its execution, and so one is required to conclude that his homicidal attack was not designed with reference to the death of his victim. The Model Penal Code extends this variety of abnormality defense to all cases where evidence of mental disease or defect is relevant to the question of whether the accused had a required state of mind at the time of the crime, so that even recklessness or negligence may be disproved by evidence of appropriate abnormality.

In both of these "criminal intent" challenges based on mental abnormality, it is not responsibility that properly is said to be diminished. Culpability is what is really claimed to be diminished, and diminished to a point where the conduct is less culpable than is required for the offense charged.

VI

The excuse of insanity has presented far greater difficulties than any other for the criminal process. The main reason is that the point of the proceedings is lost sight of and confusion arises in deciding who may appropriately answer the very different kinds of questions involved, and also in deciding what the consequences of accepting or rejecting the excuse ought to be.

Much of the controversy in which medical and legal views of the insanity defense appear to be at odds results from a failure to appreciate that the law must ultimately be concerned not with who is sick but with whose conduct is excusable. Deciding that issue requires several subsidiary decisions that fall peculiarly within either medical or legal competence. There must, in the first place, be standards which set forth generally the nature of the incapacities that render a person not responsible. It is these standards that constitute the rules of the insanity defense, and deciding upon them is the responsibility of those with legislative and judicial authority who must make the law. It bears emphasis that what is called for here is not some general description of relevant clinical abnormalities in language lawyers are used to. What is required is a statement of the kinds of mental failures (due to mental illness or defectiveness)

that entitle us to conclude for purposes of criminal liability that the accused could not help doing what he did. Once there are such standards of mental abnormality, proceedings to judge the abnormalities of a particular defendant with reference to such standards are possible. Then it is the opinion of medical experts which must first be looked to in order to determine the nature of the defendant's debilitation and the extent to which it affects capacities necessary for responsible conduct. Such expert opinion may be critically examined by lawyers, as indeed any expert opinion may be in a legal proceeding to determine a disputed issue. But that is not a means of substituting an inexpert for an expert opinion, but only a way of ensuring that its acceptance is ultimately based on reason rather than authority. There is finally a decision of vast discretion that is normally made by the jury. It is a conclusion about whether, according to the expert account of the mental condition that is finally accepted, there is debilitation sufficient to excuse according to the legal standards. Asking psychiatrists for expert opinions about whether such standards of incapacity are met is asking them to perform a role which is not within their special professional competence. But the job to be done in making the ultimate determination does require specialized skill in sifting among psychiatric opinions to arrive at a sound appreciation of the defendant's mental condition with reference to those features that are significant for judgments of responsibility. The paramount procedural problem of the insanity defense is to combine this specialist's appreciation with the layman's considered views about when choices to act are no longer meaningful or even possible. There is for this reason a great deal to recommend in principle suggestions, such as H. L. A. Hart's, that we adopt an "apparently coarser grained technique of exempting persons from liability to punishment if they fall into certain recognized categories of mental disorder", on the model of exemption from liability for persons under a specified age. But the establishment of a comprehensive scheme of clear categories seems at the present state of medical art a remote prospect.

Another sort of misapprehension deflects concern from responsibility to other matters, at the cost of both justice and humaneness in the administration of the criminal law. It is assumed that determining the accused to be responsible and so liable to have his conduct judged culpable is a warrant for treating him punitively rather than therapeutically. But in fact, it is said, many persons who meet legal standards for responsible conduct are nevertheless quite sick and sending them to a prison rather than a hospital is uncivilized. It is urged that the mentally ill ought therefore not to be treated as criminally responsible.

The mistake here is in giving priority to existing institutional arrangements and then attempting to have rules of liability which are humane in their effect under those arrangements. A rational and morally concerned society designs its institutions to treat in a humane way those who are liable according to just principles of liability. When a person who is liable according to proper standards of responsibility and culpability is also sick, principles of humane treatment, which are in no way inferior moral considerations, require that he be treated as sick. To the extent that inappropriate treatment may at present be expected under existing institutional arrangements and regimes, that is cause for reform of institutional arrangements and regimes, not of the rules of criminal liability.

D U R H A M v. U N I T E D S T A T E S

United States Court of Appeals, D.C. Cir., 1954*

BAZELON, Circuit Judge.

Monte Durham was convicted of housebreaking,[1] by the District Court sitting without a jury. The only defense asserted at the trial was that Durham was of unsound mind at the time of the offense. We are now urged to reverse the conviction (1) because the trial court did not correctly apply existing rules governing the burden of proof on the defense of insanity, and (2) because existing tests of criminal responsibility are obsolete and should be superseded.[2]

I.

Durham has a long history of imprisonment and hospitalization. In 1945, at the age of 17, he was discharged from the Navy after a psychiatric examination had shown that he suffered "from a profound personality disorder which renders him unfit for Naval service." In 1947 he pleaded guilty to violating the National Motor Theft Act[3] and was placed on probation for one to three years. He attempted suicide, was taken to Gallinger Hospital for observation, and was transferred to St. Elizabeths Hospital, from which he was discharged after two months. In January of 1948, as a result of a conviction in the District of Columbia Municipal Court for passing bad checks, the District Court revoked his probation and he commenced service of his Motor Theft sentence. His conduct within the first few days in jail led to a lunacy inquiry in the Municipal Court where a jury found him to be of unsound mind. Upon commitment to St. Elizabeths, he was diagnosed as suffering from "psychosis with psychopathic personality." After 15 months of treatment, he was discharged in July 1949 as "recovered" and was returned to jail to serve the balance of his sentence. In June 1950 he was conditionally released. He violated the conditions by leaving the District. When he learned of a warrant for his arrest as a parole violator, he fled

*214 F. 2d 862 (1954). Excerpts only. The footnotes are numbered here as in the original.

to the "South and Midwest obtaining money by passing a number of bad checks." After he was found and returned to the District, the Parole Board referred him to the District Court for a lunacy inquisition, wherein a jury again found him to be of unsound mind. He was readmitted to St. Elizabeths in February 1951. This time the diagnosis was "without mental disorder, psychopathic personality." He was discharged for the third time in May 1951. The housebreaking which is the subject of the present appeal took place two months later, on July 13, 1951.

According to his mother and the psychiatrist who examined him in September 1951, he suffered from hallucinations immediately after his May 1951 discharge from St. Elizabeths. Following the present indictment, in October 1951, he was adjudged of unsound mind in proceedings under § 4244 of Title 18 U.S.C., upon the affidavits of two psychiatrists that he suffered from "psychosis with psychopathic personality." He was committed to St. Elizabeths for the fourth time and given subshock insulin therapy. This commitment lasted 16 months—until February 1953—when he was released to the custody of the District Jail on the certificate of Dr. Silk, Acting Superintendent of St. Elizabeths, that he was "mentally competent to stand trial and. . . . able to consult with counsel to properly assist in his own defense."

He was thereupon brought before the court on the charge involved here. The prosecutor told the court:

"So I take this attitude, in view of the fact that he has been over there [St. Elizabeths] a couple of times and these cases that were charged against him were dropped, I don't think I should take the responsibility of dropping these cases against him; then Saint Elizabeths would let him out on the street, and if that man committed a murder next week then it is my responsibility. So we decided to go to trial on one case, that is the case where we found him right in the house, and let him bring in the defense, if he wants to, of unsound mind at the time the crime was committed, and then Your Honor will find him on that, and in your decision send him back to Saint Elizabeths Hospital, and then if they let him out on the street it is their responsibility."

Shortly thereafter, when the question arose whether Durham could be considered competent to stand trial merely on the basis of Dr. Silk's ex parte statement, the court said to defense counsel:

"I am going to ask you this, Mr. Ahern: I have taken the position that if once a person has been found of unsound mind after a lunacy hearing, an ex parte certificate of the superintendent of Saint Elizabeths is not sufficient to set aside that finding and I have held another lunacy hearing. That has been my custom. However, if you want to waive that you may do it, if you admit that he is now of sound mind."

The court accepted counsel's waiver on behalf of Durham, although it had been informed by the prosecutor that a letter from Durham claimed need of further hospitalization, and by defense counsel that ". . . . the defendant does say that even today he thinks he does need hospitalization; he told me that this morning."[4] Upon being so informed, the court said, "Of course, if I hold he is not mentally competent to stand trial I send him back to Saint Elizabeths Hospital and they will send him back again in two or three months."[5] In this atmosphere Durham's trial commenced.

II.

. . . It has been ably argued by counsel for Durham that the existing tests in the District of Columbia for determining criminal responsibility, that is, the so-called right-wrong test supplemented by the irresistible impulse test, are not satisfactory criteria for determining criminal responsibility. We are urged to adopt a different test to be applied on the retrial of this case. This contention has behind it nearly a century of agitation for reform.

A. The right-wrong test, approved in this jurisdiction in 1882,[13] was the exclusive test of criminal responsibility in the District of Columbia until 1929 when we approved the irresistible impulse test as a supplementary test in Smith v. Unites States.[14] The right-wrong test has its roots in England. There, by the first quarter of the eighteenth century, an accused escaped punishment if he could not distinguish "good and evil," that is, if he "doth not know what he is doing, no more than. . . . a wild beast."[15] Later in the same century, the "wild beast" test was abandoned and "right and wrong" was substituted for "good and evil."[16] And toward the middle of the nineteenth century, the House of Lords in the famous M'Naghten case[17] restated what had become the accepted "right-wrong" test[18] in a form which has since been followed, not only in England[19] but in most American jurisdictions,[20] as an exclusive test of criminal responsibility:

". . . . the jurors ought to be told in all cases that every man is to be presumed to be sane, and to possess a sufficient degree of reason to be responsible for his crimes, until the contrary be proved to their satisfaction; and that, to establish a defence on the ground of insanity, it must be clearly proved that, at the time of the committing of the act, the party accused was labouring under such a defect of reason, from disease of the mind, as not to know the nature and qulaity of the act he was doing, or, if he did know it, that he did not know he was doing what was wrong."[21]

As early as 1838, Isaac Ray, one of the founders of the American Psychiatric Association, in his now classic Medical Jurisprudence of Insanity, called knowledge of right and wrong a "fallacious" test of criminal responsibility.[22] This view has long since been substantiated by enormous developments in knowledge of mental life.[23] In 1928 Mr. Justice Cardozo said to the New York Academy of Medicine: "Everyone concedes that the present [legal] definition of insanity has little relation to the truths of mental life."[24]

Medico-legal writers in large numbers,[25] The Report of the Royal Commission on Capital Punishment 1949–1953,[26] and The Preliminary Report by the Committee on Forensic Psychiatry of the Group for the Advancement of Psychiatry[27] present convincing evidence that the right-and-wrong test is "based on an entirely obsolete and misleading conception of the nature of insanity."[28] The science of psychiatry now recognizes that a man is an integrated personality and that reason, which is only one element in that personality, is not the sole determinant of his conduct. The right-wrong test, which considers knowledge or reason alone, is therefore an inadequate guide to mental responsibility for criminal behavior. As Professor Sheldon Glueck of the Harvard Law School points out in discussing the right-wrong tests, which he calls the knowledge tests:

"It is evident that the knowledge tests unscientifically abstract out of the mental make-up but one phase or element of mental life, the cognitive, which, in this era of dynamic psychology, is beginning to be regarded as not the most important factor in conduct and its disorders. In brief, these tests proceed upon the following questionable assumptions of an outworn era in psychiatry: (1) that lack of knowledge of the 'nature or quality' of an act (assuming the meaning of such terms to be clear), or incapacity to know right from wrong, is the sole or even the most important symptom of mental disorder; (2) that such knowledge is the sole instigator and guide of conduct, or at least the most important element therein, and consequently should be the sole criterion of responsibility when insanity is involved; and (3) that the capacity of knowing right from wrong can be completely intact and functioning perfectly even though a defendant is otherwise demonstrably of disordered mind."[29]

Nine years ago we said:
"The modern science of psychology. . . . does not conceive that there is a separate little man in the top of one's head called reason whose function it is to guide another unruly little man called instinct, emotion, or impulse in the way he should go."[30]

By its misleading emphasis on the cognitive, the right-wrong test requires court and jury to rely upon what is, scientifically speaking, inadequate, and most often, invalid[31] and irrelevant testimony in determining criminal responsibility.[32]

The fundamental objection to the right-wrong test, however, is not that criminal irresponsibility is made to rest upon an inadequate, invalid or indeterminable symptom or manifestation, but that it is made to rest upon *any* particular symptom.[33] In attempting to define insanity in terms of a symptom, the courts have assumed an impossible role,[34] not merely one for

which they have no special competence.[35] As the Royal Commission emphasizes, it is dangerous "to abstract particular mental faculties, and to lay it down that unless these particular faculties are destroyed or gravely impaired, an accused person, whatever the nature of his mental disease, must be held to be criminally responsible. . . ."[36] In this field of law as in others, the fact finder should be free to consider all information advanced by relevant scientific disciplines.[37]

Despite demands in the name of scientific advances, this court refused to alter the right-wrong test at the turn of the century.[38] But in 1929, we considered in response to "the cry of scientific experts" and added the irresistible impulse test as a supplementary test for determining criminal responsibility. Without "hesitation" we declared, in Smith v. United States, "it to be the law of this District that, in cases where insanity is interposed as a defense, and the facts are sufficient to call for the application of the rule of irresistible impulse, the jury should be so charged."[39] We said:

". . . . The modern doctrine is that the degree of insanity which will relieve the accused of the consequences of a criminal act must be such as to create in his mind an uncontrollable impulse to commit the offense charged. This impulse must be such as to override the reason and judgment and obliterate the sense of right and wrong to the extent that the accused is deprived of the power to choose between right and wrong. The mere ability to distinguish right from wrong is no longer the correct test either in civil or criminal cases, where the defense of insanity is interposed. The accepted rule in this day and age, with the great advancement in medical science as an enlightening influence on this subject, is that the accused must be capable, not only of distinguishing between right and wrong, but that he was not impelled to do the act by an irresistible impulse, which means before it will justify a verdict of acquittal that his reasoning powers were so far dethroned by his diseased mental condition as to deprive him of the will power to resist the insane impulse to perpetrate the deed, though knowing it to be wrong."[40]

As we have already indicated, this has since been the test in the District.

Although the Smith case did not abandon the right-wrong test, it did liberate the fact finder from exlusive reliance upon that discredited criterion by allowing the jury to inquire also whether the accused suffered from an undefined "diseased mental condition [which] deprive[d] him of the will power to resist the insane impulse. . . ."[41] The term "irresistible impulse," however, carries the misleading implication that "diseased mental condition[s]" produce only sudden, momentary or spontaneous inclinations to commit unlawful acts.[42] As the Royal Commission found:

". . . . In many cases . . . this is not true at all. The sufferer from [melancholia, for example] experiences a change of mood which alters the whole of his existence. He may believe, for instance, that a future of such degradation and misery awaits both him and his family that death for all is a less dreadful alternative. Even the thought that the acts he contemplates are murder and suicide pales into insignificance in contrast with what he otherwise expects. The criminal act, in such circumstances, may be the reverse of impulsive. It may be coolly and carefully prepared; yet it is still the act of a madman. This is merely an illustration; similar states of mind are likely to lie behind the criminal act when murders are committed by persons suffering from schizophrenia or paranoid psychoses due to disease of the brain.

We find that as an exclusive criterion the right-wrong test is inadequate in that (a) it does not take sufficient account of psychic realities and scientific knowledge, and (b) it is based upon one symptom and so cannot validly be applied in all circumstances. We find that the "irresistible impulse" test is also inadequate in that it gives no recognition to mental illness characterized by brooding and reflection and so relegates acts caused by such illness to the application of the inadequate right-wrong test. We conclude that a broader test should be adopted.[44]

In the District of Columbia, the formulation of tests of criminal responsibility is entrusted to the courts[45] and, in adopting a new test, we invoke our inherent power to make the change prospectively.[46]

The rule we now hold must be applied on the retrial of this case and in future cases is not unlike that followed by the New Hampshire court since 1870.[47] It is simply that an accused is not criminally responsible if his unlawful act was the product of mental disease or mental defect.[48]

We use "disease" in the sense of a condition which is considered capable of either improving or deteriorating. We use "defect" in the sense of a condition which is not considered capable of either improving or deteriorating and which may be either congenital, or the result of injury, or the residual effect of a physical or mental disease.

Whenever there is "some evidence" that the accused suffered from a diseased or defective mental condition at the time the unlawful act was committed, the trial court must provide the jury with guides for determining whether the accused can be held criminally responsible. We do not, and indeed could not, formulate an instruction which would be either appropriate or binding in all cases. But under the rule now announced, any instruction should in some way convey to the jury the sense and substance of the following: If you the jury believe beyond a reasonable doubt that the accused was not suffering from a diseased or defective mental condition at the time he committed the criminal act charged, you may find him guilty. If you believe he was suffering from a diseased or defective mental condition when he committed the act, but believe beyond a reasonable doubt that the act was not the product of such mental abnormality, you may find him guilty. Unless you believe beyond a reasonable doubt either that he was not suffering from a diseased or defective mental condition, or that the act was not the product of such abnormality, you must find the accused not guilty by reason of insanity. Thus your task would not be completed upon finding, if you did find, that the accused suffered from a mental disease or defect. He would still be responsible for his unlawful act if there was no causal connection between such mental abnormality and the act.[49] These questions must be determined by you from the facts which you find to be fairly deducible from the testimony and the evidence in this case.[50]

The questions of fact under the test we now lay down are as capable of determination by the jury as, for example, the questions juries must determine upon a claim of total disability under a policy of insurance where the state of medical knowledge concerning the disease involved, and its effects, is obscure or in conflict. In such cases, the jury is not required to depend on arbitrarily selected "symptoms, phases or manifestations"[51] of the disease as criteria for determining the ultimate questions of fact upon which the claim depends. Similarly, upon a claim of criminal irresponsibility, the jury will not be required to rely on such symptoms as criteria for determining the ultimate question of fact upon which such claim depends. Testimony as to such "symptoms, phases or manifestations," along with other relevant evidence, will go to the jury upon the ultimate questions of fact which it alone can finally determine. Whatever the state of psychiatry, the psychiatrist will be permitted to carry out his principal court function which, as we noted in Holloway v. U.S., "is to inform the jury of the character of [the accused's] mental disease [or defect]."[52] The jury's range of inquiry will not be limited to, but may include, for example, whether an accused, who suffered from a mental disease or defect did not know the difference between right and wrong, acted under the compulsion of an irresistible impulse, or had "been deprived of or lost the power of his will. . . ."[53]

Finally, in leaving the determination of the ultimate question of fact to the jury, we permit it to perform its traditional function which, as we said in Holloway, is to apply "our inherited ideas of moral responsibility to individuals prosecuted for crime. . . .[54] Juries will continue to make moral judgments, still operating under the fundamental precept that "Our collective conscience does not allow punishment where it cannot impose blame."[55] But in making such judgments, they will be guided by wider horizons of knowledge concerning mental life. The question will be simply whether the accused acted because of a mental disorder, and not whether he displayed particular symptoms which medical science has long recognized do not necessarily, or even typically, accompany even the most serious mental disorder.[56]

The legal and moral traditions of the western world require that those who, of their own free will and with evil intent (sometimes called *mens rea*), commit acts which violate the law, shall be criminally responsible for those acts. Our traditions also require that where such acts stem from and are the product of a mental disease or defect as those terms are used herein, moral blame shall not attach, and hence there will not be criminal responsibility.[57] The rule we state in this opinion is designed to meet these requirements.

Reversed and remanded for a new trial.

NOTES

1.   D.C. Code §§ 22–1801, 22–2201 and 22–2202 (1951).
2.   Because the questions raised are of general and crucial importance, we called upon the Government and counsel whom we appointed for the indigent appellant to brief and argue this case a second time. Their able presentations have been of great assistance to us. On the question of the adequacy of prevailing tests of criminal responsibility, we received further assistance from the able brief and argument of Abram Chayes, *amicus curiae* by appointment of this Court, in Stewart v. United States, 94 U.S.App. D.C.—, 214 F.2d 879.
3.   18 U.S.C. § 408 (1946). 1948 Revision, 18 U.S.C. §§ 10, 2311–2313.
4.   Durham showed confusion when he testified. These are but two examples:
"Q. Do you remember writing it? A. No. Don't you forget? People get all mixed up in machines.
"Q. What kind of a machine? A. I don't know, they just get mixed up.
"Q. Are you cured now? A. No, sir.
"Q. In your opinion? A. No. sir.
"Q. What is the matter with you? A. You hear people bother you.
"Q. What? You say you hear people bothering you? A. Yes.
"Q. What kind of people? What do they bother you about? A. (No response.)"
Although we think the court erred in accepting counsel's admission that Durham was of sound mind, the matter does not require discussion since we reverse on other grounds and the principles governing this issue are fully discussed in our decision today in Gunther v. United States, 94 U.S.App.D.C. —, 215 F.2d 493.
5.   The court also accepted a waiver of trial by jury when Durham indicated, in response to the court's question, that he preferred to be tried without a jury and that he waived his right to a trial by jury.
13.   1882, 12 D.C. 498, 550, 1 Mackey 498, 550. The right-wrong test was reaffirmed in United States v. Lee, 1886, 15 D.C. 489, 496, 4 Mackey 489, 496.
14.   1929, 59 App.D.C. 144, 36 F.2d 548, 70 A.L.R. 654.
15.   Glueck, Mental Disorder and the Criminal Law 138–39 (1925), citing Rex v. Arnold, 16 How.St.Tr. 695, 764 (1724).
16.   Id. at 142–52, citing Earl Ferrer's case, 19 How.St.Tr. 886 (1760). One writer has stated that these tests originated in England in the 13th or 14th century, when the law began to define insanity in terms of intellect for purposes of determining capacity to manage feudal estates. Comment, *Lunacy and Idiocy—The Old Law and Its Incubus,* 18 U. of Chi.L. Rev. 361 (1951).
17.   8 Eng.Rep. 718 (1843).

18.   Hall, Principles of Criminal Law 480, n. 6 (1947).
19.   Royal Commission on Capital Punishment 1949–1953 Report (Cmd. 8932) 79 (1953) (hereinafter cited as Royal Commission Report).
20.   Weihofen, *The M'Naghten Rule in Its Present Day Setting,* Federal Probation 8 (Sept. 1953); Weihofen, Insanity as a Denense in Criminal Law 15, 64–68, 109–47 (1933); Leland v. State of Oregon, 1952, 343 U.S. 790, 800, 72 S.Ct. 1002, 96 L.Ed. 1302.
"In five States the M'Naghten Rules have been in substance re-enacted by statute." Royal Commission Report 409; see, for example, "Sec. 1120 of the [New York State] Penal Law [McK.Consol. Laws, c. 40] [which] provides that a person is not excused from liability on the grounds of insanity, idiocy or imbecility, except upon proof that at the time of the commission of the criminal act he was laboring under such a defect or reason as (1) not to know the nature and quality of the act he was doing or (2) not to know that the act was wrong." Ploscowe, *Suggested Changes in the New York Laws and Procedures Relating to the Criminally Insane and Mentally Defective Offenders,* 43 J. Crim.L., Criminology & Police Sci. 312, 314 (1952).
21.   8 Eng.Rep. 718, 722 (1843). "Today, Oregon is the only state that requires the accused, on a plea of insanity, to establish that defense beyond a reasonable doubt. Some twenty states, however, place the burden on the accused to establish his insanity by a preponderance of the evidence or some similar measure of persuasion." Leland v. State of Oregon, supra, note 20, 343 U.S. at page 798, 72 S.Ct. 1002. Since Davis v. United States, 1895, 160 U.S. 469, 484, 16 S.Ct. 353, 40 L.Ed. 499, a contrary rule of procedure has been followed in the Federal courts. For example, in compliance with Davis, we held in Tatum v. Unites States, supra, note 8, 88 U.S. App.D.C. 386, 389, 190 F.2d 612, 615, and text, "as soon as 'some evidence of mental disorder is introduced, . . . sanity, like any other fact, must be proved as part of the prosecution's case beyond a reasonable doubt.' "
22.   Ray, Medical Jurisprudence of Insanity 47 and 34 et seq. (1st ed. 1838). "That the insane mind is not entirely deprived of this power of moral discernment, but in many subjects is perfectly rational, and displays the exercise of a sound and well balanced mind is one of those facts now so well established, that to question it would only betray the height of ignorance and presumption." Id. at 32.
23.   See Zilboorg, *Legal Aspects of Psychiatry* in One Hundred Years of American Psychiatry 1844–1944, 507, 552 (1944).
24.   Cardozo, What Medicine Can Do For the Law 32 (1930).
25.   For a detailed bibliography on Insanity as a Defense to Crime, see 7 The Record of the Association of the Bar of the City of New York 158–62 (1952). And see. for example, Alexander, the Criminal, the Judge and the Public 70 et seq. (1931); Cardozo, What Medicine Can Do For the Law 28 et seq. (1930); Cleckley, the Mask of Sanity 491 et seq. (2d ed.1950); Deutsch, The Mentally Ill In America 389–417 (2d ed.1949); Glueck, Mental Disorder and the Criminal Law (1925). Crime and Justice 96 et seq. (1936); Guttmacher & Weihofen, Psychiatry and the Law 218, 403–23 (1952); Hall, Principles of Criminal Law 477–538 (1947); Menninger, The Human Mind 450 (1937); Hall & Menninger, *"Psychiatry and the Law"—A Dual Review,* 38 Iowa L.Rev. 687 (1953); Overholser, The Psychiatrist and the Law 41–43 (1953); Overholser & Richmond, Handbook of Psychiatry 208–15 (1947); Ploscowe, *Suggested Changes in the New York Laws and Procedures Relating to the Criminally Insane and Mentally Defective Offenders,* 43 J.Crim.L., Criminology & Police Sci. 312, 314 (1952); Ray, Medical Jurisprudence of Insanity (1st

ed.1838) (4th ed.1860); Reik, *The Doc-Ray Correspondence: A Pioneer Collaboration in the Jurisprudence of Mental Disease,* 63 Yale L.J. 183 (1953); Weihofen, Insanity as a Defense in Criminal Law (1933), *The M'Naghten Rule in Its Present Day Setting,* Federal Probation 8 (Sept. 1953); Zilboorg, Mind, Medicine and Man 246–97 (1943), *Legal Aspects of Psychiatry,* American Psychiatry 1844–1944, 507 (1944).

26. Royal Commission Report 73–129.

27. The Committee on Forensic Psychiatry (whose report is hereinafter cited as Gap Report) was composed of Drs. Philip Q. Roche, Frank S. Curran, Lawrence Z. Freedman and Manfred S. Guttmacher. They were assisted in their deliberations by leading psychiatrists, jurists, law professors, and legal practitioners.

28. Royal Commission Report 80.

29. Glueck, *Psychiatry and the Criminal Law,* 12 Mental Hygiene 575, 580 (1928), as quoted in Deutsch, The Mentally Ill in America 396 (2d ed. 1949); and see, for example, Menninger, The Human Mind 450 (1937); Guttmacher & Weihofen, Psychiatry and the Law 403–08 (1952).

30. Holloway v. United States, 1945, 80 U.S.App.D.C. 3, 5, 148 F.2d 665, 667, certiorari denied, 1948, 334 U.S. 852, 68 S.Ct. 1507, 92 L.Ed. 1774.

More recently, the Royal Commission, after an exhaustive survey of legal, medical and lay opinion in many Western countries, including England and the United States made a similar finding. It reported: "The gravamen of the charge against the M'Naghten Rules is that they are not in harmony with modern medical science, which, as we have seen, is reluctant to divide the mind into separate compartments—the intellect, the emotions and the will—but looks at it as a whole and considers that insanity distorts and impairs the action of the mind as a whole." Royal Commission Report 113. The Commission lends vivid support to this conclusion by pointing out that "It would be impossible to apply modern methods of care and treatment in mental hospitals, and at the same time to maintain order and discipline, if the great majority of the patients, even among the grossly insane, did not know what is forbidden by the rules and that, if they break them, they are liable to forfeit some privilege. Examination of a number of guilty but insane [the nearest English equivalent of our acquittal by reason of insanity] was returned, and rightly returned, has convinced us that there are few indeed where the accused can truly be said not to have known that his act was wrong." Id. at 103.

31. See Guttmacher & Weihofen, Psychiatry and the Law 421, 422 (1952). The M'Naghten rules "constitute not only an arbitrary restriction on vital medical data, but also impose an improper onus of decision upon the expert witness. The Rules are unanswerable in that they have no consensus with established psychiatric criteria of symptomatic description save for the case of disturbed consciousness or of idiocy,. . . ." From statement by Dr. Philip Q. Roche, quited id. at 407. See also United States ex rel. Smith v. Baldi, 3 Cir., 1951, 192 F.2d 540, 567 (dissenting opinion).

32. In a very recent case, the Supreme Court of New Mexico recognized the inadequacy of the right-wrong test, and adopted what it called an "extension of the M'Naghten Rules." Under this extension, lack of knowledge of right and wrong is not essential for acquittal "if, by reason of disease of the mind, defendant has been deprived of or lost the power of his will. . . ." State v. White, N.M., 270 P.2d 727, 730.

33. Deutsch, The Mentally Ill in America 400 (2d ed.1949); Keedy, *Irresistible Impulses as a Defense in Criminal Law,* 100 U. of Pa.L.Rev. 956, 992 (1952).

34. Professor John Whitehorn of the Johns Hopkins Medical School, who recently prepared an informal memo-

randum on this subject for a Commission on Legal Psychiatry appointed by the Governor of Maryland, has said: "Psychiatrists are challenged to set forth a crystal-clear statement of what constitutes insanity. It is impossible to express this adequately in words, alone, since such diagnostic judgments involve clinical skill and experience which cannot wholly be verbalized. . . . The medical profession would be baffled if asked to write into the legal code universally valid criteria for the diagnosis of the many types of psychotic illness which may seriously disturb a person's responsibility, and even if this were attempted, the diagnostic criteria would have to be rewritten from time to time, with the progress of psychiatric knowlwdge." Quoted in Guttmacher & Weihofen, Psychiatry and the Law 419–20 (1952).

35. ". . . . the legal profession were invading the province of medicine, and attempting to install old exploded medical theories in the place of facts established in the progress of scientific knowledge." State v. Pike, 1870, 49 N.H. 399, 438.

36. Royal Commission Report 114. And see State v. Jones, 1871, 50 N.H. 369, 392–393.

37. Keedy, *Irresistible Impulse as a Defense in Criminal Law,* 100 U. of Pa.L. Rev. 956, 992–93 (1952).

38. See, for example, Taylor v. United States, 1895, 7 App.D.C. 27, 41–44, where we rejected "emotional insanity" as a defense, citing with approval the following from the trial court's instruction to the jury: "Whatever may be the cry of scientific experts, the law does not recognize, but condemns the doctrine of emotional insanity—that a man may be sane up until a moment before he commits a crime, insane while he does it, and sane again soon afterwards. Such a doctrine would be dangerous in the extreme. The law does not recognize it; and a jury cannot without violating their oaths." This position was emphatically reaffirmed in Snell v. United States, 1900, 16 App.D.C. 501, 524.

39. 1929, 59 App.D.C. 144, 146, 36 F.2d 548, 550, 70 A.L.R. 654.

40. 59 App.D.C. at page 145, 36 F.2d at page 549.

41. 59 App.D.C. at page 145, 36 F.2d at page 549.

42. Impulse, as defined by Webster's New International Dictionary (2d ed.1950), is:

"1. Act of impelling, or driving onward with *sudden* force; impulsion, esp., force so communicated as to produce motion *suddenly,* or *immediately.* . . .

"2. An incitement of the mind or spirit, esp. in the form of an *abrubt* and vivid suggestion, prompting some *unpremeditated* action or leading to unforeseen knowledge or insight; a *spontaneous* inclination. . . .

3. . . . motion produced by a *sudden* or *momentary* force. . . ." [Emphasis supplied.]

43. Royal Commission Report 110; for additional comment on the irresistible impulse test, see Glueck, Crime and Justice 101–03 (1936); Guttmacher & Weihofen, Psychiatry and the Law 410–12 (1952); Hall, General Principles of Criminal Law 505–26 (1947); Keedy, *Irresistible Impulse as a Defense in Criminal Law,* 100 U. of Pa.L.Rev. 956 (1952); Wertham, The Show of Violence 14 (1949).

The New Mexico Supreme Court in recently adopting a broader criminal insanity rule, note 32, supra, observed: ". . . insanity takes the form of the personality of the individual and, if his tendency is toward depression, his wrongful act may come at the conclusion of a period of complete lethargy, thoroughly devoid of excitement."

44. As we recently said, ". . . former common law should not be followed where changes in conditions have made it obsolete. We have never hesitated to exercise the usual judicial function of revising and enlarging the common law." Linkins v. Protestant Episcopal Cathedral Foundation, 1950,

87 U.S.App.D.C. 351, 355, 187 F.2d 357, 361, 28 A.L.R.2d 521. Cf. Funk v. United States, 1933, 290 U.S. 371, 381–382, 54 S.Ct. 212, 78 L.Ed. 369.

45.   Congress, like most State legislatures, has never undertaken to define insanity in this connection, although it recognizes the fact that an accused may be acquitted by reason of insanity. See D.C. Code § 24–301 (1951). And as this court made clear in Hill v. United States, Congress has left no doubt that "common-law procedure, in all matters relating to crime . . . still continues in force here in all cases except where special provision is made by statute to the exclusion of the common-law procedure." 22 App. D.C. 395, 401 (1903), and statutes cited therein; Linkins v. Protestant Episcopal Cathedral Foundation, 87 U.S. App.D.C. at pages 354–55, 187 F.2d at pages 360–361; and see Fisher v. United States, 1946, 328 U.S. 463, 66 S.Ct. 1318, 90 L. Ed. 1382.

46.   See Great Northern R. v. Sunburst Oil & Refining Co., 1932, 287 U.S. 358, 53 S. Ct. 145, 77 L.Ed. 360; National Labor Relations Board v. Guy F. Atkinson Co., 9 Cir., 1952, 195 F.2d 141, 148; Concurring opinion of Judge Frank in Aero Spark Plug Co. v. B. G. Corporation, 2 Cir., 1942, 130 F.2d 290, 298, and note 24; Warring v. Colpoys, 1941, 74 App.D.C. 303, 122 F.2d 642, 645, 136 A.L.R. 1025; Moore & Oglebay, *The Supreme Court, Stare Decisis and Law of the Case,* 21 Texas L.Rev. 514, 535 (1943); Carpenter, *Court Decisions and the Common Law,* 17 Col.L.Rev. 593, 606–07 (1917). But see von Moschzisker, *Stare Decisis in Courts of Last Resort.* 37 Harv.L.Rev. 409, 426 (1924). Our approach is similar to that of the Supreme Court of California in People v. Maughs, 1906, 149 Cal. 253, 86 P. 187, 191, where the court prospectively invalidated a previously accepted instruction, saying:

". . . we think the time has come to say that in all future cases which shall arise, and where, after this warning, this instruction shall be given, this court will hold the giving of it to be so prejudicial to the rights of a defendant, secured to him by our Constitution and laws, as to call for the reversal of any judgment which may be rendered against him."

47.   State v. Pike, 1870, 49 N.H. 399.

48.   Cf. State v. Jones, 1871, 50 N.H. 369, 398.

49.   "There is no *a priori* reason why every person suffering from any form of mental abnormality or disease, or from any particular kind of mental disease, should be treated by the law as not answerable for any criminal offence which he may commit, and be exempted from conviction and punishment. Mental abnormalities vary infinitely in their nature and intensity and in their effects on the character and conduct of those who suffer from them. Where a person suffering from a mental abnormality commits a crime, there must always be some likelihood that the abnormality has played some part in the causation of the crime; and, generally speaking, the graver the abnormality, . . . the more probable it must be that there is a causal connection between them. But the closeness of this connection will be shown by the facts brought in evidence in individual cases and cannot be decided on the basis of any general medical principle." Royal Commission Report 99.

50.   The court may always, of course, if it deems it advisable for the assistance of the jury, point out particular areas of agreement and conflict in the expert testimony in each case, just as it ordinarily does in summing up any other testimony.

51.   State v. Jones, 1871, 50 N.H. 369, 398.

52.   1945, 80 U.S.App.D.C. 3, 5, 148 F.2d 665, 667.

53.   State v. White, see n. 32, supra.

54.   80 U.S.App.D.C. at page 5, 148 F.2d at page 667.

55.   80 U.S.App.D.C. at pages 4–5, 148 F.2d at pages 666–667.

56.   See text, supra, 214 F.2d 870–872.

57.   An accused person who is acquitted by reason of insanity is presumed to be insane, Orencia v. Overholser, 1947, 82 U.S.App.D.C. 285, 163 F.2d 763; Barry v. White, 1933, 62 App.D.C. 69, 64 F.2d 707, and may be committed for an indefinite period to a "hospital for the insane." D.C.Code § 24–301 (1951).

We think that even where there has been a specific finding that the accused was competent to stand trial and to assist in his own defense, the court would be well advised to invoke this Code provision so that the accused may be confined as long as "the public safety and . . . [his] welfare" require. Barry v. White, 62 App.D.C. at page 71, 64 F.2d at page 709.

UNITED STATES v. BRAWNER

United States Court of Appeals, D.C. Cir., 1972*

Leventhal, Circuit Judge:

Passing by various minor disagreements among the witnesses, the record permits us to reconstruct the events of September 8, 1967, as follows: After a morning and afternoon of wine-drinking, appellant Archie W. Brawner, Jr. and his uncle Aaron Ross, went to a party at the home of three acquaintances. During the evening, several fights broke out. In one of them, Brawner's jaw was injured when he was struck or pushed to the ground. The time of the fight was approximately 10:30 p.m. After the fight, Brawner left the party. He told Mr. Ross that some boys had jumped him. Mr. Ross testified that Brawner "looked like he was out of his mind". Other witnesses who saw him after the fight testified that Brawner's mouth was bleeding and that his speech was unclear (but the same witness added, "I heard every word he said"); that he was staggering and angry; and that he pounded on a mailbox with his fist. One witness testified that Brawner said, "[I'm] going to get my boys" and come back, and that "someone is going to die tonight."

Half an hour later, at about eleven p.m., Brawner was on his way back to the party with a gun. One witness testified that Brawner said he was going up there to kill his attackers or be killed.

Upon his arrival at the address, Brawner fired a shot into the ground and entered the building. He proceeded to the apartment where the party was in progress and fired five shots through the closed metal hallway door. Two of the shots struck Billy Ford, killing him. Brawner was arrested a few minutes later, several blocks away. The arresting officer testified that Brawner appeared normal, and did not appear to be drunk, that he spoke clearly, and had no odor of alcohol about him.

After the Government had presented the evidence of its non-expert witnesses, the trail judge ruled that there was insufficient evidence on "deliberation" to go to the jury: accordingly, a verdict of acquittal was directed on first degree murder.

The expert witnesses, called by both defense and prosecution, all agreed that Brawner was suffering from an abnormality of a psychiatric or neurological nature. The medical labels were variously given as "epileptic personality disorder," "psychologic brain syndrome associated with a convulsive disorder," "personality disorder associated with epilepsy," or, more simply, "an explosive personality." There was no disagreement that the epileptic condition would be exacerbated by alcohol, leading to more frequent episodes and episodes of greater intensity, and would also be exacerbated by a physical blow to the head. The experts agreed that epilepsy *per se* is not a mental disease or defect, but a neurological disease which is often associated with a mental disease or defect. They further agreed that Brawner had a mental, as well as a neurological, disease.

Where the experts disagreed was on the part which that mental disease or defect played in the murder of Billy Ford. The position of the witnesses called by the Government is that Brawner's behavior on the night of September 8 was not consistent with an epileptic seizure, and was not suggestive of an explosive reaction in the context of a psychiatric disorder. In the words of Dr. Platkin of St. Elizabeths Hospital, "He was just mad."

The experts called by the defense maintained the contrary conclusion. Thus, Dr. Eugene Stanmeyer, a psychologist at St. Elizabeths, was asked on direct by counsel for defense, whether, assuming accused did commit the act which occurred, there was a causal relationship between the assumed act and his mental abnormality. Dr. Stanmeyer replied in the affirmative, that there was a cause and effect relationship.

Later, the prosecutor asked the Government's first expert witness Dr. Weickhardt: "Did you ... come to any opinion concerning whether or not the crimes in this case were causally related to the mental illness which you diagnosed?" An objection to the form of the question was overruled. The witness then set forth that in his opinion there was no causal relationship between the mental disorder and the alleged offenses. Brawner claims that the trial court erred when it permitted a prosecution expert to testify in this manner. He relies

*471 F. 2d 969 (1972). Excerpts only. The footnotes are numbered here as in the original.

on our opinion in Washington v. United States, 129 U.S.App.D.C. 29, 390 F.2d 444 (1967).

INSANITY RULE IN OTHER CIRCUITS

The American Law Institute's Model Penal Code expressed a rule which has become the dominant force in the law pertaining to the defense of insanity. The ALI rule is eclectic in spirit, partaking of the moral focus of *M'Naghten,* the practical accommodation of the "control rules" (a term more exact and less susceptible of misunderstanding than "irresistible impulse" terminology), and responsive, at the same time, to a relatively modern, forward-looking view of what is encompassed in "knowledge."

For convenience, we quote again the basic rule propounded by the ALI's Model Penal Code:

A person is not responsible for criminal conduct if at the time of such conduct as a result of mental disease or defect he lacks substantial capacity either to appreciate the criminality [wrongfulness] of his conduct or to conform his conduct to the requirements of the law.

COMMENTS CONCERNING REASON FOR ADOPTION OF ALI RULE AND SCOPE OF RULE AS ADOPTED BY THIS COURT

In the foreglimpse stating that we had determined to adopt the ALI rule we undertook to set forth comments stating our reasons, and also the adjustments and understandings defining the ALI rule as adopted by this Court. Having paused to study the rulings in the other circuits, we turn to our comments, and to our reflections following the extensive, and intensive, exposure of this court to insanity defense issues.[9]

1. NEED TO DEPART FROM "PRODUCT" FORMULATION AND UNDUE DOMINANCE BY EXPERTS.

A principal reason for our decision to depart from the *Durham* rule is the undesirable characteristic, surviving even the *McDonald* modification, of undue dominance by the experts giving testimony. The underlying problem was identified, with stress on different facets, in the *Carter, Blocker* (concurring), and *Washington* opinions. The difficulty is rooted in the circumstance that there is no generally accepted understanding, either in the jury or the community it represents, of the concept requiring that the crime be the "product" of the mental disease.

When the court used the term "product" in *Durham* it likely assumed that this was a serviceable, and indeed a natural, term for a rule defining criminal responsibility—a legal reciprocal, as it were, for the familiar term "proximate cause," used to define civil responsibility.

But if concepts like "product" are, upon refinement, reasonably understood, or at least appreciated, by judges and lawyers, and perhaps philosophers, difficulties developed when it emerged that the "product" concept did not signify a reasonably identifiable common ground that was also shared by the nonlegal experts,[10] and the laymen serving on the jury as the representatives of the community.

The doctrine of criminal responsibility is such that there can be no doubt "of the complicated nature of the decision to be made—intertwining moral, legal, and medical judgments," see King v. United States, 125 U.S.App.D.C. 318, 324, 372 F.2d 383, 389 (1967) and *Durham* and other cases cited *supra,* note 6. Hence, as *King* and other opinions have noted, jury decisions have been accorded unusual deference even when they have found responsibility in the face of a powerful record, with medical evidence uncontradicted, pointing toward exculpation.[11] The "moral" elements of the decision are not defined exclusively by religious considerations but by the totality of underlying conceptions of ethics and justice shared by the community as expressed by its jury surrogate. The essential feature of a jury "lies in the interposition between the accused and his accuser of the commonsense judgment of a group of laymen, and in the community participation and shared responsibility that results from the group's determination of guilt or innocence." Williams v. Florida, 399 U.S. 78, 100, 90 S.Ct. 1893, 1906, 26 L.Ed.2d 466 (1970).

The expert witnesses—psychiatrists and psychologists—are called to adduce relevant information concerning what may for convenience be referred to as the "medical" component of the responsibility issue. But the difficulty—as emphasized in *Washington*—is that the medical expert comes, by testimony given in terms of a non-medical construct ("product"), to express conclusions that in essence embody ethical and legal conclusions. There is indeed, irony in a situation under which the *Durham* rule, which was adopted in large part to permit experts to testify in their own terms concerning matters within their domain which the jury should know, resulted in testimony by the experts in terms not their own to reflect unexpressed judgments in a domain that is properly not theirs but the jury's. The irony is heightened when the jurymen, instructed under the esoteric "product" standard, are influenced significantly by "product" testimony of expert witnesses really reflecting ethical and legal judgments rather than a conclusion within the witnesses' particular expertise.

It is easier to identify and spotlight the irony than to eradicate the mischief. The objective of *Durham* is still sound—to put before the jury the information that is within the expert's domain, to aid the jury in making a broad and comprehensive judgment. But when the instructions and appellate decisions define the "product" inquiry as the ultimate issue, it is like stopping the tides to try to halt the emergence of this term in the language of those with a central role in the trial—the lawyers who naturally seek to present testimony that will influence the jury who will be charged under the ultimate "product" standard, and the expert witnesses who have an awareness, gained from forensic psychiatry and related disciplines, of the ultimate "product" standard that dominates the proceeding.

The experts have meaningful information to impart, not only on the existence of mental illness or not, but also on its relationship to the incident charged as an offense. In the interest of justice this valued information should be available, and should not be lost or blocked by requirements that unnaturally restrict communication between the experts and the jury. The more we have pondered the problem the more convinced we have become that the sound solution lies not in further shaping of the *Durham* "product" approach in more refined molds, but in adopting the ALI's formulation as the linchpin of our jurisprudence.

The ALI's formulation retains the core requirement of a meaningful relationship between the mental illness and the incident charged. The language in the ALI rule is sufficiently in the common ken that its use in the courtroom, or in preparation for trial, permits a reasonable three-way communication—between (a) the law-trained, judges and lawyers; (b) the experts and (c) the jurymen—without insisting on a vocabulary that is either stilted or stultified, or conducive to a testimonial mystique permitting expert dominance and encroachment on the jury's function. There is no indication in the available literature that any such untoward development has attended the reasonably widespread adoption of the ALI rule in the Federal courts and a substantial number of state courts.

2. RETENTION OF McDONALD DEFINITION OF "MENTAL DISEASE OR DEFECT."

Our ruling today includes our decision that in the ALI rule as adopted by this court the term "mental disease or defect" includes the definition of that term provided in our 1962 en banc *McDonald* opinion, as follows:

[A] mental disease or defect includes any abnormal condition of the mind which substantially affects mental or emotional processes and substantially impairs behavior controls.

McDonald v. United States, 114 U.S.App.D.C. at 124, 312 F.2d at 851.

We take this action in response to the problem, identified by amicus comments of Mr. Dempsey and the D.C. Bar Association, that the ALI's rule, lacking definition of "mental disease or defect," contains an inherent ambiguity. These comments consider this a reason for avoiding the ALI rule. We find more merit in the suggestion of Mr. Flynn, counsel appointed to represent appellant, that the *McDonald* definition be engrafted on to the ALI rule.[12]

In our further discussion of ALI and *McDonald,* we shall sometimes refer to "mental disease" as the core concept, without specifically referring to the possibility of exculpation by reason of a non-altering "mental defect."

The *McDonald* Rule has helped accomplish the objective of securing expert testimony needed on the subject of mental illness, while guarding against the undue dominance of expert testimony or specialized labels. It has thus permitted the kind of communication without encroachment, as between experts and juries, that has prompted us to adopt the ALI rule, and hence will help us realize our objective. This advantage overrides the surface disadvantage of any clumsiness in the blending of the *McDonald* component, defining mental disease, with the rest of the ALI rule, a matter we discuss further below.

3. INTEREST OF UNIFORMITY OF JUDICIAL APPROACH AND VOCABULARY, WITH ROOM FOR VARIATIONS AND ADJUSTMENTS

Adoption of the ALI rule furthers uniformity of judicial approach—a feature eminently desirable, not as a mere glow of "togetherness," but as an appreciation of the need and value of judicial communication. In all likelihood, this court's approach under *Durham,* at least since *McDonald,* has differed from that of other courts in vocabulary more than substance. Uniformity of vocabulary has an important value, however, as is evidenced from the familiar experience of meanings that "get lost in translation." No one court can amass all the experience pertinent to the judicial administration of the insanity defense. It is helpful for courts to be able to learn from each other without any blockage due to jargon. It is an impressive virtue of the common law, that its distinctive reliance on judicial decisions to establish the corpus of the law furthers a multiparty conversation between men who have studied a problem in various places at various times.

The value of uniformity of central approach is not shattered by the circumstance that in various particulars the different circuits have inserted variations in the ALI rule. Homogeneity does not mean rigidity, and room for local variation is likely a strength, providing a basis for comparison,[13] not a weakness. Nor is the strength of essential uniformity undercut by the caution of our appointed amicus that the formulation of the ALI rule provides extremely broad flexibility.[14] Flexibility and ductility are inherent in the insanity defense, as in any judicial rule with an extensive range —say, negligence, or proximate cause—and the ALI rule permits appropriate guidance of juries.

In prescribing a departure from *Durham* we are not unmindful of the concern that a change may generate uncertainties as to corollaries of the change.[15] While the courts adopting the ALI rule have stated variations, as we have noted, these were all, broadly, in furtherance of one or more of the inter-related goals of the insanity defense:

    (a) a broad input of pertinent facts and opinions
    (b) enhancing the information and judgment
    (c) of a jury necessarily given latitude in light of its functioning as the representative of the entire community.

We are likewise and for the same objectives defining the ALI rule as adopted by the court, with its contours and corollaries given express statement at the outset so as to minimize uncertainty. We postpone this statement to a subsequent phase of the opinion (see. 990 et seq.) in order that we may first consider other alternatives, for in some measure our adaptation may obviate or at least blunt objections voiced to the ALI rule.

4. CONSIDERATION AND REJECTION OF OTHER SUGGESTIONS

a. *Proposal to abolish insanity defense*

A number of proposals in the journals recommend that the insanity defense be abolished altogether.[16] This is advocated in the amicus brief of the National District Attorneys Association as both desirable and lawful.[17] The amicus brief of American Psychiatric Association concludes it would be desirable, with appropriate safeguards, but would require a constitutional amendment. That a constitutional amendment would be required is also the conclusion of others, generally in opposition to the proposal.[18]

This proposal has been put forward by responsible judges for consideration, with the objective of reserving psychiatric overview for the phase of the criminal process concerned with disposition of the person determined to have been the actor.[19] However, we are convinced that the proposal cannot properly be imposed by judicial fiat.

The courts have emphasized over the centuries that "free will" is the postulate of responsibility under our jurisprudence. 4 Blackstone's Commentaries 27. The concept of "belief in freedom of the human will and a consequent ability and duty of the normal individual to choose between good and evil" is a core concept that is "universal and persistent in mature systems of law."

Morissette v. United States, 342 U.S. 246, 250, 72 S.Ct. 240, 243, 96 L.Ed. 288 (1952). Criminal responsibility is assessed when through "free will" a man elects to do evil. And while, as noted in *Morissette*, the legislature has dispensed with mental element in some statutory offenses, in furtherance of a paramount need of the community, these instances mark the exception and not the rule, and only in the most limited instances has the mental element been omitted by the legislature as a requisite for an offense that was a crime at common law.

The concept of lack of "free will" is both the root of origin of the insanity defense and the line of its growth.[20] This cherished principle is not undercut by difficulties, or differences of view, as to how best to express the free will concept in the light of the expansion of medical knowledge. We do not concur in the view of the National District Attorneys Association that the insanity defense should be abandoned judicially, either because it is at too great a variance with popular conceptions of guilt[21] or fails "to show proper respect for the personality of the criminal [who] is liable to resent pathology more than punishment."[22]

These concepts may be measured along with other ingredients in a legislative re-examination of settled doctrines of criminal responsibility, root, stock and branch. Such a reassessment, one that seeks to probe and appraise the society's processes and values is for the legislative branch, assuming no constitutional bar. The judicial role is limited, in Justice Holmes's figure, to action that is molecular, with the restraint inherent in taking relatively small steps, leaving to the other branches of government whatever progress must be made with seven-league leaps. Such judicial restraint is particularly necessary when a proposal requires, as a mandatory ingredient, the kind of devotion of resources, personnel and techniques that can be accomplished only through whole-hearted legislative commitment.

To obviate any misunderstanding from our rejection of the recommendation of those proposing judicial abolition of the insanity defense, we expressly commend their emphasis on the need for improvement of dispositional resources and programs. The defense focuses on the kind of impairment that warrants exculpation, and necessarily assigns to the prison walls many men who have serious mental impairments and difficulties. The needs of society—rooted not only in humanity but in practical need for attempting to break the recidivist cycles, and halt the spread of deviant behavior—call for the provision of psychiatrists, psychologists and counselors to help men with these mental afflictions and difficulties, as part of a total effort toward a readjustment that will permit re-integration in society.

b. *Proposal for defense if mental disease impairs capacity to such an extent that the defendant cannot "justly be held responsible."*

We have also pondered the suggestion that the jury be instructed that the defendant lacks criminal responsibility if the jury finds that the defendant's mental disease impairs his capacity or controls to such an extent that he cannot "justly be held responsible."

This was the view of a British commission,[23] adapted and proposed in 1955 by Professor Wechsler, the distinguished Reporter for the ALI's Model Penal Code, and sustained by some, albeit a minority, of the members of the ALI's Council.[24] In the ALI, the contrary view prevailed because of a concern over presenting to the jury questions put primarily in the form of "justice."

The proposal is not to be condemned out of hand as a suggestion that the jury be informed of an absolute prerogative that it can only exercise by flatly disregarding the applicable rule of law. It is rather a suggestion that the jury be informed of the matters the law contemplates it will take into account in arriving at the community judgment concerning a composite of factors.[25]

However, there is a substantial concern that an instruction overtly cast in terms of "justice" cannot feasibly be restricted to the ambit of what may properly be taken into account but will splash with unconfinable and malign consequences. The Government cautions that "explicit appeals to 'justice' will result in litigation of extraneous issues and will encourage improper arguments to the jury phrased solely in terms of 'sympathy' and 'prejudice.' "

Nor is this solely a prosecutor's concern.

Mr. Flynn, counsel appointed to represent defendant, puts it that even though the jury is applying community concepts of blameworthiness "the jury should not be left at large, or asked to find out for itself what those concepts are."

The amicus submission of the Public Defender Service argues that it would be beneficial to focus the jury's attention on the moral and legal questions intertwined in the insanity defense. It expresses concern, however, over a blameworthiness instruction without more, saying (Br. 19) "it may well be that the 'average' American condemns the mentally ill."[26] It would apparently accept an approach not unlike that proposed by the ALI Reporter, under which the justice standard is coupled with a direction to consider the individual's capacity to control his behavior. Mr. Dempsey's recommendation is of like import, with some simplification.[27] But the problem remains, whether, assuming justice calls for the exculpation and treatment of the mentally ill, that is more likely to be gained from a jury, with "average" notions of mental illness, which

is explicitly set at large to convict or acquit persons with impaired mental capacity according to its concept of justice.

The brief of the D.C. Bar Association as amicus submits that with a "justly responsible" formulation the test of insanity "would be largely swallowed up by this consideration." And it observes that the function of giving to the jury the law to be applied to the facts is not only the duty of the court, see Sparf v. United States, 156 U.S. 51, 102, 15 S.Ct. 273, 39 L.Ed. 343 (1895), but is also "a bedrock right of every citizen"—and, possibly, his "only protection," citing Justice Story in United States v. Battiste, 2 Sumn. 240, 244, Fed.Cas. No. 14,545 (C.C.D.Mass. 1835).

We are impressed by the observation of Professor Abraham S. Goldstein, one of the most careful students of the problem:

[The] overly general standard may place too great a burden upon the jury. If the law provides no standard, members of the jury are placed in the difficult position of having to find a man responsible for no other reason then their personal feeling about him. Whether the psyches of individual jurors are strong enough to make that decision, or whether the "law" should put that obligation on them, is open to serious question. It is far easier for them to perform the role assigned to them by legislature and courts if they know—or are able to rationalize—that their verdicts are "required" by law.[28]

Professor Goldstein was referring to the board "justice" standard recommended by the Royal Commission. But the problems remain acute even with the modifications in the proposal of the ALI Reporter, for that still leads to "justly responsible" as the ultimate and critical term.

There may be a tug of appeal in the suggestion that law is a means to justice and the jury is an appropriate tribunal to ascertain justice. This is a simplistic syllogism that harbors the logical fallacy of equivocation, and fails to take account of the different facets and dimensions of the concept of justice. We must not be beguiled by a play on words. The thrust of a rule that in essence invites the jury to ponder the evidence on impairment of defendant's capacity and appreciation, and then do what to them seems just, is to focus on what seems "just" as to the particular individual. Under the centuries-long pull of the Judeo-Christian ethic, this is likely to suggest a call for understanding and forgiveness of those who have committed crimes against society, but plead the influence of passionate and perhaps justified grievances against that society, perhaps grievances not wholly lacking in merit. In the domain of morality and religion, the gears may be governed by the particular instance of the individual seeking salvation. The judgment of a court of law must further justice to the community, and safeguard it against undercutting and evasion from overconcern for the individual. What this reflects is not the rigidity of retributive justice—an eye for an eye—but awareness how justice in the broad may be undermined by an excess of compassion as well as passion. Justice to the community includes penalties needed to cope with disobedience by those capable of control, undergirding a social environment that broadly inhibits behavior destructive of the common good. An open society requires mutual respect and regard, and mutually reinforcing relationships among its citizens, and its ideals of justice must safeguard the vast majority who responsibly shoulder the burdens implicit in its ordered liberty. Still another aspect of justice is the requirement for rules of conduct that establish reasonable generality, neutrality and constancy. Cf. L. Fuller, The Morality of Laws 33–94 (1964). This concept is neither static nor absolute, but it would be sapped by a rule that invites an ad hoc redefinition of the "just" with each new case.

It is the sense of justice propounded by those charged with making and declaring the law—legislatures and courts—that lays down the rule that persons without substantial capacity to know or control the act shall be excused. The jury is concerned with applying the community understanding of this broad rule to particular lay and medical facts. Where the matter is unclear it naturally will call on its own sense of justice to help it determine the matter. There is wisdom in the view that a jury generally understands well enough that an instruction composed in flexible terms gives it sufficient latitude so that, without disregarding the instruction, it can provide that application of the instruction which harmonizes with its sense of justice.[29] The ALI rule generally communicates that meaning. Wade v. United States, *supra,* 426 F.2d at 70–71. This is recognized even by those who might prefer a more explicit statement of the matter.[30] It is one thing, however, to tolerate and even welcome the jury's sense of equity as a force that affects its application of instructions which state the legal rules that crystallize the requirements of justice as determined by the lawmakers of the community. It is quite another to set the jury at large, without such crystallization, to evolve its own legal rules and standards of justice. It would likely be counter-productive and contrary to the larger interest of justice to become so explicit—in an effort to hammer the point home to the very occasional jury that would otherwise be too rigid—that one puts serious strains on the normal operation of the system of criminal justice.

Taking all these considerations into account we conclude that the ALI rule as announced is not productive of injustice, and we decline to proclaim the broad "justly responsible" standard.

5. ALI RULE IS CONTEMPLATED AS IMPROVING THE PROCESS OF ADJUDICATION, NOT AS AFFECTING NUMBER OF INSANITY ACQUITTALS

Amicus Dempsey is concerned that a change by this court from *Durham-McDonald* to ALI will be taken as an indication that this court intends that the number and percentage of insanity acquittals be modified. That is not the intendment of the rule adopted today, nor do we have any basis for forecasting that effect.

a. Statistical data concerning the use of insanity in criminal trials in this jurisdiction were presented in the December 15, 1966, Report of the President's Commission on Crime in the District of Columbia.[31] These data have been up-dated in Mr. Dempsey's brief, with the aid of data helpfully supplied by the United States Attorney's office. At least since *Durham* was modified by *McDonald,* insanity acquittals have run at about 2% of all cases terminated. In the seven years subsequent to *McDonald* jury verdicts of not guilty by reason of insanity averaged only 3 per annum.[32] In trials by the court, there has been an annual average of about 38 verdicts of not guilty by reason of insanity; these typically are cases where the Government psychiatrists agreed that the crime was the product of mental illness.[33] We perceive no basis in these data for any conclusion that the number of percentage of insanity acquittals has been either excessive or inadequate.

We have no way of forecasting what will be the effect on verdicts, of juries or judges, from the reduction in influence of expert testimony on "productivity" that reflects judgments outside the domain of expertise.[34] Whatever its effect, we are confident that the rule adopted today provides a sounder relationship in terms of the giving, comprehension and application of expert testimony. Our objective is not to steer the jury's verdict but to enhance its deliberation.[35]

b. Some judges have viewed the ALI test as going beyond *Durham* in enlarging the category of persons who may win acquittals.[36] The 1966 report of the President's Crime Commission (*supra* note 15) apparently concludes that the debate over *Durham* was stilled by *McDonald,* and that *Durham-McDonald* is not significantly different in content from the ALI test. In contrast, Mr. Dempsey is concerned that a person's ability to control his behavior could be "substantially impaired" by mental condition, thus qualifying the defense under *McDonald,* while still leaving him with "substantial capacity," rendering the defense unavailable under the ALI rule. We have no way of knowing whether psychiatrists giving testimony would draw such a distinction, and moreover there would be no difference in result unless one also indulges the assumption, which is dubious, that the jury would reason that the crime may have been the "product" of the mental condition of a man even though he retained substantial capacity.

In the last analysis, however, if there is a case where there would be a difference in result—and it would seem rare—we think the underlying freedom of will conception renders it just to assign responsibility to a person, even though his controls have been impaired, if his residual controls give him "substantial capacity" both to appreciate the wrongfulness of his conduct and to conform it to the requirement of law. Whether the ALI standard is to be given a narrow or broad conception rests not on abstract analysis[37] but on the application reflecting the underlying sense of responsibility of the jury, as the community's surrogate.[38]

6. ELEMENTS OF THE ALI RULE ADOPTED BY THIS COURT

Though it provides a general uniformity, the ALI rule leaves room for variations. Thus, we have added an adjustment in the *McDonald* definition of mental disease, which we think fully compatible with both the spirit and text of the ALI rule. In the interest of good administration, we now undertake to set forth, with such precision as the subject will permit, other elements of the ALI rule as adopted by this court.

The two main components of the rule define (1) mental disease, (2) the consequences thereof that exculpate from responsibility.

a. *Intermesh of components*

The first component of our rule, derived from *McDonald,* defines mental disease or defect as an abnormal condition of the mind, and a condition which substantially (a) affects mental or emotional processes and (b) impairs behavioral controls. The second component, derived from the Model Penal Code, tells which defendant with a mental disease lacks criminal responsibility for particular conduct: it is the defendant who, as a result of this mental condition, at the time of such conduct, either (i) lacks substantial capacity to appreciate that his conduct is wrongful, or (ii) lacks substantial capacity to conform his conduct to the law.

The first component establishes eligibility for an instruction concerning the defense for a defendant who presents evidence that his abnormal condition of the mind has substantially impaired behavioral controls. The second component completes the instruction and defines the ultimate issue, of exculpation in terms of whether his behavioral controls were not only substantially impaired but impaired to such an extent that he lacked substantial capacity to conform his conduct to the law.[39]

b. *The "result" of the mental disease*

The rule contains a requirement of causality, as is clear from the term "result." Exculpation is estab-

lished not by mental disease alone but only if "as a result" defendant lacks the substantial capacity required for responsibility. Presumably the mental disease of a kleptomaniac does not entail as a "result" a lack of capacity to conform to the law prohibiting rape.

c. *At the time of the conduct*

Under the Ali rule the issue is not whether defendant is so disoriented or void of controls that he is never able to conform to external demands, but whether he had that capacity at the time of the conduct. The question is not properly put in terms of whether he would have capacity to conform in some untypical restraining situation—as with an attendant or policeman at his elbow. The issue is whether he was able to conform in the unstructured condition of life in an open society, and whether the result of his abnormal mental condition was a lack of substantial internal controls. These matters are brought out in the ALI's comments to § 4.01 of the Model Penal Code Tentative Draft #4, p. 158:

The schizophrenic . . . is disoriented from reality; the disorientation is extreme; but it is rarely total. Most psychotics will respond to a command of someone in authority within the mental hospital; they thus have some capacity to conform to a norm. But this is very different from the capacity to conform to requirements that are not thus immediately symbolized by an attendant or policeman at the elbow. Nothing makes the inquiry into responsibility more unreal for the psychiatrist than limitation of the issue to some ultimate extreme of total incapacity, when clinical experience reveals only a graded scale with marks along the way.

d. *Capacity to appreciate wrongfulness of his conduct*

As to the option of terminology noted in the ALI code, we adopt the formulation that exculpates a defendant whose mental condition is such that he lacks substantial capacity to appreciate the wrongfulness of his conduct. We prefer this on pragmatic grounds to "appreciate the criminality of his conduct" since the resulting jury instruction is more like that conventionally given to and applied by the jury. While such an instruction is of course subject to the objection that it lacks complete precision, it serves the objective of calling on the jury to provide a community judgment on a combination of factors. And since the possibility of analytical differences between the two formulations is insubstantial in fact in view of the control capacity test, we are usefully guided by the pragmatic considerations pertinent to jury instructions.[40]

In adopting the ALI formulation, this court does not follow the *Currens* opinion of the Third Circuit, which puts it that the sole issue in every case is defendant's capacity to control his behavior, and that as a matter of analysis a person who lacks substantial capacity to appreciate the wrongfulness [criminality] of his conduct necessarily lacks substantial capacity to control his behavior. Like the other circuits, we resist the *Currens* lure of logic in order to make certain that the jury will give heed to the substantiality of a defense of lack of substantial capacity to appreciate wrongfulness, a point that may elude a jury instructed solely in terms of control capacity. In a particular case, however, defendant may have reason to request omission of the phrase pertaining to lack of capacity to appreciate wrongfulness, if that particular matter is not involved on the facts, and defendant fears that a jury that does not attend rigorously to the details of the instruction may erroneously suppose that the defense is lost if defendant appreciates wrongfulness. Here again, it is not enough to rely solely on logic, when a simple change will aid jury understanding. In such a case, if defendant requests, the judge should limit the instruction to the issue involved in that case, and charge that the jury shall bring in a verdict of not guilty if as a result of mental illness defendant lacked substantial capacity to conform his conduct to the requirements of the law.

e. Caveat paragraph

Section 4.01 of the Model Penal Code as promulgated by ALI contains in subsection (2) what has come to be known as the "caveat paragraph":

(2) The terms "mental disease or defect" do not include an abnormality manifested only by repeated criminal or otherwise anti-social conduct.

The purpose of this provision was to exclude a defense for the so-called "psychopathic personality."[41]

There has been a split in the Federal circuits concerning this provision. Some of the courts adopting the ALI rule refer to both subsections but without separate discussion of the caveat paragraph—as in the *Chandler* and *Blake* opinions. As to the decisions considering the point, those of the Second and Third Circuits conclude the paragraph should be retained (in *Freeman* and *Currens*), while the *Smith* and *Wade* decisions, of the Sixth and Ninth Circuits, conclude it should be omitted. The Sixth Circuit's position is (404 f.2d at 727, fn.8) that there is "great dispute over the psychiatric soundness" of the caveat paragraph. The *Wade* opinion considers the matter at great length and puts forward three grounds for rejecting the caveat paragraph: (1) As a practical matter, it would be ineffectual in keeping sociopaths out of the definition of insanity; it is always possible to introduce some evidence, other than past criminal behavior, to support a plea of insanity. (2) The criminal sanction ought not be sought for criminal psychopaths—constant recidivists—because such people should be taken off the streets indefinitely, and not merely for a set term of years. (3) Its third ground is stated thus (426 F.2d at 73):

It is unclear whether [the caveat paragraph] would require that a defendant be considered legally sane if, although the only overt acts manifesting his disease or defect were "criminal or otherwise anti-social," there arises from his acts a reasonable inference of mental derangement either because of the nature of the acts or because of credible medical or other evidence.

Our own approach is influenced by the fact that our rule already includes a definition of mental disease (from *McDonald*). Under that definition, as we have pointed out, the mere existence of "a long criminal record does not excuse crime." Williams v. United States, 114 U.S.App.D.C. 135, 137, 312 F.2d 862, 864 (1962). We do not require the caveat paragraph as an insurance against exculpation of the deliberate and persistent offender.[42] Our *McDonald* rule guards against the danger of misunderstanding and injustice that might arise, say, from an expert's classification that reflects only a conception[43] defining all criminality as reflective of mental illness. There must be testimony to show both that the defendant was suffering from an abnormal condition of the mind and that it substantially affected mental or emotional processes and substantially impaired behavioral controls.

In this context, our pragmatic approach is to adopt the caveat paragraph as a rule for application by the judge, to avoid miscarriage of justice, but not for inclusion in instructions to the jury.

The judge will be aware that the criminal and antisocial conduct of a—person on the street, in the home, in the ward—is necessarily material information for assessment by the psychiatrist. On the other hand, rarely if ever would a psychiatrist base a conclusion of mental disease solely on criminal and anti-social acts. Our pragmatic solution provides for reshaping the rule for application by the court as follows: The introduction or proffer of past criminal and anti-social actions is not admissible as evidence of mental disease unless accompanied by expert testimony, supported by a showing of the concordance of a responsible segment of professional opinion, that the particular characteristics of these actions constitute convincing evidence of an underlying mental disease that substantially impairs behavioral controls.

This formulation retains the paragraph as a "caveat" rather than an inexorable rule of law. It should serve to obviate distortions of the present state of knowledge that would constitute miscarriages of justice. Yet it leaves the door open—on shouldering the "convincing evidence" burden—to accommodate our general rule to developments that may lie ahead. It is the kind of imperfect, but not unfeasible, accommodation of the abstract and pragmatic that is often found to serve the administration of justice.

We do not think it desirable to use the caveat paragraph as a basis for instructions to the jury. It would be difficult for a juryman—or anyone else—to reconcile the caveat paragraph and the basic (*McDonald*) definition of mental disease if a psychiatrist testified that he discerned from particular past criminal behavior a pattern that established defendant as suffering from an abnormal condition of the mind that substantially impaired behavioral controls. If there is no such testimony, then there would be no evidence that mere misconduct betokens mental illness, it would be impermissible for defense counsel to present such a hypothesis to the jury, and there would be very little likelihood that a jury would arrive at such a proposition on its own. On the other hand, an instruction along the lines of the caveat paragraph runs the risk of appearing to call for the rejection of testimony that is based materially, but only partially, on the history of criminal conducts.

f. *Broad presentation to the jury*

Our adoption of the ALI rule does not depart from the doctrines this court has built up over the past twenty years to assure a broad presentation to the jury concerning the condition of defendant's mind and its consequences. Thus we adhere to our rulings admitting expert testimony of psychologists,[44] as well as psychiatrists, and to our many decisions contemplating that expert testimony on this subject will be accompanied by presentation of the facts and premises underlying the opinions and conclusions of the experts,[45] and that the Government and defense may present, in Judge Blackmun's words, "all possibly relevant evidence" bearing on cognition, volition and capacity.[46] We agree with the amicus submission of the National District Attorneys Association that the law cannot "distinguish between physiological, emotional, social and cultural sources of the impairment"—assuming, of course, requisite testimony establishing exculpation under the pertinent standard—and all such causes may be both referred to by the expert and considered by the trier of fact.[47]

Breadth of input under the insanity defense is not to be confused with breadth of the doctrines establishing the defense. As the National District Attorneys Association brief points out, the latitude for salient evidence of, for example, social and cultural factors pertinent to an abnormal condition of the mind significantly affecting capacity and controls, does not mean that such factors may be taken as establishing a separate defense for persons whose mental condition is such that blame can be imposed. We have rejected a broad "injustice" approach that would have opened the door to expositions of for example, cultural deprivation, unrelated to any abnormal condition of the mind.

We have recognized that "Many criminologists point out that even normal human behavior is influenced by such factors as training, environment, poverty and the like, which may limit the understanding and options of the individual." King v. United States, *supra*, 125 U.S.App.D.C.at 323, 372 F.2d at 388. Determinists may contend that every man's fate is ultimately sealed by his genes and environment, over which he has no control. Our jurisprudence, however, while not oblivious to deterministic components, utimately rests on a premise of freedom of will. This is not to be viewed as an exercise in philosophic discourse, but as a governmental fusion of ethics and necessity, which takes into account that a system of rewards and punishments is itself part of the environment that influences and shapes human conduct. Our recognition of an insanity defense for those who lack the essential, threshold free will possessed by those in the normal range is not to be twisted, directly or indirectly, into a device for exculpation of those without an abnormal condition of the mind.

Finally, we have not accepted suggestions to adopt a rule that disentangles the insanity defense from a medical model, and announces a standard exculpating anyone whose capacity for control is insubstantial, for whatever cause or reason. There may be logic in these submissions, but we are not sufficiently certain of the nature, range and implications of the conduct involved to attempt an all-embracing unified field theory. The applicable rule can be discerned as the cases arise in regard to other conditions—somnambulism or other automatisms; blackouts due, for example, to overdose of insulin; drug addiction. Whether these somatic conditions should be governed by a rule comparable to that herein set forth for mental disease would require, at a minimum, a judicial determination, which takes medical opinion into account, finding convincing evidence of an ascertainable condition characterized by "a broad consensus that free will does not exist." Salzman v. United States, 131 U.S.App.D.C. 393, 400, 405 F.2d 358, 365 (1968) (concurring opinion of Judge Wright).

MENTAL CONDITION, THOUGH INSUFFICIENT TO EXONERATE, MAY BE RELEVANT TO SPECIFIC MENTAL ELEMENT OF CERTAIN CRIMES OR DEGREES OF CRIME.

Our decision accompanies the redefinition of when a mental condition exonerates a defendant from criminal responsibility with the doctrine that expert testimony as to a defendant's abnormal mental condition may be received and considered, as tending to show, in a responsible way, that defendant did not have the specific mental state required for a particular crime or degree of crime—even though he was aware that his act was wrongful and was able to control it, and hence was not entitled to complete exoneration.

Some of the cases following this doctrine use the term "diminished responsibility," but we prefer the example of the cases that avoid this term (for example, note 57, *infra*), for its convenience is outweighed by its confusion: Our doctrine has nothing to do with "diminishing" responsibility of a defendant because of his impaired mental condition,[52] but rather with determining whether the defendant had the mental state that must be proved as to all defendants.

Procedurally, the issue of abnormal mental condition negativing a person's intent may arise in different ways: For example, the defendant may offer evidence of mental condition not qualifying as mental disease under *McDonald.* Or he may tender evidence that qualifies under *McDonald,* yet the jury may conclude from all the evidence that defendant has knowledge and control capacity sufficient for responsibility under the ALI rule.

The issue often arises with respect to mental condition tendered as negativing the element of premeditation in a charge of first degree premeditated murder. As we noted in Austin v. United States, 127 U.S. App.D.C. 180, 382 F.2d 129 (1967), when the legislature modified the common law crime of murder so as to establish degrees, murder in the first degree was reserved for intentional homicide done deliberately and with premeditation, and homicide that is intentional but "impulsive," not done after "reflection and meditation," was made murder only in the second degree. (127 U.S.App.D.C. at 187, 382 F.2d at 135).

An offense like deliberated and premeditated murder requires a specific intent that cannot be satisfied merely by showing that defendant failed to conform to an objective standard.[53] This is plainly established by the defense of voluntary intoxication. In Hopt v. Utah, 104 U.S. 631, 634, 26 L.Ed. 873 (1881), the Court, after stating the familiar rule that voluntary intoxication is no excuse for crime, said:

[W]hen a statute establishing different degrees of murder requires deliberate premeditation in order to constitute murder in the first degree, the question of whether the accused is in such a condition of mind, by reason of drunkenness or otherwise, as to be capable of deliberate premeditation, necessarily becomes a material subject of consideration by the jury.

In Bishop v. United States, 71 App.D.C. 132, 136, 107 F.2d 297, 301 (1939), Justice Vinson noted that while voluntary intoxication per se is no defense to guilt, "the stated condition of a defendant's mind at the time of the killing . . . is now a proper subject for consideration, inquiry, and determination by the jury." Thus "voluntary intoxication will not excuse murder, but it may negative the ability of the defendant" as to premeditation, and hence effect "a reduction to second degree murder."

Enlarging on *Hopt* and *Bishop,* Judge Burger's opinion in Heideman v. United States, 104 U.S.App.D.C. 128, 131, 259 F.2d 943, 946 (1958), points out:

Drunkenness is not per se an excuse for crime, but nevertheless it may in many instances be relevant to the issue of intent. One class of cases where drunkenness may be relevant on the issue of intent is the category of crimes where specific intent is required. Robbery falls into this category, and a defendant accused of robbery is entitled to an instruction on drunkenness as bearing on intent if the evidentiary groundwork has been adequately laid.

As Judge Burger points out there must be a showing of drunkenness that does more than remove inhibitions, and is such an "incapacitating state" as to negate intent. But he also notes, citing *Hopt,* and *Bishop,* that a lesser state of drunkenness, insufficient to negate the specific intent required for robbery, may suffice to negate the premeditation required for first degree murder.

Neither logic nor justice can tolerate a jurisprudence that defines the elements of an offense as requiring a mental state such that one defendant can properly argue that his voluntary drunkenness removed his capacity to form the specific intent but another defendant is inhibited from a submission of his contention that an abnormal mental condition, for which he was in no way responsible, negated his capacity to form a particular specific intent, even though the condition did not exonerate him from all criminal responsibility.

In Fisher v. United States, 80 U.S.App.D.C. 96, 149 F.2d (1946), the court upheld the trial court's refusal to instruct the jury that on issues of premeditation and deliberation "it should consider the entire personality of the defendant, his mental, nervous, emotional and physical characteristics as developed by the evidence in the case." Justice Arnold's abbreviated opinion was evidently premised on two factors: (1) that the instruction confused the issue of insanity with the issue of deliberation; (2) that "To give an instruction like the above is to tell the jury they are at liberty to acquit one who commits a brutal crime because he has the abnormal tendencies of persons capable of such crimes." His opinion made no effort to come to terms with the *Hopt* opinion, stressed by Fisher's counsel.

Fisher went to the Supreme Court and there was affirmed, but on the limited ground of disinclination to "force" this court in a choice of legal doctrine for the District of Columbia, 328 U.S. 463, 66 S.Ct. 1318, 90 L.Ed. 1382 (1946). The Court said (at 476, 66 S.Ct. at 1325) that such a change was "more properly a subject for the exercise of legislative power or at least for the discretion of the courts of the District."

In *Stewart I,* Stewart v. United States, 94 U.S. App.D.C. 293, 214 F.2d 879 (1954) which issued only two weeks after *Durham* was announced, we said that "reconsideration of our decision in Fisher should wait until we can appraise the results [of Durham]." In Stewart v. United States, 107 U.S.App.D.C. 159, 275 F.2d 617 (1960), the court en banc again stated that more experience with *Durham* was required to evaluate *Fisher,* and the matter was appropriate for legislative consideration. That was *Stewart II.*[54]

Today we are again *en banc,* and we have the benefit of many years of experience with *Durham-McDonald.* We are changing the insanity rule, on a prospective basis, to take into account intervening scholarship and court opinions. As a corollary, we deem it appropriate to change the rule of *Fisher* on a prospective basis, and to accept the approach which the Supreme Court declined to "force" upon us in 1946, but which has been adopted by the overwhelming majority of courts that have recently faced the question. We are convinced by the analysis set forth in the recent opinions of the highest courts of California,[55] Colorado,[56] New Jersey,[57] Iowa,[58] Ohio,[59] Idaho,[60] Connecticut,[61] Nebraska,[62] New Mexico[63] and Nevada.[64] They have joined the states that spoke out before *Fisher*—New York, Rhode Island, Utah, Wisconsin and Wyoming.[65]

The pertinent reasoning was succinctly stated by the Colorado Supreme Court as follows:[66]

The question to be determined is not whether defendant was insane, but whether the homicidal act was committed with deliberation and premeditation. The evidence offered as to insanity may or may not be relevant to that issue. * * * "A claim of insanity cannot be used for the purpose of reducing a crime of murder in the first degree to murder in the second degree or from murder to manslaughter. If the perpetrator is responsible at all in this respect, he is responsible in the same degree as a sane man; and if he is not responsible at all, he is entitled to an acquittal in both degrees. However, . . . *evidence of the condition of the mind* of the accused at the time of the crime, together with the surrounding circumstances, may be introduced, not for the purpose of establishing insanity, but to prove that the situation was such that a specific intent was not entertained—that is, *to show absence of any deliberate or premeditated design.*" (Emphasis in original.)

On the other side of the coin, very few jurisdictions which have recently considered this question have held to the contrary position.[67]

Intervening developments within our own jurisdiction underscore the soundness of a doctrine for consideration of abnormal mental condition on the issue of specific intent. In the *Fisher* opinion of 1946, the court was concerned lest such a doctrine "tell the jury that they are at liberty to acquit one who commits a brutal crime because he has the abnormal tendencies of persons capable of such crimes." That a man's abnormal mental condition short of legal insanity may be material as negativing premeditation and deliberation does not set him "at liberty" but reduces the degree of the criminal homicide. Our 1967 opinion in *Austin, supra,* clarifies that even "a particularly frightful and horrible murder" may not be murder in the first degree, that "many murders most brutish and bestial are committed in a consuming frenzy or heat of passion, and that these are in law only murder in the second degree."[68] Indeed the action of the trial judge in acquitting defendant of first degree murder indicates how the refinement of *Austin* has undercut the *Fisher* approach. Though the defendant went back to get his gun,[69] the judge concluded that the evidence as a whole—including defendant's broken jaw, the blood streaming down his face, and his irrational pounding on the mailbox—did not establish a reasonable foundation for inferring a calculated, deliberate mind at the time of shooting. We are not called upon to consider whether that action was proper in this case; what we do take note of is the inevitable implication of *Austin.*

There has also been a material legislative development since both *Fisher* and *Stewart II.* In 1964, after extensive hearings, Congress enacted the Hospitalization of the Mentally Ill Act, which provides civil commitment for the "mentally ill" who are dangerous to themselves or others.[70] Both the terminology and the underlying conception of this statute reflected a deliberate change from the 1939 law and its use of the term "insanity," which prior to *Durham* tended to be equated to psychosis and to disorientations like delusions. The enlarged conception underlying the 1964 law has been accorded a "liberal construction"[71] for the protection of the community, going so far as to include commitment of a disturbed mental defective with behavioral reactions resulting in danger-productive behavior.[72] The law is broad enough to include not only mental illness requiring confinement in St. Elizabeths, but also conditions of mental illness calling for placement in nursing homes,[73] or, where appropriate, halfway houses or requirement of outpatient care.[74] These statutory provisions provide a shield against danger from persons with abnormal mental condition—a danger which in all likelihood bolstered, or even impelled, the draconic *Fisher* doctrine.

Further, to the extent that the 1970 law (*supra,* note 48) leads to a conviction of first degree murder when the evidence is in equipoise on the issue of insanity, there would be an additional miscarriage of justice if the evidence were not available for consideration as raising a reasonable doubt on the issue of premeditation and deliberation.

In providing for the admission and consideration of expert testimony on abnormal mental condition insufficient for complete exoneration, we insert some observations prompted by State v. Sikora, 44 N.J. 453, 210 A.2d 193 (1965), *supra,* note 57. The doctrine does not permit the receipt of psychiatric testimony based on the conception that mental disorder is only a relative concept and that the behavior of every individual is dictated by forces—ultimately, his genes and lifelong environment—that are unconscious and beyond his control. As we have already made clear, we are not embarked on enquiry that must yield to tenets of the philosophy of determinism. The law accepts free will and blameworthiness as a general premise. Expert psychiatric testimony negativing blameworthiness for a crime—whether on ground of general exoneration or lack of requisite specific intent—must rest on the premise of an exception due to abnormal mental condition.

Our rule permits the introduction of expert testimony as to abnormal condition if it is relevant to negative, or establish, the specific mental condition that is an element of the crime. The receipt of this expert testimony to negative the mental condition of specific intent requires careful administration by the trial judge. Where the proof is not offered in the first instance as evidence of exonerating mental disease or defect within the ALI rule the judge may, and ordinarily would, require counsel first to make a proffer of the proof to be adduced outside the presence of the jury. The judge will then determine whether the testimony is grounded in sufficient scientific support to warrant use in the courtroom, and whether it would aid the jury in reaching a decision on the ultimate issues.[75]

NOTES

9. Ten years ago Judge Burger said: "While the time span since 1954 is brief, our total study and collective ease consideration of the problem is equal perhaps to as much a half century of case review of this problem in most jurisdictions." Blocker v. United States, 110 U.S.App.D.C. at 52, 288 F.2d at 864 (en banc, 1961) (concurring opinion).

10. A difference in language perception probably contributed to the development that psychiatric testimony concerning "product" causal relationship did not develop along the lines presaged by legal students of the problem. Early critiques in journals asserted that a but-for test of "product" would rarely, if ever, permit a psychiatrist to testify as to the existence of mental illness coexisting with a lack of "product" causal relationship to the crime. See, for example, Wechsler, The Criteria of Criminal Responsibility, 22 U.Chi.L.Rev. 367, 371 (1955); De Grazia. The Distinction of Being Mad, 22 U.Chi.L.Rev. 339, 343 (1955). Presumably, the force of this analysis was strengthened when "mental disease or defect" was defined and tightened in McDonald. As events have developed, however, it has become almost commonplace that psychiatrists testifying as to the presence of mental disease have nevertheless found an absence of "product" causal relation with the crime, or at least expressed substantial doubt as to such relationship. Perhaps more to the point, it has become commonplace for psychiatrists called by Government and defense to be in agreement on the mental disease aspects of their testimony and to differ on the issue of "product" relationship. This is not intended, in any way, as a criticism of any particular testimony. There is often a genuine and difficult

question as to the relationship between a particular mental disease and particular offense. What is our concern, however, is that the inherent difficulty of his core problem has been intensified, and the sources of confusion compounded, by a kind of mystique that came to surround the "product" test, and testimony cast in that language.

11. For example, Hawkins v. United States, 114 U.S. App.D.C. 44, 310 F.2d 849 (1962); Isaac v. United States, 109 U.S.App.D.C. 34, 284 F.2d 168 (1960).

12. This was also the suggestion of the National District Attorneys Association subject to caveats, as the test recommended if the court did not accept its submission that the insanity defense should be abolished entirely.

13. Compare New State Ice Co. v. Liebmann, 285 U.S. 262, 280, 52 S.Ct. 371, 76 L.Ed. 747 (1932) (dissenting opinion of Brandeis, J.).

14. Amicus points out that in Freeman the Second Circuit referred to the fact that the Third and Tenth Circuits "have employed their own language approaching the objectives of the Model Penal Code formulation," and then offered a discussion of guiding policy considerations, including Senator Dodd's espousal of an approach sending "marginal" cases to a hospital rather than prison, that, as amicus puts it, "strikes quite a different tone than, say, the analogous discussion of the Tenth Circuit in Wion."

15. See, for example, Report of President's D.C. Crime Commission at pp. 550 ff. A majority of the members of the Commission preferred the ALI rule, but were concerned lest departure from Durham-McDonald spawn confusion.

16. "[I]t may be that psychiatry and the other social and behavioral sciences cannot provide sufficient data relevant to a determination of criminal responsibility no matter what our rules of evidence are. If so, we may be forced to eliminate the insanity defense altogether, or refashion it in a way which is not tied so tightly to the medical model." Washington v. United States, 129 U.S.App.D.C. at 42, n. 33, 390 F.2d at 457 (1967).

17. It suggests that a mental condition be exculpatory solely as it negatives mens rea.

18. For example, Mr. Dempsey. To the same general effect is the position in the research memorandum from the University of Virginia Law School Research Group to Mr. Flynn, appellant's appointed counsel attached to his brief.

19. See for example, Burger, then Circuit Judge, Proceedings of the Sixth Annual Meeting of the National Conference of State Trial Judges, Chicago, Illinois, Aug. 9–11, 1963, quoted in Wion v. United States, 325 F.2d at 428, n. 10; Bazelon, Chief Judge, in Washington v. United States, 129 U.S.App.D.C. at 42, n. 33, 390 F.2d at 457 (1967); Haynesworth, Chief Judge, in en banc opinion in United States v. Chandler, 393 F.2d at 928 (1968); see also remarks of Chief Justice Weintraub (of New Jersey) in Insanity as a Defense—Panel Discussion, Annual Judicial Conference, Second Circuit, 37 F.R.D. 365, 369 (1964).

20. Davis v. United States, 160 U.S. 469. 484–485, 16 S.Ct. 353, 40 L.Ed. 499 (1895); Durham v. United States, supra, 94 U.S.App.D.C. at 242, 214 F.2d at 876.

21. Amicus argues that penal systems can only survive so long as they "accord substantially with the popular estimate of the enormity of guilt," citing 1 W. Lecky, History of the Rise and Influence of the Spirit of Rationalism in Europe 336–337 (1891).

22. Citing Harris, Respect for Persons in Ethics and Society 129–130 (R. DeGeorge ed. 1966).

23. In 1953 the British Royal Commission on Capital Punishment proposed: [A person is not responsible for his unlawful act if] at the time of the act the accused was suffering

from disease of the mind (or mental deficiency) *to such a degree that he ought not to be held responsible.*

24. The minority, together with the Reporter for the Model Penal Code (Professor Herbert Wechsler), propsed the following test of insanity:

A person is not responsible for criminal conduct if at the time of such conduct as a result of mental disease or defect his capacity either to appreciate the criminality of his conduct or to conform his conduct to the requirements of law is *so substantially impaired that he cannot justly be held responsible.*

This proposal appears as alternative (a) to paragraph (1) of Model Penal Code § 4.01 (Tent. Draft No. 4, 1955) (emphasis added).

25. See authorities cited *supra,* note 6.

26. See, for example, Szasz, Psychiatry, Ethics and the Criminal Law, 58 Colum.L.Rev. 183, 195 (1958) "[To] have a 'psychopathic' personality is only a more elegant way of expressing moral condemnation." See also, Star, "The Public's Ideas About Mental Illness" (National Opinion Research Center, 1955); H. Kalven and H. Zeisel, The American Jury 405 (1966).

27. He proposes (Br. 78) an instruction with this crucial sentence: "It is up to you to decide whether defendant had such an abnormal mental condition, and if he did whether the impairment was substantial enough, and was so related to the commission of the crime, *that he ought not be held responsible.*" (Emphasis added.).

28. A Goldstein, The Insanity Defense 81–82 (1967).

29. See H. Kalven and H. Zeisel. The American Jury (1966), passim, and particularly Chapters 5, 8, 12, 15 et seq. See also, Rifkind, Follow-up: The Jury. The Center Magazine 59, 64 (July, 1970).

30. See for example, the response of the Attorney General in Ramer v. United States, 390 F.2d 564, 575, n. 10 (9th Cir. en banc, 1968).

31. See ch. 7, section III: The Mentally Ill Offender, subsection "Experience Under the Durham Rule," at p. 534 ff of the Report, including Tables 1–10.

32. *McDonald* was decided in 1962. For fiscal years ending June 30, 1964–1970, there were 21 verdicts of not guilty by reason of insanity in trials by jury, 265 such verdicts in trials by court. These data appear in Appendix C of Mr. Dempsey's brief, as revised by submission of Sept. 21, 1971.

Mr. Dempsey provides data on all terminations for fiscal 1964–1968. The data for these five years show 7537 terminations, and 194 verdicts of not guilty by reason of insanity. The other terminations are: 3500 verdicts of guilty on plea, 1567 verdicts of guilty after trial, and 629 verdicts of not guilty.

33. These trials are discussed in the amicus submission of David Chambers, consultant, who prepared a report on the John Howard Pavilion at St. Elizabeths Hospital, submitted to the Hospital and the National Institutes of Mental Health. Professor Chambers characterizes most insanity trials to the courts as more nearly comparable to the taking of guilty pleas—consisting of a stipulated statement of facts; a conclusory Hospital report that the crime was the product of mental illness; and brief supporting testimony from a single John Howard psychiatrist—all in a context of a "tacit or explicit understanding" that the defendant will not contest his indefinite commitment to the Hospital.

34. Any such analysis of the productivity testimony and verdicts nor only would require prodigious time and effort, but might well be inconclusive in view of the way experts testifying on the "product" issues come to diametric differences in the same trial.

35. We do not share the cynical view that treats the instruction as devoid of consequence. In a study of the reactions of more than a thousand jurors to two experimental trials involving a defense of insanity, it was found that juries deliberated significantly longer when instructed under *Durham* than under *M'Naghten.* Yet this did not undercut consensus; there was no significant difference in the percentages of hung juries. R. Simon, The Jury and the Defense of Insanity 213 *ff.* (1967).

36. See the opinion of Trask, J., for six of the 13 judges on the Ninth Circuit, in Wade v. United States, 426 F.2d 64, 75, 79.

37. Mr. Dempsey is concerned lest the ALI test assigns responsibility unless capacity has been reduced "to the vagrant and trivial dimensions characteristic of the most severe afflictions of the mind," *see* Wechsler, Codification of Criminal Law in the United States: The Model Penal Code, 68 Colum.L.Rev. 1425. 1443 (1968). But the application in fact will depend in the last analysis on the jury's application of community standards to the evidence adduced.

38. Even under *McDonald* the jury has frequently brought in a verdict of guilty, when the exculpatory rules would plainly permit, or even contemplate, a verdict of not guilty by reason of insanity. King v. United States, *supra.*

39. Defendant is also exculpated if he lacks substantial capacity to appreciate the conduct is wrongful.

40. In *M'Naghten's* case, 10 Cl. & F. 200, 211, 8 Eng.Rep. 718, 722 (H.L.1843), the majority opinion of Lord Chief Justice Tindal ruled that the jury should be instructed in terms of the ability of the accused "to know that he was doing an act that was wrong." adding: "If the question were to be put as to the knowledge of the accused solely and exclusively with reference to the law of the land, it might tend to confound the jury, by inducing them to be believe that an actual knowledge of the law of the land was essential in order to lead to a conviction."

When the question arose as to whether "wrong" means moral or legal wrong, the American courts split. One group, following *M'Naghten,* held the offender sane if he knew the act was prohibited by law. A second group, following the lead of Judge Cardozo in People v. Schmidt, 216 N.Y. 324, 110 N.E. 945, 948–950 (1915) ruled that, for example, the defense was available to a defendant who knew the killing was legally wrong but thought it morally right because he was so ordered by God. The issue is discussed and authorities collected in A. Goldstein, The Insanity Defense, and notes thereto. In Sauer v. United States, 241 F.2d 640, 649 (9th Circ. 1957), Judge Barnes summed up the practicalities: "[The] practice has been to state merely the word 'wrong' and leave the decision for the jury. While not entirely condonable, such practice is explained in large measure by an awareness that the jury will eventually exercise a moral judgment as to the sanity of the accused."

This issue rarely arose under *M'Naghten,* and its substantiality was reduced if not removed by the control capacity test, since anyone under a delusion as to God's mandate would presumably lack substantial capacity to conform his conduct to the requirements of the law.

We are not informed of any case where a mental illness left a person with capacity to appreciate wrongfulness but not a capacity to appreciate criminality. If such a case ever arises, supported by credible evidence, the court can then consider its correct disposition more meaningfully, in the light of a concrete record.

41. See Comments to Fourth Draft, p. 160:

6. Paragraph (2) of section 4.01 is designed to exclude from the concept of "mental disease or

defect" the case of so-called "psychopathic personality." The reason for the exclusion is that, as the Royal Commission put it, psychopathy "is a statistical abnormality: that is to say, the psychopath differs from a normal person only quantitatively or in degree, nor qualitatively: and the diagnosis of psychopathic personality does not carry with it any explanation of the causes of the abnormality." While it may not be feasible to formulate a definition of "disease," there is much to be said for excluding a condition that is manifested only by the behavior phenomena that must, by hypothesis, be the result of disease for irresponsibility to be established. Although British psychiatrists had agreed, on the whole, that psychopathy should not be called "disease," there is considerable difference of opinion on the point in the United States. Yet it does not seem useful to contemplate the litigation of what is essentially a matter of terminology: nor is it right to have the legal result rest upon the resolution of a dispute of this kind.

42.   We note that the Second Circuit adopted the caveat paragraph on the ground that

a contrary holding would reduce to absurdity a test designed to encourage full analysis of all psychiatric data and would exculpate those who knowingly and deliberately seek a life of crime. (*Freeman,* 357 F.2d at 625).

43.   See, for example, D. Abrahamsen, Who Are the Guilty? 125 (1952).

44.   Jenkins v. United States, 113 U.S. App.D.C. 300, 307 F.2d 637 (en banc, 1962) (assuming substantial experience in the diagnosis of disease in association with psychiatrists or neurologists).

45.   For example, the opinions in *Durham, Carter, McDonald* and *Washington,* and Judge Burger's concurring opinion in *Blocker.*

46.   Pope v. United States, 372 F.2d 710, 736 (8th Cir. 1967).

47.   The Association points out that "the effects of poverty, historical factors and prejudice may well have an adverse effect upon an individual's mental condition."

52.   Our doctrine is different from the doctrine of "partial responsibility" that permits a jury to find that a defendant's mental condition was such that he is only "partly responsible," and therefore entitled to a verdict reducing the degree of the offense. See Model Penal Code, Comments to Art. 201, app. B at 111 (Tentative Draft No. 9, 1959), quoting the English Homicide Act of 1957, 5 & 6 Eliz. 2, c. 11.

53.   The term "malice" in second degree murder has been extended to include recklessness where defendant had awareness of a serious danger to life and displayed wanton disregard for human life. Lee v. United States, 72 App.D.C. 147, 150–151, 112 F.2d 46, 49–50 (1949): Austin v. United States, *supra,* 127 U.S.AppD.C. at 184, 382 F.2d at 133; United States v. Dixon, 135 U.S.App.D.C. 401, 405, 419 F.2d 288, 292 (1969) (concurring opinion).

54.   There was no independent consideration in Stewart v. United States, 129 U.S.App.D.C. 303, 394 F.2d 778 (1968), which was not an en banc court, and merely cited the earlier cases.

55.   People v. Nicolaus, 65 Cal.2d 866, 56 Cal.Rptr. 635, 423 P.2d 787 (1967); People v. Goedecke, 65 Cal.2d 850, 56 Cal.Rptr. 625, 423 P.2d 777 (1967); People v. Ford, 65 Cal.2d 41, 52 Cal.Rptr. 228, 416 P.2d 132 (1966); People v. Conley, 64 Cal.2d 310, 49 Cal.Rptr. 815, 411 P.2d 795, 40 Cal.Rptr. 271, 394 P.2d 959 (1964); People v. Gorshen, 51 Cal.2d 716, 336 P.2d 492 (1959); People v. Wells, 33 Cal.2d 330, 202 P.2d 53 (1949).

56.   Schwickrath v. People. 159 Colo. 390, 411 P.2d 961 (1966); Gallegos v. People, 159 Colo. 379, 411 P.2d 956 (1966); Becksted v. People, 133 Colo. 72, 292 P.2d 189 (1956); Battalino v. People, 118 Colo. 587, 199 P.2d 897 (1948); Ingles v. People, 95 Colo. 518, 22 P.2d 1109 (1933).

57.   State v. Di Paolo, 34 N.J. 279, 168 A.2d 401 (1961), clarified in State v. Sikora, 44 N.J. 453, 210 A.2d 193 (1965).

58.   State v. Gramenz, 256 Iowa 134, 126 N.W.2d 285 (1964).

59.   State v. Nichols, 3 Ohio App.2d 182, 209 N.E.2d 750 (1965).

60.   State v. Clokey, 83 Idaho 322, 364 P.2d 159 (1961).

61.   State v. Donahue, 141 Conn. 656, 109 A.2d 364 (1954).

62.   Starkweather v. State, 167 Neb. 477, 93 N.W.2d 619 (1958).

63.   State v. Padilla, 66 N.M. 289, 347 P.2d 312 (1959).

64.   Fox v. State, 73 Nev. 241, 316 P.2d 924 (1957).

65.   New York, People v. Moran, 249 N.Y. 179, 163 N.E. 553 (1928); Rhode Island, State v. Fenik, 45 R.I. 309, 121 A. 218 (1923); Utah, State v. Green, 78 Utah 580, 6 P.2d 177 (1931); Wisconsin, Hempton v. State, 111 Wis. 127, 86 N.W. 596 (1901) and Wyoming, State v. Pressler, 16 Wyo. 214, 92 P. 806 (1907).

66.   Battalino v. People, 118 Colo. 587, 199 P.2d 897, 901 (1948).

67.   State v. Janovic, 101 Ariz. 203, 417 P.2d 527 (1966); Armstead v. State. 227 Md. 73, 175 A.2d 24 (1961); State v. Flint, 142 W.Va. 509, 96 S.E.2d 677 (1957); Ezzell v. State, 88 So.2d 280 (Fla.1956).

68.   127 U.S.App.D.C. at 189–190, 382 F.2d at 138–139.

69.   *See* Belton v. United States, 127 U.S.App.D.C. 201, 203, 382 F.2d 150, 152 (1967).

70.   78 Stat. 944 (1960), 21D.C.Code § 501 et seq.

71.   Millard v. Harris, 132 U.S.App. D.C. 146, 150, 406 F.2d 964, 968 (1968).

72.   In re Alexander, 124 U.S.App.D.C. 352, 372 F.2d 925 (1967).

73.   Lake v. Cameron, 124 U.S.App.D.C. 264, 364 F.2d 657 (1966).

75.   S.Rep.No.925, 88th Cong., 2d sess., 31 (1964).

Suggestions for Further Reading

Allen, F. A., *The Borderland of Criminal Justice* (1964)

American Law Institute, *Model Penal Code, Pt. I, Porposed Official Draft* (1962).

American Law Institute, *Restatement of the Law of Torts* (1934), and supplements (1948, 1954).

Anderson, J., "The Problem of Causality," *Australasian Jour. of Phil.,* Vol. 16, (1938), pp. 127–42.

Brant, Richard, "A Utilitarian Theory of Excuses," *Philosophical Review,* Vol. 78 (1969), pp. 337–361.

Cohen, M. R., "Moral Aspects of the Criminal Law," 49 *Yale L.J.* 987 (1940), pp. 128–129.

Comment, "Admissibility of Subjective Abnormality to Disprove Criminal Mental States," 12 *Stan. L. Rev.* 226 (1959), pp. 588–589.

Comment Note, "Mental or Emotional Condition as Diminishing Responsibility for Crime," 22 *A.L.R.* 3d 1228 (1968).

Dershowitz, Alan M., "Psychiatry in the Legal Process: A Knife That Cuts Both Ways," 4 *Trial* 29 (1968).

Edgerton, H., "Legal Cause," 72 *U. of Pa. L. Rev.,* 211–44, 343–75 (1924).

Feinberg, Joel, "Causing Voluntary Actions", in *Doing and Deserving* (1970), pp. 152–186.

Feinberg, Joel, "Crime, Clutchability, and Individuated Treatment," in *Doing and Deserving* (1970), pp. 252–71.

Feinberg, Joel, "What Is So Special About Mental Illness?" in *Doing and Deserving* (1970), pp. 272–92.

Feldbrugge, F. J. M. "Good and Bad Samaritans, A Comparative Study of Criminal Law Provisions Concerning Failure to Rescue," 14 *Am. J. Comp. L.* 630 (1966).

Fine and Cohen, "Is Criminal Negligence a Defensible Basis for Penal Liability?" 16 *Buffalo L. Rev.* 749 (1967).

Fingarette, H., "The Concept of Mental Disease in Criminal Law Insanity Tests," 33 *U. Chi. L. Rev.* 229 (1966).

Fitzgerald, P. J., "Voluntary and Involuntary Acts" in *Oxford Essays in Jurisprudence,* ed. A. G. Guest (1961).

Fletcher, George P., "Fairness and Utility in Tort Theory," 85 *Harv. L. Rev.* 537 (1972).

Fletcher, George P., "Theory of Criminal Negligence: A Comparative Analysis," 119 *U. Pa. L. Rev.* 401 (1971).

Friedrich, C. J., ed. *Nomos III, Responsibility* (1960).

Glover, Jonathan, *Responsibility* (1970)

Goldstein, A., *The Insanity Defense* (1967).

Goldstein, J., and Katz, J. "Abolish the 'Insanity Defense'—Why Not?" 72 *Yale L. J.* 853 (1963).

Green, L., "Are Negligence and 'Proximate' Cause Determined by the Same Text?" 1 *Texas L. Rev.,* 242–60, 423–45 (1923).

Gregory, C. O., "Proximate Cause in Negligence—A Retreat from Rationalization,'" 6 *Univ. of Chi. L. Rev.,* 36 (1938).

Griffiths, John, "Ideology in Criminal Procedure," 79 *Yale L. J.* 359 (1970).

Gross, Hyman, "Some Unacceptable Excuses," 19 *Wayne L. Rev.* 997 (1973).

Hall, J., *General Principles of Criminal Law 2d ed. (1960).*

Hall, J., "Negligent Behavior Should Be Excluded from Penal Liability," 63 *Colum. L. Rev.* 632 (1963).

Halleck, Seymour L., *Psychiatry and the Dilemmas of Crime* (1967).

Harper, F. V., "Liability Without Fault and Proximate Cause," 30 *Michigan L. Rev.,* 1001 (1932).

Hart, H. L. A., Review of *Crime and the Criminal Law* by Barbara Wootton, 74 *Yale L. J.* 1325 (1965).

Hart, H. L. A., *The Morality of the Criminal Law* (1964).

Hart, H. L. A., *Punishment and Responsibility* (1968).

Holmes, Oliver W., Jr., *The Common Law, Lectures I, II, III* (1881).

Howard, Colin, *Strict Liability* (1963).

Hughes, Graham, "Criminal Omissions," 67 *Yale L. J.* 590 (1958).

James, F., Jr. "The Nature of Negligence," 3 *Utah L. Rev.,* 275 (1953).

James, F., Jr. and R. F. Perry, "Legal Cause," 60 *Yale L. J.* 761 (1954).

Kadish, S. H., "The Decline of Innocence," 26 *Camb. L. J.* 273 (1968).

Kelsen, H., "Causality and Retribution," in *What is Justice?* (1957).

Kenny, Anthony, "Intention and Purpose," *Journal of Philosophy*, Vol. 63 (1966), pp. 642–651.

Lewis, H. D., "Collective Responsibility," *Philosophy*, Vol. 23 (1948), pp. 3–18.

Livermore, J. M. and P. E. Meehl, "The Virtues of M'Naghten," 51 *Minn. L. Rev.* 789 (1967).

Louisell, D. W. and G. C. Hazard, "Insanity as a Defense: The Bifurcated Trial," 49 *Calif. L. Rev.* 805 (1961).

Lyons, David, "On Sanctioning Excuses," *Journal of Philosophy*, Vol. 66 (1969), pp. 646–660.

Macaulay and Other Indian Law Commissioners, *A Penal Code Prepared by the Indian Law Commissioners* (1837).

Michael, J., and H. Wechsler, *Criminal Law and Its Administration* (1940).

Moreland, R., "Rationale of Criminal Negligence," 32 *Kentucky L. J.*, 1–40, 127–92, 221–61 (1943–44).

Morris, Herbert, ed., *Freedom and Responsibility* (1961).

Morris, Herbert, "Punishment for Thoughts," 49 *The Monist* 342 (1965).

Note, "Amnesia: A Case Study in the Limits of Particular Justice," 71 *Yale L. J.* 109 (1961).

Note, "Justification for the Use of Force in the Criminal Law," 13 *Stan. L. Rev.* 506 (1961).

Packer, H. "Mens Rea and the Supreme Court," (1962) *Sup. Ct. Rev.* 107.

Plamenatz, J., "Responsibility, Blame and Punishment" in *Philosophy, Politics, and Society* (ed. P. Laslett and W. G. Runciman, 1967).

Prosser, W. L., *Handbook of the Law of Torts*, 2d. ed. (1955).

Ratcliff, James M. ed., *The Good Samaritan and the Law* (1966).

Sayre, F. B., "Criminal Attempts," 41 *Harv. L. Rev.* 55 (1933).

Silber, J. "Being and Doing: A Study of Status Responsibility and Voluntary Responsibility," 35 *U. Chi. L. Rev.* 47 (1967).

Szasz, Thomas S., *Law, Liberty, and Psychiatry* (1962).

Wasserstrom, Richard, "H. L. A. Hart and the Doctrines of Mens Rea and Criminal Responsibility," 35 *U. Chi. L. Rev.* 92 (1967).

Wasserstrom, Richard "Strict Liability in the Criminal Law" 12 *Stan. L. Rev.* 730 (1960).

Wechsler, H. and J. Michael, "A Rationale of the Law of Homicide," 37 *Colum. L. Rev.* 701 (1937).

Williams, G., "Absolute Liability in Traffic Offenses," [1967] *Crim. L. Rev.* 194.

Williams, G., "Causation in Homicide," [1957] *Crim. L. Rev.* 429.

Williams, G., *The Mental Element in Crime* (1965).

Wootton, Barbara, "Diminished Responsibility: A Layman's View," 76 *Law Quarterly Review* (1960).

Wootton, Barbara, *Social Science and Social Pathology*, Part II (1959).

The traditional debate among philosophers over the justification of legal punishment has been between partisans of the "retributive" and "utilitarian" theories. Neither the term "retributive" nor the term "utilitarian" has been used with perfect uniformity and precision, but by and large, those have been called utilitarians who have insisted that punishment of the guilty is at best a necessary evil justified only as a means to the prevention of evils even greater than itself. "Retributivism," on the other hand, has been the name of a large miscellany of theories united only in their opposition to the utilitarian theory. It may well best serve clarity, therefore, to define the utilitarian theory with relative precision (as above) and then define retributivism as its logical contradictory, so that the two theories are not only mutually exclusive but jointly exhaustive as well. Discussion of the various varieties of retributivism can then proceed.

Perhaps the leading form of the retributive theory is that whose major elements are caught in the following formulations:

It is an end in itself that the guilty should suffer pain ... The primary justification of punishment is always to be found in the fact that an offense has been committed which deserves the punishment, not in any future advantage to be gained by its infliction.[1]

Punishment is justified only on the ground that wrongdoing merits punishment. It is morally fitting that a person who does wrong should suffer in proportion to his wrongdoing. That a criminal should be punished follows from his guilt, and the severity of the appropriate punishment depends on the depravity of the act. The state of affairs where a wrongdoer suffers punishment is morally better than one where he does not, and is so irrespective of consequences.[2]

Justification, according to these accounts, must look backward in time to guilt rather than forward to "advantages"; the formulations are rich in moral terminology ("merits," "morally fitting," "wrongdoing," "morally better"); there is great emphasis on *desert*. For those reasons, we might well refer to this as a "moralistic" version of the retributive theory. As such it can be contrasted with a "legalistic" version, according to which punishment is for lawbreaking, not (necessarily) for wrongdoing. Legalistic retributivism holds that the justification of punishment is always to be found in the fact that a rule has been broken for the violation of which a certain penalty is specified, whether or not the offender incurs any moral guilt. The offender, properly apprised in advance of the penalty, voluntarily assumes the risk of punishment, and when he receives his comeuppance, he can have no complaint. As one recent legalistic retributivist put it,

> Punishment is a corollary not of law but of lawbreaking. Legislators do not choose to punish. They hope no punishment will be needed. Their laws would succeed even if no punishment occurred. The criminal makes the essential choice: he "brings it on himself."[3]

Both moralistic and legalistic retributivism have "pure" and "impure" variants. In their pure formulations, they are totally free of utilitarian admixture. Moral or legal guilt (as the case may be) is not only a necessary condition for justified punishment, it is quite sufficient "irrespective of consequences." In the impure formulation, both guilt (moral or legal) and conducibility to good consequences are necessary for justified punishment, but neither is sufficient without the other. This mixed theory could with some propriety be called "impure utilitarianism" as well as "impure retributivism," but since we have stipulated that a retributive theory is one which is not wholly utilitarian, we are committed to the latter usage.

A complete theory of punishment will not only specify the conditions under which punishment should and should not be administered; it will also provide a general criterion for determining the amount or degree of punishment. It is not only unjust to be punished undeservedly and to be let off although meriting punishment; it is also unfair to be punished severely for a minor offense or lightly for a heinous one. What is the right amount of punishment? There is one kind of answer especially distinctive of retributivism in all of its forms: an answer in terms of fittingness or proportion. The punishment must *fit* the crime; its degree must be *proportionate* to the seriousness or moral gravity of the offense. Retributivists are often understandably vague about the practical interpretations of the key notions of fittingness, proportion, and moral gravity. Sometimes aesthetic analogies are employed (such as matching and clashing colors, or harmonious and dissonant chords). Some retributivists, including Immanuel Kant, attempt to apply the ancient principle of *lex talionis* (the law of retaliation), that the punishment should match the crime not only in the degree of harm inflicted on its victim, but also in the mode and manner of infliction: fines for larceny, physical beatings for battery, capital punishment for murder. Other retributivists, however, explicitly reject the doctrine of retaliation in kind; hence that doctrine is better treated as a logically independent thesis commonly associated with retributivism than as an essential component of the theory.

Defined as the exhaustive class of alternatives to the utilitarian theory, retributivism of course is subject to no simple summary. It will be useful to subsequent discussion, however, to summarize that popular variant of the theory which can be called *pure moralistic retributivism* as consisting (at least) of the following propositions:

1. Moral guilt is a necessary condition for justified punishment.
2. Moral guilt is a sufficient condition ("irrespective of consequences") for justified punishment.
3. The proper amount of punishment to be inflicted upon the morally guilty offender is that amount which fits, matches, or is proportionate to the moral gravity of the offense.

That it is never justified to punish a morally blameless person for his "offense" (thesis 1) may not be quite self-evident, but it does find strong support in moral common sense. Thesis 2, however, is likely to prove an embarrassment for the pure retributivist, for it would have him approve the infliction of suffering on a person (albeit a *guilty* person) even when no good to the offender, his victim, or society at large is likely to result. "How can two wrongs make a right, or two evils a good?" he will be asked by the utilitarian, and in this case it is the utilitarian who will claim to speak for "moral common sense." In reply, the pure retributivist is likely to concede that inflicting suffering on an offender is not "good in itself," but will also point out that single acts cannot be judged simply "in themselves" with no concern for the context in which they fit and the events proceding them which are their occasion. Personal sadness is not a "good in itself" either, and yet when it is a response to the perceived sufferings of another it has a unique appropriateness. Glee, considered "in itself," looks much more like an intrinsically good mental state, but glee does not morally fit the perception of another's pain any more than an orange shirt aesthetically fits shocking pink trousers. Similarly, it may be true (the analogy is admittedly imperfect) that "while the moral evil in the offender and the pain of the punishment are each considered separately evils, it is intrinsically good that a certain relation exist or be established between them."[4] In this way the pure retributivist, relying on moral intuitions, can deny that a deliberate imposition of suffering on a human being is either good in itself or good as a means, and yet find it justified, nevertheless, as an essential component of an intrinsically good relation. Perhaps that is to put the point too strongly. All the retributivist needs to establish is that the complex situation preceding the infliction of punishment can be made better than it otherwise would be by the addition to it of the offender's suffering.

The utilitarian is not only unconvinced by arguments of this kind, he is also likely to find a "suspicious connection" between philosophical retributivism and the primitive lust for vengeance. The moralistic retributivist protests that he eschews anger or any other passion and seeks not revenge, but justice and the satisfaction of desert. Punishment, after all, is not the only kind of treatment we bestow upon persons simply because we think they deserve it. Teachers give students the grades they have earned with no thought of "future advantage," and with eyes firmly fixed on past performance. There is no necessary jubilation at good performance or vindictive pleasure in assigning low grades. And much the same is true of the assignments of rewards, prizes, grants, compensation, civil liability, and so on. Justice requires assignment on the basis of desert alone. To be sure, there is

a great danger of revengeful and sadistic tendencies finding vent under the unconscious disguise of a righteous indignation calling for just punishment, since the evil desire for revenge, if not identical with the latter, bears a resemblance to it sufficiently close to deceive those who want an excuse.[5]

Indeed, it is commonly thought that our modern notions of retributive justice have grown out of earlier practices, like the vendetta and the law of deodand, that were through and through expressions of the urge to vengeance.[6] Still, the retributivist replies, it is unfair to *identify* a belief with one of its corruptions, or a modern practice with its historical antecedents. The latter mistake is an instance of the "genetic fallacy" which is committed whenever one confuses an account of how a thing came to be the way it is with an analysis of the thing it has become.

The third thesis of the pure moralistic retributivist has also been subject to heavy attack. Can it really be the business of the state to see to it that happiness and unhappiness are distributed among citizens in proportion to their moral deserts? Think of the practical difficulties involved in the attempt simply to apportion pain to moral guilt in a given case, with no help from utilitarian considerations. First of all, it is usually impossible to punish an offender without inflicting suffering on those who love or depend upon him and may themselves be entirely innocent, morally speaking. In that way punishing the guilty is self-defeating from the moralistic retributive point of view. It will do more to increase than to diminish the disproportion between unhappiness and desert throughout society. Secondly, the aim of apportioning pain to guilt would in some cases require punishing "trivial" moral offenses, like rudeness, as heavily as more socially harmful crimes, since there can be as much genuine wickedness in the former as the latter. Thirdly, there is the problem of accumulation. Deciding the right amount of suffering to inflict in a given case would entail an assessment of the character of the offender as manifested throughout his whole life (and not simply at one weak moment) and also an assessment of his total lifelong balance of pleasure and pain. Moreover, there are inevitably inequalities of moral guilt in the commission of the same crime by different offenders, as well as inequalities of suffering from the same punishment. Application of the pure retributive theory then would require the abandonment of fixed penalties for various crimes and the substitution of individuated penalities selected in each case by an authority to fit the offender's uniquely personal guilt and vulnerability.

The utilitarian theory of punishment holds that punishment is never good in itself, but is (like bad-tasting medicine) justified when, and only when, it is a means to such future goods as *correction* (reform) of the offender, *protection* of society against other offenses from the same offender, and *deterrence* of other would-be offenders. (The list is not exhaustive.) Giving the offender the pain he deserves because of his wickedness is either not a coherent notion, on this theory, or else not a morally respectable independent reason for punishing. In fact, the utilitarian theory arose in the eighteenth century as part of a conscious reaction to cruel and uneconomical social institutions (including prisons) that were normally defended, if at all, in righteously moralistic terms.

For purposes of clarity, the utilitarian theory of punishment should be distinguished from utilitarianism as a general moral theory. The standard of right conduct generally, according to the latter, is conducibility to good consequences. Any act at all, whether that of a private citizen, a legislator, or a judge, is morally right if and only if it is likely, on the best evidence, to do more good or less harm all around than any alternative conduct open to the actor. (The standard for judging the goodness of consequences, in turn, for Jeremy Bentham and the early utilitarians was the amount of human happiness they contained, but many later utilitarians had more complicated conceptions of intrinsic value.) All proponents of general utilitarianism, of course, are also supporters of the utilitarian theory of punishment, but there is no logical necessity that a utilitarian in respect to punishment be a general utilitarian across the board.

The utilitarian theory of punishment can be summarized in three propositions parallel to those used above to summarize pure moralistic retributivism. According to this theory:

1. Social utility (correction, prevention, deterrence, etcetera) is a necessary condition for justified punishment.
2. Social utility is a sufficient condition for justified punishment.
3. The proper amount of punishment to be inflicted upon the offender is that amount which will do the most good or the least harm to all those who will be affected by it.

The first thesis enjoys the strongest support from common sense, though not so strong as to preclude controversy. For the retributivist, as has been seen, punishing the guilty is an end in itself quite apart from any gain in social utility. The utilitarian is apt to reply that if he could secure reform of the criminal with no loss of deterrence by simply giving him a pill that would have that effect, then nothing would be lost by not punishing him, and the substitute treatment would be "sheer gain."

Thesis 2, however, is the utilitarian's greatest embarrassment. His retributivist opponent argues forcefully against it that in certain easily imaginable circumstances it would justify punishment of the (legally) innocent, a consequence which all would regard as a moral abomination. Some utilitarians deny that punishment of the innocent could *ever* be the alternative that has the best consequences in social utility, but this reply seems arbitrary and dogmatic. Other utilitarians claim that "punishment of the innocent" is a self-contradiction. The concept of punishment, they argue,[7] itself implies hard treatment imposed upon the guilty as a conscious and deliberate response to their guilt. That guilt is part of the very definition of punishment, these writers claim, is shown by the absurdity of saying "I am punishing you for something you have not done," which sounds very much like "I am curing you even though you are not sick." Since all punishment is understood to be for guilt, they conclude, they can hardly be understood to be advocating punishing without guilt. H. L. A. Hart[8] calls this move a "definitional stop," and charges that it is an "abuse of definition," and indeed it is, if put forward by a proponent of the general utilitarian theory. If the right act in all contexts is the one which is likely to have the best consequences, then conceivably the act of framing an innocent man could sometimes be right; and the question of whether such mistreatment of the innocent party could properly be called "punishment" is a mere question of words having no bearing on the utilitarian's embarrassment. If, on the other hand, the definitional stop is employed by a defender of the utilitarian theory of the justification of punishment who is not a utilitarian across the board, then it seems to be a legitimate argumentative move. Such a utilitarian is defending official infliction of hard treatment (deprivation of liberty, suffering, et cetera) on *those who are legally guilty,* a practice to which he refers by using the word "punishment," as justified when and only when there is probable social utility in it.

No kind of utilitarian, however, will have plausible recourse to the definitional stop in defending thesis 3 from the retributivist charge that it would, in certain easily imaginable circumstances, justify excessive and/or insufficient penalties. The appeal again is to moral common sense: It would be manifestly unfair to inflict a mere two dollar fine on a convicted murderer or life imprisonment, under a balance of terror policy, for parking offenses. In either case, the punishment imposed would violate the retributivist's thesis 3, that the punishment be proportional to the moral gravity of the offense. And yet, if these were the penalties likely to have the best effects generally, the utilitarian in the theory of punishment would be committed to their support. He could not argue that excessive or deficient penalties are not "really" punishments. Instead he would have to argue, as Jeremy Bentham and Stanley Benn do with great subtlety and conviction in their writings included here, that the proper employment of the utilitarian method simply could not lead to penalties so far out of line with our moral intuitions as the retributivist charges.

So far vengeance has not been mentioned except in the context of charge and countercharge between theorists who have no use for it. There are writers, however, who have kind words for vengeance and give it a central role in their theories of the justification of punishment. We can call these approaches the Vindictive Theory of Punishment (to distinguish them from legalistic and moralistic forms of retributivism) and then subsume its leading varieties under either the utilitarian or the retributive rubrics. Vindictive theories are of three different kinds: (1) The *escape-valve version,* commonly associated with the names of James Fitzjames Stephen and Oliver Wendell Holmes, Jr., and currently in favor with some psychoanalytic writers, holds that legal punishment is an orderly outlet for aggressive feelings, which would otherwise demand satisfaction in socially disruptive ways. The prevention of private vendettas through a state monopoly on vengeance is one of the chief ways in which legal punishment has social utility. The escape-valve theory is thus easily assimilated by the utilitarian theory of punishment. (2) The *hedonistic version* of the vindictive theory finds the justification of punishment in the pleasure it gives people (particularly the victim of the crime and his loved ones) to see the criminal suffer for his crime. For most utilitarians, and certainly for Bentham, any kind of pleasure—even spiteful, sadistic, or vindictive pleasure, just insofar as it *is* pleasure—counts as a good in the computation of social utility, just as pain—any kind of pain—counts as an evil. (This is sufficient to discredit hedonistic utilitarianism thoroughly, according to its retributivist critics). The hedonistic version of the vindictive theory, then, is also subsumable under the utilitarian rubric. Finally, (3) the *romantic version* of the vindictive theory, very popular among the uneducated, holds that the justification of punishment is to be found in the emotions of hate and anger it expresses, these emotions being those allegedly felt by all normal or right-thinking people. I call this theory "romantic," despite certain misleading associations of that word, because, like any theory so labeled, it holds that certain emotions and the actions they inspire are self-certifying, needing no further justification. It is therefore not a kind of utilitarian theory and must be classified as a variety of retributivism, although in its emphasis on feeling it is in marked contrast to more typical retributive theories that eschew emotion and emphasize proportion and desert.

Many anthropologists have traced vindictive feelings and judgments to an origin in the "tribal morality" which universally prevails in primitive cultures, and which presumably governed the tribal life of our own prehistoric ancestors. If an anthropologist turned his attention to our modern criminal codes, he would discover evidence that tribalism has never entirely vacated its position in the criminal law. There are some provisions for which the vindictive theory (in any of its forms) would provide a ready rationale, but for which the utilitarian and moralistic retributivist theories are hard put to discover a plausible defense. Completed crimes, for example, are punished more severely than attempted crimes that fail for accidental reasons. This should not be surprising since the more harm caused the victim, his loved ones, and those of the public who can identify imaginatively with him, the more anger there will be at the criminal. If the purpose of punishment is to satisfy that anger, then we should expect that those who succeed in harming will be punished more than the bunglers who fail, even if the motives and intentions of the bunglers were every bit as wicked.

The classical sources of the retributive theory, at least in the modern period, are in the writings of the great German philosophers, Immanuel Kant (1724–1804) and Georg Wilhelm Friedrich Hegel (1770–1831). Those writings in their English translations are notoriously difficult and obscure, and yet their historical influence, particularly on the development of retributivism in Great Britain and America, is undeniable. This section opens with a remarkably perspicuous interpretation of Kant, Hegel, and the classical retributive theory from the important recent book, *The Rationale of Legal Punishment,* by Edmund Pincoffs. The classical source of the utilitarian theory of punishment, and indeed of the general utilitarian ethical theory as well, is *Introduction to the Principles of Morals and Legislation* by Jeremy Bentham, first published in 1776. Bentham's prose is clear and his approach unmetaphysical, so he is quite able to speak for himself to the modern student. Bentham refers often to "the principle of utility," his supreme moral principle. He does not formally define that principle in his selection here, but it finds essential expression in his first sentence: "The general object which all laws . . . ought to have . . . is to augment the total happiness of the community . . ." Bentham proceeds to apply that principle to the determination of those actions which ought, and those which ought not, to be crimes, and to the problems of selecting penalties to go with the various crimes and the various circumstances in which crimes are committed. The selection from Bentham presents the classic utilitarian interpretation of the maxim made so much of by retributivists, that the punishment should fit the crime.

The American courts have had a difficult time determining the constitutional relevance of the moral requirement that the severity of punishment should be proportional to the moral gravity of the offense. Some courts have held that the Eighth Amendment's ban on cruel and unusual punishments proscribes, among other things, heavy fines and long imprisonments for offenses that are relatively trivial from the moral point of view. (On this view, the United States Constitution could be understood as incorporating some of the strictures of Kantian retributivism). Many more courts have held, on the other hand, that the Eighth Amendment proscribes only modes and types of punishment that are physically torturous, but implies nothing about the necessity for proportionality between the offense and the duration of a "noncruel" mode of punishment such as imprisonment. In the 1909 United State Supreme Court case of *Weems v. United States*, the court overturned the conviction of Weems on the grounds that the minimum sentence specified in the statute he violated was patently disproportionate to the gravity of his offense, thus violating the Eighth Amendment's ban on cruel and unusual punishments. The fault being in the law and not in the sentence delivered by the lower court, and there being no other law under which sentence could be imposed, the Court found that it had no choice but to declare the law void and order the prisoner released. In a vigorous dissenting opinion, Mr. Justice White argued that a legislature is not restricted to the matter of proportionality in specifying the penalties in criminal statutes, but may (indeed must) consider "local conditions" and how they affect the achievement of the law's purposes. He then enumerates various factors that philosophers have called "utilitarian considerations": How widespread is the tendency at a given time and place to commit the offense in question, the difficulty or ease of detecting such crimes, and "how far it is necessary to impose stern remedies to prevent" their commission. The reader should compare and contrast this list of relevent factors with that contained in the majority opinion of Mr. Justice McKenna. (The Philippine statute, as evidenced by such terms as *cadena temporal*,—"temporary chains"—was of Spanish origin, but was revalidated as law by the United States Congress which assumed jurisdiction when the Philippines became part of the territories of the United States following the Spanish-American War of 1898. The Philippine Bill of Rights was pronounced at that time to be identically the same as that in the United States Constitution.)

Each of the next three items in this section is in its own way concerned, among other things, with the feelings or attitudes that may be expressed in an act of punishment, or indeed essentially expressed in the very institution of punishment. The Anglican Bishop and philosopher Joseph Butler (1692–1752) in his famous sermon, "Upon Resentment," preached at the Rolls Chapel in 1729, takes punishment to be the natural expression of "deliberate" (as opposed to instinctive) resentment, and then inquires after the "final cause" (that is, purpose or function) of that kind of feeling or "passion." Butler shrewdly charts the various ways in which resentment may be abused and righteousness may be self-deceptive but concludes that resentment, like the other basic "elements of human nature," has a proper social function.

For the eminent Victorian jurist, James Fitzjames Stephen (1829–1894), punishment of certain offenses expresses and solemnly ratifies the hatred excited by the offense, so that "the criminal law proceeds upon the principle that it is morally right to hate criminals. . . ." Stephen regards hatred of criminals to be a "healthy, natural sentiment," and the desire for vengeance a socially useful phenomenon, though in the end, he cannot demonstrate its rationality, since, "it is useless to argue upon questions of sentiment."

The 1960 Supreme Court case of *Flemming v. Nestor* is not explicitly about the attitudes, feelings, or judgments expressed in an act of punishment, but it indirectly gives rise to speculation about those matters. It also illustrates dramatically how important it is to have a *definition* of "punishment" as a means not only to the fruitful settlement of philosophical questions but also to the determination of the constitutional validity of certain governmental acts. The question at issue was whether or not the deprivation by the government of Mr. Nestor's social security benefits was the exercise of a "regulative" or a "punitive" sanction. If the latter, it was *ex post facto* punishment, which is unconstitutional. If the former, it was merely incidental to the regulation of an activity. It has been said, in a commentary on this case,[9] that there clearly was congressional intent to punish but that judicial confusion was caused by the fact that the sanction selected was outside the scope of the criminal law and lacked the conventional reprobative symbolism distinctive of all genuine legal punishments.

The great impasse between the utilitarian and retributive theories described in the earlier paragraphs of this introduction was largely undisturbed by a century-and-a-half of disputation, until a rash of quite original articles in the 1950s and 1960s appeared which seemed to many to make a genuine breakthrough. The articles by Rawls and Benn included here were among the more important of these articles. Their common tactic was to make more and better distinctions, for example, between definition and justification, moral and legal guilt, necessary and sufficient conditions, single acts and general practices, and to hold to these distinctions rigorously, thus permitting new and sharper questions to be formulated about punishment, so that retributivism and utilitarianism could be put forward as complementary answers to different questions, rather than conflicting answers to the same question. In Benn's article, though, the spirit is much closer to that of Bentham than Kant, and the new "rule-utilitarianism" defended there will not convince many old-style retributivists.

J. F.

Earlier, in Part Four of this volume, a powerful attack was launched by Lady Barbara Wootton against the view that the liability of those who committed crimes should be liability to punishment. In her view, the criminal process should have as its purpose the prevention of further harm, and treatment rather than punishment is the way to accomplish that. In sharp contrast, Herbert Morris in "Persons and Punishment," argues that we have a right to punishment. It is a most fundamental human right—natural, inalienable, absolute—and deriving from the very right to be treated as a person. Deny this right, says Morris, and you deny all moral rights and duties. Admittedly, most of us would gladly forego enjoyment of the right, at least until the implications of our rejection are brought home to us. And we need not look far for that. The most sophisticated modern views of correctional treatment deny that punishment is the proper thing for those who have committed crimes. Instead, it is assumed that when a person does harm he manifests a symptom of a pathological condition. The appropriate course, therefore, is to correct what is wrong with him, or at least to keep him from infecting others. "The logic of sickness implies the logic of therapy," as Morris observes. Therapy differs from punishment in focusing on the present rather than the past, in seeking to confer benefit and help, and in having no concern with any debt that may be owed to society for violating its rules. Since therapy is avowedly beneficial, a therapeutic regime is bolder in inflicting necessary suffering, in determining occasions that justify administration of it, and is less concerned about niceties of procedure to determine who may be made subject to it. These differences make considerations of personal rights, and particularly those associated with liberty, less important when therapy rather than punishment is administered. But there are even more profound differences between the two ways of treating harmdoers that relate to how *persons* are to be treated. If a person is treated not as the author of his actions but as a mere instrument of happenings that constitute his actions, he is deprived of his role as a creator, and perhaps most important, his role as a creator of himself. The satisfactions of his own achievements are closed to him. Since he can take credit for nothing, nothing is earned, and he is either the fortunate beneficiary of others' favorable regard or is treated as an afflicted creature and made subject to the control of others. His values and his will must be bent to conform to those of the therapist as represented by therapeutic standards of normality, without respect for his independent moral status. Finally, the regime of therapy regards as recalcitrant behavior the harmdoer's attempt to justify or explain away what he did, to be noted only for its pathological significance, and this again is a refusal to accord him the respect due a person.

Professor Morris, then, is arguing implicitly for the thesis that only harmdoing that is wrongdoing should be punished, and explicitly that there is a right which is of the very essence of personhood to punitive rather than therapeutic treatment for wrongdoing. It is well established in our jurisprudence that some harmdoers who are not wrongdoers may be subjected to involuntary restraint and regimes of therapy. Persons who are abnormal in ways that put their ability to avoid doing harm in serious doubt are legitimate candidates for such treatment. Those persons are not beneficiaries of a right to be punished for reasons that Professor Morris makes clear enough. But just how is the line to be drawn? What conditions must be satisfied to meet the test of pathology, and even when it is met, what capabilities of cure must be available to legitimate a regime of therapy? Are there special "social diseases" that individuals suffer whose symptoms a penal code catalogues in its definitions of crimes, and for which therapy is more appropriate not only because it is more expedient but also because it is more humane?

Further critical questions suggest themselves. Are there really no alternatives to punishment as ways of treating harmdoers except therapy? Perhaps for certain kinds of crimes it would be sufficient to impose a disability short of punishment. A person who embezzles money might be disqualified from occupying a fiduciary position, just as a person with defective eyesight might be disqualified from serving in the army. Such a person is neither punished nor cured by being excluded. On this model, there would be an initial presumption of qualification that is rebutted by criminal conviction. Instead of being either punished or cured, however, a person is simply deemed unqualified, at least until there is good reason to believe that his deficiency or abnormality no longer exists. Certainly this is not unrealistic for at least some persons who commit some crimes; and perhaps a more humane, economical, and just system for dealing with such crimes could be devised along these lines. In that case what shall we say about a right to punishment? If that right appears somewhat less universal than Professor Morris suggests, we may learn even more about it by considering why in some cases punishment still seems more appropriate than any other kind of response, including the nontherapeutic alternatives.

"The Crime of Treatment" presents an account of the evils of a therapeutic regime in operation. The modern rehabilitative ideal of treating a convicted person in ways that are good for him and at the same time good for society must compel everyone's enthusiastic support in principle. But according to this report, what goes on in the correctional system is both inhumane and unjust in the extreme. Through the mechanism of indeterminate sentences, a vast discretion is commonly conferred on administrative officials to deprive convicted persons of their liberty for virtually whatever period the administrator's notions about the person suggest is desirable. Not only is there incompetence and indifference in reaching such decisions—indeed, how could one ever expect even under optimal conditions that such an awesome and burdensome responsibility would be properly discharged?—but the discretion is regularly abused as an instrument of prison discipline. Beyond the incompetence and abuse lies the truth about these programs of rehabilitation. Insofar as they operate at all, they are a cosmetic sham to justify a system of purposeless detention, and more, a way to maximize detention. One may well reflect in this regard on the author's discussion of involuntary psychotherapy. It is well known that any benefits to be gained in psychotherapy depend upon the patient's endeavor to achieve them. Yet the authoritarian regime of a prison makes such endeavor virtually impossible. One then must ask what sort of professionals will lend themselves—even more, will devote their professional lives—to an enterprise that they know must fail. If in fact the benefits of psychotherapy are sought, an institutional setting that makes such goals at least possible should be the first order of business for those who espouse the rehabilitative ideal.

The two previous selections question in different ways the form that the rehabilitative ideal of criminal justice has taken. Another common aim of the criminal justice system is brought into question in "Prediction of Criminal Conduct and Preventive Confinement of Convicted Persons." Andrew von Hirsch points out that detention of a person accused but not yet convicted is widely regarded as a serious injustice even when it is predicted that the accused if left free may engage in further crimes. Once a person has been convicted, however, such concern evaporates, and there is general acceptance of sentences based on equally unreliable predictions of future conduct that are calculated to keep confined for a longer period than otherwise a person who is thought to be dangerous. Whether such preventive confinement is justifiable, even when practiced in a sophisticated way, is the question that is explored in this selection. As it turns out, standards of dangerousness are vague, the reliability of prediction is untested, and commitment procedures do not provide adequate safeguards for the individual whose commitment is proposed. Beyond these threshold objections to existing practice, there are even more formidable objections in principle. There is a theoretical difficulty in actual prediction—the false positive problem—that virtually ensures erroneous confinements that are unacceptable under principles of justice fundamental in our criminal jurisprudence. Even if ideal methods of prediction were possible and the hazard of false positives no longer existed, there are even more basic objections. A system of preventive confinement represents a grave threat to personal autonomy and to liberty of the citizen in his relations with the state. The consequences of a determination that a person is dangerous deprives him of the opportunity of choosing to act in ways that do not cause harm. Such a system lends itself to ready abuse by the organs of public power under the influence of unenlightened though widely accepted notions about crime and criminals, or to serve even more sinister political ends. These objections apply equally to a system that purports to confine dangerous persons before they have committed crimes and a system that deals only with those already convicted. Furthermore, preventive confinement cannot pass muster as (additional) punishment, since considerations of proportionality between an offense and the punishment imposed for it (discussed in earlier selections) preclude that. Nor can the avowed goal of "rehabilitative treatment" justify confinement of those who have been determined to be dangerous, since the availability of therapeutic programs does not cancel the objectionable deprivation of liberty. Not only do the same objections obtain, but there are then the additional objections to the unjustifiable compulsory therapy because of the suffering and deprivation which attend it.

The evil of preventive confinement is to be found, as the author suggests, in the conventional sentencing practices of judges everywhere as well as in the correctional systems of those few jurisdictions that have institutionalized such confinement. Indeed it is the largely unnoticed influence on the sentencing judge of his own crude notions of dangerousness that exert the greatest power for injustice in this regard. At the present time it seems clear that the need to take risks in the interest of liberty and justice must be recognized, just as the need to take risks to preserve other things we value is recognized in other areas of social life. Perhaps the best we can hope for at this point are criteria of dangerousness that identify those about whom there can be no disagreement—criteria that need no validation as predictive devices since they derive their validity from what we already know. There are, after all, persons who are dangerous beyond any doubt, and from these clear cases we may by careful consideration derive general standards for defining the class of persons who are certainly dangerous. It is important to note that clear cases are not cases bearing features that warrant predictions with a very high degree of probability. Rather, they are cases in which there has been behavior (perhaps criminal, perhaps not) that, according to universally accepted ideas about threats of harm, unmistakably mark the person as dangerous. These criteria of dangerousness are of the same general sort as criteria for identifying dangerous situations—not based on superstition or unsupported impressions, yet not based on selective abstractions and disinterested observation of consequences either. Rather, it is a resource of collective social intelligence—common sense about harm. This suggests that the very concept of a dangerous person that is developed statistically is the wrong one. For one thing, using the statistical concept we would be bound to pay attention to the wrong kind of factors to determine who is dangerous—racial, social, economic, and general psychopathological categories into which persons may be sorted. Our commonsense criteria, however, are designed to identify dangerous persons differently. Under these criteria, even the dangerous person himself is bound to acknowledge that his abnormality marks him as dangerous, just as though he carried a contagious disease or was driving while intoxicated. It is always open to experiment and orderly observation to disclose that what common sense indicates to be dangerous is in fact innocuous. Indeed it is essential that common sense be constantly tested and revised in this way. But doing that works a correction among the types properly included as dangerous persons, and is not the substitution of a statistical idea of a dangerous person for a common sense one.

Among all the issues that criminal punishment raises, none has been the subject of greater public controversy than capital punishment. Only utopian views conceive a society without the need for some form of meaningful condemnation of persons who wrongfully do harm that is of serious public concern. The most dramatic form that such public response may take is now exciting great debate in the United States and elsewhere, as it has for several centuries throughout the civilized world. Two selections dealing with capital punishment have been chosen from opposing speeeches delivered in Parliament in 1868 by a now obscure member and by the most distinguished philosopher ever to have contributed to its debates. Mr. Gilpin, in advocating abolition of capital punishment, sounds the major themes so frequently heard today. He suggests that the one ultimate punishment is at different times meted out for offenses whose just deserts are of very different measure. "Unequal treatment" is an expression of this objectionable practice that is familiar to modern ears; and in the recent United States Supreme Court capital punishment case that follows these selections, we shall see that the Court is concerned above all else with precisely this point. Mr. Gilpin alludes to other matters that are equally familiar as points of objection—the inhumanity of capital punishment, the incorrigibility of mistaken execution of the innocent, and the brutalizing effect throughout society that official disregard for the sanctity of life must have.

The reply of John Stuart Mill presents some familiar arguments regarding deterrence in support of capital punishment. But it also advances arguments that are quite out of the ordinary, and upon which the greatest weight seems to be placed by Mill. He concedes that the death penalty should be restricted to the most serious varieties of murder, and that even then if judges, jurors, or government officials regularly refuse because of popular feeling to give effect to it, it should be abandoned. Two arguments favoring capital punishment are then advanced. The first points to the only acceptable alternative to the death penalty—life imprisonment at hard labor—and concludes that since death is certainly a kinder fate, it is not to be objected to on grounds of inhumanity. The second argument again stresses the comparative lenity of the death sentence, this time not by comparing it to an alternative punishment but by comparing its reality to what it appears to be. Death is not nearly so awful as it is generally thought to be, yet because it is so dreaded there is great deterrent power in the threat of it. One sees here the utilitarian theorist discerning a considerable social benefit to be gained at a quite small cost in suffering. To the point that the death penalty makes an erroneous conviction into a fatal mistake, Mill replies that whatever merit that argument may have in legal systems that are less scrupulous than the English in safeguarding the innocent, it is unpersuasive in a system whose safeguards even cause guilty persons regularly to go unpunished. To the further point that the death penalty violates the sanctity of life and destroys respect for it, Mill responds by pointing out that property and freedom are taken away by sentences imposing fine and imprisonment, yet respect for property and freedom remains unimpaired.

Several critical points directed to Mill's argument suggest themselves. In the first place, the lesser concern about death that Mill advocates has other interesting consequences. "The man would have died at any rate," says Mill speaking of the one to be executed. But so indeed would his victim, and by a parity of reasoning we must then view murder as not so serious as we thought. Murder then seems not to call for life imprisonment at hard labor, and so if other considerations make the death penalty undesirable, a more moderate punishment might be inflicted for an act that now turns out to have caused a much less serious harm than we thought. Further, one wonders whether Mill, in conjuring the case of the perpetrator of an "aggravated murder," has included all the relevant details that are actually to be found in such cases, as his antagonist Mr. Gilpin evidently has. Perhaps the greatest obstacle to rational consideration of capital punishment is the disposition of those who are considering its merit to contrive in the imagination a fit object for it, and then to assume that among the most serious crimes there must be actual cases mete for the death penalty. But almost invariably actual cases include exculpating elements that are crucially important in determining the extent of condemnation that is proper, and these elements have of course been excluded in the imagined case. Another point is that Mill's faith in the safeguards of a heavy burden on the prosecution to prevent error seems historically unsupported, and the effect of a single innocent's death at the hands of the state is regularly a matter of public concern far more grave than Mill suggests. Finally, the view that capital punishment tends to diminish respect for life is as prominent now as it was in Mill's time, and seems to be something more than humanitarian rhetoric. Yet one cannot help being intrigued by Mill's countering argument that analagous deprivation of property or freedom as punishment does not diminish respect for those things. Perhaps the analogy is flawed, and in a way that points up the unique value that human life has for us.

In 1972, the Supreme Court of the United States held that the imposition and carrying out of the death penalty in one case of murder and two of rape was unconstitutional because violative of the "cruel and unusual punishment" restriction of the Eighth Amendment. There was nothing special about the sentence, the proceedings, or the law under which the defendants were sentenced in these cases, and the Supreme Court's decision was based on general considerations regarding the death penalty. The selections from four of the nine separate opinions in *Furman* v. *Georgia* that are included here present all of the important arguments that were advanced. Two themes are sounded with special prominence, and they have appeared earlier in this volume in other contexts. One is the issue of arbitrary and even discriminatory application of the capital provisions of the law by judges and (even more) by juries. It is the unprincipled (though perhaps well-meaning) exercise of discretionary power that is objected to, and the objection is especially weighty because of the awful consequences that attend such abuse. The other theme recurring in the opinions addresses the moral sentiments of the community. Justices Brennan and White, as well as the Chief Justice, all seem to accept the premise that Mill voiced as a concession. If there is general disinclination in the community to invoke the death penalty, then that should count conclusively against its continued existence. There is disagreement among members of the Court only about what the sentiment of the community is.

The state of the law following *Furman* is unclear. If only arbitrariness is a fatal objection, which is what some state legislatures and proponents of congressional bills have since assumed, it would seem that in principle, at least, suitable remedies could be found. There are ways of specifying the extreme culpability that would set the capital crime apart, and of framing specific questions bearing on culpability for jurors to answer in determining whether the death penalty is warranted. If it were mandatory whenever warranted, that would seem to preclude arbitrariness. One suspects, however, that such a consequence would ordinarily cause jurors to shrink from following their instructions, with the result that unconstitutional arbitrariness would again exist for the occasional death sentence; or the death penalty would in effect become a dead letter on the books. Those concerned to preserve the death penalty advocate a Draconian resort to simple-minded mandatory death penalties which do not provide opportunity for all matters bearing on culpability to be considered. The preclusion of exculpatory considerations by such stark provisions would seem to introduce a new arbitrariness far worse than the old. It would indeed avoid the evil of discriminatory imposition of the death penalty of which Justice Douglas speaks, but would institute a regime of equal *injustice* by requiring its infliction on all members of a class regardless of culpability —all those who intentionally and without justification kill a police officer, for example, regardless of what reason there might have been which the law does not recognize as a defense.

The community sentiment argument seems not to have been fully appreciated in the *Furman* opinions. Certainly it is wrong to require jurors to condemn to death those they find guilty if something more than the natural distaste and regret that would ordinarily accompany the performance of such a duty is generally experienced. If revulsion normally overcomes those citizens who are asked as jurors to do their duty under the law, we may expect that only when there is a passionate hatred of the convicted person will capital punishment be imposed, and that would surely result in many irrational decisions that constitute precisely the injustice of discriminatory sentences which are objectionable on separate grounds. But an even more basic consideration is whether, according to principles of right and wrong that are universally invoked in the community, the death penalty is wrong. The answer is by no means plain on the face of things, and only extended moral argument can make it plain. Strong popular feeling of revulsion by itself counts only as evidence that the practice of killing a person for the crime he committed *may be* morally unacceptable. In spite of such feeling, it may not be morally unacceptable. Slaughter of animals for food may evoke such feelings, yet it may turn out not to be morally wrong, in which case the public revulsion is reason to carry on the activity discreetly, but not to prohibit it. Superficial evidence of possible general moral objection to capital punishment, such as polls that elicit unfavorable attitudes toward it, are only the first word and not the last. What justification there is for such attitudes is the question whose answer will tell us whether the death penalty is morally wrong.

H. G.

NOTES

1. A. C. Ewing, *The Morality of Punishment* (London: Kegan Paul, 1929), p. 13.
2. John Rawls, "Two Concepts of Rules," *The Philosophical Review*, LXIV (1955), pp. 4, 5.
3. J. D. Mabbott, "Punishment," *Mind*, XLVIII (1939), p. 161.
4. A. C. Ewing, *Ethics*, (New York: Macmillan, 1953), pp. 169–70.
5. A. C. Ewing, *The Morality of Punishment* (London: Kegan Paul, 1929), p. 27.
6. See O. W. Holmes, Jr., *The Common Law* (Boston: Little, Brown, 1881) and Henry Maine, *Ancient Law*. 1861 Reprint. (Boston: Beacon Press, 1963).
7. See, for example, Anthony Quinton, "On Punishment," *Analysis*, XIV (1954), pp. 1933–42.
8. H. L. A. Hart, *Punishment and Responsibility* (New York and Oxford: Oxford University Press, 1968), pp. 5, 6.
9. Joel Feinberg, *Doing and Deserving* (Princeton: Princeton University Press, 1970), pp. 106–09.

EDMUND L. PINCOFFS

Classical Retributivism*

I

The classification of Kant as a retributivist[1] is usually accompanied by a reference to some part of the following passage from the *Rechtslehre,* which is worth quoting at length.

Juridical punishment can never be administered merely as a means for promoting another good either with regard to the criminal himself or to civil society, but must in all cases be imposed only because the individual on whom it is inflicted *has committed a crime.* For one man ought never to be dealt with merely as a means subservient to the purpose of another, nor be mixed up with the subjects of real right. Against such treatment his inborn personality has a right to protect him, even though he may be condemned to lose his civil personality. He must first be found guilty and *punishable* before there can be any thought of drawing from his punishment any benefit for himself or his fellow-citizens. The penal law is a categorical imperative; and woe to him who creeps through the serpent-windings of utilitarianism to discover some advantage that may discharge him from the justice of punishment, or even from the due measure of it, according to the Pharisaic maxim: "It is better that *one* man should die than the whole people should perish." For if justice and righteousness perish, human life would no longer have any value in the world. . . .

But what is the mode and measure of punishment which public justice takes as its principle and standard? It is just the principle of equality, by which the pointer of the scale of justice is made to incline no more to the one side than the other. It may be rendered by saying that the undeserved evil which any one commits on another, is to be regarded as perpetrated on himself. Hence it may be said: "If you slander another, you slander yourself; if you steal from another, you steal from yourself; if you strike another, you strike yourself; if you kill another, you kill yourself." This is the Right of RETALIATION *(jus talionis);* and properly under-stood, it is the only principle which in regulating a public court, as distinguished from mere private judgment, can definitely assign both the quality and the quantity of a just penalty. All other standards are wavering and uncertain; and on account of other considerations involved in them, they contain no principle conformable to the sentence of pure and strict justice.[2]

Obviously we could mull over this passage for a long time. What, exactly, is the distinction between the Inborn and the Civil Personality? How is the Penal Law a Categorical Imperative: by derivation from one of the five formulations in the *Grundlegung,* or as a separate formulation? But we are on the trail of the traditional retributive theory of punishment and do not want to lose ourselves in niceties. There are two main points in this passage to which we should give particular attention:

    i. The only acceptable reason for punishing a man is that he has committed a crime.

    ii. The only acceptable reason for punishing a man in a given manner and degree is that the punishment is "equal" to the crime for which he is punished.

These propositions, I think it will be agreed, express the main points of the first and second paragraphs respectively. Before stopping over these points, let us go on to a third. It is brought out in the following passage from the *Rechtslehre,* which is also often referred to by writers on retributivism.

Even if a civil society resolved to dissolve itself with the consent of all its members—as might be supposed in the case of a people inhabiting an island resolving to separate and scatter themselves throughout the whole world—the last murderer lying in prison ought to be executed before the resolution was carried out. This ought to be done in order that every one may realize the desert of his deeds, and that bloodguiltiness may not remain upon the people; for otherwise they will all

*From *The Rationale of Legal Punishment* by Edmund L. Pincoffs (New York: Humanities Press, Inc., 1966), pp. 2–16. Reprinted by permission of the author and the publisher.

be regarded as participators in the murder as a public violation of justice.[3]

It is apparent from this passage that, so far anyway as the punishment of death for murder is concerned, the punishment awarded not only may but must be carried out. If it must be carried out "so that everyone may realize the desert of his deeds," then punishment for deeds other than murder must be carried out too. We will take it, then, that Kant holds that:

    iii. Whoever commits a crime must be punished in accordance with his desert.

Whereas (i) tells us what kind of reason we must have *if* we punish, (iii) now tells us that we must punish *whenever* there is desert of punishment. Punishment, Kant tells us elsewhere, is "The *juridical* effect or consequence of a culpable act of Demerit."[4] Any crime is a culpable act of demerit, in that it is an "*intentional* transgression— that is, an act accompanied with the consciousness that it is a transgression."[5] This is an unusually narrow definition of crime, since crime is not ordinarily limited to intentional acts of transgression, but may also include unintentional ones, such as acts done in ignorance of the law, and criminally negligent acts. However, Kant apparently leaves room for "culpable acts of demerit" outside of the category of crime. These he calls "faults," which are unintentional transgressions of duty, but "are nevertheless imputable to a person."[6] I can only suppose, though it is a difficulty in the interpretation of the *Rechtslehre,* that when Kant says that punishment must be inflicted "only because he has committed a crime," he is not including in "crime" what he would call a fault. Crime would, then, refer to any *intentional* imputable transgressions of duty; and these are what must be punished as involving ill desert. The difficulties involved in the definition of crime as the transgression of duty, as opposed to the mere violation of a legal prohibition, will be taken up later.

Taking the three propositions we have isolated as expressing the essence of the Kantian retributivistic position, we must now ask a direct and obvious question. What makes Kant hold this position? Why does he think it apparent that consequences should have *nothing to do* with the decision whether, and how, and how much to punish? There are two directions an answer to this question might follow. One would lead us into an extensive excursus on the philosophical position of Kant, the relation of this to his ethical theory, and the relation of his general theory of ethics to his philosophy of law. It would, in short, take our question as one about the consistency of Kant's position concerning the justification of punishment with the whole of the Kantian philosophy. This would involve discussion of Kant's reasons for believing that moral laws must be universal and categorical in virtue of their form alone, and divorced from any empirical content; of his attempt to make out a moral decision-procedure based upon an "empty" categorical imperative; and, above all, of the concept of freedom as a postulate of practical reason, and as the central concept of the philosophy of law. This kind of answer, however, we must forego here; for while it would have considerable interest in its own right, it would lead us astray from our purpose, which is to understand as well as we can the retributivist position, not as a part of this or that philosophical system but for its own sake. It is a position taken by philosophers with diverse philosophical systems; we want to take another direction, then, in our answer. Is there any *general* (nonspecial, nonsystematic) reason why Kant rejects consequences in the justification of punishment?

Kant believes that consequences have nothing to do with the justification of punishment partly because of his assumptions about the *direction* of justification; and these assumptions are, I believe, also to be found underlying the thought of Hegel and Bradley. Justification is not only *of* something, it is also *to* someone: it has an addressee. Now there are important confusions in Kant's and other traditional justifications of punishment turning on the question what the "punishment" *is* which is being justified. In Chapter IV, we will examine some of these. But if we are to feel the force of the retributivist position, we can no longer put off the question of the addressee of justification.

To whom is the Kantian justification of punishment directed? The question may seem a difficult one to answer, since Kant does not consider it himself as a separate issue. Indeed, it is not the kind of question likely to occur to a philosopher of Kant's formalistic leanings. A Kantian justification or rationale stands, so to speak, on its own.

It is a structure which can be examined, tested, probed by any rational being. Even to speak of the addressee of justification has an uncomfortably relativistic sound, as if only persuasion of A or B or C is possible, and proof impossible. Yet, in practice, Kant does not address his proffered justification of punishment so much to any rational being (which, to put it otherwise, is to address it not at all), as to the being most affected: the criminal himself.

It is the criminal who is cautioned not to creep through the serpent-windings of utilitarianism. It is the criminal's rights which are in question in the debate with Beccaria over capital punishment. It is the criminal we are warned not to mix up with property or things: the "subjects of Real Right." In the *Kritik der Praktischen Vernunft,* the intended direction of justification becomes especially clear.

Now the notion of punishment, as such, cannot be united with that of becoming a partaker of happiness; for although he who inflicts the punishment may at the same time have the benevolent purpose of directing this punishment to this end, yet it must be justified in itself as punishment, that is, as mere harm, so that if it stopped there, and the person punished could get no glimpse of kindness hidden behind this harshness, he must yet admit that justice was done him, and that his reward was perfectly suitable to his conduct. In every punishment, as such, there must first be justice, and this constitutes the essence of the notion. Benevolence may, indeed, be united with it, but the man who has deserved punishment has not the least reason to reckon upon this.[7]

Since this matter of the direction of justification is central in our understanding of traditional retributivism, and not generally appreciated, it will be worth our while to pause over this paragraph. Kant holds here, as he later holds in the *Rechtslehre,* that once it has been decided that a given "mode and measure" of punishment is justified, then "he who inflicts punishment" may do so in such a way as to increase the long-term happiness of the criminal. This could be accomplished, for example, by using a prison term as an opportunity for reforming the criminal. But Kant's point is that reforming the criminal has nothing to do with justifying the infliction of punishment. It is not inflicted because it will give an opportunity for reform, but because it is merited.

The passage does not need my gloss; it is transparently clear. Kant wants the justification of punishment to be such that the criminal "who could get no glimpse of kindness behind this harshness" would have to admit that punishment is warranted.

Suppose we tell the criminal, "We are punishing you for your own good." This is wrong, because it is then open to him to raise the question whether he deserves punishment, and what you consider good to be. If he does not deserve punishment, we have no right to inflict it, especially in the name of some good of which the criminal may not approve. So long as we are to treat him as rational—a being with dignity—we cannot force our judgments of good upon him. This is what makes the appeal to supposedly good consequences "wavering and uncertain." They waver because the criminal has as much right as anyone to question them. They concern ends which he may reject, and means which he might rightly regard as unsuited to the ends.

In the "Supplementary Explanations of the Principles of Right" of the *Rechtslehre,* Kant distinguishes between "punitive justice *(justitia punitiva),* in which the ground of the penalty is moral *(quia peccatum est),*" and "punitive *expediency,* the foundation of which is merely pragmatic *(ne peccetur)* as being grounded upon the experience of what operates most effectively to prevent crime." Punitive justice, says Kant, has an "entirely distinct place *(locus justi)* in the topical arrangement of the juridical conceptions." It does not seem reasonable to suppose that Kant makes this distinction merely to discard punitive expediency entirely, that he has no concern at all for the *ne peccetur.* But he does hold that there is no place for it in the justification of punishment proper: for this can only be to show the criminal that the punishment is just.

How is this to be done? The difficulty is that on the one hand the criminal must be treated as a rational being, an end in himself; but on the other hand the justification we offer him cannot be allowed to appear as the opening move in a rational discussion. It cannot turn on the criminal's acceptance of some premise which, as rational being, he has a perfect right to question. If the end in question is the well-being of society, we are assuming that the criminal will not have a different view of what that well-being consists in, and we are telling him that he should sacrifice himself *to* that end. As a rational being, he can question whether any end we propose is a good end. And we have no right to demand that he sacrifice himself to the public well-being, even supposing he agrees with us on what that consists in. No man has a duty, on Kant's view, to be benevolent.[8]

The way out of the quandary is to show the criminal that we are not inflicting the punishment on him for some questionable purpose of our own choice, but that he, as a free agent, has exercised *his* choice in such a way as to make the punishment a necessary consequence. "His own evil deed draws the punishment upon himself."[9] "The undeserved evil which anyone commits on another, is to be regarded as perpetuated on himself."[10] But may not the criminal rationally question this asserted connection between crime and punishment? Suppose he wishes to regard the punishment *not* as "drawn upon himself" by his own "evil deed?" Suppose he argues that no good purpose will be served by punishing him? But this line of thought leads into the "serpent-windings of utilitarianism," for if it is good consequences that govern, then justice goes by the board. What may not be done to him in the name of good consequences? What proportion would remain between what he has done and what he suffers?[11]

But punishment is *inflicted.* To tell the criminal that he "draws it upon himself" is all very well, only how do we justify *to ourselves* the infliction of it? Kant's answer is found early in the *Rechtslehre.*[12] There he relates punishment to crime *via* freedom. Crime consists in compulsion or constraint of some kind: a hindrance of freedom.[13] If it is wrong that freedom should be hindered, it is right to block this hindrance. But to block the constraint of freedom it is necessary to apply constraint. Punishment is a "hindering of a hindrance of freedom." Compulsion of the criminal is, then, justified only to the extent that it hinders his compulsion of another.

But how are we to understand Kant here? Punishment comes after the crime. How can it hinder the crime? The reference cannot be to the hindrance of future crime, or Kant's doctrine reduces to a variety of utilitarianism. The picture of compulsion *vs.* compulsion is clear enough, but how are we to apply it? Our answer must be somewhat speculative, since there is no direct answer to be found in the *Rechtslehre.* The answer

must begin from yet another extension of the concept of a crime. For the crime cannot consist merely in an act. What is criminal is acting in accordance with a wrong maxim: a maxim which would, if made universal, destroy freedom. The adoption of the maxim is criminal. Should we regard punishment, then, as the hindrance of a wrong maxim? But how do we hinder a maxim? We show, exhibit, its wrongness by taking it at face value. If the criminal has adopted it, he is claiming that it can be universalized. But if it is universalized it warrants the same treatment of the criminal as he has accorded to his victim. So if he murders he must be executed; if he steals we must "steal from" him.[14] What we do to him he willed, in willing to adopt his maxim as universalizable. To justify the punishment to the criminal is to show him that the compulsion we use on him proceeds according to the same rule by which he acts. This is how he "draws the punishment upon himself." In punishing, we are not adopting his maxim but demonstrating its logical consequences if universalized: We show the criminal *what* he has willed. This is the positive side of the Kantian rationale of punishment.

II

Hegel's version of this rationale has attracted more attention, and disagreement, in recent literature. It is the Hegelian metaphysical terminology which is in part responsible for the disagreement, and which has stood in the way of an understanding of the retributivist position. The difficulty turns around the notions of "annulment of crime," and of punishment as the "right" of the criminal. Let us consider "annulment" first.

In the *Philosophie des Rechts*[15] Hegel tells us that

Abstract right is a right to coerce, because the wrong which transgresses it is an exercise of force against the existence of my freedom in an external thing. The maintenance of this existent against the exercise of force therefore itself takes the form of an external act and an exercise of force annulling the force originally brought against it.[16]

Holmes complains that by the use of his logical apparatus, involving the negation of negations (or annulment), Hegel professes to establish what is only a mystic (though generally felt) bond between wrong and punishment.[17] Hastings Rashdall asks how any rational connection can be shown between the evil of the pain of punishment, and the twin evils of the suffering of the victim and the moral evil which "pollutes the offender's soul," unless appeal is made to the probable good consequences of punishment. The notion that the "guilt" of the offense must be, in some mysterious way, wiped out by the suffering of the offender does not seem to provide it.[18] Crime, which is an evil, is apparently to be "annulled" by the addition to it of punishment, which is another evil. How can two evils yield a good?[19]

But in fact Hegel is following the *Rechtslehre* quite closely here, and his doctrine is very near to Kant's. In the notes taken at Hegel's lectures,[20] we find Hegel quoted as follows:

If crime and its annulment . . . are treated as if they were unqualified evils, it must, of course, seem quite unreasonable to will an evil merely because "another evil is there already.". . . But it is not merely a question of an evil or of this, that, or the other good; the precise point at issue is wrong, and the righting of it. . . . The various considerations which are relevant to punishment as a phenomenon and to the bearing it has on the particular consciousness, and which concern its effects (deterrent, reformative, etcetera) on the imagination, are an essential topic for examination in their place, especially in connection with modes of punishment, but all these considerations presuppose as their foundation the fact that punishment is inherently and actually just. In discussing this matter the only important things are, first, that crime is to be annulled, not because it is the producing of an evil, but because it is the infringing of the right as right, and secondly, the question of what that positive existence is which crime possesses and which must be annulled; it is this existence which is the real evil to be removed, and the essential point is the question of where it lies. So long as the concepts here at issue are not clearly apprehended, confusion must continue to reign in the theory of punishment.[21]

While this passage is not likely to dethrone confusion, it does bring us closer to the basically Kantian heart of Hegel's theory. To "annul crime" should be read "right wrong." Crime is a wrong which consists in an "infringement of the right as right."[22] It would be unjust, says Hegel, to allow crime, which is the invasion of a right, to go unrequited. For to allow this is to admit that the crime is "valid": that is, that it is not in conflict with justice. But this is what we do want to admit, and the only way of showing this is to pay back the deed to the agent: coerce the coercer. For by intentionally violating his victim's rights, the criminal in effect claims that the rights of others are not binding on him; and this is to attack *das Recht* itself: the system of justice in which there are rights which must be respected. Punishment not only keeps the system in balance, it vindicates the system itself.

Besides talking about punishment's "annulment" of crime, Hegel has argued that it is the "right of the criminal." The obvious reaction to this is that it is a strange justification of punishment which makes it someone's right, for it is at best a strange kind of right which no one would ever want to claim! McTaggart's explanation of this facet of Hegel's theory is epitomized in the following quotation:

What, then, is Hegel's theory? It is, I think, briefly this: In sin, man rejects and defies the moral law. Punishment is pain inflicted on him because he has done this, and in order that he may, by the fact of his punishment, be forced into recognizing as valid the law which he rejected in sinning, and so repent of his sin—really repent, and not merely be frightened out of doing it again.[23]

If McTaggart is right, then we are obviously not going to find in Hegel anything relevant to the justification of legal punishment, where the notions of sin and repentance are out of place. And this is the conclusion McTaggart of course reaches. "Hegel's view of punishment," he insists, "cannot properly be applied in jurisprudence, and . . . his chief mistake regarding it lay in supposing that it could."[24]

But though McTaggart may be right in emphasizing the theological aspect of Hegel's doctrine of punishment, he is wrong in denying it a jurisprudential aspect. In fact, Hegel is only saying what Kant emphasized: that to justify punishment to the criminal is to show him that *he* has chosen to be treated as he is being treated.

The injury (the penalty) which falls on the criminal is not merely *implicitly* just—as just, it is *eo ipso* his implicit will, an embodiment of his freedom, his right; on the contrary, it is also a right *established* within the criminal himself, that is, in his objectively embodied will, in his action. The reason for this is that his action is the action of a rational being and this implies that it is something universal and that by doing it the criminal has laid down a law which he has explicitly recognized in his action and under which in consequence he should be brought as under his right.[25]

To accept the retributivist position, then, is to accept a thesis about the burden of proof in the justification of punishment. Provided we make the punishment "equal" to the crime it is not up to us to justify it to the criminal, beyond pointing out to him that it is what he willed. It is not that he initiated a chain of events likely to result in his punishment, but that in willing the crime he willed that he himself should suffer in the same degree as his victim. But what if the criminal simply wanted to commit his crime and get away with it (break the window and run, take the funds and retire to Brazil, kill but live?) Suppose we explain to the criminal that *really* in willing to kill he willed to lose his life; and, unimpressed, he replies that *really* he wished to kill and save his skin. The retributivist answer is that to the extent that the criminal understands freedom and justice he will understand that his punishment was made inevitable by his own choice. No moral theory can hope to provide a justification of punishment which will seem such to the criminal merely as a nexus of passions and desires. The retributivist addresses him as a rational being, aware of the significance of his action. The burden of proof, the retributivist would argue, is on the theorist who would not start from this assumption. For to assume from the beginning that the criminal is not rational is to treat him, from the beginning, as merely a "harmful animal."

What is involved in the action of the criminal is not only the concept of crime, the rational aspect present in crime as such whether the individual wills it or not, the aspect which the state has to vindicate, but also the abstract rationality of the individual's *volition*. Since that is so, punishment is regarded as containing the criminal's right and hence by being punished he is honored as a rational being. He does not receive this due of honor unless the concept and measure of his punishment are derived from his own act. Still less does he receive it if he is treated as a harmful animal who has to be made harmless, or with a view to deterring and reforming him.[26]

To address the criminal as a rational being aware of the significance of his action is to address him as a person who knows that he has not committed a "bare" act; to commit an act is to commit oneself to the universalization of the rule by which one acted. For a man to complain about the death sentence for murder is as absurd as for a man to complain that when he pushes down one tray of the scales, the other tray goes up; whereas the action, rightly considered, is of pushing down *and* up. "The criminal gives his consent already by his very act."[27] "The Eumenides sleep, but crime awakens them, and hence it is the very act of crime which vindicates itself."[28]

F. H. Bradley's contribution to the retributive theory of punishment adds heat but not much light. The central, and best-known, passage is the following:

If there is any opinion to which the man of uncultivated morals is attached, it is the belief in the necessary connection of Punishment and guilt. Punishment is punishment, only where it is deserved. We pay the penalty because we owe it, and for no other reason; and if punishment is inflicted for any other reason whatever than because it is merited by wrong, it is a gross immorality, a crying injustice, an abominable crime, and not what it pretends to be. We may have regard for whatever considerations we please—our own convenience, the good of society, the benefit of the offender; we are fools, and worse, if we fail to do so. Having once the right to punish, we may modify the punishment according to the useful and the pleasant; but these are external to the matter, they cannot give us a right to punish, and nothing can do that but criminal desert. This is not a subject to waste words over; if the fact of the vulgar view is not palpable to the reader, we have no hope, and no wish, to make it so.[29]

Bradley's sympathy with the "vulgar view" should be apparent.[30] And there is at least a seeming variation between the position he expresses here and that we have attributed to Kant and Hegel. For Bradley can be read here as leaving an open field for utilitarian reasoning, when the question is how and how much to punish. Ewing interprets Bradley this way, and argues at some length that Bradley is involved in an inconsistency.[31] However, it is quite possible that Bradley did not mean to allow kind and quantity of punishment to be determined by utilitarian considerations. He could mean, as Kant meant, that once punishment is awarded, then "it" (what the criminal must suffer: time in jail, for example) may be made use of for utilitarian purposes. But, it should by this time go without saying, the retributivist would then wish to insist that we not argue backward from the likelihood of attaining these good purposes to the rightness of inflicting the punishment.

Bradley's language is beyond question loose when he speaks, in the passage quoted, of our "modifying" the punishment, "having once the right to punish." But when he says that "we pay the penalty because we owe it, and for no other reason," Bradley must surely be credited with the insight that we may owe more or less according to the gravity of the crime. The popular view, he says, is "that punishment is justice; that justice implies the giving what is due."[32] And, "punishment is the complement of criminal desert; is justifiable only so far as deserved."[33] If Bradley accepts this popular view, then Ewing must be wrong in attributing to him the position that kind and degree of punishment may be determined by utilitarian considerations.[34]

III

Let us sum up traditional retributivism, as we have found it expressed in the paradigmatic passage we have examined. We have found no reason, in Hegel or Bradley, to take back or qualify importantly the *three propositions* we found central in Kant's retributivism:

i. The only acceptable reason for punishing a man is that he has committed a crime.

ii. The only acceptable reason for punishing a man in a given manner and degree is that the punishment is "equal" to the crime.

iii. Whoever commits a crime must be punished in accordance with his desert.

To these propositions should be added *two underlying assumptions:*

i. An assumption about the direction of justification: to the criminal.

ii. An assumption about the nature of justification: to show the criminal that it is he who has willed what he now suffers.

Though it may have been stated in forbidding metaphysical terms, traditional retributivism cannot be dismissed as unintelligible, or absurd, or implausible.[35] There is no obvious contradic-

tion in it; and there are no important disagreements among the philosophers we have studied over what it contends. Yet in spite of the importance of the theory, no one has yet done much more than sketch it in broad strokes. If, as I have surmised, it turns mainly on an assumption concerning the direction of justification, then this assumption should be explained and defended.

And the key concept of "desert" is intolerably vague. What does it mean to say that punishment must be proportionate to what a man *deserves?* This seems to imply, in the theory of the traditional retributivists, that there is some way of measuring desert, or at least of balancing punishment against it. How this measuring or balancing is supposed to be done, we will discuss later. What we must recognize here is that there are alternative criteria of "desert," and that it is not always clear which of these the traditional retributivist means to imply.

When we say of a man that he "deserves severe punishment" how, if at all, may we support our position by arguments? What kinds of considerations tend to show what a man does or does not deserve? There are at least two general sorts: those which tend to show that what he has done is a member of a class of actions which is especially heinous; and those which tend to show that his doing of this action was, in (or because of) the circumstances, particularly wicked. The argument that a man deserves punishment may rest on the first kind of appeal alone, or on both kinds. Retributivists who rely on the first sort of consideration alone would say that anyone who would do a certain sort of thing, no matter what the circumstances may have been, deserves punishment. Whether there are any such retributivists I do not know. Kant, because of his insistence on *intention* as a necessary condition of committing a crime, clearly wishes to bring in considerations of the second sort as well. It is not, on his view, merely *what* was done, but the intention of the agent which must be taken into account. No matter what the intention, a man cannot commit a crime deserving punishment if his deed is not a transgression. But if he does commit a transgression, he must do so intentionally to commit a crime; and all crime is deserving of punishment. The desert of the crime is a factor both of the seriousness of the transgression, considered by itself, and the degree to which the intention to transgress was present. If, for Kant, the essence of morality consists in knowingly acting from duty, the essence of immorality consists in knowingly acting against duty.

The retributivist can perhaps avoid the question of how we decide that one crime is morally more heinous than another by hewing to his position that no such decision is necessary so long as we make the punishment "equal" to the crime. To accomplish this, he might argue, it is not necessary to argue to the *relative* wickedness of crimes. But at best this leaves us with the problem how we *do* make punishments equal to crimes, a problem which will not stop plaguing retributivists. And there is the problem *which* transgressions, intentionally committed, the retributivist is to regard as crimes. Surely not every morally wrong action![36]

And how is the retributivist to fit in appeals to punitive expediency? None of our authors denies that such appeals may be made, but where and how do they tie into punitive justice? It will not do simply to say that justifying punishment to the criminal is one thing, and justifying it to society is another. Suppose we must justify in both directions at once? And who are "we" anyway—the players of which roles, at what stage of the game?[37] And has the retributivist cleared himself of the charge, sure to arise, that the theory is but a cover for a much less commendable motive than respect for justice: elegant draping for naked revenge?[38]

NOTES

1. ... since in our own time there are few defenders of retributivism, the position is most often referred to by writers who are opposed to it. This does not make for clarity. In the past few years, however, there has been an upsurge of interest, and some good articles have been written. Cf. esp. J. D. Mabbott, "Punishment," *Mind,* XLVIII (1939), pp. 152–67; C. S. Lewis, "The Humanitarian Theory of Punishment," *20th Century* (Australian), March, 1949; C. W. K. Mundle, "Punishment and Desert," *The Philosophical Quarterly,* IV (1954), pp. 216–228; A. S. Kaufman, "Anthony Quinton on Punishment," *Analysis,* October, 1959; and K. G. Armstrong, "The Retributivist Hits Back," LXX (1961), pp. 471–90.
2. *Rechtslehre,* Part Second, 49, E. Hastie translation, Edinburgh, 1887, pp. 195–7.
3. *Ibid.,* p. 198. Cf. also the passage on p. 196 beginning "What, then, is to be said of such a proposal as to keep a Criminal alive who has been condemned to death ..."
4. *Ibid.,* Prolegomena, General Divisions of the Metaphysic of Morals, IV. (Hastie, p. 38).
5. *Ibid.,* p. 32.
6. *Ibid.,* p. 32.

7. Book I, Ch. I, Sect. VIII, Theorem IV, Remark II (T. K. Abbott translation, 5th ed., revised, London, 1898, p. 127).
8. *Rechtslehre.*
9. "Supplementary Explanation of The Principles of Right," V.
10. Cf. long quote from the *Rechtslehre,* above.
11. How can the retributivist allow utilitarian considerations even in the administration of the sentence? Are we not then opportunistically imposing our conception of good on the convicted man? How did we come by this right, which we did not have when he stood before the bar awaiting sentence? Kant would refer to the loss of his "Civil Personality;" but what rights remain with the "Inborn Personality," which is not lost? How is human dignity modified by conviction of crime?
12. Introduction to The Science of Right, General Definitions and Divisions, D. Right is Joined with the Title to Compel. (Hastie, p. 47).
13. This extends the definition of crime Kant has given earlier by specifying the nature of an imputable transgression of duty.
14. There are serious difficulties in the application of the "Principle of Equality" to the "mode and measure" of punishment. This will be considered ...
15. I shall use this short title for the work with the formidable double title of *Naturrecht und Stattswissenchaft in Grundrisse; Grundlinien der Philosophie des Rechts (Natural Law and Political Science in Outline; Elements of The Philosophy of Right.)* References will be to the T. M. Knox translation (*Hegel's Philosophy of Right,* Oxford, 1942).
16. *Philosophie des Rechts,* Sect. 93 (Knox, p. 67).
17. O. W. Holmes, Jr., *The Common Law,* Boston, 1881, p. 42.
18. Hastings Rashdall, *The Theory of Good and Evil,* 2nd. Edn., Oxford, 1924, vol. 1, pp. 285–6.
19. G. E. Moore holds that, consistently with his doctrine of organic wholes, they might; or at least they might yield that which is less evil than the sum of the constituent evils. This indicates for him a possible vindication of the Retributive theory of punishment. (*Principia Ethica,* Cambridge, 1903, pp. 213–214).
20. Included in the Knox translation.
21. Knox translation, pp. 69–70.
22. There is an unfortunate ambiguity in the German word *Recht,* here translated as "right." The word can mean either that which is a right or that which is in accordance with the law. So when Hegel speaks of "infringing the right as right" it is not certain whether he means a right as such or the law as such, or whether, in fact, he is aware of the ambiguity. But to say that the crime infringes the law is analytic, so we will take it that Hegel uses *Recht* here to refer to that which is right. But what the criminal does is not merely to infringe a right, but "the right *(das recht)* as right," that is, to challenge by his action the whole system of rights. (On *"Recht,"* Cf. J. Austin, *The Province of Jurisprudence Determined,* London, Library of Ideas end., 1954), Note 26, pp. 285–288 esp. pp. 287–8).
23. J. M. E. McTaggart, *Studies in The Hegelian Cosmology,* Cambridge, 1901, Ch. V, p. 133.
24. *Ibid.,* p. 145.
25. *Op. Cit.,* Sect. 100 (Hastie, p. 70.)
26. *Ibid.,* Lecture-notes on Sect. 100, Hastie, p. 71.
27. *Ibid.,* Addition to Sect. 100, Hastie, p. 246.
28. *Ibid.,* Addition to Sect. 101, Hastie, p. 247. There is something ineradicably *curious* about retributivism. We keep coming back to the metaphor of the balance scale. Why is the metaphor powerful and the same time strange? Why do we

agree so readily that "the assassination" cannot "trammel up the consequence," that "even-handed justice comments th' ingredients of our poisoned chalice to our own lips?"

29. F. H. Bradley, *Ethical Studies,* Oxford, 1952, pp. 26–7.

30. Yet it may not be amiss to note the part played by the "vulgar view" in Bradley's essay. In "The Vulgar Notion of Responsibility in Connection with the Theories of Free Will and Necessity," from which this passage is quoted, Bradley is concerned to show that neither the "Libertarian" nor the "Necessitarian" position can be accepted. Both of these "two great schools" which "divide our philosophy" "stand out of relation to vulgar morality." Bradley suggests that perhaps the truth is to be found not in either of these "two undying and opposite one-sidednesses but in a philosophy which "thinks what the vulgar believe." Cf. also the contrasting of the "ordinary consciousness" with the "philosophical" or "debauched" morality (p. 4). On p. 3 he says that by going to "vulgar morality" we "gain in integrity" what we "lose in

refinement." Nevertheless, he does say (p. 4) "seeing the vulgar are after all the vulgar, we should not be at pains to agree with their superstitions."

31. A. C. Ewing, *The Morality of Punishment,* London, 1929, pp. 41–42.

32. *Op. Cit.,* p. 29.

33. *Ibid.,* p. 30.

34. *Op. Cit.,* p. 41.

35. Or, more ingeniously, "merely logical," the "elucidation of the use of a word;" answering the question, "When (logically) *can* we punish?" as opposed to the question answered by the utilitarians, "When (morally) *may* or *ought* we to punish?" (Cf. A. M. Quinton, "On Punishment," *Analysis,* June, 1954, pp. 133–142)

36. Cf. Ch. V. [of *The Rationale of Legal Punishment*-eds.]

37. Distinction to be made in Chapter III. [*id.*-eds.]

38. To be discussed in the next chapter. [*id.*-eds.]

JEREMY BENTHAM

The Utilitarian Theory of Punishment*

OF THE PROPERTIES TO BE GIVEN TO A LOT OF PUNISHMENT

I. It has been shown what the rules are, which ought to be observed in adjusting the proportion between the punishment and the offence. The properties to be given to a lot of punishment, in every instance, will of course be such as it stands in need of, in order to be capable of being applied, in conformity to those rules: the *quality* will be regulated by the *quantity.*

II. The first of those rules, we may remember, was, that the quantity of punishment must not be less, in any case, than what is sufficient to outweigh the profit of the offence: since, as often as it is less, the whole lot (unless by accident the deficiency should be supplied from some of the other sanctions) is thrown away: it is *ineffica-*

*From *Introduction to the Principles of Morals and Legislation.* First published in 1776. Footnotes in the original deleted.

cious. The fifth was, that the punishment ought in no case to be more than what is required by the several other rules: since, if it be, all that is above that quantity is *needless.* The fourth was, that the punishment should be adjusted in such manner to each individual offence, that every part of the mischief of that offence may have a penalty (that is, a tutelary motive) to encounter it: otherwise, with respect to so much of the offence as has not a penalty to correspond to it, it is as if there were no punishment in the case. Now to none of those rules can a lot of punishment be conformable, unless, for every variation in point of quantity, in the mischief of the species of offence to which it is annexed, such lot of punishment admits of a correspondent variation. To prove this, let the profit of the offence admit of a multitude of degrees. Suppose it, then, at any one of these degrees: if the punishment be less than what is suitable to that degree, it will be *inefficacious;* it will be so much thrown away: if it be more, as far as the difference extends, it will be *needless;* it will therefore be thrown away also in that case.

The first property, therefore, that ought to be given to a lot of punishment, is that of being variable in point of quantity, in conformity to every variation which can take place in either the profit or mischief of the offence. This property might, perhaps, be termed, in a single word, *variability.*

III. A second property, intimately connected with the former, may be styled *equability.* It will avail but little, that a mode of punishment (proper in all other respects) has been established by the legislator; and that capable of being screwed up or let down to any degree that can be required; if, after all, whatever degree of it be pitched upon, that same degree shall be liable, according to circumstances, to produce a very heavy degree of pain, or a very slight one, or even none at all. In this case, as in the former, if circumstances happen one way, there will be a great deal of pain produced which will be *needless:* if the other way, there will be no pain at all applied, or none that will be *efficacious.* A punishment, when liable to this irregularity, may be styled an unequable one: when free from it, an equable one. The quantity of pain produced by the punishment will, it is true, depend in a considerable degree upon circumstances distinct from the nature of the punishment itself: upon the condition which the offender is in, with respect to the circumstances by which a man's sensibility is liable to be influenced. But the influence of these very circumstances will in many cases be reciprocally influenced by the nature of the punishment: in other words, the pain which is produced by any mode of punishment, will be the joint effect of the punishment which is applied to him, and the circumstances in which he is exposed to it. Now there are some punishments, of which the effect may be liable to undergo a greater alteration by the influence of such foreign circumstances, than the effect of other punishments is liable to undergo. So far, then, as this is the case, equability or unequability may be regarded as properties belonging to the punishment itself.

IV. An example of a mode of punishment which is apt to be unequable, is that of *banishment,* when the *locus a quo* (or place the party is banished from) is some determinate place appointed by the law, which perhaps the offender cares not whether he ever see or no. This is also the case with *pecuniary,* or *quasi-pecuniary* punishment, when it respects some particular species of property, which the offender may have been possessed of, or not, as it may happen. All these punishments may be split down into parcels, and measured out with the utmost nicety: being divisible by time, at least, if by nothing else. They are not, therefore, any of them defective in point of variability: and yet, in many cases, this defect in point of equability may make them as unfit for use as if they were.

V. The third rule of proportion was, that where two offences come in competition, the punishment for the greater offence must be sufficient to induce a man to prefer the less. Now, to be sufficient for this purpose, it must be evidently and uniformly greater: greater, not in the eyes of some men only, but of all men who are liable to be in a situation to take their choice between the two offences; that is, in effect, of all mankind. In other words, the two punishments must be perfectly *commensurable.* Hence arises a third property, which may be termed *commensurability:* to wit, with reference to other punishments.

VI. But punishments of different kinds are in very few instances uniformly greater one than another; especially when the lowest degrees of that which is ordinarily the greater, are compared with the highest degrees of that which is ordinarily the less: in other words, punishments of different kinds are in few instances uniformly commensurable. The only certain and universal means of making two lots of punishment perfectly commensurable, is by making the lesser an ingredient in the composition of the greater. This may be done in either of two ways. I. By adding to the lesser punishment another quantity of punishment of the same kind. 2. By adding to it another quantity of a different kind. The latter mode is not less certain than the former: for though one cannot always be absolutely sure, that to the same person a given punishment will appear greater than another given punishment; yet one may be always absolutely sure, that any given punishment, so as it does but come into contemplation, will appear greater than none at all.

VII. Again: Punishment cannot act any farther than in as far as the idea of it, and of its connection with the offence, is present in the mind. The idea of it, if not present, cannot act at all; and then the punishment itself must be *inefficacious*. Now, to be present, it must be remembered, and to be remembered it must have been learnt. But of all punishments that can be imagined, there are none of which the connection with the offence is either so easily learnt, or so efficaciously remembered, as those of which the idea is already in part associated with some part of the idea of the offence: which is the case when the one and the other have some circumstance that belongs to them in common. When this is the case with a punishment and an offence, the punishment is said to bear an *analogy* to, or to be *characteristic* of, the offence. *Characteristicalness* is, therefore, a fourth property, which on this account ought to be given, whenever it can conveniently be given, to a lot of punishment.

VIII. It is obvious, that the effect of this contrivance will be the greater, as the analogy is the closer. The analogy will be the closer, the more *material* that circumstance is, which is in common. Now the most material circumstance that can belong to an offence and a punishment in common, is the hurt or damage which they produce. The closest analogy, therefore, that can subsist between an offence and the punishment annexed to it, is that which subsists between them when the hurt or damage they produce is of the same nature: in other words, that which is constituted by the circumstance of identity in point of damage. Accordingly, the mode of punishment, which of all others bears the closest analogy to the offence, is that which in the proper and exact sense of the word is termed *retaliation*. Retaliation, therefore, in the few cases in which it is practicable, and not too expensive, will have one great advantage over every other mode of punishment.

IX. Again: It is the idea only of the punishment (or, in other words, the *apparent* punishment) that really acts upon the mind; the punishment itself (the *real* punishment) acts not any farther than as giving rise to that idea. It is the apparent punishment, therefore, that does all the service, I mean in the way of example, which is the principal object. It is the real punishment that does all the mischief. Now the ordinary and obvious way of increasing the magnitude of the apparent punishment, is by increasing the magnitude of the real. The apparent magnitude, however, may to a certain degree be increased by other less expensive means: whenever, therefore, at the same time that these less expensive means would have answered that purpose, an additional real punishment is employed, this additional real punishment is *needless*. As to these less expensive means, they consist, 1. In the choice of a particular mode of punishment, a punishment of a particular quality, independent of the quantity. 2. In a particular set of *solemnities* distinct from the punishment itself, and accompanying the execution of it.

X. A mode of punishment, according as the appearance of it bears a greater proportion to the reality, may be said to be the more *exemplary*. Now as to what concerns the choice of the punishment itself, there is not any means by which a given quantity of punishment can be rendered more exemplary, than by choosing it of such a sort as shall bear an *analogy* to the offence. Hence another reason for rendering the punishment analogous to, or in other words characteristic of, the offence.

XI. Punishment, it is still to be remembered, is in itself an expense: it is in itself an evil. Accordingly the fifth rule of proportion is, not to produce more of it than what is demanded by the other rules. But this is the case as often as any particle of pain is produced, which contributes nothing to the effect proposed. Now if any mode of punishment is more apt than another to produce any such superfluous and needless pain, it may be styled *unfrugal;* if less, it may be styled *frugal. Frugality,* therefore, is a sixth property to be wished for in a mode of punishment.

XII. The perfection of frugality, in a mode of punishment, is where not only no superfluous pain is produced on the part of the person punished, but even that same operation, by which he is subjected to pain, is made to answer the purpose of producing pleasure on the part of some other person. Understand a profit or stock of pleasure of the self-regarding kind: for a pleasure of the dissocial kind is produced almost of course, on the part of all persons in whose breasts the offence has excited the sentiment of ill-will. Now this is the case with pecuniary punishment, as also with such punishments of the *quasi-pecuniary* kind as consist in the subtraction of such a species of possession as is transferable from one party to another. The pleasure, indeed, produced by such an operation, is not in general equal to the pain: it may, however, be so in particular circumstances, as where he, from whom the thing is taken, is very rich, and he, to whom it is given, very poor: and, be it what it will, it is always so much more than can be produced by any other mode of punishment.

XIII. The properties of exemplarity and frugality seem to pursue the same immediate end, though by different courses. Both are occupied in diminishing the ratio of the real suffering to the apparent: but exemplarity tends to increase the apparent; frugality to reduce the real.

XIV. Thus much concerning the properties to be given to punishments in general, to whatsoever offences they are to be applied. Those which follow are of less importance, either as referring only to certain offences in particular, or depending upon the influence of transitory and local circumstances.

In the first place, the four distinct ends into which the main and general end of punishment is divisible, may give rise to so many distinct properties, according as any particular mode of punishment appears to be more particularly adapted to the compassing of one or of another of those ends. To that of *example,* as being the principal one, a particular property has already been adapted. There remains the three inferior ones of *reformation, disablement,* and *compensation.*

XV. A seventh property, therefore, to be wished for in a mode of punishment, is that of *subserviency to reformation,* or *reforming tendency.* Now any punishment is subservient to reformation in proportion to its *quantity:* since the greater the punishment a man has experienced, the stronger is the tendency it has to create in him an aversion towards the offence which was the cause of it: and that with respect to all offences alike. But there are certain punishments which, with regard to certain offences, have a particular tendency to produce that effect by reason of their *quality:* and where this is the case, the punishments in question, as applied to the offences in question, will *pro tanto* have the advantage over all others. This influence will depend upon the nature of the motive which is the cause of the offence: the punishment most subservient to reformation will be the sort of punishment that is best calculated to invalidate the force of that motive.

XVI. Thus, in offences originating from the motive of ill-will, that punishment has the strongest reforming tendency, which is best calculated to weaken the force of the irascible affections. And more particularly, in that sort of offence which consists in an obstinate refusal, on the part of the offender, to do something which is lawfully required of him, and in which the obstinacy is in great measure kept up by his resentment against those who have an interest in forcing him to compliance, the most efficacious punishment seems to be that of confinement to spare diet.

XVII. Thus, also, in offences which owe their birth to the joint influence of indolence and pecuniary interest, that punishment seems to possess the strongest reforming tendency, which is best calculated to weaken the force of the former of those dispositions. And more particularly, in the cases of theft, embezzlement, and every species of defraudment, the mode of punishment best adapted to this purpose seems, in most cases, to be that of penal labour.

XVIII. An eighth property to be given to a lot of punishment in certain cases, is that of *efficacy with respect to disablement,* or, as it might be styled more briefly, *disabling efficacy.* This is a property which may be given in perfection to a lot of punishment; and that with much greater certainty than the property of subserviency to reformation. The inconvenience is, that this property is apt, in general, to run counter to that of frugality: there being, in most cases, no certain way of disabling a man from doing mischief, without, at the same time, disabling him, in a great measure, from doing good, either to himself or others. The mischief therefore of the offence must be so great as to demand a very considerable lot of punishment, for the purpose of example, before it can warrant the application of a punishment equal to that which is necessary for the purpose of disablement.

XIX. The punishment, of which the efficacy in this way is the greatest, is evidently that of death. In this case the efficacy of it is certain. This accordingly is the punishment peculiarly adapted to those cases in which the name of the offender, so long as he lives, may be sufficient to keep a whole nation in a flame. This will now and then be the case with competitors for the sovereignty, and leaders of the factions in civil wars: though, when applied to offences of so questionable a nature, in which the question concerning criminality turns more upon success than anything else; an infliction of this sort may seem more to savour of hostility than punishment. At the same time this punishment, it is evident, is in an eminent degree *unfrugal;* which forms one among the many objections there are against the use of it, in any but very extraordinary cases.

XX. In ordinary cases the purpose may be sufficiently answered by one or other of the various kinds of confinement and banishment: of which, imprisonment is the most strict and efficacious. For when an offence is so circumstanced that it cannot be committed but in a certain place, as is the case, for the most part, with offences against the person, all the law has to do, in order to disable the offender from committing it, is to prevent his being in that place. In any of the offences which consist in the breach or the abuse of any kind of trust, the purpose may be compassed at a still cheaper rate, merely by forfeiture of the trust: and in general, in any of those offences which can only be committed under favour of some relation in which the offender stands with reference to any person, or sets of persons, merely by forfeiture of that relation: that is, of the right of continuing to reap the advantages belonging to it. This is the case, for instance, with any of those offences which consist in an abuse of the privileges of marriage, or of the liberty of carrying on any lucrative or other occupation.

XXI. The *ninth* property is that of *subserviency to compensation.* This property of punishment, if it be *vindictive* compensation that is in view, will, with little variation, be in proportion to the quantity: if *lucrative,* it is the peculiar and characteristic property of pecuniary punishment.

XXII. In the rear of all these properties may be introduced that of *popularity;* a very fleeting and indeterminate kind of property, which may belong to a lot of punishment one moment, and be lost by it the next. By popularity is meant the property of being acceptable, or rather not unacceptable, to the bulk of the people, among whom it is proposed to be established. In strictness of speech, it should rather be called *absence of unpopularity:* for it cannot be expected, in regard to such a matter as punishment, that any species or lot of it should be positively acceptable and grateful to the people: it is sufficient, for the most part,

if they have no decided aversion to the thoughts of it. Now the property of characteristicalness, above noticed, seems to go as far towards conciliating the approbation of the people to a mode of punishment, as any; insomuch that popularity may be regarded as a kind of secondary quality, depending upon that of characteristicalness.[1] The use of inserting this property in the catalogue, is chiefly to make it serve by way of memento to the legislator not to introduce, without a cogent necessity, any mode or lot of punishment, towards which he happens to perceive any violent aversion entertained by the body of the people.

XXIII. The effects of unpopularity in a mode of punishment are analogous to those of unfrugality. The unnecessary pain which denominates a punishment unfrugal, is most apt to be that which is produced on the part of the offender. A portion of superfluous pain is in like manner produced when the punishment is unpopular: but in this case it is produced on the part of persons altogether innocent, the people at large. This is already one mischief; and another is, the weakness which it is apt to introduce into the law. When the people are satisfied with the law, they voluntarily lend their assistance in the execution: when they are dissatisfied, they will naturally withhold that assistance; it is well if they do not take a positive part in raising impediments. This contributes greatly to the uncertainty of the punishment; by which, in the first instance, the frequency of the offence receives an increase. In process of time that deficiency, as usual, is apt to draw on an increase in magnitude: an addition of a certain quantity which otherwise would be *needless.*

XXIV. This property, it is to be observed, necessarily supposes, on the part of the people, some prejudice or other, which it is the business of the legislator to endeavour to correct. For if the aversion to the punishment in question were grounded on the principle of utility, the punishment would be such as, on other accounts, ought not to be employed: in which case its popularity or unpopularity would never be worth drawing into question. It is properly therefore a property not so much of the punishment as of the people: a disposition to entertain an unreasonable dislike against an object which merits their approbation. It is the sign also of another property, to wit, indolence or weakness, on the part of the legislator: in suffering the people, for the want of some instruction, which ought to be and might be given them, to quarrel with their own interest. Be this as it may, so long as any such dissatisfaction subsists, it behoves the legislator to have an eye to it, as much as if it were ever so well grounded. Every nation is liable to have its prejudices and its caprices, which it is the business of the legislator to look out for, to study, and to cure.

XXV. The eleventh and last of all the properties that seem to be requisite in a lot of punishment, is that of *remissibility*. The general presumption is, that when punishment is applied, punishment is needful: that it ought to be applied, and therefore cannot want to be *remitted*. But in very particular, and those always very deplorable cases, it may by accident happen otherwise. It may happen that punishment shall have been inflicted, where, according to the intention of the law itself, it ought not to have been inflicted: that is, where the sufferer is innocent of the offence. At the time of the sentence passed he appeared guilty: but since then, accident has brought his innocence to light. This being the case, so much of the destined punishment as he has suffered already, there is no help for. The business is then to free him from as much as is yet to come. But *is* there any yet to come? There is very little chance of there being any, unless it be so much as consists of *chronical* punishment: such as imprisonment, banishment, penal labour, and the like. So much as consists of *acute* punishment, to wit where the penal process itself is over presently, however permanent the punishment may be in its effects, may be considered as *ir*remissible. This is the case, for example, with whipping, branding, mutilation, and capital punishment. The most perfectly irremissible of any is capital punishment. For though other punishments cannot, when they are over, be remitted, they may be compensated for; and although the unfortunate victim cannot be put into the same condition, yet possibly means may be found of putting him into as good a condition, as he would have been in if he had never suffered. This may in general be done very effectually where the punishment has been no other than pecuniary.

There is another case in which the property of remissibility may appear to be of use: this is, where, although the offender has been justly punished, yet on account of some good behaviour of his, displayed at a time subsequent to that of the commencement of the punishment, it may seem expedient to remit a part of it. But this it can scarcely be, if the proportion of the punishment is, in other respects, what it ought to be. The purpose of example is the more important object, in comparison of that of reformation. It is not very likely, that less punishment should be required for the former purpose than for the latter. For it must be rather an extraordinary case, if a punishment, which is sufficient to deter a man who has only thought of it for a few moments, should not be sufficient to deter a man who has been feeling it all the time. Whatever, then, is required for the purpose of example, must abide at all events: it is not any reformation on the part of the offender, that can warrant the remitting of any part of it: if it could, a man would have nothing to do but to reform immediately, and so free himself from the greatest part of that punishment which was deemed necessary. In order, then, to warrant the remitting of any part of a punishment upon this ground, it must first be supposed that the punishment at first appointed was more than was necessary for the purpose of example, and consequently that a part of it was *needless* upon the whole. This, indeed, is apt enough to be the case, under the imperfect systems that are as yet on foot: and therefore, during the continuance of those systems, the property of remissibility may, on this second ground likewise, as well as on the former, be deemed a useful one. But this would not be the case in any new-constructed system, in which the rules of proportion above laid down should be observed. In such a system, therefore, the utility of this property would rest solely on the former ground.

XXVI. Upon taking a survey of the various possible modes of punishment, it will appear evidently, that there is not any one of them that possesses all the above properties in perfection. To do the best that can be done in the way of punishment, it will therefore be necessary, upon most occasions, to compound them, and make them into complex lots, each consisting of a number of different modes of punishment put together: the nature and proportions of the constituent parts of each lot being different, according to the nature of the offence which it is designed to combat.

XXVII. It may not be amiss to bring together, and exhibit in one view, the eleven properties above established. They are as follows:

Two of them are concerned in establishing a proper proportion between a single offence and its punishment; viz.

1. Variability.
2. Equability.

One, in establishing a proportion, between more offences than one, and more punishments than one; viz.

3. Commensurability.

A fourth contributes to place the punishments in that situation in which alone it can be efficacious; and at the same time to be bestowing on it the two farther properties of exemplarity and popularity; viz.

4. Characteristicalness.

Two others are concerned in excluding all useless punishment; the one indirectly, by heightening the efficacy of what is useful; the other in a direct way; viz.

5. Exemplarity.
6. Frugality.

Three others contribute severally to the three inferior ends of punishment; viz.

7. Subserviency to reformation.
8. Efficacy in disabling.
9. Subserviency to compensation.

Another property tends to exclude a collateral mischief, which a particular mode of punishment is liable accidentally to produce; viz.

10. Popularity.

The remaining property tends to palliate a mischief, which all punishment, as such, is liable accidentally to produce; viz.

11. Remissibility.

The properties of commensurability, characteristicalness, exemplarity, subserviency to reformation, and efficacy in disabling, are more particularly calculated to augment the *profit* which is to be made by punishment: frugality, subserviency to compensation, popularity, and remissibility, to diminish the *expense:* variability and equability are alike subservient to both those purposes.

XXVIII. We now come to take a general survey of the system of *offences:* that is, of such *acts* to which, on account of the mischievous *consequences* they have a *natural* tendency to produce, and in the view of putting a stop to those consequences, it may be proper to annex a certain *artificial* consequence, consisting of punishment, to be inflicted on the authors of such acts, according to the principles just established.

NOTE

1. The property of characteristicalness, therefore, is useful in a mode of punishment in three different ways: 1. It renders a mode of punishment, before infliction, more easy to be borne in mind: 2. It enables it, especially after infliction, to make the stronger impression, when it is there; that is, renders it the more *exemplary:* 3. It tends to render it more acceptable to the people, that is, it renders it the more *popular.*

WEEMS v. UNITED STATES

United States Supreme Court, 1909*

Mr. Justice McKenna delivered the opinion of the court.

This writ of error brings up for review the judgment of the Supreme Court of the Philippine Islands, affirming the conviction of plaintiff in error for falsifying a "public and official document."

In the "complaint," by which the prosecution was begun, it was charged that the plaintiff in error, "a duly appointed, qualified and acting disbursing officer of the Bureau of Coast Guard and Transportation of the United States Government of the Philippine Islands," did, as such, "corruptly and with intent, then and there, to deceive and defraud the United States Government of the Philippine Islands, and its officials, falsify a public and official document, namely, a cash book of the captain of the Board of Manila, Philippine Islands, and the Bureau of Coast Guard and Transportation of the United States Government of the Philippine Islands," kept by him as disbursing officer of that bureau. The falsification, which is alleged with much particularity, was committed by entering as paid out, "as wages of employés of the Light House Service of the United States Government of the Philippine Islands," at the Capul Light House of 208 pesos, and for like service at the Matabriga Light House of 408 pesos, Philippine currency. A demurrer was filed to the "complaint," which was overruled.

He was convicted, and the following sentence was imposed upon him: "To the penalty of fifteen years of Cadena, together with the accessories of section 56 of the Penal Code, and to pay a fine of four thousand pesetas, but not to serve imprisonment as a subsidiary punishment in case of his insolvency, on account of the nature of the main penalty, and to pay the costs of this cause."

The judgment and sentence were affirmed by the Supreme Court of the islands.

The assignment of error is that "A punishment of fifteen years' imprisonment was a cruel and unusual punishment, and, to the extent of the sentence, the judgment below should be reversed on this ground." Weems was convicted, as we have seen, for the falsifica-

*217 U.S. 357 (1909). Excerpts only.

tion of a public and official document, by entering therein, as paid out, the sums of 208 and 408 pesos, respectively, as wages to certain employés of the Light House service. In other words, in entering upon his cash book those sums as having been paid out when they were not paid out, and the "truth," to use the language of the statute, was thereby perverted "in the narration of facts."

A false entry is all that is necessary to constitute the offense. Whether an offender against the statute injures any one by his act or intends to injure any one is not material, the trial court held. The court said: "It is not necessary that there be any fraud nor even the desire to defraud, nor intention of personal gain on the part of the person committing it, that a falsification of a public document be punishable; it is sufficient that the one who committed it had the intention to pervert the truth and to falsify the document, and that by it damage might result to a third party." The court further, in the definition of the nature of the offense and the purpose of the law, said, "in public documents the law takes into consideration not only private interests, but also the interests of the community," and it is its endeavor (and for this a decision of the Supreme Court of Spain, delivered in 1873, was quoted) "to protect the interest of society by the most strict faithfulness on the part of a public official in the administration of the office intrusted to him," and thereby fulfill the "responsibility of the State to the community for the official or public documents under the safeguard of the State." And this was attempted to be secured through the law in controversy. It is found in § 1 of chapter IV of the Penal Code of Spain. The caption of the section is "falsification of official and commercial documents and telegraphic dispatches." Article 300 provides as follows: "The penalties of *cadena temporal* and a fine of from 1,250 to 12,500 pesetas shall be imposed on a public official who, taking advantage of his authority, shall commit a falsification. . . . by perverting the truth in the narration of facts. . . ."

By other provisions of the code we find that there are only two degrees of punishment higher in scale than *cadena temporal,* death, and *cadena perpetua.* The punishment of *cadena temporal* is from twelve years and one day to twenty years (arts. 28 and 96), which "shall be served" in certain "penal institutions." And it is provided that "those sentenced to *cadena temporal* and *cadena perpetua* shall labor for the benefit of the state. They shall always carry a chain at the ankle, hanging from the wrists; they shall be employed at hard and painful labor, and shall receive no assistance whatsoever from without the institution." Arts. 105, 106. There are besides certain accessory penalties imposed, which are defined to be (1) civil interdiction; (2) perpetual absolute disqualification; (3) subjection to surveillance during life. These penalties are defined as follows:

"Art. 42. Civil interdiction shall deprive the person punished as long as he suffers it, of the rights of parental authority, guardianship of person or property, participation in the family council, marital authority, the administration of property, and the right to dispose of his own property by acts *inter vivos*. Those cases are excepted in which the law explicitly limits its effects.

"Art. 43. Subjection to the surveillance of the authorities imposes the following obligations on the persons punished.

"1. That of fixing his domicil and giving notice thereof to the authority immediately in charge of his surveillance, not being allowed to change it without the knowledge and permission of said authority in writing.

"2. To observe the rules of inspection prescribed.

"3. To adopt some trade, art, industry, or profession, should he not have known means of subsistence of his own.

"Whenever a person punished is placed under the surveillance of the authorities, notice thereof shall be given to the government and to the governor general."

The penalty of perpetual absolute disqualification is the deprivation of office, even though it be held by popular election, the deprivation of the right to vote or to be elected to public office, the disqualification to acquire honors, etc., and the loss of retirement pay, etc.

These provisions are attacked as infringing that provision of the bill of rights of the islands which forbids the infliction of cruel and unusual punishment. It must be confessed that they, and the sentence in this case, excite wonder in minds accustomed to a more considerate adaptation of punishment to the degree of crime. In a sense the law in controversy seems to be independent of degrees. One may be an offender against it, as we have seen, though he gain nothing and injure nobody. It has, however, some human indulgence—it is not exactly Draconian in uniformity. Though it starts with a severe penalty, between that and the maximum penalty it yields something to extenuating circumstances. Indeed, by article 96 of the Penal Code the penalty is declared to be "divisible," and the legal term of its "duration is understood as distributed into three

parts forming the three degrees—that is, the minimum, medium, and maximum," being respectively from twelve years and one day to fourteen years and eight months, from fourteen years eight months and one day to seventeen years and four months, from seventeen years four months and one day to twenty years. The law therefore allows a range from twelve years and a day to twenty years, and the Government in its brief ventures to say that "the sentence of fifteen years is well within the law." But the sentence is attacked as well as the law, and what it is to be well within the law a few words will exhibit. The minimum term of imprisonment is twelve years, and that, therefore, must be imposed for "perverting the truth" in a single item of a public record, though there be no one injured, though there be no fraud or purpose of it, no gain or desire of it. Twenty years is the maximum imprisonment, and that only can be imposed for the perversion of truth in every item of an officer's accounts, whatever be the time covered and whatever fraud it conceals or tends to conceal. Between these two possible sentences, which seem to have no adaptable relation, or rather in the difference of eight years for the lowest possible offense and the highest possible, the courts below selected three years to add to the minimum of twelve years and a day for the falsification of two items of expenditure, amounting to the sums of 408 and 204 pesos. And the fine and "accesories" must be brought into view. The fine was four thousand pesetas, an excess also over the minimum. The "accesories" we have already defined. We can now give graphic description of Weems' sentence and of the law under which it was imposed. Let us confine it to the minimum degree of the law, for it is with the law that we are most concerned. Its minimum degree is confinement in a penal institution for twelve years and one day, a chain at the ankle and wrist of the offender, hard and painful labor, no assistance from friend or relative, no marital authority or parental rights or rights of property, no participation even in the family council. These parts of his penalty endure for the term of imprisonment. From other parts there is no intermission. His prison bars and chains are removed, it is true, after twelve years, but he goes from them to a perpetual limitation of his liberty. He is forever kept under the shadow of his crime, forever kept within voice and view of the criminal magistrate, not being able to change his domicil without giving notice to the "authority immediately in charge of his surveillance," and without permission in writing. He may not seek, even in other scenes and among other people, to retrieve his fall from rectitude. Even that hope is taken from him and he is subject to tormenting regulations that, if not so tangible as iron bars and stone walls, oppress as much by their continuity, and deprive of essential liberty. No circumstance of degradation is omitted. It may be that even the cruelty of pain is not omitted. He must bear a chain night and day. He is condemned to painful as well as hard labor. What painful labor may mean we have no exact measure. It must be something more than hard labor. It may be hard labor pressed to the point of pain. Such penalties for such offenses amaze those who have formed their conception of the relation of a state to even its offending citizens from the practice of the American commonwealths, and believe that it is a precept of justice that punishment for crime should be graduated and proportioned to offense. . . .

What constitutes a cruel and unusual punishment has not been exactly decided. It has been said that ordinarily the terms imply something inhuman and barbarous, torture and the like. *McDonald* v. *Commonwealth*, 173 Massachusetts, 322. The court, however, in that case conceded the possibility "that imprisonment in the State prison for a long term of years might be so disproportionate to the offense as to constitute a cruel and unusual punishment." . . .

In *Hobbs* v. *State*, and in other cases, prominence is given to the power of the legislature to define crimes and their punishment. We concede the power in most of its exercises. We disclaim the right to assert a judgment against that of the legislature of the expediency of the laws or the right to oppose the judicial power to the legislative power to define crimes and fix their punishment, unless that power encounters in its exercise a constitutional prohibition. In such case not our discretion but our legal duty, strictly defined and imperative in its direction, is invoked. Then the legislative power is brought to the judgment of a power superior to it for the instant. And for the proper exercise of such power there must be a comprehension of all that the legislature did or could take into account, that is, a consideration of the mischief and the remedy. However, there is a certain subordination of the judiciary to the legislature. The function of the legislature is primary, its exercises fortified by presumptions of right and legality, and is not to be interfered with lightly, nor by any judicial conception of their wisdom or propriety. They have no limitation, we repeat, but constitutional ones, and what those are the judiciary must judge. We have expressed these elementary truths to avoid the misapprehension that we do not recognize to the fullest the wide range of power that the legislature possesses to adapt its penal laws to conditions as they may exist and punish the crimes of men according to their forms and frequency. We do not intend in this opinion to express anything that contravenes those propositions.

Our meaning may be illustrated. For instance, in *Territory* v. *Ketchum*, 10 N.M. 718, a case that has been brought to our attention as antagonistic to our views of cruel and unusual punishments, a statute was sustained which imposed the penalty of death upon any person who should make an assault upon any railroad train, car or locomotive for the purpose and with the intent to commit murder, robbery or other felony upon a passenger or employé, express messenger or mail agent. The Supreme Court of the Territory discussed the purpose of the Eighth Amendment and expressed views opposed to those we announce in this opinion, but finally rested its decision upon the conditions which existed in the Territory and the circumstances of terror and danger which accompanied the crime denounced. So also may we mention the legislation of some of the States enlarging the common-law definition of burglary, and dividing it into degrees, fixing a severer punishment for that committed in the night time from that committed in the day time, and for arson of buildings in which human beings may be from arson of buildings which may be vacant. In all such cases there is something more to give character and degree to the crimes than the seeking of a felonious gain and it may properly become an element in the measure of their punishment.

From this comment we turn back to the law in controversy. Its character and the sentence in this case may be illustrated by examples even better than it can be represented by words. There are degrees of homicide that are not punished so severely, nor are the following crimes: misprision of treason, inciting rebellion, conspiracy to destroy the Government by force, recruiting soldiers in the United States to fight against the United States, forgery of letters patent, forgery of bonds and other instruments for the purpose of defrauding the United States, robbery, larceny and other crimes. Section 86 of the Penal Laws of the United States, as revised and amended by the act of Congress of March 4, 1909, c. 321 (35 Stat. 1088), provides that any person charged with the payment of any appropriation made by Congress who shall pay to any clerk or other employé of the United States a sum less than that provided by law and require a receipt for a sum greater than that paid to and received by him shall be guilty of embezzlement, and shall be fined in double the amount so withheld and imprisoned not more than two years. The offense described has similarity to the offense for which Weems was convicted, but the punishment provided for it is in great contrast to the penalties of *cadena temporal* and its "accesories." If we turn to the legislation of the Philippine Commission we find that instead of the penalties of *cadena temporal*, medium degree, (fourteen years eight months and one day to seventeen years and four months, with fine and "accessories"), to *cadena perpetua*, fixed by the Spanish penal code for the falsification of bank notes and other instruments authorized by the law of the kingdom, it is provided that the forgery of or counterfeiting the obligations or securities of the United States or of the Philippine Islands shall be punished by a fine of not more than ten thousand pesos and by imprisonment of not more than fifteen years. In other words, the highest punishment possible for a crime which may cause the loss of many thousand of dollars, and to prevent which the duty of the State should be as eager as to prevent the perversion of truth in a public document, is not greater than that which may be imposed for falsifying a single item of a public account. And this contrast shows more than different exercises of legislative judgment. It is greater than that. It condemns the sentence in this case as cruel and unusual. It exhibits a difference between unrestrained power and that which is exercised under the spirit of constitutional limitations formed to establish justice. The State thereby suffers nothing and loses no power. The purpose of punishment is fulfilled, crime is repressed by penalties of just, not tormenting, severity, its repetition is prevented, and hope is given for the reformation of the criminal.

. . .

It follows from these views that, even if the minimum penalty of *cadena temporal* had been imposed, it would have been repugnant to the bill of rights. In other words, the fault is in the law, and, as we are pointed to no other under which a sentence can be imposed, the judgment must be reversed, with directions to dismiss the preceedings.

So ordered.

Mr. Justice White, dissenting.

. . . Of course, in every case where punishment is inflicted for the commission of crime, if the suffering of the punishment by the wrongdoer be alone regarded the sense of compassion aroused would mislead and render the performance of judicial duty impossible. And it is to be conceded that this natural conflict between the sense of commiseration and the commands of duty is augmented when the nature of the crime defined by the Philippine law and the punishment which that law prescribes is only abstractly considered, since the impression is at once produced that the legislative authority has been severely exerted. I say only abstractly considered, because the first impression produced by the merely abstract view of the subject is met by the admonition that the duty of defining and punishing crime has never in any civilized country been exerted upon mere abstract considerations of the inherent nature of the crime punished, but has always involved the most practical consideration of the tendency at a particular time to commit certain crimes, of the difficulty of repressing the same, and of how far it is necessary to impose stern remedies to prevent the commission of such crimes. 'And, of course, as these considerations involve the necessity for a familiarity with local conditions in the Philippine Islands which I do not possess, such want of knowledge at once additionally admonishes me of the wrong to arise from forming a judgment upon insufficient data or without a knowledge of the subject-matter upon which the judgment is to be exerted. Strength, indeed, is added to this last suggestion by the fact that no question concerning the subject was raised in the courts below or there considered, and, therefore, no opportunity was afforded those courts, presumably, at least, relatively familiar with the local conditions, to express their views as to the considerations which may have led to the prescribing of the punishment in question. Turning aside, therefore, from mere emotional tendencies and guiding my judgment alone by the aid of the reason at my command, I am unable to agree with the ruling of the court. As, in my opinion, that ruling rests upon an interpretation of the cruel and unusual punishment clause of the Eighth Amendment, never before announced, which is repugnant to the natural import of the language employed in the clause, and which interpretation curtails the legislative power of Congress to define and punish crime by asserting a right of judicial supervision over the exertion of that power, in disregard of the distinction between the legislative and judicial departments of the Government, I deem it my duty to dissent and state my reasons.

To perform this duty requires at the outset a precise statement of the construction given by the ruling now made to the provision of the Eighth Amendment. My inability to do this must, however, be confessed, because I find it impossible to fix with precision the meaning which the court gives to that provision. Not for the purpose of criticising, but solely in order to indicate my perplexity on the subject, the reasons for my doubt are briefly given. Thus to my mind it appears as follows: First. That the court interprets the inhibition against cruel and unusual punishment as imposing upon Congress the duty of proportioning punishment according to the nature of the crime, and casts upon the judiciary the duty of determining whether punishments have been properly apportioned in a particular statute, and if not to decline to enforce it. This seems to me to be the case, because of the reference made by the court to the harshness of the principal punishment (imprisonment), and its comments as to what it deems to be the severity, if not inhumanity, of the accessories which result from or accompany it, and the declaration in substance that these things offend against the just principle of proportioning punishment to the nature of the crime punished, stated to be a fundamental precept of justice and of American criminal law. That this is the view now upheld, it seems to me, is additionally demonstrated by the fact that the punishment for the crime in question as imposed by the Philippine law is compared with other Philippine punishments for crimes deemed to be less heinous, and the conclusion is deduced that this fact in and of itself serves to establish that the punishment imposed in this case is an exertion of unrestrained power condemned by the cruel and unusual punishment clause.

Second. That this duty of apportionment compels not only that the lawmaking power should adequately apportion punishment for the crimes as to which it legislates, but also further exacts that the performance of the duty of apportionment must be discharged by taking into view the standards, whether lenient or severe, existing in other and distinct jurisdictions, and that a failure to do so authorizes the courts to consider such standards in their discretion and judge of the validity of the law accordingly. I say this because, although the court expressly declares in the opinion, when considering a case decided by the highest court of one of the Territories of the United States, that the legislative power to define and punish crime committed in a Territory, for the purpose of the Eighth Amendment, is separate and distinct from the legislation of Congress, yet in testing the validity of the punishment affixed by the law here in question, proceeds to measure it not alone by the Philippine legislation, but by the provisions of several acts of Congress punishing crime and in substance declares such Congressional laws to be a proper standard, and in effect holds that the greater proportionate punishment inflicted by the Philippine law over the more lenient punishments prescribed in the laws of Congress establishes that the Philippine law is repugnant to the Eighth Amendment.

Third. That the cruel and unusual punishment clause of the Eighth Amendment controls not only the exertion of legislative power as to modes of punishment, proportionate or otherwise, but addresses itself also to the mainspring of the legislative motives in enacting legislation punishing crime in a particular case, and therefore confers upon courts the power to refuse to enforce a particular law defining and punishing crime if in their opinion such law does not manifest that the lawmaking power, in fixing the punishment, was sufficiently impelled by a purpose to effect a reformation of the criminal. This is said because of the statements contained in the opinion of the court as to the legislative duty to shape legislation not only with a view to punish but to reform the criminal, and the inferences which I deduce that it is conceived that the failure to do so is a violation of constitutional duty.

Fourth. That the cruel and unusual punishment clause does not merely limit the legislative power to fix the punishment for crime by excepting out of that authority the right to impose bodily punishments of a cruel kind, in the strict acceptation of those terms, but

limits the legislative discretion in determining to what degree of severity an appropriate and usual mode of punishment may in a particular case be inflicted, and therefore endows the courts with the right to supervise the exercise of legislative discretion as to the adequacy of punishment, even although resort is had only to authorized kinds of punishment, thereby endowing the courts with the power to refuse to enforce laws punishing crime if in the judicial judgment the legislative branch of the Government has prescribed a too severe punishment.

Not being able to assent to these, as it to me seems, in some respects conflicting, or at all events widely divergent propositions, I shall consider them all as sanctioned by the interpretation now given to the prohibition of the Eighth Amendment, and with this conception in mind shall consider the subject.

Before approaching the text of the Eighth Amendment to determine its true meaning let me briefly point out why in my opinion it cannot have the significance which it must receive to sustain the propositions rested upon it. In the first place, if it be that the lawmaker in defining and punishing crime is imperatively restrained by constitutional provisions to apportion punishment by a consideration alone of the abstract heinousness of the offenses punished, it must result that the power is so circumscribed as to be impossible of execution, or at all events is so restricted as to exclude the possibility of taking into account in defining and punishing crime all those considerations concerning the condition of society, the tendency to commit the particular crime, the difficulty of detecting the same, the necessity for resorting to stern measures of repression, and various other subjects which have at all times been deemed essential to be weighed in defining and punishing crime. And certainly the paralysis of the discretion vested in the lawmaking authority which the propositions accomplish is immeasurably magnified when it is considered that this duty of proportioning punishment requires the taking into account of the standards prevailing in other or different countries or jurisdictions, thereby at once exacting that legislation on the subject of crime must be proportioned, not to the conditions to which it is intended to apply, but must be based upon conditions with which the legislation when enacted will have no relation or concern whatever. And when it is considered that the propositions go further and insist that if the legislation seems to the judicial mind not to have been sufficiently impelled by motives of reformation of the criminal, such legislation defining and punishing crime is to be held repugnant to constitutional limitations, the impotency of the legislative power to define and punish crime is made manifest. When to this result is added the consideration that the interpretation by its necessary effect does not simply cause the cruel and unusual punishment clause to carve out of the domain of legislative authority the power to resort to prohibited kinds of punishments, but subjects to judicial control, the degree of severity with which authorized modes of punishment may be inflicted, it seems to me that the demonstration is conclusive that nothing will be left of the independent legislative power to punish and define crime, if the interpretation now made be pushed in future application to its logical conclusion.

But let me come to the Eighth Amendment, for the purpose of stating why the clause in question does not, in my opinion, authorize the deductions drawn from it, and therefore does not sanction the ruling now made . . .

That no such meaning as is now ascribed to the Amendment was attributed to it at the time of its adoption is shown by the fact that not a single suggestion that it had such a meaning is pointed to, and that on the other hand the practise from the very beginning shows directly to the contrary and demonstrates that the very Congress that adopted the Amendment construed it in practice as I have construed it. This is so, since the first crimes act of the United States prescribed a punishment for crime utterly without reference to any assumed rule of proportion or of a conception of a right in the judiciary to supervise the action of Congress in respect to the severity of punishment, excluding always the right to impose as a punishment the cruel bodily punishments which were prohibited. What clearer demonstration can there be of this than the statement made by this court in *Ex parte Wilson,* 114 U.S. 427, of the nature of the first crimes act, as follows:

"By the first Crimes Act of the United States, forgery of public securities, or knowingly uttering forged public securities with intent to defraud, as well as treason, murder, piracy, mutiny, robbery, or rescue of a person convicted of a capital crime, was punishable with death; most other offences were punished by fine and imprisonment; whipping was part of the punishment of stealing or falsifying records, fraudulently acknowledging bail, larceny of goods, or receiving stolen goods; disqualification to hold office was part of the punishment of bribery; and those convicted of perjury or subornation of perjury, besides being fined and imprisoned, were to stand in the pillory for one hour, and rendered incapable of testifying in any court of the United States. Act of April 30, 1790, ch. 9; 1 Stat. 112–117; Mr. Justice Wilson's Charge to the Grand Jury in 1791, 3 Wilson's Works, 380, 381."

And it is, I think, beyond power even of question that the legislation of Congress from the date of the first crimes act to the present time but exemplifies the truth of what has been said, since that legislation from time to time altered modes of punishment, increasing or diminishing the amount of punishment as was deemed necessary for the public good, prescribing punishments of a new character, without reference to any assumed rule of apportionment or the conception that a right of judicial supervision was deemed to obtain. It is impossible with any regard for brevity to demonstrate these statements by many illustrations. But let me give a sample from legislation enacted by Congress of the change of punishment. By § 14 of the first crimes act (Art. April 30, 1790, ch. 9, 1 Stat. 115), forgery, etcetera, of the public securities of the United States, or the knowingly uttering and offering for sale of forged or counterfeited securities of the United States with intent to defraud, was made punishable by death. The punishment now is a fine of not more than $5,000, and imprisonment at hard labor for not more than fifteen years.

By the first crimes act also, as in numerous others since that time, various additional punishments for the commission of crime were imposed, prescribing disqualification to hold office, to be a witness in the courts, etcetera, and as late as 1865 a law was enacted by Congress which prescribed as a punishment for crime the disqualification to enjoy rights of citizenship.

Here, again, it is true to say, time forbidding my indulging in a review of the statutes, that the legislation of all the States is absolutely in conflict with and repugnant to the construction now given to the clause, since that legislation but exemplifies the exertion of legislative power to define and punish crime according to the legislative conception of the necessities of the situation, without the slightest indication of the assumed duty to proportion punishments, and without the suggestion of the existence of judicial power to control the legislative discretion, provided only that the cruel bodily punishments forbidden were not resorted to. And the decisions of the state courts of last resort, it seems to me, with absolute uniformity and without a single exception from the beginning, proceed upon this conception. It is true that when the reasoning employed in the various cases is critically examined a difference of conception will be manifested as to the occasion for the adoption of the English bill of rights and of the remedy which it provided. Generally speaking, when carefully analyzed, it will be seen that this difference was occasioned by treating the provision against cruel and unusual punishment as conjunctive instead of disjunctive, thereby overlooking the fact, which I think has been previously demonstrated to be the case, that the term unusual, as used in the clause, was not a qualification of the provision against cruel punishments, but was simply synonymous with illegal, and was mainly intended to restrain the courts, under the guise of discretion, from indulging in an unusual and consequently illegal exertion of power. Certain it is, however, whatever may be these differences of reasoning, there stands out in bold relief in the State cases, as it is given to me to understand them, without a single exception, the clear and certain exclusion of any prohibition upon the lawmaking power to determine the adequacy with which crime shall be punished, provided only the cruel bodily punishments of the past are not resorted to. Let me briefly refer to some of the cases . . .

Until 1865 there was no provision in the constitution of Georgia expressly guaranteeing against cruel and unusual punishments. The constitution of that year, however, contained a clause identical in terms with the Eighth Amendment, and the scope of the guarantee arose for decision in 1872 in *Whitten* v. *State,* 47 Georgia, 297. The case was this: Upon a conviction for assault and battery Whitten had been sentenced to imprisonment or the payment of a fine of $250 and costs. The contention was that this sentence was so disproportionate to the offense committed as to be cruel and unusual and repugnant to the guarantee. In one of its immediate aspects the case involved the guarantee against excessive fines, but as the imprisonment was the coercive means for the payment of the fine, in that aspect the case involved the cruel and unusual punishment clause, and the court so considered, and, in coming to interpret the clause said (p. 301):

"Whether the law is unconstitutional, a violation of that article of the Constitution which declares excessive fines shall not be imposed nor cruel and unusual punishments inflicted, is another question. The latter clause was, doubtless, intended to prohibit the barbarities of quartering, hanging in chains, castration, etcetera. When adopted by the framers of the Constitution of the United States, larceny was generally punished by hanging; forgeries, burglaries, etcetera, in the same way, for, be it remembered, penitentiaries are of modern origin, and I doubt if it ever entered into the mind of men of that day that a crime such as this witness makes the defendant guilty of deserved a less penalty than the judge has inflicted. It would be an interference with matters left by the Constitution to the legislative department of the government for us to undertake to weigh the propriety of this or that penalty fixed by the legislature for specific offenses. So long as they do not provide cruel and unusual punishments, such as disgraced the civilization of former ages, and made one shudder with horror to read of them, as drawing, quartering, burning, etcetera, the Constitution does not put any limit upon legislative discretion."

In *State* v. *White* (1890), 44 Kansas, 514, it was sought to reverse a sentence of five years' imprisonment in the penitentiary, imposed upon a boy of sixteen for statutory rape. The girl was aged sixteen, and had consented. It was contended that if the statute applied it was unconstitutional and void, "for the reason that it conflicts with section 9 of the bill of rights, because it inflicts cruel and unusual punishment, and is in conflict with the spirit of the bill of rights generally, and is in violation of common sense, common reason, and common justice."

The court severely criticised the statute. After deciding that the offense was embraced in the statute, the court said:

"With respect to the severity of the punishment, while we think it is true that it is a severer one than has ever before been provided for in any other State or county for such an offense, yet we cannot say that the statute is void for that reason. Imprisonment in the penitentiary at hard labor is not of itself a cruel or unusual punishment, within the meaning of section 9 of the bill of rights of the Constitution, for it is a kind of punishment which has been resorted to ever since Kansas has had any existence, and is a kind of punishment common in all civilized countries. That section of the Constitution probably, however, relates to the kind of punishment to be inflicted, and not to its duration. Although the punishment in this case may be considered severe, and much severer indeed than the punishment for offenses of much greater magnitude, as adultery, or sexual intercourse coupled with seduction, yet we cannot say that the act providing for it is unconstitutional or void."

In *State* v. *Hogan* (1900), 63 Ohio St. 218, the court sustained a "tramp law," which prescribed, as the punishment to be imposed on a tramp for threatening to do injury to the person of another, imprisonment in the penitentiary not more than three years nor less than one year. In the course of the opinion the court said:

"The objection that the act prescribes a cruel and unusual punishment we think not well taken. Imprisonment at hard labor is neither cruel nor unusual. It may be severe in the given instance, but that is a question for the lawmaking power. *In re Kemmler,* 136 U.S. 436; *Cornelison* v. *Com.,* 84 Kentucky, 583. The punishment, to be effective, should be such as will prove a deterrent. The tramp cares nothing for a jail sentence. Often he courts it. A workhouse sentence is less welcome, but there are but few workhouses in the State. A penitentiary sentence is a real punishment. There he has to work, and cannot shirk."

In Minnesota a register of deeds was convicted of misappropriating the sum of $62.50, which should have been turned over by him to the country treasurer. He was sentenced to pay a fine of $500 and be imprisoned at hard labor for one year. The contention that the sentence was repugnant to the state constitutional guarantee against cruel and unusual punishment was considered and disposed of by the court in *State* v. *Borgstrom,* 69 Minnesota, 508, 520. Among other things the court said:

"It is claimed that the sentence imposed was altogether disproportionate to the offense charged, and of which the defendant was convicted, and comes within the inhibition of Const. art. 1, § 5, that no cruel or unusual punishments be inflicted. ... We are not unmindful of the importance of this question, and have given to it that serious and thorough examination which such importance demands. ... In England there was a time when punishment was by torture, by loading him with weights to make him confess. Traitors were condemned to be drowned, disemboweled, or burned. It was the 'law that the offender shall be drawn, or rather dragged, to the gallows; he shall be hanged and cut down alive; his entrails shall be removed and burned while he yet lives; his head shall be decapitated; his body divided into four parts.' Browne, Bl. Comm. 617. For certain other offenses the offender was punished by cutting off the hands or ears, or boiling in oil, or putting in the pillory. By the Roman law a parricide was punished by being sewed up in a leather sack with a live dog, a cock, a viper, and an ape, and cast into the sea. These punishments may properly be termed cruel, but happily the more humane spirit of this nation does not permit such punishment to be inflicted upon criminals. Such punishments are not warranted by the laws of nature or society, and we find that they are prohibited by our Constitution. But, within this limitation or restriction, the legislature is ordinarily the judge of the expediency of creating new crimes and of prescribing the penalty. ... While the amount of money misappropriated in this instance was not great, the legislature evidently had in mind the fact that the misappropriation by a public official of the public money was destructive of the public rights and the stability of our government. But fine and imprisonment are not ordinarily cruel and unusual punishments. ..."

In *Territory* v. *Ketchum,* 10 N.M. 721, the court considered whether a statute which had recently been put in force and which imposed the death penalty instead of a former punishment of imprisonment, for an attempt at train robbery, was cruel and unusual. In sustaining the validity of the law the court pointed out the conditions of society which presumably had led the lawmaking power to fix the stern penalty, and after a lengthy discussion of the subject it was held that the law did not impose punishment which was cruel or unusual.

The cases just reviewed are typical, and I therefore content myself with noting in the margin many others to the same general effect. ...

From all the considerations which have been stated I can deduce no ground whatever which to my mind sustains the interpretation now given to the cruel and unusual punishment clause. On the contrary, in my opinion, the review which has been made demonstrates that the word cruel, as used in the Amendment, forbids only the lawmaking power, in prescribing punishment for crime and the courts in imposing punishment from inflicting unnecessary bodily suffering through a resort to inhuman methods for causing bodily torture, like or which are of the nature of the cruel methods of bodily torture which had been made use of prior to the bill of rights of 1689, and against the recurrence of which the word cruel was used in that instrument. To illustrate. Death was a well-known method of punishment prescribed by law, and it was of course painful, and in that sense was cruel. But the infliction of this punishment was clearly not prohibited by the word cruel, although that word manifestly was intended to forbid the resort to barbarous and unnecessary methods of bodily torture, in executing even the penalty of death.

In my opinion the previous considerations also establish that the word unusual accomplished only three results: First, it primarily restrains the courts when acting under the authority of a general discretionary power to impose punishment, such as was possessed at common law, from inflicting lawful modes of punishment to so unusual a degree as to cause the punishment to be illegal because to that degree it cannot be inflicted without express statutory authority; second, it restrains the courts in the exercise of the same discretion from inflicting a mode of punishment so unusual as to be impliedly not within its discretion and to be consequently illegal in the absence of express statutory authority; and, third, as to both the foregoing it operated to restrain the lawmaking power from endowing the judiciary with the right to exert an illegal discretion as to the kind and extent of punishment to be inflicted.

JOSEPH BUTLER

Upon Resentment*

"Ye have heard that it hath been said, Thou shalt love thy neighbour, and hate thine enemy: but I say unto you, Love your enemies, bless them that curse you, do good to them that hate you, and pray for them which despitefully use you and persecute you."—Matt. v. 43, 44.

(1) Since perfect goodness in the Deity is the principle from whence the universe was brought into being, and by which it is preserved; and since general benevolence is the great law of the whole moral creation: it is a question which immediately occurs, *Why had man implanted in him a principle, which appears the direct contrary to benevolence?* Now the foot upon which inquiries of this kind should be treated is this: to take human nature as it is, and the circumstances in which it is placed as they are; and then consider the correspondence between that nature and those circumstances, or what course of action and behaviour, respecting those circumstances, any particular affection or passion leads us to. This I mention to distinguish the matter now before us from disquisitions of quite another kind; namely, *Why we are not made more perfect creatures, or placed in better circumstances?* these being questions which we have not, that I know of, anything at all to do with. God Almighty undoubtedly foresaw the disorders, both natural and moral, which would happen in this state of things. If upon this we set ourselves to search and examine why he did not prevent them; we shall, I am afraid, be in danger of running into somewhat worse than impertinent curiosity. But upon this to examine how far the nature which he hath given us hath a respect to those circumstances, such as they are; how far it leads us to act a proper part in them; plainly belongs to us: and such inquiries are in many

*From *Fifteen Sermons Preached at the Rolls Chapel* by Joseph Butler, Bishop of Durham, (London: G. Bell & Sons, Ltd., 1914). "Upon Resentment" is Sermon VIII.

ways of excellent use. Thus the thing to be considered is, not, *Why we were not made of such a nature, and placed in such circumstances, as to have no need of so harsh and turbulent a passion as resentment;* but, taking our nature and condition as being what they are, *Why, or for what end such a passion was given us:* and this chiefly in order to shew what are the abuses of it.

(2) The persons who laid down for a rule, *Thou shalt love thy neighbour and hate thine enemy,* made short work with this matter. They did not, it seems, perceive anything to be disapproved in hatred, more than in good-will: and, according to their system of morals, our enemy was the proper natural object of one of these passions, as our neighbour was of the other of them. This was all they had to say, and all they thought needful to be said, upon the subject. But this cannot be satisfactory; because hatred, malice and revenge are directly contrary to the religion we profess, and to the nature and reason of the thing itself. Therefore, since no passion God hath endued us with can be in itself evil; and yet since men frequently indulge a passion in such ways and degrees that at length it becomes quite another thing from what it was originally in our nature; and those vices of malice and revenge in particular take their occasion from the natural passion of resentment: it will be needful to trace this up to its original, that we may see *what it is in itself, as placed in our nature by its Author;* from which it will plainly appear, *for what ends it was placed there.* And when we know what the passion is in itself, and the ends of it, we shall easily see, *what are the abuses of it, in which malice and revenge consist;* and which are so strongly forbidden in the text, by the direct contrary being commanded.

(3) Resentment is of two kinds: *hasty and sudden, or settled and deliberate.*[1] The former is

called anger, and often *passion;* which, though a general word, is frequently appropriated and confined to the particular feeling, sudden anger, as distinct from deliberate resentment, malice and revenge. In all these words is usually implied somewhat vicious; somewhat unreasonable as to the occasion of the passion, or immoderate as to the degree or duration of it. But that the natural passion itself is indifferent, St. *Paul* has asserted in that precept, *Be ye angry and sin not;*[2] which though it is by no means to be understood as an encouragement to indulge ourselves in anger, the sense being certainly this, *Though ye be angry, sin not;* yet here is evidently a distinction made between anger and sin; between the natural passion, and sinful anger.

(4) *Sudden anger* upon certain occasions is mere instinct: as merely so, as the disposition to close our eyes upon the apprehension of somewhat falling into them; and no more necessarily implies any degree of reason. I say, *necessarily:* for to be sure *hasty,* as well as *deliberate,* anger may be occasioned by injury or contempt; in which cases reason suggests to our thoughts that injury and contempt, which is the occasion of the passion: but I am speaking of the former only so far as it is to be distinguished from the latter. The only way in which our reason and understanding can raise anger is by representing to our mind injustice or injury of some kind or other. Now momentary anger is frequently raised, not only without any real, but without any apparent reason; that is, without any appearance of injury, as distinct from hurt or pain. It cannot, I suppose, be thought that this passion, in infants; in the lower species of animals; and, which is often seen, in men towards them; it cannot, I say, be imagined that these instances of this passion are the effect of reason: no, they are occasioned by mere sensation and feeling. It is opposition, sudden hurt, violence, which naturally excites the passion; and the real demerit or fault of him who offers that violence, or is the cause of that opposition or hurt, does not in many cases so much as come into thought.

(5) The reason and end, for which man was made thus liable to this passion, is, that he might be better qualified to prevent, and likewise (or perhaps chiefly) to resist and defeat, sudden force, violence and opposition, considered merely as such, and without regard to the fault or demerit of him who is the author of them. Yet, since violence may be considered in this other and further view, as implying fault; and since injury, as distinct from harm, may raise sudden anger; sudden anger may likewise accidentally serve to prevent, or remedy, such fault and injury. But, considered as distinct from settled anger, it stands in our nature for self-defence, and not for the administration of justice. There are plainly cases, and in the uncultivated parts of the world, and, where regular governments are not formed, they frequently happen, in which there is no time for consideration, and yet to be passive is certain destruction; in which sudden resistance is the only security.

(6) But from *this, deliberate anger or resentment* is essentially distinguished, as the latter is not naturally excited by, or intended to prevent mere harm without appearance of wrong or injustice. Now, in order to see, as exactly as we can, what is the natural object and occasion of such resentment; let us reflect upon the manner in which we are touched with reading, suppose, a feigned story of baseness and villainy, properly worked up to move our passions. This immediately raises indignation, somewhat of a desire that it should be punished. And though the designed injury be prevented, yet that it was designed is sufficient to raise this inward feeling. Suppose the story true, this inward feeling would be as natural and as just: and one may venture to affirm, that there is scarce a man in the world, but would have it upon some occasions. It seems *in us* plainly connected with a sense of virtue and vice, of moral good and evil. Suppose further, we knew both the person who did and who suffered the injury: neither would this make any alteration, only that it would probably affect us more. The indignation raised by cruelty and injustice, and the desire of having it punished, which persons unconcerned would feel, is by no means malice. No, it is resentment against vice and wickedness: it is one of the common bonds, by which society is held together; a fellow feeling, which each individual has in behalf of the whole species, as well as of himself. And it does not appear that this, generally speaking, is at all too high amongst mankind. Suppose now the injury I have been speaking of to be done against ourselves; or those whom we consider as ourselves. It is plain, the way in which we should be affected would be

exactly the same in kind: but it would certainly be in a higher degree, and less transient; because a sense of our own happiness and misery is most intimately and always present to us; and, from the very constitution of our nature, we cannot but have a greater sensibility to, and be more deeply interested in, what concerns ourselves. And this seems to be the whole of this passion which is, properly speaking, natural to mankind: namely, a resentment against injury and wickedness in general; and in a higher degree when towards ourselves, in proportion to the greater regard which men naturally have for themselves, than for others. From hence it appears, that it is not natural, but moral evil; it is not suffering, but injury, which raises that anger or resentment, which is of any continuance. The natural object of it is not one, who appears to the suffering person to have been only the innocent occasion of his pain or loss; but one, who has been in a moral sense injurious either to ourselves or others. This is abundantly confirmed by observing what it is which heightens or lessens resentment; namely, the same which aggravates or lessens the fault: friendship and former obligations, on one hand; or inadvertency, strong temptations and mistake on the other. All this is so much understood by mankind, how little soever it be reflected upon, that a person would be reckoned quite distracted, who should coolly resent an harm, which had not to himself the appearance of injury or wrong. Men do indeed resent what is occasioned through carelessness; but then they expect observance as their due, and so that carelessness is considered as faulty. It is likewise true, that they resent more strongly an injury done, than one which, though designed, was prevented, in cases where the guilt is perhaps the same: the reason however is, not that bare pain or loss raises resentment, but, that it gives a new, and, as I may speak, additional sense of the injury or injustice. According to the natural course of the passions, the degrees of resentment are in proportion, not only to the degree of design and deliberation in the injurious person; but in proportion to this, joined with the degree of the evil designed or premeditated; since this likewise comes in to make the injustice greater or less. And the evil or harm will appear greater when they feel it, than when they only reflect upon it: so therefore will the injury: and consequently the resentment will be greater.

(7) The natural object or occasion of settled resentment then being injury, as distinct from pain or loss; it is easy to see, that to prevent and to remedy such injury, and the miseries arising from it, is the end for which this passion was implanted in man. It is to be considered as a weapon, put into our hands by nature, against injury, injustice and cruelty: how it may be innocently employed and made use of shall presently be mentioned.

(8) The account which has been now given of this passion is, in brief, that sudden anger is raised by, and was chiefly intended to prevent or remedy, mere harm distinct from injury; but that it *may* be raised by injury, and *may* serve to prevent or to remedy it; and then the occasions and effects of it are the same with the occasions and effects of deliberate anger. But they are essentially distinguished in this, that the latter is never occasioned by harm, distinct from injury; and its natural proper end is to remedy or prevent only that harm, which implies, or is supposed to imply, injury or moral wrong. Every one sees that these observations do not relate to those, who have habitually suppressed the course of their passions and affections, out of regard either to interest or virtue; or who, from habits of vice and folly, have changed their nature. But, I suppose, there can be no doubt but this, now described, is the general course of resentment, considered as a natural passion, neither increased by indulgence, nor corrected by virtue, nor prevailed over by other passions or particular habits of life.

(9) As to the abuses of anger, which it is to be observed may be in all different degrees, the first which occurs is what is commonly called *passion;* to which some men are liable, in the same way as others are to the *epilepsy,* or any sudden particular disorder. This distemper of the mind seizes them upon the least occasion in the world, and perpetually without any real reason at all: and by means of it they are plainly, every day, every waking hour of their lives, liable and in danger of running into the most extravagant outrages. Of a less boisterous, but not of a less innocent kind, is *peevishness;* which I mention with pity, with real pity to the unhappy creatures, who, from their inferior station, or other circumstances and relations, are obliged to be in the way of, and to serve for a supply to it. Both these, for aught that I can see, are one and the same principle: but, as it

takes root in minds of different makes, it appears differently, and so is come to be distinguished by different names. That which in a more feeble temper is peevishness, and languidly discharges itself upon everything which comes in its way; the same principle, in a temper of greater force and stronger passions, becomes rage and fury. In one, the humour discharges itself at once; in the other, it is continually discharging. This is the account of *passion* and *peevishness,* as distinct from each other, and appearing in different persons. It is no objection against the truth of it, that they are both to be seen sometimes in one and the same person.

(10) With respect to deliberate resentment, the chief instances of abuse are: when, from partiality to ourselves, we imagine an injury done us, when there is none: when this partiality represents it to us greater than it really is: when we fall into that extravagant and monstrous kind of resentment, towards one who has innocently been the occasion of evil to us; that is, resentment upon account of pain or inconvenience, without injury; which is the same absurdity, as settled anger at a thing that is inanimate: when the indignation against injury and injustice rises too high, and is beyond proportion to the particular ill action it is exercised upon: or lastly, when pain or harm of any kind is inflicted merely in consequence of, and to gratify, that resentment, though naturally raised.

(11) It would be endless to descend into and explain all the peculiarities of perverseness and wayward humour which might be traced up to this passion. But there is one thing, which so generally belongs to and accompanies all excess and abuse of it, as to require being mentioned: a certain determination, and resolute bent of mind, not to be convinced or set right; though it be ever so plain, that there is no reason for the displeasure, that it was raised merely by error or misunderstanding. In this there is doubtless a great mixture of pride; but there is somewhat more, which I cannot otherwise express than that resentment has taken possession of the temper and of the mind, and will not quit its hold. It would be too minute to inquire whether this be anything more than bare obstinacy: it is sufficient to observe, that it, in a very particular manner and degree, belongs to the abuses of this passion.

(12) But, notwithstanding all these abuses; "Is not just indignation against cruelty and wrong one of the *instruments of death* which the Author of our nature hath provided? Are not cruelty, injustice and wrong the natural objects of that indignation? Surely then it may one way or other be innocently employed against them." True. Since therefore it is necessary for the very subsistence of the world, that injury, injustice and cruelty should be punished; and since compassion, which is so natural to mankind, would render that execution of justice exceedingly difficult and uneasy; indignation against vice and wickedness is, and may be allowed to be, a balance to that weakness of pity, and also to anything else which would prevent the necessary methods of severity. Those who have never thought upon these subjects, may perhaps not see the weight of this: but let us suppose a person guilty of murder, or any other action of cruelty, and that mankind had naturally no indignation against such wickedness and the authors of it; but that everybody was affected towards such a criminal in the same way as towards an innocent man: compassion, amongst other things, would render the execution of justice exceedingly painful and difficult, and would often quite prevent it. And notwithstanding that the principle of benevolence is denied by some, and is really in a very low degree, that men are in great measure insensible to the happiness of their fellow-creatures; yet they are not insensible to their misery, but are very strongly moved with it: insomuch that there plainly is occasion for that feeling which is raised by guilt and demerit, and as a balance to that of compassion. Thus much may, I think, justly be allowed to resentment, in the strictest way of moral consideration.

(13) The good influence which this passion has in fact upon the affairs of the world, is obvious to every one's notice. Men are plainly restrained from injuring their fellow-creatures by fear of their resentment; and it is very happy that they are so, when they would not be restrained by a principle of virtue. And after an injury is done, and there is a necessity that the offender should be brought to justice; the cool consideration of reason, that the security and peace of society requires examples of justice should be made, might indeed be sufficient to procure laws to be enacted, and sentence passed: but is it that cool reflection in the injured person, which, for the most part, brings the offender to justice? Or is it not resent-

ment and indignation against the injury and the author of it? I am afraid there is no doubt, which is commonly the case. This however is to be considered as a good effect, notwithstanding it were much to be wished that men would act from a better principle, reason and cool reflection.

(14) The account now given of the passion of resentment, as distinct from all the abuses of it, may suggest to our thoughts the following reflections.

(15) *First,* That vice is indeed of ill desert, and must finally be punished. Why should men dispute concerning the reality of virtue, and whether it be founded in the nature of things, which yet surely is not matter of question; but why should this, I say, be disputed, when every man carries about him this passion, which affords him demonstration, that the rules of justice and equity are to be the guide of his actions? For every man naturally feels an indignation upon seeing instances of villainy and baseness, and therefore cannot commit the same without being self-condemned.

(16) *Secondly,* That we should learn to be cautious, lest we *charge God foolishly,* by ascribing that to him, or the nature he has given us, which is owing wholly to our own abuse of it. Men may speak of the degeneracy and corruption of the world, according to the experience they have had of it; but human nature, considered as the divine workmanship, should methinks be treated as sacred: for *in the image of God made he man.* That

passion, from whence men take occasion to run into the dreadful vices of malice and revenge; even that passion, as implanted in our nature by God, is not only innocent, but a generous movement of mind. It is in itself, and in its original, no more than indignation against injury and wickedness: that which is the only deformity in the creation, and the only reasonable object of abhorrence and dislike. How manifold evidence have we of the divine wisdom and goodness, when even pain in the natural world, and the passion we have been now considering in the moral, come out instances of it!

NOTES

1. [This distinction between hasty and deliberate resentment has been credited, by Whewell and others, to Butler as an original observation. Dr. Bernard however suggests that Butler is indebted to his adversary Hobbes for the idea (cf. *Dissertation on Virtue,* § 1). In *Leviathan* i. 6 Hobbes distinguishes between anger (="sudden courage") and indignation aroused by injury. But notice that Hobbes seems to confine the object of indignation to injuries done *to another.* Modern psychology recognizes that the foundation of anger is a primitive unreflecting reaction against hurt or obstacles, parallel with Butler's "hasty resentment," and also that the emotion becomes more complex and rational in the higher developments of mind (cf. Butler's "deliberate resentment"). For short summaries of modern views see Stout, *Manual of Psychology* (1907), pp. 296–323, and art. "Anger" in Hastings' *Dictionary of Religion and Ethics.*]

2. Ephes. iv. 26.

3. [Aristotle makes much the same distinction between the choleric (ακροχλο) and the sulky (πικρος): both are examples of anger in excess. See the whole discussion of Gentleness in *Eth. Nic.* iv. 5.]

JAMES FITZJAMES STEPHEN

Punishment and Public Morality*

The relation between criminal law and morality is not in all cases the same. The two may harmonize; there may be a conflict between them, or they may be independent. In all common cases they do, and, in my opinion, wherever and so far as it is possible, they ought, to harmonize with, and support one another.

In some uncommon but highly important cases there is a possibility that they may to a certain extent come into conflict, inasmuch as a minority of the nation more or less influential and extensive may disapprove morally of the objects which the criminal law is intended to promote, and may regard as virtuous actions what it treats as crimes. There is a third class of cases in which the criminal law is supported by moral sentiment, in so far as moral sentiment recognizes obedience to the law as a duty, but no further. This is where it enjoins or forbids acts, which if no law existed in relation to them would be regarded as matters of indifference. The laws which forbid the cultivation of tobacco, and which require marriages to be celebrated at certain times and places only, are instances of legislation of this kind. A consideration of these three classes of laws creating offences will, I think, throw considerable light not only upon the subject of criminal responsibility, in other words upon the question what excuses ought to be admitted for acts falling within the definition of crimes, but also upon the whole question of the principles which ought to regulate legal punishments.

First I will consider the normal case, that in which law and morals are in harmony, and ought to and usually do support each other. This is true of all the gross offences which consist of instances of turbulence, force, or fraud. Whatever may be the nature or extent of the differences which exist as to the nature of morals, no one in this country regards murder, rape, arson, robbery, theft, or the like, with any feeling but detestation. I do not think it admits of any doubt that law and morals powerfully support and greatly intensify each other in this matter. Everything which is regarded as enhancing the moral guilt of a particular offence is recognised as a reason for increasing the severity of the punishment awarded to it. On the other hand, the sentence of the law is to the moral sentiment of the public in relation to any offence what a seal is to hot wax. It converts into a permanent final judgment what might otherwise be a transient sentiment. The mere general suspicion or knowledge that a man has done something dishonest may never be brought to a point, and the disapprobation excited by it may in time pass away, but the fact that he has been convicted and punished as a thief stamps a mark upon him for life. In short, the infliction of punishment by law gives definite expression and a solemn ratification and justification to the hatred which is excited by the commission of the offence, and which constitutes the moral or popular as distinguished from the conscientious sanction of that part of morality which is also sanctioned by the criminal law. The criminal law thus proceeds upon the principle that it is morally right to hate criminals, and it confirms and justifies that sentiment by inflicting upon criminals punishments which express it.

I think that whatever effect the administration of criminal justice has in preventing the commission of crimes is due as much to this circumstance as to any definite fear entertained by offenders of undergoing specific punishment. If this is doubted, let any one ask himself to what extent a man would be deterred from theft by the knowl-

*From *A History of the Criminal Law of England,* (London: 1883), Vol. II, pp. 80–87 and 90–93. The selections are from Chap. XVII, "Of Crimes in General and of Punishments."

edge that by committing it he was exposed, say, to one chance in fifty of catching an illness which would inflict upon him the same amount of confinement, inconvenience, and money loss as six months' imprisonment and hard labour. In other words, how many people would be deterred from stealing by the chance of catching a bad fever? I am also of opinion that this close alliance between criminal law and moral sentiment is in all ways healthy and advantageous to the community. I think it highly desirable that criminals should be hated, that the punishments inflicted upon them should be so contrived as to give expression to that hatred, and to justify it so far as the public provision of means for expressing and gratifying a healthy natural sentiment can justify and encourage it.

These views are regarded by many persons as being wicked, because it is supposed that we never ought to hate, or wish to be revenged upon, any one. The doctrine that hatred and vengeance are wicked in themselves appears to me to contradict plain facts, and to be unsupported by any argument deserving of attention. Love and hatred, gratitude for benefits, and the desire of vengeance for injuries, imply each other as much as convex and concave. Butler vindicated resentment which cannot be distinguished from revenge and hatred except by name, and Bentham included the pleasures of malevolence amongst the fifteen which, as he said, constitute all our motives of action. The unqualified manner in which they have been denounced is in itself a proof that they are deeply rooted in human nature. No doubt they are peculiarly liable to abuse, and in some states of society are commonly in excess of what is desirable, and so require restraint rather than excitement, but unqualified denunciations of them are as ill-judged as unqualified denunciations of sexual passion. The forms in which deliberate anger and righteous disapprobation are expressed, and the execution of criminal justice is the most emphatic of such forms, stand to the one set of passions in the same relation in which marriage stands to the other. I also think that in the present state of public feeling, at all events amongst the classes which principally influence legislation, there is more ground to fear defect than excess in these passions. Whatever may have been the case in periods of greater energy, less knowledge, and less sensibility than ours, it is now far more likely that people should witness acts of grievous cruelty, deliberate fraud, and lawless turbulence, with too little hatred and too little desire for deliberate measured revenge than that they should feel too much.

The expression and gratification of these feelings is however only one of the objects for which legal punishments are inflicted. Another object is the direct prevention of crime, either by fear, or by disabling or even destroying the offender, and this which is I think commonly put forward as the only proper object of legal punishments is beyond all question distinct from the one just mentioned and of coordinate importance with it. The two objects are in no degree inconsistent with each other, on the contrary they go hand in hand, and may be regarded respectively as the secondary and the primary effects of the administration of criminal justice. The only practical result in the actual administration of justice of admitting each as a separate ground for punishment is that when a discretion as to the punishment of an offence is placed in the judge's hands, as it is in almost all cases by our law, the judge in the exercise of that discretion ought to have regard to the moral guilt of the offence which he is to punish as well as to its specific public danger. In criminal legislation the distinction is of greater importance, as one of the arguments in favour of exemplary punishments (death, flogging, and the like) is that they emphatically justify and gratify the public desire for vengeance upon such offenders.

The views expressed above are exposed to an objection which may be regarded as the converse of the one which I have just tried to answer. Many persons, who would not say that hatred and punishments founded on it are wicked, would say that both the feeling itself and the conduct which it suggests are irrational, because men and human conduct are as much the creatures of circumstance as things, and that it is therefore as irrational to desire to be revenged upon a man for committing murder with a pistol as to desire to be revenged on the pistol with which the man commits murder. The truth of the premise of this argument I neither assert nor deny. It is certainly true that human conduct may be predicted to a great extent. It is natural to believe that an omniscient observer of it might predict not only every act, but every modification of every thought and feeling, of every human being born or to be born;

but this is not inconsistent with the belief that each individual man is an unknown something,—that as such he is other and more than a combination of the parts which we can see and touch,—and that his conduct depends upon the quality of the unknown something which he is.

However this may be, the conclusion drawn from the premise of the argument just stated does not appear to follow from it. There is nothing to show that if all conduct could be predicted praise and blame would cease to exist. If, notwithstanding the doctrine of philosophical necessity, love and hatred are as powerful as ever, and not less powerful in those who are most firmly convinced of that doctrine than in other persons, it follows that there is no real inconsistency between that doctrine and those passions, however the apparent inconsistency, if any, is to be explained. If the doctrine in question should ever be so completely established as to account for the whole of human life (and no one will assert that this has as yet been done), it will account for love and hatred as well as for other things, and will no more disturb them than other things are disturbed by being accounted for. Till it does so account for them, it is incomplete. Human life and philosophical explanations of it move in different planes till the explanation has become so complete as not to interfere with the thing to be explained. When they coincide, they cannot affect each other. One test of the truth of a philosophical explanation of human conduct is its complete harmony with human feeling.

I am, however, unable to see even an apparent conflict between the theory of philosophical necessity and the fact that men love and hate each other, and I think that the supposed difficulty arises from want of attention to the grounds on which love and hatred respectively are founded. They depend upon sympathy and antipathy; not upon theories as to the freedom of the will and the contingency or necessity of future events. Human beings love and hate each other because every man can mentally compare his neighbour's actions, thoughts, and feelings with his own. If there were any ground for ascribing intention, will, and consciousness to inanimate matter, we should approve of or condemn its behaviour in proportion as we were able to understand and sympathise with it, however accurately we might be able to predict it. If the pistol had the same knowledge and will as the murderer, the mere fact that he used it as a tool would not prevent the friends of the murdered man from hating it. This appears from the imperfect sympathy and antipathy which we feel towards the lower animals, the quasi-praise and quasi-blame which we award to the fidelity and spirit of a dog and the cruelty of a cat.

It is in reference to the grosser class of crimes, those in which law and morals are always in harmony, that the subject of excuses for conduct *primâ facie* criminal most frequently comes under consideration, and it will be found that whatever is recognised by the law of this country as an excuse for crime is something which deprives the act inquired into of its moral enormity, though it is by no means true that whatever deprives conduct of its moral enormity is a legal excuse for crime ... Full proof of this will be given in the following chapter.

The second class of offences which illustrate the relation between criminal law and morals are those in which there is a possibility of a conflict between the two. This class consists principally of political and religious offences. As regards political offences, it is obviously impossible that any government should exist at all which did not protect itself by law from open attacks on its existence or on its peace. Some of these offences, and above all high treason, have usually been stigmatised by legal writers as being the most heinous of all crimes. In modern times there has been an inclination to look upon them in a different light, instances having, or being supposed to have, occurred in which resistance to constituted authority has not only succeeded permanently, but has also been generally recognised as having introduced a better state of things than that which it destroyed or forcibly altered. Instances in the history of many countries must present themselves to the recollection of every one. It is, perhaps, less commonly remembered that almost innumerable instances might be given of political offences, involving every kind of moral guilt, presumptuous lawless turbulence, indifference to every interest except the gratification of a desire to seize political power, and in many cases to gratify, at all hazards, personal vanity, to say nothing of personal hatred, cupidity, or other passions. Even in the case of revolutions which have succeeded, and which, speaking broadly, may be described as having been beneficial, mischiefs of a terrible kind have followed from the fact that they were effected by force, and that they did constitute triumphs by unlawful violence over constituted authority. It was a true instinct which led the Parliament in the seventeenth century to condescend almost to quibble in order to keep the law on their side, and the evil effects of the temporary anarchy which the Civil War produced left deep traces in our later history. The same might be said of the American and the French Revolutions. The theories asserted by the successful parties were essentially as absurd as any theory put forward on the other side, and their success in each case filled the successful party with conceit and nonsense. The doctrines of non-resistance and of the divine right of kings are of course easily refuted, but the counter doctrines of the sovereignty of the people and the rights of man may be refuted just as easily; and so indeed may all ethical doctrines which claim absolute truth. If, however, it is alleged that armed resistance to constituted authorities is almost always most injurious, and that even in the extreme cases in which it is necessary it produces all sorts of evil results—especially evil moral results, the assertion is strictly true; and I do not know that those who maintained the divine right of kings, and the sinfulness of resistance in all cases, really meant more than to give a theoretical justification for this statement. It must also be remembered that the rebel must, by the very fact of his rebellion, condemn and stigmatise as intolerably bad the institutions against which he rebels. He is thus the declared enemy of all who regard those institutions as being, at the very least, tolerably good. He puts himself in armed opposition to their strongest convictions and most energetic feelings, and thus naturally earns their moral condemnation. A man who regards England and its institutions with deep affection and profound respect, notwithstanding their faults, must naturally look on the domestic enemies of either as a deadly and wicked enemy.

My own opinion is, that the cases in which armed resistance to English authority have been either morally innocent, or in the long run advantageous to the community, have been rare exceptions, and that, in the immense majority of cases, rebellions are both wicked and mischievous. The law must of course treat them as being so in all cases, and the possibility of a conflict on this subject between law and morals is an incident inseparable from the conditions under which we live . . .

As to this, it must be remembered that it is practically impossible to lay down an inflexible rule by which the same punishment must in every case be inflicted in respect of every crime falling within a given definition, because the degrees of moral guilt and public danger involved in offences which bear the same name and fall under the same definition must of necessity vary. There must therefore be a discretion in all cases as to the punishment to be inflicted. This discretion must, from the nature of the case, be vested either in the judge who tries the case, or in the executive government, or in the two acting together . . .

No one, I think, could fail to be struck with the way in which a definition apparently simple covers crimes utterly dissimilar, and deserving, on every ground, of widely different punishment. This is peculiarly true in cases in which the offence consists in the infliction of personal injuries. Every circumstance must be known in such cases before anything approaching to a real judgment on the offence can be formed, especially when the two elements of moral guilt and public danger are taken into account. To give illustrations on the subject would occupy more space than I can afford; but I may just observe that a drunken brawl between two or three people coming out of a publichouse, ending in the emptying of the pockets of one of the party in a manner differing little from rough horseplay, and the very worst case of highway robbery with violence, would constitute the same offence. Arson, again, may be the worst private crime that a man can commit. It may be little more than half-childish mischief.

My other observation is that, in my opinion, the importance of the moral side of punishment, the importance that is of the expression which it gives to a proper hostility to criminals, has of late years been much underestimated. The extreme severity of the old law has been succeeded by a sentiment which appears to me to be based upon the notion that the passions of hatred and revenge should be eliminated from law as being simply bad.

It is useless to argue upon questions of sentiment. All that any one can do is to avow the sentiments which he holds and denounce those which he dislikes. I have explained my own view. Those which commonly prevail upon the subject appear to me to be based on a conception of human life which refuses to believe that there are in the world many bad men who are the natural enemies of inoffensive men, just as beasts of prey are the enemies of all men.

My own experience is that there are in the world a considerable number of extremely wicked people, disposed, when opportunity offers, to get what they want by force or fraud, with complete indifference to the interests of others, and in ways which are inconsistent with the existence of civilized society. Such persons, I think, ought in extreme cases to be destroyed.

The view which I take of the subject would involve the increased use of physical pain, by flogging or otherwise, by way of a secondary punishment. It should, I think, be capable of being employed at the discretion of the judge in all cases in which the offence involves cruelty in the way of inflicting pain, or in which the offender's motive is lust. In each of these cases the infliction of pain is what Bentham called a characteristic punishment. The man who cruelly inflicts pain on another is made to feel what it is like. The man who gratifies his own passions at the expense of a cruel and humiliating insult inflicted on another is himself shamefully and painfully humiliated. This principle is recognised in a partial and unsatisfactory way in reference to robbery with violence, and attempts to strangle with intent to commit a crime. I think it should be extended in the manner stated. It seems absurd that if a man attempting to ravish a woman squeezes her throat to prevent her from crying out he should be liable to be flogged, but that he should not be liable to be flogged if he puts one hand over her mouth and with the other beats her about the head with a heavy stone.

I think, too, that the punishment of flogging should be made more severe. At present it is little, if at all, more serious than a birching at a public school.

Crime is no doubt far less important than it formerly was, and the means now available for disposing of criminals, otherwise than by putting them to death, are both more available and more effectual than they formerly were. In the days of Coke it would have been impossible practically to set up convict establishments like Dartmoor or Portland, and the expense of establishing either police or prisons adequate to the wants of the country would have been regarded as exceedingly burdensome, besides which the subject of the management of prisons was not understood. Hence, unless a criminal was hanged, there was no way of disposing of him. Large numbers of criminals accordingly were hanged whose offences indicated no great moral depravity. The disgust excited by this indiscriminate cruelty ought not to blind us to the fact that there is a kind and degree of wickedness which ought to be regarded as altogether unpardonable, just as there may be political offences which make it clear that the safety of particular institutions is inconsistent with the continued life of particular persons. Let any one read carefully such stories as those of Thurtell, Rush, Palmer, or other wretches of the same order, and ask himself under what circumstances or in what sort of society they could be trusted, and he will, I think, find it hard to deny that to allow such men to live, when their true character was known, would be like leaving wolves alive in a civilized country. Or take such a case as that of the reign of Louis Philippe. He was so so sickened and horrorstruck by the reign of terror, that he shrank from vindicating his own power at the expense of the lives of his enemies. If he had been less scrupulous on this matter, and in particular if he had put to death Louis Napoleon for his attempt at Boulogne, the Orleans family might still have been reigning in France. Great and indiscriminate severity in the law no doubt defeats itself, but temperate, discriminating, calculated severity is, within limits, effective, and I am not without hopes that in time the public may be brought to understand and to act upon this sentiment; though at present a tenderness prevails upon the subject which seems to me misplaced and exaggerated. It cannot, however, be denied that it springs from very deep roots, and that no considerable change in it can be expected unless the views current on several matters of deep importance should be greatly modified in what must at present be called an unpopular direction.

FLEMMING v. NESTOR

United States Supreme Court, 1960[*]

Mr. Justice HARLAN delivered the opinion of the Court.

From a decision of the District Court for the District of Columbia holding § 202(n) of the Social Security Act unconstitutional, the Secretary of Health, Education, and Welfare takes this direct appeal pursuant to 28 U.S.C. § 1252, 28 U.S. C.A. § 1252. The challenged section, set forth in full in the margin,[1] provides for the termination of old-age, survivor, and disability insurance benefits payable to, or in certain cases in respect of, an alien individual who, after September 1, 1954 (the date of enactment of the section), is deported under § 241(a) of the Immigration and Nationality Act on any one of certain grounds specified in § 202(n).

Appellee, an alien, immigrated to this country from Bulgaria in 1913, and became eligible for old-age benefits in November 1955. In July 1956 he was deported pursuant to § 241(a) (6) (C) (i) of the Immigration and Nationality Act for having been a member of the Communist Party from 1933 to 1939. This being one of the benefit-termination deportation grounds specified in § 202(n), appellee's benefits were terminated soon thereafter, and notice of the termination was given to his wife, who had remained in this country.[2]

III.

... The remaining, and most insistently pressed, constitutional objections rest upon Art. I, § 9, cl. 3, and Art. III, 3, of the Constitution, and the Sixth Amendment.[3] It is said that the termination of appellee's benefits amounts to punishing him without a judicial trial, see Wong Wing v. United States, 163 U.S. 228, 16 S.Ct. 977, 41 L.Ed. 140; that the termination of benefits constitutes the imposition of punishment by legislative act, rendering § 202(n) a bill of attainder, see United States v. Lovett, 328 U.S. 303, 66 S.Ct. 1073, 90 L.Ed. 1252; Cummings v. Missouri, 4 Wall. 277, 18 L.Ed. 356; and that the punishment exacted is imposed for past conduct not unlawful when engaged in, thereby violating the constitutional prohibition on *ex post facto* laws, see Ex parte Garland, 4 Wall. 333, 18 L.Ed. 366.[4]

[*]80 S. Ct. 1367 (1960). Excerpts only. Footnotes renumbered.

Essential to the success of each of these contentions is the validity of characterizing as "punishment" in the constitutional sense the termination of benefits under § 202(n).

In determining whether legislation which bases a disqualification on the happening of a certain past event imposes a punishment, the Court has sought to discern the objects on which the enactment in question was focused. Where the source of legislative concern can be thought to be the activity or status from which the individual is barred, the disqualification is not punishment even though it may bear harshly upon one affected. The contrary is the case where the statute in question is evidently aimed at the person or class of persons disqualified. In the earliest case on which appellee relies, a clergyman successfully challenged a state constitutional provision barring from that profession—and from many other professions and offices—all who would not swear that they had never manifested any sympathy or support for the cause of the Confederacy. Cummings v. Missouri, supra. The Court thus described the aims of the challenged enactment:

"The oath could not * * * have been required as a means of ascertaining whether parties were qualified or not for their respective callings or the trusts with which they were charged. *It was required in order to reach the person, not the calling.* It was exacted, not from any notion that the several acts designated indicated unfitness for the callings, but because it was thought that the several acts deserved punishment * * *." Id., 4 Wall. at page 320. (Emphasis supplied.)

Only the other day the governing inquiry was stated, in an opinion joined by four members of the Court, in these terms:

"The question in each case where unpleasant consequences are brought to bear upon an individual for prior conduct, is whether the legislative aim was to punish that individual for past activity, or whether the restriction of the individual comes about as a relevant incident to a regulation of a present situation, such as the proper qualifications for a profession." De Veau v. Braisted, 363 U.S. 144, 160, 80 S.Ct. 1146, 1155 (plurality opinion).

In Ex parte Garland, supra, where the Court struck down an oath—similar in content to that involved in

Cummings—required of attorneys seeking to practice before any federal court, as also in Cummings, the finding of punitive intent drew heavily on the Court's first-hand acquaintance with the events and the mood of the then recent Civil War, and "the fierce passions which that struggle aroused." Cummings v. Missouri, supra, 4 Wall. at page 322.[5] Similarly, in United States v. Lovett, supra, where the Court invalidated, as a bill of attainder, a statute forbidding—subject to certain conditions—the further payment of the salaries of three named government employees, the determination that a punishment had been imposed rested in large measure on the specific Congressional history which the court was at pains to spell out in detail. See 328 U.S. at pages 308–312, 66 S.Ct., at pages 1075–1077. Most recently, in Trop v. Dulles, 356 U.S. 86, 78 S.Ct. 590, 2 L.Ed. 2d 630, which held unconstitutional a statute providing for the expatriation of one who had been sentenced by a court-martial to dismissal or dishonorable discharge for wartime desertion, the majority of the Court characterized the statute as punitive. However, no single opinion commanded the support of a majority. The plurality opinion rested its determination, at least in part, on its inability to discern any alternative purpose which the statute could be thought to serve. Id., 356 U.S. at page 97, 78 S.Ct. at page 596. The concurring opinion found in the specific historical evolution of the provision in question compelling evidence of punitive intent. Id., 356 U.S. at pages 107–109, 78 S.Ct. at pages 601–602.

It is thus apparent that, though the governing criterion may be readily stated, each case has turned on its own highly particularized context. Where no persuasive showing of a purpose "to reach the person, not the calling," Cummings v. Missouri, supra, 4 Wall. at page 320, has been made, the Court has not hampered legislative regulation of activities within its sphere of concern, despite the often-severe effects such regulation has had on the persons subject to it.[6] Thus, deportation has been held to be not punishment, but an exercise of the plenary power of Congress to fix the conditions under which aliens are to be permitted to enter and remain in this country. Fong Yue Ting v. United States, 149 U.S. 698, 730, 13 S. Ct. 1016, 1028, 37 L.Ed. 905; see Galvan v. Press, 347 U.S. 522, 530–531, 74 S.Ct. 737, 742–743, 98 L.Ed. 911. Similarly, the setting by a State of qualifications for the practice of medicine, and their modification from time to time, is an incident of the State's power to protect the health and safety of its citizens, and its decision to bar from practice persons who commit or have committed a felony is taken as evidencing an intent to exercise that regulatory power, and not a purpose to add to the punishment of ex-felons. Hawker v. New York, 170 U.S. 189, 18 S.Ct. 573, 42 L.Ed. 1002. See De Veau v.

Braisted, supra (regulation of crime on the waterfront through disqualification of ex-felons from holding union office). Cf. Helvering v. Mitchell, 303 U.S. 391, 397–401, 58 S.Ct. 630, 632–634, 82 L.Ed. 917, holding that, with respect to deficiencies due to fraud, a 50 percent addition to the tax imposed was not punishment so as to prevent, upon principles of double jeopardy, its assessment against one acquitted of tax evasion.

Turning, then, to the particular statutory provision before us, appellee cannot successfully contend that the language and structure of § 202(n), or the nature of the deprivation, requires us to recognize a punitive design. Cf. Wong Wing v. United States, supra (imprisonment, at hard labor up to one year, of person found to be unlawfully in the country). Here the sanction is the mere denial of a noncontractual governmental benefit. No affirmative disability or restraint is imposed, and certainly nothing approaching the "infamous punishment" of imprisonment, as in Wong Wing, on which great reliance is mistakenly placed. Moreover, for reasons already given (363 U.S. at pages 611–612, 80 S. Ct. at pages 1372–1373), it cannot be said, as was said of the statute in Cummings v. Missouri, supra, 4 Wall. at page 319; see Dent v. West Virginia, 129 U.S. 114, 126, 9 S.Ct. 231, 235, 32 L.Ed. 623, that the disqualification of certain deportees from receipt of Social Security benefits while they are not lawfully in this country bears no rational connection to the purposes of the legislation of which it is a part, and must without more therefore be taken as evidencing a Congressional desire to punish. Appellee argues, however, that the history and scope of § 202(n) prove that no such postulated purpose can be thought to have motivated the legislature, and that they persuasively show that a punitive purpose in fact lay behind the statute. We do not agree.

We observe initially that only the clearest proof could suffice to establish the unconstitutionality of a statute on such a ground. Judicial inquiries into Congressional motives are at best a hazardous matter, and when that inquiry seeks to go behind objective manifestations it becomes a dubious affair indeed. Moreover, the presumption of constitutionality with which this enactment, like any other, comes to us forbids us lightly to choose that reading of the statute's setting which will invalidate it over that which will save it. "[I]t is not on slight implication and vague conjecture that the legislature is to be pronounced to have transcended its powers, and its acts to be considered as void." Fletcher v. Peck, 6 Cranch 87, 128, 3 L.Ed. 162.

Section 202(n) was enacted as a small part of an extensive revision of the Social Security program. The provision originated in the House of Representatives. H.R. 9366, 83d Cong., 2d Sess., § 108. The discussion in the House Committee Report, H.R.Rep. No. 1698,

83d Cong., 2d Sess., pp. 5, 25, 77, does not express the purpose of the statute. However, it does say that the termination of benefits would apply to those persons who were "deported from the United States because of illegal entry, conviction of a crime, or subversive activity * * *." Id., at 25. It was evidently the thought that such was the scope of the statute resulting from its application to deportation under the 14 named paragraphs of § 241(a) of the Immigration and Nationality Act. Id., at 77.[7]

The Senate Committee rejected the proposal, for the stated reason that it had "not had an opportunity to give sufficient study to all the possible implications of this provision, which involves termination of benefit rights under the contributory program of old-age and survivors insurance * * *." S. Rep. No. 1987, 83d Cong., 2d Sess., p. 23; see also id., at 76. However, in Conference, the proposal was restored in modified form,[8] and as modified was enacted as § 202(n). See H.R.Conf.Rep. No. 2679, 83d Cong., 2d Sess., p. 18.

[16, 17] Appellee argues that this history demonstrates that Congress was not concerned with the *fact* of a beneficiary's deportation—which it is claimed alone would justify this legislation as being pursuant to a policy relevant to regulation of the Social Security system—but that it sought to reach certain *grounds* for deportation, thus evidencing a punitive intent.[9] It is impossible to find in this meagre history the unmistakable evidence of punitive intent which, under principles already discussed, is required before a Congressional enactment of this kind may be struck down. Even were that history to be taken as evidencing Congress' concern with the grounds, rather than the fact, of deportation, we do not think that this, standing alone, would suffice to establish a punitive purpose. This would still be a far cry from the situations involved in such cases as Cummings, Wong Wing, and Garland (see 363 U.S. at page 617, 80 S.Ct. at page 1376), and from that in Lovett, supra, where the legislation was on its face aimed at particular individuals. The legislative record, however, falls short of any persuasive showing that Congress was in fact concerned alone with the grounds of deportation. To be sure Congress did not apply the termination provision to all deportees. However, it is evident that neither did it rest the operation of the statute on the occurrence of the underlying act. The fact of deportation itself remained an essential condition for loss of benefits, and even if a beneficiary were saved from deportation only through discretionary suspension by the Attorney General under § 244 of the Immigration and Nationality Act (66 Stat. 214, 8 U.S.C. § 1254, 8 U.S.C.A. § 1254), § 202(n) would not reach him.

Moreover, the grounds for deportation referred to in the Committee Report embrace the great majority of those deported, as is evident from an examination of the four omitted grounds, summarized in the margin.[10] Inferences drawn from the omission of those grounds cannot establish, to the degree of certainty required, that Congressional concern was wholly with the acts leading to deportation, and not with the fact of deportation.[11] To hold otherwise would be to rest on the "slight implication and vague conjecture" against which Chief Justice Marshall warned. Fletcher v. Peck, supra, 6 Cranch at page 128.

The same answer must be made to arguments drawn from the failure of Congress to apply § 202(n) to beneficiaries voluntarily residing abroad. But cf. § 202(t), ante, note 5. Congress may have failed to consider such persons; or it may have thought their number too slight, or the permanence of their voluntary residence abroad too uncertain, to warrant application of the statute to them, with its attendant administrative problems of supervision and enforcement. Again, we cannot with confidence reject all those alternatives which imaginativeness can bring to mind, save that one which might require the invalidation of the statute.

Reversed.

Mr. Justice BLACK, dissenting.

IV.

... The Court in part III of its opinion holds that the 1954 Act is not an *ex post facto* law or bill of attainder even though it creates a class of deportees who cannot collect their insurance benefits because they were once Communists at a time when simply being a Communist was not illegal. The Court also puts great emphasis on its belief that the Act here is not punishment. Although not believing that the particular label "punishment" is of decisive importance, I think the Act does impose punishment even in a classic sense. The basic reason for Nestor's loss of his insurance payments is that he was once a Communist. This man, now 69 years old, has been driven out of the country where he has lived for 43 years to a land where he is practically a stranger, under an Act authorizing his deportation many years after his Communist membership. Cf. Galvan v. Press, 347 U.S. 522, 532, 533, 74 S.Ct. 737, 743, 744, 98 L.Ed. 911 (dissenting opinions). Now a similar *ex post facto* law deprives him of his insurance, which, while petty and insignificant in amount to this great Government, may well be this exile's daily bread, for the same reason and in accord with the general fashion of the day—that is, to punish in every way possible anyone who ever made the mistake of being a Communist in this country or who is supposed ever to have been associated with anyone who made that mistake. See, e.g., Barenblatt v. United States, 360 U.S. 109, 79 S.Ct. 1081, 3 L.Ed.2d 1115, and Uphaus v. Wyman, 360 U.S. 72, 79 S.Ct. 1040, 3 L.Ed.2d 1090. In United States v. Lovett, 328

U.S. 303, 315–316, 66 S.Ct. 1073, 1079, 90 L.Ed. 1252, we said:

"* * * legislative acts, no matter what their form, that apply either to named individuals or to easily ascertainable members of a group in such a way as to inflict punishment on them without a judicial trial are bills of attainder prohibited by the Constitution."

Faithful observance of our holdings in that case, in Ex parte Garland, 4 Wall. 333, 18 L.Ed. 366, and in Cummings v. Missouri, 4 Wall. 277, 18 L.Ed. 356, would, in my judgment, require us to hold that the 1954 Act is a bill of attainder. It is a congressional enactment aimed at an easily ascertainable group; it is certainly punishment in any normal sense of the word to take away from any person the benefits of an insurance system into which he and his employer have paid their moneys for almost two decades; and it does all this without a trial according to due process of law. It is true that the Lovett, Cummings and Garland Court opinions were not unanimous, but they nonetheless represent positive precedents on highly important questions of individual liberty which should not be explained away with cobwebbery refinements. If the Court is going to overrule these cases in whole or in part, and adopt the views of previous dissenters, I believe it should be done clearly and forthrightly.

A basic constitutional infirmity of this Act, in my judgment, is that it is a part of a pattern of laws all of which violate the First Amendment out of fear that this country is in grave danger if it lets a handful of Communist fanatics or some other extremist group make their arguments and discuss their ideas. This fear, I think, is baseless. It reflects a lack of faith in the sturdy patriotism of our people and does not give to the world a true picture of our abiding strength. It is an unworthy fear in a country that has a Bill of Rights containing provisions for fair trials, freedom of speech, press and religion, and other specific safeguards designed to keep men free. I repeat once more that I think this Nation's greatest security lies, not in trusting to a momentary majority of this Court's view at any particular time of what is "patently arbitrary," but in wholehearted devotion to and observance of our constitutional freedoms. See Wieman v. Updegraff, 344 U.S. 183, 192, 73 S.Ct. 215, 219, 97 L.Ed. 216 (concurring opinion).

I would affirm the judgment of the District Court which held that Nestor is constitutionally entitled to collect his insurance.

Mr. Justice DOUGLAS, dissenting.

Appellee came to this country from Bulgaria in 1913 and was employed, so as to be covered by the Social Security Act, from December 1936 to January 1955—a period of 19 years. He became eligible for retirement and for Social Security benefits in November 1955 and was awarded $55.60 per month. In July 1956 he was deported for having been a member of the Communist Party from 1933 to 1939. Pursuant to a law, enacted September 1, 1954, he was thereupon denied payment of further Social Security benefits.

This 1954 law seems to me to be a classic example of a bill of attainder, which Art. I, § 9 of the Constitution prohibits Congress from enacting. A bill of attainder is a legislative act which inflicts punishment without a judicial trial. Cummings v. Missouri, 4 Wall. 277, 323, 18 L.Ed. 356.

In the old days punishment was meted out to a creditor or rival or enemy by sending him to the gallows. But as recently stated by Irving Brant,[12]

"* * * By smiting a man day after day with slanderous words, by taking away his opportunity to earn a living, you can drain the blood from his veins without even scratching his skin.

"Today's bill of attainder is broader than the classic form, and not so tall and sharp. There is mental in place of physical torture, and confiscation of tomorrow's bread and butter instead of yesterday's land and gold. What is perfectly clear is that hate, fear and prejudice play the same role today, in the destruction of human rights in America that they did in England when a frenzied mob of lords, judges, bishops and shoemakers turned the Titus Oates blacklist into a hangman's record. Hate, jealousy and spite continue to fill the legislative attainder lists just as they did in the Irish Parliament of ex-King James."

Bills of attainder, when they imposed punishment less than death, were bills of pains and penalties and equally beyond the constitutional power of Congress. Cummings v. Missouri, supra, 4 Wall. at page 323.

Punishment in the sense of a bill of attainder includes the "deprivation or suspension of political or civil rights." Cummings v. Missouri, supra, at page 322. In that case it was barring a priest from practicing his profession. In Ex parte Garland, 4 Wall. 333, 18 L.Ed. 366, it was excluding a man from practicing law in the federal courts. In United States v. Lovett, 328 U.S. 303, 66 S.Ct. 1073, 90 L.Ed. 1252, it was cutting off employees' compensation and barring them permanently from government service. Cutting off a person's livelihood by denying him accrued social benefits—part of his property interests—is no less a punishment. Here, as in the other cases cited, the penalty exacted has one of the classic purposes of punishment[13]—"to reprimand the wrongdoer, to deter others." Trop v. Dulles, 356 U.S. 86, 96, 78 S.Ct. 590, 595, 2 L.Ed.2d 630.

Social Security payments are not gratuities. They are products of a contributory system, the funds being raised by payment from employees and employers alike, or in case of self-employed persons, by the individual alone. See Social Security Board v. Nierotko, 327 U.S. 358, 364, 66 S.Ct. 637, 640, 90 L.Ed. 718. The funds are placed in the Federal Old-Age and Survivors Insurance Trust Fund, 42 U.S.C. § 401(a), 42 U.S.C.A. § 401(a); and only those who contribute to the fund are entitled to its benefits, the amount of benefits being related to the amount of contributions made. See Stark, Social Security: Its Importance to Lawyers, 43 A.B. A.J. 319, 321 (1957). As the late Senator George, long Chairman of the Senate Finance Committee and one of the authors of the Social Security system, said:

"There has developed through the years a feeling both in and out of Congress that the contributory social insurance principle fits our times—that it serves a vital need that cannot be as well served otherwise. It comports better than any substitute we have discovered with the American concept that free men want to earn their security and not ask for doles— that what is due as a matter of earned right is far better than a gratuity. * * *

"Social security is not a handout; it is not charity; it is not relief. It is an earned right based upon the contributions and earnings of the individual. As an earned right, the individual is eligible to receive his benefit in dignity and self-respect." 102 Cong.Rec. 15110.

Social Security benefits have rightly come to be regarded as basic financial protection against the hazards of old age and disability. As stated in a recent House Report:

"The old-age and survivors insurance system is the basic program which provides protection for America's families against the loss of earned income upon the retirement or death of the family provider. The program provides benefits related to earned income and such benefits are paid for by the contributions made with respect to persons working in covered occupations." H.R.Rep. No. 1189, 84th Cong., 1st Sess. 2.

Congress could provide that only people resident here could get Social Security benefits. Yet both both the House and the Senate rejected any residence requirements. See H.R.Rep. No. 1698, 83d Cong., 2d Sess. 24–25; S.Rep. No. 1987, 83d Cong., 2d Sess. 23. Congress concededly might amend the program to meet new conditions. But may it take away Social Security benefits from one person or from a group of persons for vindictive reasons? Could Congress on deporting an alien for having been a Communist confiscate his home, appropriate his savings accounts, and thus send him out of the country penniless? I think not. Any such Act would be a bill of attainder. The difference, as I see it, between that case and this is one merely of degree. Social Security benefits, made up in part of this alien's own earnings, are taken from him because he once was a Communist.

The view that § 202(n), with which we now deal,

imposes a penalty was taken by Secretary Folsom, appellant's predecessor, when opposing enlargement of the category of people to be denied benefits of Social Security, e.g., those convicted of treason and sedition. He said:

"Because the deprivation of benefits as provided in the amendment is in the nature of a penalty and based on considerations foreign to the objectives and provisions of the old-age and survivors insurance program, the amendment may well serve as a precedent for extension of similar provisions to other public programs and to other crimes which, while perhaps different in degree, are difficult to distinguish in principle.
"The present law recognizes only three narrowly limited exceptions[14] to the basic principle that benefits are paid without regard to the attitudes, opinions, behavior, or personal characteristics of the individual * * *." Hearings Senate Finance Committee on Social Security Amendments of 1955, 84th Cong., 2d Sess. 1319.

The Committee Reports, though meagre, support Secretary Folsom in that characterization of § 202(n). The House Report tersely stated that termination of the benefits would apply to those persons who were deported "because of illegal entry, conviction of a crime, or subversive activity." H.R.Rep. No. 1698, 83d Cong., 2d Sess. 25. The aim and purpose are clear—to take away from a person by legislative *fiat* property which he has accumulated because he has acted in a certain way or embraced a certain ideology. That is a modern version of the bill of attainder—as plain, as direct, as effective as those which religious passions once loosed in England and which later were employed against the Tories here.[15] I would affirm this judgment.

Mr. Justice BRENNAN, with whom THE CHIEF JUSTICE and Mr. Justice DOUGLAS join, dissenting.

When Nestor quit the Communist Party in 1939 his past membership was not a ground for his deportation. Kessler v. Strecker, 307 U.S. 22, 59 S.Ct. 694, 83 L.Ed. 1082. It was not until a year later that past membership was made a specific ground for deportation.[16] This past membership has cost Nestor dear. It brought him expulsion from the country after 43 years' residence— most of his life. Now more is exacted from him, for after he had begun to receive benefits in 1955—having worked in covered employment the required time and reached age 65—and might anticipate receiving them the rest of his life, the benefits were stopped pursuant to § 202(n) of the Amended Social Security Act.[17] His predicament is very real—an aging man deprived of the means with which to live after being separated from his family and exiled to live among strangers in a land he quit 47 years ago. The common sense of it is that he has been punished severely for his past conduct.

Even the 1950 statute deporting aliens for past membership raised serious questions in this Court whether the prohibition against *ex post facto* laws was violated.

In Galvan v. Press, 347 U.S. 522, 531, 74 S.Ct. 737, 742, 98 L.Ed. 911, we said "since the intrinsic consequences of deportation are so close to punishment for crime, it might fairly be said also that the *ex post facto* Clause, even though applicable only to punitive legislation, should be applied to deportation." However, precedents which treat deportation not as punishment, but as a permissible exercise of congressional power to enact the conditions under which aliens may come to and remain in this country, governed the decision in favor of the constitutionality of the statute.

However, the Court cannot rest a decision that § 202(n) does not impose punishment on Congress' power to regulate immigration. It escapes the common-sense conclusion that Congress has imposed punishment by finding the requisite rational nexus to a granted power in the supposed furtherance of the Social Security program "enacted pursuant to Congress' power to 'spend money in aid of the "general welfare." ' " I do not understand the Court to deny that but for that connection, § 202(n) would impose punishment and not only offend the constitutional prohibition on *ex post facto* laws but also violate the constitutional guarantees against imposition of punishment without a judicial trial.

The Court's test of the constitutionality of § 202(n) is whether the legislative concern underlying the statute was to regulate "the activity or status from which the individual is barred" or whether the statute "is evidently aimed at the person or class of persons disqualified." It rejects the inference that the statute is "aimed at the person or class of persons disqualified" by relying upon the presumption of constitutionality. This presumption might be a basis for sustaining the statute if in fact there were two opposing inferences which could reasonably be drawn from the legislation, one that it imposes punishment and the other that it is purposed to further the administration of the Social Security program. The Court, however, does not limit the presumption to that use. Rather the presumption becomes a complete substitute for any supportable finding of a rational connection of § 202(n) with the Social Security program. For me it is not enough to state the test and hold that the presumption alone satisfies it. I find it necessary to examine the Act and its consequences to ascertain whether there is ground for the inference of a congressional concern with the administration of the Social Security program. Only after this inquiry would I consider the application of the presumption.

The Court seems to acknowledge that the statute bears harshly upon the individual disqualified, but states that this is permissible when a statute is enacted as a regulation of the activity. But surely the harshness of the consequences is itself a relevant consideration to the inquiry into the congressional purpose.[18] Cf. Trop v. Dulles, 356 U.S. 86, 110, (concurring opinion).

It seems to me that the statute itself shows that the sole legislative concern was with "the person or class of persons disqualified." Congress did not disqualify for benefits all beneficiaries residing abroad or even all dependents residing abroad who are aliens. If that had been the case I might agree that Congress' concern would have been with "the activity or status" and not with the "person or class of persons disqualified." The scales would then be tipped toward the conclusion that Congress desired to limit benefit payments to beneficiaries residing in the United States so that the American economy would be aided by expenditure of benefits here. Indeed a proposal along those lines was submitted to Congress in 1954, at the same time § 202(n) was proposed,[19] and it was rejected.[20]

Perhaps, the Court's conclusion that regulation of "the activity or status" was the congressional concern would be a fair appraisal of the statute if Congress had terminated the benefits of all alien beneficiaries who are deported. But that is not what Congress did. Section 202(n) applies only to aliens deported on one or more of 14 of the 18 grounds for which aliens may be deported.[21]

H.R.Rep No. 1698, 83d Cong., 2d Sess. 25, 77, cited by the Court, describes § 202(n) as including persons who were deported "because of unlawful entry, conviction of a crime, or subversive activity." The section, in addition, covers those deported for such socially condemned acts as narcotic addiction or prostitution. The common element of the 14 grounds is that the alien has been guilty of some blameworthy conduct. In other words Congress worked its will only on aliens deported for conduct displeasing to the lawmakers.

This is plainly demonstrated by the remaining four grounds of deportation, those which do not result in the cancellation of benefits.[22] Two of those four grounds cover persons who become public charges within five years after entry for reasons which predated the entry. A third ground covers the alien who fails to maintain his nonimmigrant status. The fourth ground reaches the alien who, prior to or within five years after entry, aids other aliens to enter the country illegally.

Those who are deported for becoming public charges clearly have not, by modern standards, engaged in conduct worthy of censure. The Government's suggestion that the reason for their exclusion from § 202(n) was an unarticulated feeling of Congress that it would be unfair to the "other country to deport such destitute persons without letting them retain their modicum of social security benefits" appears at best fanciful, especially since, by hypothesis, they are deportable because the conditions which lead to their becoming public charges existed prior to entry.

The exclusion from the operation of § 202(n) of aliens deported for failure to maintain nonimmigrant status rationally can be explained, in the context of the whole statute, only as evidencing that Congress considered that conduct less blameworthy. Certainly the Government's suggestion that Congress may have thought it unlikely that such persons would work sufficient time in covered employment to become eligible for Social Security benefits cannot be the reason for this exclusion. For frequently the very act which eventually results in the deportation of persons on that ground is the securing of private employment. Finally, it is impossible to reconcile the continuation of benefits to aliens who are deported for aiding other aliens to enter the country illegally, except upon the ground that Congress felt that their conduct was less reprehensible. Again the Government's suggestion that the reason might be Congress' belief that these aliens would not have worked in covered employment must be rejected. Five years after entry would be ample time within which to secure employment and qualify. Moreover the same five-year limitation applies to several of the 14 grounds of deportation for which aliens are cut off from benefits and the Government's argument would apply equally to them if that in fact was the congressional reason.

This appraisal of the distinctions drawn by Congress between various kinds of conduct impels the conclusion, beyond peradventure that the distinctions can be understood only if the purpose of Congress was to strike at "the person or class of persons disqualified." The Court inveighs against invalidating a statute on "implication and vague conjecture." Rather I think the Court has strained to sustain the statute on "implication and vague conjecture," in holding that the congressional concern was "the activity or status from which the individual is barred." Today's decision sanctions the use of the spending power not to further the legitimate objections of the Social Security program but to inflict hurt upon those who by their conduct have incurred the displeasure of Congress. The Framers ordained that even the worst of men should not be punished for their past acts or for any conduct without adherence to the procedural safeguards written into the Constitution. Today's decision is to me a regretful retreat from Lovett, Cummings and Garland.

Section 202(n) imposes punishment in violation of the prohibition against *ex post facto* laws and without a judicial trial.[23] I therefore dissent.

NOTES

1. Section 202(n) provides as follows:

"(n) (1) If any individual is (after the date of enactment of this subsection) deported under paragraph (1), (2), (4), (5), (6), (7), (10), (11), (12), (14), (15), (16), (17), or (18), of section 241 (a) of the Immigration and Nationality Act, then, notwithstanding any other provisions of this title—

"(A) no monthly benefit under this section or section 223 [42 U.S.C. § 423, relating to "disability insurance benefits"] shall be paid to such individual, on the basis of his wages and self-employment income, for any month occurring (i) after the month in which the Secretary is notified by the Attorney General that such individual has been so deported, and (ii) before the month in which such individual is thereafter lawfully admitted to the United States for permanent residence,

"(B) if no benefit could be paid to such individual (or if no benefit could be paid to him if he were alive) for any month by reason of subparagraph (A), no monthly benefit under this section shall be paid, on the basis of his wages and self-employment income, for such month to any other person who is not a citizen of the United States and is outside the United States for any part of such month, and

"(C) no lump-sum death payment shall be made on the basis of such individual's wages and self-employment income if he dies (i) in or after the month in which such notice is received, and (ii) before the month in which he is thereafter lawfully admitted to the United States for permanent residence.

"Section 203(b) and (c) of this Act shall not apply with respect to any such individual for any month for which no monthly benefit may be paid to him by reason of this paragraph.

"(2) As soon as practicable after the deportation of any individual under any of the paragraphs of section 241(a) of the Immigration and Nationality Act enumerated in paragraph (1) in this subsection, the Attorney General shall notify the Secretary of such deportation."

The provisions of § 241(a) of the Immigration and Nationality Act are summarized in notes 10, 13, post, 363 U.S. at pages 618, 620, 80 S.Ct. at pages 1376, 1378.

2.   Under paragraph (1) (B) of § 202(n) (see note 1, ante), appellee's wife, because of her residence here, has remained eligible for benefits payable to her as the wife of an insured individual. See § 202(b), 53 Stat. 1364, as amended, 42 U.S.C. § 402(b), 42 U.S.C.A. § 402(b).

3.   Art. I, § 9, cl. 3:

"No Bill of Attainder or *ex post facto* Law shall be passed." Art. III, § 2, cl. 3:

"The Trial of all Crimes, except in Cases of Impeachment, shall be Jury; and such Trial shall be held in the State where the said Crimes shall have been committed * * *."

Amend. VI:

"In all criminal prosecutions, the accused shall enjoy the right to a speedy and public trial, by an impartial jury of the State and district wherein the crime shall have been committed, which district shall have been previously ascertained by law, and to be informed of the nature and cause of the accusation; to be confronted with the witnesses against him; to have compulsory process for obtaining witnesses in his favor, and to have the assistance of counsel for his defence."

4.   Apellee also adds, but hardly argues, the contention that he has been deprived of his rights under the First Amendment, since the adverse consequences stemmed from "mere past membership" in the Communist Party. This contention, which is no more than a collateral attack on appellee's deportation, is not open to him.

5.   See also Pierce v. Carskadon, 16 Wall. 234, 21 L.Ed. 276. A West Virginia statute providing that a nonresident who had suffered a judgment in an action commenced by attachment, but in which he had not been personally served and did not appear, could within one year petition the court for a reopening of the judgment and a trial on the merits, was

amended in 1865 so as to condition that right on the taking of an exculpatory oath that the defendant had never supported the Confederacy. On the authority of Cummings and Garland, the amendment was invalidated.

6.   As prior decisions make clear, compare Ex parte Garland, supra, with Hawker v. New York, supra, the severity of a sanction is not determinative of its character as "punishment."

7.   Paragraphs (1), (2), and (10) of § 241 (a) relate to unlawful entry, or entry not complying with certain conditions; paragraphs (6) and (7) apply to "subversive" and related activities; the remainder of the included paragraphs are concerned with convictions of designated crimes, or the commission of acts related to them, such as narcotics addiction or prostitution.

8.   For example, under the House version termination of benefits of a deportee would also have terminated benefits paid to secondary beneficiaries based on the earning records of the deportee. The Conference proposal limited this effect to secondary beneficiaries who were nonresident aliens. See note 2, ante.

9.   Appellee also relies on the juxtaposition of the proposed § 108 and certain other provisions, some of which were enacted and some of which were not. This argument is too conjectural to warrant discussion. In addition, reliance is placed on a letter written to the Senate Finance Committee by appellant's predecessor in office, opposing the enactment of what is now § 202(u) of the Act, 70 Stat. 838, 42 U.S.C. § 402(u), 42 U.S.C.A. § 402(u), on the ground that the section was "in the nature of a penalty and based on considerations foreign to the objectives" of the program. Social Security Amendments of 1955. Hearings before the Senate Committee on Finance, 84th Cong., 2d Sess., p. 1319. The Secretary went on to say that "present law recognizes only three narrowly limited exceptions [of which § 202(n) is one] to the basic principle that benefits are paid without regard to the attitudes, opinions, behavior, or personal characteristics of the individual * * *." It should be observed, however, that the Secretary did not speak of § 202(n) as a penalty, as he did of the proposed § 202(u). The latter provision is concededly penal, and applies only pursuant to a judgment of a court in a criminal case.

10.   They are: (1) persons institutionalized at public expense within five years after entry because of "mental disease, defect, or deficiency" not shown to have arisen subsequent to admission (§ 241(a) (3)); (2) persons becoming a public charge within five years after entry from causes not shown to have arisen subsequent to admission § 241(a) (8)); (3) persons admitted as nonimmigrants (see § 101(a) (15), 66 Stat. 167, 8 U.S.C. § 1101(a) (15), 8 U.S.C.A. § 1101(a) (15)) who fail to maintain, or comply with the conditions of, such status (§ 241(a) (9)); (4) persons knowingly and for gain inducing or aiding, prior to or within five years after entry, any other alien to enter or attempt to enter unlawfully (§ 241 (a) (13)).

11.   Were we to engage in speculation, it would not be difficult to conjecture that Congress may have been led to exclude these four grounds of deportation out of compassionate or *de minimis* considerations.

12.   Address entitled Bills of Attainder in 1787 and Today. Columbia Law Review dinner 1954, published in 1959 by the Emergency Civil Liberties Committee, under the title Congressional Investigations and Bills of Attainder.

13.   The broad sweep of the idea of punishment behind the concept of the bill of attainder was stated as follows by Irving Brant, op. cit. supra, note 1, 9–10:

"In 1794 the American people were in a state of excitement comparable to that which exists today. Supporters of the French Revolution had organized the Democratic Societies—blatantly adopting that subversive title. Then the Whisky Rebellion exploded in Western Pennsylvania. The Democratic Societies were blamed. A motion censuring the Societies was introduced in the House of Representatives.

"There, in 1794, you had the basic division in American thought—on one side the doctrine of political liberty for everybody, with collective security resting on the capacity of the people for self-government; on the other side the doctrine that the people could not be trusted and political liberty must be restrained.

"James Madison challenged this latter doctrine. The investigative power of Congress over persons, he contended, was limited to inquiry into the conduct of individuals in the public service. 'Opinions,' he said, 'are not the subjects of legislation.' Start criticizing people for abuse of their reserved rights, and the censure might extend to freedom of speech and press. What would be the effect on the people thus condemned? Said Madison:

" 'It is in vain to say that this indiscriminate censure is no punishment. * * * Is not this proposition, if voted, a bill of attainder?'

"Madison won his fight, not because he called the resolution a bill of attainder, but because it attainted too many men who were going to vote in the next election. The definition, however, was there—a bill of attainder—and the definition was given by the foremost American authority on the principles of liberty and order underlying our system of government."

14.   The three exceptions referred to were (1) § 202(n); (2) Act of September 1, 1954, 68 Stat. 1142, 5 U.S.C. §§ 2281–2288, 5 U.S.C.A. §§ 2281–2288; (3) Regulation of the Social Security Administration, 20 CFR § 403.409—denying dependent's benefits to a person found guilty of felonious homicide of the insured worker.

15.   Brandt, op cit., supra, note 1, states at p. 9:

"What were the framers aiming at when they forbade bills of attainder? They were, of course, guarding against the religious passions that disgraced Christianity in Europe. But American bills of attainder, just before 1787, were typically used by Revolutionary assemblies to rid the states of British Loyalists. By a curious coincidence, it was usually the Tory with a good farm who was sent into exile, and all too often it was somebody who wanted that farm who induced the legislature to attaint him. Patriotism could serve as a cloak for greed as easily as religion did in that Irish Parliament of James the Second.

"But consider a case in which nothing could be said against the motive. During the Revolution, Governor Patrick Henry induced the Virginia legislature to pass a bill of attainder condemning Josiah Phillips to death. He was a traitor, a murderer, a pirate and an outlaw. When ratification of the new Constitution came before the Virginia convention, Henry inveighed against it because it contained no Bill of Rights. Edmund Randolph taunted him with his sponsorship of the Phillips bill of attainder. Henry then made the blunder of defending it. The bill was warranted, he said, because Phillips was no Socrates. That shocking defense of arbitrary condemnation may have produced the small margin by which the Constitution was ratified."

16.   The Alien Registration Act, 1940, 54 Stat. 673, made membership in an organization which advocates the overthrow of the government of the United States by force or violence a ground for deportation even though the membership was terminated prior to the passage of that statute. See Harisiades v. Shaughnessy, 342 U.S. 580, 72 S.Ct. 512, 96 L. Ed. 586. Until the passage of the Internal Security Act of

1950, 64 Stat. 1006, 1008, it was necessary for the Government to prove in each case in which it sought to deport an alien because of membership in the Communist Party that that organization in fact advocated the violent overthrow of the Government. The 1950 Act expressly made deportable aliens who at the time of entry, or at any time thereafter were "members of or affiliated with * * * the Communist Party of the United States." See Galvan v. Press, 347 U.S. 522, 529, 74 S.Ct. 737, 742, 98 L.Ed. 911.

17. A comparable annuity was worth, at the time appellee's benefits were canceled, approximately $6,000. To date he has lost nearly $2,500 in benefits.

18. The Court, recognizing that Cummings v. Missouri, 4 Wall. 277, 18 L.Ed. 356, and Ex parte Garland, 4 Wall. 333, 18 L.Ed. 366, strongly favor the conclusion that § 202(n) was enacted with punitive intent, rejects the force of those precedents as drawing "heavily on the Court's firsthand acquaintance with the events and the mood of the then recent Civil War, and 'the fierce passions which that struggle aroused.' " This seems to me to say that the provision of § 202(n) which cuts off benefits from aliens deported for past Communist Party membership was not enacted in a similar atmosphere. Our judicial detachment from the realities of the national scene should not carry us so far. Our memory of the emotional climate stirred by the question of communism in the early 1950's cannot be so short.

19. See H.R.Rep. No. 1698, 83d Cong., 2d Sess. 24–25.

20. See S.Rep. No. 1987, 83d Cong., 2d Sess. 23; H.R.Conf.Rep. No. 2679, 83d Cong., 2d Sess. 4.

21. See Court's opinion, ante, note 1.

22. See the Court's opinion, ante, note 13.

23. It is unnecessary for me to reach the question whether the statute also constitutes a bill of attainder.

JOHN RAWLS

Punishment*

TWO CONCEPTS OF RULES‡

In this paper I want to show the importance of the distinction between justifying a practice[1] and justifying a particular action falling under it, and I want to explain the logical basis of this distinction and how it is possible to miss its significance. While the distinction has frequently been made,[2] and is now becoming commonplace, there remains the task of explaining the tendency either to overlook it altogether, or to fail to appreciate its importance.

To show the importance of the distinction I am going to defend utilitarianism against those objections which have traditionally been made against it in connection with punishment and the obligation to keep promises. I hope to show that if one uses the distinction in question then one can state utilitarianism in a way which makes it a much better explication of our considered moral judgments than these traditional objections would seem to admit.[3] Thus the importance of the distinction is shown by the way it strengthens the utilitarian view regardless of whether that view is completely defensible or not.

To explain how the significance of the distinction may be overlooked, I am going to discuss two conceptions of rules. One of these conceptions conceals the importance of distinguishing between the justification of a rule or practice and the justification of a particular action falling under it. The other conception makes it clear why this distinction must be made and what is its logical basis.

The subject of punishment, in the sense of attaching legal penalties to the violation of legal rules, has always been a troubling moral question.[4] The trouble about it has not been that people disagree as to whether or not punishment is

*From "Two Concepts of Rules" by John Rawls, *The Philosophical Review*, Vol. 64 (1955), pp. 3–13. Reprinted by permission of the author and the publisher.

‡This is a revision of a paper given at the Harvard Philosophy Club on April 30, 1954.

justifiable. Most people have held that, freed from certain abuses, it is an acceptable institution. Only a few have rejected punishment entirely, which is rather surprising when one considers all that can be said against it. The difficulty is with the justification of punishment: various arguments for it have been given by moral philosophers, but so far none of them has won any sort of general acceptance; no justification is without those who detest it. I hope to show that the use of the aforementioned distinction enables one to state the utilitarian view in a way which allows for the sound points of its critics.

For our purposes we may say that there are two justifications of punishment. What we may call the retributive view is that punishment is justified on the grounds that wrongdoing merits punishment. It is morally fitting that a person who does wrong should suffer in proportion to his wrongdoing. That a criminal should be punished follows from his guilt, and the severity of the appropriate punishment depends on the depravity of his act. The state of affairs where a wrongdoer suffers punishment is morally better than the state of affairs where he does not; and it is better irrespective of any of the consequences of punishing him.

What we may call the utilitarian view holds that on the principle that bygones are bygones and that only future consequences are material to present decisions, punishment is justifiable only by reference to the probable consequences of maintaining it as one of the devices of the social order. Wrongs committed in the past are, as such, not relevant considerations for deciding what to do. If punishment can be shown to promote effectively the interest of society it is justifiable, otherwise it is not.

I have stated these two competing views very roughly to make one feel the conflict between them: one feels the force of *both* arguments and one wonders how they can be reconciled. From my introductory remarks it is obvious that the resolution which I am going to propose is that in this case one must distinguish between justifying a practice as a system of rules to be applied and enforced, and justifying a particular action which falls under these rules; utilitarian arguments are appropriate with regard to questions about practices, while retributive arguments fit the application of particular rules to particular cases.

We might try to get clear about this distinction by imagining how a father might answer the question of his son. Suppose the son asks, "Why was *J* put in jail yesterday?" The father answers, "Because he robbed the bank at *B*. He was duly tried and found guilty. That's why he was put in jail yesterday." But suppose the son had asked a different question, namely, "Why do people put other people in jail?" Then the father might answer, "To protect good people from bad people" or "To stop people from doing things that would make it uneasy for all of us; for otherwise we wouldn't be able to go to bed at night and sleep in peace." There are two very different questions here. One question emphasizes the proper name: It asks why *J* was punished rather than someone else, or it asks what he was punished for. The other question asks why we have the institution of punishment: Why do people punish one another rather than, say, always forgiving one another?

Thus the father says in effect that a particular man is punished, rather than some other man, because he is guilty, and he is guilty because he broke the law (past tense). In his case the law looks back, the judge looks back, the jury looks back, and a penalty is visited upon him for something he did. That a man is to be punished, and what his punishment is to be, is settled by its being shown that he broke the law and that the law assigns that penalty for the violation of it.

On the other hand we have the institution of punishment itself, and recommend and accept various changes in it, because it is thought by the (ideal) legislator and by those to whom the law applies that, as a part of a system of law impartially applied from case to case arising under it, it will have the consequence, in the long run, of furthering the interests of society.

One can say, then, that the judge and the legislator stand in different positions and look in different directions: one to the past, the other to the future. The justification of what the judge does, *qua* judge, sounds like the retributive view; the justification of what the (ideal) legislator does, *qua* legislator, sounds like the utilitarian view. Thus both views have a point (this is as it should be since intelligent and sensitive persons have been on both sides of the argument); and one's initial confusion disappears once one sees that these views apply to persons holding different offices with different duties, and situated differently with respect to the system of rules that make up the criminal law.[5]

One might say, however, that the utilitarian view is more fundamental since it applies to a more fundamental office, for the judge carries out the legislator's will so far as he can determine it. Once the legislator decides to have laws and to assign penalties for their violation (as things are there must be both the law and the penalty) an institution is set up which involves a retributive conception of particular cases. It is part of the concept of the criminal law as a system of rules that the application and enforcement of these rules in particular cases should be justifiable by arguments of a retributive character. The decision whether or not to use law rather than some other mechanism of social control, and the decision as to what laws to have and what penalties to assign, may be settled by utilitarian arguments; but if one decides to have laws then one has decided on something whose working in particular cases is retributive in form.[6]

The answer, then, to the confusion engendered by the two views of punishment is quite simple: One distinguishes two offices, that of the judge and that of the legislator, and one distinguishes their different stations with respect to the system of rules which make up the law; and then one notes that the different sorts of considerations which would usually be offered as reasons for what is done under the cover of these offices can be paired off with the competing justifications of punishment. One reconciles the two views by the time-honored device of making them apply to different situations.

But can it really be this simple? Well, this answer allows for the apparent intent of each side. Does a person who advocates the retributive view necessarily advocate, as an *institution,* legal machinery whose essential purpose is to set up and preserve a correspondence between moral turpitude and suffering? Surely not.[7] What retributionists have rightly insisted upon is that no man can be punished unless he is guilty, that is, unless he has broken the law. Their fundamental criticism of the utilitarian account is that, as they interpret it, it sanctions an innocent person's being punished (if one may call it that) for the benefit of society.

On the other hand, utilitarians agree that punishment is to be inflicted only for the violation of law. They regard this much as understood from the concept of punishment itself.[8] The point of the utilitarian account concerns the institution as a system of rules: utilitarianism seeks to limit its use by declaring it justifiable only if it can be shown to foster effectively the good of society. Historically it is a protest against the indiscriminate and ineffective use of the criminal law.[9] It seeks to dissuade us from assigning to penal institutions the improper, if not sacrilegious, task of matching suffering with moral turpitude. Like others, utilitarians want penal institutions designed so that, as far as humanly possible, only those who break the law run afoul of it. They hold that no official should have discretionary power to inflict penalties whenever he thinks it for the benefit of society; for on utilitarian grounds an institution granting such power could not be justified.[10]

The suggested way of reconciling the retributive and the utilitarian justifications of punishment seems to account for what both sides have wanted to say. There are, however, two further questions which arise, and I shall devote the remainder of this section to them.

First, will not a difference of opinion as to the proper criterion of just law make the proposed reconciliation unacceptable to retributionists? Will they not question whether, if the utilitarian principle is used as the criterion, it follows that those who have broken the law are guilty in a way which satisfies their demand that those punished deserve to be punished? To answer this difficulty, suppose that the rules of the criminal law are justified on utilitarian grounds (it is only for laws that meet his criterion that the utilitarian can be held responsible). Then it follows that the actions which the criminal law specifies as offenses are such that, if they were tolerated, terror and alarm would spread in society. Consequently, retributionists can only deny that those who are punished deserve to be punished if they deny that such actions are wrong. This they will not want to do.

The second question is whether utilitarianism doesn't justify too much. One pictures it as an engine of justification which, if consistently adopted, could be used to justify cruel and arbitrary institutions. Retributionists may be supposed to concede that utilitarians *intend* to reform the law and to make it more humane; that utilitarians do not *wish* to justify any such thing as punishment of the innocent; and that utilitarians may appeal to the fact that punishment presupposes guilt in the sense that by punishment one understands an institution attaching penalties to the infraction of legal rules, and therefore that it is logically absurd to suppose that utilitarians in justifying *punishment* might also have justified punishment (if we may call it that) of the innocent. The real question, however, is whether the utilitarian, in justifying punishment, hasn't used arguments which commit him to accepting the infliction of suffering on innocent persons if it is for the good of society (whether or not one calls this punishment). More generally, isn't the utilitarian committed in principle to accepting many practices which he, as a morally sensitive person, wouldn't want to accept? Retributionists are inclined to hold that there is no way to stop the utilitarian principle from justifying too much except by adding to it a principle which distributes certain rights to individuals. Then the amended criterion is not the greatest benefit of society *simpliciter* [simply], but the greatest benefit of society subject to the constraint that no one's rights may be violated. Now while I think that the classical utilitarians proposed a criterion of this more complicated sort, I do not want to argue that point here.[11] What I want to show is that there is *another* way of preventing the utilitarian principle from justifying too much, or at least of making it much less likely to do so: namely, by stating utilitarianism in a way which accounts for the distinction between the justification of an institution and the justification of a particular action falling under it.

I begin by defining the institution of punishment as follows: a person is said to suffer punishment whenever he is legally deprived of some of the normal rights of a citizen on the ground that he has violated a rule of law, the violation having been established by trial according to the due process of law, provided that the deprivation is carried out by the recognized legal authorities of the state, that the rule of law clearly specifies both the offense and the attached penalty, that the courts construe statutes strictly, and that the statute was on the books prior to the time of the offense.[12] This definition specifies what I shall understand by punishment. The question is whether utilitarian arguments may be found to justify institutions widely different from this and such as one would find cruel and arbitrary.

This question is best answered, I think, by taking up a particular accusation. Consider the following from Carritt:

... the utilitarian must hold that we are justified in inflicting pain always and only to prevent worse pain or bring about greater happiness. This, then, is all we need to consider in so-called punishment, which must be purely preventive. But if some kind of very cruel crime becomes common, and none of the criminals can be caught, it might be highly expedient, as an example, to hang an innocent man, if a charge against him could be so framed that he were universally thought guilty; indeed this would only fail to be an ideal instance of utilitarian 'punishment' because the victim himself would not have been so likely as a real felon to commit such a crime in the future; in all other respects it would be perfectly deterrent and therefore felicific.[13]

Carritt is trying to show that there are occasions when a utilitarian argument would justify taking an action which would be generally condemned; and thus that utilitarianism justifies too much. But the failure of Carritt's argument lies in the fact that he makes no distinction between the justification of the general system of rules which constitutes penal institutions and the justification of particular applications of these rules to particular cases by the various officials whose job it is to administer them. This becomes perfectly clear when one asks who the "we" are of whom Carritt speaks. Who is this who has a sort of absolute authority on particular occasions to decide that an innocent man shall be "punished" if everyone can be convinced that he is guilty? Is this person the legislator, or the judge, or the body of private citizens, or what? It is utterly crucial to know who is to decide such matters, and by what authority, for all of this must be written into the rules of the institution. Until one knows these things one doesn't know what the institution is whose justification is being challenged; and as the utilitarian principle applies to the institution one doesn't know whether it is justifiable on utilitarian grounds or not.

Once this is understood it is clear what the countermove to Carritt's argument is. One must describe more carefully what the *institution* is which his example suggests, and then ask oneself whether or not it is likely that having this institution would be for the benefit of society in the long run. One must not content oneself with the vague thought that, when it's a question of *this* case, it would be a good thing if *somebody* did something even if an innocent person were to suffer.

Try to imagine, then, an institution (which we may call "telishment") which is such that the officials set up by it have authority to arrange a trial for the condemnation of an innocent man whenever they are of the opinion that doing so would be in the best interests of society. The discretion of officials is limited, however, by the rule that they may not condemn an innocent man to undergo such an ordeal unless there is, at the time, a wave of offenses similar to that with which they charge him and telish him for. We may imagine that the officials having the discretionary authority are the judges of the higher courts in consultation with the chief of police, the minister of justice, and a committee of the legislature.

Once one realizes that one is involved in setting up an *institution,* one sees that the hazards are very great. For example, what check is there on the officials? How is one to tell whether or not their actions are authorized? How is one to limit the risks involved in allowing such systematic deception? How is one to avoid giving anything short of complete discretion to the authorities to telish anyone they like? In addition to these considerations, it is obvious that people will come to have a very different attitude towards their penal system when telishment is adjoined to it. They will be uncertain as to whether a convicted man has been punished or telished. They will wonder whether or not they should feel sorry for him. They will wonder whether the same fate won't at any time fall on them. If one pictures how such an institution would actually work, and the enormous risks involved in it, it seems clear that it would serve no useful purpose. A utilitarian justification for this institution is most unlikely.

It happens in general that as one drops off the defining features of punishment one ends up with an institution whose utilitarian justification is highly doubtful. One reason for this is that punishment works like a kind of price system: By altering the prices one has to pay for the performance of actions, it supplies a motive for avoiding some actions and doing others. The defining features are essential if punishment is to work in this way; so that an institution which lacks these features, for example, an institution which is set up to "punish" the innocent, is likely to have about as much point as a price system (if one may call

it that) where the prices of things change at random from day to day and one learns the price of something after one has agreed to buy it.[14]

If one is careful to apply the utilitarian principle to the institution which is to authorize particular actions, then there is *less* danger of its justifying too much. Carritt's example gains plausibility by its indefiniteness and by its concentration on the particular case. His argument will only hold if it can be shown that there are utilitarian arguments which justify an institution whose publicly ascertainable offices and powers are such as to permit officials to exercise that kind of discretion in particular cases. But the requirement of having to build the arbitrary features of the particular decision into the institutional practice makes the justification much less likely to go through.

NOTES

1. I use the word "practice" throughout as a sort of technical term meaning any form of activity specified by a system of rules which defines offices, roles, moves, penalties, defenses, and so on, and which gives the activity its structure. As examples one may think of games and rituals, trials and parliaments.

2. The distinction is central to Hume's discussion of justice in *A Treatise of Human Nature,* bk. III, pt. ii, esp. secs. 2–4. It is clearly stated by John Austin in the second lecture of *Lectures on Jurisprudence* (4th ed.; London, 1873), I, 116ff. (1st ed., 1832). Also it may be argued that J. S. Mill took it for granted in *Utilitarianism;* on this point cf. J. O. Urmson, "The Interpretation of the Moral Philosophy of J. S. Mill," *Philosophical Quarterly,* vol. III (1953). In addition to the arguments given by Urmson there are several clear statements of the distinction in *A System of Logic* (8th ed.; London, 1872), bk. VI, ch. xii pars. 2, 3, 7. The distinction is fundamental to J. D. Mabbott's important paper, "Punishment," *Mind,* n.s., vol. XLVIII (April, 1939). More recently the distinction has been stated with particular emphasis by S. E. Toulmin in *The Place of Reason in Ethics* (Cambridge, 1950), see esp. ch. xi, where it plays a major part in his account of moral reasoning. Toulmin doesn't explain the basis of the distinction, nor how one might overlook its importance, as I try to in this paper, and in my review of this book (*Philosophical Review,* vol. LX [October, 1951]), as some of my criticisms show, I failed to understand the force of it. See also H. D. Aiken, "The Levels of Moral Discourse," *Ethics,* vol. LXII (1952), A. M. Quinton, "Punishment," *Analysis,* vol. XIV (June, 1954), and P. H. Nowell-Smith, *Ethics* (London, 1954), pp. 236–239, 271–273.

3. On the concept of explication see the author's paper *Philosophical Review,* vol. LX (April, 1951).

4. While this paper was being revised, Quinton's appeared; footnote 2 supra. There are several respects in which my remarks are similar to his. Yet as I consider some further questions and rely on somewhat different arguments, I have retained the discussion of punishment and promises together as two test cases for utilitarianism.

5. Note the fact that different sorts of arguments are suited to different offices. One way of taking the differences

between ethical theories is to regard them as accounts of the reasons expected in different offices.

6. In this connection see Mabbott, *op. cit.,* pp. 163–164.

7. On this point see Sir David Ross, *The Right and the Good* (Oxford, 1930), pp. 57–60.

8. See Hobbes's definition of punishment in *Leviathan,* ch. xxviii; and Bentham's definition in *The Principle of Morals and Legislation,* ch. xii, par. 36, ch. xv, par. 28, and in *The Rationale of Punishment,* (London, 1830), bk. I, ch. i. They could agree with Bradley that: "Punishment is punishment only when it is deserved. We pay the penalty, because we owe it, and for no other reason; and if punishment is inflicted for any other reason whatever than because it is merited by wrong, it is a gross immorality, a crying injustice, an abominable crime, and not what it pretends to be." *Ethical Studies* (2nd ed.; Oxford, 1927), pp. 26–27. Certainly by definition it isn't what it pretends to be. The innocent can only be punished by mistake; deliberate "punishment" of the innocent necessarily involves fraud.

9. Cf. Leon Radzinowicz, *A History of English Criminal Law: The Movement for Reform 1750–1833* (London, 1948), esp. ch. xi on Bentham.

10. Bentham discusses how corresponding to a punitory provision of a criminal law there is another provision which stands to it as an antagonist and which needs a name as much as the punitory. He calls it, as one might expect, the *anaetiosostic,* and of it he says: "The punishment of guilt is the object of the former one: the preservation of innocence that of the latter." In the same connection he asserts that it is never thought fit to give the judge the option of deciding whether a thief (that is, a person whom he believes to be a thief, for the judge's belief is what the question must always turn upon) should hang or not, and so the law writes the provision: "The judge shall not cause a thief to be hanged unless he have been duly convicted and sentenced in course of law" (*The Limits of Jurisprudence Defined,* ed. C. W. Everett [New York, 1945], pp. 238–239).

11. By the classical utilitarians I understand Hobbes, Hume, Bentham, J. S. Mill, and Sidgwick.

12. All these features of punishment are mentioned by Hobbes; cf. *Leviathan,* ch. xxviii.

13. *Ethical and Political Thinking* (Oxford, 1947), p. 65.

14. The analogy with the price system suggests an answer to the question how utilitarian considerations insure that punishment is proportional to the offense. It is interesting to note that Sir David Ross, after making the distinction between justifying a penal law and justifying a particular application of it, and after stating that utilitarian considerations have a large place in determining the former, still holds back from accepting the utilitarian justification of punishment on the grounds that justice requires that punishment be proportional to the offense, and that utilitarianism is unable to account for this. Cf. *The Right and the Good,* pp. 61–62. I do not claim that utilitarianism can account for this requirement as Sir David might wish, but it happens, nevertheless, that if utilitarian considerations are followed penalties will be proportional to offenses in this sense: the order of offenses according to seriousness can be paired off with the order of penalties according to severity. Also the absolute level of penalties will be as low as possible. This follows from the assumption that people are rational (i.e., that they are able to take into account the "prices" the state puts on actions), the utilitarian rule that a penal system should provide a motive for preferring the less serious offense, and the principle that punishment as such is an evil. All this was carefully worked out by Bentham in *The Principles of Morals and Legislation,* chs. xiii–xv.

STANLEY I. BENN

An Approach to the Problems of Punishment*

I shall develop, in this article, certain distinctions suggested by recent contributions to the philosophical discussion of punishment, which help to clarify the issues involved. Having separated out what I consider the four central philosophical questions, I shall suggest an approach to

*From *Philosophy,* Vol. XXXIII (1958), pp. 325–41. Reprinted by permission of the Royal Institute of Philosophy, London, and the author. This material was incorporated into *Social Principles and the Democratic State* by R. S. Peters and Stanley I. Benn (London: George Allen & Unwin Ltd., 1959).

them, which, while mainly utilitarian, takes due account, I believe, of the retributivist case where it is strongest, and meets the main retributivist objections.

I make three key distinctions:

(1) Between justifying punishment in general (that is, as an institution), and justifying particular penal decisions as applications of it;

(2) Between what is implied in postulating guilt as a necessary, and as a sufficient, condition for punishment;

(3) Between postulating guilt in law and guilt in morals, as a condition for punishment.

I distinguish, further, four philosophical questions, to which a complete and coherent approach to punishment would have to provide answers:

What formal criteria must be satisfied in justifying:

(1) Punishment in general, that is, as an institution?

(2) Any particular operation of the institution?

(3) The degrees of punishment attached to different classes of offense?

(4) The particular penalty awarded to a given offender?

PRELIMINARIES

A. "PUNISHMENT" DEFINED

Prof. Flew[1] has suggested five criteria for the use of "punishment" in its primary sense, that is, five conditions satisfied by a standard case to which the word would be applied:

(i) It must involve an "evil, an unpleasantness to the victim";

(ii) It must be for an offense (actual or supposed);

(iii) It must be of an offender (actual or supposed);

(iv) It must be the work of personal agencies (that is, not merely the natural consequences of an action);

(v) It must be imposed by authority (real or supposed), conferred by the system of rules (hereafter referred to as "law") against which the offense has been committed.

It is not a misuse to talk, for example, of "punishing the innocent," or of a boxer "punishing his opponent"; but since these usages, though related to the primary one, disregard one or more of the criteria ordinarily satisfied, they are extensions, or secondary usages. In considering the justification for punishment, I shall confine the word to the primary sense, unless I indicate otherwise.

B. THE DISTINCTION BETWEEN JUSTIFYING PUNISHMENT IN GENERAL, AND JUSTIFYING THE PARTICULAR APPLICATION

There would seem, on the face of it, to be a real difference between utilitarian and retributivist ap-

proaches to the justification of punishment, the former looking to its beneficent consequences, the latter exclusively to the wrongful act. It remains to be seen whether the gulf can be bridged. The first step is to distinguish between a rule, or an institution constituted by rules, and some particular application thereof. To ask what can justify punishment in general is to ask why we should have the sort of rules that provide that those who contravene them should be made to suffer; and this is different from asking for a justification of a particular application of them in punishing a given individual. Retributivist and utilitarian have tried to furnish answers to both questions, each in his own terms; the strength of the former's case rests on his answer to the second, of the latter's on his answer to the first. Their difficulties arise from attempting to make one answer do for both.

I. WHAT FORMAL CRITERIA MUST BE SATISFIED IN JUSTIFYING PUNISHMENT IN GENERAL, AS AN INSTITUTION?

The retributivist refusal to look to consequences for justification makes it impossible to answer this question within his terms. Appeals to authority apart, we can provide ultimate justification for rules and institutions, only by showing that they yield advantages.[2] Consequently, what pass for retributivist justifications of punishment in general, can be shown to be either denials of the need to justify it, or mere reiterations of the principle to be justified, or disguised utilitarianism.

Assertions of the type "it is fitting (or justice requires) that the guilty suffer" only reiterate the principle to be justified—for "it is fitting" means only that it ought to be the case, which is precisely the point at issue. Similarly, since justification must be in terms of something other than the thing in question, to say that punishment is a good in itself is to deny the need for justification. For those who feel the need, this is no answer at all. Given that punishment would not be justified for the breach of *any* rule, but only of legal rules, what is the peculiar virtue of law that makes it particularly fitting for breaches of just this type of rule? Even if we make punishment a definitional characteristic of "a legal system," so that "law" entails "punishment," we are still entitled to ask why we should have rule systems of precisely this sort.

Some retributivists argue that while punishment is a prima facie evil, and thus in need of justification, it is less objectionable than that the wicked should prosper. This is to subsume the rule "Crimes ought to be punished" under a more general rule: either "The wicked ought to be less well off than the virtuous" or "The wicked ought not to profit from their crimes." Now "wickedness" involves assessment of character; we do not punish men for their wickedness, but for particular breaches of law. There may be some ignoble but prudent characters who have never broken a law, and never been punished, and noble ones who have—our system of punishment is not necessarily the worse for that. We may have to answer for our characters on the Day of Judgment, but not at Quarter Sessions. The state is not an agent of cosmic justice; it punishes only such acts as are contrary to legal rules, conforming to which, even from unworthy motives like fear, is considered of public importance. And if we offer the narrower ground, that the wicked ought not to profit from their *crimes,* we are bound to justify the distinction between crimes and offenses against morals in general. What is the special virtue of legal rules that a breach of them alone warrants punishment? It seems that the wicked are to be prevented from prospering only if their wickedness manifests itself in selected ways; but how is the selection made, unless in terms of its consequences? In any case, if we permit the subsumption of "Crime ought to be punished" under the more general "The wicked ought not to prosper," it would still be proper to seek justification for the latter. It would not help to say "Justice requires it," for this would only deny the right to ask for justification. I see no answer possible except that in a universe in which the wicked prospered, there would be no inducement to virtue. The subsumption, if allowed, would defer the utilitarian stage of justification; it would not render it superfluous.

A veiled utilitarianism underlies Hegel's treatment of punishment, as annulling a wrong. For if punishment could annul the wrong, it would be justified by the betterment of the victim of the crime or of society in general. Not indeed that the argument is a good one; for the only way to annul a wrong is by restitution or compensation, and

neither of these is punishment. A man may be sent to prison for assault, and *also* be liable for damages. Similarly with the argument that punishment reaffirms the right. Why should a reaffirmation of right take precisely the form of punishment? Would not a formal declaration suffice? And even if the reaffirmation necessarily involved a need, right, or duty to punish, the justification would be utilitarian, for why should it be necessary to reaffirm the right, if not to uphold law for the general advantage?[3]

Others have treated punishment as a sort of reflex, a reaction of the social order to the crime following in the nature of things, like a hangover.[4] This is to confuse rules with scientific laws. The penal consequences of a breach of a rule follow only because men have decided to have rules of precisely this sort. Laws of nature, unlike rules, need no justification (except perhaps in theology) because they are independent of human choice. To treat punishment as a natural unwilled response to a breach of law is to deny the need for justification, not to justify.[5] Once we agree to have penal rules, any particular punishment might be justified (though not necessarily sufficiently justified) by reference to a rule. But this is to answer a different question from that at present under consideration.

For Bosanquet, punishment was retributive in the sense that, ideally at least, it was the returning upon the offender of "his own will, implied in the maintenance of a system to which he is a party," in the form of pain. It tends to "a recognition of the end by the person punished"; it is "his right, of which he must not be defrauded."[6] Now while a criminal may not seek to destroy the entire social order, and may even agree in principle that law-breakers should be punished, his efforts to elude the police are evidence that he does not will his own punishment in any ordinary sense. He may be unreasonable and immoral in making exceptions in his own favor—but we cannot therefore construct a theory of punishment on a hypothetical will that would be his were he reasonable and moral, for then he might not be a criminal. To say that punishment is his "right" is to disregard one of the usual criteria for the use of that word, namely, that it is something which will be enforced only if its subject so chooses, the corollary being that it operates to his advantage. Only by pretending that punishment is self-imposed can we think of the criminal as exercising choice; and only by treating it as reformative can we regard it as to his advantage. By claiming that punishment tends "to a recognition of the end by the person punished," Bosanquet introduces such a reformative justification; but to that extent the argument is utilitarian.

To sum up: Retributive justifications of punishment in general are unsatisfactory for the very reason that they refuse to look to the consequences of a rule, thereby denying a necessary part of the procedure for justifying it. To look to the consequences does not entail treating the criminal merely as a means to a social end, as critics have asserted; for in weighing advantages and disadvantages, the criminal, too, must "count for one." But equally, he must count "for no more than one." While we must not lose sight of his welfare altogether, we are not bound to treat him as our sole legitimate concern.

Bentham's case is that punishment is a technique of social control, justified so long as it prevents more mischief than it produces. At the point where damage to criminals outweighs the expected advantage to society, it loses the justification. It operates by reforming the criminal, by preventing a repetition of the offense, and by deterring others from imitating it. (These need not exhaust the possibilities of advantage—Bentham included the satisfaction of vengeance for the injured party.)

Not all theories dealing with the reform of criminals are theories of punishment. Prison reformers concerned with moral reeducation offer theories of punishment only if they expect the suffering involved in loss of liberty, et cetera, itself to lead to reformation. Reformative treatment might cure criminal inclinations by relaxing the rigors of punishment; it might nevertheless defeat its purpose by reducing the deterrent effect for others. "Reformation" is in any case ambiguous. A man would be "a reformed character" only if he showed remorse for his past misdeeds, and determined not to repeat them, not through fear of further punishment, but simply because they were wrong. A criminal who decides that "crime does not pay" is merely deterred by his own experience which is as much "an example" to himself as to others.

Sentences of preventive detention, transportation, deportation, and the death penalty may all be examples of punishment operating as a preventive. Punishment might be aimed at preventing repetitions of an offense by the criminal himself where there are good grounds (for example, a long criminal record) for supposing him undeterrable.

The strongest utilitarian argument for punishment in general is that it serves to deter potential offenders by inflicting suffering on actual ones. On this view, punishment is not the main thing; the technique works by threat. Every act of punishment is to that extent an admission of failure; we punish only that the technique may retain a limited effectiveness for the future. Thus the problem of justifying punishment arises only because it is not completely effective; if it were, there would be no suffering to justify.

Retributivists do not deny that punishment may act in these ways, nor that it has these advantages. They maintain only that they are incidental; that a system of punishment constructed entirely on these principles would lead to monstrous injustices. These I consider below. It is evident, however, that while *some* sort of justification can be offered within the utilitarian framework, the retributivist is at best denying the need for justification, or offering utilitarianism in disguise. I conclude, therefore, that any justification for punishment in general must satisfy the formal condition that the consequences for everyone concerned of adopting the technique shall be preferable to the consequences of not doing so. If the main advantage arises from a lower incidence of crime (by way of reform, prevention, deterrence, or otherwise), this must be weighed against the penal suffering actually inflicted, and these together must be preferable to a higher incidence of crime, but with no additional suffering inflicted as punishment. This is a frankly utilitarian conclusion. The strength of the retributivist position lies in its answer to the second question to which I now turn.

II. WHAT FORMAL CRITERIA MUST BE SATISFIED IN JUSTIFYING ANY PARTICULAR APPLICATION OF THE TECHNIQUE OF PUNISHMENT?

Critics of the utilitarian approach contend that a justification of punishment in terms of deterrence, prevention, and reform could be extended to justify (i) punishing the innocent, providing they were widely believed to be guilty (in the interest of deterrence); (ii) making a show of punishment, without actually inflicting it (again, deterrence, but this time on the cheap); (iii) punishment in anticipation of the offense (in the interests of prevention or reform). These criticisms, if just, would surely be conclusive. They are based, however, on a misconception of what the utilitarian theory is about. "Punishment" implies, in its primary sense, inflicting suffering only under specified conditions, of which one is that it must be for a breach of a rule. Now if we insist on this criterion for the word, "punishment of the innocent" is a logical impossibility, for by definition, suffering inflicted on the innocent, or in anticipation of a breach of the rule, cannot be "punishment." It is not a question of what is morally justified, but of what is logically possible. (An analogous relation between "guilt" and "pardon" accounts for the oddity of granting "a free pardon" to a convicted man, later found to be innocent.) When we speak of "punishing the innocent," we may mean: (i) "pretending to punish," in the sense of manufacturing evidence, or otherwise imputing guilt, while knowing a man to be innocent. This would be to treat him as *if* he were guilty, and involve the lying assertion that he was. It is objectionable, not only as a lie, but also because it involves treating an innocent person differently from others without justification, or for an irrelevant reason, the reason offered being falsely grounded;[7] (ii) We may mean, by "punish," simply "cause to suffer," that is, guilt may not be imputed. This would be a secondary use of the word. In that case, it could not be said that, as a matter of logical necessity, it is either impossible or wrong to punish the innocent. To imprison members of a subversive party (that is, under Defense Regulation 18B) treating them *in that respect* like criminals, though no offense is even charged, would not necessarily be immoral. Critics might describe it as "punishing the innocent," but they would be illegitimately borrowing implications of the primary sense to attack a type of action to which these did not apply. It is only necessarily improper to "punish the innocent" if we pretend they are guilty, that is, if we accept all the primary usage criteria; in any looser sense, there need be nothing wrong in any given case. For in exceptional conditions it may be legitimate to deprive people of their liberty as part of a

control technique, without reference to an offense (for example, the detention of lunatics or enemy aliens). Similar arguments apply in the case of the show of punishment. A utilitarian justification of punishment cannot be extended to cover lies, or the making of distinctions where there are no relevant differences; it would be impossible merely to pretend to punish *every* criminal—and unless a relevant criterion could be found, there could be no grounds for treating some differently from others.

The short answer to the critics of utilitarian theories of punishment is that they are theories of *punishment,* not of *any* sort of technique involving suffering.

We may now turn to the retributivist position itself. F. H. Bradley asserted "the necessary connection of punishment and guilt. Punishment is punishment, only where it is deserved . . . if punishment is inflicted for any other reason whatever than because it is merited by wrong, it is a gross immorality, a crying injustice, an abominable crime, and not what it pretends to be."[8] Now, we must distinguish between legal and moral guilt. If the necessary connection asserted is between punishment and legal guilt, then this is a definition of "punishment" masquerading as a moral judgment. It would be more accurate to write "Punishment is 'punishment' only when it is deserved," for the sentence is then about the use of a word, not about the rightness of the act. "The infliction of suffering on a person is only properly described as punishment if that person is guilty. The retributivist thesis, therefore, is not a moral doctrine, but an account of the meaning of the word 'punishment.' "[9]

But this is not the only form of retributive thesis. There are at least four possibilities:

(i) That guilt (that is, a breach of law) is a *necessary* condition of punishment (this is the position just examined);

(ii) That guilt (that is, a breach of a *moral* rule) is a *necessary* condition of punishment;

(iii) That guilt (*legal*) is a *sufficient* condition of punishment;

(iv) That guilt (*moral*) is a *sufficient* condition of punishment.

Position (iii) is *not* logically necessary, for it does not follow from the definition of punishment; we *cannot* "punish" where there has been no breach, but we can, and often do, let off with a caution where there has. Other conditions besides guilt may have to be satisfied before punishment is wholly justified in a given case.

The introduction, in (ii) and (iv), of moral guilt puts a new complexion on retributive theory. A person who is morally guilty deserves blame, and the conditions for blameworthiness could be listed. But it is in no sense necessary that a person who is blameworthy should also be punishable. We may blame liars, but unless, for example, they make false tax returns, or lie to a court of law, we should not feel bound to punish them. If the conditions of blameworthiness cannot be assimilated completely to the conditions for punishment, moral guilt cannot be a sufficient condition for punishment.

Position (ii) might be supported in two ways:

(*a*) A prima facie moral duty to obey law may yield, in the case of an immoral law, to a stronger duty; a breach of law would not then entail moral guilt, and we should question the justice of the punishment.[10]

(*b*) Certain conditions, like unavoidable ignorance or mistake of fact, lunacy, infancy, and irresistible duress, would exonerate from blame; offenses committed under these conditions should not be punishable—and are not in fact punished, though the deterrent effects of the punishment would be no less in these cases than in others. Therefore, in a negative sense at least, the criteria of blameworthiness must be satisfied, if the necessary conditions for punishment are to be satisfied. Punishment is retribution for such moral lapses as the law recognizes.

The first argument (*a*) might be met in two ways. From the judge's standpoint, so long as he continued in office, it would be his duty to enforce the law, whatever his opinion of it.[11] For him, at least, the absence of moral guilt would not be a bar to punishment. Secondly, criticism of a rule is only indirectly criticism of the justice of a punishment inflicted for a breach of it. The utilitarian could argue that a law that is itself mischievous (in Bentham's sense of "mischief") cannot justify the further mischief of punishment; no good can come of it anyway. This is not, therefore, a defense of a retributive theory of punishment so much as a statement of conditions that a rule must satisfy if punishment is properly to attach to it.

The second argument (*b*) is inconclusive. If the technique of punishment operates primarily by deterrence, it can serve its purpose only in respect of deliberate acts. No act committed under any of the above conditions would be deliberate. If, therefore, offenses of these types are left unpunished, the threat in relation to other offenses remains unimpaired, for the sane potential murderer gets no comfort from mercy extended to the homicidal maniac, and other homicidal maniacs will be unaffected either way. Consequently to punish in such cases would be a pointless mischief. In any case, because some of the conditions for blame and punishment coincide, it does not follow that the satisfaction of the former is a necessary condition for the satisfaction of the latter.[12] I shall return to this point later in relation to motive.

Of the four possible interpretations of the retributivist relation of guilt to punishment, it is the first only, whereby guilt in law is a necessary condition for punishment, that is completely persuasive; and this is precisely because it is a definition and not a justification. Consequently, it need not conflict with a utilitarian view.

For a utilitarian to require, for every case of punishment, that it be justified in terms of preventing more mischief than it causes, would be to miss the point of punishment as an institution. Indeed, any rule would be pointless if every decision still required to be justified in the light of its expected consequences. But this is particularly true of penal rules; for the effectiveness of punishment as a deterrent depends on its regular application, save under conditions sufficiently well understood for them not to constitute a source of uncertainty. Legal guilt once established, then, the initial utilitarian presumption against causing deliberate suffering has been overcome, and a case for a penalty has been made out. But it may still be defeated; for since guilt is not a sufficient condition, there may well be other relevant considerations (for example, that this is a first offense). The following formal criterion may be postulated, however, which any consideration must satisfy, namely that to recognize it as a general ground for waiving the penalty would not involve any otherwise avoidable mischief to society *greater* than the mischief of punishing the offender.

One of the criticisms leveled against utilitarianism is that by relating the justification of punishment to its expected consequences, rather than to the crime itself, it would justify penalties divorced from the relative seriousness of crimes, permitting severe penalties for trivial offenses, if that were the only way to reduce their number. A serious but easily detected crime might warrant lesser penalties than a minor but secret one. This conclusion being intolerable, the retributivist contends that to escape it we must seek the measure of the penalty in the crime itself, according to the degree of wickedness involved in committing it.

Again, I distinguish the justification of rules from the justification of particular applications. To ask "How much punishment is appropriate to a given offense?" is ambiguous: It may refer either to the punishment allotted by a rule to a *class* of acts, or to a particular award for a given act, within that class. The distinction is pointed by the practice of laying down only maximum (and sometimes minimum) penalties in the rule, leaving particular determinations to judicial discretion.

III. WHAT FORMAL CRITERIA MUST BE SATISFIED IN JUSTIFYING THE DEGREES OF PUNISHMENT ATTACHED TO DIFFERENT CLASSES OF OFFENSE?

"The only case" (said Kant) "in which the offender cannot complain that he is being treated unjustly is if his crime recoils upon himself and he suffers what he has inflicted on another, if not in a literal sense, at any rate according to the spirit of the law." "It is only *the right of requital (jus talionis)* which can fix definitely the quality and the quantity of the punishment." This is the most extreme retributive position; its essential weakness is present, however, in more moderate attempts to seek the determinants of punishment exclusively in the offense itself.

If retaliatory punishment is not to be effected "in a literal sense" (which might well be intolerably cruel, and in some cases physically impossible), but rather "according to the spirit of the law," it involves a sort of arithmetical equation of suffering as impracticable as the hedonistic calculus. Suffering of one sort cannot be *equated* with another, though it may be possible to prefer one to another (or to be indifferent as between one and another). I can certainly say that I would rather see A suffer in one way, than B in another,

or that there is really nothing to choose between the two. But this is quite different from saying that A ought to be made to suffer in exactly the same degree as B, whom he has injured; for this involves not a preference enunciated by some third person, but a quasi-quantitative comparison of the sufferings of two different people, treated as objective facts. And there is no way of making this comparison, even though the external features of their suffering may be identical. It is even more evidently impossible when the suffering of one is occasioned by, say, blackmail, and of the other by imprisonment.[13]

The difficulty remains in the compromise between a utilitarian and retaliatory position attempted by W. D. Ross. While admitting that the legislator must consider the deterrent ends of punishment in assessing penalties, he maintains that the injury inflicted by the criminal sets an upper limit to the injury than can legitimately be inflicted on him. "For he has lost his prima facie rights to life, liberty, or property, only insofar as these rested on an explicit or implicit undertaking to respect the corresponding rights in others, and insofar as he has failed to respect those rights."[14] But how are we to make this equation between the rights invaded and consequently sacrificed and the amount of suffering so justified—unless there is already available a scale, or rule, fixing the relation? But then how is the scale to be justified?

J. D. Mabbott admits there can be no direct relation between offense and penalty, but seeks, by comparing one crime with another, to make an estimate of the penalties *relatively* appropriate. "We can grade crimes in a rough scale and penalties in a rough scale, and keep our heaviest penalties for what are socially the most serious wrongs regardless of whether these penalties . . . are exactly what deterrence would require."[15] But what are we to understand by "socially the most serious wrongs"? On the one hand, they might be those that shock us most deeply—we could then construct a shock scale, and punish accordingly. There are some shocking acts, however, that we should not want to punish at all (for example, some sexual offenses against morality); at the same time, we should be hard put to it to know what penalties to attach to new offenses against, say, currency control regulations, where the initial shock reaction is either negligible, because the rule is unsupported by a specific rule of conventional morality, or where it is of a standard mild variety accompanying any offense against the law as such, irrespective of its particular quality. On the other hand, "the most serious wrongs" may be simply those we are least ready to tolerate. That, however, would be to introduce utilitarian considerations into our criteria of "seriousness." For to say that we are not prepared to tolerate an offense is to say that we should feel justified in imposing heavy penalties to deter people from committing it. But in making deterrent considerations secondary to the degree of "seriousness," Mr. Mabbott implicitly excludes this interpretation.

The retributivists' difficulties arise from seeking the measure of the penalty in the crime, without first assuming a scale or a rule relating the two. Given the scale, any given penalty would require justification in terms of it; but the scale itself, like any rule, must in the end be justified in utilitarian terms. It remains to be seen whether this necessarily opens the way to severe penalties for trivial offenses.

For the utilitarian, arguing in deterrent terms, it is the threat rather than the punishment itself which is primary. Could we rely on the threat being completely effective, there could be no objection to the death penalty for every offense, since *ex hypothesi* it would never be inflicted. Unhappily, we must reckon to inflict some penalties, for there will always be some offenders, no matter what the threatened punishment. We must suppose, then, for every class of crime, a scale of possible penalties, to each of which corresponds a probable number of offenses, and therefore of occasions for punishment, the number probably diminishing as the severity increases. Ultimately, however, we should almost certainly arrive at a hard core of undeterrables. We should then choose, for each class of offense, that penalty at which the marginal increment of mischief inflicted on offenders would be just preferable to the extra mischief from which the community is protected by this increment of punishment. To inflict any heavier penalty would do more harm than it would prevent. (This is Bentham's principle of "frugality."[16])

This involves not a quasi-quantitative comparison of suffering by the community and the offender, but only a preference. We might say something like this: To increase the penalty for

parking offenses to life imprisonment would reduce congestion on the roads; nevertheless the inconvenience of a large number of offenses would not be serious enough to justify disregarding in so great a measure the prima facie case for liberty, even of a very few offenders. With blackmail, or murder, the possibility of averting further instances defeats to a far greater extent the claims of the offender. One parking offense more or less is not of great moment; one murder more or less is.

In retaliatory theory we are asked to estimate the damage done by the crime, and to inflict just that amount (or no more than that amount) on the criminal; here we are required only to choose between one combination of circumstances and another. The choice may not always be easy; but it is not impossible, or even unusual. For we are well accustomed to choosing between things incapable of quantitative comparison; what is impossible is to assess what one man has suffered from blackmail, and then to impose its equivalent on the blackmailer in terms of a prison sentence. The difference is between a prescription and a description. To say, as I do above, that the right penalty is that at which the marginal increment of mischief inflicted is just preferable to the mischief thereby avoided, is to invite the critic to choose (or prescribe) one state of affairs rather than another. But to say that the penalty should equal (or should not exceed) the suffering of the victim of the crime is to invite him to prescribe a course dependent not on his own preferences, but on a factual comparison of incomparables, on an equation of objective conditions.

The utilitarian case as I have now put it is not open to the objection that it would justify serious penalties for trivial offenses. For to call an offense "trivial" is to say that we care less if this one is committed than if others are, that is, we should be unwilling to inflict so much suffering to prevent it, as to prevent others. "Relatively serious crimes" are those relatively less tolerable, that is, we prefer to inflict severer penalties rather than to suffer additional offenses. If this is so, "Trivial crimes do not deserve severe penalties" is analytic, consequently a utilitarian justification could not be extended to cover a contrary principle.[17]

Some penalties we are unwilling to inflict whatever their deterrent force. We are less ready to torture offenders than to suffer their offenses.

And there are people who would rather risk murders than inflict the death penalty, even supposing it to be "the unique deterrent." To kill, they say, is absolutely wrong. Now this may mean only that no circumstances are imaginable in which its probable consequences would make it right, that is, in which the mischief done would not outweigh the mischief prevented—not that it could *never* be right, only that in any imaginable conditions it would not be. This would not exclude justification by consequences, and is therefore compatible with the view of punishment I am advancing. On the other hand, if the absolutist denies altogether the relevance of consequences, he is making an ultimate judgment for which, in the nature of the case, justification can be neither sought nor offered, and which is therefore undiscussible.

I conclude, from this discussion, that any justification for the nature and degree of punishment attached to a given class of offense must satisfy the following formal criterion: that the marginal increment of mischief inflicted should be preferable to the mischief avoided by fixing that penalty rather than one slightly lower. Assuming that the advantages of punishment derive mainly from upholding rules, this means that the conformity secured, weighed against the suffering inflicted, should be preferable to a lower level of conformity, weighed against the suffering inflicted by imposing a lesser penalty. (This entails neither that a very few offenders suffering heavy penalties must be preferred to a larger number of offenders suffering lighter penalties, nor the converse; preferences are not settled by multiplication.)

IV. WHAT FORMAL CRITERIA MUST BE SATISFIED IN JUSTIFYING THE PARTICULAR PENALTY AWARDED TO A GIVEN OFFENDER?

Two men guilty of what is technically the same offense (that is, who have broken the same rule) are not necessarily punished alike. This could be justified only be reference to relevant criteria, other than simple guilt, by which their cases are distinguished. Provocation, temptation, duress, and a clean record may all make a difference. But these are also relevant to the determination of blame. From these considerations arise two possible objections to the view I am advancing:

(a) Is it consistent with utilitarianism that in determining the sentence, we should look to the particular conditions of the crime, rather than to the consequences of the penalty? Should we not look forward to the exemplary advantages of the maximum penalty, rather than backward to extenuating circumstances?

(b) Since we do look backward, and assess the penalty in the light of criteria also relevant to an assessment of blameworthiness, can we not say that men deserve punishment only in the measure that they deserve blame?

As to (a); a rule once accepted, there is no need to justify every application in terms of its consequences; it is necessary to justify in utilitarian terms only the criteria of extenuation, not every application of them. Now precisely because an offense has been committed under exceptional circumstances (for example, severe temptation, provocation, duress), leniency would not seriously weaken the threat, since offenders would expect similar leniency only in similar circumstances, which are such, in any case, that a man would be unlikely to consider rationally the penal consequences of his act. Given that, the full measure of the penalty would be unjustifiable.[18]

As to (b); while some criteria tend to mitigate both blame and punishment, the latter need not depend on the degree of the former. The question of motive is crucial. We generally regard a man as less blameworthy if he breaks a rule "from the highest motives," rather than selfishly or maliciously. A traitor from conscientious conviction may be blamed for wrongheadedness, but, if we respect his integrity, we blame him less than a merely mercenary one. But honest motives will not always mitigate punishment. It may be vital for the effectiveness of government that conscientious recalcitrants (for example, potential fifth columnists acting from political conviction) be deterred from action. But since strong moral convictions are often less amendable to threats than other motives, they could scarcely be admitted in such cases in extenuation of punishment. On the other hand, if the mischief of the penalty needed for a high degree of conformity exceeds its advantages, it may be reasonable to give up punishing conscientious offenders altogether, provided they can be discerned from the fakes.[19] We no longer punish conscientious objectors to military service, having found by experience that they are rarely amendable to threats, that they are unsatisfactory soldiers if coerced, and that, given a rigorous test of conscientiousness, their numbers are not likely to be so great as to impair the community purpose.

The considerable overlapping of the factors tending to mitigate blame and punishment nevertheless demands explanation. Morality and law are alike rule systems for controlling behavior, and what blame is to one, punishment is to the other. Since they are closely analogous as techniques for discouraging undesirable conduct, by making its consequences in different ways disagreeable, the principles for awarding them largely coincide. But it does not follow that because we usually also blame the man we punish, we should punish in the light of criteria determining moral guilt. Morality operates as a control not only by prescribing or prohibiting acts, but also by conditioning character (and therefore conduct in general). We blame men for being bad tempered; we punish them only for assault. Furthermore, punishment is administered through formal machinery of investigation, proof, conviction, sentence, and execution; blame by informal and personal procedures which may well take account of evidence of character that might nevertheless be rightly inadmissible in a court of law. To the extent that the techniques are analogous, they may be expected to employ similar criteria; but the analogy cannot be pushed all the way.

CONCLUSION

The quarrel between retributivist and utilitarian is primarily about procedures of justification, about how to go about defending or attacking punishment, in general or in particular, about the formal criteria that together form a schema to which any justification must conform. I have maintained that when what is wanted is a justification of a rule, or an institution, of punishment in general, or of the scale of punishments assigned to different classes of offense, it must be sought in terms of the net advantages gained or mischiefs avoided. When the particular sentence is in question, the first consideration is guilt, without which punishment in a strict sense is impossible, but which once established constitutes a prima facie case for it. The second consideration must be the legally prescribed limits, within which the penalty must fall. Beyond that, decision must be made in the light of criteria tending

to mitigate if not totally defeat the presumption in favor of the maximum penalty. These criteria must themselves be justified in terms of the net advantages, or mischief avoided, in adopting them as general principles.

These are formal principles only. To make out a substantial justification, we must postulate first the sort of advantages we expect from punishment as an institution. I have assumed that its principal advantage is that it secures conformity to rules (though others might conceivably be offered, for example, that it reformed criminal characters, which could be regarded as a good thing in itself; or that it gave the injured person the satisfaction of being revenged). Further, I have assumed that it operates primarily by way of deterence. These are in part assumptions of fact, in part moral judgments. I maintain that these being given, the criteria by which the prima facie case for punishment may be defeated, wholly or in part, are generally justifiable in utilitarian terms; that they do not weaken the deterrent threat, that they avoid inflicting suffering which would not be justified by the resultant additional degree of conformity. Further, the total assimilation to the system of punishment of criteria tending to defeat or mitigate blameworthiness, is unjustifiable in theory and is not made in practice. We do not punish men because they are morally guilty, nor must we *necessarily* refrain because they are morally guiltless, nor mitigate the punishment in the same degree for all the same reasons that we mitigate blame. This is not to say that the justifications sought are not *moral* justifications; it is simply that they must be made in the light of criteria different from those governing blame, since however close the analogy may be between the two techniques of control, there are still significant differences between them.

NOTES

1. A. Flew, "The Justification of Punishment," *Philosophy,* XXIX, (1954), 291–307.
2. Admittedly, a rule might be justified *in the first place* by reference to one more general, under which it is subsumed as a particular application—e.g., "It is wrong to pick flowers from public gardens because it is wrong to steal—and this is a special case of stealing." But this would not be conclusive. It could be countered by making a distinction between private and public property, such that while the more general rule prohibits stealing the former, it does not extend to the latter. Whether the distinction can be accepted as relevant must depend on the reasons for the more general rule, understood

in terms of its expected advantages, and on whether to allow the exception would tend to defeat them. Consider "Euthanasia is wrong because it is wrong to kill." It could be argued that the latter does not require the former; that a proper distinction can be made between killings generally, and those satisfying the conditions: (i) that the patient wants to be killed; (ii) that the purpose is to put him out of pain; (iii) that there is no hope for his recovery. Suppose the reason for the general prohibition is to ensure that the life of man shall not be "solitary, poor, nasty, brutish, and short"; then exceptions satisfying the above criteria might be admissible, on the grounds that not only would they not defeat the objectives of the rule, but that advantages would follow from distinguishing on the basis of these criteria, that would otherwise be missed. On the other hand, it might be said that it is *absolutely* wrong to kill—which is to deny the need for justification in terms of purpose or consequences, but is also to deny the need for *any* moral (as opposed to authoritative) justification. But in that case, how are we to decide whether "Thou shalt not kill" does, or does not, extend to a duty "officiously to keep alive"?

3. Cf. Lord Justice Denning, in evidence to the Royal Commission on Capital Punishment: "The ultimate justification of any punishment is not that it is a deterrent but that it is the emphatic denunciation by the community of a crime." Cmd. 8932, § 53 (1953). But "denunciation" does not imply the deliberate imposition of suffering, which is the feature of punishment usually felt to need justification.

4. Cf. Sir Ernest Barker, in *Principles of Social and Political Theory*, p. 182: "the mental rule of law which pays back a violation of itself by a violent return, much as the natural rules of health pay back a violation of themselves by a violent return."

5. For J. D. Mabbott, too, punishment is a kind of automatic response, though in a different sense. "Punishment is a corollary not of law but of lawbreaking. Legislators do not *choose* to punish. They hope no punishment will be needed. The criminal makes the essential choice; he 'brings it on himself.'" ("Punishment," in *Mind*, Vol. 48, 1939, p. 161. He reaffirms the position in "Freewill and Punishment," in *Contemporary British Philosophy*, 3d Series, ed. H. D. Lewis, 1956, p. 303.) But legislators choose to make *penal* rules, and it is this choice that needs justification.

6. *The Philosophical Theory of the State*, 4th ed. (1923), p. 211.

7. Cf. A. Quinton, "On Punishment," in *Analysis*, Vol. 14, reprinted in *Philosophy, Politics, and Society*, ed. P. Laslett, 1956.

8. *Ethical Studies*, 2d ed. 1927, pp. 26–27.

9. A. Quinton, *op cit.*, in *Analysis*, p. 137, in *Philosophy, Politics, and Society*, p. 86.

10. Cf. C. W. K. Mundle, "Punishment and Desert," in *Philosophical Quarterly*, Vol. 4, 1954: "the retributive theory implies that punishment of a person by the state is morally justifiable if, and only if he has done something which is both a legal and moral offense, and only if the penalty is proportionate to the moral gravity of his offense," p. 227.

11. This is roughly Mabbott's view *(op. cit.)*. He is a rare example of a retributivist who dissociates punishment and moral guilt.

12. A man who had broken a law (say, an import regulation), of the existence of which he was ignorant (but avoidably so), would be liable to punishment. It would be to counsel perfection to say that everyone has a moral duty to know of *every* law that might affect him. I should say, in this case, that the offender had been imprudent, but not immoral, in not ascertaining his legal position. I should impute no moral guilt either for his ignorance or for his breach of the rule; but I should not feel, on that account, that he was an injured innocent entitled to complain that he had been wrongly punished.

13. Hegel virtually admits the impossibility of answering this question rationally (*Philosophy of Right*, § 101) but insists nevertheless that there must be a right answer (§ 214) to which we must try empirically to approximate. But by what test shall we judge whether our shots at justice are approaching or receding from the target?

14. *The Right and the Good*, 1930, pp. 62–63.

15. *Op. cit.*, p. 162.

16. *Introduction to the Principles of Morals and Legislation*, Chap. XV, §§ 11–12.

17. We could say "Some trivial crimes deserve serious penalties" if we wished to imply that some crimes are a good deal more serious than they are generally held to be. But the sentence would be better punctuated: "Some 'trivial' crimes . . .," for they are "trivial" in the view of others, not of the speaker. Consider, in this connection, the difference of opinion between pedestrians and motorists' associations on the gravity of driving offenses—and on the penalties appropriate. A pedestrian might not think a prison sentence too severe a penalty for speeding—but neither is it, for him, a trivial offense.

18. Grading sentences according to the number of previous convictions might be justified by the failure, *ex hypothesi*, of lesser penalties on earlier occasions, to act as deterrents. Possible imitators with similar records may possibly require a similarly severe deterrent example. For most of the rest of us, with little criminal experience, lighter penalties awarded to less hardened offenders are sufficient deterrents. A case can therefore be made for reserving the severest penalties for the class of criminals least easily deterred.

19. Consider, in this connection, the difficulty of distinguishing the genuine survivor of a suicide pact, who has been unable to carry out his side of the bargain, from the cheat who relies on a counterfeit pact to evade the maximum penalty for murder. (See the Report on Capital Punishment, referred to above §§ 163–176.) The same applies to "mercy-killing": "How, for example, were the jury to decide whether a daughter had killed her invalid father from compassion, from a desire for material gain, from a natural wish to bring to an end a trying period of her life, or from a combination of motives?" (*Ibid.*, § 179). Nevertheless, where we feel reasonably sure that the motive was merciful, we expect leniency. A mercy-killing is not in the same class as a brutal murder for profit, and we may feel justified in tolerating a few examples rather than inflict the maximum penalty on this type of offender.

HERBERT MORRIS

Persons and Punishment*

They acted and looked ... at us, and around in our house, in a way that had about it the feeling—at least for me—that we were not people. In their eyesight we were just things, that was all. [Malcolm X]

We have no right to treat a man like a dog. [Governor Maddox of Georgia]

Alfredo Traps in Durrenmatt's tale discovers that he has brought off, all by himself, a murder involving considerable ingenuity. The mock prosecutor in the tale demands the death penalty "as reward for a crime that merits admiration, astonishment, and respect." Traps is deeply moved; indeed, he is exhilarated, and the whole of his life becomes more heroic, and, ironically, more precious. His defense attorney proceeds to argue that Traps was not only innocent but incapable of guilt, "a victim of the age." This defense Traps disavows with indignation and anger. He makes claim to the murder as his and demands the prescribed punishment—death.

The themes to be found in this macabre tale do not often find their way into philosophical discussions of punishment. These discussions deal with large and significant questions of whether or not we ever have the right to punish, and if we do, under what conditions, to what degree, and in what manner. There is a tradition, of course, not notable for its present vitality, that is closely linked with motifs in Durrenmatt's tale of crime and punishment. Its adherents have argued that justice requires a person be punished if he is guilty. Sometimes—though rarely—these philosophers have expressed themselves in terms of the criminal's *right to be punished*. Reaction to the claim that there is such a right has been astonishment combined, perhaps, with a touch of con-

*Reprinted from *The Monist*, Volume 52:4 (October, 1968), LaSalle, Illinois, with the permission of the publisher and the author.

tempt for the perversity of the suggestion. A strange right that no one would ever wish to claim! With that flourish the subject is buried and the right disposed of. In this paper the subject is resurrected.

My aim is to argue for four propositions concerning rights that will certainly strike some as not only false but preposterous: first, that we have a right to punishment; second, that this right derives from a fundamental human right to be treated as a person; third, that this fundamental right is a natural, inalienable, and absolute right; and, fourth, that the denial of this right implies the denial of all moral rights and duties. Showing the truth of one, let alone all, of these large and questionable claims, is a tall order. The attempt or, more properly speaking, the first steps in an attempt, follow.

1. When someone claims that there is a right to be free, we can easily imagine situations in which the right is infringed and easily imagine situations in which there is a point to asserting or claiming the right. With the right to be punished, matters are otherwise. The immediate reaction to the claim that there is such a right is puzzlement. And the reasons for this are apparent. People do not normally value pain and suffering. Punishment is associated with pain and suffering. When we think about punishment we naturally think of the strong desire most persons have to avoid it, to accept, for example, acquittal of a criminal charge with relief and eagerly, if convicted, to hope for pardon or probation. Adding, of course, to the paradoxical character of the claim of such a right is difficulty in imagining circumstances in which it would be denied one. When would one rightly demand punishment and meet with any threat of the claim being denied?

So our first task is to see when the claim of such a right would have a point. I want to approach this task by setting out two complex types of institutions both of which are designed to maintain some degree of social control. In the one a central concept is punishment for wrongdoing and in the other the central concepts are control of dangerous individuals and treatment of disease.

Let us first turn attention to the institutions in which punishment is involved. The institutions I describe will resemble those we ordinarily think of as institutions of punishment; they will have, however, additional features we associate with a system of just punishment.

Let us suppose that men are constituted roughly as they now are, with a rough equivalence in strength and abilities, a capacity to be injured by each other and to make judgments that such injury is undesirable, a limited strength of will, and a capacity to reason and to conform conduct to rules. Applying to the conduct of these men are a group of rules, ones I shall label 'primary', which closely resemble the core rules of our criminal law, rules that prohibit violence and deception and compliance with which provides benefits for all persons. These benefits consist in noninterference by others with what each person values, such matters as continuance of life and bodily security. The rules define a sphere for each person, then, which is immune from interference by others. Making possible this mutual benefit is the assumption by individuals of a burden. The burden consists in the exercise of self-restraint by individuals over inclinations that would, if satisfied, directly interfere or create a substantial risk of interference with others in proscribed ways. If a person fails to exercise self-restraint even though he might have and gives in to such inclinations, he renounces a burden which others have voluntarily assumed and thus gains an advantage which others, who have restrained themselves, do not possess. This system, then, is one in which the rules establish a mutuality of benefit and burden and in which the benefits of noninterference are conditional upon the assumption of burdens.

Connecting punishment with the violation of these primary rules, and making public the provision for punishment, is both reasonable and just. First, it is only reasonable that those who voluntarily comply with the rules be provided some assurance that they will not be assuming burdens which others are unprepared to assume. Their disposition to comply voluntarily will diminish as they learn that others are with impunity renouncing burdens they are assuming. Second, fairness dictates that a system in which benefits and burdens are equally distributed have a mechanism designed to prevent a maldistribution in the benefits and burdens. Thus, sanctions are attached to noncompliance with the primary rules so as to induce compliance with the primary rules among those who may be disinclined to obey. In this way the likelihood of an unfair distribution is diminished.

Third, it is just to punish those who have violated the rules and caused the unfair distribution of benefits and burdens. A person who violates the rules has something others have—the benefits of the system—but by renouncing what others have assumed, the burdens of self-restraint, he has acquired an unfair advantage. Matters are not even until this advantage is in some way erased. Another way of putting it is that he owes something to others, for he has something that does not rightfully belong to him. Justice—that is punishing such individuals—restores the equilibrium of benefits and burdens by taking from the individual what he owes, that is, exacting the debt. It is important to see that the equilibrium may be restored in another way. Forgiveness—with its legal analogue of a pardon—while not the righting of an unfair distribution by making one pay his debt is, nevertheless, a restoring of the equilibrium by forgiving the debt. Forgiveness may be viewed, at least in some types of cases, as a gift after the fact, erasing a debt, which had the gift been given before the fact, would not have created a debt. But the practice of pardoning has to proceed sensitively, for it may endanger in a way the practice of justice does not, the maintenance of an equilibrium of benefits and burdens. If all are indiscriminately pardoned less incentive is provided individuals to restrain their inclinations, thus increasing the incidence of persons taking what they do not deserve.

There are also in this system we are considering a variety of operative principles compliance with which provides some guarantee that the system of punishment does not itself promote an unfair distribution of benefits and burdens. For one thing, provision is made for a variety of defenses, each one of which can be said to have as its object diminishing the chances of forcibly depriving a person of benefits others have if that person has not derived an unfair advantage. A person has not derived an unfair advantage if he could not have restrained himself or if it is unreasonable to expect him to behave otherwise than he did. Sometimes the rules preclude punishment of classes of persons such as children. Sometimes they provide a defense if on a particular occasion a person lacked the capacity to conform his conduct to the rules. Thus, someone who in an epileptic seizure strikes another is excused. Punishment in these cases would be punishment of the innocent, punishment of those who do not voluntarily renounce a burden others have assumed. Punishment in such cases, then, would not equalize but rather cause an unfair distribution in benefits and burdens.

Along with principles providing defenses there are requirements that the rules be prospective and relatively clear so that persons have a fair opportunity to comply with the rules. There are, also, rules governing, among other matters, the burden of proof, who shall bear it and what it shall be, the prohibition on double jeopardy, and the privilege against self-incrimination. Justice requires conviction of the guilty, and requires their punishment, but in setting out to fulfill the demands of justice we may, of course, because we are not omniscient, cause injustice by convicting and punishing the innocent. The resolution arrived at in the system I am describing consists in weighing as the greater evil the punishment of the innocent. The primary function of the system of rules was to provide individuals with a sphere of interest immune from interference. Given this goal, it is determined to be a greater evil for society to interfere unjustifiably with an individual by depriving him of good than for the society to fail to punish those that have unjustifiably interfered.

Finally, because the primary rules are designed to benefit all and because the punishments prescribed for their violation are publicized and the defenses respected, there is some plausibility in the exaggerated claim that in choosing to do an act violative of the rules an individual has chosen to be punished. This way of putting matters brings to our attention the extent to which, when the system is as I have described it, the criminal "has brought the punishment upon himself" in contrast to those cases where it would be misleading to say "he has brought it upon himself," cases, for example, where one does not know the rules or is punished in the absence of fault.

To summarize, then: First, there is a group of rules guiding the behavior of individuals in the community which establish spheres of interest immune from interference by others: second, provision is made for what is generally regarded as a deprivation of some thing of value if the rules are violated; third, the deprivations visited upon any person are justified by that person's having violated the rules: fourth, the deprivation, in this just system of punishment, is linked to rules that fairly distribute benefits and burdens and to procedures that strike some balance between not punishing the guilty and punishing the innocent, a class defined as those who have not voluntarily done acts violative of the law, in which it is evident that the evil of punishing the innocent is regarded as greater than the nonpunishment of the guilty.

At the core of many actual legal systems one finds, of course, rules and procedures of the kind I have sketched. It is obvious, though, that any ongoing legal system differs in significant respects from what I have presented here, containing 'pockets of injustice'.

I want now to sketch an extreme version of a set of institutions of a fundamentally different kind, institutions proceeding on a conception of man which appears to be basically at odds with that operative within a system of punishment.

Rules are promulgated in this system that prohibit certain types of injuries and harms.

In this world we are now to imagine, when an individual harms another his conduct is to be regarded as a symptom of some pathological condition in the way a running nose is a symptom of a cold. Actions diverging from some conception of the normal are viewed as manifestations of a disease in the way in which we might today regard the arm and leg movements of an epileptic during a seizure. Actions conforming to what is normal are assimilated to the normal and healthy functioning of bodily organs. What a person does, then, is assimilated, on this conception, to what we believe today, or at least most of us believe today, a person undergoes. We draw a distinction between the operation of the kidney and raising an arm on request. This distinction between mere events or happenings and human actions is erased in our imagined system.[1]

There is, however, bound to be something strange in this erasing of a recognized distinction, for, as with metaphysical suggestions generally, and I take this to be one, the distinction may be reintroduced but given a different description, for example, 'happenings with X type of causes' and 'happenings with Y type of causes'. Responses of different kinds, today legitimated by our distinction between happenings and actions may be legitimated by this new manner of description. And so there may be isomorphism between a system recognizing the distinction and one erasing it. Still, when this distinction is erased certain tendencies of thought and responses might naturally arise that would tend to affect unfavorably values respected by a system of punishment.

Let us elaborate on this assimilation of conduct of a certain kind to symptoms of a disease. First, there is something abnormal in both the case of conduct, such as killing another, and a symptom of a disease such as an irregular heart beat. Second, there are causes for this abnormality in action such that once we know of them we can explain the abnormality as we now can explain the symptoms of many physical diseases. The abnormality is looked upon as a happening with a causal explanation rather than an action for which there were reasons. Third, the causes that account for the abnormality interfere with the normal functioning of the body, or, in the case of killing with what is regarded as a normal functioning of an individual. Fourth, the abnormality is in some way a part of the individual, necessarily involving his body. A well going dry might satisfy our three foregoing conditions of disease symptoms, but it is hardly a disease or the symptom of one. Finally, and most obscure, the abnormality arises in some way from within the individual. If Jones is hit with a mallet by Smith, Jones may reel about and fall on James who may be injured. But this abnormal conduct of Jones is not regarded as a symptom of disease. Smith, not Jones, is suffering from some pathological condition.

With this view of man the institutions of social control respond, not with punishment, but with either preventive detention, in case of 'carriers', or therapy in the case of those manifesting pathological symptoms. The logic of sickness implies the logic of therapy. And therapy and punishment differ widely in their implications. In bringing out some of these differences I want again to draw attention to the important fact that while the distinctions we now draw are erased in the therapy world, they may, in fact, be reintroduced but under different descriptions. To the extent they are, we really have a punishment system combined with a therapy system. I am concerned now, however, with what the implications would be were the world indeed one of therapy and not a disguised world of punishment and therapy, for I want to suggest tendencies of thought that arise when one is immersed in the ideology of disease and therapy.

First, punishment is the imposition upon a person who is believed to be at fault of something commonly believed to be a deprivation where that deprivation is justified by the person's guilty behavior. It is associated with resentment, for the guilty are those who have done what they had no right to do by failing to exercise restraint when they might have and where others have. Therapy is not a response to a person who is at fault. We respond to an individual, not because of what he has done, but because of some condition from which he is suffering. If he is no longer suffering from the condition, treatment no longer has a point. Punishment, then, focuses on the past; therapy on the present. Therapy is normally associated with compassion for what one undergoes, not resentment for what one has illegitimately done.

Second, with therapy, unlike punishment, we do not seek to deprive the person of something acknowledged as a good, but seek rather to help and to benefit the individual who is suffering by ministering to his illness in the hope that the person can be cured. The good we attempt to do is not a reward for desert. The individual suffering has not merited by his disease the good we seek to bestow upon him but has, because he is a creature that has the capacity to feel pain, a claim upon our sympathies and help.

Third, we saw with punishment that its justification was related to maintaining and restoring a fair distribution of benefits and burdens. Infliction of the prescribed punishment carries the implication, then, that one has 'paid one's debt' to society, for the punishment is the taking from the person of something commonly recognized as valuable. It is this conception of 'a debt owed' that may permit, as I suggested earlier, under certain conditions, the nonpunishment of the guilty, for operative within a system of punishment may be a concept analogous to forgiveness, namely pardoning. Who it is that we may pardon and under what conditions—contrition with its elements of self-punishment no doubt plays a role —I shall not go into though it is clearly a matter of the greatest practical and theoretical interest. What is clear is that the conceptions of 'paying a debt' or 'having a debt forgiven' or pardoning have no place in a system of therapy.

Fourth, with punishment there is an attempt at some equivalence between the advantage gained by the wrongdoer—partly based upon the seriousness of the interest invaded, partly on the state of mind with which the wrongful act was performed—and the punishment meted out. Thus, we can understand a prohibition on 'cruel and unusual punishments' so that disproportionate pain and suffering are avoided. With therapy attempts at proportionality make no sense. It is perfectly plausible giving someone who kills a pill and treating for a lifetime within an institution one who has broken a dish and manifested accident proneness. We have the concept of 'painful treatment'. We do not have the concept of 'cruel treatment'. Because treatment is regarded as a benefit, though it may involve pain, it is natural that less restraint is exercised in bestowing it, than in inflicting punishment. Further, protests with respect to treatment are likely to be assimilated to the complaints of one whose leg must be amputated in order for him to live, and, thus, largely disregarded. To be sure, there is operative in the therapy world some conception of the "cure being worse than the disease," but if the disease is manifested in conduct harmful to others, and if being a normal operating human being is valued highly, there will naturally be considerable pressure to find the cure acceptable.

Fifth, the rules in our system of punishment governing conduct of individuals were rules violation of which involved either direct interference with others or the creation of a substantial risk of such interference. One could imagine adding to this system of primary rules other rules proscribing preparation to do acts violative of the primary rules and even rules proscribing thoughts. Objection to such suggestions would have many sources but a principal one would consist in its

involving the infliction of punishment on too great a number of persons who would not, because of a change of mind, have violated the primary rules. Though we are interested in diminishing violations of the primary rules, we are not prepared to punish too many individuals who would never have violated the rules in order to achieve this aim. In a system motivated solely by a preventive and curative ideology there would be less reason to wait until symptoms manifest themselves in socially harmful conduct. It is understandable that we should wish at the earliest possible stage to arrest the development of the disease. In the punishment system, because we are dealing with deprivations, it is understandable that we should forbear from imposing them until we are quite sure of guilt. In the therapy system, dealing as it does with benefits, there is less reason for forbearance from treatment at an early stage.

Sixth, a variety of procedural safeguards we associate with punishment have less significance in a therapy system. To the degree objections to double jeopardy and self-incrimination are based on a wish to decrease the chances of the innocent being convicted and punished, a therapy system, unconcerned with this problem, would disregard such safeguards. When one is out to help people there is also little sense in urging that the burden of proof be on those providing the help. And there is less point to imposing the burden of proving that the conduct was pathological beyond a reasonable doubt. Further, a jury system which, within a system of justice, serves to make accommodations to the individual situation and to introduce a human element, would play no role or a minor one in a world where expertise is required in making determinations of disease and treatment.

In our system of punishment an attempt was made to maximize each individual's freedom of choice by first of all delimiting by rules certain spheres of conduct immune from interference by others. The punishment associated with these primary rules paid deference to an individual's free choice by connecting punishment to a freely chosen act violative of the rules, thus giving some plausibility to the claim, as we saw, that what a person received by way of punishment he himself had chosen. With the world of disease and therapy all this changes and the individual's free choice ceases to be a determinative factor in how others respond to him. All those principles of our own legal system that minimize the chances of punishment of those who have not chosen to do acts violative of the rules tend to lose their point in the therapy system, for how we respond in a therapy system to a person is not conditioned upon what he has chosen but rather on what symptoms he has manifested or may manifest and what the best therapy for the disease is that is suggested by the symptoms.

Now, it is clear I think, that were we confronted with the alternatives I have sketched, between a system of just punishment and a thoroughgoing system of treatment, a system, that is, that did not reintroduce concepts appropriate to punishment, we could see the point in claiming that a person has a right to be punished, meaning by this that a person had a right to all those institutions and practices linked to punishment. For these would provide him with, among other things, a far greater ability to predict what would happen to him on the occurrence of certain events than the therapy system. There is the inestimable value to each of us of having the responses of others to us determined over a wide range of our lives by what we choose rather than what they choose. A person has a right to institutions that respect his choices. Our punishment system does; our therapy system does not.

Apart from those aspects of our therapy model which would relate to serious limitations on personal liberty, there are clearly objections of a more profound kind to the mode of thinking I have associated with the therapy model.

First, human beings pride themselves in having capacities that animals do not. A common way, for example, of arousing shame in a child is to compare the child's conduct to that of an animal. In a system where all actions are assimilated to happenings we are assimilated to creatures—indeed, it is more extreme than this—whom we have always thought possessed of less than we. Fundamental to our practice of praise and order of attainment is that one who can do more—one who is capable of more and one who does more is more worthy of respect and admiration. And we have thought of ourselves as capable where animals are not of making, of creating, among other things, ourselves. The conception of man I have outlined would provide us with a status that

today, when our conduct is assimilated to it in moral criticism, we consider properly evocative of shame.

Second, if all human conduct is viewed as something men undergo, thrown into question would be the appropriateness of that extensive range of peculiarly human satisfactions that derive from a sense of achievement. For these satisfactions we shall have to substitute those mild satisfactions attendant upon a healthy well-functioning body. Contentment is our lot if we are fortunate; intense satisfaction at achievement is entirely inappropriate.

Third, in the therapy world nothing is earned and what we receive comes to us through compassion, or through a desire to control us. Resentment is out of place. We can take credit for nothing but must always regard ourselves—if there are selves left to regard once actions disappear—as fortunate recipients of benefits or unfortunate carriers of disease who must be controlled. We know that within our own world human beings who have been so regarded and who come to accept this view of themselves come to look upon themselves as worthless. When what we do is met with resentment, we are indirectly paid something of a compliment.

Fourth, attention should also be drawn to a peculiar evil that may be attendant upon regarding a man's actions as symptoms of disease. The logic of cure will push us toward forms of therapy that inevitably involve changes in the person made against his will. The evil in this would be most apparent in those cases where the agent, whose action is determined to be a manifestation of some disease, does not regard his action in this way. He believes that what he has done is, in fact, 'right' but his conception of 'normality' is not the therapeutically accepted one. When we treat an illness we normally treat a condition that the person is not responsible for. He is 'suffering' from some disease and we treat the condition, relieving the person of something preventing his normal functioning. When we begin treating persons for actions that have been chosen, we do not lift from the person something that is interfering with his normal functioning but we change the person so that he functions in a way regarded as normal by the current therapeutic community. We have to change him and his judgments of value. In doing this we display a lack of respect for the moral status of individuals, that is, a lack of respect for the reasoning and choices of individuals. They are but animals who must be conditioned. I think we can understand and, indeed, sympathize with a man's preferring death to being forcibly turned into what he is not.

Finally, perhaps most frightening of all would be the derogation in status of all protests to treatment. If someone believes that he has done something right, and if he protests being treated and changed, the protest will itself be regarded as a sign of some pathological condition, for who would not wish to be cured of an affliction? What this leads to are questions of an important kind about the effect of this conception of man upon what we now understand by reasoning. Here what a person takes to be a reasoned defense of an act is treated, as the action was, on the model of a happening of a pathological kind. Not just a person's acts are taken from him but also his attempt at a reasoned justification for the acts. In a system of punishment a person who has committed a crime may argue that what he did was right. We make him pay the price and we respect his right to retain the judgment he has made. A conception of pathology precludes this form of respect.

It might be objected to the foregoing that all I have shown—if that—is that if the only alternatives open to us are a *just* system of punishment or the mad world of being treated like sick or healthy animals, we do in fact have a right to a system of punishment of this kind. But this hardly shows that we have a right *simpliciter* to punishment as we do, say, to be free. Indeed, it does not even show a right to a just system of punishment, for surely we can, without too much difficulty, imagine situations in which the alternatives to punishment are not this mad world but a world in which we are still treated as persons and there is, for example, not the pain and suffering attendant upon punishment. One such world is one in which there are rules but responses to their violation is not the deprivation of some good but forgiveness. Still another type of world would be one in which violation of the rules were responded to by merely comparing the conduct of the person to something commonly regarded as low or filthy, and thus, producing by this mode of moral criticism, feelings of shame rather than feelings of guilt.

I am prepared to allow that these objections have a point. While granting force to the above objections I want to offer a few additional comments with respect to each of them. First, any existent legal system permits the punishment of individuals under circumstances where the conditions I have set forth for a just system have not been satisfied. A glaring example of this would be criminal strict liability which is to be found in our own legal system. Nevertheless, I think it would be difficult to present any system we should regard as a system of punishment that would not still have a great advantage over our imagined therapy system. The system of punishment we imagine may more and more approximate a system of sheer terror in which human beings are treated as animals to be intimidated and prodded. To the degree that the system is of this character it is, in my judgment, not simply an unjust system but one that diverges from what we normally understand by a system of punishment. At least some deference to the choice of individuals is built into the idea of punishment. So there would be some truth in saying we have a right to any system of punishment if the only alternative to it was therapy.

Second, people may imagine systems in which there are rules and in which the response to their violation is not punishment but pardoning, the legal analogue of forgiveness. Surely this is a system to which we would claim a right as against one in which we are made to suffer for violating the rules. There are several comments that need to be made about this. It may be, of course, that a high incidence of pardoning would increase the incidence of rule violations. Further, the difficulty with suggesting pardoning as a general response is that pardoning presupposes the very responses that it is suggested it supplant. A system of deprivations, or a practice of deprivations on the happening of certain actions, underlies the practice of pardoning and forgiving, for it is only where we possess the idea of a wrong to be made up or of a debt owed to others, ideas we acquire within a world in which there have been deprivations for wrong acts, that we have the idea of pardoning for the wrong or forgiving the debt.

Finally, if we look at the responses I suggested would give rise to feelings of shame, we may rightly be troubled with the appropriateness of this response in any community in which each person assumes burdens so that each may derive benefits. In such situations might it not be that individuals have a right to a system of punishment so that each person could be assured that inequities in the distribution of benefits and burdens are unlikely to occur and if they do, procedures exist for correcting them? Further, it may well be that, everything considered, we should prefer the pain and suffering of a system of punishment to a world in which we only experience shame on the doing of wrong acts, for with guilt there are relatively simple ways of ridding ourselves of the feeling we have, that is, gaining forgiveness or taking the punishment, but with shame we have to bear it until we no longer are the person who has behaved in the shameful way. Thus, I suggest that we have, wherever there is a distribution of benefits and burdens of the kind I have described, a right to a system of punishment.

I want also to make clear in concluding this section that I have argued, though very indirectly, not just for a right to a system of punishment, but for a right to be punished once there is in existence such a system. Thus, a man has the right to be punished rather than treated if he is guilty of some offense. And, indeed, one can imagine a case in which, even in the face of an offer of a pardon, a man claims and ought to have acknowledged his right to be punished.

2. The primary reason for preferring the system of punishment as against the system of therapy might have been expressed in terms of the one system treating one as a person and the other not. In invoking the right to be punished, one justifies one's claim by reference to a more fundamental right. I want now to turn attention to this fundamental right and attempt to shed light—it will have to be little, for the topic is immense—on what is meant by 'treating an individual as a person'.

When we talk of not treating a human being as a person or 'showing no respect for one as a person' what we imply by our words is a contrast between the manner in which one acceptably responds to human beings and the manner in which one acceptably responds to animals and inanimate objects. When we treat a human being merely as an animal or some inanimate object our responses to the human being are determined, not by his choices, but ours in disregard of or with indifference to his. And when we 'look upon' a

person as less than a person or not a person, we consider the person as incapable of rational choice. In cases of not treating a human being as a person we interfere with a person in such a way that what is done, even if the person is involved in the doing, is done not by the person but by the user of the person. In extreme cases there may even be an elision of a causal chain so that we might say that X killed Z even though Y's hand was the hand that held the weapon, for Y's hand may have been entirely in X's control. The one agent is in some way treating the other as a mere link in a causal chain. There is, of course, a wide range of cases in which a person is used to accomplish the aim of another and in which the person used is less than fully free. A person may be grabbed against his will and used as a shield. A person may be drugged or hypnotized and then employed for certain ends. A person may be deceived into doing other than he intends doing. A person may be ordered to do something and threatened with harm if he does not and coerced into doing what he does not want to. There is still another range of cases in which individuals are not used, but in which decisions by others are made that affect them in circumstances where they have the capacity for choice and where they are not being treated as persons.

But it is particularly important to look at coercion, for I have claimed that a just system of punishment treats human beings as persons; and it is not immediately apparent how ordering someone to do something and threatening harm differs essentially from having rules supported by threats of harm in case of noncompliance.

There are affinities between coercion and other cases of not treating someone as a person, for it is not the coerced person's choices but the coercer's that are responsible for what is done. But unlike other indisputable cases of not treating one as a person, for example using someone as a shield, there is some choice involved in coercion. And if this is so, why does the coercer stand in any different relation to the coerced person than the criminal law stands to individuals in society?

Suppose the person who is threatened disregards the order and gets the threatened harm. Now suppose he is told, "Well, you did after all bring it upon yourself." There is clearly something strange in this. It is the person doing the threatening and not the person threatened who is responsible. But our reaction to punishment, at least in a system that resembles the one I have described, is precisely that the person violating the rules brought it upon himself. What lies behind these different reactions?

There exist situations in the law, of course, which resemble coercion situations. There are occasions when in the law a person might justifiably say "I am not being treated as a person but being used" and where he might properly react to the punishment as something "he was hardly responsible for." But it is possible to have a system in which it would be misleading to say, over a wide range of cases of punishment for noncompliance, that we are using persons. The clearest case in which it would be inappropriate to so regard punishment would be one in which there were explicit agreement in advance that punishment should follow on the voluntary doing of certain acts. Even if one does not have such conditions satisfied, and obviously such explicit agreements are not characteristic, one can see significant differences between our system of just punishment and a coercion situation.

First, unlike the case with one person coercing another 'to do his will', the rules in our system apply to all, with the benefits and burdens equally distributed. About such a system it cannot be said that some are being subordinated to others or are being used by others or gotten to do things by others. To the extent that the rules are thought to be to the advantage of only some or to the extent there is a maldistribution of benefits and burdens, the difference between coercion and law disappears.

Second, it might be argued that at least any person inclined to act in a manner violative of the rules stands to all others as the person coerced stands to his coercer, and that he, at least, is a person disadvantaged as others are not. It is important here, I think, that he is part of a system in which it is commonly agreed that forbearance from the acts proscribed by the rules provides advantages for all. This system is the accepted setting; it is the norm. Thus, in any coercive situation, it is the coercer who deviates from the norm, with the responsibility of the person he is attempting to coerce, defeated. In a just punishment situation, it is the person deviating from the norm, indeed he might be a coercer, who is responsible, for it is the norm to restrain oneself

from acts of that kind. A voluntary agent diverging in his conduct from what is expected or what the norm is, on general causal principles, regarded as the cause of what results from his conduct.

There is, then, some plausibility in the claim that, in a system of punishment of the kind I have sketched, a person chooses the punishment that is meted out to him. If, then, we can say in such a system that the rules provide none with advantages that others do not have, and further, that what happens to a person is conditioned by that person's choice and not that of others, then we can say that it is a system reponding to one as a person.

We treat a human being as a person provided: first, we permit the person to make the choices that will determine what happens to him and second, when our responses to the person are responses respecting the person's choices. When we respond to a person's illness by treating the illness, it is neither a case of treating or not treating the individual as a person. When we give a person a gift we are neither treating or not treating him as a person, unless, of course, he does not wish it, chooses not to have it, but we compel him to accept it.

3. This right to be treated as a person is a fundamental human right belonging to all human beings by virtue of their being human. It is also a natural, inalienable, and absolute right. I want now to defend these claims so reminiscent of an era of philosophical thinking about rights that many consider to have been seriously confused.

If the right is one that we possess by virtue of being human beings, we are immediately confronted with an apparent dilemma. If, to treat another as a person requires that we provide him with reasons for acting and avoid force or deception, how can we justify the force and deception we exercise with respect to children and the mentally ill? If they, too, have a right to be treated as persons are we not constantly infringing their rights? One way out of this is simply to restrict the right to those who satisfy the conditions of being a person. Infants and the insane, it might be argued, do not meet these conditions, and they would not then have the right. Another approach would be to describe the right they possess as a prima facie right to be treated as a person. This right might then be outweighed by other considerations. This approach generally seems to me, as I shall later argue, inadequate.

I prefer this tack. Children possess the right to be treated as persons but they possess this right as an individual might be said in the law of property to possess a future interest. There are advantages in talking of individuals as having a right though complete enjoyment of it is postponed. Brought to our attention, if we ascribe to them the right, is the legitimacy of their complaint if they are not provided with opportunities and conditions assuring their full enjoyment of the right when they acquire the characteristics of persons. More than this, all persons are charged with the sensitive task of not denying them the right to be a person and to be treated as a person by failing to provide the conditions for their becoming individuals who are able freely and in an informed way to choose and who are prepared themselves to assume responsibility for their choices. There is an obligation imposed upon us all, unlike that we have with respect to animals, to respond to children in such a way as to maximize the chances of their becoming persons. This may well impose upon us the obligation to treat them as persons from a very early age, that is, to respect their choices and to place upon them the responsibility for the choices to be made. There is no need to say that there is a close connection between how we respond to them and what they become. It also imposes upon us all the duty to display constantly the qualities of a person, for what they become they will largely become because of what they learn from us is acceptable behavior.

In claiming that the right is a right that human beings have by virtue of being human, there are several other features of the right, that should be noted, perhaps better conveyed by labelling them 'natural'. First, it is a right we have apart from any voluntary agreement into which we have entered. Second, it is not a right that derives from some defined position or status. Third, it is equally apparent that one has the right regardless of the society or community of which one is a member. Finally, it is a right linked to certain features of a class of beings. Were we fundamentally different than we now are, we would not have it. But it is more than that, for the right is linked to a feature of human beings which, were

that feature absent—the capacity to reason and to choose on the basis of reasons—, profound conceptual changes would be involved in the thought about human beings. It is a right, then, connected with a feature of men that sets men apart from other natural phenomena.

The right to be treated as a person is inalienable. To say of a right that it is inalienable draws attention not to limitations placed on what others may do with respect to the possessor of the right but rather to limitations placed on the dispositive capacities of the possessor of the right. Something is to be gained in keeping the issues of alienability and absoluteness separate.

There are a variety of locutions qualifying what possessors of rights may and may not do. For example, on this issue of alienability, it would be worthwhile to look at, among other things, what is involved in abandoning, abdicating, conveying, giving up, granting, relinquishing, surrendering, transferring, and waiving one's rights. And with respect to each of these concepts we should also have to be sensitive to the variety of uses of the term 'rights'. What it is, for example, to waive a Hohfeldian 'right' in his strict sense will differ from what it is to waive a right in his 'privilege' sense.

Let us look at only two concepts very briefly, those of transferring and waiving rights. The clearest case of transferring rights is that of transferring rights with respect to specific objects. I own a watch and owning it I have a complicated relationship, captured in this area rather well I think by Hohfeld's four basic legal relationships, to all persons in the world with respect to the watch. We crudely capture these complex relationships by talking of my 'property rights' in or with respect to the watch. If I sell the watch, thus exercising a capacity provided by the rules of property, I have transferred rights in or with respect to the watch to someone else, the buyer, and the buyer now stands, as I formerly did, to all persons in the world in a series of complex relationships with respect to the watch.

While still the owner, I may have given to another permission to use it for several days. Had there not been the permission and had the person taken the watch, we should have spoken of interfering with or violating or, possibly, infringing my property rights. Or, to take a situation in which transferring rights is inappropriate, I may say to another "go ahead and slap me—you have my permission." In these types of situations philosophers and others have spoken of 'surrendering" rights or, alternatively and, I believe, less strangely, of 'waiving one's rights'. And recently, of course, the whole topic of 'waiving one's right to remain silent' in the context of police interrogation of suspects has been a subject of extensive litigation and discussion.

I confess to feeling that matters are not entirely perspicuous with respect to what is involved in 'waiving' or 'surrendering' rights. In conveying to another permission to take a watch or slap one, one makes legally permissible what otherwise would not have been. But in saying those words that constitute permission to take one's watch one is, of course, exercising precisely one of those capacities that leads us to say he has, while others have not, property rights with respect to the watch. Has one then waived his right in Hohfeld's strict sense in which the correlative is a duty to forebear on the part of others?

We may wish to distinguish here waiving the right to have others forbear to which there is a corresponding duty on their part to forbear, from placing oneself in a position where one has no legitimate right to complain. If I say the magic words "take the watch for a couple of days" or "go ahead and slap me," have I waived my right not to have my property taken or a right not to be struck or have I, rather, in saying what I have, simply stepped into a relation in which the rights no longer apply with respect to a specified other person? These observations find support in the following considerations. The right is that which gives rise, when infringed, to a legitimate claim against another person. What this suggests is that the right is that sphere interference with which entitles us to complain or gives us a right to complain. From this it seems to follow that a right to bodily security should be more precisely described as 'a right that others not interfere without permission'. And there is the corresponding duty not to interfere unless provided permission. Thus when we talk of waiving our rights or 'giving up our rights' in such cases we are not waiving or giving up our right to property nor our right to bodily security, for we still, of course, possess the right not to have our watch taken without permission. We have rather placed ourselves in a position where we do not possess the capacity,

sometimes called a right, to complain if the person takes the watch or slaps us.

There is another type of situation in which we may speak of waiving our rights. If someone without permission slaps me, there is an infringement of my right to bodily security. If I now acquiesce or go further and say "forget it" or "you are forgiven," we might say that I had waived my right to complain. But here, too, I feel uncomfortable about what is involved. For I do have the right to complain (a right without a corresponding duty) in the event I am slapped and I have that right whether I wish it or not. If I say to another after the slap, "you are forgiven" what I do is not waive the right to complain but rather make illegitimate my subsequent exercise of that right.

Now, if we turn to the right to be treated as a person, the claim that I made was that it was inalienable, and what I meant to convey by that word of respectable age is that (a) it is a right that cannot be transferred to another in the way one's right with respect to objects can be transferred and (b) that it cannot be waived in the ways in which people talk of waiving rights to property or waiving, within certain limitations, one's right to bodily security.

While the rules of the law of property are such that persons may, satisfying certain procedures, transfer rights, the right to be treated as a person logically cannot be transferred anymore than one person can transfer to another his right to life or privacy. What, indeed, would it be like for another to have our right to be treated as a person? We can understand transferring a right with respect to certain objects. The new owner stands where the old owner stood. But with a right to be treated as a person what could this mean? My having the right meant that my choices were respected. Now if I transfer it to another this will mean that he will posses the right that my choices be respected? This is nonsense. It is only each person himself that can have his choices respected. It is no more possible to transfer this right than it is to transfer one's right to life.

Nor can the right be waived. It cannot be waived because any agreement to being treated as an animal or an instrument does not provide others with the moral permission to so treat us. One can volunteer to be a shield, but then it is one's choice on a particular occasion to be a shield. If without our permission, without our choosing it, someone used us as a shield, we may, I should suppose, forgive the person for treating us as an object. But we do not thereby waive our right to be treated as a person, for that is a right that has been infringed and what we have at most done is put ourselves in a position where it is inappropriate any longer to exercise the right to complain.

This is the sort of right, then, such that the moral rules defining relationships among persons preclude anyone from morally giving others legitimate permissions or rights with respect to one by doing or saying certain things. One stands, then, with respect to one's person as the nonowner of goods stands to those goods. The nonowner cannot, given the rule-defined relationships, convey to others rights and privileges that only the owner possesses. Just as there are agreements nonenforceable because void is contrary to public policy, so there are permissions our moral outlook regards as without moral force. With respect to being treated as a person, one is 'disabled' from modifying relations of others to one.

The right is absolute. This claim is bound to raise eyebrows. I have an innocuous point in mind in making this claim.

In discussing alienability we focused on incapacities with respect to disposing of rights. Here what I want to bring out is a sense in which a right exists despite considerations for refusing to accord the person his rights. As with the topic of alienability there are a host of concepts that deserve a close look in this area. Among them are according, acknowledging, annulling, asserting, claiming, denying, destroying, exercising, infringing, insisting upon, interfering with, possessing, recognizing and violating.

The claim that rights are absolute has been construed to mean that 'assertions of rights cannot, for any reason under any circumstances be denied'. When there are considerations which warrant refusing to accord persons their rights, there are two prevalent views as to how this should be described: There is, first, the view that the person does not have the right, and second, the view that he has rights but of a prima facie kind and that these have been outweighed or overcome by the other considerations. "We can conceive times when such rights must give way, and, therefore, they are only prima facie and not absolute rights." (Brandt)

Perhaps there are cases in which a person claims a right to do a certain thing, say with his property, and argues that his property rights are absolute, meaning by this he has a right to do whatever he wishes with his property. Here, no doubt, it has to be explained to the person that the right he claims he has, he does not in fact possess. In such a case the person does not have and never did have, given a certain description of the right, a right that was prima facie or otherwise, to do what he claimed he had the right to do. If the assertion that a right is absolute implies that we have a right to do whatever we wish to do, it is an absurd claim and as such should not really ever have been attributed to political theorists arguing for absolute rights. But, of course, the claim that we have a prima facie right to do whatever we wish to do is equally absurd. The right is not prima facie either, for who would claim, thinking of the right to be free, that one has a prima facie right to kill others, if one wishes, unless there are moral considerations weighing against it?

There are, however, other situations in which it is accepted by all that a person possesses rights of a certain kind, and the difficulty we face is that of according the person the right he is claiming when this will promote more evil than good. The just act is to give the man his due and giving a man what it is his right to have is giving him his due. But it is a mistake to suppose that justice is the only dimension of morality. It may be justifiable not to accord to a man his rights. But it is no less a wrong to him, no less an infringement. It is seriously misleading to turn all justifiable infringements into noninfringements by saying that the right is only prima facie, as if we have, in concluding that we should not accord a man his rights, made out a case that he had none. To use the language of 'prima facie rights' misleads, for it suggests that a presumption of the existence of a right has been overcome in these cases where all that can be said is that the presumption in favor of according a man his rights has been overcome. If we begin to think the right itself is prima facie, we shall, in cases in which we are justified in not according it, fail sufficiently to bring out that we have interfered where justice says we should not. Our moral framework is unnecessarily and undesirably impoverished by the theory that there are such rights.

When I claim, then, that the right to be treated as a person is absolute what I claim is that given that one is a person, one always has the right so to be treated, and that while there may possibly be occasions morally requiring not according a person this right, this fact makes it no less true that the right exists and would be infringed if the person were not accorded it.

4. Having said something about the nature of this fundamental right I want now, in conclusion, to suggest that the denial of this right entails the denial of all moral rights and duties. This requires bringing out what is surely intuitively clear that any framework of rights and duties presupposes individuals that have the capacity to choose on the basis of reasons presented to them, and that what makes legitimate actions within such a system are the free choices of individuals. There is, in other words, a distribution of benefits and burdens in accord with a respect for the freedom of choice and freedom of action of all. I think that the best way to make this point may be to sketch some of the features of a world in which rights and duties are possessed.

First, rights exist only when there is some conception of some things valued and others not. Secondly, and implied in the first point, is the fact that there are dispositions to defend the valued commodities. Third, the valued commodities may be interfered with by others in this world. A group of animals might be said to satisfy these first three conditions. Fourth, rights exist when there are recognized rules establishing the legitimacy of some acts and ruling out others. Mistakes in the claim of right are possible. Rights imply the concepts of interference and infringement, concepts the elucidation of which requires the concept of a rule applying to the conduct of persons. Fifth, to possess a right is to possess something that constitutes a legitimate restraint on the freedom of action of others. It is clear, for example, that if individuals were incapable of controlling their actions we would have no notion of a legitimate claim that they do so. If, for example, we were all disposed to object or disposed to complain, as the elephant seal is disposed to object when his territory is invaded, then the objection would operate in a causal way, or approximating a causal way, in getting the behavior of noninterference. In a system of rights, on the other hand, there is a point to appealing to the rules in legitimating one's complaint. Implied,

then, in any conception of rights is the existence of individuals capable of choosing and capable of choosing on the basis of considerations with respect to rules. The distribution of freedom throughout such a system is determined by the free choice of individuals. Thus any denial of the right to be treated as a person would be a denial undercutting the whole system, for the system rests on the assumption that spheres of legitimate and illegitimate conduct are to be delimited with regard to the choices made by persons.

This conclusion stimulates one final reflection on the therapy world we imagined.

The denial of this fundamental right will also carry with it, ironically, the denial of the right to treatment to those who are ill. In the world as we now understand it, there are those who do wrong and who have a right to be responded to as persons who have done wrong. And there are those who have not done wrong but who are suffering from illnesses that in a variety of ways interfere with their capacity to live their lives as complete persons. These persons who are ill have a claim upon our compassion. But more than this they have, as animals do not, a right to be treated as persons. When an individual is ill he is entitled to that assistance which will make it possible for him to resume his functioning as a person. If it is an injustice to punish an innocent person, it is no less an injustice, and a far more significant one in our day, to fail to promote as best we can through adequate facilities and medical care the treatment of those who are ill. Those human beings who fill our mental institutions are entitled to more than they do in fact receive; they should be viewed as possessing the right to be treated as a person so that our responses to them may increase the likelihood that they will enjoy fully the right to be so treated. Like the child the mentally ill person has a future interest we cannot rightly deny him. Society is today sensitive to the infringement of justice in punishing the innocent; elaborate rules exist to avoid this evil. Society should be no less sensitive to the injustice of failing to bring back to the community of persons those whom it is possible to bring back.

NOTES

1. "When a man is suffering from an infectious disease, he is a danger to the community, and it is necessary to restrict his liberty of movement. But no one associates any idea of guilt with such a situation. On the contrary, he is an object

of commiseration to his friends. Such steps as science recommends are taken to cure him of his disease, and he submits as a rule without reluctance to the curtailment of liberty involved meanwhile. The same method in spirit ought to be shown in the treatment of what is called 'crime.' "

Bertrand Russell, *Roads to Freedom* (London: George Allen and Unwin Ltd., 1918), p. 135.

"We do not hold people responsible for their reflexes—for example, for coughing in church. We hold them responsible for their operant behavior—for example, for whispering in church or remaining in church while coughing. But there are variables which are responsible for whispering as well as coughing, and these may be just as inexorable. When we recognize this, we are likely to drop the notion of responsibility altogether and with it the doctrine of free will as an inner causal agent."

B. F. Skinner, *Science and Human Behavior* (1953), pp. 115–6.

"Basically, criminality is but a symptom of insanity, using the term in its widest generic sense to express unacceptable social behavior based on unconscious motivation flowing from a disturbed instinctive and emotional life, whether this appears in frank psychoses, or in less obvious form in neuroses and unrecognized psychoses. . . . If criminals are products of early environmental influences in the same sense that psychotics and neurotics are, then it should be possible to reach them psychotherapeutically."

Benjamin Karpman, "Criminal Psychodynamics," *Journal of Criminal Law and Criminology*, 47 (1956), p. 9.

"We, the agents of society, must move to end the game of tit-for-tat and blow-for-blow in which the offender has foolishly and futilely engaged himself and us. We are not driven, as he is, to wild and impulsive actions. With knowledge comes power, and with power there is no need for the frightened vengeance of the old penology. In its place should go a quiet, dignified, therapeutic program for the rehabilitation of the disorganized one, if possible, the protection of society during the treatment period, and his guided return to useful citizenship, as soon as this can be effected."

Karl Menninger, "Therapy, Not Punishment," *Harper's Magazine* (August 1959), pp. 63–64.

AMERICAN FRIENDS SERVICE COMMITTEE

The Crime of Treatment*

Most if not all the assumptions that underpin the treatment model are unsubstantiated or in conflict with basic humanitarian values. Despite these shortcomings the treatment approach receives nearly unanimous support from those working in the field of criminal justice, even the most progressive and humanitarian. How can this solid support be explained? Many persons admit the shortcomings we describe but nevertheless support treatment practices out of a belief that, if nothing else, they do help some prisoners.

*Reprinted with the permission of Hill and Wang, a division of Farrar, Straus & Giroux, Inc. from *Struggle for Justice, A Report On Crime and Punishment in America*, prepared for the American Friends Service Committee. Copyright © 1971 by Hill and Wang, Inc. "The Crime of Treatment" is Chapter 6 of *Struggle for Justice*, pp. 83–99.

Is this the case? Does what passes for treatment actually help? Does prison rehabilitate?

Much of our discussion will be devoted to the California correctional system, which has pushed further toward full implementation of the rehabilitative idea than any other correctional system in the United States. For example, Norman S. Hayner, in comparing correctional systems in various countries, says that California "easily ranks at the top from the standpoint of emphasis on treatment with a score of 122 points out of a possible 140."[1]

Before examining the impact of rehabilitation on convicts, we will sketch briefly some of the major contours of "rehabilitation" itself.

Rehabilitation as a direction for penal systems introduced three new characteristics: individualization, indeterminancy, and discretionary power. Individualization was needed because the focus of scientific perspective was not on law violation but on the criminal. The criminal is a different type of person, his infraction merely a manifestation of this difference. Decisions had to be tailored to the individual case to make the rehabilitative routine possible. This led to the indeterminate sentence system whereby the individual is released only when he has been "cured" of his criminality. Implementation of the rehabilitative system also demanded greatly expanded discretionary powers for the persons making decisions, such as judges, district attorneys, prison administrators, parole-board members, and parole officers.

Nevertheless, prisons never became hospitals and criminals have never been treated merely as sick persons. Interested segments of society have demanded that other goals be pursued in the handling of a convicted person. What was remarkable about the emergence of the rehabilitative ideal in the correctional world is that it was able to take contradictory ideas and, through intellectual gymnastics and a great deal of hypocrisy, combine these into a system that for the time being made everyone happy—except the criminal!

Despite its failure, the rehabilitative ideal has received overwhelming acceptance. Here we will examine attitudes toward it by three groups within our society: the humanitarian reformers, the punitively oriented citizens, and the prison administrators.

The eighteenth-century humanitarian's attitude of reform through penance was replaced in the late nineteenth century by the attitude of cure through rehabilitation. In both attitudes the criminal is seen as an undesirable person, formerly a moral inferior, later a mental or emotional inferior. These attitudes were considered humanitarian because they viewed some criminals as redeemable.

It did not disturb reformers pursuing the rehabilitative ideal that the person who was identified as sick or abnormal was forced into a treatment routine and that he might experience this not as help but as punishment. It was society's motives that counted. Since they were doing it for his own good and society's protection, it was treatment not punishment. (Isn't this similar to the handling of the mentally ill in mental hospitals?)

An important force in the reform movement was the mixture of hatred, fear, and revulsion that white, middle-class, Protestant reformers felt toward lower-class persons, particularly foreign-born lower-class persons who did not share their Christian ethic. These difficult feelings were disguised as humanitarian concern for the "health" of threatening subculture members. Imprisonment dressed up as treatment was a particularly suitable response for reformers' complicated and inconsistent feelings.

The treatment-oriented correctional routine, with its serious theoretical inconsistencies, was embraced wholeheartedly by most persons involved in the administration of criminal justice, even the punitively oriented. District attorneys, police officers, and correctional administrators saw in the rehabilitative ideal increased latitude to imprison for longer periods of time criminals they viewed as especially dangerous. Previously, uniformly applied statutory sentences, specifying the maximum penalty, forced them to release prisoners they considered extremely dangerous. Indeterminate sentencing, however, allows them to avoid this. Furthermore, they are able to keep a released prisoner under surveillance by placing him on parole, another logical outgrowth of a rehabilitative correctional system. Indeterminate sentencing has increased the length of imprisonment for most crimes.

Prison administrators also embraced the rehabilitative ideal. Their enthusiasm and their concrete efforts in state legislatures helped bring about the shift from prisons that delivered straight-forward punishment to the rehabilitative prison with treatment added. Academic penal theoreticians supplied the rhetoric and correctional workers won the political battles.

However, it wasn't treatment that excited them. It was the prospect of having greater control over their prisons. This increased control took two forms. Formerly corporal punishment was the main control mechanism, but this technique was becoming troublesome because outside parties were increasingly critical of it. The rehabilitative system, particularly indeterminate sentencing, offered them a highly effective and less objectionable control method. Today prison routines are manipulated largely to maximize conformity to prison regulations. The second area of control that the rehabilitative system offered prison administrators is that of the size and flow of the prison population. Today they can increase or reduce the prison population as suits their purposes.

The rehabilitative prison satisfies nearly everybody except the uninformed general public. Not recognizing the sophistication of the system and believing the rhetoric generated and disseminated by the professionals, some portion of the public thinks criminals are being treated too well. Treatment-oriented prisons are perceived as "country clubs," where convicts are coddled and pampered. Courts are perceived as "too permissive." It is felt that the criminal is living better than ordinary hardworking folk. Politicians and prison administrators are far from insensitive to these sentiments, which are certainly a factor in preventing adherents of the treatment model from implementing it more fully.

CLASSIFICATION

Classification is the initial phase of the modern correctional routine. The earliest classifications and differentiations were on the basis of sex and age. The first was done to preserve the morals of prisoners. When it was recognized that young offenders were corrupted by older offenders, the two age groups were separated. From this point on there has been a steady movement in modern correctional institutions toward greater and greater differentiation of prisoners.

This differentiation is presently not only for segregation, but more for implementing different rehabilitative strategies. This is consistent with the contemporary view that the criminal has *something* wrong with him. This something is different from person to person. Therefore, a prison routine designed to treat the prisoner must have various rehabilitative strategies to treat the different kinds of problems and sicknesses of individual prisoners.

This classificatory routine might appear sound on paper; in actuality it does not come close to fulfilling its stated purposes. The diagnostic interviews are short, about half an hour per man. Evaluation made in this setting is of questionable validity. This is not simply a fault of time or of the particular instrument; we do not have the techniques for classifying offenders in a meaningful way—that is, in a manner that is related to their future criminal propensities or their treatment needs. Furthermore, there is considerable evidence that various treatment strategies do not make *any* significant difference in the future criminal behavior of inmates.

To some extent the classification process fails because of the basic conflict in the goals of the prison, that is, surveillance and treatment. Custody and housekeeping concerns usually take precedence over treatment matters. Even if it were possible to diagnose a particular offender's needs properly and recommend a treatment strategy, the actual recommendation would be based on the availability of space in the prison system or the custody level of the individual. For instance, about six thousand inmates in California are housed in San Quentin and Folsom, the two maximum-security prisons. The treatment and educational and vocational training programs in these prisons can serve only a small minority of the inmates. The rest are there for surveillance. Furthermore, in recent years California has been expanding its conservation camps program. There are two Conservation Centers, which are the focal point for clusters of camps. It has been found that it is cheaper for the state to put more of the inmate population in this kind of situation, so it appears that the trend will grow. The purpose of sending people there is in no way related to treatment strategies. There are virtually no rehabilitative programs in the camps, unless one construes hard work as rehabilitation. Even in the California system, then, the primary factors in deciding where a man serves his time and what he does are custodial concerns. This appears to be the case in all prison systems.

PROGRAMMING

"I'm going to get a program."
"Get a program and you'll get a parole."
"Look at——, he's programming."
Such statements, heard frequently in California prisons, reflect a general consensus of inmates and staff that inmates must participate in treatment programs in order to be paroled. The undisguised cynicism they exhibit implies that the programs are regarded as phony and that the motivation for participation is to manipulate the parole process.

A wide variety of therapeutic programs has been experimented with in California. Group counseling was introduced about 1955 and now involves a majority of inmates. Most convicts participate in these sessions only because they feel they have to. They lack commitment and are fearful that anything meaningful revealed in these sessions might be used against them and damage their chances of receiving a parole. Consequently, the sessions seldom move beyond the bland and the trivial. The essence of such sessions is perfectly captured in a novel by a former San Quentin inmate:

He found his group already gathered, sitting in the usual symbolic circle. The therapist, a Dr. Erlenmeyer, occupied what was intended as just one more chair, but the group automatically polarized wherever he seated himself. He was dressed entirely in shades of brown, and his shirt was darker than his coat. His glasses were tinted a pale tan, and his head full of hair seemed soft and dusty.

'You're late, Paul,'' he said, in a tone that didn't admit the obvious quality of his remark. His voice was opaque.

"I lost track of the day," Juleson said.

This hung in the air for a moment like a palpable lie, then settled into the heavy silence. The group had nothing going. No one, as they said, was coming out with anything. Juleson settled around in his chair, careful not to look at Erlenmeyer, who might try to make him feel responsible for this wasteful silence. Once Erlenmeyer had stressed how therapy was working on them even while they sat dumb, as sometimes happened, for the entire hour. But he didn't like their silences. . . .

Finally, Erlenmeyer cleared his throat to ask, "Why do you suppose Paul is late so often?"

They looked at each other to see if anyone was going to attempt an answer. Bernard only shrugged; he didn't care. After a moment Zekekowski said quietly, "He's got better sense than the rest of us."[2]

More ambitious therapeutic experiments have also been tried in California. Generally these have not been successful from the administration's point of view—that is, they have not had any measurable effect on recidivism. Often they have been disastrous from the inmates' viewpoint.

Educational-vocational programs have fared somewhat better. In California theoretically a person may learn the following trades: cooking, baking, butchering, dry cleaning, sewing-machine repair, auto mechanics, printing, auto body and fender, sheet metal, machinist, plumbing, painting, welding, and hospital techniques. In fact, however, few learn these trades. Though there has been great expenditure for vocational programs, there are only enough openings in these programs for a small percentage of the in-

mate population. Also, the training routine, actually an appendage of the prison housekeeping enterprise, is not related to outside occupational settings. For instance, men working in a prison bakery are ostensibly in a vocational bakery program; actually, however, they spend most of their time merely baking food to be consumed in the prison. After years of experience in the prison bakery, a person would have to learn a considerable part of the trade after leaving. In programs designed primarily for vocational training, such as the body and fender shop or some machine shops, often the equipment, the techniques, and the knowledge of the instructor are obsolete. As evidence that these programs are not effective, an unpublished study conducted by a regional office of the California Parole Agency discovered that only 36 percent of parolees receive any trade training and only 12 percent of that group later work in a field related to that training. The figures would probably be lower in other states.

PAROLE

The terminating program in the rehabilitative routine is parole. In many ways it epitomizes the treatment-punishment mixture. Theoretically the parole agent aids the parolee's transition back into the community by mixing the two functions help and surveillance. On the one hand he enforces (with considerable leniency) special rules of conduct—the conditions of parole. In this way he protects the parolee from slipping back into harmful behavior patterns and likewise helps the community by keeping the parolee out of trouble. On the other hand he "works with the parolee," giving him counseling, moral support, and some concrete help, such as aid in securing employment and residence.

In practice there is a serious flaw in this helping-surveillance relationship. The parole agent is in theory required to enforce very restrictive rules of conduct, so restrictive that the parolee's life chances would be seriously reduced if he were forced to live by them. For instance, one of the rules in California is that the parolee must not "associate" with other ex-convicts or persons with bad reputations. For a person who lives among other working- and lower-class persons, which is the case of most parolees, not associating with ex-convicts or persons with "bad reputations" is clearly unrealistic. Furthermore, the California parolee may not leave the county of residence, drive a car, or change jobs without his agent's permission. And he may not drink "to excess."

In actuality, the agent, in order to prevent having to "violate" the majority of his case load and in order to increase the life chances of the parolee, enforces a much more lenient set of informal rules. The problem with this is that the formal rules still exist and are invoked when some outside attention is directed toward a particular parolee. When this occurs, the parolee is often held to answer for behavior that the parole agent had known about and had explicitly condoned.

Moreover, the agent is not in a good position to help the parolee. He is not a professional therapist (if this would help) and has few resources to supply concrete help, such as a job, which the parolee often needs desperately. At best, parole is an obstacle the ex-convict has to contend with among the many other obstacles in his path. At worst, it is a trap that when sprung intensifies his feelings of injustice toward the hypocritical, unpredictable rehabilitative system.

IMPACT OF CONVICTS

Three trends are significant in appraising the consequences of California's adoption of the rehabilitative ideal. First, the length of sentences has steadily increased. From 1959 to 1969 the median time served has risen from twenty-four to thirty-six months, *the longest in the country.* Second, the number of persons incarcerated per 100,-000 has continued to rise, from 65 in 1944 to 145 in 1965. This figure too is the highest in the country. During a period when the treatment idea was maximized, when vocational training programs, group and individual therapy programs, milieu therapy, and many other rehabilitative experiments were introduced, more than twice as many persons served twice as much time. Third, there is evidence that people are not being helped any more by a median stay of three years in a rehabilitatively oriented prison than they were by approximately two years in a basically punitively oriented prison. One indicator of this lack of change is the consistent recidivist rates. Through the years approximately 40 percent of the persons released on parole in California have been returned to confinement two to three years after release.

So that we can see how the California system works, let us briefly examine the procedure for determining length of sentence. This decision is absolutely the most important to the prisoner. California, having one of the most indeterminate forms of the indeterminate sentence system, leaves the final determination of length of sentence and time of parole release in the hands of a government-appointed nine-man panel—the Adult Authority. This parole board has wide margins within which to work. For instance, the statutory limits for second-degree burglary are one to fifteen years; first-degree robbery, five years to life. The most frequently occurring statutory sentence is one to fifteen years. The general procedure for determining the sentence is for the prisoner to appear annually before a panel, which will have one or two members of the Adult Authority and one or two "representatives"—persons of civil service rank whose decisions must be approved by the Adult Authority members. Before the prisoner makes his annual appearance, one of the members of the panel reads his "jacket"—a compilation of information, such as test results, psychiatric and psychological evaluations, work and disciplinary reports, and probation and arresting-officer reports. Key information from this file has been summarized in a fifteen- to twenty-page "Cumulative Summary" for the board appearance and the board member usually confines his examination to this "Cum Sum." Moreover, this five- or ten-minute perusal is being done while another board member questions another prisoner.

During the actual hearing the discussion, led by the panel member who is the chief examiner in a particular case, covers a variety of topics, such as the crime, the prison record of the inmate, and his future plans. The hearing lasts on an average of fourteen minutes, after which there is a determination of his sentence and a granting of a parole date or a "denial."

Several aspects of this process are worthy of mention. First, extraordinary power is lodged in the Adult Authority. It not only has the power to make the final determination of sentence; it can also rescind this determination after it has been made; for example, it can release on parole, rescind the determination, return to prison, and again refix the inmate's sentence. None of these powers can be checked by judicial review.

Second, in a rehabilitatively oriented system, those who determine a release date should be a panel of experts in the behavioral sciences. That such individuals actually have the required expertise is, as already emphasized, unlikely, but the supposition is that they do. In California the law that originally constituted the Adult Authority in 1946 specified that there would be three board members, one with a background in the social sciences, one with a legal background, and one from the correctional field. As the board grew, this initial conception of its composition remained unrealized. At present, six of its nine members have police work backgrounds.

Many prisoners are convinced that there are no valid or consistent criteria operative in this sentencing hearing. The decisions seem arbitrary and unjust. For instance, often one or more members will recommend that a prisoner follow some program for the next year. At his next annual board appearance the prisoner discovers an entirely different panel, uninterested in last year's hearing, which denies him parole even though the previous board's instructions were followed to the letter. Until recently no record was kept of the yearly recommendations of panel members.

There is considerable evidence, mainly in the form of testimony from prisoners and ex-prisoners of various California prisons, that indefinite sentences are one of the most painful aspects of prison life. Here is the opinion of a woman imprisoned at Frontera:

> The total waste of time spent while here and the constant mental torture of never really knowing how long you'll be here. The indeterminate sentence structure gives you no peace of mind and absolutely nothing to work for.
> The total futility of this time is the most maddening thing to bear. You realize nothing but frustration from the beginning to the end of your confinement. This situation is compounded by the "never knowing" system of the indeterminate sentencing law.[3]

Moreover the determination of sentence and many other facets of the California rehabilitative routine strike many prisoners as hypocritical. They feel that denial of parole for the stated purpose of pursuing some treatment program often hides other reasons for the denial, including not having enough time served for a particular crime, suspicion of other crimes, outside concern over certain types of crime, or for factors having little o do with him or her, such as administrative exigencies. Prisoners react strongly to such injustice.

The suffering caused by indeterminacy and the hypocrisy of the newer systems may be different from that experienced in earlier, more openly punitive systems, but it is not necessarily any less severe, nor has the suffering really been alleviated by the introduction of various comforts, such as television and recreation programs. Those who were concerned about removing earlier forms of suffering have shown a curious insensitivity to the newer forms. The middle-class person who blanches at the thought of the cat-o'-nine-tails apparently accepts without undue feelings of guilt the cat-and-mouse game whereby the prisoner never knows whether the sentence is three years or ten and discipline is maintained by the threat of more time.

Besides suffering from the indeterminacy and the hypocrisy in the penal situation, convicts in rehabilitative prisons experience a more profound form of suffering. This is the pain of being treated unjustly. Probably many prisoners have always felt some diffuse sense of injustice about the way they have been treated, but in recent years this has grown. There is increasing sophistication among prisoners in understanding basic legal rights. There is a growing tendency among prisoners to view procedures based on the rehabilitative ideal as clever strategies for stripping them of constitutional rights. Several of these rights from the convict's perspective are regularly violated. The following case reported by a convict is an example in which the convict felt that he was being denied due process.

> S. was convicted for second degree burglary and served two years. While on parole, he states that his relations with his parole agent were not good even though he was working steadily and conforming to parole regulations. After completing eighteen months on parole he was arrested two blocks from his home at 11:00 p.m. He was on his way home from a nearby bar where he had just spent two or three hours. The police were looking for someone who had committed a burglary several blocks away about an hour earlier. When they discovered that S. had a record for burglary he was taken to jail and charged with this crime. When his alibi was established and there was no evidence to connect him with the crime except for his being in the neighborhood, the judge dismissed the charge and admonished the arresting officers.
> S.'s parole was cancelled, however, and he was returned to prison. When he appeared before the Adult Authority for a parole violation hearing he was asked

if he knew why he had been returned. He replied that he did not. The Adult Authority member became irritated with him and told him that just because he "beat the charge" in court did not mean that he was not guilty, and that the best thing he could do was to admit that he was guilty. He refused to do this and tried to explain to the member that the judge clearly believed him to be innocent and that he could prove this from the transcript of the preliminary hearing.

S. was denied parole consideration and postponed for another year. The next year he brought the transcript of his case to the hearing and the member said that he did not want to read it and that it made no difference to him anyway. He was guilty as far as they were concerned. Once again he was denied parole and scheduled for another hearing in a year.

Many convicts serving time under the indeterminate sentence system feel that the crimes of others aggravate their own crimes. The following is an example in which the convict felt that this had taken place.

D., an armed robbery offender, appeared before the Adult Authority after serving 4½ years. He felt that because of his crime, the time served and his institutional record, he should be paroled at this time. However, approximately two months prior to this board appearance an armed robbery had occurred which, because of having excessive violence, received considerable news media coverage. Furthermore, many statements by law enforcement officers and political leaders had followed which requested harsher treatment of armed robbers. At D.'s appearance very little was said about his progress in prison; instead the conversation turned to the recent violent robbery and the attendant publicity given to this crime. D. was not granted a parole at this time and was scheduled to return for another board appearance when he had served 5½ years. Needless to say, D. felt that he was being punished for the acts of other persons.

Another complaint of persons living under rehabilitative routines is that parole authorities regularly are guilty of ex post facto law enforcement. They do this by increasing a person's penalty after he has been convicted and sentenced because in the meantime more stringent legislation has been passed.

In most rehabilitative prison systems that employ an indeterminate sentence system, the majority of the convicts serve a sentence very close to the median sentence. A minority, however, serve longer sentences for reasons they feel are vague, invalid, not constitutional, or not legally admissible in the sentencing procedure. For this, they and others around them feel a sense of injustice. This sense of injustice is contagious and its effects are profound.

Suffering within the penal system has not decreased. The opposite seems to be the case: rehabilitation has introduced a new form of brutality, more subtle and elusive. That rehabilitation is less disturbing to the deliverers who, consequently, have spread it among a much larger number of persons is also true.

TREATMENT AND COERCION

Mixing treatment with coercion in the penal system not only lengthens sentences and increases the suffering and the sense of injustice, it also vitiates the treatment programs that are its justification.

Many have pointed to the difficulties inherent in implementing treatment in prison. For instance, David Powelson and Reinhard Bendix,[4] writing in 1951 about the rapidly expanding California system, identified a basic therapeutic flaw in the prisoner situation, in which custody concerns were necessarily primary and the moral depravity of the prisoner must be assumed in order to legitimate custody. They further warned of the danger that existed in disguising custody concerns as treatment, which inevitably happens. Donald Cressey and Lloyd Ohlin[5] recognized potential difficulties in implementing treatment in prison because of organizational obstacles stemming from the multiple and possibly conflicting goals of the prison.

Beyond the special problems of effecting "treatment" in prisons, is it possible to coerce people into "treatment" in any setting? Is the necessary therapeutic relationship between the helper and the helped possible if the person to be helped is forced into the relationship? Psychiatrists have argued that in order for psychotherapy to be effective, the client must enter the relationship voluntarily. When he is coerced, resentment, suspicion of the motives of the therapist, and lack of commitment to the therapeutic goals destroy any chances of success.

Though perhaps not universally true, such a criticism probably applies to most forms of help offered through the criminal justice system. Persons forced into group therapy, group counseling, "therapeutic communities," vocational training, or education probably resent the coercion, are suspicious of the motives of the helpers, or lack commitment to such a degree that the programs do not accomplish their explicit purpose, even though some of the programs may be very good.

There is another dimension to coerced help. "Coerced" does not simply mean that a person is ordered to do something. He is ordered to do so *or else*. The "or else" is usually a penal sanction, such as a jail sentence or a lengthened jail sentence. In rehabilitative prisons the person's release may be effected by the quantity and quality of his participation in "treatment programs." Since he knows this is true, he is greatly influenced to enter these programs not simply to help himself, but in order to manipulate the release system. In doing so he usually corrupts the treatment value of the programs.

VOLUNTARY PROGRAMS

Let us look briefly at the other side of the problem. Would help for convicts be more useful if it were completely voluntary? There is a belief held by many, especially experts in the social service fields, that lower-class, emotionally disturbed, "deviant" or "criminal" persons most often are not aware of their real problems and will not seek services that can help them. We disagree totally with this proposition. In the first place, help must be defined from the viewpoint of the person in need, and in the second place, the reason a person in need turns his back on help is, by and large, that the services offered are shabby substitutes for help. When real services are available, those in need literally line up at the door.

We cannot stress too strongly the necessity that help be voluntary and be truly accessible to all elements of the population. After all, the needs of the defendant or prisoner are not unique. Because of stigmatization he may have special difficulties in securing a job. Because of long imprisonment he may have difficulties reentering society. But by and large the needs of the defendant and the prisoner are the same as those of most people. He or she has the need of good pay, meaningful work, leisure time and the resources to enjoy it, and perhaps counseling on special personal, vocational, or family problems. Beyond this, what is offered the defendant or prisoner, out of our sense of justice, should not be unavailable to other segments of the population. To do otherwise would encourage law violations as a way of seeking help. It would be yet another instance of the discriminatory distribution of available services.

The range of voluntary services that could be made available either to defendants or prisoners is endless. To substitute real helping services for the puny, the ineffective, or the somewhat harmful services that exist for both free persons in need and prisoners will require a major investment of public resources. As we stressed in our opening chapters, however, the prerequisite to an equitable criminal justice system is social justice, and social justice will be predicated upon a more equitable distribution of the goods and services in society.

An example of some of the concrete services that should be considered are such things as crisis centers for free persons, where counseling, job training, temporary housing, emergency funds, and temporary retreat could be sought. During imprisonment, education, vocational training, salaries for work performed, and a variety of counseling services are minimum items that could be offered.

We find it important that such services be voluntary not only on the part of those receiving aid, but also from the standpoint of those offering the services. Voluntary groups sometimes have the flexibility to meet human needs in ways that can only be approximated by institutionalized agencies. The freshness and compassion of a volunteer with only a few hours of training often outweighs the expertise of professionals.

In social service agencies, especially those run by government, bureaucracy and red tape tend to pyramid. Human concern tends to be replaced by a detachment that grows eventually into contempt for those the agency is intended to serve. This is as destructive to those offering the supposed help as it is to those receiving it. Witness the coldness and inefficiency of most big-city welfare departments and medical clinics.

NOTES

1.   "Correctional Systems and National Values," *British Journal of Criminology,* October 1962.
2.   Malcolm Braly, *On the Yard* (Boston, Little, Brown, 1967), pp. 103–104.
3.   David A. Ward and Gene G. Kassebaum, *Women's Prison* (Chicago, Aldine, 1965).
4.   "Psychiatry in Prison," *Psychiatry,* 1951.
5.   Donald Cressey, "Limitations on Organization of Treatment in the Modern Prison," and Lloyd Ohlin, "Conflicting Interests in Correctional Objectives," in *Theoretical Studies in Social Organization in the Prison* (pamphlet, Social Science Research Council, March 1960).

ANDREW VON HIRSCH

Prediction of Criminal Conduct and Preventive Confinement of Convicted Persons*

I. INTRODUCTION

Preventive confinement—incapacitating an allegedly dangerous individual in order to prevent him from engaging in predicted criminal conduct —is a concept that seems rather foreign to our traditions of justice. We would be prone to assert that a person may be deprived of his liberty, not on the basis of a prediction of criminal behavior, but only on the basis of a determination of guilt for a past offense. As the recent controversy over pretrial preventive detention in the District of Columbia illustrates,[1] it can arouse our concern or alarm when the state seeks to incarcerate preventively those suspected of criminal tendencies, even for brief periods. While predictions of dangerousness have historically been used to justify confining mentally ill persons, this practice also is beginning to generate criticism and doubts.[2]

Yet once a person has been convicted of a crime, our scruples about preventive confinement seem to disappear. Predictions of criminal conduct regularly enter into decisions concerning the disposition of convicted criminal offenders. With little public notice and few voiced objections, the state has been free to impose prolonged terms of confinement upon convicted persons predicted to be dangerous, for the express or implied purpose of incapacitating them from engaging in future criminal conduct; the duration of these individu-

als' confinement may far exceed what would ordinarily seem justified as punishment for their past offenses. Thus one is tempted to ask: "If we are so distrustful of preventive confinement in cases where there has been no conviction for a crime, why should we so readily accept it after there has been a conviction?" This paper will attempt to deal with that question.

A. PREVALENCE OF THE PRACTICE OF PREVENTIVE CONFINEMENT

Numerous examples could be cited in existing law involving essentially preventive confinement of convicted persons predicted to be dangerous. I shall mention just a few.

Canada has adopted a system explicitly termed "Preventive Detention," authorizing the imprisonment of convicted multiple offenders for an indeterminate term if:

[T]he court is of the opinion that because the accused is an habitual criminal, it is expedient for the protection of the public to sentence him to preventive detention.[3]

England, having had a system of Preventive Detention similar to the Canadian one until 1967, still permits a judge to sentence an offender for a term well beyond the maximum term for his last offense, if, in the words of the statute, the court is satisfied, by reason of his previous conduct and of the likelihood of his committing further offences, that it is expedient to protect the public from him for a substantial time . . .[4].

One of the most overt schemes of preventive confinement in this country is the Maryland Defective Delinquent Law.[5] Under the Maryland statute, an individual who has been convicted for the first time of any of a wide variety of offenses

*From the *Buffalo Law Review,* Vol. 21 (1972), pp. 717–58. Copyright © 1972 by Buffalo Law Review. Reprinted by permission of the author and the publisher.

This article is based upon a staff paper prepared by the author for the Committee for the Study of Incarceration. The Committee is an interdisciplinary study group that is conducting a general conceptual inquiry into incarceration and its alternatives, operating under grants from the Field Foundation and the New World Foundation. . . .

The author wishes to note his particular indebtedness to the writings, comments and suggestions of Professor Alan Dershowitz, who is currently conducting an extensive inquiry into the role of predictions of deviant conduct in the law.

(some rather minor), may be indefinitely confined if he is found by a court, on the basis of recommendations by a state medical board, to be a "defective delinquent." To be classified as such, the individual must meet two sets of criteria, one predictive and one quasi-psychiatric. The predictive criterion is that the individual

by the demonstration of persistent aggravated antisocial or criminal behavior, evidences a propensity toward criminal activity . . . as to clearly demonstrate an actual danger to society so as to require such confinement and treatment, when appropriate, as may make it reasonably safe for society to terminate the confinement and treatment.[6]

The quasi-psychiatric criterion is that the individual, *though legally sane,* manifests "emotional unbalance" or "intellectual deficiency."[7] If the individual is found to meet these criteria, then he will be confined in a special institution for defective delinquents, Patuxent Institution. The term of his confinement is indeterminate, can exceed the maximum term of punishment for the offense of which he was convicted, and can even be for life.[8] He is entitled to release only when it is determined that he no longer meets the criteria for "defective delinquency" that justified his confinement.[9] During confinement, he is supposed to be subjected to an intensive program of rehabilitative treatment, although a Maryland court has recently found that such treatment is not being made available to the more recalcitrant prisoners.[10]

Colorado authorizes the preventive confinement of persons convicted for sexual offenses, if the court finds that such individuals constitute "a threat of bodily harm to members of the public."[11] Confinement is for an indeterminate term, up to the lifetime of the defendant.[12] According to a recent survey conducted under the auspices of the American Bar Foundation, seventeen other jurisdictions authorize the indeterminate confinement of sex offenders or so-called "sexual psychopaths," with or without a prior conviction.[13]

The Model Sentencing Act proposes that a felony offender convicted of certain serious crimes be sentenced for an extended term of up to thirty years (thrice the maximum term of confinement he otherwise could receive for such offenses) if the court, after ordering a psychiatric examination, finds that "because of the dangerousness of the defendant, such period of confined correctional treatment or custody is required for the protection of the public" and if it further finds that he "is suffering from a severe personality disorder indicating a propensity toward criminal activity."[13a] The Model Penal Code provides that a trial judge, in sentencing a person convicted of a felony, may extend the term of his imprisonment well beyond the maximum provided for that category of felony, when "the defendant is a dangerous, mentally abnormal person whose commitment for an extended term is necessary for protection of the public."[13b]

The California indeterminate sentence law gives an independent sentencing board—the Adult Authority—plenary discretion to determine release dates within the widest maximum and minimum statutory limits.[14] The Adult Authority may—and apparently does—determine the duration of an offender's confinement in part upon the basis of informal estimates of his supposed individual dangerousness.[15]

Essentially predictive judgments are also frequently made in conventional parole situations. Since 1933, Illinois has made regular use of statistical prediction techniques in its parole system. An actuarial prediction table of parole outcomes has been prepared for each of the major institutions in the state. A sociologist-actuary at each institution prepares a routine prediction report based upon the tables for each inmate appearing at a parole hearing. He computes the prisoner's statistical chances for making a successful adjustment on parole; the final sentence in the report reads: "This inmate is in a class in which —% may be expected to violate the parole agreement." Together with sociological, psychiatric and psychological reports and interviews by the parole board, the predictive score is used to determine whether the prisoner is granted or denied parole.[16]

Based on the Illinois experience, several noted criminologists have advocated more extensive and systematic use of prediction tables in sentencing and parole decisions.[17] According to a nationwide survey conducted in 1962,[18] three other states—Ohio, California and Colorado—had developed formal prediction tables for application in individual parole decisions. While not using tables, parole boards in other states regularly make informal estimates of individual inmates' potential for future antisocial conduct in determining whether to grant or deny parole; a recent American Bar Foundation survey of sentencing and parole procedures found that "the principal consideration in the decision to grant or deny parole is the probability that the inmate will violate the criminal law if he is released."[19]

B. SCOPE OF THE INQUIRY

Before proceeding, it is appropriate to define the scope of this inquiry more precisely. Imprisonment has or may have as one of its functions, the prevention of future crimes—even without any attempt at prediction of individual dangerousness. *Any* decision to confine a person convicted of a crime incapacitates him from committing, during his period of confinement, any criminal acts he might otherwise choose to commit against the outside community. That is true even if the decision to confine is made *solely* with reference to his past criminal conduct, and no effort is made to forecast his individual future behavior. So long as it is assumed that *some* convicted robbers (never mind which individual ones) would be inclined to commit further offenses if allowed to remain at large, imprisoning *all* convicted robbers for a specified period of time might prevent *some* future robberies from occurring. This kind of prevention is what might be called prevention in the *collective* sense. It raises some important questions, worthy of careful study.[20] However, it is outside the scope of the present article.

Instead, this article has a narrower scope. It is concerned with prevention in the *individual, predictive* sense—where decisions to confine persons turn upon official forecasts of their particular future conduct. More exactly, it focuses on this specific question: *Is it appropriate to decide whether and how long to confine a sane adult who has been convicted of a crime, on the basis that he is deemed likely to engage in certain criminal conduct in the future?*

This topic is of particular interest for two reasons. It raises questions of the reliability of predictions of individual dangerousness and of the policy consequences of erroneous predictions. It also raises questions of the propriety of confining an individual who is deemed of sound mind and full age for what he *will* do, not what he has done.

It is to this kind of prevention—in the individual, predictive sense—that I will be referring in this article when I use the term "preventive confinement."

C. CONCEPTUAL NATURE OF THE INQUIRY

Techniques for predicting criminal behavior are still relatively primitive, and existing schemes of preventive confinement generally lack even minimal legal safeguards, as the discussion below indicates. Thus it is easy enough to criticize preventive confinement in the state in which it exists today.

The more difficult question—and the one with which this article will primarily be concerned—is whether the *concept* of preventive confinement is a sound one, assuming that prediction techniques and legal safeguards are improved. If the *concept* is sound,[21] then preventive confinement may be an important and fruitful area for further innovation and development. If not, it may be a dangerous blind alley. In making this conceptual analysis, theoretical models have been found helpful and will be used.

II. PREVENTIVE CONFINEMENT—A THEORETICAL MODEL

We might start our analysis by examining the following theoretical model:

The Preventive Confinement Model. In an imaginary jurisdiction, a person convicted of a criminal offense would be subject to preventive confinement for an indeterminate term, if specified predictive criteria indicated a high probability of his committing a serious offense in the future. Following completion of his term in prison for the offense of which he was convicted, he would be transferred to and confined in a special facility designed solely for preventive purposes, in which living conditions would be made as "pleasant," that is, as little punitive, as possible, consistent with the fact of incarceration itself. The individual would not be subjected to mandatory rehabilitative treatment during confinement in this special facility. The duration of confinement could substantially exceed the maximum statutory term of punishment prescribed for the offense of which he had been convicted. He would be released only at such time as he is found no longer to meet the predictive criteria for dangerousness.

In actual practice, preventive confinement frequently is mixed with other elements. The

Maryland Defective Delinquent Law combines preventive confinement with mandatory treatment.[22] By giving the Adult Authority plenary discretion to determine an adult offender's release date, the California indeterminate sentence law allows preventive considerations to be mixed with judgments concerning punishment, treatment and institutional convenience.[23] In these contexts, it is difficult to isolate and analyze the preventive component of decisions to confine.

In our theoretical model, however, the preventive component is separately identified. The offender serves an indeterminate term in a special facility in which confinement is *for preventive purposes only*. The duration of confinement in that facility would be set *solely on the basis of a prediction of his individual future dangerousness, without regard to the nature of his past offense*.

Thus the model gives us the opportunity to evaluate preventive confinement in its more or less "pure state." Once we have done that, we will examine the effect of adding other components to the model, such as mandatory rehabilitative treatment.

A. THRESHOLD REQUIREMENTS: EXPLICIT LEGAL STANDARDS OF DANGEROUSNESS; VALIDATION OF PREDICTION METHOD; PROCEDURAL SAFEGUARDS

To have any possible merit, the model should satisfy three important threshold requirements: (1) There must be reasonably precise legal standards of dangerousness; (2) the prediction methods used must be subjected to careful and continuous validation; and (3) the procedure for commitment must provide the defendant with certain minimal procedural safeguards. These requirements, however, are seldom met by current practices of preventive confinement.

1. *Explicit Legal Standards of Dangerousness.* As Dershowitz[24] and Goldstein and Katz[25] have pointed out in connection with the law of commitment of the insane, a supposedly "dangerous" person should never be preventively confined, unless the "danger" he poses is of sufficient gravity —and sufficient likelihood—to warrant deprivation of his freedom. That determination—of the seriousness and likelihood of the predicted misconduct required to justify confinement—is a value judgment the *law* should make; it is not a

factual judgment within the professional competence of psychiatrists or other expert witnesses. Failure to provide explicit legal standards of "dangerousness" creates the unacceptable situation where, for example, one psychiatrist can decide that only those mental patients who are likely to perpetrate violent crimes ought to be confined, while another psychiatrist, depending upon his personal philosophy, can employ the concept of "dangerousness" to confine potential minor offenders, as well.

These considerations apply with equal force to the preventive incarceration of convicted persons. Yet existing preventive confinement schemes seldom, if ever, provide legal standards of dangerousness which have any definiteness. The Maryland Defective Delinquent Law, for example, authorizes commitment of individuals who demonstrate an "actual danger" to society.[26] No definition is supplied of what constitutes such a danger; nor is there even a statutory requirement that the supposed "dangerousness" be seriously criminal in character.

Unless "dangerousness" is defined by law with some minimal degree of precision, the entire preventive model may well be unconstitutional on grounds of vagueness.[27] Thus a threshold requirement for acceptability of the model would be a reasonably precise statutory definition of "dangerousness": one that specifies what kind of future criminal conduct, and what degree of likelihood of that conduct, warrants preventive confinement.

2. *Validating the Predictive Method.* In commitment proceedings for the mentally ill, there is rarely any effort made to check the accuracy of psychiatric predictions of dangerousness by following up and tabulating their results.[28] The same absence of validation pervades the existing preventive confinement practice for some offenders. No systematic follow-up is made, for example, of the predictions of dangerousness under the Maryland Defective Delinquent Law. Even among states that utilize prediction tables as an aid to parole decisions, validation is not always attempted.[29]

Not surprisingly under these circumstances, unverified predictions of dangerousness prove fallible, indeed, when their accuracy is subsequently examined by scholars. In his ongoing study of the accuracy of psychiatric prediction in commitment proceedings for the mentally ill, Dershowitz notes:

[I] was able to discover fewer than a dozen studies which followed up psychiatric predictions of antisocial conduct. And even more surprisingly, these few studies strongly suggest that psychiatrists are rather inaccurate predictors; inaccurate in an absolute sense, and even less accurate when compared with other professionals, such as psychologists, social workers and correctional officials, and when compared to actuarial devices, such as prediction or experience tables. Even more significant for legal purposes: it seems that psychiatrists are particularly prone to one type of error—overprediction. In other words, they tend to predict antisocial conduct in many instances where it would not, in fact, occur. Indeed, our research suggests that for every correct psychiatric prediction of violence, there are numerous erroneous predictions.[30]

Predictions by supposedly "expert" correctional personnel show the same proneness to error, as a study by Hakeem suggests.[31] He requested ten trained parole officers and ten laymen with no correctional experience to make a series of predictions of parole survival on the basis of case summaries of 200 parolees, half of whom had been recommitted for parole violations and half of whom had not. He found that the laymen were substantially *more* accurate predictors than the parole officers. Moreover, both groups combined made fewer correct identifications of the nonviolators than would have been made by random selection.[32]

Aside from inaccuracy, hazards of class and racial discrimination inhere in giving psychiatrists, correctional officials or other supposed "experts" *carte blanche* powers to make predictive determinations of dangerousness—unless the predictive criteria used are first carefully validated. Psychiatrists or parole board members of middle class backgrounds can and do, all too easily, misinterpret lower-class or nonconforming styles and attitudes as symptoms of supposed "dangerousness."[33]

If this kind of laxity is carried over to the model system of preventive confinement, that alone would be sufficient to condemn it.

Thus a second threshold requirement for acceptability of the model would be that its predictive method carefully be validated *in advance* of

being applied in actual decisions to confine; and be subject to continual follow-up and review.

Adequate validation studies of the predictive technique in the model are required, regardless of whether the predictive method is purely statistical, purely clinical, or a mixture of the two.[34] Clinical evaluation avoids statistics in the projection itself, but the statistician must always have the last word in judging the accuracy and utility of the evaluation method; as Meehl points out in his *Clinical vs. Statistical Prediction:*

All clinicians should make up their minds that of the two uses of statistics (structural and validating), the validating use is unavoidable. Regardless of one's theory about personality and regardless of one's choice of data . . .; regardless of how these data are fused for predictive purposes—by intuition, table, equation, or rational hypotheses developed in a case conference—the honest clinician cannot avoid the question 'Am I doing better than I could do by flipping pennies?'. . .

Is any clinician infallible? No one claims to be. Hence, sometimes he is wrong. If he is sometimes wrong, why should we pay any attention to him? There is only one possible reply to this 'silly' question. It is simply that he *tends* (read: 'is likely') to be right. 'Tending' to be right means just one thing—'being right in the long run.'. . . [We thus] have no recourse except to record our predictions at the time, allow them to accumulate, and ultimately tally them up. . . . If the clinical utility is really established and not merely proclaimed, it will have been established by procedures which have all the earmarks of an acceptable validation study.[35]

3. *Procedural Safeguards.* Certain basic procedural safeguards—too often lacking today—should be built into the preventive model.

At minimum, a full hearing should be required before any convicted individual is committed for preventive confinement. That hearing should be separate from the trial for his past offense, because the issues involved (for example, his supposed dangerousness) are distinct from the issues at trial. At this hearing, he must have the rights of counsel, confrontation and cross-examination of witnesses, and the right to call his own witnesses.[36] The Supreme Court has struck down a sexual psychopath law which denied such a hearing,[37] but many such state laws still abridge full implementation of these rights.[38] The Maryland Defective Delinquent Law, while providing a hearing and a right to counsel at the hearing, denies the defendant the right to confront and cross-examine staff psychiatrists whose reports are used in determining his status as a defective delinquent.[39]

A requirement more difficult to satisfy but equally important relates to indigents' right of representation. To conduct any kind of effective defense, an indigent defendant would not only need to have competent counsel provided for him but also to have access to competent expert witnesses able to challenge the state's prediction of his supposed dangerousness.[40] That would involve very considerable expense, which would have to be assumed by the state. The defendant's expert witnesses, to testify effectively on behalf of their client, would need, for example, to conduct extended psychiatric observations of the defendant, or run validation studies to check the accuracy of past predictions of dangerousness made by the state's expert witnesses. This will require a very much more ambitious and costly legal services program than is available today. But without it, indigent defendants will be virtually helpless to defend themselves, and the entire model would violate basic standards of procedural fairness.

A still more difficult question relates to the privilege against self-incrimination. If the privilege applies to preventive confinement under the model—and there are arguments to suggest that it should[41]—then the individual could be confined only if a prediction could be made on the basis of independently obtained data; the individual could not be compelled to cooperate with psychiatric investigations designed to determine whether he is dangerous. If that were so, the preventive model probably could not be implemented unless and until the predictive art had progressed to the point where it could rely safely upon "objective" data and dispose with psychiatric investigations in making predictions.

B. THEORETICAL IMPEDIMENTS TO PREDICTION: THE FALSE POSITIVE PROBLEM

Even if these threshold requirements are satisfied, however, the preventive model will encounter a formidable theoretical impediment to prediction: the false positive problem.

1. *The Significance of False Positives.* Starting in the early 1920s with S. B. Warner's statistical study of recidivism among prisoners paroled from the Massachusetts State Reformatory and with the Gluecks' widely publicized prediction studies, an extensive literature has developed concerning the statistical prediction of parole recidivism and of delinquency.[42]

As Wilkins points out in his perceptive *Evaluation of Penal Measures,*[43] there has been a tendency in this predictive literature to adopt a rather one-sided criterion for success. A prediction table for delinquency or recidivism is thought effective if it can correctly forecast a relatively high proportion of those individuals who actually become delinquent or recidivist. The other side of the coin is less often considered: the so-called *false positives*—those mistakenly predicted to engage in such deviant conduct. There has been an inclination to overlook how many nondelinquents or nonrecidivists a prediction table incorrectly classifies as potentially deviant.

In certain types of prediction, the criteria for success need not be too seriously concerned with false positives. If, for example, we develop a prediction table for recruitment into the army,[44] the table may well be useful if it successfully identifies a high percentage of individuals actually unsuitable for the service, who can then be screened out. If the manpower pool is ample, it does not really matter that the predictive index also yields a substantial number of false positives—individuals actually suitable for the service who are rejected as a result of a mistaken prediction of unsuitability. For the Army does not need to recruit all suitable persons; and the impact upon affected individuals of a mistaken prediction of unsuitability generally is not damaging.

In predicting criminal conduct, however, the consequences of ignoring the false positives are much more serious. As Wilkins points out:

Taking a sample of offenders and showing that a large proportion would have scored in the delinquent category does not validate the prediction. Yet claims of this kind are frequently found. If decisions are made upon the basis of prediction statements, it is to be expected that the consequences of errors in each class will be different. It may be more damaging to regard (predict) a person as delinquent or recidivist when this is incorrect, than to incorrectly regard a person as nondelinquent or nonrecidivist. Some recent writers have claimed that the first kind of error can lead to a self-fulfilling prophecy—the labeling process of classification as "likely delinquent" may change the perception of the person by others, and through this, his own self-image.[45]

In the context of our model system of preventive incarceration, we can afford little tolerance, indeed, of prediction methods that show a high yield of false positives. Here, mistakenly predicting nondangerous individuals to be dangerous is gravely damaging—for it can lead to their prolonged incarceration.

Because of the historical lack of concern with the question, the existing prediction indices for juvenile delinquency and parole recidivism seldom tabulate the actual rate of false positives. Yet where the false positive rate has been calculated for existing prediction tables, it turns out to be disturbingly high.[46]

It has sometimes been suggested that statistical predictive indices should be used only to identify the *risk category* in which offenders are located; and that selection of individuals within a given risk category for release or continued confinement should then be made by the parole board on the basis of clinical observation.[47] However, this suggestion does not solve the problem of false positives in the model. Given what we know of the fallibility of psychiatrists' and correctional officials' clinical forecasts,[48] there is no reason to expect that *their* predictive choices—even within statistically defined risk categories—will be dramatically free of false positives, where the prediction tables themselves are not. As Wilkins states:

It is sometimes claimed that subjective judgment can help in regard to these kinds of error. Where the tables may fail to find the ten who will succeed in the 90 percent failure group, the human intelligence will be able to identify them. This is sometimes claimed by those who recognize that the human subjective intelligence is not adequate in any other part of the range of assessment. They want to cooperate with the tables, helping them when they fail. These kinds of claims for clinical supplementation of statistical tables have not been supported by any evidence. Their belief that something of this kind of supplementation *should* be possible seems again to originate in an inability to come to terms with uncertainty. For them, probability must

be supplemented so that a deterministic model is provided—then a decision can be made![49]

The false positive issue, therefore, must squarely be faced.

2. *The Rare Event and False Positives: The Rosen Suicide Model.* It might be hoped that with increased attention to the false positive problem and sufficient expenditure of time, money and effort, superior predictive indices could be developed which would be relatively free of false positives. That hope, however, may be misplaced—for there exist theoretical impediments to prediction of criminal conduct notwithstanding such efforts at improvement.

Generally speaking, criminal conduct tends to have two characteristics which make it resistant to accurate prediction:

(1) It is comparatively rare. The more dangerous the conduct is, the rarer it is. Violent crime —perhaps the most dangerous of all—is the rarest of all.

(2) It has no known, clearly identifiable symptoms. Prediction therefore becomes a matter of developing statistical correlations between observed characteristics of offenders and subsequent criminal conduct. Where those two conditions obtain, false positives show a high degree of persistence, even in a theoretical predictive model.

In a valuable 1954 article, Albert Rosen[50] of the University of Minnesota developed a theoretical model for predicting suicide among mental patients, that illustrates this problem. Rosen constructed a hypothetical suicide detection index for an assumed population of 12,000 mental patients. On the basis of existing suicide statistics, he assumed that the rate of suicides was very low —one third of one percent of the total patient population. With this low rate, only 40 patients out of the initial population of 12,000 would actually commit suicide. Thus, without any test, *all* patients in this population could be predicted to be nonsuicidal, and the prediction would be right in 99⅔% of all cases. A hypothetical suicide detection index would have to perform better than this in identifying the potential suicides.

Rosen assumes such a hypothetical index is developed as follows: (1) The patient population is divided into two groups—patients who actually committed suicide during confinement (suicide population), and patients who did not (nonsuicide population); (2) a random sample is selected and analyzed from each population; (3) a predictive index is developed, based upon the test data which significantly differentiate the two criterion samples; (4) a cutting line is established—that is, a differentiating score on the index, so that patients testing above that score would be classified as suicidal and patients testing below that score would be classified as nonsuicidal; and (5) the cutting line is cross-validated—for example, it is validated with new suicide and nonsuicide samples, every psychiatric patient over a period of years being scored on the index.[51]

Such an index, Rosen finds, can identify a significant number of true positives only by misidentifying a very much larger number of false positives. If an effort is made to reduce the false positives to a manageable number, only a tiny fraction of the true positives can be spotted—and even then, there are many more false positives than true positives.[52]

Suppose the cutting line is established at a point where, after cross-validation, the index will correctly identify 75% of the patients in both the suicide and the nonsuicide populations, respectively. Using this cutting line, the index *will correctly identify 30 of the 40 actual suicides.* However, Rosen indicates, *it will also incorrectly identify 2,990 nonsuicidal patients as potentially suicidal.*[53] The false positive rate here is so high as to make the prediction, in his words "[of] no appreciable value, for it would be impractical to treat as suicidal the prodigious number of misclassified cases."[54]

Suppose, then, a much higher cutting line is established—one which, when cross-validated, will correctly identify 90% of the nonsuicide cases. It is assumed that the new cutting line reduces to 60% (regarded by Rosen as a liberal estimate) the proportion of correctly classified suicidal patients. Using this new cutting line, the index *will correctly identify 24 out of 40 actual suicides,* but still *will mis-identify as suicidal 1,196 false positives.* This is still "an impractical instrument because of the large number of false positives."[55]

With every elevation of the cutting line, Rosen shows, there would be some reduction in the number of false positives. However, there would be a corresponding shrinkage in the number of true positives. And the false positives will continue to greatly outnumber the true.

If the cutting line is raised to the point where it screens out 99.5% of the nonsuicide cases, then, Rosen estimates, the predictive index will be able to spot only 2.5% of the actual suicides. Thus the problem remains unsolved. *Only 1 out of 40 actual suicides is correctly identified; and to achieve this meagre result, 60 false positives will still have to be predicted.*

To achieve a better result, the experimenter might try to seek to develop a predictive index for a special diagnostic subgroup that has a substantially higher suicide rate than the general mental patient population. But, as Rosen points out,[56] there are inherent limitations in this approach. Any such diagnostic subgroup would be unlikely to have a suicide rate much higher than two percent, and that still would yield an excessive number of false positives. Moreover, a considerable proportion of the actual suicidal patients in the entire sample population would then be *excluded* from the diagnostic subgroup.

3. *Violent Crimes and False Positives.* Like suicide, crimes of violence are infrequent events. They are rare not only among the general population, but also (as will be discussed below) among previous offenders who have been released. The Rosen model thus has applicability to violent crimes, as well as to suicide. Predictions of violence tend to yield large numbers of false positives.

What makes violence so particularly difficult to predict is not merely its rarity, but its situational quality. Deterministic models to the contrary notwithstanding, violence generally is not a quality which inheres in certain "dangerous" individuals: it is an occurrence which may erupt—or may not—in certain crisis situations. Whether it does erupt, whether it is reported, whether the perpetrator is apprehended and punished, depend upon a wide variety of fortuitous circumstances, largely beyond the actor's control. Not only the actor's proclivities, but the decisions of other individuals—the victim, the bystanders, the police, the magistrate—may determine whether an act of violence occurs and whether it comes to be included in the criminal statistics. Trying to predict violence on the basis of information concerning only the supposedly violence-prone individual—

without taking these numerous external contingencies into account—is trying to solve a multi-variable problem by keeping track of only one variable. It is a hazardous undertaking, indeed.

The difficulty of predicting violent criminal behavior is strikingly illustrated by a recent study by Wenk and Robison of violent recidivism among California Youth Authority wards.[57] Wenk and Robison examined the records of all juvenile offenders who were processed during 1964–66 through the Deuel Reception-Guidance Center, a diagnostic unit that examines older juvenile offenders at the time they are committed to the Youth Authority. A follow-up study was made of their behavior on parole for a period of 15 months after release from confinement—with a view to determining how many were recommitted for a violent offense. As nearly one quarter of the sample had originally been committed for a violent offense or had a history of known violent behavior, the violence potential of the group might have been expected to be relatively high. Nevertheless, the investigators found that of this entire group, the incidence of violent recidivism during the 15-month follow-up period was only 2.4%.[58] As Rosen's analysis of his suicide model indicates, constructing a hypothetical predictive index upon a base rate as low as that—only 2.4% —would yield an unmanageable number of false positives.

Wenk and Robison's own tentative analysis supports this conclusion. They requested a psychologist and a statistician to project hypothetical predictive indices for violent recidivism, based upon the data in their sample. The *less* pessimistic projection—that of the psychologist—was that a multi-variable multiple regression equation could be developed from the data, which could identify about one-half of the true positives, *but in which the false positives would outnumber the true positives by a discouraging eight to one.*[59]

4. *Selection of High-Risk Subgroups.* One strategy mentioned by Rosen[60] for avoiding the false positive problem was to develop a predictive index only for narrowly defined subgroups of the original sample population, which manifest a considerably higher rate of the behavior to be tested. Applying this strategy to predictions of violent crime, we might try to construct a predictive instrument only for special subgroups of the

convicted offender population, which manifest a substantially higher rate of violence.

The Wenk and Robison study suggests, however, that there may be serious obstacles to such a strategy. Their investigation identified five subgroups which manifested higher rates of violent recidivism than the general sample population.[61] The subgroups were: (1) offenders with known histories of violence; (2) offenders originally committed on a violent offense charge; (3) offenders committed to the Youth Authority for the fourth time or more (that is, multiple recidivists); (4) offenders with histories of "moderate to serious" opiate involvement; and (5) offenders referred to a psychiatrist for violence potential upon commitment to the Youth Authority.[62] The investigators' results indicated that *none* of these subgroups manifested a high enough incidence of violent recidivism to avoid the false positive problem. The highest rate (for category 5) was 6.2%; the other categories showed rates of about 5% or less.[63] These rates are well below the frequency needed for constructing an instrument relatively free of false positives—which, as Meehl and Rosen[64] estimate, should be closer to 50%.

Moreover, Wenk and Robison found that all these subgroups, except the first, account for a rather small fraction of the total incidence of violent recidivism in the sample population. For example, offenders in category (5), which manifests the highest rate of violence, account for only 15% of the total incidence of violence on parole in the entire group. This creates another difficulty. If to construct an accurate predictive index, we are forced to limit its application to defined, high-risk subgroups that account for only a small fraction of the total occurrence of violence, then the public obtains little additional protection from preventive confinement so limited in scope.

5. *Inclusion of Lesser Offenses.* Another avoidance strategy might be to include nonviolent offenses—since they are much more frequent. In the Wenk and Robison study, for example, if all parole violations are considered—which include not only violent crimes but also property crimes and other lesser offenses—then the recidivism rate climbs to a more statistically manageable 39.9%. Another serious objection is encountered here, however. To obtain the needed higher offense rates, we find ourselves fast descending the scale of seriousness toward the minor

offenses. Then, it becomes increasingly difficult to demonstrate a need for societal protection of the degree of urgency that could conceivably warrant the kind of deprivation of liberty contemplated in the model. It should be recalled that the model involves incarceration for an indeterminate period that may be quite prolonged, perhaps lifelong.[65]

6. *Concealing Overprediction.* Even were we to extricate ourselves from this last difficulty we face another formidable theoretical problem: any system of preventive incarceration *conceals errone-ous confinements, while revealing erroneous releases.*[66] The individual who is wrongly identi-fied as dangerous is confined, and thus has little or no opportunity to demonstrate that he would not have committed the crime had he been re-leased. The individual who is wrongly identified as nondangerous remains at large, so it comes to public attention if he later commits a crime. Thus, once a preventive system is established, it creates the illusion of generating only one kind of evidence: *evidence of erroneous release, that prompts decision-makers to expand the categories of persons who are preventively confined.* In short, a system of preventive confinement creates a self-fulfilling prophecy for the need of *more* preven-tive incarceration.[67]

Preventive confinement will also make it diffi-cult to determine with any degree of confidence when a person ceases to be dangerous, and may be released. For the predictive criteria, in all like-lihood, will largely rely upon the individual's be-havior patterns in the relatively recent past. Incarceration itself will temporarily distort or suppress those behavior patterns, thus leaving few accurate clues concerning his probable be-havior upon release.

Moreover, the problem of distortion of evi-dence would greatly be compounded by political-bureaucratic pressures. Under a system of preventive confinement, the public undoubtedly would hold officials responsible if they fail to in-carcerate (or if they release) persons who subse-quently do commit violent criminal acts. This would create overwhelming pressures upon offi-cials to overpredict—since it would entail much less risk to the institution and to their own careers for them to confine (or fail to release) persons who actually are or have become harmless, than to release persons who are actually dangerous and do subsequently perpetrate crimes.

C. EVALUATION OF THE MODEL— WITH FALSE POSITIVES

We are now ready to evaluate our model of preventive confinement. Let us begin by assuming that the technique of prediction used in the model manifests a relatively high incidence of false posi-tives. More specifically, let us suppose that the prediction method *generates false positives at a rate which substantially exceeds the rate of errone-ous convictions under the existing system of crimi-nal justice for those categories of offenses.* (Since there is little available evidence concerning the rate of mistaken convictions, it is difficult to con-firm that any given rate of false positives would, or would not, substantially exceed it. But if the rate of false positives is of the high order of mag-nitude discussed in the preceding analysis—say, the eight false positives to every one true positive suggested by the Wenk and Robison study—it is fairly safe to conjecture that, in Dershowitz' words, "any system of predicting future crimes would result in a vastly larger number of errone-ous confinements"[68] than could be expected to occur under the present criminal justice system.) Later, we will go on to make an evaluation of the model in the context of a hypothetical "ideal" predictive technique that is relatively "free" of false positives.

1. *Inappropriateness of Cost-Benefit Rationale.* To sustain the model where false positives are present, a cost-benefit rationale must be assumed. Proponents of preventive confinement must argue in terms of "balancing" the individual's interest in not being mistakenly confined against society's need for protection from the actually dangerous person. It has to be contended that the "benefit" of preventing the really dangerous in-dividual from committing future crimes exceeds, in the aggregate, the "cost" of mistakenly identi-fying and confining the nondangerous one.

Even if this kind of cost-benefit thinking were appropriate, it is highly questionable whether the preventive confinement model could be justified in its terms—once the magnitude of the "cost" of confining large numbers of false positives is fully taken into account. That is especially true be-cause—for reasons just noted—strategies de-signed to minimize the number of false positives also sharply reduce the number of true positives that can be identified—and hence, minimize the social benefits of the system as a crime prevention device.

The more basic point, however, is that *cost-benefit thinking is wholly inappropriate here.* If a system of preventive incarceration is known systematically to generate mistaken confinements, then it is unacceptable in absolute terms because it violates the obligation of society to do *individual* justice. Such a system cannot be justified by arguing that its aggregate social benefits exceed the aggregate amount of injustice done to mistakenly confined individuals.

2. *The Parallel of Conviction of the Innocent.* In our criminal law, a whole variety of safeguards exist—most notably, the requirement of proof of guilt beyond a reasonable doubt—designed to assure that an innocent person is not convicted or punished. There, aggregate cost-benefit theories would definitely be inappropriate. Would reducing the standard of proof in criminal cases to a "preponderance of the evidence" yield favorable cost-benefit results—in terms of yielding a greater increase in numbers of convictions of the guilty than in numbers of additional convictions of the innocent? Perhaps so, perhaps not; but it does not really matter. A reduction in the standard of proof is absolutely unacceptable if it would materially increase convictions of the innocent. As Tribe states:

Indeed, the very enterprise of formulating a tolerable ratio of false convictions to false acquittals puts an explicit price on an innocent man's liberty and defeats the concept of a human person as an entity with claims that cannot be extinguished, however great the payoff to society.

This argument does not imply that we do or should insist on absolute certainty; we properly instruct juries to convict if they believe that guilt has been established "beyond a reasonable doubt" rather than "beyond all doubt." We do so, however, only because total certainty is incompatible with the human condition, and we do not wish to immobilize the system by demanding the impossible. Thus, guilt beyond a reasonable doubt represents not a lawyer's fumbling substitute for a specific percentage, but a standard that seeks to come as close to certainty as human knowledge allows—one that refuses to take a deliberate risk of punishing any innocent man.[69]

The Supreme Court has recently held that "the Due Process Clause protects the accused against conviction except upon proof beyond a reasonable doubt of every fact necessary to constitute the crime with which he is charged."[70] The Court cited three reasons for its decision. Its first reason was that of simple fairness (an individual should not be subjected to the deprivations of punishment if there is any reasonable doubt he deserved it):

The accused during a criminal prosecution has at stake interests of immense importance, both because of the possibility that he may lose his liberty upon conviction and because of the certainty that he would be stigmatized by the conviction. Accordingly, a society that values the good name and freedom of every individual should not condemn a man for commission of a crime when there is reasonable doubt about his guilt . . .;[71]

its second, the need to uphold the moral force of the law:

Moreover, use of the reasonable-doubt standard is indispensable to command the respect and confidence of the community in applications of the criminal law. It is critical that the moral force of the criminal law not be diluted by a standard of proof which leaves people in doubt whether innocent men are being condemned . . .;[72]

and its third, the need to preserve citizens' sense of security from wrongful state interference:

It is also important in our free society that every individual going about his ordinary affairs have confidence that his government cannot adjudge him guilty of a criminal offense without convincing a proper factfinder of his guilt with utmost certainty.[73]

Assuming for the sake of argument that the state is entitled to confine *actually* dangerous individuals (an assumption to be examined below), the *mistaken* preventive confinement of actually nondangerous persons can no more be tolerated than the conviction of the innocent. We are speaking here, of course, of persons who have already been convicted of crimes. But by hypothesis in our model, they have already served the full punishment for their past offense, and are being preventively confined for an additional time designed expressly and solely to incapacitate them from committing future crimes. Hence, the past conviction would not cure the unfairness inherent in preventively incarcerating nondangerous persons. After all, if a man is convicted of robbery and serves the maximum term in prison, we *still* would object to further imprisoning him for an alleged past murder of which he was wholly innocent. Why should we be more tolerant of taking a man who has been convicted and has served the full time for the robbery and confining him for more years to prevent a future murder which in fact he would never commit if given his freedom?

Even if preventive confinement is not officially labelled "punishment," the deprivations of prolonged preventive confinement would be much like those of prolonged imprisonment. The loss of liberty would be the same. So would many of the other unpleasant aspects of confinement, such as forced association with other persons, some of whom may well be actually dangerous. The social obloquy of confinement would be similar—since labeling someone a potential criminal would have much the same stigmatizing effect as labeling him a past offender.[74]

3. *Reduced Trial Safeguards.* If accused of a crime, an individual has recourse to various traditional trial safeguards that enable him to defend himself against a false charge. The prosecution has to meet a standard of proof beyond a reasonable doubt. It cannot show that the defendant had a propensity to commit criminal acts,[75] but must establish that he had the opportunity to commit, and did actually commit a specific crime. Thus the defendant, if he has effective counsel, can escape conviction by casting doubt upon the evidence connecting him with the offense.

These safeguards would not be available in a preventive proceeding. A standard of proof beyond a reasonable doubt would be virtually meaningless, and could not be applied. Given all the contingencies affecting future occurrences, how can any future event be predicted beyond a reasonable doubt? We can at least imagine what it would be like to be sure beyond reasonable question that X has committed a murder; but how could we imagine being so sure he *will* do so, since he could always change his mind, be arrested beforehand, be killed in an accident, etc.? How, particularly, could we be so sure if we know our predictive method yields false positives and there is no way of ascertaining whether *he* is one of the false or one of the true positives? Moreover, evidence of a mere propensity to commit criminal acts would, necessarily, have to be sufficient to incarcerate. The defendant would have no way of

challenging his actual connection with the crime —for the crime would be in the future. (How, for example, could he establish an alibi for an offense which has not yet occurred?)[76]

D. EVALUATION OF THE MODEL— MINUS THE FALSE POSITIVES

Thus far, the objection to preventive confinement has centered upon the false positive issue— the injustice inflicted upon those wrongly confined on the basis of an erroneous prediction of dangerousness. Is this, however, the only objection? If it is, then it might be worthwhile to labor to overcome the obstacles to prediction, formidable as they are, with a view ultimately to establishing a system of preventive confinement when and if the accurate prediction of criminal conduct can be achieved.

Or do more fundamental evils inhere in the preventive concept—even if the false positive problem is assumed not to be present? If so, the entire concept deserves to be scrapped.

To answer these questions, we should inquire: How would we judge the preventive model described earlier, were we to assume that a predictive technique had been developed which is reasonably free of false positives? More specifically, let us hypothesize that the predictive technique misidentifies false positives at a rate which is *no greater* than the rate of convictions of innocent persons for past crimes which are assumed to occur under the existing system of criminal justice.[77]

1. *Universal Preventive Confinement.* To evaluate the model assuming such a "foolproof" predictive technique, we might start by inquiring: "If our predictions are so accurate, why limit the model to previously convicted persons; why not preventively confine *anybody* found to be potentially dangerous?" If, as we shall find, there are serious objections to such a universal scheme of preventive confinement, then we should ask: "What, if anything, is there about a prior conviction that renders our preventive model any more acceptable?"

What are the objections, then, to a universal system of preventive confinement, assuming we can predict criminal conduct with a high degree of accuracy? Suppose a preventive system is established which is similar to our model in all major respects but one—it is not limited to persons who have already been convicted of crimes. If any individual meets specified standards of probable cause for being dangerous, the state could initiate commitment proceedings against him. After a full hearing, with maximum feasible procedural safeguards, he would be preventively confined for an indeterminate term if the predictive criteria indicate that he can be expected to commit a serious crime if permitted to remain at large.

Even with an accurate predictive technique, such an Orwellian scheme would be unacceptable, for two major reasons.

(1) Universal preventive confinement would run counter to basic concepts of individual liberty: it would deny individuals the fair opportunity to make their own decisions and order their own lives. A system of criminal justice which imposes specified punishments for specified crimes gives us some degree of assurance that we can, in Hart's words,

predict and plan the future course of our lives within the coercive framework of the law. For the system which makes liability to the law's sanctions dependent upon a voluntary act not only maximizes the power of the individual to determine by his choice his future fate; it also maximizes his power to identify in advance the space which will be left open to him free from the law's interference.[78]

In a system of preventive confinement, this safeguard would be lost; an individual would have little choice as to whether he is confined or remains at large. His liberty would depend not upon his voluntary acts, but upon his *propensities* for future conduct as they are seen by the state. Far from being able "to identify in advance the space which would be left free to him from the law's interference," his liberty would depend upon predictive determinations which he would have little ability to foretell, let alone alter by his own choices.

Our constitutional scheme assigns a high value to the right of individual choice; this is reflected, for example, in the guarantees of free speech, free assembly and free association. It is likewise reflected in the basic rule of our criminal jurisprudence, that a sane adult may not be deprived of his liberty except as punishment for a crime of which he has been convicted.[79] The law thus

warns that specified modes of antisocial conduct will be met by unpleasant consequences, including incarceration for a specified time. But the choice—whether to engage in such conduct and chance the punishment—is left up to the individual; the state will not intervene unless he has been found to have violated the law. By giving him that choice, society risks that the individual will make the wrong selection, to the community's detriment. Similar hazards are entailed by other constitutional guarantees. Free speech risks incitement to violence; free assembly risks riot; free association risks criminal conspiracy. Nevertheless, we choose to withhold the coercive power of the law until *after* the event. In so doing, we may incur the costs of certain antisocial conduct that might have been precluded by state preventive action. But that is felt to be well worth the assurance given to individual freedom.

Universal preventive confinement is inconsistent with this concept of individual choice. Because a prescient and paternalistic state is assumed to know that certain individuals will make the wrong choice, it confines them precisely for the purpose of depriving them of the opportunity of choosing at all. Even if the state's predictions are imagined to be highly accurate, such a scheme would entail undue sacrifice of individual freedom and dignity.

The force of this argument, it should be noted, does not depend upon any particular psychological or philosophical view of individual choice. Do individuals consciously weigh the risks when they decide whether or not to comply with the law—or do they act upon impulse, habit and social pressure? Are individuals really free to choose between legal and illegal conduct, or is their choice determined by their backgrounds and experiences? Interesting as these questions may be in themselves, they are of no relevance here. As Herbert Packer points out, we are not describing the process of individual choice, but expressing a value preference for limiting *state* intrusion into citizens' lives:

Neither philosophic concepts nor psychological realities are actually at issue in the criminal law. The idea of free will in relation to conduct is not, in the legal system, a statement of fact, but rather a value preference having very little to do with the metaphysics of determinism and free will. The fallacy that legal values describe physical reality is a very common one. . . . But we need to dispose of it here, because it is such a major impediment to rational thought about the criminal law. Very simply, the law treats man's conduct as autonomous and willed, not because it is, but because it is desirable to proceed as if it were. It is desirable because the capacity of the individual human being to live his life in reasonable freedom from socially imposed external constraints (the only kind with which the law is concerned) would be fatally impaired unless the law provided a *locus poenitentiae,* a point of no return beyond which external constraints may be imposed but before which the individual is free—not free of whatever compulsions determinists tell us he labors under but free of the very specific social compulsions of the law.[80]

(2) Preventive confinement also would entail unjustified risks of abuse. If the government had the power to designate any individual as dangerous and to confine him preventively regardless of any prior determination of guilt, it could misuse that power to incarcerate for racial, social or political ends. Granted, we are assuming here that a highly accurate predictive technique has been developed. However, the mere fact that such a technique is known to exist provides no guarantee that government—once it has the power of universal preventive confinement—will opt for that technique alone and will not resort to biased prediction devices. Prediction being such a highly technical matter, the difference between an accurate and a distorting predictive instrument could depend upon subtle shifts in the data base, the sampling and validation methods, and the prediction variables and equations employed. It would be difficult, indeed, to develop workable constitutional or legal safeguards, that could effectively be administered by the courts, to assure that such distortions not be made. Nor could there be an effective popular check on abuses, given the arcane nature of the entire subject.

Of course, any human institution is susceptible to abuse. However, our tolerance for abuse diminishes as the institution's potential intrusiveness into citizens' lives increases. Universal preventive confinement has great potential intrusiveness. By abandoning the requirement of a prior criminal act, it reduces the protections and immunities available to individuals against state interference, and permits the state to confine a larger number of individuals, at an earlier time,

and for a longer period than the criminal law would allow. Where the degree of intrusion can be so great, the risks of abuse implicit in a scheme of preventive confinement seem truly unacceptable.

2. *Preventive Confinement for Those Convicted.* If a scheme of universal preventive confinement is unacceptable, why is our model any better? It differs from the universal scheme in only one significant respect: It is applicable solely to persons who have been convicted of a crime. The fact of a prior conviction, however, gives no additional sustenance to the scheme.

It cannot be argued that the fact of the prior conviction justifies the preventive confinement in the model *as punishment.* For we are assuming in the model that the individual has already served the maximum statutory term of punishment for the past offense, and is now serving extra time that is expressly intended to be preventive, not punitive.

Nor can it be asserted that the supposed greater dangerousness of convicted persons justifies their preventive incarceration. A universal system of preventive confinement would not be rendered acceptable if its application were limited to the most dangerous individuals. With an accurate method of prediction—which we assume to be available—a finding of dangerousness would not have to depend upon the presence or absence of a prior conviction. Some persons who had never been convicted might well be found to be *more* dangerous than their convicted brethren.

The two major policy objections to universal preventive confinement, just described, would seem equally applicable to our model.

Objection (1)—the individual's loss of the fair opportunity "to identify in advance the space which will be left open to him free of the state's interference"—applies as well to the model. An individual who commits an offense will have no way of determining whether, in addition to being liable to punishment if he is apprehended, he will be subject to indeterminate and possibly lifelong confinement on the basis of a prediction of dangerousness. The possible result—the indeterminate confinement—is well beyond the reasonably foreseeable risk involved in committing an offense. True, he may be on notice that if he commits the offense, there is *some* possibility of his being subjected to indeterminate preventive confinement, whereas none exists if he complies with the law. However, the degree of likelihood of his being so confined if he commits an offense depends not upon the nature and quality of his chosen acts, but upon the state's determination of his proclivities.

A violation of law may warrant punishment and punishment involves the temporary suspension of certain rights, including in some instances the right to liberty. In the model, however, we are speaking of the offender at a point in time where he has fully served his punishment; where he once again should be able to regain most, if not all of the ordinary rights of a citizen—including at least the right to remain free from seizure of his person by the state unless and until he has committed another offense.

Objection (2)—risk of abuse—applies a fortiori to the class of convicted offenders. Widely feared because of their past conduct[81] and drawn predominantly from the most underprivileged segments of society, convicted persons would have the most to fear from a deliberate "slanting" of the predictive criteria.

E. PREVENTIVE CONFINEMENT AS "PUNISHMENT"

It is worth exploring more thoroughly whether a scheme of preventive confinement could be supported by resort to the concept of punishment. To do so, let us vary our original model slightly as follows:

Variation 1 of the Model. The legislature provides general maximum terms of imprisonment for various offenses. However, it provides that where any convicted offender meets specified predictive criteria for future dangerousness, he will be subject to an indeterminate term of confinement, possibly exceeding the normal maximum penalty, until he is adjudged no longer dangerous. The additional confinement would be classified by law as punishment and as an addition to the sentence for the crime of which he has been convicted; it would be served in a regular prison, rather than a special, less rigorous preventive facility.

Thus in the revised model—unlike the original model—preventive confinement is officially labelled as *punishment* for the prior offense and is served under conventional punitive conditions, for example, in a regular prison. This change in the model is designed to enable us to focus

squarely on the issue: Can preventive confinement be *justified* as punishment for the prior offense?[82]

It is a basic principle of justice that the severity of punishment should not unduly exceed the gravity of the offense. While the legislature has wide discretion in defining the seriousness of offenses and determining the severity of punishments, it is subject to some moral and constitutional limits. The old English practice of hanging pickpockets would now be regarded as repugnant. On at least one occasion, the Supreme Court has invalidated a criminal statute that imposed excessive fines and an extended prison term for a relatively minor crime. The Court in *Weems v. United States*[83] ruled the Eighth Amendment ban on cruel and unusual punishments extended not only to barbaric punishments, but also to prolonged punishments that were in no way proportional to the offense committed.

It is likewise a basic principle of justice—although one widely ignored in practice in our criminal justice system—that persons guilty of equally serious offenses should not be subjected to grossly unequal punishments.[84]

These are what Hart[85] calls principles of distribution—that is, principles limiting the way punishment may properly be distributed among individuals. As Hart points out, they should apply whether or not one adopts a retributive theory of the general aim of punishment.[86]

Suppose, for example, we reject the view that retribution for moral guilt is the main purpose of punishment, and hold instead that punishment serves the object of deterring the general public from engaging in criminal activity. Even with this deterrence philosophy, we should still—in fairness to the individuals affected—insist that punishment not be disproportionately severe in relation to the gravity of the offense. That being so, we should oppose the infliction of severe exemplary punishments upon certain individuals convicted of minor offenses, however useful that might be in deterring that type of offense.[87]

If we consider prevention to be the main purpose of punishment, the same principles of justice still limit the manner in which we distribute punishment among individuals. Punishments of grossly disproportionate severity, and grossly unequal punishments for similar offenses, would still be objectionable.

Obviously, the application of these principles depends upon how we judge the seriousness of the offense. (Their application may also depend upon the extent to which we take into consideration the personal culpability of the offender. Should there, for example, be uniform penalties for each category of offense, disregarding the actor's state of mind except insofar as necessary to ascertain whether his conduct was intentional, negligent, accidental, etcetera, as some reformers have recently recommended?[88] Or should we continue to permit judges and parole boards to vary the punishment for an offense in order to reflect the actor's personal culpability, as indicated by his apparent motives, character or personal history?[89]) Without needing to resolve these difficult questions, it is fairly evident that the revised model violates the two principles of justice of which we are speaking. This is so because the revised model authorizes the imposition of indeterminate, even lifelong imprisonment, *without regard to the seriousness of the offender's past offense*—however such seriousness may be defined.

Consider the example of robbery. Under the revised model, the ordinary robber could be confined for no more than a specified number of years. But the robber who has the misfortune of being predicted to be dangerous would be subject to imprisonment for as much as his entire life. This would be objectionable for the two reasons just stated: 1) confinement for as much as a lifetime for the crime of robbery would, by any humane standards, be disproportionately severe in relation to the character of the offense, and 2) such prolonged confinement would be discriminatory against the robbers classified as dangerous, because their punishment would far exceed the penalty suffered by equally culpable robbers who happen not to be predicted to be dangerous.

Here, assuming the prediction of dangerousness to be accurate would not cure these objections. For the individual is, by hypothesis, serving the additional time as *punishment,* under punitive conditions. The punishment can be imposed only for the past offense—the robbery. If the extra time cannot be justified as punishment for the past robbery, then it cannot be justified with reference to the predicted crime, regardless of its prospective heinousness. For it likewise offends basic concepts of justice to *punish* someone—if

confinement is seriously intended as punishment —except for a past offense.[90] Hence the revised version of the model would be unacceptable, whether one assumes false positives are involved or not.[91]

F. ADDITION OF REHABILITATIVE TREATMENT

It has been suggested that the imposition of compulsory rehabilitative treatment gives justification to a scheme of preventive confinement.[92] This suggestion is worth critical examination.

To do so, let us again vary our original model, this time to provide the additional element of compulsory individualized treatment.

Variation 2 of the Model. The legislature provides maximum terms of imprisonment for various criminal offenses. It prescribes, however, that where any convicted offender meets the predictive criteria for dangerousness, he will be subject to preventive confinement for an indeterminate period that may exceed the maximum statutory term of imprisonment for his offense. Preventive confinement would be served in a special facility under conditions of minimum rigorousness; there, he would be required to undergo psychological, educational and vocational rehabilitative treatment. Either the offender would first serve a prison term for his past offense and then be transferred to this special facility; or else he could be sent immediately to the special facility. In either case, he would not be released from the special facility until he no longer met the criteria for dangerousness.[93]

Here, the individual's alleged need for treatment, alone, could not justify his being preventively confined—even were it supposed that he is suffering from an emotional or personality disturbance and could be genuinely helped by the treatment. For he is assumed to be an adult and— despite his psychological troubles—legally sane. Without the added elements of the prior conviction and the prediction of dangerousness, it could hardly be contended that the state had the right to confine *any* sane adult (even if he is somewhat disturbed) solely for therapeutic treatment, against his will.

Nor would the prior conviction alone justify his confinement. For we are assuming, again, that the period during which the individual is being confined for treatment exceeds the maximum statutory term of punishment for the offense of which he was convicted.

The justification of the mandatory treatment must depend, therefore, upon the prediction of dangerousness itself. The individual is being committed for treatment *because* he is thought to be dangerous, *precisely for the purpose of "curing" him of his dangerousness.* Were he not found dangerous he would not have to be treated.

The only functional difference between the original model of preventive confinement and this revised model of treatment-oriented confinement, is the manner by which they are designed to protect the community from individuals who are deemed dangerous. Pure preventive confinement operates only by incapacitating the individual; whatever his propensities for injuring the community, he is rendered incapable of exercising them because he is isolated. Treatment-oriented confinement operates by trying to eliminate these propensities in the individual, through a program of rehabilitative therapy; the individual is confined in order to assure his availability for the treatment program, and also in order to incapacitate him from doing harm during the interim period while the treatment is being administered and is supposedly taking effect.

Treatment could permit earlier release, assuming—and this assumption itself has been questioned[94]—that it can be effective. Under the preventive model, the individual simply remains in confinement until such time as he changes sufficiently of his own accord so that he ceases to meet the criteria of dangerousness. Under the revised, treatment-oriented model, an effort would be made to hasten the process of change—and hence the prospects of his release—by application of the appropriate rehabilitative therapy. Despite these differences, however, both models have essentially the same purpose: to safeguard society against persons who have been identified by specified predictive criteria as individually dangerous if permitted to remain at large.

Thus the treatment-oriented model ultimately rests upon the same assumption as the purely preventive model: that society has the right to deprive persons of their freedom on the basis of individual predictions of future dangerousness. If for the reasons earlier explained, that assumption is unacceptable as applied to the original preventive model, it cannot sustain the treatment-oriented model either. (The false positive problem, for example, does not disappear merely because we choose to impose treatment upon the individuals who are mistakenly identified as dangerous.)

G. IMPLICATIONS FOR CURRENT PRACTICE

It is wise to be cautious in translating conclusions developed from a theoretical model to the real world; for the question can always be asked: "How do you know the real world is similar to the model in all the relevant respects?" In the field of preventive confinement, sufficient data concerning current practices is not available to enable us to answer this question with any certainty. However, some tentative conclusions might be ventured.

First, the foregoing analysis calls into serious doubt the rationality and fairness of overt schemes of preventive confinement in existing law —such as the Canadian Preventive Detention statute, the Maryland Defective Delinquent Law and the Colorado sexual offender statute, described at the beginning of this paper. Any such system—which takes legally sane individuals who have been convicted of crimes, makes predictions of their individual future dangerousness, and subjects them on the basis of such predictions to prolonged confinement, in excess of what could legally be imposed as punishment for their prior offenses—shares the essential defects of the models we have been analyzing. This conclusion holds also for the recommendations of the Model Sentencing Act and the Model Penal Code which would impose extended terms of confinement upon certain "dangerous" offenders.

Second, the analysis raises questions concerning the use of predictions of dangerousness in sentencing and parole decisions. Are sentencing judges and parole boards attempting to make individual assessments of the supposed dangerousness of convicted persons coming before them? To what extent do these assessments affect decisions concerning imposition and duration of confinement or grant or denial of parole? Is there evidence that individuals predicted to be dangerous receive materially *longer* sentences or serve materially *longer* terms of confinement than other offenders with similar offense histories not so predicted? Do individuals predicted to be dangerous receive terms of confinement of a duration that substantially exceeds what would ordinarily be regarded as appropriate as punishment for the past offense, if its seriousness alone is considered? A definitive answer to these questions would require a much more detailed investigation of existing law and practice than the scope of this theoretical analysis permits. However, if the answers to these questions are affirmative (as one might well suspect to be often the case) then the law is being used to create *de facto* preventive confinement—that would be subject to essentially the same objections as apply to the theoretical models discussed in this paper.

III. CONCLUSION

In this article, the following question was considered: "Is it appropriate to decide whether and how long to confine a person convicted of a crime on the basis of a prediction of his supposed individual dangerousness?"

To examine this question, we constructed a hypothetical model where a person convicted of a criminal offense is subjected to preventive confinement for an indeterminate term—possibly well in excess of the maximum statutory term of punishment for the crime of which he was convicted—if specified predictive criteria indicated a high probability of his committing a serious offense in the future. It was assumed that the model met certain threshold criteria, namely: that there would be a reasonably precise legal definition of "dangerousness"; that the predictive criteria would be adequately validated in advance; and that certain minimum procedural safeguards would be adopted.

Our analysis indicated that predictions of dangerousness would, because of the infrequency of the events to be predicted, generally yield a high incidence of false positives—that is, persons *mistakenly* predicted to be dangerous. Where numerous false positives are confined, the model was found to offend fundamental conceptions of individual justice.

Even if the predictive methods were assumed to be highly accurate, preventive confinement in the model was found not sustainable, because it infringed the right of individual choice and entailed significant risks of abuse. The preventive confinement could not, moreover, be justified by reference to concepts of punishment for the prior offense.

The addition of mandatory rehabilitative treatment, likewise, did not sustain the model, for the function of treatment itself was dependent upon the prior finding of individual dangerousness.

Thus, under our analysis, the model scheme of preventive confinement failed. The consequence of that failure for current practice has been examined.

Preventive confinement requires the assumption that conviction of a crime relegates the offender, even after he has completed the punishment for his prior offense, to *permanent* second-class status. The erroneous incarceration of false positives; the risk of abuse of prediction methods; and the abdication of concepts of personal choice which are inherent in such a scheme can be excused only if it is assumed that their infliction upon convicted persons does not matter—because, as a class, these persons are expendable. As Caleb Foote stated:

It is a prerequisite for any system of preventive detention that you assume that those detained are going to be second-class citizens. The false positives are viewed as more expendable in the debates on preventive detention. Judges and psychiatrists who support preventive detention assume that a mistaken identification of one actually safe person who is predicted to be dangerous is much less serious than the release of one actually dangerous person. The operating rationale, therefore, is much like that of a search-and-destroy mission. Some dangerous Viet Cong may be eliminated, and the civilians and children are expendable.[95]

NOTES

1.   For a summary of arguments against pre-trial preventive detention, see Ervin, *Foreward: Preventive Detention—A Step Backward for Criminal Justice,* 6 Harv. Civ. Rights-Civ. Lib. L. Rev. 291 (1971); Tribe, *An Ounce of Detention: Preventive Justice in the World of John Mitchell,* 56 Va. L. Rev. 371 (1970).

2.   For critical analyses of the use of psychiatric predictions in civil commitment proceedings for the mentally ill, see Dershowitz, *The Law of Dangerousness: Some Fictions About Predictions,* 23 J. Legal Ed. 24 (1970) [hereinafter cited as Dershowitz, *The Law of Dangerousness*]; Dershowitz, *Psychiatry in the Legal Process: A Knife That Cuts Both Ways,* 4 Trial 29 (Feb.–Mar. 1968); Livermore, Malmquist & Meehl, *On the Justifications for Civil Commitment,* 117 U. Pa. L. Rev. 75 (1968); Note, *Civil Commitment of the Mentally Ill: Theories and Procedures,* 79 Harv. L. Rev. 1288 (1966).

3.   Can. Rev. Stat. c. 34, § 688 (1970). According to the statute, an "habitual criminal" is one who has been previously convicted of three separate offenses punishable by five years or more of imprisonment, and who is "leading persistently a criminal life." For a description and history of the Canadian Preventive Detention law see MacDonald, *A Critique of Habitual Criminal Legislation in Canada and England,* 4 U.B.C. L. Rev. 87 (1969).

4. Gr. Brit., Criminal Justice Act of 1967, §§ 37–38. For a history of the British Preventive Detention law prior to 1967 see MacDonald, *supra* note 3.

5. Md. Ann. Code art. 31B (Supp. 1971). For a useful analysis of the Maryland statute, see Note, *"Defective Delinquent" and Habitual Criminal Offender Statutes—Required Constitutional Safeguards,* 20 Rutgers L. Rev. 756 (1966) [hereinafter cited as *Rutgers Note*]. The Supreme Court has recently granted certiorari on a constitutional challenge to the Maryland law in Tippett v. Maryland, 436 F.2d 1153 (4th Cir. 1971), *cert. granted sub nom.* Murel v. Baltimore City Court, 92 S. Ct. 567 (1971).

6. Md. Ann Code art. 31B, § 5 (1971).

7. *Id.*

8. *Id.* § 9(b).

9. *Id.* § 9(a).

10. McCray v. Maryland, Misc. Pet. No. 4363 (Md. Cir. Ct., Montgomery County, Nov. 11, 1971).

11. Colo. Rev. Stat. Ann. § 39-19-11(2) (Supp. 1969). This is the current version of the Colorado statute, revised since the U.S. Supreme Court held an earlier version unconstitutional, in Specht v. Patterson, 386 U.S. 605 (1967). For comment on the Colorado statute, see Note, *Indiana's Sexual Psychopath Law,* 44 Ind. L.J. 242 (1969).

12. Colo. Rev. Stat. Ann. § 39-19-3 (1969 Supp.).

13. S. Brakel & R. Rock, The Mentally Disabled and the Law ch. 10 (American Bar Foundation rev. ed. 1971). According to this survey, these jurisdictions are Alabama, California, Florida, Illinois, Indiana, Iowa, Kansas, Massachusetts, Missouri, Nebraska, New Hampshire, Oregon, Pennsylvania, Tennessee, Washington, West Virginia, and the District of Columbia. The statutory definitions of "sexual psychopath," along with the statute citations, are set forth in this survey. Generally, the term "sexual psychopath" is used to refer to an individual who is not legally insane, is suffering from some kind of emotional or mental disturbance that makes him "disposed" to commit sex crimes, and is deemed to constitute a danger to the community if permitted to remain at large.

13a. Advisory Council of Judges, National Council on Crime and Delinquency, Model Sentencing Act § 5 (1963); National Council on Crime and Delinquency, Guides to Sentencing the Dangerous Offender (1969).

13b. Model Penal Code § 7.03(3) (Proposed Official Draft, 1962).

14. Cal. Penal Code §§ 1168, 3020 (West 1970).

15. *See* Johnson, *Multiple Punishment and Consecutive Sentences: Reflections on the Neal Doctrine,* 58 Calif. L. Rev. 357, 379–83 (1970); Mitford, *Kind and Usual Punishment in California,* The Atlantic, March 1971, at 46.

16. Evjen, *Current Thinking on Parole Prediction Tables,* 8 Crime and Delin. 215 (1962).

17. L. Ohlin, Selection for Parole (1951); Glaser, *Prediction Tables as Accounting Devices for Judges and Parole Boards,* 8 Crime and Delin. 239 (1962). Ohlin and Glaser developed the prediction tables in use in Illinois. Evjen, *supra* note 16.

For a valuable analysis and summary of prediction studies, see, H. Mannheim & L. Wilkins, Prediction Methods in Relation to Borstal Training (1955).

18. Evjen, *supra* note 16, at 216–17.

19. R. Dawson, Sentencing ch. 11, at 263 (American Bar Foundation, Administration of Criminal Justice Series, 1969).

20. If a specified term of confinement is imposed upon persons convicted of a criminal offense, without any attempt at predicting individual dangerousness, that will (by temporarily incapacitating such of those offenders as would otherwise be disposed to commit further offenses) prevent *some* crimes from occurring. The question remains, however, whether the use of imprisonment will prevent a sufficient number of offenses from occurring (considering only its incapacitating effect, and leaving general deterrence aside) to provide the public with a significant degree of net protection against crime. It also might be asked whether the public protection that is achieved is sufficient to warrant the costs and other negative side effects of the institution of imprisonment. Here, the following issues might be explored in further detail:

(a) What percentage of the total number of actual offenders are apprehended, convicted and incarcerated for a given offense? For most types of crimes—except, perhaps, murder, bank robbery and a few others—the percentage appears to be quite small. If this percentage is small, then the public may obtain little added protection from the incapacitating effect of incarceration upon confined criminals.

(b) What is the average rate at which persons incarcerated for a specified crime could be expected to commit further offenses, if permitted to remain at large? If the rate is low, again, little public protection is achieved by incarceration. Generally, the rate is relatively low for the more serious offenses.

(c) To what extent does the experience of imprisonment *increase* the propensity of those confined to commit criminal acts upon release? If imprisonment is criminogenic—as some studies suggest it might be—it may have a *counter-preventive* effect, by prompting more crimes after release than are prevented during confinement.

(d) How cost-effective is imprisonment as a device for preventing crime by incapacitating criminals, in view of the high per prisoner cost of confinement?

For a useful analysis of these issues, with some empirical data, see J. Robison, The California Prison, Parole and Probation System (Tech. Supp. 2, Cal. Assembly, Preliminary Report on the Costs and Effects of the California Criminal Justice System, April, 1969).

21. In evaluating the soundness of the concept of preventive confinement, I will be examining its broad implications for social policy, rather than the narrower question of its compliance or lack of compliance with legal and constitutional standards under the present state of the law.

22. *See* text accompanying *supra* note 5.

23. *See supra* note 15.

24. Dershowitz, *The Law of Dangerousness, supra* note 2.

25. Goldstein & Katz, *Dangerousness and Mental Illness: Some Observations on the Decision to Release Persons Acquitted by Reason of Insanity,* 70 Yale L.J. 225 (1960).

26. *See* text accompanying *supra* note 6.

27. *See Rutgers Note, supra* note 5. This 1966 *Rutgers Law Review* Note argues that the Maryland Defective Delinquent Law is void for vagueness because the criterion for dangerousness—"actual danger to society"—is so imprecise as to leave the crucial decision of what kind of future conduct warrants incarceration wholly to the discretion of individual psychiatrists, without giving the courts any workable criteria for decision-making. The Note contends that the law's invalidity for vagueness does not depend upon whether it is classified as a civil or criminal statute. The vagueness question may be considered in the coming Supreme Court test of the constitutionality of the statute, Tippett v. Maryland, 436 F.2d 1153 (4th Cir. 1971), *cert. granted sub nom.* Murel v. Baltimore City Court, 92 S. Ct. 567 (1971). *See also* Schreiber, *Indeterminate Therapeutic Incarceration of Dangerous Criminals: Perspectives and Problems,* 56 Va. L. Rev. 602 (1970).

28. Dershowitz, *The Law of Dangerousness, supra* note 2.

29. Glaser, *supra* note 17, at 257.

30. Dershowitz, *The Law of Dangerousness, supra* note 2, at 46. *See also,* J. Rappeport, Clinical Evaluation of the Dangerousness of the Mentally Ill (1967); Morris, *The Confusion of Confinement Syndrome: An Analysis of the Confinement of Mentally Ill Criminals and Ex-Criminals by the Department of Correction of the State of New York,* 17 Buffalo L. Rev. 651 (1968).

31. Hakeem, *Prediction of Parole Outcome from Summaries of Case Histories,* 52 J. Crim. L.C. & P.S. 145 (1961).

32. *Id.* at 149–50.

33. American Friends Service Committee, Struggle for Justice ch. 5 (1971) [hereinafter cited as AFSC Report].

34. *See* text accompanying note 47, *infra.*

35. P. Meehl, Clinical vs. Statistical Prediction 136–38 (1954).

36. *See* Specht v. Patterson, 386 U.S. 605 (1967).

37. *Id.*

38. For a summary of state court decisions concerning the applicability of procedural due process safeguards in sexual psychopath proceedings, see Annot., 34 A.L.R.3d 652 (1970).

39. Md. Ann. Code art. 31B (Supp. 1971); Tippett v. Maryland, 436 F.2d 1153 (4th Cir. 1971).

40. The Maryland Defective Delinquent Law provides an indigent defendant with a psychiatric witness at state expense, but no provision is made to enable the witness to conduct the kind of extended psychiatric observation needed to challenge the state's psychiatrists—who have had the defendant confined under prolonged observation. Md. Code Ann. art. 31B § 7(b) (Supp. 1971); *Rutgers Note, supra* note 5.

41. *See* S. Brakel & R. Rock, *supra* note 13, ch. 10, and Note, *Indiana's Sexual Psychopath Law, supra* note 11, arguing that the privilege against self-incrimination should apply in sexual psychopath proceedings; People v. Potter, 85 Ill. App. 2d 151, 228 N.E.2d 238 (1967), holding that, on the basis of the Supreme Court's reasoning in Specht v. Patterson, 386 U.S. 605 (1967), the privilege against self-incrimination should be applicable to proceedings under the Illinois Sexual Offender Act. *Contra, Rutgers Note, supra* note 5; Haskett v. Marion Criminal Court, 250 Ind. 229, 234 N.E.2d 636 (1968).

42. The Warner, Glueck and other studies are summarized in H. Mannheim & L. Wilkins, *supra* note 17, ch. 1.

43. L. Wilkins, Evaluation of Penal Measures ch. 5 (1969).

44. For an example of such a prediction study designed for Army recruitment purposes, see Danielson & Clark, *A Personality Inventory for Induction Screening,* 10 J. Clin. Psychol. 137 (1954). The design of that study, however, was criticized in Meehl & Rosen, *Antecedent Probability and the Efficiency of Psychometric Signs, Patterns and Cutting Scores,* 52 Psychol. Bull. 194 (1955).

45. L. Wilkins, *supra* note 43, at 69–70.

46. For example: Gottfredson developed a prediction table for parole recidivism, based upon California Base Expectancy scores, and applied it to a validation sample of 2,132 California male parolees. The lowest score category (Base Expectancy scores 0–4)—which indicated the highest expectancy of recidivism—correctly identified slightly under 10% of all violators in the sample; but 26% of those in this category were false positives. Those scoring in the lowest third of the sample (in percentile terms) constituted 46% of the actual violators; but 33% of those in this low scoring group were false positives. Gottfredson, *The Base Expectancy Approach,* in The Sociology of Punishment and Correction 807–13 (N. Johnston, L. Savitz & M. Wolfgang eds. 1970). Wenk and Robison applied more elaborate prediction tables for parole recidivism, developed by Gough, Wenk and Rozynko and based upon the California Psychological Inventory and Min-

nesota Multiphasic Personality Inventory scores, to a large group of paroled California Youth Authority wards (the sample used in this study is described in the text accompanying note 57, *infra).* Again, the results were disappointing, with over 50% of those predicted to be violators being false positives, and with the incidence of correct predictions being lower than it would be by random selection. E. Wenk & J. Robison, Assaultive Experience and Assaultive Potential, May 1971 (unpublished paper, National Council on Crime and Delinquency Research Center, Davis, Cal.). *See also* Gough, Wenk & Rozynko *Parole Outcome as Predicted from the CPI, the MMPI, and a Base Expectancy Table,* 70 J. Abnormal Psychol. 432 (1965).

47. Glaser, *supra* note 17, at 247–48.

48. *See* text accompanying *supra* notes 30 and 31.

49. L. Wilkins, *supra* note 43, at 128–29.

50. Rosen, *Detection of Suicidal Patients: An Example of Some Limitations in the Prediction of Infrequent Events,* 18 J. Consulting Psych. 397 (1954).

51. *Id.* at 398.

52. *Id.* at 399–400.

53. *Id.* at 399.

54. *Id.*

55. *Id.* at 400.

56. *Id.*

57. E. Wenk & J. Robison, Assaultive Experience and Assaultive Potential, May 1971 (unpublished paper, National Council on Crime and Delinquency Research Center, Davis, Cal.).

58. *Id.* at 27.

59. *Id.* at 47.

60. *See* text accompanying *supra* note 56.

61. Wenk & Robison, *supra* note 57, at 27–38.

62. *Id.*

63. *Id.*

64. Meehl & Rosen, *supra* note 44.

65. As will be recalled, indeterminate terms of confinement are utilized in the model in order to assure that an individual predicted to be dangerous remains confined—and thus unable to harm the community—until he is found no longer dangerous.

66. Dershowitz, *On Preventive Detention,* in Crime, Law and Society 307–19 (A.S. Goldstein & J. Goldstein eds. 1971); Tribe, *supra* note 1, at 372–73.

67. To avoid this distortion of the evidence, it has been suggested that a random sample of the population of those preventively confined be released from time to time, and the accuracy of the prediction be tested upon that sample. That may get us involved, however, in the problem of infrequent events. If we are trying to predict violent crimes, where the offense rate is very low, a substantial number of persons would have to be released at random in order to be able to measure the effectiveness of the criteria. This would pose serious problems of fairness for those who remain subject to confinement. Also, any large-scale random release could reduce the effectiveness of the system as a measure of public protection—and rekindle much of the public anxiety that the preventive system is designed to alleviate. *But see* Dershowitz, *On Preventive Detention, supra* note 66.

68. Dershowitz, *supra* note 66, at 313.

69. Tribe, *supra* note 1, at 387–88.

70. *In re* Winship, 397 U.S. 358, 364 (1970). The Court held that the requirement of proof beyond a reasonable doubt applied both to criminal and juvenile delinquency proceedings.

71. *Id.* at 363–64.

72. *Id.* at 364.

73. *Id.*

74. The force of this argument—that preventive confinement of the false positives is essentially unjust—does not, in fact, depend upon whether such confinement is classified as punishment. Even if it is regarded as a precautionary, rather than a punitive measure, the justification of preventively confining an individual would depend upon his *actually* being dangerous. The individual is being deprived of his liberty because, if he were to remain at large, he would interfere with the liberty of others by committing crimes. If he is *not* in fact dangerous, this justification simply collapses; and what we have left is gratuitous suffering imposed upon a harmless individual.

See also In re Winship, 397 U.S. 358 (1970), where the Supreme Court ruled that the mere fact that juvenile delinquency proceedings were legislatively designated as civil, instead of criminal, did not obviate the need for criminal due process safeguards, including proof beyond reasonable doubt.

For comment on reasons for the different treatment of the insane, see note 79 *infra.*

75. Generally, evidence of a defendant's propensity for criminal conduct is not even admissible in a criminal trial. *See* Comment, *Procedural Protections of the Criminal Defendant —A Reevaluation of the Privilege Against Self-Incrimination and the Rule Excluding Evidence of Propensity to Commit Crimes,* 78 Harv. L. Rev. 426, 435–43 (1964).

76. Dershowitz has also pointed out that in a criminal trial, imperfect as it is, the judge and jurors have "some sense of what it means to decide whether a specifically charged act probably was or was not committed . . . some basis for sorting out the relevant from the irrelevant, the believable from the incredible, the significant from the trivial." Dershowitz, *supra* note 66, at 315. In a preventive proceeding, the regular participants in the judicial process would be ill-equipped to judge the validity of the prediction. In a traditional courtroom, one might imagine what predictive trials would become when they were contested: baffling arguments between prosecution and defense expert witnesses, each claiming superior expertise and offering contrasting clinical or statistical judgements. A lay judge and jury (if there is a jury) will find such evidence much harder to evaluate intelligently than evidence of past crimes.

To provide greater expertise to the decision-makers, preventive confinement might be decided upon by specialists. That, however, would remove the traditional safeguard of lay control over the judicial process. If the experts decide, who chooses the experts and judges their performance?

77. *But see* Tribe, *supra* note 1, at 385–88.

78. H.L.A. Hart, Punishment and Responsibility 181–82 (1968).

79. An exception has historically been made of the insane —who have been subjected to preventive confinement without the requirement of a prior conviction, if deemed to be "dangerous to themselves or others." Little concern has been shown with safeguarding mental patients' rights of individual choice—because, in part, they have been regarded as persons incapable of choosing: that is, so cognitively and emotionally deranged that, for them, choice has little or no meaning. As one commentary put it:

Another explanation might be found in the assumption that society's rules cannot deter the mentally ill from acting dangerously. Whether persons who are not mentally ill commit dangerous acts or avoid them is thought to depend on a process of choice. This process is respected and valued; only by not confining even those who can be accurately predicted to be dangerous can all persons be permitted to make the choice. On the other hand, whether mentally ill persons act dangerously is thought to depend not on their own choice but on the chance effects of their disease. Confining them hinders no respected process.

Note, *Civil Commitment of the Mentally Ill, supra* note 2, at 1291. This view of mental illness has been questioned, *see* Livermore, Malmquist & Meehl, *On the Justifications for Civil Commitment, supra* note 2. Whatever its merits, this justification points up the high value assigned to individual choice, in the case of persons not deemed insane.

80. H. Packer, The Limits of The Criminal Sanction 74–75 (1968).

81. *See* Harris poll on public attitudes toward convicted offenders in Joint Commission on Correctional Manpower and Training, The Public Looks at Crime and Corrections (1968).

82. *See* H.L.A. Hart, *supra* note 78, ch. 1, at 4–6.

83. 217 U.S. 349 (1910), invalidating a statute imposing a penalty of from 12 to 20 years imprisonment at hard and painful labor for the crime of falsifying official records. For a comment on this case, see *Rutgers Note, supra* note 5; Katkin, *Habitual Offender Laws: A Reconsideration,* 21 Buffalo L. Rev. 99 (1971).

84. *See* H.L.A. Hart, *supra* note 78, ch. 1; AFSC Report, *supra* note 33, ch. 3, 9. *See also* United States v. Wiley, 278 F.2d 500 (7th Cir. 1960); President's Commission on Law Enforcement and Administration of Criminal Justice, Task Force Report: The Courts 23–24 (1967); S. Kadish & M. Paulsen, Criminal Law and its Processes 1284–87 (1969).

85. H.L.A. Hart, *supra* note 78, ch. 1.

86. *Id.* at 11–13.

87. Hart explains this point as follows:

The further principle that different kinds of offence of different gravity (however that is assessed) should not be punished with equal severity is one which like other principles of Distribution may qualify the pursuit of our General Aim and is not deducible from it. Long sentences of imprisonment might effectually stamp out car parking offences, yet we think it wrong to employ them; *not* because there is for each crime a penalty "naturally" fitted to its degree of iniquity (as some Retributionists in General Aim might think); not because we are convinced that the misery caused by such sentences (which might indeed be slight because they would rarely need to be applied) would be greater than that caused by the offences unchecked (as a Utilitarian might argue). The guiding principle is that of a proportion within a system of penalties between those imposed for different offences where these have a distinct place in a commonsense scale of gravity. This scale itself no doubt consists of very broad judgments both of relative moral iniquity and harmfulness of different types of offence: it draws rough distinctions like that between parking offences and homicide, or between 'mercy killing' and murder for gain, but cannot cope with any precise assessment of an individual's wickedness in committing a crime (Who can?). Yet maintenance of proportion of this kind may be important: for where the legal gradation of crimes expressed in the relative severity of penalties diverges sharply from this rough scale, there is a risk of either confusing common morality or flouting it and bringing the law into contempt.

H.L.A. Hart, *supra* note 78, ch. 1, at 25. *See also* American Bar Association, Project on Minimum Standards for Criminal Justice, Standards Relating to Sentencing Alternatives and Procedures 56–61 (1968).

88. *See* AFSC Report, *supra* note 33, ch. 9.

89. *See, e.g.,* R. Dawson, *supra* note 19, at 79–93.

90. *See* H.L.A. Hart, *supra* note 78, ch. 7. *See also* H. Packer, *supra* note 80, at 73–79.

91. The concept of punishment might justify imposing longer sentences upon multiple offenders than upon first

offenders—on the ground that a persistent course of criminal conduct evidences a greater degree of culpability. However, the model cannot be rescued by limiting its application to recidivists. Even for second robbery offenders, for example, an indeterminate and possible lifelong sentence would seem excessive; and selecting *some* second robbery offenders (namely, those predicted to be dangerous) and not others (namely, those not so predicted) for such harsh treatment would, again, be discriminatory. For a useful analysis of habitual offender laws, see Katkin, *supra* note 83.

92.   *See, e.g.,* Sas v. Maryland, 334 F2d 506 (4th Cir. 1964), upholding the Maryland Defective Delinquent Law.

93.   This revised model closely resembles Maryland's Defective Delinquent Law-described in the text accompanying *supra* notes 5–9—except that the procedures and predictive criteria would be improved to meet the threshold requirements described in part II-A of this article.

94.   Several studies have shown that existing rehabilitative treatment programs have had little or no measurable success in reducing recidivism rates. *See* G. Kassebaum, D. Ward & D. Wilner, Prison Treatment and Parole Survival (1971); Robison & Smith, *The Effectiveness of Correctional Programs,* 17 Crime & Delin. (1971). The concept of mandatory rehabilitative treatment has also been attacked as having functioned almost exclusively as a pretext for widening the discretion of law enforcement and correctional officials, and having aggravated the repressive and discriminatory features of the correctional system. AFSC Report *supra* note 33, chs. 3, 6.

95.   Foote, *Comments on Preventive Detention, 23* J. Legal Ed. 48, 52–53 (1970).

THE HON. MR. GILPIN

Speech Against Capital Punishment (1868)*

CAPITAL PUNISHMENT WITHIN PRISONS BILL—[BILL 36.]

Mr. Gilpin said, he rose to move the Amendment of which he had given notice—

"That, in the opinion of this House, it is expedient, instead of carrying out the punishment of death within prisons, that Capital Punishment should be abolished."

He felt some difficulty and hesitation in asking the attention of the House to the Motion of which he had given notice. In the first instance, he would express his extreme regret at the absence of his hon. Friend and Member for Dumfries (Mr. Ewart), whose name had been so closely connected with the amelioration of the criminal law, and who had done so much to abolish capital punishment. His reason for bringing forward this Motion now was, that he had a strong conviction that capital punishment was inexpedient and unnecessary; that it did not ensure the purposes for which it was enacted; that it was unjust in principle; that it involved not unfrequently the sacrifice of innocent human life; and further, that it afforded an escape for many guilty of atrocious crimes. Holding these opinions, he could not permit to pass an Act which proposed to reenact the punishment of death without entering his solemn protest against it, and submitting the reasons why he thought it inexpedient that capital punishment should be inflicted. The late division on this question was no test whatever of the feeling of the House on the question of capital punishment. He was now asked. "Will you bring forward a Motion for the abolition of capital punishment in the face of the frequent murders, of the increase of the crime of murder—at a time when no doubt there are influences at work"—to which he would not particularly allude—"which aggravate the crime to an extent almost unprecedented?" He unhesitatingly replied, "Yes, I will bring it forward now, because, if my principle is good for

*The Honorable Mr. Gilpin, "Parliamentary Debate on Capital Punishment Within Prisons Bills," *Hansard's Parliamentary Debates,* 3rd Series, April 21, 1868 (London: Hansard, 1868).

anything, it is good at all times and under all circumstances." He would remind the House that the atrocious murders which were now being committed, and which they all so much deplored, were murders which were committed under the present law, and he believed would not be committed under the altered state of the law which he desired to introduce. The question he had to deal with was—by what means could they best stop the crime of murder? He disavowed emphatically any sympathy with crime—he disavowed any maudlin sentimentality with respect to this question. He was sure his right hon. Friend opposite (Mr. Gathorne Hardy) would agree with him that the question between them was, how best to prevent the crime of murder. He said, without fear of contradiction, that almost in every instance in which capital punishment had ceased to be inflicted for certain crimes those crimes had lessened in frequency and enormity since its abolition; yet, as regarded murder, where the punishment of death was still retained, the crime had increased not only in number but enormity. In proof of that allegation he might quote statistics; but the fact was well known, and he would not take up the time of the House by doing so. It was also not to be denied that this was a question upon which there had been a very considerable change in public opinion within a comparatively short period of time. Some of those who had the administration of the law in their hands, and some of those who had occupied the position of the right hon. Gentlemen opposite (Mr. Gathorne Hardy), had come to the conclusion, at which he arrived many years ago, that capital punishment was undesirable—that it was unnecessary—and that the time had arrived when some other system ought to be adopted. Surely they were not succeeding in putting down murder. They had for centuries tried the *lex talionis* —the life for life principle—and they had miserably failed, and murder still stalked abroad. Earl Russell, in the introduction in the new edition of his work on the *English Constitution,* thus expressed himself as being favorable to the abolition of capital punishment—

"For my own part, I do not doubt for a moment either the right of a community to inflict the punishment of death, or the expediency of exercising that right in certain states of society. But when I turn from that abstract right and that abstract expediency to our own state of society—when I consider how difficult it is for any Judge to separate the case which requires inflexible justice from that which admits the force of mitigating circumstances—how invidious the task of the Secretary of State in dispensing the mercy of the Crown—how critical the comments made by the public—how soon the object of general horror becomes the theme of sympathy and pity—how narrow and how limited the examples given by this condign and awful punishment —how brutal the scene of execution—I come to the conclusion that nothing would be lost to justice, nothing lost in the preservation of innocent life, if the punishment of death were altogether abolished. In that case a sentence of a long term of separate confinement, followed by another term of hard labor and hard fare, would cease to be considered as an extension of mercy. If the sentence of the Judge were to that effect, there would scarcely ever be a petition for remission of punishment, in cases of murder, sent to the Home Office. The guilty, unpitied, would have time and opportunity to turn repentant to the Throne of Mercy."

Now, the first objection which he (Mr. Gilpin) had to the punishment of death was its essential injustice. They gave the same punishment to the crime of a Rush or a Manning as they did to that of a Samuel Wright, and other less guilty persons. They had, under the present law, constant occurrences in which the feeling, intellect, judgment, and Christianity of the public were against carrying out the extreme penalty, even in cases where the law was clear and unmistakable as to the matter and there was every reason to believe that it had been justly administered by the Judge who had condemned the criminal. Take, for instance, the case of the woman Charlotte Harris. She was sentenced to death, being *enceinte* at the time. According to custom she was reprieved until her babe was born, and then if the sentence of the law had taken its course she would have been hanged; but public opinion in the meantime had become so strong that the Home Office, even, he believed, in opposition to the judgment of the Secretary of State, had to give way, though the case was a fearful and atrocious one, and her life was spared. Richard Cobden, writing to him (Mr. Gilpin) with reference to this case, said—

"You are right. It is truly horrible to think of nursing a woman through her confinement, and then with her first returning strength to walk her to the scaffold! What is to become of the baby at its birth? Is it to lie upon the mother's breast until removed by the hand of Calcraft? Oh, horrible! horrible! Could you not have a meeting to shame the authorities."

Well, there were several meetings—one of 40,000 women, headed by Mary Howitt—and they petitioned the Throne for mercy, and mercy was extended. Then there was the case of Alice Holt. She, too, was pregnant; but the Home Office, having got wiser by this time, would not bring her to trial until after the birth of her child. Then they brought her to trial, sentenced her to death, and carried out the execution. Against the injustice of such a proceeding he had at the time most earnestly protested. A practical point most serious to the interests of society was this: numbers of criminals had escaped from the punishment due to their crimes, because of the unwillingness of juries to incur the possibility of convicting the innocent. He believed it was on this ground that Mr. Waddington, the former Under Secretary at the Home Office, came almost to the opinions that he (Mr. Gilpin) entertained. He knew it did not appear in his evidence before the Royal Commission; but Mr. Waddington told him though looking at the matter from a different standpoint and urged by different arguments, still he had very nearly come to his (Mr. Gilpin's) opinions that it would be desirable for the interests of society at large that the abolition of capital punishment should take place. He (Mr. Gilpin) believed it was not too much to say that there were men and women walking about red-handed amongst us—persons unquestionably guilty of the most atrocious murders—who, had the punishment for their crimes been other than capital, would be now immured in prison, utterly unable to repeat such crimes as those for which they had been already tried. This arose from the unwillingness of juries to convict—an unwillingness which did them honour—unless they had evidence positive and indisputable. It was right that evidence which would suffice to convict a man where the punishment would be fourteen years, or imprisonment for life, should be regarded as utterly insufficient to convict a man when the sentence would send him out of the world. Some twenty years ago Charles Dickens wrote a series of letters in *The Daily News* on the subject of capital punishment; and in one, headed "How Jurymen Feel," he said—

"Juries, like society, are not stricken foolish or motionless. They have, for the most part, an objection to the punishment of death; and they will, for the most part, assert it by such verdicts. As jurymen in the forgery cases (where jurors found a £10 note to be worth 39s., so as not to come under capital punishment) would probably reconcile their verdict to their consciences by calling to mind that the intrinsic value of a banknote was almost nothing; so jurymen, in cases of murder, probably argue that grave doctors have said all men are more or less mad, and therefore they believe the prisoner mad. This is a great wrong to society; but it arises out of the punishment of death. And the question will always suggest itself in jurors' minds, however earnestly the learned Judge presiding may discharge his duty—which is the greater wrong to society?—to give this man the benefit of the possibility of his being mad, or to have another public execution, with all its depraving and hardening influences? Imagining myself a juror, in a case of life or death, and supposing that the evidence had forced me from every other ground of opposition to this punishment in the particular case than a possibility of immediate mistake or otherwise, I would go over it again on this ground, and, if I could by any reasonable special pleading with myself find him mad rather than hang him, I think I would."

He had alluded to the numbers of persons who had escaped justice altogether, because juries could not make up their minds to convict under such circumstances; but there was another view of the case, and that was the execution of innocent persons, and when he said innocent persons, he meant persons innocent of the crimes with which they were charged. He would not delay the House by quoting what he quoted on a former occasion—the evidence of Daniel O'Connell, or the evidence of the present Lord Chief Baron, as to the frequency of the execution of innocent persons. But he would call the attention of the House to a case which occurred in 1865—that was the Italian Pollizioni, who was tried for the Saffron Hill murder, when one of the most humane of our Judges expressed his entire belief that the conviction was right. Pollizioni was sentenced, and was within a few days of being hanged. Law had done its best and its worst, when Mr. Negretti—of the firm of Negretti and Zambra—heard of the case, and became convinced that the man was innocent. He busied himself in getting evidence, which at last satisfied the Home Secretary, not that the prisoner deserved secondary punishment, but that he was absolutely innocent, and then he was taken out of the condemned cell. But for the interference of a private individual this man would have been hanged. It might be said that a case like this was very exceptional, and God forbid that it should be frequent; but within a few months there was the case of another man at Swansea, Giardinieri—oddly enough, also an Italian—who was sentenced to death, and was within a short time of being hanged. Evidence was, however, procured which showed him to be innocent. These were solemn facts. Charles Dickens said—

"I entreat all who may chance to read this letter to pause for an instance, and ask themselves whether they can remember any occasion on which they have in the broad day, and under circumstances the most favorable to recognition, mistaken one person for another, and believed that in a perfect stranger they have seen going away from them, or coming towards them, a familiar friend."

Hence there should be a reasonable hesitation as to an irrevocable verdict. The frequency of cases of mistaken identity were notorious. Mr. Visschers, who held a high position in the Government of the King of the Belgians, stated that in his experience three men convicted of murder appealed to the Court of Cassation, when the conviction was confirmed. The King, however, commuted their sentence into one of perpetual imprisonment; but their innocence being afterwards established, they were liberated, and granted annuities for life. Mr. Serjeant Parry stated, in reply to a Question by Mr. Waddington—

"I could mention six or eight instances within my own knowledge in which men have been acquitted, purely upon the ground that the punishment was capital."

And in reply to Mr. Bright, the learned gentleman said—

"I know that juries have acquitted men clearly and beyond all doubt guilty of murder, and some of the very worst murders that have ever been committed in this country, and have done so simply because the punishment has been the punishment of death. They would have convicted if the punishment had been imprisonment for life, or any punishment short of taking the life of the man, and they have seized hold of any excuse rather than be agents in putting capital punishment into operation."

This was not unreasonable; because a man, if wrongly transported, as in the case of Mr. Barber, the solicitor, could have compensation made to him, but not so if wrongly hanged. Many years ago Sir James Mackintosh stated before a Committee on the Criminal Laws that during a long cycle of years an average of one person was executed every three years whose innocence was afterwards proved. And Sir Fitz Roy Kelly stated, in 1839, that there were no less than fourteen innocent persons within the first forty years of this century who had been convicted, and whose innocence since their death had been fully established. And doubtless the average of one innocent person every three years was much too low, because it should be remembered that after the person was executed there was no motive to discover whether he or she was innocent or not. It was only necessary again to refer to the well-known case of Samuel Wright, a working carpenter in Southwark, to show the inequality of the law, and that, too, resulting simply from the character of the punishment. He believed no jury would have found Wright guilty on the charge of murder, and that no Judge but one would have left him for execution. The prisoner, it was true, pleaded guilty to the crime, and neither the counsel nor the Court could induce him to retract the plea; but it was clear from the facts of the case that this was not a case of wilful murder. The man was awoke in the night, and was dragged out of bed by a violent woman with whom he lived. He struggled with her, and seizing his razor, which was lying in his way, without premeditation he killed her. He was brought up for trial, and he pleaded guilty. They could not expect a carpenter to be trained to the niceties of the law, and it could not be wondered at that he, a conscientious man, determined to plead guilty. Almost at the last moment a very large body of his fellow working men came up to the Home Office to plead that his life might be spared. The present Government was not then in office. [Mr. Buxton: Who was the Home Secretary?] His right hon. Friend the Member for Morpeth (Sir George Grey). It was thought, most unwisely in his opinion, that the appearance of so large a body of working men on such a subject was an attempt to terrorise the Home Office, and a deaf ear was turned to their pleadings, which might wisely have been granted. Samuel Wright was executed, and that in the face of Charlotte Windsor, the hired murderess of babies, who, to solve some of the subtleties of law, was brought from one part of England to another, and after all was only imprisoned for life. He could never forget the morning of that execution. The people in the neighbourhood, instead of rushing to see the execution, had their blinds drawn down. It was a case which it would take a long time to wipe out from the memories of the people of that neighbourhood. That happened about the time that Townley, another murderer, was acquitted on the ground of insanity—a plea which his subsequent suicide showed to be true. But the question of insanity was one of the most uncertain character; the dividing line was disputed by doctors, and even by doctors in divinity; and the result was that in the case of men who were executed no time was allowed to show whether the crime was the result of a diseased brain, or of that moral obliquity which was rightly the subject of punishment. He felt grateful to the House for the indulgence they had shown him on a subject which had occupied his attention for twenty years. Now, he would ask, what was capital punishment? The punishment of death? No, it was not that. The sentence of death was decreed upon all of us by a higher than a mortal Judge. We but antedated the sentence, and by how much this was done no man could know. A man might be sent to the gallows who, according to medical opinion, could not live three months—and, in fact, a man had been recently executed, of whom the medical man said he could not live three months if he died in course of nature, and another man with a prospect of a long life. But what was the punishment? It was not death; it was antedating the sentence passed upon us all by the Most High. From ten thousand pulpits in the land, they were told, and rightly told, that for the repentant sinner the gates of Heaven were open, whether his death was a violent one or not; and yet in the face of those sermons they said—he did not mean that the Judges say it in so many words—"Your crime is so great that there can be no forgiveness with man; but appeal unto God and he may forgive you if you appeal in the right way and pay due attention to your religious advisers." We told the criminal in one breath that his crime was too great for man to forgive—that he was not fit to live on earth, but we commended him to the mercy of the Highest. We said, in effect, that those feet "which would leave no stain on the pure pavements of the New Jerusalem would leave the polluting mark of blood upon the ground that mortals tread." He knew not how to escape from this argument. If criminals were fit to die the time of their going to Heaven was hastened; and if not fit to die, they were allowed to go with all their unexpiated crimes on their heads before their final Judge. If we believed that faith which we professed, then the greater the sin the greater the need for repentance; and it was something monstrous that we should set ourselves up to decide that a fortnight from the date of his sentence was enough time for the worst murderer to make his peace with God. If we believed there was need for that peacemaking, let us give the murderer the time which God would give him to make his peace with Him. If we wanted to teach mercy, let us set an example of that mercy, and at all events stop short of shedding human blood. And if we would teach reverence for human life, let us not attempt to teach it by showing how it may be speedily taken away. He therefore moved the Amendment of which he had given notice, convinced that by the entire abolition of capital punishment, and the removal from their criminal code of the principle of revenge—the life for life principle—they would inaugurate an era in which the sanctity of human life would be regarded more highly than it had hitherto been, and in which the sense of that sanctity, permeating through society, would result in a great lessening of the crime of murder, and consequently in increased security to the public of his country.

JOHN STUART MILL

Speech in Favor of Capital Punishment (1868)*

. . . It would be a great satisfaction to me if I were able to support this Motion. It is always a matter of regret to me to find myself, on a public question, opposed to those who are called—sometimes in the way of honour, and sometimes in what is intended for ridicule—the philanthropists. Of all persons who take part in public affairs, they are those for whom, on the whole, I feel the greatest amount of respect; for their characteristic is, that they devote their time, their labour, and much of their money to objects purely public, with a less admixture of either personal or class selfishness, than any other class of politicians whatever. On almost all the great questions, scarcely any politicians are so steadily and almost uniformly to be found on the side of right; and they seldom err, but by an exaggerated application of some just and highly important principle. On the very subject that is now occupying us we all know what signal service they have rendered. It is through their efforts that our criminal laws—which within my memory hanged people for stealing in a dwelling house to the value of 40s.—laws by virtue of which rows of human beings might be seen suspended in front of Newgate by those who ascended or descended Ludgate Hill—have so greatly relaxed their most revolting and most impolitic ferocity, that aggravated murder is now practically the only crime which is punished with death by any of our lawful tribunals; and we are even now deliberating whether the extreme penalty should be retained in that solitary case. This vast gain, not only to humanity, but to the ends of penal justice, we owe to the philanthropists; and if they are mistaken, as I cannot but think they are, in the present instance, it is only in not perceiving the right time and place for stopping in a career hitherto so

eminently beneficial. Sir, there is a point at which, I conceive, that career ought to stop. When there has been brought home to any one, by conclusive evidence, the greatest crime known to the law; and when the attendant circumstances suggest no palliation of the guilt, no hope that the culprit may even yet not be unworthy to live among mankind, nothing to make it probable that the crime was an exception to his general character rather than a consequence of it, then I confess it appears to me that to deprive the criminal of the life of which he has proved himself to be unworthy—solemnly to blot him out from the fellowship of mankind and from the catalogue of the living—is the most appropriate, as it is certainly the most impressive, mode in which society can attach to so great a crime the penal consequences which for the security of life it is indispensable to annex to it. I defend this penalty, when confined to atrocious cases, on the very ground on which it is commonly attacked—on that of humanity to the criminal; as beyond comparison the least cruel mode in which it is possible adequately to deter from the crime. If, in our horror of inflicting death, we endeavour to devise some punishment for the living criminal which shall act on the human mind with a deterrent force at all comparable to that of death, we are driven to inflictions less severe indeed in appearance, and therefore less efficacious, but far more cruel in reality. Few, I think, would venture to propose, as a punishment for aggravated murder, less than imprisonment with hard labor for life; that is the fate to which a murderer would be consigned by the mercy which shrinks from putting him to death. But has it been sufficiently considered what sort of a mercy this is, and what kind of life it leaves to him? If, indeed, the punishment is not really inflicted—if it becomes the sham which a few years ago such punishments were rapidly becoming—then, indeed, its adoption would be almost

*John Stuart Mill, "Parliamentary Debate on Capital Punishment Within Prisons Bill," in *Hansard's Parliamentary Debates*, 3rd Series, April 21, 1868 (London: Hansard, 1868).

tantamount to giving up the attempt to repress murder altogether. But if it really is what it professes to be, and if it is realized in all its rigour by the popular imagination, as it very probably would not be, but as it must be if it is to be efficacious, it will be so shocking that when the memory of the crime is no longer fresh, there will be almost insuperable difficulty in executing it. What comparison can there really be, in point of severity, between consigning a man to the short pang of a rapid death, and immuring him in a living tomb, there to linger out what may be a long life in the hardest and most monotonous toil, without any of its alleviations or rewards—debarred from all pleasant sights and sounds, and cut off from all earthly hope, except a slight mitigation of bodily restraint, or a small improvement of diet? Yet even such a lot as this, because there is no one moment at which the suffering is of terrifying intensity, and, above all, because it does not contain the element, so imposing to the imagination, of the unknown, is universally reputed a milder punishment than death—stands in all codes as a mitigation of the capital penalty, and is thankfully accepted as such. For it is characteristic of all punishments which depend on duration for their efficacy—all, therefore, which are not corporal or pecuniary—that they are more rigorous than they seem; while it is, on the contrary, one of the strongest recommendations a punishment can have, that it should seem more rigorous than it is; for its practical power depends far less on what it is than on what it seems. There is not, I should think, any human infliction which makes an impression on the imagination so entirely out of proportion to its real severity as the punishment of death. The punishment must be mild indeed which does not add more to the sum of human misery than is necessarily or directly added by the execution of a criminal. As my hon. Friend the Member for Northampton (Mr. Gilpin) has himself remarked, the most that human laws can do to anyone in the matter of death is to hasten it; the man would have died at any rate; not so very much later, and on the average, I fear, with a considerably greater amount of bodily suffering. Society is asked, then, to denude itself of an instrument of punishment which, in the grave cases to which alone it is suitable, effects it purposes at a less cost of human suffering than any other; which, while it inspires more terror, is less cruel in actual fact than any punishment that

we should think of substituting for it. My hon. Friend says that it does not inspire terror, and that experience proves it to be a failure. But the influence of a punishment is not to be estimated by its effect on hardened criminals. Those whose habitual way of life keeps them, so to speak, at all times within sight of the gallows, do grow to care less about it; as, to compare good things with bad, an old soldier is not much affected by the chance of dying in battle. I can afford to admit all that is often said about the indifference of professional criminals to the gallows. Though of that indifference one-third is probably bravado and another third confidence that they shall have the luck to escape, it is quite probable that the remaining third is real. But the efficacy of a punishment which acts principally through the imagination, is chiefly to be measured by the impression it makes on those who are still innocent; by the horror with which it surrounds the first promptings of guilt; the restraining influence it exercises over the beginning of the thought which, if indulged, would become a temptation; the check which it exerts over the graded declension towards the state—never suddenly attained—in which crime no longer revolts, and punishment no longer terrifies. As for what is called the failure of death punishment, who is able to judge of that? We partly know who those are whom it has not deterred; but who is there who knows whom it has deterred, or how many human beings it has saved who would have lived to be murderers if that awful association had not been thrown round the idea of murder from their earliest infancy? Let us not forget that the most imposing facts loses its power over the imagination if it is made too cheap. When a punishment fit only for the most atrocious crimes is lavished on small offences until human feeling recoils from it, then, indeed, it ceases to intimidate, because it ceases to be believed in. The failure of capital punishment in cases of theft is easily accounted for; the thief did not believe that it would be inflicted. He had learnt by experience that jurors would perjure themselves rather than find him guilty; that Judges would seize any excuse for not sentencing him to death, or for recommending him to mercy; and that if neither jurors nor Judges were merciful, there were still hopes from an authority above both. When things had come to this pass it was high time to give up the vain attempt. When it is impossible to inflict a punishment, or when its infliction becomes a public scandal, the idle threat cannot too soon disappear from the statute book. And in the case of the host of offences which were formerly capital, I heartily rejoice that it did become impracticable to execute the law. If the same state of public feeling comes to exist in the case of murder; if the time comes when jurors refuse to find a murderer guilty; when Judges will not sentence him to death, or will recommend him to mercy; or when, if juries and Judges do not flinch from their duty, Home Secretaries, under pressure of deputations and memorials, shrink from theirs, and the threat becomes, as it became in the other cases, a mere *brutum fulmen;* then, indeed, it may become necessary to do in this case what has been done in those—to abrogate the penalty. That time may come—my hon. Friend thinks that it has nearly come. I hardly know whether he lamented it or boasted of it; but he and his Friends are entitled to the boast; for if it comes it will be their doing, and they will have gained what I cannot but call a fatal victory, for they will have achieved it by bringing about, if they will forgive me for saying so, an enervation, an effeminancy, in the general mind of the country. For what else than effeminancy is it to be so much more shocked by taking a man's life than by depriving him of all that makes life desirable or valuable? Is death, then, the greatest of all earthly ills? *Usque adeone mori miserum est?* Is it, indeed, so dreadful a thing to die? Has it not been from of old one chief part of a manly education to make us despise death—teaching us to account it, if an evil at all, by no means high in the list of evils; at all events, as an inevitable one, and to hold, as it were, our lives in our hands, ready to be given or risked at any moment, for a sufficiently worthy object? I am sure that my hon. Friends know all this as well, and have as much of all these feelings as any of the rest of us; possibly more. But I cannot think that this is likely to be the effect of their teaching on the general mind. I cannot think that the cultivating of a peculiar sensitiveness of conscience on this one point, over and above what results from the general cultivation of the moral sentiments, is permanently consistent with assigning in our own minds to the fact of death no more than the degree of relative importance which belongs to it among the other incidents of our humanity. The men of old cared too little about death, and gave their own lives or took those of others with equal recklessness. Our

danger is of the opposite kind, lest we should be so much shocked by death, in general and in the abstract, as to care too much about it in individual cases, both those of other people and our own, which call for its being risked. And I am not putting things at the worst, for it is proved by the experience of other countries that horror of the executioner by no means necessarily implies horror of the assassin. The stronghold, as we all know, of hired assassination in the 18th century was Italy; yet it is said that in some of the Italian populations the infliction of death by sentence of law was in the highest degree offensive and revolting to popular feeling. Much has been said of the sanctity of human life, and the absurdity of supposing that we can teach respect for life by ourselves destroying it. But I am surprised at the employment of this argument, for it is one which might be brought against any punishment whatever. It is not human life only, not human life as such, that ought to be sacred to us, but human feelings. The human capacity of suffering is what we should cause to be respected, not the mere capacity of existing. And we may imagine somebody asking how we can teach people not to inflict suffering by ourselves inflicting it? But to this I should answer—all of us would answer—that to deter by suffering from inflicting suffering is not only possible, but the very purpose of penal justice. Does fining a criminal show want of respect for property, or imprisoning him, for personal freedom? Just as unreasonable is it to think that to take the life of a man who has taken that of another is to show want of regard for human life. We show, on the contrary, most emphatically our regard for it, by the adoption of a rule that he who violates that right in another forfeits it for himself, and that while no other crime that he can commit deprives him of his right to live, this shall. There is one argument against capital punishment, even in extreme cases, which I cannot deny to have weight—on which my hon. Friend justly laid great stress, and which never can be entirely got rid of. It is this—that if by an error of justice an innocent person is put to death, the mistake can never be corrected; all compensation, all reparation for the wrong is impossible. This would be indeed a serious objection if these miserable mistakes—among the most tragical occurrences in the whole round of human affairs—could not be made extremely rare. The argument is invincible where the mode of criminal procedure is dangerous to the innocent, or where the Courts of Justice are not trusted. And this probably is the reason why the objection to an irreparable punishment began (as I believe it did) earlier, and is more intense and more widely diffused, in some parts of the Continent of Europe than it is here. There are on the Continent great and enlightened countries, in which the criminal procedure is not so favorable to innocence, does not afford the same security against erroneous conviction, as it does among us; countries where the Courts of Justice seem to think they fail in their duty unless they find somebody guilty; and in their really laudable desire to hunt guilt from its hiding places, expose themselves to a serious danger of condemning the innocent. If our own procedure and Courts of Justice afforded ground for similar apprehension, I should be the first to join in withdrawing the power of inflicting irreparable punishment from such tribunals. But we all know that the defects of our procedure are the very opposite. Our rules of evidence are even too favorable to the prisoner; and juries and Judges carry out the maxim, "It is better that ten guilty should escape than that one innocent person should suffer," not only to the letter, but beyond the letter. Judges are most anxious to point out, and juries to allow for, the barest possibility of the prisoner's innocence. No human judgment is infallible; such sad cases as my hon. Friend cited will sometimes occur; but in so grave a case as that of murder, the accused, in our system, has always the benefit of the merest shadow of a doubt. And this suggests another consideration very germane to the question. The very fact that death punishment is more shocking than any other to the imagination, necessarily renders the Courts of Justice more scrupulous in requiring the fullest evidence of guilt. Even that which is the greatest objection to capital punishment, the impossibility of correcting an error once committed, must make, and does make, juries and Judges more careful in forming their opinion, and more jealous in their scrutiny of the evidence. If the substitution of penal servitude for death in cases of murder should cause any declaration in this conscientious scrupulosity, there would be a great evil to set against the real, but I hope rare, advantage of being able to make reparation to a condemned person who was afterwards discovered to be innocent. In order that the possibility of correction may be kept open wherever the chance of

this sad contingency is more than infinitesimal, it is quite right that the Judge should recommend to the Crown a commutation of the sentence, not solely when the proof of guilt is open to the smallest suspicion, but whenever there remains anything unexplained and mysterious in the case, raising a desire for more light, or making it likely that further information may at some future time be obtained. I would also suggest that whenever the sentence is commuted the grounds of the commutation should, in some authentic form, be made known to the public. Thus much I willingly concede to my hon. Friend; but on the question of total abolition I am inclined to hope that the feeling of the country is not with him, and that the limitation of death punishment to the cases referred to in the Bill of last year will be generally considered sufficient. The mania which existed a short time ago for paring down all our punishments seems to have reached its limits, and not before it was time. We were in danger of being left without any effectual punishment, except for small offences. What was formerly our chief secondary punishment—transportation—before it was abolished, had become almost a reward. Penal servitude, the substitute for it, was becoming, to the classes who were principally subject to it, almost nominal, so comfortable did we make our prisons, and so easy had it become to get quickly out of them. Flogging—a most objectionable punishment in ordinary cases, but a particularly appropriate one for crimes of brutality, especially crimes against women—we would not hear of, except, to be sure, in the case of garotters, for whose peculiar benefit we reestablished it in a hurry, immediately after a Member of Parliament had been garrotted. With this exception, offences, even of an atrocious kind, against the person, as my hon. and learned Friend the Member for Oxford (Mr. Neate) well remarked, not only were, but still are, visited with penalties so ludicrously inadequate, as to be almost an encouragement to the crime. I think, Sir, that in the case of most offences, except those against property, there is more need of strengthening our punishments than of weakening them; and that severer sentences, with an apportionment of them to the different kinds of offences which shall approve itself better than at present to the moral sentiments of the community, are the kind of reform of which our penal system now stands in need. I shall therefore vote against the Amendment.

FURMAN v. GEORGIA

United States Supreme Court, 1972*

Mr. Justice Douglas, concurring.

In these three cases the death penalty was imposed, one of them for murder, and two for rape. In each the determination of whether the penalty should be death or a lighter punishment was left by the State to the discretion of the judge or of the jury. In each of the three cases the trial was to a jury. They are here on petitions for certiorari which we granted limited to the question whether the imposition and execution of the death penalty constitutes "cruel and unusual punishment" within the meaning of the Eighth Amendment as applied to the States by the Fourteenth. I vote to vacate each judgment, believing that the exaction of the death penalty does violate the Eighth and Fourteenth Amendments.

... We cannot say from facts disclosed in these records that these defendants were sentenced to death because they were black. Yet our task is not restricted to an effort to divine what motives impelled these death penalties. Rather, we deal with a system of law and of justice that leaves to the uncontrolled discretion of judges or juries the determination whether defendants committing these crimes should die or be imprisoned. Under these laws no standards govern the selection of the penalty. People live or die, dependent on the whim of one man or of 12.

... In a Nation committed to equal protection of the laws there is no permissible "caste" aspect[18] of law enforcement. Yet we know that the discretion of judges and juries in imposing the death penalty enables the penalty to be selectively applied, feeding prejudices against the accused if he is poor and despised, and lacking political clout, or if he is a member of a suspect or unpopular minority, and saving those who by social position may be in a more protected position. In ancient Hindu law a Brahman was exempt from capital punishment,[19] and in those days, "[g]enerally, in the law books, punishment increased in severity as social status diminished."[20] We have, I fear, taken in practice the same position, partially as a result of making the death penalty discretionary and partially as a result of

the ability of the rich to purchase the services of the most respected and most resourceful legal talent in the Nation.

The high service rendered by the "cruel and unusual" punishment clause of the Eighth Amendment is to require legislatures to write penal laws that are evenhanded, nonselective, and nonarbitrary, and to require judges to see to it that general laws are not applied sparsely, selectively, and spottily to unpopular groups.

A law that stated that anyone making more than $50,000 would be exempt from the death penalty would plainly fall, as would a law that in terms said that blacks, those who never went beyond the fifth grade in school, those who made less than $3,000 a year, or those who were unpopular or unstable should be the only people executed. A law which in the overall view reaches that result in practice[21] has no more sanctity than a law which in terms provides the same.

Thus, these discretionary statutes are unconstitutional in their operation. They are pregnant with discrimination and discrimination is an ingredient not compatible with the idea of equal protection of the laws that is implicit in the ban on "cruel and unusual" punishments.

Any law which is nondiscriminatory on its face may be applied in such a way as to violate the Equal Protection Clause of the Fourteenth Amendment. *Yick Wo* v. *Hopkins*, 118 U.S. 356. Such conceivably might be the fate of a mandatory death penalty, where equal or lesser sentences were imposed on the elite, a harsher one on the minorities or members of the lower castes. Whether a mandatory death penalty would otherwise be constitutional is a question I do not reach.

I concur in the judgments of the Court.

Mr. Justice Brennan, concurring.

... There are, then, four principles by which we may determine whether a particular punishment is "cruel and unusual." The primary principle, which I believe supplies the essential predicate for the application of the others, is that a punishment must not by its severity be degrading to human dignity. The paradigm violation of this principle would be the infliction of a torturous punishment of the type that the Clause has always prohibited. Yet "[i]t is unlikely that any State at this

*408 U.S. 238 (1972). Excerpts only. Footnotes numbered as in the original. Two cases from Georgia and one from Texas were considered and decided together by the Supreme Court.

moment in history," *Robinson* v. *California,* 370 U.S., at 666, would pass a law providing for the infliction of such a punishment. Indeed, no such punishment has ever been before this Court. The same may be said of the other principles. It is unlikely that this Court will confront a severe punishment that is obviously inflicted in wholly arbitrary fashion; no State would engage in a reign of blind terror. Nor is it likely that this Court will be called upon to review a severe punishment that is clearly and totally rejected throughout society; no legislature would be able even to authorize the infliction of such a punishment. Nor, finally, is it likely that this Court will have to consider a severe punishment that is patently unnecessary; no State today would inflict a severe punishment knowing that there was no reason whatever for doing so. In short, we are unlikely to have occasion to determine that a punishment is fatally offensive under any one principle.

Since the Bill of Rights was adopted, this Court has adjudged only three punishments to be within the prohibition of the Clause. See *Weems* v. *United States,* 217 U.S. 349 (1910) (12 years in chains at hard and painful labor); *Trop* v. *Dulles,* 356 U.S. 86 (1958) (expatriation); *Robinson* v. *California,* 370 U.S. 660 (1962) (imprisonment for narcotics addiction). Each punishment, of course, was degrading to human dignity, but of none could it be said conclusively that it was fatally offensive under one or the other of the principles. Rather, these "cruel and unusual punishments" seriously implicated several of the principles, and it was the application of the principles in combination that supported the judgment. That, indeed, is not surprising. The function of these principles, after all, is simply to provide means by which a court can determine whether a challenged punishment comports with human dignity. They are, therefore, interrelated, and in most cases it will be their convergence that will justify the conclusion that a punishment is "cruel and unusual." The test, then, will ordinarily be a cumulative one: If a punishment is unusually severe, if there is a strong probability that it is inflicted arbitrarily, if it is substantially rejected by contemporary society, and if there is no reason to believe that it serves any penal purpose more effectively than some less severe punishment, then the continued infliction of that punishment violates the command of the Clause that the State may not inflict inhuman and uncivilized punishments upon those convicted of crimes.

. . . The question, then, is whether the deliberate infliction of death is today consistent with the command of the Clause that the State may not inflict punishments that do not comport with human dignity. I will analyze the punishment of death in terms of the principles set out above and the cumulative test to which they lead: It is a denial of human dignity for the State arbitrarily to subject a person to an unusually severe punishment that society has indicated it does not regard as acceptable, and that cannot be shown to serve any penal purpose more effectively than a significantly less drastic punishment. Under these principles and this test, death is today a "cruel and unusual" punishment.

Death is a unique punishment in the United States. In a society that so strongly affirms the sanctity of life, not surprisingly the common view is that death is the ultimate sanction. This natural human feeling appears all about us. There has been no national debate about punishment, in general or by imprisonment, comparable to the debate about the punishment of death. No other punishment has been so continuously restricted, see *infra,* at 296–298, nor has any State yet abolished prisons, as some have abolished this punishment. And those States that still inflict death reserve it for the most heinous crimes. Juries, of course, have always treated death cases differently, as have governors exercising their communication powers. Criminal defendants are of the same view. "As all practicing lawyers know, who have defended persons charged with capital offenses, often the only goal possible is to avoid the death penalty." *Griffin* v. *Illinois,* 351 U.S. 12, 28 (1956) (Burton and Minton, JJ., dissenting). Some legislatures have required particular procedures, such as two-stage trials and automatic appeals, applicable only in death cases. "It is the universal experience in the administration of criminal justice that those charged with capital offenses are granted special considerations." *Ibid.* See *Williams* v. *Florida,* 399 U.S. 78, 103 (1970) (all States require juries of 12 in death cases). This Court, too, almost always treats death cases as a class apart.[34] And the unfortunate effect of this punishment upon the functioning of the judicial process is well known; no other punishment has a similar effect.

The only explanation for the uniqueness of death is its extreme severity. Death is today an unusually severe punishment, unusual in its pain, in its finality, and in its enormity. No other existing punishment is comparable to death in terms of physical and mental suffering. Although our information is not conclusive, it appears that there is no method available that guarantees an immediate and painless death.[35] Since the discontinuance of flogging as a constitutionally permissible punishment, *Jackson* v. *Bishop,* 404 F. 2d 571 (CA8 1968), death remains as the only punishment that may involve the conscious infliction of physical pain. In addition, we know that mental pain is an inseparable part of our practice of punishing criminals by death for the prospect of pending execution exacts a frightful toll during the inevitable long wait between the imposition of sentence and the actual infliction of death. Cf *Ex parte Medley,* 134 U.S. 160, 172 (1890). As the California Supreme Court pointed out, "the process of carrying out a verdict of death is often so degrading and brutalizing to the human spirit as to constitute psychological torture." *People* v. *Anderson,* 6 Cal. 3d 628, 649, 493 P. 2d 880, 894 (1972).[36] Indeed, as Mr. Justice Frankfurter noted, "the onset of insanity while awaiting execution of a death sentence is not a rare phenomenon." *Solesbee* v. *Balkcom,* 339 U.S. 9, 14 (1950) (dissenting opinion). The "fate of ever-increasing fear and distress" to which the expatriate is subjected, *Trop* v. *Dulles,* 356 U.S., at 102, can only exist to a greater degree for a person confined in prison awaiting death.[37]

The unusual severity of death is manifested most clearly in its finality and enormity. Death, in these respects, is in a class by itself. Expatriation, for example, is a punishment that "destroys for the individual the political existence that was centuries in the development," that "strips the citizen of his status in the national and international political community," and that puts "[h]is very existence" in jeopardy. Expatriation thus inherently entails "the total destruction of the individual's status in organized society." *Id.,* at 101. "In short, the expatriate has lost the right to have rights." *Id.,* at 102. Yet, demonstrably, expatriation is not "a fate worse than death." *Id.,* at 125 (Frankfurther, J., dissenting).[38] Although death, like expatriation, destroys the individual's "political existence" and his "status in organized society," it does more, for, unlike expatriation, death also destroys "[h]is very existence." There is, too at least the possibility that the expatriate will in the future regain "the right to have rights." Death forecloses even that possibility.

Death is truly an awesome punishment. The calculated killing of a human being by the State involves, by its very nature, a denial of the executed person's humanity. The contrast with the plight of a person punished by imprisonment is evident. An individual in prison does not lose "the right to have rights." A prisoner retains, for example, the constitutional rights to the free exercise of religion, to be free of cruel and unusual punishments, and to treatment as a "person" for purposes of due process of law and the equal protection of the laws. A prisoner remains a member of the human family. Moreover, he retains the right of access to the courts. His punishment is not irrevocable. Apart from the common charge, grounded upon the recognition of human fallibility, that the punishment of death must inevitably be inflicted upon innocent men, we know that death has been the lot of men whose convictions were unconstitutionally secured in view of later, retroactively applied, holdings of this Court. The punishment itself may have been unconstitutionally inflicted, see *Witherspoon* v. *Illinois,* 391 U.S. 510

(1968), yet the finality of death precludes relief. An executed person has indeed 'lost the right to have rights." As one 19th century proponent of punishing criminals by death declared, "When a man is hung, there is an end of our relations with him. His execution is a way of saying, 'You are not fit for this world, take your chance elsewhere.' "[39]

In comparison to all other punishments today, then, the deliberate extinguishment of human life by the State is uniquely degrading to human dignity. I would not hesitate to hold, on that ground alone, that death is today a "cruel and unusual" punishment, were it not that death is a punishment of longstanding usage and acceptance in this country. I therefore turn to the second principle—that the State may not arbitrarily inflict an unusually severe punishment.

... When the punishment of death is inflicted in a trivial number of the cases in which it is legally available, the conclusion is virtually inescapable that it is being inflicted arbitrarily. Indeed, it smacks of little more than a lottery system. The States claim, however, that this rarity is evidence not of arbitrariness, but of informed selectivity: Death is inflicted, they say, only in "extreme" cases.

Informed selectivity, of course, is a value not to be denigrated. Yet presumably the States could make precisely the same claim if there were 10 executions per year, or five, or even if there were but one. That there may be as many as 50 per year does not strengthen the claim. When the rate of infliction is at this low level, it is highly implausible that only the worst criminals or the criminals who commit the worst crimes are selected for this punishment. No one has yet suggested a rational basis that could differentiate in those terms the few who die from the many who go to prison. Crimes and criminals simply do not admit of a distinction that can be drawn so finely as to explain, on that ground, the execution of such a tiny sample of those eligible. Certainly the laws that provide for this punishment do not attempt to draw that distinction; all cases to which the laws apply are necessarily "extreme." Nor is the distinction credible in fact. If, for example, petitioner Furman or his crime illustrates the "extreme," then nearly all murderers and their murders are also "extreme."[48] Furthermore, our procedures in death cases, rather than resulting in the selection of "extreme" cases for this punishment, actually sanction an arbitrary selection. For this Court has held that juries may, as they do, make the decision whether to impose a death sentence wholly unguided by standards governing that decision. *McGautha* v. *California,* 402 U.S. 183, 196–208 (1971). In other words, our procedures are not constructed to guard against the totally capricious selection of criminals for the punishment of death.

Although it is difficult to imagine what further facts would be necessary in order to prove that death is, as my Brother Stewart puts it, "wantonly and . . . freakishly" inflicted, I need not conclude that arbitrary infliction is patently obvious. I am not considering this punishment by the isolated light of one principle. The probability of arbitrariness is sufficiently substantial that it can be relied upon, in combination with the other principles, in reaching a judgment on the constitutionality of this punishment.

When there is a strong probability that an unusually severe and degrading punishment is being inflicted arbitrarily, we may well expect that society will disapprove of its infliction. I turn, therefore, to the third principle. An examination of the history and present operation of the American practice of punishing criminals by death reveals that this punishment has been almost totally rejected by contemporary society.

. . . The progressive decline in, and the current rarity of, the infliction of death demonstrate that our society seriously questions the appropriateness of this punishment today. The States point out that many legislatures authorize death as the punishment for certain crimes and that substantial segments of the public, as reflected in opinion polls and referendum votes, continue to support it. Yet the availability of this punishment through statutory authorization, as well as the polls and referenda, which amount simply to approval of that authorization, simply underscores the extent to which our society has in fact rejected this punishment. When an unusually severe punishment is authorized for wide-scale application but not, because of society's refusal, inflicted save in a few instances, the inference is compelling that there is a deep-seated reluctance to inflict it. Indeed, the likelihood is great that the punishment is tolerated only because of its disuse. The objective indicator of society's view of an unusually severe punishment is what society does with it, and today society will inflict death upon only a small sample of the eligible criminals. Rejection could hardly be more complete without becoming absolute. At the very least, I must conclude that contemporary society views this punishment with substantial doubt.

The final principle to be considered is that an unusually severe and degrading punishment may not be excessive in view of the purposes for which it is inflicted. This principle, too, is related to the others. When there is a strong probability that the State is arbitrarily inflicting an unusually severe punishment that is subject to grave societal doubts, it is likely also that the punishment cannot be shown to be serving any penal purpose that could not be served equally well by some less severe punishment.

The States' primary claim is that death is a necessary punishment because it prevents the commission of capital crimes more effectively than any less severe punishment. The first part of this claim is that the infliction of death is necessary to stop the individuals executed from committing further crimes. The sufficient answer to this is that if a criminal convicted of a capital crime poses a danger to society, effective administration of the State's pardon and parole laws can delay or deny his release from prison, and techniques of isolation can eliminate or minimize the danger while he remains confined.

The more significant argument is that the threat of death prevents the commission of capital crimes because it deters potential criminals who would not be deterred by the threat of imprisonment. The argument is not based upon evidence that the threat of death is a superior deterrent. Indeed, as my Brother Marshall establishes, the available evidence uniformly indicates, although it does not conclusively prove, that the threat of death has no greater deterrent effect than the threat of imprisonment. The States argue, however, that they are entitled to rely upon common human experience, and that experience, they say, supports the conclusion that death must be a more effective deterrent than any less severe punishment. Because people fear death the most, the argument runs, the threat of death must be the greatest deterrent.

It is important to focus upon the precise import of this argument. It is not denied that many, and probably most, capital crimes cannot be deterred by the threat of punishment. Thus the argument can apply only to those who think rationally about the commission of capital crimes. Particularly is that true when the potential criminal, under this argument, must not only consider the risk of punishment, but also distinguish between two possible punishments. The concern, then, is with a particular type of potential criminal, the rational person who will commit a capital crime knowing that the punishment is long-term imprisonment, which may well be for the rest of his life, but will not commit the crime knowing that the punishment is death. On the face of it, the assumption that such persons exist is implausible.

In any event, this argument cannot be appraised in the abstract. We are not presented with the theoretical question whether under any imaginable circumstances the threat of death might be a greater deterrent to the commission of capital crimes than the threat of imprisonment. We are concerned with the practice of punishing criminals by death as it exists in the United States today. Proponents of this argument necessarily admit that its validity depends upon the existence of a system in which the punishment of death is invariably and swiftly imposed. Our system, of course, satisfies neither condition. A rational person contemplating a murder or rape is confronted, not with the certainty of a speedy death, but with the slightest possibility that he will be executed in the distant future. The risk of death is remote and improbable; in contrast, the risk of long-term imprisonment is near and great. In short, whatever the speculative validity of the assumption that the threat of death is a superior deterrent, there is no reason to believe that as currently administered the punishment of death is necessary to deter the commission of capital crimes. Whatever might be the case were all or substantially all eligible criminals quickly put to death, unverifiable possibilities are an insufficient basis upon which to conclude that the threat of death today has any greater deterrent efficacy than the threat of imprisonment.[54]

There is, however, another aspect to the argument that the punishment of death is necessary for the protection of society. The infliction of death, the States urge, serves to manifest the community's outrage at the commission of the crime. It is, they say, a concrete public expression of moral indignation that inculcates respect for the law and helps assure a more peaceful community. Moreover, we are told, not only does the punishment of death exert this widespread moralizing influence upon community values, it also satisfies the popular demand for grievous condemnation of abhorrent crimes and thus prevents disorder, lynching, and attempts by private citizens to take the law into their own hands.

The question, however, is not whether death serves these supposed purposes of punishment, but whether death serves them more effectively than imprisonment. There is no evidence whatever that utilization of imprisonment rather than death encourages private blood feuds and other disorders. Surely if there were such a danger, the execution of a handful of criminals each year would not prevent it. The assertion that death alone is a sufficiently emphatic denunciation for capital crimes suffers from the same defect. If capital crimes require the punishment of death in order to provide moral reinforcement for the basic values of the community, those values can only be undermined when death is so rarely inflicted upon the criminals who commit the crimes. Furthermore, it is certainly doubtful that the infliction of death by the State does in fact strengthen the community's moral code; if the deliberate extinguishment of human life has any effect at all, it more likely tends to lower our respect for life and brutalize our values. That, after all, is why we no longer carry out public executions. In any event, this claim simply means that one purpose of punishment is to indicate social disapproval of crime. To serve that purpose our laws distribute punishments according to the gravity of crimes and punish more severely the crimes society regards as more serious. That purpose cannot justify any particular punishment as the upper limit of severity.

Mr. Justice White, concurring.
... Most important, a major goal of the criminal law —to deter others by punishing the convicted criminal —would not be substantially served where the penalty is so seldom invoked that it ceases to be the credible threat essential to influence the conduct of others. For present purposes I accept the morality and utility of punishing one person to influence another. I accept also the effectiveness of punishment generally and need not reject the death penalty as a more effective deterrent than a lesser punishment. But common sense and experience tell us that seldom-enforced laws become ineffective measures for controlling human conduct and that the death penalty, unless imposed with sufficient frequency, will make little contribution to deterring those crimes for which it may be exacted.

The imposition and execution of the death penalty are obviously cruel in the dictionary sense. But the penalty has not been considered cruel and unusual punishment in the constitutional sense because it was thought justified by the social ends it was deemed to serve. At the moment that it ceases realistically to further these purposes, however, the emerging question is whether its imposition in such circumstances would violate the Eighth Amendment. It is my view that it would, for its imposition would then be the pointless and needless extinction of life with only marginal contributions to any discernible social or public purposes. A penalty with such negligible returns to the State would be patently excessive and cruel and unusual punishment violative of the Eighth Amendment.

It is also my judgment that this point has been reached with respect to capital punishment as it is presently administered under the statutes involved in these cases. Concededly, it is difficult to prove as a general proposition that capital punishment, however administered, more effectively serves the ends of the criminal law than does imprisonment. But however that may be, I cannot avoid the conclusion that as the statutes before us are now administered, the penalty is so infrequently imposed that the threat of execution is too attenuated to be of substantial service to criminal justice.

I need not restate the facts and figures that appear in the opinions of my Brethren. Nor can I "prove" my conclusion from these data. But, like my Brethren, I must arrive at judgment; and I can do no more than state a conclusion based on 10 years of almost daily exposure to the facts and circumstances of hundreds and hundreds of federal and state criminal cases involving crimes for which death is the authorized penalty. That conclusion, as I have said, is that the death penalty is exacted with great infrequency even for the most atrocious crimes and that there is no meaningful basis for distinguishing the few cases in which it is imposed from the many cases in which it is not. The short of it is that the policy of vesting sentencing authority primarily in juries—a decision largely motivated by the desire to mitigate the harshness of the law and to bring community judgment to bear on the sentence as well as guilt or innocence—has so effectively achieved its aims that capital punishment within the confines of the statutes now before us has for all practical purposes run its course.

Mr. Chief Justice Burger, with whom Mr. Justice Blackmun, Mr. Justice Powell, and Mr. Justice Rehnquist join, dissenting.

. . . There are no obvious indications that capital punishment offends the conscience of society to such a degree that our traditional deference to the legislative judgment must be abandoned. It is not a punishment such as burning at the stake that everyone would ineffably find to be repugnant to all civilized standards. Nor is it a punishment so roundly condemned that only a few aberrant legislatures have retained it on the statute books. Capital punishment is authorized by statute in 40 States, the District of Columbia, and in the federal courts for the commission of certain crimes.[7] On four occasions in the last 11 years Congress has added to the list of federal crimes punishable by death.[8] In looking for reliable indicia of contemporary attitude, none more trustworthy has been advanced.

One conceivable source of evidence that legislatures have abdicated their essentially barometric role with respect to community values would be public opinion polls, of which there have been many in the past decade addressed to the question of capital punishment. Without assessing the reliability of such polls, or intimating that any judicial reliance could ever be placed on them, it need only be noted that the reported results have shown nothing approximating the universal condemnation of capital punishment that might lead us to suspect that the legislatures in general have lost touch with current social values.[9]

Counsel for petitioners rely on a different body of empirical evidence. They argue, in effect, that the number of cases in which the death penalty is imposed, as compared with the number of cases in which it is statutorily available, reflects a general revulsion toward the penalty that would lead to its repeal if only it were more generally and widely enforced. It cannot be gainsaid that by the choice of juries—and sometimes judges[10]—the death penalty is imposed in far fewer than half the cases in which it is available.[11] To go further and characterize the rate of imposition as "freakishly rare," as petitioners insist, is unwarranted hyperbole. And regardless of its characterization, the rate of imposition does not impel the conclusion that capital punishment is now regarded as intolerably cruel or uncivilized.

It is argued that in those capital cases where juries have recommended mercy, they have given expression to civilized values and effectively renounced the legislative authorization for capital punishment. At the same time it is argued that where juries have made the awesome decision to send men to their deaths, they have acted arbitrarily and without sensitivity to prevailing standards of decency. This explanation for the infrequency of imposition of capital punishment is unsupported by known facts, and is inconsistent in principle with everything this Court has ever said about the functioning of juries in capital cases.

In *McGautha* v. *California,* decided only one year ago, the Court held that there was no mandate in the Due Process Clause of the Fourteenth Amendment that juries be given instructions as to when the death penalty should be imposed. After reviewing the autonomy that juries have traditionally exercised in capital cases and noting the practical difficulties of framing manageable instructions, this Court concluded that judicially articulated standards were not needed to insure a responsible decision as to penalty. Nothing in *McGautha* licenses capital juries to act arbitrarily or assumes that they have so acted in the past. On the contrary, the assumption underlying the *McGautha* ruling is that juries "will act with due regard for the consequences of their decision." 402 U.S., at 208.

The responsibility of juries deciding capital cases in our system of justice was nowhere better described than in *Witherspoon* v. *Illinois, supra:*

"[A] jury that must choose between life imprisonment and capital punishment can do little more—and must do nothing less—than express *the conscience of the community* on the ultimate question of life or death."
"And one of the most important functions any jury can perform in making such a selection is to maintain a link between contemporary community values and the penal system—a link without which the determination of punishment could hardly reflect 'the evolving standards of decency that mark the progress of a maturing society' " 391 U.S., at 519 and n. 15 (emphasis added).

The selectivity of juries in imposing the punishment of death is properly viewed as a refinement on rather than a repudiation of, the statutory authorization for that penalty. Legislatures prescribe the categories of crimes for which the death penalty should be available, and, acting as "the conscience of the community,' juries are entrusted to determine in individual cases that the ultimate punishment is warranted. Juries are undoubtedly influenced in this judgment by myriad factors. The motive or lack of motive of the perpetrator, the degree of injury or suffering of the victim or victims, and the degree of brutality in the commission of the crime would seem to be prominent among these factors. Given the general awareness that death is no longer a routine punishment for the crimes for which it is made available, it is hardly surprising that juries have been increasingly meticulous in their imposition of the penalty. But to assume from the mere fact of relative infrequency that only a random assortment of pariahs are sentenced to death, is to cast grave doubt on the basic integrity of our jury system.

It would, of course, be unrealistic to assume that juries have been perfectly consistent in choosing the cases where the death penalty is to be imposed, for no human institution performs with perfect consistency. There are doubtless prisoners on death row who would not be there had they been tried before a different jury or in a different State. In this sense their fate has been controlled by a fortuitous circumstance. However, this element of fortuity does not stand as an indictment either of the general functioning of juries in capital cases or of the integrity of jury decisions in individual cases. There is no empirical basis for concluding that juries have generally failed to discharge in good faith the responsibility described in *Witherspoon*—that of choosing between life and death in individual cases according to the dictates of community values.[12]

. . . It seems remarkable to me that with our basic trust in lay jurors as the keystone in our system of criminal justice, it should now be suggested that we take the most sensitive and important of all decisions away from them. I could more easily be persuaded that mandatory sentences of death, without the intervening and ameliorating impact of lay jurors, are so arbitrary and doctrinaire that they violate the Constitution. The very infrequency of death penalties imposed by jurors attests their cautious and discriminating reservation of that penalty for the most extreme cases. I had thought that nothing was clearer in history, as we noted in *McGautha* one year ago, than the American abhorrence of "the common-law rule imposing a mandatory death sentence on all convicted murderers." 402 U.S., at 198. As the concurring opinion of Mr. Justice Marshall shows, *ante,* at 339, the 19th century movement away from mandatory death sentences marked an enlightened introduction of flexibility into the sentencing process. It recognized that individual culpability is not always measured by the category of the crime committed. This change in sentencing practice was greeted by the Court as a humanizing development. See *Winston v. United States,* 172 U.S. 303 (1899); cf. *Calton v. Utah,* 130 U.S. 83 (1889). See also *Andres v. United States,* 333 U.S. 740, 753 (1948) (Frankfurter, J., concurring). I do not see how this history can be ignored and how it can be suggested that the Eighth Amendment demands the elimination of the most sensitive feature of the sentencing system.

As a general matter, the evolution of penal concepts in this country has not been marked by great progress, nor have the results up to now been crowned with significant success. If anywhere in the whole spectrum of criminal justice fresh ideas deserve sober analysis, the sentencing and correctional area ranks high on the list. But it has been widely accepted that mandatory sentences for crimes do not best serve the ends of the criminal justice system. Now, after the long process of drawing away from the blind imposition of uniform sentences for every person convicted of a particular offense, we are confronted with an argument perhaps implying that only the legislatures may determine that a sentence of death is appropriate, without the intervening evaluation of jurors or judges. This approach threatens to turn back the progress of penal reform, which has moved until recently at too slow a rate to absorb significant setbacks.

NOTES

1. The opinion of the Supreme Court of Georgia affirming Furman's conviction of murder and sentence of death is reported in 225 Ga. 253, 167 S. E. 2d 628, and its opinion affirming Jackson's conviction of rape and sentence of death is reported in 225 Ga. 790, 171 S. E. 2d 501. The conviction of Branch of rape and the sentence of death were affirmed by the Court of Criminal Appeals of Texas and reported in 447 S. W. 2d 932.

18. See Johnson, The Negro and Crime, 217 Annals Amer. Acad. Pol. & Soc. Sci. 93 (1941).

19. See J. Spellman, Political Theory of Ancient India 112 (1964).

20. C. Drekmeier, Kingship and Community in Early India 233 (1962).

21. Cf. B. Prettyman, Jr., Death and The Supreme Court 296–297 (1961). "The disparity of representation in capital cases raises doubts about capital punishment itself, which has been abolished in only nine states. If a James Avery [345 U.S. 559] can be saved from electrocution because his attorney made timely objection to the selection of a jury by the use of yellow and white tickets, while an Aubry Williams [349 U.S. 375] can be sent to his death by a jury selected in precisely the same manner, we are imposing our most extreme penalty in an uneven fashion.

"The problem of proper representation is not a problem of money, as some have claimed, but of a lawyer's ability, and it is not true that only the rich have able lawyers. Both the rich and the poor usually are well represented—the poor because more often than not the best attorneys are appointed to defend them. It is the middle-class defendant, who can afford to hire an attorney but not a very good one, who is at a disadvantage. Certainly William Fikes [352 U.S. 191], despite the anomalous position in which he finds himself today, received as effective and intelligent a defense from his court-appointed attorneys as he would have received from an attorney his family had scraped together enough money to hire.

"And it is not only a matter of ability. An attorney must be found who is prepared to spend precious hours—the basic commodity he has to sell—on a case that seldom fully compensates him and often brings him no fee at all. The public has no conception of the time and effort devoted by attorneys to indigent cases. And in a first-degree case, the added responsibility of having a man's life depend upon the outcome exacts a heavy toll."

34. "That life is at stake is of course another important factor in creating the extraordinary situation. The difference between capital and non-capital offenses is the basis of differentiation in law in diverse ways in which the distinction becomes relevant." *Williams* v. *Georgia,* 349 U.S. 375, 391 (1955) (Frankfurter, J.). "When the penalty is death, we, like state court judges, are tempted to strain the evidence and even, in close cases, the law in order to give a doubtfully condemned man another change." *Stein* v. *New York,* 346 U.S. 156, 196 (1953) (Jackson, J.). "In death cases doubts such as those presented here should be resolved in favor of the accused." *Andres* v. *United States,* 333 U.S. 740, 752 (1948) (Reed, J.). Mr. Justice Harlan expressed the point strongly: "I do not concede that whatever process is 'due' an offender faced with a fine or a prison sentence necessarily satisfies the requirements of the Constitution in a capital case. The distinction is by no means novel, . . . nor is it negligible, being literally that between life and death." *Reid* v. *Covert,* 354 U.S. 1, 77 (1957) (concurring in result). And, of course, for many years this Court distinguished death cases from all others for purposes of the constitutional right to counsel. See *Powell* v. *Alabama,* 287 U.S. 45 (1932); *Betts* v. *Brady,* 316 U.S. 455 (1942); *Bute* v. *Illinois,* 333 U.S. 640 (1948).

35. See Report of Royal Commission on Capital Punishment 1949–1953, ¶¶ 700–789, pp. 246–273 (1953); Hearings on S. 1760 before the Subcommittee on Criminal Laws and Procedures of the Senate Committee on the Judiciary, 90th Cong., 2d Sess., 19–21 (1968) (testimony of Clinton Duffy); H. Barnes & N. Teeters, New Horizons in Criminology 306–309 (3d ed. 1959); C. Chessman, Trial by Ordeal 195–202 (1955); M. DiSalle, The Power of Life and Death 84–85 (1965); C. Duffy, 88 Men and 2 Women 13–14 (1962); B. Eshelman, Death Row Chaplain 26–29, 101–104, 159–164 (1962); R. Hammer, Between Life and Death 208–212 (1969); K. Lamott, Chronicles of San Quentin 228–231 (1961); L. Lawes, Life and Death in Sing Sing 170–171 (1928); Rubin, The Supreme Court, Cruel and Unusual Punishment, and the Death Penalty, 15 Crime & Delin. 121, 128–129 (1969); Comment, The Death Penalty Cases, 56 Calif. L. Rev. 1268, 1338–1341 (1968); Brief *amici curiae* filed by James V. Bennett, Clinton T. Duffy, Robert G. Sarver, Harry C. Tinsley, and Lawrence E. Wilson 12–14.

36. See H. Barnes & N. Teeters, New Horizons in Criminology 309–311 (2d ed. 1959); Camus, Reflections on the Guillotine, in A. Camus, Resistance, Rebellion, and Death 131, 151–156 (1960); C. Duffy, 88 Men and 2 Women 68–70, 254 (1962); R. Hammer, Between Life and Death 222–235, 244–250, 269–272 (1969); S. Rubin, The Law of Criminal Correction 340 (1963); Bluestone & McGahee, Reaction to Extreme Stress: Impending Death by Execution, 119 Amer. J. Psychiatry 393 (1962); Gottlieb, Capital Punishment, 15 Crime & Delin. 1, 8–10 (1969); West, Medicine and Capital Punishment, in Hearings on S. 1760 before the Subcommittee on Criminal Laws and Procedures of the Senate Committee on the Judiciary, 90th Cong., 2d Sess., 124 (1968); Ziferstein, Crime and Punishment, The Center Magazine 84 (Jan. 1968); Comment, The Death Penalty Cases, 56 Calif. L. Rev. 1268, 1342 (1968); Note, Mental Suffering under Sentence of Death: A Cruel and Unusual Punishment, 57 Iowa L. Rev. 814 (1972).

37. The State, of course, does not purposely impose the lengthy waiting period in order to inflict further suffering. The impact upon the individual is not the less severe on that account. It is no answer to assert that long delays exist only because condemned criminals avail themselves of their full panoply of legal rights. The right not to be subjected to inhuman treatment cannot, of course, be played off against the right to pursue due process of law, but, apart from that, the plain truth is that it is society that demands, even against the wishes of the criminal, that all legal avenues be explored before the execution is finally carried out.

38. It was recognized in *Trop* itself that expatriation is a "punishment short of death." 356 U.S., at 99. Death, however, was distinguished on the ground that it was "still widely accepted." *Ibid.*

39. Stephen, Capital Punishments, 69 Fraser's Magazine 753–763 (1864).

48. The victim surprised Furman in the act of burglarizing the victim's home in the middle of the night. While escaping, Furman killed the victim with one pistol shot fired through the closed kitchen door from the outside. At the trial, Furman gave his version of the killing:

"They got me charged with murder and I admit, I admit going to these folks' home and they did caught me in there and I was coming back out, backing up and there was a wire down there on the floor. I was coming out backwards and fell back and I didn't intend to kill nobody. I didn't know they was behind the door. The gun went off and I didn't know nothing about no murder until they arrested me, and when the gun went off I was down on the floor and I got up and ran. That's all to it." App. 54–55.

The Georgia Supreme Court accepted that version:

"The admission in open court by the accused . . . that during the period in which he was involved in the commission of a criminal act at the home of the deceased, he accidentlly tripped over a wire in leaving the premises causing the gun to go off, together with other facts and circumstances surrounding the death of the deceased by violent means, was sufficient to support the verdict of guilty of murder. . . ." *Furman* v. *State,* 225 Ga. 253, 254, 167 S. E. 2d 628, 629 (1969).

About Furman himself, the jury knew only that he was black and that, according to his statement at trial, he was 26 years old and worked at "Superior Upholstery." App. 54. It took the jury one hour and 35 minutes to return a verdict of guilt and a sentence of death. *Id.,* at 64–65.

54. There is also the more limited argument that death is a necessary punishment when criminals are already serving or subject to a sentence of life imprisonment. If the only punishment available is further imprisonment, it is said, those criminals will have nothing to lose by committing further crimes, and accordingly the threat of death is the sole deterrent. But "life" imprisonment is a misnomer today. Rarely, if ever, do crimes carry a mandatory life sentence without possibility of parole. That possibility ensures that criminals do not reach the point where further crimes are free of consequences. Moreover, if this argument is simply an assertion that the threat of death is a more effective deterrent than the threat of increased imprisonment by denial of release on parole, then, as noted above, there is simply no evidence to support it.

7. See Department of Justice, National Prisoner Statistics No. 46, Capital Punishment 1930–1970, p. 50 (Aug. 1971). Since the publication of the Department of Justice report, capital punishment has been judicially abolished in California, *People* v. *Anderson,* 6 Cal. 3d 628, 493 P. 2d 880, cert. denied, 406 U.S. 813 (1972). The States where capital punishment is no longer authorized are Alaska, California, Hawaii, Iowa, Maine, Michigan, Minnesota, Oregon, West Virginia, and Wisconsin.

8. See Act of Jan. 2, 1971, Pub. L. 91–644, Tit. IV, § 15, 84 Stat. 1891, 18 U.S.C. § 351; see Act of Oct. 15, 1970, Pub. L. 91–452, Tit. XI, § 1102 (a), 84 Stat. 956, 18 U.S.C. § 844 (f) (i); Act of Aug. 28, 1965, 79 Stat. 580, 18 U.S.C. § 1751;

Act of Sept. 5, 1961, § 1, 75 Stat. 466, 49 U.S.C. § 1472 (i). See also opinion of Mr. Justice Blackmun, *post,* at 412–413.

9. A 1966 poll indicated that 42% of those polled favored capital punishment while 47% opposed it, and 11% had no opinion. A 1969 poll found 51% in favor, 40% opposed, and 9% with no opinion. See Erskine, The Polls: Capital Punishment, 34 Public Opinion Quarterly 290 (1970).

10. The jury plays the predominant role in sentencing in capital cases in this country. Available evidence indicates that where the judge determines the sentence, the death penalty is imposed with a slightly greater frequency than where the jury makes the determination. H. Kalven & H. Zeisel, The American Jury 436 (1966).

11. In the decade from 1961–1970, an average of 106 persons per year received the death sentence in the United States, ranging from a low of 85 in 1967 to a high of 140 in 1961; 127 persons received the death sentence in 1970. Department of Justice, National Prisoner Statistics No. 46, Capital Punishment 1930–1970, p. 9. See also Bedau, The Death Penalty in America, 35 Fed. Prob., No. 2, p. 32 (1971). Although accurate figures are difficult to obtain, it is thought that from 15% to 20% of those convicted of murder are sentenced to death in States where it is authorized. See, for example, McGee, Capital Punishment as Seen by a Correctional Administrator, 28 Fed. Prob., No. 2, pp. 11, 12 (1964); Bedau, Death Sentences in New Jersey 1907–1960, 19 Rutgers L. Rev. 1, 30 (1964); Florida Division of Corrections, Seventh Biennial Report (July 1 1968, to June 30, 1970) 82

(1970); H. Kalven & H. Zeisel, The American Jury 435–436 (1966). The rate of imposition for rape and the few other crimes made punishable by death in certain States is considerably lower. See, for example, Florida Division of Corrections, Seventh Biennial Report, *supra,* at 83; Partington, The Incidence of the Death Penalty for Rape in Virginia, 22 Wash. & Lee L. Rev. 43–44, 71–73 (1965).

12. Counsel for petitioners make the conclusory statement that "[t]hose who are selected to die are the poor and powerless, personally ugly and socially unacceptable." Brief for Petitioner in No. 68–5027, p. 51. However, the sources cited contain no empirical findings to undermine the general premise that juries impose the death penalty in the most extreme cases. One study has discerned a statistically noticeable difference between the rate of imposition on blue collar and white collar defendants; the study otherwise concludes that juries do follow rational patterns in imposing the sentence of death. Note, A Study of the California Penalty Jury in First-Degree-Murder Cases, 21 Stan. L. Rev. 1297 (1969). See also H. Kalven & H. Zeisel, The American Jury 434–449 (1966).

Statistics are also cited to show that the death penalty has been imposed in a racially discriminatory manner. Such statistics suggest, at least as a historical matter, that Negroes have been sentenced to death with greater frequency than whites in several States, particularly for the crime of interracial rape. See, for example, Koeninger, Capital Punishment in Texas, 1924–1968, 15 Crime & Delin. 132 (1969).

Suggestions for Further Reading

American Bar Association Project on Minimum Standards for Criminal Justice, "Standards Relating to Appellate Review of Sentences," (Tent. Draft 1967).

American Law Institute, *Model Penal Code, Part III* "Treatment and Correction", *Proposed Official Draft* (1962).

Acton, H. B., ed., *Philosophy of Punishment* (1969).

Andenaes, J., "General Prevention," 43 *J. Crim. L.C. & P.S.* 176 (1952).

Andenaes, J., "The General Preventive Effects of Punishment," 114 *U. Pa. L. Rev.* 949 (1966).

Baier, K., "Is Punishment Retributive?" *Analysis,* Vol. 16, (1955) pp. 25–32.

Beccaria, Cesare, *On Crimes and Punishment,* trans. H. Paolucci, (1963).

Bedau, Hugo A., ed., *The Death Penalty in America* (1964).

Bok, C., *Star Wormwood* (1959).

Butler, Samuel, *Erewhon* (1872).

Cohen, Bernard L., *Law Without Order: Capital Punishment and the Liberals* (1970).

Dershowitz, Alan M., "The Law of Dangerousness: Some Fictions About Predictions," 23 *J. Legal Ed.* 24 (1970).

Dershowitz, Alan M., "On Preventive Detention," in *Crime, Law and Society* eds. A. S. Goldstein & J. Goldstein. (1971), pp. 307–19.

Ewing, A. C., *The Morality of Punishment* (1929).

Ezorsky, Gertrude, ed., *Philosophical Perspectives on Punishment* (1972).

Feinberg, Joel, "The Expressive Function of Punishment," reprinted in *Doing and Deserving* (1970), pp. 95–118.

Feinberg, Joel, "On Justifying Punishment," in *Responsibility,* ed. Friedrich (*Nomos III*) 152 (1960).

Fitzgerald, P. J., *Criminal Law and Punishment,* (1962).

Flew, A., "The Justification of Punishment," *Philosophy,* Vol. 24 (1954), pp. 291–307.

Frankel, Marvin E., *Criminal Sentences* (1973).

Glenn, "The California Penalty Trial," 52 *Cal. L. Rev.* 386 (1964).

Green, T. H., "State's Right to Punish," *Jour. of Crim. L. and Criminol.*, Vol. 1, (1910), pp. 19–43.

Hall, J., *General Principles of Criminal Law,* 2d ed. (1960).

Hall-Williams, J. E., "Publications on Sentencing," 10 *Brit. J. Delinq.* 145 (1959).

Hart, H. L. A., *Punishment and Responsibility* (1968).

Hart, H. M., "The Aims of the Criminal Law," 23 *Law & Contemp.* Prob. 401 (1958).

Hegel, G. F., *Philosophy of Right,* trans. Knox., (1942).

Honderick, T., *Punishment, Its Supposed Justifications* (1970).

Kadish, S. H., "Some Observations on the Use of Criminal Sanctions in Enforcing Economic Regulations," 30 *U. Chi. L. Rev.* 423 (1963).

Knowlton, R. E., "Problems of Jury Discretion in Capital Cases," 101 *U. Pa. L. Rev.* 1099 (1953).

Koestler, Arthur, *Reflections on Hanging* (1956).

Lewis, C. S. "Humanitarian Theory of Punishment," *Res Judicatae,* VI (1953), pp. 224–30. Reply by N. Morris and D. Bucke, VI (1953), pp. 231–37. Comment by J. J. C. Smart, VI (1954), pp. 368–71. Reply by C. S. Lewis, VI (1954), pp. 519–23.

Loftsgordon, D., "Present-Day British Philosophers on Punishment," *Journal of Philosophy,* Vol. 63 (1966), pp. 341 ff.

Longford, F. P., *The Idea of Punishment* (1961).

Mabbott, J. D., "Freewill and Punishment," in *Contemporary British Philosophy,* 3rd ser. ed. H. D. Lewis. (1956), pp. 287–370.

Mabbott, J. D., "Punishment," *Mind,* Vol. 48, (1939), pp. 152–67.

McCloskey, H. J., "Utilitarianism and Retributive Punishment," *Journal of Philosophy,* Vol. 64 (1967), pp. 91 ff.

Michael, J., and H. Wechsler, *Criminal Law and Its Administration* (1940).

Mitford, Jessica, *Kind and Usual Punishment* (1973).

Moberly, Walter, *The Ethics of Punishment* (1968).

Mundle, C. W. K., "Punishment and Desert," *Philos. Q.,* Vol. 4 (1954), p. 216.

Note, "Consecutive Sentences in Single Prosecutions: Judicial Multiplication of Statutory Penalties," 67 *Yale L. J.* 916 (1958).

Note, "Cruel and Unusual Punishment Clause and the Substantive Criminal Law," 79 *Harv. L. Rev.* 635 (1966).

Note, "Due Process and Legislative Standards in Sentencing," 101 *U. Pa. L. Rev.* 257 (1952).

Note, "The Effectiveness of the Eighth Amendment: An Appraisal of Cruel and Unusual Punishment," 36 *N.Y. U.L. Rev.* 846 (1961).

Note, "Revival of the Eighth Amendment: Development of Cruel-Punishment Doctrine by the Supreme Court," 16 *Stan. L. Rev.* 996 (1964).

Note, "Statutory Multiple Punishment and Multiple Prosecution," 50 *Minn. L. Rev.* 1102 (1966).

Note, "Statutory Structures for Sentencing Felons to Prison," 60 *Colum. L. Rev.* 1134 (1960).

Note, "A Trial Judge's Freedom and Responsibility in Administering Probation, 71 *Yale L. J.* 551 (1962).

Packer, Herbert, *The Limits of the Criminal Sanction* (1968).

Packer, Herbert, "Making the Punishment Fit the Crime," 77 *Harv. L. Rev.* 1071 (1964).

Packer, Herbert, "Two Models of the Criminal Process," 113 *U. Pa. L. Rev.* 1 (1964).

Pincoffs, Edmund, *The Rationale of Legal Punishment* (1966).

President's Commission on Law Enforcement and the Administration of Justice, *Task Force Report: Corrections* (1967).

Rashdall, H., *Theory of Good and Evil,* Vol. I, (1924), Chap. 9.

Ross, W. D., *The Right and the Good,* (1930), pp. 56–64.

Royal Commission on Capital Punishment, 1949–53, *Report* (1953).

Sellin, J. T., "The Law and Some Aspects of Criminal Conduct," in *Aims and Methods of Legal Research,* ed. J. J. Conard. (1955).

Sharp, Frank C., *Ethics* (1928).

Shaw, G. B. *The Crime of Imprisonment* (1924).

de Tarde, G., *Penal Philosophy* (1912).

Van den Haag, E., "On Deterrence and the Death Penalty," *Ethics,* Vol. 78 (1968).

Wasserstrom, Richard, "Why Punish the Guilty?" *Princeton Univ. Mag.,* Vol. 20 (1964), pp. 14–19.

Wechsler, H., "Sentencing, Correction, and the Model Penal Code," 109 *U. Pa. L. Rev.* 465 (1961).